Journey of Remembering

Belfast Book of Honour

This project would not have been possible without the help of:

News Letter

Belfast Telegraph

THE IRISH NEWS

Belfast Book of Honour Committee
37-41 May, Street, Belfast BT1 4DN

www.journeyofremembering.org

Our website will be expanded and revised to include all new information

If you wish to correct any errors or omissions please write
or email the Committee on **Info@ journeyofremembering.org**

© Copyright 2009 Johnston Publishing NI

ISBN: 978-0-9549715-8-8

Published in conjunction with the Belfast Book of Honour Committee

All rights reserved

No part of this book may be reproduced, stored in a retrieval system, or transmitted in any form or by any means – electronic, mechanical, photocopy, recorfing, or otherwise – without written permission of the publisher, except for brief quotation in written reviews.

Contents

Foreword	I
Belfast Book of Honour Committee	II
Introduction	III
Acknowledgements	IV
List of Belfast Great War Dead	1 – 680
The Great War Dead of Belfast by Country	V
The Great War Dead of Belfast by Year	VI
Some Military Terms	VII

Foreword

This book represents a further significant step in a journey of remembrance and discovery. Throughout Ireland there has been in recent years a growing recognition that, regardless of subsequent political or other divisions, due acknowledgement should be paid to the sacrifice of Irish soldiers who fought and died in the Great War. In individual families, the loss of loved ones has long been remembered. In many households there rests a treasured sepia photograph of a uniformed figure from another era. Now, though, we see in so many places a heartening move forward from individual to communal recognition.

Sir Kenneth Bloomfield

This change in atmosphere and attitudes was recognised when a Peace Park was opened at Messines by Queen Elizabeth, President McAleese and the King of the Belgians. Thanks in particular to Paddy Harte of Donegal, who had joined hands in this initiative with Glenn Barr of Londonderry, Books of Honour were published for Donegal and Dublin. Closer to home, meticulous research and cross-community support led to the publication of written memorials to the dead of Newry and Mourne and Cookstown.

It seemed to many of us that our great city of Belfast, which sent so many of its sons and daughters to the fronts of the Great War and mourned their loss in all too many cases, deserved nothing less than a comprehensive book of remembrance.

The present publication would not have been possible without the support of many individuals and organisations. I have been privileged to chair a steering group whose members sought to define the task and rally support for it The "Belfast Telegraph" and "Irish News" gave us a kick-start by generously funding an initial conference in Lisburn. Ulster Garden Villages and its then chairman Sir Desmond Lorimer enabled us to retain the services of Derek Smyth, a passionate student of the period and the subject, as our researcher and author. For him this has been a labour of love. Now at last, after much time and effort, and with the heartening and generous support of the Belfast City Council, the "News Letter", "Irish News" and " Belfast Telegraph" we have been able to bring our book to publication.

Experience shows that the task of identifying all those who fell so many years ago can never be complete. Inevitably some readers will note an absence. Happily we have established alongside the book, with the generous support of the Ireland Funds, a website, www.journeyofremembering.org, where names can be added over time.

We hope, of course, that councils and other bodies and individuals will take up this torch in areas not yet covered by our own work .

This publication is not intended to glorify or justify war, but rather to underline the cost of conflict in human terms. Behind it lies a tragic but noble history of stoicism, courage, endurance and sacrifice. We are all familiar with dedications to " Our Glorious Dead". Death itself can never be glorious, and least of all in the mud and chaos of endless slaughter. But what truly was glorious was that so many men, and many brave women too, brought to this crisis in our world's turbulent history qualities which transcend all other considerations. To them and their memory we dedicate this book. We hope it will bring pride and comfort to the descendants of those named in it. together with a recognition that the sons and daughters of Belfast, when put to this ultimate test, were amongst the bravest of the brave.

Belfast Book of Honour Committee

Sir Kenneth Bloomfield (Chairman)

Monsignor Thomas Toner (vice Chairman)

Valerie Adams

Jack Allen

Bill Canning

Colonel Robin Charley

Jim Hendron

Brian McKenna

Leslie Morrell

Sir Robert Porter

Derek Smyth

Ian Elliott (Secretary)

Introduction

This book records over 6,700 Belfast servicemen and women who perished in the Great War. Their remains lie in 33 different countries, in every continent and in every ocean and are commemorated in 621 cemeteries or memorials across the globe. These lost citizens of Belfast had served in The British Army, The Royal Navy, (including The Royal Marines), The Merchant Navy and, after 1 April 1918, The Royal Air Force. They also served in the armed forces of Australia, Canada, New Zealand and South Africa.

The Committee of the Belfast Book of Honour project stipulated that for inclusion in the Book a serviceman or woman should have been born or resident in the City of Belfast. It had to be accepted that the appearance in the records or memorial of a work place, church, school, sports club, society or lodge did not necessarily mean that a person had been born or was resident within the city. Then there remained the difficulty of actually defining the City of Belfast. There have been several boundary changes over the last century and these were compounded by the major population shift in Belfast in the events of 1969 and subsequent years. In the end, the Committee decided to follow the lead of the Commonwealth War Graves Commission where they declared a casualty to be from Belfast

The example of the Commonwealth War Graves Commission has also been followed in regard to the range of dates covered by the book. The CWGC regards almost all service deaths from August 1914 to the 31st August 1921 as attributable to the Great War. Many former servicemen did indeed succumb to wounds in the years, and even the decades, following the armistice. In addition, the Spanish Influenza pandemic which emerged in the latter part of the War and lasted until at least 1920 cut a broad swathe through the ranks of the military as it did through the civil population.

This book is incomplete as it has not always been possible to establish a link between some of the dead and the City of Belfast. Other names simply remain undiscovered. Sifting personal information on Great War fatal casualties can, at times, prove frustrating. A principal difficulty is the loss of World War One service records during the Second World War. In September 1940 a Luftwaffe raid during the London Blitz destroyed some 60% of the documents. Those surviving were partially burned or damaged by smoke or water. Fortunately, other sources such as; The Commonwealth War Graves Commission, The National Archives in London, The National Archives of Ireland , and the Public Record Office of Northern Ireland proved more productive. These were supplemented by Soldiers Died in the Great War 1914-1919, Ireland's Memorial Records and World War 1 Irish Soldiers - their Final Testament.

Church records and other memorials, monuments and plaques were useful but, in some cases, offered scant or sometimes misleading data. Local and regional newspapers of the period were a rich source of information if not always entirely accurate. Spelling variations of surnames was a particular difficulty. The launch of a web site and the lodging of an initial list in six public libraries across the city began the process of gleaning information. Two public appeals made through, and with the enthusiastic support of, the local press, yielded a wealth of information. The present day citizens of Belfast demonstrated their characteristic generosity by offering, not only information, but the loan of treasured letters, documents and photographs. Sadly, these had to be declined because of the pressure on space. This book is about one third larger than envisaged and the original plan of including personal material had to be abandoned. Otherwise the information would have expanded beyond a single volume.

Some of the entries are very brief, simply verifying the connection with the City. Others are more expansive but an effort has been made to equalize the emphasis on each entry. Some entries have been included which lack burial details or other information if it was thought that the individual did indeed die in the Great War and had an appropriate Belfast connection. The information on officers and winners of bravery awards has been curbed. The default phrase, "Died in War", equates with the notion that the individual died because of enemy action even if the alternative and explicit phrases such as, "Killed in Action" or "Died of Wounds" are not used. Where it is known that someone died as a result of an accident or disease this has been stated. Some nine per cent of deaths on the Western Front were from sickness or accident. The figures for Gallipoli, the Middle East, and Africa are much higher. Also included are those sad episodes when a soldier was executed by firing squad following a Court Martial. These are already a matter of public record but the few references to death by suicide have been removed, in deference to any surviving relatives.

Research into the origins of local World War I deaths also, quite incidentally, offered a glimpse at early twentieth century Belfast society. Many parents of soldiers, and indeed the soldiers themselves, had originated in rural areas and then settled in Belfast in the search for work. It was a time when the linen industry and production engineering, including shipbuilding, employed enormous numbers of young men. It was also a period when families moved house more often than today, sometimes at the frequency of every few months. It is not difficult to imagine households of abject poverty in the cramped mill streets and fetid alleys of the city. Yet what also can also be identified is the emergence of the new and growing, third level educated, professional middle class. Economically confident they were often occupying newly built villas on the leafier fringes of Belfast.

Belfast men served in every Corps and in almost every regiment in the British Army. Overwhelmingly they filled the ranks of Irish regiments. Yet given the economic and family connections with western Scotland, and also the recruiting efforts of Scots units in Belfast, many choose to soldier in the kilt. The Seaforth Highlanders, the Black Watch and the Highland Light Infantry were particularly popular. Again, reflecting traditional links and economic migration, the regiments of Lancashire, Yorkshire, Northumberland and the London area also attracted a number of Belfast soldiers.

Many of the families who had emigrated to Australia, Canada, New Zealand and South Africa produced a significant number of recruits. Some returned home to serve in Irish regiments. Others soldiered with the army of their adopted country. For example, on the great Canadian Memorial at Vimy in Northern France thirty five of the names are of men who had been born in Belfast.

It was the infantry that bore the brunt of the fighting and, accordingly, sustained the bulk of the casualties, over four thousand. The Royal Irish Rifles suffered particularly with over two thousand, three hundred dead. Figures such as these mask the plight of numbed families, sorrowing parents and grieving widows. Even if not explicit it is possible to identify members of the same family, brothers and, in some cases, fathers and sons. Although some young boys did succeed in enlisting illegally the median age, at twenty three, was much higher than often thought. At the time of death 80% of all casualties were aged 21 or over. There were also many soldiers who were mature men in their thirties, forties and even fifties. The Merchant Navy provided the extremes of the age range, from James Erikson at 14 and Henry Grogan at 68.

Then there is, inevitably, the question of religious and political allegiance. This had not been included except in the case of the Canadians where it shown on their enlistment details. However, Belfast readers may choose to make their own deductions from names, addresses, schools and membership of clubs, lodges and societies. Yet the great religious monolithic divide was not entirely exclusive. Over 320 Jews, from all parts of the then United Kingdom served in Irish infantry regiments. By 1918 the small Belfast Hebrew community had 35 men in the forces. These included Arthur Jaffe the son of Sir Otto, the former Lord Mayor of Belfast. The Jewish fighting men were also supported at home. The Belfast Synagogue organized a monthly collection for war charities while mothers, wives and sisters formed the, "Jewish Ladies War Sewing and Knitting Guild".

The motives for joining the forces were as varied as the men themselves. Rich or poor, highly educated or barely literate, Protestant, Catholic, Jewish and those of other faiths or of none, it matters not. All were citizens of our great City of Belfast and are equally deserving of honour.

Acknowledgements

Paddy Harte, with characteristic enthusiasm and dedication set the standard with his book of the war dead of Donegal. This example was followed by several counties, towns and areas of local government, both north and south. This is the latest, as well as the largest, of these projects.

Sir Kenneth Bloomfield, chairman of the Belfast Book of Honour Committee was the driving force throughout the entire undertaking. I would thank him for his support, understanding and forbearance. The Committee was equally resolute in its purpose. The Secretary of the Committee, Ian Elliott, Chief Executive of Oaklee Housing, was unfailingly helpful, resourceful and patient. The Communications Manager of Oaklee, Brian McKenna, demonstrated great tolerance in dealing with one with such lamentable computer skills. This was also true of his staff, Gerry Ward and Majella Boyd as well as the IT consultant, Dominic Griffith.

I should like to thank all those who contributed in any way in the preparation of this book. These include Valerie Adams of the Public Record Office of Northern Ireland, Jim Adamson, Desmond Blackadder of the Ballymena Times, Martin Brennan of Cookstown, Tom Burke MBE of the Royal Dublin Fusiliers Association, Oliver Fallon and Frank Higgins of the Connaught Rangers Association, Hazel Francey of Belfast City Council, Sheila Gallagher, Keith Haines formerly of Campbell College, Donal Hall of Dundalk, Steven Jaffe of the Belfast Jewish Community, Captain (Retd) Jaki Knox MBE and Terence Nelson of the Royal Ulster Rifles Museum, Philip Lee, Amanda Marino of the Royal Irish Fusiliers Association, John McVicar of the Shankill Mirror, Sir Robert Porter QC, Robin Sadlier OBE, Carol Walker and Noel Kane of the Somme Heritage Centre, Mary Wilmont and Mrs Jackie Withers of the Commonwealth War Grave Comission.

Colin Moffett of Newry and Mourne Council gave valuable early guidance and Billy Donald and Gerry Ward produced some quite excellent photographs. Karen Fitzmaurice of Johnston Press was unfailingly helpful in preparing the work for publication and Joel Byers, also of Johnston Press, contributed his considerable skill in designing the volume. Billy Ervine, formerly of the Somme Heritage Centre, was kind enough to offer sound advice and to examine parts of the work. Dr Richard Grayson, Head of Politics at Goldsmiths College London, most generously shared his early research for his forthcoming major book on West Belfast. James W Taylor, the military historian from Wexford contributed, quite selflessly, not only his deep knowledge of the subject but also research materials and, without complaint, months of his free time. Numerous other people kindly contributed and to all of them I am deeply grateful.

Most of all I would thank my wife, Brenda Smyth, who sustained me throughout every stage of the work and without whom this book would not have been possible. The work on this volume has been a truly collaborative effort. Nevertheless, errors and omissions are, and will remain, mine.

Derek Smyth, Belfast

March 2009

Journey of Remembering

Abbott, Vivian Hartley Church - Private
646187 Canadian Infantry (British Columbia Regiment) "D" Company 29th Battalion
Age 36 Died in War on 21 August 1917
VIMY MEMORIAL, France
Son of the Venerable the late Archdeacon of Clogher, Ireland, and his wife, the late Charlotte E. Church; husband of Eleanor Bell Abbott (née Riddell), of 51, Myrtlefield Park, Belfast.
Former student at Trinity College Dublin.

Abernethy, John - Rifleman
60 Royal Irish Rifles 15th Battalion *Killed in Action on 11 June 1916*
HAMEL MILITARY CEMETERY, BEAUMONT-HAMEL, France
Born and enlisted in Belfast.

Abraham, Sydney Herbert - Corporal
16803 Royal Irish Rifles 1st Battalion *Age 20 Killed in Action on 7 February 1916*
RUE-DU-BOIS MILITARY CEMETERY, FLEURBAIX, France
Son of Charlotte Browne (formerly Abraham), of 4, Zetland Street, Belfast. Native of Nenagh, County Tipperary.

Ackinson, Robert - Rifleman
40201 Royal Irish Rifles 2nd Battalion *Age 32 Killed in Action on 22 October 1918*
TYNE COT MEMORIAL, Belgium
Son of Thomas and Phoebe Ackinson, of 46, Lawther Street, Belfast. Formerly R/21548 King's Royal Rifle Corps.

Adair, Alexander - Private
241194 Seaforth Highlanders 1/5th Battalion *Age 23 Died in War on 15 March 1918*
GREVILLERS BRITISH CEMETERY, France
Son of Alexander and Jane Adair, of 31, Comber Street, Belfast.

Adair, Francis - Rifleman
5766 Royal Irish Rifles 2nd Battalion *Killed in Action on 22 August 1916*
LONSDALE CEMETERY AUTHUILE, France
14 Wimbledon Street, Belfast. A member of Agnes Street Presbyterian Church.

Adair, Hugh - Trooper
11/959 Wellington Mounted Rifles New Zealand Expeditionary Force *Died in War on 3 October 1915*
PIETA MILITARY CEMETERY, Malta
Member of Cooke Centenary Presbyterian Church. Son of Hugh and Mary Adair of Spring Hill, Bangor.

Adair, John - Private
27699 Wiltshire Regiment Depot *Age 23 Died as a result of war on 13 March 1919*
BELFAST CITY CEMETERY, United Kingdom
A factory worker and the son of Robert Hunter Adair, 84 Brussels Street, Belfast and the late Elizabeth Adair.

Adair, John Thomas - Lieutenant
Bedfordshire Regiment attached 1st Battalion Border Regiment *Age 31 Buried at sea on 22 August 1915*
HELLES MEMORIAL, Turkey
A factory manager. Son of Mrs. Elizabeth Adair, of 2, Century Street, Belfast.

Adair, Robert - Sergeant
9204 Royal Irish Rifles 2nd Battalion *Killed in Action on 25 October 1914*
LE TOURET MEMORIAL, France
1 Great Patrick Street, Belfast. Member of Clifton Street Presbyterian Church.

JOURNEY OF REMEMBERING

Adair, Robert James - Rifleman
8955 Royal Irish Rifles 2nd Battalion *Age 24 Killed in Action on 11 November 1914*
YPRES (MENIN GATE) MEMORIAL, Belgium
Son of Robert Hunter Adair, of 84, Brussels Street, Belfast, and the late Elizabeth Adair. A building labourer.

Adair, Robert Moore - Rifleman
509 Royal Irish Rifles 8th Battalion *Killed in Action on 7 June 1917*
YPRES (MENIN GATE) MEMORIAL, Belgium
8 Elizabeth Street, Belfast.

Adair, William - Rifleman
5\5481 Royal Irish Rifles 7th Battalion *Age 23 Died in War on 9 September 1916*
LA NEUVILLE BRITISH CEMETERY, CORBIE, France
Son of Mrs. Adair, of 15, Cromwell Street, Belfast.

Adams, Adolphus - Rifleman
13945 Royal Irish Rifles 15th Battalion *Age 21 Died in War on 2 May 1918*
BAILLEUL COMMUNAL CEMETERY EXTENSION (NORD), France
Son of Mary Ann Robinson (formerly Adams), of 49, Lisburn Road, Belfast, and the late James Adams.

Adams, Albert - Rifleman
13944 Royal Irish Rifles 8th Battalion *Killed in Action on 4 August 1916*
BAILLEUL COMMUNAL CEMETERY EXTENSION (NORD), France
Born in Belfast.

Adams, Charles - Rifleman
13969 Royal Irish Rifles 14th Battalion *Age 19 Killed in Action on 1 July 1916*
THIEPVAL MEMORIAL, France
Son of Mary Ann Robinson (formerly Adams), of 49, Lisburn Road, Belfast, and the late James Adams.

Adams, Charles - Rifleman
1990 Royal Irish Rifles 2nd Battalion *Killed in Action on 14 October 1914*
LE TOURET MEMORIAL, France
22 Osman Street, Belfast.

Adams, Dominick - Private
2904 Royal Inniskilling Fusiliers 2nd Battalion *Died in War on 16 May 1915*
LE TOURET MEMORIAL, France
Son of David and Elizabeth Adams, of 12, Varna Street, Belfast.

Adams, Edward - Rifleman
16158 Royal Irish Rifles 14th Battalion *Killed in Action on 6 May 1916*
AUTHUILE MILITARY CEMETERY, France
32 Cullingtree Street, Belfast. Killed by shrapnel in the trench. He was survived by his sister, Nellie.
An Orangeman and a Mason he was also a member of the Young Citizen Volunteers.

Adams, Edward - Rifleman
7944 Royal Irish Rifles 2nd Battalion *Killed in Action on 14 October 1914*
LE TOURET MEMORIAL, France
Son of John Adams, of the 3rd Battalion Leinster Regiment and of 13, Plevna Street, Belfast.
He also had a brother serving with the Royal Army Medical Corps. A reservist, he had previously worked in Gallaher's Tobacco Factory.

Journey of Remembering

Adams, Ernest - Private
22623 Royal Inniskilling Fusiliers "D" Company 9th Battalion *Age 22 Killed in Action on 1 July 1916*
THIEPVAL MEMORIAL, France
Son of Charles J. and Mary Adams, of 21, Willowfield Drive, Belfast. One of the first to enlist in 1914.

Adams, George - Rifleman
12497 Royal Irish Rifles 8th Battalion *Died in War on 2 July 1916*
THIEPVAL MEMORIAL, France
8 Witham Street, Belfast.

Adams, James - Private
59790 Royal Army Medical Corps 36th Field Ambulance *Age 19 Died in War on 30 August 1918*
DAOURS COMMUNAL CEMETERY EXTENSION, France
Son of William J. and Fanny Adams, of 31, Third Avenue, Strandtown, Belfast.

Adams, James Alexander - Lance Corporal
3694 Royal Inniskilling Fusiliers "D" Company 1st Battalion *Age 18 Killed in Action on 11 June 1916*
BEAUVAL COMMUNAL CEMETERY, France
Son of William and Mary Jane Adams, of 34, Lime Street, Belfast.

Adams, John - Driver
119855 Royal Horse Artillery and Royal Field Artillery *Died in War on 11 August 1917*
BELGIUM BATTERY CORNER CEMETERY, France
Born and enlisted in Belfast.

Adams, John - Rifleman
9249 Royal Irish Rifles 1st Battalion *Age 32 Killed in Action on 9 May 1915*
PLOEGSTEERT MEMORIAL, Belgium
Son of David and Elizabeth Adams, of 12, Varna Street, Belfast.

Adams, Joseph - Rifleman
10025 Royal Irish Rifles 2nd Battalion *Killed in Action on 6 September 1918*
MESSINES RIDGE BRITISH CEMETERY, Belgium
Son of John and Ellen Adams, of 16, Keegan Street, Belfast.

Adams, Samuel - Private
63065 Canadian Infantry (Central Ontario Regiment) 4th Battalion *Age 34 Died in War on 8 October 1916*
VIMY MEMORIAL, France
Son of the late Samuel and Eliza Adams, of 82, Shankill Road, Belfast; husband of
Theodosia Johns (formerly Adams), of 1313, Third Street, Estevan, Saskatchewan, Canada.

Adams, William Hanna - Corporal
40635 Royal Inniskilling Fusiliers "B" Company 10th Battalion *Age 30 Died in War on 8 August 1917*
YPRES (MENIN GATE) MEMORIAL, Belgium
Son of John Adams, of Strandtown, Belfast; husband of Maggie Adams, of Brook Street, Coleraine.

Adamson, George - Private
6105 Royal Irish Fusiliers 1st Battalion *Died in War on 1 November 1917*
YPRES (MENIN GATE) MEMORIAL, Belgium
Son of Robert and Melissa Adamson of Portadown. A resident of Belfast.

Adderley, Lee - Gunner
Royal Garrison Artillery *Died of sickness contracted on active service on 25 May 1918*
Survived by his wife Mary and children. 39 Servia Street, Belfast.

Addis, Henry - Rifleman
17126 Royal Irish Rifles 11th Battalion *Age 21 Died in War on 8 June 1917*
BAILLEUL COMMUNAL CEMETERY EXTENSION NORD, France
Born in Derriaghy, enlisted Lisburn and resident Belfast. A labourer, he was the grandson of Edward Addis, Derriaghy, a farmer.

Addison, Robert - Private
50842 Royal Army Medical Corps 108th Field Ambulance *Age 23 Killed in Action at Lindenhoek on 7 June 1917*
DRANOUTRE MILITARY CEMETERY, Belgium
Son of William and Ellen Addison, of 87, Grove Street East, Belfast. Enlisted January 1915.

Addley, W J - Lance Corporal
64342 Royal Engineers Training Centre (Newark) *Age 32 Died in War on 1 November 1917*
BELFAST CITY CEMETERY, United Kingdom
Husband of Florence Addley, of 5, Majestic Street, Belfast.

Adrain, William Kearns - Second Lieutenant
Royal Irish Regiment 5th Battalion Attached 1st Battalion Royal Irish Rifles *Age 20 Killed in Action on 24 August 1916*
VERMELLES BRITISH CEMETERY, France
Son of Robert and Jane Adrian. Educated at the Model School and RBAI and a member of Queen's University Officer Training Corps. Reported to have been killed whilst digging out soldiers who had been buried in the debris of an artillery attack.

Agar, John - Rifleman
17/789 Royal Irish Rifles "A" Company 15th Battalion *Age 26 Died in War on 1 October 1918*
DADIZEELE NEW BRITISH CEMETERY, Belgium
Son of Margaret Agar, of 81, Northbrook Street, Lisburn Road, Belfast, and Andrew Agar.

Agnew, Alexander - Fireman And Trimmer
Mercantile Marine S.S. "Madura" (Glasgow)
Age 47 Drowned, as a result of an attack by enemy submarine in the English Channel on 18 October 1917
TOWER HILL MEMORIAL, United Kingdom
Son of Martha Agnew (née Brown), of 9, Seaview Street, Belfast, and the late John Agnew; Born in Belfast.

Agnew, George - Rifleman
1372 Royal Irish Rifles 10th Battalion *Died in War on 22 November 1917*
CAMBRAI MEMORIAL LOUVERVAL, France
Born Ballyclare, Resident of Belfast.

Agnew, James - Leading Stoker
308866 Royal Navy HMS "Indefatigable" *Age 29 Killed in Action at the Battle of Jutland on 31 May 1916*
CHATHAM NAVAL MEMORIAL, United Kingdom
Son of Martha Agnew, of Seaview Street, Belfast, and John Agnew.

Agnew, James - Rifleman
42470 Royal Irish Rifles 14th Battalion *Age 19 Killed in Action on 16 August 1917*
TYNE COT MEMORIAL, Belgium
Son of Samuel and Maria Agnew, of 147, Dee Street, Belfast.

Agnew, James - Rifleman
5037 Royal Irish Rifles 7th Battalion *Killed in Action on 16 August 1917*
TYNE COT MEMORIAL, Belgium
Born in Belfast and enlisted in Lisburn.

Agnew, John - Rifleman
587 Royal Irish Rifles 9th Battalion *Killed in Action on 1 July 1916*
THIEPVAL MEMORIAL, France
Born and enlisted in Belfast.

Agnew, Joseph McCann - Rifleman
16 Royal Irish Rifles 10th Battalion *Age 19 Killed in Action on 1 July 1916*
THIEPVAL MEMORIAL, France
Son of James Graham Agnew and Elizabeth Agnew, of 19, Ravenscroft Street, Belfast.
A month later his brother, William, was killed with the Seaforth Highlanders.

Agnew, Kenneth Malcolm - Rifleman
20459 Royal Irish Rifles 1st Battalion *Died as a Prisoner of War on 25 June 1918*
HAMBURG CEMETERY, Germany
Born in Belfast. Lived in Philadelphia USA before enlisting.

Agnew, Nathaniel - Stoker First Class
SS/105083 Royal Navy HMS "Hawke" *Age 26 Died in War on 15 October 1914*
CHATHAM NAVAL MEMORIAL, United Kingdom
Son of Nathaniel and Elizabeth Agnew, of 18, Westminster Avenue, Belfast. Signed the Covenant in 1912.
His brother, William, a soldier, also fell.

Agnew, Thomas Rainey - Stoker First Class
SS/113435 Royal Navy HMS "Vanguard" *Age 25 Died in War on 9 October 1917*
CHATHAM NAVAL MEMORIAL, United Kingdom
Son of Samuel and Dorothy Agnew, of 138, Spamount Street, Belfast.

Agnew, William - Rifleman
903 Royal Irish Rifles 15th Battalion *Age 41 Died as a POW on 5 August 1918*
BERLIN SOUTH-WESTERN CEMETERY, Germany
Son of Nathaniel and Elizabeth Agnew, of 18, Westminster Avenue, Strandtown, Belfast. His brother, a sailor, also fell.

Agnew, William - Private
4150 Seaforth Highlanders 5th Battalion *Age 23 Killed in Action on 2 August 1916*
THIEPVAL MEMORIAL, France
Son of James Graham Agnew and Elizabeth Agnew, of 19, Ravenscroft Street, Belfast.
His brother, Joseph, had been killed a month earlier, on the first day of the Somme.

Agnew, William - Rifleman
19372 Royal Irish Rifles 14th Battalion *Killed in Action on 1 July 1916*
THIEPVAL MEMORIAL, France
21 Ulsterville Street, Belfast.

Agnew, William - Rifleman
8204 Royal Irish Rifles 2nd Battalion *Died in War on 19 November 1914*
LE MANS WEST CEMETERY, France
Born and enlisted in Belfast.

Aiken, James - Fireman And Trimmer
Mercantile Marine S.S. "Artist" (Liverpool) *Age 30 Drowned, as a result of an attack by an enemy submarine on 27 January 1917*
TOWER HILL MEMORIAL, *United Kingdom*
Husband of Hannah Aiken of 30, Bridgewater Street, Liverpool. Born in Belfast.

Aiken, James - Rifleman
12504 Royal Irish Rifles 15th Battalion *Age 22 Killed in Action on 20 January 1916*
SUCRERIE MILITARY CEMETERY, COLINCAMPS, *France*
Son of Eliza Aitken, of 22, Ayr Street, Belfast, and John Aiken.

Aiken, Samuel - Private
5723 Royal Irish Regiment Depot *Age 33 Died of pneumonia on 24 March 1919*
BELFAST CITY CEMETERY, *United Kingdom*
Son of William and Margaret Aiken of Belfast.

Aiken, Walter Edmond - Private
3396 Royal Inniskilling Fusiliers 7th Battalion *Died in War on 9 September 1916*
THIEPVAL MEMORIAL, *France*
14 Ardiluan Street, Belfast.

Aikin, David - Private
880497 Canadian Infantry (Western Ontario Regiment) 18th Battalion *Age 24 Died in War on 21 August 1917*
AIX-NOULETTE COMMUNAL CEMETERY EXTENSION, *France*
Son of David and Jane Aikin; husband of Myrtle Fitzpatrick Loop (formerly Aikin),
of Wheatley, Ontario, Canada. Born in Belfast, Ireland.

Ainslie, John Ellist - Second Lieutenant
Royal Scots 12th (Service) Battalion *Age 19 Killed in Action on 28 September 1915*
LOOS MEMORIAL, *France*
Son of Rev W J Ainslie, a Congregational minister, and his wife Sara.
Born in Belfast and killed at the Battle of Loos.

Aitcheson, Thomas - Private
18391 Machine Gun Corps (Infantry) *Died in War on 23 October 1917*
DOCHY FARM NEW BRITISH CEMETERY, *Belgium*
Born in Belfast, enlisted Musselburgh, Scotland. Formerly 13548, Royal Scots.

Albert, Barry - Private
10130 Royal Dublin Fusiliers 1st Battalion *Died in War on 25 August 1915*
V BEACH CEMETERY, *Turkey*
Brother of Mary Barry, 13 Warren Street, Belfast.

Albin, Albert - Private
6445 Sherwood Foresters (Nottinghamshire and Derbyshire Regiment) 2nd Battalion
Died in War on 26 December 1915
LIJSSENTHOEK MILITARY CEMETERY, *Belgium*
Born in Richhill, County Armagh, resident of Belfast.

Alderdice, Norman - Private
G/6613 Queen's (Royal West Surrey Regiment) 6th Battalion *Died in War on 12 May 1917*
ARRAS MEMORIAL, *France*
Born in Belfast, enlisted in Guildford, Surrey.

Alderdice, William - Rifleman
3 Royal Irish Rifles 9th Battalion *Killed in Action on 1 July 1916*
MILL ROAD CEMETERY, THIEPVAL, *France*
Born and enlisted in Belfast.

Alexander, James - Drummer
9332 Royal Inniskilling Fusiliers 1st Battalion *Killed in Action on 21 August 1915*
GREEN HILL CEMETERY, *Turkey*
Born in Belfast.

Alexander, Joseph - Private
22807 Royal Inniskilling Fusiliers 9th Battalion *Killed in Action on 1 July 1916*
THIEPVAL MEMORIAL, *France*
Born and enlisted in Belfast.

Alexander, Samuel - Private
2358 Connaught Rangers "C" Company 6th Battalion *Age 23 Killed in Action on 16 August 1917*
TYNE COT MEMORIAL, *Belgium*
Son of Robert Hugh and Jane Alexander, of 106, Butler Street, Belfast; husband of Catherine Alexander, of 54, Butler Street, Belfast.

Alexander, Samuel Hill - Private
23362 Cameronians (Scottish Rifles) 3rd Battalion *Age 40 Died as a result of war on 1 March 1920*
BOTHWELL (BELLSHILL) CEMETERY, *United Kingdom*
Son of Thomas and Mary Alexander; husband of Mary Morran Alexander, of 27, Douglas Place, Bothwellhaugh, Glasgow. Born at Belfast.

Allan, George - Private
6140 Queen's Own Cameron Highlanders 2nd Battalion *Died in War on 23 April 1915*
YPRES (MENIN GATE MEMORIAL), *Belgium*
Born in Belfast, enlisted in Glasgow.

Allely, George - Rifleman
18852 Royal Irish Rifles 13th Battalion *Died in War on 18 October 1917*
ROCQUIGNY-EQUANCOURT ROAD BRITISH CEMETERY, MANANCOURT, *France*
Born in Belfast, enlisted in Newry.

Allely, William - Private
145474 Canadian Infantry (Western Ontario Regiment) 47th Battalion *Died in War on 21 August 1917*
VIMY MEMORIAL, *France*
His mother-in-law lived at 331 Donegall Road, Belfast.

Allely, William - Sergeant
4843 Royal Irish Rifles 2nd Battalion *Age 32 Killed in Action on 5 January 1916*
TANCREZ FARM CEMETERY, *Belgium*
Son of Mrs. Mary E. Allely, of Belfast, and the late William Allely; husband of Agnes Ann Allely, of 104, Saunders Street, Belfast.

Allen, Alexander - Boatswain (Bosun)
Mercantile Marine S.S. "Taplow" (London) *Age 59 Presumed drowned on 5 June 1917*
TOWER HILL MEMORIAL, *United Kingdom*
Son of the late Robert and Mary Allen; husband of Letitia Allen (née Armstrong), of 8, Northam Street, Southampton. Born at Belfast.

Allen, Alexander - Private
13077 Royal Irish Fusiliers "A" Company 7th Battalion *Age 22 Died in War on 9 September 1916*
THIEPVAL MEMORIAL, *France*
Son of Mrs. Margaret Allen, of 54, Clementine Street, Belfast.

Allen, Campbell - Private
350466 Highland Light Infantry 18th Battalion (4th Glasgow) *Died in War on 26 October 1917*
TYNE COT MEMORIAL, *Belgium*
Born in Belfast, enlisted Glasgow.

Allen, Charles - Private
1535 Irish Guards 1st Battalion *Died in War on 18 November 1914*
YPRES (MENIN GATE), *Belgium*
Born in Belfast. Lived in Ballymena, County Antrim, when enlisted.

Allen, George - Lance Corporal
17447 Queen's Own Cameron Highlanders 5th Battalion *Died in War on 11 July 1916*
THIEPVAL MEMORIAL, *France*
Born in Belfast, enlisted in Chester, Cheshire.

Allen, George - Private
23847 Royal Inniskilling Fusiliers 9th Battalion *Killed in Action on 16 August 1917*
BRANDHOEK NEW MILITARY CEMETERY, *Belgium*
Resident of Belfast he lived at 62 Glenwood Street. The son of William and Rebecca Allen of Londonderry.

Allen, Henry - Boy First Class
J/34509 Royal Navy HMS "Black Prince" *Age 15 Killed in Action at the Battle of Jutland on 31 May 1916*
PLYMOUTH NAVAL MEMORIAL, *United Kingdom*
Son of Samuel and Margaret Allen, of Belfast.

Allen, Hugh - Rifleman
11457 Royal Irish Rifles 1st Battalion *Age 37 Died in War on 22 March 1916*
SAILLY-SUR-LA-LYS CANADIAN CEMETERY, *France*
Son of James and Margaret Allen, of Belfast.

Allen, Hugh Charles - Second Lieutenant
Black Watch (Royal Highlanders) 1st/7th Battalion *Age 27 Died in War on 23 April 1917*
BROWN'S COPSE CEMETERY, ROEUX, *France*
Son of Hugh Allen and the late Charlotte Allen of Belfast. Awarded the Distinguished Conduct Medal.

Allen, James - Rifleman
11633 Royal Irish Rifles 15th Battalion *Age 42 Died in War on 28 June 1916*
BELFAST (DUNDONALD) CEMETERY, *United Kingdom*
Son of Samuel Allen; husband of Mary Ann Allen of 81, Fortingale Street, Belfast. Born in Coleraine.

Allen, John - Regimental Sergeant Major
724001 Canadian Infantry 124th Battalion *Age 36 Died in War on 9 August 1918*
LINDSAY (RIVERSIDE) CEMETERY, *Canada*
Son of Mrs. Ellen Aitken, of 22, St. Leonard Street, Belfast, Ireland; husband of Clara Helen Allen, of 68, Adelaide Street South, Lindsay, Ontario, Canada.

Allen, James - Private
17152 Royal Dublin Fusiliers 2nd Battalion *Age 39 Died in War on 27 October 1918*
THIEPVAL MEMORIAL, *France*
Brother of Mrs Charlotte Moore, of Glenrosa House, Glenrosa Street South, Belfast.

Allen, James - Private
7648 Royal Inniskilling Fusiliers 3rd Battalion *Age 34 Died as a result of war on 6 March 1919*
KNOCKBREDA CHURCH OF IRELAND CHURCHYARD, *United Kingdom*
Son of James Allen; husband of Lena Allen, of 51, Rathmore Street, Belfast.

Allen, James - Private
S/10160 Princess Louise's (Argyll & Sutherland Highlanders) 11th Battalion *Died in War on 29 March 1918*
AUBIGNY COMMUNAL CEMETERY EXTENSION, *France*
Born in Belfast, enlisted Newtowngrange, Scotland.

Allen, James - Rifleman
8731 Royal Irish Rifles 1st Battalion *Killed in Action on 16 August 1917*
TYNE COT MEMORIAL, *Belgium*
Born in Belfast, enlisted in Ballykinler, County Down.

Allen, James Giffin - Private
7563 Princess Victoria's (Royal Irish Fusiliers) 1st Battalion *Killed in Action on 16 February 1917*
FINS NEW BRITISH CEMETERY, SOREL-LE-GRAND, *France*
Born and enlisted in Belfast.

Allen, John - Rifleman
3409 Royal Irish Rifles 15th Battalion *Age 24 Died in War on 2 November 1916*
BAILLEUL COMMUNAL CEMETERY EXTENSION (NORD), *France*
Husband of Elizabeth Allen, of 14, Haddow Street, Belfast.

Allen, Robert - Rifleman
17143 Royal Irish Rifles 13th Battalion *Killed in Action on 1 July 1916*
THIEPVAL MEMORIAL, *France*
Born in Belfast, enlisted in Comber, County Down.

Allen, Robert Henry - Private
DM2/221143 Army Service Corps Mechanical Transport Training Depot
Age 26 Died in War on 23 May 1917
BELFAST (DUNDONALD) CEMETERY, *United Kingdom*
Son of John T. and Sarah E. Allen, of 47, Woodcot Avenue, Bloomfield, Belfast.

Allen, Samuel - Rifleman
18/1199 Royal Irish Rifles "A" Company 12th Battalion *Age 34 Died in War on 7 March 1917*
ST. QUENTIN CABARET MILITARY CEMETERY, *Belgium*
Son of Edward and Mary Allen, of Lisburn; husband of Agnes Boyd (formerly Allen),
of 39, Ardoyne Road, Belfast.

Allen, Thomas James - Private
S/21822 Gordon Highlanders 1st Battalion *Age 19 Died in War on 27 September 1916*
LOWRIE CEMETERY, HAVRINCOURT, *France*
Son of James and Mary Allen, of 17, South Bridge Street, St. Andrews. Native of Belfast.

Allen, Thomas Joseph - Rifleman
3978 Royal Irish Rifles 8th Battalion *Age 38 Died in War on 2 July 1916*
THIEPVAL MEMORIAL, France
Husband of Margaret Allen, of 50, Spring Street, Belfast. Holder of the Military Medal.

Allison, Frederick Herbert - Rifleman
11079 Royal Irish Rifles 2nd Battalion *Died in War on 30 September 1918*
DADIZEELE NEW BRITISH CEMETERY, Belgium
Born and enlisted in Belfast.

Allison, George - Private
25251 Royal Inniskilling Fusiliers 10th Battalion *Age 20 Killed in Action on 10 September 1916*
POND FARM CEMETERY, Belgium
Son of James Allison, of 7, Skipton Street, Belfast.

Allister, David - Sapper
357995 Corps of Royal Engineers *Died in War on 15 February 1918*
HAM BRITISH CEMETERY, MUILLE-VILLETTE, France
Born and enlisted in Belfast. Formerly 12521, Royal Irish Regiment.

Allman, George - Corporal
8568 Cheshire Regiment 1st Battalion *Died in War on 16 November 1914*
YPRES (MENIN GATE) MEMORIAL, Belgium
Husband of Kathleen Allman, of 181, Leopold Street, Belfast.

Allsopp, Matthew - Rifleman
2739 Royal Irish Rifles 14th Battalion *Shot while saving a wounded comrade on 1 November 1916*
POND FARM CEMETERY, Belgium
Son of William, (who also served), and S. A. Allsopp, 6 Sancroft Street Belfast.

Amos, Harry - Corporal
28279 Royal Welsh Fusiliers 19th Battalion *Died in War on 25 December 1917*
CROISILLES RAILWAY CEMETERY, France
Born in Belfast enlisted in Wallasey, Cheshire.

Anderson, Benjamin - Rifleman
588 Royal Irish Rifles 9th Battalion *Killed in Action on 1 July 1916*
THIEPVAL MEMORIAL, France
Husband of Annie Anderson, of 113, Mountcollyer Road, Belfast.

Anderson, Bowie - Private
7257 Royal Inniskilling Fusiliers 2nd Battalion *Age 33 Died of Wounds on 17 November 1914*
CITE BONJEAN MILITARY CEMETERY, ARMENTIERES, France
Son of James and Margaret Anderson; husband of Elizabeth Anderson, of 3, Paris Street, Belfast.

Anderson, David - Private
12085 Royal Irish Fusiliers 5th Battalion *Died of Wounds on 10 August 1915*
HELLES MEMORIAL, Turkey
61 Berlin Street. One brother served in the Royal Navy and another in the 2nd Inniskilling Fusiliers.

Anderson, Edward - Private
5246 Royal Munster Fusiliers 7th Battalion *Died in War on 21 August 1915*
HELLES MEMORIAL, *Turkey*
Born and enlisted in Belfast. Formerly 12960 Royal Inniskilling Fusiliers.

Anderson, Edward - Rifleman
7778 Royal Irish Rifles 2nd Battalion *Killed in Action on 7 July 1916*
THIEPVAL MEMORIAL, *France*
Born Ballymacarrett, Belfast.

Anderson, George - Rifleman
1815 Royal Irish Rifles 10th Battalion *Died of Wounds on 1 July 1916*
THIEPVAL MEMORIAL, *France*
Survived by his mother at 24 Crosby Street, Belfast.

Anderson, Heaney - Private
23813 Royal Dublin Fusiliers 4th Battalion *Died of Wounds on 23 October 1916*
DARTMOOR CEMETERY, BECORDEL-BECOURT, *France*
Son of Mrs. Mary Anderson, of 248, Upper Meadow Street Belfast.

Anderson, Henry McDonnell - Lieutenant
Northumberland Fusiliers 5th Battalion *Died in War on 30 May 1918*
BAGNEUX BRITISH CEMETERY, GEZAINCOURT, *France*
Fitzwilliam Street, Belfast. Born in Portaferry, the son of John and Mary Anderson. Awarded the Military Cross.

Anderson, Hugh - Lance Corporal
17/706 Royal Irish Rifles 15th Battalion *Died of Wounds on 4 July 1916*
PUCHEVILLERS BRITISH CEMETERY, *France*
Holder of the Military Medal, the son of William and Jane Anderson of Belfast.

Anderson, Hugh - Rifleman
20 Royal Irish Rifles 14th Battalion *Age 20 Killed in Action on 1 July 1916*
THIEPVAL MEMORIAL, *France*
Son of Mrs. Margaret Kelly, of 25, Derry Street, Belfast.

Anderson, James - Private
1009021 Canadian Infantry 46th Battalion *Killed in Action on 26 October 1917*
YPRES (MENIN GATE) MEMORIAL, *Belgium*
Son of Jane Anderson, of 38, Broadway Road, Belfast, and the late William Anderson.

Anderson, James - Sailor
Mercantile Marine S.S. "Cheviot Range" (West Hartlepool)
Age 28 Drowned as a result of an attack by an enemy submarine on 21 February 1918
TOWER HILL MEMORIAL, *United Kingdom*
Son of James Anderson; husband of Elizabeth Ann Anderson (née Wiseman), of 11, Stanhope Street, Sunderland. Born at Belfast

Anderson, James - Sapper
253905 Corps of Royal Engineers *Died in War on 1 November 1918*
ST SEVER CEMETERY EXTENSION, ROUEN, *France*
Born and enlisted in Larne. Resident of Belfast. Formerly 100817, Royal Field Artillery.

Anderson, James Hill - Corporal
16842 Royal Inniskilling Fusiliers 11th Battalion *Killed in Action on 1 July 1916*
MILL ROAD CEMETERY, THIEPVAL, *France*
Born in Belfast, enlisted in Finner Camp, County Donegal.

Anderson, James Joseph - Private
7426 Royal Inniskilling Fusiliers 2nd Battalion *Killed in Action on 20 October 1914*
PLOEGSTEERT MEMORIAL, *Belgium*
Born in Belfast.

Anderson, James Walker - Private
13334 Cameronians (Scottish Rifles) 10th Battalion *Died in War on 12 May 1916*
LOOS MEMORIAL, *France*
Born in Belfast. Enlisted in Clydebank, Scotland.

Anderson, John - Private
13581 Royal Scots Fusiliers 7th Battalion *Died in War on 26 September 1915*
LOOS MEMORIAL, *France*
Born in Belfast. Enlisted in Kilwinning, Ayr, Scotland.

Anderson, Richard - Private
3430 Royal Inniskilling Fusiliers 2nd Battalion *Age 19 Died in War on 16 May 1915*
LE TOURET MEMORIAL, *France*
Cousin of Catherine Mulholland, of 22, Edith Street, Belfast.

Anderson, Robert - Private
10382 Royal Inniskilling Fusiliers 2nd Battalion *Age 19 Died in War on 31 October 1914*
PLOEGSTEERT MEMORIAL, *Belgium*
Son of Mrs. Mary Anderson, of 15, Chatsworth Street, Belfast.

Anderson, Robert - Private
16153 Royal Irish Rifles 9th Battalion *Killed in Action on 1 July 1916*
THIEPVAL MEMORIAL, *France*
He was the son of Sergeant R Anderson, also on active service.

Anderson, Robert - Private
4662 Royal Inniskilling Fusiliers 1st Battalion *Age 18 Died in War on 20 November 1917*
CAMBRAI MEMORIAL, LOUVERVAL, *France*
Son of William and Agnes Anderson, of 3, Foxglove Street, Belfast.

Anderson, Robert - Rifleman
G/3562 Royal Irish Rifles 9th Battalion *Age 26 Died in War on 8 August 1917*
LIJSSENTHOEK MILITARY CEMETERY, *Belgium*
Son of William and Mary Anderson, of 15, Connswater Street, Belfast.

Anderson, Robert - Stoker First Class
K/28798 Royal Navy HMS "Pembroke" *Killed in an air raid on 3 September 1917*
GILLINGHAM (WOODLANDS) CEMETERY, *United Kingdom*
25 Ghent Street, Belfast. Was an Army Reservist called up when the war broke out. He went through the battles of Mons and the Marne unscathed. He completed his time, and instead of re-enlisting in the Army he joined the Navy. He served on mine sweeper and patrol boats, and was at least three times torpedoed.

Anderson, Robert George Kyle McCloud - Company Quartermaster Sergeant
186969 Royal Engineers 570th Army Troops Company *Age 27 Died of pneumonia on 19 January 1920*
HAIFA WAR CEMETERY, Israel
Son of R. G. and T. Anderson; husband of E. A. Anderson, of 58, Pearson Street, Queen's Road, Manchester. Born in Belfast

Anderson, Thomas - Lance Corporal
9398 Royal Irish Rifles 1st Battalion *Died in War on 10 March 1915*
LE TOURET MEMORIAL, France
Son of Agnes Anderson 31 Clonallan Street, Belfast.

Anderson, William - Private
21099 Royal Irish Fusiliers 7/8th Battalion *Age 19 Died in War on 8 August 1917*
YPRES (MENIN GATE) MEMORIAL, Belgium
Son of William and Mary Ellen Anderson, of 214, Leeson Street, Belfast. Enlisted along with his brother James. Mentioned in Despatches twice for brave conduct.

Anderson, William - Rifleman
12512 Royal Irish Rifles 14th Battalion *Died in War on 26 March 1918*
POZIERES MEMORIAL, France
Born and enlisted in Belfast.

Andison, James Stewart - Private
6902 King's Own Scottish Borderers 4th Battalion *Age 24 Died in War on 12 July 1915*
LANCASHIRE LANDING CEMETERY, Turkey
Son of Thomas B. and Jane Andison, of 230, Cliftonville Road, Belfast. Native of Galashiels, Scotland.

Andrews, David - Lance Corporal
16168 Royal Irish Rifles 14th Battalion *Killed in Action on 16 August 1917*
TYNE COT MEMORIAL, Belgium
Born and enlisted in Belfast.

Andrews, Hugh - Lance Corporal
1179 Royal Irish Rifles 8th Battalion *Age 21 Died in War on 2 July 1916*
THIEPVAL MEMORIAL, France
A bobbin turner and Plymouth Brethren, he was the son of Ellen Andrews, 23 Tobergill Street, Belfast.

Andrews, James - Rifleman
9980 Royal Irish Rifles 1st Battalion *Died in War on 8 June 1918*
THIEPVAL MEMORIAL, France
Born and enlisted in Belfast.

Andrews, James Allfrey - Captain
Devonshire Regiment 2nd Battalion *Age 26 Killed in Action on 1 July 1916*
SERRE ROAD CEMETERY No.2, France
Native of Belfast. Son of the late Lieutenant Colonel J W and Emily Andrews of "Bantony", Robertsbridge, Sussex.

Andrews, John Walker - Sapper
64417 Royal Engineers 150th Field Company *Age 32 Killed in Action on 1 July 1916*
THIEPVAL MEMORIAL, France
Son of Thomas and Elizabeth Andrews, of 17, Elswick Street, Belfast.

Andrews, Matthew - Rifleman
9162 Royal Irish Rifles 2nd Battalion *Killed in Action on 6 September 1918*
WULVERGHEM-LINDENHOEK ROAD MILITARY CEMETERY, Belgium
Husband of Annie Matthew, 19 Harrison Street, Belfast.

Andrews, Robert - Rifleman
19/28 Royal Irish Rifles 14th Battalion *Age 19 Died in War on 16 August 1917*
NEW IRISH FARM CEMETERY, Belgium
Survived by his brother Thomas, 27 Crosby Street, Belfast.

Andrews, Robert - Rifleman
5694 Royal Irish Rifles 2nd Battalion *Age 17 Killed in Action on 20 April 1915*
ELZENWALLE BRASSERIE CEMETERY, Belgium
Son of Mrs. Alice J. Andrews, of 62, Mountjoy Street, Belfast.

Angus, Thomas - Private
260207 Seaforth Highlanders (Ross-shire Buffs, the Duke of Albany's) 5th Battalion Seaforth Highlanders
Died in War on 17 October 1917
WANCOURT BRITISH CEMETERY, France
Born in Belfast, enlisted in Glasgow. Formerly 5709, Argyll & Sutherland Highlanders.

Annesley, James Ferguson St John - Captain
Royal Army Medical Corps *Died in War on 19 May 1917*
EUSTON ST. GENEVIEVE CHURCHYARD, United Kingdom
Born Belfast, the son of a Church of Ireland Rector. Educated at Armagh Royal School and the
Royal University of Ireland. An army doctor he died, aged 53, in an airfield accident in
Norfolk leaving a widow, Geraldine, and four children.

Anton, Charles - Private
202334 Princess Louise's (Argyll & Sutherland Highlanders) 1st/7th Battalion *Died in War on 13 July 1917*
YPRES (MENIN GATE) MEMORIAL, Belgium
Born in Belfast, enlisted Glasgow.

Apsimon, Arthur Tryweryn - Lieutenant
Royal Welsh Fusiliers 14th Battalion *Age 34 Died in War on 4 August 1917*
BARD COTTAGE CEMETERY, Belgium
Born in Belfast. Son of Thomas and Anna Elizabeth Apsimon, 107 Liscard Road, Wallasey, Cheshire.

Arbuckle, Hubert Hugh - Second Lieutenant
Royal Irish Regiment 2nd Battalion Age 26 *Died in War on 2 September 1918*
QUEANT ROAD CEMETERY, BUISSY, France
Son of the late Hugh and Mrs. Arbuckle, of Londonderry; husband of Mary Helen Arbuckle,
of 131, Belmont Road, Belfast.

Archer, Arthur Patrick - Sergeant
10044 Dorsetshire Regiment 5th Battalion *Died in War on 8 August 1915*
HELLES MEMORIAL, Turkey
Born in Belfast, enlisted in Aldershot, Hampshire.

Archer, George - Private
1481 Leinster Regiment 7th Battalion *Died in War on 9 September 1916*
LA NEUVILLE BRITISH CEMETERY, CORBIE, France
Born and enlisted in Belfast.

Archer, John - Rifleman
8938 Royal Irish Rifles 1st Battalion *Died in War on 18 December 1914*
RUE-DU-BACQUEROT (13th LONDON) GRAVEYARD, LAVENTIE, France
21 Ormeau Street, Belfast. Born in Ballymacarrett and enlisted in Belfast.

Archer, John C - Private
4597 Royal Inniskilling Fusiliers 2nd Battalion *Died in War on 16 May 1915*
LE TOURET MEMORIAL, France
56 Turin Street, Belfast. Eldest son of Thomas Archer. Formerly employed by the Durham Street Weaving Company.

Archer, R - Lance Corporal
14322 Manchester Regiment 24th Battalion *Age 21 Died in War on 4 May 1917*
MORY ABBEY MILITARY CEMETERY, MORY, France
Son of William E. Archer, of 36, Ivan Street, Belfast.

Archer, William - Private
438346 Canadian Infantry (Quebec Regiment) 87th Battalion *Age 37 Killed in Action on 24 March 1918*
SUCRERIE CEMETERY, ABLAIN-ST. NAZAIRE, France
Son of Emily Archer, of 81, Antrim Road, Belfast, Ireland, and the late Edward Archer. Native of Caledon, County Tyrone.

Archer, William John - Rifleman
13958 Royal Irish Rifles "A" Company 10th Battalion *Age 19 Died in War on 1 July 1916*
SERRE ROAD CEMETERY No.2, France
Son of William and Ellen Archer, of 17, Conduit Street, Belfast.

Ard, Hugh - Private
14877 Royal Irish Fusiliers 5th Battalion *Killed in Action on 16 August 1915*
HELLES MEMORIAL, Turkey
Born in Belfast, enlisted in Belfast.

Ardis, James - Private
CH/336(S) Royal Marine Light Infantry *Age 21 Died ashore on 6 June 1915*
HELLES MEMORIAL, Turkey
Son of James and Sarah Ardis, of 76, Mervue Street, Belfast

Armour, Thomas - Lance Corporal
12518 Royal Irish Rifles 8th Battalion *Killed in Action on 23 November 1917*
CAMBRAI MEMORIAL, LOUVERVAL, France
Son of Mrs. M. Armour, of 10, Bendigo Street, Belfast.

Armstrong, William - Private
9196 Black Watch 1st Battalion *Age 31 Died in War on 29 October 1914*
YPRES (MENIN GATE) MEMORIAL, Belgium
Ribble Street, Belfast. Born at Ballymena, County Antrim.

Journey of Remembering

Armstrong, William Wilberforce - Second Lieutenant
Black Watch 7th (Territorial) Battalion *Killed in Action on 27 December 1917*
JERUSALEM WAR CEMETERY, Israel
Born Belfast the son of a linen merchant, William and Mrs Elizabeth Armstrong.

Armstrong, Adam - Private
36003 Royal Army Service Corps *Age 34 Died as a result of war on 13 January 1920*
SOUTHAMPTON (HOLLYBROOK) CEMETERY, United Kingdom
Husband of Rosina Armstrong, of 3 Edith Street, Belfast

Armstrong, Alexander - Private
830031 Canadian Infantry 144th Battalion *Age 44 Died as a result of war on 9 May 1921*
WINNIPEG (BROOKSIDE) CEMETERY, Canada
Son of the late Thomas and Margaret Armstrong, of The Commons, Carrickfergus, Ireland; husband of Margaret Barkley Armstrong, of 44, River Terrace, Ormeau Road, Belfast.

Armstrong, George - Lance Corporal
9185 Royal Irish Rifles 1st Battalion *Killed in Action on 25 March 1918*
POZIERES MEMORIAL, France
Born and enlisted in Belfast. Formerly 6371, Army Cyclist Corps.

Armstrong, Isaiah - Private
12270 Royal Irish Regiment 2nd Battalion *Died in War on 27 September 1918*
VIS-EN-ARTOIS MEMORIAL, France
Brother of Mrs Orr 10 Silvergrove Street, Belfast

Armstrong, James - Private
10128 Royal Inniskilling Fusiliers 1st Battalion *Age 29 Died in War on 22 May 1915*
HELLES MEMORIAL, Turkey
Son of Walter and Sarah Jane Armstrong, of 88, Brookfield Street, Crumlin Road, Belfast.

Armstrong, John - Private
19195 Labour Corps transferred from the Royal Munster Fusiliers *Age 45 Died of sickness on 2 March 1919*
BELFAST CITY CEMETERY, United Kingdom
Son of Isaac and Mary Ann Armstrong, of Carrickmore, County Tyrone; husband of Ellen Armstrong, of 42, Danube Street, Belfast.

Armstrong, John - Private
23389 Royal Irish Fusiliers *Died in War on 6 September 1916*
SERRE ROAD CEMETERY No. 2, France
Husband of Mary Armstrong, 22, Hamilton Place, Belfast.

Armstrong, John - Rifleman
6929 Royal Irish Rifles 7th Battalion *Age 21 Killed in Action on 16 August 1917*
TYNE COT MEMORIAL, Belgium
Son of Isabella Armstrong, of 27, Ashdale Street, Connswater, Belfast, and James Armstrong.

Armstrong, John Leslie - Company Sergeant Major
16175 Royal Irish Rifles 14th Battalion *Age 24 Killed in Action on 16 August 1917*
TYNE COT MEMORIAL, Belgium
Son of William and Emily Armstrong, of Erin View, 179, Cliftonpark Avenue, Belfast.

Journey of Remembering

Armstrong, Patrick - Lance Corporal
9109 Royal Irish Rifles 15th Battalion *Killed in action on 1 July 1916*
THIEPVAL MEMORIAL, *France*
Brother of Mrs Rice, 10 Sunnyside Street, Ballynafeigh, Ormeau Rd, Belfast.

Armstrong, Thomas - Private
62978 Royal Fusiliers (City of London Regiment) 13th Battalion *Died in War on 2 October 1917*
TYNE COT MEMORIAL, *Belgium*
Born and enlisted in Belfast. Formerly 230216, Army Service Corps.

Armstrong, Thomas - Sapper
320850 Corps of Royal Engineers *Died in War on 30 September 1917*
MARGATE CEMETERY, *United Kingdom*
Born in Belfast. Lived in New York, USA, before enlisting

Armstrong, William - Private
12311 Royal Irish Fusiliers 1st Battalion *Died in War on 23 November 1917*
CAMBRAI MEMORIAL, LOUVERVAL, *France*
Husband of Katherine, 585, Falls Road, Belfast.

Armstrong, William J - Private
M/320012 Royal Army Service Corps *Age 23 Died as a result of war on 14 March 1920*
BELFAST (DUNDONALD) CEMETERY, *United Kingdom*
Son of William Armstrong, of 20, Memel Street, Belfast, and Margaret Jane Armstrong.

Armstrong, William John - Rifleman
14/16176 Royal Irish Rifles 14th Battalion *Age 27 Killed in Action on 7 June 1917*
SPANBROEKMOLEN BRITISH CEMETERY, *Belgium*
Son of Thomas and Margaret Armstrong, of Belfast.

Arneill, Willie John - Rifleman
13959 Royal Irish Rifles 2nd Battalion *Age 29 Killed in Action on 15 October 1918*
DADIZEELE NEW BRITISH CEMETERY, *Belgium*
A packer, he was the brother of Minnie and Maggie Arneill, of 33, Lindsay Street, Belfast.

Arnold, Henry Carpenter - Private
20100 Duke of Cornwall's Light Infantry 1st Battalion *Died in War on 14 April 1917*
ARRAS MEMORIAL
Born in Belfast. Formerly 10836, Somerset Light Infantry.

Arnold, James - Private
1522 Northumberland Fusiliers 1st/5th Battalion (Territorial) *Died in War on 26 April 1915*
BAILLEUL COMMUNAL CEMETERY (NORD), *France*
Born at Belfast, enlisted on Tyneside.

Arnold, Samuel - Private
4598 Royal Inniskilling Fusiliers 1st Battalion *Age 21 Died in War on 19 June 1915*
TWELVE TREE COPSE CEMETERY, *Turkey*
Son of William and Agnes Arnold, of 25, Wilton Street, Belfast.

Arnold, William - Sergeant
25225 Royal Dublin Fusiliers 10th Battalion *Age 31 Killed in Action at Beaumont Hamel on 13 November 1916*
ANCRE BRITISH CEMETERY, BEAUMONT-HAMEL, France
Son of William and Emma Arnold, of 11, Easton Crescent, Cliftonville, Belfast.
Born at the Diamond, Donegal Town.

Arthur, Edward J. - Private
7975 Highland Light Infantry 1st Battalion *Died in War on 21 December 1914*
LE TOURET MEMORIAL, France
Son of Mr E J Arthur, of Belfast.

Arthur, Robert - Rifleman
8759 Royal Irish Rifles 1st Battalion *Killed in Action on 13 May 1915*
MERVILLE COMMUNAL CEMETERY, France
Born and enlisted in Belfast.

Arthur, William John - Private
28811 Cameronians (Scottish Rifles) 1st/8th Battalion *Age 34 Died in War on 27 October 1918*
TERLINCTHUN BRITISH CEMETERY, WIMILLE, France
Born in Scotland and a carpenter he was the son of Mr and Mrs Arthur, of Belfast.
Awarded the Croix de Guerre.

Arthurs, Francis - Rifleman
11256 Royal Irish Rifles 6th Battalion *Died in War on 10 August 1915*
HELLES MEMORIAL, Turkey
Born and enlisted in Belfast.

Arthurs, James - Private
11758 Highland Light Infantry 1st Battalion *Died in War on 7 November 1914*
YPRES (MENIN GATE) MEMORIAL, Belgium
10 Dunvegan Street, Belfast. Born in Scotland.

Arthurs, Robert J - Rifleman
8759 Royal Irish Rifles 1st Battalion *Killed in Action on 13 March 1915*
MERVILLE COMMUNAL CEMETERY, France
Husband of T Arthurs, of 54, North Thomas Street, Belfast.

Ashe, William G - Rifleman
16157 Royal Irish Rifles 10th Battalion *Killed in Action on 1 July 1916*
CONNAUGHT CEMETERY THIEPVAL, France
His wife, Jane Ashe, lived at 41, Connswater Street, Belfast. He had signed the 1912 Ulster Covenant.

Ashfield, Joseph - Private
3534 Royal Inniskilling Fusiliers 2nd Battalion *Died in War on 7 June 1915*
LILLERS COMMUNAL CEMETERY, France
Born Sixmilecross, County Tyrone, enlisted Omagh, resident Belfast.

Ashley, A - Rifleman
Royal Irish Rifles *Died in War*
107, Roden Street Belfast

Journey of Remembering

Ashley, Claude - Second Lieutenant
15th Battalion attached 22nd (Tyneside Scottish) Battalion Northumberland Fusiliers
Age 21 Killed in Action on 1 July 1916
THIEPVAL MEMORIAL, *France*
Only son of Frederick Ashley, of 65, Wandsworth Road, Belfast, and the late Annie Ashley.

Atcheson, David - Fireman
914382 Mercantile Marine Reserve HMS "Pembroke" *Age 22 Died as a result of war on 26 March 1920*
DONEGORE CHURCH OF IRELAND CHURCHYARD, *United Kingdom*
Son of James Atcheson, of 17, Craigavad Street, Belfast, and the late Agnes Atcheson.

Atcheson, James A - First Class Petty Officer
165519 Royal Navy HMS "Pheasant" *Died in War on 1 March 1917*
PLYMOUTH NAVAL MEMORIAL, *United Kingdom*
17, Bellevue Street, Belfast.

Atkinson, A - Private
Royal Irish Rifles *Died in War*
20, Enfield Street, Belfast.

Atkinson, Eric - Private
30170 Royal Army Medical Corps 60th Field Ambulance *Age 28 Died in War on 1 July 1918*
PLAINE FRENCH NATIONAL CEMETERY, *France*
Son of John and Elizabeth Atkinson, of Belfast.

Atkinson, Hugh - Rifleman
13962 Royal Irish Rifles "A" Company 8th Battalion *Age 22 Died in War on 5 August 1917*
YPRES (MENIN GATE) MEMORIAL, *Belgium*
Son of Hugh and Lavina Atkinson, of 19, Mersey Street, Belfast.

Atkinson, Hugh - Second Lieutenant
Royal Irish Rifles 10th Battalion *Age 24 Died in War on 22 November 1917*
CAMBRAI MEMORIAL, LOUVERVAL, *France*
Son of Edward A. and Honoria J. Atkinson, of 617, Lisburn Road, Belfast.
Enlisted in 1914. Mentioned in Despatches.

Atkinson, James - Lance Corporal
12 Royal Irish Rifles 10th Battalion *Age 28 Killed in Action on 1 July 1916*
THIEPVAL MEMORIAL, *France*
Husband of Wilhelmina Atkinson, of 3, Convention Street, Belfast.

Atkinson, James - Private
523564 Canadian Army Medical Corps 3rd Field Ambulance
Age 29 Died of wounds, received at Etaples on 15 June 1918
BROOKWOOD MILITARY CEMETERY, *United Kingdom*
Son of James and Juanita Atkinson, of Willow Bank Street, Belfast; husband of Nellie Atkinson,
of 134, Spamount Street, Belfast.

Atkinson, John Mercier - Private
17000 Royal Inniskilling Fusiliers 2nd Battalion *Died in War on 10 July 1916*
THIEPVAL MEMORIAL, *France*
Born in Belfast, enlisted Liverpool.

Atkinson, Robert - Rifleman
8/12520 Royal Irish Rifles 8th Battalion *Age 25 Died in War on 2 July 1916*
AVELUY WOOD CEMETERY, MESNIL-MARTINSART, France
Son of Andrew and Elizabeth Atkinson, of 44, Woodcot Avenue, Belfast.

Atkinson, Thomas - Lance Corporal
5863 Royal Irish Rifles 2nd Battalion *Age 29 Killed in Action on 25 September 1915*
YPRES (MENIN GATE) MEMORIAL, Belgium
Son of the late William and Eliza Atkinson; husband of Margaret Atkinson, of 15, Blaney Street, Belfast.

Atkinson, Thomas - Rifleman
184 Royal Irish Rifles 8th Battalion *Died in War on 2 July 1916*
THIEPVAL MEMORIAL, France
Born Ballymacarrett, Belfast. Enlisted in Belfast.

Atkinson, William - Gunner
5844 Royal Garrison Artillery *Died in War on 9 March 1917*
ASSEVILLERS NEW BRITISH CEMETERY, France
Born and enlisted in Belfast.

Atkinson, William - Rifleman
23837 Royal Irish Rifles "D" Company 3rd Battalion *Age 19 Died as a result of war on 16 August 1919*
CARNMONEY CEMETERY, United Kingdom
Son of William James and Mary Atkinson, of 101, Mountcollyer Road, Belfast.

Auld, Hermon Robert - Private
1605 Army Cyclist Corps "X" Corps Cyclist Battalion *Age 22 Killed in Action on 20 June 1917*
RENINGHELST NEW MILITARY CEMETERY, Belgium
A brass finisher and the son of John and Louise Auld, of 46, Fitzroy Avenue, Belfast.

Austin, Edgar - Private
S/25499 Queen's Own Cameron Highlanders 7th Battalion *Died in War on 28 April 1917*
ARRAS MEMORIAL, France
Born and enlisted in Belfast.

Austin, Hubert Morrell - Second Lieutenant
Highland Light Infantry 12th Battalion *Age 25 Died in War on 3 August 1916*
ADANAC MILITARY CEMETERY, MIRAUMONT, France
Son of Hugh Austin, of 8, Cranmore Avenue, Belfast. His brother, James, also fell.

Austin, James - Second Lieutenant
Manchester Regiment 13th Battalion *Died in War on 21 June 1917*
SALONIKA (LEMBET ROAD) MILITARY CEMETERY, Greece
Son of Hugh Austin, of 8, Cranmore Avenue, Belfast. His brother, Hubert, also fell.

Austin, John - Rifleman
9017 Royal Irish Rifles 1st Battalion *Killed in Action on 24 February 1915*
MERVILLE COMMUNAL CEMETERY, France
1, James Street, Belfast.

Ayer, George - Corporal
7988 Royal Inniskilling Fusiliers *Died in War on 26 August 1914*
LA FERTE-SOUS-JOUARRE MEMORIAL, France
22, Lisburn Avenue, Belfast. Born in County Antrim, enlisted in Belfast.

Aynscomb, Charles Richard - Rifleman
14/6607 Royal Irish Rifles "C" Company 14th Battalion *Age 20 Died of wounds on 5 May 1917*
DRANOUTRE MILITARY CEMETERY, Belgium
Son of George and Annie Aynscomb, of 52, Richardson Sreet, Ravenhill Road, Belfast.
Native of Heathfield, Sussex.

Ayre, David - Bugler
7453 Royal Irish Rifles 2nd Battalion *Killed in Action on 7 June 1917*
YPRES (MENIN GATE) MEMORIAL, Belgium
Only son of Samuel and May Ayre 25 Coates Street, Belfast.

Ayre, David - Lance Corporal
267476 Seaforth Highlanders (Ross-shire Buffs, the Duke of Albany's) 6th Battalion
Died in War on 25 March 1918
ARRAS MEMORIAL, France
Born in Belfast, enlisted Bradford, Yorkshire.

Babes, William - Rifleman
5165 Royal Irish Rifles 2nd Battalion *Killed In Action on 2 June 1915*
AUBERS RIDGE BRITISH CEMETERY, France
Born in Belfast.

Babington, Samuel - Private
5141 Royal Munster Fusiliers 2nd Battalion *Age 37 Died in War on 5 October 1918*
DOINGT COMMUNAL CEMETERY EXTENSION, France
Son of Mary Babington, of 11, Annesley Street, Antrim Road, Belfast, and William Babington.

Bagley, Alexander - Rifleman
S/5955 Rifle Brigade (The Prince Consort's Own) 11th Battalion *Died in War on 8 November 1915*
ROYAL IRISH RIFLES GRAVEYARD, LAVENTIE, France
Born in Belfast, enlisted in Barrow-in-Furness.

Bailey, Alexander - Lance Corporal
1570 Princess Patricia's Canadian Light Infantry (Eastern Ontario Regiment) *Died of Wounds on 7 May 1915*
YPRES (MENIN GATE) MEMORIAL, Belgium
Son of the Rev Robert Taylor Bailey M.A, a Presbyterian minister, and Mrs Alice Bailey. Born at Strangford, County Down. He worked as a clerk and had served previously in the Canadian Militia. Native of Belfast.

Bailey, James - Private
8852 Royal Inniskilling Fusiliers 1st Battalion *Age 28 Died in War on 29 June 1915*
HELLES MEMORIAL, Turkey
Son of James and Margaret Bailey, of 79, Cambrai Street, Belfast.

Bailey, Robert - Sergeant
5376 Royal Garrison Artillery 379th Siege Battery *Age 36 Killed in Action on 25 September 1917*
GAZA WAR CEMETERY, Israel
Husband of Annie Bailey of 13, St. Kilda Street, Ravenhill Road, Belfast. Served in the South African War.

Bailey, Samuel McCutcheon - Engine Room Artificer
M/11615 Royal Navy HM Torpedo Boat Number 10 *Age 22 Died in War on 10 June 1915*
CHATHAM NAVAL MEMORIAL, United Kingdom
Loxey Villa, Donegall Road, Belfast.

Bailie, Arthur - Rifleman
11870 Royal Irish Rifles 7th Battalion *Died in War on 16 February 1916*
SUCRERIE MILITARY CEMETERY, COLINCAMPS, France
Born and enlisted in Belfast.

Bailie, David - Rifleman
14050 Royal Irish Rifles 15th Battalion *Died in War on 23 November 1917*
THIEPVAL MEMORIAL, France
Eldest son of Martha and David Bailie, 20 Emerson Street, Belfast.

Bailie, Hugh - Private
6981 South Lancashire Regiment 2nd Battalion *Age 31 Died in War on 26 August 1914*
LA FERTE-SOUS-JOUARRE MEMORIAL, France
Son of Hugh and Martha Bailie of 21, Wolff Street, Belfast; husband of Sarah Bailie, of Toronto, Canada.

Bailie, James - Rifleman
1176 Royal Irish Rifles 15th Battalion *Died in War on 18 August 1918*
BRANDHOEK NEW MILITARY CEMETERY No.3, *Belgium*
Born Ballymacarrett and enlisted in Belfast.

Bailie, Matthewson - Sergeant
9721 Royal Irish Fusiliers 1st Battalion *Age 34 Killed while a prisoner of war on 6 June 1918*
HAM BRITISH CEMETERY, MUILLE-VILLETTE, *France*
Husband of Margaret Bailie, of I, William Street, Milford, Armagh. Born in Belfast.

Baillie, David - Private
10533 Machine Gun Corps (Infantry) *Died in War on 30 May 1917*
KEMMEL CHATEAU MILITARY CEMETERY, *Belgium*
Born in Belfast enlisted Lisburn. Formerly 9496, Royal Irish Rifles.

Baillie, Hugh Montgomery - Captain
Royal Irish Rifles "A" Company 16th Battalion *Age 25 Killed in Action on 21 March 1918*
POZIERES MEMORIAL, *France*
Son of Robert and Sara Baillie, of "Ellerslie", Ravenhill Park, Belfast. A trainee lawyer with the legal firm of Carson and McDaid. Educated at RBAI and a former member of the old UVF.

Baillie, John - Private
2483 Argyll & Sutherland Highlanders 5th Battalion *Age 21 Died in War on 10 April 1917*
BELFAST (DUNDONALD) CEMETERY, *United Kingdom*
Son of Robert McDonald Baillie and Isabella Baillie of 35, Vicarage Street, Belfast.

Baillie, R McD - Stoker
K/53085 Royal Navy HMS "Hercules" *Died as a result of War on 3 December 1919*
BELFAST (DUNDONALD) CEMETERY, *United Kingdom*
Son of Robert Baillie, of 55, Vicarage Street, Belfast.

Baily, Wilhelmina Maude Isabel - Nurse
Voluntary Aid Detachment British Red Cross Society *Age 40 Died as a result of Spanish Influenza on 23 September 1918*
STAGLIENO CEMETERY, GENOA, *Italy*
Widow of Samuel Edward Baily, California USA and youngest of the eleven children of
William Charley JP DL and Ellen Anna Matilda (née Johnson). Born at Seymour Hill, Dunmurry, Belfast.

Bain, David - Rifleman
13980 Royal Irish Rifles 8th Battalion *Killed in Action on 2 July 1916*
CONNAUGHT CEMETERY, THIEPVAL, *France*
Son of Edward and Mary Ann Bain, of Belfast; husband of Elizabeth Bain,
of 4, Mountain View Street, Ligoneil, Belfast.

Bainbridge, Robert John - Sapper
WR/296491 Corps of Royal Engineers Railways *Died in War on 23 September 1918*
MIKRA BRITISH CEMETERY, KALAMARIA, *Greece*
Born in Darlington, enlisted Gateshead, resident Belfast. Formerly T/2249, Royal Army Service Corps.

Baird, Alexander - Ordinary Seaman
J/134064 Royal Navy HMS "Vanguard" *Died in War on 9 July 1917*
PLYMOUTH NAVAL MEMORIAL, *United Kingdom*
Son of William and Ellen Baird, of Belfast. Killed when his ship accidently exploded at anchor in Scapa Flow.

Baird, David - Rifleman
3899 Royal Irish Rifles 15th Battalion *Killed in Action on 1 July 1916*
THIEPVAL MEMORIAL, France
Born and enlisted in Belfast.

Baird, James - Rifleman
15/11886 Royal Irish Rifles 15th Battalion *Died in War on 24 December 1915*
SUCRERIE MILITARY CEMETERY, COLINCAMPS, France
Son of James and Elizabeth Baird, 23 Arlington Street, Belfast. Killed on Christmas Eve.

Baird, John - Rifleman
17166 Royal Irish Rifles 14th Battalion *Died in War on 7 February 1917*
BERKS CEMETERY EXTENSION, France
Born in Belfast. Lived in Belfast when enlisted.

Baird, Samuel - Rifleman
5039 Royal Irish Rifles 1st Battalion *Killed in Action on 16 November 1914*
LE TOURET MEMORIAL, France
Son of Edward and Ellen Baird of 16 Worcester Terrace, Belfast.

Baird, Samuel - Sergeant
11548 Royal Irish Rifles 2nd Battalion *Killed in Action on 24 November 1916*
HYDE PARK CORNER (ROYAL BERKS) CEMETERY, France
Born and enlisted in Belfast.

Baird, William - Private
21577 Princess Victoria's (Royal Irish Fusiliers) 9th Battalion *Age 35 Killed in Action on 16 August 1917*
TYNE COT MEMORIAL, Belgium
Born and enlisted in Belfast.

Baker, John - Private
12608 Royal Irish Fusiliers 6th Battalion *Age 40 Died in War on 15 August 1915*
HELLES MEMORIAL, Turkey
Husband of Mrs S Annie Baker, of 32, Kingswood Street, Belfast.

Baker, Robert - Private
4457 The King's Hussars *Died in War on 13 October 1914*
VIEILLE-CHAPELLE NEW MILITARY CEMETERY, LACOUTURE, France
73 Frome Street, Belfast.

Baker, Thomas - Lance Corporal
8744 Royal Irish Rifles 2nd Battalion *Killed by shellfire on 3 May 1915*
RIDGE WOOD MILITARY CEMETERY, Belgium
5 Kingswood Street, Belfast.

Ballagh, Samuel - Private
24125 Canterbury Regiment New Zealand Expeditionary Force 1st Battalion
Age 34 Died in War on 12 October 1917
TYNE COT MEMORIAL, Belgium
Son of William and Margaret Ballagh, of "Glenview", Ligoneil, Belfast, Ireland.

JOURNEY OF REMEMBERING

Ballard, Claude - Private
S/20035 Queen's Own Cameron Highlanders 5th Battalion *Died in War on 5 May 1918*
NEWTOWNHAMILTON CHURCH OF IRELAND CHURCHYARD, *United Kingdom*
Born in Newtownhamilton, enlisted Liverpool, resident Belfast. Awarded the Military Medal.

Ballard, Robert - Private
10632 King's (Liverpool Regiment) 1st Battalion *Died in War on 10 March 1915*
LE TOURET MEMORIAL, *France*
128 Cliftonpark Avenue, Belfast. Born in Armagh.

Ballentine, Samuel - Corporal
9310 Argyll and Sutherland Highlanders 2nd Battalion *Age 28 Died in War on 21 October 1914*
PLOEGSTEERT MEMORIAL, *Belgium*
Son of Thomas J. and Elizabeth Ballentine, of 83, Willowfield Street, Belfast.

Banford, C - Private
PLY/17001 Royal Marine Light Infantry *Age 21 Died of wounds received at the Dardanelles on 11 December 1916*
BELFAST CITY CEMETERY, *United Kingdom*
Husband of Maud Banford, of 18, Excise Street, Belfast. Mrs Banford subsequently married his brother.

Bankhead, Samuel - Private
S/40153 Queen's Own Cameron Highlanders 1st Battalion *Died in War on 12 July 1917*
BAILLEUL COMMUNAL CEMETERY EXTENSION (NORD), *France*
Born in Monkstown, resident Belfast.

Banks, John - Sergeant
1501 Leinster Regiment 2nd Battalion *Died of Wounds on 26 June 1917*
ETAPLES MILITARY CEMETERY, *France*
Husband of Margaret, 12 Dunstan Street, Belfast.

Banks, Joseph - Private
3/6307 Cameronians (Scottish Rifles) 2nd Battalion *Died in War on 29 January 1915*
LE TOURET MEMORIAL, *France*
Born in Belfast, enlisted in Lanark, Scotland.

Bannister, Herbert Stanley - Lieutenant
Canadian Infantry (Alberta Regiment) 10th Battalion *Age 30 Died in War on 21 June 1918*
BOULOGNE EASTERN CEMETERY, *France*
Son of Peter and Jane Bannister, of Belfast. Educated at RBAI and trained as a dentist.
He enlisted in the Canadian army before transferring to the Royal Air Force. Killed in an accident
whilst flying a Sopwith Camel aircraft.

Bannon, Patrick - Private
8988 Royal Irish Rifles 2nd Battalion *Age 24 Killed in Action on 25 October 1914*
LE TOURET MEMORIAL, *France*
Son of Peter and Mary Bannon, of 25, Milton Street, Belfast.

Barham, Henry - Rifleman
9341 Royal Irish Rifles 1st Battalion *Age 24 Died of wounds on 29 January 1915*
ROYAL IRISH RIFLES GRAVEYARD, LAVENTIE, *France*
Son of Mr and Mrs Arthur Barham, of Belfast.

Barker, Cecil Massey Arbuthnot - Second Lieutenant
Royal Irish Fusiliers 6th (Service) Battalion *Age 19 Killed in Action on 17 August 1915*
HELLES MEMORIAL, Greece
Son of Samuel and Mrs Catherine Maud Lindsey-Bucknal Barker. Born at Belfast and educated at Campbell College and Trinity College Dublin. Killed at Suvla Bay, Gallipoli.

Barker, Francis Sydney - Rifleman
1645 Royal Irish Rifles 2nd Battalion *Died of Wounds on 17 August 1918*
THIEPVAL MEMORIAL, France
Born in Belfast, enlisted in London.

Barker, George - Rifleman
6722 Royal Irish Rifles 16th Battalion *Age 23 Died in War on 31 July 1917*
YPRES (MENIN GATE) MEMORIAL, Belgium
Son of Maria Barker of 8 Roundhill Street, Mount Pottinger, Belfast, and George Barker.

Barklay, George - Private
G/53857 Duke of Cambridge's Own (Middlesex Regiment) 19th London Battalion *Died in War on 26 October 1918*
ESTAIRES COMMUNAL CEMETERY, France
Born in Adavoyle, Ireland. Enlisted in Grove Park, Kent. Resident of Belfast.
Formerly M/270965, Army Service Corps, awarded the Military Medal.

Barkley, James - Private
36427 Machine Gun Corps (Infantry) 13th Company *Age 18 Died in War on 31 August 1916*
THIEPVAL MEMORIAL, France
Son of Alexander and Sarah Barkley of 122, Earl Street, Belfast.

Barkley, James - Rifleman
5778 Royal Irish Rifles 2nd Battalion *Age 35 Died in War on 9 September 1917*
BROOKWOOD MILITARY CEMETERY, United Kingdom
Son of Mr and Mrs. Barkley. Native of Belfast.

Barnes, Edward - Corporal
12575 Royal Irish Rifles 2nd Battalion *Age 22 Died in War on 28 September 1918*
TYNE COT MEMORIAL, Belgium
Son of Benjamin and Mary Ann Barnes of 74, Bloomfield Avenue, Connswater, Belfast.

Barnes, G - Rifleman
12616 Royal Irish Rifles 9th Battalion *Age 30 Died in War on 15 June 1916*
AUTHUILE MILITARY CEMETERY, France
A general labourer he was the son of Margaret Barnes of 121, Lawnbrook Avenue, Belfast, and the late Peter Barnes.

Barnes, Herbert Edward Kerley - Private
4356 (Queen's Own) Hussars *Died of pneumonia on 22 February 1919*
BELFAST CITY CEMETERY, United Kingdom
Son of Joseph and Emily Jane Barnes; husband of Lillian Towers Barnes, of 55, Brougham Street, Belfast. Born in Leeds. His family served in the 4th Hussars continuously from about 1716 to World War One.

Barnett, Ernest C - Private
S/40453 Black Watch (Royal Highlanders) 8th Battalion *Died in War on 9 April 1917*
CABARET-ROUGE BRITISH CEMETERY, SOUCHEZ, France
1, Lyle Street Belfast.

Barnett, John - Corporal
3941 Connaught Rangers *Age 34 Died of sickness following wounds on 14 August 1920*
BELFAST CITY CEMETERY, United Kingdom
(Served as Hasson). Son of John and Mary Barnett; husband of Elizabeth Barnett, of 13, Brennan Street, Belfast.

Barnett, Samuel - Private
40916 Royal Army Medical Corps *Died in War on 1 April 1917*
CARNMONEY CEMETERY, United Kingdom
Born and enlisted in Belfast.

Barnett, William - Stoker First Class
SS/109372 Royal Navy HMS "Pathfinder"
Age 30 Killed in Action with submarine off the Firth of Forth on 5 September 1914
CHATHAM NAVAL MEMORIAL, United Kingdom
(Served as Swann). Son of Jane Swann (formerly Barnett) of 2, Orchard Street, Belfast, and the late Charles Alfred Barnett.

Barnhill, David - Lance Sergeant
14673 Royal Inniskilling Fusiliers 11th Battalion *Killed in Action on 1 July 1916*
THIEPVAL MEMORIAL, France
Son of Mrs. Margaret Barnhill of 174, Connsbrook Avenue, Strandtown, Belfast.

Barr, Henry (Harry) Victor - Sapper
64517 Royal Engineers 36th Signal Company *Died in War on 16 August 1917*
BRANDHOEK NEW MILITARY CEMETERY No.3, Belgium
Son of Henry and Agnes Barr of Belfast.

Barr, Hugh Joseph - Private
3566 Connaught Rangers 6th Battalion *Died in War on 3 February 1916*
NOEUX-LES-MINES COMMUNAL CEMETERY, France
Husband of Mrs E. Barr of 55, Hardinge Street, Belfast.

Barr, Joseph J - Stoker First Class
SS/108937 Royal Naval Division Hood Battalion 2nd Naval Brigade *Died in War on 27 May 1915*
SKEW BRIDGE CEMETERY, Turkey
46 Sancroft Street, Belfast.

Barr, William - Private
7466 Labour Corps Transferred from the Seaforth Highlanders *Died in War on 9 January 1918*
DUNHALLOW A.D.S. CEMETERY, Belgium
Born in Belfast, enlisted in Glasgow.

Barrett, David - Private
8244 Royal Inniskilling Fusiliers 1st Battalion *Killed in Action on 9 August 1916*
POTIJZE CHATEAU WOOD CEMETERY, Belgium
Husband of Sarah, Ashmore Street, Belfast.

Barrett, John Henry - Private
40918 Royal Army Medical Corps 109th Field Ambulance *Died in War on 16 August 1917*
TYNE COT MEMORIAL, Belgium
22, Carnan Street, Belfast.

Barrett, Samuel - Corporal
10214 Prince of Wales's Volunteers (South Lancashire Regiment) 2nd Battalion
Killed in Action on 25 September 1915
YPRES (MENIN GATE) MEMORIAL, Belgium
Born and enlisted in Belfast.

Barron, Robert - Rifleman
1159 Royal Irish Rifles 16th Battalion *Died in War on 11 August 1917*
YPRES (MENIN GATE) MEMORIAL, Belgium
17 Limestone Road, Belfast.

Barry, John - Rifleman
7844 Royal Irish Rifles 6th Battalion *Died of Wounds on 3 October 1916*
Born in Portadown, County Armagh, enlisted Clydebank, Scotland, resident Belfast.

Barry, Malcolm - Lance Sergeant
8770 Royal Scots Fusiliers 1st Battalion *Died in War on 16 June 1915*
YPRES (MENIN GATE) MEMORIAL, Belgium
Born in Belfast, enlisted Kilmarnock, Scotland.

Bartlett, Thomas - Gunner
2196 Royal Garrison Artillery Transferred to Private 283645 619th Home Service Employment Company
Age 41 Died in War on 10 July 1918
BELFAST (MILLTOWN) ROMAN CATHOLIC CEMETERY, United Kingdom
Husband of Elizabeth, 54, Unity Street, Belfast.

Barton, Henry - Lance Corporal
S/43406 Black Watch (Royal Highlanders) 9th Battalion *Age 22 Died in War on 25 August 1917*
TYNE COT MEMORIAL, Belgium
Son of Henry and Sarah Barton of 58, Solway Street, Belfast.

Bartrop, Benjamin - Corporal
42477 Royal Welsh Fusiliers 26th Battalion *Died of disease on active service on 5 October 1918*
RATION FARM MILITARY CEMETERY, LA CHAPELLE-D'ARMENTIERES, France
Son of William Bartrop; husband of Mary Emma Snowden (formerly Bartrop)
of 32, Bickerton Road, Wadsley Bridge, Sheffield. Resident of Belfast.

Bashford, John - Rifleman
963 Royal Irish Rifles 8th Battalion *Died in War on 2 July 1916*
THIEPVAL MEMORIAL, France
Son of Thomas George and Annie Bashford of 4, Maria Place, Belfast.

Bassett, Robert - Private
L/8557 Royal Sussex Regiment 2nd Battalion *Age 27 Died in War on 9 May 1915*
LE TOURET MEMORIAL, France
Son of William Bassett, of Southborough, Tunbridge Wells; husband of Mary T. McDowell (formerly Bassett),
of 1, Elm Street, Belfast.

Batchelor, David - Private
200371 Black Watch (Royal Highlanders) 6th (Perthshire) Battalion (Territorial) *Died in War on 1 July 1917*
VLAMERTINGHE NEW MILITARY CEMETERY, Belgium
Born in Belfast, enlisted in Dundee, Scotland.

Bates, James Fitzgerald - Private
24649 Manchester Regiment 11th Battalion *Age 18 Died of Wounds on 15 October 1916*
ST. SEVER CEMETERY, ROUEN, France
Son of James and Jane Isabella Bates of 72, Havana Street, Belfast.

Bateson, Hugh - Private
29637 East Yorkshire Regiment 1st Battalion *Age 22 Died in War on 22 March 1918*
POZIERES MEMORIAL, France
Son of Thomas and Jessie Bateson of 34, Thalia Street, Belfast.

Baxter, Edward - Private
12199 Royal Inniskilling Fusiliers 6th Battalion *Age 39 Died in War on 7 November 1917*
GAZA WAR CEMETERY, Israel
Son of Hugh and Mary Ann Baxter of Belfast. His brother also fell.

Baxter, George - Private
4536 Royal Inniskilling Fusiliers 3rd Battalion *Age 21 Died in War on 16 May 1915*
LE TOURET MEMORIAL, France
Son of the late James and Agnes Baxter. His brother also fell.

Baxter, George - Rifleman
6769 Royal Irish Rifles 2nd Battalion *Killed in Action on 9 July 1916*
THIEPVAL MEMORIAL, France
Born in Belfast, enlisted in Clonmel, Tipperary.

Baxter, James - Private
10170 Royal Inniskilling Fusiliers 1st Battalion *Died of Wounds on 11 September 1915*
ALEXANDRIA (CHATBY) MILITARY AND WAR MEMORIAL CEMETERY, Egypt
22, Dewey Street, Belfast.

Baxter, James - Sergeant
10701 Duke of Wellington's (West Riding Regiment) 8th Battalion *Died in War on 14 September 1916*
THIEPVAL MEMORIAL, France
Born in Belfast enlisted and resident in Yorkshire.

Baxter, John Edward - Rifleman
14063 Royal Irish Rifles "B" Company 10th Battalion *Age 22 Killed in Action on 1 July 1916*
THIEPVAL MEMORIAL, France
Son of Isabella Baxter of 63, Windsor Road, Belfast, and the late Thomas Edward Baxter.

Baxter, Robert - Private
16168 Kings Own Scottish Borderers 1st Battalion *Died in War on 2 July 1916*
ACHEUX BRITISH CEMETERY, France
Son of Mrs J Baxter, 4, Boyne Square, Belfast.

Baxter, Richard James - Rifleman
47450 Royal Irish Rifles 12th Battalion *Died in War on 22 November 1917*
CAMBRAI MEMORIAL, LOUVERAL, France
Born and enlisted in Belfast. Formerly T/4/059038, Army Service Corps.

Baxter, William - Rifleman
19877 Royal Irish Rifles 14th Battalion *Killed in Action on 21 March 1918*
HAM BRITISH CEMETERY, MUILLE-VILLETTE, *France*
Born Ballymacarrett, Belfast. Enlisted in Belfast.

Baxter, William Henry - Rifleman
12604 Royal Irish Rifles 8/9th Battalion *Died in War on 23 November 1917*
CAMBRAI MEMORIAL, LOUVERAL, *France*
Born and enlisted in Belfast.

Beastall, John - Lance Corporal
14066 Royal Irish Rifles 10th Battalion *Age 22 Died in War 25 June 1917*
DERRY HOUSE CEMETERY No.2, *Belgium*
Son of William and Marian Beastall of 15 Parkgate Avenue, Strandtown, Belfast.
Had signed the Covenant in 1912 and been one of the first to enlist in 1914.

Beatson, James - Regimental Sergeant Major
1469 Royal Irish Rifles 13th Battalion *Killed in Action on 28 June 1916*
MARTINSART BRITISH CEMETERY, *France*
Born at Hillsborough but living at Bromley Street, Shankill, Belfast. One of 14 men killed, (9 died later), when a powerful German shell devastated a platoon preparing to move into the front line.

Beattie, Albert - Rifleman
17242 Royal Irish Rifles 14th Battalion *Age 20 Died in War on 6 May 1916*
AUTHUILE MILITARY CEMETERY, *France*
Son of the late Mr D A and Mrs. D Beattie, of Belfast.

Beattie, David Henry - Private
201844 Seaforth Highlanders 1st/4th Battalion *Died in War on 10 April 1917*
NINE ELMS MILITARY CEMETERY, THELUS, *France*
Son of Mrs Kathleen Beattie, 51 Springvale Terrace, Ballysillan, Belfast.

Beattie, Hugh H. - Private
278731 Princess Louise's (Argyll & Sutherland Highlanders) 1/7th Battalion *Died in War on 22 March 1918*
ARRAS MEMORIAL, *France*
Born in Belfast, enlisted in London. Formerly G/29179, Middlesex Regiment.

Beattie, Norman - Sergeant
14148 Royal Irish Rifles "B" Company 10th Battalion *Age 30 Died in War on 19 December 1915*
DOULLENS COMMUNAL CEMETERY EXTENSION No.1, *France*
Son of William Thomas and Mary Beattie, of Belfast.

Beattie, R - Gunner
57330 Royal Field Artillery 44th Battery *Age 31 Died of dysentery on 27 September 1917*
BAGHDAD (NORTH GATE) WAR CEMETERY, *Iraq*
Son of Robert and the late Margaret Beattie; husband of Sarah Elizabeth Beattie of 38 Teutonic Street, Belfast.

Beattie, Robert - Pioneer
18385 South Wales Borderers 5th Battalion *Died in War on 30 July 1916*
THIEPVAL MEMORIAL, *France*
Son of Paymaster-Sergeant Beattie, 99, Broom Street, Belfast.

Beattie, Robert - Private
3350 Royal Inniskilling Fusiliers "D" Company 2nd Battalion *Age 21 Died in War on 16 May 1915*
LE TOURET MEMORIAL, France
Son of Robert and Rebecca Beattie of 29, Kenilworth Street, Belfast.

Beattie, Robert James - Driver
76765 Royal Field Artillery 29th Division Artillery
Drowned. Was on board the transport ship, "Manitou", attacked by Turkish torpedo boat on 14 April 1915
HELLES MEMORIAL, Turkey
Born and enlisted in Belfast.

Beattie, Samuel - Rifleman
12619 Royal Irish Rifles "D" Company 8th Battalion *Age 28 Killed in Action on 14 November 1915*
SUCRERIE MILITARY CEMETERY, COLINCAMPS, France
Son of James and Jane Beattie, of Belfast.

Beattie, Thomas - Private
24569 Royal Irish Fusiliers 2nd Battalion *Age 22 Died of jaundice on 26 August 1919*
KANTARA WAR MEMORIAL CEMETERY, Egypt
Son of John and Sarah Beattie of 5, Oregon Street, Belfast.

Beattie, William - Private
18708 Machine Gun Corps (Infantry) *Died in War on 10 November 1917*
TYNE COT MEMORIAL, Belgium
Born and enlisted in Belfast. Formerly 14/16221, Royal Irish Rifles.

Beattie, William - Private
40637 Royal Inniskilling Fusiliers 10th Battalion *Age 19 Died of Wounds on 16 August 1917*
LIJSSENTHOEK MILITARY CEMETERY, Belgium
Son of Archibald and Emma Beattie of 132 Mountcollyer Street, Alexandra Park, Belfast.

Beattie, William - Private
9828 Royal Inniskilling Fusiliers 6th Battalion *Died in War on 10 September 1916*
STRUMA MILITARY CEMETERY, Greece
Son of William Beattie and brother of Alice and Catherine of 37 Coolbeg Street, Donegall Road, Belfast.

Beattie, William - Rifleman
4396 Royal Irish Rifles 10th Battalion *Died in War on 24 December 1915*
MAILLY-MAILLET COMMUNAL CEMETERY EXTENSION, France
Born and enlisted in Belfast. Killed on Christmas Eve.

Beattie, William - Rifleman
238 Royal Irish Rifles 8th Battalion *Died in War on 17 August 1917*
TYNE COT MEMORIAL, Belgium
Born St Anne's Belfast and enlisted in the city.

Beckett, Robert - Private
789 Army Cyclist Corps *Died of Wounds on 12 June 1917*
LIJSSENTHOEK MILITARY CEMETERY, Belgium
Born in Belfast.

Beggins, Edward John - First Mate
Mercantile Marine S.S. "Ventmoor" (London)
Age 36 Drowned, as a result of an attack by an enemy submarine on 14 February 1918
TOWER HILL MEMORIAL, United Kingdom
Son of the late Daniel and Mary Beggins; husband of Clara Beggins (née Howes) of 11, Stanley Street, Seacombe, Cheshire. Born at Belfast.

Beggs, John - Rifleman
7108 Royal Irish Rifles 2nd Battalion *Killed in Action on 25 November 1914*
PLOEGSTEERT MEMORIAL, Belgium
202 Blythe Street, Belfast.

Beggs, Robert - Private
4493 Connaught Rangers 5th Battalion *Died in War on 21 August 1915*
HELLES MEMORIAL, Turkey
Born and enlisted in Belfast. Formerly 13822, Royal Inniskilling Fusiliers.

Beggs, Samuel - Private
23634 Royal Inniskilling Fusiliers 9th Battalion *Killed in Action on 1 July 1916*
THIEPVAL MEMORIAL, France
Born and enlisted in Belfast.

Beggs, William John - Sapper
64330 Royal Engineers *Age 43 Died of pneumonia on 3 December 1915*
BELFAST CITY CEMETERY, United Kingdom
Husband of Martha Beggs of 10 Swift Street, Belfast. Born at Larne.

Begley, Peter - Private
15669 Machine Gun Corps (Infantry) 87th Company *Died in War on 21 November 1916*
THIEPVAL MEMORIAL, France
10 Alton Street, Belfast.

Bell, Alexander - Rifleman
136 Royal Irish Rifles 8/9th Battalion *Killed in Action on 1 July 1916*
THIEPVAL MEMORIAL, France
Born and enlisted in Belfast.

Bell, Andrew - Private
3735 Royal Irish Rifles 11th Battalion *Died of Wounds on 15 July 1916*
HAMBURG CEMETERY, Germany
80 McTier Street, Belfast.

Bell, Arthur - Rifleman
8363 Royal Irish Rifles 1st Battalion *Age 19 Died in War on 14 December 1914*
MONS COMMUNAL CEMETERY, Belgium
Born and enlisted in Belfast.

Bell, Charles - Lance Corporal
8256 Royal Irish Fusiliers 1st Battalion *Died in War on 25 April 1915*
YPRES (MENIN GATE) MEMORIAL, Belgium
Husband of Mary Bell of 11, Upton Cottages, Glen Road, Belfast.

JOURNEY OF REMEMBERING

Bell, David - Stoker First Class
SS/108915 Royal Navy HMS "Hawke" *Killed in Action with submarine in North Sea on 15 October 1914*
CHATHAM NAVAL MEMORIAL, United Kingdom
Son of Edmond and Jane Bell, of Belfast; husband of Annie McCauley.

Bell, G - Airman
53490 Royal Flying Corps 76th Home Defence Squadron *Died in War on 20 January 1917*
RIPON CEMETERY, United Kingdom
Husband of Jane Bell of 47, Sheriff Street, Belfast.

Bell, George - Rifleman
1894 Royal Irish Rifles; 10th Battalion *Age 18 Killed in Action on 1 July 1916*
THIEPVAL MEMORIAL, France
Son of John Bell of 194, Donegall Avenue, Belfast.

Bell, George Sinclair - Stoker First Class
308909 Royal Navy HMS "Pathfinder" *Age 28 Killed in Action with submarine off the Firth of Forth on 5 September 1914*
CHATHAM NAVAL MEMORIAL, United Kingdom
Son of the late Henry A and Elizabeth Bell, of Belfast.

Bell, Henry - Private
8628 Irish Guards 2nd Battalion *Age 19 Died in War on 15 September 1916*
THIEPVAL MEMORIAL, France
Son of Robert John and Margaret Ann Bell of 50, McClure Street, Belfast.

Bell, Henry - Rifleman
11248 Royal Irish Rifles 2nd Battalion *Killed in Action on 24 March 1918*
POZIERES MEMORIAL, France
37, Lawnbrook Avenue, Belfast.

Bell, Hugh Ernest - Trimmer
2351/ST Royal Naval Reserve HMS "Redoubtable" *Age 42 Died in War on 25 May 1916*
HASLAR ROYAL NAVAL CEMETERY, United Kingdom
Son of John and Catherine Bell, of Belfast; husband of Jessie Bell of 34, Ardilaun Street, Belfast.

Bell, James - Private
14027 Princess Victoria's (Royal Irish Fusiliers) 9th Battalion *Killed in Action on 1 July 1916*
THIEPVAL MEMORIAL, France
Born in Belfast. Lived in Belfast when enlisted.

Bell, James - Private
16811 Royal Scots Fusiliers 7th Battalion *Died in War on 26 September 1915*
LOOS MEMORIAL, France
Born in Belfast, enlisted Coatbridge, Scotland.

Bell, James - Private
5993 Princess Victoria's (Royal Irish Fusiliers) 1st Battalion *Died in War on 26 June 1915*
NEW IRISH FARM CEMETERY, Belgium
Born and enlisted in Belfast.

BELFAST BOOK OF HONOUR

Bell, James - Rifleman
516 Royal Irish Rifles 8th Battalion *Died in War on 13 August 1917*
ST. SEVER CEMETERY EXTENSION, France
Born Ballymacarrett, Belfast. Enlisted in Belfast.

Bell, James McD - Rifleman
4420 Royal Irish Rifles 14th Battalion *Age 22 Died in War on 10 October 1916*
POND FARM CEMETERY, Belgium
Son of Mr W Bell of 80 McTier Street, Belfast.

Bell, John - Gunner
32885 Royal Field Artillery *Died in War on 24 July 1916*
THIEPVAL MEMORIAL, France
Born in County Down. Enlisted Belfast where he worked on the Tramway system.

Bell, John - Private
27551 Royal Inniskilling Fusiliers 7/8th Battalion *Died in War on 18 March 1918*
Born and enlisted in Belfast. Formerly 7/1510, Leinster Regiment.

Bell, John - Rifleman
5775 Royal Irish Rifles 10th Battalion *Killed in Action on 6 August 1917*
YPRES (MENIN GATE) MEMORIAL, Belgium
Born and enlisted in Belfast.

Bell, John K - Sergeant
14078 Royal Irish Rifles 9th Battalion *Died of Wounds on 29 March 1916*
MIRAUMONT COMMUNAL CEMETERY, France
Son of Thomas and Jane Bell of 40, Wigton Street, Belfast. Died in a German prison camp after being wounded and captured while on a patrol. A former member of the old UVF.

Bell, Joseph - Private
10045 Royal Irish Fusiliers 2nd Battalion *Died in War on 25 May 1915*
HOP STORE CEMETERY, Belgium
Born Ballymacarrett, Belfast. Enlisted in Belfast.

Bell, Joseph - Private
17500 Royal Inniskilling Fusiliers 9th Battalion *Age 30 Killed in Action on 1 July 1916*
THIEPVAL MEMORIAL, France
Husband of Maud Bell of 73, Utility Street, Belfast.

Bell, Joseph - Trimmer
7603TS Royal Naval Reserve HMS "Bittern" *Age 19 Drowned through collision in English Channel on 4 April 1918*
PORTSMOUTH NAVAL MEMORIAL, United Kingdom
(Served as GREEN) Joseph, Son of William Bell, of 2, Shaftesbury Street, Belfast.

Bell, Michael - Private
12235 Princess Victoria's (Royal Irish Fusiliers) 5th Battalion *Died in War on 5 October 1915*
ALEXANDRIA (CHATBY) MILITARY AND WAR MEMORIAL CEMETERY, Egypt
Born and enlisted in Belfast.

Bell, Robert - Rifleman
7842 Royal Irish Rifles 2nd Battalion *Age 35 Killed in Action on 26 October 1914*
LE TOURET MEMORIAL, France
Son of Mrs Sarah Trimble of 31, Connswater Street, Belfast.

Bell, Robert Gaw - Private
40452 Black Watch (Royal Highlanders) "C" Company 8th Battalion
Age 27 Died of wounds on 14 October 1917
DOZINGHEM MILITARY CEMETERY, Belgium
Son of William James and Margaret Bell of 63, Bloomfield Avenue, Belfast.

Bell, Robert H - Corporal
2872 Irish Guards 1st Battalion *Died in War on 1 February 1915*
CUINCHY COMMUNAL CEMETERY, France
Born and enlisted in Belfast. Husband of M Bell of 86, Nelson Road, Crouch End, London.

Bell, Robert John - Rifleman
8743 Royal Irish Rifles 1st Battalion *Died of Wounds on 10 April 1918*
ST. SEVER CEMETERY EXTENSION, ROUEN, France
Born and enlisted in Belfast.

Bell, Robert Rea - Private
46396 Royal Scots 5/6th Battalion *Age 20 Killed in Action on 11 August 1918*
BOUCHOIR NEW BRITISH CEMETERY, France
Son of Thomas and Rachel Bell of Belfast.

Bell, Samuel E - Corporal
9818 Royal Irish Rifles 1st Battalion *Died of Wounds on 24 July 1916*
BOULOGNE EASTERN CEMETERY, France
Son of Thomas and Elizabeth Bell of 111, Fortingale Street, Belfast.

Bell, Thomas - Gunner
10588 Royal Horse Artillery and Royal Field Artillery *Died in War on 2 October 1917*
HOOGE CRATER CEMETERY, Belgium
Born and enlisted in Belfast.

Bell, William - Private
10742 Royal Inniskilling Fusiliers 3rd Battalion
Age 17 Drowned while on guard at Buncrana on 7 December 1914
LOWER FAHAN (CHRIST CHURCH) CHURCHYARD, Republic of Ireland
Son of Richard Samuel and Martha Bell, of Ligoneil, Belfast.

Bell, William - Private
16490 Manchester Regiment 2nd Battalion *Age 36 Died in War on 25 March 1915*
LA LAITERIE MILITARY CEMETERY, Belgium
Son of William and Selina Bell, of Belfast; husband of Sarah Elizabeth Bell of 3, Aughrim Street, Belfast.

Bell, William J - Corporal
12606 Royal Irish Rifles 9th Battalion *Shot in head by a sniper on 8 March 1916*
BERTRANCOURT MILITARY CEMETERY, France
Son of Abraham and Charlotte Bell, of Belfast. By a coincidence, the chaplain who officiated at the graveside was his own minister in Belfast, Rev. James Quinn, of St.Michael's, Shankill Road.

Bell, William James - Rifleman
264 Royal Irish Rifles 15th Battalion *Age 21 Died in War on 17 August 1917*
LIJSSENTHOEK MILITARY CEMETERY, Belgium
Son of James and Sarah Bell of 28, Nore Street, Belfast.

Bell, William James - Rifleman
565 Royal Irish Rifles 10th Battalion *Age 18 Killed in Action on 1 July 1916*
THIEPVAL MEMORIAL, France
Son of William James and Annie Bell, of 4, Bristol Street, Belfast. William Bell, known as 'Wullie', an apprentice tailor, had managed to enlist aged 15 - only to be discharged when his true age was discovered. He then joined the West Belfast battalion of the old UVF. Aged 17 he rejoined the army and, like many of his age and outlook was killed on the first day of the Battle of the Somme. He has no known grave and the name 'William' has been passed down through subsequent generations of his family.

Belshaw, James - Corporal
2575 Royal Inniskilling Fusiliers 4th Battalion *Age 21 Died in War on 24 September 1914*
LONDONDERRY CITY CEMETERY, United Kingdom
Son of William and Elizabeth Belshaw, of 35, Jennymount Street, Belfast.

Belshaw, Robert - Rifleman
9430 Royal Irish Rifles 6th Battalion *Killed in Action on 16 May 1917*
STRUMA MILITARY CEMETERY, Greece
Son of Sarah Jane Belshaw of 105, Matilda Street, Belfast.

Belton, William - Rifleman
7440 Royal Irish Rifles 2nd Battalion *Age 20 Died of Wounds on 27 March 1918*
POZIERES MEMORIAL, France
Son of Thomas H. Belton, of 51, Tyrone Street, Belfast, and the late Kathleen Belton.

Bennet, Charles Hoskins - Lieutenant
Royal Field Artillery *Age 20 Died as a result of war on 25 February 1919*
NORTHHAM (ST MARGARET) CEMETERY, DEVON, United Kingdom
Born at Belfast. Educated at Marlborough and the Royal Military Academy, Woolwich. Lived in North Devon and died of pneumonia as result of active service.

Bennet, Trevor Moutray - Lieutenant
Royal Flying Corps 70th Squadron and Royal Irish Rifles *Age 19 Killed in Action on 10 November 1916*
HERMIES HILL BRITISH CEMETERY, France
Son of James Bennet, of 1, Chlorine Place, University Road, Belfast. Educated at Methodist College and RBAI. Member of the old Ulster Volunteer Force. Won the Military Cross on the Somme serving with the Royal Irish Rifles. Thereafter transferred to the Royal Flying Corps and was shot down and killed over German lines.

Bennett, Alexander - Rifleman
17257 Royal Irish Rifles 14th Battalion *Age 19 Killed in Action on 1 July 1916*
THIEPVAL MEMORIAL, France
Son of Mrs. Margaret Bennett of 18, Grampian Street, Belfast.

Bennett, Edward Hermann - Private
19/1256 Northumberland Fusiliers 19th Battalion (Tyneside Pioneers) *Died in War on 1 January 1915*
NEWCASTLE ON TYNE (ST ANDREWS AND JESMOND) CEMETERY, United Kingdom
Born in Belfast, enlisted in North Shields, England.

Journey of Remembering

Bennett, Frederick - Sergeant
1221 Royal Irish Rifles 12th Battalion *Age 33 Died in War on 18 April 1918*
TYNE COT MEMORIAL, Belgium
Son of the late James and Annie Bennett, of 23, Rosevale Street, Belfast.

Bennett, Hugh - Private
3335 Royal Inniskilling Fusiliers 1st Battalion *Age 21 Killed in Action on 1 July 1916*
THIEPVAL MEMORIAL, France
Brother of John Bennett of 35, Springfield Village, Belfast. A member of Edenderry Brass Band and the old UVF.

Bennett, James - Private
18099 Royal Inniskilling Fusiliers 11th Battalion *Killed in action on 1 July 1916*
CONNAUGHT CEMETERY, THIEPVAL, France
Husband of Lizzie Bennett, Capital Street, Belfast.

Bennett, James - Rifleman
14080 Royal Irish Rifles 9th Battalion *Killed in Action on 1 July 1916*
THIEPVAL MEMORIAL, France
35 Springfield Village, Belfast.

Bennett, John - Private
9343 Royal Inniskilling Fusiliers 1st Battalion *Died in War on 8 July 1916*
BELFAST (MILLTOWN) ROMAN CATHOLIC CEMETERY, United Kingdom
Son of Mrs Margaret Bennett, of 26, Moira Street, Belfast.

Bennett, Joseph - Company Sergeant Major
8996 Royal Irish Rifles 9th Battalion *Killed in Action on 1 July 1916*
CONNAUGHT CEMETERY, THIEPVAL, France
Born and enlisted in Belfast. Holder of the Military Medal.

Bennon, Edward - Private
2006 Australian Infantry 12th Battalion *Age 31 Died of disease on 1 April 1917*
ETAPLES MILITARY CEMETERY, France
Son of Michael and Annie Bennon. Native of Belfast, Ireland.

Benson, Ernest - Private
13176 Royal Inniskilling Fusiliers 5th Battalion *Age 31 Died in War on 15 August 1915*
HELLES MEMORIAL, Turkey
Son of David and Agnes Benson of 36, Eia Street, Belfast.

Benson, James - Private
198631 Canadian Infantry (Manitoba Regiment) 52nd Battalion *Age 30 Died in War on 2 April 1917*
ECOIVRES MILITARY CEMETERY, MONT-ST. ELOI, France
Born in Belfast the son of William and Esther Benson of Drumherriff, Portadown, Ireland.

Benson, John Joseph - Driver
25553 Royal Engineers 3rd Pontoon Park *Died in War on 24 March 1918*
DOULLENS COMMUNAL CEMETERY, EXTENSION No 1, France
12 Bangor Street, Belfast.

Benson, William James - Private
S/17560 Black Watch (Royal Highlanders) 8th (Service) Battalion *Died in War on 1 January 1917*
FAUBOURG D'AMIENS CEMETERY, ARRAS, France
Born in Belfast, enlisted in Paisley, Scotland. Formerly 1735, Argyll and Sutherland Highlanders.

Bentley, Thomas Herbert - Sergeant
506 Australian Infantry 23rd Battalion *Age 23 Died of wounds on 19 June 1916*
BAILLEUL COMMUNAL CEMETERY EXTENSION (NORD), France
Son of Thomas Herbert and Margaret Ann Wemyss Bentley 59, High Street, Ardersier, Inverness, Scotland. Native of Belfast, Ireland.

Bentley, Thomas James - Rifleman
437 Royal Irish Rifles 10th Battalion *Killed in Action on 1 July 1916*
THIEPVAL MEMORIAL, France
Only son of Mr Thomas Bentley, 10 Westminster Avenue, Belfast.
Had worked in the Shipyard before enlistment.

Berkeley, William Lowry - Lance Corporal
7610 South African Infantry 3rd Regiment *Died in War on 24 April 1917*
CABARET-ROUGE BRITISH CEMETERY, SOUCHEZ, France
Son of Lowry and Margaret Berkeley, of Belfast, Ireland.

Berry, Christopher Barnett - Boy Artificer
M/11326 Royal Navy HMS "Indus" *Age 16 Died in War on 17 March 1915*
FORD PARK CEMETERY (FORMERLY PLYMOUTH OLD CEMETERY) (PENNYCOMEQUICK), United Kingdom
Son of Robert and Arabella Berry, 304 Springfield Road, Belfast.

Berry, Frederick Ernest - Rifleman
42469 Royal Irish Rifles 1st Battalion *Age 19 Died in War on 14 October 1918*
TYNE COT MEMORIAL, Belgium
Son of Mr. and Mrs. C. M. Berry of 14, Chambers Street, Belfast. Educated at Mountpottinger School and a keen member of the Boy Scout movement. His family think he managed to join the army aged 15. Two brothers, Maurice and Henry, also served. Both survived but Henry never entirely recovered from being gassed.

Berry, John - Rifleman
7844 Royal Irish Rifles 6th Battalion *Age 43 Died of sickness on 3 October 1916*
STRUMA MILITARY CEMETERY, Greece
Son of the late James and Annie Berry of Mullantine, County Armagh; husband of Margaret Berry of 69, Grove Street, Belfast.

Berry, Malcolm - Lance Sergeant
8770 Royal Scots Fusiliers 1st Battalion *Died in War on 16 June 1915*
YPRES (MENIN GATE) MEMORIAL, Belgium
21, Rugby Avenue, Belfast.

Best, James Gardiner - Private
14374 Wellington Regiment, New Zealand Expeditionary Force 2nd Battalion
Age 24 Killed in Action at La Basseville on 31 July 1917
MESSINES RIDGE (N.Z.) MEMORIAL, Belgium
Son of William John Best, of Moa Street, Otahuhu, Auckland. Native of Belfast, Ireland.

Journey of Remembering

Best, John - Rifleman
1379 Royal Irish Rifles 2nd Battalion *Killed in Action on 24 March 1918*
POZIERES MEMORIAL, France
Survived by his mother from 67 Brussels Street, Belfast.

Best, Robert - Rifleman
652 Royal Irish Rifles 9th Battalion *Age 20 Killed in Action on 7 June 1917*
YPRES (MENIN GATE) MEMORIAL, Belgium
Husband of Margaret Best, of 33, Ghent Street, Belfast.

Best, Thomas - Private
6416 King's Own Scottish Borderers 2nd Battalion *Died in War on 2 March 1915*
POPERINGHE OLD MILITARY CEMETERY, Belgium
Born in Belfast, enlisted Glasgow.

Best, Thomas W A - Rifleman
7298 Royal Irish Rifles "B" Company 2nd Battalion *Age 21 Killed in Action on 2 August 1916*
VERMELLES BRITISH CEMETERY, France
Son of Thomas William Alexander Best and Annie Vickers Best of 49, Jennymount Street, Belfast.

Bickerstaff, William - Private
51063 Eastern Ontario Regiment Princess Patricia's Canadian Light Infantry
Age 29 Died as a result of war on 17 July 1919
CARNMONEY CEMETERY, United Kingdom
Son of William and Agnes Bickerstaff of 19, Lawther Street, Belfast.

Bidmead, Frederick - Lance Corporal
22937 King's Own (Yorkshire Light Infantry) 2nd Battalion *Killed in Action on 1 July 1916*
THIEPVAL MEMORIAL, France
Born in Belfast. Formerly 17984, Durham Light Infantry.

Bill, John Alexander Patterson - Second Lieutenant
Royal Irish Rifles 18th Battalion attached 12th Battalion *Age 22 Died in War on 16 August 1917*
TYNE COT MEMORIAL, Belgium
61 University Street, Belfast. The son of Samuel Alexander and Grace Bill, both missionaries. Educated at RBAI and Queen's University.

Bill, Thomas - Private
17594 Royal Inniskilling Fusiliers 9th Battalion *Died of Wounds on 17 May 1916*
BEAUVAL COMMUNAL CEMETERY, France
Born in Belfast.

Bingam, Alfred - Rifleman
14088 Royal Irish Rifles 9th Battalion *Age 18 Died in War on 5 February 1916*
MAILLY-MAILLET COMMUNAL CEMETERY EXTENSION, France
Son of Thomas and Annie Bingam of 51, Sugarfield Street, Belfast.

Bingham, Alexander - Quartermaster Sergeant (Brigade)
15/12571 Royal Irish Rifles 15th Battalion *Age 29 Killed in Action on 27 November 1915*
FORCEVILLE COMMUNAL CEMETERY AND EXTENSION, France
Eldest son of Julia and the late Thomas Bingham, of Belfast.

BELFAST BOOK OF HONOUR

Bingham, Frederick - Private
124013 Machine Gun Corps (Infantry) 54th Battalion *Accidentally killed on 17 January 1919*
CAIRO WAR MEMORIAL CEMETERY, Egypt
Son of John and Agnes Bingham, of 31, Castlereagh Place, Belfast.

Bingham, Henry - Rifleman
19398 Royal Irish Rifles 15th Battalion *Killed in Action on 21 March 1918*
POZIERES MEMORIAL, France
Born and enlisted in Belfast.

Bingham, John Warnock - Captain
Royal Army Medical Corps 10th Field Ambulance *Age 39 Died as a result of war on 10 March 1919*
MONS COMMUNAL CEMETERY, Belgium
Son of Henry Bingham, M.D., and Letitia Bingham, of Belfast; husband of Alison Bingham of 3, Ulsterville Avenue, Belfast.

Bingham, Robert - Private
53919 Royal Dublin Fusiliers and King's Own Yorkshire Light Infantry (9168)
Age 20 Died of wounds (gas) on 4 October 1919
BELFAST CITY CEMETERY, United Kingdom
Son of Samuel Bingham, of Belfast.

Bingham, Robert James - Sergeant
10/14003 Royal Irish Rifles 10th Battalion *Died in War on 21 January 1917*
ST. QUENTIN CABARET MILITARY CEMETERY, Belgium
Husband of Annie Marie Bingham, 37 Delhi Street, Belfast.

Bingham, Samuel - Private
4581 Royal Inniskilling Fusiliers 2nd Battalion *Age 32 Died in War on 16 May 1915*
LE TOURET MEMORIAL, France
Son of Joseph and Ellen Bingham of 28, Dundela Street, Strandtown, Belfast.
Father and son had signed the 1912 Ulster Covenant.

Bingham, Thomas - Corporal
16191 Royal Irish Rifles 10th Battalion *Died in War on 6 August 1917*
YPRES (MENIN GATE) MEMORIAL, Belgium
46 Medway Street, Belfast.

Bingham, Thomas - Lance Corporal
11650 Royal Inniskilling Fusiliers 6th Battalion *Age 16 Died in War on 17 August 1915*
HELLES MEMORIAL, Turkey
Son of Mrs Janet Bingham of 16, Medway Street, Belfast. His father also fell.

Bingham, Thomas Hugh - Private
240954 Seaforth Highlanders 5th Battalion *Killed in Action on 21 March 1918*
ARRAS MEMORIAL, FRANCE
105, Solway Street, Belfast.

Bingham, William James - Rifleman
16190 Royal Irish Rifles 10th Battalion *Died in War on 6 August 1918*
BELFAST CITY CEMETERY, United Kingdom
His wife lived at 64, Rowland Street, Belfast.

Birney, Patrick - Private
2883 Connaught Rangers 5th Battalion *Died in War on 9 September 1915*
PLYMOUTH (WESTON MILL) CEMETERY, United Kingdom
Born in Dungannon, resident Belfast.

Birney, Patrick Joseph - Private
10669 Royal Inniskilling Fusiliers 1st Battalion *Age 18 Died in War on 30 January 1917*
THIEPVAL MEMORIAL, France
Son of Mary Birney of 16, Oranmore Street, Belfast, and the late Patrick Birney.

Birnie, Robert - Rifleman
172 Royal Irish Rifles 12th Battalion *Killed in Action on 1 July 1916*
THIEPVAL MEMORIAL, France
Husband of Jennie Birnie, of 3, Broom Street, Belfast.

Bishop, Alexander - Drummer
10824 Welsh Regiment 2nd Battalion *Died in War on 18 July 1916*
THIEPVAL MEMORIAL, France
Born in Aldershot, resident Belfast.

Bissett, Andrew - Corporal
5367 Royal Irish Rifles 7th Battalion *Age 18 Died in War on 9 July 1916*
BOIS-CARRE MILITARY CEMETERY, HAISNES, France
Son of Andrew and Sarah Bissett of 34, Sandhurst Gardens, Belfast.

Black, Adam - Lance Corporal
201058 Seaforth Highlanders 1st/4th Battalion *Died of Wounds on 6 December 1917*
ROCQUIGNY-EQUANCOURT ROAD BRITISH CEMETERY, MANANCOURT, France
48, Brussels Street, Belfast.

Black, Alfred - Bombardier
5591 Royal Garrison Artillery *Died in War on 4 July 1917*
BAGHDAD (NORTH GATE) WAR CEMETERY, Iraq
Born and enlisted in Belfast.

Black, Davidson Grant - Rifleman
19/349 Royal Irish Rifles Battalion 8th Battalion *Age 21 Died of Wounds on 6 August 1917*
LIJSSENTHOEK MILITARY CEMETERY, Belgium
Son of Ellen Black of 21, Lyle Street, Belfast, and the late James Black.

Black, Edward - Rifleman
17269 Royal Irish Rifles 13th Battalion *Killed in Action on 1 July 1916*
MILL ROAD CEMETERY, THIEPVAL, France
Survived by his sister, Mrs Templeton, 29 Glenwood Street, Belfast.

Black, George - Lance Corporal
834 Royal Irish Rifles 1st Battalion *Killed in Action on 15 July 1918*
RETHEL FRENCH NATIONAL CEMETERY, France
Born and enlisted in Belfast.

Black, James - Lance Corporal
5846 Manchester Regiment 13th Battalion *Died in War on 25 April 1917*
KARASOULI MILITARY CEMETERY, Greece
Born in Belfast.

Black, James - Private
Royal Irish Rifles 15th Battalion *Killed in Action on 21 March 1918*
237 Cambrai Street, Belfast.

Black, James D. - Sergeant
8/14091 Royal Irish Rifles 8th Battalion *Age 20 Died in War on 19 August 1916*
RATION FARM (LA PLUS DOUVE) ANNEXE, Belgium
Son of John William and Isabella J Black, of Irwin Avenue, Strandtown, Belfast.

Black, John - Driver
6818 Royal Horse Artillery and Royal Field Artillery *Died in War on 11 January 1918*
ACHIET-LE-GRAND COMMUNAL EXTENSION, France
Born and enlisted in Belfast.

Black, John - Private
26853 Royal Dublin Fusiliers 9th Battalion *Died in War on 17 August 1917*
TYNE COT CEMETERY, Belgium
Born in Belfast, enlisted in London.

Black, John - Private
7673 Royal Inniskilling Fusiliers 2nd Battalion *Died in War on 1 November 1914*
PLOEGSTEERT MEMORIAL, Belgium
Brother of Grace Tate, 247 Newtownards Road, Belfast.

Black, John Clarence - Rifleman
14090 Royal Irish Rifles "A" Company 10th Battalion *Age 22 Killed in Action at Cambrai on 11 December 1917*
THIEPVAL MEMORIAL, France
Son of John and Elizabeth Black, of 36, Albion Street, Belfast.

Black, Peter - Private
3168 Irish Guards 1st Battalion *Died in War on 16 November 1916*
THIEPVAL MEMORIAL, France
Born and enlisted in Belfast.

Black, Richard - Private
10462 Royal Dublin Fusiliers 2nd Battalion *Died in War on 27 August 1914*
HONNECHY BRITISH CEMETERY, France
Born and enlisted in Belfast.

Black, Robert - Rifleman
908 Royal Irish Rifles 15th Battalion *Died in War on 2 March 1918*
POZIERES MEMORIAL, France
Born and enlisted in Belfast.

Black, Robert Henry - Rifleman
1739 Royal Irish Rifles 9th Battalion *Killed in Action on 1 July 1916*
THIEPVAL MEMORIAL, *France*
Born and enlisted in Belfast.

Black, T - Private
Deal/13809(S) Royal Marine Labour Corps *Age 48 Died of sickness on 1 February 1919*
BELFAST CITY CEMETERY, *United Kingdom*
Son of Samuel and Jane Black; husband of Sarah Taylor (formerly Black), of 102, Urney Street, Belfast.

Black, William - Rifleman
5946 Royal Irish Rifles "B" Company 1st Battalion *Age 23 Died of sickness on 13 October 1918*
DADIZEELE NEW BRITISH CEMETERY, *Belgium*
Son of Thomas and Mary Black, of 12, Mill Row, Dunmurry, Belfast.

Black, William Colman - Sapper
57654 Royal Engineers 150th Field Company *Died in War on 16 August 1916*
BEDFORD HOUSE CEMETERY, *Belgium*
14 Kenbaan Street, Belfast.

Black, William Wesley - Private
3179 Royal Inniskilling Fusiliers "C" Company 2nd Battalion *Age 20 Died of wounds received 22nd July on 1 August 1915*
CHOCQUES MILITARY CEMETERY, *France*
Son of William and the late Fanny Black, of 16, Euston Street, Belfast.

Blackadder, Thomas - Rifleman
17/709 Royal Irish Rifles 9th Battalion *Age 32 Died in War on 24 March 1917*
POND FARM CEMETERY, *Belgium*
Son of Mrs. Annie Blackadder of 34, Tobergill Street, Belfast and formerly of Urney Street.

Blackman, George - Private
L/8043 Royal Sussex Regiment 2nd Battalion *Died in War on 14 September 1914*
VENDRESSE BRITISH CEMETERY, *France*
25 Lothair Street, Belfast.

Blackmore, Herbert - Corporal
17273 Royal Irish Rifles 12th Battalion *Died in War on 12 January 1918*
HARINGHE (BANDAGHEM) MILITARY CEMETERY, *Belgium*
Born Ballymacarrett, Belfast. Son of George Blackmore of Quay Road, Ballycastle, County Antrim.

Blackmore, William - Private
16996 Royal Inniskilling Fusiliers 11th Battalion *Killed in Action on 16 August 1917*
TYNE COT MEMORIAL, *Belgium*
Born Ballyhackamore, Belfast. Enlisted in Belfast.

Blackstock, Thomas - Rifleman
23893 Royal Irish Rifles "C" Company 2nd Battalion *Age 19 Died of wounds on 22 August 1920*
BAGHDAD (NORTH GATE) WAR CEMETERY, *Iraq*
Son of Thomas and Mary Blackstock of 5, Mersey Street, Belfast.

Blackwood, George - Rifleman
1662 Royal Irish Rifles 9th Battalion *Killed in Action on 1 July 1916*
THIEPVAL MEMORIAL, France
43 Beechpark Street, Belfast. A member of Agnes Street, Presbyterian Church.

Blackwood, James - Private
12201 Royal Inniskilling Fusiliers 5th Battalion *Age 22 Died in War on 3 September 1915*
GREEN HILL CEMETERY, Turkey
Born in Belfast.

Blackwood, James - Private
2901 Royal Inniskilling Fusiliers 2nd Battalion *Age 18 Died in War on 16 May 1915*
LE TOURET MEMORIAL, France
Son of Mr. and Mrs. George Blackwood of 72, Pound Street, Belfast.

Blackwood, John - Lance Corporal
20555 Royal Inniskilling Fusiliers 8th Battalion *Died of Wounds on 29 April 1916*
LOOS MEMORIAL, France
Survived by his wife and mother, 22, Woodford Street, Belfast.

Blain, Joseph - Rifleman
8877 Royal Irish Rifles 1st Battlion *Killed in Action on 26 October 1916*
THIEPVAL MEMORIAL, France
His parents, Thomas and Sarah lived at 35, Joseph Street, Belfast. His brother also served.

Blair, Alexander - Private
71699 North Irish Horse *Age 25 Died of wounds on 2 September 1918*
VARENNES MILITARY CEMETERY, France
Son of Alexander and Mary Blair. Born at Belfast.

Blair, Bryce Smith - Second Officer
Mercantile Marine S.S. "Artist" (Liverpool)
Age 36 Drowned as a result of an attack by an enemy submarine on 27 January 1917
TOWER HILL MEMORIAL, United Kingdom
Son of Eleanor Louisa Blair (née O'Neill), of 9, Springfield Road, Bangor, and the late Thomas Blair. Born in Belfast.

Blair, David - Private
10278 South Lancashire Regiment 2nd Battalion *Died of Wounds on 5 June 1915*
BEDFORD HOUSE CEMETERY, Belgium
66 Pernau Street, Belfast. His brother also fell.

Blair, Henry Robert - Rifleman
14/68 Royal Irish Rifles 14th Battalion *Killed in action on 7 June 1917*
SPANBROEKMOLEN BRITISH CEMETERY, Belgium
Son of Mrs M J Blair, 65 Kimberley, Belfast.

Blair, James - Lance Corporal
773 Royal Irish Rifles 8th Battalion *Died in War on 2 July 1916*
THIEPVAL MEMORIAL, France
Born Ballymacarrett, Belfast. Enlisted in Belfast, the son of Thomas and Bella Boyle.

Blair, James - Private
29184 Royal Inniskilling Fusiliers 6th Battalion *Age 19 Killed in Action on 4 November 1918*
FONTAINE-AU-BOIS COMMUNAL CEMETERY, France
Son of Samuel and Sarah Blair, of 82, Paris Street, Belfast.

Blair, James - Sapper
108392 Royal Engineers Base Signal Depot *Age 39 Died in War on 16 September 1916*
NAIROBI BRITISH AND INDIAN MEMORIAL, Kenya
Son of James and Margaret Ann Blair; husband of Isabella Blair, of 6, Copperfield Street, Belfast.

Blair, John - Rifleman
9092 Royal Irish Rifles 1st Battalion *Killed in Action on 12 March 1915*
LE TOURET MEMORIAL, France
98, Wilton Street, Belfast. Two brothers also served.

Blair, John Kirkwood - Lance Corporal
17275 Royal Irish Rifles 14th Battalion *Age 23 Killed in Action on 16 August 1917*
NEW IRISH FARM CEMETERY, Belgium
Son of Hugh and Elise Blair, of 57, Candahar Street, Ormeau Road, Belfast.
Native of Holywood, County Down.

Blair, Mark - Private
7363 Royal Scots Fusiliers 2nd Battalion *Died in War on 12 March 1915*
LE TOURET MEMORIAL, France
Born in Belfast, enlisted in Ayr, Scotland.

Blair, Richard - Lance Corporal
6706 Royal Irish Rifles 10th Battalion *Killed in Action on 1 July 1916*
CONNAUGHT CEMETERY, THIEPVAL, France
Born and enlisted in Belfast.

Blair, Samuel - Gunner
951466 Royal Field Artillery *Died in War on 1 December 1917*
METZ-EN-COUTURE COMMUNAL CEMETERY BRITISH EXTENSION, France
Fourth Street, Belfast.

Blair, Thomas - Private
1239 Royal Irish Rifles 14th Battalion *Killed in Action on 1 July 1916*
CONNAUGHT CEMETERY, THIEPVAL, France
64 Cumberland Street, Belfast.

Blair, William John - Rifleman
1691 Royal Irish Rifles 15th Battalion *Died in War on 27 March 1918*
POZIERES MEMORIAL, France
Born and enlisted in Belfast.

Blake, Charles - Rifleman
6397 Royal Irish Rifles 14th Battalion *Killed In Action on 7 June 1916*
SPANBROEKMOLEN BRITISH CEMETERY, Belgium
Born in Belfast.

Blake, Henry - Rifleman
1284 Royal Irish Rifles 15th Battalion *Killed In Action on 1 July 1916*
THIEPVAL MEMORIAL, France
Born in Belfast.

Blake, Paul Francis - Rifleman
7470 Royal Irish Rifles 1st Battalion *Killed in Action on 15 August 1917*
YPRES RESERVOIR CEMETERY, Belgium
Born and enlisted in Belfast.

Blakeley, Robert - Private
T.F.293393 Duke of Cambridge's Own (Middlesex Regiment) 2/10th Battalion *Died in War on 19 February 1918*
JERUSALEM WAR CEMETERY, Israel
Born in Belfast, enlisted in Middlesex, England.

Blakely, Bertie - Corporal
9437 Royal Inniskilling Fusiliers 7th Battalion *Died in War on 9 September 1916*
THIEPVAL MEMORIAL, France
Born in Belfast, enlisted in Ballykinler.

Bleakely, John - Stoker First Class
213143 Royal Navy HMS "Monmouth" *Age 33 Killed in Action at Battle of Coronel on 1 November 1914*
PLYMOUTH NAVAL MEMORIAL, United Kingdom
Son of Robert Bleakely, of 34, Ballynure Street, Belfast.

Bleakley, Edward - Private
3669 Royal Inniskilling Fusiliers 7/8th Battalion *Killed in Action on 16 August 1917*
TYNE COT MEMORIAL, Belgium
Born and enlisted in Belfast.

Bleakley, Robert - Private
17/1738 Royal Irish Rifles 9th Battalion *Killed in Action on 25 December 1916*
ST. QUENTIN CABARET MILITARY CEMETERY, Belgium
86 Argyle Street, Belfast. Died on Christmas Day.

Bleakley, Westley - Private
11735 Royal Irish Fusiliers "C" Company 5th Battalion *Age 29 Died in War on 7 December 1915*
DOIRAN MEMORIAL, Greece
Son of Mr. and Mrs R. Bleakley, of Clounagh, Portadown; husband of Mary Bleakley,
of 86, Methuen Street, Belfast.

Bloomer, Andrew - Private
2402 Connaught Rangers 6th Battalion *Killed in Action on 21 March 1918*
POZIERES MEMORIAL, France
Survived by his sister, Mrs McGurk, 61 Norfolk Street, Belfast.

Bloomer, Robert - Rifleman
12209 Royal Irish Rifles 8th Battalion *Died in War on 2 July 1916*
THIEPVAL MEMORIAL, France
Born and enlisted in Belfast.

Bloomer, William - Private
4623 Royal Inniskilling Fusiliers 5th Battalion *Age 32 Died in War on 15 August 1915*
HELLES MEMORIAL, Turkey
Husband of Mrs. Henrietta Bloomer, of 228, Matilda Street, Belfast.

Bloomer, William John - Private
266283 Black Watch (Royal Highlanders) 4/5th (Angus and Dundee) Battalion (Territorial)
Died in War on 1 April 1918
POZIERES MEMORIAL, France
Born and enlisted in Belfast.

Boal, Adam - Private
54340 Manchester Regiment 12th Battalion formerly 088434 Army Service Corps
Killed In Action on 26 August 1918
ADANAC MILITARY CEMETERY, MIRAUMONT, France
Born in Belfast.

Boal, John - Private
8817 Machine Gun Corps (Infantry) formerly 1937 Manchester Regiment *Died in War on 20 September 1917*
TYNE COT MEMORIAL, Belgium
Born in Belfast. Enlisted in England.

Boas, Ernest George - Second Lieutenant
Royal Irish Rifles 5th Battalion attached 13th Battalion *Age 19 Killed in Action on 1 July 1916*
THIEPVAL MEMORIAL, France
Son of May L. Boas, of 31, Sans Souci Park, Belfast, and Ernest A. Boas. A member of Queen's University Officer Training Corps. Worked in the Loopbridge Weaving Factory which his father owned.

Bodel, Edward - Lance Corporal
5446 6th Dragoons (Inniskilling) attached 1st Life Guards *Age 28 Died in War on 2 June 1915*
YPRES TOWN CEMETERY EXTENSION, Belgium
Son of the late Henry Bodel and of Annie Bodel, of 7, Catherine Place, Greencastle, Belfast.

Boden, John - Corporal
70 4th (Queen's Own) Hussars) *Age 30 Died in War on 30 March 1918*
POZIERES MEMORIAL, France,
Son of John Boden, of 13, Brandon Terrace, Park Gate Avenue, Strandtown, Belfast, and the late Agnes Boden; husband of Jane Boden of 85, Willowfield Street, Belfast.

Body, John - Private
450 Middlesex Regiment 11th Battalion *Age 24 Died in War on 14 August 1917*
MONCHY BRITISH CEMETERY, MONCHY-LE-PREUX, France
Son of Joseph and Sarah Body, of Chenies, Buckinghamshire; husband of E. M. Porter (formerly Body) of 82, Thistle Street, Belfast.

Boggs, Robert - Private
18027 Leinster Regiment 2nd Battalion *Died in War on 27 April 1918*
CINQ RUES BRITISH CEMETERY, HAZEBROUCK, Belgium
Resident in Belfast, born in County Tyrone. Formerly 4682 Connaught Rangers.

Bogne, Douglas Hill - Sergeant
King's Royal Irish Hussars *Died in War on 4 October 1916*
BURIED IN YPRES, Belgium
Born Belfast in 1890. Son of Douglas and Magaret Bogne of Greenore County Louth. Educated at Wilson Grammar School and worked as a bank clerk before enlisting in 1916.

Boland, Alexander - Rifleman
14098 Royal Irish Rifles 10th Battalion *Age 20 Killed in Action on 1 July 1916*
THIEPVAL MEMORIAL, France
Son of Charles and Martha Boland of 21, Gosford Street, Belfast.

Boland, James - Private
20852 Royal Inniskilling Fusiliers 1st Battalion *Died in War on 13 August 1915*
HELLES MEMORIAL, Turkey
35 Raglan Street, Belfast. Survived by his mother.

Boland, William - Rifleman
8/14099 Royal Irish Rifles "B" Company 8th Battalion *Age 19 Died in War on 12 June 1916*
AUTHUILE MILITARY CEMETERY, France
Born in Scotland his father was a mattress maker. Son of James and Mary Elizabeth Boland of 49, Ogilvie Street, Belfast.

Bolton, William - Private
59395 Royal Army Medical Corps *Age 46 Died of sickness on 22 March 1918*
BELFAST (DUNDONALD) CEMETERY, United Kingdom
Discharged from the army in 1916 and issued with the Silver War Badge. Husband of Annie Bolton of 6, Conlon Street, Belfast. Born in County Antrim.

Bond, Joseph - Rifleman
9461 Royal Irish Rifles 2nd Battalion *Died of Wounds on 4 April 1918*
MAUBEUGE-CENTRE CEMETERY, France
Husband of Mrs. A Bond, of 9, Conlig Street, Belfast.

Bond, Samuel - Sergeant
16248 Royal Irish Rifles "A" Company 14th Battalion *Age 23 Killed in Action on 1 July 1916*
THIEPVAL MEMORIAL, France
Son of Margaret Bond, of 6, Manor Drive, Belfast, and the late William Bond (Royal Navy).

Bond, Thomas Morgan - Second Lieutenant
Royal Irish Rifles 11th Battalion *Age 18 Died in War on 17 August 1915*
PLOEGSTEERT MEMORIAL, Belgium
Born in Belfast. the son of Major Thomas and Mrs Martha Frances Bond. Initially served in the 5th London Rifle Brigade before being commisioned into the Royal Irish Rifles. Killed at the second Battle of Ypres.

Bone, Thomas - Sapper
64598 Royal Irish Rifles *Died in War on 9 October 1917*
BARD COTTAGE CEMETERY, Belgium
Husband of Mrs Agnes Bone, 4 Earl Street, Belfast.

Bonnar, William - Private
201087, Seaforth Highlanders 1st/5th Battalion *Age 19 Killed in Action on 23 July 1918*
MARFAUX BRITISH CEMETERY, France
Son of George Bonnar of 2, Oldpark Village, Belfast, and Helen Bonnar. Awarded the Military Medal.

Bonynge, Stephen - Private
25113 Royal Dublin Fusiliers 10th Battalion *Died in War on 31 August 1916*
BULLY-GRENAY COMMUNAL CEMETERY, BRITISH EXTENSION, France
Husband of Susan Bonynge of 7, Britannic Street, Sandy Row, Belfast.

Boorman, James - Private
B/8364 Cameronians (Scottish Rifles) 2nd Battalion *Died in War on 20 November 1915*
SAILLY-SUR-LA-LYS CANADIAN CEMETERY, France
Born in Dunloy, County Antrim, resident in Belfast.

Booth, Henry - Rifleman
937 Royal Irish Rifles *Age 45 Died in War on 8 September 1916*
BELFAST CITY CEMETERY, United Kingdom
Husband of Annie Margaret Booth of 13, Colchester Street, Donegall Road, Belfast.

Booth, Henry Maxwell - Lance Corporal
237918 Canadian Infantry 204th Battalion *Age 40 Died of phthisis on 7 June 1919*
TORONTO (PROSPECT) CEMETERY, Canada
Son of Thomas Rogers Booth and Mary Ann Booth of 165, Ormeau Street, Belfast; husband of Hannah Mayall Booth, of 23, Verrall Avenue, Toronto, Ontario, Canada.

Booth, Hudson - Rifleman
3969 Royal Irish Rifles 14th Battalion *Age 21 Killed in Action on 1 July 1916*
THIEPVAL MEMORIAL, France
Son of Mrs. Isabella Booth of 11, Wimbledon Street, Belfast.

Booth, Robert - Rifleman
2354 Royal Irish Rifles 1st Battalion *Age 18 Killed in Action on 20 April 1918*
TYNE COT MEMORIAL, Belgium
Son of William Thomas Booth of 22, Lawyer Street, Belfast.

Booth, Thomas - Quartermaster Sergeant
S/15284 Army Service Corps "A" Supply Company *Age 37 Died suddenly at home on 19 October 1915*
CARNMONEY CEMETERY, United Kingdom
Eighteen years service, the son of the late Robert Stephen Booth; husband of Jane Booth of 167, Tennent Street, Belfast.

Boston, John Joseph - Private
139521 Canadian Infantry (Quebec Regiment) "A" Company 87th Battalion
Age 43 Died as a Prisoner of War on 4 January 1918
COLOGNE SOUTHERN CEMETERY, Germany
Son of Joseph and Elizabeth Boston, of 7 Leroy Street, Belfast, Ireland.

Boston, J Joseph - Private
11697 Loyal North Lancashire Regiment 6th *Age 24 Died in War on 9 August 1915*
HELLES MEMORIAL, Turkey
A draper, he was the son of Samuel Boston; husband of Ann Boston, of 8 Florida Street, Belfast.

Boston, Samuel - Private
6095 South Lancashire Regiment 2nd Battalion *Died in War on 15 July 1916*
THIEPVAL MEMORIAL, *France*
His parents, Samuel and Christina lived at 22 Bromley Street, Belfast. His brother was also killed.

Boston, Thomas - Lieutenant
Machine Gun Corps (Infantry) 10th Battalion *Age 26 Died of pneumonia on 25 December 1918*
CAIRO WAR MEMORIAL CEMETERY, *Egypt*
Son of John and Margaret Boston, of 76, The Mount, Mountpottinger, Belfast.
Educated at RBAI he was a member of the old UVF.

Bothwell, Arthur William - Private
12757 Royal Inniskilling Fusiliers "C" Company 6th Battalion *Age 35 Died in War on 13 September 1916*
SALONIKA (LEMBET ROAD) MILITARY CEMETERY, *Greece*
Son of the late Jonathan and Agnes A. Bothwell, of Derry, Dromara, County Down; husband of
Mary Bothwell of 10, Ashfield Street, Belfast. Served in the South African Campaign.

Bothwell, Samuel James - Major
1st Canadian Mounted Rifles (Saskatchewan Regiment) *Age 41 Died in War on between 9 - 12 April 1917*
NINE ELMS MILITARY CEMETERY, THELUS, *France*
Son of Samuel and Susan Bothwell of Mosside, Alberta Canada, and formerly of Belfast, Ireland.
Husband of Alice Hannah Bothwell (now Morris), of Stewartfield, Alberta, Canada.

Bourke, Albert William - Second Lieutenant
Royal Irish Fusiliers attached Royal Irish Rifles 1st Battalion *Age 23 Killed in Action on 9 May 1915*
LE TROU AID POST CEMETERY, FLEURBAIX, *France*
Son of Charles Edward and Sophia Bourke, of Kensington House, Kensington Road, Knock, Belfast.
Educated at Methodist College and Queen's University where he studied medicine and was a member
of the Officer Training Corps. Shot through the head whilst leading an attack on enemy lines.

Boville, James - Private
724650 Canadian Infantry (Central Ontario Regiment) 20th Battalion *Age 30 Died in War on 5 April 1917*
ECOIVRES MILITARY CEMETERY, MONT-ST. ELOI, *France*
Son of James and Margaret Boville, of 7 Leroy Street, Belfast. Husband of Margaret Boville,
of 21, Cambridge Avenue, Toronto, Canada. Enlisted in 1915, he was a brother of Robert.

Boville, Robert - Private
163291 Canadian Infantry (Central Ontario Regiment) 75th Battalion *Age 36 Died in War on 18 November 1916*
VIMY MEMORIAL, *France*
Son of James Boville, of 7, Leroy Street, Ballysillan, Belfast, husband of Sarah Boville
of 295, Ashdale Avenue, Toronto. Like his brother he enlisted in 1915.

Bowers, James - Lance Corporal
1172 The Loyal North Lancashire Regiment 1st Battalion *Age 24 Died in War on 31 December 1914*
LE TOURET MEMORIAL, *France*
Son of John and Mary Bowers, of 9, Cambridge Street, Belfast.

Bowman, Hugh David - Corporal
S/17481 Black Watch (Royal Highlanders) 2nd Battalion *Age 29 Died in War on 14 March 1917*
BASRA MEMORIAL, *Iraq*
Husband of M A Bowman, of 7, Rockdale Street, Belfast.

Bowman, James - Rifleman
12601 Royal Irish Rifles 8th Battalion *Age 21 Died in War on 2 July 1916*
THIEPVAL MEMORIAL, *France*
Son of John Bowman, of 30, Sandown Road, Ballyhackamore, Belfast.

Bowman, John - Private
11013 Highland Light Infantry 2nd Battalion *Died in War on 19 December 1914*
His parents, George, a stonecutter, and Martha lived at 9 Crosby Street and previously Hopewell Street, Belfast.

Bowman, Samuel - Private
2960 Royal Inniskilling Fusiliers "C" Company 2nd Battalion *Age 21 Died in War on 22 July 1915*
BETHUNE TOWN CEMETERY, *France*
Son of Isabella Bowman of 51, Witham Street, Belfast, and the late Samuel Bowman.

Boyce, John McMaster - Rifleman
17292 Royal Irish Rifles 12th Battalion *Killed in Action on 1 July 1916*
THIEPVAL MEMORIAL, *France*
Born and enlisted in Belfast.

Boyd, Alexander - Lance Corporal
7784 Royal Irish Rifles 2nd Battalion *Killed in Action on 27 October 1914*
LE TOURET MEMORIAL, *France*
His widow lived at 63 Lawnbrook Avenue, Belfast. He was an army reservist and a member of the old UVF.

Boyd, Alexander - Sergeant
17303 Royal Irish Rifles 12th Battalion *Age 20 Killed in Action on 16 August 1917*
TYNE COT CEMETERY, *Belgium*
Son of William John Boyd, of 107, East Bread Street, Belfast. Native of Whiteabbey, Belfast.

Boyd, Arthur - Private
40927 Royal Army Medical Corps 108th Field Ambulance *Age 24. Died in War on 16 September 1918*
ARNEKE BRITISH CEMETERY, *France*
Brother of Mrs. Mary Stewart, of Dundela Park Cottages, Strandtown, Belfast.

Boyd, Brian - Second Lieutenant
Royal Irish Rifles 14th Battalion *Age 19 Killed in Action on 7 June 1917*
BAILLEUL COMMUNAL CEMETERY EXTENSION (NORD), *France*
Son of William A. and Lizzie M. Boyd, of 10, Cyprus Gardens, Belfast. Educated at RBAI and then apprenticed in the linen trade. Initially joined in the ranks, won the Military Medal for bravey and was subsequently commissioned.

Boyd, Cecil Vincent - Second Lieutenant
Royal Irish Rifles *Died in War on 23 November 1917*
CAMBRAI MEMORIAL, LOUVERVAL, *France*
Claremont, Ardenleee Avenue, Belfast.

Boyd, David - Able Seaman
229233 Royal Navy HMS "Good Hope" *Age 28 Killed in Action at the Battle of Coronel on 1 November 1914*
PORTSMOUTH NAVAL MEMORIAL, *United Kingdom*
Son of David and Mary Boyd, of 40, Jerusalem Street, Belfast.

Boyd, David - Rifleman
6841 Royal Irish Rifles 2nd Battalion *Killed in action on 1 July 1916*
FORCEVILLE COMMUNAL CEMETERY AND EXTENSION, France
Husband of Elizabeth Boyd, 61 Skipton Street, Belfast.

Boyd, David Thomas - Second Lieutenant
Cameronians (Scottish Rifles) 6th Battalion *Age 26 Died in War on 3 May 1917*
ETAPLES MILITARY CEMETERY, France
Son of David and Jane Harvie Boyd, of 53, Fitzwilliam Street, Belfast.

Boyd, George - Stoker First Class
SS/107749 Royal Navy HMS "Pembroke" *Died in War on 3 September 1917*
GILLINGHAM (WOODLANDS) CEMETERY, United Kingdom
11 Cultra Street, Belfast.

Boyd, Harry - Sergeant
S/33833 Army Service Corps General Headquarters (Cairo) *Age 21 Drowned at sea
(from H.T. "Ivernia") on 1 January 1917*
MIKRA MEMORIAL, Greece
Son of Robert and Margaret Boyd, of 78, Hillman Street, Belfast. Awarded the Obilitch Silver Medal (Serbia).

Boyd, Henry - Lieutenant
Royal Air Force 100th Squadron *Age 19 Died in War on 25 August 1918*
CHARMES MILITARY CEMETERY, ESSEGNEY, France
Son of William G. and M. Boyd, of Holway Drive, Santa Cruz, California, USA. Native of Belfast.

Boyd, James - Lance Corporal
2953 Black Watch (Royal Highlanders) 6th (Perthshire) Battalion (Territorial) *Died in War on 30 July 1916*
THIEPVAL MEMORIAL, France
Born in Belfast. Enlisted Perth, Scotland.

Boyd, James - Private
291511 Welsh Regiment *Age 24 Died as a result of war on 29 April 1920*
CARNMONEY CEMETERY, United Kingdom
Son of James and Annie Boyd; husband of Margaret Boyd, of 8, Summerhill Street, Belfast.

Boyd, James - Rifleman
11848 Royal Irish Rifles 15th Battalion *Died in War on 16 February 1916*
SUCRERIE MILITARY CEMETERY, COLINCAMPS, France
8 Lever Street Ligoneil, Belfast.

Boyd, James - Rifleman
5221 Royal Irish Rifles 1st Battalion *Age 42 Died of wounds on 13 January 1915*
BOULOGNE EASTERN CEMETERY, France
Son of Mary Boyd, of 15, Malcolm Street, Belfast.

Boyd, James - Sergeant
10400 Royal Irish Fusiliers 1st Battalion *Age 24 Died of wounds on 11 October 1918*
DADIZEELE NEW BRITISH CEMETERY, Belgium
Son of William and Esther Boyd, of 3, Barrow Street, Oldpark Road Belfast. Awarded the Military Medal.

Boyd, John - Private
201336 Argyll and Sutherland Highlanders 1st/5th Battalion *Age 29 Died in War on 24 June 1918*
LIGNY-ST. FLOCHEL BRITISH CEMETERY, AVERDOINGT, France
Native of Belfast.

Boyd, John - Private
9499 King's (Liverpool Regiment) 4th Battalion *Died in War on 1 May 1915*
YPRES (MENIN GATE) MEMORIAL, Belgium
Born in Portadown, enlisted Liverpool, resident Belfast.

Boyd, John - Rifleman
3199 Royal Irish Rifles 8th Battalion *Killed In Action on 2 July 1916*
THIEPVAL MEMORIAL, France
Son of the late Hugh and Elizabeth Boyd.

Boyd, John - Sergeant
12581 Royal Irish Rifles 8th Battalion *Age 22 Died in War on 11 June 1916*
THIEPVAL MEMORIAL, France
Son of Robert and Agnes Boyd of 17, Titania Street, Cregagh Road, Belfast.

Boyd, Robert - Rifleman
582 Royal Irish Rifles 10th Battalion *Age 37 Killed in Action on 1 July 1916*
THIEPVAL MEMORIAL, France
Son of Mrs Jeannie Boyd, of 17, India Street, Belfast.

Boyd, Robert - Rifleman
5823 Royal Irish Rifles 2nd Battalion *Killed in Action on 20 June 1917*
YPRES (MENIN GATE) MEMORIAL, Belgium
Born in Belfast, enlisted at Ballykinler.

Boyd, Robert - Rifleman
9142 Royal Inniskilling Fusiliers 2nd Battalion *Died in War on 1 November 1914*
PLOEGSTEERT MEMORIAL, Belgium
Born and enlisted in Belfast.

Boyd, Samuel - Rifleman
14/16264 Royal Irish Rifles 14th Battalion *Died in War on 31 January 1917*
BERKS CEMETERY EXTENSION, Belgium
Enlisted and resident in Belfast.

Boyd, Thomas - Rifleman
17/653 Royal Irish Rifles 8th Battalion *Age 27 Died in War on 2 July 1916*
THIEPVAL MEMORIAL, France
Husband of Agnes Boyd, of 43, Mineral Street, Belfast.

Boyd, Thomas - Rifleman
8948 Royal Irish Rifles 2nd Battalion *Died of Wounds on 3 May 1916*
MERICOURT-L'ABBE COMMUNAL CEMETERY EXTENSION, France
Born in Belfast.

Boyd, Willaim - Sergeant
73 Middlesex Regiment Age 52 *Died as a result of war on 27 January 1920*
FINCHLEY (HOLY TRINITY) CHURCHYARD, United Kingdom
Son of the late David Boyd, of Belfast; husband of Margaret Boyd of 14, New Trinity Road, East Finchley. Holder of the Distinguished Conduct Medal.

Boyd, William (Willie) - Private
8143 South African Infantry 3rd Regiment *Died of Wounds on 24 December 1917*
FINS NEW BRITISH CEMETERY, SOREL-LE-GRAND, France
Son of Mina and the late David Boyd.

Boyd, William - Corporal
12215 Royal Irish Rifles 15th Battalion *Age 28 Died in War on 2 July 1916*
SERRE ROAD CEMETERY No.2, France
Son of William Boyd; husband of M A Bull (formerly Boyd), of 41, James Street, Belfast.

Boyd, William - Gunner
16897 Royal Garrison Artillery 1st/2nd (Lancs) Heavy Battery *Age 35 Died in War on 15 June 1917*
ETAPLES MILITARY CEMETERY, France
Son of Mary Boyd, of 8, Chamberlain Street, Belfast, and the late William Boyd.

Boyd, William - Lance Sergeant
6453 Irish Guards 2nd Battalion *Died in War on 6 October 1915*
JANVAL CEMETERY, DIEPPE, France
Craven Street, Belfast. A former member of the Royal Irish Constabulary.

Boyd, William - Private
17/401 Royal Irish Rifles 15th Battalion *Died in War on 17 December 1916*
ST. QUENTIN CABARET MILITARY CEMETERY, Belgium
Husband of Jeannie, 83 Disraeli Street, Belfast.

Boyd, William - Rifleman
7025 Royal Irish Rifles 1st Battalion *Killed in Action on 16 December 1915*
STE MARIE CEMETERY, LE HAVRE, France
Born in Belfast, enlisted in Holywood.

Boyd, William Bruce - Private
14574 South African Infantry 4th Regiment *Died in War on 24 March 1918*
POZIERES MEMORIAL, France
Son of Bryce and Florence Boyd 55 Tennent Street.

Boyd, William Hatchell - Second Lieutenant
Royal Dublin Fusiliers *Age 29 Died in War on 9 September 1916*
THIEPVAL MEMORIAL, France
Native of Belfast; an accountant, he was the son of the Rev Samuel Boyd, a Methodist minister in Dublin.

Boyd, William James - Rifleman
12214 Royal Irish Rifles 15th Battalion *Killed in Action on 1 July 1916*
THIEPVAL MEMORIAL, France
Husband of Maggie and father of a small daughter, 22 Sancroft Street, Belfast.

Boyde, Joseph - Sergeant
16200 Royal Irish Rifles 9th Battalion *Killed in Action on 1 July 1916*
THIEPVAL MEMORIAL, France
17, Bromley Street, Belfast.

Boyes, George - Private
4633 Royal Inniskilling Fusiliers 6th Battalion *Died of Wounds on 8 November 1917*
BEERSHEBA WAR CEMETERY, Israel
Born and enlisted in Belfast.

Boylan, John - Rifleman
12558 Royal Irish Rifles 15th Battalion *Age 20 Killed in Action on 1 July 1916*
THIEPVAL MEMORIAL, France
Son of John and Annie Boylan, of 166, Alexandra Park Avenue, Belfast.

Boylan, John - Rifleman
8751 Royal Irish Rifles 1st Battalion *Killed in Action on 25 September 1915*
PLOEGSTEERT MEMORIAL, Belgium
Born and enlisted in Belfast.

Boyle, Arthur - Pioneer
WR/342896 Corps of Royal Engineers Inland Water Transport *Died on 17 July 1918*
NEWPORT (ST. WOOLOS) CEMETERY, United Kingdom
Born and enlisted in Belfast.

Boyle, Augustine Hugh - Private
10759 Royal Inniskilling Fusiliers 1st Battalion *Killed in action on 22 March 1918*
POZIERES MEMORIAL, France
Son of Mrs Sarah Ann Boyle, 96 Donegall Road, Belfast

Boyle, Bernard - Rifleman
7443 Royal Irish Rifles 6th Battalion *Died in War on 11 August 1915*
HELLES MEMORIAL, Turkey
Husband of Margaret Boyle, of 7, Ross Place, Belfast.

Boyle, Daniel Leo - Private
61515 Royal Army Medical Corps *Died in War on 12 May 1917*
POPERINGHE NEW MILITARY CEMETERY, Belgium
Born in Belfast, enlisted in Dublin.

Boyle, Edward James - Sergeant
9002 Princess Victoria's (Royal Irish Fusiliers) 1st Battalion *Died in War on 18 December 1917*
DOULLENS COMMUNAL CEMETERY EXTENSION No.1, France
Born and enlisted in Belfast.

Boyle, Frederick - Lance Corporal
20098 Royal Inniskilling Fusiliers 7th/8th Battalion *Age 24 Killed in Action on 16 August 1917*
TYNE COT MEMORIAL, Belgium
Son of Jane Boyle, of 68, Walmer Street, Belfast.

Boyle, Henry - Private
10309 Royal Irish Fusiliers 1st Battalion *Age 22 Killed in Action on 18 October 1914*
HOUPLINES COMMUNAL CEMETERY EXTENSION, France
Son of Patrick and Margaret J. Boyle, of 52, St. John's Park, Upper Holloway, London. Born in Belfast.

Boyle, Hugh - Private
265491 Cameronians (Scottish Rifles) 1st/7th Battalion *Age 23 Died in war on 20 April 1917*
GAZA WAR CEMETERY, Israel
Son of Hugh and Sarah Boyle, of 13, Argowan Street, South Side, Glasgow. Born at Belfast.

Boyle, James - Private
12653 Royal Irish Fusiliers "A" Company 1st Battalion *Age 30 Killed in Action on 11 April 1917*
BROWN'S COPSE CEMETERY, ROEUX, France
Husband of Mary Bridget Boyle, of 17, Middlepath Street, Belfast.

Boyle, James - Private
29187 Royal Inniskilling Fusiliers 2nd Battalion *Died in War on 29 November 1917*
DOZINGHEM MILITARY CEMETERY, Belgium
Born in Whiteabbey, enlisted Port Glasgow, resident in Belfast.

Boyle, James - Private
7152 Princess Victoria's (Royal Irish Fusiliers) 1st Battalion *Killed in Action on 21 March 1918*
POZIERES MEMORIAL, France
Born and enlisted in Belfast.

Boyle, John - Private
28380 Royal Inniskilling Fusiliers 9th Battalion *Killed in Action on 1 July 1916*
THIEPVAL MEMORIAL, France
Born Ballyhackamore, Belfast. Enlisted in Belfast.

Boyle, John - Sapper
2055599 Corps of Royal Engineers Inland Water Transport *Died on 13 November 1917*
BASRA WAR CEMETERY, Iraq
Born in Belfast.

Boyle, John Joseph - Third Engineer
Mercantile Marine S.S. Zara (Hull) *Drowned, as a result of an attack by an enemy submarine, on 13 April 1917*
TOWER HILL MEMORIAL, United Kingdom
Husband of Elizabeth Boyle, of 2, Bedeque Street, Belfast.

Boyle, Jonanthan - Sergeant
9066 Royal Army Medical Corps *Died as a result of war on 26 February 1919*
BELFAST CITY CEMETERY, United Kingdom
Husband of Elizabeth Boyd, 22 Twickenham Street, Belfast.

Boyle, Robert - Lance Corporal
1370 Royal Irish Rifles 1st Battalion *Age 19 Killed in Action on 21 March 1918*
GRAND-SERAUCOURT BRITISH CEMETERY, France
Son of Robert and Margaret Boyle, of Belfast.

Journey of Remembering

Boyle, Thomas - Private
S/4955 Argyll and Sutherland Highlanders 12th Battalion *Age 25 Died in War on 9 May 1917*
DOIRAN MEMORIAL, Greece
Son of Hugh Boyle, of 97, Nelson Street, South Side, Glasgow, and the late S Boyle. Born at Belfast.

Boylen, John - Rifleman
12558 Royal Irish Rifles 15th Battalion *Killed in Action on 1 July 1916*
THIEPVAL MEMORIAL, France
Born and enlisted in Belfast.

Boyles, Ferran - Lance Corporal
17/806 Royal Irish Rifles 10th Battalion *Age 28 Died of Wounds on 20 January 1918*
HAM BRITISH CEMETERY, MUILLE-VILLETTE, France
Son of John, a shipwright, and Eliza Boyles, 15 Excise Street, Belfast.

Boyles, James - Fourth Engineer Officer
Mercantile Marine S.S. "Don Arturo" (London) *Age 47 Presumed drowned on 17 June 1917*
TOWER HILL MEMORIAL, United Kingdom
Born at Belfast.

Boyles, John - Rifleman
566 Royal Irish Rifles 10th Battalion *Killed In Action on 20 January 1918*
THIEPVAL MEMORIAL, France
25 Cosgrave Street, Belfast.

Boyles, William J - Private
22644 Royal Irish Fusiliers 9th Battalion *Killed in Action on 1 July 1916*
THIEPVAL MEMORIAL, France
22 Arkwright Street, Belfast.

Bracken, Robert - Driver
T4/160143 Royal Army Service Corps *Died in War on 30 September 1917*
BELAST CITY CEMETERY, United Kingdom
Born and enlisted in Belfast.

Braden, Thomas - Private
775445 Canadian Infantry 21st (Eastern Ontario Regiment) *Age 39 Died in War on 15 August 1917*
VIMY MEMORIAL, France
Son of Martha Braden, of 13, Glentilt Street, Belfast, and Thomas Braden. Two brothers were also serving.

Bradford, Robert - Rifleman
5465 Royal Irish Rifles 2nd Battalion *Killed in Action on 8 May 1915*
YPRES (MENIN GATE) MEMORIAL, Belgium
Born and enlisted in Belfast.

Bradley, George - Sergeant
206144 Machine Gun Corps (Motors) "D" Battalion Heavy Branch *Age 26 Killed in Action on 3 May 1917*
MORY ABBEY MILITARY CEMETERY, MORY, France
Originally served in the 12th Battalion Royal Irish Rifles and later the Tank Corps.
Son of Robert and Margaret Ann Bradley, of 34, Greenmount Villa, Henderson Avenue, Belfast.
Awarded the Military Medal.

Bradley, James - Acting Sergeant
33917 Loyal North Lancashire Regiment 10th Battalion *Died in War on 28 April 1917*
ARRAS MEMORIAL, France
Born and enlisted in Belfast. Formerly 13083, Royal Inniskilling Fusiliers.

Bradley, John - Private
4871 Labour Corps *Died in War on 14 October 1918*
BEAULENCOURT BRITISH CEMETERY, LIGNY-THILLOY, France
Born in Belfast, enlisted in Glasgow. Formerly 26790, Royal Scots Fusiliers.

Bradley, John - Rifleman
10005 Royal Irish Rifles 1st Battalion *Killed in Action on 16 June 1915*
PLOEGSTEERT MEMORIAL, Belgium
Born and enlisted in Belfast.

Bradley, Patrick - Private
H/31787 Reserve Cavalry Regiment *Age 17 Died in War on 8 December 1916*
BELFAST (MILLTOWN) ROMAN CATHOLIC CEMETERY, United Kingdom
Son of Thomas, a dealer in fowl, and Catherine Bradley, of 6, Stanfield Court, Belfast.

Bradley, Thomas - Private
202590 Argyll & Sutherland Highlanders 1st/7th Battalion *Died in War on 20 September 1916*
TYNE COT MEMORIAL, Belgium
Born Ballymacarrett, Belfast. Enlisted in Belfast.

Bradley, William John - Private
23009 Royal Irish Fusiliers 8th Battalion *Killed in Action on 17 August 1917*
TYNE COT MEMORIAL, Belgium
Born Ballymacarrett, Belfast. Enlisted in Belfast.

Bradshaw, John - Private
7797 Cameronians (Scottish Rifles) 2nd Battalion *Age 25 Died of wounds on 11 June 1915*
MERVILLE COMMUNAL CEMETERY, France
Son of John and Matilda Bradshaw, of 25, Yarrow Street, Belfast.

Bradshaw, Joseph - Private
6334 Royal Inniskilling Fusiliers 2nd Battalion *Age 33 Died in War on 28 October 1914*
PLOEGSTEERT MEMORIAL, Belgium
Husband of Elizabeth Bradshaw, of 1, Ratcliffe Street, Donegall Pass, Belfast. Served in the South African Campaign.

Bradshaw, Joseph - Private
775242 Canadian Infantry 129th Battalion *Age 44 Died of sickness on 25 December 1919*
TORONTO (PROSPECT) CEMETERY, Canada
Son of Martha Bradshaw, of 52, Fairview Street, Belfast, Ireland and the late William Bradshaw; husband of Elizabeth Bradshaw, of 63, Ellsworth Avenue, Toronto, Canada.

Bradshaw, Robert Oliver - Sergeant
74295 Canadian Infantry (Saskatchewan Regiment) 28th Battalion *Age 36 Died in War on 11 August 1916*
RENINGHELST NEW MILITARY CEMETERY, Belgium
Son of Caroline Bradshaw, Great Victoria Street, Belfast. Had previously served twelve years with the 1st Battalion Scots Guards. A carpenter by trade.

Bradshaw, Samuel - Rifleman
19/780 Royal Irish Rifles 10th Battalion *Age 21 Died in War on 22 November 1917*
CAMBRAI MEMORIAL, LOUVERVAL, France
Son of Henry and Rachel Bradshaw, of 4, Courtrai Street, Belfast.

Bradshaw, Thomas - Corporal
15/12542 Royal Irish Rifles 15th Battalion *Age 18 Died of Wounds on 23 December 1915*
MAILLY-MAILLET COMMUNAL CEMETERY EXTENSION, France
Son of Thomas and Sarah Bradshaw, of 48, Upper Townsend Street, Belfast.

Bradshaw, Thomas - Lance Corporal
4319 Royal Irish Rifles 15th Battalion *Died in War on 2 October 1918*
YPRES RESERVOIR CEMETERY, Belgium
Husband of Martha Bradshaw, 25 Scott Street, Belfast.

Bradshaw, William - Lance Corporal
9355 Royal Irish Rifles 1st Battalion *Age 23 Killed in Action on 21 April 1916*
THIEPVAL MEMORIAL, France
Son of Mrs. Margaret Belshaw, of 47, Broadbent Street, Old Lodge Road, Belfast.

Bradshaw, William - Private
41190 North Staffordshire Regiment 1st Battalion formerly 204130 Norfolk Regiment
Killed in Action on 21 March 1918
BELLICOURT BRITISH CEMETERY, France
Born in Belfast.

Brady, James - Rifleman
3/1569 Royal Irish Rifles 1st Battalion *Age 21 Killed in Action on 4 August 1915*
ST. SEVER CEMETERY, ROUEN, France
Son of James and Bridget Brady, of 10, King's Court, Lancaster Street, Belfast.

Brady, James - Rifleman
6695 Royal Irish Rifles 1st Battalion *Killed in Action on 9 May 1915*
PLOEGSTEERT MEMORIAL, Belgium
Born in Downpatrick, enlisted Newtownards, resident Belfast.

Brady, James P - Private
23756 Royal Inniskilling Fusiliers 7th Battalion *Age 38 Died of Wounds on 27 April 1916*
CLACTON CEMETERY, United Kingdom
Son of Catherine and the late B Brady (Sergeant Royal Irish Constabulary), of 141 McDonnell Street, Belfast.

Brady, John Joseph - Trimmer
7759/TS Royal Naval Reserve HMS "Nesmar" *Age 25 Died of pneumonia on 15 July 1918*
BELFAST (MILLTOWN) ROMAN CATHOLIC CEMETERY, United Kingdom
Son of William and Catherine Brady, of Belfast; husband of Mary Brady, of 68, McDonnell Street, Belfast.

Brady, Patrick - Private
27573 Royal Inniskilling Fusiliers 7th Battalion *Died in War on 19 July 1916*
PHILOSOPHE BRITISH CEMETERY, MAZINGARBE, France
Born and enlisted in Belfast. Formerly 1500, Leinster Regiment.

Brady, Robert - Rifleman
596613 London Regiment 18th (County of London) Battalion (London Irish Rifles)
Died in War on 6 September 1918
WULVERGHEM-LINDENHOEK ROAD MILITARY CEMETERY, *Belgium*
Born and enlisted in Belfast. Formerly 3680, Seaforth Highlanders.

Branagh, Robert - Private
6687 Royal Inniskilling Fusiliers 2nd Battalion *Killed in Action on 6 August 1915*
LE TOURET MEMORIAL, *France*
Born in Belfast.

Braniff, James - Private
32974 Sherwood Foresters (Notts and Derby Regiment) 16th Battalion *Age 17 Died in War on 10 October 1916*
THIEPVAL MEMORIAL, *France*
Son of Thomas K Braniff, of 63, High Street, Holywood, County Down.
Also lived at 113 Snugville Street, Belfast.

Brankin, George - Sergeant
14/16204 Royal Irish Rifles 14th Battalion *Age 29 Died of Wounds on 8 June 1917*
HAZEBROUCK COMMUNAL CEMETERY, *France*
Son of James and Agnes Brankin; husband of Mary Brankin, of 18 Seventh Street, Belfast.
Born at Newtownards, County Down.

Brannigan, Henry J - Lance Corporal
4633 Irish Guards 2nd Battalion *Died on 15 December 1915*
GREAT WARLEY (CHRIST CHURCH) CEMETERY, *United Kingdom*
Born in Belfast.

Bratton, George - Private
3352 Royal Irish Regiment 8th Battalion *Age 22 Killed in Action on 12 August 1918*
LE GRAND HASARD MILITARY CEMETERY, MORBECQUE, *France*
Son of Margaret Bratton, of 28, Pine Street, Belfast.

Bready, Richard - Rifleman
9402 Royal Irish Rifles 2nd Battalion *Died in War on 18 June 1917*
YPRES (MENIN GATE) MEMORIAL, *BELGIUM*
32 Mervue Street, Belfast.

Breen, John - Private
1483 Leinster Regiment 7th Battalion *Age 25 Died in War on 3 September 1916*
DELVILLE WOOD CEMETERY, LONGUEVAL, *France*
Husband of Mary Breen, of 5, Bow Street, Belfast.

Breen, John - Private
4057 Connaught Rangers 5th Battalion *Age 25 Died in War on 18 October 1918*
BROOKWOOD MILITARY CEMETERY, *United Kingdom*
Born in County Cork. Enlisted and resident in Belfast.

Breen, Robert - Rifleman
5767 Royal Irish Rifles 7th Battalion *Age 18 Died in War on 3 June 1916*
DUD CORNER CEMETERY, LOOS, *France*
Son of Sarah McCormick, of 87, Glenwood Street, Belfast.

Breen, William Henry - Rifleman
44 Royal Irish Rifles 1st Battalion *Age 30 Killed in Action on 23 March 1918*
POZIERES MEMORIAL, France
Son of James and Annie Breen; husband of Eleanor Breen, of I, Sugarfield Street, Belfast.

Breene, Thomas Frederick - Lieutenant
Royal Warwickshire Regiment 1st Battalion *Age 28 Killed in Action on 1 July 1916*
THIEPVAL MEMORIAL, France
Son of T J and Mary Breene, of 99, Fitzroy Avenue, Belfast.

Brennan, Charles - Private
12787 Royal Inniskilling Fusiliers 8th Battalion *Age 27 Killed in Action on 29 April 1916*
BETHUNE TOWN CEMETERY, France
Son of Mrs. Elizabeth Brennan, of 5, Carrington Street, Belfast; husband of Annie Lewis (formerly Brennan), of 42, Glentoran Street, Belfast.

Brennan, George P - Lance Sergeant
3536 Irish Guards 1st Battalion *Died in War on 9 November 1914*
YPRES (MENIN GATE) MEMORIAL, Belgium
A reservist from 30 Nansen Street, Belfast. Son Mrs Geraldine and Mr J Brennan, who was formerly a member of the Royal Irish Constaulary.

Brennan, John - Private
G/52034 Middlesex Regiment 2nd Battalion *Died in War on 5 August 1917*
LIJSSENTHOEK MILITARY CEMETERY, Belgium
Son of John Brennan, of 59, McDonnell Street, Belfast.

Brennan, Peter - Private
8045 Leinster Regiment 2nd Battalion *Died in War on 20 October 1914*
PLOEGSTEERT MEMORIAL, Belgium
Born in Belfast. Enlisted in Greenock, Scotland.

Brennan, Thomas - Private
64791 Machine Gun Corps (Infantry) *Died in War on 7 August 1917*
LONDONTHORPE (ST JOHN THE BAPTIST) CHURCHYARD, United Kingdom
Born in Belfast. Enlisted in Brecon, Wales. Formerly 33961, South Wales Borderers

Brereton, Samuel - Private
36337 Yorkshire Regiment 10th Battalion *Age 21 Died in War on 4 October 1917*
TYNE COT MEMORIAL, Belgium
Son of William Henry Brereton, of 25, Dunvegan Street, Belfast.

Bretherick, Thomas - Lance Corporal
58339 Corps of Royal Engineers *Died in War on 1 November 1916*
GUARDS CEMETERY LESBOEUFS, France
Born in Belfast. Enlisted in Burnley, Lancashire. Formerly 86176, Royal Field Artillery

Brewer, Albert - Stoker First Class
K/15525 Royal Navy HMS "Penshurst" *Age 23 Killed in Action with submarine on 24 December 1917*
CHATHAM NAVAL MEMORIAL, United Kingdom
Son of Charles and the late Mary Brewer, of 108 Bellvue Street, Belfast.

Brewis, Charles M - Sergeant
116851 Canadian Infantry (Western Ontario Regiment) 47th Battalion
Age 30 Died in War on 20 January 1918
AUBIGNY COMMUNAL CEMETERY EXTENSION, France
Born in Belfast. Husband of Eleanor Brewis, of 959, Broadway East, Vancouver, British Columbia.

Brewster, James - Rifleman
18996 Royal Irish Rifles 2nd Battalion *Died in War on 20 November 1915*
TANCREZ FARM CEMETERY, Belgium
Father John lived at 17 Bedeque Street, Belfast.

Breze, William - Private
G/5119 Queen's Own (Royal West Kent Regiment) 1st Battalion *Died in War on 23 April 1915*
YPRES (MENIN GATE) MEMORIAL, Belgium
Born in Belfast, enlisted London.

Brickley, Alexander - Rifleman
9140 Royal Irish Rifles 1st Battalion *Age 24 Killed in Action on 10 March 1915*
LE TOURET MEMORIAL, France
Son of Mrs. M. Brickley, of 29, Bisley Street, Belfast.

Bridgett, William T. H. - Sergeant
1213 Royal Irish Rifles "D" Company 9th Battalion *Age 20 Killed in Action on 7 June 1917*
SPANBROEKMOLEN BRITISH CEMETERY, Belgium
Son of William and Annie Bridgett, of 98, Great Victoria Street, Belfast.

Brien, John - Private
13545 Royal Scots Fusiliers 1st Battalion *Age 35 Died in War on 16 June 1915*
YPRES (MENIN GATE) MEMORIAL, Belgium
Husband of Mary C Doherty (formerly Brien), of 46, Colinward Street, Springfield Street, Belfast.

Briggs, Thomas - Rifleman
7385 Royal Irish Rifles 1st Battalion *Age 21 Died of Wounds on 10 March 1916*
SAILLY-SUR-LA-LYS-CANADIAN CEMETERY, France
Formerly employed in the Workman Clark Shipyard. Husband of Sarah Briggs,
of 1, Paris Street, Shankill Road, Belfast.

Briggs, William - Private
32736 Royal Scots Fusiliers 11th Battalion *Age 34 Died of peritonitis on 24 April 1919*
DUNKIRK TOWN CEMETERY, France
Son of William J. Briggs, of Belfast; husband of Elizabeth K. Briggs, of 154, Rosebery Street, Belfast.

Bright, R - Private
M/21498 Royal Army Service Corps *Age 20 Died as a result of war on 9 April 1921*
KIRKEE 1914-1918 MEMORIAL, India
Son of Elizabeth Bright, of 18, Turin Street, Belfast.

Bristow, Thompson - Rifleman
14118 Royal Irish Rifles 9th Battalion *Died in War on 23 November 1917*
CAMBRAI MEMORIAL, LOUVERVAL, France
His parents were John and Susan. Two brothers also served.

Brizzell, Samuel - Pioneer
116648 Royal Engineers 5th Labour Battalion *Age 46 Died in War on 20 October 1915*
DIVISIONAL CEMETERY, Belgium
Husband of Martha Brizzell, of 12, Trafalgar Street, Belfast, his son, William also fell.

Brizzell, William - Rifleman
11416 Royal Irish Rifles "D" Company 6th Battalion *Age 20 Died in War on 11 August 1915*
HELLES MEMORIAL, Turkey
Son of Martha Brizzell, of 12, Trafalgar Street, Belfast, and Samuel Brizzell who, himself, was killed in the war .

Broad, James - Sick Berth Steward Second Class
351213 Royal Navy HMS "Formidable"
Age 28 Killed in Action with submarine in English Channel on 1 January 1915
CHATHAM NAVAL MEMORIAL, United Kingdom
Son of James and Lucy Broad, of Wantage, Berkshire husband of Priscilla F. Hughes (formerly Broad), of 28, Stranmillis Gardens, Belfast.

Broadley, Harry - Captain
Royal Inniskilling Fusiliers 2nd Battalion *Age 35 Died in War on 6 August 1917*
POTIJZE CHATEAU GROUNDS CEMETERY, Belgium
Husband of Agnes Broadley, of 12, Egeria Street, Belfast.

Broderick, Alfred - Private
4697 Connaught Rangers 6th Battalion *Died in War on 3 September 1916*
THIEPVAL MEMORIAL, France
Born, enlisted and resident in Belfast.

Brolly, William, John - Corporal
7679 Royal Inniskilling Fusiliers 2nd Battalion *Died in War on 16 May 1915*
LE TOURET MEMORIAL, France
4 Pittsburg Street Belfast. Born in County Antrim.

Brooks, George - Private
2798 Northumberland Fusiliers 2nd Battalion *Died in War on 17 February 1915*
YPRES (MENIN GATE) MEMORIAL, Belgium
Born in Belfast enlisted Bradford, Yorkshire. Formerly King's Own Yorkshire Light Infantry.

Brooks, Robert - Private
3356 Royal Inniskilling Fusiliers 2nd Battalion *Age 23 Died in War on 27 February 1918*
POELCAPELLE BRITISH CEMETERY, Belgium
Son of Mrs. Margaret Brooks, of 53, Hooker Street, Crumlin Road, Belfast.

Brooks, Robert - Private
6980 King's Own (Yorkshire Light Infantry) 2nd Battalion *Died in War on 1 November 1914*
LE TOURET MEMORIAL, France
Born in Belfast, enlisted County Antrim.

Brooks, William Davidson - Private
7252 Royal Inniskilling Fusiliers 2nd Battalion *Died in War on 5 September 1914*
VERBERIE COMMUNAL CEMETERY, France
Son of John and Matilda Brooks, of 6, Tramway Street, Belfast.

Brough, Hugh - Stoker First Class
Royal Navy HMS "Good Hope" *Died in War on 1 November 1914*
PORTSMOUTH NAVAL MEMORIAL, United Kingdom
23 Lake Street, Belfast.

Brown, Adam - Driver
TH/045350 Army Service Corps Attached 1st/4th Battalion The Loyal North Lancashire Regiment
Age 24 Died of disease on 4 November 1918
TERLINCTHUN BRITISH CEMETERY, WIMILLE, France
Son of James and Eliza Jane Brown, of Torneroy, Hannahstown, Belfast.

Brown, Albert Victor - Rifleman
7439 Royal Irish Rifles 1st Battalion *Killed in Action on 31 July 1917*
YPRES (MENIN GATE) MEMORIAL, Belgium
Born and enlisted in Belfast.

Brown, Alexander - Private
6913 South Lancashire Regiment 2nd Battalion *Died of Wounds on 20 October 1914*
NETLEY MILITARY CEMETERY, United Kingdom
Copeland Street Belfast. Born in Newry.

Brown, Alexander - Rifleman
14120 Royal Irish Rifles 10th Battalion *Age 20 Killed in Action on 1 July 1916*
THIEPVAL MEMORIAL, France
Son of Margaret Brown, of 2, Walnut Place, Belfast.

Brown, Charles - Rifleman
9472 Royal Irish Rifles 1st Battalion *Killed in Action on 13 March 1915*
LE TOURET MEMORIAL, France
Born and enlisted in Belfast.

Brown, David - Battery Quartermaster Sergeant
28047 Royal Garrison Artillery *Died in War on 7 October 1917*
MENIN ROAD SOUTH MILITARY CEMETERY, Belgium
Born in Lurgan, County Armagh. Enlisted in Manchester, resident in Belfast. Awarded the Military Medal.

Brown, David - Rifleman
8877 Royal Irish Rifles 2nd Battalion *Age 23 Killed in Action on 15 September 1914*
LA FERTE-SOUS-JOUARRE MEMORIAL, France
Son of Mrs. Sarah J. Murphy, of 35, Winchester Street, Belfast.

Brown, David Alexander - Private
30004 Yorkshire Regiment 9th Battalion *Died in War on 10 October 1918*
CROSS ROADS CEMETERY, FONTAINE-AU-BOIS, France
Son of John Brown, of 37, Fraser Street, Belfast. Born in Newry, County Down.

Brown, Edward - Corporal
4654 Royal Irish Rifles 7th Battalion *Killed in Action on 16 August 1917*
TYNE COT CEMETERY, Belgium
Born in Belfast. Enlisted in Girvan, Scotland.

Brown, Edward - Lance Corporal
10105 Royal Inniskilling Fusiliers 1st Battalion *Age 21 Killed in Action on 1 July 1916*
ANCRE BRITISH CEMETERY, BEAUMONT-HAMEL, *France*
Son of William and Isabella Brown, of Belfast. Previously wounded at the Dardanelles.

Brown, Francis - Lance Corporal
57412 Royal Engineers Q Depot Company *Age 41 Died of pneumonia on 6 November 1918*
FORT PITT MILITARY CEMETERY, *United Kingdom*
Son of the late Robert Brown; husband of Margaret Brown, of 5, Ambrose Street, Belfast.

Brown, Francis - Rifleman
1148 Royal Irish Rifles "A" Company 4th Battalion *Died of Wounds on 14 July 1916*
CARNMONEY CEMETERY, *United Kingdom*
Husband of Elizabeth Brown, of 148, Cupar Street, Belfast.

Brown, George - Private
3366 Royal Inniskilling Fusiliers 1st Battalion *Age 20 Died in War on 23 April 1917*
ARRAS MEMORIAL, *France*
Son of George and Sarah Brown, of 4, Central Street, Belfast.

Brown, Harold George - Rifleman
9543 Royal Irish Rifles 1st Battalion *Killed in Action on 11 March 1915*
LE TOURET MEMORIAL, *France*
Born in Belfast, enlisted in Dublin.

Brown, Hugh - Second Lieutenant
Royal Irish Rifles 1st Battalion *Killed in Action on 31 July 1917*
DOVER (ST. JAMES'S) CEMETERY, *Belgium*
Son of Commander John Brown Royal Naval Reserve, the Captain of HMS "City of Oxford". Educated at RBAI he originally had been a merchant seaman when, on the outbreak of war, he enlisted in the Hampshire Regiment before being commissioned into the Royal Irish Rifles. His brother, Corporal John Brown, was also killed.

Brown, J - Rifleman
174 Royal Irish Rifles 10th Battalion *Killed in Action on 19 June 1916*
HAMEL MILITARY CEMETERY, BEAUMONT-HAMEL, *France*
20 Weir Street, Belfast.

Brown, James - Private
1958 Army Cyclist Corps *Died in War on 19 August 1917*
VOORMEZEELE ENCLOSURES No 1 and No 2, *Belgium*
Born Ballymacarrett, Belfast. Enlisted in Belfast.

Brown, James - Private
4669 Connaught Rangers 6th Battalion *Died in War on 3 September 1917*
THIEPVAL MEMORIAL, *France*
Born at St Matthew's Belfast, enlisted and resident in Belfast

Brown, James - Private
7538 Princess Victoria's (Royal Irish Fusiliers) 1st Battalion *Died in War on 7 May 1917*
ARRAS MEMORIAL, *France*
Born and enlisted in Belfast.

Brown, James - Private
S2/SR/04727 Army Service Corps 20th Field Bakery *Died on 15 October 1916*
BOULOGNE EASTERN CEMETERY, France
58 Esmond Street, Belfast.

Brown, James - Rifleman
9189 Royal Irish Rifles 10th Battalion formerly 7509 A.C.C. *Killed In Action on 6 August 1917*
YPRES (MENIN GATE) MEMORIAL, Belgium
Born in Belfast.

Brown, John - Captain
Royal Irish Rifles 8th Battalion attached 1st Battalion *Age 23 Killed in Action on 21 March 1918*
POZIERES MEMORIAL, France
Son of Samuel Stuart and Agnes Brown of Ailsa Crescent Standtown, Belfast. Enlisted into the 8th Royal Irish Rifles at the the beginning of the war and was later promoted to sergeant. He was then commissioned and subsequently wounded on the first dayof the Somme. Whilst recovering on home leave he received the Royal Humane Society's Bronze Medal for saving an individual from drowning in the River Lagan. On return to the front he commanded a platoon and then "C" Company. Twice awarded the Military Cross for bravery on the battlefield.

Brown, John - Company Sergeant Major
R/10826 King's Royal Rifle Corps 21st Battalion *Died in War on 10 October 1916*
THIEPVAL MEMORIAL, France
Born in Belfast, enlisted in Winchester, England.

Brown, John - Corporal
240483 Hampshire Regiment 1st/4th Battalion *Died in War on 21 January 1916*
BASRA MEMORIAL, Iraq
Born in Belfast.

Brown, John - Corporal
9437 Royal Irish Rifles 2nd Battalion *Killed in Action on 13 May 1916*
ECOIVRES MILITARY CEMETERY, MONT-ST. ELOI, France
Born in Belfast, enlisted Glasgow.

Brown, John - Engineer Lieutenant
Royal Naval Reserve M.F.A. "Whitehead"
Age 41 Killed in Action with submarine in Mediterranean on 15 October 1917
PORTSMOUTH NAVAL MEMORIAL, United Kingdom
Son of John and Jane Brown, of Belfast, Ireland; husband of Rosina Brown, of "Olive Bank",
49, Perkin Street, Newcastle, New South Wales.

Brown, John - Lance Sergeant
9/17316 Royal Irish Rifles 9th Battalion *Age 21 Killed in Action on 7 June 1917*
LONE TREE CEMETERY, Belgium
Son of John and Jane Brown of 43, Bellevue Street, Belfast.

Brown, John - Private
2718 Royal Inniskilling Fusiliers 2nd Battalion *Age 22 Died in War on 19 November 1914*
STRAND MILITARY CEMETERY, Belgium
Son of the late John and Mary Brown; husband of Margaret McCleave (formerly Brown),
of 36, Pernau Street, Belfast.

Brown, John - Private
7236 Prince of Wales's Volunteers (South Lancashire Regiment) 2nd Battalion
Killed in Action on 25 December 1914
YPRES (MENIN GATE) MEMORIAL, Belgium
See "McCANN" the true family name. Born in Shankill. Enlisted in Belfast.

Brown, John - Rifleman
18/1568 Royal Irish Rifles 1st Battalion formerly 7509 Army Cyclist Corps *Killed in Action on 20 July 1918*
GODEWAERSVELDE BRITISH CEMETERY, France
Husband of Mrs. E Brown, of 21, Israel Street, Belfast.

Brown, John - Sergeant
17316 Royal Irish Rifles 9th Battalion *Died in War on 7 June 1917*
LONE TREE CEMETERY, France
Born and enlisted in Belfast.

Brown, John Edward - Company Quartermaster Sergeant
4821 King's Own Scottish Borderers 1st Battalion *Died in War on 29 May 1915*
PIETA MILITARY CEMETERY, Malta
Born in Belfast, enlisted in Dublin.

Brown, Joseph - Private
21756 Cameronians (Scottish Rifles) 11th Battalion *Age 40 Died in War on 18 May 1917*
SALONIKA (LEMBET ROAD) MILITARY CEMETERY, Greece
Son of David and Mary Brown, of Belfast; husband of Hannah Brown, of 42, Marine Street, Belfast.

Brown, Joseph - Rifleman
47189 Royal Irish Rifles 15th Battalion *Died in War on 22 November 1917*
THIEPVAL MEMORIAL, France
Born and enlisted in Belfast. Formerly 030833 Army Service Corps.

Brown, Martin - Company Sergeant Major
1149 Royal Irish Rifles "B" Company 17th Battalion *Age 52 Died in War on 22 March 1916*
BLARIS OLD BURIAL GROUND, United Kingdom
Son of Mr W. and Mrs S. Brown of Lisburn; husband of M. Brown, of 94, Marlborough Park, Belfast.

Brown, Michael - Private
70767 Machine Gun Corps 19th Battalion *Died as a result of war on 1 December 1918*
AWOINGT BRITISH CEMETERY, France
Native of Belfast. Son of Mrs A Brown, 13 Breffini Terrace, Cavan. Formerly 3195 Royal Irish Fusiliers.

Brown, Robert - Private
20928 Royal Irish Fusiliers 8th Battalion *Age 20 Died of Wounds on 8 May 1916*
ABBEVILLE COMMUNAL CEMETERY, France
Youngest son of Catherine and Robert Brown, of Belfast. An elder brother was also serving.

Brown, Robert - Rifleman
1313 Royal Irish Rifles "D" Company 8th Battalion *Age 18 Died in War on 2 July 1916*
THIEPVAL MEMORIAL, France
Son of Robert and Elizabeth Brown, of 118, Blythe Street, Belfast.

Brown, Robert - Rifleman
180 Royal Irish Rifles 1st Garrison Battalion *Died in War on 9 July 1918*
NETLEY MILITARY CEMETERY, United Kingdom
Born Belfast, enlisted in Lurgan.

Brown, Robert - Rifleman
3620 Royal Irish Rifles 10th Battalion *Age 28 Died in War on 1 July 1917*
THIEPVAL MEMORIAL, France
Son of Debora Brown, of 200, Roden Street, Belfast, and the late Henry Brown.

Brown, Robert William - Private
11941 Royal Inniskilling Fusiliers 9th Battalion *Age 25 Killed in Action on 1 July 1916*
THIEPVAL MEMORIAL, France
Son of William R. Smyley, of 2, Dunraven Avenue, Belfast.

Brown, Samuel G - Private
27114 Royal Inniskilling Fusiliers 1st Battalion *Died in War on 15 October 1918*
DADIZEELE NEW BRITISH CEMETERY, Belgium
Brother of Mrs. L. Wilson, of 9, Sydney Street West, Belfast.

Brown, Samuel Leslie - Rifleman
19402 Royal Irish Rifles 14th Battalion *Died on 11 July 1916*
READING CEMETERY, United Kingdom
Son of Mrs. James Brown, of 115, Agincourt Avenue, Belfast.

Brown, Thomas - Private
6749 Royal Scots Fusiliers 6th/7th Battalion *Age 33 Died in War on 15 September 1916*
THIEPVAL MEMORIAL, France
Son of Thomas Kerr, of 7, Ritchie Street, Belfast, and Agnes Kerr.

Brown, Thomas Fletcher - Second Lieutenant
Manchester Regiment 7th Battalion *Age 20 Killed in Action on 30 May 1915*
REDOUBT CEMETERY, HELLES, Turkey
Educated at RBAI and later a member of Queen's University Officers Training Corps.
Son of William and Lizzie Brown, of 204, Shankill Road, Belfast.

Brown, William - Driver
57628 Royal Engineers 121st Field Company *Died in War on 15 November 1915*
BEAUVAL COMMUNAL CEMETERY, France
11 Little George's Street, Belfast.

Brown, William - Lance Corporal
14/14124 Royal Irish Rifles 14th Battalion *Age 25 Died of wounds on 16 August 1917*
BRANDHOEK NEW MILITARY CEMETERY No.3, Belgium
Son of James and the late Isabella Brown, of Belfast.

Brown, William - Private
330082 Royal Scots (Lothian Regiment) 8th Battalion *Died in War on 22 July 1916*
THIEPVAL MEMORIAL, France
Born in Belfast, enlisted in Midlothian, Scotland.

Brown, William - Private
41451 Royal Irish Fusiliers 9th (North Irish Horse) Battalion *Age 23 Died in War on 11 - 12 August 1918*
MONT NOIR MILITARY CEMETERY, ST. JANS-CAPPEL, France
Son of John and Sarah Brown, of 51, Lichfield Avenue, Bloomfield, Belfast.
Assistant Librarian, Central Library, Belfast.

Brown, William Balfour - Private
S/40125 Black Watch (Royal Highlanders) 1st Battalion *Age 25 Died in War on 20 April 1918*
LOOS MEMORIAL, France
Brother of Miss Jennie Brown, of 111, Rosebery Road, Belfast.

Brown, Willaim Charles - Private
40929 Royal Army Medical Corps *Died in War on 30 June 1917*
BELFAST CITY CEMETERY, United Kingdom
Son of Mary Ann and Edwin Charles Brown of Ballynaveigh, Belfast.

Brown, William Henry - Rifleman
9457 Royal Irish Rifles 1st Battalion *Killed in Action on 9 May 1915*
PLOEGSTEERT MEMORIAL, Belgium
Born and enlisted in Belfast.

Brown, William James - Private
3981 Seaforth Highlanders 3rd/4th Battalion *Age 36 Died in War on 15 February 1918*
BELFAST CITY CEMETERY, United Kingdom
Son of John and Eliza A. Brown; husband of Ellen Jane Brown, of 19, Riversdale Street, Belfast.

Brown, William Thomas - Able Seaman
J/31938 Royal Navy HMS "Glatton" *Died of accidental injuries on 21 September 1918*
DOVER (ST. JAMES'S) CEMETERY, United Kingdom
Son of Thomas Brown, of 7, Jonesboro' Street, Belfast, and the late Agnes Brown.

Browne, Albert Victor - Rifleman
7439 Royal Irish Rifles 1st Battalion *Age 20 Killed in Action on 31 July 1917*
YPRES (MENIN GATE) MEMORIAL, Belgium
Son of Alice Jane Browne, of 70, Argyle Street, Belfast, and the late James Browne.

Browne, George - Private
25/1675 Otago Regiment, New Zealand Expeditionary Force 2nd Battalion
Age 27 Died of Wounds on 1 October 1916
CATERPILLAR VALLEY (NEW ZEALAND) MEMORIAL, France
Son of James and Margaret Jane Browne, of 109, Beechfield Street, Mountpottinger Road, Belfast, Ireland.

Browne, James - Private
10415 Royal Inniskilling Fusiliers 2nd Battalion *Age 20 Died in War on 26 August 1914*
LA FERTE-SOUS-JOUARRE MEMORIAL, France
Son of Robert and Emily Browne, of 16, Hillview Street, Belfast.

Browne, John - Master
Mercantile Marine "Strathnairn" *Age 39 Drowned, as a result of an attack by an enemy submarine on 15 June 1915*
TOWER HILL MEMORIAL, United Kingdom
Son of Thomas and Mary Browne, of Islandmagee, County Antrim; husband of Elizabeth Browne, of 2, Spring Gardens, Knock, Belfast.

Browne, Llewellyn Albert - Gunner
64785 Royal Field Artillery 3rd/7th Trench Mortar Battery *Age 23 Killed in Action on 8 May 1916*
CITADEL NEW MILITARY CEMETERY, FRICOURT, France
Son of James Browne, of 4, Zetland Street, Belfast. Born in King's County.

Browne, Maximillian Herbert - Captain
Royal Irish Rifles attached 108th Trench Mortar Battery *Died in War on 21 June 1918*
ESQUELBECQ MILITARY CEMETERY, France
Holder of the Military Cross, the son of George Burrowes Browne and Margaret Browne, of "Lisnamaul" Ormeau Road, Belfast. Educated at RBAI and a member of Queen's University OTC. Killed in an accidental explosion during training.

Browne, Rennie - Rifleman
445 Royal Irish Rifles 8th/9th Battalion *Age 19 Died in War on 23 November 1917*
CAMBRAI MEMORIAL, LOUVERVAL, France
Son of John Browne, of "Glenmore" Bloomfield Road, Belfast, and the late Dessa Browne.

Browne, Robert - Lance Corporal
200978 Seaforth Highlanders 1st/4th Battalion *Age 20 Killed in Action on 8 - 10 April 1917*
NINE ELMS MILITARY CEMETERY, THELUS, France
Son of Robert and Margaret Browne, of I, St. Jude's Avenue, Belfast.

Browne, Samuel Leslie - Rifleman
19402 Royal Irish Rifles "A" Company 14th Battalion *Age 31 Died of Wounds on 11 July 1916*
READING CEMETERY, United Kingdom
Son of Mrs. James Browne, of 115, Agincourt Avenue, Belfast.

Browne, William - Lance Corporal
9093 Royal Irish Fusiliers 1st Battalion *Age 30 Died in War on 6 July 1916*
SUCRERIE MILITARY CEMETERY, COLINCAMPS, France
Son of Joseph and Elizabeth Browne, of Upper Ballysillan, Ligoneil, Belfast.

Browne, William - Rifleman
4555 Royal Irish Rifles 2nd Battalion *Age 20 Killed in Action on 18 August 1918*
BERTENACRE MILITARY CEMETERY, FLETRE, France
Son of William and Margaret Browne, of 35, City Street, Belfast. Awarded the Military Medal.

Browning, George Albert - Private
29472 Royal Irish Fusiliers 1st Battalion *Age 19 Died of Wounds on 5 September 1918*
TERLINCTHUN BRITISH CEMETERY, WIMILLE, France
Son of Margaret Browning, of 8, Stratheden Street, Antrim Road, Belfast.

Brownlee, John - Private
14019 Royal Irish Fusiliers 9th Battalion *Age 33 Killed in Action on 1 July 1916*
THIEPVAL MEMORIAL, France
Son of Robert and Susan Brownlee, of 2 Robert Street, Lurgan; husband of Frances Brownlee, of 2, Combermere Street, Belfast.

Bruce, Adam - Second Engineer
Mercantile Marine Reserve H.M. Tug "Labour" *Age 30 Died of pneumonia on 29 November 1918*
CARNMONEY CEMETERY, United Kingdom
Son of Donald and Isabella Bruce, of 73, Glasgow Street, Belfast. Born in Dumbartonshire, Scotland.

Bruce, James - Rifleman
912286 Royal Irish Rifles 8th Battalion *Age 31 Killed in Action on 7 June 1917*
LONE TREE CEMETERY, Belgium
Husband of Isabella Bruce, of 54, Hunter Street, Belfast.

Bruce, Thomas Walter - Private
S/43194 Black Watch (Royal Highlanders) 8th Battalion *Age 19 Died in War on 3 May 1917*
ARRAS MEMORIAL, France
Son of Sarah Bruce, of 6, Derlett Street, Belfast, and the late Thomas Bruce.

Bruce, William - Rifleman
1117204 Royal Irish Rifles 12th Battalion *Age 24 Died in War on 23 October 1918*
HARLEBEKE NEW BRITISH CEMETERY, Belgium
Son of John and Frances Cosby Bruce; husband of Mary Jane Bruce, of Edgebank, Deramore Park South, Belfast.

Brush, Joshua - Rifleman
3068 Royal Irish Rifles "A" Company 2nd Battalion *Age 40 Killed in Action on 21 March 1918*
POZIERES MEMORIAL, France
Husband of Rachel Brush of 85, Matilda Street, Sandy Row, Belfast. Served in the South African Campaign.

Bryans, Alfred - Lance Corporal
13911 Royal Inniskilling Fusiliers 9th Battalion *Age 19 Killed and Action on 1 July 1916*
CONNAUGHT CEMETERY, THIEPVAL, France
Son of John, a ship's blacksmith, and Jane Bryans, of 39, Sugarfield Street, Belfast.

Bryans, Frederick - Rifleman
12583 Royal Irish Rifles 15th Battalion *Age 19 Died in War on 21 November 1917*
CAMBRAI MEMORIAL, LOUVERVAL, France
Son of Samuel and Rachel Bryans, of 150, Cambrai Street, Belfast.

Bryans, George - Stoker First Class
226076 Royal Navy HMS "Indefatigable" *Age 30 Killed in Action on 31 May 1916*
PLYMOUTH NAVAL MEMORIAL, United Kingdom
Brother of Mary Bryans, of 71, Northumberland Street, Belfast.

Bryans, Henry - Private
8793 4th (Queen's Own) Hussars C Squadron *Age 21 Killed in Action on 11 September 1914*
LA FERTE-SOUS-JOUARRE MEMORIAL, France
Son of Samuel and Rachel Bryans, of 150, Cambrai Street, Belfast.

Bryans, Samuel - Lance Corporal
14130 Royal Irish Rifles 9th Battalion *Died in War on 8 July 1916*
CAUDRY OLD COMMUNAL CEMETERY, France
39 Sugarfield Street, Belfast. A former member of the old UVF. His brother also fell.

Bryans, William John - Able Seaman
J/18455 Royal Navy HMS "Violet" *Age 22 Died of influenza on 10 July 1918*
DOVER (ST. JAMES'S) CEMETERY, United Kingdom
Son of John and Sarah Bryans, of 40, Hardcastle Street, Belfast

Brydon, Walter - Major
South African Heavy Artillery 73rd Siege Battery *Age 38 Died in War on 12 April 1918*
NOEUX-LES-MINES COMMUNAL CEMETERY EXTENSION, France
Son of Jenny Hay Brydon, of Richmond House, 36 Blessington Road, Lewisham, London, and the late William Walter Brydon. Native of Belfast. Award the Distinguished Service Order for leadership in battle.

Bryon, George Henry - Private
302519 Durham Light Infantry 12th Battalion *Died in War on 21 September 1917*
HOOGE CRATER CEMETERY, Belgium
Born in Belfast, enlisted in Winchester.

Buchanan, John - Corporal
10638 Royal Irish Rifles 6th Battalion *Died in War on 10 August 1915*
HELLES MEMORIAL, Turkey
Born and enlisted in Ballymena. Resident of Belfast.

Buchanan, Richard - Private
50545 Prince of Wales's (North Staffordshire Regiment) 1/6th Battalion *Died in War on 2 May 1918*
BEUVRY COMMUNAL CEMETERY EXTENSION,, France
Born in Drumbeg, enlisted in Newtownards, resident in Belfast.
Awarded the Military Medal, formerly T/32714, Army Service Corps.

Buller, William J - Rifleman
8858 Royal Irish Rifles 1st Battalion *Age 22 Killed in Action on 1 July 1916*
THIEPVAL MEMORIAL, France
Son of William and Margaret Buller, 24 Langford Street.

Bunting , David - Private
257919 Royal Inniskilling Fusiliers 9th Battalion *Died of Wounds on 14 June 1917*
BAILLEUL COMMUNAL CEMETERY EXTENSION (NORD), France
Born in Belfast.

Bunting, James - Private
12611 Royal Inniskilling Fusiliers 6th Battalion *Died in War on 18 March 1918*
JERUSALEM WAR CEMETERY, Israel
Born Ballymacarrett, Belfast. Enlisted in Belfast.

Bunting, William - Rifleman
12589 Royal Irish Rifles 15th Battalion *Killed In Action on 17 August 1918*
TYNE COT MEMORIAL, Belgium
Born in Belfast.

Bunting, William John - Signal Boy
2086SB Royal Naval Reserve HMS "Vivid" *Age 17 Died of pneumonia on 29 June 1918*
FORD PARK CEMETERY (FORMERLY PLYMOUTH OLD CEMETERY) (PENNYCOMEQUICK), United Kingdom
Son of Joseph and Mary Ann Bunting, of 80, Seaview Street, Belfast.

Burdge, David E - Rifleman
14/2736 Royal Irish Rifles 1st Battalion *Age 19 Killed in Action on 4 October 1918*
DADIZEELE NEW BRITISH CEMETERY, Belgium
Son of David and Jane E. Burdge, of 43, Battenberg Street, Belfast. Enlisted at age 15 and survived several major battles, including the Somme.

Burgin, Charles - Sergeant
2331 Royal Inniskilling Fusiliers 2nd Battalion *Age 22 Died in War on 17 November 1914*
PLOEGSTEERT MEMORIAL, Belgium
Son of Mrs. Annie Burgin, of 15, Nelson Street, Belfast.

Burke, George - Private
DM2/164128 Royal Army Service Corps *Died in War on 8 July 1917*
BAILLEUL COMMUNAL CEMETERY EXTENSION (NORD), France
Born in Belfast, enlisted in Birkenhead.

Burke, George - Rifleman
986 Royal Irish Rifles 11th Battalion *Killed in Action on 1 July 1916*
THIEPVAL MEMORIAL, France
8 Sackville Street, Belfast.

Burland, Dominick J - Corporal
8737 East Yorkshire Regiment 1st Battalion *Died of Wounds on 3 July 1916*
HEILLY STATION CEMETERY, MERICOURT-L'ABBE, France
24 Lime Street, Belfast.

Burnett, Henry Wilmer - Lance Corporal
241186 Seaforth Highlanders 4th Battalion *Died in War on 23 November 1917*
CAMBRAI MEMORIAL, LOUVERVAL, France
Enlisted in Belfast and a member of Knock Presbyterian Church.
Son of the Revd Lawson Burnett and Mrs Jane Burnett.

Burns, Alexander Gibson - Private
17488 Royal Inniskilling Fusiliers 5th Battalion *Died in War on 15 August 1915*
HELLES MEMORIAL, Turkey
75 Emerson Street, Belfast. Two brothers also served.

Burns, David - Lance Corporal
27566 Royal Inniskilling Fusiliers 7th Battalion *Died of Wounds on 31 May 1916*
NETLEY MILITARY CEMETERY, United Kingdom
3 Milford Street, Belfast.

Burns, Edward - Corporal
4654 Royal Irish Rifles 7th Battalion *Age 24 Killed in Action on 16 August 1917*
TYNE COT MEMORIAL, Belgium
(Served as BROWN). Son of Susan Burns, of 30, Little Georges Street, Belfast.

Burns, Frank - Corporal
9402 Royal Inniskilling Fusiliers 1st Battalion *Died in War on 7 June 1915*
ALEXANDRIA (CHATBY) MILITARY AND WAR MEMORIAL CEMETERY, Egypt
16 Ravensdale Street Belfast. Born in Lisburn.

Burns, George - Lance Corporal
16279 Royal Irish Rifles 14th Battalion *Died in War on 28 May 1917*
DRANOUTRE MILITARY CEMETERY, Belgium
Born and enlisted in Belfast.

Burns, George - Rifleman
14042 Royal Irish Rifles 9th Battalion *Age 34 Killed in Action on 1 July 1916*
THIEPVAL MEMORIAL, France
Husband of Ellen Burns, of 23, Nile Street, Belfast.

Burns, Isaac - Rifleman
11644 Royal Irish Rifles 15th Battalion *Age 38 Died in War on 22 November 1917*
THIEPVAL MEMORIAL, France
Husband of Sarah Jane Burns, of 63, Brownlow Street, Belfast.

Burns, James - Driver
T4/038836 Army Service Corps 251st H.Q. Company 36th Division Train *Age 19 Died in War on 5 May 1916*
NEWCASTLE-UPON-TYNE (ST. ANDREW'S AND JESMOND) CEMETERY, United Kingdom
Son of James and Minnie Burns, of Belfast.

Burns, James - Private
4261 Seaforth Highlanders 5th Battalion *Died in War on 19 May 1916*
AUBIGNY COMMUNAL CEMETERY EXTENSION, FRANCE
Native of Belfast.

Burns, James - Private
9064 Highland Light Infantry 2nd Battalion *Died in War on 14 November 1914*
YPRES (MENIN GATE) MEMORIAL, Belgium
Born in Newcastle, Northumberland, enlisted in Edinburgh, resident of Belfast.

Burns, James - Rifleman
6844 Royal Irish Rifles 2nd Battalion *Died in War on 8 January 1915*
YPRES (MENIN GATE) MEMORIAL, Belgium
41, Fraser Street, Belfast.

Burns, John - Private
12679 Royal Inniskilling Fusiliers 6th Battalion *Died in War on 14 July 1917*
BELFAST CITY CEMETERY, United Kingdom
Born Ballymacarrett, enlisted in Belfast.

Burns, John - Private
17501 Royal Inniskilling Fusiliers 9th Battalion *Killed in Action on 1 July 1916*
THIEPVAL MEMORIAL, France
Born in Belfast, enlisted Finner Camp, County Donegal.

Burns, John - Private
2411 Connaught Rangers 6th Battalion *Died in War on 25 March 1916*
DUD CORNER CEMETERY, LOOS, France
Born, enlisted and resident in Belfast.

Burns, John - Rifleman
11355 Royal Irish Rifles 1st Battalion *Killed in Action on 21 March 1918*
POZIERES MEMORIAL, OVILLERS-LA BOISSELLE, France
Born and enlisted in Belfast.

Burns, John - Sailmaker
182612 Royal Navy HMS "Queen Mary" *Age 38 Killed in Action on 31 May 1916*
PORTSMOUTH NAVAL MEMORIAL, United Kingdom
(Served as O'Brien), son of Bridget Burns, of Crumlin Road, Belfast; husband of Rachel Burns, of 59, Cottage View, Landport, Portsmouth. Served in the South African War.

Burns, John Joseph - Private
26930 Royal Inniskilling Fusiliers 7th Battalion *Age 25 Died of Wounds on 5 April 1916*
BETHUNE TOWN CEMETERY, France
Only son of Margaret Burns, of 26, Seymour Street, Belfast, and the late John Burns.

Burns, Joseph L (Joe) - Lance Corporal
1514 Connaught Rangers 6th Battalion *Died of Wounds on 8 September 1916*
ST. SEVER CEMETERY, ROUEN, France
24 Upton Street, Belfast. Survived by his mother, Elizabeth, five sisters and a brother.

Burns, Rodger - Company Sergeant Major
16017 Highland Light Infantry 52nd (Grad) Battalion *Died in War on 16 January 1918*
BROOKWOOD 1914-18 MEMORIAL, United Kingdom
Born in Belfast. Enlisted Hamilton, Scotland.

Burns, Thomas - Private
7310 Royal Dublin Fusiliers 2nd Battalion *Killed In Action on 25 April 1915*
YPRES (MENIN GATE) MEMORIAL, Belgium
Born and enlisted in Belfast.

Burns, William - Rifleman
1248 Royal Irish Rifles 9th Battalion *Age 26 Died in War on 8 August 1917*
YPRES (MENIN GATE) MEMORIAL, Belgium
Son of William Burns, of "Willowbank" Knockbreda Road, Cregagh, Belfast.

Burns, William - Rifleman
9248 Royal Irish Rifles 1st Battalion *Age 22 Killed in Action on 16 March 1915*
BOULOGNE EASTERN CEMETERY, France
Son of George and Margaret Burns, of Belfast.

Burns, William James - Rifleman
7854 Royal Irish Rifles 2nd Battalion *Age 20 Killed in Action on 28 September 1916*
LONSDALE CEMETERY, AUTHUILE, France
Son of William and Elizabeth Burns, of 14, Derby Street, Belfast.

Burnside, Edward Edmond - Second Lieutenant
Royal Irish Rifles 16th Battalion *Age 19 Killed in Action on 21 March 1918*
GRAND-SERAUCOURT BRITISH CEMETERY, France
Son of Ingram and M E Burnside, of Malone and later, Greenisland. Educated at RBAI and Queen's University. Member of Fitzroy Avenue Presbyterian Church, Belfast.

Burnside, Matthew - Rifleman
17/103 Royal Irish Rifles 9th Battalion *Age 17 Died of wounds on 21 September 1916*
ST. QUENTIN CABARET MILITARY CEMETERY, Belgium
Son of Matthew and Jane Burnside, of 43, Ewarts Row, Belfast.

Burnside, Samuel - Private
M2/113718 Army Service Corps 108th Army Field Artillery Brigade Park Section
Age 31 Accidentally killed on 25 October 1917
POPERINGHE NEW MILITARY CEMETERY, Belgium
Son of John and Rebecca Burnside, of County Monaghan; husband of Maggie E. Burnside, of 270, Cupar Street, Belfast.

Burrows, Robert - Rifleman
17207 Royal Irish Rifles 14th Battalion *Killed in Action on 1 July 1916*
THIEPVAL MEMORIAL, France
Husband of Susannah. 49 Sixth Street, Belfast.

Burrows, Robert - Sapper
57416 Royal Engineers 150th Field Company *Killed in Action on 1 July 1916*
THIEPVAL MEMORIAL, France
Member of Megain Memorial Presbyterian Church Belfast. Born at Drumreagh, County Down.

Burton, John - Sergeant
16282 Royal Irish Rifles 14th Battalion *Killed in Action on 1 July 1916*
THIEPVAL MEMORIAL, France
Tassagh, Cranmore Park, Belfast.

Burton, Robert - Lance Corporal
12202 Royal Inniskilling Fusiliers 5th Battalion *Age 22 Died in War on 15 August 1915*
HELLES MEMORIAL, Turkey
Son of Agnes C. Burton, of 1, Perry Street, Mountpottinger, Belfast, and the late Andrew Burton.

Burton, Robert - Private
47098 King's Own Scottish Borderers 10th Battalion *Died in War on 12 October 1918*
ERQUINGHEM-LYS CHURCHARD EXTENSION, France
Born in Drumbo, resident in Belfast.

Burton, Thomas J - Private
3485 Royal Inniskilling Fusiliers 1st Battalion *Died in War on 2 July 1915*
HELLES MEMORIAL, Turkey
Left a widow at 97 Wilton Street, Belfast.

Busby, Isaac - Private
G/597 Middlesex Regiment 18th Battalion *Age 38 Died in War on 26 September 1917*
HOOGE CRATER CEMETERY, Belgium
Son of Samuel Busby, of 82, Henry Street, Belfast, and the late Catherine Busby.

Busby, John - Private
43003 Royal Dublin Fusiliers 2nd Battalion *Died in War on 23 October 1916*
THIEPVAL MEMORIAL, France
27 Pound Street, Belfast.

Bushe, Samuel - Rifleman
4796 Royal Irish Rifles 11th Battalion *Killed in Action on 1 July 1916*
THIEPVAL MEMORIAL, France
Born in Glenavy County Antrim, enlisted in Clandeboye, County Down, resident Belfast.

Bustard, John - Lance Corporal
17208 Royal Irish Rifles 14th Battalion *Killed In Action on 1 July 1916*
THIEPVAL MEMORIAL, France
Born in Belfast, husband of Evelyn Bustard.

Bustard, Robert - Rifleman
11891 Royal Irish Rifles 7th Battalion *Age 21 Died in War on 31 March 1915*
CARNMONEY CEMETERY, United Kingdom
A mechanic, he was son of Martha Bustard, of 16, Baden Powell Street, Belfast, and the late William Bustard.

Bustard, William Ewart - Lance Corporal
19411 Royal Irish Rifles 14th Battalion *Killed In Action on 1 July 1916*
CONNAUGHT CEMETERY, THIEPVAL, France
Born in Belfast.

Butler, Daniel - Rifleman
9065 Royal Irish Rifles 2nd Battalion *Killed in Action on 28 March 1918*
POZIERES MEMORIAL, France
34 Milan Street, Belfast.

Butler, Frederick - Private
21047 Royal Irish Fusiliers 7th/8th Battalion *Age 25 Died in War on 17 August 1917*
TYNE COT MEMORIAL, Belgium
Brother of William John Butler, of 23, Bank Street, Belfast.

Butler, James - Rifleman
40203 Royal Irish Rifles 10th Battalion formerly 6792, King's Shropshire Light Infantry
Died of Wounds on 21 March 1917
BAILLEUL COMMUNAL CEMETERY EXTENSION (NORD), France
Husband of Elizabeth Butler of 54 Skipton Street, Belfast.

Butler, James - Rifleman
6008 Royal Irish Rifles 1st Battalion *Killed in Action on 7 August 1916*
BETHUNE TOWN CEMETERY, France
Born and enlisted in Belfast.

Butler, Michael - Rifleman
5865 Royal Irish Rifles "D" Company 5th Battalion *Age 22 Died in War on 24 March 1918*
SAVY BRITISH CEMETERY, France
Son of Patrick and Annie Butler, of 33, New Andrew Street, Belfast.

Byrne, Andrew - Rifleman
7005 Royal Irish Rifles 1st Battalion *Killed in Action on 14 January 1916*
Y FARM MILITARY CEMETERY, BOIS-GRENIER, France
25 Ton Street, Belfast. Survived by his mother.

Byrne, Hugh - Corporal
13357 Royal Inniskilling Fusiliers 8th Battalion *Killed in Action on 17 April 1916*
LOOS MEMORIAL, France
Born at Belfast.

Byrne, L - Fireman And Trimmer
Mercantile Marine S.S. "Tasso" (Bristol)
Age 29 Drowned, as a result of an attack by an enemy submarine on 17 March 1917
TOWER HILL MEMORIAL, United Kingdom
Born at Belfast.

Byrne, Patrick - Private
23047 Royal Irish Fusiliers 8th Battalion *Age 33 Died in War on 19 August 1916*
BOIS-CARRE MILITARY CEMETERY, HAISNES, France
Born and enlisted in Belfast. Husband of Alice A. O'Hara (formerly Byrne),
of 4, John Street, Lurgan, County Armagh.

Byrne, Thomas Francis - Private
29539 Royal Inniskilling Fusiliers 7th Battalion *Age 19 Died in War on 4 October 1916*
SHEFFIELD (ST. MICHAEL'S) ROMAN CATHOLIC CEMETERY, United Kingdom
Son of Richard and Bridget Byrne, of 36, Roe Street, Belfast. Born in County Wexford.

Cabrey, William John - Rifleman
17435 Royal Irish Rifles 10th Battalion *Age 45 Died in War on 9 March 1916*
DOULLENS COMMUNAL CEMETERY EXTENSION No.1, France
Worked in the shipyard as a plater's helper, Husband of Catherine A. Cabrey and father of Catherine and Robert of 5, Pitt Street, Belfast.

Cadden, William - Rifleman
5704 Royal Irish Rifles 1st Battalion *Age 17 Killed in Action on 1 July 1916*
THIEPVAL MEMORIAL, France
Son of Bernard, a blacksmith, and Lucy Cadden, of 24, Lake Street, Ormeau Road, Belfast.

Cahill, Joseph - Private
13156 Royal Inniskilling Fusiliers 1st Battalion *Died in War on 14 May 1915*
HELLES MEMORIAL, Turkey
192 Leeson Street, Belfast. Another brother also served.

Cahoon, Charles - Lance Corporal
9126 Royal Irish Rifles 1st Battalion *Age 27 Died of wounds on 17 July 1916*
ST. SEVER CEMETERY, ROUEN, France
Son of Charles and Annie Cahoon, of 17, Liffey Street, Belfast.

Cain, Charles - Seaman
3573B Royal Naval Reserve HMS "Alcantara"
Age 39 Killed in Action with the raider "Greif" in the North Sea on 29 February 1916
PORTSMOUTH NAVAL MEMORIAL, United Kingdom
Husband of Margaret Cain, 13, Hanna Street, Belfast.

Cairley, Robert Frank - Squadron Quartermaster Sergeant
1036 Army Pay Corps *Died of Malaria on 20 July 1917*
MIKRA BRITISH CEMETERY, KALAMARIA, Greece
Long Service and Good Conduct Medal. Serbian Gold Medal. Son of Robert and Jane Cairley, of Saskatchewan, Canada; husband of Catherine Cairley, of 5, Pacific Avenue, Antrim Road, Belfast, Ireland. Served in the South African war.

Cairns, Albert - Stoker First Class
SS/112841 Royal Navy HMS "Pembroke" *Age 23 Died in War on 3 September 1917*
GILLINGHAM (WOODLANDS) CEMETERY, United Kingdom
Son of Wilson and Maria Cairns, of 22, Beechnut Street, Oldpark Road, Belfast.

Cairns, Alexander - Private
1982 Hussars 4th (Queen's Own) *Age 26 Died of Wounds on 6 April 1916*
PICQUIGNY BRITISH CEMETERY, France
Son of Robert and Matilda Cairns, of 36, Cosgrove Street, Belfast.

Cairns, Duncan Morrison - Rifleman
14272 Royal Irish Rifles 8th/9th Battalion *Age 35 Died of Wounds on 11 December 1917*
ROCQUIGNY-EQUANCOURT ROAD BRITISH CEMETERY, MANANCOURT, France
Husband of Charlotte Cairns, of 5, Tyne Street, Belfast.

Cairns, George - Private
201281 Seaforth Highlanders 4th Battalion *Died in War on 9 April 1917*
ROCLINCOURT VALLEY CEMETERY, France
Son of Charles and Frances, 174 Roden Street, Belfast. A member of the old UVF and employed in the shipyard. He enlisted, with another brother, at the outbreak of the war.

Cairns, Herbert - Corporal
6394 Royal Irish Rifles 1st Battalion *Killed in Action on 9 May 1915*
PLOEGSTEERT MEMORIAL, Belgium
From 209 Matilda Street. Awarded the Distinguished Conduct Medal.

Cairns, Herbert - Private
19484 Machine Gun Corps (Infantry) *Died in War on 23 March 1918*
VILLERS-FAUCON COMMUNAL CEMETERY EXTENSION, France
Born and enlisted in Belfast. Formerly 9/14196, Royal Irish Fusiliers.

Cairns, Isaac - Rifleman
14181 Royal Irish Rifles 10th Battalion *Age 25 Died in War on 9 June 1918*
BELFAST (DUNDONALD) CEMETERY, United Kingdom
Son of James and Agnes Cairns, of 53, Jerusalem Street, Belfast.

Cairns, James - Private
572648 Labour Corps 33rd Prisoner of War Company *Age 40 Died of influenza on 15 April 1919*
MAZARGUES WAR CEMETERY, MARSEILLES, France
Son of Mrs. Mary Cairns; husband of Martha Cairns, of 33, Wall Street, Belfast.

Cairns, John - Battery Sergeant Major
50810 Royal Field Artillery 102nd Brigade *Died in War on 28 May 1917*
RAILWAY DUGOUTS BURIAL GROUND, Belgium
1 Mayo Street, Belfast.

Cairns, John - Private
133378 Royal Fusiliers 46th Battalion *Age 33 Died as a result of war on 29 August 1919*
ARCHANGEL ALLIED CEMETERY (BURIED OBOZERSKAYA BURIAL GROUND), Russian Federation
Husband of Elizabeth Cairns, of 24, Kingston Street, Belfast.

Cairns, John - Sapper
57420 Corps of Royal Engineers 150th Field Company *Died of accidental injuries on 6 August 1917*
WIELTJE FARM CEMETERY, Belgium
Born and enlisted in Belfast.

Cairns, William - Private
24044 Royal Inniskilling Fusiliers 1st Battalion *Died in War on 7 January 1916*
HELLES MEMORIAL, Turkey
Born in Belfast, resident in Larne.

Cairns, Wilson - Private
3392 Royal Inniskilling Fusiliers B Company 2nd Battalion *Age 25 Died in War on 23 November 1916*
WAGGON ROAD CEMETERY, BEAUMONT-HAMEL, France
Son of Wilson and Maria, 22 Beechnut Street, Belfast.

Calderwood, William - Private
419 Australian Infantry 11th Battalion *Died in War on 25 April 1915*
LONE PINE MEMORIAL, *Turkey*
Son of James and Esther, 32 Beverley Street, Belfast.

Caldwell, David - Private
48216 Royal Inniskilling Fusiliers 13th Battalion *Died in War on 27 August 1918*
NIEPPE-BOIS (RUE-DU-BOIS) BRITISH CEMETERY,VIEUX-BERQUIN, *France*
Born and enlisted in Belfast.

Caldwell, George - Private
DM2/196174 Royal Army Service Corps *Died in War on 3 May 1917*
PERONNE COMMUNAL CEMETERY EXTENSION, *France*
Born in Bessbrook, County Armagh. Enlisted and resident in Belfast.

Caldwell, James - Rifleman
8566 Royal Irish Rifles 1st Battalion *Age 28 Died of Wounds on 23 March 1915*
MERVILLE COMMUNAL CEMETERY, *France*
Son of Thomas and Elizabeth Caldwell, of 22, Mackey Street, Belfast.

Caldwell, John - Private
42658 Royal Army Medical Corps *Died as a result of war on 6 January 1918*
BELFAST CITY CEMETERY, *United Kingdom*
Husband of Elizabeth Caldwell, 61 Mackey Street, Belfast.

Caldwell, John - Rifleman
1862 Royal Irish Rifles 8th Battalion *Died in War on 2 July 1916*
THIEPVAL MEMORIAL, *France*
Born and enlisted in Belfast.

Caldwell, Robert - Rifleman
11456 Royal Irish Rifles 6th Battalion *Died in War on 11 August 1915*
HELLES MEMORIAL, *Turkey*
Born and enlisted in Belfast.

Caldwell, Thomas James - Private
13597 Cameronians (Scottish Rifles) 2nd Battalion *Died in War on 19 May 1916*
AVELUY COMMUNAL CEMETERY EXTENSION, *France*
Born in Belfast, enlisted in Glasgow.

Caldwell, Walter James - Pioneer
147284 Corps of Royal Engineers formerly 6272 Royal Irish Rifles *Killed in Action on 22 August 1917*
RAMSCAPPELLE ROAD MILITARY CEMETERY, *Belgium*
Born in Belfast.

Callon, William - Private
201406 Loyal North Lancashire Regiment 7th Battalion *Died in War on 15 June 1917*
YPRES (MENIN GATE) MEMORIAL, *Belgium*
Born in Belfast, enlisted in Preston, England.

Calvert, Albert - Private
16480 Machine Gun Corps 10th Battalion *Died in War on 16 October 1916*
THIEPVAL MEMORIAL, *France*
Native of Belfast. Formerly 5762 Royal Irish Fusiliers.

Calvert, William Henry - Sergeant
14264 Royal Irish Rifles 14th Battalion *Age 24 Accidentally killed by bomb explosion on 7 February 1916*
STE. MARIE CEMETERY, LE HAVRE, *France*
Son of W. H. and Margaret Calvert, of Cliftonville, Belfast.

Calvin, William Findlay - Private
3413 Royal Inniskilling Fusiliers 1st Battalion *Age 18 Died in War on 2 July 1915*
HELLES MEMORIAL, *Turkey*
Son of Mrs. Elizabeth Calvin, of 55, East Bread Street, Newtownards Road, Belfast.

Calwell, Theophilus Legate - Lieutenant
Royal Fusiliers 9th Battalion *Age 23 Died in War on 7 October 1916*
THIEPVAL MEMORIAL, *France*
Born in Belfast. the son of Walter and Rebecca Calwell. Commissioned into the Royal Fusiliers
(City of London Regiment). Awarded the Military Cross for bravery. His brother, Lieutenant W H Calwell,
was killed serving with the Royal Irish Rifles.

Calwell, Walter Henry - Lieutenant
Royal Irish Rifles 5th Battalion attached 2nd Battalion *Age 33 Died of Wounds on 27 August 1918*
ARNEKE BRITISH CEMETERY, *France*
Born in Belfast. the son of Walter and Rebecca Calwell. He was in Vancouver when the war started
and initially enlisted in the Canadian Forces. He was later commissioned into the Royal Irish Rifles.
He died three days after being severely wounded. His brother, Lieutenant T L Calwell MC,
was also killed, serving with the 9th Battalion Royal Fusiliers.

Cambridge, Robert - Sergeant
33162 New Zealand Training Unit *Age 33 Died in War on 12 February 1917*
CHRISTCHURCH (LINWOOD) CEMETERY, *New Zealand*
Native of Belfast, Ireland. Husband of Mrs A Cambridge, Christchurch, New Zealand.

Cameron, Donald - Private
302838 Princess Louise's (Argyll & Sutherland Highlanders) 1/8th Battalion *Died in War on 17 March 1917*
ARRAS MEMORIAL, *France*
Born in Belfast, enlisted in Greenock, Scotland.

Cameron, James - Sergeant
160496 Canadian Infantry (Alberta Regiment) 50th Battalion *Age 25 Died of Wounds on 5 June 1917*
BARLIN COMMUNAL CEMETERY EXTENSION, *France*
Son of James and Sarah Cameron, of 52, Brookhill Avenue, Antrim Road, Belfast, Ireland.
Formerly of Ballymena, County Antrim. Awarded the Military Medal.

Cameron, John - Rifleman
5362 Royal Irish Rifles 1st Battalion *Killed in Action on 28 March 1918*
POZIERES MEMORIAL, *France*
Born and enlisted in Belfast.

Journey of Remembering

Cameron, John - Sergeant
305686 King's (Liverpool Regiment) 8th Battalion *Died in War on 8 August 1916*
THIEPVAL MEMORIAL, *France*
Born in Belfast, enlisted Liverpool.

Cameron, Robert - Gunner
78638 Royal Field Artillery No. 7 Depot *Age 22 Died in War on 1 February 1918*
BELFAST CITY CEMETERY, *United Kingdom*
Son of John Cameron, of 33, Cosgrave Street, Belfast. Had been badly wounded, repatriated and died at home. A Presbyterian he had worked as a steam engineer.

Camlin, Joseph - Private
103277 Canadian Infantry 67th Battalion *Age 28 Died of endocarditis on 16 July 1918*
VICTORIA (ROSS BAY) CEMETERY, *Canada*
Son of James Camlin, of 75, Windsor Road, Belfast, Ireland.

Cammock, Thomas - Private
12591 Princess Victoria's (Royal Irish Fusiliers) 6th Battalion *Died in War on 9 August 1915*
HELLES MEMORIAL, *Turkey*
Born and enlisted in Belfast.

Campbell, A - Private
5727 Royal Irish Regiment 1st Garrison Battalion *Age 47 Died as a result of war on 8 April 1919*
CAIRO WAR MEMORIAL CEMETERY, *Egypt*
Husband of Margaret Campbell, of 98, Dundela Street, Strandtown, Belfast.

Campbell, Albert Edward - Air Mechanic Third Class
284636 Royal Air Force 5th Aircraft Repair Depot *Age 19 Died as a result of war on 20 March 1919*
BELFAST CITY CEMETERY, *United Kingdom*
Son of John and Jane Campbell, of 12, Ambrose Street, Belfast.

Campbell, Alexander - Private
3385 Princess Victoria's (Royal Irish Fusiliers) 1st Battalion *Died in War on 30 April 1916*
BERLES-AU-BOIS CHURCHYARD EXTENSION, *France*
Born and enlisted in Belfast.

Campbell, Alexander - Rifleman
14173 Royal Irish Rifles 14th Battalion *Died in War on 7 April 1916*
FORCEVILLE COMMUNAL CEMETERY AND EXTENSION, *France*
Born and enlisted in Belfast.

Campbell, Alexander - Rifleman
6983 Royal Irish Rifles 2nd Battalion *Killed in Action on 27 October 1914*
LE TOURET MEMORIAL, *France*
Born in Kilkenny, enlisted Newtownards, resident in Belfast.

Campbell, Alfred John - Private
10478 Royal Inniskilling Fusiliers 2nd Battalion *Age 21 Died in War on 16 May 1915*
LE TOURET MEMORIAL, *France*
Brother of Mrs. Sarah Jane Hussen, of 4, Connswater Street, Belfast.

Campbell, Andrew - Private
3438 Royal Inniskilling Fusiliers 2nd Battalion *Age 38 Died in War on 31 January 1917*
BELFAST CITY CEMETERY, United Kingdom
Husband of Matilda Campbell, of 31, Ottawa Street, Belfast.

Campbell, Archibald - Rifleman
17404 Royal Irish Rifles 13th Battalion *Killed in Action on 1 July 1916*
THIEPVAL MEMORIAL, France
Born in Belfast, enlisted in Newtownards.

Campbell, Colin - Rifleman
1076 Royal Irish Rifles 16th Battalion *Age 23 Killed in Action on 31 July 1917*
YPRES (MENIN GATE) MEMORIAL, Belgium
Son of John and Isobel Campbell, of 63, Surrey Street, Lisburn Road, Belfast.

Campbell, David - Rifleman
10403 Royal Irish Rifles 1st Battalion *Killed in Action on 31 July 1917*
YPRES (MENIN GATE) MEMORIAL, Belgium
Born and enlisted in Belfast.

Campbell, Frank - Rifleman
19422 Royal Irish Rifles 15th Battalion *Died in War on 9 April 1918*
CEMENT HOUSE CEMETERY, Belgium
Lived at Laganvale, Stranmillis, Belfast.

Campbell, Frederick - Rifleman
249 Royal Irish Rifles 8th Battalion *Died in War on 2 July 1916*
THIEPVAL MEMORIAL, France
107 East Bread Street, Belfast.

Campbell, Fredrick Ewen - Private
839 (Eastern Ontario Regiment) Princess Patricia's Canadian Light Infantry *Age 25 Died in War on 9 April 1917*
ECOIVRES MILITARY CEMETERY, MONT-ST. ELOI, France
Son of William and Jennie Campbell, of Belfast. A single man and a Presbyterian he had previously served in the British Army.

Campbell, George - Lance Corporal
64211 Royal Engineers (Aldershot) *Age 40 Died in War on 27 May 1918*
BELFAST CITY CEMETERY, United Kingdom
Husband of Sarah Campbell, of 51, Conlon Street, Belfast.

Campbell, George Jackson - Stoker First Class
Royal Navy HMS "Hawke" *Died in War on 15 October 1915*
CHATHAM NAVAL MEMORIAL, United Kingdom
69 East Bread Street, Belfast.

Campbell, Herbert - Leading Seaman
213144 Royal Navy HMS "Monmouth" *Age 28 Killed in Action at Battle of Coronel on 1 November 1914*
PLYMOUTH NAVAL MEMORIAL, United Kingdom
Son of John and Marguerite Campbell (née Peters), of Belfast.

Campbell, Herbert Ernest - Rifleman
1567 Royal Irish Rifles 10th Battalion *Age 18 Killed in Action on 1 July 1916*
THIEPVAL MEMORIAL, France
Son of Thomas and Ellen Campbell, of 50, Battenberg Street, Shankill Road, Belfast.

Campbell, Hugh - Private
16989 Royal Army Medical Corps 33rd Company *Died on 16 January 1917*
CAIRO WAR MEMORIAL CEMETERY, Egypt
99 Chief Street, Belfast.

Campbell, Hugh - Private
24829 Royal Inniskilling Fusiliers "D" Company 1st Battalion *Age 26 Died in War on 9 August 1916*
YPRES (MENIN GATE) MEMORIAL, Belgium
Son of Hugh and Maggie Campbell, of 14, Ewart's Row, Belfast. Husband of Mary Campbell (née McConnell), of Mullaghmore, Omagh, County Tyrone.

Campbell, James - Private
84569 Machine Gun Corps (Infantry) 12th Company *Killed in Action on 3 May 1917*
ARRAS MEMORIAL, France
His uncle, Mr P Campbell, lived at 94 Turin Street, Belfast.

Campbell, James - Private
S/9448 Black Watch (Royal Highlanders) 8th (Service) Battalion *Died in War on 14 July 1916*
THIEPVAL MEMORIAL, France
Born in Belfast. Lived in Glasgow when enlisted.

Campbell, James - Private
21456 Royal Dublin Fusiliers 6th Battalion *Died in War on 8 October 1917*
KIRECHKOI-HORTAKOI MILITARY CEMETERY, Greece
Husband of Agnes Campbell of 11 Ardilea Street, Belfast.

Campbell, James - Rifleman
9199 Royal Irish Rifles 9th Battalion *Age 30 Died in War on 8 August 1917*
YPRES (MENIN GATE) MEMORIAL, Belgium
Son of William and Mary Campbell, of "Island Vale", King's Road, Knock, Belfast.

Campbell, John - Lance Corporal
14547 Royal Inniskilling Fusiliers 9th Battalion *Killed in Action on 16 August 1917*
TYNE COT MEMORIAL, Belgium
33 Rosebank Street, Belfast.

Campbell, John - Private
11702 Royal Inniskilling Fusiliers 1st Battalion *Killed in Action on 22 March 1918*
POZIERES MEMORIAL, France
Born in Belfast.

Campbell, John - Private
164066 Canadian Infantry (Central Ontario Regiment) 75th Battalion *Age 23*
Died of Wounds on 25 November 1916
ETAPLES MILITARY CEMETERY, France
Son of John and Jean Campbell, of 26, Montrose Street, Belfast.

Campbell, John - Private
M/299865 Royal Army Service Corps *Age 21 Died as a result of war on 25 February 1919*
BELFAST (MILLTOWN) ROMAN CATHOLIC CEMETERY, United Kingdom
Son of John Campbell, of 15, Mountain View Street, Belfast.

Campbell, John - Regimental Sergeant Major
5629 Princess Charlotte of Wales's (Royal Berkshire Regiment) 2nd Battalion *Died in War on 15 October 1917*
PROWSE POINT MILITARY CEMETERY, Belgium
Born in Belfast, enlisted in London. Son of Sarah and Daniel Campbell and husband of Louise Campbell.

Campbell, John - Rifleman
5414 Royal Irish Rifles 1st Battalion
Age 36 Died of Wounds received at Neuve Chapelle 10th March on 21 April 1915
LE TOUQUET-PARIS PLAGE COMMUNAL CEMETERY, France
Son of Thomas and Martha Campbell, of 20, Hollycroft Avenue, Bloomfield, Belfast. Nineteen years service. Served in the South African Campaign. Native of Portadown, County Armagh.

Campbell, John - Rifleman
6100 Royal Irish Rifles 1st Battalion *Age 40 Killed in Action on 10 March 1915*
LE TOURET MEMORIAL, France
Husband of Harriett Campbell, of 7, Roxburgh Street, Belfast.

Campbell, John - Rifleman
7073 Royal Irish Rifles 2nd Battalion *Age 23 Killed in Action on 27 October 1914*
LE TOURET MEMORIAL, France
Son of William Campbell, of 49, Annette Street, Belfast.

Campbell, John F. - Sergeant
271242 Royal Scots (Lothian Regiment) 16th Battalion *Died in War on 4 May 1918*
TOURNAI COMMUNAL CEMETERY ALLIED EXTENSION, France
Born in Knockbreda, Belfast. Lived in Glasgow when enlisted. Formerly 1470, Scottish Rifles.

Campbell, Joseph - Lance Corporal
9408 Royal Irish Rifles 1st Battalion *Died of Wounds on 9 May 1915*
LE TROU AID POST CEMETERY, FLEURBAIX, France
Son of John and Gertrude Campbell, of 15, Mountain View Street, Ligoneil, Belfast.

Campbell, Joseph - Private
7003 Cavalry 9th (Queen's Royal) Lancers *Died in War on 27 March 1918*
POZIERES MEMORIAL, France
Born in Belfast, enlisted in Northampton, England.

Campbell, Joseph - Rifleman
12229 Royal Irish Rifles "A" Company 8th Battalion *Age 50 Died in War on 2 July 1916*
THIEPVAL MEMORIAL, France
Son of William Campbell; husband of Martha Campbell, of 19, Convention Street, Belfast.

Campbell, Kenneth M - Corporal
17101 Canadian Infantry (British Columbia Regiment) *Died in War on 25 May 1915*
VIMY MEMORIAL, France
Born Dublin and lived at Belmont, Belfast. A Presbyterian he worked as a locomotive fireman and had served in the militia.

Campbell, Lawford Burne - Lieutenant
Royal Irish Rifles "C" Company 12th Battalion *Age 20 Killed in Action on 1 July 1916*
THIEPVAL MEMORIAL, France
Son of Robert Garrett Campbell and Alicia Anna Campbell, of Coolgreany, Fortwilliam Park, Belfast.

Campbell, Nathaniel - Rifleman
10606 Royal Irish Rifles 6th Battalion *Died in War on 10 August 1915*
HELLES MEMORIAL, Turkey
Argylle Street, Belfast.

Campbell, Nesbitt - Rifleman
759 Royal Irish Rifles 9th Battalion *Age 18 Died in War on 13 October 1917*
NEUVILLE-BOURJONVAL BRITISH CEMETERY, France
Son of James and Mary Campbell, of 108, Duncairn Gardens, Belfast.

Campbell, Randolph Churchill Bestall - Rifleman
14168 Royal Irish Rifles 14th Battalion *Age 21 Killed in Action on 6 April 1916*
HAMEL MILITARY CEMETERY, BEAUMONT-HAMEL, France
Son of Mr. H. A. and Mrs. C. E. Campbell, of 16, Cyprus Park, Belfast. Native of Ballynahinch, County Down where he had signed the Covenant in 1912.

Campbell, Robert - Sergeant
410245 Canadian Infantry (Eastern Ontario Regiment) 38th Battalion
Age 23 Died in War on 9 April 1917
VIMY MEMORIAL, France
Son of Hugh and Margaret Campbell, of Belfast, Ireland. Born in County Tyrone he worked as a book-keeper and was a member of the Presbyterian Church.

Campbell, Robert Blair - Rifleman
14159 Royal Irish Rifles 12th Battalion *Age 22 Died in War on 15 April 1918*
TYNE COT MEMORIAL, Belgium
Son of William J. and Maggie Blair Campbell, of 222, Upper Meadow Street, Belfast.

Campbell, Samuel - Private
29640 East Yorkshire Regiment 1st Battalion *Age 30 Died in War on 7 November 1918*
VIS-EN-ARTOIS MEMORIAL, France
Husband of Margaret Campbell, of 41, Lindsay Street, Belfast.

Campbell, Stewart - Private
37843 Machine Gun Corps 95th Company *Age 21 Died in War on 23 April 1917*
LA CHAUDIERE MILITARY CEMETERY, VIMY, France
Son of Robert and Martha Campbell, of 20, Dromara Street, Belfast.

Campbell, Thomas - Private
2794 6th Dragoons (Inniskilling) *Died in War on 7 July 1917*
TEMPLEUX-LE-GUERARD BRITISH CEMETERY, France
Born and enlisted in Belfast.

Campbell, Thomas - Private
3772 Royal Irish Fusiliers 8th Battalion *Died in War on 8 July 1916*
ST PATRICK'S CEMETERY, LOOS, France
Born Ballymacarrett, Belfast. Enlisted in Belfast.

Campbell, Thomas Callender - Lieutenant
Royal Engineers *Died in War on 8 October 1915(Soldier buried at sea)*
HELLES MEMORIAL Turkey
Son of the late William Howard Campbell and Mrs. Campbell, of Wellington Park, Belfast; husband of Georgia S. Campbell, of 6, The Mount, Mountpottinger, Belfast.

Campbell, Thomas Hugh - Ordinary Seaman
Mercantile Marine S.S. "Middleton" (Hull) *Age 16 Died, as a result of an attack by an enemy submarine on 1 December 1915*
TOWER HILL MEMORIAL, United Kingdom
Son of Leah Campbell, of 16, Mountcollyer Avenue, Belfast, and the late George Campbell.

Campbell, Thomas James - Gunner
24603 Royal Garrison Artillery 154th Siege Battery *Age 27 Killed in Action on 15 June 1917*
VLAMERTINGHE NEW MILITARY CEMETERY, Belgium
Only son of Andrew and the late E. J. M. Campbell; husband of Elizabeth Campbell, of 2, Bandon Street, Belfast. Native of Coleraine.

Campbell, William - Bombardier
65619 Royal Field Artillery 119th Battery *Age 25 Died of phthisis on 9 August 1918*
BELFAST (DUNDONALD) CEMETERY, United Kingdom
Son of Nathaniel and Emily Campbell, of 53, Farnham Street, Belfast. Was a Prisoner of War for three years.

Campbell, William - Private
3913 Seaforth Highlanders (Ross-shire Buffs, the Duke of Albany's) 4th Battalion
Died in War on 8 June 1916
LOUEZ MILITARY CEMETERY, DUISANS, France
Born and enlisted in Belfast.

Campbell, William - Rifleman
1096 Royal Irish Rifles 16th Battalion *Age 17 Died in War on 16 July 1916*
DOULLENS COMMUNAL CEMETERY EXTENSION No.1, France
Son of Susan and the late Robert Campbell, of 99, Chief Street, Belfast.

Campbell, William - Rifleman
11159 Royal Irish Rifles 6th Battalion *Age 21 Died in War on 13 August 1915*
HELLES MEMORIAL, Turkey
Son of William and Margret Campbell, of 28, Walbeck Street, Antrim Road, Belfast.

Campbell, William - Rifleman
17409 Royal Irish Rifles 14th Battalion *Age 23 Killed in Action on 1 July 1916*
THIEPVAL MEMORIAL, France
Son of Mr. and Mrs. W. Campbell, of Authuille House, 71, Hillsborough Drive, Castlereagh Road, Belfast.

Campbell, William - Rifleman
7223 Royal Irish Rifles 4th attached 2nd Battalion *Died in War on 30 April 1917*
BELFAST CITY CEMETERY, United Kingdom
Husband of Eleanor McCrory (formerly Campbell), of 11, Enniskillen Street, Belfast. Discharged and awarded the Silver War Badge.

Journey of Remembering

Campbell, William Henry - Private
PLY/13623 Royal Marine Light Infantry SS "Baykerran"
Age 30 Drowned in the loss of his ship off Nova Scotia on 23 January 1918
PLYMOUTH NAVAL MEMORIAL, United Kingdom
Son of the late John and Margaret Campbell, of 26, Fingal Street, Belfast.

Campbell, William John - Lance Corporal
16290 Royal Irish Rifles 9th Battalion *Killed in Action on 1 July 1916*
THIEPVAL MEMORIAL, France
35 Silvio Street, Belfast.

Campbell, William Joseph - Sergeant
5554 Royal Irish Rifles 2nd Battalion *Killed in Action on 7 June 1917*
WULVERGHEM-LINDENHOEK ROAD MILITARY CEMETERY, Belgium
Born in Belfast. Lived in Glasgow when enlisted.

Campfield, Frederick - Corporal
1521 Leinster Regiment 7th Battalion *Died in War on 3 September 1916*
THIEPVAL MEMORIAL, France
Born in Stockport Lancashire, resident in Belfast.

Campion, John James - Staff Sergeant Major
T/18474 Royal Army Service Corps 55th Division *Age 32 Died of pneumonia on 1 March 1919*
HEVERLEE WAR CEMETERY, Belgium
Son of James and Esther Campion, of 29, Atlantic Avenue, Belfast.

Canavan, James Patrick - Private
2364 Connaught Rangers 6th Battalion *Died in War on 3 February 1916*
ABBEVILLE COMMUNAL CEMETERY, France
Son of Mr. and Mrs. Canavan, of Belfast. Had six brothers and two sisters. His father was on active service.

Canavan, Patrick - Private
8372 Royal Irish Fusiliers 1st Battalion *Age 28 Killed in Action on 10 May 1915*
ST. SEVER CEMETERY, ROUEN, France
Husband of Rose Canavan, of 45, Kashmir Road, Belfast.

Canavan, Patrick - Rifleman
10541 Royal Irish Rifles 6th Battalion *Age 28 Died in War on 11 August 1915*
HELLES MEMORIAL, Turkey
Son of Edward and Brigid Canavan (née McKenna); husband of Mary Teresa Canavan, of 36, Servia Street, Belfast.

Cannell, Ernest Charles - Gunner
1736 Australian Field Artillery 41st Battery 11th Brigade *Age 27 Died of Wounds on 15 June 1917*
KANDAHAR FARM CEMETERY, Belgium
Son of Benjamin and Lucy Cannell, of 3, Saltwell Street, Gateshead, Durham, England. Native of Belfast, Ireland.

Canney, Patrick - Corporal
46209 Labour Corps *Died in War on 20 June 1918*
OLDHAM (GREENACRES) CEMETERY), United Kingdom
Born in Belfast. Enlisted in Oldham Lancashire. Formerly 5316,Lancashire Fusiliers

Canning, Albert - Gunner
81925 Royal Field Artillery 103rd Battery *Age 40 Died of Wounds on 7 May 1915*
BEDFORD HOUSE CEMETERY, *Belgium*
Husband of Annie Canning, of 64, Moira Street, Belfast. Holder of the Silver War Badge.

Canning, James - Trimmer
7611TS Royal Naval Reserve HMS "Bittern" *Age 28 Drowned through collision in English Channel on 4 April 1918*
PORTSMOUTH NAVAL MEMORIAL, *United Kingdom*
Son of Mr. and Mrs. Canning, of Belfast; husband of E. Canning, of 52, Stanhope Street, Belfast.

Canning, John - Private
21104 Princess Victoria's (Royal Irish Fusiliers) 8th Battalion *Died in War on 26 April 1916*
LOOS BRITISH CEMETERY, *France*
Born and enlisted in Belfast. Formerly 3746,Connaught Rangers

Canning, Patrick - Rifleman
7067 Royal Irish Rifles 1st Battalion *Killed in Action on 1 July 1916*
THIEPVAL MEMORIAL, *France*
Son of Mrs. Catherine Canning, of 146, Ross Street, Belfast.

Capper, Adam Clarke - Second Lieutenant
Royal Irish Rifles attached 7th Battalion *Age 23 Killed in Action on 9 September 1916*
DELVILLE WOOD CEMETERY, LONGUEVAL, *France*
Son of Adam Clarke Capper and Rebecca Capper, of "Malvern", Malone Road, Belfast. Educated at RBAI he was suffering from measles when the 36th Division departed for France and thus missing the first phase of the Somme battle. He subsequently transferred to the 16th (Irish) Division and was killed in the later stages of the battle.

Capper, Bass Durant - Captain
Royal Flying Corps *Age 29 Killed while flying on 6 December 1917*
BELFAST CITY CEMETERY, *United Kingdom*
Son of Bass and Alice Capper of Lennoxvale, Belfast.

Carabine, Patrick - Private
10644 Royal Inniskilling Fusiliers 1st Battalion *Age 20 Died in War on 21 August 1915*
HELLES MEMORIAL, *Turkey*
Son of Thomas and Annie Carabine, of 135, Cavendish Street, Belfast.

Cardwell, J - Private
180596 Canadian Infantry (Western Ontario Regiment) 47th Battalion *Killed in Action on 4 February 1917*
VILLERS STATION CEMETERY, VILLERS-AU-BOIS, *France*
A labourer, he born in County Tyrone and then resident in Belfast. His, sister, Mrs Greer, lived at 47 Tennent Street, Belfast. He was a member of the Church of Ireland and lived with his wife, Margaret, in British Columbia. He had served with the Imperial Yeomanry in the Boer War and later with the Gordon Highlanders of Canada.

Cardwell, John - Private
3/6745 Gordon Highlanders 2nd Battalion *Died in War on 11 March 1915*
LE TOURET MEMORIAL, *France*
Born in Belfast. Lived in Glasgow when enlisted.

Journey of Remembering

Carey, Rondaine - Private
17359 Royal Inniskilling Fusiliers 11th Battalion *Died in War on 27 February 1915*
BALLYMENA NEW CEMETERY, United Kingdom
Born in Liverpool, resident Belfast and enlisted in Finner Camp, County Donegal.

Carey, Thomas James - Lance Corporal
866 Australian Infantry 15th Battalion *Killed in Action on 9 - 10 May 1915*
BEACH CEMETERY, ANZAC, Turkey
Father of Master E. C. Carey. Native of Belfast, Ireland.

Cargo, Hugh - Rifleman
49267 Rifle Brigade 1st Battalion *Died as result of war on 28 March 1919*
LES BARAQUES MILITARY CEMETERY, SANGATTE, France
Son of Mary Jane Cargo 122, Matilda Street, Belfast.

Carleton, John - Leading Stoker
K/11026 Royal Navy HMS."Princess Irene" *Age 24 Killed by internal explosion of vessel off Sheerness on 27 May 1915*
CHATHAM NAVAL MEMORIAL, United Kingdom
Son of William and Mary Carleton, of 44, Belgrave Street, Belfast.

Carlile, George H. P. - Private
241011 Seaforth Highlanders 7th Battalion *Age 24 Killed in Action on 22 October 1918*
TERLINCTHUN BRITISH CEMETERY, WIMILLE, France
Son of Samuel M. and Jane Carlile, of 3, Twickenham Street, Belfast. Holder of the Military Medal.

Carlin, John M. - Private
101223 Royal Army Medical Corps *Died in War on 3 December 1917*
GLASNEVIN (OR PROSPECT) CEMETERY, DUBLIN, Republic of Ireland
Born in Belfast. Lived in Dublin when enlisted.

Carlisle, David - Rifleman
6043 Royal Irish Rifles 1st Battalion *Died in War on 12 March 1915*
YPRES (MENIN GATE) MEMORIAL, Belgium
Husband of Ellen Jane Carlisle, of 21, Bristol Street, Belfast.

Carlisle, Herbert - Private
4106 Irish Guards 1st Battalion *Age 21 Died in War on 14 September 1914*
LA FERTE-SOUS-JOUARRE MEMORIAL, France
Son of Mary Jane Carlisle, of 24, Dorchester Street, Donegall Road, Belfast, and the late Samuel Carlisle.

Carlisle, Richard - Gunner
51506 Royal Field Artillery 94th Battery *Killed in Action on 25 October 1914*
GUARDS CEMETERY, WINDY CORNER, CUINCHY, France
Survived by his mother at 16 Cargill Street, Belfast.

Carlisle, Robert - Rifleman
1209 Royal Irish Rifles 16th Battalion *Age 20 Killed in Action on 21 March 1918*
POZIERES MEMORIAL, France
Son of John and Jane Carlisle, of 67, Utility Street, Belfast.

Carlisle, Robert - Rifleman
8199 Royal Irish Rifles 2nd Battalion *Age 27 Killed in Action on 27 October 1914*
LE TOURET MEMORIAL, France
Son of Mrs. Mary Ann Carlisle, of 13, St. Leonard Street, Belfast.

Carlisle, William - Private
29818 Yorkshire Regiment 13th Battalion *Died in War on 3 July 1916*
BETHUNE TOWN CEMETERY, France
Son of William James Carlisle, of 76, Ravenhill Avenue, Belfast.

Carlisle, William - Rifleman
1060 Royal Irish Rifles 14th Battalion *Age 19 Killed in Action on 16 August 1917*
TYNE COT MEMORIAL, Belgium
Son of Robert and Sarah Bella Carlisle, of 101, Bloomfield Avenue, Belfast.

Carlisle, William - Rifleman
11211 Royal Irish Rifles 1st Battalion *Age 24 Killed in Action on 23 October 1916*
THIEPVAL MEMORIAL, France
Husband of Elizabeth Carlisle, of 14, Court Street, Belfast.

Carmichael, Andrew Wilson - Private
187025 Canadian Infantry (Manitoba Regiment) 8th Battalion *Died of Wounds on 28 September 1916*
CONTAY BRITISH CEMETERY, CONTAY, France
2 Bracken Street, Belfast. A Presbyterian, he worked as a machinist in Canada.
His brother, William, was killed with the Irish Rifles.

Carmichael, Robert - Sergeant
12655 Royal Irish Rifles 15th Battalion *Died in War on 22 November 1917*
THIEPVAL MEMORIAL, France
Born and enlisted in Belfast.

Carmichael, William - Private
10927 Royal Irish Rifles 6th Battalion *Died in War on 11 August 1915*
HELLES MEMORIAL, Turkey
Survived by his mother at 2 Bracken Street, Belfast.
His brother, Andrew was killed serving with the Canadians.

Carolan, Neal - Private
7324 South Lancashire Regiment 2nd Battalion *Killed in Action on 24 October 1914*
LE TOURET MEMORIAL, France
Son of Patrick and Maragaret Carolan of 3 Merkland Street, Belfast.

Carr, James - Rifleman
10523 Royal Irish Rifles 6th Battalion *Died in War on 28 August 1915*
HELLES MEMORIAL, Turkey
Born and enlisted in Belfast.

Carr, Wilfred - Private
7211 Royal Irish Rifles 16th Battalion *Killed in Action on 21 March 1918*
POZIERES MEMORIAL, France
Son of William James and Annie Carr, of 10 Woodcote Avenue, Belfast.

Carracher, Francis - Private
18414 Royal Irish Fusiliers 8th Battalion *Died in War on 6 September 1916*
THIEPVAL MEMORIAL, *France*
Sister of Mary Ann Carragher, 28, Ormeau Road, Belfast.

Carran, Thomas H (Harry) - Sergeant
57806 Royal Engineers 36th Signal Company *Killed in Action on 6 July 1916*
YPRES (MENIN GATE) MEMORIAL, *Belgium*
Lived at 89, Deramore Avenue, Belfast.

Carroll, Henry - Rifleman
11910 Royal Irish Rifles 7th Battalion *Died in War on 1 July 1918*
LOOS MEMORIAL, *France*
Born and enlisted in Belfast.

Carroll, Patrick Joseph - Rifleman
7421 Royal Irish Rifles 2nd Battalion *Killed in Action on 8 July 1916*
THIEPVAL MEMORIAL, *France*
Born in Belfast, enlisted Holywood.

Carruth, John - Lieutenant
Royal Dublin Fusiliers attached 1st Royal Irish Rifles *Died of Wounds on 10 October 1918*
TINCOURT NEW BRITISH CEMETERY, *France*
Husband of Vera Maude Carruth of Stewartstown. A member of Queen's University Officer Training Corps.
His brother, Matthew, was also killed.

Carruth, Matthew - Second Lieutenant
Royal Irish Regiment attached 6th Connaught Rangers *Age 26 Died in War on 9 September 1918*
THIEPVAL MEMORIAL, *France*
Born at Belfast. Son of Elisha Carruth and Jane Carruth of 'The Haven', Mallusk.
His brother, John, was also killed.

Carruthers, Josiah - Private
10113 Royal Inniskilling Fusiliers 1st Battalion *Age 22 Died in War on 14 May 1915*
TWELVE TREE COPSE CEMETERY, *Turkey*
4 Glenbrook Avenue, Belfast.

Carson, Andrew - Private
430533 Canadian Infantry (British Columbia Regiment) 7th Battalion
Age 31 Died in War on 10 August 1918
VILLERS-BRETONNEUX MILITARY CEMETERY, *France*
Son of David and Sarah Carson, of 163, Barton Lane, Eccles, Manchester, England. Native of Belfast, Ireland.
A Presbyterian he worked as a ship's carpenter and served in the Canadian Militia.
Awarded the Military Medal.

Carson, Charles - Private
725 Royal Irish Rifles 8th Battalion *Died of Wounds on 3 July 1916*
CONNAUGHT CEMETERY, THIEPVAL, *France*
Husband of Lucy and father of three children. 45 McCandless Street, Belfast.

Carson, David - Private
281582 Highland Light Infantry 7th (Blythswood) Battalion (Territorial) *Died in War on 7 August 1918*
ROCLINCOURT MILITARY CEMETERY, France
Born in Belfast. Lived in Glasgow when enlisted.

Carson, John - Rifleman
11899 Royal Irish Rifles 15th Battalion *Age 19 Killed in Action on 21 March 1918*
POZIERES MEMORIAL, France
Son of John and Isabella Carson, of 17, North Queen Street, Belfast.

Carson, John - Rifleman
24/991 New Zealand Rifle Brigade 2nd Battalion *Died in War on 15 October 1917*
LIJSSENTHOEK MILITARY CEMETERY, Belgium
Member of St Enoch's Presbyterian Church Belfast.

Carson, Patrick - Private
21979 Royal Dublin Fusiliers 6th Battalion *Died in War on 9 December 1915*
DOIRAN MEMORIAL, Greece
Born in Belfast enlisted Omagh. Formerly 3496, Connaught Rangers.

Carson, Patrick - Private
2766 Royal Irish Fusiliers 6th Battalion *Died in War on 5 June 1916*
DUD CORNER CEMETERY, LOOS, France
Husband of Helen Jane Carson, 50 Mayfair Street, Belfast.

Carson , Samuel - Company Sergeant Major
6869 Royal Inniskilling Fusiliers 2nd Battalion *Died in War on 28 January 1917*
THIEPVAL MEMORIAL, France
Awarded the Distinguished Conduct Medal. Sister of Frances Carson, 41 Fortwilliam Parade, Belfast.

Carson, William John White - Second Lieutenant
Royal Irish Rifles 14th Battalion *Age 29 Killed in Action on 1 July 1916*
THIEPVAL MEMORIAL, France
Only Son of William McRobert Carson and Sarah Carson, of Tareen House, Old Cavehill Road, Belfast.

Cartlidge, Frederick - Private
10296 Cheshire Regiment 2nd Battalion *Age 19 Died in War on 3 October 1915*
LOOS MEMORIAL, France
Brother of William Percy Cartlidge, of 149 Tates Avenue, Belfast.

Casement, John - Private
13502 Princess Victoria's (Royal Irish Fusiliers) 6th Battalion *Died in War on 7 August 1915*
HELLES MEMORIAL, Turkey
Born and enlisted in Belfast.

Casey, Edward - Private
4346 Connaught Rangers 6th Battalion *Died in War on 26 December 1917*
TINCOURT NEW BRITISH CEMETERY, France
Enlisted and resident in Belfast. Native of Lurgan.

Casey, Francis - Private
3474 Royal Inniskilling Fusiliers 7th Battalion *Killed in Action on 9 October 1916*
THIEPVAL MEMORIAL, *France*
Born in Belfast.

Caskey, David - Rifleman
17420 Royal Irish Rifles 15th Battalion *Died in War on 2 May 1918*
BARD COTTAGE CEMETERY, *Belgium*
Born and enlisted in Belfast.

Cassells, Alexander - Rifleman
9816 Royal Irish Rifles 1st Battalion *Killed in Action on 9 May 1915*
PLOEGSTEERT MEMORIAL, *Belgium*
8 Belgrave Street, Belfast.

Cassells, Samuel - Rifleman
17/1032 Royal Irish Rifles 8th Battalion *Age 20 Died of Wounds on 20 March 1916*
BERTRANCOURT MILITARY CEMETERY, *France*
Son of William and Mary Jane Cassells, of Belfast.

Cassidy, Felix - Lance Corporal
20599 Royal Inniskilling Fusiliers 8th Battalion *Died in War on 29 March 1916*
LOOS MEMORIAL, *France*
Born and enlisted in Belfast. Formerly 2405 Connaught Rangers.

Cassidy, Harry - Private
RC/96 South African Road Corps 2nd Battalion *Age 60 Died in War on 5 July 1918*
LUMBO BRITISH CEMETERY, *Mozambique*
Husband of E. Bennett (formerly Cassidy), of 58, Davies Street, Doornfontein, Johannesburg. Served in the South African War. Born in Belfast, Ireland.

Cassidy, James - Private
23236 Royal Irish Fusiliers 8th Battalion *Died in War on 17 November 1916*
BAILLEUL COMMUNAL CEMETERY EXTENSION (NORD), *France*
Son of Margaret Cassidy of Belfast.

Cassidy, James - Rifleman
11527 Royal Irish Rifles 6th Battalion *Age 27 Died in War on 11 August 1915*
HELLES MEMORIAL, *Turkey*
Son of Rose Ann Cassidy, of 131, New Lodge Road, Belfast, and the late Thomas Cassidy.

Cassidy, James - Rifleman
23889 The King's (Liverpool Regiment) formerly, 5th Dragoon Guards 3rd/5th Battalion *Age 58 Died in War on 21 December 1915*
PRESTON (NEW HALL LANE) CEMETERY, *United Kingdom*
Son of John and Maria Cassidy. Born in Belfast.

Cassidy, James - Rifleman
8980 Royal Irish Rifles "A" Company 2nd Battalion *Age 26 Killed in Action on 15 September 1914*
LA FERTE-SOUS-JOUARRE MEMORIAL, *France*
Son of John and Mary Jane Cassidy, of 101, Ardilea Street, Oldpark Road, Belfast.

Cassidy, John Malachi - Lance Corporal
3170 Loyal North Lancashire Regiment 6th Battalion *Died in War on 9 March 1917*
BASRA MEMORIAL, Iraq
Born in Belfast, enlisted Liverpool. Formerly 11218, Liverpool Regiment.

Cassidy, Joseph - Private
25618 Royal Scots 17th Battalion *Age 21 Died in War on 8 June 1916*
HARPONVILLE COMMUNAL CEMETERY EXTENSION, France
Nephew of Susanna Shields, of 76, Falls Road, Belfast.

Cassidy, William Lindsay - Private
526924 Canadian Army Medical Corps 2nd Field Ambulance *Age 28 Killed in Action on 2 September 1918*
QUEBEC CEMETERY, CHERISY, France
Son of John and Anna Cassidy, of Belfast, Ireland. He was studying as a theological student for the Congregational Church when he enlisted.

Castles, William - Sergeant
5983 Duke of Cornwall's Light Infantry 1st Battalion *Died in War on 15 September 1914*
LA FERTE-SOUS-JOUARRE MEMORIAL, France
51 Sandy Row Belfast. Born in Waterford.

Caswell, William - Sergeant
16328 Royal Irish Rifles 1st Battalion *Killed in Action on 24 March 1918*
POZIERES MEMORIAL, France
Born and enlisted in Belfast.

Cathcart, David - Rifleman
17424 Royal Irish Rifles 11th Battalion *Died in War on 1 September 1916*
YPRES (MENIN GATE) MEMORIAL, Belgium
Born in Belfast. Lived in Lisburn when enlisted.

Cathcart, Henry - Private
8442 Royal Inniskilling Fusiliers 1st Battalion *Age 29 Died in War on 30 June 1915*
TWELVE TREE COPSE CEMETERY, Turkey
51, Ivan Street, Belfast. His brother, Herbert, also fell.

Cathcart, Herbert - Rifleman
7106 Royal Irish Rifles 2nd Battalion *Age 20 Killed in Action on 7 June 1917*
WULVERGHEM-LINDENHOEK ROAD MILITARY CEMETERY, Belgium
Son of John Cathcart, of 51, Ivan Street, York Road, Belfast. His brother, Henry, also fell.

Cathcart, John - Private
67377 The Queen's (Royal West Surrey Regiment) 6th Battalion *Age 18 Died in War on 14 August 1918*
MORLANCOURT BRITISH CEMETERY No.2, France
Son of Mrs. Margaret Cathcart, of 111, Ardilea Street, Oldpark Road, Belfast.

Catherwood, Hugh - Rifleman
1760 Royal Irish Rifles 10th Battalion *Age 22 Died in War on 4 August 1917*
WIMEREUX COMMUNAL CEMETERY, France
Son of Sarah Jane and Hugh Catherwood, of Belfast.

Journey of Remembering

Catherwood, Joseph - Private
11409 Royal Inniskilling Fusiliers 9th Battalion *Died in War on 1 July 1917*
CONNAUGHT CEMETERY, THIEPVAL, France
Born in Belfast, enlisted Omagh.

Catherwood, Joseph - Rifleman
9097 Royal Irish Rifles 2nd Battalion *Died in War on 11 July 1915*
HAZEBROUCK COMMUNAL CEMETERY, France
Father of Josephine Catherwood, 30 Hopefield Street, Belfast.

Caughley, Percy - Sapper
64075 Royal Engineers 121st Field Company *Age 23 Died of Wounds on 20 March 1916*
FORCEVILLE COMMUNAL CEMETERY AND EXTENSION, France
Son of James and Sarah Caughley, of Victoria Terrace, Limestone Road, Belfast.

Cavanagh, Charles - Rifleman
8290 Royal Irish Rifles 3rd Battalion *Died in War on 3 March 1916*
MILLTOWN (ROMAN CATHOLIC) CEMETERY, United Kingdom
Born and enlisted in Belfast.

Cavanagh, Edward - Private
11131 Princess Victoria's (Royal Irish Fusiliers) 2nd Battalion *Died in War on 14 May 1915*
YPRES (MENIN GATE) MEMORIAL, Belgium
Born and enlisted in Armagh. A resident of Belfast.

Caves, Edward - Private
8155 Royal Inniskilling Fusiliers 2nd Battalion *Age 28 Died in War on 16 May 1915*
LE TOURET MEMORIAL, France
Son of Mrs. Elizabeth Caves, of 76, Cosgrave Street, Belfast. Killed at the Battle of Loos.

Caves, Thomas R. - Private
2068 Irish Guards 1st Battalion *Died in War on 6 November 1914*
ST SOUPLET BRITISH CEMETERY, France
Born and enlisted in Belfast.

Cecil, Robert Angus Malcolm - Pioneer
WR/209016 Royal Engineers Railway Construction Troops Depot *Age 33 Died in War on 1 November 1918*
BORDON MILITARY CEMETERY, United Kingdom
Son of Jeanette McKee (formerly Cecil), of Tulnavern House, Andersonstown, Belfast, and the late Robert Cecil. Born in Dublin.

Cesar, Robert - Private
9404 Royal Inniskilling Fusiliers *Died in War on 22 May 1915*
TWELVE TREE COPSE CEMETERY, Turkey
95 Tildarg Street, Belfast.

Chambers, George - Lance Corporal
14065 Royal Irish Fusiliers 9th Batttalion *Age 19 Died in War on 1 July 1916*
ANCRE BRITISH CEMETERY, BEAUMONT-HAMEL, France
90 Britannic Street, Belfast. Born County Tyrone.

Chambers, James - Lance Corporal
20160 Princess Victoria's (Royal Irish Fusiliers) 8th Battalion *Died in War on 20 November 1917*
ARRAS MEMORIAL, France
Born and enlisted in Belfast.

Chambers, Joseph - Rifleman
609 Royal Irish Rifles 1st Battalion *Killed in Action on 23 December 1916*
BAILLEUL COMMUNAL CEMETERY EXTENSION (NORD), France
Son of Joseph and Mary Chambers, Stewartstown Road, Belfast.

Chambers, Joseph - Sergeant
47236 Royal Field Artillery "B" Battery 276th West Lancs Brigade *Died in War on 10 April 1918*
BELFAST CITY CEMETERY, United Kingdom
Husband of Margaret Chambers, of 11, Renfrew Street, Belfast. Had been discharged and awarded the Silver War Badge.

Chambers, Richmond J. T. - Private
103844 Royal Army Medical Corps *Died in War on 29 October 1918*
DROMORE (BANBRIDGE ROAD) PRESBYTERIAN CHURCHYARD, United Kingdom
Born and enlisted in Belfast.

Chambers, Robert - Private
59303 Machine Gun Corps (Infantry) formerly 5345 Liverpool Regiment Died in War *on 17 April 1917*
HOLLYBROOK MEMORIAL, SOUTHAMPTON, United Kingdom
Born in Belfast. Son of John and Catherine Chambers, of Liverpool; husband of Susan Chambers, of 11, Lune Street, Great Crosby, Liverpool.

Chambers, Thomas - Rifleman
12661 Royal Irish Rifles 8th Battalion attached 107th Trench Mortar Battery *Died in War on 2 June 1917*
POND FARM CEMETERY, Belgium
Son of Mr. D. Chambers, of 40, Roslyn Street, Belfast.

Chambers, Thomas - Lance Corporal
16333 Machine Gun Corps 15th Company *Died in War on 27 July 1916*
SERRE ROAD CEMETERY No.2, France
Son of Mrs. Charlotte Chambers, of 59, Charles St. South, Belfast.

Chambers, William - Rifleman
1351 Royal Irish Rifles 8th/9th Battalion *Age 21 Died in War on 21 March 1918*
HAM BRITISH CEMETERY, MUILLE-VILLETTE, France
Grandson of James and Sarah Robinson, of 29, Lee Street, Belfast. Awarded the Military Medal.

Chancellor, Samuel - Stoker First Class
SS/110580 Royal Navy HMS "Cressy" *Age 22 Killed in Action with submarine in North Sea on 22 September 1914*
CHATHAM NAVAL MEMORIAL, United Kingdom
Son of John and Emily Chancellor, of Belfast.

Chapman, Edward - Rifleman
6459 Royal Irish Rifles 12th Battalion *Died in War on 17 May 1918*
ROYE NEW BRITISH CEMETERY, France
Born in Aghalee, enlisted Lisburn, resident Belfast.

Journey of Remembering

Chapman, Nicholas - Rifleman
10170 Royal Irish Rifles 2nd Battalion *Died in War 10 May 1918*
VEVEY (ST. MARTIN'S) CEMETERY, Switzerland
Born in Belfast.

Charles, Daniel - Private
21318 Canadian Infantry (Alberta Regiment) *Died in War 22 May 1915*
VIMY MEMORIAL, France
35 Burmah Street, Belfast.

Charters, James - Corporal
12663 Royal Irish Rifles "C" Company 15th Battalion *Age 28 Died of Wounds on 21 March 1918*
GRAND-SERAUCOURT BRITISH CEMETERY, France
Son of Margaret Charters, of 8, Marine Street, Belfast, and the late Henry Percy Charters.

Cheasty, Martin - Private
2126 Lancashire Fusiliers 1st Battalion *Died in War on 15 April 1918*
PLOEGSTEERT MEMORIAL, Belgium
Born in Belfast, enlisted in Bury, Lancashire.

Cheddy, Thomas - Rifleman
47486 Royal Irish Rifles 10th Battalion *Age 22 Died of Wounds on 11 December 1917*
SUNKEN ROAD CEMETERY, VILLERS-PLOUICH, France
Son of James Cheddy, a coachman, of 35, Queen Victoria Gardens, Belfast.
Formerly S/4/111283 Army Service Corps.

Cherry, William - Rifleman
8830 Royal Irish Rifles 1st Battalion *Killed in Action on 9 May 1915*
PLOEGSTEERT MEMORIAL, Belgium
Born and enlisted in Belfast.

Cheyne, Edward Emmerson - Private
8409 Royal Irish Fusiliers 1st Battalion *Age 26 Died in War on 25 April 1915*
YPRES (MENIN GATE) MEMORIAL, Belgium
Son of George and Susan Cheyne, of 102, McClure Street, Belfast.

Chiplin, William Henry - Captain
Royal Irish Rifles 15th Battalion *Age 30 Killed in Action on 1 July 1916*
THIEPVAL MEMORIAL, France
Son of William John and Frances Annie Chiplin, "Rosenalea", Cyprus Gardens, Bloomfield, Belfast.

Chisim, John - Stoker First Class
SS/105949 Royal Navy HMS "Hawke" *Age 25 Killed in Action with submarine in North Sea on 15 October 1914*
CHATHAM NAVAL MEMORIAL, United Kingdom
Son of the late John and Mary Eleanor Chisim, of Belfast.

Christie, John Francis - Private
25106 Royal Dublin Fusiliers 10th Battalion *Age 24 Died in War on 26 February 1917*
THIEPVAL MEMORIAL, France
Son of John and Isabella Christie, of 12, Stranmillis Park, Belfast.

Christie, Thomas Henry - Rifleman
1115 Royal Irish Rifles 12th Battalion *Age 25 Killed in Action on 16 August 1917*
TYNE COT MEMORIAL, Belgium
Son of William Henry Christie; husband of Sarah Jane Christie, of Cottonmount, Mallusk, Belfast.

Christie, William - Private
17846 Royal Inniskilling Fusiliers 9th Battalion *Killed in Action on 1 July 1916*
CONNAUGHT CEMETERY, THIEPVAL, France
Son of Mrs. E. Christie, of 54, Raby Street, Ormeau Road, Belfast.

Christie, William - Private
30041 Yorkshire Regiment 4th Battalion *Age 20 Died in War on 28 October 1917*
TYNE COT MEMORIAL, Belgium
Son of Mrs. Jane Christie, of 49, Baker Street, Belfast.

Christy, James - Private
18014 Royal Irish Regiment 2nd Battalion *Died in War on 3 September 1916*
THIEPVAL MEMORIAL, France
Born and enlisted in Belfast. Formerly 4241, Royal Munster Fusiliers.

Chubb, Ernest Edward - Lance Corporal
8/12665 Royal Irish Rifles 15th Battalion *Age 25 Died of pneumonia while a POW 12 April 1918*
NIEDERZWEHREN CEMETERY, Germany
Son of Herbert Chubb, of 78, Thistle Street, Belfast. Mentioned in Despatches

Church, Edwin Charles - Private
25421 Duke of Wellington's (West Riding Regiment) 10th Battalion *Died in War on 30 September 1917*
TYNE COT MEMORIAL, Belgium
Born in Belfast, enlisted in Kingston-upon-Thames, England. Formerly 2596, Norfolk Regiment.

Church, Joseph - Rifleman
9445 Royal Irish Rifles 2nd Battalion *Age 39 Killed in Action on 26 April 1916*
ECOIVRES MILITARY CEMETERY, MONT-ST. ELOI, France
Son of Joseph and Mary Church, of Belfast; husband of Sarah E. Church, of 79, Donegall Road, Belfast.

Cinnamond, Frederick Charles - Rifleman
12666 Royal Irish Rifles 8th Battalion *Age 21 Died in War on 2 July 1916*
THIEPVAL MEMORIAL, France
Son of F. W. and Harriet Alice Cinnamond, of 103, Belmont Road, Belfast.

Cinnamond, Isaac - Fireman And Trimmer
Mercantile Marine S.S. "Rathlin Head" (Belfast)
Age 40 Killed, as a result of an attack by an enemy submarine on 26 May 1918
TOWER HILL MEMORIAL, United Kingdom
Son of James and Eliza Cinnamond; husband of Sarah Cinnamond (née Edgar), of 8, Garston Street, Belfast.

Cinnamond, James - Private
21996 Royal Dublin Fusiliers 6th Battalion *Age 23 Died in War on 10 August 1915*
HELLES MEMORIAL, Turkey
Son of Mrs. Margaret Cinnamond, of 31, Tyrone Street, Belfast.

Clair, William - Stoker
1406U Royal Navy HMS "Hogue" *Died in War on 22 September 1914*
CHATHAM NAVAL MEMORIAL, United Kingdom
7 Ardmore Avenue, Belfast.

Clare, James - Rifleman
2835 Royal Irish Rifles "D" Company 15th Battalion *Age 22 Killed in Action on 24 March 1918*
POZIERES MEMORIAL, France
Son of James and Caroline Clare, of 27, Coniston Street, Belfast.

Clark, David - Rifleman
592130 London Regiment 18th (County of London) Battalion (London Irish Rifles)
Died in War on 27 November 1917
JERESALEM WAR CEMETERY, Israel
Born and enlisted in Belfast.

Clark, George - Lieutenant
Royal Naval Reserve H.M. Yacht "Kethailes" *Age 25 Drowned through collision on 11 October 1917*
CHATHAM NAVAL MEMORIAL, United Kingdom
Son of Robert Dawson Clark and Jane Clark, of West Hartlepool; husband of Lilian Jane Clark,
of Flush House, Knockbreda Road, Belfast.

Clark, Herbert Cameron Russell. - Captain
Canadian Infantry (British Columbia Regiment) 7th Battalion *Age 28 Died of Wounds on 20 November 1918*
ETAPLES MILITARY CEMETERY, France
Son of Mr. and Mrs. James Murray Clark, of Vancouver, British Columbia, late of Belfast, Ireland.
Awarded the Military Cross twice.

Clarke, Andrew - Rifleman
6647 Royal Irish Rifles 1st Battalion *Died in War on 24 August 1916*
VERMELLES BRITISH CEMETERY, France
Husband of Mrs S Clarke, 34 Chamberlain Street, Belfast.

Clarke, Camillus - Private
27608 Royal Inniskilling Fusiliers 8th Battalion *Age 38 Died of Wounds (gas) on 3 May 1916*
BETHUNE TOWN CEMETERY, France
Son of Patrick and Mary Clarke; husband of Mary Clarke, of 12, Parkview Street, Oldpark Road, Belfast.

Clarke, Charles - Rifleman
1745 Royal Irish Rifles 7th Battalion *Age 19 Died in War on 8 August 1917*
YPRES (MENIN GATE) MEMORIAL, Belgium
Son of Charles Clarke, of 27, Little Charlotte Street, Belfast.

Clarke, Francis - Rifleman
5855 Royal Irish Rifles 2nd Battalion *Killed In Action on 17 May 1916*
ARRAS MEMORIAL, France
Born in Belfast.

Clarke, Frank - Private
12820 Manchester Regiment 20th Battalion *Died in War on 15 July 1916*
ST SEVER CEMETERY ROUEN, France
Born in Belfast. Lived in Manchester when enlisted.

Clarke, Hugh - Rifleman
14208 Royal Irish Rifles 10th Battalion *Age 44 Killed in Action on 1 July 1916*
THIEPVAL MEMORIAL, France
Son of Hugh and Esther Clarke, of 22, Irwell Street, Belfast.

Clarke, James - Rifleman
17/1042 Royal Irish Rifles 14th Battalion *Died in War on 3 July 1916*
BOULOGNE EASTERN CEMETERY, France
Born Ballymacarrett, Belfast. Enlisted in Belfast.

Clarke, John - Private
161113 Canadian Infantry (Alberta Regiment) 10th Battalion *Age 28 Died in War on 26 September 1916*
POZIERES BRITISH CEMETERY, OVILLERS-LA BOISSELLE, France
Son of John Clarke, Upper Crescent, Belfast. A fitter by trade he enlisted in Calgary, Canada.

Clarke, John - Rifleman
7011 Royal Irish Rifles 2nd Battalion *Killed in Action on 20 September 1914*
LA FERTE-SOUS-JOUARRE MEMORIAL, France
Born in Belfast.

Clarke, John - Rifleman
7016 Royal Irish Rifles 1st Battalion *Killed in Action on 1 July 1916*
THIEPVAL MEMORIAL, France
The son of Mary and the late James, 43 Derry Street, Belfast.

Clarke, John K - Second Lieutenant
Royal Air Force 103rd Squadron *Died in War on 22 July 1918*
CABARET-ROUGE BRITISH CEMETERY, SOUCHEZ, France
Member of Duncairn Presbyterian Church. Son of Rev Edward and Janie Clarke.

Clarke, Patrick - Private
9020 Royal Irish Rifles 2nd Battalion *Age 37 Killed in Action on 27 October 1914*
LE TOURET MEMORIAL, France
Husband of the late Elizabeth Clarke, 55 Springview Street, Belfast.

Clarke, Robert - Private
12969 Royal Inniskilling Fusiliers 1st Battalion *Killed in Action on 1 July 1916*
THIEPVAL MEMORIAL, France
Born and enlisted in Belfast.

Clarke, Samuel - Rifleman
R/14105 King's Royal Rifle Corps 13th Battalion *Died in War on 5 August 1917*
DERRY HOUSE CEMETERY No 2, Belgium
Born in Belfast, enlisted in Barrow-in-Furness.

Clarke, Samuel James - Rifleman
14207 Royal Irish Rifles 2nd Battalion *Age 25 Killed in Action on 30 July 1918*
PLOEGSTEERT MEMORIAL, Belgium
Son of William Clarke of 16, Gaffikin Street, Sandy Row, Belfast.

Clarke, Thomas Henry - Lance Corporal
7146 West Yorkshire Regiment (Prince of Wales's Own) "B" Company 2nd Battalion
Age 34 Died in War on 24 April 1918
POZIERES MEMORIAL, France
Son of the late Thomas and Mary Clarke, of Goole, Yorkshire; husband of Jeanie Clarke,
of 26, Legann Street, Ballysillan, Belfast.

Clarke, Wilfred - Rifleman
6386 Royal Inniskilling Fusiliers *Killed in Action on 1 July 1916*
THIEPVAL MEMORIAL, France
70 Rosevale Street, Belfast.

Clarke, William - Gunner
277171 Royal Garrison Artillery *Died in War on 13 July 1917*
ADDOLORATA CEMETERY, Malta
Born in England, enlisted Carrickfergus, resident in Belfast.

Clarke, William - Gunner
3910 Royal Garrison Artillery 20th Siege Battery *Age 36 Died in War on 28 September 1917*
MENDINGHEM MILITARY CEMETERY, Belgium
Son of David Clarke; husband of Wilhelmina Clarke, of 28, Ulverston Street, Belfast.

Clarke, William - Private
17928 Royal Irish Fusiliers 9th Battalion *Killed in Action on 1 July 1916*
THIEPVAL MEMORIAL, France
20, Christopher Street, Belfast.

Clarke, William - Private
18818 Royal Inniskilling Fusiliers 2nd Battalion *Age 22 Died in War on 3 July 1916*
THIEPVAL MEMORIAL, France
Only son of Robert and Agnes Clarke, of 40, Christopher Street, Belfast.

Clarke, William - Private
8908 Highland Light Infantry 2nd Battalion *Died in War on 29 October 1914*
YPRES (MENIN GATE) MEMORIAL, Belgium
Born in Belfast. Enlisted in Glasgow .

Clarke, William - Sergeant
19414 Royal Irish Rifles "D" Company 12th Battalion
Age 40 Died of Wounds on 12 April 1918
LIJSSENTHOEK MILITARY CEMETERY, Belgium
Son of Thomas and Sarah Clarke, of Crumlin, County Antrim; husband of Catherine Graham
(formerly Clarke) of 19, Malt Street, Grosvenor Road, Belfast.

Clarke, William - Stoker First Class
SS/100711 Royal Navy HMS "Hawke"
Age 28 Killed in Action with submarine in North Sea on 15 October 1914
CHATHAM NAVAL MEMORIAL, United Kingdom
Son of John and Sarah McConnell, of 26, Foreman Street, Belfast.

Clarke, William Donald - Rifleman
9200 Royal Irish Rifles 11/13th Battalion *Died in War on 29 March 1918*
POZIERES MEMORIAL, France
Born in Belfast, enlisted Dublin. Formerly 2654, Army Cyclist Corps.

Clarkin, John - Private
20931 Royal Irish Fusiliers 8th Battalion *Age 33 Died of Wounds on 9 May 1916*
BETHUNE TOWN CEMETERY, France
Son of John and Mary Clarkin of Belfast; husband of Mary Clarkin of Conway Steet, Belfast.

Classon, Ermot - Private
260074 Royal Warwickshire Regiment 2/6th Battalion *Died in War on 4 September 1917*
TYNE COT MEMORIAL, Belgium
Born in Belfast, enlisted in Liverpool. Formerly 41432, Liverpool Regiment and 5089, Monmouthshire Regiment.

Clawson, Sydney - Rifleman
16335 Royal Irish Rifles 14th Battalion *Died in War on 6 December 1917*
CAMBRAI MEMORIAL, France
Born and enlisted in Belfast.

Clayton, Joseph - Private
32665 Royal Warwickshire Regiment 10th Battalion *Age 37 Died in War on 19 April 1918*
TYNE COT MEMORIAL, Belgium
Son of George Clayton, of Huddersfield; husband of Ada Clayton, of 29, Rosebery Gardens, Willowfield, Belfast. Served 16 years with 1st and 5th Dragoon Guards.

Clegg, Alfred - Rifleman
9974 Royal Irish Rifles 2nd Battalion *Died of Wounds on 10 May 1915*
PONT-DU-HEM MILITARY CEMETERY, LA GORGUE, France
Born in Belfast, enlisted in Cork.

Clegg, Fred - Private
19538 East Lancashire Regiment 2nd Battalion *Killed in Action on 9 May 1915*
PLOEGSTEERT MEMORIAL, Belgium
Brother of James Clegg, of 14, Baltic Avenue, Antrim Road, Belfast.

Clegg, William Hamilton - Private
S/43008 Cameron Highlanders "A" Company 1st Battalion *Age 22 Died in War on 16 November 1917*
TYNE COT MEMORIAL, Belgium
Son of John and Anne Jane Clegg, of 2, Sturgeon Street, Sandy Row, Belfast.

Cleland, Matthew - Stoker First Class
SS/105670 Royal Navy HMS "Aboukir"
Age 23 Killed in Action with submarine in North Sea on 22 September 1914
CHATHAM NAVAL MEMORIAL, United Kingdom
Son of James Cleland, of 58, Beersbridge Road, Belfast.

Cleland, Richard - Private
740 Irish Guards 1st Battalion *Age 37 Killed in Action on 1 November 1914*
OXFORD ROAD CEMETERY, Belgium
Son of Richard Cleland, of Belfast; husband of Eliza Cleland, of 115, Riga Street, Belfast.

Cleland, Robert J. - Private
871175 Canadian Infantry (New Brunswick Regiment) 44th Battalion *Age 36*
Died of sickness on 28 March 1921
WINNIPEG (BROOKSIDE) CEMETERY, Canada
Son of Thomas and Mary Cleland, of 136, Utility Street, Belfast, Ireland; husband of Margaret Cleland, of Cartier, Ontario. An Anglican, he worked as a machinist in Canada.

Clements, Edmund - Private
3050 Royal Inniskilling Fusiliers 1st Battalion *Age 21 Died in War on 28 June 1915*
TWELVE TREE COPSE CEMETERY, Turkey
Son of Annie Soutter (formerly Clements), of 101, Lilliput Street, Belfast, and the late William Clements.

Clements, John - Private
19802 Cameronians (Scottish Rifles) 9th Battalion *Died in War on 4 August 1916*
ARRAS MEMORIAL, France
Born in Belfast, enlisted in Scotland.

Clements, John - Private
28101 Royal Inniskilling Fusiliers 8th Battalion *Age 19 Died in War on 16 May 1917*
BELFAST CITY CEMETERY, United Kingdom
Son of Mrs. Mary Clements, of 13, Wensley Street, Belfast.

Clements, William - Private
10721 Royal Inniskilling Fusiliers 1st Battalion *Age 19 Died in War on 10 August 1915*
HELLES MEMORIAL, Turkey
Son of William and Annie Clements, of 101, Lilliput Street, Belfast.

Clements, William - Private
14456 Royal Inniskilling Fusiliers 11th Battalion *Killed in Action on 1 July 1916*
CERISY-GAILLYFRENCH NATIONAL CEMETERY, France
Born Belfast, enlisted Londonderry.

Clements, William - Sergeant
10/14302 Royal Irish Rifles 3rd Battalion *Died in War on 5 July 1918*
BELFAST CITY CEMETERY, United Kingdom
Husband of M. Clements, of 64, Egmont Street, Belfast. Awarded the Silver War Badge.

Clements, William Hunter - Second Lieutenant
Royal Inniskilling Fusiliers 11th Battalion *Age 24 Died in War on 16 August 1917*
NEW IRISH FARM CEMETERY, Belgium
Son of Andrew Clements, LL.D., and Margaret B. Clements, of 28, Knutsford Drive, Cliftonville, Belfast. Awarded the Meritorious Service Medal.

Clendinning, John George - Sapper
504231 Canadian Engineers 7th Field Company *Age 21 Died in War on 17 December 1916*
VIMY MEMORIAL, France
Son of John and Catherine Clendinning, of 64, Ardenlee Avenue, Belfast, Ireland.

Clendinning, Robert Alexander - Corporal
18890 Royal Irish Rifles 3rd Battalion *Age 45 Died as a result of war on 11 November 1920*
DUNDROD PRESBYTERIAN CHURCH, Uniited Kingdom
A native of Belfast and husband of Agnes Clendinning, Riverside, Glenavy, Lisburn.
His death was possibly the result of gassing. Two brothers also served. His son, David, was killed in World War II when his ship, HMS "Whirlwind", was torpedoed by the German submarine, U34.

Clewlo, William - Rifleman
14/6513 Royal Irish Rifles 8th Battalion *Killed in Action on 11 June 1916*
AUTHUILE MILITARY CEMETERY, France
Husband of Teresa, 15 Ninth Street, Belfast.

Clifford, William George - Rifleman
239 Royal Irish Rifles 10th Battalion *Age 21 Died in War on 24 November 1917*
CAMBRAI MEMORIAL, LOUVERVAL, France
Son of William and Annie Clifford, of 7, Wayland Street, Castlereagh Road, Belfast.

Clifford, William John - Greaser
Mercantile Marine S.S. "Donegal" (Belfast)
Age 29 Drowned as a result of an attack by an enemy submarine on 17 April 1917
TOWER HILL MEMORIAL, United Kingdom
Son of Letitia Clifford, of Lancastrian Street, Carrickfergus, County Antrim, and the late Robert Clifford. Born at Belfast.

Clifton, Joseph Richard - Corporal
G/13868 Royal Sussex Regiment 3rd Battalion *Age 42 Died of sickness on 15 August 1920*
CHICHESTER CEMETERY, United Kingdom
Husband of Mrs. A. Clifton, of 4, Parchment Street, Chichester.

Clingan, Edward - Private
99729 The King's (Liverpool Regiment) 4th Battalion *Age 19 Died in War on 19 October 1918*
ROCQUIGNY-EQUANCOURT ROAD BRITISH CEMETERY, MANANCOURT, France
Son of the late William and Mary Clingan, of Belfast.

Clinton, John - Private
11909 Royal Inniskilling Fusiliers 9th Battalion *Age 31 Died in War on 10 August 1917*
YPRES (MENIN GATE) MEMORIAL, Belgium
Husband of Jane Clinton, of 2, Oswald Street, Belfast.

Clinton, Thomas - Corporal
23777 Royal Inniskilling Fusiliers 7th Battalion *Died in War on 19 April 1916*
PHILOSOPHE BRITISH CEMETERY, MAZINGARBE, France
Husband of Maggie, 97 Cupar Street, Belfast. Formerly employed at the Blackstaff Mill.

Clokey, J - Private
2378705 Canadian Infantry (Manitoba Regiment) 52nd Battalion *Age 23 Died in War on 29 May 1918*
ETAPLES MILITARY CEMETERY, France
Son of John and Margaret Clokey of Belfast, Ireland.

Close, Edward - Private
Royal Irish Rifles 1st Battalion *Killed in Action on 10 March 1915*
Son of John and Mary Close, 14 Lower Urney Street, Belfast.

Journey of Remembering

Close, James - Private
202712 Seaforth Highlanders 4th Battalion *Age 32 Died of Wounds on 26 April 1917*
ETAPLES MILITARY CEMETERY, France
Son of Hugh and Mary Jane Close, of Braniel, Castlereagh; husband of Lavinia Close, of 254, Castlereagh Road, Belfast.

Close, James - Rifleman
17/603 Royal Irish Rifles 8th Battalion *Died in War on 11 June 1916*
AUTHUILE MILITARY CEMETERY, France
Canton Street, Belfast.

Close, James - Rifleman
8879 Royal Irish Rifles 2nd Battalion *Age 17 Died of Wounds on 2 June 1915*
CHICHESTER CEMETERY, United Kingdom
Son of the late Alexander and Mary Close, of 25 Eastland Street, Belfast.

Close, John - Able Seaman
216280 Royal Navy HMS "Indefatigable" *Died suddenly on 2 August 1915*
DALMENY AND QUEENSFERRY CEMETERY, United Kingdom
32 Ashmore Street, Belfast. A veteran of 14 years service he was survived by his widowed mother.

Close, John - Private
4258 Royal Inniskilling Fusiliers 1st Battalion *Age 23 Died as POW on 23 September 1918*
NIEDERZWEHREN CEMETERY, Germany
Son of John and Matilda Close, of 115, Cambrai Street, Belfast.
Native of Galgorm, Ballymena, County Antrim.

Close, William - Private
14506 Royal Inniskilling Fusiliers 9th Battalion *Killed in Action on 8 May 1916*
AUTHUILE MILITARY CEMETERY, France
Born Belfast, enlisted Finner Camp, County Donegal.

Clucas , Robert - Private
26329 Royal Inniskilling Fusiliers 7th Battalion *Killed in Action on 27 April 1916*
LOOS MEMORIAL, France
Native of Wicklow, resident of Belfast.

Clugston, Andrew - Corporal
26305 Royal Inniskilling Fusiliers 5th Battalion *Age 22 Died in War on 8 October 1918*
BEAUREVOIR BRITISH CEMETERY, France
Son of the late Andrew and Mary Clugston, of Belfast.

Clugston, Frederick - Corporal
11628 Royal Inniskilling Fusiliers 6th Battalion *Age 19 Died in War on 17 August 1915*
HELLES MEMORIAL, Turkey
Son of William and Agnes Clugston, of 109, My Lady's Road, Belfast.

Clulow, Edward - Private
D/19464 5th Dragoon Guards (Princess Charlottes) "C" Squadron *Age 36 Died of Wounds on 27 March 1918*
ST. SEVER CEMETERY EXTENSION, ROUEN, France
Son of Mr. and Mrs. James Evitt Clulow, of Belfast; husband of Sarah Jane Clulow, of 52, Clementine Street, Belfast. Served in the South African Campaign. An Army Reservist.

Clulow, Thomas - Private
6829 South Lancashire Regiment *Age 30 Died in War on 19 September 1916*
BELFAST CITY CEMETERY, United Kingdom
Husband of Eleanor Clulow, of 10, Renfrew Street, Sandy Row, Belfast.

Clyde, John - Rifleman
93181 Royal Irish Rifles 9th Battalion *Killed in Action on 1 July 1916*
THIEPVAL MEMORIAL, France
Brother of Isasbella Clyde and Annnie Jackson of 35 Renfrew Street, Belfast.

Clydesdale, Samuel Thomas - Private
PLY/17576 Royal Marine Light Infantry 2nd R.M. Battalion Royal Naval Division
Age 19 Died in War on 19 February 1917
THIEPVAL MEMORIAL, France
Son of Samuel and Georgina Clydesdale, of 41, Douglas Street, Belfast.

Coard, Samuel - Trimmer
487/ST Royal Naval Reserve H.M. Trawler "Nellie Dodds" *Age 35 Died in War on 8 November 1918*
CARNMONEY CEMETERY, United Kingdom
Husband of Rose Ann Coard, of 6, Garston Street, Belfast.

Coates, George Washington Tate - Second Lieutenant
Royal Field Artillery 33rd Battery *Age 19 Died in War on 10 March 1915*
LE TOURET MEMORIAL, France
Son of George D. Coates, manager of the Northern Bank in Royal Avenue and who lived at Fruit Hill, Andersonstown, Belfast. Mentioned in Despatches.

Coates, Matthew - Private
26276 Royal Inniskilling Fusiliers 1st Battalion *Died in War on 28 January 1917*
THIEPVAL MEMORIAL, France
175 Sidney Street West, Belfast. His brother, William, was killed with the Irish Rifles in 1915.

Coates, Robert - Rifleman
8205 Royal Irish Rifles 2nd Battalion *Age 31 Killed in Action on 7 July 1917*
YPRES (MENIN GATE) MEMORIAL, Belgium
Son of Margaret Coates, of 24, Argyle Street, Belfast.

Coates, William - Lance Corporal
9176 Royal Irish Rifles 1st Battalion *Killed in Action on 9 May 1915*
PLOEGSTEERT MEMORIAL, France
Born in Lisburn. Enlisted and resident in Belfast.

Coates, William John - Private
2562375 Canadian Infantry (Central Ontario Regiment) 116th Battalion
Age 28 Died in War on 12 August 1918
VIMY MEMORIAL,France
Son of Mrs. Margretta Clydesdale (formerly Coates), of 683, Elm Street, Arlington, Kearny, New Jersey, U.S.A., and the late Robert James Coates. Born in Belfast, Ireland.

Journey of Remembering

Cobain, James - Rifleman
16340 Royal Irish Rifles 14th Battalion *Died in War on 17 February 1915*
CARNMONEY (HOLY EVANGELISTS) CHURCH OF IRELAND CHURCHYARD EXTENSION, *United Kingdom*
3, Evelyn Gardens, Belfast.

Coburn, John - Private
3206414 Canadian Infantry (Alberta Regiment) *Age 26 Died of sickness on 5 April 1920*
EDMONTON (MOUNT PLEASANT) CEMETERY, *Canada*
Son of John Coburn, of 122, Cambrai Street, Belfast, Ireland, and the late Elizabeth Coburn. Worked as a labourer in Canada, an Anglican.

Coburn, Robert - Rifleman
3904 Royal Irish Rifles 2nd Battalion *Killed in Action on 19 January 1916*
TRANCREZ CEMETERY, *Belgium*
Born in Hillsborough, enlisted in Ballykinler, resident of Belfast.

Cochrane, Hugh - Corporal
46075 Royal Engineers 97th Field Company *Age 24 Died in War on 28 May 1918*
POZIERES MEMORIAL, *France*
Son of Hugh and Elizabeth Cochrane, of 23, Fleet Street, Belfast.

Cochrane, J - Rifleman
5537 Royal Irish Rifles 1st Battalion *Age 30 Died of Wounds on 25 April 1915*
MERVILLE COMMUNAL CEMETERY, *France*
Son of Thomas and Mary Cochrane; husband of Sarah Cochrane, of 9, Linfield Street, Belfast.

Cochrane, James - Sapper
64302 Corps of Royal Engineers(150th Field Company) *Died in War on 30 April 1918*
DUHALLOW A.D.S. CEMETERY, *Belgium*
Born and enlisted in Belfast.

Cochrane, John Dawson - Petty Officer
196429 Royal Navy HMS "Nestor" *Killed in action on 31 May 1916*
PORTSMOUTH NAVAL MEMORIAL, *United Kingdom*
Born in Belfast. Killed during the Battle of Jutland.

Cochrane, Joseph - Rifleman
1099 Royal Irish Rifles 15th Battalion *Died in War on 22 November 1917*
THIEPVAL MEMORIAL, *France*
Husband of Sarah, 102 Palmer Street, Belfast.

Cochrane, Joseph Maxwell - Rifleman
14229 Royal Irish Rifles 14th Battalion *Age 32 Died of Wounds on 2 July 1916*
PUCHEVILLERS BRITISH CEMETERY, *France*
Son of George and Mary Maxwell Cochrane. Native of Belfast.

Cochrane, Patrick - Private
9180 King's Own Scottish Borderers 2nd Battalion *Died in War on 18 April 1915*
YPRES (MENIN GATE) MEMORIAL, *Belgium*
Born in Belfast, enlisted in Lanark, Scotland.

Cochrane, Robert - Driver
48765 Royal Horse Artillery and Royal Field Artillery *Died in War on 3 March 1917*
BASRA MEMORIAL, Iraq
Born and enlisted in Belfast. May have lived in Dundela Street.

Cochrane, T - Ordinary Seaman
CH/SS/5098 Royal Navy HMS "St. George" *Age 19 Drowned on 12 November 1915*
BELFAST CITY CEMETERY, United Kingdom
Son of Hugh and Elizabeth Cochrane, of 23, Fleet Street, Belfast.

Cochrane, William - Rifleman
1656 Royal Irish Rifles 9th Battalion *Age 20 Died in War on 23 November 1917*
CAMBRAI MEMORIAL, LOUVERVAL, France
Son of Robert J. and Ellen Cochrane, of 172, Blythe Street, Belfast.

Coghlan, Joseph James - Petty Officer Stoker
303132 Royal Navy HMS "Indefatigable" *Age 34 Killed in Action at Battle of Jutland on 31 May 1916*
PLYMOUTH NAVAL MEMORIAL, United Kingdom
Son of James and Catherine Coghlan, of County Waterford; husband of Minnie Coghlan, of 84, Butler Street, Belfast.

Coid, Andrew - Private
10413 Royal Inniskilling Fusiliers 2nd Battalion *Died of Wounds on 21 March 1918*
GRAND-SERAUCOURT BRITISH CEMETERY, France
Born and enlisted in Belfast.

Coid, James - Lance Corporal
5314 Royal Irish Rifles 7th Battalion *Age 21 Died in War on 29 April 1916*
LOOS MEMORIAL, France
Son of Mrs. Jane McCloy, of 17, Shipbouy Street, Belfast.

Coleman, Arthur H - Sergeant
7942 Royal Fusiliers 1st Battalion *Age 28 Died in War on 25 January 1915*
CHAPELLE-D'ARMENTIERES OLD MILITARY CEMETERY, France
Son of Mrs. M. H. Coleman, of 128, Woodvale Road, Belfast.

Coleman, Thomas - Private
3587 Royal Inniskilling Fusiliers 11th Battalion *Age 27 Died of Wounds on 1 February 1917*
BAILLEUL COMMUNAL CEMETERY EXTENSION (NORD), France
Son of Thomas and Sarah Coleman, of Belfast; husband of Elizabeth Coleman, of 19, Spring Street, Belfast.

Coles, Charles Archibald - Private
40237 Lincolnshire Regiment 1st Battalion, formerly 1606 Cambridgeshire Regiment *Died in War on 16 April 1918*
MAGNABOSCHI BRITISH CEMETERY, Italy
Born in Belfast, enlisted in Cambridge.

Colgan, James - Rifleman
6907 Royal Irish Rifles 16th Battalion *Age 18 Died in War on 9 September 1917*
VLAMERTINGHE NEW MILITARY CEMETERY, Belgium
Son of William and Jane Colgan, of 11, Bute Street, Belfast.

Collier, David - Company Sergeant Major
12235 Royal Irish Rifles 8th Battalion *Age 34 Died in War on 5 August 1917*
YPRES (MENIN GATE) MEMORIAL, Belgium
Husband of Annie Collier, of 19, Belvoir Street, Belfast.

Collier, Reginald John - Second Lieutenant
Royal Flying Service *Age 19 Killed while flying (crashed) on 12 February 1918*
BANGOR CEMETERY, United Kingdom
Born in Belfast the son of William and Marion Collier of Bangor. Originally served in the Royal Irish Rifles. Transferred to the Royal Flying Corps and died in a flying accident in England.

Collins, Charles Albert - Company Sergeant Major
10658 Royal Munster Fusiliers 1st Battalion *Died in War on 22 July 1916*
PHILOSOPHE BRITISH CEMETERY, MAZINGARBE, France
Born at sea aboard the ship "Shinwara", enlisted in India, resident in Belfast.
Formerly 6045 Royal Inniskilling Fusiliers. Holder of the Distinguished Conduct Medal

Collins, David - Private
265756 Black Watch (Royal Highlanders) 6th Battalion *Age 20 Died in War on 17 May 1917*
BAILLEUL ROAD EAST CEMETERY, ST. LAURENT-BLANGY, France
Son of Robert and Mrs. J. A. Collins, of "Maryburn", Andersonstown, Belfast.

Collins, David - Private
7701 Royal Inniskilling Fusiliers 2nd Battalion *Age 32 Died in War on 16 May 1915*
LE TOURET MEMORIAL, France
Son of Alexander Collins, of 123, Millfield, Belfast.

Collins, Edward - Rifleman
9183 Royal Irish Rifles 1st Battalion *Age 27 Killed in Action on 11 March 1915*
MERVILLE COMMUNAL CEMETERY, France
Son of the late John and Sarah Ann Collins, of Belfast. Also served in India

Collins, George - Private
PLY/16508 Royal Marine Light Infantry Plymouth Battalion Naval Division
Age 19 Killed in Action on 2 July 1915
SKEW BRIDGE CEMETERY, Turkey
Son of John and Elizabeth Collins, of 26, Fortuna Street, Belfast. Enlisted in 1913.

Collins, Herbert - Rifleman
3962 Royal Irish Rifles 2nd Battalion *Age 18 Killed in Action on 8 September 1915*
YPRES (MENIN GATE) MEMORIAL, Belgium
Son of James Collins, of 76, Pernau Street, Belfast.

Collins, John - Seaman
Mercantile Marine S.S. "Eveleen" (Belfast) *Age 29 Presumed drowned on 6 May 1918*
TOWER HILL MEMORIAL, United Kingdom
Son of Jane Collins (née McGann), of 61, Corporation Street, Belfast, and the late Michael Collins.
Born in Belfast.

Collins, Joseph - Lance Corporal
21418 Machine Gun Corps (Infantry) *Age 28 Died of Wounds on 26 March 1917*
BELFAST (MILLTOWN) ROMAN CATHOLIC CEMETERY, United Kingdom
Son of James and M. A. Collins, of 17, Granville Street, Belfast. Born at Drogheda, County Louth. Awarded the Military Medal.

Collins, Leslie James Stanley - Rifleman
8/12674 Royal Irish Rifles 15th Battalion *Age 28 Died of wounds on 18 September 1918*
TERLINCTHUN BRITISH CEMETERY, WIMILLE, France
Son of Robert Henry and Kate Collins, of Rathverde, Knock, Belfast.

Collins, Michael - First Mate
Mercantile Marine S.S. "Eveleen" (Belfast) *Age 60 Presumed drowned on 6 May 1918*
TOWER HILL MEMORIAL, United Kingdom
Son of the late Owen and Eliza Collins; husband of Jane Collins, (née McGann),
of 61, Corporation Street, Belfast. Born at Portaferry, County Down.

Collins, Percy - Able Bodied Seaman
180045 Royal Navy HMS "Tiger" *Age 38 Killed in action on 31 May 1916*
PLYMOUTH NAVAL MEMORIAL, United Kingdom
Born in Belfast. Husband of Emma Jane Collings, Cornwall.

Collins, Richard - Private
41545 Royal Scots (Lothian Regiment) 2nd Battalion *Died in War on 12 April 1918*
PLOEGSTEERT MEMORIAL, Belgium
Born and enlisted in Belfast. Formerly 34965, Highland Light Infantry

Collins, Robert - Private
18962 Royal Inniskilling Fusiliers 11th Battalion *Killed in Action on 1 July 1916*
THIEPVAL MEMORIAL, France
Born and enlisted in Belfast.

Collins, Robert - Sergeant
34346 Royal Field Artillery 57th Battery *Age 27 Died in War on 25 December 1916*
BRONFAY FARM MILITARY CEMETERY, BRAY-SUR-SOMME, France
Son of William and Mary Jane Collins, of 48, Agincourt Avenue, Belfast.

Collins, William - Rifleman
12/11411 Royal Irish Rifles 12th Battalion *Age 21 Died in War on 12 April 1918*
ST. SEVER CEMETERY EXTENSION, ROUEN, France
Son of Frederick Charles and Lily Jane Collins, of 41, Disraeli Street, Belfast.
Formerly employed at Ewart's Mill.

Colville, Samuel - Rifleman
49330 Rifle Brigade (The Prince Consort's Own) 1st Battalion *Died in War on 20 October 1918*
HASPRES COPPICE CEMETERY, France
Born and enlisted in Belfast. Formerly 22354, Royal Irish Rifles

Colville, William - Lance Corporal
10147 Royal Inniskilling Fusiliers 2nd Battalion *Died in War on 25 November 1914*
BOULOGNE EASTERN CEMETERY, France
Born Ballymacarrett, Belfast. Enlisted in Belfast. Formerly 9478 Royal Irish Rifles.

Journey of Remembering

Comiskey, John - Private
1519 Leinster Regiment 7th Battalion *Died in War on 17 February 1916*
CAMBRIN CHURCHYARD EXTENSION, France
Born and enlisted in Belfast.

Commack, Edward - Lance Corporal
8968 Royal Irish Rifles 2nd Battalion *Age 30 Killed in Action on 7 July 1916*
THIEPVAL MEMORIAL, France
Son of Margaret Commack, of 220, Leopold Street, Belfast, and the late James Commack.

Common, James - Private
2943 Northumberland Fusiliers 1/7th Battalion (Territorials) *Killed in Action on 12 May 1916*
CHATTON (HOLY CROSS) CHURCHYARD, United Kingdom
Born in Belfast, enlisted in Northumberland.

Condon, Patrick - Lance Corporal
6545 Royal Irish Rifles 2nd Battalion *Killed in Action on 16 June 1915*
YPRES (MENIN GATE) MEMORIAL, Belgium
56 Clementine Street, Belfast. Born in County Cork.

Conkey, Henry Dominick - Private
PLY/16188 Royal Marine Light Infantry 4th Royal Marine Battalion
Age 19 Killed in Action during the sea raid on Zeebrugge on 23 April 1918
DOVER (ST. JAMES'S) CEMETERY, United Kingdom
Served as CAMPBELL. Son of Thomas F. and Catherine Conkey, of 100, Foundry Street, Belfast.
Five years' service.

Conlon, Owen - Rifleman
10931 Royal Irish Rifles 6th Battalion *Age 20 Died in War on 10 August 1915*
HELLES MEMORIAL, Turkey
Son of Owen and Margaret Conlon, of 8, Omar Street, Belfast.

Conn, William G - Rifleman
20342 Royal Irish Rifles 5th Battalion *Age 19 Died in War on 9 July 1918*
BELFAST CITY CEMETERY, United Kingdom
Son of the late Thomas and Isabella Conn of Wardlow Street, Belfast.

Connal, John - Private
67213 Machine Gun Corps (Infantry) *Died in War on 26 October 1917*
TYNE COT MEMORIAL, Belgium
Born in Belfast. Lived in Glasgow when enlisted. Formerly 33115 Highland Light Infantry

Connell, William - Boy First Class
J/23481 Royal Navy HMS "Monmouth" *Age 17 Killed in Action at Battle of Coronel on 1 November 1914*
PLYMOUTH NAVAL MEMORIAL, United Kingdom
Son of John Connell of 14, Fitzroy Avenue, Belfast, and the late Mary Jane Connell.
Native of Skibbereen, County Cork.

Connelly, David Rutherford - Lance Corporal
2813 Royal Irish Rifles 15th Battalion *Age 19 Killed in Action on 1 July 1916*
MILL ROAD CEMETERY, THIEPVAL, France
Son of the late Edward and Jemima Connelly, of 2, Dewey Street, Belfast.

Journey of Remembering

Connolly, Patrick J - Private
1397 Irish Guards 1st Battalion *Killed in Action on 6 November 1914*
YPRES (MENIN GATE) MEMORIAL, Belgium
Born and resident in Belfast.

Connolly, Alexander - Private
5991 Irish Guards 2nd Battalion *Age 26 Died in War on 3 November 1916*
BELFAST CITY CEMETERY, United Kingdom
Son of John and Jane Connolly. Member of Shankill Road Mission, Belfast.

Connolly, Arthur Joseph - Private
2903 Royal Inniskilling Fusiliers 2nd Battalion *Age 18 Died in War on 16 May 1915*
LE TOURET MEMORIAL, France
Son of the late Arthur and Mary Connolly, of 2, Grosvenor Place, Belfast.

Connolly, Hugh A - Second Lieutenant
Irish Guards Attached Guards Machine Gun Company *Died in War on 27 August 1918*
H.A.C. CEMETERY, ECOUST-ST. MEIN, France
Survived by his sister who lived at 172 Old Lodge Road.

Connolly, John - Lance Corporal
5692 Royal Irish Rifles 2nd Battalion *Killed in Action on 20 September 1914*
LA FERTE-SOUS-JOUARRE MEMORIAL, France
Husband of Elizabeth Connolly. Born in Belfast. the son of James Connolly.

Connolly, Joseph - Second Engineer
Mercantile Marine S.S. "Aylevarroo" (Limerick) *Age 44 Presumed drowned on 7 October 1917*
TOWER HILL MEMORIAL, United Kingdom
Son of Martin and Mary Connolly, of 20, Berkley Street, Liverpool. Born in Belfast.

Connolly, Peter - Rifleman
11360 Royal Irish Rifles 6th Battalion *Died in War on 12 August 1915*
HELLES MEMORIAL, Turkey
Born and enlisted in Belfast.

Connolly, Robert John - Rifleman
6925 Royal Irish Rifles 1st Battalion *Killed in Action on 25 September 1915*
PLOEGSTEERT MEMORIAL, Belgium
Born in Belfast, enlisted Holywood.

Connolly, Thomas - Rifleman
11377 Royal Irish Rifles 1st Battalion *Killed in Action on 30 November 1917*
YPRES RESERVOIR CEMETERY, Belgium
Born and enlisted in Belfast.

Connor, Alexander William - First Engineer
Mercantile Marine S.S. "Eskmere" (Liverpool)
Age 33 Drowned, as a result of an attack by an enemy submarine on 13 October 1917
TOWER HILL MEMORIAL, United Kingdom
Son of James and Jane Connor (née Ewing), of 5, Wandsworth Road, Belmont, Belfast.

Journey of Remembering

Connor, Charles - Gunner
80588 Royal Horse Artillery and Royal Field Artillery *Died in War on 23 March 1916*
ETAPLES MILITARY CEMETERY, France
Born and enlisted in Belfast.

Connor, David - Private
2/25277 Royal Inniskilling Fusiliers 1st Battalion *Died in War on 30 May 1917*
LONDON CEMETERY, NEUVILLE-VITASSE, France
66 Pound Street, Belfast.

Connor, Dominick - Private
27552 Royal Inniskilling Fusiliers 7th Battalion *Died in War on 1 April 1917*
BAILLEUL COMMUNAL CEMETERY EXTENSION (NORD), France
Born and enlisted in Belfast. Formerly 1525 Leinster Regiment.

Connor, Frederick - Gunner
150182 Royal Garrison Artillery 49th Siege Battery *Age 30 Died in War on 6 September 1917*
WHITE HOUSE CEMETERY, Belgium
Son of Sarah and the late William Connor; husband of Annie May Connor,
of 64, Three But Lane, West Derby, Liverpool. Native of Belfast.

Connor, George - Private
S/15950 Cameron Highlanders 2nd Battalion *Killed in Action on 16 February 1915*
VOORMEZEELE ENCLOSURES No 1 and No 2, Belgium
46 Donegall Avenue, Belfast.

Connor, Harry - Private
16295 Canadian Infantry (British Columbia Regiment) 7th Battalion *Died in War on 24 April 1915*
TYNE COT CEMETERY, Belgium
Son of David and Elizabeth, of 92 Snugville Street, Belfast.

Connor, Hugh - Rifleman
8484 Royal Irish Rifles 2nd Battalion *Age 26 Killed in Action on 26 October 1914*
LE TOURET MEMORIAL, France
Born and enlisted in Belfast The son of Hugh Connor and husband of Mary Ann Connor,
of 9, Bullocks Court, Bridge Street, Lisburn. An Army Reservist.

Connor, John - Gunner
22871 Royal Field Artillery 15th Brigade *Died in War on 9 October 1917*
RUISSEAU FARM CEMETERY, Belgium
Son of David and Elizabeth of 92 Snugville Street, Belfast.

Connor, John - Private
4716 Princess Victoria's (Royal Irish Fusiliers) 1st Battalion *Died in War on 14 October 1914*
METEREN MILITARY CEMETERY, France
Born in Belfast, enlisted Lurgan.

Connor, John - Rifleman
16348 Royal Irish Rifles 10th Battalion *Killed in Action on 1 July 1916*
THIEPVAL MEMORIAL, France
31 Havana Street, Belfast. Enlisted in Belfast.

Belfast Book of Honour

Connor, Robert - Rifleman
3642 Royal Irish Rifles 10th Battalion *Died in War on 9 October 1916*
ST QUENTIN CABARET MILITARY CEMETERY, Belgium
Born and enlisted in Belfast. Attached 107th Trench Mortar Battery.

Connor, Samuel - Rifleman
10/14312 Royal Irish Rifles 15th Battalion *Age 26 Died in War on 26 August 1918*
METEREN MILITARY CEMETERY, France
Son of Elizabeth Wallace, of 47, Egmont Street, Belfast.

Connor, Thomas - Sapper
57421 Royal Engineers 150th Company *Age 22 Died of Wounds on 10 February 1916*
MAILLY-MAILLET COMMUNAL CEMETERY EXTENSION, France
Son of David and Ellen Connor, of 27, James Street, Belfast.

Connor, William H. - Private
12497 Royal Irish Fusiliers 6th Battalion *Age 25 Died in War on 15 August 1915*
HELLES MEMORIAL, Turkey
Son of Elizabeth Connor, of 20, Clifton Drive, Belfast, and the late Alexander Connor; husband of Margaret Connor, of Oldpark Cottage, Ballysillan, Belfast.

Conroy, Charles Wellesley - Third Engineer
Mercantile Marine S.S. "Cento" (Liverpool)
Age 26 Killed, as a result of an attack by an enemy submarine on 4 June 1918
TOWER HILL MEMORIAL, United Kingdom
Son of Mrs. Maria Thompson (formerly Conroy), of 16, Bandon Street, Belfast. Born at Dublin.

Convill, Alexander - Private
3536 Royal Inniskilling Fusiliers 1st Battalion *Killed in Action on 21 August 1915*
HELLES MEMORIAL, Turkey
Born and enlisted in Belfast.

Conway, Alexander - Sergeant
3230 Royal Inniskilling Fusiliers "A" Company 7th Battalion *Age 21 Killed in Action on 21 March 1918*
POZIERES MEMORIAL, France
Son of Matthew and Agnes Conway, of 57, Thistle St. Belfast. Awarded the Croix de Guerre (Belgium).

Conway, Charles - Lance Sergeant
16974 Royal Inniskilling Fusiliers 8th Battalion *Died in War on 12 May 1916*
CHOCQUES MILITARY CEMETERY, France
Born in Belfast, enlisted in Omagh.

Conway, George - Private
1688 Irish Guards 1st Battalion *Died in War on 27 December 1914*
LE TOURET MILITARY CEMETERY RICHEROURG-L'AVOUE, France
Born in County Tipperary, enlisted in Mulligar, resident Belfast.

Conway, James - Private
3923 Connaught Rangers 6th Battalion *Died of Wounds on 3 September 1916*
A.I.F. BURIAL GROUND, FLERS, France
Born at Dublin. Son of John and Margaret Conway, of Belfast. His brother served with the same regiment.

JOURNEY OF REMEMBERING

Conway, John - Rifleman
12680 Royal Irish Rifles 8th Battalion *Age 24 Died in War on 2 July 1916*
THIEPVAL MEMORIAL, France
Son of Matthew and Agnes Conway, of 57, Thistle Street, Belfast. Holder of the Military Medal.

Conway, William - Corporal
S/6003 Black Watch (Royal Highlanders) 7th (Fife) Battalion (Territorial) *Died in War on 26 March 1918*
ARRAS MEMORIAL, France
Born in Belfast, enlisted Ardrossan, Scotland.

Coogan, Denis - Rifleman
8114 Royal Irish Rifles 1st Battalion *Age 24 Killed in Action on 9 May 1915*
PLOEGSTEERT MEMORIAL, Belgium
Husband of Isabella Brennan (formerly Coogan), of 10, Frederick Lane, Belfast.

Coogan, John - Private
463 Highland Light Infantry 11th (Service) Battalion *Died in War on 25 September 1915*
LOOS MEMORIAL, France
Born in Belfast, enlisted Scotland.

Cook, Ernest - Rifleman
16306 Royal Irish Rifles 15th Battalion *Died in War on 31 May 1918*
DUHALLOW A.D.S. CEMETERY, Belgium
Born and enlisted in Belfast.

Cook, Samuel Arthur - Sapper
3135455 Canadian Engineers Reinforcement Pool *Age 23 Died in War on 3 October 1918*
ETAPLES MILITARY CEMETERY, France
A native of Belfast the was the son of Mr and Mrs Samuel Cross, Ontario.
A member of Belfast Orange Lodge No. 499.

Cooke, Charles Ernest - Second Lieutenant
Royal Irish Fusiliers 3rd Battalion *Age 30 Died in War on 25 May 1915*
YPRES (MENIN GATE) MEMORIAL, Belgium
A member of the old UVF and son of Alexander and Mrs E. J. Cooke, of Notting Hill, Belfast.
Mentioned in Despatches.

Cooke, Frederick St. G. - Private
41694 Royal Irish Fusiliers formerly (2182), North Irish Horse 9th Battalion *Died in War on 19 April 1918*
TYNE COT MEMORIAL, Belgium
Son of the late Francis and Anne Cooke, of Gortermone House, Carrigallen, County Leitrim;
husband of Jeannie C. Cooke, of "Norton" 6, Hawthornden Road, Knock, Belfast.

Cooke, George - Rifleman
47442 Royal Irish Rifles 1st Battalion *Killed in Action on 22 November 1917*
TYNE COT MEMORIAL, Belgium
27 Upper Mervue Street, Belfast.

Cooke, George - Rifleman
6563 Royal Irish Rifles 1st Battalion *Killed in Action on 13 March 1915*
LE TOURET MEMORIAL, France
Born and enlisted in Belfast.

Cooke, James H - Lance Corporal
S/2448 Gordon Highlanders 8/10th Battalion *Age 25 Died in War on 20 April 1918*
WANQUETIN COMMUNAL CEMETERY EXTENSION, *France*
Son of Mr. and Mrs. George Cooke, of Kimberley Street, Belfast; husband of Margaret Cooke, of 35, Dunn Street, Bridgeton, Glasgow.

Cooke, Robert Francis - Private
15423 Royal Inniskilling Fusiliers 10th Battalion *Killed in Action on 1 July 1916*
THIEPVAL MEMORIAL, *France*
Awarded the Military Medal. Parents lived at 152 My Lady's Road, Belfast.

Cooley, John - Private
3412 Leinster Regiment 7th Battalion *Died in War on 27 June 1916*
ST PATRICK'S CEMETERY LOOS, *France*
Born and enlisted in Belfast.

Cooley, Robert - Rifleman
7369 Royal Irish Rifles 6th Battalion *Died in War on 11 August 1915*
HELLES MEMORIAL, *Turkey*
Son of Robert Cooley; husband of Elizabeth Cooley, of 22, Bow Street, Cullingtree Road, Belfast.

Cooper, John O - Corporal
8013 Leinster Regiment 2nd Battalion *Died in War on 20 October 1914*
PLOEGSTEERT MEMORIAL, *Belgium*
Son of George and Susan Cooper, 17 Marlborough Gardens.

Cooper, Richard - Rifleman
8362 Royal Irish Rifles "E" Company 1st Battalion *Age 27 Died of disease on 28 November 1914*
BOIS GUILLAUME COMMUNAL CEMETERY, *France*
Son of Thomas and Annie Cooper, of 19, Oregon Street, Belfast.

Coote, William James - Rifleman
12236 Royal Irish Rifles 8th Battalion *Died in War on 2 July 1916*
THIEPVAL MEMORIAL, *France*
Born and enlisted in Belfast.

Colquhoun, William - Rifleman
1794 Royal Irish Riles 15th Battalion *Died in War on 23 March 1918*
POZIERES MEMORIAL, *France*
Son of Mrs Rebeccsa Colquhoun, 10 Broadbent Street, Belfast.

Cope, George - Rifleman
14/438 Royal Irish Rifles 16th Battalion *Age 19 Killed in Action on 31 January 1917*
VLAMERTINGHE MILITARY CEMETERY, *Belgium*
Son of James and Mary Elizabeth Cope, of 60, Skipton Street, Belfast.

Copeland, George - Private
3185 Manchester Regiment 13th Battalion *Died in War on 24 October 1916*
KARASOULI MILITARY CEMETERY, *Greece*
Born in Belfast. Lived in Manchester when enlisted.

Copeland, James - Private
11679 Irish Guards 1st Battalion *Died of Wounds on 29 October 1918*
GREVILLERS BRITISH CEMETERY, France
Born and enlisted in Belfast.

Copeland, John - Private
6484 Royal Irish Fusiliers 1st Battalion *Age 36 Died in War on 26 April 1915*
YPRES (MENIN GATE) MEMORIAL, Belgium
Son of Frank Copeland, of 54, Sheriff Street, Belfast; Husband of Isabella Copeland.

Copeland, William - Sergeant
100520 Royal Field Artillery 398th Battery *Age 24 Died in War on 1 November 1918*
ST. SEVER CEMETERY EXTENSION, ROUEN, France
Son of Robert and Mary Copeland, of 24, Hanover Street, Portadown, County Armagh; husband of Alice Copeland of 2, Little Victoria Street, Belfast.

Corbett, Arthur - Rifleman
8939 Royal Irish Rifles 1st Battalion *Killed in Action on 17 January 1915*
ROYAL IRISH RIFLES GRAVEYARD, LAVENTIE, France
Husband of M. Corbett, of 19, Lesley Street, Ligoneil, Belfast.

Corbett, David - Private
4347 Connaught Rangers 6th Battalion *Died in War on 4 March 1916*
QUARRY CEMETERY VERMELLES, France
Born in St. Patrick's, Belfast. Enlisted and resident in in the city.

Corbett, David Bertram - Second Lieutenant
Royal Irish Rifles 17th Battalion *Died in War on 3 July 1916*
MARTINSART BRITISH CEMETERY, France
Son of John Corbett, of Ardsallagh, Derryvolgie, Belfast.

Corbett, J - Private
81345 The Queen's (Royal West Surrey Regiment) 19th Battalion
Age 19 Died as a result of war on 9 March 1919
KNOCK CEMETERY, United Kingdom
Son of John Corbett, of 27, Cuba Street, Newtownards Road, Belfast.

Corbett, Patrick - Rifleman
8024 Royal Irish Rifles 6th Battalion *Died in War on 29 November 1916*
SALONIKA (LEMBET ROAD) MILITARY CEMETERY, Greece
Born and enlisted in Belfast.

Cordner, James - Lieutenant
Royal Irish Rifles 17th Battalion attached 2nd Battalion *Killed in Action (shellfire) on 16 August 1918*
MINTY FARM CEMETERY, Belgium
Awarded the Military Cross and a member of St Enoch's Presbyterian Church, Belfast.
Formerly of the Manse, Drumbo, County Down.

Cordner, James - Private
1880 Lancashire Fusiliers 1/7th Battalion *Died in War on 27 September 1918*
RIBECOURT ROAD CEMETERY TRESAULT, France
Born in Belfast, enlisted in England.

Cordner, James Henry - Lieutenant
Tank Corps 15th Battalion *Age 22 Died in War on 16 April 1918*
CERISY-GAILLY MILITARY CEMETERY, France
Son of William John and Sarah Cordner, of South Park Villas, Park Road, Belfast.

Corken, Robert John - Corporal
17674 Machine Gun Corps (Infantry) 108th Company *Age 24 Killed in Action on 1 July 1916*
THIEPVAL MEMORIAL, France
Son of James and Jane Corken, of Antrim Road, Lisburn. A book keeper employed with Messrs. Abraham Neill, Castalia Mills, Belfast.

Corr, George - Private
4154 Australian Infantry 54th Battalion *Age 34 Killed in Action on 20 July 1916*
RUE-DU-BOIS MILITARY CEMETERY, FLEURBAIX, France
Son of James and Eleanor Alice Corr, of 107, Ormeau Road, Belfast, Ireland.

Corr, Herbert Garfield - Private
143901 Machine Gun Corps (Infantry) *Died in War on 16 April 1918*
READING CEMETERY, United Kingdom
Born and enlisted in Belfast. Formerly 19/242 Royal Irish Rifles

Corr, Patrick J - Private
20532 Royal Irish Fusiliers 8th Battalion *Age 21 Died in War on 18 July 1916*
ST. PATRICK'S CEMETERY, LOOS, France
Son of Patrick and Martha Corr, of 24, Slate Street, Belfast. Formerly 2439 6th Battalion Connaught Rangers.

Corrigan, Patrick - Private
7134 Royal Irish Fusiliers 1st Battalion *Age 34 Died in War on 25 April 1915*
YPRES (MENIN GATE) MEMORIAL, Belgium
Husband of Ellen Corrigan, of 92, Cullingtree Road, Belfast.

Corrigan, Thomas Patrick - Private
6965 Royal Munster Fusiliers 6th Battalion *Age 20 Died in War on 28 December 1917*
JERUSALEM WAR CEMETERY, Israel
Son of Patrick and Bridget Corrigan, of 71, Herbert Street, Crumlin Road, Belfast. Native of Lisburn.

Corrigan, William Henry - Private
26306 Royal Inniskilling Fusiliers 7/8th Battalion *Died in War on 16 August 1917*
TYNE COT MEMORIAL, Belgium
Son of Mrs Shane 20 Canmore Street, Belfast.

Corry, Alexander - First Engineer (Engineer Lieutenant R.N.R.)
Mercantile Marine S.S. "W. M. Barkley" (Belfast)
Age 48 Drowned as a result of an attack by an enemy submarine on 12 October 1917
TOWER HILL MEMORIAL, United Kingdom
Husband of Mrs. Corry, of 3, Victoria Villas, Dublin. Born at Belfast.

Corry, James - Private
7243 South Lancashire Regiment "A" Company 2nd Battalion *Age 29 Died in War on 24 October 1914*
LE TOURET MEMORIAL, France
Husband of Mary Jane Corry, of 20, Cable Street, Newtownards Road, Belfast.

Journey of Remembering

Corry, James Alexander - Rifleman
1088 Royal Irish Rifles "C" Company 14th Battalion *Age 26 Killed in Action on 16 August 1917*
TYNE COT MEMORIAL, Belgium
Son of Agnes Corry, of 93, Rugby Avenue, Belfast.

Corry, John - Rifleman
17372 Royal Irish Rifles 12th Battalion *Age 45 Died in War on 12 April 1918*
TYNE COT MEMORIAL, Belgium
Son of Henry Corry; husband of Jane Corry, of 151, Dunluce Avenue, Lisburn Road, Belfast.
Served in the South African Campaign. Nine years' service in 2nd Battalion.

Corry, William - Corporal
8252 Machine Gun Corps (Infantry) 29th Battalion *Age 20 Died of Wounds on 29 September 1918*
HARINGHE (BANDAGHEM) MILITARY CEMETERY, Belgium
Son of Robert and Annie Corry, of 4, Bethany Street, Ballyhackamore, Belfast.
Awarded the Military Medal. Formerly 4/26522 Royal Inniskilling Fusiliers.

Cosgrove, John - Private
23920 Royal Inniskilling Fusiliers 1st Battalion *Age 33 Died in War on 9 August 1916*
YPRES (MENIN GATE) MEMORIAL, Belgium
Son of John and Mary Cosgrove, of Millfield, Belfast; husband of Mary Cosgrove,
of 9, Whifflet Street, Coatbridge, Lanarkshire, Scotland.

Cosgrove, William - Private
19551 Machine Gun Corps (Infantry) *Killed in Action on 1 July 1916*
THIEPVAL MEMORIAL, France
Born and enlisted in Belfast. Formerly 11896 Royal Irish Rifles.

Costello , Joseph - Private
11655 Royal Inniskilling Fusiliers 2nd Battalion *Killed in Action on 27 November 1917*
TYNE COT MEMORIAL, Belgium
Born in Belfast.

Costello, Patrick R - Private
21987 Royal Dublin Fusiliers 6th Battalion *Age 24 Died in War on 9 August 1915*
HELLES MEMORIAL, Turkey
Son of Robert and Mary Costello, of 12, Lady Street, Belfast.

Costello, Robert - Rifleman
5717 Royal Irish Rifles 2nd Battalion *Died in War on 14 January 1918*
LISBURN (HOLY TRINITY) ROMAN CATHOLIC CEMETERY, United Kingdom
46 Iris Street, Belfast.

Cotter, Edward - Rifleman
7021 Royal Irish Rifles 2nd Battalion *Killed in Action on 16 January 1915*
BAILLEUL COMMUNAL CEMETERY EXTENSION (NORD), France
Byron Place, Belfast.

Cotter, James Prentice - Sergeant
11911 Royal Irish Rifles 15th Battalion *Died of Wounds on 8 July 1916*
PUCHEVILLERS BRITISH CEMETERY, France
Son of George Cotter, 105 Broom Street, Belfast.

Belfast Book of Honour

Cotter, Thomas - Sapper
41667 Royal Engineers *Age 32 Died in War on 29 January 1918*
CARNMONEY CEMETERY, United Kingdom
Son of William and Mary Jane Cotter; husband of Mary Ann Cotter, of 37, Upper Mervue Street, Belfast. Born at Aughnacloy, County Tyrone.

Cotter, William - Rifleman
5849 Royal Irish Rifles 2nd Battalion *Age 35 Killed in Action on 16 June 1915*
YPRES (MENIN GATE) MEMORIAL, Belgium
Brother of Mrs. Mary Hunter, of 7, Copperfield Street, Belfast.

Coubery, John James - Sergeant
16739 Royal Irish Rifles 14th Battalion *Died in War on 23 June 1917*
MESSINES RIDGE BRIDGE CEMETERY, Belgium
Born and enlisted in Belfast.

Coulter, Allan Alexander - Private
670162 Canadian Labour Corps 1st Battalion *Age 43 Died in War on 26 May 1917*
STE. MARIE CEMETERY, LE HAVRE, France
Eldest son of the late James and Jane Coulter, of Belfast, Ireland; husband of Annie M. Coulter, of 1018, Woodbine Avenue, Toronto, Canada. Late of "The Mail and Empire" Toronto. A Church of Ireland member he was born in County Donegal.

Coulter, James George - Rifleman
10101 Royal Irish Rifles 2nd Battalion *Age 21 Killed in Action on 20 September 1914*
LA FERTE-SOUS-JOUARRE MEMORIAL, France
Son of George and Elizabeth Coulter, of 42, Boundary Street, Belfast.

Coulter, James H - Private
14592 Royal Inniskilling Fusiliers 9th Battalion *Killed in Action on 1 July 1916*
THIEPVAL MEMORIAL, France
Born in Belfast, enlisted in Finner Camp, County Donegal.

Coulter, Joseph - Corporal
14350 Royal Irish Rifles 14th Battalion *Killed in Action on 24 March 1918*
POZIERES MEMORIAL, France
Born and enlisted in Belfast.

Coulter, Samuel - Corporal
3768 Royal Irish Rifles 12th Battalion *Killed in Action on 7 June 1917*
SPANBROEKMOLEN BRITISH CEMETERY, Belgium
61 Matchett Street, Belfast.

Courtney, Samuel - Rifleman
14252 Royal Irish Rifles 2nd Battalion *Age 25 Killed in Action on 18 August 1918*
BERTENACRE MILITARY CEMETERY, FLETRE, France
Son of William and Jane Courtney, of 3, Rowland Street, Belfast.

Courtney, Alexander - Rifleman
9167 Royal Irish Rifles 1st Battalion *Killed in action on 21 March 1918*
POZIERES MEMORIAL, France
Son of Mrs Mary Courtney, 54 Donegall Road, Belfast.

Courtney, Thomas - Rifleman
43023 Royal Irish Rifles 2nd Battalion *Killed in Action on 23 November 1917*
CAMBRAI MEMORIAL, LOUVERVAL, France
22 Glenwood Street, Belfast. An Army Reservist he had worked in Mackie's Foundry. Awarded the Military Medal. His father also served.

Courtney, William - Private
769901 (Eastern Ontario Regiment) Princess Patricia's Canadian Light Infantry
Age 41 Died in War on 7 June 1918
BELFAST (DUNDONALD) CEMETERY, United Kingdom
Son of William and Jane Courtney, of Dundonald, Belfast; husband of Elizabeth Courtney, of 189, Rhodes Avenue, Toronto. A Presbyterian he had worked as a teamster in Canada.

Courtney, William Boomer - Private
1015402 Canadian Infantry (British Columbia Regiment) 72nd Battalion
Age 38 Died in War on 30 October 1917
TYNE COT CEMETERY, Belgium
Son of Joseph Courtney and Mary Jane Boomer (his wife) of Belfast, Ireland. A Methodist, he had worked as clerk in Canada.

Couser, John - Lance Corporal
7424 Royal Irish Rifles 1st Battalion *Age 29 Killed in Action on 14 June 1916*
ALBERT COMMUNAL CEMETERY EXTENSION, France
Son of William and Rose Couser. Born in Belfast, Ireland.

Cousins, Isaac - Private
22641 Royal Irish Fusiliers 9th Battalion *Killed in Action on 1 July 1916*
THIEPVAL MEMORIAL, France
52 Sixth Street, Belfast. Survived by his mother, brothers and sisters.

Cousins, John - Rifleman
16355 Royal Irish Rifles 14th Battalion *Age 21 Killed in Action on 16 August 1917*
TYNE COT MEMORIAL, Belgium
Son of Eveline Cousins, of 131, Madrid Street, Mountpottinger, Belfast, and the late John Cousins.

Cousins, Peter - Private
20918 East Lancashire Regiment 2nd Battalion *Died in War on 14 March 1916*
ARRAS MEMORIAL, France
Born in Belfast. Lived in Liverpool when enlisted.

Cowan, M - Private
PO/13739 Royal Marine Light Infantry HMS "Blake" *Died in War on 8 November 1918*
DUNFERMLINE CEMETERY, United Kingdom
Husband of F. Cowan, of 77, Tobergill Street, Belfast.

Cowan, Marshall - Rifleman
9944 Royal Irish Rifles 1st Battalion *Killed in Action on 8 April 1917*
ST SEVER CEMETERY EXTENSION ROUEN, France
Born and enlisted in Belfast.

Cowan, William John - Seaman
5266B Royal Naval Reserve H.M. Trawler "Hawk"
Age 31 Killed in Action with submarine in Mediterranean on 17 February 1917
PORTSMOUTH NAVAL MEMORIAL, United Kingdom
Son of Thomas and Margaret Cowan, of 62, Parkmount Street, Belfast.

Cowden, Alexander - Sergeant
5801 Royal Irish Rifles 15th Battalion *Died in War on 22 November 1917*
THIEPVAL MEMORIAL, France
Born and enlisted in Belfast.

Cowden, William - Rifleman
10295 Royal Irish Rifles 2nd Battalion *Killed In Action on 25 September 1915*
YPRES (MENIN GATE) MEMORIAL, Belgium
Born and enlisted in Belfast.

Cox, Frederick - Private
5628 Royal Munster Fusiliers 1st Battalion *Died in War on 21 August 1915*
HELLES MEMORIAL, Turkey
Born in Belfast, enlisted in Wales. Formerly 8499 Lancers of the Line

Cox, James Joseph - Private
1972 Irish Guards 1st Battalion *Died of Wounds on 28 October 1914*
BOULOGNE EASTERN CEMETERY, France
Husband of Mary Cox, of 65, Servia Street, Belfast.

Cox, William - Lieutenant
Royal Navy HM "Progress" *Died in War on 21 December 1916*
CHATHAM NAVAL MEMORIAL, United Kingdom
Lived at Balmoral, Belfast.

Coyle, Patrick - Private
28580 Royal Scots Fusiliers 2nd Battalion *Died in War on 7 May 1918*
ARNEKE BRITISH CEMETERY, France
Lived in Belfast, enlisted in Glasgow.

Craig, Alexander - Private
14727 Highland Light Infantry 16th (Service) Battalion (2nd Glasgow) *Killed in Action on 1 July 1916*
LONSDALE CEMETERY, AUTHUILE, France
Lived in Belfast, enlisted in Glasgow.

Craig, Archibald - Driver
37613 Royal Horse Artillery and Royal Field Artillery *Died in War on 21 April 1915*
LONGUENESSE (ST. OMER) SOUVENIR CEMETERY, France
Lived in Belfast, enlisted in Glasgow.

Craig, Daniel - Private
1673968 Gordon Highlanders 8th/10th Battalion *Died in War on 30 July 1916*
THIEPVAL MEMORIAL, France
Native of Belfast.

Craig, David - Private
3024 Royal Inniskilling Fusiliers 1st Battalion *Age 23 Died in War on 8 February 1917*
THIEPVAL MEMORIAL, France
Son of William and Sarah Craig, of 42, Lendrick Street, Belfast.

Craig, David - Rifleman
4305 Royal Irish Rifles 10th Battalion *Died in War on 15 August 1916*
RATION FARM CEMETERY, Belgium
Husband of Annie Craig, 67 Hunter Street, Belfast.

Craig, James - Lance Corporal
20965 Royal Inniskilling Fusiliers 1st Battalion *Died in War on 27 August 1917*
BLEUET FARM CEMETERY, Belgium
103 Upper Canning Street, Belfast.

Craig, John - Corporal
2338 Loyal North Lancashire Regiment 1st Battalion *Died in War on 26 January 1915*
LIEVIN COMMUNAL CEMETERY EXTENSION, France
Born in Belfast, enlisted in Liverpool.

Craig, John - Private
11410 Royal Inniskilling Fusiliers 9th Battalion *Killed in Action on 16 August 1917*
TYNE COT MEMORIAL, Belgium
Born Belfast and enlisted in Belfast.

Craig, John - Private
2357 Leinster Regiment 2nd Battalion *Died in War on 31 March 1917*
AIX-NOULETTE COMMUNAL CEMETERY EXTENSION, France
Son of Patrick and Agnes Craig, of 22, Lady Street, Cullingtree Road, Belfast.

Craig, John Ross - Driver
52662 Royal Horse Artillery and Royal Field Artillery *Died in War on 1 January 1916*
HOP STORE CEMETERY, Belgium
Born in Belfast, enlisted in Glasgow.

Craig, Samuel - Company Sergeant Major
13210 Royal Irish Fusiliers 7th/8th Battalion *Age 27 Died in War on 20 November 1917*
CROISILLES BRITISH CEMETERY, France
Husband of Sarah Craig, of 12, Gosford Place, McClure Street, Ormeau Road, Belfast.
Awarded the Distinguished Conduct Medal.

Craig, Samuel - Rifleman
5373 Royal Irish Rifles 2nd Battalion *Killed in Action on 16 April 1917*
YPRES (MENIN GATE) MEMORIAL, Belgium
Born and enlisted in Belfast.

Craig, Thomas - Private
13204 Princess Victoria's (Royal Irish Fusiliers) 4th Battalion *Died in War on 27 October 1917*
BELFAST CITY CEMETERY, United Kingdom
Born and enlisted in Belfast.

JOURNEY OF REMEMBERING

Craig, Thomas - Private
42355 Highland Light Infantry 17th (Service) Battalion (3rd Glasgow) *Died in War on 1 April 1917*
FORESTE COMMUNAL CEMETERY, France
Born and enlisted in Belfast. Formerly 24779 Royal Scots Fusiliers

Craig, Thomas - Rifleman
14/3970 Royal Irish Rifles 14th Battalion *Age 23 Killed in Action on 7 June 1917*
LONE TREE CEMETERY, Belgium
Son of Thomas and Hannah Kennedy. Native of Belfast.

Craig, William - Master
Mercantile Marine S.S. "Harbury" *Age 56 Drowned, as a result of an attack by an enemy submarine on 9 June 1917*
TOWER HILL MEMORIAL, United Kingdom
Son of the late Hugh Craig; husband of Jeannie H. Craig, of "Shalimar" Waterloo Gardens, Antrim Road, Belfast.

Craig, William - Private
10092 South Lancashire Regiment 2nd Battalion *Killed in Action on 20 October 1914*
LE TOURET MEMORIAL, France
10 Mountjoy Street, Belfast. Formerly employed by the New Northern Spinning and Weaving Company. The only son of Gawn Craig.

Craig, William - Rifleman
1137 Royal Irish Rifles 1st Battalion *Killed in Action on 24 March 1918*
POZIERES MEMORIAL, France
Born and enlisted in Belfast.

Craig, William John - Corporal
9975 Royal Irish Fusiliers 2nd Battalion *Age 24 Died of Wounds on 10 November 1916*
SALONIKA (LEMBET ROAD) MILITARY CEMETERY, Greece
Son of William and Elizabeth Craig, of 195, Upper Meadow Street, Belfast.

Crainey, William John - Rifleman
9087 Royal Irish Rifles 2nd Battalion *Killed in Action on 11 November 1914*
YPRES (MENIN GATE) MEMORIAL, Belgium
25 Ewart's Row, Belfast. Born in Carrickfergus.

Crangle, Albert - Rifleman
17492 Royal Irish Rifles 13th Battalion *Died in War on 28 June 1916*
MARTINSART BRITISH CEMETERY, France
Born in Belfast. Lived in Lisburn, when enlisted.

Crangle, John - Private
16377 Royal Irish Fusiliers 1st Battalion *Age 21 Died in War on 30 April 1915*
YPRES (MENIN GATE) MEMORIAL, Belgium
Son of John Crangle, of 91, Ardenlee Avenue, Belfast.

Cranston, William James - Private
40951 Royal Army Medical Corps 109th Field Ambulance *Died in War on 2 August 1917*
VLAMERTINGHE NEW MILITARY CEMETERY
Husband of Mary Ann Cranston, 130 Boundary Street, Belfast.

Journey of Remembering

Crawford, Alexander - Rifleman
17/79 Royal Irish Rifles 2nd Battalion *Killed in Action on 29 September 1917*
METZ-EN-COUTURE COMMUNAL CEMETERY BRITISH EXTENSION, France
Husband of Minnie Crawford, 71 Urney Street, Belfast.

Crawford, David - Private
6368 Manchester Regiment 2nd Battalion *Died in War on 19 April 1915*
CHESTER FARM CEMETERY, Belgium
Born in Belfast, enlisted in England.

Crawford, Hampton - Private
25239 Royal Inniskilling Fusiliers 9th Battalion *Killed in Action on 1 July 1916*
THIEPVAL MEMORIAL, France
Son of Samuel Crawford, 14 Fortingale Street, Belfast.

Crawford, Hugh - Able Seaman
SS/2908 Royal Navy HMS "Hawke" *Age 26 Killed in Action with submarine in North Sea on 15 October 1914*
CHATHAM NAVAL MEMORIAL, United Kingdom
Son of Jonathan and Sarah Crawford, of 3, Coyle's Place, Ormeau Road, Belfast; husband of Isabella Crawford, of 15, Wigton Street, Belfast.

Crawford, James - Private
4640 Connaught Rangers 6th Battalion *Died in War on 5 March 1916*
LOOS MEMORIAL, France
Born, enlisted and resident in Belfast.

Crawford, James - Rifleman
3852 Royal Irish Rifles 2nd Battalion *Killed in Action on 16 July 1916*
OVILLERS MILITARY CEMETERY, France
Born in Ballymena, enlisted Ballykinler, resident Belfast.

Crawford, James - Stoker
7821S Royal Naval Reserve HMS "Black Prince" *Killed in Action on 31 May 1916*
PORTSMOUTH NAVAL MEMORIAL, United Kingdom
Survived by his sister, Mrs E Lemon, 60 Sidney Street West, Belfast.

Crawford, John - Corporal
12703 Royal Inniskilling Fusiliers 12th Battalion *Killed in Action on 21 March 1918*
POZIERES MEMORIAL, France
Born and enlisted in Belfast.

Crawford, Richard - Company Sergeant Major
27026 Northumberland Fusiliers 2nd Garrison Battalion *Died in War on 18 July 1917*
BASRA WAR CEMETERY, Iraq
Born Kilkeel, County Down. Resident of Belfast.

Crawford, Robert - Lance Corporal
6100 Royal Irish Rifles 1st Battalion *Age 24 Killed in Action on 10 April 1918*
DUHALLOW A.D.S. CEMETERY, Belgium
Son of James and J. Crawford, of 2, Shankill Road, Belfast. Born Cairncastle, County Antrim.

Crawford, Samuel - Private
41273 Royal Irish Fusiliers *Age 21 Died as a result of war on 2 November 1920*
BELFAST CITY CEMETERY, United Kingdom
Husband of Margaret Crawford of 14 Downing Street, Belfast. His brother also fell.

Crawford, Thomas - Private
3010 Royal Inniskilling Fusiliers 1st Battalion *Age 23 Killed in Action on 1 July 1916*
THIEPVAL MEMORIAL, France
Son of Thomas Crawford, of 23, Willow Street, Belfast.

Crawford, Thomas James - Able Seaman
933204 Mercantile Marine Reserve HMS "Victory" *Died as a result of War on 14 June 1919*
CARNMONEY CEMETERY, United Kingdom
Husband of Annie Crawford, of 240, Donegall Road, Belfast.

Crawford, William - Sergeant
Royal Irish Rifles *Died in War on 16 July 1916*
65,Wall Street, Belfast.

Crawford, William J - Private
16482 Machine Gun Corps (Infantry) *Age 26 Died of Wounds on 11 May 1920*
BELFAST CITY CEMETERY, United Kingdom
Husband of Isabella Crawford, of 14, Downing Street, Belfast. His brother also fell.
Previously 11511 Royal Irish Fusiliers.

Crawley, Richard - Gunner
5839 Royal Garrison Artillery 120th Siege Battery *Age 31 Killed in Action on 7 August 1916*
THIEPVAL MEMORIAL, France
Son of the late John and Mary Crawley, of Blairs, Aberdeen; husband of Margaret Crawley, of 98, Blythe Street, Belfast.

Creaney, Cecil - Corporal
10031 Royal Inniskilling Fusiliers *Age 24 Died in War on 21 August 1915*
HELLES MEMORIAL, Turkey
Son of Staff Sergeant. William Creaney (Royal Inniskilling Fusiliers) and Edith Creaney.

Creaney, John - Private
14113 Princess Victoria's (Royal Irish Fusiliers) 9th Battalion *Killed in Action on 1 July 1916*
THIEPVAL MEMORIAL, France
Born in Belfast, enlisted Armagh.

Cree, Arthur - Sapper
18291 Royal Engineers17th Field Company *Age 21 Died in War on 12 May 1915*
YPRES (MENIN GATE) MEMORIAL, Belgium
Son of Arthur and M. J. Cree, of 116, Limestone Road, Belfast.

Cree, Henry Greer - Rifleman
10011 Royal Irish Rifles 2nd Battalion *Age 20 Killed in Action on 26 October 1914*
LE TOURET MEMORIAL, France
Son of Henry and Hannah Jane Cree, of 52, Chadolly Street, Belfast.

Cree, Samuel - Sergeant
6622 Royal Inniskilling Fusiliers 2nd Battalion *Age 30 Died in War on 15 December 1914*
STE. MARIE CEMETERY, LE HAVRE, France
Son of Mary Cree, of Belfast, and the late William Cree; husband of Agnes Cree, of 3, Druse Street, Belfast.

Creen, Archibald - Third Steward
Mercantile Marine S.S. "Garron Head" (Belfast) *Age 18 Killed by mine on 16 November 1917*
TOWER HILL MEMORIAL, United Kingdom
Son of Agnes Creen (née Ferguson), of 47, Pilot Street, Belfast, and the late William James Creen.

Creevy, William - Corporal
12704 Royal Irish Rifles 15th Battalion *Died on 28 June 1917*
HARTLEPOOL WEST VIEW CEMETERY, United Kingdom
Born in Belfast.

Creighton, Edward Henry - First Engineer
Mercantile Marine S.S. "Garron Head" (Belfast) *Age 32 Killed by mine on 16 November 1917*
TOWER HILL MEMORIAL, United Kingdom
Son of David and Anna Creighton; husband of Marie Evelyn Creighton (née Rankin), of "Mervue" Whitehead, County Antrim. Born in Belfast.

Creighton, James - Private
241560 Seaforth Highlanders 2nd Battalion *Age 41 Died in War on 14 November 1917*
ARRAS MEMORIAL, France
Brother of Hugh Creighton, of 3, Hampden Street, Belfast.

Creighton, John - Sergeant
753 Royal Irish Rifles 8th Battalion *Died in War on 2 July 1916*
THIEPVAL MEMORIAL, FRANCE
Born in Glasgow, enlisted in Belfast. A member of Westbourne Presbyterian Church.

Creighton, Robert - Stoker First Class
SS/107757 Royal Navy HMS "Hawke" *Age 22 Killed in Action with submarine in North Sea on 15 October 1914*
CHATHAM NAVAL MEMORIAL, United Kingdom
Son of Maggie Creighton, of I, Mountcollyer Street, Belfast; and the late Thomas H. Creighton.

Cresswell, Ernest Henry - Private
9227 Cheshire Regiment 2nd Battalion *Died in War on 2 March 1915*
WULVERGHEM-LINDEHOEK ROAD MILITARY CEMETERY, Belgium
87 York Lane, Belfast.

Cresswell, John Leonard - Chief Engineer
Mercantile Marine S.S. "Huntsmoor" (London)
Age 34 Drowned, as a result of an attack by an enemy submarine on 20 February 1918
TOWER HILL MEMORIAL, United Kingdom
Son of Eliza Jane Cresswell (née Thompson), of "Craigmore" Kirkliston Drive, Belfast, and the late William James Cresswell. Born at St. John's Place, Larne.

Crichton, John Bell - Sergeant
753 Royal Irish Rifles 8th Battalion *Age 42 Died in War on 2 July 1916*
THIEPVAL MEMORIAL, France
Husband of Margaret Jane Crichton, of 30, McMaster Street, Belfast.

Crilly, Daniel - Rifleman
17/294 Royal Irish Rifles 9th Battalion *Died of Wounds on 8 December 1915*
SUCRERIE MILITARY CEMETERY, COLINCAMPS, France
Husband of Martha Crilly, of 60, King Street, Belfast. A former shipyard worker and a member of the old UVF. He was never to receive the Christmas gifts and cards which had been sent by his family.

Crilly, Thomas - Corporal
8917 Royal Munster Fusiliers 2nd Battalion *Died in War on 22 March 1918*
EPEHY WOOD FARM CEMETERY, EPEHY, France
Born and enlisted in Belfast.

Crockett, Walter - Private
15434 Royal Inniskilling Fusiliers 10th Battalion *Killed in Action on 1 July 1916*
THIEPVAL MEMORIAL, France
Born Belfast, enlisted Londonderry.

Croft, Robert Albert - Corporal
78300 Tank Corps 5th Battalion *Died in War on 8 August 1918*
HANGARD COMMUNAL CEMETERY EXTENSION, France
Son of James and Susan Croft, of The Cottages, Clandeboye. Born at Belfast.

Croft, William John Hillis - Rifleman
19/49 Royal Irish Rifles 1st Battalion *Age 20 Killed in Action on 2 October 1918*
DADIZEELE NEW BRITISH CEMETERY, Belgium
Son of Joseph and Sarah Croft, of 7, Warkworth Street, Belfast.

Croll, Ninian - Rifleman
14224 Royal Irish Rifles 9th Battalion *Killed in Action on 1 July 1916*
MILL ROAD CEMETERY, THIEPVAL, France
Husband of Sarah Jane Croll, 68 Sugarfield Street, Belfast.

Cromie, David - Rifleman
989 Royal Irish Rifles 8th Battalion *Died in War on 2 July 1916*
THIEPVAL MEMORIAL, France
Son of David Cromie; husband of Margaret Cromie, of 35, Rathmore Street, Belfast.

Cromien, Laurence - Private
7716 Royal Inniskilling Fusilers *Died in War on 30 June 1915*
HELLES MEMORIAL, Turkey
22 Edlingham Street, Belfast. Born in Dublin and husband of Martha Matilda Lambert Cromien of Kingston, Ontario, Canada.

Crone, George - Bombardier
4930 Royal Garrison Artillery 43rd Siege Battery *Died in War on 1 January 1916*
HELLES MEMORIAL, Turkey
Survived by his wife, 4 Boomer Street, Belfast. He had served for twenty one years.

Cross, Frederick - Private
5657 Royal Munster Fusiliers 1st Battalion *Died in War on 8 August 1915*
LANCASHIRE LANDING CEMETERY, Turkey
Born in Belfast, enlisted Lancashire. Formerly 4480, Lancers of the Line.

Cross, John A. - Rifleman
16360 Royal Irish Rifles "A" Company 14th Battalion *Age 25 Died in War on 6 December 1917*
CAMBRAI MEMORIAL, LOUVERVAL, France
Son of William A. and Sarah A. Cross, of 174, Cliftonville Road, Belfast. Enlisted August, 1914.

Cross, Joseph - Private
9639 Royal Inniskilling Fusiliers 2nd Battalion *Killed in Action on 23 November 1916*
THIEPVAL MEMORIAL, France
Born in Belfast, enlisted Armagh.

Cross, William - Private
8060 Cavalry 4th Dragoon Guards (Royal Irish) *Died in War on 24 August 1914*
LA-FERTE-SOUS JOUARRE MEMORIAL, France
Born and enlisted in Belfast.

Crossan, John - Rifleman
14221 Royal Irish Rifles 9th Battalion *Died in War on 2 July 1916*
THIEPVAL MEMORIAL, France
32 Keswick Street, Belfast.

Crossan, John - Rifleman
911 Royal Irish Rifles 15th Battalion *Age 30 Died in War on 23 March 1918*
POZIERES MEMORIAL, France
Husband of Mary Ann Crossan, of 3, Legnavea Street, Ligoneil, Belfast.

Crossan, Thomas - Rifleman
10818 Royal Irish Rifles 6th Battalion *Died in War on 11 August 1915*
HELLES MEMORIAL, Turkey
Born and enlisted in Belfast.

Crossen, John - Rifleman
11113 Royal Irish Rifles 6th Battalion *Died in War on 11 August 1915*
HELLES MEMORIAL,, Turkey
93 Derwent Street, Belfast.

Crossett, John - Rifleman
8015 Royal Irish Rifles 2nd Battalion *Age 23 Killed in Action on 27 October 1914*
LE TOURET MEMORIAL, France
Son of Henry and Mary Ann Crossett, of 116, Carnan Street, Belfast.

Crossey, Charles - Private
27102 Royal Inniskilling Fusiliers 2nd Battalion *Died in War on 23 November 1916*
WAGGON ROAD CEMETERY, BEAUMONT-HAMEL, France
Father of Catherine Crossey, 200 Argyle Steet, Belfast.

Crossey, Edward - Lance Corporal
21107 Princess Victoria's (Royal Irish Fusiliers) 8th Battalion *Died in War on 10 August 1917*
YPRES (MENIN GATE) MEMORIAL, Belgium
Born and enlisted in Belfast. Formerly 2268, Connaught Rangers

Crossey, Oliver - Rifleman
16353 Royal Irish Rifles 13th Battalion *Died in War on 30 June 1916*
PUCHEVILLERS BRITISH CEMETERY, *France*
Born and enlisted in Belfast.

Crothers, David - Rifleman
20889 Royal Irish Rifles 2nd Battalion *Age 18 Killed in Action on 6 September 1918*
PLOEGSTEERT MEMORIAL, *Belgium*
Son of William and Margaret Crothers, of 136, Disraeli Street, Belfast.

Crothers, David Walter - Rifleman
11014 Royal Irish Rifles 2nd Battalion *Killed In Action on 7 July 1916*
THIEPVAL MEMORIAL, *France*
Born in Belfast the son of William John and Ellen Crothers. Also served at Dardanelles with 6th Battalion and was wounded in August 1915.

Crothers, George Soran Frazer - Rifleman
12709 Royal Irish Rifles 15th Battalion *Age 20 Died in War on 20 October 1918*
HARLEBEKE NEW BRITISH CEMETERY, *Belgium*
Son of Joseph and Mary Ann Crothers, of 6, Beechnut Street, Belfast.

Crothers, James A - Private
1152 Australian Infantry, A.I.F. 18th Battalion *Killed in Action on 22 August 1915*
LONE PINE MEMORIAL, *Turkey*
Son of Thomas, Glenfarne Street, Belfast.

Crothers, John - Seaman
6583A Royal Naval Reserve HMS "Defence" *Died in War on 31 May 1916*
PORTSMOUTH NAVAL MEMORIAL, *United Kingdom*
Member of Shankill Road Mission, Belfast.

Crothers, Josiah - Private
10113 Royal Inniskilling Fusiliers 1st Battalion *Killed in Action on 3 May 1915*
Born Ballymacarrett, Belfast. Enlisted Glasgow.

Crothers, Robert - Private
249560 Canadian Infantry (Central Ontario Regiment) 54th Battalion
Age 27 Died in War on 30 September 1918
CANADA CEMETERY, TILLOY-LES-CAMBRAI, *France*
Son of William and Rose Crothers, of 12, McGee Street, Toronto, Canada. Native of Belfast, Ireland. A Catholic, he was unmarried and worked as a labourer in Canada.

Crothers, Robert - Stoker First Class
SS/108396 Royal Navy HMS "Invincible" *Age 27 Killed in Action on 31 May 1916*
PORTSMOUTH NAVAL MEMORIAL, *United Kingdom*
Son of Johnston Crothers, of 35, Ivan Street, Belfast. One brother in the Navy was also killed. Three additional brothers served with the Army.

Crothers, Samuel - Company Sergeant Major
6880 South Lancashire Regiment 2nd Battalion *Age 32 Killed in Action on 20 January 1917*
LONDON RIFLE BRIGADE CEMETERY, Belgium
Son of Henry and Ellen Crothers, of Belfast; husband of Cissie Wagner (formerly Crothers), of 829, Pottsville Street, Pottsville, Pennsylvania, U.S.A.

Crothers, Thomas - Rifleman
9/130 Royal Irish Rifles 15th Battalion *Died in War on 15 October 1918*
DADIZEELE NEW BRITISH CEMETERY, Belgium
Born and enlisted in Belfast.

Crothers, Thomas - Rifleman
9679 Royal Irish Rifles 1st Battalion *Killed in Action on 9 May 1915*
PLOEGSTEERT MEMORIAL, Belgium
Born and enlisted in Belfast.

Crotty, Richard Alfred - Private
265795 Black Watch (Royal Highlanders) *Killed in Action on 21 March 1918*
ARRAS MEMORIAL, France
Born in Belfast, enlisted in Perth, Scotland. Member of Belfast Masonic Lodge 609.

Crowe, Charles - Lance Corporal
6632 Royal Inniskilling Fusiliers 1st Battalion *Died in War on 21 August 1915*
HELLES MEMORIAL, Turkey
Husband of Janet Crowe, 66 Orkney Street, Belfast.

Crowe, Thomas - Sergeant
1274 Royal Irish Rifles 2nd Battalion *Age 26 Killed in Action on 24 March 1918*
POZIERES MEMORIAL, France
Son of Mrs. E. Crowe, of 9, Courtrai Street, Belfast.

Crowley, James Edward - Able Seaman
Mercantile Marine S.S. "Garron Head" (Belfast) *Age 40 Killed by mine on 19 November 1917*
TOWER HILL MEMORIAL, United Kingdom
Son of Daniel Crowley and the late Honor Crowley; husband of Kathleen Crowley (née Rea), of 91, Spamount Street, Belfast. Born in U.S.A.

Crowley, Joseph - Private
4232 Connaught Rangers 6th Battalion *Died in War on 3 September 1916*
THIEPVAL MEMORIAL, France
Born County Cavan. Enlisted and resident in Belfast.

Crozier, George - Rifleman
G/7178 Royal Fusiliers (City of London Regiment) 3rd Battalion *Died in War on 12 March 1915*
KEMMEL CHATEAU MILITARY CEMETERY, Belgium
Born in Belfast, enlisted London.

Crozier, Jack - Private
6080 Royal Irish Rifles 1st Battalion *Killed in Action on 9 May 1915*
PLOEGSTEERT MEMORIAL, Belgium
Husband of Jeannie Crozier, 127 Bellevue Street, Belfast.

Crozier, James - Private
14218 Royal Irish Rifles 9th Battalion *Died in War on 27 February 1916*
SUCRERIE MILITARY CEMETERY, COLINCAMPS, France
Son of Mrs. Elizabeth Crozier, of 80, Battenberg Street, Belfast. Executed by firing squad for desertion.

Crozier, Thomas - Sergeant
11062 Royal Inniskilling Fusiliers 9th Battalion *Age 22 Killed in Action on 1 July 1916*
THIEPVAL MEMORIAL, France
Son of James Crozier, of Strathearne, Dunmurry, Belfast.

Crumlin, William Robert - Rifleman
11143 Royal Irish Rifles 2nd Battalion *Killed in Action on 17 May 1916*
ECOIVRES MILITARY CEMETERY, MONT-ST. ELOI, France
Husband of Ellen Frances Crumlin, of 52, River Terrace, Ormeau Road, Belfast.

Crumpton, Thomas - Rifleman
7285 Royal Irish Rifles 2nd Battalion *Age 26 Died of Wounds on 19 July 1916*
ETAPLES MILITARY CEMETERY, France
Husband of Mary Crumpton, of 24, McAuley Street, Belfast.

Crymble, Cecil Reginald - Lieutenant
Royal Irish Fusiliers 3rd Battalion attached 1st Battalion *Age 29 Died in War on 20 November 1914*
PLOEGSTEERT MEMORIAL Belgium
Son of George Gordon Crymble and Agnes Templeton Crymble, of Gordon House, Annadale. B.A., D.Sc., Queen's University, Belfast. He was a member of the OTC and had been appointed a lecturer in Chemistry at University College, London.

Crymble, Charles - Rifleman
7301 Royal Irish Rifles 2nd Battalion *Killed in Action on 8 July 1916*
THIEPVAL MEMORIAL, France
Mountjoy Street. Born and enlisted in the city.

Crymble, John Gordon - Second Lieutenant
Royal Irish Fusiliers 9th Battalion *Age 19 Died of Wounds on 28 December 1916*
BAILLEUL COMMUNAL CEMETERY EXTENSION (NORD), France
Son of Samuel Gordon Crymble and Elizabeth Emily Crymble (née Agnew), of 12, College Green, Belfast.

Crymble, Thomas - Rifleman
9380 Royal Irish Rifles 1st Battalion *Killed in Action on 10 March 1915*
LE TOURET MEMORIAL, France
38 Rosapenna Street, Belfast.

Culbert, James - Sergeant
11525 Royal Irish Rifles 6th Battalion *Died in War*
DOIRAN MEMORIAL, Greece
21 Dunn Street, Belfast. Born in Lurgan, enlisted and resident in Belfast.
Commemorated in Shankill Road Orange Hall.

Cull, James Herbert - Lance Corporal
14260 Royal Irish Rifles 14th Battalion *Killed in Action on 16 August 1917*
TYNE COT MEMORIAL, Belgium
Born and enlisted in Belfast.

Cull, Samuel - Private
5214 Seaforth Highlanders 6th Battalion *Died in War on 8 December 1916*
OVILLERS MILITARY CEMETERY, *France*
3 Colville Street, Belfast.

Cullen, Cyril - Lance Corporal
23604 Princess Victoria's (Royal Irish Fusiliers) 9th Battalion *Killed in Action on 16 August 1917*
DOCHY FARM NEW BRITISH CEMETERY, *Belgium*
Born in Londonderry, enlisted Lurgan, resident Belfast.

Cullen, Daniel - Trimmer
7508TS Royal Naval Reserve HMS "Bittern" *Age 20 Drowned through collision in English Channel on 4 April 1918*
PORTSMOUTH NAVAL MEMORIAL, *United Kingdom*
Son of the late Daniel and Sarah Cullen, of Belfast; brother of Margaret O'Neill,
of 26, Henrietta Street, Belfast.

Cullen, James - Private
8112 Cameronians (Scottish Rifles) 2nd Battalion *Died in War on 20 February 1915*
LE TOURET MEMORIAL, *France*
Born in Belfast and enlisted Glasgow.

Cullen, Joseph - Private
G/1015 Princess Victoria's (Royal Irish Fusiliers) 2nd Garrison Battalion *Died in War on 25 April 1916*
GRANGEGORMAN MILTARY CEMETERY, *Republic of Ireland*
Born and enlisted in Belfast. Formerly 4550 Royal Irish Rifles.

Cullen, Patrick - Rifleman
S/24012 Rifle Brigade (The Prince Consort's Own) 13th Battalion *Died in War on 5 August 1917*
YPRES (MENIN GATE) MEMORIAL, *Belgium*
Born in Dublin, enlisted in London and resident of Belfast.

Cullen, Thomas - Rifleman
7845 Royal Irish Rifles 2nd Battalion *Age 22 Killed in Action on 8 July 1916*
THIEPVAL MEMORIAL, *France*
Husband of Mrs. Julia Cromer (formerly Cullen), of 23, Frederick Lane, Belfast.

Cully, George - Private
9419 Royal Inniskilling Fusiliers 1st Battalion *Age 29 Killed in Action on 13 June 1915*
TWELVE TREE COPSE CEMETERY, *Turkey*
Son of Sarah Cully of Belfast.

Cully, Joseph - Sapper
97659 Royal EngineersTraining Centre (Newark) *Age 30 Died of Wounds on 28 November 1916*
BELFAST CITY CEMETERY, *United Kingdom*
Son of James and Margret Cully; husband of Elizabeth Cully, of 19, Lawnbrook Avenue, Belfast.

Cummings, David Ernest - Rifleman
16369 Royal Irish Rifles 14th Battalion *Age 25 Died in War on 11 June 1917*
BAILLEUL COMMUNAL CEMETERY EXTENSION (NORD), *France*
Son of Mr. and Mrs. D. Cummings, of Belfast.

Cummins, Daniel - Private
11377 Royal Irish Fusiliers 2nd Battalion *Killed in Action on 15 March 1915*
YPRES (MENIN GATE) MEMORIAL, *Belgium*
95 North Queen Street, Belfast.

Cummins, James - Rifleman
1639 Royal Irish Rifles 8th Battalion *Died in War on 2 July 1916*
THIEPVAL MEMORIAL, *France*
Born and enlisted in Belfast.

Cummins, Moses - Rifleman
4935 Royal Irish Rifles 1st Battalion *Killed in Action on 19 July 1915*
Y FARM MILITARY CEMETERY BOIS-GRENIER, *France*
Born in Belfast, enlisted Waringstown.

Cummins, Patrick - Rifleman
9110 Royal Irish Rifles 2nd Battalion *Killed In Action on 27 November 1914*
ROYAL IRISH RIFLES GRAVEYARD, LAVENTIE, *France*
Born and enlisted in Belfast.

Cummins, William - Private
9218 Royal Inniskilling Fusiliers 1st Battalion *Died in War on 4 July 1915*
LANCASHIRE LANDING CEMETERY, *Turkey*
Son of George and the Elizabeth Cummins, 56 Beverley Street, Belfast.

Cummins, William J - Lance Sergeant
14341 Royal Irish Rifles 10th Battalion *Killed in Action on 25 December 1915*
SUCRERIE MILITARY CEMETERY, COLINCAMPS, *France*
Born and enlisted in Belfast. Lost his life on Christmas day.

Cunniffe, Michael - Rifleman
8553 Royal Irish Rifles "D" Company 1st Battalion *Age 26 Killed in Action on 9 May 1915*
PLOEGSTEERT MEMORIAL, *Belgium*
Brother of Mrs. Mary Keenan, of 9, Lepper Street, Belfast.

Cunningham, Charles - Sergeant
19240 Royal Irish Fusiliers Depot *Age 41 Died as a result of war on 22 April 1919*
BELFAST (DUNDONALD) CEMETERY, *United Kingdom*
Husband of Fanny Cunningham, of 54, Craigmore Street, Belfast. Formerly 14345 Royal Irish Rifles.

Cunningham, Edward - Private
2336 Leinster Regiment 7th Battalion *Died in War on 2 November 1916*
BELFAST (MILLTOWN) ROMAN CATHOLIC CEMETERY, *United Kingdom*
Son of Mrs. M. Cunningham, of 15, Upper Library Street, Belfast.

Cunningham, James - Driver
45464 Royal Field Artillery *Died in War on 24 April 1915*
YPRES (MENIN GATE) MEMORIAL, *Belgium*
35 Comber Street, Belfast.

Cunningham, James - Rifleman
1629 Royal Irish Rifles 15th Battalion *Killed in Action on 1 July 1916*
THIEPVAL MEMORIAL, France
Born Ballymacarrett, Belfast and enlisted in Belfast. Possibly resided at 36 Emerald Street.
Brother and sister lived at 32 Lendrick Street.

Cunningham, John - Private
2403 Royal Irish Fusiliers 2nd Battalion *Age 24 Died in War on 14 March 1915*
VOORMEZEELE ENCLOSURE No.3, Belgium
Brother of Mrs. Jane Russell, of 8, Coates Street, Belfast.

Cunningham, Joseph - Private
9336 Connaught Rangers 2nd Battalion *Age 22 Died in War on 29 October 1914*
YPRES (MENIN GATE) MEMORIAL, Belgium
Son of Stephen and Anne Cunningham, of Mountpottinger Street, Belfast.

Cunningham, Robert - Mate
Mercantile Marine S.S. "Castlebar" (Belfast) *Age 30 Presumed drowned on 13 March 1918*
TOWER HILL MEMORIAL, United Kingdom
Son of Eliza Cunningham (née Brooks), of 4, Spamount Street, Belfast, and the late James Cunningham.
Born at Belfast.

Cunningham, Robert - Rifleman
8114268 Royal Irish Rifles 8th Battalion *Died in War on 7 July 1916*
ETAPLES MILITARY CEMETERY, France
Son of Thomas and Rebecca Cunningham, of 47, Glenbrook Avenue, Belfast.

Cunningham, Samuel - Private
3318 Royal Inniskilling Fusiliers 2nd Battalion *Killed in Action on 22 December 1915*
CERISY-GAILLY MILITARY CEMETERY, France
Son of Samuel and Margaret Cunningham, of 29, Langford Street, Belfast.

Cunningham, Samuel - Private
S/17494 Queen's Own Cameron Highlanders 2nd Battalion *Died in War on 3 October 1916*
STURMA MILITARY CEMETERY, Greece
Born in Belfast. Enlisted Greenock, Scotland.

Cunningham, William - Private
9894 Royal Irish Fusiliers 2nd Battalion *Age 23 Died in War on 4 May 1915*
YPRES (MENIN GATE) MEMORIAL, Belgium
Son of Richard and Elizabeth Cunningham, of 11, Athens Street, Woodstock Road, Belfast.

Cunningham, William Andrew - Lance Corporal
811 Royal Irish Rifles 8th Battalion *Died in War on 5 August 1917*
YPRES (MENIN GATE) MEMORIAL, Belgium
Son of Robert and Jane Cunningham 330 Shankill Road, Belfast.
An Orangeman and Shipyard worker he was also a member of the old UVF.

Cupples, William - Captain
Royal Inniskilling Fusiliers 3rd Battalion *Age 20 Died in War on 25 September 1915*
YPRES (MENIN GATE) MEMORIAL, Belgium
Son of Mr. and Mrs. W. Cupples, of 124, Malone Avenue, Belfast. Educated at Methodist College and studied medicine at Queen's University. Served in the OTC. At first posted missing and only confirmed dead in March 1919.

Curley, Francis - Lieutenant
Royal Engineers Royal Anglesey *Age 24 Died in War on 25 September 1915*
LOOS MEMORIAL, France
Son of Mrs. R. Curley, of "Mentmore", Lisburn Road, Belfast, and the late Alexander Curley. Educated at Queen's University, Belfast. Graduated B.Sc. Engineering (1912). Member of the University Officer Training Corps. Gazetted as an officer 1914.

Curlis, Roland - Private
273 Australian Light Horse *Died in War on 19 May 1915*
SHRAPNEL VALLEY CEMETERY, Turkey
583 Ormeau Road, Belfast.

Curran, Edward - Private
12468 Royal Inniskilling Fusiliers 6th Battalion *Killed in Action on 3 October 1918*
VIS-EN-ARTOIS MEMORIAL, France
Born and enlisted in Belfast.

Curran, Francis - Private
416360 5th Canadian Mounted Rifles (Quebec Regiment) *Killed in Action on 1 - 2 October 1916*
REGINA TRENCH CEMETERY, GRANDCOURT, France
Next of kin was his sister, Martha Curran, 4 Linwood Street, Belfast.
A Presbyterian, he had previous military service.

Curran, Francis - Private
25053 Royal Inniskilling Fusiliers 9th Battalion *Age 20 Died of Wounds on 5 July 1916*
STE. MARIE CEMETERY, LE HAVRE, France
Son of James and Eliza Jane Curran, of 3, Pim Street, Antrim Road, Belfast.

Curran, Herbert - Private
2101 Royal Fusiliers 24th Battalion *Age 21 Killed in Action on 7 May 1916*
TRANCHEE DE MECKNES CEMETERY, AIX-NOULETTE, France
Son of Miles and Edith Curran, of 9, Myrtlefield Park, Belfast. Educated at RBAI.

Curran, Patrick - Private
1523 Leinster Regiment "D" Company 7th Battalion *Age 24 Killed in Action on 24 June 1916*
ST. PATRICK'S CEMETERY, LOOS, France
Son of John and Martha Curran, of 8, Saul Street, Belfast.

Currie, Albert B - Private
28465 Hampshire Regiment 2nd Battalion *Died in War on 4 September 1918*
OUTTERSTEENE COMMUNAL CEMETERY EXTENSION BAILLEUL, France
Born Belfast. Enlisted in Belfast, formally D/9305, Royal Irish Rifles.

Currie, David - Private
42513 Royal Irish Fusiliers 9th Battalion *Age 19 Died of Wounds on 8 October 1918*
LIJSSENTHOEK MILITARY CEMETERY, Belgium
Son of Richard and Agnes Currie, of 6, Dickson Street, Belfast.

Currie, David - Rifleman
12644 Royal Irish Rifles 8th Battalion *Killed in action on 7 June 1917*
LONE TREE CEMETERY, Belgium
Husband of Mrs Agnes Currie, 48 Brighton Street, Belfast.

Currie, James Alexander Vance. - Second Lieutenant
London Regiment 10th Battalion *Age 28 Killed in Action on 13 March 1917*
LE FERMONT MILITARY CEMETERY, RIVIERE, France
Husband of E. V. Currie, of "Ermington", Chaucer Road, Broadstairs, Kent. Native of Belfast.

Currie, James - Rifleman
12643 Royal Irish Rifles 8th Battalion *Died in War on 2 July 1916*
THIEPVAL MEMORIAL, FRANCE
14 Canton Street, Belfast.

Currie, James Graham - Private
54553 Royal Army Medical Corps 109th Field Ambulance *Age 31 Died of Wounds on 22 August 1917*
WIMEREUX COMMUNAL CEMETERY, France
Son of Thomas H. Currie, of Belfast; husband of Mary Ellen Currie, of 74, Northumberland Street, Belfast. In 1971 a squad of soldiers from the Queen's Own Highlanders carried out a search for arms in a derelict house in Northumberland Street. No weapons were found but a World War 1 Medal was discovered. It had belonged to a James Currie. The medal was handed over to the medical Sergeant, an Irishman from Galway, (now a retired Major and an MBE), who presented it to the Royal Army Medical Corps Museum. There it remains today.

Currie, Robert - Rifleman
3036 Royal Irish Rifles 14th Battalion *Died in War on 5 October 1918*
POZIERES MEMORIAL, France
Born in Belfast, enlisted Lisburn.

Currie, Samuel - Private
44342 Royal Army Ordnance Corps No. 9 Section (York) *Age 28 Died in War on 11 November 1918*
BARROW-IN-FURNESS CEMETERY, United Kingdom
Husband of Martha Currie, of 20, Island Street, Belfast. Lost his life on the last day of the war.

Currie, Thomas - Private
20257 Royal Inniskilling Fusiliers 9th Battalion *Died in War on 18 October 1918*
DUHALLOW A.D.S. CEMETERY, Belgium
Born and enlisted in Belfast.

Currie, Thomas - Rifleman
17/605 Royal Irish Rifles 9th Battalion *Died of suffocation - cause not stated in official notice on 21 October 1915*
VIGNACOURT BRITISH CEMETERY, France
Born and enlisted in Belfast. A former member of the old UVF he left a widow and four children.

Curry, Charles John - First Engineer
Mercantile Marine S.S. "Bray Head" (Belfast) *Age 37 Drowned, as a result of an attack by an enemy submarine on 14 March 1917*
TOWER HILL MEMORIAL, United Kingdom
Son of the late William and Jane Curry. Born in Belfast.

Curry, Francis - Rifleman
23616 Royal Irish Rifles 3rd Battalion *Age 23 Drowned on 5 August 1919*
BELFAST CITY CEMETERY, United Kingdom
Son of Thomas and Sarah Curry, of 30, Warkworth Street, Belfast.

Curry, Nathaniel - Gunner
78667 Royal Field Artillery 27th Division Ammunition Column *Age 24 Died in War on 27 August 1918*
CARNMONEY CEMETERY, United Kingdom
Son of John H. Curry, of 6, Aberdeen Street, Belfast.

Curry, Robert Joseph - Private
829402 Canadian Infantry (New Brunswick Regiment) 44th Battalion *Age 20 Died in War on 26 April 1917*
VILLERS STATION CEMETERY, VILLERS-AU-BOIS, France
Son of William and Elizabeth Curry, of 248, Crumlin Road, Belfast, Ireland. A Presbyterian, he had worked as a farm labourer.

Curry, William - Rifleman
8965 Royal Irish Rifles 1st Battalion *Age 22 Killed in Action on 25 March 1915*
PLOEGSTEERT MEMORIAL, Belgium
Son of William and Emily Curry, of 41, Royal Avenue, Belfast.

Curry, William Gordon - Second Lieutenant
Cheshire Regiment 12th Battalion attached 13th Battalion *Age 24 Killed in Action on 7 June 1917*
WULVERGHEM-LINDENHOEK ROAD MILITARY CEMETERY, Belgium
Son of Mr & Mrs David Curry, 2 Gordon Terrace, Agincourt Terrace. Educated at RBAI, killed at the attack on Messines Ridge.

Curtis, Bernard - Private
23517 Royal Inniskilling Fusiliers 7th Battalion *Killed in Action on 27 April 1916*
PHILOSOPHE BRITISH CEMETERY, MAZINGARBE, France
Born and enlisted in Belfast.

Curtis, John - Rifleman
1637443 Royal Irish Rifles 6th Battalion *Died in War on 29 September 1915*
EAST MUDROS MILITARY CEMETERY, Greece
Son of Rose and Thomas Curtis, 42 River Terrace, Belfast

Curtis, Michael - Rifleman
8954 Royal Irish Rifles 1st Battalion *Killed in Action on 10 March 1916*
LE TOURET MEMORIAL, France
Born in Belfast but later moved to Cookstown, County Tyrone.

Cushnahan, Thomas - Private
29000 Royal Inniskilling Fusiliers 1st Battalion *Died in War on 19 April 1917*
ARRAS MEMORIAL, France
46 Conway Street, Belfast.

Cutler, John Isaac - Colour Sergeant
G/1228 Royal Irish Fusiliers 2nd (Garrison) Battalion *Died of heart disease on 12 October 1916*
SALONIKA (LEMBET ROAD) MILITARY CEMETERY, Greece
Husband of Kathleen Cutler, of 61, Belvoir Street, Belfast

Culbert, Robert Gilliland - Lance Corporal
14/7149 Royal Irish Rifles 8th Battalion *Age 20 Killed in Action on 2 July 1916*
THIEPVAL MEMORIAL, France
Son of Thomas Henry and Emily Culbert of Antrim Road, Belfast.

Journey of Remembering

Dady, Richard - Driver
77461 Royal Horse Artillery and Royal Field Artillery *Died in War on 9 April 1918*
HAVERSKERQUE BRITISH CEMETERY, France
Born and enlisted in Belfast.

Daglin, Frank - Rifleman
11610 Royal Irish Rifles 6th Battalion *Age 35 Died in War on 12 June 1916*
MIKRA BRITISH CEMETERY, KALAMARIA, Greece
Husband of Mary Daglin, of 366, Ligoniel Road, Belfast.

Dale, John Henry - Regimental Sergeant Major
14407 Royal Irish Rifles 21st Entrenching Battalion, late 10th Battalion *Died in War on 21 March 1918*
POZIERES MEMORIAL, France
13 Belvoir Street, Belfast. Holder of the Military Medal.

Dales, Andrew - Private
22180 Cameronians (Scottish Rifles) *Killed in Action on 18 August 1916*
THIEPVAL MEMORIAL, France
Born and enlisted in Belfast.

Daley, Thomas - Private
11907 Royal Scots Fusiliers 6th Battalion *Died in War on 29 September 1915*
LOOS MEMORIAL, France
Born in Belfast, enlisted Glasgow.

Daley, William Lorenzo - Rifleman
311 Royal Irish Rifles 9th Battalion *Died in War on 30 April 1917*
SHORNCLIFFE MILITARY CEMETERY, United Kingdom
Born and enlisted in Belfast.

Dalton, Alexander - Fireman
865477 Mercantile Marine Reserve HMS "Eaglet" *Age 25 Died as a result of war on 2 March 1919*
BLARIS OLD BURIAL GROUND, United Kingdom
Son of William Dalton, of 128, Bristol Street, Belfast.

Dalton, Thomas J - Rifleman
9033 Royal Irish Rifles 2nd Battalion *Age 21 Died of Wounds on 19 June 1915*
BAILLEUL COMMUNAL CEMETERY EXTENSION (NORD), France
Son of Thomas and Martha Dalton, of 48, Hopeton Street, Shankill Road, Belfast.

Daly, Bernard - Corporal
8145 King's Shropshire Light Infantry "B" Company 2nd Battalion
Age 35 Died in War on 12 February 1915
YPRES (MENIN GATE) MEMORIAL, Belgium
Son of Captain. B. Daly, of "Braefoot" Waterloo Gardens, Antrim Road, Belfast.
Husband of Jane Frances Daly, of 13, Bradshaw Street, Lancaster.

Daly, Hugh - Private
20198 Royal Irish Fusiliers 8th Battalion *Died in War on 25 May 1916*
ST. PATRICK'S CEMETERY, LOOS, France
Brother of Miss M. A. Daly, of 33, Cavendish Street, Belfast.

Daly, John E. - Lance Sergeant
6463 Irish Guards 1st Battalion *Age 24 Killed in Action on 25 September 1916*
THIEPVAL MEMORIAL, France
Son of William and Bridget Teresa Daly, of 26, Gloucester Street, Belfast.

Daly, John Joseph - Private
4594 Royal Inniskilling Fusiliers 1st Battalion *Age 22 Died in War on 8 August 1916*
YPRES (MENIN GATE) MEMORIAL, Belgium
Son of John and Julia Daly, of 68, Herbert Street, Crumlin Road, Belfast.

Daly, Peter - Lance Corporal
16388 Royal Inniskilling Fusiliers 3rd Battalion *Died suddenly at home on 27 July 1915*
LONDONDERRY CITY CEMETERY, United Kingdom
His widow, Margaret, lived at 20 Kane Street, Belfast.

Dalzell, Ernest Victor - Third Engineer
Mercantile Marine S.S. "Teelin Head" (Belfast)
Age 28 Drowned, as a result of an attack by an enemy submarine on 21 January 1918
TOWER HILL MEMORIAL, United Kingdom
Son of John Dalzell, and the late Rosina Dalzell; husband of Elizabeth Maud Dalzell, of 55, Abbott Street, Belfast. Born at Belfast.

Dalzell, Hugh - Private
24114 Royal Irish Fusiliers 9th Battalion *Age 20 Killed in Action on 16 August 1917*
TYNE COT MEMORIAL, Belgium
Son of Mr. and Mrs. Hugh Dalzell, of 76, Paris Street, Belfast.

Dalzell, James - Private
8104 Royal Inniskilling Fusiliers 2nd Battalion *Died in War on 21 October 1914*
STRAND MILITARY CEMETERY, Belgium
Born and enlisted in Belfast.

Dalzell, Richard - Driver
T4/036423 Royal Army Service Corps *Died in War on 24 March 1917*
BELFAST (DUNDONALD) CEMETERY, United Kingdom
Born in County Cavan, resident in Belfast.

Dalzell, Robert - Stoker
2100/T Royal Naval Reserve HMS "Lancaster" *Age 43 Died in War on 23 July 1915*
GILLINGHAM (WOODLANDS) CEMETERY, United Kingdom
Husband of Matilda Dalzell, of 14, Ulverston Street, Belfast.

Dalzell, Robert James - Private
3202 Royal Inniskilling Fusiliers 1st Battalion *Age 18 Died in War on 21 August 1915*
HELLES MEMORIAL, Turkey
Son of Mrs. S. Dalzell, of 99, Donegall Road, Belfast.

Dalzell, Thomas Robinson - Rifleman
47182 Royal Irish Rifles 15th Battalion formerly 831201, Army Service Corps
Age 21 Died in War on 22 November 1917
THIEPVAL MEMORIAL, France
Son of Hugh and Mary Dalzell, of 9, Derwent Street, Belfast.

Journey of Remembering

Darby, Peter - Private
26162 Royal Inniskilling Fusiliers 8th Battalion *Age 25 Died in War on 29 April 1916*
LOOS MEMORIAL, France
Son of Peter and Rose Darby of County Down. Husband of Rosaleen Darby, of 216, Falls Road, Belfast.

Darcy, Joseph - Private
21051 Royal Irish Fusiliers 2nd Battalion *Died in War on 6 February 1918*
BROOKWOOD MILITARY CEMETERY, United Kingdom
(Served as DAWSON). Son of Eliza Darcy, of 3, Park Street, Belfast.

Darling, Patrick - Private
26094 Royal Irish Fusiliers 7th/8th Battalion *Died of Wounds on 21 November 1917*
BUCQUOY ROAD CEMETERY, FICHEUX, France
74, Servia Street, Belfast.

Darling, Roland Harry - Lance Corporal
516 Royal Irish Rifles 14th Battalion *Killed In Action on 16 March 1917*
TYNE COT MEMORIAL, Belgium
Born and enlisted in Belfast. A former member of the old UVF he left a widow and four children.

Darragh, Henry - Private
9985 Royal Inniskilling Fusiliers 1st Battalion *Died in War on 28 September 1916*
VLAMERTINGHE MILITARY CEMETERY, Belgium
Brother of George Darragh, of 57, Northumberland Street, Belfast.

Darragh, Joseph - Driver
T/423571 Royal Army Service Corps *Age 25 Died as result of war on 8 March 1919*
BELFAST CITY CEMETERY, United Kingdom
Husband of Elizabeth Darragh, of 112, Brookmount Street, Belfast. Formerly 3464 Royal Irish Rifles.

Darragh, Richard - Rifleman
14411 Royal Irish Rifles 9th Battalion *Died in War on 24 February 1915*
CARNMONEY (HOLY EVANGELISTS) CHURCH OF IRELAND EXTENSION, United Kingdom
Born and enlisted in Belfast. A former member of the old UVF he left a widow and four children.

Darragh, William James - Rifleman
5748 Royal Irish Rifles 2nd Battalion *Killed in Action on 25 September 1915*
YPRES (MENIN GATE) MEMORIAL, Belgium
Husband of Lillie 245 Springfield Road, Belfast. His brother also served.

Darroch, Duncan - Sergeant
14393 Royal Irish Rifles 14th Battalion *Age 24 Killed in Action on 1 July 1916*
THIEPVAL MEMORIAL, France
Son of the late Duncan and Letitia Darroch of Belfast.

Davey, William Edwin - Private
9485 Royal Fusiliers 9th Battalion *Age 22 Died in War on 7 October 1916*
THIEPVAL MEMORIAL, France
Son of the Rev. Charles Davey, D.D., and Margaret Davey, of 3, College Park, Belfast.

Davidson, Duncan - Rifleman
16427 Royal Irish Rifles 14th Battalion attached 109th Trench Mortar Battery
Age 26 Killed in Action on 16 August 1917
TYNE COT MEMORIAL, Belgium
Son of Thomas C. Davidson, of 3, South View Cottages, Rugby Road, Belfast.

Davidson, Frederick - Private
8557 Royal Inniskilling Fusiliers 2nd Battalion *Age 27 Died in War on 7 November 1914*
PLOEGSTEERT MEMORIAL, Belgium
Son of Robert Davidson, of Maymount Street, Belfast; husband of Lily Davidson,
of 25, Fairview Street, Crumlin Road, Belfast.

Davidson, James Johnston - Rifleman
355 Royal Irish Rifles 12th Battalion *Age 19 Killed in Action on 21 March 1918*
POZIERES MEMORIAL, France
Son of Benjamin Adair Davidson and Elizabeth Johnston Davidson, of Carnmoney, Belfast.

Davidson, Samuel - Rifleman
992 Royal Irish Rifles "D" Company 12th Battalion *Age 21 Killed in Action on 21 March 1918*
POZIERES MEMORIAL, France
Brother of Andrew Davidson, of 45, Island Street, Belfast.

Davidson, Thomas - Private
24882 Manchester Regiment 16th Battalion *Died in War on 28 December 1917*
HOOGE CRATER CEMETERY, Belgium
Husband of Minnie, 14 Malt Street, Belfast.

Davidson, Thomas - Sergeant
8/12716 Royal Irish Rifles 8th Battalion *Died of Wounds on 15 July 1916*
CAUDRY OLD COMMUNAL CEMETERY, France
Husband of Elizabeth Davidson, of 38, Avoniel Road, Belfast.

Davidson, William Robert - Private
28827 Royal Inniskilling Fusiliers 11th Battalion *Died in War on 30 January 1917*
MAPLE LEAF CEMETERY, Belgium
Born in Belfast, enlisted Enniskillen.

Davies, Edward - Private
16197 Coldstream Guards 2nd Battalion *Age 26 Died of meningitis on 21 October 1917*
DOZINGHEM MILITARY CEMETERY, Belgium
Son of Joseph and Mary Davies, of Rednal, Shropshire; husband of Edith Davies,
of 9, Annadale Street, Antrim Road, Belfast.

Davies, George William - Private
7984 Royal Fusiliers (City of London Regiment) 1st Battalion *Died in War on 13 August 1916*
THIEPVAL MEMORIAL, France
Son of Joseph and Minnie Davies, born in Belfast and enlisted in Finsbury, London.

Davies, William - Rifleman
14361 Royal Irish Rifles 10th Battalion *Age 34 Died of Wounds on 8 August 1917*
BRANDHOEK NEW MILITARY CEMETERY, Belgium
Son of James and Elizabeth Davies, of Belfast.

Davis, James - Private
10554 Royal Inniskilling Fusiliers 2nd Battalion *Killed in Action on 20 October 1914*
PLOEGSTEERT MEMORIAL, Belgium
Born and enlisted in Belfast.

Davis, Henry Ouseley - Captain
Royal Irish Rifles *Age 30 Killed in Action on 27 October 1914*
LE TOURET MEMORIAL, France
Educated at Portora Royal School, and Campbell College, Belfast; from which he passed direct to R.M.C. Sandhurst. Gazetted Second Lieutenant Royal Dublin Fusiliers, 15th August, 1905. Resigned commission, 1910. Rejoined the army and gazetted Captain, Royal Irish Rifles, 31st August, 1914.

Davis, James - Private
10554 Royal Inniskilling Fusiliers 2nd Battalion *Killed in Action on 20 October 1914*
PLOEGSTEERT MEMORIAL, Belgium
Son of Samuel and Margaret Davis, 45 Durham Street, Belfast.

Davis, John - Private
84040 Royal Army Medical Corps attached River Sick Convoy Unit *Age 38 Died of heatstroke on 22 July 1917*
AMARA WAR CEMETERY, Iraq
Son of the Rev. John Davis, of Ballynahinch Manse, County Down; husband of Margaret Davis (née Kernahan), of "Grasmere" Lansdowne Road, Belfast. Parish Minister of Buittle, Castle Douglas, Kirkcudbrightshire.

Davis, John Henry - Captain
Royal Army Medical Corps *Age 51 Died of accidental injuries on 21 June 1916*
BELFAST CITY CEMETERY, United Kingdom
Son of Robert Davis of Belfast.

Davis, Joseph Steele - Private
249720 Canadian Infantry 58th Battalion *Died in War on 27 August 1918*
VIS-EN-ARTOIS BRITISH CEMETERY, HAUCOURT, France
Native of Belfast.

Davis, Laurence - Gunner
59292 Royal Garrison Artillery *Died in War on 18 April 1917*
TILLOY BRITISH CEMETERY, TILLOY-LES-MOFFLAINES, France
Born in Belfast enlisted Staffordshire. Husband of Teresa Clyne (formerly Davis).

Davis, Maxwell - Rifleman
20291 Royal Irish Rifles 14th Battalion *Died in War on 30 June 1918*
DRUMBO PRESBYTERIAN CHURCHYARD, United Kingdom
Born and enlisted in Belfast.

Davis, Robert - Private
27794 Wiltshire Regiment 6th Battalion *Age 19 Died in War on 10 April 1918*
TYNE COT MEMORIAL, Belgium
Son of Thomas Davis, of 1, Gotha Street, Belfast.

Davis, Thomas - Private
18656 Princess Victoria's (Royal Irish Fusiliers) 4th Battalion *Died in War on 25 April 1916*
BELFAST(MILLTOWN) ROMAN CATHOLIC CEMETERY, United Kingdom
Born in Belfast, enlisted Armagh.

Davies, Thomas Skidmore - Company Sergeant Major
172 Prince of Wales Volunteers (South Lancashire Regiment) 14th Battalion *Age 36 Died in War on 28 November 1915*
DICKEBUSCH NEW MILITARY CEMETERY EXTENSION, Belgium
Born in Belfast. Enlisted Warrington, Lancashire. Husband of Margaret Davies, 7, Lexden Street, Lovely Lane, Warrington.

Davis, William - Rifleman
16411 Labour Corps transferred from Royal Irish Rifles 411151 *Age 47 Died in War on 21 November 1918*
BELFAST CITY CEMETERY, United Kingdom
Husband of Fanny Davis, of 103, Charles Street South, Sandy Row, Belfast.

Davison, Alexander - Private
7339 Royal Scots Fusiliers 1st Battalion *Died in War on 16 June 1915*
YPRES (MENIN GATE) MEMORIAL, Belgium
Born in Belfast, enlisted Glasgow.

Davison, Daniel - Sapper
64575 Royal Engineers 122nd Field Company *Age 36 Killed in Action on 1 July 1916*
THIEPVAL MEMORIAL, France
Son of Robert and Elizabeth Davison, of 391, Donegall Road, Belfast.

Davison, Henry - Private
2609 Manchester Regiment 2nd Battalion *Killed in Action on 26 August 1914*
LA FERTE-SOUS-JOUARRE MEMORIAL, France
Born and enlisted in Belfast.

Davison, Hugh - Private
A/4056 Canadian Infantry (Central Ontario Regiment) 3rd Battalion *Age 29 Died of wounds on 14 June 1916*
LIJSSENTHOEK MILITARY CEMETERY, Belgium
Son of Mr. and Mrs. Hugh M. Davison; husband of Alma Davison, of 35, Ashdale Avenue, Toronto.
Native of Belfast, Ireland. Had previous military service with the Royal Irish Rifles, a Presbyterian.

Davison, James Smyth - Sapper
19729 Royal Engineers 59th Field Company *Age 25 Died in War on 16 June 1915*
BELFAST CITY CEMETERY, United Kingdom
Son of Thomas and Agnes Davison, of Lake Glen, Andersonstown, Belfast.
Holder of the Distinguished Conduct Medal.

Davison, Robert - Lieutenant
The King's (Liverpool Regiment) 12th Battalion *Age 20 Died of Wounds received at Geudecourt on 8 October 1916*
GROVE TOWN CEMETERY, MEAULTE, France
Son of John Robert Davison, M.D. and Lizzie Davison, of "Romanov" Ormeau Road, Belfast.
Awarded the Military Cross.

Davison, Samuel - Private
6962 Princess Victoria's (Royal Irish Fusiliers) 6th Battalion *Died in War on 29 September 1916*
STRUMA MILITARY CEMETERY, Greece
Born and enlisted in Belfast.

Davison, Thomas - Private
102535 Canadian Infantry 67th Battalion *Died in War on 11 July 1916*
BRAMSHOTT (ST MARY) CHURCHYAROAD, United Kingdom
Spamount Street, Belfast.

JOURNEY OF REMEMBERING

Davison, Thomas - Rifleman
16812 Royal Irish Rifles 1st Battalion *Age 29 Killed in Action on 12 March 1915*
LE TOURET MEMORIAL, France
Son of Mr. and Mrs. Hugh Davison, of 5, Spamount Street, Belfast; husband of Jane Davison, of 13, Ohio Street, Belfast. General Post Office employee for 13 years.

Davitt, Joseph - Private
26333 Royal Inniskilling Fusiliers 8th Battalion *Killed in Action on 16 August 1917*
BEDFORD HOUSE CEMETERY, Belgium
Born in Belfast, enlisted Omagh.

Dawson, Edward - Rifleman
9206 Royal Irish Rifles 7th Battalion *Age 35 Killed in Action on 16 August 1917*
TYNE COT MEMORIAL, Belgium
Son of William Edward Dawson, of 7, Bleakley Street, Belfast.

Dawson, Edward - Rifleman
957 Royal Irish Rifles 8th Battalion *Died in War on 23 November 1917*
CAMBRAI MEMORIAL, LOUVERVAL, France
9, Magnetic Street Belfast. Grandparents Mary M & Henry Cassells.

Dawson, Frederick - Rifleman
19/533 Royal Irish Rifles 9th Battalion *Age 32 Killed in Action on 7 June 1917*
SPANBROEKMOLEN BRITISH CEMETERY, Belgium
Son of James and Mary Dawson, of Caledon, County Tyrone; husband of Anna Helen Dawson (née Hughey), of 93, Cavehill Road, Belfast.

Dawson, John - Private
21051 Princess Victoria's (Royal Irish Fusiliers) 2nd Battalion *Died in War on 6 February 1918*
BROOKWOOD MILITARY CEMETERY, United Kingdom
Born and enlisted in Belfast. Formerly 2598, Connaught Rangers.

Dawson, John Thomas Gibson - Able Seaman
SS/2426 Royal Navy HMS "Hawke" *Age 24 Killed in Action with submarine in North Sea on 15 October 1914*
CHATHAM NAVAL MEMORIAL, United Kingdom
Son of Henry and Denah Dawson, of 356, Donegall Road, Belfast.

Dawson, Thomas - Private
28855 Royal Inniskilling Fusiliers 1st Battalion *Died in War on 9 August 1916*
YPRES MENIN GATE MEMORIAL, Belgium
Born and enlisted in Belfast.

Dawson, William - Corporal
9138 Royal Irish Rifles 6th Battalion *Died of pleurisy in hospital on 18 September 1917*
PIETA MILITARY CEMETERY, Malta
10, Townsend Street, Belfast.

Deane, Arthur Denham - Second Lieutenant
Royal Irish Regiment 1st Battalion attached 2nd Battalion *Died in War on 14 July 1916*
THIEPVAL MEMORIAL, France
Educated at RBAI and lived in Knockdene Park, he was a member of Knock Rugby Club. Served in the ranks of the Royal Engineers before being commissioned.

BELFAST BOOK OF HONOUR

Deane, Robert - Sergeant
14419 Royal Irish Rifles 10th Battalion *Killed in Action on 1 July 1916*
CONNAUGHT MEMETERY THIEPVAL, France
Husband of Jane Deane, 82, Roslyn Street.

Dearden, Alfred Boyd - Lance Corporal
17569 Royal Irish Rifles 14th Battalion *Age 29 Killed in Action on 1 July 1916*
THIEPVAL MEMORIAL, France
Son of Minnie Dearden, of 63, Burmah Street, Belfast, and the late Alfred Dearden.

Deddis, Thomas - Lance Corporal
5066 Royal Irish Rifles 6th Battalion *Died in War on 5 June 1917*
STRUMA MILITARY CEMETERY, Greece
Born in Hillsborough, enlisted Downpatrick, resident in Belfast.

Deighan, Michael - Private
11361 5th Dragoon Guards (Princess Charlottte's Own) *Died in War on 5 August 1916*
FRICOURT BRITISH CEMETERY, France
Born in Belfast, enlisted Edinburgh.

Delaney, James - Gunner
4978 Royal Garrison Artillery Base Depot *Age 48 Died in War on 24 December 1916*
STE. MARIE CEMETERY, LE HAVRE, France
Son of Charles and Mary A Delaney; husband of Ellen Delaney,
of 1, Columbus Street, Great Georges Street, Belfast.

Delaney, Thomas - Rifleman
4618 Royal Irish Rifles 2nd Battalion *Age 36 Died in War on 11 March 1917*
GLASGOW (CRAIGTON) CEMETERY, United Kingdom
Son of Charles and Mary Ann Delaney, of 36, Little Georges Street, Belfast;
husband of Mary Delaney, of 29, Albert Street, Govan, Glasgow.

Delany, Michael - Gunner
99757 Royal Field Artillery 95th Brigade *Age 26 Killed in Action on 4 July 1916*
NORFOLK CEMETERY, BECORDEL-BECOURT, France
Son of Mrs. E. Delany, of 3, New Lodge Road, Belfast.

Dempsey, Hugh - Private
8532 Royal Inniskilling Fusiliers 2nd Battalion *Died in War on 16 May 1915*
LE TOURET MEMORIAL, France
Born and enlisted in Belfast.

Dempsey, James Joseph - Rifleman
8625 Royal Irish Rifles "A" Company 1st Battalion *Age 36 Died of wounds on 25 February 1917*
BRAY MILITARY CEMETERY, France
Son of James and Catherine Dempsey, of Belfast; husband of Lizzie Dempsey, of 31, English Street, Belfast.

Dempsey, Samuel - Rifleman
14402 Royal Irish Rifles 14th Battalion *Killed In Action on 17 October 1917*
HERMIES BRITISH CEMETERY, France
Born and Enlisted in Belfast.

Journey of Remembering

Dempsey, The Rev. John - Chaplain
Australian Army Chaplains Department *Age 36 Died in War on 13 June 1917*
CAIRO WAR MEMORIAL CEMETERY, *Egypt*
Son of Patrick and Martha Dempsey; husband of Lily E. Dempsey of Ethel Street, Burwood, New South Wales. Born in Belfast, Ireland.

Dempster, George - Stoker
1714 (S) Royal Naval Reserve HMS "Sirlus" *Died in War on 16 April 1915*
BROOKWOOD MILITARY CEMETERY, *United Kingdom*
Born at Belfast.

Dempster, Robert - Rifleman
16412 Royal Irish Rifles 14th Battalion *Killed in Action on 1 July 1916*
THIEPVAL MEMORIAL, *France*
Husband of Mary C. Dempster, of 22, Dover Street, Belfast.

Dempster, Robert - Rifleman
9623 Royal Irish Rifles 1st Battalion *Killed in Action on 19 November 1914*
LE TOURET MEMORIAL, *France*
Son of Hugh and Mary Dempster, of 17, Arundel Street, Belfast.

Dempster, Samuel - Private
7237 Royal Irish Fusiliers 1st Battalion *Died in War on 25 April 1915*
YPRES (MENIN GATE) MEMORIAL, *Belgium*
Husband of Mary Jane Dempster, of 65, Montreal Street, Crumlin Road, Belfast.

Dempster, William J - Sapper
64562 Royal Engineers 150th Field Company *Killed in Action on 1 July 1916*
THIEPVAL MEMORIAL, *France*
Born Ballymacarrett, Belfast. Enlisted in Belfast. Resident Hillsborough, County Down.

Dempster, Hugh - Sapper
64563 Royal Engineers 121st Field Company *Age 48 Died in War on 5 June 1916*
MAGHULL (SAINT ANDREW) CHURCHYARD, *United Kingdom*
Born Ballymacarrett, Belfast. Enlisted in Belfast. Resident Hillsborough, County Down.

Denison, Samuel - Private
42234 Manchester Regiment 18th Battalion *Died in War on 14 December 1917*
YPRES RESERVOIR CEMETERY, *Belgium*
16 Jennymount Street, Belfast.

Denny, James - Second Lieutenant
Royal Irish Fusiliers 1st Battalion *Age 27 Died in War on 23 October 1918*
HARLEBEKE NEW BRITISH CEMETERY, *Belgium*
Son of William Denny, of 30/31, Smithfield Square, Belfast.

Derby, Michael - Sapper
414172 Royal Engineers *Died as a result of war on 27 September 1920*
BELFAST (MILLTOWN) ROMAN CATHOLIC CEMETERY, *United Kingdom*
Son of Annie Derby, of 40, Raglan Street, Belfast, and the late Bernard Derby.

BELFAST BOOK OF HONOUR

Derragh, Robert - Rifleman
1021 Royal Irish Rifles 7th Battalion *Died in War on 6 May 1916*
DUD CORNER CEMETERY, LOOS, *France*
Born and enlisted in Belfast.

Despard, Charles Beauclerk - Captain
6th Dragoons (Inniskilling) attached 9th Battalion Royal Irish Fusiliers *Age 37 Died in War on 18 April 1918*
TYNE COT MEMORIAL, *Belgium*
Son of William and Mary Despard, of "Sheelagh" Malone Park, Belfast; husband of Josephine Despard, of The Acacias, Portarlington, Queen's County. Educated at RBAI. Awarded the Distinguished Service Order for "conpicuous gallantry and devotion to duty" in holding back the German advance on Kemmel Hill near Ypres.

Devine, James - Corporal
2855 Royal Inniskilling Fusiliers 1st Battalion *Died in War on 20 June 1915*
LANCASHIRE LANDING CEMETERY, *Turkey*
16 Lower Urney Street, Belfast, left a widow, Margaret.

Devine, John - Stoker
1427S Royal Naval Reserve HMS "Vanguard" *Age 30 Killed by internal explosion of vessel at Scapa Flow on 9 July 1917*
PORTSMOUTH NAVAL MEMORIAL, *United Kingdom*
Son of Hugh and Ellen Devine, of Ballymoney, County Antrim; husband of Nellie Devine,
of 21, Artillery Street, Belfast.

Devlin, James - Private
368269 Labour Corps *Died in War on 29 October 1918*
THIEPVAL MEMORIAL, *France*
Born and enlisted in Ayrshire, Scotland. Resident in Belfast. Formerly 14689 Royal Scots Fusiliers.

Devlin, John - Gunner
95897 Royal Horse Artillery and Royal Field Artillery *Died in War on 19 December 1915*
YPRES RESERVOIR CEMETERY, *Belgium*
Born in Belfast, enlisted in Yorkshire.

Devlin, Patrick James Joseph - Private
21054 Princess Victoria's (Royal Irish Fusiliers) 1st Battalion *Died in War on 29 October 1916*
THIEPVAL MEMORIAL, *France*
Born and enlisted in Belfast. Formerly C/2509, Connaught Rangers.

Devlin, Robert - Private
2794 Royal Irish Regiment 5th Battalion *Died in War on 16 August 1915*
HELLES MEMORIAL, *Turkey*
Born and enlisted in Belfast. Formerly 11168, Royal Irish Rifles.

Devlin, Samuel - Private
2554 Royal Inniskilling Fusiliers 1st Battalion *Died in War on 21 August 1915*
HELLES MEMORIAL, *Turkey*
17 Colin Street, Belfast.

Devlin, Thomas - Private
18536 Royal Irish Regiment 2nd Battalion *Died in War on 20 July 1918*
HAWTHORN RIDGE CEMETERY No.1, AUCHONVILLERS, *France*
Brother of Mr A Devlin, 14 Hardcatle Street, Belfast.

Devlin, William - Lance Corporal
17570 Royal Irish Rifles 14th Battalion *Killed in Action on 1 July 1916*
CONNAUGHT CEMETERY, THIEPVAL, *France*
90, Hanover Street, Belfast.

Devlin, William - Private
7469 Royal Inniskilling Fusiliers 6th Battalion attached 5th Battalion *Age 38 Died of pleurisy on 26 October 1916*
SALONIKA (LEMBET ROAD) MILITARY CEMETERY, *Greece*
Son of Samuel and Bella Devlin, of Belfast; husband of Annie Devlin, of 48, Irwin Street, Belfast.

Dewar, James - Private
1010112 Canadian Infantry 46th Battalion *Died in War on 23 November 1917*
ST. SEVER CEMETERY EXTENSION, ROUEN, *France*
109, University Street, Belfast.

Diamond, Robert - Rifleman
8918 Royal Irish Rifles 1st Battalion *Killed in Action on 21 March 1915*
BAILLEUL COMMUNAL CEMETERY (NORD), *France*
Born and enlisted in Belfast.

Dick, Ingram - Lance Corporal
20441 Royal Irish Fusiliers 9th Battalion *Age 38 Drowned on 30 December 1919*
BELFAST CITY CEMETERY, *United Kingdom*
Son of Ingram and Janet Dick. Born in Belfast. Awarded both the Military Medal and the Croix de Guerre (Belgium).

Dickey, James - Stoker First Class
SS/104940 Royal Navy HMS "Hawke" *Died in War on 15 October 1914*
CHATHAM NAVAL MEMORIAL, *United Kingdom*
12 Canton Street, Belfast.

Dickey, James H - Corporal
8995 Royal Irish Rifles 2nd Battalion *Age 24 Killed in Action on 11 November 1914*
YPRES (MENIN GATE) MEMORIAL, *Belgium*
Son of William and Letitia Dickey, of 6, Dayton Street, Belfast.

Dickey, John - Private
7585 Royal Inniskilling Fusiliers *Age 28 Died of sickness on 28 January 1916*
CARNMONEY CEMETERY, *United Kingdom*
Son of the late William and Jane Dickey; husband of Susan Jane Dickey, of 53, Cosgrave Street, Belfast. Born at Ballyclare.

Dickinson, Frederick - Trooper
731 Household Cavalry Household Battalion *Died in War on 8 July 1917*
CRUMP TRENCH BRITISH CEMETERY FAMBOUX, *France*
Born in Belfast, enlisted in York. Formerly 3875 1st Life Guards.

Dickinson, Robert Edward - Private
152646 Machine Gun Corps (Infantry) *Died in War on 17 October 1918*
QUIETISTE MILITARY CEMETERY LE CATEAU, *France*
Born in Belfast, enlisted in Sunderland. Formerly 44994 Yorkshire Regiment

Dickson, Francis - Rifleman
915 Royal Irish Rifles "C" Company 10th Battalion *Age 27 Killed in Action on 1 July 1916*
THIEPVAL MEMORIAL, France
Son of Robert James and Margaret Dickson, of 35, Farnham Street, Ormeau Road, Belfast.

Dickson, Hugh - Private
3427 Highland Light Infantry 9th (Glasgow Highland) Battalion (Territorial) *Died in War on 12 October 1918*
HIGHLAND CEMETERY LE CATEAU, France
Born in Belfast, enlisted Glasgow.

Dickson, James - Lance Corporal
14370 Royal Irish Rifles 10th Battalion *Age 20 Killed in Action on 1 July 1916*
THIEPVAL MEMORIAL, France
Son of James Dickson of 10, Walnut Place, Belfast. and the late Ellen Dickson.

Dickson, James - Private
72877 Royal Welsh Fusiliers 13th Battalion *Age 19 Died in War on 31 July 1917*
DRAGOON CAMP CEMETERY, Belgium
Son of Robert and Sarah J. Dickson, of 92 and 94, Sandy Row, Belfast.

Dickson, James - Rifleman
16437 Royal Irish Rifles 14th Battalion attached 109th Trench Mortar Battery
Age 22 Died of disease on 28 June 1916
WARLOY-BAILLON COMMUNAL CEMETERY EXTENSION, France
Son of Alexander Dickson, of Belfast.

Dickson, James - Sapper
126265 Corps of Royal Engineers *Died on 24 November 1916*
MINSTER (THANET) CEMETERY, United Kingdom
Born and enlisted in Belfast.

Dickson, John Hetherington - Second Lieutenant
Royal Air Force 27th Squadron *Age 22 Died in War on 14 August 1918*
WANQUETIN COMMUNAL CEMETERY EXTENSION, France
A pilot of a bombing aircraft, he was the only son of Martha Elizabeth and the late John Dickson, of "Clifton", Shandon Park, Knock, Belfast.

Dickson, Robert - Rifleman
10/14369 Royal Irish Rifles 10th Battalion *Age 19 Died in War on 25 November 1915*
SUCRERIE MILITARY CEMETERY, COLINCAMPS, France
Son of Robert and Sarah J. Dickson, of 92 and 94, Sandy Row, Belfast.

Dickson, Robert Adair - Second Lieutenant
Royal Irish Regiment 6th Battalion *Age 36 Died in War on 2 August 1917*
YPRES (MENIN GATE) MEMORIAL, Belgium
Son of John Mitchel Dickson and Mary Gamble Dickson, of 28, Stranmillis Road, Belfast.

Dickson, Robert Fletcher - Private
628042 Canadian Infantry (47th Battalion Western Ontario Regiment) *Died in War on 21 August 1917*
VIMY MEMORIAL, France
10 St Paul's Street, Belfast.

Dickson, Samuel James - Able Seaman
J/8265 Royal Navy HMS "Monmouth" *Age 20 Killed in Action on 1 November 1914*
PLYMOUTH NAVAL MEMORIAL, *United Kingdom*
Son of Matilda Dickson, of 31, Rosebank Street, Belfast, and the late Robert Dickson.
Native of Edenderry, King's County.

Dickson, Thomas - Corporal
48763 Corps of Royal Engineers 18th Division Signal Company *Died in War on 6 August 1917*
YPRES (MENIN GATE) MEMORIAL, *Belgium*
Born in Belfast, enlisted in Glasgow.

Dickson, Thomas - Gunner
41431 Royal Field Artillery 47th Battery *Died in War on 29 August 1918*
VIS-EN-ARTOIS BRITISH CEMETERY, HAUCOURT, *France*
Born in Dromara. Son of William and Agnes Dickson and lived at 30 Peveril Street, Ormeau Road, Belfast

Dickson, Thomas - Private
12772 Royal Irish Rifles 9th Battalion *Killed in Action on 1 July 1916*
THIEPVAL MEMORIAL, *France*
103, Lawnbrook Avenue, Belfast.

Dickson, William - Private
17503 Royal Inniskilling Fusiliers 9th Battalion *Age 29 Died of sickness on 17 November 1918*
BELFAST CITY CEMETERY, *United Kingdom*
Husband of Agnes Dickson, of 92, Matilda Street, Belfast. Had been discharged due to illness.

Dickson, William John - Corporal
12723 Royal Irish Rifles 8th Battalion *Died in War on 11 June 1916*
AUTHUILE MILITARY CEMETERY, *France*
Born and enlisted in Belfast.

Dillon, Joseph - Rifleman
8818 Royal Irish Rifles 2nd Battalion *Died in War on 15 May 1916*
ECOIVRES MILITARY CEMETERY, MONT-ST. ELOI, *France*
Son of Joseph Dillon, of Belfast; husband of Frances Annie Dillon, of 127, Sidney Street West, Belfast.

Dinsmore, Charles - Sergeant
1553 Leinster Regiment 7th Battalion *Age 24 Died in War on 3 August 1917*
YPRES (MENIN GATE) MEMORIAL, *Belgium*
Son of John Dinsmore, of 97, New Lodge Road, Belfast, and the late Margaret Dinsmore.

Dinsmore, William - Driver
T4/127909 Royal Army Service Corps *Died in War on 4 March 1918*
HAZEBROUCK COMMUNAL CEMETERY, *France*
Born and enlisted in Belfast.

Ditty, Albert - Private
19487 Machine Gun Corps (Infantry) 36th Battalion *Age 22 Killed in Action on 21 March 1918*
POZIERES MEMORIAL, *France*
Son of Thomas J. and Mary Ann Ditty, of 5, Everton Street, Belfast.

Dixon, George - Private
1590 Princess Louise's (Argyll & Sutherland Highlanders) 1/5th Battalion
Died in War on 12 July 1915
HELLES MEMORIAL, *Turkey*
Born in Belfast, enlisted in Port Glasgow.

Dixon, Hugh - Private
53357 Royal Army Medical Corps *Died in War on 4 August 1915*
BELFAST CITY CEMETERY, *United Kingdom*
Husband of Hannah Dixon, of 5, Verdun Terrace, Ballygomartin Road, Belfast.

Dixon, James - Leading Stoker
278285 Royal Navy HMS "Vivid" *Age 46 Died of pneumonia on 7 September 1918*
PLYMOUTH NAVAL MEMORIAL, *United Kingdom*
Son of Jane Dixon, of 31, Sandown Road, Belfast, and the late James Dixon.

Dixon, John Harvey - Lance Corporal
14396 Royal Irish Rifles "B" Company 14th Battalion *Age 25 Killed in Action on 16 August 1917*
TYNE COT MEMORIAL, *Belgium*
Son of Joseph and Elizabeth Dixon, of 51, Ormeau Road, Belfast.

Dixon, Richard - Rifleman
19/837 Royal Irish Rifles 10th Battalion *Age 22 Killed in Action on 7 June 1917*
LONE TREE CEMETERY, *Belgium*
Son of John and Eliza Dixon, of 49, Kendal Street, Belfast.

Dixon, Thomas George - Private
24019 Royal Irish Fusiliers 9th Battalion *Age 20 Killed in Action on 30 September 1918*
DUHALLOW A.D.S. CEMETERY, *Belgium*
Son of William and Mary J. Dixon. of 67, Delhi Street, Belfast.

Dixon, Wesley - Lance Corporal
12725 Royal Irish Rifles "C" Company 8th Battalion *Age 23 Died in War on 23 November 1917*
CAMBRAI MEMORIAL, LOUVERVAL, *France*
Son of Mr and Mrs W J Dixon, of 32, Mount Street, Belfast.

Dixon, William James - Private
10849 Alexandra, Princess of Wales's Own (Yorkshire Regiment) 6th Battalion
Died in War on 22 August 1915
HELLES MEMORIAL, *Turkey*
Born in Belfast, enlisted Middlesbrough.

Dobbin, Albert - Aircraftman Second Class
298101 Royal Air Force *Age 18 Died as a result of war on 28 May 1919*
DRUMBO (HOLY TRINITY) CHURCH OF IRELAND CHURCHYARD, *United Kingdom*
Son of Hugh and Jane Scott Dobbin, of 115, Hillman Street, Belfast.

Dobbin, William Kinnear - Private
SPTS/266 Royal Fusiliers 23rd Battalion *Age 26 Died in War on 27 July 1916*
THIEPVAL MEMORIAL, France
Son of Florence Brandon (formerly Dobbin), of "Roseville", of 258, Antrim Road, Belfast, and the late John Muir Dobbin. A Chartered Accountant.

Dobson, Alexander - Driver
Royal Engineers *Died in War*
16, Roe Street Belfast.

Dobson, Eric Trist - Lieutenant
124th Duchess of Connaught's Own Baluchistan Infantry 2nd Battalion *Age 23 Died as a result of war on 8 June 1920*
PORT SAID WAR MEMORIAL CEMETERY, Egypt
Born in Belfast. Son of William James and Violet Mary Dobson, of the Provincial Bank of Ireland, Kilkeel, County Down.

Dobson, John - Second Lieutenant
Royal Irish Fusiliers *Age 26 Died in War on 4 May 1917*
AUBIGNY COMMUNAL CEMETERY EXTENSION, France
Son of William and Jane Dobson; husband of Mary Hopper Dobson of "Oakland", Chichester Park, Belfast.

Dobson, Parke - Private
2513 Lancers 5th (Royal Irish) *Age 24 Died in War on 8 September 1914*
PERREUSE CHATEAU FRANCO BRITISH NATIONAL CEMETERY, France
Son of William H. and Eleanor Dobson, of Roden Terrace, Woodstock Road, Belfast.

Docherty, Charles - Private
16959 Highland Light Infantry 10th (Service) Battalion *Killed in Action on 25 September 1915*
LOOS MEMORIAL, France
Born in Belfast, enlisted Lanarkshire, Scotland.

Dodds, James - Rifleman
14381 Royal Irish Rifles 10th Battalion *Died in War on 17 August 1917*
POTIJZE CHATEAU WOOD CEMETERY, Belgium
Born and enlisted in Belfast.

Dodds, John - Private
6945 Royal Inniskilling Fusiliers 1st Battalion *Died of Wounds on 31 August 1915*
CAIRO WAR MEMORIAL CEMETERY, Egypt
45 Disraeli Street, Belfast.

Dodds, William - Rifleman
5796 Royal Irish Rifles 1st Battalion *Age 18 Died in War on 11 April 1916*
BECOURT MILITARY CEMETERY, BECORDEL-BECOURT, France
Son of James and Annie Dodds, of 62, Seaview Street, Belfast.

Doey, Henry Cooke - Second Mate
Mercantile Marine S.S. "Queen" (London)
Age 60 Drowned, as a result of an attack by an enemy submarine on 28 June 1918
TOWER HILL MEMORIAL, United Kingdom
Son of Hugh Doey; husband of Constance Doey (née Dawn), of 27, Rake Lane, Liscard, Cheshire. Born at Belfast.

Doggart, Alexander - Rifleman
389 Royal Irish Rifle 2nd Battalion *Died in War on 19 June 1917*
YPRES (MENIN GATE) MEMORIAL, Belgium
Brother of Mr Adam Doggart, 2 Matlock Street, Belfast.

Doggart, James - Rifleman
17575 Royal Irish Rifles 13th Battalion *Killed in Action on 1 July 1916*
THIEPVAL MEMORIAL, France
Born in Belfast, enlisted Holywood.

Doggart, William - Rifleman
329 Royal Irish Rifles 12th Battalion *Died in War on 22 November 1917*
CAMBRAI MEMORIAL, France
Born and enlisted in Holywood, resident in Belfast.

Doggart, William Lemon - Private
679060 Canadian Infantry (Central Ontario Regiment) 15th Battalion
Age 44 Died of Wounds received 23rd July on 26 July 1917
LILLERS COMMUNAL CEMETERY, France
Son of the late Isaac and Alice Doggart, of Belfast, Ireland; husband of Agnes Doggart, of 4, Commodore Avenue, Silverthorn, Toronto. Enlisted in February 1916. An Anglican, he had worked in Canada as a painter.

Dogherty, Patrick - Private
28897 Royal Irish Fusiliers 1st Battalion *Age 20 Died in War on 1 October 1918*
TYNE COT MEMORIAL, Belgium
Son of John and Elizabeth Dogherty, of 44, Conway Street, Belfast.

Doherty, Charles - Private
1552 Leinster Regiment 7th Battalion *Died in War on 3 September 1916*
THIEPVAL MEMORIAL, France
87 Albert Street, Belfast.

Doherty, Charles - Private
22006 Royal Dublin Fusiliers 6th Battalion *Died in War on 9 December 1915*
DOIRAN MEMORIAL, Greece
Survived by a widow and young daughter. 25 Getty Street, Belfast.

Doherty, Francis - Private
20202 Princess Victoria's (Royal Irish Fusiliers) 8th Battalion *Died in War on 9 December 1916*
LOKER CHURCHYARD, Belgium
Born in Belfast, enlisted Glasgow.

Doherty, George - Private
9163 Royal Inniskilling Fusiliers 1st Battalion *Died in War on 24 August 1915*
HELLES MEMORIAL, Turkey
Born in Belfast, enlisted Ballykinlar.

Doherty, George - Rifleman
7876 Royal Irish Rifles 2nd Battalion *Age 19 Killed in Action on 8 July 1916*
THIEPVAL MEMORIAL, France
Son of George and Margaret Doherty, of 9, Cromac Square, Belfast.

Journey of Remembering

Doherty, John - Private
12586 Highland Light Infantry 10/11th Battalion *Died in War on 9 April 1918*
PLOEGSTEERT MEMORIAL, Belgium
Born in Belfast, enlisted Lanarkshire, Scotland.

Doherty, R - Private
32012 Royal Inniskilling Fusiliers "A" Company 1st Battalion
Age 20 Died as a result of war on 9 September 1920
KARACHI 1914-1918 WAR MEMORIAL, Pakistan
Son of Alexander and Annie Doherty, of Belfast, Ireland.

Doherty, William - Gunner
2166 Royal Garrison Artillery "X" Trench Mortar Battery *Killed by a shell splinter on 28 March 1916*
YPRES (MENIN GATE) MEMORIAL, Belgium
Husband of Annie Doherty, 40 Roumania Street, Belfast.

Doherty, William - Sergeant
4476 Royal Irish Rifles 1st Battalion *Killed in Action on 16 August 1917*
TYNE COT MEMORIAL, Belgium
Born and enlisted in Belfast.

Dolan, James - Rifleman
9010 Royal Irish Rifles 2nd Battalion *Killed In Action on 20 May 1916*
ECOIVRES MILITARY CEMETERY, MONT-ST. ELOI, France
Born and enlisted in Belfast.

Doloughan, James - Corporal
3/24785 Royal Inniskilling Fusiliers 5th Battalion *Age 34 Killed in Action on 27 December 1917*
JERUSALEM WAR CEMETERY, Israel
Son of John and Eliza Jane Doloughan, of Belfast. Formerly a diver, Royal Navy.

Donaghy, Edward - Private
23452 Princess Victoria's (Royal Irish Fusiliers) 1st Battalion *Died in War on 11 April 1917*
HERVIN FARM BRITISH CEMETERY ST LAURENT-BLANGY, France
Born and enlisted in Belfast.

Donaghy, Owen - Private
22543 Machine Gun Corps (Infantry) *Died in War on 27 December 1917*
BELFAST (MILLTOWN) ROMAN CATHOLIC CEMETERY, United Kingdom
Born in Belfast, enlisted Barrow-in-Furness, England. Formerly 2367 Lancashire Regiment.

Donaghy, Patrick James - Private
3846 Princess Victoria's (Royal Irish Fusiliers) 1st Battalion *Died in War on 15 April 1917*
ARRAS MEMORIAL, France
Born and enlisted in Belfast.

Donaldson, David - Private
9455 Royal Inniskilling Fusiliers 3rd Battalion *Died in War on 12 July 1917*
BELFAST (MILLTOWN) ROMAN CATHOLIC CEMETERY, United Kingdom
Son of Mrs Mary Donaldson, 19 Foundry Street, Belfast.

Donaldson, Frederick - Rifleman
6052 Royal Irish Rifles 7th Battalion *Age 18 Died in War on 5 September 1916*
THIEPVAL MEMORIAL, France
Son of Mrs. Agnes Donaldson, of 2, Dickson Street, Belfast.

Donaldson, James - Lance Corporal
6920 Royal Irish Rifles 2nd Battalion *Age 22 Died of Wounds on 10 August 1917*
LONGUENESSE (ST. OMER) SOUVENIR CEMETERY, France
Son of James and Jane Donaldson, of 32, Ton Street, Belfast.

Donaldson, Robert - Rifleman
14/17579 Royal Irish Rifles 13th Battalion *Age 26 Died of Wounds on 4 November 1916*
WIMEREUX COMMUNAL CEMETERY, France
Son of George and Jane Donaldson, of St. Ives Gardens, Stranmillis, Belfast.
Late of Magherana, Waringstown, County Down.

Donaldson, Samuel - Rifleman
14401 Royal Irish Rifles 14th Battalion *Age 22 Killed in Action on 1 July 1916*
THIEPVAL MEMORIAL, France
Son of Jane Donaldson, of "Hillcrest" 82 Woodvale Road, Belfast, and the late William Donaldson.

Donaldson, Thomas - Private
22693 Royal Irish Fusiliers 7th Battalion *Age 19 Died in War on 27 April 1916*
LOOS MEMORIAL, France
Son of William and Mary Donaldson, of 38, Butler Street, Belfast.

Donegan, Patrick - Private
8567 Royal Dublin Fusiliers 1st Battalion *Died in War on 1 January 1916*
HELLES MEMORIAL, Turkey
Born and enlisted in Dublin, resident in Belfast.

Donnan, John - Private
42411 Royal Irish Fusiliers 1st Battalion *Age 38 Died in War on 1 October 1918*
DADIZEELE NEW BRITISH CEMETERY, Belgium
Son of Francis Donnan, of 6, Henryville Street, Belfast.

Donnell, Charles - Private
15280 Connaught Rangers 5th Battalion *Died in War on 8 October 1918*
BEAUREVOIR BRITISH CEMETERY, France
Born in Castlewellan County Down, resident in Belfast. Formerly 14868, Royal Irish Fusiliers.

Donnelly Hugh, - Stoker First Class
SS/105635 Royal Navy HMS "Aboukir" *Died in War on 22 September 1914*
CHATHAM NAVAL MEMORIAL, United Kingdom
22 College Square North, Belfast.

Donnelly Hugh, Frederick - Rifleman
14512 Royal Irish Rifles 10th Battalion *Killed in Action on 1 July 1916*
THIEPVAL MEMORIAL, France
Born in Stewartstown, County Tyrone. Enlisted and resident in Belfast.
Member of Fisherwick Presbyterian Church.

Donnelly, Daniel - Private
8752 Royal Irish Fusiliers 1st Battalion *Age 27 Died in War on 14 November 1914*
HOUPLINES COMMUNAL CEMETERY EXTENSION, France
Son of William and Jane Donnelly, of 12, Getty Street, Belfast. Born at Dungannon, County Tyrone.

Donnelly, George - Rifleman
14379 Royal Irish Rifles 2nd Battalion *Killed In Action on 9 September 1918*
PLOEGSTEERT MEMORIAL, Belgium
Born and enlisted in Belfast.

Donnelly, Gilbert - Lieutenant
Royal Munster Fusiliers 1st Battalion *Age 20 Killed in Action on 21 March 1918*
POZIERES MEMORIAL, France,
Son of John and Mima Donnelly, of Glastonbury Avenue, Belfast.

Donnelly, Hugh - Sergeant
132353 Royal Fusiliers 47th Battalion *Age 35 Died of heart failure on 30 October 1919*
LES BARAQUES MILITARY CEMETERY, SANGATTE, France
Son of Francis and Maggie Donnelly, of 14, Milton Street, Belfast; husband of Ellen Donnelly, of 51, Seaforde Street, Belfast.

Donnelly, James - Rifleman
6971 Royal Irish Rifles 2nd Battalion *Died in War on 18 November 1918*
NIEDERZWEHREN CEMETERY, Germany
Brother of Michael Donnelly, 95 Albert Street, Belfast.

Donnelly, James Alexander - Second Lieutenant
Royal Flying Corps 59th Squadron and General List *Age 44 Died of Wounds on 31 March 1918*
DOULLENS COMMUNAL CEMETERY EXTENSION No.1, France
Husband of Sarah A. Donnelly, of 12, Willowbank Street, Belfast.

Donnelly, James Joseph - Private
25282 Royal Inniskilling Fusiliers 1st Battalion *Killed in Action on 19 May 1917*
ARRAS MEMORIAL, France
Born and enlisted in Belfast.

Donnelly, John - Private
17036 Royal Scots Fusiliers 6/7th Battalion *Died in War on 11 April 1917*
ARRAS MEMORIAL, France
Born in Belfast. Lived in Glasgow when enlisted.

Donnelly, John - Private
3444 Royal Irish Fusiliers 7th/8th Battalion *Age 26 Died in War on 24 January 1918*
STE. EMILIE VALLEY CEMETERY, VILLERS-FAUCON, France
Son of Patrick Donnelly of Belfast; husband of Mary J. Donnelly, of Ballytrudden, Blackwatertown, County Armagh.

Donnelly, John - Rifleman
7735 Royal Irish Rifles 6th Battalion *Age 25 Died of dysentery on 20 July 1916*
SALONIKA (LEMBET ROAD) MILITARY CEMETERY, Greece
Husband of Elizabeth Donnelly, of 70, Bellevue Street, Belfast.

Donnelly, John Joseph - Fireman
914303 Mercantile Marine Reserve H.M.M.S. "Blackmorevale" *Age 19 Killed by mine explosion off Montrose on 1 May 1918*
PLYMOUTH NAVAL MEMORIAL, *United Kingdom*
Son of Margaret Milligan (formerly Donnelly), of 41, York Lane, Belfast, and the late John Donnelly.

Donnelly, Joseph - Petty Officer Motor Mechanic
F/9833 Royal Naval Air Service HMS "President II" *Age 28 Drowned on 11 June 1916*
HAIDAR PASHA MEMORIAL, *Turkey*
Son of Thomas and Margaret Donnelly, of 77, Alexandra Park Avenue, Belfast.

Donnelly, Joseph - Private
3470 Royal Inniskilling Fusiliers 2nd Battalion *Died in War on 27 March 1915*
BETHUNE TOWN CEMETERY, *France*
Survived by his mother at 1 Grosvenor Place, Belfast. Employed by Combe Barbours he was a member of the Irish National Volunteers. Two brothers also served.

Donnelly, Joseph - Private
9563 Royal Dublin Fusiliers 2nd Battalion *Age 20 Died in War on 24 May 1915*
YPRES (MENIN GATE) MEMORIAL, *Belgium*
Son of Mr. and Mrs. B. Donnelly, of 20, Springview Street, Belfast.

Donnelly, Patrick J - Lance Corporal
10814 Royal Inniskilling Fusiliers 2nd Battalion *Age 22 Killed in Action on 8 August 1917*
COXYDE MILITARY CEMETERY, *Belgium*
Son of Edward and Eliza Jane Donnelly (née Grant), of 42, Amon Street, Old Lodge Road, Belfast. Also served at the Dardanelles.

Donnelly, Robert - Private
21055 Royal Irish Fusiliers "B" Company 8th Battalion *Age 36 Died of Wounds on 9 June 1916*
ETRETAT CHURCHYARD, *France*
Son of Daniel and Mary Donnelly, of 84, Brookfield Street, Crumlin Road, Belfast.

Donnelly, Thomas - Private
12925 Royal Scots Fusiliers 7th Battalion *Died in War on 26 September 1915*
LOOS MEMORIAL, *France*
Born in Derrynoose, County Armagh Enlisted in Uddington, Lanarkshire, Scotland. Resident in Belfast.

Donnelly, Thomas - Private
16399 Royal Irish Fusiliers 5th Battalion *Died in War on 7 August 1915*
HELLES MEMORIAL, *Turkey*
A native of Armagh he lived at 10 Inkerman Street, Belfast. His older brother, Patrick, a member of the Irish National Volunteers also served and survived.

Donnelly, Thomas - Private
8220 Royal Inniskilling Fusiliers 2nd Battalion *Killed in Action on 26 August 1914*
ESNES COMMUNAL CEMETERY, *France*
Born and enlisted in Belfast.

Donnelly, William - Lance Corporal
2600 Royal Inniskilling Fusiliers 1st Battalion *Killed in Action on 1 July 1916*
ANCRE BRITISH CEMETERY, BEAUMONT-HAMEL, *France*
222 Leopold Street, Belfast.

Donnelly, William - Private
3385 Royal Inniskilling Fusiliers 2nd Battalion *Killed in Action on 23 August 1918*
MONT NOIR MILITARY CEMETERY, ST. JANS-CAPPEL, France
Born and enlisted in Belfast.

Donnelly, William John - Private
305510 Tank Corps 7th Battalion *Age 21 Died in War on 13 April 1918*
LOOS MEMORIAL, France
Son of Alexander and Ellen Donnelly, of 14, Locan Street, Belfast. His father also served.

Donohoe, John - Sapper
19714 Royal Engineers 57th Field Company *Died in War on 9 September 1914*
LE TOURET MEMORIAL, France
Son of ex-Head Constable Donohoe of 10 Pim Street, Belfast.

Donohue, James - Private
10315 Royal Inniskilling Fusiliers "A" Company 1st Battalion *Age 32 Killed in Action on 1 July 1916*
THIEPVAL MEMORIAL, France
Son of the late Mr. and Mrs. I. M. Donohue, of 76, Servia Street, Belfast.

Donovan, John Charles - Sergeant
457114 Canadian Infantry (Quebec Regiment) 87th Battalion *Age 38 Died in War on 31 May 1918*
PERNES BRITISH CEMETERY, France
Son of James and Frances Donovan, of Tralee, County Kerry; husband of Alice Donovan, of 29, Derryvolgie Avenue, Malone Road, Belfast, Ireland. A member of Church of Ireland he was born at Tarbert, County Kerry. Worked originally as a clerk.

Dooley, James - Lance Corporal
9075 Irish Guards 2nd Battalion *Died in War on 9 October 1917*
ARTILLERY WOOD CEMETERY, Belgium
Mother lived at 47 Altcar Street, Belfast.

Doran, Arthur - Corporal
7451 Royal Irish Rifles 2nd Battalion *Killed in Action on 27 August 1914*
CAUDRY OLD COMMUNAL CEMETERY, France
Husband of Sarah Doran, 12, Merkland Street, Belfast. One of the first Belfast men to die in the war. Active in politics, his death was marked by a press notice from the Independent Labour Party.

Doran, Bernard - Private
7228 Royal Irish Rifles 2nd Battalion *Died in War on 18 December 1914*
YPRES (MENIN GATE) MEMORIAL, Belgium
69 Ardilea Street, Belfast.

Doran, John R - Private
25977 Royal Irish Fusiliers 1st Battalion *Died in War on 27 September 1917*
METZ-EN-COUTURE COMMUNAL CEMETERY BRITISH EXTENSION, France
11 Boomer Street, Belfast.

Doran, Michael - Rifleman
6587 Royal Irish Rifles 2nd Battalion *Died Of Wounds on 17 April 1915*
ELZENWALLE BRASSERIE CEMETERY, France
Born in Belfast, enlisted in Newtownards.

Dorman, Albert - Sapper
25292 Royal Engineers 54th Company *Age 21 Died of wounds on 4 October 1915*
BETHUNE TOWN CEMETERY, France
Son of Teresa Dorman, of 17, Steen Street, Belfast.

Dorman, Charles Colombus - Able Seaman
SS/3434 Royal Navy HMS "Wear" *Age 24 Died in War on 31 August 1916*
GILLINGHAM (WOODLANDS) CEMETERY, United Kingdom
Son of James and Margaret Dorman, of 5, Aughrim Street, Belfast.

Dornan, Francis - Lance Corporal
9433 Royal Irish Rifles 1st Battalion *Killed in Action on 9 May 1915*
PLOEGSTEERT MEMORIAL, Belgium
Born and enlisted in Belfast.

Dornan, George - Private
9065 Scots Guards 1st Battalion *Age 26 Died in War on 25 January 1915*
LE TOURET MEMORIAL, France
Son of James and Rachel Dornan, of 95, Donegall Road, Belfast.

Dornan, George Irwin - Lance Corporal
1641 Australian Infantry 44th Battalion *Age 33 Killed in Action on 7 April 1918*
VILLERS-BRETONNEUX MILITARY CEMETERY, France
Son of James and Minnie Dornan. Born in Belfast, Ireland.

Dornan, Henry - Rifleman
20484 Royal Irish Rifles *Died in War on 11 September 1918*
UNDERHILL FARM CEMETERY, United Kingdom
66 Cambrai Street, Belfast.

Dornan, James - Private
267443 Seaforth Highlanders (Ross-shire Buffs, the Duke of Albany's) 6th Battalion
Died in War on 16 May 1917
ARRAS MEMORIAL, France
Born in Belfast, enlisted Paisley, Scotland. Resident in Belfast.

Dornan, John - Private
12779 Royal Inniskilling Fusiliers 2nd Battalion *Age 29 Killed in Action on 1 July 1916*
THIEPVAL MEMORIAL, France
Son of William and M. A. Dornan, of 19, Rosebery Street, Connswater, Belfast.

Dornan, Robert - Private
7989 Royal Inniskilling Fusiliers 2nd Battalion *Died in War on 21 October 1914*
PLOEGSTEERT MEMORIAL, Belgium
Born in Belfast, enlisted Dungannon.

Dornan, Thomas - Private
13101 Royal Inniskilling Fusiliers 11th Battalion *Killed in Action on 1 July 1916*
THIEPVAL MEMORIAL, France
Born Ballynafeigh and enlisted in Belfast.

Journey of Remembering

Dorrian, Hugh - Corporal
8065 Royal Irish Fusiliers 9th Battalion *Killed in Action on 16 August 1917*
TYNE COT CEMETERY, *Belgium*
Husband of Lizzie Dorrian, 12 Bombay Street, Belfast.

Dorrian, John - Private
95096 King's (Liverpool Regiment) 13th Battalion *Died in War on 31 August 1918*
ECCOUST-ST MEIN, BRITISH CEMETERY, *France*
Born in Belfast, enlisted in Armagh. Formerly 23339, Royal Irish Fusiliers.

Dorris, Henry (Harry) - Corporal
17584 Royal Irish Rifles 14th Battalion *Age 21 Killed in Action on 16 August 1917*
TYNE COT MEMORIAL, *Belgium*
Son of Elizabeth Dorris, of 12, Bootle Street, Belfast, and the late Henry Dorris.

Dorrity, George - Rifleman
16443 Royal Irish Rifles "B" Company 14th Battalion *Age 21 Died in War on 6 April 1916*
HAMEL MILITARY CEMETERY, BEAUMONT-HAMEL, *France*
Son of William Dorrity, of 29, Elaine Street, Stranmillis, Belfast.

Douey, Ernest - Lance Corporal
914042 Royal Irish Rifles 9th Battalion *Died of Wounds on 1 July 1916*
BAILLEUL COMMUNAL CEMETERY EXTENSION (NORD), *France*
Third son of Thomas and Isabella, 34 Penrith Street, Belfast.

Douey, Walter - Sergeant
14384 Royal Irish Rifles 9th Battalion *Age 20 Killed in Action on 1 July 1916*
THIEPVAL MEMORIAL, *France*
Son of Thomas and Isabella Douey, of 54, Penrith Street, Belfast.

Dougal, Robert Joseph - Lieutenant
Northumberland Fusiliers 21st (Tyneside Scottish) Battalion *Age 21 Killed in Action on 1 July 1916*
THIEPVAL MEMORIAL, *France*
Son of Susan Dougal, of 34, May Street, Belfast, and the late Hugh Dougal.
A member of Andrew Dougal & Son, Belfast.

Dougall, John - Private
25514 Highland Light Infantry 2nd Battalion *Died in War on 13 November 1916*
REDAN RIDGE CEMETERY No 2, *France*
Born in Belfast. Enlisted in Leith, Scotland.

Dougan, Alexander - Rifleman
10983 Royal Irish Rifles 1st Battalion *Age 19 Killed in Action on 11 September 1918*
UNDERHILL FARM CEMETERY, *Belgium*
Son of William and Elizabeth Dougan, of 88, Roden Street, Belfast.

Dougan, Hugh - Lance Corporal
6512 Royal Irish Rifles 16th Battalion *Age 22 Killed in Action on 21 March 1918*
POZIERES MEMORIAL, *France*
Son of John and Sarah Dougan, of 4, Benburb Street, Belfast.

Dougherty, Patrick Joseph - Rifleman
3994 Royal Irish Rifles 2nd Battalion *Age 30 Killed in Action on 5 May 1916*
ECOIVRES MILITARY CEMETERY, MONT-ST. ELOI, France
Son of the late John and Cecilia Dougherty, of Belfast.

Dougherty, Timothy - Rifleman
5480 Royal Irish Rifles 2nd Battalion *Age 35 Died of Wounds on 4 May 1918*
BELFAST (MILLTOWN) ROMAN CATHOLIC CEMETERY, United Kingdom
The husband of Mary Dougherty, his second wife, of 12, Cairns Street, Belfast. Had peacetime service with the Royal Irish Fusiliers and, possibly, the Royal Garrison Artillery. In any case, he rejoined the Army at the start of the Great War. By May of 1918, probably as the result of gassing, he was admitted to the Clifton Street, Belfast Military Hospital. He died there of septicaema.

Douglas, Arthur James - Cadet
182273 Royal Air Force 8th Cadet Wing *Age 30 Died of pneumonia on 29 September 1918*
SHORNCLIFFE MILITARY CEMETERY, United Kingdom
Son of Richard and Elizabeth Douglas, of 4, Glengareff Terrace, Three Anchor Bay, Cape Town. Born in Belfast, Ireland

Douglas, David - Private
5225 Royal Munster Fusiliers (formerly 12974 Royal Inniskilling Fusiliers) "B" Company 6th Battalion *Age 34 Died in War on 29 December 1917*
RAMLEH WAR CEMETERY, Israel
Son of Thomas and Grace Douglas; husband of the late Agnes McVeigh Douglas, 67 Dunvegan Street.

Douglas, Fred - Private
CH/19888 Royal Marine Light Infantry HMS "Newcastle" *Age 20 Died in War on 2 April 1918*
BELFAST CITY CEMETERY, United Kingdom
Son of John and Jane Douglas, of 35, Danube Street, Belfast.

Douglas, Hugh - Private
3061 Royal Inniskilling Fusiliers 1st Battalion *Age 22 Killed in Action on 1 July 1916*
THIEPVAL MEMORIAL, France
Son of the late Jane Douglas, of 23, Malcolm Street, Belfast.

Douglas, R - Rifleman
18/767 Royal Irish Rifles 11th Battalion *Age 20 Died in War on 1 September 1916*
RATION FARM (LA PLUS DOUVE) ANNEXE, Belgium
Son of John and Agnes Douglas, of 13, Eversleigh Street, Belfast.

Douglas, Richard - Rifleman
16446 Royal Irish Rifles 14th Battalion *Age 22 Killed in Action on 16 August 1917*
TYNE COT MEMORIAL, Belgium
Son of John and Hannah Douglas, of 24, Malone Avenue, Belfast.

Douglas, Samuel - Able Seaman
226243 Royal Navy HMS "Magic" *Died in War on 10 April 1918*
PLYMOUTH NAVAL MEMORIAL, United Kingdom
67 Dunvegan Street, Belfast.

Journey of Remembering

Douglas, William John - Private
25189 Royal Irish Fusiliers 1st Battalion *Age 19 Killed in Action on 1 October 1918*
DADIZEELE NEW BRITISH CEMETERY, Belgium
Son of John and Alice Douglas, of 42, Theodore Street, Belfast.

Dowdall, John - Lance Bombardier
4107 Royal Garrison Artillery *Died in War on 10 September 1918*
WEYMOUTH CEMETERY, United Kingdom
Born in Birkenhead, enlisted Carrickfergus, resident Belfast.

Dowds, Henry - Rifleman
1762 Royal Irish Rifles 15th Battalion *Killed in Action on 1 July 1916*
CONNAUGHT CEMETERY, THIEPVAL, France
Husband of Minnie Bertha Dowds of 15, Jonesboro' Street, Belfast. A member of the Salvation Army. He left a son, Horace.

Dowie, James - Private
10047 Royal Irish Fusiliers 1st Battalion *Age 24 Killed in Action on 26 August 1914*
LA FERTE-SOUS-JOUARRE MEMORIAL, France
Son of Mrs. Elizabeth Dowie, of 37, Devonshire Street, Belfast.

Downey, Andrew - Rifleman
644 Royal Irish Rifles 9th Battalion *Died in War on 30 November 1917*
CAMBRAI MEMORIAL, LOUVERVALE, France
1, Maryville Avenue, Belfast. A native of Newry.

Downey, Joseph - Private
3554 Seaforth Highlanders 3rd/4th Battalion *Died in War on 28 January 1916*
BELFAST (MILLTOWN) ROMAN CATHOLIC CEMETERY, United Kingdom
Husband of Annie Downey, of 228, York Street, Belfast.

Downey, James - Rifleman
9/14495 Royal Irish Rifles 9th Battalion *Killed by a sniper on 15 October 1916*
ST QUENTIN CABARET MILITARY CEMETERY, Belgium
Born in Ballyclare County Antrim, thereafter lived in Ballysillan, Belfast when enlisted. Shot by a sniper. He was the only fatal casualty suffered by his unit on that day.

Downey, John - Lance Corporal
12446 Royal Irish Fusiliers 2nd Battalion *Age 23 Killed in Action on 7 November 1917*
GAZA WAR CEMETERY, Israel
Son of the late Robert and Annie Downey; husband of Christina Downey (née Burgess), of 10, Grove Road, Portobello, Dublin. Born at Belfast.

Downey, John - Private
19347 Royal Inniskilling Fusiliers 9th Battalion *Killed in Action on 1 July 1916*
THIEPVAL MEMORIAL, France
Born in Belfast. Enlisted Bundoran, Co Donegal.

Downey, John - Private
5067 Royal Munster Fusiliers 2nd Battalion *Died in War on 10 November 1917*
TYNE COT MEMORIAL, Belgium
Born in Gilford, County Down. Enlisted and resident in Belfast. Formerly 13709, Royal Inniskilling Fusiliers.

Belfast Book of Honour

Downey, Sydney James Livingston - Second Lieutenant
Royal Irish Rifles 14th Battalion *Age 21 Killed in Action on 17 June 1917*
SPANBROEKMOLEN BRITISH CEMETERY, Belgium
Son of James Livingston and Marion Louisa Downey, of 7, Hampden Terrace, Rugby Street, Belfast. Killed at the Battle of Messines Ridge.

Dowey, Thomas - Sergeant
9948 Royal Inniskilling Fusiliers 2nd Battalion *Died in War on 5 January 1917*
PORTE-DE-PARIS CEMETERY, CAMBRAI, France
Son of Mrs M Dowey, 38, Mervue Street, Belfast.

Downey, William Clarence - Private
4773 Australian Infantry, A.I.F. 15th Battalion *Killed in Action on 23 September 1918*
STOURBRIDGE CEMETERY, United Kingdom
Son of Michael and Jane Downey; husband of Martha Downey, of 31, Third Street, Belfast, Ireland. Born in Australia.

Downing, James - Second Lieutenant
Royal Irish Regiment *Died in War on 3 September 1916*
THIEPVAL MEMORIAL, France
South Parade, Belfast. Son of John and Rebecca Downing, Hollyhouse, Hill Hall, Lisburn.

Dowse, Robert Joseph Gordon - Captain
Royal Army Service Corps VIII Corps Troops M.T. Company *Age 32 Died as a result of war on 19 December 1918*
DOUAI BRITISH CEMETERY, CUINCY, France
Eldest son of the Very Rev. William Dowse, Dean of Connor, of St. Thomas' Rectory, Belfast; husband of Kathleen Dowse, of 27, Gordon Place, Kensington, London.

Doyle, Andrew - Lance Corporal
8102 Royal Irish Rifles 2nd Battalion *Killed in Action on 27 October 1914*
LE TOURET MEMORIAL, France
Born in Belfast. Enlisted in Brighton, England.

Doyle, Andrew - Sergeant
1377 Leinster Regiment 7th Battalion *Age 32 Killed in Action on 24 June 1916*
ST. PATRICK'S CEMETERY, LOOS, France
Husband of Margaret Doyle, of 297, Crumlin Road, Belfast.

Doyle, Daniel - Private
3848 Princess Victoria's (Royal Irish Fusiliers) 1st Battalion *Died in War on 11 April 1917*
ARRAS MEMORIAL, France
Born and enlisted in Belfast.

Doyle, Patrick - Rifleman
6397 Royal Irish Rifles 1st Battalion *Age 28 Killed in Action on 9 May 1915*
PLOEGSTEERT MEMORIAL, Belgium
Son of Catherine Doyle, of 44, Ton Street, Belfast, and the late Michael Doyle.

Dragonetti, M - Private
24770 Royal Irish Fusiliers 1st Battalion *Age 18 Died in War on 11 April 1917*
BROWN'S COPSE CEMETERY, ROEUX, France
Son of Pasquale Dragonetti, of 70, Great Patrick Street, Belfast.

Drain, John - Private
2337 Connaught Rangers 6th Battalion *Died in War on 9 September 1916*
THIEPVAL MEMORIAL, France
Eldest son of James and Annie Drain, 25, Peel Street, Belfast.

Drain, Robert - Private
43079 Royal Irish Fusiliers 8th Battalion *Died in War on 21 September 1916*
ETAPLES MILITARY CEMETERY, France
Foster-son of Mary McCarthy, of 6, Hillview Terrace, Greencastle, Belfast.

Draper, Charles - Private
37688 Royal Berkshire Regiment 8th Battalion *Died of pneumonia on 23 February 1917*
ST. SEVER CEMETERY EXTENSION, ROUEN, France
230, Conway Street, Belfast.

Drennan, David - Rifleman
18/4 Royal Irish Rifles 11th Battalion *Age 37 Killed in Action on 1 September 1916*
RATION FARM (LA PLUS DOUVE) ANNEXE, Belgium
Son of James and Eliza Drennan, of Belfast; husband of Hester Drennan, of 42, Vernon Street, Belfast.

Duff, Daniel - Private
18342 Leinster Regiment 2nd Battalion *Killed in Action on 14 October 1918*
DADIZEELE NEW BRITISH CEMETERY, Belgium
Husband of Mrs. J. Duff, of 7, Portland Place, Belfast. Formerly 2512 6th Battalion Connaught Rangers.

Duff, John - Second Lieutenant
Royal Inniskilling Fusiliers 3rd Battalion attached 1st Battalion *Killed in Action on 25 August 1918*
BERTENACRE MILITARY CEMETERY, FLETRE, France
15 Deacon Street, Belfast.

Duff, Walter Shaw - Stoker First Class
K/9746 Royal Navy HMS "Coquette" *Age 23 Killed by mine explosion in North Sea on 7 March 1916*
CHATHAM NAVAL MEMORIAL, United Kingdom
Son of Mr. and Mrs. James Duff, of 202, Oldpark Road, Belfast.

Duff, William - Rifleman
6607 Royal Irish Rifles "C" Company 2nd Battalion *Age 21 Killed in Action at Hill 60 on 8 May 1915*
DIVISIONAL COLLECTING POST CEMETERY AND EXTENSION, Belgium
Son of David and Cathrine Duff, of 45, Gertrude Street, Newtownards Road, Belfast.

Duffield, Christopher - Rifleman
13143 Royal Irish Rifles 8th Battalion *Died in War on 1 April 1915*
BELFAST CITY CEMETERY, United Kingdom
(Served as McPHERSON). Son of Elizabeth Dougherty (formerly Duffield, née McPherson), of 180, Woodstock Road, Belfast, and the late Christopher Duffield.

Duffin, Patrick - Private
1547 Leinster Regiment 7th Battalion *Died of Wounds on 5 September 1916*
CORBIE COMMUNAL CEMETERY EXTENSION, France
10 Varna Street, Belfast.

Duffy, Alexander Thomas - Petty Officer Stoker
310731 Royal Navy HMS "Mary Rose"
Age 29 Killed in Action protecting convoy in North Sea on 17 October 1917
CHATHAM NAVAL MEMORIAL, *United Kingdom*
Husband of Agnes Duffy, of 29, Mackey Street, Belfast.

Duffy, Francis - Rifleman
4253 Royal Irish Rifles 2nd Battalion *Died in War on 17 December 1914*
YPRES (MENIN GATE) MEMORIAL, *Belgium*
Born in Armagh, enlisted at Ballykinler, resident Belfast.

Duffy, Henry - Third Steward
Mercantile Marine S.S. "War Clover" (London)
Age 18 Drowned, as a result of an attack by an enemy submarine on 19 October 1917
TOWER HILL MEMORIAL, *United Kingdom*
Son of Francis and Elizabeth Duffy, of 14, Arlington Street, Belfast.

Duffy, James - Gunner
86428 Royal Horse Artillery and Royal Field Artillery *Died in War on 27 September 1918*
ST SEVER CEMETERY EXTENSION ROUEN, *France*
Born in Belfast, enlisted Manchester.

Duffy, John - Rifleman
5600 Royal Irish Rifles 2nd Battalion *Killed in Action on 7 July 1916*
THIEPVAL MEMORIAL, *France*
Husband of Maggie Duffy, of 2, Ormond Place, Belfast.

Duffy, Joseph - Private
48521 Royal Scots Fusiliers 1/4th Battalion *Died in War on 19 April 1917*
GAZA WAR CEMETERY, *Israel*
Born, the son of James and Annie Duffy in County Antrim. Lived in Hamilton, Scotland when enlisted, resident of Belfast.

Duffy, Michael - Lance Corporal
11588 Highland Light Infantry 1st Battalion *Died in War on 11 January 1917*
BASRA MEMORIAL, *Iraq*
Born in Belfast, enlisted Edinburgh.

Duffy, Peter - Private
11252 King's Own Scottish Borderers 1st Battalion *Died in War on 29 June 1916*
ENGLEBELMER COMMUNAL CEMETERY, *France*
Born in Edinburgh, enlisted and resident in Belfast.

Duffy, William - Sergeant
280564 Highland Light Infantry 7th (Blythswood) Battalion (Territorial)
Died in War on 16 November 1917
KANTARA WAR MEMORIAL CEMETERY, *Egypt*
Born in Belfast, enlisted Glasgow.

Journey of Remembering

Duggan, Archibald Reginald - Sergeant
23337 Canadian Garrison Artillery 1st Heavy Battery *Age 42 Died in War on 1 March 1915*
LE GRAND BEAUMART BRITISH CEMETERY, STEENWERCK, France
Holder of Long Service and Good Conduct Medal. Son of Mr. Alfred Duggan, of Belfast; husband of Mrs. Lillie Duggan (née Smith), of 218, Oliver Street, Quebec. Before re-enlisting he had 21 years army service. An Anglican he had worked as a fitter.

Duggan, Humphrey Griffith - Rifleman
9/14364 Royal Irish Rifles 15th Battalion *Age 21 Died of Wounds on 27 October 1918*
DUHALLOW A.D.S. CEMETERY, Belgium
Son of Humphrey Griffith Duggan and Mary Ann Duggan, of 41, Seventh Street, Belfast.

Duggan, Richard - Private
20834 Princess Victoria's (Royal Irish Fusiliers) 7th Battalion *Died in War on 29 April 1916*
LOOS MEMORIAL, France
Enlisted in London, resident of Belfast.

Duke, Samuel - Rifleman
7315 Royal Irish Rifles 1st Battalion *Died in War on 10 March 1918*
BELFAST CITY CEMETERY, United Kingdom
Born and enlisted in Belfast.

Dumigan, Robert - Rifleman
4325 Royal Irish Rifles 10th Battalion *Age 30 Killed in Action on 1 July 1916*
THIEPVAL MEMORIAL, France
Husband of the late Margaret Dumigan.

Dunbar, William - Rifleman
12732 Royal Irish Rifles 8th Battalion *Age 19 Died in War on 2 July 1916*
BEAUMONT-HAMEL BRITISH CEMETERY, France
Son of William H. Dunbar, of 12, Downpatrick Street, Belfast.

Duncan, Benjamin - Rifleman
14356 Royal Irish Rifles 10th Battalion *Age 20 Killed in Action on 1 July 1916*
THIEPVAL MEMORIAL, France
Son of James and Agnes Duncan, of 275, Donegall Road, Belfast.

Duncan, James - Rifleman
4/7580 Royal Irish Rifles 6th Battalion *Age 21 Killed in Action on 5 March 1918*
JERUSALEM WAR CEMETERY, Israel
Son of John and Susan Duncan, of 3, Broadbent Street, Belfast.

Duncan, John - Second Engineer
Mercantile Marine S.S. "Crispin" (Liverpool)
Age 35 Drowned, as a result of an attack by an enemy submarine on 29 March 1917
TOWER HILL MEMORIAL, United Kingdom
Son of the late Thomas and Ellan Duncan; husband of Edith Duncan (née Hughes), of 21, Arnold Street, Liverpool. Born at Belfast.

Journey of Remembering

Duncan, Victor Alexander - Private
6059 Royal Irish Rifles 7th Battalion *Died of Wounds on 8 September 1916*
LA NEUVILLE BRITISH CEMETERY, CORBIE, France
Son of James and Mary, 45, Lorton Street, Belfast.

Duncan, William - Private
11173 Royal Inniskilling Fusiliers 6th Battalion *Age 23 Died in War on 22 August 1915*
HELLES MEMORIAL, Turkey
Son of Mrs. Annie Duncan, of 37, Thorndale Avenue, Belfast.

Duncan, William - Private
25161 Princess Victoria's (Royal Irish Fusiliers) 7/8th Battalion *Died in War on 22 December 1917*
THIEPVAL MEMORIAL, France
Born and enlisted in Belfast. Formerly 691434, Army Service Corps.

Dunlop, Charles - Lieutenant
Royal Inniskilling Fusiliers 2nd Battalion
Age 22 Died of wounds received at the Battle of the Aisne on 22 October 1914
LES GONARDS CEMETERY, VERSAILLES, France
Son of Elizabeth Dunlop, of Edenderry House, Ballylesson, Belfast, and the late James Dunlop, F.S.R.N.

Dunlop, David G - Private
11574 Royal Irish Fusiliers 5th Battalion *Died in War on 16 August 1915*
HELLES MEMORIAL, Turkey
9 Maryville Street, Belfast.

Dunlop, Henry - Private
24572 Royal Irish Fusiliers 7/8th Battalion *Age 21 Died in War on 15 August 1917*
TYNE COT CEMETERY, Belgium
Son of David and Annie Dunlop, of 32, Frederick Lane, Belfast.

Dunlop, John - Private
5813 Royal Irish Fusiliers 1st Battalion *Died in War on 25 April 1915*
POELCAPELLE BRITISH CEMETERY, Belgium
26 Pittsburg Street, Belfast. Born in Ballycastle.

Dunlop, Quenton - Corporal
18950 Royal Irish Rifles 11th Battalion *Killed in Action on 1 July 1916*
THIEPVAL MEMORIAL, France
Born in Belfast, enlisted Lisburn.

Dunlop, Robert - Private
6937 Royal Inniskilling Fusiliers 2nd Battalion *Died in War on 24 November 1914*
PLOEGSTEERT MEMORIAL, Belgium
Son of John and Elizabeth Dunlop, of 12, Craigmore Street, Belfast.

Dunlop, Samuel - Gunner
80564 Royal Field Artillery 364th Battery *Age 21 Died of Wounds on 11 November 1916*
STRUMA MILITARY CEMETERY, Greece
Son of Samuel and Mary Dunlop, of 29, Wilson Street, Belfast.

Journey of Remembering

Dunlop, William - Gunner
81877 Royal Field Artillery *Age 27 Died of sickness following wounds (gas) on 4 August 1921*
BELFAST CITY CEMETERY, United Kingdom
Son of Mary Dunlop, of 29, Wilson Street, Belfast, and the late Samuel Dunlop.

Dunlop, William - Rifleman
8723 Royal Irish Rifles 1st Battalion *Killed in Action on 2 September 1918*
STE. MARIE CEMETERY, LE HAVRE, France
Born and enlisted in Belfast.

Dunlop, William James - Second Lieutenant
Royal Field Artillery *Died in War on 21 September 1916*
ALBERT COMMUNAL CEMETERY EXTENSION, France
Commemorated in St Paul's Church, York Road, Belfast.

Dunn, David Andrew - Donkeyman
Mercantile Marine S.S. "Garron Head" (Belfast) *Age 39 Killed by mine on 16 November 1917*
TOWER HILL MEMORIAL, United Kingdom
Son of the late John and Alice Dunn; husband of Henrietta Matilda Winifred Dunn (née Flood), of 128, Agincourt Avenue, Belfast. Born at Brookeborough County Fermanagh.

Dunn, John - Private
3114 Royal Inniskilling Fusiliers 2nd Battalion *Killed in Action on 1 April 1917*
SAVY BRITISH CEMETERY, France
Born and elisted in Belfast.

Dunn, Joseph - Rifleman
R/20247 King's Royal Rifle Corps 2nd Battalion *Died in War on 23 July 1916*
THIEPVAL MEMORIAL, France
Born and enlisted in Belfast.

Dunne, Thomas - Rifleman
9406 Royal Irish Rifles 2nd Battalion *Age 25 Killed in Action on 11 November 1914*
YPRES (MENIN GATE) MEMORIAL, Belgium
Son of John and Eliza Dunne, of 25, Steens Row, Belfast.

Dunning, David J - Rifleman
3180 Royal Irish Rifles 12th Battalion *Age 22 Died as a Prisoner of War on 3 August 1918*
BERLIN SOUTH-WESTERN CEMETERY, Germany
A linen spinner, he was the son of David and Lavinia Dunning, of 15, Northland Street, Belfast.

Dunning, Thomas John - Rifleman
9/14506 Royal Irish Rifles 9th Battalion *Age 21 Killed in Action on 2 March 1916*
SUCRERIE MILITARY CEMETERY, COLINCAMPS, France
Husband of Margaret Dunning, of 16, Haddow Street, Belfast.

Dunseith, William - Sapper
64399 Royal Engineers Lancs Field Company *Died from illness contracted in France on 31 January 1918*
BELFAST CITY CEMETERY, United Kingdom
26, Bisley Street, Belfast. Discharged from the army through illness, in early 1918.

Dunville, George - Sergeant
158 Royal Flying Corps *Age 23 Killed while flying on 5 September 1917*
CARNMONEY CEMETERY, United Kingdom
Son of Mr. and Mrs. Dunville, of Shankill Road, Belfast; husband of Susannah Vance (formerly Dunville), of 184, Grosvenor Road, Belfast.

Dunwoodie, Alexander - Lance Corporal
20/1646 Northumberland Fusiliers 20th Battalion (Tyneside Scottish) *Killed in Action on 1 July 1916*
THIEPVAL MEMORIAL, France
Born in Belfast, enlisted on Tyneside.

Dunwoody, George - Private
1574 Royal Irish Rifles 9th Battalion *Age 23 Killed in Action on 1 July 1916*
THIEPVAL MEMORIAL, France
Son of Joseph and Sarah Dunwoody, of 27, Fingal Street, Woodvale, Belfast.

Dunwoody, Hugh Henderson - Second Lieutenant
Royal Irish Fusiliers 10th Battalion attached 9th Battalion *Age 26 Died in War on 31 July 1916*
RATION FARM (LA PLUS DOUVE) ANNEXE, Belgium
Youngest son of Robert and Eliza Ann Dunwoody, of 92, Holywood Road, Strandtown, Belfast.
Educated at Campbell College. Served on the Somme and later killed in Belgium.

Dunwoody, John - Private
26979 Royal Inniskilling Fusiliers 7th Battalion *Died in War on 27 April 1916*
PHILOSOPHE BRITISH CEMETERY, MAZINGARBE, France
Born and enlisted in Belfast .

Dunwoody, Robert Andrew - Private
2805 Irish Guards 1st Battalion *Age 22 Died in War on 6 November 1914*
YPRES (MENIN GATE) MEMORIAL, Belgium
Son of Agnes Dunwoody and husband of Mary Ellen Dunwoody, of 61, Gaffikin Street, Belfast.

Dunwoody, William - Rifleman
14405 Royal Irish Rifles 10th Battalion *Killed In Action on 1 July 1916*
THIEPVAL MEMORIAL, France
Son of the late John and Eliza Ann Dunwoody. Sister lived at 216 Blythe Street, Belfast.

Dyer, Frank - Private
2760 Gloucestershire Regiment 1/6th Battalion *Died in War on 31 May 1915*
LANCASHIRE COTTAGE CEMETERY, Belgium
Born in Belfast, enlisted in Bristol.

Dyer, John - Rifleman
2846 Royal Irish Rifles 11th Battalion *Age 20 Killed in Action on 1 July 1916*
THIEPVAL MEMORIAL, France
Son of James and Francis Dyer, of 37, Hudson Street, Belfast.

Dyer, Joseph - Rifleman
R/27552 King's Royal Rifle Corps 13th Battalion *Age 34 Killed in Action on 24 December 1916*
PONT-DU-HEM MILITARY CEMETERY, LA GORGUE, France
Son of John and Mary Dyer (née McCann), of Belfast; husband of the late Mary Ann Dyer.

Dynes, David William - Private
10747 Royal Inniskilling Fusiliers 1st Battalion *Age 19 Died in War on 21 August 1915*
HELLES MEMORIAL, Turkey
Son of Valentine and Susannah Dynes, of 4, Rathmore Street, Belfast.

Dynes, John - Rifleman
1112 Royal Irish Rifles 9th Battalion *Age 48 Killed in Action on 1 July 1916*
THIEPVAL MEMORIAL, France
Husband of Elizabeth Dynes, of 8, Lecale Street, Donegall Road, Belfast.

Eagle, John - Rifleman
12751 Royal Irish Rifles 8th Battalion *Died in War on 3 August 1917*
BRANDHOEK NEW MILITARY CEMETERY, Belgium
Born and enlisted in Belfast.

Eakin, Frederick Wllliam - Company Sergeant Major
71255 Canadian Infantry (Manitoba Regiment) 27th Battalion *Died in War on 26 July 1917*
FOSSE No.10 COMMUNAL CEMETERY EXTENSION, SAINS-EN-GOLHELLE, France
Brother of Mrs McClenaghan, Belfast.

Eakins, John - Private
23767 Royal Irish Fusiliers 5th Battalion *Age 18 Died in War on 10 September 1916*
DOIRAN MEMORIAL, Greece
Son of James Eakins, of 8, Medway Street, Dee Street, Belfast.

Eakins, Joseph - Rifleman
5576 Royal Irish Rifles 7th Battalion *Died in War on 6 September 1916*
THIEPVAL MEMORIAL, France
73 Hudson Street, Belfast.

Earle, Charles - Private
10633 Royal Inniskilling Fusiliers 2nd Battalion *Accidentally killed on 10 October 1918*
HAGLE DUMP CEMETERY, Belgium
Son of David and Maggie Earle, 117 Canmore Street, Belfast.

Earles, Patrick - Rifleman
7006 Royal Irish Rifles 2nd Battalion *Killed in Action on 25 September 1915*
YPRES (MENIN GATE) MEMORIAL, Belgium
Born in Belfast, enlisted Hamilton, Scotland.

Easton, Samuel - Rifleman
181874 Royal Irish Rifles 11th Battalion *Age 27 Killed in Action on 1 July 1916*
MILL ROAD CEMETERY, THIEPVAL, France
Son of Mrs. Agnes Easton, of 65, Matchett Street, Belfast.

Easton, Samuel - Rifleman
9258 Royal Irish Rifles 2nd Battalion *Age 36 Killed in Action on 26 October 1914*
LE TOURET MEMORIAL, France
Son of the late William and Sarah Easton, of Warwick Street, Belfast. Husband of the late Rose Ann Easton.
Next of kin was Mr S R Easton, 68 Lousia Street, Belfast.

Easton, Thomas - Rifleman
5634 Royal Irish Rifles 2nd Battalion *Killed in Action on 27 October 1914*
LE TOURET MEMORIAL, France
60 Belgrave Street, Belfast.

Eccleston, Sidney - Rifleman
1578 Royal Irish Rifles 10th Battalion *Killed in action on 21 March 1918*
BOUCHOIR NEW BRITISH CEMETERY, France
Son of Henry Eccleston, 25 Cherryville Street, Belfast.

Edens, James - Private
7553 Royal Inniskilling Fusiliers 2nd Battalion *Killed in Action on 21 October 1914*
PLOEGSTEERT MEMORIAL, Belgium
Born and resident in Belfast.

Edens, James - Rifleman
10961 Royal Irish Rifles 6th Battalion *Died in War on 11 August 1915*
HELLES MEMORIAL, Turkey
Born and enlisted in Belfast.

Edgar, Hamilton - Private
20583 Grenadier Guards 2nd Battalion *Died in War on 6 April 1915*
GUARDS CEMETERY, WINDY CORNER, CUINCHY, France
Wife and parents resided at 7, Walnut Place, Belfast.

Edgar, John Hammond - Lieutenant
Durham Light Infantry 9th Battalion *Died in War on 24 February 1916*
RAILWAY DUGOUTS BURIAL GROUND, Belgium
Born in Belfast.

Edgar, James - Rifleman
11141 Royal Irish Rifles 6th Battalion *Age 25 Died in War on 11 August 1915*
HELLES MEMORIAL, Turkey
Husband of Isabella Edgar, of 6, Disraeli Street, Belfast.

Edgar, Thomas - Rifleman
10624 Royal Irish Rifles 6th Battalion *Died in War on 11 August 1915*
HELLES MEMORIAL, Turkey
26 Shankill Road Belfast. A native of County Armagh.

Edgar, Thomas William Gallamore - Private
3537 Irish Guards 1st Battalion *Age 21 Died in War on 1 November 1914*
YPRES (MENIN GATE) MEMORIAL, Belgium
Son of Elizabeth Edgar, of 7, Princess Terrace, Cregagh Road, Belfast, and the late Joseph Edgar (Chemist). Native of Dromore, County Down.

Edmond, James Chalmers - Private
7085 South African Infantry "A" Company 2nd Regiment *Age 26 Killed in Action on 12 April 1917*
BROWN'S COPSE CEMETERY, ROEUX, France
Son of John and Margaret Edmond, of Belfast, Ireland; husband of Mary Roy Edmond, of East Worldham, Hampshire, England. Served with South African Irish Horse in German South West Africa, 1914, and in the Boer Rebellion.

Edmonds, Edwin Edmund - Able Seaman
SS/3266 Royal Navy HMS "Otranto"
Age 27 Drowned through collision and wreck of vessel off Isle of Islay on 6 October 1918
CHATHAM NAVAL MEMORIAL, United Kingdom
Son of William Edmonds, of 214, Roden Street, Belfast.

Edmonds, George Edgar - Rifleman
10707 Royal Irish Rifles 7th Battalion *Age 24 Died in War on 8 August 1917*
TYNE COT CEMETERY, Belgium
Son of William Edmonds, of 214, Roden Street, Belfast.

Edmonds, William Barnewall - Private
CH/483(S) Royal Marine Light Infantry 1st R.M. Battalion Royal Naval Division *Age 28 Died of Wounds on 13 November 1916*
VARENNES MILITARY CEMETERY, France
Son of William Edmonds, of 214, Roden Street, Belfast.

Edmondson, John - Rifleman
17598 Royal Irish Rifles 7th Battalion *Age 45 Died in War on 5 November 1918*
BELFAST CITY CEMETERY, United Kingdom
Husband of Margaret Jane Edmondson, of 20, Beggs Street, Sandy Row, Belfast.

Edmondson, Samuel C - Private
51151 Princess Patricia's Canadian Light Infantry (Eastern Ontario Regiment) *Age 21 Died in War on 4 June 1916*
YPRES (MENIN GATE) MEMORIAL, Belgium
Son of Eliza Edmondson, of 18, Tyne Street, Belfast, Ireland, and the late William J. Edmondson.
A Prebyterian, he had worked in Canada as a ship plater.

Edmondson, William - Private
20071 Royal Inniskilling Fusiliers *Died in War on 10 July 1916*
THIEPVAL MEMORIAL, France
Born and enlisted in Belfast. Member of Fountainville Presbyterian Church.

Edwards, James - Private
699 Army Cyclist Corps 28th Division Cyclist Company *Age 19 Died in War on 3 May 1915*
YPRES (MENIN GATE) MEMORIAL, Belgium
Son of Henrietta Edwards, of 59, Lepper Street, Belfast. Formerly 4th Battalion Royal Inniskilling Fusiliers.

Edwards, John - Gunner
20814 Royal Garrison Artillery *Died in War on 6 April 1917*
ST NICOLAS BRITISH CEMETERY, France
Born and resident in Belfast.

Edwards, William Victor - Captain
Royal Dublin Fusiliers 7th Battalion *Age 30 Died in War on 29 December 1917*
JERUSALEM WAR CEMETERY, Israel
Son of Mary Edwards, of The Laurels, Strandtown, Belfast, and the late Alfred Edwards. An accountant, he was educated at Campbell College and Queen's University. A keen rugby and water polo player he was the first man to swim across Belfast Lough.

Ekin, Frederick William - Private
4705 Regiment, Corp Royal Fusiliers (City of London Regiment) 20th Battalion *Died in War on 18 August 1916*
BELFAST CITY CEMETERY, United Kingdom
Born and enlisted in Belfast.

Elder, Charles - Private
71585 Cavalry North Irish Horse *Died in War on 7 November 1918*
DOURLERS COMMUNAL CEMETERY EXTENSION, France
Born in Antrim, resident of Belfast.

Elder, John - Sergeant
12144 Royal Irish Regiment 2nd Battalion formerly 10464 Royal Inniskilling Fusiliers
Killed In Action on 20 May 1918
VARENNES MILITARY CEMETERY, France
Born and resident in Belfast.

Journey of Remembering

Elder, Robert Craig - Petty Officer Stoker
311202 Royal Navy HMS "Turbulent" *Age 27 Killed in Action at Battle of Jutland on 1 June 1916*
CHATHAM NAVAL MEMORIAL, *United Kingdom*
Son of John and Isabella Elder, of Belfast; husband of Agnes McKittrick (formerly Elder), of 31, East Bread Street, Belfast.

Elliott, Alexander - Rifleman
13566 Royal Irish Rifles 1st Battalion *Killed in Action on 10 March 1915*
MERVILLE COMMUNAL CEMETERY, *France*
Husband of S. Elliott, of 9, Ravensdale Street, Belfast.

Elliott, Charles - Rifleman
2706 Royal Irish Rifles 8th Battalion *Age 24 Died in War on 8 August 1917*
YPRES (MENIN GATE) MEMORIAL, *Belgium*
Husband of Josephine Elliott, of 13, Disraeli Street, Crumlin Road, Belfast.

Elliott, David - Rifleman
2350 Royal Irish Rifles 14th Battalion *Age 29 Killed in Action on 24 March 1918*
POZIERES MEMORIAL, *France*
Son of Hugh and Mary Jane Elliott, of 14, Lindsay Street, Belfast; husband of Mary Elliott, of 20, Hunter Street, Belfast.

Elliott, Francis - Rifleman
10709 Royal Irish Rifles "B" Company 6th Battalion *Age 32 Died in War on 18 June 1917*
LAHANA MILITARY CEMETERY, *Greece*
Struck and killed by lightning. Born at Cogrey, County Antrim.
Son of George and Jane Elliott, of 21, Oregon Street, Belfast.

Elliott, Frank - Sergeant
2492841 Royal Irish Rifles 2nd Battalion *Age 27 Died of Wounds on 7 August 1917*
LIJSSENTHOEK MILITARY CEMETERY, *Belgium*
Awarded the Croix de Guerre (France). Son of Joshua and Mary Elliott, of 12, Sullivan Street, Holywood; husband of Elizabeth McVeigh (formerly Elliott), of 53, Seaview Street, York Road, Belfast.

Elliott, James - Private
288 Irish Guards 1st Battalion *Age 44 Died of Wounds on 27 March 1916*
BRIGHTON (BEAR ROAD) BOROUGH CEMETERY, *United Kingdom*
Originally a brick maker and engine driver. Joined the army in 1899 and thereafter transferred to the Irish Guards. On the Reserve when called up in 1914. Son of Mr. J. Elliott, of 60, Gibson Street, Belfast and husband of Rose.

Elliott, James - Rifleman
14522 Royal Irish Rifles 14th Battalion *Age 26 Killed in Action on 1 July 1916*
THIEPVAL MEMORIAL, *France*
Husband of Anna Elliott, of 10, Alexandra Park Avenue, Belfast.

Elliott, John - Rifleman
3965 Royal Irish Rifles 2nd Battalion *Age 20 Died of Wounds on 8 June 1917*
BAILLEUL COMMUNAL CEMETERY EXTENSION (NORD), *France*
Son of Maria Russell (formerly Elliott), of 101, Howard Street, South, Belfast, and the late Joseph Elliott.

Elliott, John - Rifleman
1401 Royal Irish Rifles 10th Battalion *Died in War on 22 November 1917*
CAMBRAI MEMORIAL, LOUVERVAL, *France*
Son of Samuel Elliott, 47 Fraser Street, Belfast.

Elliott, John - Stoker First Class
SS/104009 Royal Navy HMS "Hawke" *Died in War on 15 October 1914*
CHATHAM NAVAL MEMORIAL, United Kingdom
Hardinge Street, Belfast.

Elliott, Joseph - Private
3285 Leinster Regiment "B" Company 2nd Battalion *Age 35 Died in War on 3 September 1916*
THIEPVAL MEMORIAL, France
Son of William Elliott, of 35, Leeson Street, Belfast; husband of Susan McCallan (formerly Elliott), of 41, Sultan Street, Belfast.

Elliott, Robert - Private
44585 Labour Corps *Died in War on 9 January 1918*
TYNE COT MEMORIAL, Belgium
Born in Belfast, enlisted Manchester. Formerly 68035, Liverpool Regiment.

Elliott, Samuel - Rifleman
9004 Royal Irish Rifles 2nd Battalion *Age 41 Killed in Action on 25 October 1914*
CABARET-ROUGE BRITISH CEMETERY, SOUCHEZ, France
Son of James and Alice Elliott; husband of M. L. Elliott, of 12, Pitt Street, Belfast.

Elliott, Thomas - Rifleman
552 Royal Irish Rifles "C" Company 6th Battalion *Age 38 Died in War on 1 January 1917*
DOIRAN MEMORIAL, Greece
Husband of Mary Ann Elliott, of 9, Pitt Street, Belfast. Born at Newry.

Elliott, Thomas Brignall - Second Lieutenant
Royal Irish Rifles 10th Battalion *Age 29 Killed in Action on 1 July 1916*
THIEPVAL MEMORIAL, France
A former pupil of RBAI he was the son of Thomas and Annie Elliott, of Knockdene Park and later of "Sandowne", Chichester Park, Belfast. He had originally joined as a private and was later commissioned.

Elliott, William James - Rifleman
14532 Royal Irish Rifles 10th Battalion *Killed In Action on 1 July 1916*
THIEPVAL MEMORIAL, France and Flanders
Born and enlisted in Belfast.

Ellis, James Graves St John - Second Lieutenant
Royal Engineers *Age 28 Killed in Action on 11 October 1915*
HILL 10 CEMETERY, Turkey
Son of William Edward Ellis L.L D., L.L.B., and Edith Annie Ellis, of Dublin; husband of Florence Kathleen Ellis, of 4, Rugby Terrace, Rugby Road, Belfast. Assistant Engineer, C.P.R

Ellis, William - Corporal
4612 Royal Irish Rifles 11th Battalion *Age 36 Died in War on 1 September 1916*
YPRES (MENIN GATE) MEMORIAL, Belgium
Son of Richard and Hannah Ellis, of Yorkshire; husband of Alice Mary Ellis, of 24, St. Kilda Street, Belfast.

Ellis, William - Rifleman
6064 Royal Irish Rifles 5th Battalion *Age 32 Died in War on 20 January 1917*
BELFAST (DUNDONALD) CEMETERY, United Kingdom
Son of John Rowles Ellis and Jennie Ellis, of Eastbourne; husband of Angelina Ellis, of Belfast.

Ellison, Robert Arthur Alexander - Corporal
11575 Lancashire Fusiliers "C" Company 16th Battalion *Age 23 Killed in enemy air-raid on 29 November 1917*
HARINGHE (BANDAGHEM) MILITARY CEMETERY, Belgium
Son of Robert and Agnes Ellison, of 4, Albyns Avenue, Cheetham Hill Road, Manchester. Native of Belfast.

Ellison, William - Private
19504 Royal Inniskilling Fusiliers 10th Battalion *Age 29 Killed in Action on 1 July 1916*
CONNAUGHT CEMETERY, THIEPVAL, France
Son of James and Letitia Ellison; husband of Annie Ellison, of 87, Methuen Street, Belfast.

Elphick, Robert John - Corporal
9719 Royal Irish Rifles 2nd Battalion *Age 22 Died of wounds received at Neuve Chapelle on 7 November 1914*
NOTTINGHAM GENERAL CEMETERY, United Kingdom
Son of Robert and Elizabeth Elphick, of 143, Dunluce Street, Belfast.

Elwood, David - Private
19488 Machine Gun Corps (Infantry) formerly 218967 Royal Irish Rifles *Died of Wounds on 16 April 1918*
HARINGHE (BANDAGHEM) MILITARY CEMETERY, Belgium
Born and enlisted in Belfast.

Elwood, Henry - Private
21919 Royal Dublin Fusiliers 7th Battalion *Age 19 Died in War on 1 September 1915*
HELLES MEMORIAL, Turkey
Son of Henry Elwood, 23 Huss Street, Belfast. Formerly employed in the Shipyard.

Elwood, Henry - Private
42319 Princess Victoria's (Royal Irish Fusiliers) 1st Battalion *Died in War on 2 November 1918*
LONGUENESSE (ST. OMER) SOUVENIR CEMETERY, France
Born in Belfast. Enlisted in Perth, Scotland. Formerly 11072 Royal Irish rifles

Emerson, Joseph - Private
19449 Machine Gun Corps (Infantry) 107th Company *Age 18 Killed in Action on 1 July 1916*
THIEPVAL MEMORIAL, France
Son of James Emerson, of 45, Paxton Street, Belfast, and the late Harriett Annie Emerson.

Emerson, Thomas Henry - Rifleman
497 Royal Irish Rifles "C" Company 14th Battalion *Age 23 Died in War on 20 June 1917*
LOCRE HOSPICE CEMETERY, Belgium
Son of William and Agnes Emerson, of 11, Zetland Street, Belfast. Native of Hillsborough, County Down.

England, Fredrick - Rifleman
1646 Royal Irish Rifles 15th Battalion *Age 18 Killed in Action on 11 June 1916*
HAMEL MILITARY CEMETERY, BEAUMONT-HAMEL, France
Son of William and Mary England, of 16, Penrose Street, Belfast.

English, Alexander - Sapper
101013 Corps of Royal Engineers 225th Field Company *Died in War on 4 July 1916*
LOOS MEMORIAL, France
Born in Belfast, enlisted in County Durham.

English, Alexander - Private
12690 Royal Inniskilling Fusiliers 1st Battalion *Killed in Action on 1 July 1916*
ANCRE BRITISH CEMETERY, BEAUMONT-HAMEL, France
60 Foreman Street, Belfast.

English, David - Sergeant
14/16471 Royal Irish Rifles 14th Battalion *Died in War on 14 June 1917*
MESSINES RIDGE BRITISH CEMETERY, Belgium
"Buncrana", Ormeau Road, Belfast. Born in Glenarm County Antrim.

English, Nathaniel Joseph - Master
Mercantile Marine "Fenay Lodge"
Age 41 Drowned, as a result of an attack by an enemy submarine on 7 March 1917
TOWER HILL MEMORIAL, United Kingdom
Son of the late John and Sarah English, of Folkestone; husband of Annie Proudfoot (formerly English), of 44, Malone Avenue, Belfast.

English, Thomas - Private
2564 Connaught Rangers 6th Battalion *Died in War on 3 August 1917*
YPRES (MENIN GATE) MEMORIAL, Belgium
Son of Bridget and the late Thomas English, 9 Balaclava Street, Belfast.

Ennis, David - Rifleman
8238 Royal Irish Rifles 2nd Battalion *Age 26 Killed in Action on 17 February 1915*
KEMMEL CHATEAU MILITARY CEMETERY, Belgium
Son of Elizabeth Ennis, of 36, Constance Street, Albert Bridge, Belfast

Ennis, Thomas - Donkeyman And Greaser
Mercantile Marine S.S. "War Clover" (London)
Age 43 Drowned, as a result of an attack by an enemy submarine on 19 October 1917
TOWER HILL MEMORIAL, United Kingdom
Son of William John Ennis and the late Agnes Ennis; husband of Annie Ennis (née Cuthbert), of 52, Willowfield Street, Belfast. Born at Belfast.

Entwistle, James - Private
45627 Lincolnshire Regiment 11th Labour Company *Age 34 Killed in Action on 21 August 1917*
FOSSE NO. 10 COMMUNAL CEMETERY EXTENSION, SAINS-EN-GOHELLE, France
Son of Elizabeth and the late Thomas Entwistle, of Belfast; husband of Mary Entwistle, of 62, Argyle Street, Belfast.

Eogan, John F - Lance Corporal
3038 Irish Guards 1st Battalion *Died in War on 6 September 1914*
MONTREUIL-AUX-LIONS BRITISH CEMETERY, France
Plevna Street, Belfast.

Eppleston, Hugh - Rifleman
10111 Royal Irish Rifles 2nd Battalion *Age 19 Killed in Action on 27 October 1914*
LE TOURET MEMORIAL, France
Son of William and Mary Eppleston, of 19, Southwell Street, Belfast.

Eppleston, James Henry - Private
31385 Machine Gun Corps 55th Battalion *Age 34 Died of Wounds on 3 September 1918*
PERNES BRITISH CEMETERY, France
Son of William and Mary Eppleston, of 19, Southwell Street, Belfast.

JOURNEY OF REMEMBERING

Erikson, James - Second Mate
Mercantile Marine S.S. "Castlebar" (Belfast) *Age 14 Presumed drowned on 13 March 1918*
TOWER HILL MEMORIAL, United Kingdom
Son of Frances Erikson (née Kearney), of 18, Hartwell Street, Belfast, and the late John Erikson.
Born in Belfast. Two brothers on the same boat.

Erikson, John - Second Engineer
Mercantile Marine S.S. "Castlebar" (Belfast) *Age 34 Presumed drowned on 13 March 1918*
TOWER HILL MEMORIAL, United Kingdom
Son of Frances Erikson and the late John Erikson; husband of Margaret Erikson (née Harte),
of 30, Spamount Street, Belfast. Born at Belfast. Two brothers on the same boat.

Erskine, Alexander - Lance Corporal
41235 Royal Irish Fusiliers 9th Battalion *Age 22 Died of wounds on 10 October 1918*
LIJSSENTHOEK MILITARY CEMETERY, Belgium
Son of E. J. Erskine, of 111, Cavehill Road, Belfast, and the late Alec Erskine. Enlisted 5th October, 1914
Formerly 1284 North Irish Horse.

Erskine, George - Corporal
8644 Royal Irish Rifles 2nd Battalion *Killed in Action on 23 November 1915*
LE BIZET CEMETERY, ARMENTIERES, France
Born Ballymacarrett, Belfast. Enlisted in Belfast.

Erskine, Walter - Rifleman
7006 Royal Irish Rifles 2nd Battalion *Age 21 Killed in Action on 23 November 1917*
CAMBRAI MEMORIAL, LOUVERVAL, France
Son of William Erskine, 43 Sancroft Street, Belfast.

Erskine, William - Private
47516 Royal Fusiliers (City of London Regiment) 1st Battalion *Died in War on 30 December 1916*
PHILOSOPHE BRITISH CEMETERY, MAZINGARBE, France
Born in Belfast, enlisted in Romford, Essex.

Erskine, William Alexander - Rifleman
12758 Royal Irish Rifles 15th Battalion *Age 27 Killed in Action on 21 March 1918*
POZIERES MEMORIAL, France
Son of William B. Erskine, of 14, Sealands Parade, Seaview, Belfast.

Ervine, Charles James - Second Lieutenant
Northumberland Fusiliers 27th (Tyneside Irish) Battalion *Age 22 Died of Wounds on 6 April 1916*
BAILLEUL COMMUNAL CEMETERY EXTENSION (NORD), France
Son of Robert and Mary Ervine, of "Moylena" 190, Cregagh Road, Belfast.
His father had a business address in Ocean Buildings, Donegall Square East, Belfast.

Ervine, William - Sergeant
12757 Royal Irish Rifles 8th Battalion *Age 21 Died in War on 2 July 1916*
THIEPVAL MEMORIAL, France
Son of William James and Susan Ervine, of 4, Rugby Street, Belfast.

Etheridge, Leonard - Sergeant Major
8971 Dorset Regiment 1st Battalion *Died of gassing on 2 May 1915*
BAILLEUL COMMUNAL CEMETERY EXTENSION (NORD), France
29 Burnaby Street, Belfast.

Evans, Andrew - Private
1622 King's Own (Royal Lancaster Regiment) 1st/4th Battalion *Died in War on 18 August 1916*
ST SEVER CEMETERY EXTENSION ROUEN, *France*
Born in Belfast, enlisted in Barrow-in-Furness.

Evans, Joseph - Mechanic
306289 Royal Navy HMS "Hampshire" *Age 35 Killed by mine explosion off Orkneys on 5 June 1916*
PORTSMOUTH NAVAL MEMORIAL, *United Kingdom*
Son of W. and J. Evans, of 13, McClure Street, Belfast; husband of Alice J. Vickery (formerly Evans), of 65, Hunter Street, Burton-on-Trent.

Evans, Robert - Private
71586 North Irish Horse *Died in War on 9 November 1918*
DERRYAGHY (CHRIST CHURCH) CHURCH OF IRELAND CHURCHYARD, *United Kingdom*
Son of Thomas Evans, of Suffolk, Dunmurry, Belfast. Awarded the Silver War Badge.

Evans, Samuel - Private
10190 Highland Light Infantry 2nd Battalion *Died in War on 28 December 1914*
LE TOURET MEMORIAL
Born in Belfast, enlisted Hamilton, Scotland.

Evans, Thomas - Private
17716 Machine Gun Corps (Infantry) *Age 23 Died as a result of war on 21 March 1920*
DERRYAGHY (CHRIST CHURCH) CHURCH OF IRELAND CHURCHYARD, *United Kingdom*
Son of Thomas Evans, of Suffolk, Dunmurry, Belfast.

Everett, Alexander Frazer - Rifleman
552328 London Regiment 16th (County of London) Battalion (Queen's Westminster Rifles)
Died in War on 14 April 1917
ARRAS MEMORIAL, *France*
Born in Belfast, enlisted London.

Everett, Reginald Jess - Lance Corporal
43863 Lincolnshire Regiment 7th Battalion *Died in War on 18 September 1918*
GOUZEAUCOURT NEW BRITISH CEMETERY, *France*
Born in South Tottenham, London. Enlisted in Harrow and resident in Belfast.

Evitt, William - Lance Corporal
7196 Gordon Highlanders 2nd Battalion *Died in War on 2 November 1915*
CAMBRIN CHURCHYARD EXTENSION, *France*
28 Stanley Street, Belfast.

Ewing, W G - Rifleman
23426 Royal Irish Rifles 2nd Battalion *Age 20 Died as a result of war on 25 August 1920*
BAGHDAD (NORTH GATE) WAR CEMETERY, *Iraq*
Born in Scotland the son of Thomas and Isabella Ewing, of 28, Beverley Street, Belfast.

Ewing, William - Private
19138 Royal Inniskilling Fusiliers 10th Battalion *Killed in Action on 7 June 1917*
YPRES (MENIN GATE) MEMORIAL, *Belgium*
Born in Belfast the son of Robert and Martha Ann Ewing, of Conchillas, Colonia, Uruguay, South America.

Fagan, James - Rifleman
20461 Royal Irish Fusiliers 1st Battalion *Age 20 Died of pneumonia while a POW on 20 July 1918*
NIEDERZWEHREN CEMETERY, Germany
Son of James and Catherine Fagan, of 53, Mountpottinger Road, Belfast.

Fairbairn, William - Lance Corporal
H/6139 8th King's (Royal Irish) Hussars *Age 23 Died in War on 13 June 1915*
PERTH CEMETERY (CHINA WALL), Belgium
Son of Thomas and Margaret Fairbairn, of McKee's Terrace, Dungannon, County Tyrone. Resident of Belfast.

Fallon, Samuel - Lance/Corporal
10243 Royal Inniskilling Fusiliers 1st Battalion *Killed in Action on 2 August 1915*
HELLES MEMORIAL, Turkey
Born, enlisted and resident in Belfast.

Falloon, Albert - Private
PLY/16053 Royal Marine Light Infantry HMS "Exmouth" *Age 21 Died in War on 1 December 1916*
PIRAEUS NAVAL AND CONSULAR CEMETERY, Greece
Son of Albert Victor and Louie Falloon, of 3, Bay Road, Larne Harbour, County Antrim.
Born at Ballysillan, Belfast.

Falloon, James Huston - Driver
64034 Royal Engineers 122nd Field Company *Died in War on 9 October 1915*
BOULOGNE EASTERN CEMETERY, France
Son of Albert and Louisa Falloon, 896 Crumlin Road, Belfast.

Falls, Thomas - Rifleman
10934 Royal Irish Rifles 6th Battalion *Age 19 Died in War on 10 August 1915*
HELLES MEMORIAL, Turkey
Son of John Falls, of 162, Cambrai Street, Belfast, and the late Charlotte Falls.

Faloon, William - Corporal
170 Royal Irish Rifles 15th Battalion *Killed in Action on 21 March 1918*
POZIERES BRITISH MEMORIAL, France
Born and enlisted in Belfast.

Farley, Andrew - Rifleman
8785 Royal Irish Rifles 1st Battalion *Killed in Action on 9 March 1917*
BRAY MILITARY CEMETERY, France
Born and enlisted in Belfast.

Farley, Patrick - Rifleman
9460 Royal Irish Rifles 1st Battalion *Age 21 Died of wounds on 15 March 1915*
BOULOGNE EASTERN CEMETERY, France
Son of John and Elizabeth Farley of Belfast.

Farmer, Hugh - Rifleman
9119 Royal Irish Rifles 1st Battalion *Killed in Action on 23 April 1916*
MILLENCOURT MILITARY CEMETERY EXTENSION, France
Born and enlisted in Belfast.

Farnon, Hugh - Private
1013 Royal Army Medical Corps *Age 42 Died as a result of war on 13 July 1919*
BELFAST CITY CEMETERY, United Kingdom
Husband of Roseanna Farnon, of 27, Fourth Street, Conway Street, Belfast.

Farrell, Edward - Private
3645 Royal Inniskilling Fusiliers 2nd Battalion *Died of Wounds on 29 October 1916*
LIVERPOOL (KIRKDALE) CEMETERY, United Kingdom
Born and enlisted in Belfast.

Farrell, Francis - Lieutenant
Royal Irish Rifles "D" Company 15th Battalion *Age 24 Died of pneumonia on 23 February 1919*
BELFAST CITY CEMETERY, United Kingdom
Son of Frances Helen Farrell (née Rea), of 28, Ardoyne Village, Belfast.

Farrell, John - Private
2392 Leinster Regiment 7th Battalion *Died in War on 3 August 1917*
LIJSSENTHOEK MILITARY CEMETERY, Belgium
Born and enlisted in Belfast.

Farrell, John - Rifleman
9200 Royal Irish Rifles 1st Battalion *Killed in Action on 31 July 1917*
BUTTES NEW BRITISH CEMETERY, POLYGON WOOD, Belgium
Born and enlisted in Belfast. Father of Miss Sarah Farrell, of Murlaggan, Roy Bridge, Inverness-shire.

Farrell, Patrick - Private
8183 Royal Dublin Fusiliers 8th Battalion *Age 25 Died in War on 27 April 1916*
LOOS MEMORIAL, France
Son of Rose Farrell, of Ashdale Street, Belfast; husband of Mary Farrell,
of 1, Stephens Lane, Lower Mount Street, Dublin.

Farrell, Stanley Knox - Second Lieutenant
Black Watch (Royal Highlanders) 1st/6th Battalion *Age 20 Died in War on 20 July 1918*
LA NEUVILLE-AUX-LARRIS MILITARY CEMETERY, France
Son of James and Marion Farrell, of 15, Bathgate Drive, Strandtown, Belfast.
Joined in the ranks and later commissioned.

Faulkner, James - Acting Sergeant Major
6624 Royal Garrison Artillery *Died in War on 5 November 1916*
PIETA MILITARY CEMETERY, Malta
Born in Belfast, enlisted Devonport, Engand.

Faulkner, John - Rifleman
17626 Royal Irish Rifles 13th Battalion *Killed in Action on 1 July 1916*
THIEPVAL MEMORIAL, France
Born in Belfast. Lived in Lisburn when enlisted.

Faulkner, Robert - Private
26920 Royal Inniskilling Fusiliers 7th Battalion *Age 20 Died in War on 6 March 1916*
LAPUGNOY MILITARY CEMETERY, France
(served as CRIGLINGTON). Son of Mrs. M. Faulkner, of 61, Fraser Street, Belfast.

Faulkner, Thomas - Private
1885 Irish Guards 1st Battalion *Age 33 Died in War on 18 May 1915*
LE TOURET MEMORIAL, France
Son of Alexander and Annie Faulkner, of Ahoghill, Ballymena, County Antrim; husband of Sarah Faulkner, of 10, Somerset Street, Belfast.

Fausset, Stuart Simon - Lieutenant
The King's (Liverpool Regiment) 9th Battalion *Age 26 Killed in Action on 31 July 1917*
YPRES (MENIN GATE) MEMORIAL, Belgium
Son of Charles Simon and Isabella Fausset, of 16, Chichester Avenue, Belfast, an Architect.
Joined 1914, from Queen's University Officer Training Corps Belfast.

Fay, Michael - Private
19827 Royal Dublin Fusiliers 9th Battalion *Age 27 Died in War on 27 April 1916*
LOOS MEMORIAL, France
Son of Thomas and Kathleen Fay, of 22, Dromara Street, Belfast.

Fee, Samuel - Stoker First Class
SS/102801 Royal Navy HMS "Hawke" *Age 25 Killed in Action with submarine in North Sea on 15 October 1914*
CHATHAM NAVAL MEMORIAL, United Kingdom
Husband of Catherine Fee, of 24, Harrisburg Street, Belfast.

Fee, William - Rifleman
568 Royal Irish Rifles 10th Battalion *Age 17 Died in War on 22 November 1917*
CAMBRAI MEMORIAL, LOUVERVAL, France
Son of Samuel Fee, of 53, Kilronan Street, Belfast.

Fegan, John - Private
21822 Royal Inniskilling Fusiliers 1st Battalion *Killed in Action on 22 March 1918*
OVILLERS MILITARY CEMETERY, France
Born in Belfast, enlisted in Hamiliton, Scotland.

Fell, David - Rifleman
14594 Royal Irish Rifles 15th Battalion attached 107th Trench Mortar Battery *Age 23 Died in War on 29 March 1918*
POZIERES MEMORIAL, France
Son of Thomas and Helen Fell, of 20, Hanna Street, Belfast.

Fenning, Thomas - Private
3143 Irish Guards 1st Battalion *Age 23 Died in War on 6 November 1914*
YPRES (MENIN GATE) MEMORIAL, Belgium
Son of George J. and Ann Jane Fenning, of 113, Northumberland Street, Belfast.

Fenton, James Andrew - Lieutenant
Royal Air Force 209th Squadron *Age 21 Died in War on 28 September 1918*
CHAPEL CORNER CEMETERY, SAUCHY-LESTREE, France
Son of Mr. D. J. and Mrs. A. M. Fenton, of 27, Thorndale Avenue, Belfast.

Fenton, William Joseph - Private
46835 Canadian Infantry (Central Ontario Regiment) 15th Battalion *Age 30 Died of Wounds on 3 June 1916*
YPRES (MENIN GATE) MEMORIAL, Belgium
Son of James and Alice Fenton; husband of Annie Fenton, of 19, Herbert Street, Crumlin Road, Belfast, Ireland. Worked as a clerk and had 6 years service in the Royal Inniskilling Fusiliers.

Ferguson, Daniel - Private
622324 Canadian Infantry (New Brunswick Regiment) "D" Company 44th Battalion
Age 28 Died in War on 23 August 1917
VIMY MEMORIAL, France
Son of Jane Ferguson of 33, The Mount, Belfast, Ireland, and the late Thomas Ferguson.
Born in Falkirk, Scotland he was a fitter by trade. A Presbyterian, he lived in Winnipeg, Canada.

Ferguson, David - Rifleman
14599 Royal Irish Rifles 9th Battalion *Killed in Action on 1 July 1916*
SERRE ROAD CEMETERY No.2, France
Born and enlisted in Belfast.

Ferguson, John - Private
4591 Connaught Rangers 1st Battalion *Died in War on 11 July 1917*
BAGHDAD (NORTH GATE) WAR CEMETERY, Iraq
Born in Belfast.

Ferguson, Mary - Worker
33682 Queen Mary's Army Auxiliary Corps *Age 35 Died of pneumonia on 9 February 1919*
STE. MARIE CEMETERY, LE HAVRE, France
Daughter of Captain Matthew and Mrs. Rosanna Ferguson, of 47, Cedar Avenue, Belfast.

Ferguson, Matthew Henry - Corporal
11929 Royal Irish Rifles 15th Battalion *Killed in Action on 21 March 1918*
POZIERES MEMORIAL, France
Born and enlisted in Belfast.

Ferguson, Thomas - Gunner
721 South African Heavy Artillery 73rd Battery *Age 27 Died in War on 4 August 1917*
DICKEBUSCH NEW MILITARY CEMETERY EXTENSION, Belgium
Son of Thomas Hugh Ferguson, of 109, Killowen Street, Belfast.

Ferguson, Walter - Lance Corporal
14/14596 Royal Irish Rifles 14th Battalion *Age 24 Died in War on 8 July 1916*
CAUDRY OLD COMMUNAL CEMETERY, France
Son of Mr. W. H. Ferguson, of 2, Collingwood Road, Belfast.

Ferguson, William - Private
17847 Royal Inniskilling Fusiliers 9th Battalion *Died in War on 5 December 1916*
POND FARM CEMETERY, Belgium
48 Canning Street, Belfast. Native of Whitehouse.

Ferguson, William - Private
7480 Irish Guards 2nd Battalion *Age 20 Died in War on 15 September 1916*
THIEPVAL MEMORIAL, France
Son of Mrs. Ezena Malcolm, of 74, Burnaby Street, Belfast.

Ferguson, William Burroughs - Private
97334 Royal Army Medical Corps *Died whilst on demobilization leave on 31 December 1919*
TAUKKYAN MEMORIAL, Myanmar
Husband of Eleanor Ferguson of 16, Charlotte Street, Belfast.

Ferguson, William G. - Gunner
248325 Royal Field Artillery 464th Battery 179th Brigade *Age 18 Killed in Action on 4 July 1918*
CRUCIFIX CORNER CEMETERY, VILLERS-BRETONNEUX, France
Son of James and Ellen Ferguson, of Parkmount Lodge, Parkmount Road, Belfast.

Ferguson, William James - Private
G/14433 Buffs (East Kent Regiment) 7th Battalion *Died in War on 24 August 1918*
DAOURS COMMUNAL CEMETERY EXTENSION, France
Born in Belfast, enlisted in Hounslow, England.

Ferguson, William James - Stoker First Class
308717 Royal Navy Nelson Battalion *Age 29 Died in War on 17 May 1915*
ALEXANDRIA (CHATBY) MILITARY AND WAR MEMORIAL CEMETERY, Egypt
Son of Leah Ferguson, of 20, Bryson Street, Belfast, and the late James Ferguson.

Ferguson, William Joseph - Trimmer
7543/TS Royal Naval Reserve HMS "Pekin" *Age 19 Died as a result of war on 13 December 1918*
GRIMSBY (SCARTHO ROAD) CEMETERY, United Kingdom
Son of Joseph and Margaret Ferguson, of Whitehouse, Belfast.

Ferran, James - Private
9615 Northumberland Fusiliers 1st Battalion *Died of Wounds on 21 June 1915*
BAILLEUL COMMUNAL CEMETERY EXTENSION (NORD), France
Husband of Bella Ferran, 29 Springview Street, Belfast.

Ferrar, Walter Hughes - Captain and Adjutant
2nd Battalion Welsh Regiment *Age 38 Killed in Action on 31 October 1914*
YPRES TOWN CEMETERY, Belgium
Son of A. M. Ferrar, D.L., and Mrs. R. C. Ferrar, of "Torwood", Windsor, Belfast.
Order of the Osmanieh, 4th Class (Turkey).

Ferres, Joseph - Private
43457 Highland Light Infantry 12th Battalion *Died in War on 13 January 1917*
ETRETAT CHURCHYARD EXTENSION, France
Born in Belfast, enlisted Hamilton, Scotland. Formerly 1366, Lanarkshire Yeomanry.

Ferrie, Francis - Private
16910 King's Own Scottish Borderers 2nd Battalion *Age 27 Died in War on 7 May 1915*
YPRES (MENIN GATE) MEMORIAL, Belgium
Son of Francis Ferrie, of Foundry Street, Belfast; husband of Isabella Ferrie,
of 52, James Street, Mile End, Glasgow.

Ferrie, Gordon - Rifleman
6069 Royal Irish Rifles 7th Battalion *Died in War on 21 April 1916*
DUD CORNER CEMETERY, LOOS, France
Born in Belfast. Enlisted in Holywood.

Ferrin, Alexander - Rifleman
10052 Royal Irish Rifles 1st Battalion *Killed in Action on 2 October 1918*
TYNE COT MEMORIAL, Belgium
Born and enlisted in Belfast.

Ferrin, John - Private
S/43051 Queen's Own Cameron Highlanders 1st Battalion *Died in War on 2 December 1916*
WARLENCOURT BRITISH CEMETERY, *France*
Born and enlisted in Belfast.

Ferris, David - Private
64 Australian Infantry 28th Battalion *Died in War on 29 July 1916*
VILLERS-BRETONNEUX MEMORIAL, *France*
Son of James and Margaret Gagburn Ferris; husband of Bertha Ferris,
of 203, Barker Road, Subiaco, Western Australia. Born in Belfast, Ireland.

Ferris, George - Private
14174 Royal Irish Fusiliers 9th Battalion *Age 18 Killed in Action on 1 July 1916*
MILL ROAD CEMETERY, THIEPVAL, *France*
Son of George and Annie E. Ferris, of 6, Crosby Street, Belfast. Native of Tandragee, County Armagh.

Ferris, Herbert - Private
7739 Canadian Infantry (Eastern Ontario Regiment) *Died in War on 22 April 1915*
YPRES (MENIN GATE) MEMORIAL, *Belgium*
Born in Belfast the son of James and Rebecca Ferris. An Anglican he worked as a steam fitter in Canada.

Ferris, Joseph F - Private
3557 Seaforth Highlanders 4th Battalion *Age 18 Died of Wounds on 23 September 1915*
MERVILLE COMMUNAL CEMETERY, *France*
Son of William and Mary A. Ferris, of 28, Silvergrove Street, Belfast.

Ferris, Richard - Private
17826 Highland Light Infantry 1st Battalion attached 107th Trench Mortar Battery *Died of Wounds on 1 November 1918*
BAGHDAD (NORTH GATE) WAR CEMETERY, *Iraq*
277 Cupar Street, Belfast.

Ferris, Robert - Rifleman
1436 Royal Irish Rifles 8th Battalion *Age 28 Died in War on 2 July 1916*
THIEPVAL MEMORIAL, *France*
Son of William Ferris and the late Margaret Ferris; husband of Martha Rock (formerly Ferris),
of 6, Bradford Street, Belfast.

Ferris, Samuel - Lance Corporal
14/17616 Royal Irish Rifles 14th Battalion *Killed in Action on 9 October 1916*
POND FARM CEMETERY, *Belgium*
Husband of Mrs. E. Flanagan (formerly Ferris), of 49, Coolderry St Belfast.

Ferris, Samuel - Rifleman
9153 Royal Irish Rifles 2nd Battalion *Age 40 Died in War on 11 November 1914*
YPRES (MENIN GATE) MEMORIAL, *Belgium*
Husband of Catherine Ferris, of 914, Crumlin Road, Ballysillan, Belfast.
A career soldier he re-joined the Army at the beginning of the war.

Ferris, Wesley - Stoker First Class
SS/114263 Royal Navy HMS "Racoon" *Age 24 Drowned in wreck of vessel on the Irish coast on 9 January 1918*
CHATHAM NAVAL MEMORIAL, *United Kingdom*
Son of William J. and Elizabeth Ferris, of 84, North Howard Street, Belfast. Mentioned in Despatches.

Ferris, William - Private
4414 Connaught Rangers 6th Battalion *Died in War on 3 September 1916*
THIEPVAL MEMORIAL, *France*
53 Silvio Street, Belfast.

Ferris, William - Sapper
59104 Royal Engineers *Age 39 Died as a result of war on 2 January 1920*
WANDSWORTH (STREATHAM) CEMETERY, *United Kingdom*
Husband of Florence Alice White (formerly Ferris), of 13C, Theatre Street, Battersea, London.
Served in the South African Campaign. Born in Belfast.

Ferris, William Small - Second Lieutenant
Royal Irish Rifles 12th Battalion *Age 29 Killed in Action on 7 June 1917*
LONE TREE CEMETERY, *Belgium*
Son of the Rev J. C. Ferris and Elizabeth Ferris, 4 Sandown Park, Knock, Belfast.

Fetherston, John McDonald - Sub-Lieutenant
Royal Navy H.M.M.L. "218" *Age 21 Died as a result of War on 6 December 1918*
EAST MUDROS MILITARY CEMETERY, *Greece*
Son of John William Fetherston, of Montono, Malone Park, Belfast.

Field, William - Trimmer
Mercantile Marine S.S. "Lusitania" (Liverpool)
Age 31 Drowned, as a result of an attack by an enemy submarine on 7 May 1915
TOWER HILL MEMORIAL, *United Kingdom*
Son of Alexander and Elizabeth Field; husband of Catherine Field (née Doran),
of 38, Ship Street, Belfast. Born in Scotland.

Fields, Robert Dickie - Private
M/282816 Royal Army Service Corps *Died in War on 24 March 1917*
GLASGOW (RIDDRIE PARK) CEMETERY, *United Kingdom*
Born in Belfast, enlisted Glasgow.

Findlay, William. - Watchman
Mercantile Marine H.M.H.S. "Llandovery Castle" (London)
Age 18 Drowned, as a result of an attack by an enemy submarine on 27 June 1918
TOWER HILL MEMORIAL, *United Kingdom*
Son of the late William and Esther Findlay. Born at Belfast.

Finlay, Alexander - Private
3582 Royal Inniskilling Fusiliers 2nd Battalion *Age 24 Died in War on 10 July 1916*
THIEPVAL MEMORIAL, *France*
Son of John Finlay, of 52, Carrington Street, Belfast.

Finlay, David - Private
7755 Royal Inniskilling Fusiliers 2nd Battalion
Age 28 Died of wounds, received at Richebourge L'Avoue on 17 May 1915
BETHUNE TOWN CEMETERY, *France*
Brother of Mrs. Elizabeth A. Irwin, of 63, Seaview Street, Belfast.

Finlay, John - Rifleman
10573 Royal Irish Rifles 6th Battalion *Died in War on 11 August 1915*
HELLES MEMORIAL, Turkey
Born and enlisted in Belfast.

Finlay, Patrick - Sergeant
4756 Royal Irish Rifles 1st Battalion *Killed in Action on 25 September 1915*
WHITE CITY CEMETERY, BOIS-GRENIER, France
The son of Hugh and Jane Finlay of Belfast. Had also served in the Boer War.

Finlay, Walter James - Writer First Class
343795 Royal Navy HMS "Bulwark" *Died in War on 26 November 1914*
PORTSMOUTH NAVAL MEMORIAL, United Kingdom
2 Oakland Villas, Upper Beersbridge Road, Belfast.

Finlay, William - Sergeant
16488 Royal Irish Rifles 16th Battalion *Age 24 Killed in Action on 21 March 1918*
POZIERES MEMORIAL, France
Son of Mrs. Sarah Finlay, of 18, Snugville Street, Belfast, and the late William J. Finlay.

Finlay, William James - Private
1657 North Irish Horse *Age 19 Died in War on 23 June 1916*
FONCQUEVILLERS MILITARY CEMETERY, France
Son of William James and Mareia Concetta Finlay, of 28. Glenallen Street, Belfast.

Finn, Michael - Private
21113 Royal Irish Fusiliers 8th Battalion formerly 2520 Connaught Rangers
Died in War on 16 March 1916
MAROC BRITISH CEMETERY, GRENAY, France
Son of Maurice Finn, 18 Milliken Street, Belfast.

Finn, Thomas - Rifleman
15/12781 Royal Irish Rifles Depot *Age 24 Died as a result of war on 23 November 1918*
BELFAST CITY CEMETERY, United Kingdom
Son of William and Annie Finn, of 19, Shipbuoy Street, Belfast.

Finn, William John - Rifleman
9997 Royal Irish Rifles 2nd Battalion *Age 24 Killed in Action on 7 June 1917*
YPRES (MENIN GATE) MEMORIAL, Belgium
Son of Henry and Margaret A. Finn, of 11, Paris Street, Shankill Road, Belfast.

Finnegan, Joseph - Private
27577 Northamptonshire Regiment 7th Battalion *Died in War on 10 June 1917*
YPRES (MENIN GATE) MEMORIAL, Belgium
Brother of Maggie Finnegan of Belfast.

Finnegan, Robert Thompson - Private
M2/274193 Royal Army Service Corps *Died of Wounds on 21 March 1918*
POZIERES MEMORIAL, France
Son of John Maxwell and Susan Wilson Finnegan.

Fisher, Benjamin - Gunner
71400 Royal Field Artillery 66th Battery *Age 25 Died of sickness on 18 November 1917*
BELFAST (DUNDONALD) CEMETERY, *United Kingdom*
Son of Benjamin and Annie Fisher, of 9, Constance Street, Albertbridge Road, Belfast.
Discharged in 1916 and awarded the Silver War Badge.

Fisher, Charles Heath - Second Lieutenant
East Surrey Regiment 4th Battalion attached 12th Battalion *Age 27 Died in War on 14 October 1918*
DADIZEELE NEW BRITISH CEMETERY, *Belgium*
Son of Mr. and Mrs. C. E. Fisher, of 8, Cromwell Rd. Wimbledon, London; husband of
Nora E. Fisher, of Ashleigh, Newtownbreda, Belfast. Awarded the Military Cross

Fisher, Frederick - Private
S/10526 Queen's Own Cameron Highlanders 5th Battalion *Killed in Action on 22 March 1918*
POZIERES MEMORIAL, *France*
Born in Belfast, enlisted Glasgow.

Fisher, George - Private
724696 Canadian Infantry (Eastern Ontario Regiment) 38th Battalion
Age 28 Died of wounds received at Vimy Ridge on 16 April 1917
BELFAST (DUNDONALD) CEMETERY, *United Kingdom*
Husband of Elizabeth Fisher, of 67, Lord Street, Belfast. An Anglican he had previous
military experience and had worked as a labourer.

Fisher, Hugo Bell - Lieutenant
Royal Munster Fusiliers 2nd Battalion *Age 19 Died of wounds on 23 November 1917*
HARLEBEKE NEW BRITISH CEMETERY, *Belgium*
Only son of Dr. Elizabeth Bell Fisher, of 4, College Gardens, Belfast, and the late Dr. Hugh Fisher.

Fisher, John - Private
PLY/12264 Royal Marine Light Infantry 1st R.M. Battalion Royal Naval Division
Age 30 Died in War on 13 November 1916
THIEPVAL MEMORIAL, *France*
Son of Mrs. Isabella Fisher, of 20, Baltic Avenue, Belfast.

Fisher, Thomas - Lance Corporal
8264 Queen's Own Cameron Highlanders 2nd Battalion *Died in War on 23 April 1915*
YPRES (MENIN GATE) MEMORIAL, *Belgium*
Born in Belfast, enlisted Glasgow.

Fisher, Thomas - Private
12300 Princess Victoria's (Royal Irish Fusiliers) 6th Battalion *Died in War on 15 August 1915*
HELLES MEMORIAL, *Turkey*
Born and enlisted in Belfast.

Fisher, Thomas - Private
17530 Royal Inniskillings Fusiliers 9th Battalion *Killed in Action on 1 July 1916*
THIEPVAL MEMORIAL, *France*
62 Templemore Street, Belfast.

Fitzgerald, David - Lance Corporal
7356 Royal Irish Rifles 2nd Battalion *Age 19 Killed in Action on 23 November 1917*
CAMBRAI MEMORIAL, LOUVERVAL, France
Son of Robert and Maggie Fitzgerald, of Upper Ballysillan, Ligoneil, Belfast.

Fitzgerald, Patrick - Private
9440 Highland Light Infantry 2nd Battalion *Killed in Action on 25 September 1915*
PONT-DU-HEM MILITARY CEMETERY, LA GORGUE, France
Born in Belfast, enlisted Edinburgh.

Fitzgerald, Robert - Private
11325 Royal Warwickshire Regiment 1st Battalion *Died in War on 10 October 1915*
NORFOLK CEMETERY, BECORDEL-BECOURT, France
Born in Belfast enlisted in Hereford, England.

Fitzgerald, Robert - Rifleman
11066 Royal Irish Rifles 6th Battalion *Age 20 Killed in Action on 24 February 1916*
MIKRA BRITISH CEMETERY, KALAMARIA, Greece
Son of William and Brigid Fitzgerald, of 122, Dover Street, Belfast.
Two brothers also served and his father was a former soldier.

Fitzgerald, William - Rifleman
14602 Royal Irish Rifles 9th Battalion *Age 36 Killed in Action on 1 July 1916*
THIEPVAL MEMORIAL, France
Son of David and Jane Fitzgerald, of Ligoneil, Belfast; husband of Margaret Elizabeth Fitzgerald,
of Church Street, Dromore, County Down.

Fitzgerald, William Wilks - Second Lieutenant
Royal Flying Corps 25th Squadron *Age 22 Killed in Action on 27 July 1917*
LAPUGNOY MILITARY CEMETERY, France
Son of Maurice F. and Anna M. Fitzgerald, of "Fairholme" Kill-O'-the-Grange, Blackrock, County Dublin.
Native of Belfast.

Fitzpatrick, Thomas - Corporal
1952 Leinster Regiment 7th Battalion *Died in War on 2 August 1917*
YPRES (MENIN GATE) MEMORIAL, Belgium
Eldest son of Thomas and Margaret Fitzpatrick, of 135 Cullingtree Road, Belfast.

Fitzsimmons, James - Rifleman
5367 Royal Irish Rifles "C" Company 2nd Battalion *Age 31 Killed in Action on 12 December 1916*
HYDE PARK CORNER (ROYAL BERKS) CEMETERY, Belgium
Son of James and Mary Anne Fitzsimmons (née Hilden), of Lisburn; husband of Catherine Fitzsimmons,
of 22, Shore Street, Belfast.

Fitzsimmons, James - Rifleman
5510 Royal Irish Rifles 2nd Battalion *Age 20 Killed in Action on 16 June 1915*
YPRES (MENIN GATE) MEMORIAL, Belgium
Son of Mrs. Ellen Fitzsimmons, of 37, Skipton Street, Belfast.

Journey of Remembering

Fitzsimmons, John - Lance Corporal
14610 Royal Irish Rifles 10th Battalion *Died in War on 22 March 1916*
BELFAST CITY CEMETERY, United Kingdom
Native of Belfast.

Fitzsimmons, Patrick - Rifleman
6322 Royal Irish Rifles "G" Company 2nd Battalion *Age 35 Killed in Action on 16 June 1915*
YPRES (MENIN GATE) MEMORIAL, Belgium
An Army reservist he had been employed by Messrs WW Kennedy & Co of Academy Street, Belfast. He is listed among the missing on the Menin Gate Memorial, Ypres. However, it is also suggested that he actually occupies the grave at Poelcappelle attributed to Prviate John Condon of the Royal Irish Regiment. John Condon is often accepted as the youngest soldier to be killed in the Great War and is thought to have been just 14.

Fitzsimmons, Thomas John - Private
24854 Royal Irish Fusiliers 2nd Battalion *Age 31 Died of pneumonia on 13 March 1917*
STRUMA MILITARY CEMETERY, Greece
Son of James and Margaret Fitzsimmons, of 36, Pound Street, Belfast.

Fitzsimmons, William - Private
3455 Royal Inniskilling Fusiliers 1st Battalion *Killed in Action on 22 March 1918*
POZIERES MEMORIAL, France
Born and enlisted in Belfast.

Fitzsimmons, William John - Private
12551 Princess Victoria's (Royal Irish Fusiliers) 9th Battalion *Died in War on 25 October 1918*
HARLEBEKE NEW BRITISH CEMETERY, Belgium
Born and enlisted in Belfast. Formerly 22093 Royal Irish Rifles.

Fitzsimons, Charles - Private
8077 Royal Irish Fusiliers 1st Battalion *Age 39 Died in War on 5 June 1915*
YPRES (MENIN GATE) MEMORIAL, Belgium
Husband of Bridget Fitzsimons, of 3, Grosvenor Place, Belfast.

Fitzsimons, Hugh - Rifleman
9400 Royal Irish Rifles 1st Battalion *Killed in Action on 10 March 1915*
ESTAIRES COMMUNAL CEMETERY, France
Son of a butcher, John of Spamount Street, Belfast. Two brothers also served but survived. A great uncle of the broadcaster, Eamonn Holmes.

Fitzsimons, James - Rifleman
5367 Royal Irish Rifles 2nd Battalion *Died in War on 12 December 1916*
HYDE PARK CORNER (ROYAL BERKS) CEMETERY, Belgium
Born in Lambeg, enlisted in Lisburn, resident of Belfast.

Fitzsimons, John H - Corporal
14603 Royal Irish Rifles 14th Battalion *Killed in Action on 1 July 1916*
CONNAUGHT CEMETERY, THIEPVAL, France
172 Roden Street, Belfast. His father, Mr C. E. Fitzsimons, was a former Sergeant in the Royal Irish Constabulary.

Fitzsimons, Robert - Lance Corporal
6581 Royal Irish Rifles 2nd Battalion *Age 40 Killed in Action on 17 October 1916*
THIEPVAL MEMORIAL, France
Son of Henry and Rosanna Fitzsimons, of Belfast; husband of Harriette Fitzsimons,
of Ballymorran, Killinchy, County Down.

Flack, David William Barnet - Lance Corporal
939 Royal Irish Rifles 13th Battalion *Killed in Action on 16 August 1917*
TYNE COT MEMORIAL, Belgium
Born and enlisted in Belfast.

Flaherty, James - Private
19828 Princess Victoria's (Royal Irish Fusiliers) 5th Battalion *Died in War on 19 March 1918*
KANTARA WAR MEMORIAL CEMETERY, Egypt
Born in Athlone, enlisted Waterford, resident in Belfast.

Flanagan, Alexander - Sergeant
11932 Royal Irish Rifles 15th Battalion *Killed in Action on 1 July 1916*
THIEPVAL MEMORIAL, France
Born and enlisted in Belfast.

Flanagan, Dominic - Private
3171 Leinster Regiment 7th Battalion *Died in War on 18 November 1917*
GREVILLERS BRITISH CEMETERY, France
Born and enlisted in Belfast.

Flanagan, Edward - Private
3326 Leinster Regiment 7th Battalion *Died in War on 27 June 1916*
LOOS MEMORIAL, France
Born and enlisted in Belfast.

Flanagan, Hugh - Lance Corporal
41229 Royal Irish Fusiliers 9th Battalion *Age 21 Died in War on 22 November 1917*
CAMBRAI MEMORIAL, LOUVERVAL, France
Son of R. H. and Martha Flanagan, of 129, Dunluce Avenue, Belfast.

Flanagan, James - Corporal
19902 Royal Irish Rifles 6th Battalion *Age 38 Died in War on 16 May 1917*
BELFAST (MILLTOWN) ROMAN CATHOLIC CEMETERY, United Kingdom
Born and enlisted in Dundalk, resident in Belfast. Died in Victoria Barracks.
His brother, who also served, lived at Mary Street South, Dundalk

Flanagan, Robert - Private
48743 Machine Gun Corps (Infantry) 30th Company *Age 33 Died of Wounds on 7 October 1916*
MIKRA BRITISH CEMETERY, KALAMARIA, Greece
Son of Michael and Mary Jane Flanagan, of 59, McDonnell St. Belfast.

Flanagan, Robert - Sergeant
4843 Royal Irish Rifles 2nd Battalion *Killed in Action on 19 January 1916*
Born in Seapatrick, County Down, enlisted in Banbridge. Resident of Belfast.

Flanagan, William Henry Murray - Rifleman
10310 Royal Irish Rifles 12th Battalion *Age 23 Died in War on 13 April 1918*
TYNE COT MEMORIAL, Belgium
Son of Robert Henry and Martha Flanagan, of 129, Dunluce Avenue, Belfast.

Flanigan, Edmund Hughes - Lieutenant
Royal Army Medical Corps 102nd Field Ambulance *Age 33 Died in War on 17 June 1916*
BANBRIDGE ROMAN CATHOLIC CEMETERY, United Kingdom
Son of Patrick and Ellen Flanigan, of Duivelskloof, Northern Transvaal. Born at Belfast, Ireland.

Flanigan, Gerald - Private
21832 Canadian Infantry (Central Ontario Regiment) 4th Battalion *Age 29 Died in War on 20 April 1916*
LIJSSENTHOEK MILITARY CEMETERY, Belgium
Son of Patrick and Ellen Flanigan, of 46, Great Victoria Street, Belfast. An architect by profession, he emigrated to Canada in 1913, joining the Forces at Regina, Saskatchewan

Flavell, George - Private
L/15691 Royal Fusiliers (City of London Regiment) 4th Battalion *Died in War on 26 October 1914*
LE TOURET MEMORIAL, France
Born and enlisted in Belfast.

Fleming, Thomas - Rifleman
3076 Royal Irish Rifles 14th Battalion *Age 21 Killed in Action on 16 August 1917*
NEW IRISH FARM CEMETERY, Belgium
Son of George and Elizabeth Fleming, of 15, Mountcashel Street, Belfast.

Fleming, William Joseph - Rifleman
S/10035 Royal Irish Rifles 7th Battalion transferred to 386907 61st Company Labour Corps
Age 23 Died of Wounds on 14 October 1918
UNDERHILL FARM CEMETERY, Belgium
Son of William Fleming, of Belfast, and the late Mary Fleming.

Fletcher, James - Corporal
14303 Royal Inniskilling Fusiliers 8th Battalion *Died in War on 27 December 1916*
KEMMEL CHATEAU MILITARY CEMETERY, Belgium
13, Oakley Street, Belfast.

Fletcher, Robert - Stoker
1422U Royal Naval Reserve HMS "Queen Mary" *Killed in Action on 31 May 1916*
PORTSMOUTH NAVAL MEMORIAL, United Kingdom
Son of Robert and Jane Fletcher, of Belfast; husband of Margaret Fletcher, of 5, Eighth Street, Belfast.

Fletcher, William - Driver
49996 Royal Horse Artillery and Royal Field Artillery *Died in War on 13 September 1916*
BAGHDAD (NORTH GATE) WAR CEMETERY, Iraq
Born and enlisted in Belfast.

Floyd, Charles - Private
11367 Royal Inniskilling Fusiliers 6th Battalion *Died in War on 16 August 1915*
HELLES MEMORIAL, Turkey
Brother of Mrs Cochrane, 16, Lawnview Street, Belfast.

Flynn, Felix - Private
B/8515 Highland Light Infantry 2nd Battalion *Age 39 Killed in Action on 12 September 1916*
EUSTON ROAD CEMETERY, COLINCAMPS, *France*
Son of John and Hannah Flynn, of 32, Mountpottinger Road, Belfast.

Flynn, Henry - Private
6882 Royal Irish Rifles 1st Battalion *Killed in Action on 1 January 1915*
ESTAIRES COMMUNAL CEMETERY AND EXTENSION, *France*
30 Ghent Street, Belfast. A Boer War veteran.

Flynn, Patrick - Private
24279 Royal Irish Fusiliers 7th/8th Battalion *Age 24 Died in War on 21 November 1917*
BUCQUOY ROAD CEMETERY, FICHEUX, *France*
Son of Patrick Flynn, of 77, North Queen Street, Belfast; husband of Mary Jane Leneghan (formerly Flynn).

Flynn, Patrick - Private
P.W.2892 Duke of Cambridge's Own (Middlesex Regiment) 1st Battalion *Died in War on 7 May 1918*
CANTERBURY CEMETERY, *Kent, United Kingdom*
Born in Belfast. Enlisted in Inverkeithing, Scotland.

Flynn, William - Private
7189 Royal Irish Fusiliers 1st Battalion *Died of Wounds on 20 October 1914*
CITE BONJEAN MILITARY CEMETERY, ARMENTIERES, *France*
13 Waterville Street, Belfast.

Flynn, William George Acheson - Rifleman
18981 Royal Irish Rifles 12th Battalion *Age 22 Died in War on 11 August 1917*
YPRES (MENIN GATE) MEMORIAL, *Belgium*
Son of William George Wade Flynn, of Glenbank, Ballysillan, Belfast, and the late Sarah Flynn.

Foley, Robert James - Rifleman
7180 Royal Irish Rifles 2nd Battalion *Age 29 Killed in Action on 26 October 1914*
LE TOURET MEMORIAL, *France*
Son of Patrick and Mary Ellen Foley, of 59, Servia Street, Belfast.

Forbes, Hugh - Private
53348 Royal Army Medical Corps *Died in War on 25 February 1915*
BELFAST CITY CEMETERY, *United Kingdom*
Native of Belfast.

Forbes, John Donald - Second Lieutenant
Lancashire Fusiliers 10th Battalion *Age 20 Died of Wounds on 29 September 1915*
LIJSSENTHOEK MILITARY CEMETERY, *Belgium*
Son of John Forbes, and Annie Cladwell Forbes of "Sunbury" Cadogan Park, Belfast. Previously 72 Eglantine Avenue. His brothers Murray and Robert served as officers with the 1st Royal Irish Rifles.

Forbes, William F - Lance Corporal
178 Royal Irish Rifles "D" Company 14th Battalion *Age 20 Died in War on 1 November 1916*
POND FARM CEMETERY, *Belgium*
Son of Sarah Forbes, of "Glenderown" Kingsmere Avenue, Belfast, and the late Alexander Forbes. Native of Dunadry, County Antrim.

Ford, James - Private
3501 Royal Inniskilling Fusiliers 2nd Battalion *Died in War on 29 November 1917*
MENDINGHEM MILITARY CEMETERY, Belgium
Born Belfast. Enlisted in Barrow-in-Furness.

Fordyce, William - Rifleman
17647 Royal Irish Rifles 1st Battalion *Age 21 Killed in Action on 7 September 1918*
PLOEGSTEERT MEMORIAL, Belgium
Son of Mrs. S. Fordyce, of 56, Posnett Street, Belfast.

Foreman, Ernest - Private
29480 Princess Victoria's (Royal Irish Fusiliers) 1st Battalion *Died in War on 14 April 1918*
TYNE COT MEMORIAL, Belgium
Born and enlisted in Belfast. Formerly 4494, Seaforth Highlanders.

Foreman, Robert - Lance Corporal
576 Royal Irish Rifles 2nd Battalion *Died in War on 22 April 1918*
LA CAPELLE-EN-THIERACHE COMMUNAL CEMETERY, France
Born and enlisted in Belfast.

Forrest, George Henry - Private
27735 Worcestershire Regiment 1st Battalion *Age 40 Died in War on 28 March 1918*
POZIERES MEMORIAL, France
Son of Samuel and Lavinia Mary Wheldon Forrest, of "Bordesley", Haddington Gardens, Cregagh, Belfast.

Forrest, John - Gunner
128 Royal Garrison Artillery *Died in War on 28 July 1916*
PEAKE WOOD CEMETERY FRICOURT, France
Born in Belfast, enlisted Port Glasgow.

Forrester, George - Rifleman
619 Royal Irish Rifles 15th Battalion *Died in War on 15 June 1918*
GWALIA CEMETERY, Belgium
Born and enlisted in Belfast.

Forster, George - Private
10138 Connaught Rangers 1st Battalion *Died in War on 23 November 1914*
LE TOURET MEMORIAL, France
Born in Belfast.

Forsyth, William - Stoker First Class
305407 Royal Navy HMS "Defence" *Age 35 Killed in Action on 31 May 1916*
PLYMOUTH NAVAL MEMORIAL, United Kingdom
Son of Charles and Sarah Forsyth, of Belfast.

Forsythe, Alexander - Private
2686 Royal Inniskilling Fusiliers 1st Battalion *Killed in Action on 1 July 1916*
THIEPVAL MEMORIAL, France
Husband of Elizabeth, 69 Silvio Street, Belfast.

Forsythe, George - Rifleman
47126 Royal Irish Rifles 2nd Battalion *Died in War on 6 September 1918*
WULVERGHEM-LINDENHOEK ROAD MILITARY CEMETERY, Belgium
Born and enlisted in Belfast. Formerly168, Royal Irish Rifles.

Forsythe, Hugh - Lance Corporal
19451 Machine Gun Corps 107th Company Ulster Division
Age 22 Died of wounds on 11 September 1916
BOULOGNE EASTERN CEMETERY, France
Son of Robert and Elizabeth Forsythe, of 3, Bryson Street, Belfast. Formerly served in 8th Battalion Royal Irish Rifles. An engineer employed at Harland and Wolff.

Forsythe, James McMullan - Rifleman
12787 Royal Irish Rifles 8th Battalion *Age 20 Died in War on 7 June 1917*
SPANBROEKMOLEN BRITISH CEMETERY, Belgium
Son of Stanfield and Elizabeth Forsythe, of 55, Belvoir Street, Belfast.

Forsythe, John Alexander - Rifleman
1770 Royal Irish Rifles 10th Battalion *Killed in Action on 1 July 1916*
THIEPVAL MEMORIAL, France
Son of Agnes Patterson, 42 Roundhill Street, Belfast.

Forsythe, William Robert - Lance Corporal
19414 Highland Light Infantry 10/11th Battalion *Age 26 Killed in Action on 15 September 1916*
DERNANCOURT COMMUNAL CEMETERY EXTENSION, France
Son of the late William George and Sarah Jane Forsythe, of Belfast.

Foster, Andrew - Lance Corporal
3302 Royal Inniskilling Fusiliers "B" Company 1st Battalion *Age 21 Died in War on 19 May 1917*
ARRAS MEMORIAL, France
Son of Mrs. Bridget Foster, of 73, Brookfield Street, Belfast.

Foster, Crawford - Corporal
6853 South Lancashire Regiment 2nd Battalion *Age 27 Died of wounds on 28 August 1915*
BRANDHOEK MILITARY CEMETERY, Belgium
Son of Robert and Maria Foster, of 13, Rutland Street, Belfast.

Foster, George - Rifleman
14619 Royal Irish Rifles 14th Battalion *Age 21 Died in War on 6 April 1916*
HAMEL MILITARY CEMETERY, BEAUMONT-HAMEL, France
Son of Alexander and Susan Foster, of 76A, Beechfield Street, Belfast. A Boiler Maker.

Foster, Henry - Sergeant
12770 Royal Irish Rifles 9th Battalion *Age 45 Killed in Action on 1 July 1916*
THIEPVAL MEMORIAL, France
Husband of Annie Foster, of 128, Canmore Street, Belfast.

Foster, J - Rifleman
Royal Irish Rifles *Died of Wounds*
19, Wigton Street, Belfast.

Journey of Remembering

Foster, John - Private
14177 Royal Inniskilling Fusiliers 5th Battalion *Died of Wounds on 15 August 1915*
HELLES MEMORIAL, Greece
Born and enlisted in Belfast.

Foster, John - Rifleman
5623 Royal Irish Rifles 2nd Battalion Age 56 *Killed in Action on 18 December 1914*
YPRES (MENIN GATE) MEMORIAL, Belgium
Husband of Rose Ann Foster of 35, Tyne Street, Belfast.

Foster, John - Stoker First Class
SS104740 Royal Navy HMS "Aboukir" *Died in War on 22 September 1914*
CHATHAM NAVAL MEMORIAL, United Kingdom
Son of Jane Foster, 29 Spring Street, Belfast.

Foster, Robert McKibben - Rifleman
19914 Royal Irish Rifles 7th Battalion *Died in War on 27 March 1916*
DUD CORNER CEMETERY, LOOS, France
Born and enlisted in Belfast.

Foster, William - Private
394176 Labour Corps Formerly 1344 Royal Irish Fusiliers *Died in War on 8 July 1918*
SALONKIA (LEMBET ROAD) MILITARY CEMETERY, Greece
Native of Belfast.

Fowler, George - Private
3303 Royal Inniskilling Fusiliers 1st Battalion *Killed in Action on 1 July 1916*
THIEPVAL MEMORIAL, France
Born and enlisted in Belfast.

Fowler, James - Rifleman
14587 Royal Irish Rifles 9th Battalion *Died in War on 6 June 1916*
AUTHUILE MILITARY CEMETERY, France
Husband of Eleanor, 30 Stanley Street, Belfast.

Fox, James - Private
8639 Royal Inniskilling Fusiliers 1st Battalion *Died in War on 28 April 1915*
HELLES MEMORIAL, Turkey
Born and enlisted in Belfast.

Foy, David - Lance Corporal
17621 Royal Irish Rifles 14th Battalion *Killed in Action on 1 July 1916*
MILL ROAD CEMETERY, THIEPVAL, France
Son of David W. and Agnes Foy; husband of Ellen Rodgers Foy, of 6, Pakenham Street, Belfast.

Foy, James - Private
349378 Labour Corps *Died in War on 2 February 1918*
BLACKBURN CEMETERY, United Kingdom
Born in Belfast, enlisted in London. Formerly 21935 Army Service Corps.

Frame, James Russell Granger Allen - Fireman
884616 Mercantile Marine Reserve HMS "Paxton" *Age 17 Killed in Action with submarine on 20 May 1917*
PLYMOUTH NAVAL MEMORIAL, United Kingdom
Son of James and Sarah Frame, of 110, Agnes Street, Belfast.

Frame, Thomas - Bombardier
Royal Artillery 48th Brigade *Died of Wounds on 17 November 1917*
DUHALLOW A.D.S. CEMETERY, Belgium
Son of James and the late Sarah Frame,110 Agnes Street, Belfast.

Frame, William Allen - Bombardier
38816 Royal Field Artillery 74th Brigade *Died in War on 3 September 1917*
CANADA FARM CEMETERY, Belgium
Son of James and the late Sarah Frame, of 110, Agnes Street, Belfast.

Francey, Thomas - Private
8061 Royal Inniskilling Fusiliers "A" Company 2nd Battalion *Age 29 Died in War on 16 May 1915*
LE TOURET MEMORIAL, France
Son of William John and Mary A. Francey, of 21, Paxton Street, Belfast; husband of Mary Jane Francey, of 117, Thorndyke Street, Belfast.

Francey, William - Private
12261 Royal Inniskilling Fusiliers 5th Battalion *Age 19 Died in War on 15 April 1915*
HELLES MEMORIAL, Turkey
Son of William John and Mary Ann Francey, of 21, Paxton Street, Belfast.

Fraser, Frederick - Sergeant
8381 King's (Liverpool Regiment) 4th Battalion *Died in War on 28 March 1916*
CAMBRIN MILITARY CEMETERY, France
Born in Belfast. Enlisted and was resident in Manchester.

Fraser, James - Private
53045 King's (Liverpool Regiment) 1st Battalion *Died in War on 15 November 1916*
MAILLY WOOD CEMETERY, MAILLY MAILLET, France
Born in Belfast. Lived in Manchester when enlisted.

Fraser, Richard - Lance Corporal
16494 Royal Irish Rifles 13th Battalion *Killed in Action on 1 July 1916*
THIEPVAL MEMORIAL, France
Born and enlisted in Belfast.

Fraser, Thomas - Private
24930 Cameronians (Scottish Rifles) 1st Battalion *Died in War on 21 September 1918*
VILLERS HILL BRITISH CEMETERY, VILLERS-GUISLAIN, France
92 Montrose Street, Belfast.

Fraser, William - Private
14169 Northunberland Fusiliers 10th Battalion *Died in War on 17 July 1916*
THIEPVAL MEMORIAL, France
92 Montrose Street, Belfast.

Fraser, William - Second Lieutenant
Black Watch (Royal Highlanders) 1st Battalion
Age 23 Died, of wounds, received at Loos 26th September on 29 September 1915
LAPUGNOY MILITARY CEMETERY, France
Native of Inverness-shire and a noted athelete. Son of Ewen and Christina Fraser, of "Bunloit" Deerpark Road and of 15 Willowbank Gardens, both Belfast.

Fraser, William - Sergeant
7587 Highland Light Infantry 8th (Lanark) Battalion (Territorial) *Died in War on 26 July 1916*
DANTZIG ALLEY BRITISH CEMETERY MAMETZ, France
Born in Belfast, enlisted in Lanark, Scotland.

Frazer, William - Rifleman
14589 Royal Irish Rifles 9th Battalion *Age 35 Killed in Action on 7 June 1917*
YPRES (MENIN GATE) MEMORIAL, Belgium
Husband of Alice Frazer, of 101, Northumberland Street, Belfast.

Frazer, Willoughby - Private
9852 Royal Irish Fusiliers 9th Battalion *Age 30 Died in War on 16 August 1918*
ARNEKE BRITISH CEMETERY, France
Son of David and Elizabeth Frazer, of 12, Windsor Road, Lisburn Road, Belfast.

Freebairn, George - Private
6739 Princess Louise's (Argyll & Sutherland Highlanders) 2/6th Battalion
Died in War on 5 December 1916
BELFAST CITY CEMETERY, United Kingdom
Born in Springburn, Renfrew, enlisted Stirling, resident Belfast.

Freeburn, David - Private
4106 Princess Victoria's (Royal Irish Fusiliers) 1st Battalion *Died in War on 25 May 1915*
Born in Portadown, enlisted Finner Camp, County Donegal, resident Belfast.

Freel, Wiliam John - Private
2983 Royal Inniskilling Fusiliers 2nd Battalion *Age 21 Died in War on 23 November 1916*
SERRE ROAD CEMETERY No.2, France
Son of William and Selina Freel, of 17, Wilton Square, Belfast.

Freeman, John - Rifleman
16495 Royal Irish Rifles 15th Battalion *Age 21 Killed in Action on 24 December 1915*
SUCRERIE MILITARY CEMETERY, COLINCAMPS, France
Son of Samuel and Elizabeth Freeman, of 27, Trafalgar Street, Belfast.

Freeman, Michael Isaac - Private
15579 Highland Light Infantry 17th Battalion *Age 34 Killed in Action on 1 July 1916*
BOUZINCOURT COMMUNAL CEMETERY EXTENSION, France
Son of Rhoda Freeman, of 51, Avoca Street, Belfast, and the late Abraham Freeman. A Jew, his Rabbi, Isaac Herzog, (whose own son, Chaim, would be elected President of Israel), praised his character and sense of patriotism and duty.

French, Frederick George - Private
874792 Canadian Infantry (Manitoba Regiment) 27th Battalion *Age 31 Died in War on 10 April 1917*
NINE ELMS MILITARY CEMETERY, THELUS, France
Son of Thomas and Anne Jane French. Member of Belfast Masonic Lodge No 166.
A Presbyterian he worked in Canada as an accountant.

French, Joseph - Private
20705 Royal Scots Fusiliers Depot *Died in War on 24 September 1916*
AYR CEMETERY, United Kingdom
Born in Belfast. Enlisted in Kilmarnock, Scotland.

French, Robert James - Rifleman
398 Royal Irish Rifles "A" Company 8th Battalion *Age 31 Died in War on 2 July 1916*
THIEPVAL MEMORIAL, France
Husband of Catherine French, of 13, Legane Street, Ballysillan, Belfast.

French, William - Private
8741 Irish Guards 1st Battalion *Age 38 Died in War on 8 February 1916*
MERVILLE COMMUNAL CEMETERY, France
Son of William and Ellen French, of 4, Belair Street, Belfast.

French, William Halliday - Private
59 Royal Irish Rifles 9th Battalion *Killed in Action on 1 July 1916*
THIEPVAL MEMORIAL, France
Son of William and Anna French, of 18, Rosevale Street, Cliftonville, Belfast.

Frizelle, Edwin Samuel - Second Lieutenant
Lancashire Fusiliers 5th Battalion *Age 21 Died in War on 3 August 1915*
LANCASHIRE LANDING CEMETERY, Turkey
Educated at Antrim Road Baptist School and Queen's University. He was the son of William and Janie Frizelle, Alliance Avenue, and latterly of Knutsford House, Cliftonville, Belfast.

Frizzell, John - Private
Royal Army Medical Corps 13th Field Ambulance *Died in War on 27 August 1916*
PERONNE ROAD COMMUNAL CEMETERY MARICOURT, France
21, Clonard Street, Belfast.

Frizzell, Joseph - Private
24189 Machine Gun Corps (Infantry) *Died of Wounds on 29 November 1917*
ROCQUIGNY-EQUANCOURT ROAD BRITISH CEMETERY, MANANCOURT, France
His Aunt, Mrs Robinson, lived at 10 Arundel Street, Belfast.

Fry, Frederick Samuel - Company Sergeant Major
L/5733 Royal Sussex Regiment "B" Company 2nd Battalion *Age 35 Died in War on 25 September 1915*
LOOS MEMORIAL, France
Son of the late Albert Edward and Harriett Annie Fry, of Hartfield, Sussex; husband of Alice Maud Fry, of 4, Dromore Street, Cregagh, Belfast.

Fry, John - Private
2112 Manchester Regiment 11th Battalion *Age 20 Died of Wounds on 19 November 1916*
LIVERPOOL (TOXTETH PARK) CEMETERY, United Kingdom
Son of Sarah Fry, of Kenaston, Saskatchewan, Canada, and the late Robert Fry. Native of Belfast.

Journey of Remembering

Fryer, Edward - Rifleman
14627 Royal Irish Rifles "B" Company 9th Battalion *Age 22 Killed in Action on 1 July 1916*
THIEPVAL MEMORIAL, *France*
Son of Robert and Sarah Fryer, of 8, Tenth Street, Belfast.

Fryer, William John - Lance Corporal
41089 Royal Irish Rifles 12th Battalion *Age 27 Killed in Action on 2 September 1918*
NIEUWKERKE CHURCHYARD, *Belgium*
Son of David and Annie Fryer, of Belfast.

Fryers, William - Rifleman
14/7567 Royal Irish Rifles 2nd Battalion *Age 33 Died of Wounds on 11 April 1918*
HARINGHE (BANDAGHEM) MILITARY CEMETERY, *Belgium*
Son of Agnes and the late Robert Fryers; husband of Elizabeth Fryers,
of 36, Upper Movilla Street, Newtownards. Native of Belfast.

Fullarton, Kenneth - Lieutenant
Royal Naval Volunteer Reserve Motor Launch "43" *Age 31 Died of pneumonia on 17 November 1918*
LOWESTOFT (BECCLES ROAD) CEMETERY, *United Kingdom*
Son of Robert and Ada Fullarton, of Belfast.

Fullerton, Henry - Private
4019 Royal Inniskilling Fusiliers 2nd Battalion *Died in War on 16 May 1915*
LE TOURET MEMORIAL, *France*
Brother of Sarah Brooks, 1 Lawnbrook Avenue, Belfast.

Fullerton, James Archer - Gunner
L/35892 Royal Field Artillery 1st Battery 45th Brigade *Died in War on 13 November 1916*
GROVE TOWN CEMETERY, MEAULTE, *France*
Nephew of Annie Turner, of 19, Evolina Street, Belfast.

Fullerton, Matthew - Driver
23630 Royal Engineers 2nd Signal Group *Age 22 Died of disease on 29 November 1918*
TERLINCTHUN BRITISH CEMETERY, WIMILLE, *France*
Son of Matthew and Agnes Fullerton, of Belfast.

Fulton, David - Sapper
64453 Royal Engineers 150th Field Company *Killed in Action on 1 July 1916*
CONNAUGHT CEMETERY, THIEPVAL, *France*
11 Langley Street, Belfast.

Fulton, James - Corporal
S3/030877 Army Service Corps Staff Supply Company *Age 40 Died of malaria on 7 July 1918*
KIRECHKOI-HORTAKOI MILITARY CEMETERY, *Greece*
Son of Henry and Mary Fulton, of Lisburn Road, Belfast; husband of Margaret Fulton,
of 38, Brookland Street, Lisburn Road, Belfast.

Fulton, Joseph - Private
2549 Royal Army Medical Corps *Age 33 Died in War on 31 January 1917*
CARNMONEY CEMETERY, *United Kingdom*
Son of Joseph and Annie Fulton; husband of Annie Fulton, of 33, Jennymount Terrace, York Road, Belfast.

Fulton, Samuel - Corporal
32014 South Lancashire Regiment 2nd Battalion *Age 35 Died in War on 21 August 1918*
LOCRE No.10 CEMETERY, Belgium
Husband of Minnie Fulton, of 48, Glentoran Street, Belfast.

Fulton, Samuel - Rifleman
7239 Royal Irish Rifles 10th Battalion *Age 18 Killed in Action on 1 July 1916*
THIEPVAL MEMORIAL, France
Son of the late John Fulton, of 16, Maralin Street, Belfast.

Furphy, James - Rifleman
10838 Royal Irish Rifles 2nd Battalion *Died in War on 7 July 1916*
THIEPVAL MEMORIAL, France
Son of Lizzie Furphy, 25 Braemar Street, Belfast.

Fury, Joseph - Sergeant
694 Royal Fusiliers (City of London Regiment) 9th Battalion *Died in War on 27 August 1915*
LE TREPORT MILITARY CEMETERY, France
Born in Belfast, enlisted in London.

Gabbey, James - Private
27524 Royal Inniskilling Fusiliers 9th Battalion *Killed in Action on 20 October 1918*
HARLEBEKE NEW BRITISH CEMETERY, Belgium
Born Belfast, enlisted Newtownards, son of James Gabbey, of 27, Railway Street, Comber, County Down.

Gaffikin, Robert - Sapper
59434 Canadian Engineers 3rd Tunnelling Company *Age 22 Died of Wounds on 15 September 1916*
PUCHEVILLERS BRITISH CEMETERY, France
Son of Mary Ellen and the late John Gaffikin, of 20, Cawnpore Street, Belfast, Ireland.
A Catholic, he worked as a steam fitter in Canada.

Gaffikin, William Bertram - Private
2265976 Eastern Ontario Regiment Princess Patricia's Canadian Light Infantry
Age 36 Died in War on 28 September 1918
DRUMMOND CEMETERY, RAILLENCOURT, France
Born at Belfast, Ireland. Son of John and Mary Jane Gaffikin; husband of Elsie Garton Gaffikin
(née Faulkner), of 13, Doncliffe Drive, Toronto 12, Ontario, Canada.

Gageby, Robert - Private
406719 Canadian Infantry (Western Ontario Regiment) 18th Battalion *Age 33 Died in War on 2 March 1916*
RIDGE WOOD MILITARY CEMETERY, Belgium
Son of Robert Gageby, of 45, Brookhill Avenue, Belfast, Ireland. Had 3 years service in the
Royal Irish Fusiliers and he later worked as a tinsmith, an Anglican.

Galbraith, George - Private
41188 Princess Victoria's (Royal Irish Fusiliers) 9th Battalion *Died in War on 24 November 1917*
GREVILLERS BRITISH CEMETERY, France
Born in Dunadry, County Antrim, resident of Belfast. Formerly 1601 North Irish Horse.

Galbraith, John Lee - Rifleman
1113 Royal Irish Rifles *Died in War on 2 July 1916*
A I F BURIAL GROUND, France
Born and enlisted in Belfast.

Galbraith, Joseph - Private
M/349543 Army Service Corps 12th Mobile Company (Lanark) *Age 21 Died in War on 6 February 1918*
CARNMONEY CEMETERY, United Kingdom
Son of William and Elizabeth Galbraith, of 1, Annalee Street, Belfast.

Gale, Thomas - Private
10049 Rifles Irish Rifles *Killed in Action on 8 May 1915*
YPRES (MENIN GATE) MEMORIAL, Belgium
7 Glenpark Street, Belfast.

Gallagher, Edward - Leading Fireman
867246 Mercantile Marine Reserve HMS "Marmora"
Age 26 Killed in Action with submarine off the South Coast of Ireland on 23 July 1918
PLYMOUTH NAVAL MEMORIAL, United Kingdom
Son of James and Sophia Gallagher, of 27, Beersbridge Road, Belfast; husband of Nancy H. Gallagher,
of 2, Whitewell Road, Belfast.

Gallagher, James - Rifleman
9/14684 Royal Irish Rifles 9th Battalion *Age 19 Died in War on 24 December 1915*
MIRAUMONT COMMUNAL CEMETERY, France
Son of Mary Gallagher, of Belfast, and the late James Gallagher.

Gallagher, John - Rifleman
6220 Royal Irish Rifles 2nd Battalion *Age 30 Killed in Action on 14 October 1914*
LE TOURET MEMORIAL, France
Husband of Maggie Gallagher, of 17, Sheriff Street, Belfast.

Gallagher, John - Rifleman
7210 Royal Irish Rifles 2nd Battalion *Died of Wounds on 17 September 1914*
LA FERTE-SOUS-JOUARRE MEMORIAL, France
Born in Belfast. Enlisted in Belfast.

Gallagher, John - Rifleman
7355 Royal Irish Rifles "A" Company 6th Battalion *Age 43 Died of Wounds on 10 August 1915*
7th FIELD AMBULANCE CEMETERY, Turkey
Son of John and Margaret Gallagher, of Cavan; husband of Annie Gallagher, of 112, Utility Street, Belfast.

Gallagher, Joseph G - Corporal
Royal Inniskilling Fusiliers *Died in War*
Youngest son of John Gallagher, 129 McDonnell Street, Belfast.

Gallagher, Michael - Private
3486 Royal Inniskilling Fusiliers 5th Battalion *Died on 12 November 1916*
STRUMA MILITARY CEMETERY, Greece
Born and enlisted in Belfast.

Gallagher, Robert James - Rifleman
6997 Royal Irish Rifles 1st Battalion *Age 19 Died of Wounds on 15 October 1915*
SAILLY-SUR-LA-LYS-CANADIAN CEMETERY, France
Son of Mrs. Eliza Jane Gallagher, of 150, My Lady's Road, Belfast.

Gallagher, Thomas James - Private
20937 Princess Victoria's (Royal Irish Fusiliers) 1st Battalion *Died in War on 3 May 1917*
ARRAS MEMORIAL, France
Born and enlisted in Belfast. Formerly 43619 Connaught Rangers.

Gallery, Henry - Rifleman
4925 Royal Irish Rifles 2nd Battalion *Died in War on 25 July 1915*
PERTH CEMETERY (CHINA WALL), Belgium
Born in Belfast, enlisted in Ballykinler.

Gallery, Henry Frederick - Rifleman
8868 Royal Irish Rifles 1st Battalion *Killed in Action on 25 September 1915*
YPRES (MENIN GATE) MEMORIAL, Belgium
Born and enlisted in Belfast.

Galloway, Robert - Private
22941 Princess Victoria's (Royal Irish Fusiliers) 7/8th Battalion *Killed in Action on 7 June 1917*
YPRES (MENIN GATE) MEMORIAL, Belgium
Born and enlisted in Belfast.

Galloway, Robert Harrison - Private
4156 Seaforth Highlanders 5th Battalion *Age 20 Died in War on 17 September 1916*
BELFAST (DUNDONALD) CEMETERY, United Kingdom
Son of Robert and Matilda Galloway, of 3, Ravenscroft Street, Belfast.

Galway, Charles - Private
25508 Royal Inniskilling Fusiliers 9th Battalion *Age 23 Killed in Action on 1 July 1916*
THIEPVAL MEMORIAL, France
Husband of Lena Galway, of 46, Belgrave Street, Belfast.

Galway, James Leathem - Private
101545 Canadian Infantry (Alberta Regiment) 31st Battalion *Age 20 Died of Wounds on 25 September 1916*
BOULOGNE EASTERN CEMETERY, France
Son of J. L. Galway, of Ballinavally, Neills Hill, Belfast, Ireland. Native of County Down, Ireland.
A Presbyterian and a marine engineer he had served for a year in the old UVF.

Galway, William - Sapper
57446 Royal Engineers 121st Field Company *Killed in Action on 27 March 1918*
POZIERES MEMORIAL, France
Husband of Mary Galway, 153 Urney Street, Belfast.

Gamble, Hugh - Rifleman
14686 Royal Irish Rifles 10th Battalion *Killed in Action on 1 July 1916*
THIEPVAL MEMORIAL, France
Son of John and Margaret Jane Gamble. Brothers and sisters lived at 19 Rowland Street, Belfast.

Gamble, William H - Private
22673 Royal Irish Fusiliers *Died in War on 18 September 1918*
BELFAST CITY CEMETERY, United Kingdom
Son of Catherine Gamble and the late Hugh Gamble; husband of Ellen Gamble,
of 12, James Street, Belfast. Holder of the Silver War Badge.

Gardiner, Arthur - Lance Corporal
9206 Royal Irish Rifles 1st Battalion *Died in War on 10 March 1915*
LE TOURET MEMORIAL, France
9 Roe Street, Belfast.

Gardiner, David - Rifleman
5566 Rifle Brigade 3rd Battalion *Age 21 Killed by shell fire on 13 February 1916*
MENIN ROAD SOUTH MILITARY CEMETERY, Belgium
Brother of Mrs Moore, 80 Broom Street, Belfast.

Gardiner, Joseph - Rifleman
7634 Royal Irish Rifles 2nd Battalion *Killed in Action on 16 October 1914*
LE TOURET MEMORIAL, France
Born and enlisted in Belfast.

Gardner, Aaron Wason - Private
SS/1503 Army Service Corps 3rd Cavalry Division Supply Column
Age 25 Died in War on 9 November 1914
RAILWAY CHATEAU CEMETERY, Belgium
Son of Joseph and Margaretta Gardner, of 39, Hattan Drive, Woodstock Road, Belfast.

Gardner, James - Private
70770 Machine Gun Corps (Infantry) *Age 28 Died as a result of war on 14 February 1919*
BELFAST CITY CEMETERY, United Kingdom
Husband of Margaret Brennan (formerly Gardner), of 31, Saunders Street, Belfast.
Formerly 10140 Royal Irish Fusiliers.

Gardner, James Nelson - Rifleman
17/1111 Royal Irish Rifles 10th Battalion *Age 33 Killed in Action on 31 December 1916*
ST. QUENTIN CABARET MILITARY CEMETERY, Belgium
Son of Mr. and Mrs. R. Gardner, of 60, Coolbeg Street, Belfast; husband of Elizabeth Gardner, of 102, Bentham Street, Belfast.

Gardner, John - Private
145401 Canadian Infantry (Western Ontario Regiment) "D" Company 47th Battalion
Age 26 Killed in Action on 3 January 1917
VILLERS STATION CEMETERY, VILLERS-AU-BOIS, France
Son of Samuel and Eliza Wilson Gardner, of Belfast, Ireland.
A Presbyterian, he had previous military service and had worked as a printer.

Gardner, Joseph - Rifleman
7634 Royal Irish Rifles 2nd Battalion *Age 28 Killed in Action on 16 October 1914*
LE TOURET MEMORIAL, France
Husband of Mary Crooks (formerly Gardner), of 33, Glenallen Street, Belfast.

Gardner, Stewart Henry - Private
8658 Royal Inniskilling Fusiliers *Age 26 Accidentally killed on 31 March 1915*
RUGBY (CLIFTON ROAD) CEMETERY, United Kingdom
Son of George and Elizabeth Gardner, of Belfast.

Gardner, William - Drummer
9933 Royal Inniskilling Fusiliers 1st Battalion *Killed in Action on 21 August 1915*
HELLES MEMORIAL, Turkey
Born and enlisted in Belfast.

Garrett, Joseph - Lance Corporal
6861 Royal Inniskilling Fusiliers 8th Battalion *Killed in Action on 11 July 1917*
KEMMEL CHATEAU MILITARY CEMETERY, Belgium
Born and enlisted in Belfast.

Garrett, Robert - Private
12932 Royal Irish Fusiliers 6th Battalion *Died in War on 15 August 1915*
HELLES MEMORIAL, Turkey
Husband of Mrs. M. Haslett (formerly Garrett), of 6, Ariel Street, Belfast.

JOURNEY OF REMEMBERING

Garrett, Robert - Private
8422 Royal Inniskilling Fusiliers 1st Battalion *Died in War on 22 May 1915*
TWELVE TREE COPSE CEMETERY, Turkey
Born Magheraculmony, County Fermanagh, enlisted Irvinestown, resident Belfast.

Garry, Arthur Foley - Engine Room Artificer First Class
268538 Royal Navy HMS "Nottingham" *Age 47 Killed in Action with submarine in North Sea on 19 August 1916*
PLYMOUTH NAVAL MEMORIAL, United Kingdom
Son of Charles Septimus Garry and Alicia Garry, of Birkenhead; husband of Mary E. Vitty (formerly Garry), of 89, Park Avenue, Belfast.

Garry, Joseph - Private
2942 Royal Inniskilling Fusiliers 2nd Battalion *Age 20 Died in War on 16 May 1915*
LE TOURET MEMORIAL, France
Son of Philip and Catherine Garry, of 31, Artillery Street, Belfast.

Garston, James - Private
404755 Canadian Infantry (Saskatchewan Regiment) 46th Battalion *Age 36 Died in War on 5 May 1917*
VILLERS STATION CEMETERY, VILLERS-AU-BOIS, France
Son of Thomas and Eliza Jane Garston, of Belfast, Ireland. Had 8 years service in the British Army. In Canada he was an iron worker and a member of the Salvation Army.

Garvey, Thomas - Driver
T4/045364 Royal Army Service Corps *Died in War on 4 October 1915*
NETLEY MILITARY CEMETERY, United Kingdom
Born in Lisburn, enisted and resident in Belfast. Formerly 1570 7th Leinster Regiment.

Garvey, William J - Private
Royal Irish Fusiliers *Killed in Action on 16 August 1917*
13 Upton Street, Belfast.

Garville, John - Rifleman
10469 Royal Irish Rifles 2nd Battalion *Killed In Action on 9 July 1916*
THIEPVAL MEMORIAL, France
Born in Belfast.

Garvin, Samuel - Lieutenant
Royal Welsh Fusiliers 9th Battalion attached 1/7th Battalion *Age 20 Died in War on 27 March 1917*
GAZA WAR CEMETERY, Israel
Son of William and Sara Garvin, of 16, Landscape Terrace, Belfast.

Gaskin, James - Private
6391 Royal Irish Fusiliers "B" Company 9th Battalion *Age 19 Killed in Action on 16 August 1917*
TYNE COT MEMORIAL, Belgium
Son of Annie Gaskin, of 129, Leeson Street, Belfast and the late James Gaskin.

Gaston, Samuel - Private
2940 Royal Scots 12th Battalion *Died of Wounds on 1 August 1916*
ETAPLES MILITARY CEMETERY, France
35 Carnan Street, Belfast.

Gatchell, James Harcourt Cecil - Captain
Royal Army Medical Corps attached 11th Battalion Royal Sussex Regiment
Killed in Action on 27 September 1917
BEDFORD HOUSE CEMETERY, *Belgium*
Son of the Rev. J. H. Gatchell, D.D., and Louisa J. Gatchell, of 30, Cliftonville Avenue, Belfast.
Born in Earl's Gift, Donemana, County Tyrone.

Gatensby, Samuel - Lieutenant
Royal Irish Rifles 15th Battalion *Died of pneumonia following wounds (gas) on 24 November 1918*
BELFAST CITY CEMETERY, *United Kingdom*
Son of the late Thomas and Mary Gatensby, of Belfast. Awarded the Military Cross.

Gates, Samuel - Rifleman
17/1044 Royal Irish Rifles 15th Battalion *Killed in Action on 11 June 1916*
HAMEL MILITARY CEMETERY, BEAUMONT-HAMEL, *France*
62 Sidney Street, Belfast.

Gault, Hugh - Rifleman
3773 Royal Irish Rifles 9th Battalion *Died as a Prisoner of War on 1 April 1918*
COLOGNE SOUTHERN CEMETERY, *Germany*
Born and enlisted in Belfast.

Gault, James - Lance Corporal
14692 Royal Irish Rifles 14th Battalion *Died in War on 8 December 1917*
LE CATEAU MILITARY CEMETERY, *France*
1 Azamor Street, Belfast.

Gault, Joseph Birkmyre - Rifleman
12814 Royal Irish Rifles 15th Battalion *Age 18 Died in War on 11 June 1916*
HAMEL MILITARY CEMETERY, BEAUMONT-HAMEL, *France*
Son of Mrs. M. Gault, of 33, Glenbank Place, Ballysillan, Belfast.

Gault, Samuel - Lance Corporal
26651 Lancashire Fusiliers 20th Battalion *Died in War on 23 July 1916*
BRONFAY FARM MILITARY CEMETERY, BRAY-SUR-SOMME, *France*
Born in Belfast, enlisted in Liverpool.

Gault, William - Rifleman
5553 Royal Irish Rifles 2nd Battalion *Killed In Action on 10 August 1917*
YPRES (MENIN GATE) MEMORIAL, *Belgium*
Born in Belfast.

Gavin, Edward George - Private
228198 London Regiment 1st (City of London) Battalion (Royal Fusiliers) *Died in War on 7 June 1917*
YPRES (MENIN GATE) MEMORIAL, *Belgium*
Born in Belfast, enlisted in London. Formerly 3682, Sussex Yeomanry

Gavin, Hugh - Private
2638 Royal Inniskilling Fusiliers 2nd Battalion *Killed in Action on 16 May 1915*
LE TOURET MEMORIAL, *France*
Born and enlisted in Belfast.

Gavin, John - Private
6674 Royal Scots Fusiliers 1st Battalion *Died in War on 16 June 1915*
YPRES (MENIN GATE) MEMORIAL, Belgium
Born in Leith, enlisted Hamilton, both in Scotland, resident Belfast.

Gavin, Michael - Rifleman
6943 Royal Irish Rifles 1st Battalion *Killed in Action on 9 May 1915*
PLOEGSTEERT MEMORIAL, Belgium
Born in Edinburgh, enlisted Holywood, resident Belfast.

Gawley, Patrick - Private
3942 Connaught Rangers 6th Battalion *Died in War on 4 June 1917*
YPRES (MENIN GATE) MEMORIAL, Belgium
Born in Ballinderry County Antrim. Enlisted and resident in Belfast.

Gaynor, Edward - Rifleman
3959 Royal Irish Rifles 2nd Battalion *Died on 4 February 1915*
POPERINGHE OLD MILITARY CEMETERY, Belgium
Born in Belfast, enlisted Ballykinler.

Gaynor, Patrick - Private
2865 Leinster Regiment 2nd Battalion *Died in War on 31 July 1917*
YPRES (MENIN GATE) MEMORIAL, Belgium
Born in Newry. Enlisted and resident in Belfast.

Geddis, Edward Francis - Private
S/40524 Seaforth Highlanders 2nd Battalion *Age 20 Died of Wounds received at Arras on 13 April 1917*
ATHIES COMMUNAL CEMETERY EXTENSION, France
Son of Samuel and Grace Geddis, of 5, Hornby Street, Belfast.

Geddis, George - Rifleman
14696 Royal Irish Rifles *Killed in Action on 1 July 1916*
THIEPVAL MEMORIAL, France
Born and enlisted in Belfast. Member of Fisherwick Presbyterian Church.

Geelan, Robert Henry - Private
829864 Canadian Infantry (Manitoba Regiment) 8th Battalion *Age 22 Killed in Action on 9 August 1918*
MANITOBA CEMETERY, CAIX, France
Son of John Arthur and Maggie Geelan, of 48, Boston Avenue, Southend-on-Sea, England.
Born at Belfast, Ireland. Worked as a clerk in Canada, a Presbyterian.

George, George - Private
PLY/14462 Royal Marine Light Infantry *Died as a result of war on 25 November 1918*
FORD PARK CEMETERY,PLYMOUTH, United Kingdom
8 Carlton Street, Belfast.

George, James - Private
6940 Connaught Rangers 2nd Battalion *Age 38 Died of Wounds on 29 October 1914*
BOULOGNE EASTERN CEMETERY, France
Husband of Mary George, of Tullynore, Hillsborough, County Down. Born in Belfast.
An Army Reservist he had worked in the Shipyard.

Gettinby, Thomas - Sergeant
17696 Royal Irish Rifles 12th Battalion *Killed in Action on 1 July 1916*
THIEPVAL MEMORIAL, France
Brother of Mrs. Mary Donnelly, of 3, Erin Street, Ormeau Avenue, Belfast.

Gibbons, Albert John - Private
42854 Royal Inniskilling Fusiliers 1st Battalion *Died in War on 22 August 1918*
BERTENACRE MILITARY CEMETERY, FLETRE, France
Husband of Mary Jane Gibbons and father of a small daughter. 18 Coniston Street, Belfast.

Gibson, James - Rifleman
9943 Royal Irish Rifles 2nd Battalion *Killed In Action on 29 May 1915*
YPRES (MENIN GATE) MEMORIAL, Belgium
Born in Belfast.

Gibson, Albert Henry - Second Lieutenant
Royal Inniskilling Fusiliers 12th Battalion attached 9th Battalion *Age 19 Killed in Action on 1 July 1916*
THIEPVAL MEMORIAL, France
Son of Robert Gibson, J.P., and Mrs Gibson, of North Parade, Belfast.

Gibson, Alexander - Driver
57742 Royal Engineers 121st Field Company *Age 25 Died of Wounds on 22 June 1917*
BOULOGNE EASTERN CEMETERY, France
Husband of Mrs. S. Gibson, of 16, Baywood Street, Belfast.

Gibson, Chancellor - Sapper
51731 Corps of Royal Engineers 103rd Field Comapnay *Died in War on 17 June 1916*
DRANOUTRE MILITARY CEMETERY, Belgium
Born in Belfast. Enlisted in Govan, Scotland.

Gibson, Isaac - Chief Engine Room Artificer Second Class
270632 Royal Navy H.M. Submarine "K.17" *Age 39 Drowned through collision in North Sea on 31 January 1918*
PLYMOUTH NAVAL MEMORIAL, United Kingdom
Son of Samuel and Charlotte Gibson, of Belfast; husband of Ellen Duncan Gibson,
of 38, Sidney Street, Saltcoats, Ayrshire.

Gibson, James - Private
28157 Royal Inniskilling Fusiliers 1st Battalion *Age 20 Died in War on 17 May 1917*
ARRAS MEMORIAL, France
Brother of Henry Gibson, of 13, Alaska Street, Belfast.

Gibson, John - Gunner
80000 Royal Horse Artillery and Royal Field Artillery *Died in War on 19 August 1916*
HEILLY STATION CEMETERY, MERICOURT-L'ABBE, France
Born and enlisted in Belfast.

Gibson, John - Private
6344 Royal Inniskilling Fusiliers 1st Battalion *Killed in Action on 23 April 1917*
ARRAS MEMORIAL, France
Born in Belfast.

Gibson, John - Rifleman
15/11945 Royal Irish Rifles "C" Company 15th Battalion *Age 23 Killed in Action on 31 January 1916*
SUCRERIE MILITARY CEMETERY, COLINCAMPS, France
Son of the late James Gibson, and of Margaret Gibson, of 78, Lilliput Street, Belfast.

Gibson, John Alexander - Rifleman
18/452 Royal Irish Rifles 9th Battalion *Age 18 Died in War on 6 April 1917*
POND FARM CEMETERY, Belgium
Son of Alexander and Jane Gibson, of 37, Agincourt Avenue, Belfast.

Gibson, John Spence - Sergeant
14700 Royal Irish Rifles 10th Battalion *Died in War on 29 October 1917*
METZ-EN-COUTURE COMMUNAL CEMETERY BRITISH EXTENSION, France
Husband of Dora, 63 Devonshire Street, Belfast.

Gibson, Matthew Henry - Captain
Royal Irish Rifles 12th Battalion *Age 28 Killed in Action on 29 October 1918*
DUHALLOW A.D.S. CEMETERY, Belgium
Son of David and Annie E. Gibson, of 1, Chesnut Gardens, Cliftonville, Belfast.
Awarded the Military Cross twice.

Gibson, Oliver - Rifleman
4300 Royal Irish Rifles 10th Battalion *Killed in action on 1 July 1916*
THIEPVAL MEMORIAL, France
Husband of Sarah Gibson, 64 Pine Street, Belfast.

Gibson, Robert J - Private
13093 Royal Irish Fusiliers 5th Battalion *Died in War on 16 August 1915*
HELLES MEMORIAL, Turkey
Husband of Agnes L. Gibson, of 26, Brennan Street, Belfast.

Gibson, Samuel - Rifleman
11593 Royal Irish Rifles 2nd Battalion *Killed in Action on 7 June 1917*
WULVERGHEM-LINDENHOEK ROAD MILITARY CEMETERY, Belgium
Husband of Lillie Gibson and father of two young sons, 37 Beresford Street, Belfast.

Gibson, Thomas - Corporal
6957 Royal Inniskilling Fusiliers *Died in War on 21 October 1914*
PLOEGSTEERT MEMORIAL, Belgium
29 St Kilda Street, Belfast.

Gibson, Thomas - Rifleman
11943 Royal Irish Rifles 15th Battalion *Age 24 Killed in Action on 1 July 1916*
THIEPVAL MEMORIAL, France
Son of William and Elizabeth Gibson, of 16, Pittsburg Street, Belfast.

Gibson, W - Shoeing Smith
T/15310 Royal Army Service Corps *Died as a result of war on 2 July 1920*
BELFAST CITY CEMETERY, United Kingdom
Husband of M. Gibson, of 49, City Street, Belfast.

Gibson, William John - Sergeant
8846 Royal Irish Rifles 1st Battalion *Age 24 Died in War on 7 September 1918*
PLOEGSTEERT MEMORIAL, *Belgium*
Son of William John and Harriett Gibson, of 49, Donegall Avenue, Belfast.

Giffen, Thomas Alexander - Lance Corporal
139583 Canadian Infantry (Central Ontario Regiment) 3rd Battalion *Died of Wounds on 24 September 1916*
VIMY MEMORIAL, *Fance*
116 Tennent Street, Belfast. Husband of Tillie. A Presbyterian, he worked in Canada as a waggon driver and also served in the militia.

Gihon, James Henry - Lance Corporal
11944 Royal Irish Rifles 15th Battalion *Died of Wounds on 25 November 1916*
BELFAST CITY CEMETERY, *United Kingdom*
46 Sancroft Street, Belfast. A member of Cavehill Orange Lodge 1956.

Gihon, William - Lance Corporal
14701 Royal Irish Rifles "B" Company 14th Battalion *Age 24 Killed in Action on 16 August 1917*
TYNE COT CEMETERY, *Belgium*
Son of John and Jane Gihon, of 5, Adela Place, Antrim Road, Belfast.

Gilbert, William - Private
G/14760 Buffs (East Kent Regiment) 6th Battalion *Died in War on 22 August 1918*
MEAULTE MILITARY CEMETERY
Born and enlisted in Belfast.

Gilchrist, William - Private
147546 Canadian Infantry (Manitoba Regiment) 78th Battalion *Age 30 Died in War on 30 October 1917*
YPRES (MENIN GATE) MEMORIAL, *Belgium*
Son of William and Anna Maria Gilchrist, of 61, Crosscollyer Street, Belfast, Ireland.
A Presbyterian, he worked as a grocery clerk and had both regular and reserve military service.

Gilchrist, William John - Rifleman
5521 Royal Irish Rifles 2nd Battalion *Killed In Action on 16 June 1915*
YPRES (MENIN GATE) MEMORIAL, *Belgium*
Born and enlisted in Belfast.

Gildea, James - Sergeant
64253 Royal Engineers 122nd Field Company *Killed in Action on 27 March 1918*
POZIERES MEMORIAL, *France*
Husband of Margaret, 79 Brookmount Street, Belfast.

Giles, Victor Marshall - Second Lieutenant
Royal Irish Rifles 7th Battalion *Age 19 Killed in Action at Loos on 28 June 1916*
VERMELLES BRITISH CEMETERY, *France*
Son of Marshall and Ethel Giles, of 66, University Street, Belfast.
He relinquished a valuable scholarship at King's Hospital, Dublin, in order to enlist.

Gill, Daniel Lawrence - Private
6646 11th Hussars (Prince Albert's Own) *Age 28 Died in War on 13 May 1915*
YPRES (MENIN GATE) MEMORIAL, *Belgium*
Husband of Sarah A. V. Gill, of 56, Westmoreland Street, Belfast.

Journey of Remembering

Gill, David - Rifleman
428 Royal Irish Rifles 16th Battalion *Age 20 Killed in Action on 21 March 1918*
POZIERES MEMORIAL, France
Son of John and Sarah J. Gill, of 106, Belmont Road, Strandtown, Belfast. His brother, George, also fell.

Gill, George - Private
H/71502 North Irish Horse attached 9th Royal Irish Fusiliers *Age 24 Died in War on 26 August 1918*
FLATIRON COPSE CEMETERY, MAMETZ, France
Son of John and Sarah Jane Gill, of 106, Belmont Road, Strandtown, Belfast. His brother, David, also fell.

Gill, William - Private
Royal Irish Fusiliers 1st Battalion *Died in War on or before August 1915*
60 Pound Street, Belfast.

Gillespie, Alexander - Rifleman
12795 Royal Irish Rifles 15th Battalion *Died in War on 6 June 1918*
HAM BRITISH CEMETERY, MUILLE-VILLETTE, France
Wife of Mrs M J Gillespie, 5 Temple Street, Belfast.

Gillespie, Andrew - Driver
47649 Royal Field Artillery 10th Battery 4th Indian Brigade *Age 26 Died in War on 26 August 1915*
BALLINCOLLIG MILITARY CEMETERY, Republic of Ireland
Son of Mr. and Mrs. William Gillespie, of Belfast.

Gillespie, Norman Alexander - Private
27342 Canadian Infantry (Central Ontario Regiment) *Died in War on 25 April 1915*
CEMENT HOUSE CEMETERY, Belgium
Originally from the Mount, Belfast though born at Rathfriland, County Down.
He was a bank clerk and had served as member of the Militia.

Gillespie, Samuel - Rifleman
4768 Royal Irish Rifles "B" Company 2nd Battalion *Age 22 Killed in Action on 21 February 1915*
KEMMEL CHATEAU MILITARY CEMETERY, Belgium
Son of the late William George and Annie Gillespie; husband of Maria Adams (formerly Gillespie),
of 67, Lanark Street, Belfast.

Gillespie, Townley Sherwood - Private
1636 North Irish Horse *Age 27 Died in War on 13 November 1915*
BELFAST CITY CEMETERY, United Kingdom
Son of William Henry and Sarah E. Gillespie, of 52, Haddington Gardens, Belfast.

Gillespie, W J - Stoker First Class
SS/107919 Royal Navy HMS "Hawke" *Age 30 Lost at sea on 15 October 1914*
CHATHAM NAVAL MEMORIAL, United Kingdom
Son of William and Maria Gillespie, of Dunmurry, Belfast.

Gilliland, David - Private
3783 Princess Victoria's (Royal Irish Fusiliers) 1st Battalion *Died in War on 30 April 1918*
LIJSSENTHOEK MILITARY CEMETERY, Belgium
Born in Lisburn, resident in Belfast. Formerly 7248 Royal Irish Rifles.

Gilliland, Henry (Harry) - Rifleman
14704 Royal Irish Rifles 10th Battalion *Age 23 Killed in Action on 1 July 1916*
THIEPVAL MEMORIAL, France
Son of Mrs. Martha Gilliland, of 8, Milner Street, Belfast.

Gilliland, James - Lance Bombardier
201057 Royal Garrison Artillery V Anti-Aircraft Battery *Age 28 Died of influenza on 2 November 1918*
CREMONA TOWN CEMETERY, Italy
Son of William and Martha Gilliland, of 8, Milner Street, Belfast. Served at Gallipoli.

Gilliland, James - Rifleman
17/1471 Royal Irish Rifles 8th Battalion *Killed in Action on 7 June 1917*
LONE TREE CEMETERY, Belgium
Husband of Mrs. Gilliland, of 7, Crossland Street, Belfast.

Gilliland, John - Private
1082 Guards Machine Gun Regiment 4th Battalion *Age 25 Died of disease on 9 May 1918*
BOIS GUILLAUME COMMUNAL CEMETERY EXTENSION, France
Son of Elizabeth and the late John Gilliland, of Belfast.

Gilliland, Samuel Joseph - Private
24074 Royal Inniskilling Fusiliers 7th Battalion *Age 20 Died in War on 5 April 1916*
PHILOSOPHE BRITISH CEMETERY, MAZINGARBE, France
Husband of Elizabeth McVeigh (formerly Gilliland), of 25, Lower Mount Street, Albertbridge Road, Belfast.

Gilmore, (William) Henry - Rifleman
17/69 Royal Irish Rifles 9th Battalion *Age 28 Died in War on 5 August 1917*
YPRES (MENIN GATE) MEMORIAL, Belgium
Born and enlisted in Belfast. Son of Henry Gilmore.

Gilmore, Alexander William Francis - Second Lieutenant
Royal Irish Rifles 15th Battalion *Age 19 Died in War on 23 November 1917*
CAMBRAI MEMORIAL, LOUVERVAL, France
Son of Mary Jane Gilmore, of Bailieborough, County Cavan, and the late Isaiah Gibson Gilmore.
A holder the Military Cross he had been a clerk in Northern Bank, Belfast.

Gilmore, Andrew - Second Lieutenant
Royal Irish Rifles 1st Battalion *Age 35 Killed in Action on 11 March 1915*
LE TOURET MEMORIAL, France
Son of Richard and Catherine Gilmore, of 16, Unity Street, Belfast; husband of Mary Gilmore,
of "Kamptee" 6, Rosapenna Drive, Belfast. Served 17 years in India.

Gilmore, Daniel Patrick - Second Engineer
Mercantile Marine S.S. "Waverley" (West Hartlepool)
Age 43 Drowned, as the result of an attack by an enemy submarine on 20 December 1917
TOWER HILL MEMORIAL, United Kingdom
Son of Mrs. Mary Gilmore; husband of Johanna (Edith) Gilmore (née Canlan),
of Harrow Villa, King's Road, Canton, Cardiff. Born at Belfast.

Gilmore, Hugh - Private
9910 Royal Inniskilling Fusiliers 2nd Battalion *Age 24 Presumed killed on 16 May 1915*
LE TOURET MEMORIAL, France
Bother of Mrs Sara Shevlin, 57 Milford Street, Belfast.

Gilmore, James - Lance Corporal
10461 Royal Inniskilling Fusiliers 2nd Battalion *Age 20 Killed in Action on 21 October 1914*
PLOEGSTEERT MEMORIAL, *Belgium*
Son of Mr. and Mrs. W. Gilmore, of 66, Stanhope Street, Belfast.

Gilmore, Joseph - Private
3479 Royal Inniskilling Fusiliers 2nd Battalion *Killed in Action on 16 May 1915*
LE TOURET MEMORIAL, *France*
15 Keswick Street, Belfast.

Gilmore, Robert John - Rifleman
47177 Royal Irish Rifles 15th Battalion *Died in War on 22 November 1917*
THIEPVAL MEMORIAL, *France*
Born and enlisted in Belfast. Formerly 031215 Army Service Corps.

Gilmore, Robert John Richard - Lance Corporal
8/12826 Royal Irish Rifles 8th Battalion *Killed in Action on 2 July 1916*
THIEPVAL MEMORIAL, *France*
32 Hutchinson Street, Belfast.

Gilmore, William Henry - Rifleman
69 Royal Irish Rifles 9th Battalion *Died in War on 5 August 1917*
YPRES (MENIN GATE) MEMORIAL, *Belgium*
Born and enlisted in Belfast.

Gilmour, James - Rifleman
17721 Royal Irish Rifles 13th Battalion *Age 21 Killed in Action on 16 August 1917*
TYNE COT MEMORIAL, *Belgium*
Son of the late Hamilton Gilmour and Mary McMullan Gilmour, of Rockport, Craigavad, Belfast.

Gilmour, Patrick - Private
9860 Durham Light Infantry 2nd Battalion *Died in War on 1 August 1915*
LIJSSENTHOEK MILITARY CEMETERY, *Belgium*
Born in Belfast. Enlisted in Newcastle.

Gilmour, Robert James - Private
15217 Royal Scots (Lothian Regiment) 11th Battalion *Died in War on 14 July 1916*
THIEPVAL MEMORIAL, *France*
Born in Belfast, enlisted in Scotland.

Gilpin, Frederick - Private
451221 Canadian Infantry (Central Ontario Regiment) *Died in War on 8 October 1916*
ADANAC MILITARY CEMETERY, MIRAUMONT, *France*
Son of Robert and Rebecca Gilpin, 100 Duncairn Gardens, Belfast.

Gilroy, George - Private
15258 Royal Irish Fusiliers 9th (North Irish Horse) Battalion *Age 31 Killed in Action on 27 March 1918*
POZIERES MEMORIAL, *France*
Son of William and Mary Ann Gilroy; husband of Mary Jane Gilroy, of 50, Stanhope Street, Belfast.

Gilvray, James - Private
18057 Highland Light Infantry 12th Battalion *Killed in Action on 26 September 1915*
LOOS MEMORIAL, *France*
Born in Bundoran, County Donegal, enlisted Glasgow, resident of Belfast.

Ginn, Robert - Sergeant
8810 Royal Inniskilling Fusiliers 1st Battalion *Killed in Action on 1 July 1916*
THIEPVAL MEMORIAL, *France*
Born and enlisted in Belfast.

Ginn, William Henry - Sergeant
8979 Royal Inniskilling Fusiliers 1st Battalion *Died in War on 4 July 1916*
HAMEL MILITARY CEMETERY, BEAUMONT-HAMEL, *France*
Born and enlisted in Belfast. Holder of the Distinguished Conduct Medal.

Girvan, Frederick William - Captain
Devonshire Regiment 8th Battalion *Age 24 Died in War on 26 October 1917*
TYNE COT MEMORIAL, *Belgium*
Son of Robert and Isabella Girvan, of 115, Cavehill Road, Belfast.

Girvan, John James - Rifleman
10030 Royal Irish Rifles 2nd Battalion *Killed in Action on 24 March 1918*
POZIERES MEMORIAL, OVILLERS-LA BOISSELLE, *France*
Born in Belfast, enlisted Glasgow.

Girvan, Samuel - Private
26776 Royal Inniskilling Fusiliers 6th Battalion *Age 32 Died of Wounds on 10 May 1916*
MIKRA BRITISH CEMETERY, KALAMARIA, *Greece*
(Served as Rae). Son of James and Mary Ann Girvan, of 84, Clementine Street, Belfast. Born in Sixmilecross, County Tyrone.

Girvin, William David - Rifleman
11666 Royal Irish Rifles 15th Battalion *Killed In Action on 1 July 1916*
THIEPVAL MEMORIAL, *France*
Born and enlisted in Belfast.

Gittens, John - Rifleman
8922 Royal Irish Rifles 2nd Battalion *Died in War on 5 October 1918*
BERLIN SOUTHERN-WESTERN CEMETERY, *Germany*
Son of Mrs Ann Gittens, 31 Vulcan Street, Belfast.

Glackin, Leo - Private
18419 Royal Irish Fusiliers 2nd Battalion *Age 21 Died of Wounds on 8 November 1917*
BEERSHEBA WAR CEMETERY, *Israel*
Son of John and Catherine Glackin, of 10, Cuba Street, Belfast. Native of Strabane, County Tyrone.

Glasgow, Robert - Gunner
35886 Royal Field Artillery 22nd Brigade *Age 20 Killed in Action on 28 October 1917*
THE HUTS CEMETERY, *Belgium*
Son of Adam and Mary Jane Glasgow, of 34, Fourth Street, Belfast.

Journey of Remembering

Glasgow, Robert - Private
17345 Royal Dublin Fusiliers 2nd Battalion *Died in War on 4 November 1916*
ST SEVER CEMETERY EXTENSION ROUEN, France
Born in Belfast, enlisted Glasgow.

Glass, Adam - Rifleman
14651 Royal Irish Rifles 10th Battalion *Killed In Action on 1 July 1916*
MILL ROAD CEMETERY, THIEPVAL, France
Born and enlisted in Belfast.

Glass, Gilbert - Rifleman
3253 Royal Irish Rifles 15th Battalion *Killed in Action on 1 July 1916*
THIEPVAL MEMORIAL, France
17 Rushholme Street, Belfast.

Glass, Sam - Fireman
Mercantile Marine Reserve HMS "Duke of Albany"
Age 35 Killed in Action with submarine in North Sea on 24 August 1916
PLYMOUTH NAVAL MEMORIAL, United Kingdom
Son of John and Mary Ann Glass, of 69, Stratheden Street, Belfast.

Glass, William - Second Lieutenant
Black Watch 6th Battalion *Died in War on 23 April 1917*
CABARET-ROUGE BRITISH CEMETERY, SOUCHEZ, France
Parkmount Road, Belfast. Husband of Harriet Phoebe Glass, Ballaglass, Maughold, Isle of Man.

Gleeson, John - Private
5122 King's (Liverpool Regiment) 8th Battalion *Died in War on 27 September 1916*
THIEPVAL MEMORIAL, France
Born in Belfast, enlisted Liverpool.

Glencross, James - Rifleman
14708 Royal Irish Rifles 1st Battalion *Age 26 Died of Wounds on 1 October 1918*
DADIZEELE NEW BRITISH CEMETERY, Belgium
Son of David and Mary Glencross, of 119, Brookmount Street, Belfast.

Glenn, John - Private
4617 Leinster Regiment 2nd Battalion *Died in War on 16 May 1915*
FERME BUTERNE MILITARY CEMETERY HOUPLINES, France
Born in Belfast. Enlisted at Mosney Camp, Drogheda.

Glover, Joseph - Private
PLY/15628 Royal Marine Light Infantry HMS "Defence" *Age 22 Killed in Action on 31 May 1916*
PLYMOUTH NAVAL MEMORIAL, United Kingdom
Son of David and Annie Glover, of 21, Manning Avenue, Toronto, Canada. Native of Belfast, Ireland.

Godding, Patrick Harry - Private
19653 Dorsetshire Regiment 1st Battalion *Died in War on 6 March 1917*
NETLEY MILITARY CEMETERY, United Kingdom
Born in Belfast, enlisted in Bedfordshire. Formerly 7254 Bedfordshire Regiment.

Golden, John - Rifleman
6845 Royal Irish Rifles 2nd Battalion *Age 31 Killed in Action on 27 October 1914*
LE TOURET MEMORIAL, France
Son of Bridget Golden, of 44, Crumlin Street, Belfast and the late John Golden. Husband of the late Eliza Golden and father of James.

Goldie, Barney - Private
3517 Royal Irish Fusiliers 1st Battalion *Age 20 Died of Wounds on 22 October 1916*
ST. SEVER CEMETERY, ROUEN, France
Son of Louis and Sarah Goldie, of 19, Baden Powell Street. A member of the Belfast Jewish Community.

Goodfellow, Bernard - Private
20267 Leinster Regiment 1st Battalion *Died in War 19 September 1919*
RAMLEH WAR CEMETERY, Israel
Born and enlisted in Belfast. Formerly 7431 Royal Irish Rifles.

Goodfellow, James - Lance Corporal
404842 Canadian Machine Gun Corps 7th Company *Age 26 Died in War on 8 October 1916*
VIMY MEMORIAL, France
Son of Mrs. Louisa Goodfellow, of 45, Abingdon Street, Belfast, Ireland.
An Anglican he worked as a clerk in Canada.

Goodman, Francis Pasteur - Boy First Class
J/37781 Royal Navy HMS "Natal" *Age 17 Killed in Action on 30 December 1915*
PLYMOUTH NAVAL MEMORIAL, United Kingdom
Son of Thomas and Jane Goodman, of 15, Quadrant Street, Belfast.

Goodwin, James - Sergeant
2241 Connaught Rangers 6th Battalion *Killed in Action on 16 August 1917*
POTIJZE CHATEAU LAWN CEMETERY
Born, enlisted and resident in Belfast.

Goodwin, John - Rifleman
6911 Royal Irish Rifles 10th Battalion *Killed in action on 1 July 1916*
THIEPVAL MEMORIAL, France
Husband of Mary Goodwin, 22 Nelson Street, Belfast.

Gordon, David - Private
3406 Royal Inniskilling Fusiliers 2nd Battalion *Age 19 Died of Wounds received in Action on 10 August 1915*
SHORNCLIFFE MILITARY CEMETERY, United Kingdom
Son of James Gordon, of 1, Bunker Hill Court, Charlestown, Boston, Mass., U.S.A. Born in Belfast.

Gordon, Francis James - Private
27802 Wiltshire Regiment 6th Battalion *Age 19 Died in War on 10 April 1918*
TYNE COT MEMORIAL, Belgium
Son of Mrs. Elizabeth Gordon, of 35, Banbury Street, Belfast.

Gordon, Frederick - Gunner
31739 Royal Horse Artillery and Royal Field Artillery *Died in War on 14 May 1918*
BIENVILLERS MILITARY CEMETERY, France
Born and enlisted in Belfast.

Gordon, Gawn - Private
3694 Seaforth Highlanders 1st/4th Battalion *Age 20 Died in War on 26 June 1916*
LOUEZ MILITARY CEMETERY, DUISANS, France
Son of Robert and Minnie Gordon, of 33, Courtrai Street, Belfast.

Gordon, Geoffrey - Lieutenant
12th Lancers (Prince of Wales's Royal) *Age 34 Died in War on 30 April 1915*
YPRES (MENIN GATE) MEMORIAL, Belgium
Son of the Rev. Alexander Gordon M.A. and Clara Maria Gordon (née Boult), of 35, Rosemary Street, Belfast.

Gordon, James - Rifleman
895 Royal Irish Rifles 8th Battalion *Age 21 Died in War on 2 July 1916*
THIEPVAL MEMORIAL, France
Son of Joseph and Susan Gordon, of Belfast.

Gordon, John - Corporal
28989 Machine Gun Corps (Infantry) 56th Company *Age 25 Died in War on 7 November 1916*
THIEPVAL MEMORIAL, France
Son of John and Elizabeth Gordon, of 3, Ina Street, Belfast.

Gordon, John - Lance Corporal
3509 Royal Inniskilling Fusiliers 1st Battalion *Age 22 Killed in Action on 1 July 1916*
ANCRE BRITISH CEMETERY, BEAUMONT-HAMEL, France
Son of James and Elizabeth Gordon, of Whitewell, Belfast.

Gordon, John Henry - Private
22851 Canadian Army Medical Corps 12th Field Ambulance *Age 24 Died of influenza on 9 October 1918*
MONTREAL (MOUNT ROYAL) CEMETERY, Canada
Son of J. H. Gordon and Edith Pattenden, of Belfast, Ireland, husband of Mae Gordon,
of Walsingham, Ontario, Canada.

Gordon, Robert - Private
27489 Royal Inniskilling Fusiliers 1st Battalion *Died in War on 9 August 1916*
POTIJZE CHATEAU GROUNDS CEMETERY, Belgium
Born in Londonderry, resident Belfast. Formerly 8743 Royal Irish Rifles

Gordon, Robert - Rifleman
S/10824 Rifle Brigade (The Prince Consort's Own) 12th Battalion *Died in War on 12 February 1916*
YPRES (MENIN GATE) MEMORIAL, Belgium
Born in Belfast, enlisted Manchester.

Gordon, Robert John - Private
28275 Royal Inniskilling Fusliers 11th Battalion *Killed in Action on 16 August 1917*
TYNE COT MEMORIAL, Belgium
Born and enlisted in Belfast. A member of Townsend Presbyterian Church.

Gordon, Samuel - Private
27853 Royal Inniskilling Fusiliers 9th Battalion *Died in War on 23 June 1916*
AUTHUILE MILITARY CEMETERY, France
Born and enlisted in Belfast.

Gordon, Samuel - Rifleman
Royal Irish Rifles 13th Battalion *Died in War on 3 July 1916*
PUCHEVILLERS BRITISH CEMETERY, *France*
9 Charleville Street, Belfast and then 679 Runnymeade Road, Toronto, Canada.

Gordon, Thomas - Private
3192 Royal Inniskilling Fusiliers 2nd Battalion *Age 28 Died in War on 16 May 1915*
LE TOURET MEMORIAL, *France*
Son of Thomas and Jeanie Gordon, of 129, Mervue Street, Belfast.

Gordon, Thomas - Private
669955 Canadian Infantry (Quebec Regiment) 13th Battalion *Died in War on 15 April 1918*
DUISANS BRITISH CEMETERY ETRUN, *France*
47 Carnan Street, Belfast.

Gordon, William - Corporal
13447 Royal Inniskilling Fusiliers 7th Battalion *Age 28 Died in War on 8 August 1917*
YPRES (MENIN GATE) MEMORIAL, *Belgium*
Son of David and Matilda Gordon, of 21, Ottawa Street, Belfast.

Gordon, William - Private
29976 Royal Inniskilling Fusiliers 1st Battalion *Age 24 Died in War on 20 November 1917*
CAMBRAI MEMORIAL, LOUVERVAL, *France*
Son of Thomas and Anna Gordon, of Tawlaugh, Ballynarry, County Cavan; husband of May Halliday (formerly Gordon), of 2, Mornington Street, Belfast.

Gordon, William J - Private
M/335697 Army Service Corps Motor Transport *Died in War on 28 February 1918*
DURBAN (STELLAWOOD) CEMETERY, *South Africa*
Son of Mr. and Mrs. John Gordon, of 81, Derwent Street, Newtownwards Road, Belfast.

Gore, James - Private
13448 Royal Inniskilling Fusiliers 9th Battalion *Age 32 Killed in Action on 21 March 1918*
NOYON NEW BRITISH CEMETERY, *France*
Son of Robert and Lizzie Gore, of 26, Carnalea Street, Belfast.

Gore, Thomas - Rifleman
5799 Royal Irish Rifles 2nd Battalion *Killed In Action on 6 September 1918*
PLOEGSTEERT MEMORIAL, *Belgium*
Son of Robert Gore. Born and enlisted in Belfast.

Gorfunkle, Isaac - Captain
Lancashire Fusiliers 13th attached 1st Battion *Died in War on 12 August 1918*
OUTTERSTEENE COMMUNAL CEMETERY EXTENSION, BAILLEUL, *France*
A Belfast Jew, who had been wounded previously, he was killed whilst leading his men in an attack on the German positions.

Gorman, Charles John - Able Seaman
SS/2706 Royal Navy HMS "Pathfinder" *Died in War on 15 October 1914*
CHATHAM NAVAL MEMORIAL, *United Kingdom*
1 Summerhill Street, Belfast.

Journey of Remembering

Gorman, Charles John - Stoker First Class
SS/108091 Royal Navy HMS "Pathfinder"
Age 23 Killed in Action with submarine off Firth of Forth on 5 September 1914
CHATHAM NAVAL MEMORIAL, *United Kingdom*
Son of James and Fanny Gorman, of Belfast.

Gorman, Hugh - Private
11924 Royal Inniskilling Fusiliers 7th Battalion *Age 21 Killed in Action on 27 April 1916*
PHILOSOPHE BRITISH CEMETERY, MAZINGARBE, *France*
Son of Elizabeth Gorman, of 119, Walmer Street, Ballynafeigh, Belfast, and the late William Gorman.

Gorman, Hugh - Private
6884 Royal Irish Rifles 2nd Battalion *Killed in Action on 25 October 1914*
LE TOURET MEMORIAL, *France*
20 Balaclava Street, Belfast.

Gorman, James Toland - Able Seaman
SS/2796 Royal Navy HMS "Hawke" *Age 25 Killed in Action with submarine in North Sea on 15 October 1914*
CHATHAM NAVAL MEMORIAL, *United Kingdom*
Son of James and Fanny Gorman, of Belfast.

Gorman, John J - Private
3636 Seaforth Highlanders 1st/6th Battalion *Age 32 Died in War on 15 November 1916*
MAILLY WOOD CEMETERY, MAILLY-MAILLET, *France*
Husband of Catherine Gorman, of 41, Emerson Row, Ligoneil, Belfast.

Gorman, Samuel - Lance Corporal
14715 Royal Irish Rifles 9th Battalion *Age 19 Died in War on 6 June 1916*
AUTHUILE MILITARY CEMETERY, *France*
Son of Mary Gorman, of 1, Florence Terrace, Ballygomartin Road, Belfast, and the late William Matthew Gorman.

Gorman, Samuel - Rifleman
8013 Royal Irish Rifles 1st Battalion *Age 31 Died of Wounds on 21 March 1915*
MANCHESTER SOUTHERN CEMETERY, *United Kingdom*
Nephew of Marjorie Johnston, of 8, St. Paul's Street, Belfast.

Goudy, John - Rifleman
54185 King's Royal Rifle Corps 2nd Battalion *Died in War on 17 October 1918*
BUSIGNY COMMUNAL CEMETERY EXTENSION, *France*
Born and enlisted in Belfast. Formerly D/22419 Royal Irish Rifles.

Goudy, Robert Connor - Rifleman
11949 Royal Irish Rifles 15th Battalion *Age 20 Died in War on 7 June 1916*
HAMEL MILITARY CEMETERY, BEAUMONT-HAMEL, *France*
Son of Henry and Martha Goudy, of 100, Tennent Street, Belfast.

Gougerty, Patrick - Lance Corporal
3/14444 Royal Irish Rifles 2nd Battalion *Age 29 Killed in Action on 26 April 1916*
ECOIVRES MILITARY CEMETERY, MONT-ST. ELOI, *France*
Son of Jane and the late Matthew Gougerty, of 14, North Derby Street, Belfast.

Journey of Remembering

Gould, William - Lance Corporal
14/201 Royal Irish Rifles 1st Battalion *Killed in Action on 1 October 1918*
DADIZEELE NEW BRITISH CEMETERY, Belgium
Son of Mr. M. Gould, of 48, Devonshire Street, Belfast.

Goulding, Matthew - Sergeant
240901 Royal Warwickshire Regiment 2/6th Battalion *Died in War on 9 December 1917*
RIBECOURT ROAD CEMETERY TRESAULT, France
Born in Belfast, enlisted Birmingham.

Gourley, David - Private
PLY/15688 Royal Marine Light Infantry 1st R.M. Battalion Royal Naval Division
Age 27 Died in War on 2 September 1918
VIS-EN-ARTOIS MEMORIAL, France
Son of Samuel Gourley, of 6, Johnston Street, Wilson Street, Belfast.

Gourley, Francis - Rifleman
9790 Royal Irish Rifles 2nd Battalion *Died of Wounds on 27 March 1918*
POZIERES MEMORIAL, France
Born and enlisted in Belfast.

Gourley, Joseph Leo - Lance Sergeant
10072 Royal Inniskilling Fusiliers 1st Battalion *Killed in Action on 22 March 1918*
POZIERES MEMORIAL, France
His widow lived at 53 Hamill Street, Belfast.

Gourley, Samuel - Private
6214 Australian Infantry 25th Battalion *Age 26 Died of disease on 26 May 1918*
VIGNACOURT BRITISH CEMETERY, France
Son of John and Agnes Gourley, of 48, Vicarage Street, Belfast, Ireland.
Native of Ballyskeagh, Newtownards, Ireland.

Gourley, William - Private
463279 British Columbia Regiment 2nd Canadian Mounted Rifles *Age 27 Died in War on 5 June 1916*
YPRES (MENIN GATE) MEMORIAL, Belgium
Son of Stephen and Margaret Gourley, of 27, Elm Street, Belfast, Ireland. A former shipyard worker he was born at Mealough, County Down and his next-of-kin was his sister, Mrs Jessie Watt.

Gourley, William - Sapper
42062 Corps of Royal Engineers 13th Base Park Company *Died in War on 8 September 1917*
ROCHDALE CEMETERY, United Kingdom
Born in Belfast, enlisted Manchester.

Govan, William - Lance Corporal
P/8092 Military Police Corps Mounted *Age 24 Killed in Action on 22 March 1918*
POZIERES MEMORIAL, France
Son of John and Sarah Govan, of Gleniffer, Upper Ballysillan, Belfast.

Gowan, Samuel - Private
11493 Royal Inniskilling Fusiliers 9th Battalion *Killed in Action on 16 August 1917*
TYNE COT MEMORIAL, Belgium
Son of Mr. and Mrs. John Gowan, of 28, Harrybrook Street, Crumlin Road, Belfast. Previously twice wounded.

Journey of Remembering

Gowdy, Robert - Rifleman
9276 Royal Irish Rifles 2nd Battalion *Killed in Action on 14 October 1914*
LE TOURET MEMORIAL, France
Son of Robert John Gowdy, 168 Agnes Street, Belfast.

Gracey, Thomas - Private
L/12518 5th (Royal Irish) Lancers attached Machine Gun Corps
Age 20 Died as a result of war on 12 March 1919
THEUX COMMUNAL CEMETERY, Belgium
Son of William John and Mary Ellen Gracey, of 124, Tennent Street, Belfast.

Gracie, Charles - Private
12823 Highland Light Infantry 12th (Service) Battalion *Died in War on 13 August 1916*
CATERPILLAR CEMETERY VALLEY LONGUEVAL, France
Born in Belfast enlisted Lanarkshire, Scotland.

Gradwell, William - Guardsman
4876 Scots Guards 1st Battalion *Died in War on 10 April 1915*
CABARET- ROUGE BRITISH CEMETERY SOUCHEZ, France
Born and enlisted in Preston Lancashire. Resident in Belfast.

Graham, Alexander - Rifleman
2834 Royal Irish Rifles 15th Battalion *Age 21 Killed in Action on 1 July 1916*
LONDON CEMETERY AND EXTENSION, LONGUEVAL, France
Son of Jeannie Graham, of 26, Gainsborough Drive, Belfast.

Graham, Andrew - Company Quarter Master Sergeant
6203 Royal Dublin Fusiliers 2nd Battalion *Died in War on 8 November 1914*
PLOEGSTEERT MEMORIAL, Belgium
Born in Athlone, enlisted Naas, resident Belfast.

Graham, David - Private
6809 Royal Irish Fusiliers 1st Battalion *Age 32 Killed in Action on 21 October 1914*
PLOEGSTEERT MEMORIAL, Belgium
Son of John and Mary Anne Graham, of 4, Ritchie's Terrace, Whitehouse, Belfast.
Served in the South African Campaign.

Graham, David - Rifleman
7548 Royal Irish Rifles 11th Battalion *Age 21 Killed in Action on 1 July 1916*
SUZANNE MILITARY CEMETERY No.3, France
Son of Samuel and Jane Graham, of 13, Willow Street, Belfast.

Graham, Duncan - Rifleman
17759 Royal Irish Rifles 12th Battalion *Age 28 Killed in Action on 1 July 1916*
MILL ROAD CEMETERY, THIEPVAL, France
Son of John and Mary C. Graham, of Cloughfern, Whiteabbey, Belfast.

Graham, Edward - Gunner
L/958 Royal Field Artillery 173rd Brigade *Age 19 Died in War on 27 March 1917*
VLAMERTINGHE NEW MILITARY CEMETERY, Belgium
Born in Belfast. Son of Mr and Mrs Edward Graham of "The Whitehouse", Whitehouse.

Belfast Book of Honour

Graham, Edward - Private
27300 Royal Inniskilling Fusiliers 9th Battalion *Age 29 Killed in Action on 16 August 1917*
TYNE COT MEMORIAL, Belgium
Son of Robert and Elizabeth Graham of 39 Fourth Street, Belfast.

Graham, Frank - Private
17115 Royal Inniskilling Fusiliers 9th Battalion *Age 23 Killed in Action on 1 July 1916*
THIEPVAL MEMORIAL, France
Son of Mary Alexander Graham, of 16, New North Queen Street, Belfast, and the late Thomas Graham.

Graham, Fred - Private
3523 Queen's Own Cameron Highlanders 1st Battalion *Killed in Action on 17 August 1916*
THIEPVAL MEMORIAL, France
Born and enlisted in Belfast.

Graham, George - Private
7535 Cameronians (Scottish Rifles) 1st Battalion *Died in War on 3 June 1915*
ERQUINGHEM-LYS CHURCHYARD EXTENSION, Belgium
Born in Belfast, enlisted Hamilton, Scotland.

Graham, George - Rifleman
14543 Royal Irish Rifles 2nd Battalion *Killed In Action on 19 November 1916*
BERKS CEMETERY EXTENSION, Belgium
Born in Belfast, enlisted Newtownards.

Graham, George - Rifleman
189 Royal Irish Rifles 10th Battalion *Killed in Action on 1 July 1916*
THIEPVAL MEMORIAL, France
Born at Armagh, enlisted and resident of Belfast.

Graham, George Lyons - Second Lieutenant
Royal Dublin Fusiliers 6th Battalion *Age 24 Died in War on 17 August 1917*
TYNE COT MEMORIAL, Belgium
Husband of Margaret Graham, of 42, Channing Street, Castlereagh Road, Belfast.

Graham, Hamilton - A/Bombardier
6451 Royal Garrison Artillery *Died in War on 30 October 1915*
DIVISIONAL CEMETERY, Belgium
Born in Belfast.

Graham, Hedley William Brownrigg - Rifleman
14729 Royal Irish Rifles 10th Battalion *Age 22 Died in War on 22 December 1915*
MAILLY-MAILLET COMMUNAL CEMETERY EXTENSION, France
Son of Wesley Graham, of 66, Melrose Street, Belfast.

Graham, Henry - Private
5172 Queen's Own Cameron Highlanders 1st Battalion *Died in War on 11 November 1914*
TYNE COT CEMETERY, Belgium
Born in Belfast, enlisted Edinburgh.

Graham, Henry Joseph - Private
S/4310 Black Watch (Royal Highlanders) 9th Battalion *Died in War on 25 September 1915*
PHILOSOPHE BRITISH CEMETERY, MAZINGARBE, France
Born in Belfast, enlisted Glasgow.

Graham, James - Private
19297 Royal Inniskilling Fusiliers 9th Battalion *Killed in Action on 1 July 1916*
THIEPVAL MEMORIAL, *France*
His widow lived at 32 Brownlow Street, Belfast with two small daughters. A third child a small boy, Jim, died a month before his father was killed.

Graham, James - Private
23376 Machine Gun Corps (Infantry) *Age 21 Died in War on 3 August 1917*
MENIN ROAD SOUTH MILITARY CEMETERY, *Belgium*
Son of James and Margaret Graham, of 36, Limehill Street, Ligoniel, Belfast.

Graham, James Alexander - Rifleman
12840 Royal Irish Rifles 15th Battalion *Age 25 Killed in Action on 20 February 1916*
SUCRERIE MILITARY CEMETERY, COLINCAMPS, *France*
Son of Martha Graham, of 14, Groomsport Street, Belfast, and the late Hugh Graham.

Graham, James Henry - Rifleman
3451 Royal Irish Rifles 6th Battalion *Died in War on 10 May 1918*
HELLES MEMORIAL, *Turkey*
Born in Belfast enlisted Warrington, England.

Graham, James Joseph - Private
22952 Royal Inniskilling Fusiliers 8th Battalion *Died in War on 28 November 1917*
SHEFFIELD (BUNGREAVE) CEMETERY, *United Kingdom*
Born and enlisted in Belfast.

Graham, Jeremiah - Private
12792 Royal Inniskilling Fusiliers 1st Battalion *Killed in Action on 1 July 1916*
THIEPVAL MEMORIAL, *France*
Born in Belfast, enlisted Lanarkshire, Scotland.

Graham, John - Rifleman
188 Royal Irish Rifles 8/9th Battalion *Killed in Action on 23 March 1918*
POZIERES MEMORIAL, *France*
Born and enlisted in Belfast.

Graham, John - Sapper
42227 Royal Engineers 71st Field Company *Age 39 Died in War on 25 July 1915*
HELLES MEMORIAL, *Turkey*
Husband of Agnes Graham, of 11, Mayfield Street, Lisburn Road, Belfast.

Graham, Joseph - Lance Corporal
2831 Royal Irish Rifles 15th Battalion *Killed in Action on 21 March 1918*
POZIERES MEMORIAL, *France*
Awarded the Military Medal and a member of Knock Presbyterian Church. Son John and Mary Ellen Graham of Mountdarby, County Fermanagh.

Graham, Joseph James - Petty Officer Motor Mechanic (Mech.)
Royal Naval Air Service Russian Armoured Cars *Age 21 Died in War on 24 April 1917*
SLOBOZIA MILITARY CEMETERY, *Romania*
Husband of Annie Maria Graham, of 50, Glenvarlock Street, Castlereagh Road, Belfast. Awarded the Order of St. George, 4th Class (Russia).

Graham, Nathaniel - Rifleman
7282 Royal Irish Rifles 1st Battalion *Killed in Action on 15 January 1916*
Y FARM MILITARY CEMETERY, BOIS-GRENIER, *France*
Born in Ardoyne, Belfast, enlisted Holywood.

Graham, P - Lance Corporal
Royal Irish Fusiliers 2nd Battalion *Died in War on 15 May 1915*
Son of George and Maria Graham, 139 McDonnell Street, Belfast.

Graham, Robert Henry - Rifleman
13551 Royal Irish Rifles 1st Battalion *Age 20 Killed in Action on 31 July 1917*
YPRES (MENIN GATE) MEMORIAL, *Belgium*
Son of Richard and Mary Graham, of 11, Lisburn Avenue, Lisburn Road, Belfast.

Graham, Robert John - Rifleman
9628 Royal Irish Rifles "C" Company 1st Battalion *Age 27 Killed in Action on 25 September 1915*
PLOEGSTEERT MEMORIAL, *Belgium*
Son of Mrs. Margaret Graham, of 13, Little Charlotte Street, Belfast.

Graham, Thomas - Rifleman
5057 Royal Irish Rifles 1st Battalion *Killed in Action on 11 March 1915*
LE TOURET MEMORIAL, *France*
Born in Belfast, enlisted Lisburn.

Graham, Thomas John - Rifleman
6500 Royal Irish Rifles 14th Battalion *Died in War on 16 December 1917*
THIEPVAL MEMORIAL, *France*
20 Distillery Street, Belfast.

Graham, William - Lieutenant Colonel
Royal Army Medical Corps *Died in War on 5 November 1917*
DUNDROD PRESBYTERIAN GRAVEYARD, *United Kingdom*
Native of Belfast. A member of Newtownbreda Presbyterian Church.

Graham, William - Private
43566 Cameronians (Scottish Rifles) 9th Battalion *Died in War on 3 May 1917*
ARRAS MEMORIAL, *France*
Born in Belfast, enlisted in Lanarkshire, Scotland. Formerly 8689 Highland Light Infantry.

Graham, William - Private
PLY/17800 Royal Marine Light Infantry 2nd R.M. Royal Naval Division
Age 20 Died in War on 13 November 1916
ANCRE BRITISH CEMETERY, BEAUMONT-HAMEL, *France*
137 Snugville Street, Belfast.

Graham, William - Private
R4/111376 Royal Army Service Corps *Age 50 Died as a result of war on 3 June 1920*
BELFAST CITY CEMETERY, *United Kingdom*
Husband of Ellen Jane Graham, of 36, Charles Street South, Belfast. Born at Dublin. Served in the South African Campaign with 19th Royal Hussars.

Graham, William - Rifleman
8/3208 Royal Irish Rifles 1st Battalion *Age 21 Killed accidentally on 2 May 1919*
BELFAST (DUNDONALD) CEMETERY, United Kingdom
Son of Robert and Helena Graham, of 3, Coburg Street, Belfast.

Graham, William John - Fireman And Trimmer
Mercantile Marine S.S. "Excellence Pleske" (London)
Age 58 Drowned, as a result of an attack by an enemy submarine on 31 March 1918
TOWER HILL MEMORIAL, United Kingdom
Son of the late Charles and Isabella Graham; husband of Martha Graham (née O'Neill),
of 1, Ludlow Street, Belfast.

Graham, William John - Rifleman
12775 Royal Irish Rifles 15th Battalion *Killed in Action on 1 July 1916*
THIEPVAL MEMORIAL, France
Born and enlisted in Belfast.

Graham, William John - Second Lieutenant
Royal Irish Rifles 18th Battalion attached 12th Battalion *Age 26 Died in War on 22 November 1917*
CAMBRAI MEMORIAL, LOUVERVAL, France
Son of William and Mary Graham, of 67, Coolderry Street, Donegall Road, Belfast.

Graham, William Rennie - Lieutenant
Royal Irish Fusiliers 9th (North Irish Horse) Battalion *Age 26 Killed in Action on 1 October 1918*
DADIZEELE NEW BRITISH CEMETERY, Belgium
Son of John C. and Elizabeth Graham, of 43, Malone Avenue, Belfast; husband of Kathleen Graham
of 123, Fitzroy Avenue, Belfast.

Grainger, Albert - Private
S/40475 Black Watch (Royal Highlanders) 8th Battalion *Age 19 Died of Wounds on 20 October 1916*
DERNANCOURT COMMUNAL CEMETERY EXTENSION, France
Son of John Grainger, of 9, Charleville Street, Belfast.

Grainger, Hames - Driver
80493 Royal Field Artillery *Died in War on 26 April 1915*
LE TOURET MEMORIAL, France
44 Bristol Street, Belfast.

Grainger, William - Private
41209 Royal Army Medical Corps 109th Field Ambulance *Killed in Action on 1 July 1916*
THIEPVAL MEMORIAL, France
Father lived at 175 Leopold Street, Belfast.

Grainger, William Henry - Rifleman
14730 Royal Irish Rifles 14th Battalion *Killed In Action on 3 May 1916*
AUTHUILE MILITARY CEMETERY, France
Born and enlisted in Belfast.

Grant, Fred Campbell - Private
458091 Canadian Infantry 60th Battalion *Died in War on 4 October 1916*
YPRES (MENIN GATE) MEMORIAL, Belgium
Ardenlee Parade, Belfast. Later his widow, Molly, moved to Montreal, Canada.

Grant, Henry - Sapper
200337 Royal Engineers *Died in War on 19 April 1917*
CHEPSTOW CEMETERY, United Kingdom
Born Ballymacarrett, Belfast. Enlisted in Belfast.

Grant, Malcolm - Lance Sergeant
15/14659 Royal Irish Rifles 15th Battalion attached 107th Trench Mortar Battery
Age 35 Killed in Action on 3 January 1917
RATION FARM (LA PLUS DOUVE) ANNEXE, Belgium
Son of the late James and Margaret Grant, of 19, Hudson Street, Belfast; husband of Mary Grant, of 10, Hudson Street, Belfast.

Grant, William John - Private
10266 Royal Inniskilling Fusiliers 1st Battalion *Died in War on 5 July 1916*
ABBEVILLE COMMUNAL CEMETERY, France
34 Saunders Street, Belfast. Born at Lisburn.

Grassick, William G. - Private
S/9300 Gordon Highlanders 2nd Battalion *Died in War on 18 June 1915*
LE TOURET MEMORIAL, France
Born in Belfast, enlisted Leith, Scotland.

Grattan, Thomas - Sergeant
238 Royal Irish Rifles 16th Battalion *Age 32 Died in War on 7 July 1916*
LONDON CEMETERY AND EXTENSION, LONGUEVAL, France
Son of William and Mary Grattan; husband of Ellen Grattan, of 36, Meadowbank Place, Belfast

Gray, Alexander - Rifleman
14662 Royal Irish rifles 9th Battalion *Died in War on 1 July 1916*
THIEPVAL MEMORIAL, France
Husband of Jeannie Gray, 19 Broadbent Street, Belfast.

Gray, Francis (Frank) - Private
22771 2nd Canadian Mounted Rifles (British Columbia Regiment) *Age 33 Died in War on 9 April 1917*
LA CHAUDIERE MILITARY CEMETERY, VIMY, France
Back Gate Lodge, Ligoneil Avenue, Belfast. Two brothers also served.

Gray, George - Private
7144263 Connaught Rangers 1st Battalion formerly King's Own (Royal Lancaster Regiment)
Age 24 Died as a result of war on 17 August 1921
RAWALPINDI WAR CEMETERY, Pakistan
Son of George and Annie Gray, of 5, Mary's Place, Whitehouse, Belfast.

Gray, James - Private
41378 Royal Army Medical Corps 108th Field Ambulance *Age 17 Died of Wounds on 9 August 1917*
BRANDHOEK NEW MILITARY CEMETERY, Belgium
Son of Robert and Agnes Gray, of Belfast. Enlisted at the age of 14.

Gray, John - Private
CH/298(S) Royal Marine Light Infantry *Died in War on 3 June 1915*
ALEXANDRIA (CHATBY) MILITARY CEMETERY AND MEMORIAL, Egypt
94 Donegall Street, Belfast.

Gray, Louis - Private
8316 Royal Inniskilling Fusiliers 2nd Battalion *Age 27 Died in War on 12 September 1914*
LA FERTE-SOUS-JOUARRE MEMORIAL, France
Son of Thomas and Jeannie Gray, of 19, Rossmore Avenue, Ormeau Road, Belfast.

Gray, Robert - Private
201000 Seaforth Highlanders 6th Battalion *Died in War on 9 April 1918*
LOOS MEMORIAL, France
Son of Robert J. and Annie Gray, of 147, Cambria Street, Belfast.

Gray, Robert John - Corporal
PS4916 Royal Fusiliers (City of London Regiment) 20th Battalion
Died in War on 14 February 1916
CAMBRIN CHURCHYARD EXTENSION, France
Born and enlisted in Belfast. Son of Robert M. and Elizabeth M. Gray of "Lindores", of 291, Ormeau Road, Belfast.

Gray, Samuel - Rifleman
10895 Royal Irish Rifles 15th Battalion *Killed In Action on 21 March 1918*
POZIERES MEMORIAL, France
Born and enlisted in Belfast.

Gray, Samuel - Rifleman
16528 Royal Irish Rifles 9th Battalion *Killed in Action on 1 July 1916*
THIEPVAL MEMORIAL, France
Lived at 21 Suir Street, Belfast.

Gray, Thomas - Private
8583 Irish Guards 2nd Battalion *Age 40 Died in War on 2 December 1918*
BUSIGNY COMMUNAL CEMETERY EXTENSION, France
Son of John and Mary Ann Gray, of Dublin; a dock labourer and the husband of Ellen Gray, of 2, Stephen Street, Belfast.

Gray, Thomas - Rifleman
14/14732 Royal Irish Rifles 14th Battalion *Age 23 Died in War on 23 May 1916*
DRUMBO (HOLY TRINITY) CHURCH OF IRELAND CHURCHYARD, United Kingdom
Son of George and Agnes Gray, of Ballycoan, Purdysburn, Belfast.

Gray, William - Lance Corporal
9122 Royal Irish Rifles 1st Battalion *Killed in Action on 10 March 1915*
LE TOURET MEMORIAL, France
From Back Gate Lodge, Ligoneil Avenue, Belfast.

Gray, William - Rifleman
12841 Royal Irish Rifles 8th Battalion *Age 25 Died of Wounds on 12 July 1916*
BOURNEMOUTH EAST CEMETERY, United Kingdom
Son of the late William and Mary Gray, of Belfast.

Gray, William - Rifleman
G/14737 Royal Irish Rifles 9th Battalion *Age 21 Died of Wounds on 2 July 1916*
CONNAUGHT CEMETERY, THIEPVAL, France
Son of David Gray, of 15, Dover Street, Belfast.

Gray, William - Sergeant
19441 Machine Gun Corps (Infantry) 107th Company *Age 36 Killed in Action on 6 June 1917*
POND FARM CEMETERY, *Belgium*
Husband of Margaret E. Gray, of 62, Bright Street, Belfast.

Gray, William - Stoker
1979U Royal Naval Reserve HMS "Bulwark" *Died in War on 26 November 1914*
PORTSMOUTH NAVAL MEMORIAL, *United Kingdom*
3, Grove Street, Belfast.

Gray, William Blackstock - Sergeant
36080 Royal Air Force 25th Squadron *Age 19 Died of Wounds (gas) on 15 August 1918*
HUBY-ST. LEU BRITISH CEMETERY, *France*
Son of John A. and Margaret Gray, of Milltown, Shaws Bridge, Belfast.

Gray, William Francis - Private
14346 Royal Inniskilling Fusiliers 2nd Battalion *Age 20 Died in War on 1 April 1917*
SAVY BRITISH CEMETERY, *France*
Son of Hugh and Mary Jane Gray, of 33, Wilson Street, Belfast. Formerly 12279 Royal Irish Rifles

Gray, William James - Private
11366 Royal Irish Rifles 2nd Battalion *Died of Wounds on 15 July 1916*
ST. SEVER CEMETERY, ROUEN, *France*
30, Mansfield Street, Belfast.

Gray, Wilson - Corporal
S/11651 Seaforth Highlanders 9th Battalion *Age 23 Killed in Action on 24 March 1918*
POZIERES MEMORIAL, *France*
Son of Mrs. Matilda Gray, of 65, Pim's Avenue, Strandtown, Belfast.

Graydon, Charles - Aircraftman Second Class
286836 Royal Air Force *Age 17 Died as a result of War on 22 March 1919*
GALLOON (ST. COMGALL) CHURCH OF IRELAND CHURCHYARD, *United Kingdom*
Son of James Graydon and Emily Lee Graydon, of 58, Surrey Street, Belfast. Born at Newtownbutler.

Green, Arthur Vivian - Second Lieutenant
Royal Dublin Fusiliers 5th Battalion *Age 21 Killed in Action on 17 August 1917*
TYNE COT MEMORIAL, *Belgium*
Son of Herbert Percy and Jessie Green, of "Limehurst", Holland Park, Knock, Belfast.
Educated at Methodist College and Royal Academical Institution, Belfast.

Green, Charles F - Lance Corporal
9947 Royal Inniskilling Fusiliers 1st Battalion *Killed in Action on 1 July 1916*
THIEPVAL MEMORIAL, *France*
Son of Mr and Mrs F Green, 51 Glenbrook Avenue, Belfast.

Green, Edward - Private
4282 Royal Inniskilling Fusiliers 2nd Battalion *Age 18 Died in War on 10 November 1914*
PLOEGSTEERT MEMORIAL, *Belgium*
Son of Edward and Ellen Green, of 16, Spinner Street, Falls Road, Belfast.

Green, George Henry - Rifleman
7031 Royal Irish Rifles 2nd Battalion *Age 28 Killed in Action on 15 September 1914*
VAILLY BRITISH CEMETERY, France
Son of the late Charles and Jane Green; husband of Ellen McKissack (formerly Green), of 9, Paris Street, Belfast. His brother Robert was also killed.

Green, Henry - Private
6491 Royal Scots Fusiliers 1st Battalion *Died in War on 11 November 1914*
YPRES (MENIN GATE) MEMORIAL, Belgium
Brother of Edward, 6 Dunmore Street, Belfast.

Green, Joseph - Private
54182 Canadian Infantry (Western Ontario Regiment) "B" Company 18th Battalion *Age 31 Died in War on 8 April 1916*
VOORMEZEELE ENCLOSURE No.3, Belgium
Son of Joseph and Margaret Green, of 10, Hartington Street, Belfast, Ireland. Worked in Canada as a carriage painter, a Presbyterian.

Green, Percy Harold - Second Lieutenant
Royal Inniskilling Fusiliers 9th Battalion *Age 25 Killed in Action on 26 March 1918*
POZIERES MEMORIAL, France
Son of Herbert P. and Jessie Green, of "Limehurst", Holland Park, Knock, Belfast. Educated at Methodist College, Belfast. Originally enlisted in September 1914 in the 20th (Public School's Battalion) Royal Fusiliers.

Green, Robert - Private
5844 Royal Irish Rifles 2nd Battalion *Killed in Action on 24 October 1916*
LE TOURET MEMORIAL, France
Born in Ligoneil and enlisted in Belfast.

Green, Thomas - Rifleman
17766 Royal Irish Rifles "B" Company 12th Battalion *Age 24 Died in War on 10 October 1918*
HAUTMONT COMMUNAL CEMETERY, France
Son of Robert H. and Annie Green, of 57, Donegall Street, Belfast. Born in Dunmurry, Belfast.

Green, William - Private
4017 Seaforth Highlanders (Ross-shire Buffs, the Duke of Albany's) 4th Battalion *Died in War on 1 August 1916*
Born and enlisted in Belfast.

Greenan, Thomas Joseph - Gunner
6950 Australian Field Artillery 22nd Brigade *Age 25 Killed in Action on 31 July 1916*
FLATIRON COPSE CEMETERY, MAMETZ, France
Son of Peter and Ellen Greenan, of 12, Loretto Terrace, Springfield Road, Belfast, Ireland.

Greenaway, Samuel - Lance Corporal
8347 Royal Irish Rifles 2nd Battalion *Killed in Action on 20 September 1914*
LA FERTE-SOUS-JOUARRE MEMORIAL, France
Born and enlisted in Belfast.

Greene, Joseph - Private
24242 Princess Victoria's (Royal Irish Fusiliers) 1st Battalion *Killed in Action on 21 March 1918*
POZIERES MEMORIAL, France
Born and enlisted in Belfast.

Greenlee, James - Private
2328 Irish Guards 1st Battalion *Died in War on 26 July 1917*
BLEUET FARM CEMETERY, Belgium
Born and enlisted in Belfast.

Greenlee, John James - Acting Bombardier
307777 Canadian Field Artillery 43rd Battery 8th Brigade
Age 38 Killed in Action on 23 November 1917
BRANDHOEK NEW MILITARY CEMETERY No.3, Belgium
Son of Robert and Martha Greenlee, of Belfast, Ireland. A Presbyterian, he was a student in Canada.

Greenwood, John Edwin - Corporal
40997 Royal Army Medical Corps *Killed in Action on 16 August 1917*
TYNE COT MEMORIAL, Belgium
Born and enlisted in Belfast. Awarded the Military Medal.

Greer, Abraham J - Private
12867 Royal Irish Fusiliers Depot *Age 24 Died in War on 27 March 1916*
BELFAST CITY CEMETERY, United Kingdom
Son of Mrs. Annie Greer, of 45, Downing Street, Belfast.

Greer, Arthur - Trimmer
933130 Mercantile Marine Reserve HMS "Otranto"
Age 19 Drowned through collision and wreck of vessel off Isle of Islay on 6 October 1918
PLYMOUTH NAVAL MEMORIAL, United Kingdom
Son of Arthur and Catherine Greer, of 27, Harland Street, Belfast.

Greer, Arthur Joseph - Lance Corporal
9680 Royal Inniskilling Fusiliers 1st Battalion *Age 24 Died in War on 28 April 1915*
HELLES MEMORIAL, Turkey
Son of Samuel R. and Mary Greer, of 159, Donegall Road, Belfast.

Greer, Charles - Private
49744 Royal Irish Fusiliers 9th Battalion *Age 19 Died in War on 4 October 1918*
HARINGHE (BANDAGHEM) MILITARY CEMETERY, Belgium
Son of Charles Greer, of 4, Wallace Row, Ravenhill Road, Belfast.

Greer, Frederick William Martin - Rifleman
14/17771 Royal Irish Rifles 14th Battalion *Age 25 Died in War on 9 October 1916*
POND FARM CEMETERY, Belgium
Late of Ulster Bank, Belfast. Son of the late Thomas Greer. of Culvavy, Hillsborough, County Down, and of Mary Greer, of Beresford House, Coleraine.

Greer, George - Private
30236 King's (Liverpool Regiment) 20th Battalion *Died in War on 30 July 1916*
THIEPVAL MEMORIAL, France
Born in Belfast, enlisted Liverpool.

Greer, George - Private
406539 Canadian Infantry (Eastern Ontario Regiment) 2nd Battalion *Age 24 Died of Wounds on 8 November 1917*
LIJSSENTHOEK MILITARY CEMETERY, Belgium
Son of William and Elizabeth Greer; husband of Harriet Greer, of 144, Parkgate Avenue, Belfast, Ireland.

Journey of Remembering

Greer, Henry - Private
3576 Royal Inniskilling Fusiliers 1st Battalion *Died of Wounds on 5 February 1917*
ST. SEVER CEMETERY EXTENSION, ROUEN, France
Brother of Mrs Reavey, 14 Dagmar Street, Belfast.

Greer, Henry - Rifleman
556 Royal Irish Rifles 15th Battalion *Died in War on 2 December 1917*
ROCQUIGNY-EQUANCOURT ROAD BRITISH CEMETERY, MANANCOURT, France
Born and enlisted in Belfast.

Greer, James - Private
G/26349 Royal Irish Fusiliers transferred to 390371 156th Company Labour Corps
Age 42 Killed in troop train collison on 5 March 1919
BLARGIES COMMUNAL CEMETERY EXTENSION, France
Son of John and Martha Greer, of Banbridge; husband of I. P. Greer, of 22, Colchester Street, Belfast.

Greer, James - Rifleman
18/960 Royal Irish Rifles 12th Battalion *Age 19 Killed in Action on 7 June 1917*
LONE TREE CEMETERY, Belgium
Son of James and Elizabeth Greer, of 206, Blythe Street, Belfast.

Greer, James - Sapper
59804 Royal Engineers Postal Section *Died in War on 13 August 1915*
HELLES MEMORIAL, Turkey
Son of Mrs Mary Greer 10 Shaftsbury Avenue, Belfast.

Greer, John - Rifleman
10663 Royal Irish Rifles 2nd Battalion *Age 33 Killed in Action on 10 August 1917*
YPRES (MENIN GATE) MEMORIAL, Belgium
Native of Belfast. The son of James and Annie Greer, of 8, Valentia Place, Newcastle, County Down.

Greer, John - Rifleman
8747 Royal Irish Rifles 2nd Battalion *Killed In Action on 26 October 1914*
CANADIAN CEMETERY No.2, NEUVILLE-ST. VAAST, France
Born in Belfast, enlisted Dover, Kent.

Greer, John - Stoker First Class
CH/SS/113181 Royal Navy HMS "Racoon" *Age 25 Died in War on 9 January 1918*
BELFAST CITY CEMETERY, United Kingdom
Son of John and Isabella Greer, of 104, Ravenhill Road, Belfast.

Greer, Joseph - Rifleman
17772 Royal Irish Rifles 14th Battalion *Age 31 Died of Wounds on 14 December 1917*
ETRETAT CHURCHYARD EXTENSION, France
Son of Margaret Hydes (formerly Greer), of 12, Donegall Cottages, Cavehill Road, Belfast.

Greer, Robert James - Sergeant
7123 Royal Inniskilling Fusiliers 2nd Battalion *Died of Wounds on 22 July 1916*
BELFAST CITY CEMETERY, United Kingdom
1Weir Street, Belfast.

Journey of Remembering

Greer, Samuel - Private
612143 Canterbury Regiment New Zealand Expeditionary Force 1st Battalion
Age 24 Died of Wounds on 2 October 1916
ETAPLES MILITARY CEMETERY, France
Son of William and Elizabeth Greer, of Belfast, Ireland.

Greer, Thomas McNeill - Private
7126 Australian Infantry 13th Battalion *Age 21 Died of Wounds on 11 July 1917*
TROIS ARBRES CEMETERY, STEENWERCK, France
Son of John and Mary Thomasina Greer, of 272, Springfield Road, Belfast, Ireland.

Greer, William - Private
4017 Seaforth Highlanders 4th Battalion *Died of Wounds on 27 July 1916*
HEILLY STATION CEMETERY, MERICOURT-L'ABBE, France
Son of the late John and Susannah Greer, of 92, McTier Street, Belfast; husband of Elizabeth J. Greer, of 74, McTier Street, Belfast.

Greer, William - Rifleman
14738 Royal Irish Rifles 10th Battalion *Killed In Action on 1 July 1916*
THIEPVAL MEMORIAL, France
Born and enlisted in Belfast.

Greer, William - Stoker First Class
SS/103607 Royal Navy HMS "Hawke" *Died in War on 15 October 1914*
CHATHAM NAVAL MEMORIAL, United Kingdom
16 Cluan Place, Belfast.

Greer, William H - Private
30158 Machine Gun Corps (Infantry) transferred to 375633 Labour Corps
Age 26 Died in War on 29 October 1918
ST. POL BRITISH CEMETERY, ST. POL-SUR-TERNOISE, France
Son of Eliza Jane Greer, of 1, Weir Street, Belfast, and the late Robert Greer.

Greeves, Thomas Malcomson - Flight Sub-Lieutenant
Royal Naval Air Service 12th Squadron 5th Wing *Age 22 Killed whilst flying (crashed) on 23 December 1917*
DUNKIRK TOWN CEMETERY, France
Son of Alfred and Annie Frances Greeves, of "Fernbank" Strandtown, Belfast.

Gregg, James - Lance Corporal
17556 Royal Irish Fusiliers 9th Battalion *Killed in Action on 1 July 1916*
THIEPVAL MEMORIAL, France
Husband of Maggie Gregg, 74 Brussels Street, Belfast.

Gregg, William - Lance Corporal
112116 Royal Irish Fusiliers 9th Battalion *Died in War on 1 October 1918*
DADIZEELE NEW BRITISH CEMETERY, Belgium
Born and enlisted in Belfast. Awarded the Distinguished Conduct Medal.

Gregg, William Henry - Second Lieutenant
Royal Irish Rifles 5th Battalion attached 1st Battalion *Killed in Action on 1 July 1916*
THIEPVAL MEMORIAL, France
Son of John and Margaret Wynne Gregg, of 10, Deramore Park South, Belfast.

JOURNEY OF REMEMBERING

Gregory, James - Lance Corporal
10991 4th (Queen's Own) Hussars *Died in War on 10 April 1918*
ST SEVER CEMETERY EXTENSION ROUEN, France
Born in Newtownards, enlisted and resident in Belfast. Awarded the Military Medal.

Gregory, Robert - Private
S/13995 Black Watch (Royal Highlanders) 2nd Battalion *Died in War on 14 March 1917*
BASRA MEMORIAL, Iraq
Born in Belfast, enlisted in Glasgow.

Gregory, Robert - Rifleman
14748 Royal Irish Rifles 10th Battalion *Killed in Action on 1 July 1916*
THIEPVAL MEMORIAL, France
Born and enlisted in Belfast.

Gribben, Hugh - Private
1571 Leinster Regiment 7th Battalion *Died in War on 3 May 1916*
LONGUENESSE (ST. OMER) SOUVENIR CEMETERY, France
Born in Cushendun, County Antrim, enlisted and resident of Belfast.

Gribbin, Joseph - Private
201001 Seaforth Highlanders 4th Battalion *Died in War on 19 - 21 September 1917*
TYNE COT MEMORIAL, Belgium
Son of Sarah, 9 Benares Street, Belfast.

Gribbon, Hugh - Private
3232 Royal Inniskilling Fusiliers 2nd Battalion *Died in War on 16 May 1915*
LE TOURET MEMORIAL, France
Stepbrother of William McBride, of 168, Newtownards Road, Belfast.

Gribbon, Stanley - Private
5363 Highland Light Infantry 6th (City of Glasgow) Battalion (Territorial) *Died in War on 27 September 1918*
VIS-EN-ARTOIS BRITISH CEMETERY, HAUCOURT, France
Born in Belfast.

Grierson, John Bradley - Private
466531 Canadian Infantry (Saskatchewan Regiment) "A" Company 5th Battalion
Age 20 Died of Wounds on 27 September 1916
ALBERT COMMUNAL CEMETERY EXTENSION, France
Son of Jean Hay Grierson, of 9924, 114th Street, Edmonton, Alberta, and the late John Bradley Grierson. Born in Belfast, Ireland. A Methodist, he worked in Canada as a legal clerk.

Griffin, William - Fireman And Trimmer
Mercantile Marine S.S. "War Clover" (London)
Age 23 Drowned, as a result of an attack by an enemy submarine on 19 October 1917
TOWER HILL MEMORIAL, United Kingdom
Son of William Griffin, of 75, New Dock Street, Belfast, and the late Jane Griffin.

Grogan, Francis - Private
21236 Princess Victoria's (Royal Irish Fusiliers) 7/8th Battalion *Died in War on 25 May 1917*
KEMMEL CHATEAU MILITARY CEMETERY, Belgium
Born and enlisted in Belfast. Formerly 1567 Leinster Regiment.

Grogan, Henry - Able Seaman And Quartermaster
Mercantile Marine S.S. "Aburi" (London)
Age 68 Drowned, as a result of an attack by an enemy submarine on 17 April 1917
TOWER HILL MEMORIAL, *United Kingdom*
Husband of Emma Grogan (née Lizzett). Born at Belfast.

Ground, Alfred William - Private
8616 Royal Irish Fusiliers 1st Battalion *Age 32 Died of Wounds on 24 June 1915*
BAILLEUL COMMUNAL CEMETERY EXTENSION (NORD), *France*
Son of the late Quartermaster Sergeant Ground, (Royal Irish Fusiliers), of Armagh.
Husband of Elizabeth Ground, of 50, Newry Street, Belfast.

Grubb, Donald James - Second Lieutenant
Royal Inniskilling Fusiliers 5th Battalion *Age 20 Killed in Action at Suvla Bay on 15 August 1915*
HELLES MEMORIAL, *Turkey*
Only son of the Rev. James and Jessie Grubb, of Belfast. Educated at Wesley College, Dublin.
A former member of the Officer Training Corps, Queen's University, Belfast.

Grundy, Charles - Private
13731 Royal Inniskilling Fusiliers 9th Battalion *Age 33 Died of Wounds (gas) on 27 October 1918*
ETAPLES MILITARY CEMETERY, *France*
Son of John and Ellen Grundy, of 34, Rosebank Street, Belfast; husband of Annie Grundy,
of Disraeli Street, Belfast.

Guerin, Cornelius - Private
8006 Worcestershire Regiment 3rd Battalion *Died in War on 19 September 1914*
LA FERTE-SOUS-JOUARRE MEMORIAL, *France*
Born in Drumragh, County Tyrone, enlisted Lurgan, resident Belfast.

Guinness, Henry - Lance Corporal
12849 Royal Irish Rifles 8th Battalion *Age 22 Died in War on 2 July 1916*
THIEPVAL MEMORIAL, *France*
Brother of John Guinness, of 14, Belmont Street, Woodstock Road, Belfast.

Gulston, Walter Charles - Sergeant
17775 Royal Irish Rifles 15th Battalion *Age 23 Died of Wounds on 28 April 1918*
BOULOGNE EASTERN CEMETERY, *France*
Son of Henry and Ellen Gulston, of 10, Brookhill Avenue, Belfast.

Gunning, Benjamin Thomas - Corporal
Canadian Infantry (Bristish Columbia Regiment) 29th Battalion *Died in War on 6 November 1917*
YPRES (MENIN GATE) MEMORIAL, *Belgium*
Born in Belfast. Son of Samuel and Margaret Elizabeth Gunning of Vancouver Canada.

Gunning, Frank Douglas - Second Lieutenant
Royal Inniskilling Fusiliers 6th Battalion attached 11th Battalion
Age 22 Died in War on 1 July 1916
THIEPVAL MEMORIAL, *France*
Son of Mrs. Gunning, of Wheatfield Gardens, Belfast, and the late Sinclair Gunning.

Gunning, John Saint Claire - Private
Canadian Infantry (Manitoba Regiment) 16th Battalion Age 21 *Died in War on 22 April 1915*
YPRES (MENIN GATE) MEMORIAL, Belgium
Born in Belfast. Son of Samuel and Margaret Elizabeth Gunning of Vancouver Canada.

Guntley, Fred S - Sergeant
3251 Royal Irish Rifles 15th Battalion *Killed in Action on 1 July 1916*
SERRE ROAD CEMETERY No.2, France
Born in London, a resident of Belfast.

Guthrie, Henry - Private
26897 Royal Inniskilling Fusiliers 7th Battalion *Died in War on 21 October 1918*
POZIERES MEMORIAL, France
Born and enlisted in Belfast.

Guthrie, Thomas - Sergeant
6925 Lancashire Fusiliers 1/6th Battalion *Died in War on 7 August 1915*
HELLES MEMORIAL, Turkey
Born in Belfast, enlisted Rochdale, Lancashire.

Hackett, Augustine John - Sergeant
2486 Connaught Rangers 6th Battalion *Age 21 Killed in Action on 19 February 1917*
KEMMEL CHATEAU MILITARY CEMETERY, Belgium
Son of Patrick Joseph and the late Elizabeth Hackett, of 173, Albertbridge Road, Mount Pottinger, Belfast. Born at Dublin.

Hadden, Samuel Ernest - Rifleman
1697 Royal Irish Rifles 10th Battalion *Age 21 Died of Wounds on 3 July 1916*
FORCEVILLE COMMUNAL CEMETERY AND EXTENSION, France
Son of William and Sara M. Hadden, of Belfast.

Haffern, John - Private
1888 Royal Irish Rifles 14th Battalion *Killed in Action on 1 July 1916*
THIEPVAL MEMORIAL, France
54, Agnes Street, Belfast.

Haggan, Andrew - Rifleman
12/17814 Royal Irish Rifles 12th Battalion *Died in War on 15 August 1917*
YPRES (MENIN GATE) MEMORIAL, Belgium
16, Ulverston Street, Belfast.

Haggan, D - Stoker First Class
CH/SS/115481 Royal Navy HMS "Express" *Age 19 Killed in Action on 20 November 1916*
BELFAST CITY CEMETERY, United Kingdom
Son of Rose Ann Haggan, of 10, Alaska Street, Belfast, and the late David Haggan.

Haggan, Joseph - Rifleman
8679 Royal Irish Rifles 2nd Battalion *Killed in Action on 31 October 1914*
BOULOGNE EASTERN CEMETERY, France
7 Bright Street, Belfast.

Haig, Charles Wolseley - Trooper
2809 2nd Australian Light Horse *Age 44 Died in War on 6 November 1918*
JERUSALEM WAR CEMETERY, Israel
Son of Mr. J. F. and Mrs. M Haig, of 33, Bedford Street, Belfast, Ireland.

Haire, Albert Frederick - Stoker First Class
SS/101089 Royal Navy H.M. Motor Lighter "X 216" *Age 30 Died of pneumonia on 2 November 1918*
STE. MARIE CEMETERY, LE HAVRE, France
Son of Wm. John and Amelia Haire; husband of Rowena Haire, of 72, Wilgar Street, Belfast. Awarded the Order of St. Stanislas (Russian).

Haire, Thompson - Ordinary Seaman
VR/2574 Royal Naval Canadian Volunteer Reserve H.M. Canadian Drifter "96" *Drowned on 3 September 1918*
QUEBEC CITY (MOUNT HERMON) CEMETERY, Canada
Son of Edmond Haire, of 29, Gaffikin Street, Belfast, Ireland.

Hale, James H - Rifleman
15/2823 Royal Irish Rifles 15th Battalion *Age 35 Died of Wounds on 19 October 1916*
RATION FARM (LA PLUS DOUVE) ANNEXE, Belgium
Husband of Annie Hale, of 38, Chief Street, Belfast.

Journey of Remembering

Hale, Patrick - Private
124466 Quebec Regiment 5th Canadian Mounted Rifles *Age 36 Died in War on 16 September 1916*
ETAPLES MILITARY CEMETERY, *France*
Son of Peter and Mary Hale, of Belfast, Ireland; husband of Margaret Hale, of 2201, Court Street, Flint, Michigan, U.S.A. A Catholic he worked in Canada as a labourer and had 12 years service with the Royal Navy.

Hale, Sarah Rachel Orr (Sadie) - Typist
Mercantile Marine S.S. "Lusitania" (Liverpool) *Age 29 Drowned, as a result of an attack by an enemy submarine on 7 May 1915*
TOWER HILL MEMORIAL, *United Kingdom*
Daughter of John and W J Hale of Belfast. Born at Ballymena.

Halfpenny, James - Private
21118 Princess Victoria's (Royal Irish Fusiliers) 7/8th Battalion *Died in War on 7 June 1917*
YPRES (MENIN GATE) MEMORIAL, *Belgium*
Born and enlisted in Belfast. Formerly 2382 Connaught Rangers.

Halfpenny, Patrick - Private
4777 Royal Munster Fusiliers 8th Battalion *Died in War on 6 July 1916*
CALAIS SOUTHERN CEMETERY, *France*
Born in Baillieborough, County Cavan, resident Belfast.

Halfpenny, Peter - Greaser
587394 Mercantile Marine Reserve HMS "Marchioness of Bute"
Age 34 Died as a result of war on 27 February 1919
ST. SEVER CEMETERY EXTENSION, ROUEN, *France*
Son of John and Elizabeth Halfpenny; husband of Mary Halfpenny, of 2, Clyde Street, Belfast

Hall, Arthur - Company Sergeant Major
Royal Irish Rifles 8th Battalion *Died in War on 2 July 1916*
THIEPVAL MEMORIAL, *France*
57 Mourne Street, Belfast.

Hall, David - Gunner
47671 Royal Field Artillery 28th Brigade *Age 28 Died in War on 20 September 1917*
TYNE COT MEMORIAL, *Belgium*
Son of Elizabeth Hall, of 11, Drew Street, Belfast, and the late John Hall.

Hall, Ferris Jackson - Rifleman
14818 Royal Irish Rifles 1st Battalion *Age 23 Died as POW on 25 June 1918*
BERLIN SOUTH-WESTERN CEMETERY, *Germany*
Son of Alexander and Margaret Hall, of 34, Linfield, Belfast.

Hall, Francis Henry - Second Lieutenant
Royal Irish Fusiliers 1st Battalion attached 9th (North Irish Horse) Battalion *Age 29 Killed in Action on 30 September 1918*
DADIZEELE NEW BRITISH CEMETERY, *Belgium*
Native of Belfast. Son of John and Margaret Hall (née Lytle), of Glenanne, County Armagh.
A graduate of Queen's University and a teacher.

Hall, Fred - Private
79706 Welsh Regiment 11th Battalion *Age 23 Killed in Action on 18 September 1918*
DOIRAN MILITARY CEMETERY, *Greece*
Son of Alice Sinton (formerly Hall), of Kingscourt Buildings, Wellington Place, Belfast, and the late F. Hall.

Hall, George Wasson - Rifleman
2012 Royal Irish Rifles 14th Battalion *Age 19 Died in War on 16 August 1917*
POTIJZE CHATEAU GROUNDS CEMETERY, Belgium
Son of Isabella Hall, of 288, Old Lodge Road, Belfast, and the late David R. Hall (Royal Irish Constabulary).

Hall, Henry - Private
4165 Seaforth Highlanders 1/4th Battalion *Age 31 Died of Wounds on 4 May 1916*
ETAPLES MILITARY CEMETERY, France
Husband of Rebecca Hall, 6, St. Mary Street, Belfast.

Hall, John Martindale - Second Lieutenant
Border Regiment 3rd Battalion attached 8th Battalion *Age 19 Died in War on 28 August 1916*
BLIGHTY VALLEY CEMETERY, France
Son of James and Elizabeth Hall. His father owned a musical intrument business in Belfast city centre.

Hall, Samuel Patrick - Sergeant
24393 Royal Garrison Artillery *Died in War on 3 August 1918*
BEVEREN-IJZER CHURCHYARD, Belgium
Born in Belfast, enlisted in Sheerness, Kent.

Hall, Thomas - Rifleman
5558 Royal Irish Rifles 1st Battalion *Died in War on 9 May 1915*
PLOEGSTEERT MEMORIAL, Belgium
Born and enlisted in Belfast.

Hall, William - Able Seaman
234154 Royal Navy HMS"Invincible" *Age 29 Killed in Action at Battle of Jutland on 31 May 1916*
PLYMOUTH NAVAL MEMORIAL, United Kingdom
Son of Mrs. McGrogan, of 32, Canning Street, Belfast; husband of L. A. Hall, of Lilliput House, Parkstone, Dorset.

Hall, William - Rifleman
5545 Royal Irish Rifles 2nd Battalion *Died in War on 31 July 1915*
YPRES (MENIN GATE) MEMORIAL, Belgium
Brother of Joseph Hall, 60 Carlow Street, Belfast. A veteran of the Boer War and a skilled footballer who had played for Cliftonville.

Hall, William James - Private
4272 Seaforth Highlanders 5th Battalion *Age 20 Died in War on 14 November 1916*
MAILLY WOOD CEMETERY, MAILLY-MAILLET, France
Son of James and Elizabeth Hall, of 11, Avon Street, Dee Street, Belfast. Native of Seagoe, Portadown.

Hallam, Henry Richard - Private
35431 The King's (Liverpool Regiment) 16th Battalion *Age 28 Died in War on 10 July 1916*
HALE (ST. MARY) CHURCHYARD, United Kingdom
Son of Henry Richard Hallam, of Hunts Cross, Liverpool; husband of Rose Hallam, of 5, Parkhead Street, Belfast.

Halliday, John - Private
14837 Royal Inniskilling Fusiliers 1st Battalion *Killed in Action on 1 July 1916*
ANCRE BRITISH CEMETERY, BEAUMONT-HAMEL, France
163 Durham Street, Belfast.

Journey of Remembering

Halliday, Robert - Private
18226 Royal Irish Fusiliers 9th Battalion *Age 19 Killed in Action on 1 July 1916*
ANCRE BRITISH CEMETERY, BEAUMONT-HAMEL, *France*
Son of Robert and Mary J. Halliday, of 6, Mornington Street, Belfast. Born at Kilmore, County Cavan.

Halliday, Samuel - Lance Corporal
64327 Royal Engineers 150th Field Company *Died in War on 9 February 1917*
BERKS CEMETERY EXTENSION, *Belgium*
Husband of Annie Halliday, of 51, Roslyn Street, Belfast.

Halliday, Stephen - Rifleman
5525 Royal Irish Rifles 5th Battalion *Age 44 Died in War on 23 November 1917*
BELFAST CITY CEMETERY, *United Kingdom*
Husband of Caroline Halliday, of 62, Douglas Street, Belfast.

Halliday, Thomas - Rifleman
14820 Royal Irish Rifles 10th Battalion *Killed In Action on 1 July 1916*
MILL ROAD CEMETERY, THIEPVAL, *France*
Born in Belfast.

Halliday, Thomas Owens - Second Lieutenant
Royal Irish Rifles 9th Battalion *Died in War on 21 March 1918*
GRAND-SERAUCOURT BRITISH CEMETERY, *France*
Ormeau Road, Belfast.

Halpin, Matthew - Private
25476 Royal Inniskilling Fusiliers 8th Battalion transferred to 421203 Labour Corps
Age 32 Died of bronchial pneumonia on 27 February 1919
LONGUENESSE (ST. OMER) SOUVENIR CEMETERY, *France*
Son of Matthew and Mary Halpin, of Barristown, Slane, County Meath; husband of Hannah Halpin, of 105, Butler Street, Belfast.

Hamil, Robert - Corporal
8792 4th (Queen's Own) Hussars *Died in War on 20 April 1918*
GUISE (LA DESOLATION) FRENCH NATIONAL CEMETERY FLAVIGNY-LE-PETIT, *France*
Born and enlisted in Belfast. Holder of the Military Medal.

Hamill, Alexander - Sergeant
9794 Royal Irish Rifles 1st Battalion *Died in War on 31 October 1916*
THIEPVAL MEMORIAL, *France*
Son of Elizabeth and the late Robert Hamill, 14 Cairns Street, Belfast. Four of his brothers also served.

Hamill, David - Private
12945 Princess Victoria's (Royal Irish Fusiliers) 4th Battalion *Died in War on 15 November 1916*
BELFAST (CITY) CEMETERY, *United Kingdom*
Born and enlisted in Belfast.

Hamill, James - Private
241056 Seaforth Highlanders 5th Battalion *Age 38 Died of Wounds on 9 April 1917*
ARRAS MEMORIAL, *France*
Son of the late William and Matilda Hamill; husband of Jane Hamill, of 27, Beresford Street, Belfast. His brother, Samuel George, was also killed.

Hamill, James - Private
5033 Irish Guards 2nd Battalion *Died in War on 1 February 1915*
CUINCHY COMMUNAL CEMETERY, France
Son of Mrs. S. Hamel, of 13, Abercorn Street, Belfast.

Hamill, Patrick - Lance Sergeant
13073 Royal Irish Fusiliers 6th Battalion *Died in War on 9 August 1915*
HELLES MEMORIAL, Turkey
24 Alton Street, Belfast. A Boer War veteran.

Hamill, Robert - Driver
55896 Royal Field Artillery 76th Battery *Age 29 Died in War on 25 July 1916*
BAGHDAD (NORTH GATE) WAR CEMETERY, Iraq
Son of Robert and Elizabeth Hamill, of 14, Cairns Street, Belfast.

Hamill, Samuel George - Rifleman
584 Royal Irish Rifles 13th Battalion *Age 21 Died of Wounds on 6 July 1916*
DOULLENS COMMUNAL CEMETERY EXTENSION No.1, France
Son of Margaret and the late William John Hamill, of Legland Street, Ligoneil, Belfast.
His brother, James, was also killed.

Hamilton, Alexander - Rifleman
117 Royal Irish Rifles 8th Battalion *Killed in action on 2 July 1916*
THIEPVAL MEMORIAL, France
Finvoy Street, Belfast.

Hamilton, Allen - Rifleman
14477 Royal Irish Rifles 1st Battalion *Died in War on 10 March 1915*
LE TOURET MEMORIAL, France
Born and enlisted in Belfast.

Hamilton, Andrew - Rifleman
14826 Royal Irish Rifles "A" Company 15th Battalion *Age 18 Killed in Action on 1 July 1916*
THIEPVAL MEMORIAL, France
Son of W. J. and Annie Hamilton, of 32, Randon Terrace, Silvio Street, Belfast.

Hamilton, Andrew Charles Coulter - Rifleman
3127 Royal Irish Rifles 8th Battalion *Died in War on 17 August 1917*
NEW IRISH FARM CEMETERY, Belgium
Born and enlisted in Belfast.

Hamilton, Archibald (Archie) H - Captain
Royal Irish Rifles *Died in War on 4 November 1916*
BELFAST CITY CEMETERY, United Kingdom
Member of Belfast Masonic Lodge No 154.

Hamilton, Arthur - Corporal
43381 Cameronians (Scottish Rifles) 9th Battalion *Died in War on 19 September 1917*
POTIJZE CHATEAU LAWN CEMETERY, Belgium
Born in Belfast. Enlisted in Motherwell, Scotland.

Hamilton, Arthur - Private
39213 Durham Light Infantry 14th Battalion *Died in War on 27 March 1917*
NOEX-LES-MINES COMMUNAL EXTENSION, France
Orignally from Belfast. Shot by firing squad for desertion.

Hamilton, Daniel - Private
PLY/16877 Royal Marine Light Infantry 1st R.M. Battalion Royal Naval Division *Died in War on 17 February 1917*
QUEENS CEMETERY, BUCQUOY, France
Northumberland Street, Belfast.

Hamilton, David - Private
1014464 Wellington Regiment New Zealand Expeditionary Force 2nd Battalion *Age 31 Died of Wounds on 8 October 1916*
ETAPLES MILITARY CEMETERY, France
Son of Mary and the late James Hamilton, of Belfast, Ireland.

Hamilton, Edward - Lieutenant
Royal Irish Rifles 9th Battalion *Died in War on 14 April 1918*
TYNE COT MEMORIAL, Belgium
12 Cregagh Road, Belfast.

Hamilton, George - Rifleman
18/1088 Royal Irish Rifles "A" Company 12th Battalion *Age 24 Killed in Action on 7 March 1917*
ST. QUENTIN CABARET MILITARY CEMETERY, Belgium
Native of Belfast. Son of Robert and Margaret Hamilton, of 30, Moat Street, Donaghadee, County Down.

Hamilton, Herbert - Sergeant
17781 Royal Irish Rifles 12th Battalion *Killed In Action on 6 December 1917*
RIBECOURT BRITISH CEMETERY, France
Born in Belfast, enlisted in Carrickfergus.

Hamilton, Hugh - Rifleman
12920 Royal Irish Rifles 15th Battalion *Died in War on 21 March 1918*
GRAND-SERAUCOURT BRITISH CEMETERY, France
Born and enlisted in Belfast.

Hamilton, John Robertson - Private
74315 Canadian Infantry (New Brunswick Regiment) 26th Battalion
Died in War on 6 November 1917
TYNE COT CEMETERY, Belgium
Brother of Mrs Quigg, 23 Northumberland Street, Belfast.

Hamilton, James - Able Seaman
Mercantile Marine S.S. "Hollington" (London) *Age 31 Drowned, as a result of an attack by an enemy submarine on 2 June 1917*
TOWER HILL MEMORIAL, United Kingdom
Son of Minnie Hamilton and the late James Hamilton; husband of Catherine Hamilton (née Murray), of 43, Regent Road, Liverpool. Born in Belfast.

Hamilton, James - Chief Gunner
Royal Navy H.M.T.B. "No 90" *Age 46 Drowned through capsizing of vessel off Gibraltar on 25 April 1918*
PLYMOUTH NAVAL MEMORIAL, United Kingdom
Son of the late Thomas Hamilton, of Belfast; husband of Clara Jane Hamilton, of 9, Fairfield Avenue, Peverell, Plymouth. Awarded the Distinguished Service Cross.

Hamilton, James - Private
23814 Princess Victoria's (Royal Irish Fusiliers) 7th Battalion *Died in War on 9 September 1916*
THIEPVAL MEMORIAL, France
Born and enlisted in Belfast.

Hamilton, James - Rifleman
11036 Royal Irish Rifles 1st Battalion *Age 29 Died in War on 2 October 1918*
TYNE COT MEMORIAL, Belgium
Son of the late James and Isabella Hamilton, of 16, Winetavern Street, Belfast.

Hamilton, James H - Private
201146 Seaforth Highlanders 4th Battalion *Died in War on 19 September 1917*
TYNE COT MEMORIAL, Belgium
Husband of Martha, 78 Urney Street, Belfast. Awarded the Military Medal.

Hamilton, James Hope - Able Seaman
239262 Royal Navy HMS "Pheasant" *Age 25 Killed by mine explosion on 1 March 1917*
PLYMOUTH NAVAL MEMORIAL, United Kingdom
Son of Mary A. Hamilton, of 121, Mayo Street, Belfast, and the late James Hamilton.

Hamilton, John - Corporal
11974 Royal Irish Rifles 15th Battalion *Died in War on 22 November 1917*
THIEPVAL MEMORIAL, France
Born and enlisted in Belfast.

Hamilton, John - Corporal
26424 Royal Scots "C" Company 11th Battalion *Age 31 Killed in Action on 9 April 1917*
BAILLEUL ROAD WEST CEMETERY, ST. LAURENT-BLANGY, France
Husband of Eliza Jane Hamilton, of 14, Mourne Street, Belfast. Native of Belfast. Awarded the Military Medal.

Hamilton, John - Lance Corporal
2797 Leinster Regiment 7th Battalion *Died in War on 30 January 1917*
POND FARM CEMETERY, Belgium
Son-in-law of Mrs. E. Doherty, of 25, Jetty Street, Belfast.

Hamilton, John - Private
11330 Royal Inniskilling Fusiliers 9th Battalion *Died in War on 10 August 1917*
NEW IRISH FARM CEMETERY, Belgium
Born Ballymacarrett, Belfast. Enlisted in Belfast. Husband of Janet Hamilton, of 264 Pope Avenue, Toronto, Canada.

Hamilton, John - Sergeant
1660 Australian Infantry 9th Battalion *Killed in Action on 28 June 1915*
SHELL GREEN CEMETERY, Turkey
Brother of Mr. D. Hamilton, of 145, Canmore Street, Belfast, Ireland.

Hamilton, John Steen - Private
9202 Canadian Infantry (Central Ontario Regiment) 3rd Battalion *Age 24 Died in War on 8 October 1916*
ADANAC MILITARY CEMETERY, MIRAUMONT, France
33 Ottawa Street, Belfast. Son of J. S. and Margaret Hamilton, of Ballymena, Ireland. Worked as a salesman in Canada, an Anglican.

Hamilton, Joseph - Air Mechanic Third Class
263964 Royal Air Force Recruits Depot (Blandford) *Age 32 Died in War on 2 July 1918*
MIDDLETON ST. GEORGE (ST. GEORGE) CHURCHYARD, United Kingdom
Son of Francis and Jane Hamilton; husband of Florence Lilian Agar (formerly Hamilton), of 5, Old Row, Middleton St. George. Born at Belfast.

Hamilton, Michael - Sergeant
12299 Cameronians (Scottish Rifles) 9th Battalion *Died in War on 25 September 1915*
CAMBRIN CHURCHYARD EXTENSION, France
47, English Street, Belfast.

Hamilton, Robert - Private
23680 Royal Inniskilling Fusiliers 1st Battalion *Died of Wounds on 14 September 1918*
ETAPLES MILITARY CEMETERY, France
Born and enlisted in Belfast.

Hamilton, Robert - Private
4278 Royal Inniskilling Fusiliers 2nd Battalion *Died in War on 16 May 1915*
LE TOURET MEMORIAL, France
5, Houston Street, Belfast.

Hamilton, Robert John - Stoker First Class
SS/104942 Royal Navy HMS "Hawke" *Age 25 Killed in Action with submarine in North Sea on 15 October 1914*
CHATHAM NAVAL MEMORIAL, United Kingdom
Son of Joseph and Sarah Hamilton, of 38, Mersey Street, Belfast.

Hamilton, Robert Victor - Second Lieutenant
Royal Irish Rifles 9th Battalion *Age 24 Killed in Action on 1 July 1916*
THIEPVAL MEMORIAL, France
The son of James and Matilda Hamilton of 7 Charnwood Avenue, Belfast A civil servant based in Dublin Castle he had been educated at RBAI.

Hamilton, Thomas - Private
6703 Royal Inniskilling Fusiliers 2nd Battalion *Died in War on 30 November 1917*
TYNE COT MEMORIAL, Belgium
48 ,Canmore Street, Belfast.

Hamilton, William - Corporal
90547 Royal Field Artillery 61st Battery *Died of Wounds on 4 April 1917*
BAGHDAD (NORTH GATE) WAR CEMETERY, Iraq
Resident of Belfast.

Hamilton, William - Lance Corporal
3415 Royal Inniskilling Fusiliers 2nd Battalion *Died in War on 21 September 1917*
ZUYDCOOTE MILITARY CEMETERY, France
Son of John Hamiliton, 29, Alexander Street, Belfast.

Hamilton, William - Lieutenant
Connaught Rangers 1st Battalion *Died in War on 30 September 1918*
DADIZEELE NEW BRITISH CEMETERY, Belgium
Magdala Street, Belfast. Husband of Elizabeth Hamilton of 17, Salem Avenue, Toronto, Canada.

Hamilton, William - Rifleman
47169 Royal Irish Rifles 8/9th Battalion *Died in War on 23 November 1917*
CAMBRAI MEMORIAL LOUVERVAL, France
Born and enlisted in Belfast.

Hampton, Adam Stanley - Junior Fourth Engineer Officer
Mercantile Marine S.S. "Mesaba" (Liverpool)
Age 26 Drowned, as a result of an attack by an enemy submarine on 1 September 1918
TOWER HILL MEMORIAL, United Kingdom
Son of Adam and Annie Hampton (née Porter), of 68, Ailesbury Road, Belfast.

Hammond, Gerald - Private
37882 Highland Light Infantry 16th Battalion *Died in War on 27 April 1917*
ST. SEVER CEMETERY EXTENSION, ROUEN, France
Born in Belfast.

Hancock, William Edwin - Private
21661 York and Lancaster Regiment 10th (Service) Battalion *Died in War on 31 July 1917*
YPRES (MENIN GATE) MEMORIAL, Belgium
Born in Belfast, enlisted Sheffield, Yorkshire.

Hands, Robert - Private
10892 King's Own (Royal Lancaster Regiment) 1st Battalion *Age 20 Died in War on 15 May 1915*
YPRES (MENIN GATE) MEMORIAL, Belgium
Son of Annie Hands, of 58, Westland Street, Belfast. His father was also serving.

Hanlan, David - Leading Seaman
206086 Royal Navy S.S. "Ravensworth" *Age 36 Drowned on 15 September 1917*
BALLANTRAE PARISH CHURCHYARD, United Kingdom
Son of David and Ellen Hanlan; husband of Lillie Jane Hanlan, of 18, Cross Street, Holyhead.
Born at Belfast.

Hanley, David - Lance Corporal
999 Royal Irish Rifles 14th Battalion *Age 26 Died in War on 16 August 1917*
TYNE COT MEMORIAL, Belgium
Son of Agnes Hanley, of 65, Mountview Street, and the late Tom Hanley; husband of Lilias Hanley, of 10, Rosapenna Street, Belfast.

Hanley, Joseph - Rifleman
7818 Royal Irish Rifles 2nd Battalion *Died in War on 21 September 1914*
CITY OF PARIS CEMETERY, BAGNEUX, France
126 Disraeli Street, Belfast.

Hanley, Patrick - Private
3676 Princess Victoria's (Royal Irish Fusiliers) 8th Battalion *Died in War on 6 September 1916*
THIEPVAL MEMORIAL, France
Born and enlisted in Belfast.

Hanlon, Thomas - Private
4921 Royal Munster Fusiliers 2nd Battalion *Age 30 Reported missing, belived killed on 15 November 1914*
YPRES (MENIN GATE) MEMORIAL, Belgium
Brother of Mrs. Mary Jane Piddock, of 29, Kilronan Street, Duncairn Gardens, Belfast.

Hanna, Archibald McMillan - Private
12892 Royal Irish Rifles 15th Battalion *Killed in Action on 1 July 1916*
THIEPVAL MEMORIAL, France
Court Street, Belfast.

Hanna, Charles Henry - Private
760553 Canadian Infantry (British Columbia Regiment) 7th Battalion
Age 34 Killed in Action at Loos on 9 April 1918
ECOIVRES MILITARY CEMETERY, MONT-ST. ELOI, France
Native of Belfast. Son of Hugh and Amy Hanna, of 1324, 18th Avenue East, Vancouver.
A member of Church of Ireland he was a single man and had worked as a civil engineer.

Hanna, Christopher - Private
4373 3rd Dragoon Guards (Prince of Wales' Own) *Age 27 Died in War on 31 October 1914*
YPRES (MENIN GATE) MEMORIAL, Belgium
Husband of Ellen Hanna, of 9, Coolfin Street, Donegall Road, Belfast.

Hanna, David Loftus - Private
3642 Royal Inniskilling Fusiliers 1st Battalion *Age 32 Died in War on 9 August 1916*
LIJSSENTHOEK MILITARY CEMETERY, Belgium
Brother of Mrs Cavan, Essex Street, Belfast.

Hanna, Dennis - Rifleman
7210 Royal Irish Rifles 1st Battalion *Age 19 Killed in Action on 18 August 1916*
VERMELLES BRITISH CEMETERY, France
Son of Robert and Annie Hanna, of 62, Anderson Street, Belfast.

Hanna, Francis - Private
11942 Royal Scots Fusiliers 2nd Battalion *Age 19 Killed in Action on 23 April 1917*
BOOTHAM CEMETERY, HENINEL, France
Son of Mrs. Mary Jane Hanna, of 148, Matilda Street, Belfast.

Hanna, Francis - Private
15797 Royal Irish Fusiliers 6th Battalion *Age 34 Died of dysentery on 17 August 1915*
PORTIANOS MILITARY CEMETERY, Greece
Son of Hugh and Mary Hanna, of Queenstown; husband of Elizabeth Hanna,
of 67, Church Street East, Newtownards Road, Belfast.

Hanna, Frank Leslie - Lieutenant
Argyll & Sutherland Highlanders 3rd Battalion formerly Army Service Corps
Age 24 Died of nephritis on 26 July 1918
KNOCKBREDA CHURCH OF IRELAND CHURCHYARD, United Kingdom
Son of Francis and Marion Hanna, of Gayfield, Finaghy Park, Belfast. Born in Bangor, County Down.

Hanna, George - Private
12609 Royal Irish Fusiliers 1st Battalion *Age 26 Died in War 6 November 1917*
NEUVILLE-BOURJONVAL BRITISH CEMETERY, France
Thought to have been originally from Belfast, he was the son Henry and Elizabeth Hanna.
Shot by firing squad for desertion.

Hanna, Hugh - Private
171472 Canadian Infantry (Central Ontario Regiment) 3rd Battalion *Age 27 Killed in Action on 29 July 1917*
MAROC BRITISH CEMETERY, GRENAY, France
Son of Mr. and Mrs. Andrew Hanna, of Belfast, Ireland; husband of Christina Hanna, of 48, Hickson Street, Toronto, Canada.

Hanna, Isaac - Rifleman
1075 Royal Irish Rifles 15th Battalion *Killed In Action on 6 August 1917*
NEW IRISH FARM CEMETERY, Belgium
Born and enlisted in Belfast.

Hanna, James - Company Sergeant Major
7680 Royal Inniskilling Fusiliers 1st Battalion *Killed in Action on 1 July 1916*
THIEPVAL MEMORIAL, FRANCE
39 Haypark Avenue, Belfast. Born and enlisted in Belfast.

Hanna, James Reynolds - Private
24111 Canterbury Regiment New Zealand Expeditionary Force 1st Battalion
Age 20 Killed in Action on 12 October 1917
TYNE COT MEMORIAL, Belgium
Son of Joseph and Sarah Hanna, of 370, Worcester Street, Christchurch, New Zealand.
Native of Belfast, Ireland.

Hanna, John - Rifleman
6774 Royal Irish Rifles 2nd Battalion *Died in War on 28 April 1916*
GRANGEGORMAN MILITARY CEMETERY, Republic of Ireland
Born Downpatrick, enlisted Newtownards, resident Belfast

Hanna, John Clendinning - Second Engineer
Mercantile Marine S.S. "Garron Head" (Belfast) *Age 25 Killed by mine on 16 November 1917*
TOWER HILL MEMORIAL, United Kingdom
Son of Elizabeth Hanna (née Linton), of 201, Spamount Street, Belfast, and the late James George Hanna. Born in Belfast.

Hanna, Patrick - Corporal
24842 Royal Inniskilling Fusiliers 7th Battalion *Killed in Action on 27 April 1916*
LOOS MEMORIAL, France
Born and enlisted in Belfast.

Hanna, Patrick - Private
24738 Royal Inniskilling Fusiliers 7th Battalion *Died of Wounds on 1 June 1916*
PHILOSOPHE BRITISH CEMETERY, MAZINGARBE, France
Born and enlisted in Belfast.

Hanna, Samuel - Private
20942 Royal Irish Fusiliers 8th Battalion *Died in War on 4 May 1916*
BETHUNE TOWN CEMETERY, France
Son of Samuel Hanna, of 5, Eliza Street, Belfast.

Hanna, William - Rifleman
6724 Royal Irish Rifles 14th Battalion *Age 21 Killed in Action 1 July 1916*
MILL ROAD CEMETERY, THIEPVAL, France
Son of William and Mary Hanna, of 44, Glenwherry Street, Ravenhill Road, Belfast.

Journey of Remembering

Hanna, William - Rifleman
7199 Royal Irish Rifles 2nd Battalion *Killed In Action on 16 July 1916*
THIEPVAL MEMORIAL, France
Son of Samuel Hanna, of 5, Eliza Street, Belfast.

Hanna, William - Sergeant
29416 Royal Irish Fusiliers 1st Battalion *Age 23 Died in War on 5 April 1918*
TYNE COT MEMORIAL, Belgium
Son of Hugh and Bridget Hanna, of 30, Mountcollyer Street, Belfast; husband of Agnes Hanna, of The Square, Skerries, County Dublin.

Hanna, William James - Rifleman
15/2844 Royal Irish Rifles 15th Battalion *Age 26 Died in War on 29 May 1918*
CANADA FARM CEMETERY, Belgium
Son of William and Fanny Hanna, of Belfast.

Hannan, John - Private
Z/2972 Leinster Regiment 2nd Battalion *Died on 29 December 1917*
ETAPLES MILITARY CEMETERY, France
Son of Sarah Jane Hannan; husband of Mary Jane Hannan, of 50, Cullingtree Road, Belfast.

Hannan, Joseph - Private
26711 King's (Liverpool Regiment) 12th Battalion *Died in War on 10 March 1916*
YPRES (MENIN GATE) MEMORIAL, Belgium
Born in Limerick, resident Belfast.

Hannaway, Terrance - Guardsman
6644 Scots Guards 2nd Battalion *Died in War on 26 October 1914*
YPRES (MENIN GATE) MEMORIAL, Belgium
Born in Belfast, enlisted in Glasgow.

Hannigan, Thomas Gilbert - Sergeant
2969 Irish Guards 1st Battalion *Age 25 Killed in Action on 4 September 1914*
GUARDS GRAVE, VILLERS COTTERETS FOREST, France
Son of George and Hariett Hannigan, of 42, Fitzroy Avenue, Ormeau Road, Belfast.

Hannon, Hugh - Private
4954 Argyll and Sutherland Highlanders 1st/6th Battalion *Age 21 Died of meningitis on 6 September 1916*
DAOURS COMMUNAL CEMETERY EXTENSION, France
Son of Hugh J. and Mary Ann Hannon, of Hagg Cottage, Johnstone, Renfrewshire, Scotland. Native of Belfast.

Hanvey, Herbert - Lance Corporal
9658 Royal Inniskilling Fusiliers "C" Company 1st Battalion
Age 24 Died of Wounds, received at the Battle of the Somme on 2 July 1916
ACHEUX BRITISH CEMETERY, France
Son of James and Jane Hanvey, of Belfast.

Hanvey, John - Lance Corporal
19556 Machine Gun Corps (Infantry) 107th Company *Age 23 Killed in Action on 24 March 1917*
POND FARM CEMETERY, Belgium
Brother of Mrs. Sarah Jane Walker, of 5, Salisbury Place, Ligoneil, Belfast. Formerly 12280 Royal Irish Rifles.

JOURNEY OF REMEMBERING

Haraghy, John - Private
24226 Princess Victoria's (Royal Irish Fusiliers) 1st Battalion *Died in War on 10 July 1917*
CRUMP TRENCH BRITISH CEMETERY, FAMPOUX, France
Born and enlisted in Belfast.

Harding, Joseph - Private
1072 Australian Infantry 20th Battalion *Age 24 Killed in Action on 5 May 1916*
BREWERY ORCHARD CEMETERY, BOIS-GRENIER, France
Son of Joseph and Annie Steele, of 1, Mersey Street, Belfast, Ireland.

Hardy, John - Gunner
5851 Royal Garrison Artllillery 5th Trench Mortar Battery *Died in War on 9 May 1916*
BETHUNE TOWN CEMETERY, France
Father lived at 91 Craigmore Street, Belfast.

Hare, Henry - Sergeant
6745 Royal Dublin Fusiliers 5th Battalion *Age 40 Died in War on 26 April 1916*
GRANGEGORMAN MILITARY CEMETERY, Republic of Ireland
Husband of R. Hare, of 109, Cupar Street, Belfast.

Hare, Joseph - Sapper
64344 Royal Engineers 150th Field Company *Died in War on 29 May 1917*
BAILLEUL COMMUNAL CEMETERY EXTENSION (NORD), France
29 Stonyford Street, Belfast. Born at Comber, County Down.

Harfitt, Henry - Private
11302 Irish Guards 2nd Battalion *Died in War on 1 August 1917*
CANADA FARM CEMETERY, Belgium
Born in Belfast, enlisted Frome, Somerset.

Harkness, Alexander - Private
PLY/11869 Royal Marine Light Infantry HMS "Goliath" *Age 29 Died in War on 13 May 1915*
PLYMOUTH NAVAL MEMORIAL, United Kingdom
Son of the late John and Mary J. Harkness, of Knockboy, County Antrim.
Native of Ballygarvey, County Antrim. Resident of Belfast.

Harkness, George D - Rifleman
8252 Royal Irish Rifles 2nd Battalion *Died of pneumonia on 3 December 1914*
LE MANS WEST CEMETERY, France
Husband of Nellie Harkness, 30 Argyle Street, Belfast.

Harkness, Hugh
Royal Irish Rifles *Died in War*
95 Leopold Street, Belfast.

Harland, who served as "Harlin", George - Corporal
129405 Royal Engineers N Special Company *Died in War on 19 June 1917*
RAILWAY DUGOUTS BURIAL GROUND, Belgium
Husband of Edith Harlin, 26 Danube Street, Belfast.

Journey of Remembering

Harmes, Andrew - Private
25743 Royal Inniskilling Fusiliers 2nd Battalion *Age 33 Died in War on 3 April 1917*
SAVY BRITISH CEMETERY, France
Son of John Frederick Harmes, of 65, Aberdeen Street, Belfast, and the late Isabella Harmes.

Harper, Frank Leitch - Company Quartermaster Sergeant
7114767 Royal Dublin Fusiliers 7th Battalion *Age 27 Killed in Action on 3 October 1916*
STRUMA MILITARY CEMETERY, Greece
Son of Thomasina Harper, of 19, Lothair Avenue, Belfast, and the late James Harper.
Educated at Antrim Road School and Sargent's College, Belfast.

Harper, Jameson - Rifleman
14847 Royal Irish Rifles 14th Battalion *Died in War on 16 August 1917*
TYNE COT MEMORIAL, Belgium
95 Rugby Avenue, Belfast.

Harper, Joseph - Lance Sergeant
13031 Royal Inniskilling Fusiliers 8th Battalion *Age 22 Died in War on 9 September 1916*
THIEPVAL MEMORIAL, France
Son of Rebecca Harper, of 6, Coburg Street, Belfast, and the late Thomas Harper.

Harper, Paul - Rifleman
20969 Royal Irish Rifles secondary Regiment London Irish Rifles *Died in War on 5 September 1918*
PERONNE COMMUNAL CEMETERY EXTENSION, France
Born and enlisted in Belfast.

Harper, Samuel - Lance Corporal
6941 Royal Irish Rifles 1st Battalion *Died in War on 10 March 1915*
GUARDS CEMETERY, WINDY CORNER, CUINCHY, France
20 Abyssinia Street, Belfast.

Harper, William - Rifleman
3407 London Regiment 8th (City of London) Battalion (Post Office Rifles) *Died in War on 15 September 1916*
THIEPVAL MEMORIAL, France
Born and enlisted in Belfast

Harper, William - Sapper
57709 Royal Engineers 150th Company *Died as a result of war on 25 July 1919*
BELFAST CITY CEMETERY, United Kingdom
Husband of Sarah Johnston (formerly Harper), of 53, Upper Charles Street, Shankill Road, Belfast.

Harper, William James - Stoker First Class
SS/104430 Royal Navy HMS "Hawke" *Lost at sea on 15 October 1914*
CHATHAM NAVAL MEMORIAL, United Kingdom
7 Linden Street, Belfast.

Harpur, Thompson - Private
41433 Royal Irish Fusiliers "C" Company 9th (North Irish Horse) Battalion *Age 21 Died of Wounds on 18 May 1918*
AVESNES-SUR-HELPE COMMUNAL CEMETERY, France
Son of John James and Jeannie Harpur, of 10, Glandore Street, Belfast. Native of County Donegal.

JOURNEY OF REMEMBERING

Harraghy, John - Private
24226 Royal Irish Fusiliers "A" Company 1st Battalion *Age 20 Died in War on 10 July 1917*
CRUMP TRENCH BRITISH CEMETERY, FAMPOUX, France
Son of Francis and Elizabeth Harraghy, of 109, Cavendish Street, Belfast.

Harris, Alfred John - Rifleman
104 Royal Irish Rifles 15th Battalion *Age 22 Killed in Action on 21 March 1918*
POZIERES MEMORIAL, France
Son of William and Ellen Harris, of 24, Prospect Street, Belfast.

Harris, Charles William Henry - Private
7025 Worcestershire Regiment 3rd Battalion *Died in War on 20 October 1914*
LE TOURET MEMORIAL, France
Born and resident in Belfast, enlisted Dudley, England.

Harris, John - Rifleman
9185 Royal Irish Rifles 1st Battalion *Died in War on 10 March 1915*
LE TOURET MEMORIAL, France
Born and enlisted in Belfast.

Harris, Thomas - Lance Corporal
9590 Connaught Rangers 1st Battalion *Died in War on 23 November 1914*
LE TOURET MEMORIAL, France
103 Melrose Street, Belfast. Born in Newtownards.

Harris, William - Private
27780 Wiltshire Regiment 6th (Wiltshire Yeomanry) Battalion *Age 18 Died in War on 2 July 1918*
PREMONT BRITISH CEMETERY, France
Son of Elizabeth Crothers (formerly Harris), of 4, Bungalow, Ballyhenry, Belfast, and the late William Harris.

Harrison, Albert - Rifleman
19009 Royal Irish Rifles 9th Battalion *Age 30 Died in War on 26 July 1917*
COLCHESTER CEMETERY, United Kingdom
Husband of Margaret Harrison, of 200, Cupar Road, Belfast.

Harrison, Elias John - Lance Corporal
587 Royal Irish Rifles 1st Battalion *Died in War on 24 March 1918*
ST SEVER CEMETERY EXTENSION ROUEN, France
Seaview Street, Belfast. A native of Antrim.

Harrison, Frederick - Private
81582 Durham Light Infantry 15th Battalion *Age 32 Died in War on 18 April 1918*
TYNE COT MEMORIAL, Belgium
Son of David Harrison, of 7, Artana Street, Belfast, and the late Charlotte Mary Harrison.

Harrison, Henry - Lance Corporal
14560 Royal Dublin Fusiliers 10th Battalion *Died in War on 15 April 1917*
ARRAS MEMORIAL, France
Born and enlisted in Dublin, resident of Belfast.

Journey of Remembering

Harrison, James - Rifleman
7234 Royal Irish Rifles 2nd Battalion *Killed In Action on 27 October 1914*
RUE-PETILLON MILITARY CEMETERY, FLEURBAIX, France
Born and resident in Belfast.

Harrison, John George - Lance Corporal
20405 Royal Irish Rifles "B" Company 12th Battalion *Age 19 Died in War on 14 April 1918*
TYNE COT MEMORIAL, Belgium
Son of James and Elizabeth Harrison, of 167, Stranmillis Road, Belfast.

Harrison, Robert - Lance Sergeant
2249 Irish Guards 1st Battalion *Died in War on 19 May 1915*
BETHUNE TOWN CEMETERY, France
170 North Street, Belfast. Born in Newtownards County Down.

Harrison, William - Rifleman
11164 Royal Irish Rifles 6th Battalion *Age 22 Died in War on 29 October 1915*
KIRECHKOI-HORTAKOI MILITARY CEMETERY, Greece
Son of Ellen Harrison, of 3 Hill Street, Belfast, and the late Nathaniel Harrison.

Harrison, William James - Lance Corporal
1095 Royal Irish Rifles 9thBattalion *Killed in Action on 1 July 1916*
THIEPVAL MEMORIAL, France
36 Hutchinson Street Belfast.

Harrow, James - Corporal
9862 King's Royal Rifle Corps 4th Battalion *Died in War on 10 January 1915*
YPRES (MENIN GATE) MEMORIAL, Belgium
Enlisted and resident in Belfast.

Hart, John - Rifleman
6600 Royal Irish Rifles 1st Battalion *Died in War on 26 April 1916*
MERICOURT-L'ABBE COMMUNAL CEMETERY EXTENSION, France
Brother of Ellen Hart, Saul Street, Belfast.

Hart, John - Rifleman
17842 Royal Irish Rifles 14th Battalion *Age 18 Killed in Action on 1 July 1916*
THIEPVAL MEMORIAL, France
Son of Robert and Sarah Hart, of 17, Kyle Street, Sydenham, Belfast.

Hart, William - Private
10497 Royal Inniskilling Fusiliers 2nd Battalion *Killed in Action on 11 July 1916*
THIEPVAL MEMORIAL, France
Born and enlisted in Belfast.

Hart, William - Private
79 Irish Guards 1st Battalion *Died in War on 16 September 1914*
LA FERTE-SOUS-JOUARRE MEMORIAL, France
Born Ballymacarrett, Belfast. Enlisted in Belfast. Father of William A Hart of Church Row, Limehouse, London.

Harvey, Daniel - Private
18656 Royal Irish Fusiliers 4th Battalion *Died suddenly at home on 25 April 1916*
BELFAST (MILLTOWN) ROMAN CATHOLIC CEMETERY, United Kingdom
(Served as DAVIS). Son of the late Thomas and Sarah Harvey, of Belfast. A Veteran of the Boer War.

Harvey, Frederick George - Lance Corporal
9660 Royal Irish Rifles 12th Battalion *Age 18 Died of Wounds on 15 October 1918*
DUHALLOW A.D.S. CEMETERY, Belgium
Son of Joseph and Mary Harvey, of 5, Pacific Avenue, Antrim Road, Belfast, born Bedford, England.

Harvey, Harold - Private
12719 Canadian Infantry (Saskatchewan Regiment) *Died in War on 24 May 1915*
VIMY MEMORIAL, France
Born in Belfast. In Canada he worked as a clerk and was an Anglican.

Harvey, James - Private
16282 Royal Inniskilling Fusiliers "C" Company 9th Battalion *Age 17 Killed in Action on 1 July 1916*
THIEPVAL MEMORIAL, France
Son of William and Theresa Harvey, of 89, Great Northern Street, Belfast.

Harvey, John - Private
12763 Royal Inniskilling Fusiliers 6th Battalion *Died in War on 7 December 1915*
DOIRAN MEMORIAL, Greece
Son of Mary Harvey, of 10, Johnston Street, Belfast, and the late James Harvey.
A member of King William Temperance Orange Lodge 238.

Harvey, John - Rifleman
6970 Royal Irish Rifles 2nd Battalion *Died in War on 16 June 1915*
YPRES (MENIN GATE) MEMORIAL, Belgium
Born Ballymacarrett, Belfast, enlisted Holywood.

Harvey, John Forsyth - Captain
Royal Inniskilling Fusiliers 9th Battalion *Age 24 Died in War on 23 March 1918*
POZIERES MEMORIAL, France
Son of William and Elizabeth Harvey, of "Inverary", Downshire Road, Cregagh, Belfast.
He enlisted as a private soldier and was later commissioned.

Harvey, John J - Sergeant
S4/127941 Army Service Corps 36th (Ulster) Field Bakery *Age 38 Died of sickness on 10 December 1916*
STE. MARIE CEMETERY, LE HAVRE, France
Husband of Susan Harvey, of 35, Silvergrove Street, Donegall Pass, Belfast.

Harvey, Joseph Samuel - Rifleman
7290 Royal Irish Rifles 11th Battalion *Killed in Action on 1 July 1916*
THIEPVAL MEMORIAL, France
Born and enlisted in Belfast.

Harvey, Robert - Private
5/13233 Royal Inniskilling Fusiliers 5th Battalion *Died of Wounds on 27 December 1917*
JERUSALEM WAR CEMETERY, Israel
Brother of John Harvey, of 18, Avondale Street, Belfast.

Journey of Remembering

Harvey, Robert - Rifleman
19/497 Royal Irish Rifles 14th Battalion *Died in War on 7 June 1917*
LONE TREE CEMETERY, Belgium
Son of Mr. R. Harvey, of 64, Gertrude Street, Belfast.

Harvey, Thomas - Rifleman
6569 Royal Irish Rifles 2nd Battalion *Age 38 Died in War on 17 December 1914*
YPRES (MENIN GATE) MEMORIAL, Belgium
Husband of Sarah Jane Niblock (formerly Harvey), of 46, Weir Street, Belfast.

Harvey, William John - Private
10263 Royal Inniskilling Fusiliers "A" Company 2nd Battalion
Age 20 Killed in Action at Le Cateau on 26 August 1914
LA FERTE-SOUS-JOUARRE MEMORIAL, France
Son of Thomas Douglas Harvey and Ellen Jane Harvey, of 49, Convention Street, Belfast.

Haslam, Hugh Benjamin - Sergeant
9416 Connaught Rangers 6th Battalion *Age 27 Died of Wounds on 26 August 1917*
BOULOGNE EASTERN CEMETERY, France
Born Sherrygroom, County Tyrone, enlisted Clydebank, resident Belfast.

Hasley, Joseph - Rifleman
14858 Royal Irish Rifles 14th Battalion *Killed In Action on 16 August 1917*
TYNE COT MEMORIAL, Belgium
Born and enlisted in Belfast.

Hassan, Francis - Private
11727 Cameronians (Scottish Rifles) 9th Battalion *Died in War on 3 July 1916*
THIEPVAL MEMORIAL, France
Son of Margaret and the late Robert Hassan of 71, Lincoln Street, Belfast.

Hastings, Alexander - Private
41706 Royal Inniskilling Fusiliers 9th Battalion *Killed in Action on 15 October 1918*
TYNE COT MEMORIAL, Belgium
18, Matchett Street, Belfast.

Hastings, John - Lance Corporal
12908 Royal Irish Rifles 8th Battalion *Died of Wounds on 7 June 1917*
BAILLEUL COMMUNAL CEMETERY EXTENSION (NORD), France
Son of Robert Hastings 10, Fifth Street, Belfast.

Hastings, Thomas - Rifleman
9383 Royal Irish Rifles 1st Battalion *Died in War on 9 May 1915*
PLOEGSTEERT MEMORIAL, Belgium
Son of Robert Hastings 10, Fifth Street, Belfast. Four brothers served.

Haughey, David - Sapper
WR/503462 Royal Engineers *Age 45 Died as a result of war on 31 January 1920*
BELFAST CITY CEMETERY, United Kingdom
Son of Robert John and Agnes J. Haughey, of 23, Donaldson Crescent, Woodvale, Belfast.

Journey of Remembering

Haughey, Henry - Rifleman
12200 Royal Irish Rifles 10th Battalion attached Machine Gun Corps (Infantry)
Age 28. Killed in Action on 21 March 1918
POZIERES MEMORIAL, France
Son of Mrs. Margaret Haughey, of 24, Gaffikin Street, Belfast.

Haughey, Patrick - Private
601 Royal Munster Fusiliers 9th Battalion *Died in War on 27 March 1916*
DUD CORNER CEMETERY, LOOS, France
Born in Portadown, County Armagh, resident in Belfast.

Haughney, James - Private
22406 Royal Inniskilling Fusiliers 8th Battalion *Age 26 Died in War on 20 May 1916*
LOOS MEMORIAL, France
Son of Edward and Mary Ann Haughney, of 46, Donnybrook Street, Belfast.

Haveron, Daniel - Rifleman
1537 Royal Irish Rifles 8th Battalion *Age 23 Killed in Action on 17 August 1917*
TYNE COT MEMORIAL, Belgium
27 Lorton Street, Belfast.

Haveron, Patrick Joseph - Private
3017 Royal Inniskilling Fusiliers 1st Battalion *Killed in Action on 21 August 1915*
HELLES MEMORIAL, Turkey
Born and enlisted in Belfast.

Haveron, William - Private
30773 Royal Scots (Lothian Regiment) 13th Battalion *Died in War on 15 September 1916*
THIEPVAL MEMORIAL, France
Lawnbrook Avenue, Belfast.

Hawkins, William - Sergeant
12289 Royal Irish Rifles 15th Battalion *Killed in Action on 1 July 1916*
THIEPVAL MEMORIAL, France
Wife lived at 14, Limepark Street, Ballysillan, Belfast.

Hawthorne, Edward - Private
1780 Australian Infantry 11th Battalion *Died in War on 1 August 1915*
LONE PINE CEMETERY, Turkey
Parents lived at 15, Apsley Street, Belfast.

Hawthorne, George A - Rifleman
14863 Royal Irish Rifles 10th Battalion *Killed in Action on 1 July 1916*
CONNAUGHT CEMETERY, THIEPVAL, France
Son of George Hawthorne, 19, Mulhouse Street, Belfast. A former employee of the Great Northern Railway. His bother, William, also served and was wounded.

Hawthorne, James - Sergeant
9349 Royal Inniskilling Fusiliers 1st Battalion *Died in War on 2 December 1917*
CAMBRAI MEMORIAL, LOUVERVAL, France
Son of James Hawthorne, 113, Canmore Street, Belfast.

Journey of Remembering

Hawthorne, John - Rifleman
9452 Royal Irish Rifles 1st Battalion *Killed in Action on 17 March 1915*
LE TOURET MEMORIAL, France
Eldest son of John and the late Catherine, 56, Mossvale Street, Belfast.

Hay, William Stevenson Brown - Captain
Royal Army Medical Corps attached 53rd Brigade *Age 27 Killed in Action on 5 October 1918*
POTIJZE BURIAL GROUND CEMETERY, Belgium
Son of George C. and Mary F. Hay, of 9, Cameron Street, Belfast. Educated at Methodist College and Queen's University. A doctor, he was gazetted in 1915 and attached to 110th Field Ambulance 36th (Ulster) Division and later the Royal Artillery. Served in all the major battles from 1915 and was killed within a few weeks of the armistice.

Hayden, Arnold - Rifleman
14866 Royal Irish Rifles 14th Battalion *Age 23 Died of Wounds on 4 May 1916*
BEAUVAL COMMUNAL CEMETERY, France
Son of Thomas and Louisa Hayden, of 4, Ashley Avenue, Belfast.

Hayden, John - Shoeing Smith
L/994 Royal Horse Artillery and Royal Field Artillery *Died in War on 6 May 1918*
SOLFERINO FARM CEMETERY, Belgium
Born and enlisted in Belfast.

Haydock, Richard - Lance Corporal
4503 Royal Irish Rifles 6th Battalion *Age 19 Died in War on 10 August 1915*
HELLES MEMORIAL, Turkey
Son of Richard Haydock, of 84, Fortingale Street, Belfast.

Hayes, Alexander - Private
3968 Seaforth Highlanders 4th Battalion *Age 20 Died in War on 25 November 1915*
BELFAST CITY CEMETERY, United Kingdom
Son of Mr. and Mrs. Alexander Hayes, of 1138, Avenue M., South Saskatoon, Saskatchewan, Canada. Born at Belfast.

Hayes, Andrew - Quartermaster Sergeant
9067 Royal Irish Regiment *Age 41 Died in War on 6 March 1917*
BELFAST (MILLTOWN) ROMAN CATHOLIC CEMETERY, United Kingdom
Husband of Elizabeth Hayes, of 63, Manor Street, Cliftonville, Belfast.

Hayes, Charles - Air Mechanic
186357 Royal Air Force *Age 19 Died as a result of war on 24 February 1919*
CARNMONEY CEMETERY, United Kingdom
Son of Joseph and Mary Hayes, of 28, Linwood Street, Belfast.

Hayes, Frank Gordon - Lance Corporal
24047 Royal Irish Fusiliers 7/8th Battalion *Age 19 Killed in Action on 16 August 1917*
TYNE COT MEMORIAL, Belgium
Son of Frank and Annie Hayes, of 83, Ogilvie Street, Belfast.

Hayes, J L - Private
PO/18251 Royal Marine Light Infantry 1st R.M. Battalion Royal Naval Division
Age 21 Died in War on 9 October 1918
DELSAUX FARM CEMETERY, BEUGNY, France
Son of Charles and Lilian Hayes, of 2, Roberts Road, Leicester. Born at Belfast.

Hayes, John - Rifleman
7869 Royal Irish Rifles 1st Battalion *Died in War on 31 October 1916*
THIEPVAL MEMORIAL, France
Born and enlisted in Belfast.

Hayes, Joseph Charles - Stoker
K/19004 Royal Navy H.M. Submarine "K.4" *Age 24 Drowned through collision in North Sea on 31 January 1918*
CHATHAM NAVAL MEMORIAL, United Kingdom
Son of Joseph Charles Hayes, of Belfast; husband of Minnie Hayes, of 5, Shaftesbury Street, Belfast.

Hayes, Robert - Rifleman
4045 Royal Irish Rifles 11th Battalion *Died in War on 25 July 1918*
BELFAST CITY CEMETERY, United Kingdom
Brother of Mrs M Gray, 81 Urney Street, Belfast.

Hayes, Samuel - Rifleman
10/14867 Royal Irish Rifles "B" Company 10th Battalion *Age 21 Killed in Action on 5 October 1916*
ST. QUENTIN CABARET MILITARY CEMETERY, Belgium
Son of Agnes Collins (formerly Hayes), of 23, Hatfield Street, Belfast, and the late Samuel Hayes.

Hayes, Thomas - Sergeant
14496 Royal Dublin Fusiliers 8th Battalion *Age 29 Died in War on 29 April 1916*
LOOS MEMORIAL, France
Son of the late Patrick Hayes, of 21, Halcombe Street, Belfast.

Hays, Archibald - Sergeant
8204 Irish Guards 2nd Battalion *Died in War on 31 July 1917*
ARTILLERY WOOD CEMETERY, Belgium
Son of Archie and Mary Hays of 80, Beechmont Parade, Belfast, Ireland.

Hazelton, John Douglas - Corporal
883532 Canadian Infantry (Alberta Regiment) 31st Battalion *Age 33 Died of Wounds on 25 June 1918*
WANQUETIN COMMUNAL CEMETERY EXTENSION, France
Son of the Rev E. and Mrs A. Hazelton, of 6, Windsor Park, Belfast, Ireland. B.A., R.U.I. A barrister, and a Methodist, he had 2 years service with Queen's University Officer Training Corps.

Hazlett, Francis - Rifleman
17/1427 Royal Irish Rifles 14th Battalion *Age 18 Died in War on 16 October 1916*
POND FARM CEMETERY, Belgium
Son of Francis and Jane Hazlett, of 71, Kimberley Street, Belfast.

Hazlett, Henry - Pioneer
57707 Royal Engineers 122nd Field Company *Age 30 Killed in Action on 1 March 1917*
DRANOUTRE MILITARY CEMETERY, Belgium
Son of Thomas and Mary Hazlett; husband of Margaret Reaney (formerly Hazlett), of 24, Fairfax Street, Crumlin Road, Belfast. Native of Belfast.

Journey of Remembering

Healy, Michael Patrick - Private
2341 Connaught Rangers 6th Battalion *Died in War on 4 May 1916*
DUD CORNER CEMETERY, LOOS, France
13, McMillans's Place, Belfast.

Heaney, Daniel - Rifleman
89 Royal Irish Rifles 1st Battalion *Died in War on 28 September 1918*
HOOGE CRATER CEMETERY, Belgium
Born and enlisted in Belfast.

Heaney, John - Private
9416 East Lancashire Regiment 1st Battalion *Age 26 Died whilst a prisoner of war on 30 September 1914*
PORTE-DE-PARIS CEMETERY, CAMBRAI, France
Son of Robert and Sarah Heaney, of 22, Browne Street, Belfast.

Heaney, Kirkwood - Private
47217 Royal Fusiliers "B" Company 9th Battalion *Age 21 Died in War on 3 May 1917*
ARRAS MEMORIAL, France
Son of Mrs. Harriett Tilley, of 27, Coyle's Place, Belfast.

Heaney, Stanley - Rifleman
3799 Royal Irish Rifles 2nd Battalion *Age 32 Died in War on 10 May 1915*
YPRES (MENIN GATE) MEMORIAL, Belgium
Husband of Catherine Hamilton (formerly Heaney), of 20, McQuillan Street, Belfast.

Heaney, Thomas Hugh - Rifleman
8588 Royal Irish Rifles 2nd Battalion *Age 23 Died of Enteric fever on 24 January 1915*
WIMEREUX COMMUNAL CEMETERY, France
Son of Richard Heaney, of 10, Theodore Street, Belfast.

Heaphy, John Eyre - Lance Corporal
6059 Lord Strathcona's Horse *Age 33 Died in War on 7 April 1918*
MAUBEUGE-CENTRE CEMETERY, France
Husband of Jane Heaphy, of 124, Castlereagh Street, Belfast, Ireland.

Heathwood, Robert - Private
41285 Princess Victoria's (Royal Irish Fusiliers) 9th Battalion *Died in War on 3 November 1917*
THIEPVAL MEMORIAL, France
Born and enlisted in Belfast. Formerly 1135 North Irish Horse.

Heenan, Arthur - Rifleman
8966 Royal Irish Rifles 1st Battalion *Killed in Action on 9 May 1915*
PLOEGSTEERT MEMORIAL, Belgium
Born and enlisted in Belfast.

Heenan, Patrick - Sergeant
13380 Royal Inniskilling Fusiliers 8th Battalion *Died from gas on 29 April 1916*
BETHUNE TOWN CEMETERY, France
Son of Patrick Heenan, 10, Boundary Street, Belfast.

Heffernan, Edward - Private
11128 Royal Dublin Fusiliers 1st Battalion *Died in War on 7 October 1914*
MADRAS (ST PATRICKS) CEMETERY CHENNAI, India
Born in Belfast, enlisted in Dublin.

Hemphill, Andrew - Rifleman
9169 Royal Irish Rifles 1st Battalion *Age 25 Died in War on 10 March 1915*
LE TOURET MEMORIAL, France
Son of Joseph Hemphill, of 23, St. Albans Gardens, Stranmillis Road, Belfast, and the late Helen Hemphill.

Henderson , Robert - Rifleman
11682 Royal Irish Rifles 15th Battalion *Killed In Action on 8 July 1916*
CAUDRY OLD COMMUNAL CEMETERY, France
Born and enlisted in Belfast.

Henderson, George York - Lieutenant
Royal Irish Rifles 10th Battalion *Age 24 Died in War on 22 November 1917*
CAMBRAI MEMORIAL, LOUVERVAL, France
Son of the late Sir James Henderson, D.L. and of Lady Henderson, of Oakley House, Belfast. Sir James was propietor of the Belfast News Letter and had been the first Lord Mayor of Greater Belfast in 1898. Served in 36th (Ulster) Division Train, Royal Army Service Corps, as Captain and Adjutant before transferring voluntarily to the Royal Irish Rifles. Awarded the Military Cross. His brother, Captain Richard Henderson, survived service with 1st Royal Irish Rifles.

Henderson, Herman Hewitt - Lance Corporal
9247 Royal Inniskilling Fusiliers 1st Battalion *Age 20 Died in War on 2 May 1915*
HELLES MEMORIAL, Turkey
Son of William and Annie Henderson, of 45, Donaldson Crescent, Woodvale Road, Belfast.

Henderson, James - Pioneer
192562 Corps of Royal Engineers K Special Company *Died in War on 29 April 1917*
BAILLEUL COMMUNAL CEMETERY EXTENSION (NORD), France
Born and enlisted in Belfast.

Henderson, James - Private
50742 North Staffordshire Regiment 2/5th Battalion *Died of Wounds on 8 December 1917*
ROCQUIGNY-EQUANCOURT ROAD BRITISH CEMETERY, MANANCOURT, France
6, Northumberland Street, Belfast.

Henderson, James Alexander - Private
51209 East Yorkshire Regiment 10th Battalion formerly M/320158, Army Service Corps
Killed In Action on 7 September 1918
TROIS ARBRES CEMETERY, STEENWERCK, France
Born and enlisted in Belfast.

Henderson, John - Rifleman
1323 Royal Irish Rifles 11th Battalion *Died in War on 18 December 1916*
LA PLUS DOUVE FARM CEMETERY, Belgium
Born and enlisted in Belfast.

Journey of Remembering

Henderson, John - Rifleman
5835 Royal Irish Rifles 7th Battalion *Age 19 Died in War on 21 April 1916*
DUD CORNER CEMETERY, LOOS, France
Son of William and Mary Eliza Henderson, of 6, Finlay Street, Ligoneil, Belfast.

Henderson, Robert - Private
266838 Seaforth Highlanders (Ross-shire Buffs, the Duke of Albany's) 4th Battalion
Died in War on 2 August 1917
YPRES (MENIN GATE) MEMORIAL, Belgium
Born in Belfast, enlisted in Glasgow.

Henderson, Robert - Rifleman
11682 Royal Irish Rifles 15th Battalion *Died in War on 8 July 1916*
CAUDRY OLD COMMUNAL CEMETERY, France
Hanna Street, Belfast.

Henderson, Samuel - Private
240982 Seaforth Highlanders 7th Battalion *Age 22 Killed in Action on 20 September 1918*
HAGLE DUMP CEMETERY, Belgium
Son of John and Mary Henderson, of 57, Dundela Street, Strandtown, Belfast.

Henderson, Wesley - Private
Canadian Infantry (Eastern Ontario Regiment) 2nd Battalion *Died in War on 1 July 1916*
YPRES (MENIN GATE) MEMORIAL, Belgium
15 Rockville Street, Belfast. Son of William Henderson, 56 Coady Avenue, Toronto.
A single man who worked as a labourer in Canada.

Henderson, William - Private
25153 Royal Inniskilling Fusiliers 6th Battalion *Died in War on 27 December 1917*
RAMLEH WAR CEMETERY, Israel
Born and enlisted in Belfast.

Henderson, William - Rifleman
11963 Royal Irish Rifles 15th Battalion *Killed In Action on 1 July 1916*
THIEPVAL MEMORIAL, France
Born and enlisted in Belfast.

Henderson, William - Sergeant
19881 Royal Irish Rifles 13th Battalion *Age 54 Died in War on 25 August 1917*
ROCQUIGNY-EQUANCOURT ROAD BRITISH CEMETERY, MANANCOURT, France
Son of James and Jane Henderson, of Belfast; husband of Annie Henderson,
of 44, Warkworth Street, Belfast.

Henderson, William - Corporal
6528 Royal Irish Rifles "C" Company 2nd Battalion *Age 22 Killed in Action on 16 June 1915*
YPRES (MENIN GATE) MEMORIAL, Belgium
Son of Robert and Mary Henderson, of 19, Eighth Street, Shankill Road, Belfast.

Hendrick, Charles - Private
29523 Royal Inniskilling Fusiliers 1st Battalion *Died in War on 23 March 1918*
MONT HUON MILITARY CEMETERY, LE TREPORT, France
Son of William and Catherine Hendrick, 1, Lowry Street, Belfast.

Hendry, Peter - Private
11042 Highland Light Infantry 2nd Battalion *Died in War on 1 October 1914*
NETLEY MILITARY CEMETERY, United Kingdom
25, Mourne Street, Belfast.

Henerson, William - Rifleman
11963 Royal Irish Rifles 15th Battalion *Killed in Action on 1 July 1916*
THIEPVAL MEMORIAL, France
Hanna Street, Belfast.

Henry, Bertie - Private
8770 Machine Gun Corps 8th Battalion *Died in War on 24 March 1918*
GRAND-SERAUCOURT BRITISH CEMETERY, France
Native of Belfast

Henry, James - Corporal
6954 Royal Irish Rifles 2nd Battalion *Died in War on 26 October 1914*
SAINGHIN-EN-WEPPES COMMUNAL CEMETERY, France
Ashbrook, Glenburn, Belfast. Born in Downpatrick.

Henry, James - Private
75289 Northumberland Fusiliers 1/6th Battalion *Age 22 Died in War on 21 October 1918*
TERLINCTHUN BRITISH CEMETERY, WIMILLE, France
Son of Mr. and Mrs John Henry, of 13, Vere Street, Belfast.

Henry, Joseph - Private
133176 Machine Gun Corps (Infantry) 50th Battalion *Age 29 Died as a POW on 5 November 1918*
NIEDERZWEHREN CEMETERY, Germany
Son of James Henry, of Belfast; husband of Mary Henry, of 55, Hamilton Street, Govan, Glasgow. Formerly 10537 Royal Irish Rifles.

Henry, Joseph - Private
2354 Royal Inniskilling Fusiliers 2ndBattalion *Age 23 Died in War on 16 May 1915*
LE TOURET MEMORIAL, France
Son of John and Mary Henry, of 5, Spinner Street, Falls Road, Belfast. Born at Dungannon, County Tyrone.

Henry, Olivia - Stewardess
Mercantile Marine S.S. "Cork" (Dublin)
Age 55 Drowned, as a result of an attack by an enemy submarine on 26 January 1918
TOWER HILL MEMORIAL, United Kingdom
Sister of Rosalind Henry, of 31, Oakleigh, Old Swan, Liverpool. Born at Belfast.

Henry, Patrick - Private
16438 Royal Inniskilling Fusiliers 2nd Battalion *Killed in Action on 16 May 1915*
LE TOURET MEMORIAL, France
Born Belfast, enlisted Edinburgh. Brother of Joseph Henry, of 12, Flesh Wynd, Kirkcaldy, Fife.

Henry, Thomas - Corporal
16589 Royal Irish Rifles 14th Battalion attached 109th Trench Mortar Battery
Age 20 Died in War on 16 August 1917
TYNE COT MEMORIAL, Belgium
Son of Robert and Elizabeth Henry, of 88, Mount Pottinger Road, Belfast

Journey of Remembering

Henry, William R - Private
24645 Royal Irish Fusiliers transferred to 364647 Labour Corps *Age 39 Died in War on 10 February 1919*
CARNMONEY CEMETERY, *United Kingdom*
Son of the late William and Margaret Henry, of Belfast; husband of the late Rebecca Henry.

Hermon, James F - Lance Corporal
3609 Royal Inniskilling Fusiliers 2nd Battalion *Died of Wounds on 16 April 1917*
ST. SEVER CEMETERY EXTENSION, ROUEN, *France*
32, Lime Street, Belfast.

Heron, George - Rifleman
7163 Royal Irish Rifles 15th Battalion *Age 19 Died in War on 11 June 1916*
HAMEL MILITARY CEMETERY, BEAUMONT-HAMEL, *France*
Born in Ballymacarrett the son of John Heron, of 30, Ivan Street, York Road, Belfast.

Heron, John - Lance Corporal
S/40477 Black Watch (Royal Highlanders) 8th (Service) Battalion *Died in War on 13 August 1917*
RUYAULCOURT MILITARY CEMETERY, *France*
Born in Belfast, enlisted in Perth, Scotland.

Heron, John - Rifleman
9220 Royal Irish Rifles 2nd Battalion *Age 40 Died in War on 12 October 1916*
COURCELETTE BRITISH CEMETERY, *France*
Brother of William James Heron, of 2, Charlemont Street, Belfast.

Herring, Horace Dawborn - Lance Corporal
21884 Duke of Edinburgh's (Wiltshire Regiment) 1st Battalion *Died in War on 28 August 1918*
ETAPLES MILITARY CEMETERY, *France*
Born in Belfast. Lived in Exeter when enlisted.

Herring, Norman Hamilton - Sergeant
9325 Devonshire Regiment 2nd Battalion *Killed in Action on 1 July 1916*
THEIPVAL MEMORIAL, *France*
Born Belfast the son of Willie Harry Herring, a Customs official and Mrs Mary Anna Herring.
Orginally a member of the Royal Garrison Artillery later tranferring to the Devonshire Regiment.

Herriot, George Hodges - Flight Sub-Lieutenant
Royal Naval Air Service *Age 20 Died of injuries received whilst flying on 6 November 1917*
MINSTER (THANET) CEMETERY, *United Kingdom*
Son of John Scott Herriot and Jane Herriot late of Belfast.

Herron, Albert - Sergeant
8811 Royal Irish Rifles 1st Battalion *Killed in Action on 1 July 1916*
THIEPVAL MEMORIAL, *France*
Brother of Martin and Robert Herron, 187 Snugville Street, Belfast.

Herron, Hugh - Lance Corporal
12909 Royal Irish Rifles 8th Battalion *Died in War on 8 December 1917*
THIEPVAL MEMORIAL, *France*
Son of Mrs Herron, 11 Canton Street, Belfast.

BELFAST BOOK OF HONOUR

Herron, Jackson - Rifleman
11321 Royal Irish Rifles 6th Battalion *Died in War on 25 August 1915*
ALEXANDRIA (CHATBY) MILITARY AND WAR MEMORIAL CEMETERY, Egypt
Born and enlisted in Belfast.

Herron, John - Lance Corporal
S/40477 Black Watch (Royal Highlanders) "B" Company 8th Battalion *Age 21 Died in War on 13 August 1917*
RUYAULCOURT MILITARY CEMETERY, France
Son of William Herron, of 26, Lisburn Avenue, Belfast, and the late Margaret Herron.

Herron, Joseph - Lance Corporal
42364 Royal Irish Fusiliers 1st Battalion *Killed in Action on 1 October 1918*
DADIZEELE NEW BRITISH CEMETERY, Belgium
308 Crumlin Road, Belfast. Previously 12292 Royal Irish Rifles.

Hesketh, Henry - Private
2325 Connaught Rangers 1st Battalion *Age 36 Died of heat stroke on 23 August 1917*
BAGHDAD (NORTH GATE) WAR CEMETERY, Iraq
Son of John and Susan Hesketh; husband of Mary E. Hesketh, of 50, Malcolmson Street, Springfield Road, Belfast. Born at Belfast.

Heslip, Robert - Rifleman
1094 Royal Irish Rifles 15th Battalion *Age 44 Killed in Action on 1 July 1916*
THIEPVAL MEMORIAL, France
Husband of Frances Heslip, of 62, Osborne Street, Belfast.

Hewitt, David John - Corporal
14880 Royal Irish Rifles 2nd Battalion *Age 28 Died in War on 22 October 1918*
INGOYGHEM MILITARY CEMETERY, Belgium
Son of John Hewitt, of Castlereagh, Belfast, and the late Anna Mary Hewitt.

Hewitt, Ernest Henry - Lieutenant
King's Own (Royal Lancaster Regiment) 4th Battalion *Age 29 Died in War on 15 June 1915*
LE TOURET MEMORIAL, France
Born in Belfast. The son of James H and Jeannie D Hewitt of Bangor. Former pupil of Bangor Grammar School and the Royal Belfast Academical Institution. A member of Queen's University Officer Training Corps and vice captain North of Ireland Cricket and Football Club. Killed at Festubert.
One of three brothers to die in the war.

Hewitt, Holt Montgomery - Lieutenant
Machine Gun Corps (Infantry) 109 Brigade *Age 29 Killed in Action on 1 July 1916*
MILL ROAD CEMETERY, THIEPVAL, France
Born in Belfast. The son of James H and Jeannie D Hewitt of Bangor.
Member of the North of Ireland Cricket and Football Club. Killed on the first day of the Somme.
One of three brothers to die in the war.

Hewitt, John - Private
634 Australian Infantry 2nd Battalion *Died in War on 6 August 1915*
LONE PINE CEMETERY, ANZAC, Turkey
Margaret Villa, Linfield Road, Belfast.

Hewitt, John Charles - Rifleman
20835 Royal Irish Rifles 2nd Battalion *Died in War on 6 September 1918*
WULVERGHEM-LINDENHOEK ROAD MILITARY CEMETERY, *Belgium*
Born in Belfast, enlisted Scotland.

Hewitt, John J - Private
12853 Highland Light Infantry 17th (Service) Battalion (3rd Glasgow) *Died in War on 18 November 1916*
NEW MUNICH TRENCH BRITISH CEMETERY, BEAUMONT-HAMEL, *France*
Born in Belfast. Lived in Glasgow when enlisted.

Hewitt, John Morrison - Rifleman
400 Royal Irish Rifles 16th Battalion *Age 18 Died in War on 13 March 1915*
DRUMEE PRESBYTERIAN CEMETERY, *United Kingdom*
Son of Hugh and Lizzie Ann Hewitt, of 61, Bryson Street, Belfast.

Hewitt, Thomas - Private
3881 Princess Victoria's (Royal Irish Fusiliers) 2nd Battalion *Died in War on 14 April 1915*
YPRES (MENIN GATE) MEMORIAL, *Belgium*
Born in Laurelvale, County Armagh, enlisted Finner Camp, County Donegal, resident of Belfast.

Hewitt, William - Sapper
45424 Royal Engineers 2nd Field Company *Died in War on 23 October 1916*
THIEPVAL MEMORIAL, *France*
22, McDonnell Street, Belfast.

Hewitt, William Arthur - Second Lieutenant
Royal Inniskilling Fusiliers 9th Battalion *Age 23 Killed in Action on 1 July 1916*
THIEPVAL MEMORIAL, *France*
Born in Belfast. The son of James H and Jeannie D Hewitt of Bangor. Member of the North of Ireland Cricket and Football Club. One of three brothers to die in the war. Killed on the same day and place, the first day of the Somme, as his elder brother, Holt Montgomery Hewitt.

Higgens, John - Rifleman
9617 Royal Irish Rifles 1st Battalion *Died in War on 9 May 1915*
PLOEGSTEERT MEMORIAL, *Belgium*
Born in Carrickfergus, resident of Belfast.

Higgins, Edward - Rifleman
8239 Royal Irish Rifles 2nd Battalion *Died in War on 23 March 1915*
LOKER CHURCHYARD, *Belgium*
Born at Belfast. Son of Lawrence and Margaret Higgins, of 130, Beckwith Street, Birkenhead, England.

Higgins, Martin - Lance Sergeant
474 Connaught Rangers 5th Battalion *Died in War on 11 August 1915*
Born in Ballinasloe, County Galway, enlisted Clydebank Scotland, resident Belfast

Higgins, Thomas - Gunner
43155 Royal Garrison Artillery *Died in War on 21 October 1917*
ST SEVER CEMETERY EXTENSION, ROUEN, *France*
Born and enlisted in Belfast.

JOURNEY OF REMEMBERING

Higgins, William - Rifleman
12894 Royal Irish Rifles 15th Battalion *Killed in Action on 1 July 1916*
THIEPVAL MEMORIAL, France
Born Ballysillan, Belfast.

Higginson, William - Private
6870 Royal Inniskilling Fusiliers 2nd Battalion *Killed in Action on 11 September 1914*
LA FERTE-SOUS-JOUARRE MEMORIAL, France
Born in Belfast the son of James Henry and Mary Jane Higginson.

Higginson, William - Rifleman
8/12901 Royal Irish Rifles 12th Battalion *Age 30 Died of Wounds on 8 October 1918*
DADIZEELE NEW BRITISH CEMETERY, Belgium
Son of Thomas and Susan Higginson, of 11, Ribble Street, Newtownards Road, Belfast.
Also served in the Labour Corps with the number 379705.

Higgiston, James - Private
5584 Irish Guards 1st Battalion *Died in War on 17 September 1916*
THIEPVAL MEMORIAL, France
Born in County Leitrim, resident Belfast.

Higney, Maurice - Private
27497 Royal Inniskilling Fusiliers 2nd Battalion *Died in War on 22 June 1917*
RAMSCAPPELLE ROAD MILITARY CEMETERY, France
Son of Mary Ann Higney, 4 Legnavea Street, Ligoneil, Belfast.

Hildersley, Alexander - Lance Corporal
17875 Royal Irish Rifles 14th Battalion *Age 21 Killed in Action on 1 July 1916*
THIEPVAL MEMORIAL, France
Son of Alexander and Caroline Hildersley, of 61, Oldpark Road, Belfast. Awarded the Military Medal.

Hilditch, Herbert - Private
DM21/54976 Army Service Corps 596th M.T. Company *Age 17 Died in War on 2 July 1916*
AMARA WAR CEMETERY, Iraq
Son of Robert and Jane Hilditch, of I, Oak Street, Belfast.

Hiles, Hector - Stoker First Class
SS/109881 Royal Navy HMS "Goliath" *Killed in Action with Turkish destroyer in Dardanelles on 13 May 1915*
CHATHAM NAVAL MEMORIAL, United Kingdom
Husband of Catherine Hiles, of 48, Derwent Street, Newtownards Road, Belfast.

Hill, Arthur - Company Sergeant Major
9/16552 Royal Irish Rifles 9th Battalion *Died of Wounds on 24 August 1919*
BELFAST CITY CEMETERY, United Kingdom
Son of the late Arthur and Ann J. Hill; husband of Alice Hill, of 89, Enfield Street, Belfast.

Hill, David - Rifleman
9371 Royal Irish Rifles 1st Battalion *Died in War on 5 July 1915*
Y FARM MILITARY CEMETERY, BOIS-GRENIER, France
Born in Belfast, enlisted Newtownards.

Journey of Remembering

Hill, George - Private
CH/430(S) Royal Marine Light Infantry Chatham Battalion Royal Naval Division
Age 21 Died in War on 12 December 1915
REDOUBT CEMETERY, HELLES, Turkey
Son of George and Sarah Hill, of 9, Dundee Street, Belfast.

Hill, George - Private
M/337251 Royal Army Service Corps *Died in War on 4 November 1918*
BORDIGHERA BRITISH CEMETERY, Italy
Born in Derry, enlisted and resident in Belfast.

Hill, Harry - Lance Corporal
G/5243 Royal Sussex Regiment 7th Battalion *Age 25 Died in War on 25 November 1917*
CAMBRAI MEMORIAL, LOUVERVAL, France
Son of Samuel and Annie Hill, of 43, Thames Street, Broadway, Belfast.

Hill, James - Lance Corporal
3244 Royal Inniskilling Fusiliers 8th Battalion *Died in War on 10 September 1916*
CORBIE COMMUNAL CEMETERY EXTENSION, France
Born Ballymacarrett, Belfast. Enlisted in Belfast. Father of William A Hart of Church Row, Limehouse, London.

Hill, James - Private
42425 Royal Irish Fusiliers 1st Battalion formerly 3rd Battalion Royal Irish Rifles
Age 24 Died of Wounds on 1 October 1918
DADIZEELE NEW BRITISH CEMETERY, Belgium
Son of Mrs. Elizabeth Hill, of 18, St. Kilda Street, Belfast.

Hill, James - Sergeant
2669 Princess Victoria's (Royal Irish Fusiliers) 1st Battalion *Died in War on 11 May 1917*
ROEUX BRITISH CEMETERY, France
Born in Belfast, enlisted in Lurgan.

Hill, John - Sailor
Mercantile Marine S.S. "Wavelet" (West Hartlepool) *Age 42 Killed by mine on 13 February 1915*
TOWER HILL MEMORIAL, United Kingdom
Born at Belfast. Son of Lawrence and Margaret Higgins, of 130, Beckwith Street, Birkenhead, England.

Hill, Joseph - Acting Bombardier
90717 Royal Field Artillery 10th Battery *Age 22 Died in War on 22 December 1915*
HELLES MEMORIAL, Turkey
Son of Mrs. S. Hill, of 17, Rainey Street, Belfast.

Hill, Leonard - Private
3531 Royal Irish Fusiliers 8th Battalion *Age 19 Died in War on 6 September 1916*
FLATIRON COPSE CEMETERY, MAMETZ, France
Son of Joseph and Mary Jane Hill, of Belfast.

Hill, Moore - Private
14299 Royal Irish Fusiliers "D" Company 9th Battalion *Age 19 Died in War on 10 May 1916*
DRUMCREE CHURCH OF IRELAND CHURCHYARD, United Kingdom
Son of Mary Lindsay (formerly Hill), of 27, Cumberland Street, Belfast, and the late William J. Hill. Born at Portadown.

JOURNEY OF REMEMBERING

Hill, Robert - Private
16431 Royal Irish Fusiliers "B" Company Depot *Age 22 Died in War on 17 July 1916*
DRUMCREE CHURCH OF IRELAND CHURCHYARD, United Kingdom
Son of Mary Lindsay (formerly Hill), of 27, Cumberland Street, Belfast, and the late William J. Hill. Born at Portadown.

Hill, Robert Henry - Private
3518 Royal Inniskilling Fusiliers 2nd Battalion *Age 19 Died in War on 23 November 1916*
FRANKFURT TRENCH BRITISH CEMETERY, BEAUMONT-HAMEL, France
Son of James Henry and Sarah Hill, of 91, Matilda Street, Belfast.

Hill, Samuel - Rifleman
19557 Royal Irish Rifles 12th Battalion *Age 23 Died in War on 22 October 1915*
DOULLENS COMMUNAL CEMETERY EXTENSION No.1, France
Son of Samuel and Elizabeth Hill, of Rushpark, Whitehouse, Belfast.

Hill, William - Private
40675 Royal Inniskilling Fusiliers 1st Battalion *Age 27 Died in War on 22 March 1918*
POZIERES MEMORIAL, France
Son of Mrs. Margaret Mason, of 9, Hunt Street, Belfast.

Hill, William - Rifleman
19/151 Royal Irish Rifles 15th Battalion *Died in War on 19 March 1917*
POND FARM CEMETERY, Belgium
Husband of Mrs. E. Hill, of 18, Norton Street, Cromac Street, Belfast.

Hill, William Carlisle - Lieutenant
Royal Irish Rifles 2nd Battalion attached 74th Trench Mortar Battery *Age 21 Died in War on 7 June 1917*
YPRES (MENIN GATE) MEMORIAL, Belgium
Son of R. C. and Catherine Hill of Fitzroy Avenue Belfast. Enlisted as soldier in the Black Watch and then was commissioned into the Royal Irish Rifles in 1915 Awarded the Military Cross.

Hill, William Quintus Ewart - Lance Corporal
16595 Royal Irish Rifles 14th Battalion *Age 25 Died in War on 16 August 1917*
TYNE COT MEMORIAL, Belgium
Son of John and Catherine Hill, of 8, Ormeau Avenue, Belfast. Awarded the Military Medal.

Hilland, J - Stoker First Class
SS/106892 Royal Navy HMS "Cressy" *Age 24 Killed in Action with submarine in North Sea on 22 September 1914*
GRAVENZANDE GENERAL CEMETERY, Netherlands
Son of John and Esther Hilland; husband of Eliza Jane Hilland, of 43, Renfrew Street, Belfast. Born at Belfast.

Hillis, James Herbert - Leading Stoker
K/4837 Royal Navy HMS "Pathfinder" *Killed in Action with submarine off Firth of Forth on 5 September 1914*
CHATHAM NAVAL MEMORIAL, United Kingdom
Husband of Catherine Hillis, of 28, Newcastle Street, Belfast.

Hillis, John - Driver
64326 Royal Engineers 150th Field Company *Age 24 Died in War on 7 July 1916*
ALBERT COMMUNAL CEMETERY EXTENSION, France
Son of William John and Elizabeth Hillis, of 32, Lawther Place, Belfast.

Hinchie, James - Rifleman
13383 King's Royal Rifle Corps 4th Battalion *Died in War on 3 October 1918*
PROSPECT HILL CEMETERY GOUY, *France*
Born and enlisted in Boyle, County Roscommon. Resident of Belfast.

Hobbs, Thomas Henry - Private
228298 Labour Corps *Died in War on 27 April 1918*
BELFAST (MILLTOWN) ROMAN CATHOLIC CEMETERY, *United Kingdom*
Born and enlisted in Belfast. Formerly 7001 Royal Irish Fusiliers.

Hobson, David George - Rifleman
9216 Royal Irish Rifles 1st Battalion *Died in War on 3 November 1918*
Y FARM MILITARY CEMETERY, BOIS-GRENIER, *France*
Born and enlisted in Belfast. Formerly 1183 Army Catering Corps

Hodge, Samuel - Private
3619 Royal Inniskilling Fusiliers 1st Battalion *Age 32 Died in War on 22 March 1918*
POZIERES MEMORIAL, *France*
Born and enlisted in Belfast. Son of the late Thomas and Elizabeth Hodge; husband of Mary Hodge, of 37, Salisbury Avenue, Toronto, Canada.

Hodgen, James - Private
3481 Royal Inniskilling Fusiliers 1st Battalion *Died in War on 20 October 1918*
TYNE COT MEMORIAL, *Belgium*
118 Castlereagh Road, Belfast.

Hodgen, John - Rifleman
11336 Royal Irish Rifles 10th Battalion *Age 26 Died of Wounds on 2 July 1916*
FORCEVILLE COMMUNAL CEMETERY AND EXTENSION, *France*
Son of Hugh and Elizabeth Hodgen, Belfast.

Hodgen, William - Rifleman
3129 Royal Irish Rifles 8th Battalion *Age 22 Killed in Action at the Battle of the Somme on 2 July 1916*
CAYEUX MILITARY CEMETERY, *France*
Son of Mr. William Hodgen, of 34, Dee Street, Belfast.

Hodges, Henry Burden - Second Lieutenant
King's Own Yorkshire Light Infantry 2nd Battalion *Age 19 Died in War on 18 April 1915*
YPRES (MENIN GATE) MEMORIAL, *Belgium*
Son of Mr and Mrs J F W Hodges of Glenravel House, Glenravel, Ballymena. Born at Belfast. Killed near Ypres after five weeks at the front.

Hodgins, John Thomas - Private
89070 Machine Gun Corps (Infantry) 219th Company *Age 37 Killed in Action on 5 September 1917*
COXYDE MILITARY CEMETERY, *Belgium*
Son of Joseph Henry and Sarah Ann Hodgins; husband of Agnes Hodgins, of 40, Cussick Street, Lisburn Road, Belfast.

Hoey, Stewart - Private
4244 Seaforth Highlanders 5th Battalion *Age 18 Died in War on 19 April 1916*
MAROEUIL BRITISH CEMETERY, *France*
Son of William and Mary Jane Hoey, of Belfast.

Hoey, William Robert - Rifleman
14921 Royal Irish Rifles "A" Company 10th Battalion *Age 22 Died in War on 15 July 1916*
ST. SEVER CEMETERY, ROUEN, France
Son of Robert and Margaret Hoey, of 164, Grosvenor Road, Belfast; husband of Jane Hoey, of 14, Turin Street, Belfast.

Hoff, Robert J - Private
10862 Royal Inniskilling Fusiliers 1st Battalion *Died in War on 6 May 1917*
LA CLYTTE MILITARY CEMETERY, Belgium
Husband of Sarah 6 Mayo Street, Belfast. Son of Sergeant Charles Hoff of the Dorsetshire Regiment.

Hogan, Joseph - Lance Corporal
20132 Royal Inniskilling Fusiliers 1st Battalion *Killed in Action on 1 July 1916*
THIEPVAL MEMORIAL, France
Son of Mrs T Hogan, Donegall Road, Belfast.

Hogan, Patrick - Private
27211 Royal Inniskilling Fusiliers 1st Battalion *Died in War on 20 May 1917*
ARRAS MEMORIAL, France
Born and enlisted in Dublin. Resident in Belfast.

Hogan, Samuel - Lance Corporal
10751 Royal Inniskilling Fusiliers 1st Battalion *Age 22 Died of Wounds on 15 July 1916*
BRISTOL (ARNOS VALE) CEMETERY, United Kingdom
Son of Timothy Hogan, of 55, Vernon Street, Belfast, and the late Catherine Hogan.

Hogan, William Edward - Sergeant
9242 Cheshire Regiment 2nd Battalion *Died in War on 8 May 1915*
YPRES (MENIN GATE) MEMORIAL, Belgium
Husband of Susan Hogan, 88 Beersbridge Road, Belfast.

Hogg, Frank - Rifleman
8004 Royal Irish Rifles 2nd Battalion *Age 19 Died in War on 27 October 1914*
LE TOURET MEMORIAL, France
Son of Mrs. Mary Hogg, of 3, Cross Street, Belfast.

Hogg, John Ormandy - Private
6045 Army Cyclist Corps *Age 40 Died in War on 18 April 1915*
BOURNEMOUTH EAST CEMETERY, United Kingdom
Son of Margaret Hogg, of 2, Ormiston Crescent, Knock and the late Robert Hogg. Native of Belfast.

Hogg, Theodore Alan - Captain
North Staffordshire Regiment 2nd Battalion *Age 29 Died in War on 21 March 1918*
ARRAS MEMORIAL, France
Husband of Ruth Hogg, 37 Bishops Road, Highgate, London. Born in Belfast.

Hogg, Walter Gordon - Lieutenant
Royal Irish Rifles 15th Battalion *Died in War on 24 May 1917*
POND PARK CEMETERY, Belgium
Son of Walter Gordon Hogg of Mertoun, Knock, Belfast.

Journey of Remembering

Holdcroft, Robert - Sergeant
8853 Prince of Wales's (North Staffordshire Regiment) 7th Battalion *Died in War on 9 April 1916*
BASRA WAR CEMETERY, Iraq
Born and enlisted in Staffordshire. Resident in Belfast.

Holden, Henry - Rifleman
2641 Royal Irish Rifles 9th Battalion *Killed in Action on 1 July 1916*
THIEPVAL MEMORIAL, France
Born and enlisted in Belfast.

Holloway, Alfred William - Private
9454 7th Dragoon Guards (Princess Royal) *Died in War on 10 April 1915*
CLANDON (SS PETER and PAUL) CHURCH CEMETERY, United Kingdom
Born in Belfast, enlisted in London.

Holloway, George Alexander - Private
CH/416(S) Royal Marine Light Infantry Chatham Battalion Royal Naval Division
Age 20 Died in War on 19 August 1915
LANCASHIRE LANDING CEMETERY, Turkey
Son of George and Ada R. Holloway, of 35, Jameson Street, Belfast.

Holloway, William - Corporal
11961 Royal Irish Rifles 15th Battalion *Age 24 Died in War on 14 May 1918*
ST. SOUPLET BRITISH CEMETERY, France
Son of William J. and Alice Holloway, of 4, Ruth Street, Belfast. Born at Liverpool.

Hollywood, Harry - Private
4302 Seaforth Highlanders 5th Battalion *Died in War on 29 June 1916*
MAROEUIL BRITISH CEMETERY, France
Son of Edward and Mary Hollywood, 77 Utility Street, Belfast.

Holmes, Albert - Lance Corporal
11097 Princess Victoria's (Royal Irish Fusiliers) 1st Battalion *Died in War on 3 May 1917*
ARRAS MEMORIAL, France
Born in Belfast, enlisted Armagh.

Holmes, Albert - Rifleman
2742 Royal Irish Rifles 12th Battalion *Age 22 Died in War on 30 September 1918*
DADIZEELE NEW BRITISH CEMETERY, Belgium
Son of John and Mary Holmes, of 9, Southport Street, Belfast.

Holmes, Charles Adair - Third Engineer
Mercantile Marine S.S. "Garron Head" (Belfast) *Age 26 Killed by mine on 16 November 1917*
TOWER HILL MEMORIAL, United Kingdom
Son of Elizabeth Holmes, of 21, Manor Street, Belfast, and the late William John Holmes.
Born at Belfast.

Holmes, Hugh - Corporal
2616 Royal Irish Rifles 1st Battalion *Died in War on 10 May 1915*
LE TOURET MEMORIAL, France
39 Hardinge Street, Belfast.

BELFAST BOOK OF HONOUR

Holmes, John - Private
16993 Royal Inniskilling Fusiliers "D" Company 11th Battalion *Age 22 Killed in Action on 1 July 1916*
THIEPVAL MEMORIAL, France
Son of James and Jane Holmes, of 50, Edith Street, Belfast; husband of the late Elizabeth Holmes.

Holmes, John - Private
21478 Royal Irish Fusiliers "C" Company 7th Battalion *Age 21 Died in War on 5 September 1916*
THIEPVAL MEMORIAL, France
Son of Ellen McCormick (formerly Holmes), of 23, Sydney Street West, Belfast, and the late William Holmes.

Holmes, Patrick - Private
23050 Princess Victoria's (Royal Irish Fusiliers) 7th Battalion *Died in War on 10 September 1916*
THIEPVAL MEMORIAL, France
Born and enlisted in Belfast.

Holmes, William John - Lance Corporal
5812 Royal Irish Fusiliers "A" Company 1st Battalion *Age 22 Died in War on 3 May 1917*
ARRAS MEMORIAL, France
Son of John Holmes, of 84, Northbrook Street, Belfast.

Honeyford, James - Gunner
76838 Royal Horse Artillery and Royal Field Artillery *Died in War on 16 September 1914*
LA FERTE-SOUS-JOUARRE MEMORIAL, France
Born and enlisted in Belfast.

Hooks, John - Lance Corporal
S/2011 Seaforth Highlanders 8th Battalion *Age 22 Died in War on 17 March 1916*
BOIS-CARRE MILITARY CEMETERY, HAISNES, France
Son of James and Jessie Hooks, of Belfast.

Hooks, Samuel - Rifleman
9415 Royal Irish Rifles 3rd Battalion *Age 46 Killed accidentally on the railway on 30 May 1918*
TOURGEVILLE MILITARY CEMETERY, France
Husband of Martha Hooks, of 20, Caledonian Street, Belfast.

Hopkins, David - Rifleman
16555 Royal Irish Rifles 9th Battalion *Killed in Action on 1 July 1916*
THIEPVAL MEMORIAL, France
Born Ballymacarrett, Belfast. Enlisted in Belfast.

Horgan, Dennis Edmund - Driver
99785 Royal Field Artillery *Age 20 Died in War on 20 November 1918*
BLACKROCK (ST. MICHAEL) CHURCH OF IRELAND CHURCHYARD, Republic of Ireland
Son of Dennis and Anna M. Horgan, of 55, Woodvale Street, Belfast.

Horn, John - Private
464076 Canadian Infantry (British Columbia Regiment) 29th Battalion
Age 26 Died in War on 26 September 1916
VIMY MEMORIAL, France
Son of William and Margaret Horn, of 3, Delhi Street, Belfast, Ireland.
Worked as a fireman in Canada, a Presbyterian.

Hornagold, William Fordler - Private
G/11638 Duke of Cambridge's Own (Middlesex Regiment) 1st Battalion *Died in War on 15 July 1916*
THIEPVAL MEMORIAL, France
Born in Belfast, son of William Fordler Hornagold and Mrs. Hornagold, of Wembley, Middlesex.

Horner, George - Private
Seaforth Highlanders *Died in War on 3 June 1916*
44 Braemar Street, Belfast.

Horner, John - Private
9114 Leinster Regiment 1st Battalion *Died in War on 4 May 1915*
YPRES (MENIN GATE) MEMORIAL, Belgium
148 Ainsworth Avenue, Belfast.

Hosick, Joseph - Private
10979 Prince Albert's (Somerset Light Infantry) 8th Battalion *Died in War on 21 January 1916*
PLOEGSTEERT MEMORIAL, Belgium
Born in Belfast, enlisted Bristol.

Hossack, Simon - Sergeant
40686 Highland Light Infantry 10/11th Battalion *Died in War on 9 April 1918*
PLOEGSTEERT MEMORIAL, Belgium
Born in Belfast, enlisted Glasgow.

Hossick, Samuel - Rifleman
5353 Royal Irish Rifles 6th Battalion *Killed in Action on 10 March 1918*
RAMLEH CEMETERY, Israel
Son of John Hossick, 10, Blackwater Street, Belfast.

Houston, Alexander - Private
9494 Royal Inniskilling Fusiliers 1st Battalion *Killed in Action on 27 January 1917*
THIEPVAL MEMORIAL, France
Born and enlisted in Belfast.

Houston, Charles Edward - Corporal
40645 Royal Inniskilling Fusiliers 2nd Battalion *Age 24 Died in War on 2 October 1918*
DADIZEELE NEW BRITISH CEMETERY, Belgium
Son of Thomas and Sarah Houston, of Doagh Road, Whitehouse, Belfast.

Houston, Frederick - Rifleman
6323 Royal Irish Rifles 12th Battalion *Died in War on 1 October 1918*
TYNE COT MEMORIAL, Belgium
13, Albion Street, Belfast.

Houston, Robert Francis - Driver
T3/029424 Royal Army Service Corps *Died in War on 15 July 1917*
Born Londonderry, resident Belfast.

Houston, Thomas - Rifleman
12865 Royal Irish Rifles 15th Battalion *Died in War on 29 December 1915*
BERTRANCOURT MILITARY CEMETERY, France
Born and enlisted in Belfast.

Howard, Henry - Sergeant
A/10989 Canadian Machine Gun Corps 7th Company *Age 30 Died of Wounds on 30 October 1917*
YPRES (MENIN GATE) MEMORIAL, Belgium
Born in Lancashire and a member of the Church of England he was the son of Henry and Elizabeth Howard, of 2, Ebrington Gardens, Bloomfield, Belfast, Ireland. A naval daughtsman he was unmarried and had served in a medical unit of the Canadian Militia. Awarded the Military Medal.

Howatt, John - Sapper
57647 Royal Engineers 150th Field Company *Died in War on 14 October 1918*
DADIZEELE NEW BRITISH CEMETERY, Belgium
Husband of Annie Howatt, of 42, Cherry Valley Gardens, Knock Road, Belfast.

Howe, Robert - Private
602253 Canadian Infantry (Quebec Regiment) 13th Battalion *Age 27 Died of Wounds on 3 June 1916*
LIJSSENTHOEK MILITARY CEMETERY, Belgium
Son of William and Mary Jane Howe, of 22, St. Ives Gardens, Stranmillis, Belfast. Native of Coagh, County Tyrone, Ireland. An Anglican, he had served for five years in the Royal Irish Constabulary and then in the Canadian prison service.

Howell, Thomas - Driver
30698 Royal Field Artillery "C" Battery 232nd Brigade *Age 24 Died in War on 20 April 1917*
FAUBOURG D'AMIENS CEMETERY, ARRAS, France
Son of Mrs. Catherine Howell, of 30, Manderson Street, Belfast.

Howells, Hugh - Second Lieutenant
General List and Royal Flying Corps *Died in War on 10 April 1917*
CARDIFF WESTERN CEMETERY, United Kingdom
10 Ohio Street, Belfast. A member of Agnes Street Presbyterian Church. His widow lived at Barry Island, South Wales.

Howie, Alexander - Rifleman
22296 London Regiment (London Irish Rifles) 2nd/18th Battalion
Age 19 Died in War on 13 October 1918
RATION FARM MILITARY CEMETERY, LA CHAPELLE-D'ARMENTIERES, France
Son of William and Sophia Howie, of 3, Mourne Street, Belfast.

Howie, George - Private
3722 Seaforth Highlanders 1st/4th Battalion *Age 34 Killed in Action on 3 June 1916*
LOUEZ MILITARY CEMETERY, DUISANS, France
Husband of Annie Howie, of 6, Lady Street, Belfast.

Howie, Samuel - Private
202449 Gordon Highlanders 4th Battalion *Died in War on 23 April 1917*
LEVEL CROSSING CEMETERY, France
Born in Belfast, enlisted Motherwell, Scotland.

Howie, Walter - Private
4434 Irish Guards No. 1. Company 1st Battalion *Age 20 Died in War on 3 November 1914*
YPRES (MENIN GATE) MEMORIAL, Belgium
Son of Samuel and Sarah Howie, of 2 Jerusalem Street, Ormeau Road, Belfast.

Howieson, Hugh - Private
DM2/129727 Royal Army Service Corps *Died in War on 15 January 1918*
LIJSSENTHOEK MILITARY CEMETERY, Belgium
Born in Belfast, enlisted Glasgow.

Hoy, George - Rifleman
14936 Royal Irish Rifles 10th Battalion *Killed in Action on 1 July 1916*
CONNAUGHT CEMETERY, THIEPVAL, France
1 Penrith Street, Belfast.

Hoy, Hugh - Rifleman
16/1104 Royal Irish Rifles 16th Battalion *Died in War*
8 Summer Street, Belfast. A member of Agnes Street Presbyterian Church.

Hoy, John - Sapper
41727 Royal Engineers 68th Field Company *Age 38 Died in War on 18 August 1915*
HELLES MEMORIAL, Turkey
Son of John and Isabella Hoy; husband of Annie Hoy, of Matilda Street, Belfast.

Hoy, Samuel - Private
10384 Royal Inniskilling Fusiliers 2nd Battalion *Age 19 Died in War on 26 August 1914*
LA FERTE-SOUS-JOUARRE MEMORIAL, France
Son of Mrs. Margaret Hoy, of 82, Newcastle Street, Belfast.

Hoy, Samuel - Private
809 Royal Irish Rifles 11th Battalion *Killed in Action on 1 July 1916*
THIEPVAL MEMORIAL, France
Son of Allan Hoy, Ballymurphy, Springfield Road, Belfast.

Hoy, Samuel - Rifleman
40211 Royal Irish Rifles 10th Battalion formerly R/19903, King's Royal Rifle Corps
Killed In Action on 7 June 1917
YPRES (MENIN GATE) MEMORIAL, Belgium
Born and enlisted in Belfast.

Hudson, William - Rifleman
14797 Royal Irish Rifles 12th Battalion *Age 27 Died in War on 15 April 1918*
TYNE COT MEMORIAL, Belgium
Son of Mrs. N. Hudson, of 69, Sandown Road, Belfast; husband of Mrs. M. Hudson, of Hibernia Cottage, Holywood.

Hughes, Arthur - Corporal
8435 Royal Irish Rifles 1st Battalion *Died in War on 10 March 1915*
LE TOURET MEMORIAL, France
Born and enlisted in Belfast.

Hughes, Daniel - Corporal
1585 Leinster Regiment Depot *Died in War on 21 June 1917*
BELFAST (MILLTOWN) ROMAN CATHOLIC CEMETERY, United Kingdom
Born and enlisted in Belfast.

Hughes, Edward - Private
2868 Connaught Rangers 6th Battalion *Died in War on 17 May 1916*
DUD CORNER CEMETERY, LOOS, France
Born in Saul, County Down. Enlisted and resident in Belfast.

Hughes, Francis - Private
3981 Royal Inniskilling Fusiliers 2nd Battalion *Died in War on 21 October 1914*
PLOEGSTEERT MEMORIAL, Belgium
15 Fairfield Street, Belfast.

Hughes, George - Lance Corporal
1203 Royal Irish Rifles 7th Battalion *Died in War on 24 March 1917*
BOULOGNE EASTERN CEMETERY, France
Born and enlisted in Belfast.

Hughes, George Harold - Stoker First Class
K/3124 Royal Navy HMS "Recruit" *Died in War on 1 January 1915*
CHATHAM NAVAL MEMORIAL, United Kingdom
Native of Belfast.

Hughes, Henry - Private
18112 Royal Irish Regiment 2nd Battalion *Age 22 Died of Wounds on 5 February 1920*
BELFAST (MILLTOWN) ROMAN CATHOLIC CEMETERY, United Kingdom
Son of Henry Hughes, of 13, Parkview Street, Oldpark Road, Belfast.

Hughes, Isaac - Corporal
11649 Royal Inniskilling Fusiliers 8th Battalion *Died of Wounds on 29 June 1916*
LONGUENESSE (ST. OMER) SOUVENIR CEMETERY, France
Son of the late Alexander and Anna Hughes, of Belfast.

Hughes, James - Rifleman
5313 Royal Irish Rifles 2nd Battalion *Age 19 Died in War on 7 May 1915*
YPRES (MENIN GATE) MEMORIAL, Belgium
Son of David and Martha Hughes, of 19, Moscow Street, Belfast.

Hughes, James - Rifleman
5932 Royal Irish Rifles 7th Battalion *Died in War on 9 September 1916*
THIEPVAL MEMORIAL, France
52 Douglas Street, Belfast.

Hughes, James - Rifleman
2579 Royal Irish Rifles 2nd Battalion *Killed in Action on 7 June 1917*
WULVERGHEM-LINDENHOEK ROAD MILITARY CEMETERY, Belgium
Brother of Mrs Annie Baker, 79 Oldpark Road, Belfast.

Hughes, James - Sapper
64571 Royal Engineers 122nd Field Company *Killed in Action on 1 July 1916*
THIEPVAL MEMORIAL, France
A married man, he had orginally served in the Royal Navy.

Hughes, John - Private
14872 Cameronians (Scottish Rifles) 11th Battalion *Died in War on 11 April 1918*
SALONIKA (LEMBET ROAD) MILITARY CEMETERY, Greece
Born in Belfast, enlisted in Coatbridge, Scotland.

Hughes, John - Private
20170 Royal Irish Fusiliers 7th Battalion *Age 29 Died in War on 30 April 1916*
LOOS MEMORIAL, France
Son of William and Margaret Hughes, of Nail Street, Belfast; husband of Hanna Hughes, of 5, Roundhill Street, Belfast.

Hughes, John - Private
4419 Royal Inniskilling Fusiliers 1st Battalion *Killed in Action on 1 July 1916*
ANCRE BRITISH CEMETERY BEAUMONT-HAMEL, France
Born in Magherafelt, enlisted Cookstown, resident in Belfast.

Hughes, John - Sapper
99787 Royal Engineers *Died in War on 5 February 1916*
CHIPILLY COMMUNAL CEMETERY, France
Born Tullyserren, County Armagh and then resident at 69, Farnham Street, Belfast.
His brother, William, was also killed.

Hughes, Lawrence - Private
25707 Royal Scots 12th Battalion *Died in War on 10 May 1917*
AUBIGNY COMMUNAL CEMETERY EXTENSION, France
Son of Mrs. Margaret Farrell, of 49, Norfolk Street, Falls Road, Belfast.

Hughes, Patrick J - Sergeant
19971 Royal Irish Fusiliers 2nd Battalion *Died in War on 30 December 1917*
CHATBY MEMORIAL, Egypt
Husband of Mrs Margaret Hughes, 19 Maralin Street, Belfast.

Hughes, Patrick - Rifleman
6895 Royal Irish Rifles 1st Battalion *Age 33 Died in War on 6 July 1918*
BERTENACRE MILITARY CEMETERY, FLETRE, France
Son of Michael and Matilda Hughes of 49, Altcar Street, Mount Pottinger Road, Belfast.

Hughes, Patrick - Rifleman
9786 Royal Irish Rifles 2nd Battalion *Died of Wounds on 7 September 1918*
ARNEKE BRITISH CEMETERY, France
Born and enlisted in Belfast.

Hughes, Robert - Rifleman
17904 Royal Irish Rifles 14th Battalion *Killed in Action on 1 July 1916*
THIEPVAL MEMORIAL, France
Born and enlisted in Belfast.

Hughes, Robert - Rifleman
6952 Royal Irish Rifles 1st Battalion *Killed in Action on 1 July 1916*
THIEPVAL MEMORIAL, France
Born and enlisted in Belfast.

Hughes, Thomas - Rifleman
6442 Royal Irish Rifles 12th Battalion *Died in War on 13 October 1918*
LIJSSENTHOEK MILITARY CEMETERY, Belgium
Born in Belfast. Enlisted Ballinderry, County Antrim.

Hughes, Thomas Joseph - Stoker First Class
SS/103750 Royal Navy HMS "Cressy" *Age 29 Killed in Action with submarine in North Sea on 22 September 1914*
CHATHAM NAVAL MEMORIAL, United Kingdom
Son of James Hughes; husband of Mary Ann Hughes, of 58, Dunville Street, Belfast.

Hughes, William - Private
12716 Durham Light Infantry 11th Battalion *Died in War on 22 March 1918*
POZIERES MEMORIAL, OVILLERS-LA BOISSELLE, France
Born in Belfast, enlisted Darlington, England.

Hughes, William - Private
8445 Irish Guards 2nd Battalion *Died in War on 27 November 1917*
CAMBRAI MEMORIAL, LOUVERVAL, France
Born Tullyserren, County Armagh and then resident at 69, Farnham Street, Belfast.
His brother, John, was also killed.

Hughes, William - Private
S/10744 Queen's Own Cameron Highlanders 1st Battalion *Died in War on 27 January 1915*
LE TOURET MEMORIAL, France
Born in Blantyre, Lanarkshire, enlisted Glasgow, resident Belfast.

Hughes, William - Rifleman
14938 Royal Irish Rifles 14th Battalion *Killed In Action on 14 November 1916*
POND FARM CEMETERY, Belgium
Born in Belfast the son of Hugh C. and Elizabeth Tate Hughes, of 42, The Esplanade, Ballyholme, Bangor.

Hughes, William John - Petty Officer Stoker
307002 Royal Navy HMS "Invincible" *Age 30 Killed in Action at Battle of Jutland on 31 May 1916*
PORTSMOUTH NAVAL MEMORIAL, United Kingdom
Son of John and Mary Hughes, of Belfast.

Hughes, William Lamont - Rifleman
17/816 Royal Irish Rifles 10th Battalion
Age 33 Died of Wounds received at the Battle of the Somme on 3 July 1916
FORCEVILLE COMMUNAL CEMETERY AND EXTENSION, France
Son of William and Sarah Hughes of Belfast.

Hughey, James - Rifleman
2866 Royal Irish Rifles 1st Battalion *Died in War on 10 March 1915*
LE TOURET MEMORIAL, France
Born in Belfast. Enlisted in Ardrossan, Scotland.

Hull, George - Rifleman
6957 Royal Irish Rifles 16th Battalion *Age 21 Died in War on 4 July 1916*
PUCHEVILLERS BRITISH CEMETERY, France
Husband of Ethel Hull, of 40, Montrose Street, Belfast.

Hull, John - Rifleman
541 Royal Irish Rifles 16th Battalion No. 3 Company *Age 21 Died in War on 31 July 1917*
DIVISIONAL CEMETERY, Belgium
Son of David and Agnes Hull, of 49, Hatfield Street, Belfast.

Hull, John Allingham - Lance Sergeant
32114 London Regiment 6th (City of London) Battalion (Rifles) *Died in War on 22 February 1918*
NOYON NEW BRITISH CEMETERY, France
Resident in Belfast, enlisted in London.

Hull, Reginald Louis - Lance Corporal
3205 London Regiment 6th (City of London) Battalion (Rifles) *Died in War on 15 September 1916*
THIEPVAL MEMORIAL, France
Resident in Belfast, enlisted in London.

Hume, Joseph - Private
1358 Highland Light Infantry 2nd Battalion *Died in War on 30 July 1916*
THIEPVAL MEMORIAL, France
Cliftonville Road, Belfast.

Hummerston, James - Private
10619 Royal Inniskilling Fusiliers 6th Battalion *Age 21 Killed in Action on 31 December 1917*
RAMLEH WAR CEMETERY, Israel
Son of James and Elizabeth Hummerston, of 59, North Queen Street, Belfast. Born in Dublin.

Humphrey, Robert - Rifleman
11971 Royal Irish Rifles 15th Battalion *Age 19 Killed in Action on 1 July 1916*
THIEPVAL MEMORIAL, France
Son of Elizabeth Humphrey, of 47, Thompson Square, Whitehouse, Belfast, and the late Samuel Humphrey.

Humphrey, Vincent E - Lieutenant
Army Service Corps (Canteens) *Age 32 Died in War on 26 October 1918*
FILLIEVRES BRITISH CEMETERY, France
Husband of Mabel G Humphrey of Holly Villa, Winston Gardens, Knock.
Member of No 34 Masonic Lodge Belfast.

Humphreys, William - Private
5176 Royal Irish Fusiliers "C" Company 1st Battalion *Died in War on 25 April 1915*
YPRES (MENIN GATE) MEMORIAL, Belgium
Son of James and Rachel Humphreys, of 63, Ottawa Street, Belfast.

Hunsdale, Hans - Seaman
Mercantile Marine S.S. "Bray Head" (Belfast)
Age 35 Drowned, as a result of an attack by an enemy submarine on 14 March 1917
TOWER HILL MEMORIAL, United Kingdom
Son of Arthur and Sarah Ann Hunsdale; husband of Mary Jane Hunsdale (née Alexander),
of Irish Street, Killyleagh, County Down. Born in Belfast.

Hunt, Edward - Lance Corporal
2488 Connaught Rangers 6th Battalion *Died in War on 8 January 1917*
POND FARM CEMETERY, Belgium
Resident in Belfast when enlisted.

Hunt, Edward - Private
S/18893 Queen's Own Cameron Highlanders 6th Battalion *Died in War on 11 November 1915*
LOOS MEMORIAL, France
Born in Belfast, enlisted in Hamilton, Scotland.

Hunt, Henry - Air Mechanic Second Class
290035 Royal Air Force 215th Squadron *Age 18 Died in War on 25 October 1918*
CHARMES MILITARY CEMETERY, ESSEGNEY, France
Son of James and Edith Hunt, of 77, Pernau Street, Belfast.

Hunter, David - Private
3026 Royal Scots (Lothian Regiment) 2nd Battalion *Died in War on 29 December 1914*
YPRES (MENIN GATE) MEMORIAL, Belgium
Born in Alloa, enlisted Edinburgh, both Scotland, resident in Belfast.

Hunter, Duncan - Rifleman
14802 Royal Irish Rifles 10th Battalion *Age 38 Died in War on 19 June 1916*
HAMEL MILITARY CEMETERY, BEAUMONT-HAMEL, France
Son of John and Agnes Hunter; husband of Mary Hunter, of 27, Bryson Street, Belfast.

Hunter, Francis - Rifleman
7305 Royal Irish Rifles 2nd Battalion *Died in War on 10 February 1915*
LOKER CHURCHYARD, Belgium
Son of William and Jane Hunter, 22, Frome Street. Born and enlisted in Belfast.

Hunter, Frederick - Lance Corporal
8179 Royal Irish Rifles 1st Battalion *Died in War on 10 March 1915*
LE TOURET MEMORIAL, France
Son of the late James and Marion Hunter, 13, Virginia Street, Belfast.

Hunter, John - Lance Corporal
17912 Royal Irish Rifles "A" Company 13th Battalion *Age 19 Killed in Action on 1 July 1916*
SERRE ROAD CEMETERY No.2, France
Son of Thomas and Jane Hunter, of 105, Vernon Street, Belfast.

Hunter, John Edward - Sergeant
14948 Royal Irish Rifles 14th Battalion *Died in War on 1 September 1916*
YPRES (MENIN GATE) MEMORIAL, Belgium
79, Northumberland Street, Belfast.

Hunter, Robert - A/Corporal
633737 London Regiment 20th (County of London) Battalion (Blackheath and Woolwich) *Died in War on 28 May 1917*
LIJSSENTHOEK MILITARY CEMETERY, Belgium
Born in County Down, enlisted and resident in Belfast. Formerly 4344, 18th London Regiment.

Hunter, Robert - Lance Corporal
776 Royal Irish Rifles 8th Battalion *Died in War on 2 July 1916*
THIEPVAL MEMORIAL, France
12 Iveagh Street, Belfast.

Hunter, Robert - Private
454250 Canadian Infantry (Central Ontario Regiment) 20th Battalion *Age 30 Died in War on 14 February 1917*
ECOIVRES MILITARY CEMETERY, MONT-ST. ELOI, France
Son of Joseph and Eliza Jane Hunter, of 41, New North Queen Street, Belfast, Ireland.
He was unmarried, a Presbyterian and worked as a fireman.

Hunter, Robert - Stoker First Class
SS/104449 Royal Navy HMS"Hawke" *Killed in Action with submarine in North Sea on 15 October 1914*
CHATHAM NAVAL MEMORIAL, United Kingdom
Husband of Isabella Hunter, of 80, Derwent Street, Belfast.

Hunter, Samuel - Fourth Engineer Officer
Mercantile Marine S.S. "Lorca" (London) *Age 22 Presumed drowned on 29 October 1916*
TOWER HILL MEMORIAL, United Kingdom
Son of James and the late Margaret Hunter (formerly Brevings). Born at Belfast.

Hunter, Thomas - Private
19350 Royal Inniskilling Fusiliers 9th Battalion *Killed in Action on 1 July 1916*
CONNAUGHT CEMETERY, THIEPVAL, France
50, Aberdeen Street, Belfast.

Hunter, William - Rifleman
19034 Royal Irish Rifles 13th Battalion *Killed in Action on 1 July 1916*
THIEPVAL MEMORIAL, France
Born in Belfast. Enlisted in Newry.

Hunter, William - Rifleman
47464 Royal Irish Rifles 1st Battalion *Age 23 Died in War on 24 October 1917*
PROWSE POINT MILITARY CEMETERY, Belgium
Son of Samuel and Rebecca Ann Hunter, of 23, Donegore Street, Belfast. Native of Magherafelt.

Hunter, William - Rifleman
8982 Royal Irish Rifles 1st Battalion *Age 26 Died in War on 10 March 1915*
NEUVE-CHAPELLE FARM CEMETERY, France
Son of Mr. and Mrs. Hunter, of 12, Lecumpher Street, Beersbridge Road, Belfast.
Awarded the Distinguished Conduct Medal for 'gallant conduct'.

Hunter, William - Sergeant
347 Royal Irish Rifles 16th Battalion *Died in War on 29 April 1918*
HOLYWOOD CEMETERY, United Kingdom
Born in Antrim, enlisted Lurgan, resident in Belfast.

Hurley, William - Rifleman
5138 Royal Irish Rifles 2nd Battalion *Died in War on 27 October 1914*
LE TOURET MEMORIAL, France
Born in Athy, County Kildare, enlisted Dublin, resident in Belfast.

Hurrell, Ernest Henry - Corporal
5569 Royal Irish Rifles 2nd Battalion *Died in War on 30 January 1915*
YPRES (MENIN GATE) MEMORIAL, Belgium
5, Foyle Street, Belfast. Born in Brighton, Sussex.

Hussey, George Forbes - Private
13791 Australian Army Medical Corps 3rd Australian General Hospital
Age 51 Died of disease on 21 April 1917
ABBEVILLE COMMUNAL CEMETERY EXTENSION, France
Son of Edward and Elizabeth Hussey; husband of Sarah Jane Hussey, of 81, Kent Street, New Farm, Brisbane, Queensland. Native of Belfast, Ireland.

Huston, Gerald M - Corporal
28763 Corps of Royal Engineers 7th Signal Company *Died on 6 December 1915*
BEAUVAL COMMUNAL CEMETERY, France
Born in Belfast. The son of Mr. W. W. and Mrs. E. V. Huston, of Astville, Killinchy, County Down. Awarded the Distinguished Conduct Medal.

Huston, Samuel - Rifleman
14933 Royal Irish Rifles 10th Battalion transferred to 377309 Labour Corps
Age 45 Died of dysentery on 28 September 1919
BELFAST (DUNDONALD) CEMETERY, United Kingdom
Son of Hugh Huston, of 24, Lismore Street, Belfast; husband of Isabella Huston.

Huston, Samuel - Sapper
WR/553750 Corps of Royal Engineers *Died on 25 September 1918*
BASRA WAR CEMETERY, Iraq
Born in Belfast, enlisted Edinburgh.

Hutchinson, Alexander - Private
8691 Royal Inniskilling Fusiliers 1st Battalion
Died in War on 22 May 1915
TWELVE TREE COPSE CEMETERY, Turkey
4 Lawyer Street, Belfast.

Hutchinson, Charles Frederick - Private
45191 Worcestershire Regiment 3rd Battalion *Died in War on 26 October 1918*
THIEPVAL MEMORIAL, France
Born in Belfast, enlisted Birmingham.

Hutchinson, George - Rifleman
8235 Royal Irish Rifles 2nd Battalion *Died in War on 23 November 1917*
CAMBRAI MEMORIAL LOUVERVAL, France
Son of Mrs Jane Hutchinson, 30 Ewarts Row, Belfast.

Hutchinson, Isaac - Private
14537 King's (Liverpool Regiment) 4th Battalion *Died in War on 15 July 1916*
FLATIRON COPSE CEMETERY, MAMETZ, France
Born in Belfast, enlisted Liverpool.

Hutchinson, William - Gunner
78122 Royal Field Artillery 65th Howitzer Battery *Died of Wounds on 10 August 1917*
LA GORGUE COMMUNAL CEMETERY, France
Son of Elizabeth and William Hutchinson (a former soldier), 147, Crimea Street, Belfast.

Journey of Remembering

Hutchinson, William - Private
3334 Royal Inniskilling Fusiliers 2nd Battalion *Killed in Action on 1 April 1917*
ROUPY COMMUNAL CEMETERY, France
Born and enlisted in Belfast.

Hutchison, Alexander - Private
18720 Machine Gun Corps (Infantry) 109th Company *Age 27 Died in War on 1 July 1916*
THIEPVAL MEMORIAL, France
Son of Mrs. Elizabeth Hutchison, of 225, Spamount Street, Belfast.

Hutchison, Ernest E R - Private
18664 Highland Light Infantry 12th Battalion *Died in War on 26 September 1915*
LOOS MEMORIAL, FRANCE
Born in Hertfordshire, enlisted Glasgow, resident Belfast.

Hutton, James - Sapper
64457 Royal Engineers 150th Field Company *Died in War on 2 October 1918*
HARLEBEKE NEW BRITISH CEMETERY, Belgium
Born Ballymacarrett, Belfast. Enlisted in Belfast. Husband of E. J. Hutton of 12, Pound Street, Newtownards.

Hutton, John - Private
9644 Royal Inniskilling Fusiliers *Age 33 Died in War on 8 November 1916*
BELFAST CITY CEMETERY, United Kingdom
Son of Robert Hutton, of 27, Pomona Avenue, Strandtown, Belfast, and the late Annie Hutton.

Hutton, John - Rifleman
11381 Royal Irish Rifles 6th Battalion *Died in War on 11 August 1915*
HELLES MEMORIAL, Turkey
Born and enlisted in Belfast.

Hutton, Richard - Rifleman
7943 Royal Irish Rifles 1st Battalion *Age 28 Died of Wounds on 11 May 1915*
MERVILLE COMMUNAL CEMETERY, France
Son of William and Jane Hutton, of 3, Columbus Street, Belfast.

Hutton, Robert - Lance Corporal
9645 Royal Inniskilling Fusiliers 1st Battalion *Age 31 Killed in Action on 1 July 1916*
THIEPVAL MEMORIAL, France
Son of Robert and Annie Hutton, of 27, Pomona Avenue, Strandtown, Belfast.

Hutton, William - Drummer
4605 Connaught Rangers 6th Battalion *Died in War on 8 March 1917*
KEMMEL CHATEAU MILITARY CEMETERY, Belgium
4, Linview Street, Belfast.

Hyde, George - Driver
T3/031198 Army Service Corps *Died in War on 13 April 1915*
BELFAST (DUNDONALD) CEMETERY, United Kingdom
Husband of Elizabeth Hyde, of 20, Devonshire Street, Belfast.

Hyde, James - Private
11229 Royal Irish Fusiliers 1st Battalion *Age 24 Died in War on 25 April 1915*
YPRES (MENIN GATE) MEMORIAL, *Belgium*
Son of Crawford and Rachel Hyde, of 18, Bentham Street, Belfast.

Hyland, Thomas - Lance Corporal
3262 Royal Inniskilling Fusiliers 5th Battalion Age 28 *Died of Wounds on 27 December 1917*
JERUSALEM WAR CEMETERY, *Israel*
Son of William and Jane Hutton, of 3, Columbus Street, Belfast.

Hylands, John - Sapper
64071 Royal Engineers 121st Field Company *Age 36 Died in War on 10 December 1917*
METZ-EN-COUTURE COMMUNAL CEMETERY BRITISH EXTENSION, *France*
Husband of Catherine Hylands of 173, Leopold Street, Belfast.

Hyles, David - Sergeant
5/4731 King's Royal Rifle Corps 1st Battalion *Age 24 Died of Wounds (gas) on 20 August 1918*
BELFAST CITY CEMETERY, *United Kingdom*
Son of David and Margaret Hyles, of 36, Boyne Square, Belfast.
Awarded the Distinguished Conduct Medal.

Hyndman, James - Rifleman
7261 Royal Irish Rifles (Secondary regiment: Labour Corps) *Died in War on 14 November 1917*
STE. MARIE CEMETERY, LE HAVRE, *France*
Husband of Rose Hyndman, Suffolk, Belfast.

Hyndman, Val - Captain
Royal Irish Rifles 14th Battalion *Age 29 Died in War on 7 July 1916*
WIMEREUX COMMUNAL CEMETERY, *France*
Son of James Hyndman, of "Lisanore" Antrim Road, Belfast.

Hyndman, William - Private
12849 Royal Irish Fusiliers Depot *Age 25 Died in War on 31 July 1916*
BELFAST CITY CEMETERY, *United Kingdom*
Son of William and Sarah Hyndman, of 143, Crimea Street, Belfast.

Hynes, Samuel - Rifleman
909 Royal Irish Rifles "C" Company 8th Battalion *Age 21 Died in War on 23 November 1917*
CAMBRAI MEMORIAL, LOUVERVAL, *France*
Son of Hugh and Jane Hynes, of 36, Houston Street, Ballyhackamore, Belfast.

Journey of Remembering

Ingledew, Charles - Sergeant
13080 Princess Victoria's (Royal Irish Fusiliers) 9th Battalion *Died in War on 5 September 1918*
WULVERGHEM-LINDENHOEK ROAD MILITARY CEMETERY, Belgium
Born and enlisted in Belfast.

Ingram, William James - Rifleman
17/848 Royal Irish Rifles 10th Battalion *Age 22 Died in War on 14 September 1916*
ST. QUENTIN CABARET MILITARY CEMETERY, Belgium
Son of James and Alice Ingram, of 21, Lake Street, Ormeau Road, Belfast.

Ingrim, James - Private
10726 Royal Inniskilling Fusiliers 2nd Battalion *Age 19 Died in War on 16 May 1915*
LE TOURET MEMORIAL, France
Son of Mrs. Mary Ingrim, of 104, Island Street, Belfast.

Ireland, James - Rifleman
347 Royal Irish Rifles 15th Battalion *Age 18 Killed in Action on 1 July 1916*
SERRE ROAD CEMETERY No.2, France
Son of Mrs. Mary Ireland, of 274, Old Lodge Road, Belfast.

Ireland, James - Second Lieutenant
Royal Field Artillery *Age 18 Died of pneumonia on 24 July 1918*
BELFAST CITY CEMETERY, United Kingdom
Son of James Ireland of Newforge Lodge, Belfast.

Ireland, John - Private
79880 Devonshire Regiment 15th Battalion *Age 18 Accidentally drowned on 6 September 1918*
DUNDONALD (ST. ELIZABETH) CHURCH OF IRELAND CHURCHYARD, United Kingdom
Son of James and Agnes Ireland, of 18, Eton Street, Belfast.

Ireland, Ralph - Lieutenant Commander
Royal Navy HMS "Southampton" *Age 28 Drowned in North Sea.*
PORTSMOUTH NAVAL MEMORIAL, United Kingdom
Son of Adam Liddell and Isabel Ireland, of 17, Malone Park, Belfast. Took part in the Battle of Jutland. Died when washed overboard during a storm, along with three other Sailors.

Ireland, Samuel James - Second Lieutenant
The King's Liverpool Regiment 17th Battalion *Died in War on 12 October 1916*
THIEPVAL MEMORIAL, France
21, Madrid Street, Belfast or 47, Victoria Road, Belfast.

Ireland, William - Private
201379 Seaforth Highlanders 1st/4th Battalion *Age 20 Died in War on 1 August 1918*
SEZANNE COMMUNAL CEMETERY, France
Son of James and Agnes Ireland, of 18, Eton Street, Belfast. Awarded the Military Medal.

Irvine, Francis - Private
43849 Duke of Edinburgh's (Wiltshire Regiment) 1st Battalion *Died in War on 9 October 1918*
PROSPECT HILL CEMETERY, GOUY, France
Born and enlisted in Belfast. Formerly M/399095 Army Service Corps

Irvine, James - Lance Corporal
18392 King's Own Scottish Borderers 7/8th Battalion *Killed in Action on 1 August 1917*
YPRES (MENIN GATE) MEMORIAL, Belgium
191 Leopold Street, Belfast

Irvine, James - Private
21943 Royal Scots 17th Battalion *Died of Wounds on 1 August 1916*
CORBIE COMMUNAL CEMETERY EXTENSION, France
Son of Mary Jane Irvine, 38, Urney Street, Belfast.

Irvine, James - Rifleman
1204 Royal Irish Rifles 6th Battalion *Died in War on 1 November 1916*
STRUMA MILITARY CEMETERY, Greece
Born and enlisted in Belfast.

Irvine, John - Rifleman
7587 Royal Irish Rifles 2nd Battalion *Age 29 Died in War on 9 November 1914*
POPERINGHE OLD MILITARY CEMETERY, Belgium
Resident of Belfast the son of Samuel and Margaret Irvine, of 24, Upper Movilla Street, Newtownards.

Irvine, Joseph - Private
7561 Dragoon Guards *Died in War on 25 March 1918*
POZIERES MEMORIAL, France
Native of Belfast. "Irvine" was an Alias. Nixon was the true family name.

Irvine, Paul - Rifleman
802 Royal Irish Rifles 10th Battalion *Killed in Action on 1 July 1916*
THIEPVAL MEMORIAL, France
31, Lower Lockview Street, Belfast.

Irvine, Robert - Rifleman
18/1113 Royal Irish Rifles 12th Battalion *Killed in Action on 13 August 1917*
BRANDHOEK NEW MILITARY CEMETERY, Belgium
96, Agnes Street, Belfast.

Irvine, Robert - Sapper
251015 Corps of Royal Engineers *Died in War on 2 November 1918*
FORT PITT MILITARY CEMETERY, Kent
Born in Belfast, enlisted Glasgow.

Irvine, Robert R - Lance Corporal
5952 Royal Irish Rifles 7th Battalion *Died in War on 9 September 1916*
THIEPVAL MEMORIAL, France
Son of Samuel Irvine, 152, Leopold Street, Belfast.

Irvine, Samuel - Private
13314 Royal Inniskilling Fusiliers 11th Battalion *Killed in Action on 1 July 1916*
CONNAUGHT CEMETERY, THIEPVAL, France
Husband of Minnie Irvine, 61, North Boundary Street, Belfast.

JOURNEY OF REMEMBERING

Irvine, Samuel - Private
3327 Leinster Regiment 7th Battalion *Age 18 Killed in Action on 27 June 1916*
ST. PATRICK'S CEMETERY, LOOS, France
Son of John and Bridget Irvine. Born at Belfast.

Irvine, Thomas Boyce - Driver
T/327495 Army Service Corps 66th Divisional Train *Died of Wounds on 21 March 1918*
POZIERES MEMORIAL, France
Son of Margaret Jane Irvine, 25, Broadbent Street, Belfast.

Irvine, Thomas Henry - Gunner
66930 Royal Field Artillery 8th Heavy Trench Mortar Battery *Age 25 Died in War on 3 December 1917*
ETAPLES MILITARY CEMETERY, France
Son of John and Isabella Irvine, of 2, Valentine Street, Belfast.

Irvine, William - Private
3576 Royal Irish Rifles 9th Battalion *Killed in Action on 1 July 1916*
SERRE ROAD CEMETERY No.2, France
31, Brookmount Street, Belfast.

Irvine, William Joseph - Private
3693 Seaforth Highlanders 1st/4th Battalion *Age 26 Died in War on 6 October 1916*
BOULOGNE EASTERN CEMETERY, France
Husband of Sarah Irvine, of 1, Sydney Street, Belfast.

Irwin, David John - Private
29052 Border Regiment 1st Battalion *Age 20 Died in War on 30 September 1918*
TYNE COT MEMORIAL, Belgium
Son of Mrs. John Irwin, of The Cottages, Helen's Bay, Belfast.

Irwin, Edwin Johnston - Private
4222 Australian Infantry 14th Battalion *Age 25 Died in War on 11 April 1917*
VILLERS-BRETONNEUX MEMORIAL, France
Son of Mrs. Lucy Irwin, of 6, Chichester Road, Belfast, Ireland.

Irwin, Isaac - Private
12052 Cameronians (Scottish Rifles) 2nd Battalion *Died in War on 9 May 1915*
PLOEGSTEERT MEMORIAL, Belgium
Youngest brother of W J Irwin, 95 Tennent Street, Belfast.

Irwin, J - Private
3/71644 Seaforth Highlanders 2nd Battalion *Died of Wounds on 14 April 1917*
WIMEREUX COMMUNAL CEMETERY, France
95, Tennent Street, Belfast. His brother had been killed two years previously.

Irwin, John - Private
21250 Royal Irish Fusiliers 1st Battalion *Died in War on 22 October 1918*
HARLEBEKE NEW BRITISH CEMETERY, Belgium
Son of Mrs Annie Irwin, 79 Lousia Street, Belfast.

Irwin, Samuel - Corporal
8622 Royal Irish Rifles 2nd Battalion *Died in War on 16 June 1915*
YPRES (MENIN GATE) MEMORIAL, Belgium
Born Ballymacarrett, Belfast. Enlisted in Belfast.

Irwin, William - Rifleman
583 Royal Irish Rifles 2nd Battalion *Age 30 Died of Wounds on 11 November 1918*
TERLINCTHUN BRITISH CEMETERY, WIMILLE, France
Son of Hugh and Ann Irwin, of Belfast.

Irwin, William David - Corporal
16613 Royal Irish Rifles 9th Battalion *Died in War on 31 March 1916*
SUCRERIE MILITARY CEMETERY, COLINCAMPS, France
42, Battenberg Street, Belfast.

Irwin, William James - Rifleman
17931 Royal Irish Rifles 14th Battalion *Age 21 Died in War on 23 June 1917*
WIMEREUX COMMUNAL CEMETERY, France
Son of Amelia and the late William Irwin, of Belfast.

Irwin, William James - Second Lieutenant
Royal Irish Rifles 7th Battalion *Died in War on 16 June 1917*
TYNE COT MEMORIAL, Belgium
Cregagh Road, Belfast.

Ives, James Frederick - Private
50968 Royal Warwickshire Regiment 1st Battalion *Age 18 Died of Wounds on 30 August 1918*
LIGNY-ST. FLOCHEL BRITISH CEMETERY, AVERDOINGT, France
Son of Frederick and Bertha Ives, of 2, Avonbeg Street, Belfast.

Jackson, Arthur - Rifleman
16624 Royal Irish rifles 8th Battalion *Died in War on 8 June 1917*
BAILLEUL COMMUNAL CEMETERY EXTENSION (NORD), France
Son of Rachel Jackson, 4 Wellwood Street, Belfast.

Jackson, Balfour - Private
SPTS/2102 Royal Fusiliers 24th Battalion *Age 24 Died in War on 31 July 1916*
THIEPVAL MEMORIAL, France
Son of William and Jane Jackson, of 28, South Parade, Belfast, County Antrim.
His brother, George, was also killed.

Jackson, George - Private
SPTS/274 Royal Fusiliers 23rd Battalion *Age 23 Died in War on 27 July 1916*
SUCRERIE MILITARY CEMETERY, COLINCAMPS, France
Son of William and Jane Jackson, of 28, South Parade, Belfast, County Antrim.
His brother, Balfour, was also killed.

Jackson, George Wesley - Sergeant
14361 Royal Irish Fusiliers 9th Battalion *Age 21 Killed in Action on 1 July 1916*
THIEPVAL MEMORIAL, France
Son of Thomas Scott Jackson, of 36, Stranmillis Gardens, Belfast, and the late Minnie Louisa Jackson.

Jackson, Herbert Meynell - Lieutenant
Royal Flying Corps 53rd Squadron and General List *Age 22 Died in War on 18 June 1917*
ARRAS FLYING SERVICES MEMORIAL, France
Son of Matthew and Elizabeth Ann Jackson, of Greenisland Lodge, Greenisland, native of Belfast.

Jackson, Hugh - Private
436733 Canadian Infantry (Alberta Regiment) 49th Battalion *Killed in Action on 1 May 1916*
NEW IRISH FARM CEMETERY, Belgium
Son of Hugh and Maria Jackson, of 83, Cheviot Avenue, Strandtown, Belfast, Ireland.
A Presbyterian, a single man and a book keeper.

Jackson, James - Gunner
88306 Royal Horse Artillery and Royal Field Artillery *Died in War on 21 October 1916*
GUARDS CEMETERY LESBOEUFS, France
Born and enlisted in Belfast.

Jackson, James - Private
29777 Royal Irish Fusiliers 1st Battalion *Age 46 Died in War on 12 December 1918*
ST. ANDRE COMMUNAL CEMETERY, France
Husband of Emily Cotter (formerly Jackson), of 165, Bellevue Street, Belfast. Native of Gilford.

Jackson, John - Rifleman
14980 Royal Irish Rifles 15th Battalion *Killed In Action on 21 March 1918*
NOYON NEW BRITISH CEMETERY, France
Born and enlisted in Belfast.

Jackson, Lester - Sergeant
17937 Royal Irish Rifles 2nd Battalion *Died in War on 6 September 1918*
PLOEGSTEERT MEMORIAL, Belgium
Born and enlisted in Belfast.

Jackson, Samuel James - Private
28610 The Loyal North Lancashire Regiment 2/5th Battalion formerly Army Service Corps
Age 26 Died in War on 26 October 1917
TYNE COT MEMORIAL, Belgium
Son of James and Rose Anne Jackson, of 24, Arkwright Street, Belfast;
husband of Jane Jackson (née Hanna), of Drumreagh, Ballymoney, County Antrim.

Jackson, Victor - Rifleman
1266 Royal Irish Rifles 11/13th Battalion attached 22nd Entrenching Battalion
Age 19 Died in War on 29 March 1918
POZIERES MEMORIAL, France
Son of Robert Jackson, of 240, Cambrai Street, Belfast.

Jackson, William - Rifleman
17938 Royal Irish Rifles 14th Battalion *Killed in Action on 1 July 1916*
THIEPVAL MEMORIAL, France
Born Ballymacarrett, Belfast. Enlisted in Belfast.

James, Frank - Sergeant
L/4737 Royal Sussex Regiment 2nd Battalion *Died in War on 8 November 1914*
YPRES (MENIN GATE) MEMORIAL, Belgium
15 Queensland Street, Belfast.

Jameson, Alexander - Stoker First Class
308933 Royal Navy HMS "Cressy" *Died in War on 22 September 1914*
CHATHAM NAVAL MEMORIAL, United Kingdom
30 Upper Canning Street, Belfast.

Jameson, James - Corporal
10197 Royal Irish Fusiliers 2nd Battalion *Died as a result of war on 24 November 1918*
RAMLEH WAR CEMETERY, Israel
Son of Mrs E Jameson, 97 Tilbarg Street, Belfast.

Jameson, James - Stoker First Class
SS/107068 Royal Navy HMS "Raglan" *Age 28 Killed in Action at Imbros with "Goeben" and "Breslau" on 20 January 1918*
PLYMOUTH NAVAL MEMORIAL, United Kingdom
Son of James and Jane Jameson, of Belfast; husband of Annabella Jameson, of 71, Little Patrick Street, Belfast.

Jameson, Wiliam John - Lance Corporal
3105 Irish Guards 1st Battalion *Killed in Action on 6 November 1914*
YPRES (MENIN GATE) MEMORIAL, United Kingdom
Husband of Carrie, Argyle Street, Belfast. A member of the old UVF.

Jamieson, Alfred - Private
13033 Royal Inniskilling Fusiliers 7th Battalion *Died in War on 19 July 1916*
PHILOSOPHE BRITISH CEMETERY, MAZINGARBE, France
Son of Mary Jamieson, of 89, Tildarg Street, Belfast.

Jamieson, E - Lance Corporal
5563 Royal Irish Rifles 6th Battalion *Died in War on 27 April 1917*
BELFAST (DUNDONALD) CEMETERY, United Kingdom
Son of the late Edward and Fanny Jamieson, of Belfast.

Jamieson, John - Private
11663 Royal Inniskilling Fusiliers "D" Company 9th Battalion *Age 18 Died in War on 31 January 1915*
ARDSTRAW CHURCH OF IRELAND CHURCHYARD, United Kingdom
Son of Thomas and Ellen Jamieson, of 39, Colvil Street, Strandtown, Belfast. Born at Newtownstewart.

Jamieson, Robert - Lance Corporal
7554 Royal Irish Rifles 2nd Battalion *Age 26 Killed in Action on 25 October 1914*
LE TOURET MEMORIAL, France
Son of the late George Jamieson; husband of Margaret Jamieson, of 25, Heather Street, Crumlin Road, Belfast.

Jamison, James - Rifleman
11412 Royal Irish Rifles 1st Battalion *Died in War on 21 August 1918*
BERTENACRE MILITARY CEMETERY, FLETRE, France
Born and enlisted in Belfast.

Jamison, James Clawson - Captain
Royal Irish Rifles 10th Battalion *Age 32 Died in War on 22 November 1917*
CAMBRAI MEMORIAL, LOUVERVAL, France
Son of Alexander and Elizabeth Jamison, of "Florenceville" Ormeau Road, Belfast;
husband of Edith M. Jamison, of 177, Lisburn Road, Belfast.

Jamison, Robert - Rifleman
17943 Royal Irish Rifles 14th Battalion *Killed in Action on 1 July 1916*
A.I.F. BURIAL GROUND, FLERS, France
473, Ormeau Road, Belfast.

Jamison, Sydney - Rifleman
17942 Royal Irish Rifles 12th Battalion *Killed in Action on 1 July 1916*
THIEPVAL MEMORIAL, France
Born in Belfast, enlisted County Antrim.

Jamison, Thomas Edward - Rifleman
17944 Royal Irish Rifles 12th Battalion *Died in as a Prisoner of War on 26 August 1916*
HAMBURG CEMETERY, Germany
Born in Belfast, enlisted County Antrim.

Jardine, James - Sergeant
27731 Royal Artillery 17th Siege Battery *Died of Wounds on 29 October 1918*
ST. SOUPLET BRITISH CEMETERY, France
Son of David and Anne Jardine; husband of Henrietta Sarah Jardine, of 80, Mayfield Avenue, Dover.
Born at Belfast. Awarded both the Military Medal and the Meritorious Service Medal.

Jarman, Andrew Hatch - Second Lieutenant
Northumberland Fusiliers 20th (Tyneside Scottish) Battalion *Age 34 Killed in Action on 1 July 1916*
OVILLERS MILITARY CEMETERY, France
Brother of Miss Alice Joyce Jarman, of "Ivy Dene" 242, Antrim Road, Belfast.
A former manager with Workman Clark shipyard.

Jeffers, James - Gunner
63873 Royal Field Artillery 42nd Battery 2nd Brigade *Age 25 Died of Wounds on 28 March 1917*
BETHUNE TOWN CEMETERY, France
Son of John and Mary Jeffers, of 4, Fingal Street, Belfast.

Jefferson, James - Rifleman
192 Royal Irish Rifles "D" Company 10th Battalion *Age 35 Killed in Action at Thiepval Wood on 19 June 1916*
HAMEL MILITARY CEMETERY, BEAUMONT-HAMEL, *France*
Son of William and Jane Jefferson, of Dunmurry, County Antrim; husband of Jane Jefferson, of 5, Reformatory Avenue, Lisburn Road, Balmoral, Belfast.

Jefferson, Richard - Lance Corporal
432980 Canadian Infantry (Alberta Regiment) 49th Battalion *Age 26 Died in War on 2 June 1916*
YPRES (MENIN GATE) MEMORIAL, *Belgium*
Son of Robert S. and Amelia Jefferson, of 45, College Park Avenue, Belfast, Ireland.
A single man, Anglican and book keeper.

Jefferson, Victor - Private
14285 Royal Dublin Fusiliers 7th Battalion *Died in War on 23 August 1915*
Born in Belfast. Enlisted in The Curragh, County Kildare.

Jefferson, William James - Private
769361 Canadian Infantry (Quebec Regiment) 87th Battalion
Age 25 Died of Wounds received at Lens on 24 September 1917
MONS COMMUNAL CEMETERY, *Belgium*
Son of James and Isabella Jefferson, of 1, Crossland Street, Belfast.
An Anglican, he worked as a clerk in Canada.

Jeffrey, Thomas - Private
17812 Royal Inniskilling Fusiliers 9th Battalion *Killed in Action on 1 July 1916*
THIEPVAL MEMORIAL, *France*
Born Muckamore, enlisted Cookstown, resident Belfast.

Jeffries, Arthur Grace - Company Sergeant Major
16/316 Royal Irish Rifles 20th Battalion *Age 49 Died in War on 3 May 1916*
BELFAST (DUNDONALD) CEMETERY, *United Kingdom*
Born in Poona, India. Husband of Margaret Jeffries, of 21, Liffey Street, Oldpark Road, Belfast.

Jeffries, Charles - Private
5975 Royal Irish Rifles Depot *Died in War on 12 April 1917*
BELFAST (DUNDONALD) CEMETERY, *United Kingdom*
54, Tyrone Street, Belfast.

Jeffs, John - Rifleman
14985 Royal Irish Rifles "D" Company 14th Battalion *Age 21 Killed in Action on 1 July 1916*
THIEPVAL MEMORIAL, *France*
Son of Richard and Margaret Jeffs, of 23, The Mount, Belfast.

Jelly, Henry - Able Seaman
233032 Royal Navy HMS "Indefatigable" *Age 28 Killed in Action at Battle of Jutland on 31 May 1916*
PLYMOUTH NAVAL MEMORIAL, *United Kingdom*
Son of Margaret Jane Smith (formerly Jelly), of 162, New Lodge Road, Belfast, and the late Henry Jelly.

Jelly, Herbert - Private
25403 Royal Irish Regiment 7th (South Irish Horse) Battalion *Age 30 Died in War on 14 September 1918*
LE CATEAU MILITARY CEMETERY, *France*
Son of James Jelly, of 81, Delhi Street, Belfast.

Jenkins, Edward - Rifleman
14986 Royal Irish Rifles 8th Battalion *Age 21 Died in War on 17 August 1917*
TYNE COT MEMORIAL, Belgium
Son of Edward Jenkins, 5, Sixth Street, Belfast. A member of the old UVF.

Jenkins, Robert - Rifleman
2767 Royal Irish Rifles 2nd Battalion *Age 18 Died in War on 25 September 1915*
YPRES (MENIN GATE) MEMORIAL, Belgium
Son of Robert and Ann Elizabeth Jenkins, of 1, Ninon Street, Belfast.

Jenkins, William - Private
Royal Inniskilling Fusiliers *Died in War*
Son of Mrs Meharry, 15, Pernau Street, Belfast.

Jenkins, William - Rifleman
49245 Rifle Brigade 1st Battalion *Died in War on 1 November 1918*
Son of James, (a serving soldier), and Maria Jenkins. 30, Bisley Street, Belfast.

Jennett, Joseph - Rifleman
4131 Royal Irish Rifles 1st Battalion *Died in War on 11 March 1916*
YPRES (MENIN GATE) MEMORIAL, Belgium
Born in Belfast, elisted Ballykinler.

Jennings, George - Fireman And Trimmer
Mercantile Marine S.S. "War Clover" (London)
Age 37 Drowned, as a result of an attack by an enemy submarine on 19 October 1917
TOWER HILL MEMORIAL, United Kingdom
Son of Margaret Jennings, and the late Samuel Jennings; husband of Charlotte Jennings (née Carrothers), of 38, Peveril Street, Belfast. Born at Omagh.

Jennings, William - Acting Bombardier
69501 Royal Field Artillery 21st Division Ammunition Column *Died in War on 3 November 1916*
SAILLY-LABOURSE COMMUNAL CEMETERY, France
Son of Mr. J. Jennings, of 109, Solway Street, Belfast.

Jennings, William Robert - Private
152493 Canadian Infantry (Manitoba Regiment) 16th Battalion *Age 40 Died in War on 28 September 1916*
VIMY MEMORIAL, France
Son of John and Mary Jennings, of 26, Southport Street, Belfast, Ireland.
An Anglican, he became a farmer in Canada after serving 12 years with the Royal Irish Rifles.

Jervis, Harry C. - Lance Corporal
231117 Canadian Infantry (Alberta Regiment) "A" Company 10th Battalion
Age 27 Died in War on 16 August 1918
VILLERS-BRETONNEUX MILITARY CEMETERY, France
Son of Mr. and Mrs George Jervis, of Belfast, Ireland; husband of Mrs. A. Jervis, of 302, Irving Road, Victoria, British Columbia. A Presbyterian, he worked as a telephone inspector. Awarded the Military Medal.

Jess, Daniel - Private
6892 Royal Irish Rifles 10th Battalion *Age 28 Died in War on 22 October 1916*
ST. QUENTIN CABARET MILITARY CEMETERY, Belgium
Third son of John and Mary Jess, 44, Selby Street, Belfast.

Journey of Remembering

Jess, Thomas - Guardsman
4642 Scots Guards 2nd Battalion *Died in War on 14 June 1915*
LE TOURET MEMORIAL, France
Born in Belfast, enlisted Glasgow.

Jess, William George - Rifleman
1019 Royal Irish Rifles 8th Battalion *Age 25 Died of Wounds on 12 July 1916*
BELFAST (DUNDONALD) CEMETERY, United Kingdom
Son of Robert and Agnes Jess. Born at Belfast.

Job, Ernest Frederick - Private
18853 Cameronians (Scottish Rifles) 9th Battalion *Died in War on 30 November 1915*
YPRES RESERVOIR CEMETERY, Belgium
Born in Belfast, enlisted Birmingham. Formerly 49523 Royal Garrison Artillery.

Johns, John - Lance Corporal
8151 Royal Irish Rifles 2nd Battalion *Died in War on 14 October 1914*
LE TOURET MEMORIAL, France
32 Cheviot Avenue, Belfast.

Johnson, Joseph - Private
20182 Royal Irish Fusiliers 7th Battalion *Age 28 Died in War on 5 September 1916*
THIEPVAL MEMORIAL, France
Son of George and Jane Johnson; husband of Annie Johnson, of 21, Garnet Street, Belfast.

Johnson, Robert - Private
10469 The Loyal North Lancashire Regiment 1st Battalion *Age 21 Died in War on 14 September 1914*
LA FERTE-SOUS-JOUARRE MEMORIAL, France
Son of James and Elizabeth Johnson, of 9, Cromwell Street, Belfast.

Johnson, Samuel - Rifleman
2989 King's Royal Rifle Corps 1st Battalion *Died as prisoner of war (from the German camps at Baistrup) on 6 March 1915*
TINGLEV CHURCHYARD, Denmark
Born in Belfast, enlisted Lincoln, England.

Johnson, William - Rifleman
9812 Royal Irish Rifles 1st Battalion *Age 21 Died of Wounds on 12 March 1915*
ESTAIRES COMMUNAL CEMETERY, France
Son of Daniel and Mary Johnson, of 16, Taylor Street, Belfast. Born in Dublin.

Johnston Richard, - Private
14365 Royal Irish Fusiliers 9th Battalion *Killed in Action on 1 July 1916*
THIEPVAL MEMORIAL, France
Born and enlisted in Lurgan. Married in the former St Anne's church, Belfast and thought to have been resident in the city.

Johnston, Alex - Rifleman
11009 Royal Irish Rifles 6th Battalion *Died in War on 15 August 1915*
HELLES MEMORIAL, Turkey
27, Boundary Street, Belfast.

Johnston, Andrew - Private
Royal Inniskilling Fusiliers *Died in War*
77, Beverley Street, Belfast.

Johnston, Andrew - Rifleman
10004 Royal Irish Rifles 1st Battalion *Died in War on 27 May 1916*
ALBERT COMMUNAL CEMETERY EXTENSION, France
Born and enlisted in Belfast.

Johnston, Charles - Sergeant
6676 Sherwood Foresters (Notts and Derby Regiment) 1st Battalion *Age 31 Died in War on 11 March 1915*
LE TOURET MEMORIAL, France
Son of James and Mary Johnston, of 101, Killowen Street, Belfast

Johnston, Edward - Lance Corporal
9228 Royal Irish Rifles 7th Battalion *Age 25 Killed in Action on 16 August 1917*
TYNE COT CEMETERY, Belgium
Husband of Ruth Johnston, of 20, Derg Street, Belfast.

Johnston, Edward - Trimmer
1172ST Royal Naval Reserve HMS "Alert" *Age 47 Died of heatstroke on 26 June 1916*
PORTSMOUTH NAVAL MEMORIAL, United Kingdom
Son of Edward and Bridget Johnston, of Belfast; husband of Jane Johnston, of 13, Shiels Street, Belfast.

Johnston, Edward James - Corporal
3512 Royal Irish Fusiliers 7th Battalion *Age 41 Died in War on 5 September 1916*
THIEPVAL MEMORIAL, France
Husband of Rachel Helena Balmer (formerly Johnston), of 25, Bristol Street, Belfast.

Johnston, Elliott - Captain
Royal Irish Rifles *Age 28 Killed in Action on 1 July 1916*
THIEPVAL MEMORIAL, France
Son of Samuel Johnston, of 1, Deramore Park, Belfast. A former officer in the old UVF he had been awarded the Military Cross for leading a raid on enemy lines which produced thirteen German prisoners. He was killed five days later, on the first day of the Somme.

Johnston, F - Private
PLY/15664 Royal Marine Light Infantry 1st R.M. Battalion Royal Naval Division
Age 23 Died in War on 27 September 1918
MOEUVRES COMMUNAL CEMETERY EXTENSION, France
Son of Frederick Johnston, of 67, Hornby Street, Belfast.

Johnston, George - Lance Corporal
25155 Royal Inniskilling Fusiliers 9th Battalion *Died in War on 30 September 1918*
DADIZEELE NEW BRITISH CEMETERY, Belgium
Husband of Mrs. J. E. Johnston, of 20, Walton Street, Belfast.

Johnston, George - Private
27625 Royal Inniskilling Fusiliers 5th Battalion attached 8th Battalion *Age 18 Died in War on 20 May 1916*
PHILOSOPHE BRITISH CEMETERY, MAZINGARBE, France
Son of George Johnston, of 23, Abercorn Street North, Belfast.

Johnston, Henry - Lance Corporal
14993 Royal Irish Rifles 10th Battalion *Age 31 Killed in Action on 1 July 1916*
THIEPVAL MEMORIAL, France
Son of Andrew and Catherine Johnston, of 251, Donegall Road, Belfast.

Johnston, Henry - Rifleman
17971 Royal Irish Rifles 16th Battalion *Killed in Action on 21 March 1918*
POZIERES MEMORIAL, France
Born and enlisted in Belfast.

Johnston, Herbert Benjamin - Private
3023 Argyll and Sutherland Highlanders 1/6th Battalion *Age 20 Died in War on 20 June 1915*
VIEILLE-CHAPELLE NEW MILITARY CEMETERY, LACOUTURE, France
Son of Benjamin and Leana Johnston. Brother of William, 162 Ainsworth Avenue, Belfast.

Johnston, Hugh - Rifleman
14994 Royal Irish Rifles 14th Battalion *Killed In Action on 15 August 1917*
WHITE HOUSE CEMETERY, ST. JEAN-LES-YPRES, Belgium
Born in Belfast.

Johnston, Hugh - Rifleman
1627 Royal Irish Rifles 10th Battalion *Died in War on 1 July 1916*
THIEPVAL MEMORIAL, France
Born and enlisted in Belfast.

Johnston, Hugh - Rifleman
6467 Royal Irish Rifles "C" Company 2nd Battalion *Age 19 Died in War on 16 June 1915*
YPRES (MENIN GATE) MEMORIAL, Belgium
Son of Mrs. Sarah Johnston, of 2, Carew Street, Ballymacarrett, Belfast.

Johnston, James - Private
19518 Machine Gun Corps (Infantry) 107th Company *Age 24 Died in War on 17 May 1917*
DRANOUTRE MILITARY CEMETERY, Belgium
Son of Mrs. E. Johnston, of 26, Charlotte Street, Belfast.

Johnston, James - Private
2574 Leinster Regiment 7th Battalion *Died in War on 28 March 1916*
ST PATRICK'S CEMETERY LOOS, France
Born and enlisted in Belfast.

Johnston, James - Rifleman
11986 Royal Irish Rifles 10th Battalion *Age 21 Killed in Action on 1 July 1916*
THIEPVAL MEMORIAL, France
Son of Mrs. Margaret E. Johnston, of 35, Bracken Street, Belfast.

Johnston, James - Rifleman
14999 Royal Irish Rifles 10th Battalion *Killed in Action on 1 July 1916*
THIEPVAL MEMORIAL, France
Born and enlisted in Belfast.

Journey of Remembering

Johnston, James - Rifleman
664 Royal Irish Rifles 9th Battalion *Killed in Action on 1 July 1916*
THIEPVAL MEMORIAL, France
Born and enlisted in Belfast.

Johnston, James - Sergeant
3985 Irish Guards 1st Battalion *Age 25 Died in War on 1 December 1917*
ROCQUIGNY-EQUANCOURT ROAD BRITISH CEMETERY, MANANCOURT, France
Son of William and Margaret Johnston. Native of Belfast.

Johnston, James Alexander - Able Seaman
235110 Royal Navy HMS "Laforey" *Killed by mine explosion in Straits of Dover on 23 March 1917*
PLYMOUTH NAVAL MEMORIAL, United Kingdom
Brother of John Johnston, of 56, Channing Street, Belfast.

Johnston, James Barlow - Sub-Lieutenant
Royal Naval Vounteer Reserve Hawke Battalion Royal Naval Division *Age 21 Died in War on 8 October 1918*
CAMBRAI EAST MILITARY CEMETERY, France
Son of Philip and Edith Elizabeth Arden Johnston, of "Denarden", Standtown Belfast.
Educated Campbell College. Intially enlisted in the Royal Engineers, subsequently was commissioned and transferred to the Royal Naval Division.

Johnston, James Carlisle - Sapper
196711 Royal Engineers Inland Water Transport *Died of sunstroke on 23 July 1917*
KUT WAR CEMETERY, Iraq
Husband of Eliza Ann Johnston, of 25, Hamilton Place, Belfast.

Johnston, James Stevenson - Rifleman
17980 Royal Irish Rifles 13th Battalion *Killed in Action on 1 July 1916*
SERRE ROAD CEMETERY No.2, France
Born in Belfast, enlisted Downpatrick.

Johnston, John - Fireman And Trimmer
Mercantile Marine S.S. "Beacon Light" (Liverpool)
Age 51 Drowned, as a result of an attack by an enemy submarine on 19 February 1918
TOWER HILL MEMORIAL, United Kingdom
(Served as SAVAGE). Son of the late John and Mary Anne Johnston; husband of Mary Jane Johnston (née O'Reilly), of 51, Great Richmond Street, Liverpool. Born in Belfast.

Johnston, John - Lance Corporal
64664 Royal Engineers 150th Field Company *Age 35 Killed in Action on 1 July 1916*
THIEPVAL MEMORIAL, France
Son of William and Elizabeth Johnston, of Printwork Terrace, Oldpark Road; husband of Annie Johnston, of 3, Concord Street, Belfast.

Johnston, John - Private
17508 Royal Inniskilling Fusiliers 9th Battalion *Killed in Action on 1 July 1916*
THIEPVAL MEMORIAL, France
Born and enlisted in Belfast.

Johnston, John - Private
26123 Royal Inniskilling Fusiliers 8th Battalion *Killed in Action on 9 September 1916*
THIEPVAL MEMORIAL, France
Born and enlisted in Belfast.

Johnston, John - Private
3400 Machine Gun Corps (Infantry) *Died in War on 13 August 1916*
POZIERES BRITISH CEMETERY, OVILLERS-LA BOISSELLE, France
Born Ballymacarrett, Belfast. Enlisted in Belfast. Formerly 31904 Liverpool Regiment.

Johnston, John - Private
3596 Royal Inniskilling Fusiliers 1st Battalion *Age 22 Died in War on 21 August 1915*
HELLES MEMORIAL, Turkey
Son of William and Mary Johnston, of 35, Cumberland Street, Belfast.
A machinist he was Presbyterian in religion.

Johnston, John - Private
241157 Seaforth Highlanders 1/5th Battalion *Killed in action on 21 March 1918*
QUEANT ROAD CEMETERY, BUISSY, France
Brother of Martha Johnston, 1 St Andrew's Square, Belfast.

Johnston, John - Rifleman
12937 Royal Irish Rifles 8th Battalion *Died in War on 2 July 1916*
THIEPVAL MEMORIAL, France
Born and enlisted in Belfast.

Johnston, John - Rifleman
8991 Royal Irish Rifles 2nd Battalion *Died of Wounds as POW on 25 July 1918*
COLOGNE SOUTHERN CEMETERY, Germany
Born and enlisted in Belfast.

Johnston, John - Rifleman
9476 Royal Irish Rifles 1st Battalion *Age 26 Died in War on 10 March 1915*
LE TOURET MEMORIAL, France
Son of Mrs. Margaret Johnston, of 213, Matilda Street, Belfast.

Johnston, Joseph - Lance Corporal
3096 Royal Irish Rifles 1st Battalion *Killed in Action on 21 March 1918*
POZIERES MEMORIAL, France
Born in Belfast, enlisted Manchester.

Johnston, Joseph - Private
2375 Royal Inniskilling Fusiliers 1st Battalion *Died in War on 3 July 1916*
GEZAINCOURT COMMUNAL CEMETERY, France
From the Shankill area. He left a widow, Phoebe. Two sons served in the Inniskillings in the Second World War. One, Joseph, was badly wounded and the other, James, was killed at the battle of Monte Cassino, Italy.

Johnston, Joseph - Rifleman
11246 Royal Irish Rifles 6th Battalion *Died in War on 11 August 1915*
HELLES MEMORIAL, Turkey
Brother of Mary Johnston, of 176, Cambrai Street, Belfast.

JOURNEY OF REMEMBERING

Johnston, Joseph - Rifleman
8/15002 Royal Irish Rifles 8th Battalion *Died in War on 14 August 1917*
WHITE HOUSE CEMETERY, ST JEAN-LES-YPRES, Belgium
Born and enlisted in Belfast.

Johnston, Patrick - Rifleman
4434 Royal Irish Rifles 2nd Battalion *Died in War on 6 August 1917*
MENIN ROAD SOUTH MILITARY CEMETERY, Belgium
Born in Belfast, enlisted in Ballykinler.

Johnston, Robert - Lance Corporal
6359 Royal Irish Rifles 1st Battalion *Died in War on 9 May 1915*
PLOEGSTEERT MEMORIAL, Belgium
Born and enlisted in Newtownards, resident in Belfast.

Johnston, Robert - Private
10469 Loyal North Lancashire Regiment 1st Battalion *Died in War on 14 September 1914*
LA FERTE-SOUS-JOUARRE MEMORIAL, France
Born and enlisted in Belfast.

Johnston, Robert - Rifleman
12949 Royal Irish Rifles 8th Battalion *Died in War on 2 July 1916*
THIEPVAL MEMORIAL, France
Born and enlisted in Belfast.

Johnston, Robert J (Bertie) - Private
S/40752 Black Watch (Royal Highlanders) 8th Battalion *Age 19 Died in War on 9 April 1917*
CABARET-ROUGE BRITISH CEMETERY, SOUCHEZ, France
Son of James and Margaret Johnston, of 25, Avoca Street, Belfast. One of 11 children.

Johnston, Robert John - Corporal
15/12936 Royal Irish Rifles 2nd Company 15th Battalion *Age 23 Died of Wounds on 11 November 1918*
TERLINCTHUN BRITISH CEMETERY, WIMILLE, France
Son of Richard and Emma Johnston, of Ligoneil, Belfast. Died of his wounds on the last day of the war.

Johnston, Robert John - Rifleman
17985 Royal Irish Rifles 14th Battalion *Age 24 Killed in Action on 1 July 1916*
THIEPVAL MEMORIAL, France
Son of Thomas Johnston, of 15, Century Street, Belfast.

Johnston, Samuel - Lance Corporal
15007 Royal Irish Rifles 10th Battalion *Died in War on 1 July 1916*
THIEPVAL MEMORIAL, France
Born and enlisted in Belfast.

Johnston, Sidney - Private
9928 Canadian Infantry (Central Ontario Regiment) 3rd Battalion *Age 22 Died in War on 13 June 1916*
YPRES (MENIN GATE) MEMORIAL, Belgium
Son of Superintendent John A. Johnston, of the Harbour Police Force, Belfast, Ireland, and Matilda H. Johnston. A Presbyterian who worked in the shipping business.

Johnston, Thomas - Pioneer
319470 Royal Engineers Inland waterways and docks *Accidentally drowned on 20 October 1917*
TARANTO TOWN CEMETERY EXTENSION, Italy
107, East Bread, Street, Belfast.

Johnston, Thomas - Private
22803 Royal Inniskilling Fusiliers 12th Battalion *Age 35 Died in War on 18 February 1917*
SHANKILL CEMETERY, United Kingdom
Son of Thomas and Agnes Johnston, of 3, Crosby Street, Belfast.

Johnston, Thomas - Private
9279 Royal Inniskilling Fusiliers "A" Company 1st Battalion *Age 26 Died in War on 1 July 1916*
THIEPVAL MEMORIAL, France
Brother of Mrs. L. Hammond, of 8, Matilda Street, Belfast.

Johnston, Thomas - Rifleman
15009 Royal Irish Rifles 9th Battalion *Killed in Action on 1 July 1916*
THIEPVAL MEMORIAL, France
Son of Thomas and Susan Johnston, 54, Canmore Street, Belfast.
His brother, William would be killed a year later, at Ypres.

Johnston, William - Private
200349 Highland Light Infantry 9th (Glasgow Highlanders) Battalion *Age 25 Died in War on 25 September 1917*
HOOGE CRATER CEMETERY, Belgium
Son of Robert James and Charlotte Johnston, of Belfast; husband of Elizabeth Johnston, of Church Road, Lytham, England.

Johnston, Walter - Private
23345 Royal Warwickshire Regiment 10th Battalion *Age 24 Died in War on 23 March 1918*
ARRAS MEMORIAL, France
Son of John and Mary Jane Johnston, of 14, Belvoir Street, Belfast.

Johnston, William - Able Seaman
188608 Royal Navy HMS "Hawke" *Age 34 Killed in Action with submarine in North Sea on 15 October 1914*
CHATHAM NAVAL MEMORIAL, United Kingdom
Husband of Mrs. Johnston, of 2, Stewart Street, Belfast.

Johnston, William - Private
13530 Royal Inniskilling Fusiliers "C" Company 9th Battalion *Age 27 Died in War on 1 July 1916*
THIEPVAL MEMORIAL, France
Son of William and Sarah Johnston, of 94, Upper Canning Street, Belfast.

Johnston, William - Private
16637 Royal Irish Rifles 9th Battalion *Killed in Action on 1 July 1916*
THIEPVAL MEMORIAL, France
Son of Thomas and Barbara Johnston, 194, Mayo Street, Belfast.

Johnston, William - Private
23152 Canadian Infantry (Quebec Regiment) 14th Battalion *Age 33 Killed in Action on 30 April 1916*
CHESTER FARM CEMETERY, Belgium
Son of William and Mary Johnston, of 35, Cumberland Street, Belfast, Ireland.
A machinist he was Presbyterian in religion.

Johnston, William - Private
65279 Northumberland Fusiliers 1st Battalion *Age 19 Died in War on 27 April 1918*
SANDPITS BRITISH CEMETERY, FOUQUEREUIL, *France*
Son of William and Lizzie Johnston, of Belfast.

Johnston, William - Private
8166 Royal Irish Fusiliers 1st Battalion *Age 31 Died in War on 11 December 1915*
FORCEVILLE COMMUNAL CEMETERY AND EXTENSION, *France*
Son of the late Alexander and Sarah Johnston, of Ballymena, County Antrim.

Johnston, William - Rifleman
12941 Royal Irish Rifles 15th Battalion *Died of Wounds on 27 August 1918*
BERTENACRE MILITARY CEMETERY, FLETRE, *France*
Born and enlisted in Belfast.

Johnston, William - Rifleman
17976 Royal Irish Rifles 14th Battalion *Killed in Action on 1 July 1916*
THIEPVAL MEMORIAL, *France*
Born and enlisted in Belfast.

Johnston, William Henry - Rifleman
15012 Royal Irish Rifles 8th Battalion *Died in War on 6 August 1917*
YPRES (MENIN GATE) MEMORIAL, *Belgium*
Son of Thomas and Susan Johnston, 54, Canmore Street, Belfast. His brother, Thomas, had been killed a year earlier, on the Somme.

Johnston, William Holden - Second Lieutenant
The King's (Liverpool Regiment) 13th Battalion *Age 31 Died in War on 30 July 1916*
GUILLEMONT ROAD CEMETERY, GUILLEMONT, *France*
Son of John G. and Esther Johnston, of Brooklands, Annadale, Belfast; husband of Dorothy Holden Johnston, of Hoylake, Birkenhead, England.

Johnston, William J - Private
22152 Royal Irish Fusiliers 9th Battalion *Age 34 Killed in Action on 16 August 1917*
TYNE COT MEMORIAL, *Belgium*
Husband of Margaret Johnston, of 9, Upper Charleville Street, Belfast.

Johnstone, Anthony V - Sergeant
400433 Canadian Army Medical Corps 14th Field Ambulance *Died in War on 16 June 1917*
WITLEY (MILFORD) CEMETERY, *United Kingdom*
Husband of Lily Johnstone, of 19, Eglantine Gardens, Belfast. A member of Church of Ireland he was born in Galway and had worked as a druggist.

Johnstone, Joseph - Private
11877 Cameronians (Scottish Rifles) 9th Battalion *Died in War on 22 October 1915*
YPRES (MENIN GATE) MEMORIAL, *Belgium*
Born in Belfast, enlisted in Glasgow.

Johnstone, Robert - Private
9047 Royal Irish Rifles 2nd Battalion *Age 35 Died of Wounds - shot in eye in France and operated on on 7 July 1915*
DERBY (NOTTINGHAM ROAD) CEMETERY, United Kingdom
38 Aberdeen Street, Belfast. He had served throughout the Boer War and thereafter worked for Harland and Wolff. As a reservist he was recalled at the beginning of the war. His aunt, Mrs Boomer, was chief mourner at his funeral in Derby.

Johnstone, William McKelvey - Private
437709 Canadian Infantry (Saskatchewan Regiment) 46th Battalion *Died of Wounds on 26 December 1916*
VILLERS STATION CEMETERY, VILLERS-AU-BOIS, France
Born in Scotland and later lived in Belfast. A Methodist he had Regular Army service and then worked as a printer.

Jones, David - Rifleman
6857 Royal Irish Rifles 2nd Battalion *Died in War on 24 May 1915*
DICKIEBUSCH NEW MILITARY CEMETERY, Belgium
11, East Bread Street, Belfast. Born Ballymacarrett, enlisted in Holywood.

Jones, Espar - Private
295085 London Regiment (Royal Fusiliers) 4th Battalion *Age 20 Died in War on 8 April 1918*
GRAND-SERAUCOURT BRITISH CEMETERY, France
Son of Espar and Hannah Jones, of "Beltana" Greenisland, Belfast. Born at Carrickfergus, County Antrim.

Jones, Fred Lewis - Private
41564 Royal Scots 15th Battalion *Age 27 Died in War on 26 August 1917*
THIEPVAL MEMORIAL, France
Son of Robert Jones, of Cooper Street, Belfast; husband of Sarah Morrow Jones, of 25, Alma Street, Govan, Glasgow.

Jones, Henry - Private
12957 Royal Irish Rifles 9th Battalion *Died in War on 23 August 1916*
BAILLEUL COMMUNAL CEMETERY EXTENSION (NORD), France
21, Urney Street, Belfast.

Jones, Hubert Victor Edward - Second Lieutenant
Royal Irish Rifles 12th Battalion *Age 25 Died in War on 25 October 1918*
HARLEBEKE NEW BRITISH CEMETERY, Belgium
Son of Mary Jones, of 28, Bedeque Street, Belfast, and the late Hugh Jones.

Jones, James - Lance Corporal
38850 Northamptonshire Regiment 1/4th Battalion *Died in War on 3 November 1917*
DEIR EL BELAH WAR CEMETERY, Israel
Born in Belfast, enlisted in Leeds, Yorkshire. Formerly 26662, Yorkshire Light Infantry.

Jones, John - Stoker
1035U Royal Naval Reserve HMS "Goliath" *Age 42 Killed in Action with Turkish Destroyer on 13 May 1915*
PORTSMOUTH NAVAL MEMORIAL, United Kingdom
Husband of Charlotte Jones, of 11, Sugarfield Street, Belfast. His brother, Robert, was also killed, with the Royal Navy.

Jones, John Horden - Private
4123 London Regiment (Prince of Wales' Own Civil Service Rifles) 15th Battalion
Age 21 Killed in Action on 15 September 1916
CERISY-GAILLY FRENCH NATIONAL CEMETERY, France
Son of John M. and Mary E. Jones (née Horden), of 165, Inderwick Road, Hornsey, London. Born at Belfast.

Jones, Joseph - Rifleman
15018 Royal Irish Rifles "A" Company 9th Battalion *Age 34 Died in War on 5 February 1916*
MAILLY-MAILLET COMMUNAL CEMETERY EXTENSION, France
Son of John and Anne Jones, of Belfast.

Jones, Robert - Stoker
2249T Royal Naval Reserve HMS"Goliath"
Age 43 Killed in Action with Turkish Destroyer in Dardanelles on 13 May 1915
PORTSMOUTH NAVAL MEMORIAL, United Kingdom
Husband of Margaret Jones, of 37, Hurst Street, Sandy Row, Belfast.

Jones, William - Private
28179 Royal Inniskilling Fusiliers 9th Battalion *Age 19 Died of Wounds on 13 February 1919*
BIRMINGHAM (LODGE HILL) CEMETERY, United Kingdom
Son of James Jones, of 29, Bann Street, Belfast, and the late Elizabeth Jones.

Jones, William - Sergeant
17987 Royal Irish Rifles 14th Battalion *Died in War on 6 December 1917*
CAMBRAI MEMORIAL LOUVERVAL, France
Born and enlisted in Belfast. Son of Samuel and Mary Jane Jones.

Jordan, Gerald - Private
192538 Canadian Infantry (Central Ontario Regiment) 15th Battalion *Age 25 Died of Wounds on 7 July 1917*
LA TARGETTE BRITISH CEMETERY, NEUVILLE-ST. VAAST, France
Son of Samuel and Minnie Jordan, of Belfast, Ireland; husband of Helen G. Girvin McMullan (formerly Jordan), of 148, Inkster Avenue, Winnipeg, Canada. Served previously in the Royal Irish Rifles before becoming a bricklayer in Canada, a Presbyterian.

Jordan, Thomas - Private
52076 The King's (Liverpool Regiment) 19th Battalion *Died in War on 15 September 1916*
LOOS MEMORIAL, France
Native of Belfast.

Jordan, William - Private
13639 Royal Scots (Lothian Regiment) 13th Battalion *Died in War on 13 October 1916*
CONTALMAISON CHATEAU CEMETERY, France
Born in Belfast, lived in Glasgow when enlisted.

Joyce, Patrick - Private
L/13673 21st (Empress of India's) Lancers *Died of pneumonia on 1 November 1918*
DELHI 1914-1918 WAR MEMORIAL, India
10 Stanhope Street, Belast.

Junk, Robert - Private
8796 Royal Inniskilling Fusiliers 1st Battalion *Died in War on 30 May 1915*
TWELVE TREE COPSE CEMETERY, Turkey
68, Beresford Street, Belfast.

Kane, Alexander - Private
10475 Irish Guards 1st Battalion *Died in War on 6 July 1917*
BLEUET FARM CEMETERY, Belgium
Born and enlisted in Belfast.

Kane, Henry - Private
8361 Princess Victoria's (Royal Irish Fusiliers) 1st Battalion *Died in War on 21 December 1914*
WIMEREUX COMMUNAL CEMETERY, France
Born in Belfast, enlisted Armagh.

Kane, James - Corporal
17997 Royal Irish Rifles 12th Battalion *Died in War on 25 August 1918*
BAILLEUL COMMUNAL CEMETERY EXTENSION (NORD), France
Born in Belfast, enlisted Lisburn.

Kane, James - Private
25043 Royal Irish Fusiliers 1st Battalion *Age 27 Died of Wounds on 14 May 1917*
ETAPLES MILITARY CEMETERY, France
Son of Mary Hurley, of 29, Jennymount Terrace, York Road, Belfast.

Kane, James - Rifleman
15052 Royal Irish Rifles 10th Battalion *Killed In Action on 4 August 1917*
YPRES (MENIN GATE) MEMORIAL, Belgium
Born and enlisted in Belfast.

Kane, John - Private
2579 Connaught Rangers 6th Battalion *Died in War on 12 January 1917*
POND FARM CEMETERY, Belgium
Son of Mrs. C. Kane, of 59, McDonnell Street, Belfast.

Kane, John Alexander - Rifleman
1142 Royal Irish Rifles 11th Battalion attached 22nd Entrenching Battalion
Age 25 Died in War on 30 March 1918
POZIERES MEMORIAL, France
Son of Robert Kane, of 12, Joseph Street, Belfast, and Mary Kane (stepmother).

Kane, Robert - Private
12873 Princess Victoria's (Royal Irish Fusiliers) 6th Battalion *Died in War on 15 August 1915*
HELLES MEMORIAL, Turkey
Born and enlisted in Belfast. Formerly 11815 Royal Irish Fusiliers.

Kane, Samuel - Private
13715 Princess Victoria's (Royal Irish Fusiliers) 0th Battalion *Died in War on 6 September 1916*
BOUZINCOURT COMMUNAL CEMETERY EXTENSION, France
Born and enlisted in Carrickfergus, resident of Belfast.

Kane, Thomas - Private
23638 Royal Irish fusiliers 1st Battalion *Killed while a prisoner of war on 29 June 1918*
NEUF-BRISACH COMMUNITY CEMETERY EXTENSION, France
21, Clonard Street, Belfast.

Kane, William - Private
10220 Royal Inniskilling Fusiliers 1st Battalion *Age 24 Died in War on 6 December 1916*
THIEPVAL MEMORIAL, France
Son of William and Agnes Kane, of 92, Mervue Street, Belfast.

Kane, William Henry - Rifleman
5449 Royal Irish Rifles 7th Battalion *Age 18 Killed in Action on 28 June 1916*
BOIS-CARRE MILITARY CEMETERY, HAISNES, France
Son of Samuel and Sarah Kane, of 63, Joseph Street, Belfast.

Kavanagh, William - Rifleman
10999 Royal Irish Rifles 1st Battalion *Died in War on 14 September 1916*
VERMELLES BRITISH CEMETERY, France
Born in Cork, enlisted Dublin, resident of Belfast.

Kayes, George - Private
4348 Royal Inniskilling Fusiliers 1st Battalion *Killed in Action on 16 May 1915*
ROYAL IRISH RIFLES GRAVEYARD, LAVENTIE, France
Born and enlisted in Belfast.

Kayes, Samuel - Private
201204 Canadian Infantry (Central Ontario Regiment) 3rd Battalion *Age 32 Died in War on 8 October 1916*
ADANAC MILITARY CEMETERY, MIRAUMONT, France
84, Matchett Street, Belfast. Had eight years service in the British Army before becoming a general labourer, Anglican in religion.

Kealey, Thomas - Private
6256 Royal Inniskilling Fusiliers 2nd Battalion *Killed in Action on 16 May 1915*
LE TOURET MEMORIAL, France
Born and enlisted in Belfast.

Keane, Joseph - Private
3349 Leinster Regiment 7th Battalion *Died in War on 2 September 1916*
THIEPVAL MEMORIAL, France
Born in Belfast. Lived in Dublin when enlisted.

Kearney, Charles - Private
21166 Bedfordshire Regiment 2nd Battalion *Died in War on 14 July 1916*
ST SEVER CEMETERY EXTENSION, ROUEN, France
Born and enlisted in Belfast. Formerly 49746, Royal Garrison Artillery.

Kearney, Francis John - Private
3368 Royal Inniskilling Fusiliers 7th Battalion *Died of Wounds on 28 April 1916*
PHILOSOPHE BRITISH CEMETERY, MAZINGARBE, France
Born and enlisted in Belfast.

Kearney, James - Private
3722 Royal Inniskilling Fusiliers 1st Battalion *Killed in Action on 22 March 1918*
POZIERES MEMORIAL, France
Born and enlisted in Belfast.

Kearney, John - Private
21462 Royal Irish Fusiliers 7th/8th Battalion *Age 26 Died in War on 17 August 1917*
TYNE COT MEMORIAL, Belgium
Son of Mrs. Mary Kearney, of 15, Springfield Road, Belfast.

Kearney, John - Rifleman
5645 Royal Irish Rifles 2nd Battalion *Died in War on 1 August 1915*
YPRES (MENIN GATE) MEMORIAL, Belgium
Husband of Annie Kearney, 4 Leginn Street, Ligoneil, Belfast.

Kearney, Patrick - Sergeant
4957 Irish Guards 1st Battalion *Age 22 Died in War on 30 November 1917*
CAMBRAI MEMORIAL, LOUVERVAL, France
Son of Michael Kearney, of 31, New Lodge Road, Belfast, and the late Mary Ann Kearney.
Awarded the Military Medal.

Kearney, Thomas Edwin - Leading Boatswain
218553(PO) H.M. Coastguard Raffney Head Station *Age 35 Died as a result of war on 1 January 1921*
ABERDEEN (TRINITY) CEMETERY, United Kingdom
Son of William and Jane Kearney, of 128, Oldpark Avenue, Belfast; husband of Lily Maud Kearney,
of Ballyduff, Lixnaw, County Kerry. Born at Cloughmills, County Antrim.

Kearney, William Arthur - Warrant Mechanician
Royal Navy HMS "Warspite" *Age 40 Died in War on 30 August 1916*
CARNMONEY CEMETERY, United Kingdom
Son of William and Jeannie Kearney, of Inverness Terrace, Cliftonville Road, Belfast; husband of
Agnes Kearney, of "Beach Vista" Larne Harbour. Holder of the Long Service and Good Conduct Medal.

Kearney, William E - Lance Corporal
15/12313 Royal Irish Rifles 15th Battalion *Age 25 Killed in Action on 27 November 1915*
FORCEVILLE COMMUNAL CEMETERY AND EXTENSION, France
Son of William E. and Mary Kearney, of Belfast.

Keatings, David - Rifleman
7585 Royal Irish Rifles 2nd Battalion *Age 20 Died of Wounds on 22 March 1916*
ECOIVRES MILITARY CEMETERY, MONT-ST. ELOI, France
Son of David and Rose Keatings, of Belfast.

Keatings, Thomas John - Sergeant
8057 Royal Irish Rifles 1st Battalion *Age 39 Died in War on 10 May 1915*
PONT-DU-HEM MILITARY CEMETERY, LA GORGUE, France
Husband of Annie Keatings, 57, Daiseyfield Street, Belfast.

Keefe, William John - Rifleman
14/6882 Royal Irish Rifles 10th Battalion *Age 34 Killed in Action on 1 July 1916*
AVELUY WOOD CEMETERY, MESNIL-MARTINSART, France
Son of John and Mary Keefe; husband of Alice Keefe, of 42, Derwent Street, Belfast.

Journey of Remembering

Keenan, Francis - Rifleman
6948 Royal Irish Rifles 14th Battalion *Killed in Action on 1 July 1916*
THIEPVAL MEMORIAL, France
Brother of Patrick Joseph Keenan who was also killed. The familiy lived at 4, Sussex Place, Belfast and were natives of County Cork.

Keenan, George Clements - Rifleman
15054 Royal Irish Rifles 9th Battalion *Age 29 Died in War on 2 July 1916*
THIEPVAL MEMORIAL, France
Son of Annie Keenan, of 94, Dover Street, Belfast and the late George C. Keenan.

Keenan, John - Private
50312 Cameron Highlanders 11th Battalion *Age 44 Killed in Action on 21 August 1918*
LE GRAND HASARD MILITARY CEMETERY, MORBECQUE, France
Born in Lochee, Dundee. Son of Patrick and Jane Keenan, of Belfast. Husband of Mary Ann Keenan. Enlisted on 6 September 1914.

Keenan, William John - Private
106512 Royal Army Medical Corps *Died in War on 15 June 1918*
BELFAST (DUNDONALD) CEMETERY, United Kingdom
Native of Belfast.

Keenan, Patrick Joseph - Lance Corporal
9871 Royal Irish Rifles "F" Company 1st Battalion *Age 21 Died in War on 5 March 1915*
ROYAL IRISH RIFLES GRAVEYARD, LAVENTIE, France
Son of Mr. W. and Mrs. K. M. Keenan, of 4, Sussex Place, Belfast. Born at Fermoy, County Cork. His brother, Francis was also killed.

Keenan, William - Greaser
Mercantile Marine S.S. "Bray Head" (Belfast)
Age 46 Died from exposure, as a result of an attack by an enemy submarine on 14 March 1917
TOWER HILL MEMORIAL, United Kingdom
Son of the late Patrick and Mary Keenan; husband of Sarah Jane Keenan (née Gordon), of 6, Economy Place, Belfast. Born at Killyleagh, County Down.

Keenan, William - Lance Corporal
19/84 Royal Irish Rifles 14th Battalion *Died of Wounds on 16 August 1917*
BRANDHOEK NEW MILITARY CEMETERY No.3, Belgium
19, Arundel Street, Belfast. His uncle, William, was also in the Army.

Keenan, William James - Private
25598 Canadian Infantry (Quebec Regiment) 14th Battalion *Age 36 Died in War on 17 April 1915*
PERTH CEMETERY (CHINA WALL), Belgium
Son of Josiah and Mary Keenan, of 25, Shankill Road, Belfast; husband of Elizabeth Keenan. Worked as a book-keeper in Canada and was a Presbyterian.

Keenan, William John - Private
106512 Royal Army Medical Corps *Died in War on 15 June 1918*
BELFAST (DUNDONALD) CEMETERY, United Kingdon
Born in Belfast, enlisted in County Down.

Keery, James - Rifleman
15956 Royal Irish Rifles 14th Battalion *Died in War on 27 September 1916*
BAILLEUL COMMUNAL CEMETERY EXTENSION (NORD), France
Born and enlisted in Belfast.

Keightley, Absalom - Private
22841 Royal Inniskilling Fusiliers 9th Battalion *Killed in Action on 1 July 1916*
THIEPVAL MEMORIAL, France
Beresford Street, Belfast.

Keightley, Philip Charles Russell - Captain
Royal Irish Artillery 262 Siege Battery *Age 24 Died as a result of war on 2 March 1919*
DRUMBEG (ST PATRICK) CHURCH OF IRELAND CHURCHYARD, United Kingdom
Born in Belfast the son of Sir Samuel Robert Keightley, Kt., M.A. LL.D., and of Lady Keightley, of The Drum House, Drumbeg. Educated privately and at Trinity College Dublin.
He was a distinguished athelete and had published a book, "Among the Guns".

Keilty, David John - Rifleman
10117 Royal Irish Rifles 1st Battalion *Died in War on 16 September 1916*
BELFAST (DUNDONALD) CEMETERY, United Kingdom
Born and enlisted in Newtownards, resident of Belfast.

Keir, Alexander Edmund - Private
7162 Canadian Infantry (Western Ontario Regiment) 1st Battalion *Age 19 Died of Wounds on 25 April 1915*
BOULOGNE EASTERN CEMETERY, France
Son of David and Minnie Keir, of 92, Waverley Road, Kew Beach, Toronto. Native of Belfast, Ireland.
Worked in Canada as a teamster, a Presbyterian.

Kell, John - Lance Corporal
420414 Canadian Infantry (Manitoba Regiment) 16th Battalion *Age 35 Accidentally killed on 17 August 1916*
LONGUENESSE (ST. OMER) SOUVENIR CEMETERY, France
Born Belfast. Husband of Isabella Kell, of 10, Westland Street, Belfast. A Presbyterian, he worked as a labourer in Canada.

Kells, David W - Private
27915 Canadian Infantry (Central Ontario Regiment) 15th Battalion *Died in War on 3 May 1915*
DUHALLOW A.D.S. CEMETERY, Belgium
Son of James and Mary Kells, of Belfast. Worked in shipping and was an Anglican.

Kells, George - Private
16747 Royal Inniskilling Fusiliers 7th Battalion *Died in War on 14 June 1915*
TIPPERARY (ST. MARY) CHURCHYARD, Republic of Ireland
Son of Mary Jane Kells, of 54, Hillman Street, Belfast.

Kells, John - Rifleman
12314 Royal Irish Rifles 8th Battalion *Died in War on 2 July 1916*
THIEPVAL MEMORIAL, France
Husband of Annie Kells, of 159, Woodstock Road, Belfast.

Kells, Samuel - Lance Corporal
18723 Machine Gun Corps (Infantry) 109th Company *Age 21 Killed in Action on 1 July 1916*
THIEPVAL MEMORIAL, France
Son of William and Maria Kells, of 105, Cambrai Street, Belfast.

JOURNEY OF REMEMBERING

Kelly, Andrew - Private
M2/269309 Army Service Corps Mechanical Transport Heavy Artillery *Died of Wounds on 24 October 1917*
DOZINGHEM MILITARY CEMETERY, Belgium
Son of Mary Kelly, of 35, Sherbrook Street, Belfast. Formerly 15058 Royal Irish Rifles

Kelly, Bernard - Private
8238 Highland Light Infantry 10th Battalion *Age 33 Died in War on 25 September 1915*
LOOS MEMORIAL, France
Nephew of Mrs. Mary Kelly, of 51, Lepper Street, Belfast. Served in the South African Campaign. Eight years service with the Royal Inniskilling Fusiliers.

Kelly, Bernard - Sapper
258639 Corps of Royal Engineers *Died on 14 July 1917*
NETLEY MILITARY CEMETERY, United Kingdom
Born and enlisted in Belfast.

Kelly, Charles - Private
5161 Royal Munster Fusiliers 1st Battalion *Age 25 Died in War on 2 March 1917*
BAILLEUL COMMUNAL CEMETERY EXTENSION (NORD), France
Son of Charles and Mary Kelly, of 25, Derry Street, Belfast.

Kelly, Charles - Private
8984 King's (Liverpool Regiment) 1st Battalion *Died in War on 4 November 1914*
YPRES (MENIN GATE) MEMORIAL, Belgium
Born in Belfast, enlisted Liverpool.

Kelly, Edward - Sergeant
20659 Royal Inniskilling Fusiliers 8th Battalion *Died in War on 27 April 1916*
DUD CORNER CEMETERY, LOOS, France
Native of Whitehouse, Belfast.

Kelly, Francis - Private
43313 Royal Scots Fusiliers 1st Battalion *Killed in Action on 2 November 1917*
FAVREUIL BRITISH CEMETERY, France
Son of the late Thomas and Elizabeth Kelly.

Kelly, James - Company Quartermaster Sergeant
7550 Royal Irish Rifles 2nd Battalion *Died in War on 10 June 1917*
KANDAHAR FARM CEMETERY, Belgium
37, Unity Street, Belfast.

Kelly, James - Private
40622 Lancashire Fusiliers 9th Battalion *Died in War on 7 October 1917*
DOZINGHEM MILITARY CEMETERY, Belgium
Born in Belfast, enlisted Dublin. Formerly 119697, Royal Field Artillery

Kelly, James - Private
41577 Royal Irish Fusiliers 9th Battalion *Age 24 Died in War on 5 September 1918*
ARNEKE BRITISH CEMETERY, France
Son of Sampson and Ellen Kelly, of 137, Manor Street, Belfast.

BELFAST BOOK OF HONOUR

Kelly, James - Private
9726 Royal Irish Regiment 6th Battalion *Died in War on 3 September 1916*
THIEPVAL MEMORIAL, France
Born in Belfast, enlisted in Swansea, Wales.

Kelly, John - Private
1601 Princess Patricia's Canadian Light Infantry (Eastern Ontario Regiment)
Age 34 Died in War on 8 May 1915
YPRES (MENIN GATE) MEMORIAL, Belgium
Son of John Kelly, of 9, Riversdale Street, Belfast, Ireland. Served 8 years with the Army before discharge and then re-enlistment. Anglican in religion.

Kelly, John - Private
6618 Royal Munster Fusiliers 8th Battalion *Age 37 Died in War on 9 September 1916*
THIEPVAL MEMORIAL, France
Husband of Maria Kelly, of 4, Maralin Street, Belfast.

Kelly, John - Private
72270 Machine Gun Corps 31st Battalion *Killed in Action on 29 October 1918*
DIVISIONAL COLLECTING POST CEMETERY AND EXTENSION, Belgium
Son of William and Jane, 11, Perth Street, Belfast.

Kelly, Joseph - Rifleman
10399 Royal Irish Rifles 2nd Battalion *Age 20 Died in War on 1 March 1915*
LOKER CHURCHYARD, Belgium
Son of William Kelly, of 3, Frederick Lane, Belfast.

Kelly, Joseph - Rifleman
5854 Royal Irish Rifles 14th Battalion *Died in War on 16 August 1917*
NEW IRISH FARM CEMETERY, Belgium
Ward of Mrs Agnes Moore, 44, Sidney Street, Belfast.

Kelly, Joseph - Rifleman
16642 Royal Irish Rifles 9th Battalion *Age 42 Died in War on 14 December 1917*
ROCQUIGNY-EQUANCOURT ROAD BRITISH CEMETERY, MANANCOURT, France
Husband of Mary Anne Kelly, of 136, Boundary Street, Belfast.

Kelly, Patrick - Private
27781 Duke of Edinburgh's (Wiltshire Regiment) 6th Battalion *Died in War on 10 April 1918*
BETHUNE TOWN CEMETERY, France
Born in Mullingar, enlisted Monaghan, resident of Belfast. Formerly 23940 Royal Irish Fusiliers.

Kelly, Patrick J - Private
18221 Royal Irish Fusiliers 7th Battalion *Killed in Action on 29 April 1916*
LOOS MEMORIAL, France
16, Turin Street, Belfast. Commended by the Commander of the 16th (Irish) Division, General Hickie, for "outstanding gallantry".

Kelly, Peter - Private
23757 Royal Inniskilling Fusiliers 7th Battalion *Died in War on 4 April 1916*
PHILOSOPHE BRITISH CEMETERY, MAZINGARBE, France
16, Frere Street, Belfast.

JOURNEY OF REMEMBERING

Kelly, Robert - Rifleman
1049 Royal Irish Rifles 8th Battalion *Died in War on 13 July 1916*
CAUDRY OLD COMMUNAL CEMETERY, France
Born and enlisted in Belfast.

Kelsall, Joseph - Private
10526 Royal Inniskilling Fusiliers 2nd Battalion *Age 19 Died in War on 17 March 1915*
WOBURN ABBEY CEMETERY, CUINCHY, France
Son of Mrs. Elizabeth Kelsall, of 52, Ivan Street, Belfast.

Kelsey, Henry - Cook
Mercantile Marine S.S. "Eveleen" (Belfast) *Age 32 Presumed drowned on 6 May 1918*
TOWER HILL MEMORIAL, United Kingdom
Son of John and Mary Kelsey (née Larbin), of Duncairn Gardens, Belfast. Born at Dublin.

Kelso, John - Private
111 Princess Patricia's Canadian Light Infantry (Eastern Ontario Regiment) *Died in War on 8 May 1915*
YPRES (MENIN GATE) MEMORIAL, Belgium
Mother, Rachel, lived at Cupar Street Belfast. Had served 12 years in the Royal Inniskilling Fusiliers
and thereafter worked as a labourer in Canada. A Presbyterian.

Kelso, John - Private
4674 Royal Inniskilling Fusiliers 2nd Battalion *Died in War on 11 November 1914*
PLOEGSTEERT MEMORIAL, Belgium
Son of Isaac Kelso, of 6, Britton Street, Belfast.

Kelso, Thomas - Private
3296 Royal Inniskilling Fusiliers 1st Battalion *Age 18 Killed in Action on 1 July 1916*
THIEPVAL MEMORIAL, France
Son of James and Sarah Kelso, of 50, City Street, Belfast.

Kennedy, Albert Douglas - Private
688217 Canadian Mounted Rifles (British Columbia Regiment) 2nd Battalion
Age 30 Died of Wounds, received at Vimy Ridge on 19 May 1917
BOULOGNE EASTERN CEMETERY, France
Son of William Kennedy, of Belvedere, Knock, Belfast, Ireland. He was a rancher in Canada
and Unitarian in religion.

Kennedy, Ambrose - Private
4475 Connaught Rangers 1st Battalion *Died in War on 27 April 1916*
AMARA WAR CEMETERY, Iraq
Son of Ambrose Kennedy, Glen Road, Belfast.

Kennedy, Archibald - Private
11729 Royal Inniskilling Fusiliers 6th Battalion *Age 29 Died in War on 7 December 1915*
DOIRAN MEMORIAL, Greece
Son of John and Sarah Kennedy, of Belfast.

Kennedy, David - Rifleman
2821 Royal Irish Rifles 15th Battalion *Died in War on 22 November 1917*
THIEPVAL MEMORIAL, France
Member of Westbourne Presbyterian Church, Belfast. Born at Greencastle, County Antrim.

BELFAST BOOK OF HONOUR

Kennedy, James - Private
1593 Leinster Regiment 2nd Battalion *Died in War on 8 July 1918*
BLEUE MAISON MILTARY CEMETERY, EPERLECQUES, France
Born and enlisted in Belfast.

Kennedy, James - Private
9348 Royal Inniskilling Fusiliers 1st Battalion *Killed in Action on 21 August 1915*
HELLES MEMORIAL, Turkey
Born and enlisted in Belfast.

Kennedy, James - Rifleman
9146 Royal Irish Rifles 2nd Battalion *Died in War on 11 May 1915*
YPRES (MENIN GATE) MEMORIAL, Belgium
Nephew of Elizabeth Duffy, of 10, Frederick Place, Belfast.

Kennedy, James - Second Lieutenant
Royal Irish Rifles *Killed in Action on 21 March 1918*
GRAND-SERAUCOURT BRITISH CEMETERY, France
Son of the Revd Professor Samuel G Kennedy and Christine Kennedy of Cromwell Road, Belfast. Educated at RBAI. Originally joined in the ranks. He was the brother of Rifleman William Kennedy who was also killed.

Kennedy, James - Sergeant
3168 Royal Inniskilling Fusiliers 7th/8th Battalion *Age 19 Killed in Action on 29 July 1918*
GODEWAERSVELDE BRITISH CEMETERY, France
Son of John and Mary Jane Kennedy, of 22, Earlscourt Street, Belfast.

Kennedy, John - Gunner
29516 Royal Garrison Artillery *Died in War on 19 July 1916*
HEBUTERNE MILITARY CEMETERY, France
Born in Belfast, enlisted Carrickfergus.

Kennedy, John - Private
24808 Machine Gun Corps (Infantry) 107th Company *Age 27 Died in War on 16 August 1917*
TYNE COT MEMORIAL, Belgium
Son of James and Elizabeth Kennedy, of 8, Westcott Street, Connswater, Belfast.

Kennedy, Joseph - Private
2829 Royal Inniskilling Fusiliers 4th Battalion attached 1st *Age 20 Died in War on 21 August 1915*
HELLES MEMORIAL, Turkey
Son of Isabella Kennedy, of 6, Disraeli Street, Belfast.

Kennedy, Michael - Private
2457 Connaught Rangers 6th Battalion *Died in War on 8 April 1916*
LOOS MEMORIAL, France
Born in Ballinakin, Queen's County, he was resident and enlisted in Belfast.

Kennedy, Patrick Joseph - Private
3825 Royal Irish Fusiliers 8th Battalion *Age 19 Killed in Action on 25 May 1916*
VERMELLES BRITISH CEMETERY, France
Son of John and Mary Kennedy, of Belfast.

Kennedy, Patrick - Private
12398 Royal Inniskilling Fusiliers 1st Battalion *Age 35 Died in War on 9 August 1916*
BEDFORD HOUSE CEMETERY, Belgium
Son of James and Mrs Kennedy of Belfast.

Kennedy, Peter - Stoker
1836U Royal Naval Reserve HMS "Queen Mary" *Age 33 Killed in Action at Battle of Jutland on 31 May 1916*
PORTSMOUTH NAVAL MEMORIAL, United Kingdom
Son of the late Frank and Jane Kennedy, of Ballymena, County Antrim; husband of Sarah Kennedy, of 26, Ritchie Street, York Road, Belfast.

Kennedy, Richard - Private
G/33 Royal Irish Rifles 2nd Battalion transferred to 513222 Labour Corps
Age 38 Killed in Action on 2 August 1918
TERLINCTHUN BRITISH CEMETERY, WIMILLE, France
Son of John and Mary Jane Kennedy, of Belfast.

Kennedy, Robert - Private
1049 Royal Irish Rifles 11th Battalion *Killed in Action on 1 July 1916*
THIEPVAL MEMORIAL, France
Husband of Annie Kennedy and father of five children, 8, Eton Street, Belfast.

Kennedy, Robert - Private
1592 Leinster Regiment 7th Battalion *Died in War on 2 August 1917*
YPRES (MENIN GATE) MEMORIAL, Belgium
40, Irish Street, Belfast. He was secretary of the Model Junior Football Club.

Kennedy, Robert - Private
3204 Royal Inniskilling Fusiliers 7th Battalion formerly 4th Battalion *Age 20 Died in War on 9 September 1916*
THIEPVAL MEMORIAL, France
Son of Robert and Marion Kennedy of 11, St. Andrew Square North, Belfast. Enlisted January 1914.

Kennedy, Robert - Rifleman
10/15068 Royal Irish Rifles 10th Battalion *Died from cardiac failure on 30 October 1918*
DURRINGTON CEMETERY, United Kingdom
7, Malt Street, Belfast. Native of Caledon, County Tyrone.

Kennedy, Robert Henry - Rifleman
13050 Royal Irish Rifles 2nd Battalion *Killed In Action on 2 May 1915*
RIDGE WOOD MILITARY CEMETERY, Belgium
Born and enlisted in Belfast.

Kennedy, S - Sapper
19 Canadian Engineers 10th Fortress Company *Age 21 Died of pneumonia on 3 April 1916*
HALIFAX (MOUNT OLIVET) CEMETERY, Canada
Son of Mrs. Florence Kennedy, of 2, Waterproof Street, Oldpark Road, Belfast, Ireland.

Kennedy, Samuel - Lance Corporal
24852 Royal Dublin Fusiliers 8th Battalion *Died in War on 30 October 1916*
STOURBRIDGE CEMETERY, United Kingdom
Born in Belfast. Lived in Dublin when enlisted.

Kennedy, William - Rifleman
14/16657 Royal Irish Rifles 14th Battalion *Died in War on 7 June 1917*
SPANBROEKMOLEN BRITISH CEMETERY, Belgium
Son of The Rev. S. G. Kennedy, of Cromwell House, Cromwell Road, Belfast.
His brother, Second Lieutenant James Kennedy, was also killed.

Kennedy, William Edward - Company Sergeant Major
9301 Royal Inniskilling Fusiliers 1st Battalion *Age 26 Died in War on 9 August 1916*
YPRES (MENIN GATE) MEMORIAL, Belgium
Son of the late William and Elizabeth Kennedy, of 10, Derlett Street, Belfast.

Kennedy, William Wolfe - Rifleman
7223 Royal Irish Rifles 2nd Battalion *Age 25 Died in War on 11 November 1914*
YPRES (MENIN GATE) MEMORIAL, Belgium
Son of John and Sarah Kennedy, of 57, Island Street, Belfast.

Kenny, Frank - Corporal
49993 Northumberland Fusiliers *Age 26 Died as a result of war on 17 November 1918*
BELFAST (MILLTOWN) ROMAN CATHOLIC CEMETERY, United Kingdom
Son of Mrs. Mary Kenny, of 11, Walbeck Street, Belfast.

Kent, William George - Private
10135 Royal Inniskilling Fusiliers 1st Battalion *Age 25 Died in War on 22 May 1915*
TWELVE TREE COPSE CEMETERY, Turkey
Son of Richard and Harriett Kent, of 38, Perth Street, Belfast.

Kernaghan, James - Sergeant
19584 Royal Irish Rifles 15th Battalion *Died in War on 21 March 1918*
POZIERES MEMORIAL, France
Born in Muckamore, enlisted Antrim, resident of Belfast.

Kernaghan, Robert - Rifleman
8637 Royal Irish Rifles 2nd Battalion *Age 17 Died in War on 9 July 1916*
THIEPVAL MEMORIAL, France
Son of Christopher and Sarah Kernaghan, of 130, Balfour Avenue, Belfast.

Kernaghan, William J - Rifleman
9363 Royal Irish Rifles *Died in War on 7 July 1918*
BELFAST CITY CEMETERY, United Kingdom
14, Egeria Street, Belfast.

Kerr, Alexander - Rifleman
15072 Royal Irish Rifles 12th Battalion *Age 24 Killed in Action on 25 October 1918*
HARLEBEKE NEW BRITISH CEMETERY, Belgium
Son of Elizabeth Kerr, of 28, Linview Street, Grosvenor Road, Belfast, and the late Robert Kerr.

Kerr, Alfred - Rifleman
1543 Royal Irish Rifles 10th Battalion *Killed in Action on 1 July 1916*
CONNAUGHT CEMETERY, THIEPVAL, France
Born and enlisted in Belfast.

Kerr, Bernard - Private
20949 Princess Victoria's (Royal Irish Fusiliers) 9th Battalion *Died in War on 12 April 1918*
TYNE COT MEMORIAL, Belgium
Born and enlisted in Belfast. Formerly 3652 Connaught Rangers.

Kerr, Ernest - Private
22659 Royal Inniskilling Fusiliers 9th Battalion *Killed in Action on 16 August 1917*
TYNE COT MEMORIAL, Belgium
Born and enlisted in Belfast.

Kerr, Henry - Private
34192 Royal Warwickshire Regiment 1st Battalion *Died in War on 23 December 1917*
MONCHY BRITISH CEMETERY MONCHY-LE-PREUX, France
Born and enlisted in Belfast. Formerly 4209 Hussars.

Kerr, Hugh Sloan - Engine Room Artificer
1352EA Royal Naval Reserve HMS "Invincible" *Age 26 Killed in Action at Battle of Jutland on 31 May 1916*
PORTSMOUTH NAVAL MEMORIAL, United Kingdom
Son of Robert and Ellen Jane Kerr; husband of Elizabeth Catherine Kerr,
of 35, Woodcot Avenue, Bloomfield, Belfast.

Kerr, James - Lieutenant
Royal Irish Rifles 3rd Battalion attached 1st Battalion *Age 24 Killed in Action 21 March 1918*
POZIERES MEMORIAL, France
Son of Francis Kerr of Myrtlefield Park. Educated at Clongowes Wood College and later a member
of Queen's University Officer Training Corps. Had been Mentioned in Despatches.
His brother, John, was killed with the Australian Infantry in 1917.

Kerr, James - Rifleman
12985 Royal Irish Rifles 8th Battalion *Age 23 Died in War on 2 July 1916*
THIEPVAL MEMORIAL, France
Son of Mrs. Isabella Martin, of 43, Willowfield Street, Belfast.

Kerr, James - Rifleman
15039 Royal Irish Rifles 10th Battalion *Died in War on 4 December 1915*
THIEPVAL MEMORIAL, France
Born and enlisted in Belfast.

Kerr, John - Corporal
1598 Leinster Regiment 7th Battalion *Died in War on 28 March 1916*
DUD CORNER CEMETERY, LOOS, France
Born and enlisted in Belfast.

Kerr, John - Lance Corporal
25633 Royal Scots (Lothian Regiment) 11th Battalion *Died in War on 12 April 1917*
BROWN'S COPSE CEMETERY, ROEUX, France
Born and enlisted in Belfast.

Kerr, John - Private
12144 Highland Light Infantry 2nd Battalion *Age 18 Died in War on 17 May 1915*
LE TOURET MEMORIAL, France
Son of Mrs. Francis Kerr, of 23, Kenmare Street, Belfast.

Kerr, John - Private
19883 Princess Victoria's (Royal Irish Fusiliers) 6th Battalion *Died in War on 23 October 1915*
DOIRAN MEMORIAL, *Greece*
Born in Belfast, enlisted Carrickfergus.

Kerr, John - Private
3849 Australian Infantry 21st Battalion *Killed in Action on 20 March 1917*
VILLERS-BRETONNEUX MEMORIAL, *France*
Son of Frank Kerr of Myrtlefield Park, Belfast. His brother, Lieutenant James Kerr, of the Royal Irish Rifles, was killed in 1918.

Kerr, John - Third Engineer
Mercantile Marine S.S. "Llongwen" (Cardiff)
Age 34 Drowned, as a result of an attack by an enemy submarine on 18 July 1916
TOWER HILL MEMORIAL, *United Kingdom*
Husband of Constance Kerr, of 19, Fields Park Road, Cardiff. Born in Belfast.

Kerr, Joseph - Private
1596 Leinster Regiment 7th Battalion *Age 32 Died of Wounds on 23 September 1916*
BELFAST (MILLTOWN) ROMAN CATHOLIC CEMETERY, *United Kingdom*
Husband of Margaret Kerr, of 67, Vere Street, Belfast.

Kerr, Patrick - Lance Sergeant
11812 King's (Liverpool Regiment) 1st Battalion *Died in War on 1 August 1916*
THIEPVAL MEMORIAL, *France*
Born and enlisted in Belfast.

Kerr, Patrick - Private
8305 Irish Guards 1st Battalion *Died in War on 9 October 1917*
TYNE COT MEMORIAL, *Belgium*
56, Pound Street, Belfast.

Kerr, Richard - Private
10683 Royal Inniskilling Fusiliers 1st Battalion *Age 20 Killed in Action on 29 June 1915*
TWELVE TREE COPSE CEMETERY, *Turkey*
Son of John Kerr, of 12, Temple Street, Belfast.

Kerr, Robert - Private
18301 South Lancashire Regiment 6th Battalion *Died in War on 16 April 1918*
BAGHDAD (NORTH GATE) WAR CEMETERY, *Iraq*
Born in Belfast, enlisted in Warrington, Lancashire.

Kerr, Robert Ernest - Private
252109 Canadian Infantry (Alberta Regiment) 49th Battalion *Age 33 Died of Wounds on 31 August 1918*
LIGNY-ST. FLOCHEL BRITISH CEMETERY, AVERDOINGT, *France*
Son of James and Rosa M. Kerr, of 117, Wellesley Avenue, Belfast, Ireland, and of Swift Current, Saskatchewan, Canada. A single man, a Presbyterian and a painter by trade.

Kerr, Samuel Currie - Private
31560 Royal Inniskilling Fusiliers 5th Battalion *Killed in Action on 8 October 1918*
PROSPECT HILL CEMETERY, GOUY, *France*
Born and enlisted in Belfast.

Kerr, Thomas - Assistant Steward
Mercantile Marine S.S. "Agnete" (London)
Age 15 Drowned, as a result of an attack by an enemy submarine on 24 April 1918
TOWER HILL MEMORIAL, *United Kingdom*
Son of Mary Duignan (formerly Kerr), of 35, Kilronan Street, Belfast, and the late Thomas Kerr. Born at Cavan.

Kerr, Thomas - Chief Steward
Mercantile Marine S.S. "Agnete" (London)
Age 35 Drowned, as a result of an attack by an enemy submarine on 24 April 1918
TOWER HILL MEMORIAL, *United Kingdom*
Husband of Mary Kerr, of 35, Kilronan Street.

Kerr, Thomas - Driver
22900 Royal Field Artillery 129th Battery 42nd Brigade *Age 32 Died in War on 5 May 1917*
TILLOY BRITISH CEMETERY, TILLOY-LES-MOFFLAINES, *France*
Son of J. Kerr, of Belfast; husband of Florence Kerr, of 40, Manor Road, Bishopston, Bristol.

Kerr, Thomas - Greaser
Mercantile Marine S.S. "Cambric" (Hull)
Age 36 Drowned, as a result of an attack by an enemy submarine on 31 October 1917
TOWER HILL MEMORIAL, *United Kingdom*
Son of the late Alexander and Nancy Kerr. Born in Belfast.

Kerr, William - Rifleman
18022 Royal Irish Rifles 14th Battalion *Age 22 Died in War on 16 August 1917*
LIJSSENTHOEK MILITARY CEMETERY, *Belgium*
Son of the late Thomas and Jane Kerr, of Whiterock, Belfast.

Kerr, William James - Private
40296 King's Own Scottish Borderers 7/8th Battalion *Died in War on 15 September 1916*
THIEPVAL MEMORIAL, *France*
Born in Belfast, enlisted Lanark, Scotland. Formerly 7237, Highland Light Infantry

Kerr, William Johnstone - Stoker First Class
SS/105934 Royal Navy HMS "Aboukir" *Died in War on 22 September 1914*
CHATHAM NAVAL MEMORIAL, *United Kingdom*
Son of John and Mary Kerr, 12, Temple Street, Belfast.

Kershaw, William Henry - Private
8089 Royal Irish Regiment 2nd Battalion *Died in War on 24 May 1915*
VLAMERTINGHE NEW MILITARY CEMETERY, *Belgium*
Born in Belfast, enlisted Barrow-in-Furness, England.

Kertland, Edwin Blow - Second Lieutenant
Royal Irish Rifles 3rd Battalion attached 2nd Battalion *Age 19 Killed in Action on 16 June 1915*
YPRES (MENIN GATE) MEMORIAL, *Belgium*
Son of Edwin Happer Kertland and Meta Blow Kertland, of Dunnimarle, Knockdene Park, Belfast. A member of Queen's University OTC. Slightly wounded in March 1915 and then declared missing in June. Subsequently accepted as having died due to machine-gun fire.

Kidd, Frank - Rifleman
18023 Royal Irish Rifles "B" Company 12th Battalion *Age 21 Killed in Action on 1 July 1916*
SERRE ROAD CEMETERY No.2, France
Son of William and Margaret Kidd, of "Fernagh Cottage", Whiteabbey, Belfast.

Kidd, George - Rifleman
371263 London Regiment (Post Office Rifles) 8th Battalion *Age 23 Killed in Action on 20 July 1917*
OAK DUMP CEMETERY, Belgium
Son of James and Matilda Kidd, of 21, Abbot Street, Belfast, a Postman.

Kilgariff, Henry - Lance Corporal
8680 Royal Irish Rifles 2nd Battalion *Age 34 Died in War on 28 April 1916*
AUBIGNY COMMUNAL CEMETERY EXTENSION, France
Son of Mary and the late Patrick Kilgariff, of Belfast.

Killen, Edward Osborne Brice - Lieutenant
Royal Engineers 71st Field Company *Died in War on 15 January 1917*
AMARA WAR CEMETERY, Iraq
Native of Belfast.

Killip, Robert Douglas - Sergeant
26803 King's (Liverpool Regiment) 4th Battalion *Died in War on 20 May 1917*
ARRAS MEMORIAL, France
Born in Belfast, enlisted in Douglas, Isle of Man.

Killops, Joseph - Rifleman
8145 Royal Irish Rifles 1st Battalion *Age 27 Killed in Action on 7 December 1914*
RUE-DU-BACQUEROT (13th LONDON) GRAVEYARD, LAVENTIE, France
Husband of Margaret Killops, of 81, Palmer Street, Crumlin Road, Belfast.

Kilpatrick, Robert - Sergeant
28642 Canterbury Regiment New Zealand Expeditionary Force 2nd Battalion
Age 37 Killed in Action on 23 March 1917
LA PLUS DOUVE FARM CEMETERY, Belgium
Son of William and Annie Kilpatrick, of 24, Eia Street, Belfast, Ireland.

Kilpatrick, William John - Sapper
57469 Royal Engineers *Died in War on 31 March 1915*
BELFAST CITY CEMETERY, United Kingdom
Born and enlisted in Belfast.

Kincaid, Hubert George - Private
115437 Canadian Infantry (Manitoba Regiment) 27th Battalion *Died of Wounds on 8 October 1918*
BUCQUOY ROAD CEMETERY, FICHEUX, France
Husband of Margaret E. Kincaid, of Denmark, Nova Scotia. Born in Belfast, Ireland.
He had served in South Africa, thereafter worked as a book-keeper and was an Anglican.

Kincaid, William - Rifleman
197 Royal Irish Rifles 10th Battalion *Died of Wounds on 28 August 1916*
BAILLEUL COMMUNAL CEMETERY EXTENSION (NORD), France
His father and family lived at 199, Mayo Street, Belfast.

Journey of Remembering

King, Edward - Rifleman
15/12989 Royal Irish Rifles 15th Battalion *Age 18 Died in War on 22 January 1916*
SUCRERIE MILITARY CEMETERY, COLINCAMPS, France
Son of Thomas and Annie King, of 8, Hillview Street, Oldpark Road, Belfast.

King, Gerald - Sergeant
20654 Royal Inniskilling Fusiliers 7th/8th Battalion *Age 22 Killed in Action on 21 March 1918*
POZIERES MEMORIAL, France
Son of Martin King, of Kentucky, U.S.A., and Kathleen King, of Belfast.
Awarded both the Distinguished Conduct Medal and the Military Medal.

King, James - Gunner
915 Royal Garrison Artillery *Died in War on 12 September 1917*
CHESTER FARM CEMETERY, Belgium
Born in Belfast, enlisted Edinburgh.

King, John - Private
19290 Royal Scots Fusiliers 6/7th Battalion *Died in War on 24 April 1917*
ARRAS MEMORIAL, France
Born in Belfast, enlisted Glasgow.

King, John Gerald - Private
46896 Leicestershire Regiment 2/4th Battalion *Died in War on 15 April 1918*
BRAINE-LE-COMTE COMMUNAL CEMETERY, Belgium
Born in Belfast, enlisted Leeds.

King, Robert John George - Stoker First Class
SS/115695 Royal Navy HMS "Indefatigable" *Age 21 Killed in Action at Battle of Jutland on 31 May 1916*
PORTSMOUTH NAVAL MEMORIAL, United Kingdom
Son of Robert and Mary Isabella Rachel King, of 7, Ravenhill Street, Belfast.

King, Samuel - Private
5559 Royal Irish Rifles 2nd Battalion *Age 47 Died in War on 16 June 1916*
YPRES (MENIN GATE) MEMORIAL, Belgium
Son of James King, of 35, Eighth Street, Belfast.

King, William - Lance Corporal
18030 Royal Irish Rifles 14th Battalion *Age 33 Killed in Action on 1 July 1916*
THIEPVAL MEMORIAL, France
Son of the late James and Mary J. King, of Belfast.

King, William James - Corporal
148647 Canadian Infantry (Manitoba Regiment) 78th Battalion *Age 20 Died of Wounds on 14 April 1917*
LAPUGNOY MILITARY CEMETERY, France
Son of the Rev. J. L. and Mrs. King, of Roblin, Manitoba, Canada. Born at Belfast, Ireland.
A Methodist he was a single man and a school teacher.

Kingcross, G - Trimmer
7876/TS Royal Naval Reserve HMS "Crescent" *Died in War on 28 November 1919*
DUNDEE EASTERN NECROPOLIS, United Kingdom
Son of William and Mary Kingcross, of 13, Eton Street, Agnes Street, Belfast.

Kinkead, Alfred - Rifleman
12992 Royal Irish Rifles 15th Battalion *Died in War on 28 March 1918*
ROYE NEW BRITISH CEMETERY, France
Born and enlisted in Belfast.

Kinkead, John - Private
4643 Royal Inniskilling Fusiliers 1st Battalion *Killed in Action on 1 July 1916*
THIEPVAL MEMORIAL, France
80, Oregon Street, Belfast.

Kinnaird, Samuel - Sapper
45425 Corps of Royal Engineers 78th Field Company *Died in War on 31 March 1918*
BOUZINCOURT RIDGE CEMETERY, ALBERT, France
Born and enlisted in Belfast.

Kinnear, William John - Rifleman
15076 Royal Irish Rifles 8th Battalion *Died in War on 2 July 1916*
THIEPVAL MEMORIAL, France
Born and enlisted in Belfast.

Kinner, David - Driver
31191 Royal Field Artillery 17th Brigade *Died in War on 18 July 1917*
BLEUET FARM CEMETERY, Belgium
Husband of Hannah Kinner, 51, Wilton Street, Belfast. His father also served.

Kinney, James - Rifleman
9711 Royal Irish Rifles 4th Battalion attached 2nd Battalion *Age 27 Died in War on 21 May 1917*
BAILLEUL COMMUNAL CEMETERY EXTENSION (NORD), France
Son of Agnes Brady (formerly Kinney), of 28, Ivy Row, Whitehouse, Belfast, and the late John Kinney.

Kinney, Laurence - Private
6570 Royal Scots Fusiliers 1st Battalion *Died in War on 1 January 1915*
YPRES (MENIN GATE) MEMORIAL, Belgium
Born in Belfast, enlisted Kilmarnock, Scotland.

Kinnier, John - Private
640161 Canadian Infantry (Eastern Ontario Regiment) 38th Battalion *Age 24 Died in War on 30 October 1917*
YPRES (MENIN GATE) MEMORIAL, Belgium
Son of Thomas Archer Kinnier and Rose Ellen Kinnier, of 3, East Bread Street, Connswater, Belfast, Ireland. A Methodist, he worked as paper maker.

Kinsman, Cecil Henry - Second Lieutenant
Royal Engineers Cheshire Field Company *Age 30 Died in War on 28 March 1916*
RENINGHELST NEW MILITARY CEMETERY, Belgium
Originally served in the 5th Battalion Connaught Rangers. Killed at Eloi, Belgium. Son of Henry and Annie Kinsman, of 1, Ashgrove Villas, Glenburn Park, Belfast. Born Bedford, England.

Kirk, Frank - Sergeant
8642 Royal Irish Fusiliers 1st Battalion *Age 29 Died in War on 2 May 1915*
YPRES (MENIN GATE) MEMORIAL, Belgium
Son of Mrs. Ellen Kirk, of 1, Euston Street, Belfast.

Kirk, James - Rifleman
15080 Royal Irish Rifles 9th Battalion *Age 21 Killed in Action on 1 July 1916*
THIEPVAL MEMORIAL, France
Son of Thomas and Mary Kirk, of 16, Springfield Village, Belfast.

Kirk, Matthew - Rifleman
6518 Royal Irish Rifles 16th Battalion *Died in War on 25 May 1918*
POZIERES MEMORIAL, France
10, Coyle Street, Belfast. Member of Clifton Street Presbyterian Church.

Kirkland, George - Lieutenant
Australian Machine Gun Corps 4th Company *Age 27 Died in War on 13 April 1917*
HEM-LENGLET COMMUNAL CEMETERY, France
Son of James and Frances Kirkland; husband of May Kirkland, of 248, Newtownards Road, Belfast, Ireland.

Kirkpatrick, Albert V - Sapper
64090 Royal Engineers 122nd Field Company *Killed in Action on 31 August 1916*
BERKS CEMETERY EXTENSION, Belgium
Native of Belfast.

Kirkpatrick, Alexander - Lance Corporal
14882 Royal Inniskilling Fusiliers 11th Battalion *Age 24 Killed in action on 1 July 1916*
THIEPVAL MEMORIAL, France
Brother of Mary Dunlop, 37, Queen Victoria Street, Belfast.

Kirkpatrick, Daniel - Rifleman
707 Royal Irish Rifles 8th Battalion *Died in War on 11 June 1916*
AUTHUILE MILITARY CEMETERY, France
Born and enlisted in Belfast.

Kirkpatrick, David - Lance Corporal
12739 Royal Inniskilling Fusiliers 1st Battalion *Died in War on 20 October 1918*
HARLEBEKE NEW BRITISH CEMETERY, Belgium
Son of David and Mary A. Kirkpatrick, of 72, Cosgrave Street, Belfast.

Kirkpatrick, Hugh - Private
240994 Seaforth Highlanders 1st/2th Battalion *Died in War on 13 February 1917*
ETAPLES MILITARY CEMETERY, France
Son of Hugh Kirkpatrick, 10, Constance Street, Belfast.

Kirkpatrick, John - Private
PLY/17752 Royal Marine Light Infantry 2nd R.M. Battalion Royal Naval Division
Age 19 Died of Wounds on 27 November 1916
WIMEREUX COMMUNAL CEMETERY, France
Son of Margaret Kirkpatrick, 122, Disraeli Street, Belfast. Two brothers also served.

Kirkpatrick, John - Rifleman
10782 Royal Irish Rifles transferred to 333738 Southern Command Labour Corps
Age 20 Died in War on 27 December 1917
SHEFFIELD (BURNGREAVE) CEMETERY, United Kingdom
Son of James Kirkpatrick, of 59, Castlereagh Road, Belfast.

Kirkpatrick, John - Rifleman
R/515 Royal Irish Rifles 6th Battalion *Age 28 Died in War on 3 December 1915*
CARMAVEY BURIAL GROUND, COUNTY ANTRIM, United Kingdom
42, Burnaby Street, Belfast.

Kirkpatrick, John Joseph - Private
15172 Royal Irish Fusiliers 7th Battalion *Age 18 Died of Wounds on 25 July 1916*
DOULLENS COMMUNAL CEMETERY EXTENSION No.1, France
Son of John and Bridget Kirkpatrick, of 37, York Street, Belfast.

Kirkpatrick, Joseph - Rifleman
12327 Royal Irish Rifles 15th Battalion *Died in War on 21 February 1916*
SUCRERIE MILITARY CEMETERY, COLINCAMPS, France
Born and enlisted in Belfast.

Kirkpatrick, Robert - Corporal
12698 Royal Inniskilling Fusiliers 6th Battalion *Age 25 Died in War on 10 September 1916*
DOIRAN MEMORIAL, Greece
Son of Jessie Kirkpatrick, of 23, Main Street, Greencastle and the late James Kirkpatrick. Born Belfast.

Kirkpatrick, Robert - Private
213326 Canadian Infantry (Quebec Regiment) 87th Battalion *Age 27 Died in War on 16 November 1917*
NINE ELMS BRITISH CEMETERY, Belgium
Son of Hugh Warner Kirkpatrick, of Belfast, Ireland; husband of Charlotte Kirkpatrick,
of 10/3, Louis Avenue, Windsor, Ontario, Canada. He had worked as a labourer and was a Presbyterian.

Kirkpatrick, Samuel - Rifleman
9126 Royal Irish Rifles 2nd Battalion *Killed In Action on 9 July 1916*
THIEPVAL MEMORIAL, France
Born and enlisted in Belfast.

Kirkwood, George - Rifleman
15085 Royal Irish Rifles B Company 14th Battalion *Age 22 Died of Wounds on 9 May 1916*
FORCEVILLE COMMUNAL CEMETERY AND EXTENSION, France
Son of Mary and the late James Kirkwood, of Belfast.

Kirkwood, John - Lance Corporal
14/639 Royal Irish Rifles 9th Battalion *Age 39 Killed in Action on 1 July 1916*
THIEPVAL MEMORIAL, France
Husband of Elizabeth Kirkwood, of 15, Argyle Street, Belfast.

Kirkwood, William Hugh - Private
71817 Canadian Infantry (Manitoba Regiment) 27th Battalion *Age 27 Died in War on 3 May 1917*
VIMY MEMORIAL, France
Son of Mr. and Mrs. James E. Kirkwood, of Ballysillan Road, Belfast, Ireland.
A Presbyterian, he was born in County Antrim and worked as a dyer and finisher.

Knowles, Robert George - Rifleman
20529 Royal Irish Rifles 1st Battalion *Died in War on 2 October 1918*
TYNE COT MEMORIAL, Belgium
Born and enlisted in Belfast. Formerly 3793, Seaforth Highlanders.

Knox, Charles - Gunner
71959 Royal Horse Artillery and Royal Field Artillery *Died in War on 16 September 1916*
LONGUEVAL ROAD CEMETERY, France
Born and enlisted in Belfast.

Knox, Herbert - Private
32497 King's Own (Royal Lancaster Regiment) "C" Company1st/4th Battalion
Age 19 Killed in Action on 9 July 1918
HOUCHIN BRITISH CEMETERY, France
Son of Martha Knox, of 19, Ashmore Street, Belfast, and the late William Knox.

Knox, John Stanley - Second Lieutenant
Royal Inniskilling Fusiliers 7th Battalion *Age 25 Died of Wounds on 11 July 1916*
PHILOSOPHE BRITISH CEMETERY, MAZINGARBE, France
Son of Joseph Knox, of 2, York Villas, Cable Road, Whitehead, County Antrim. Native of Belfast.

Knox, William - Lance Corporal
8522 Royal Irish Rifles 2nd Battalion *Died in War on 7 September 1916*
THIEPVAL MEMORIAL, France
71, Lilliput Street, Belfast.

Kyle, Joseph - Rifleman
16661 Royal Irish Rifles 14th Battalion *Killed In Action on 1 July 1916*
THIEPVAL MEMORIAL, France
10, Belgravia Avenue, Belfast.

Kyle, Thomas - Lance Sergeant
726 Royal Irish Rifles 8th Battalion *Age 38 Killed in Action on 7 June 1917*
LONE TREE CEMETERY, Belgium
Son of the late Samuel and Jane Kyle; husband of Eveleen Kyle, of 27, Mountcashel Street, Belfast.

Kyles, James - Private
11098 Royal Inniskilling Fusiliers 2nd Battalion *Killed in Action on 16 May 1915*
LE TOURET MEMORIAL, France
Born in Belfast the son of James Kyles, of Irish Quarter, Carrickfergus.

Laird, Alexander - Sapper
43504 Royal Engineers 76th Field Company *Died in War on 8 October 1915*
LOOS MEMORIAL, France
151, Belmont Road, Belfast.

Laird, James - Rifleman
201 Royal Irish Rifles "C" Company 1st Battalion *Age 19 Died of Wounds on 23 October 1918*
DUHALLOW A.D.S. CEMETERY, Belgium
Son of William John and Jane Laird, of Belfast.

Laird, Robert - Rifleman
10585 Royal Irish Rifles "D" Company 6th Battalion *Age 22 Died in War on 11 August 1915*
HELLES MEMORIAL, Turkey
Son of Eliza Laird, of 11, Pernau Street, Belfast, and the late Richard Laird.

Laird, Thomas - Private
92224 Royal Fusiliers (City of London Regiment) 7th Battalion
Died in War on 28 September 1918
VIS-EN-ARTOIS BRITISH CEMETERY, HAUCOURT, France
Born and enlisted in Belfast. Formerly T/4/045334 Army Service Corps.

Laird, William - Private
12926 Royal Irish Fusiliers 6th Battalion *Died in War on 15 August 1915*
HELLES MEMORIAL, Turkey
Husband of Sarah Laird, 21 Richmond Street, Belfast.

Lamble, Thomas - Rifleman
S/3000 Rifle Brigade (The Prince Consort's Own) 11th Battalion
Died in War on 10 February 1917
THIEPVAL MEMORIAL, France
Born in Belfast, enlisted London.

Lamont, William - Rifleman
17/1461 Royal Irish Rifles 10th Battalion *Age 40 Killed in Action on 26 April 1916*
LOUVENCOURT MILITARY CEMETERY, France
Husband of Sarah Jane Lamont, of 21, Buller Street, Oldpark Road, Belfast.

Lane, Sidney - Corporal
3526 Irish Guards 1st Battalion *Died in War on 29 May 1915*
BOULOGNE EASTERN CEMETERY, France
11, Coolderry Street, Belfast. Born in Newtownards.

Lang, John - Fireman And Trimmer
Mercantile Marine S.S. "Cabotia" (Glasgow)
Age 43 Drowned, as a result of an attack by an enemy submarine on 20 October 1916
TOWER HILL MEMORIAL, United Kingdom
Husband of Harriet Lang (née Henry), of 34, Jennymount Street, Belfast.

Lannary, William - Sapper
155820 Corps of Royal Engineers 252nd Tunnelling Company formerly 13456 Scottish Rifles
Died in War on 13 November 1916
THIEPVAL MEMORIAL, France
Born in Belfast. Lived in Glasgow when enlisted.

Lannigan, Robert - Private
Royal Inniskilling Fusiliers *Died in War on 16 August 1917*
49 Disraeli Street, Belfast.

Lappin, Daniel - Rifleman
54047 Royal Irish Rifles 2nd Battalion *Killed In Action on 16 June 1915*
YPRES (MENIN GATE) MEMORIAL, Belgium
Born in Belfast the son of William and Jane Lappin, of 12, Millview, Chapel Hill, Lisburn.

Lappin, James - A/Corporal
49501 Royal Horse Artillery and Royal Field Artillery *Died in War on 18 October 1917*
POELCAPELLE BRITISH CEMETERY, Belgium
Born in Belfast, enlisted Glasgow.

Lappin, John George Henry - Private
7587 Suffolk Regiment 2nd Battalion *Age 28 Died in War on 20 July 1916*
THIEPVAL MEMORIAL, France
Son of John Lappin, of 3, Zetland Street, McClure Street, Belfast.

Lappin, Robert - Rifleman
14/3751 Royal Irish Rifles 1st Battalion *Died in War on 28 June 1918*
ESQUELBECQ MILITARY CEMETERY, France
Born and enlisted in Belfast.

Larkham, Harry - Rifleman
5316 Royal Irish Rifles 7th Battalion *Age 22 Died in War on 29 April 1916*
LOOS MEMORIAL, France
Son of William and Sarah Jane Larkham, of 6, Ambrose Street, Belfast.

Larkin, George - Private
15051 Royal Inniskilling Fusiliers 1st Battalion *Age 37 Died in War on 7 May 1915*
HELLES MEMORIAL, Turkey
Husband of Emma Martin Larkin, of 27, Sidney Street West, Belfast.
Sixteen years service including the South African War.

Larkin, Henry - Rifleman
15134 Royal Irish Rifles 10th Battalion *Killed in Action on 1 July 1916*
THIEPVAL MEMORIAL, France
13 Ambrose Street, Belfast.

Larkin, Patrick - Private
4744 Connaught Rangers 1st Battalion *Died in War on 18 October 1918*
HAIFA WAR CEMETERY, Israel
Born and enlisted in Belfast.

Larkin, Patrick Joseph - Rifleman
23610 Royal Irish Rifles transferred to 680957 Labour Corps
Age 17 Died as a result of war on 16 February 1919
COMPTON CHAMBERLAYNE CEMETERY, United Kingdom
Son of James and Elizabeth Larkin, of 44, Elmfield Street, Belfast.

Larkin, Robert - Rifleman
19/783 Royal Irish Rifles 10th Battalion *Age 19 Died in War on 8 August 1917*
LIJSSENTHOEK MILITARY CEMETERY, Belgium
Son of Robert and Margaret Larkin, of 15, Courtrai Street, Belfast.

Larmour, Archibald - Rifleman
15/11695 Royal Irish Rifles 15th Battalion *Died in War on 6 June 1918*
HAM BRITISH CEMETERY, MUILLE-VILLETTE, France
Husband of Margaret Larmour, of 101, Leopold Street, Belfast.

Larmour, Daniel - Private
20423 Royal Dublin Fusiliers 2nd Battalion *Killed In Action on 21 March 1918*
POZIERES MEMORIAL, France
Born and enlisted in Belfast.

Larmour, Edward Archibald Rice - Engineer Lieutenant
Royal Naval Reserve HMS "Laurentic" *Age 36 Killed by mine explosion off North Irish coast on 25 January 1917*
PLYMOUTH MEMORIAL, United Kingdom
Son of Annabella Steele (formerly Larmour), of Belfast, and the late Edward Larmour; husband of Johanna Margrietha Larmour, of I, Stretton Avenue, Wallasey, Cheshire.

Larmour, George - Rifleman
16674 Royal Irish Rifles 14th Battalion *Age 25 Killed in Action on 1 July 1916*
THIEPVAL MEMORIAL, France
Son of Susan Larmour, of 11, Fitzroy Avenue, Belfast, and the late James Larmour.

Larmour, James - Second Officer
Mercantile Marine S.S. "Saint Ninian" (Glasgow)
Age 46 Drowned, as a result of an attack by an enemy submarine on 7 February 1917
TOWER HILL MEMORIAL, United Kingdom
Son of the late Hugh and Elizabeth Larmour. Born at Belfast.

Larmour, Robert - Private
51295 Eastern Ontario Regiment Princess Patricia's Canadian Light Infantry
Age 33 Killed in Action on 8 May 1915
YPRES (MENIN GATE) MEMORIAL, Belgium
Son of the late William Larmour, of 37, Camden Street, Belfast, Ireland. Served in the South African Campaign with the 3rd Dragoon Guards. He was Presbyterian and worked as a carpenter before re-enlisting in the Army.

Larmour, William - Bugler
16675 Royal Irish Rifles 9th Battlion *Age 21 Killed in Action on 1 July 1916*
THIEPVAL MEMORIAL, France
Second son of William and Barbara Larmour, 38, Glenfarne Street, Belfast.
An apprentice at Workman and Clark shipyard, he was also a member of the old UVF.

Larmour, James - Stoker Second Class
K/24617 Royal Navy HMS "Princess Irence" *Died in War on 27 May 1915*
CHATHAM NAVAL MEMORIAL, *United Kingdom*
103, Lilliput Street, Belfast.

Latimer, Hugh - Rifleman
13010 Royal Irish Rifles 15th Battalion *Killed In Action on 22 November 1917*
THIEPVAL MEMORIAL, *France*
Born and enlisted in Belfast.

Latimer, James - Company Sergeant Major
13011 Royal Irish Rifles 15th Battalion *Died in War on 21 March 1918*
POZIERES MEMORIAL, *France*
Husband of Agnes Latimer, 11 New North Queen street, Belfast.

Latimer, Samuel Hugh - Company Sergeant Major
9307 Royal Irish Fusiliers 5thBattalion *Died in War on 1 September 1915*
GREEN HILL CEMETERY, *Turkey*
Born in Belfast, enlisted in Monaghan.

Latimer, William - Rifleman
12006 Royal Irish Rifles 15th Battalion *Killed in Action on 1 July 1916*
CONNAUGHT CEMETERY, THIEPVAL, *France*
Born and enlisted in Belfast.

Lauder, Ernest - Private
305624 Hampshire Regiment 1/7th Battalion attached 4th Battalion
Age 21 Died of Wounds on 21 January 1916
BASRA MEMORIAL, *Iraq*
Son of Henry and Miriam Lauder, of 6, Castleton Gardens, Belfast. Born at Bedford, England.

Laughlin, Albert - Private
15139 Royal Irish Rifles 14th Battalion *Killed in Action on 1 July 1916*
THIEPVAL MEMORIAL, *France*
Son of William Laughlin, 110 Battenberg Street, Belfast.

Laughlin, James Courtney - Second Lieutenant
The King's (Liverpool Regiment) 20th Battalion *Age 25 Killed in Action on 1 July 1916*
CERISY-GAILLY MILITARY CEMETERY, *France*
Son of Robert Gardiner Laughlin and Annie Laughlin, of 129, University Street, Belfast.

Laughlin, Robert - Private
23467 Border Regiment 10th Battalion *Died in War on 5 July 1917*
BELFAST CITY CEMETERY, *United Kingdom*
Son of Agnes Laughlin, 24 Lecale Street, Belfast.

Laughlin, William - Rifleman
11350 Royal Irish Rifles 6th Battalion *Died in War on 11 August 1915*
HELLES MEMORIAL, *Turkey*
Born and enlisted in Belfast.

L

Laughlin, William Donaldson - Private
3650 Irish Guards 1st Battalion *Age 21 Killed in Action on 1 November 1914*
YPRES (MENIN GATE) MEMORIAL, Belgium
Son of Arthur Richard and Mary Ann Laughlin of 329, Shankill Road, Belfast.

Laughran, Michael - Rifleman
10384 Royal Irish Rifles 2nd Battalion *Age 23 Died of Wounds on 12 August 1917*
LIJSSENTHOEK MILITARY CEMETERY, Belgium
Brother of John James Laughran, of 18, McDowell's Row, Greencastle, Belfast.

Laughton, Percy - Private
40473 Royal Inniskilling Fusiliers 2nd Battalion *Died in War on 5 April 1917*
SAVY BRITISH CEMETERY, France
Born in Northamtonshire England, resident of Belfast. Formerly 30933 Northamptonshire Regiment.

Laurison, James - Rifleman
11138 Royal Irish Rifles 6th Battalion *Age 20 Died of Wounds on 15 August 1915*
EAST MUDROS MILITARY CEMETERY, Greece
Son of John and Elinor Laurison, of 101, Charles Street South, Belfast.

Laverty, Alfred - Rifleman
6813 Royal Irish Rifles 1st Battalion *Died in War on 11 March 1915*
LE TOURET MEMORIAL, France
Husband of Minnie, 39 Central Street, Belfast.

Laverty, Arthur - Lance Corporal
12/6840 Royal Irish Rifles 12th Battalion *Died in War on 13 October 1918*
DADIZEELE NEW BRITISH CEMETERY, Belgium
Husband of Mrs. M. E. Frame (formerly Laverty), of 8, Roxburgh Street, Belfast.

Laverty, Daniel - Stoker First Class
SS/108512 Royal Navy HMS "Hawke" *Age 23 Killed in Action with submarine in North Sea on 15 October 1914*
CHATHAM NAVAL MEMORIAL, United Kingdom
Son of Jane Laverty, of 13, Ravenscroft Street, Connswater, Belfast, and the late James Laverty.

Laverty, Francis - Corporal
19/491 Royal Irish Rifles 14th Battalion *Died in War on 7 June 1917*
LONE TREE CEMETERY, Belgium
Husband of Mrs. Laverty, of 206, Blythe Street, Belfast.

Laverty, James - Rifleman
20404 Royal Irish Rifles Depot *Age 22 Died as a result of war on 22 February 1920*
BILLY CHURCH OF IRELAND CHURCHYARD, United Kingdom
Son of Francis and Margaret Laverty, of 20/117, Bouverie Street, Port Glasgow. Born at Belfast.

Laverty, William Aicken - Leading Seaman
218192 Royal Navy HMS "Laurentic"
Age 30 Killed by mine explosion off the North Irish coast on 25 January 1917
PLYMOUTH NAVAL MEMORIAL, United Kingdom
Son of James and Jane Laverty, of 13, Ravenscroft Street, Connswater, Belfast.

Journey of Remembering

Laverty, William John - Rifleman
949 Royal Irish Rifles 1st Garrison Battalion *Died in War on 10 November 1916*
MADRAS 1914 - 18 WAR MEMORIAL CHENNAI, India
Born and enlisted in Omagh, resident of Belfast.

Lavery, Frederick George - A/Corporal
M/319366 Royal Army Service Corps *Died in War on 30 December 1917*
ALEXANDRIA (CHATBY) MILITARY AND WAR MEMORIAL CEMETERY, Egypt
Enlisted in Cork, resident of Belfast.

Lavery, James - Private
5229 Connaught Rangers 1st Battalion *Died in War on 17 April 1916*
BAGHDAD (NORTH GATE) WAR CEMETERY, Iraq
Born in Belfast. Enlisted in Coatbridge, Scotland.

Lavery, James Edward - Private
21933 Royal Dublin Fusiliers 2nd Battalion *Age 34 Died in War on 7 October 1918*
VIS-EN-ARTOIS MEMORIAL, France
Son of Joseph and Mary Lavery, of 31, Lagan Street, Belfast.

Lavery, John - Private
20013 Royal Irish Fusiliers 1st Battalion *Age 39 Died in War on 11 April 1918*
TYNE COT MEMORIAL, Belgium
Husband of Mary Anne Lavery, of 32, Marchioness Street, Belfast.

Lavery, John - Private
2354 Royal Scots 5th Battalion *Age 27 Died in War on 12 June 1915*
LANCASHIRE LANDING CEMETERY, Turkey
Son of John and Mary McCann Lavery, of 3, Herron Court, Cowgate, Edinburgh. Born in Belfast.

Lavery, John - Private
2442 Connaught Rangers 6th Battalion *Died in War on 27 January 1916*
DUD CORNER CEMETERY, France
Born in Warrenpoint, enlisted and resident in Belfast.

Lavery, John - Rifleman
2847 Royal Irish Rifles 15th Battalion *Killed in Action on 1 July 1916*
THIEPVAL MEMORIAL, France
Born and enlisted in Belfast.

Lavery, Joseph - Private
8728 Royal Irish Rifles 2nd Battalion *Age 36 Killed in Action on 27 October 1914*
LE TOURET MEMORIAL, France
Husband of Catherine Murphy (formerly Lavery), of 34, Berry Street, Belfast.
Served in the South African Campaign.

Lavery, Robert - Sergeant
2748 Royal Irish Rifles 16th Battalion *Killed In Action on 6 August 1917*
WIELTJE FARM CEMETERY, Belgium
Born and enlisted in Belfast.

Lavery, Thomas - Rifleman
3983 Royal Irish Rifles 8th Battalion *Died in War on 2 July 1916*
THIEPVAL MEMORIAL, France
Born and enlisted in Belfast.

Lavery, William - Private
1774 Australian Infantry 13th Battalion *Age 30 Killed in Action on 9 August 1915*
7th FIELD AMBULANCE CEMETERY, Turkey
Son of Robert and Sarah Lavery, of Holmhurst, Richmond Park, Belfast, Ireland.
Native of County Dublin.

Lavery, William - Rifleman
17/602 Royal Irish Rifles 10th Battalion *Age 43 Died of Wounds on 16 December 1915*
MAILLY-MAILLET COMMUNAL CEMETERY EXTENSION, France
Husband of Annie Lavery, of 32, Blythe Street, Belfast.

Lavery, William John - Private
26071 Royal Inniskilling Fusiliers 5th Battalion *Killed in Action on 17 October 1918*
LE CATEAU MILITARY CEMETERY, France
Son of Samuel and Margaret Lavery; husband of Mary Harvey (formerly Lavery),
of 10, Carnan Street, Belfast.

Law, Ernest - Rifleman
15/9228 Royal Irish Rifles 15th Battalion *Age 19 Died in War on 29 April 1918*
BOULOGNE EASTERN CEMETERY, France
Son of James and Frances Emily Law, of Belfast.

Law, James - Private
13050 Royal Scots 12th Battalion *Age 32 Killed in Action on 23 August 1915*
CAMBRIN CHURCHYARD EXTENSION, France
Son of James and Ellen Law, of Dunmurry, Belfast.

Law, Joseph - Driver
64055 Royal Engineers 122nd Field Company *Died in War on 20 March 1917*
HAZEBROUCK COMMUNAL CEMETERY, France
Born in Dublin, enlisted and resident in Belfast.

Law, Michael - Private
6989 Royal Irish Rifles 2nd Battalion *Died of Wounds on 11 June 1916*
WIMEREUX COMMUNAL CEMETERY, France
30 Balaclava Street, Belfast.

Law, Robert J. - Private
253031 Princess Louise's (Argyll & Sutherland Highlanders) 1/7th Battalion *Died in War on 25 July 1918*
MARFAUX BRITISH CEMETERY, France
Born in Belfast, enlisted Huddersfield, Yorkshire.

Law, Stanley - Private
5655 Connaught Rangers "B" Company 5th Battalion *Age 24 Killed in Action on 9 October 1918*
MONTAY-NEUVILLY ROAD CEMETERY, MONTAY, France
Son of Charles Muller Law and Joyce Eaton Law, of 28, Hamilton Street, South Circular Road, Dublin.
Native of Belfast.

Lawless, James - Sergeant
1603 Leinster Regiment 2nd Battalion *Age 26 Died in War on 22 March 1918*
POZIERES MEMORIAL, France
Son of John and Bridget Lawless, of 50, Seaforde Street, Belfast.

Lawless, Robert - Private
8016 Royal Inniskilling Fusiliers 2nd Battalion *Died in War on 16 May 1915*
LE TOURET MEMORIAL, France
Born and enlisted in Cookstown, resident of Belfast.

Lawlor, James Dominick - Private
10479 Royal Inniskilling Fusiliers 2nd Battalion *Died in War on 16 May 1915*
LE TOURET MEMORIAL, France
Born and enlisted in Ballymacarrett, Belfast. For many years worked and lived in Cookstown.

Lawson, Charles Henry - Private
M2/131354 Royal Army Service Corps *Died in War on 1 November 1918*
ABBEVILLE COMMUNAL CEMETERY EXTENSION, France
Born in Nelson, enlisted Colchester, both England, resident of Belfast.

Lawther, Jack - Private
12290 South African Infantry "A" Company 1st Regiment
Age 17 Died of Wounds on 20 September 1917
NINE ELMS BRITISH CEMETERY, Belgium
Son of Mr. J. and Mrs. E. Lawther, of Belfast, Ireland.

Leach, William - Rifleman
18074 Royal Irish Rifles 14th Battalion *Died in War on 21 March 1916*
FORCEVILLE COMMUNAL CEMETERY AND EXTENSION, France
Born and enlisted in Belfast.

Leader, Hamilton - Lance Corporal
8975 Royal Irish Rifles 7th Battalion *Age 25 Killed in Action on 16 August 1917*
TYNE COT MEMORIAL, Belgium
Son of William and Elizabeth Leader, of 26, Bentham Street, Donegall Road, Belfast.
Over 8 years service.

Leahey, Hugh - Rifleman
809 Royal Irish Rifles 15th Battalion *Killed in Action on 1 July 1916*
THIEPVAL MEMORIAL, France
Son of the late Robert and Rose Leahey.

Leahy, Eugene Patrick - Captain
Royal Army Medical Corps 61st Field Ambulance *Died in War on 18 September 1916*
GROVE TOWN CEMETERY, MEAULTE, France
Son of the late David Leahy, J.P., and Mrs. Leahy, of 48, Elmwood Avenue, Belfast.

Leary, John - Private
8806 Cheshire Regiment 1st Battalion *Age 24 Died in War on 17 November 1914*
YPRES (MENIN GATE) MEMORIAL, Belgium
Husband of Catherine Leary, of 13, Duffy Street, Belfast.

Leatham, John - Bombardier
91542 Royal Field Artillery (E.E.F.) *Age 35 Died in War on 11 May 1916*
ALEXANDRIA (HADRA) WAR MEMORIAL CEMETERY, Egypt
Son of Margaret Leatham, of 29, Valentine Street, Belfast.

Leathem, James Edward - Private
M2/105568 Army Service Corps 61st Division Mechanical Transport Company
Age 27 Died in War on 18 June 1918
AIRE COMMUNAL CEMETERY, France
Husband of Martha Wilhelmina Leathem, of 1, Westminster Street, Belfast. Three years continuous service.

Leckey, Alexander - Private
8192 Grenadier Guards 2nd Battalion *Age 30 Died of Wounds on 19 October 1915*
QUATRE-VENTS MILITARY CEMETERY, ESTREE-CAUCHY, France
Son of George and Agnes Leckey of Gertrude Street, Belfast; husband of Catherine Leckey.

Leckey, Joseph - Rifleman
6177 Royal Irish Rifles 1st Battalion *Killed in Action on 1 July 1916*
THIEPVAL MEMORIAL, France
Born and enlisted in Belfast.

Leckey, Robert Nixon - Lance Corporal
5938 Royal Irish Rifles 2nd Battalion *Killed In Action on 15 July 1916*
SERRE ROAD CEMETERY No.1, France
Born and enlisted in Belfast.

Leckey, Thomas - Private
5024 Royal Munster Fusiliers 6th Battalion *Died in War on 15 August 1915*
HELLES MEMORIAL, Turkey
Born in Ballymurphy, enlisted in Belfast. Formerly 15177 Royal Inniskilling Fusiliers.

Leckey, William - Lance Corporal
40889 Royal Irish Rifles 1st Battalion *Died in War on 11 May 1918*
GWALIA CEMETERY, Belgium
Son of Samuel and Jane Leckey, of 38, Avoca Street, Belfast.

Lee, Frank Robert - Lance Corporal
8088 Royal Inniskilling Fusiliers 2nd Battalion *Died in War on 21 October 1914*
PLOEGSTEERT MEMORIAL, Belgium
82 Britannic Street, Belfast. Born in County Fermangh.

Lee, George - Bombardier
265391 Royal Field Artillery *Age 34 Died as a result of war on 14 January 1920*
BELFAST CITY CEMETERY, United Kingdom
Husband of Jennie Lee, of 11, Malcolm Street, Belfast. Awarded the Military Medal.

Lee, Isaac - Private
13174 Royal Irish Fusiliers 5th Battalion *Age 21 Died in War on 8 August 1915*
HELLES MEMORIAL, Turkey
Son of Mrs. Hughena Lee, of 62, Aberdeen Street, Belfast.

Lee, Joseph - Private
4745 Leinster Regiment 1st Battalion *Age 20 Died in War on 14 June 1915*
WIMEREUX COMMUNAL CEMETERY, France
Son of Thomas and Susan Lee, of 153, James Street, Dublin. Born in Belfast.

Lee, Michael - Private
2419 Leinster Regiment 7th Battalion *Died in War on 3 September 1916*
THIEPVAL MEMORIAL, France
Born and enlisted in Belfast.

Lee, Robert - Sergeant
9111 Royal Irish Rifles 2nd Battalion *Died in War on 27 October 1914*
LE TOURET MEMORIAL, France
Born in County Wicklow the son of a career soldier, Sergeant Joe Lee, Inniskilling Fusiliers, and Annie Lee (née McGee) lived of Ballymoney Street Belfast. Enlisted in 1908 and was a sergeant at the beginning of the war. He took part in the initial battles and by October 1914 was reported missing at Neuve Chapelle. Despite an appeal for information in the *Belfast Evening Telegraph* by his parents, then living at 279 Crumlin Road, his body was never identified. He was later officially declared to have been killed on 27 October 1914. He is shown on the rear cover of this book, as a Lance Corporal, in his barrack room in England prior to the outbreak of war.

Lee, Robert Mcmillan - Private
5833 Irish Guards *Age 22 Died in War on 24 November 1918*
BELFAST CITY CEMETERY, United Kingdom
Son of Joseph and Mary Lee, of 60, Emerson Street, Belfast.

Lee, Thomas - Rifleman
15151 Royal Irish Rifles 9th Battalion *Died in War on 29 May 1916*
AUTHUILE MILITARY CEMETERY, France
Born and enlisted in Belfast.

Lee, Thomas - Rifleman
9683 Royal Irish Rifles 1st Battalion *Died in War on 17 March 1915*
LE TOURET MEMORIAL, France
Born and enlisted in Belfast.

Lee, William J - Driver
48698 Royal Field Artillery 2nd Reserve Battery *Age 25 Died in War on 29 June 1918*
BELFAST CITY CEMETERY, United Kingdom
Son of Henry and Elizabeth Lee, of 72, Glenmachan Street, Donegall Road, Belfast.

Leebody, Robert - Rifleman
329 Royal Irish Rifles 16th Battalion *Died in War on 3 May 1917*
KEMMEL CHATEAU MILITARY CEMETERY, Belgium
Born in Ballynahinch, enlisted Lurgan, resident of Belfast.

Lees, James Lowry - Captain
Tank Corps 6th Battalion *Died in War on 23 August 1918*
BIENVILLERS MILITARY CEMETERY, France
Awarded the Military Cross, the son of Mr. J. Lees, of Drumadoon, Old Cavehill Road, Belfast.

Lees, Lowry - Sergeant
511845 London Regiment (London Scottish) 2nd/14th Battalion *Age 22 Died in War on 14 October 1918*
DERRY HOUSE CEMETERY No.2, Belgium
Son of John L. and Frances A. Lees, of 31, Hughenden Avenue, Belfast.

Legg, William Norman - Second Lieutenant
King's Shropshire Light Infantry 7th Battalion *Age 26 Died of Wounds on 24 March 1916*
ETAPLES MILITARY CEMETERY, France
Son of Sarah Ann Legg, of 41, Fitzwilliam Street, Belfast. Native of Belfast.

Leggatt, Fredrick Alexander - Gunner
317933 Canadian Field Artillery 5th Brigade *Age 23 Died in War on 3 November 1917*
VLAMERTINGHE NEW MILITARY CEMETERY, Belgium
The son of Mary and the late Charles Leggatt, of 50, Lewis Street, Belfast, Ireland.
A Methodist, he was born in Donegal and worked as a clerk.

Leggett, Samuel - Fireman
Mercantile Marine S.S. "Treverbyn" (St. Ives)
Age 25 Drowned, as a result of an attack by an enemy submarine, or killed by mine on 3 September 1917
TOWER HILL MEMORIAL, United Kingdom
Son of the late David and Elizabeth Leggett. Born at Belfast.

Leinster, David A. - Rifleman
17/128 Royal Irish Rifles "D" Company 10th Battalion *Age 19 Died in War on 24 December 1917*
BELFAST CITY CEMETERY, United Kingdom
Son of Thomas J. and Eleanor Leinster, of 35, Magnetic Street, Belfast.

Leinster, William George - Private
41266 Princess Victoria's (Royal Irish Fusiliers) 9th Battalion *Died in War on 19 April 1918*
TYNE COT MEMORIAL, Belgium
Born and enlisted in Cavan, resident of Belfast. Formerly 1469 North Irish Horse.

Leitch, William - Rifleman
14/18074 Royal Irish Rifles 14th Battalion *Age 20 Killed in Action on 21 March 1916*
FORCEVILLE COMMUNAL CEMETERY AND EXTENSION, France
Son of John and Jane T. Leitch, of Donegal Road, Belfast.

Lemon, Archie Dunlap - Lieutenant
Royal Irish Rifles "B" Company 12th Battalion *Age 41 Killed in Action on 1 July 1916*
THIEPVAL MEMORIAL, France
Son of A. D. Lemon, J.P., and Mrs. Lemon, of Edgcumbe House, Strandtown, Belfast. Educated at Methodist College and was a member of the Royal North of Ireland Yacht Club and of Belfast No 7 Masonic Lodge.

Lemon, David - Petty Officer
168749 (Dev) H.M. Coastguard Station Rosmoney HM "President IV" *Age 42 Died as a result of war on 11 March 1919*
BELFAST (DUNDONALD) CEMETERY, United Kingdom
Husband of Frances Lemon, of 144, Madrid Street, Belfast.

Lemon, Francis - Rifleman
1005 Royal Irish Rifles 8th Battalion *Died in War on 2 July 1916*
THIEPVAL MEMORIAL, France
Born and enlisted in Belfast.

Lemon, John - Lance Corporal
12650 Royal Inniskilling Fusiliers 5th Battalion *Age 22 Died in War on 15 August 1915*
HELLES MEMORIAL, Turkey
Born and enlisted in Belfast. Son of John and Elizabeth Lemon.

One of the most famous photographs of the Great War. A ration party of the Royal Irish Rifles, 36th (Ulster) Division, rest in a communication trench on the Somme. The sandbags would have contained loaves from a field bakery. (Imperial War Museum)

IWM Q1

Woodland devastated after sustained artillery bombardment. Over 60 per cent of all fatalities in the War were the result of shellfire. (Imperial War Museum)

1928: Fred Sadlier visits the grave of his brother, 2nd Lieutenant Frank Sadlier, Royal Inniskilling Fusiliers. The cemetery, at Dadizeele, Belgium, had just been completed. (Courtesy of Robin Sadlier)

2008: Eighty years later Fred Sadlier's son, Robin, visits the same grave.

The yard of a former military prison in Poperinge, Belgium. The post was used to tie soldiers before execution by firing squad.(Billy Donald)

Tyne Cot Memorial and Cemetery, Passchendaele, Belgium. This is the largest British Military Cemetery in the world with nearly 12,000 graves. On the wall to the left there are 33,000 names of soldiers whose bodies were never found or identified. 220 are from Belfast. (Billy Donald)

ABOVE: *Some of the most neglected casualties of the War were Merchant Seamen most of whom went down with their ships after submarine attacks. This is their memorial at Tower Hill, London. Almost one hundred and fifty Belfast men are commemorated here. Several of these were amongst the oldest, and youngest, deaths in the war.*

RIGHT: *A bugler on top of the Ulster Tower prepares to sound the Last Post on the 1st July 2006, the 90th anniversary of the beginning of the Somme Battle. The tower at Thiepval is the largest, and the first to be completed, divisional memorial on the Somme. (Billy Donald)*

Shankill Graveyard: The Young family headstone. It also commemorates one of the few Belfast female fatalities of the Great War. Margaret Cameron was a Voluntary Aid Detachment Nurse who died in 1918. She is buried in Terlincthun Military Cemetery, France.

Shankill Graveyard: The headstone of Walter Ambrose Sterling of the Royal Air Force, aged 14. He died from pneumonia

The gentle pastoral farm land of the Somme belies its violent past. The huge Thiepval Memorial to the missing is in the distance. (Billy Donald)

The massive Thiepval Memorial on the Somme. Opened in 1932 it bears the names of 72,000 missing soldiers. Over 800 are from Belfast. (Billy Donald)

Friar's Bush Catholic Graveyard, Stranmillis Road. The family monument to Francis Joseph Wisely. Doctor Wisely was the Medical Officer of the 1st Battalion Lancashire Fusiliers. He was mortally wounded at the Dardanelles (Gallipoli) and is buried in Alexandria, Egypt. (Gerry Ward)

The Island of Ireland Peace Park, Messines, Belgium. It was opened on 11 November 1998 by Queen Elizabeth II, President Mary McAleese and King Albert II of the Belgians. A symbol of reconciliation it marks the success of the 16th (Irish) and 36th (Ulster) Divisions at the Battle of Messines in June 1917. (Billy Donald)

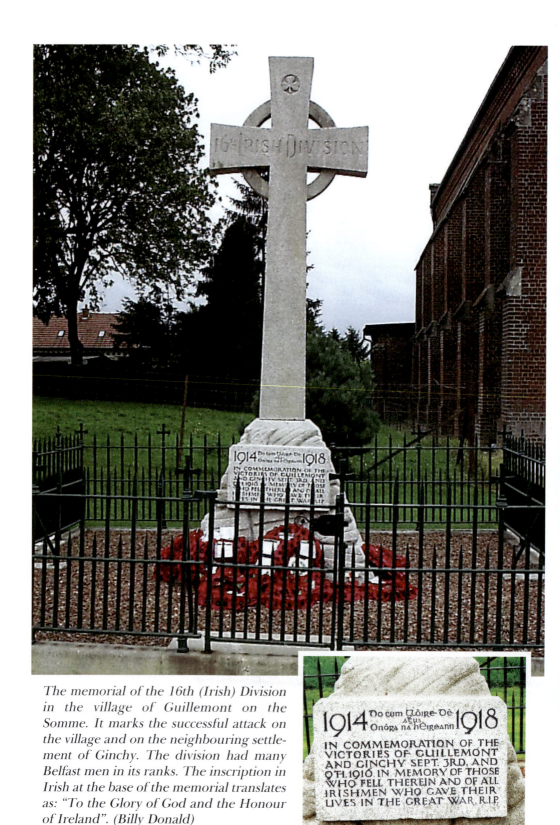

The memorial of the 16th (Irish) Division in the village of Guillemont on the Somme. It marks the successful attack on the village and on the neighbouring settlement of Ginchy. The division had many Belfast men in its ranks. The inscription in Irish at the base of the memorial translates as: "To the Glory of God and the Honour of Ireland". (Billy Donald)

ABOVE: The Menin Gate, Ypres was built in 1928 on the exit route from the town towards the front. Each evening, at 8pm the traffic is stopped and buglers from the local Fire Brigade sound the Last Post. (Billy Donald)

RIGHT: The Menin Gate looking west to the town centre. There are 55,000 names of the missing on the Gate including 400 Belfast men. (Billy Donald)

Concrete shelter built into western side of Kemmel Hill, Belgium. For a time it was part of the headquarters of the 36th (Ulster) Division. (Billy Donald)

An excavated trench in Thiepval Wood, France. It was from trenches such as these that the 36th (Ulster) Division advanced on the 1st July 1916. The figure on the right is Teddy Colligan who, with his wife Phoebe, is custodian of the Ulster Tower and Thiepval Wood. (Billy Donald)

The Germans also suffered. Four mourning figures by Emil Krieger watch over the German cemetery at Langemark, Belgium. The site has 44,000 burials including a mass grave of 25,000. (Billy Donald)

The Germans also suffered. An example of the mourning cards printed by German parents and distributed amongst relatives and friends. (Billy Donald)

Professor Mary Wilmont, her father, James Golden and her children, Colin, Katy and Jonathan. They are visiting the Le Touret Memorial in France in 1987. Her grandfather, Rifleman John Golden had been killed with the 2nd Battalion Royal Irish Rifles at Neuve Chapelle, in October 1914. His body was never identified and he is commemorated on the Memorial. Mary said; "My father was born in 1905, profoundly deaf and his mother died shortly afterwards. He was sent to a school for the deaf in Dublin. From that period he retained a faint memory of being visited by a man in uniform – my grandfather. Father grew up very conscious of his Irishness and held to strong socialist beliefs. He also spoke often, and with pride, of his father. Each November he wore his poppy which, as a teenager, used to embarrass me when we went to Mass. The visit to Le Touret, at the age of 81, to see his father's name was a deeply moving and poignant experience for him and all the family. (Photograph courtesy of Colin Wilmont senior)

"To My daughter Betty, The Gift of God". The poem written by Lieutenant Tom Kettle five days before his death in battle at 1916. This stone is the grounds of the Island of Ireland Peace Park. (Billy Donald)

Lemon, John Frazer - Corporal
64420 Royal Engineers 150th Field Company *Age 36 Died of Wounds on 14 August 1917*
BRANDHOEK NEW MILITARY CEMETERY, Belgium
Son of Sarah and the late Hugh Lemon, of Belfast.

Lemon, Moses - Private
7356 Royal Inniskilling Fusiliers *Age 43 Died of Wounds on 8 August 1917*
BELFAST (DUNDONALD) CEMETERY, United Kingdom
Son of the late James Lemon. Born at Belfast.

Lemon, Samuel - Lance Corporal
15106 Royal Irish Rifles 10th Battalion *Died in War on 14 December 1915*
SUCRERIE MILITARY CEMETERY, COLINCAMPS, France
Born and enlisted in Belfast.

Lemon, William John - Private
5323 Royal Munster Fusiliers "A" Company 2nd Battalion *Age 24 Died in War on 10 November 1917*
TYNE COT MEMORIAL, Belgium
Son of Thomas Wesley and Ellen Lemon, of 311, North Queen Street, Belfast.

Lenaghan, Thomas - Sapper
46072 Royal Engineers 97th Field Company *Age 24 Died in War on 22 March 1918*
POZIERES MEMORIAL, France
Son of Robert Lenaghan, of 60, Brookvale Street, Antrim Road, Belfast.

Lenigham, James - A/Sergeant
90808 Royal Horse Artillery and Royal Field Artillery *Died in War on 7 July 1917*
KENSAL GREEN (ALL SOULS) CEMETERY, London
Born and enlisted in Belfast.

Lennard, William Herbert - Private
9077 Dorsetshire Regiment 1st Battalion *Died in War on 12 October 1914*
LE TOURET MEMORIAL, France
29 Scott Street, Belfast. Born in St Helier, Channel Islands.

Lennon, Alexander - Private
9/15153 Royal Irish Rifles 9th Battalion *Killed in Action on 15 September 1916*
ST. QUENTIN CABARET MILITARY CEMETERY, Belgium
Only son of Mary and the late James Lennon, 58 Boyd Street, Belfast.

Lennon, James - Private
17688 Machine Gun Corps (Infantry) 108th Company *Age 22 Killed in Action on 1 July 1916*
THIEPVAL MEMORIAL, France
Son of Robert Lennon, of 52 London Street, Belfast, and the late Mrs. Lennon.

Lennon, John - Private
26221 Welsh Regiment 9th Battalion *Died in War on 20 September 1917*
TYNE COT MEMORIAL, Belgium
Born in Belfast, enlisted Monmouthshire, Wales.

Lennon, Matthew - Private
5292 Royal Munster Fusiliers 7th Battalion *Died in War on 22 August 1915*
LALA BABA CEMETERY, Turkey
Born and enlisted in Belfast. Formerly 16184 Royal Inniskilling Fusiliers.

Lennon, Robert - Private
25195 South Wales Borderers 2nd Battalion *Died in War on 28 May 1916*
AUCHONVILLERS MILITARY CEMETERY, France
Born and enlisted in Belfast. Formerly 10195 Royal Inniskilling Fusiliers.

Lennon, William - Private
2751 Connaught Rangers 5th Battalion *Died in War on 12 August 1915*
HELLES MEMORIAL, Turkey
Born in Belfast, enlisted Lurgan.

Lennox, Alexander - Lance Corporal
9484 East Lancashire Regiment 1st Battalion *Age 25 Died in War on 13 May 1915*
YPRES (MENIN GATE) MEMORIAL, Belgium
Son of Alexander Lennox, of 53, Matilda Street, Belfast.

Lennox, George Donald - Private
9157 Irish Guards 1st Battalion *Age 19 Died in War on 26 May 1918*
AYETTE BRITISH CEMETERY, France
Son of Albert George Lennox, of 22, Ranfurly Drive, Strandtown, Belfast.

Leonard, Francis Patrick Mapletoft - Lieutenant
Royal Inniskilling Fusiliers 8th Battalion *Age 26 Died in War on 29 April 1916*
LOOS MEMORIAL, France
Son of the late Francis Mapletoft Leonard, the Chief Clerk of HM Customs Belfast, and Jessie Leonard, of Salisbury Avenue Belfast. Enlisted in the University and Public Schools Battalion of the Royal Fusiliers, September 1914. Subsequently commissioned into the Royal Inniskilling Fusiliers.

Leonard, Michael - Private
4531 Connaught Rangers 6th Battalion *Died in War on 28 July 1916*
DUD CORNER CEMETERY, LOOS, France
20 Abercorn Street, Belfast.

Leonard, Patrick - Rifleman
7618 Royal Irish Rifles 1st Battalion *Killed in Action on 6 August 1918*
Born and enlisted in Belfast.

Leslie, David - Rifleman
1080 Royal Irish Rifles 16th Battalion *Died in War on 18 June 1917*
YPRES (MENIN GATE) MEMORIAL, Belgium
Born and enlisted in Belfast.

Lester, Robert - Private
24979 Royal Inniskilling Fusiliers 3rd Battalion *Died in War on 7 March 1916*
LONDONDERRY CITY CEMETERY, United Kingdom
Born and enlisted in Belfast.

Letts, Bertram Chiene - Lieutenant
Royal Army Medical Corps 13th Casualty Clearing Station *Age 27 Died in War on 21 October 1915*
ALEXANDRIA (CHATBY) MILITARY AND WAR MEMORIAL CEMETERY, Egypt
Son of the late Dr. E. A. Letts (Professor of Chemistry, Queen's College, Belfast); husband of Kathleen Mabel Whitlet Letts, of 9, Comely Bank, Perth.

Lewis, Alexander - Rifleman
34 Royal Irish Rifles 15th Battalion *Died in War on 5 August 1917*
YPRES (MENIN GATE) MEMORIAL, Belgium
Born in Carnmoney, enlisted in Belfast. Member of Ballysillan Presbyterian Church.

Lewis, David - Rifleman
13000 Royal Irish Rifles 8th Battalion *Died in War on 2 July 1916*
THIEPVAL MEMORIAL, France
Born at Barrow-in-Furness, Lancashire, enlisted in Belfast and lived at 102, Island Street, Belfast.

Lewis, David - Stoker First Class
SS/106974 Royal Navy HMS "Cressy" *Killed in Action with submarine in North Sea on 22 September 1914*
CHATHAM NAVAL MEMORIAL, United Kingdom
Husband of Rebecca Lewis, of 14, Drumfrachar Road, Greenock. Native of Belfast.

Lewis, Frederic Homer - Second Lieutenant
Royal Irish Rifles 10th Battalion attached 1st Battalion *Killed in Action on 29 April 1918*
TYNE COT MEMORIAL, Belgium
Son of Fredereick William and Lizzie Blanche Lewis of 41, Shore Road, Belfast.

Lewis, Griffith - Rifleman
4638 Royal Irish Rifles 14th Battalion *Killed In Action on 1 July 1916*
MILL ROAD CEMETERY, THIEPVAL, France
Born and enlisted in Belfast.

Lewis, Isaac - Stoker First Class
SS/108181 Royal Navy HMS "Hawke" *Age 23 Killed in Action with submarine in North Sea on 15 October 1914*
CHATHAM NAVAL MEMORIAL, United Kingdom
Son of Issac and Margaret J. Lewis, of Ballymacarrett, Belfast.

Lewis, J - Sapper
WR/311769 Royal Engineers Inland Waterways and Docks *Died as a result of War on 20 June 1919*
BROOKWOOD MILITARY CEMETERY, United Kingdom
Son of John and Jane Lewis, of Belfast; husband of A. Lewis, of 92, Bright Street, Belfast.

Lewis, James - Fireman And Trimmer
Mercantile Marine S.S. "Garron Head" (Belfast) *Age 39 Killed by mine on 16 November 1917*
TOWER HILL MEMORIAL, United Kingdom
Son of the late Samuel and Mary Lewis; husband of Margaret Anne Lewis (née Higgins), of 30A, Great Patrick Street, Belfast.

Lewis, James - Private
10551 Royal Inniskilling Fusiliers 1st Battalion *Killed in Action on 21 August 1915*
HELLES MEMORIAL, Turkey
Born and enlisted in Belfast.

Lewis, John - Rifleman
15109 Royal Irish Rifles 8th Battalion *Died in War on 2 July 1916*
THIEPVAL MEMORIAL, France
Born Barrow in Furness. Husband of Annie and father of three young children. His brother also fell. Lived at 2, Island Street, Belfast.

Lewis, John W - Private
25056 Royal Irish Fusiliers 1st Battalion *Killed in Action on 21 October 1918*
TYNE COT MEMORIAL, *Belgium*
Brother of Mrs Andrews, 19, Harrison Street, Belfast.

Lewis, Lawrence John - Rifleman
2935 Royal Irish Rifles 14th Battalion *Died of Wounds on 9 July 1916*
THIEPVAL MEMORIAL, *France*
Born and enlisted in Belfast.

Lewis, Robert - Lance Corporal
16679 Royal Irish Rifles 10th Battalion *Age 27 Killed in Action on 22 December 1915*
SUCRERIE MILITARY CEMETERY, COLINCAMPS, *France*
Son of William and Ellen Lewis, of 18, Euston Street, Belfast.

Lewis, Samuel John - Rifleman
2915 Royal Irish Rifles 14th Battalion *Age 19 Died of Wounds on 22 March 1916*
FORCEVILLE COMMUNAL CEMETERY AND EXTENSION, *France*
Son of Samuel J. and Mary Lewis, of Belfast.

Lewis, Thomas - Rifleman
15108 Royal Irish Rifles 9th Battalion *Age 33 Killed in Action on 1 July 1916*
THIEPVAL MEMORIAL, *France*
Son of Thomas Lewis; husband of Agnes Lewis, of 24, Fourth Street, Belfast.

Lewis, Thomas David - Corporal
3603 Royal Inniskilling Fusiliers 4th Battalion attached 1st Battalion *Age 21 Died in War on 14 August 1915*
HELLES MEMORIAL, *Turkey*
Son of Thomas David and Rebecca Lewis, of 6, Matchet Street, Belfast.

Lewis, William - Rifleman
15157 Royal Irish Rifles 10th Battalion *Age 18 Killed in Action on 1 July 1916*
THIEPVAL MEMORIAL, *France*
Son of William James and Ellen Lewis, of 58, Rutland Street, Belfast.

Lewis, William James - Private
140578 Canadian Infantry (Central Ontario Regiment) 3rd Battalion
Age 27 Died of Wounds, received at the Battle of the Somme on 5 October 1916
BOULOGNE EASTERN CEMETERY, *France*
Son of John and Jennie Lewis, of 169, Ormeau Road, Belfast, Ireland.
A Presbyterian, he worked in Canada as a clerk.

Liddy, James - Private
24726 Royal Dublin Fusiliers 9th Battalion *Died in War on 6 September 1916*
THIEPVAL MEMORIAL, *France*
Born in Belfast, enlisted Dublin.

Liddy, James - Private
3418 Royal Inniskilling Fusiliers 1st Battalion *Age 20 (soldier, buried at sea) on 29 August 1915*
HELLES MEMORIAL, *Turkey*
Son of Hugh and Susanah Liddy, of 16, Pinkerton Street, Belfast.

Liddy, William - Private
555 Highland Light Infantry 11th (Service) Battalion *Died in War on 25 September 1915*
LOOS MEMORIAL, France
Born in Belfast, enlisted Coatbridge, Scotland.

Liggett, George - Gunner
101062 Royal Horse Artillery and Royal Field Artillery *Died in War on 4 November 1918*
VIS-EN-ARTOIS BRITISH MEMORIAL, HAUCOURT, France
Born and enlisted in Belfast.

Lilley, Anthony - Private
10033 Gordon Highlanders 2nd Battalion *Died in War on 16 November 1914*
GRANGEGORMAN MILITARY CEMETERY, Republic of Ireland
Born in Belfast, enlisted Glasgow.

Lilly, Herbert Ewart - Private
2688 Black Watch (Royal Highlanders) 6th Battalion *Age 18 Died in War on 30 July 1916*
THIEPVAL MEMORIAL, France
Brother of Ethel Lilly, of 63, Foyle Street, Belfast.

Lindsay, George - Rifleman
90 Royal Irish Rifles 15th Battalion *Died as as a Prisoner of War on 16 November 1917*
NIEDERZWEHREN CEMETERY, Germany
Born and enlisted in Belfast.

Lindsay, Joseph - Lance Corporal
7000 Machine Gun Corps (Infantry) 111th Company *Age 19 Died in War on 11 April 1917*
ARRAS MEMORIAL, France
Son of Mr. and Mrs. H. R. Lindsay, of 102, Ormeau Road, Farnham Terrace, Belfast.

Lindsay, William - Rifleman
11245 Royal Irish Rifles 6th Battalion then 2nd Battalion *Killed in Action on 8 July 1916*
THIEPVAL MEMORIAL, France
Son of James and Sarah Lindsay, of 56, Lawnbrook Avenue, Belfast. A member of the old UVF.

Lindsay, William John - Lance Corporal
15/811 Royal Irish Rifles 15th Battalion *Died following an operation for appendicitis on 4 October 1917*
ROCQUIGNY-EQUANCOURT ROAD BRITISH CEMETERY, MANANCOURT, France
Son of Hugh C. and Agnes Lindsay, of 41, McCandless Street, Belfast.

Linton, Joseph - Private
171917 5th Canadian Mounted Rifles (Quebec Regiment) *Age 19 Died in War on 1 - 2 October 1916*
VIMY MEMORIAL, France
Son of Thomas and Susan Linton, of 5, Clara Crescent, Bloomfield, Belfast, Ireland.
A Presbyterian, he was born in Greenock, Scotland and worked as a steam fitter.

Little, Harry Hezekiah - Private
34 General and Base Depots, South African Forces General Depot Staff (Wynberg)
Age 53 Died in War on 22 May 1917
CAPE TOWN (PLUMSTEAD) CEMETERY, South Africa
Son of W. and H. Little; husband of D. Little, of 48, Loader Street, Cape Town. Born at Belfast, Ireland.

Little, Richard - Rifleman
10839 Royal Irish Rifles 2nd Battalion *Killed in Action on 17 May 1916*
ARRAS MEMORIAL, France
Born and enlisted in Belfast.

Little, Thomas - Rifleman
11121 Royal Irish Rifles 2nd Battalion *Died in War on 23 October 1918*
TYNE COT MEMORIAL, Belgium
Born and enlisted in Belfast.

Littlewood, Robert Ralph Victor - Pioneer
255365 Corps of Royal Engineers Signal Depot *Died in War on 27 March 1917*
LEAMINGTON (MILVERTON) CEMETERY
Born in Belfast, enlisted in Warwick, England.

Livingston, William - Private
GS/68544 Royal Fusiliers 17th Battalion formerly 120067 Royal Engineers *Died in War on 1 November 1918*
POIX-DU-NORD COMMUNAL CEMETERY EXTENSION, France
Born Ballymacarrett, Belfast. Enlisted in Belfast. Killed only 10 days before the war ended.

Livingstone, Charles - Private
M2/081014 Army Service Corps 621st Motor Transport Company *Died in War on 15 December 1916*
BELFAST (DUNDONALD) CEMETERY, United Kingdom
Born Belmont, Belfast. The son of George and Isabella Livingstone, Park Avenue, Dundonald.

Livingstone, Dominick - Private
24692 Royal Irish Fusiliers 9th Battalion *Killed in Action on 9 April 1918*
TYNE COT MEMORIAL, Belgium
62 Broadbent Street, Belfast.

Livingstone, James - Private
1144 Royal Irish Rifles 10th Battalion *Killed in Action on 1 July 1916*
THIEPVAL MEMORIAL, France
23, Fox Row, Belfast.

Lizars, Henry - Private
50384 King's (Liverpool Regiment) 4th Battalion *Died in War on 25 September 1917*
TYNE COT MEMORIAL, Belgium
Born and enlisted in Belfast. Formerly 47667, Manchester Regiment.

Lockard, Francis - Corporal
260377 Royal Engineers 323rd Quarrying Company *Age 42 Died in War on 14 April 1917*
BUXTON CEMETERY, United Kingdom
Son of Mrs. Annie Lockard, of 8, Laburnum Street, Connswater, Belfast.

Locke, George - Private
11946 Cheshire Regiment 2nd Battalion *Died in War on 8 May 1915*
YPRES (MENIN GATE) MEMORIAL, Belgium
Born in Belfast, enlisted Birkenhead, England.

Lockhart, Gordon William - Private
8/1277 New Zealand Expeditionary Force Otago Regiment *Age 25 Killed in Action on 8 May 1915*
TWELVE TREE COPSE (NEW ZEALAND) MEMORIAL, Turkey
Son of the late George and Henrietta Lockhart, of 13, Woodcot Avenue, Bloomfield, Belfast, Ireland.

Lockhart, Matthew John - Private
15497 South African Infantry 4th Regiment *Died in War on 20 June 1918*
LA KREULE MILITARY CEMETERY, HAZEBROUCK, Belgium
Sister of Alice Lockhart, 23 Mount Street, Belfast.

Lockington, Edward Stewart - Lance Corporal
6681 Royal Irish Rifles "C" Company 10th Battalion *Age 25 Killed in Action on 1 July 1916*
THIEPVAL MEMORIAL, France
Son of the late John and Mary Lockington, of 10, Kinallen Street, Ormeau Road, Belfast.

Lockington, William - Lance Corporal
3113 Irish Guards 2nd Battalion *Age 28 Died in War on 27 September 1916*
THIEPVAL MEMORIAL, France
Son of the late John and Mary Lockington, of Kinallen Street, Belfast; husband of Hannah Lockington, of 114, Albert Street, Belfast.

Loftus, Patrick - Private
16673 Royal Irish Fusiliers "B" Company 8th Battalion *Age 27 Died in War on 27 April 1916*
LOOS MEMORIAL, France
Son of Patrick and Ellen Loftus, of 10, Panton Street, Belfast; husband of Margaret Loftus, of 17, Spittal Street, Tipperary.

Logan, Charles - Gunner
277172 Royal Garrison Artillery 108th Heavy Battery *Age 33 Died of Wounds on 20 August 1917*
DUHALLOW A.D.S. CEMETERY, Belgium
Son of John and Matilda Logan, of Belfast.

Logan, David - Private
348351 Royal Engineers formerly 16434 Labour Corps *Died in War on 26 November 1917*
TARANTO TOWN CEMETERY, Italy
Born in Belfast.

Logan, George Henry - Sapper
156817 Royal Engineers Inland Water Transport
Age 28 Drowned as the result of the sinking of the S.S. "Connamara" on 3 November 1916
CARNMONEY CEMETERY, United Kingdom
Son of Henry and Sarah Logan, of 40, Summer Street, Belfast.

Logan, Henry - Corporal
48121 Royal Inniskilling Fusiliers 13th Battalion *Died of Wounds on 23 July 1918*
LONGUENESSE (ST. OMER) SOUVENIR CEMETERY, France
62 Westmorland Street, Belfast.

Logan, James - Private
436 Royal Inniskilling Fusiliers 2nd Battalion *Age 19 Died in War on 16 May 1915*
LE TOURET MEMORIAL, France
Son of Mrs. Margaret Logan, of 57, Glenwherry Street, Belfast.

Logan, John - Private
2314 Connaught Rangers 6th Battalion *Age 39 Died in War on 5 March 1916*
LOOS MEMORIAL, France
Son of the late John and Matilda Logan, of 111, Hardinge Street, Belfast.

Logan, John - Stoker First Class
SS/106972 Royal Navy HMS "Cressy" *Died in War on 22 September 1914*
CHATHAM NAVAL MEMORIAL, *United Kingdom*
19 Upper Meadow Street, Belfast.

Logan, Robert - Private
2466 Irish Guards 1st Battalion *Died in War on 9 October 1917*
TYNE COT MEMORIAL, *Belgium*
222 Leopold Street, Belfast.

Logan, Samuel - Private
8866 Royal Inniskilling Fusiliers 2nd Battalion *Killed in Action on 29 September 1918*
DADIZEELE NEW BRITISH CEMETERY, *Belgium*
Born in Belfast.

Logan, Samuel James - Rifleman
11073 Royal Irish Rifles 6th Battalion *Died in War on 2 July 1916*
SALONIKA (LEMBET ROAD) MILITARY CEMETERY, *Greece*
Husband of Mary C. Lavery (formerly Logan), of 44, Canning Street, York Street, Belfast.

Logue, William John - Private
24123 Royal Irish Fusiliers 1st Battalion *Died in War on 11 April 1917*
ARRAS MEMORIAL, *France*
Born and enlisted in Belfast.

Long, John - Rifleman
13031 Royal Irish Rifles 10th Battalion *Died in War on 22 November 1917*
CAMBRAI MEMORIAL, LOUVERVAL, *France*
16 Kinallon Street, Belfast.

Long, William - Private
3534 Royal Inniskilling Fusiliers 1st Battalion *Died in War on 28 June 1915*
TWELVE TREE COPSE CEMETERY, *Turkey*
Born and enlisted in Belfast.

Long, William Francis Frederick - Private
57071 Lancashire Fusiliers 1/8th Battalion *Died in War on 16 August 1918*
BERTRANCOURT MILITARY CEMETERY, *France*
Born in Belfast, enlisted Nottingham.

Longhlin, William - Private
3650 Irish Guards 1st Battalion *Died in War on 1 November 1914*
Born in Belfast, enlisted Blackburn, England.

Longmore, James - Private
15332 Princess Victoria's (Royal Irish Fusiliers) 8th Battalion *Died in War on 6 September 1916*
THIEPVAL MEMORIAL, *France*
Born in Ballymena, enlisted Tipperary, resident of Belfast.

Longmore, Wilson - Lance Sergeant
2700 Irish Guards 1st Battalion *Age 26 Died in War on 28 October 1916*
YPRES (MENIN GATE) MEMORIAL, *Belgium*
Son of the late Thomas Wilson Longmore and of Elizabeth Longmore, of 18, Jocelyn Gardens, Belfast.

Journey of Remembering

Lorimer, Andrew - Rifleman
11699 Royal Irish Rifles 8/9th Battalion attached 21st Entrenching Battalion
Age 36 Died in War on 21 March 1918
POZIERES MEMORIAL, France
Son of the late John Lorimer; husband of Emily Lorimer, of 268, Leopold Street, Belfast.

Lorimer, Frank - Driver
T/26301 Royal Army Service Corps *Died in War on 26 October 1918*
BELFAST CITY CEMETERY, United Kingdom
Born in Dundee, enlisted Perth, both Scotland, resident of Belfast.

Lorimer, William - Rifleman
18054 Royal Irish Rifles 14th Battalion *Age 24 Died of pneumonia on 13 November 1915*
BEAUVAL COMMUNAL CEMETERY, France
Son of William and Maggie Lorimer, of Belfast; husband of Mary Lorimer,
of 106, Mountcollyer Avenue, Belfast.

Lough, Robert - Rifleman
13036 Royal Irish Rifles 8th Battalion *Died in War on 2 July 1916*
KNIGHTSBRIDGE CEMETERY, MESNIL-MARTINSART, France
Born and enlisted in Belfast.

Lough, William John Companyle - Private
50789 Highland Light Infantry 9th Battalion *Died in War on 31 October 1918*
TOURNAI COMMUNAL CEMETERY ALLIED EXTENSION, Belgium
Son of William and Katherine Lough, of 95, Delhi Street, Ormeau Road, Belfast.

Loughan, Charles - Lance Corporal
8708 Leinster Regiment 1st Battalion *Died in War on 30 January 1915*
YPRES (MENIN GATE) MEMORIAL, Belgium
Born in Belfast, enlisted Coatbridge, Scotland.

Loughan, Peter - Private
S/6457 Black Watch (Royal Highlanders) 8th Battalion *Age 19 Died in War on 14 July 1916*
THIEPVAL MEMORIAL, France
Brother of Private Charles Loughan of the Leinster Regiment who was also killed.

Loughens, Ernest - Corporal
1601 Leinster Regiment 2nd Battalion *Died in War on 27 March 1918*
POZIERES MEMORIAL, France
Born and enlisted in Belfast.

Loughins, David - Private
9411 Royal Irish Rifles 1st Battalion *Died of Wounds on 5 January 1915*
ESTAIRES COMMUNAL CEMETERY AND EXTENSION, France
26 Wellwyne Street, Belfast.

Loughlin, Robert - Rifleman
5921 Royal Irish Rifles 2nd Battalion *Age 25 Died in War on 16 June 1915*
YPRES (MENIN GATE) MEMORIAL, Belgium
Son of the late Robert and Mary Loughlin; husband of Roseann Loughlin,
of 32, Clandeboye Street, Belfast.

Loughran, Joseph - Private
DM2/165456 Army Service Corps Motor Transport Depot *Age 50 Died in War on 4 July 1916*
GREENWICH CEMETERY, United Kingdom
Son of the late Charles and Annie Loughran; husband of Sarah Loughran, of 74, Mary Street, Belfast.

Loughran, Joseph William Fredrick - Private
42030 Royal Berkshire Regiment 7th Battalion *Age 20 Died in War on 16 September 1918*
KARASOULI MILITARY CEMETERY, Greece
Son of Patrick and Margaret Loughran, of 5 Mawhinney's Court, Townsend Street, Belfast.

Loughran, Michael - Rifleman
10384 Royal Irish Rifles 2nd Battalion *Died of Wounds on 12 August 1917*
Born Omagh, enlisted Glasgow, resident of Belfast.

Loughran, William - Private
W/538 Cheshire Regiment 11th Battalion *Died in War on 14 October 1918*
PLOEGSTEERT MEMORIAL, Belgium
Born in Belfast, enlisted in Port Sunlight, England.

Love, Charles Edwin - Ships Steward
209188 Royal Navy HMS "Indefatigable" *Age 36 Killed in Action at the Battle of Jutland on 31 May 1916*
PLYMOUTH NAVAL MEMORIAL, United Kingdom
Son of John and Martha Love, of Belfast; husband of Cecelia A. A. Love,
of 21, Glencairn Terrace, St. Budeaux, Devonport.

Love, James - Rifleman
5405 Royal Irish Rifles 1st Battalion *Died of Wounds on 13 April 1916*
WARLOY-BAILLON COMMUNAL CEMETERY, France
Son of William and Elizabeth Love, of 134, Balfour Avenue, Belfast.

Love, James Patrick - Rifleman
41192 3rd New Zealand Rifle Brigade 4th Battalion *Age 32 Killed in Action on 23 November 1917*
BUTTES NEW BRITISH CEMETERY, POLYGON WOOD, Belgium
Son of the late Michael Love and of Bridget Agnes Love, of 16, Chief Street, Belfast.
Born at Rathdangan, Wicklow.

Lowden, Norman - Lieutenant
Royal Inniskilling Fusiliers 9th Battalion attached 109th Trench Mortar Battery
Age 22 Killed in Action on 21 March 1918
SAVY BRITISH CEMETERY, France
Son of Mr. and Mrs. James Lowden, of 5, Easton Avenue, Belfast. Mentioned in Despatches.

Lowe, Thomas - Rifleman
7286 Royal Irish Rifles 1st Battalion *Died in War on 1 April 1917*
BRAY MILITARY CEMETERY, France
Born in Deptford, Kent, enlisted in Holywood, resident of Belfast.

Lowry, Albert - Private
22812 Royal Irish Fusiliers 8th Battalion *Died in War on 26 May 1916*
VERMELLES BRITISH CEMETERY, France
A native of Belfast and enlisted in the city.

Lowry, David - Stoker
2581T Royal Naval Reserve HMS "Queen Mary" *Died in War on 31 May 1916*
PORTSMOUTH NAVAL MEMORIAL, United Kingdom
34 Arkwright Street, Belfast. His only brother, Hugh, had been killed five months previously.

Lowry, Francis - Rifleman
20259 Royal Irish Rifles 1st Battalion *Age 21 Died of Wounds on 8 April 1918*
ST. SEVER CEMETERY EXTENSION, ROUEN, France
Son of Samuel and Elizabeth Lowry, of 20, Hamilton Place, Belfast.

Lowry, George - Private
12634 Royal Irish Fusiliers 6th Battalion *Age 21 Died in War on 9 August 1915*
HELLES MEMORIAL, Turkey
Youngest son of William Lowry of Springfield Cottage, Springfield Road, Belfast.
Two other brothers also served.

Lowry, George - Rifleman
1395 Royal Irish Rifles 13th Battalion *Age 19 Died in War on 8 December 1917*
THIEPVAL MEMORIAL, France
Son of William and Agnes Lowry, of 8, Bloomfield Street, Belfast.

Lowry, Henry Cooke - Captain
Royal Army Veterinary Corps *Age 32 Died in War on 11 July 1916*
BASRA WAR CEMETERY, Iraq
8 Candahar Street, Belfast. Only son of James Lowry JP of Larne.

Lowry, Hugh George - Rifleman
7471 Royal Irish Rifles 1st Battalion *Age 29 Died in War on 29 January 1916*
RUE-DU-BOIS MILITARY CEMETERY, FLEURBAIX, France
Son of Mr. and Mrs. William John Lowry, of 34, Arkwright Street, Belfast.
His brother, David, was killed serving in the Royal Navy.

Lowry, James - Private
4286 Royal Inniskilling Fusiliers 2nd Battalion *Killed in Action on 16 May 1915*
LE TOURET MEMORIAL, France and Flanders
Born and enlisted in Belfast.

Lowry, John - Able Seaman
Mercantile Marine S.S. "Garthwaite" (London)
Age 24 Drowned as a result of an attack by an enemy submarine on 13 December 1917
TOWER HILL MEMORIAL, United Kingdom
Son of William and Agnes Lowry, of 21, Hanover Street, Belfast.

Lowry, John - Second Lieutenant
King's Shropshire Light Infantry 9th Battalion attached 2nd Battalion *Age 23 Died in War on 4 May 1917*
SALONIKA (LEMBET ROAD) MILITARY CEMETERY, Greece
Son of John and Eleanor Lowry, of Belfast.

Lowry, Robert - Fireman
Mercantile Marine S.S. "Coquet" (London) *Drowned, as a result of an attack by an enemy submarine on 4 January 1916*
TOWER HILL MEMORIAL, United Kingdom
Born in Belfast.

Lowry, Robert Ernest - Rifleman
2897 Royal Irish Rifles 14th Battalion *Age 19 Died in War on 16 August 1917*
TYNE COT MEMORIAL, *Belgium*
Son of William and Margaret Lowry, of 212, Grosvenor Road, Belfast.

Lowry, Samuel - Sergeant
1139 Royal Irish Rifles "B" Company 8th Battalion *Age 30 Died in War on 2 July 1916*
THIEPVAL MEMORIAL, *France*
Husband of Harriet L. Lowry, of 36, Powerscourt Street, Belfast. He was a former employee of Belfast Co-Op, played soccer for Willowfield United and was a member of the old UVF. He had been Mentioned in Despatches before being awarded the Distinguished Conduct Medal.

Lowry, Thomas Edwin - Lance Corporal
10/15177 Royal Irish Rifles 10th Battalion *Died of sickness contracted in France on 12 June 1918*
BELFAST CITY CEMETERY, *United Kingdom*
Husband of Minnie Lowry, of 33, Matlock Street, Belfast. Holder of the Silver War Badge.

Lowry, William - Lance Corporal
13510 Royal Irish Fusiliers 7th Battalion *Age 28 Killed in Action on 26 April 1916*
VERMELLES BRITISH CEMETERY, *France*
Son of William and the late Mrs. Lowry, of Belfast; husband of Ellen Lowry, of 44, Vernon Street, Belfast.

Lowry, William - Rifleman
17/1530 Royal Irish Rifles 10th Battalion *Age 28 Died as a result of War on 26 May 1919*
BERLIN SOUTH-WESTERN CEMETERY, *Germany*
Son of Robert and Elizabeth Rea Lowry, of 4, Hurst Street, Belfast.

Lowry, William - Rifleman
6776 Royal Irish Rifles 2nd Battalion *Age 19 Killed in Action on 7 July 1916*
THIEPVAL MEMORIAL, *France*
Son of William and Agnes Lowry, of 8, Bloomfield Street, Connswater, Belfast.

Lucas, Joseph - Private
63719 Royal Fusiliers 1st Battalion *Age 25 Died in War on 25 March 1918*
POZIERES MEMORIAL, *France*
Son of Joseph and Elizabeth Lucas, of 46, Edenderry, Shaws Bridge, Belfast.

Lucas, Robert - Private
4241 Seaforth Highlanders 1/5th Battalion *Age 19 Died in War on 29 June 1916*
MAROEUIL BRITISH CEMETERY, *France*
Son of Joseph and Catherine Lucas, of Belfast.

Lundy, Patrick - Rifleman
10339 Royal Irish Rifles "A" Company 7th Battalion *Age 24 Died in War on 16 August 1917*
TYNE COT MEMORIAL, *Belgium*
Son of the late Arthur and Sarah Lundy; husband of Catherine Lundy, of 27, Anderson Street, Belfast.

Lyddall, Herbert Percy Sydney - Lance Corporal
L/8635 Royal Sussex Regiment 7th Battalion *Age 28 Died in War on 25 November 1917*
CAMBRAI MEMORIAL, LOUVERVAL, *France*
Son of the late George William and Alice Lyddall, of 91, Sugden Road, Clapham Common, London; husband of Jeanie Lyddall, of 59, Lavinia Street, Ormeau Road, Belfast.

Journey of Remembering

Lyle, William - Sergeant
G/40 Royal Irish Fusiliers 1st Garrison Battalion *Died of Bright's disease on 31 July 1916*
KIRKEE 1914-1918 MEMORIAL, India
Husband of Mary Jane Lyle, of Belfast.

Lynar, Edward - Private
15019 Royal Army Medical Corps 16th Field Ambulance *Age 41 Died in War on 26 October 1914*
LONGUENESSE (ST. OMER) SOUVENIR CEMETERY, France
Son of Alfred Lynar, Moorgate Street, Belfast. Husband of Hannah Carson (formerly Lynar), of 23, Clarendon Avenue, Bloomfield, Belfast.

Lynas, Francis - Private
7482 Royal Inniskilling Fusiliers 2nd Battalion *Killed in Action on 18 March 1916*
AUTHUILE MILITARY CEMETERY, France
Born and enlisted in Belfast.

Lynas, Hugh - Private
12/27169 Royal Inniskilling Fusiliers 10th Battalion *Age 35 Killed in Action on 16 August 1917*
WHITE HOUSE CEMETERY, Belgium
Son of Hugh and Jane Lynas, of Bangor, County Down; husband of Mary Lynas, of 48, Welland Street, Connswater, Belfast.

Lynas, John - Private
7800 Royal Inniskilling Fusiliers *Died in War on 4 November 1918*
BELFAST CITY CEMETERY, United Kingdom
Born in County Antrim. Resident of Belfast.

Lynas, William - Lance Corporal
9631 Royal Irish Rifles 2nd Battalion *Age 23 Died in War on 27 July 1915*
YPRES (MENIN GATE) MEMORIAL, Belgium
Son of Martha Lynas, of 63, Malvern Street, Shankill Road, Belfast.

Lynas, William John - Rifleman
17/1552 Royal Irish Rifles 12th Battalion *Age 21 Died of pneumonia on 29 June 1918*
PREMONT BRITISH CEMETERY, France
Son of William and Mary Lynas, of 219, Cambrai Street, Belfast.

Lynch, David - Rifleman
15183 Royal Irish Rifles 14th Battalion *Killed In Action on 12 April 1917*
KANDAHAR FARM CEMETERY, Belgium
Born and enlisted in Belfast.

Lynch, Herbert Valentine Mitchell - Rifleman
14/15184 Royal Irish Rifles "A" Company 14th Battalion *Age 25 Killed in Action on 1 November 1916*
POND FARM CEMETERY, Belgium
Son of Sergeant Major Denis Lynch and Elizabeth Jane Lynch, of 66, Carlisle Street, Belfast.

Lynch, John Walter - Seaman
Mercantile Marine "Umgeni" (London) *Age 28 Presumed drowned on 9 November 1917*
TOWER HILL MEMORIAL, United Kingdom
Father of Miss Gertrude Lynch, of 121, Sutton Street, Liverpool. Born at Belfast.

Lynch, Michael James - Private
3/6872 Prince Albert's (Somerset Light Infantry) 1st Battalion *Died in War on 9 August 1916*
LIJSSENTHOEK MILITARY CEMETERY, Belgium
Born in Belfast.

Lynch, Thomas - Sergeant
15165 Royal Inniskilling Fusiliers 8th Battalion *Age 21 Killed in Action on 15 July 1916*
PHILOSOPHE BRITISH CEMETERY, MAZINGARBE, France
Son of James and Mary Lynch, of 17, Fallswater Street, Belfast.

Lyness, David Andrew - Company Sergeant Major
4588 Royal Irish Rifles "A" Company 2nd Battalion *Age 34 Died in War on 15 September 1914*
LA FERTE-SOUS-JOUARRE MEMORIAL, France
Son of William and Margaret Lyness (Stepmother), of 29, Carlisle Street, Belfast; husband of Helena Lyness, of 158, New Lodge Road, Belfast. Holder of the Long Service and Good Conduct Medal.

Lyness, Harold - Second Lieutenant
Royal Irish Fusiliers 9th Battalion *Died of Wounds on 2 September 1916*
BAILLEUL COMMUNAL CEMETERY EXTENSION (NORD), France
Eldest son of Joseph and Jane Lyness, of 88, Fitzroy Avenue, Belfast. Originally enlisted in the Black Watch and in 1915 was commissioned into the Royal Irish Rifles. Mortally wounded south of Messines and died in No 2 Clearing Station, Bailleul, France.

Lyness, James - Rifleman
17/1167 Royal Irish Rifles 9th Battalion *Died in War on 7 June 1917*
LONE TREE CEMETERY, Belgium
Son of Mr. Lyness, of 34, Ghent Street, Crumlin Road, Belfast.

Lynn, Adam (Eddie) - Rifleman
6729 Royal Irish Rifles 16th Battalion *Died in War on 30 January 1917*
LA PLUS DOUVE FARM CEMETERY, Belgium
Son of Mr. J. Lynn, of 27, Excise Street, Belfast.

Lynn, Alexander - Private
16899 Royal Inniskilling Fusiliers 9th Battalion *Age 19 Killed in Action on 1 July 1916*
THIEPVAL MEMORIAL, France
Son of William John and Annie Lynn, of 23, Ferndale Street, Belfast.

Lynn, John - Lance Corporal
13177 Royal Inniskilling Fusiliers 5th Battalion *Age 20 Died in War on 15 August 1915*
AZMAK CEMETERY, SUVLA, Turkey
Son of James and Elizabeth Lynn, of 162, Spamount Street, Belfast.

Lynn, Robert - Private
17057 Royal Scots Fusiliers 2nd Battalion *Died in War on 30 September 1915*
LOOS MEMORIAL, France
Born in Belfast, enlisted Glasgow.

Lynn, William James - Private
10302 Royal Inniskilling Fusiliers 1st Battalion *Age 21 Died in War on 12 May 1915*
LANCASHIRE LANDING CEMETERY, Turkey
Son of Robert A. and Mary Ann Lynn, of 57 Bristol Street, Belfast.

Lyons, - Lieutenant Colonel (Brevet Major) William Barry
Royal Munster Fusiliers 2nd Battalion *Age 29 Died of Wounds on 4 September 1916*
ABBEVILLE COMMUNAL CEMETERY, France
Son of James Bristow Lyons and Marguerite Lyons of Belfast; grandson of W. T. B. Lyons, D.L.,
of Old Park, County Antrim.

Lyons, Archibald - Gunner
2710 Royal Field Artillery *Died in War on 2 October 1914*
LA FERTE-SOUS-JOUARRE MEMORIAL, France
Husband of Annie Lyons, 17 Little Victoria Street, Belfast.

Lyons, Henry - Sergeant
9360 Royal Inniskilling Fusiliers 2nd Battalion *Age 27 Killed in Action on 1 July 1916*
CONNAUGHT CEMETERY, THIEPVAL, France
Son of Henry and Ellen Lyons, of Belfast; husband of Charlotte Lyons,
of 24, Bonds Street, Waterside, Londonderry.

Lyons, Henry James - Second Lieutenant
King's Own (Royal Lancaster Regiment) 7th Battalion *Died in War on 23 September 1917*
DUHALLOW A.D.S. CEMETERY, Belgium
Husband of Harriet Isabella , 75 Riga Street, Belfast.

Lyons, Hugh - Private
S/40221 Seaforth Highlanders 7th Battalion *Age 21 Died in War on 30 April 1917*
ARRAS MEMORIAL, France
Son of the late William and Elizabeth Lyons.

Lyons, John - Gunner
69091 Royal Field Artillery *Died in War on 26 August 1914*
LE CATEAU COMMUNAL CEMETERY, France
Born in Belfast, enlisted in Glasgow.

Lyons, John - Petty Officer
163666 Royal Navy HMS "Flirt" *Died in War on 26 October 1916*
PORTSMOUTH NAVAL MEMORIAL, United Kingdom
Member of Berry Street Presbyterian Church.

Lyons, John - Private
2368 Connaught Rangers 6th Battalion *Died in War on 4 May 1916*
DUD CORNER CEMETERY, LOOS, France
Born, enlisted and resident in Belfast.

Lyons, Matthew - Lance Sergeant
15167 Royal Inniskilling Fusiliers 2nd Battalion *Age 21 Killed in Action on 21 March 1918*
POZIERES MEMORIAL, France
Son of Mrs. Charlotte Edith Lyons, of 8, Wesley Street, Belfast.

Lyons, Robert - Private
3496 Royal Inniskilling Fusiliers "B" Company 1st Battalion *Age 28 Died in War on 21 August 1915*
HELLES MEMORIAL, Turkey
Son of the late Alexander and Annie Lyons; husband of Martha Lyons, of 126, Cambrai Street, Belfast.

Lyons, Robert Victor - Second Lieutenant
Royal Irish Rifles 14th Battalion attached 23rd Entrenching Battalion *Age 21 Killed in Action on 24 March 1918*
POZIERES MEMORIAL, *France*
Son of Ruth Lyons, of Rosetta Park, Belfast, and the late Thomas H. Lyons.

Lyons, Thomas - Private
41325 Princess Victoria's (Royal Irish Fusiliers) 9th Battalion *Died in War on 29 March 1918*
POZIERES MEMORIAL, *France*
Born in Belfast, enlisted Antrim. Formerly 1846, North Irish Horse.

Lyons, Thomas J - Private
11501 Royal Irish Rifles 6th Battalion *Age 22 Died in War on 10 August 1915*
HELLES MEMORIAL, *Turkey*
Son of Peter and Emily Lyons, of 7, Greenland Street, Belfast.

Lyons, William - Private
DM2/138253 Royal Army Service Corps *Died in War on 22 January 1917*
SALONIKA (LEMBET ROAD) MILITARY CEMETERY, *Greece*
Born in Cork, enlisted Belfast.

Lyons, William H St J - Lieutenant
Middlesex Regiment *Age 29 Died in War on 1 November 1918*
KNOCKBREDA CHURCH OF IRELAND CHURCHYARD, *United Kingdom*
Son of the late The Right Hon W.H.H. Lyons DL and of Lily Lyons of "Newlands", Deramore Park Belfast. Born at Belfast. Member of Masonic Lodge No 10, Belfast.

Lyons, William Thomas - Captain
King's Own (Royal Lancaster Regiment) 8th Battalion *Age 24 Died in War on 18 July 1916*
THIEPVAL MEMORIAL, *France*
Son of Mr. and Mrs. T. H. Lyons, of Valere, Rosetta Park, Belfast. Had been a member of Queen's University OTC. Awarded the Military Cross for gallantry.

Lyons, William Thomas - Captain
Royal Welsh Fusiliers 10th Battalion *Age 35 Killed in Action on 3 March 1916*
SPOILBANK CEMETERY, *Belgium*
Son of Martha Lyons, of 21, Kerrsland Drive, Strandtown, Belfast, and the late William Lyons. Educated at Methodist College and the Royal School Dungannon. Adjutant of his battalion, Mentioned in Despatches.

Lyttle, John - Sailor
Mercantile Marine S.S. "Garron Head" (Belfast) *Age 20 Killed by mine on 16 November 1917*
TOWER HILL MEMORIAL, *United Kingdom*
Son of James and Lucy Ann Lyttle, of 29, Trafalgar Street, Belfast.

Lyttle, Thomas Faulkner - Sergeant
50850 Royal Army Medical Corps 108th Field Ambulance *Age 42 Died of Wounds (gas) on 20 September 1918*
LA KREULE MILITARY CEMETERY, HAZEBROUCK, *France*
Son of William and Adelaide Lyttle, of Belfast; husband of Louise Lyttle, of "Normanlea" 106, Park Crescent, Turffontein, Johannesburg. Holder of the Distinguished Conduct Medal.

Lyttle, William - Private
202718 Border Regiment 7th Battalion *Died in War on 21 September 1918*
VIS-EN-ARTOIS BRITISH MEMORIAL, HAUCOURT, *France*
Born in Belfast enlisted in Whitehaven, Cumbria.

Lyttle, William - Rifleman
13044 Royal Irish Rifles 9th Battalion *Age 18 Killed in Action on 1 July 1916*
THIEPVAL MEMORIAL, France
Son of Samuel Lyttle, of 16, Tenth Street, Belfast.

Lyttle, William Thomas - Lance Corporal
10084 Royal Inniskilling Fusiliers 1st Battalion *Killed in Action on 1 July 1916*
THIEPVAL MEMORIAL, France
Born in Belfast, enlisted Dublin. Formerly 8216 Royal Dublin Fusiliers.

Mabin, George - Private
3574 Royal Inniskilling Fusiliers 1st Battalion *Age 18 Killed in Action on 1 July 1916*
THIEPVAL MEMORIAL, France
Son of George and Margaret Mabin, of 16, Crosby Street, Belfast. The Mabin brothers, George and Jeremiah, although in different regiments and divisions, died within a mile of each other on the opening day of the Somme battle. Since 1916 the Mabin family have, each year, faithfully marked the anniversary with an insertion in the local press.

Mabin, Jeremiah - Rifleman
156 Royal Irish Rifles 9th Battalion *Age 17 Killed in Action on 1 July 1916*
THIEPVAL MEMORIAL, France
Son of George and Margaret Mabin, of 16, Crosby Street, Belfast.

MacAulay, Samuel - Corporal
14/16726 Royal Irish Rifles 14th Battalion *Age 24 Killed in Action on 7 June 1917*
SPANBROEKMOLEN BRITISH CEMETERY, Belgium
Son of Susan MacAulay, of 14, Mountcollyer Avenue, York Road, Belfast, and the late Samuel MacAulay.

MacAuley, Thomas - Private
9136 Royal Irish Rifles 2nd Battalion *Killed in Action on 12 December 1914*
YPRES (MENIN GATE) MEMORIAL, Belgium
Husband of Charlotte, Argyle Street, Belfast.

MacAuley, William Ingham - Major
Army Veterinary Corps Assistant Director of Veterinary Services *Age 38 Died in War on 14 May 1917*
BAPAUME AUSTRALIAN CEMETERY, France
Twice Mentioned in Despatches. Son of Christopher J. and Margaret G. Macauley, of 3, Easton Crescent, Cliftonville, Belfast. Native of Monaghan.

MacCabe, Robert Maxwell - Lieutenant
London Regiment (Post Office Rifles) 8th Battalion *Age 31 Died of Wounds, received at Givenchy on 23 April 1915*
BETHUNE TOWN CEMETERY, France
Son of Thomas and Magaret MacCabe, of 45, Avoca Street, Belfast; husband of Amy Constance Robb MacCabe, of 22, Landscape Terrace, Belfast. Educated at Cliftonpark National School and Queen's University where he was a member of the Officer Training Corps.

MacColl, George Edwardes - Major
Royal Irish Rifles 8th Battalion *Age 44 Died in War on 5 August 1917*
YPRES (MENIN GATE) MEMORIAL, Belgium
Son of the late Hector and Mary MacColl, of Belfast; husband of Margaret P. MacColl, of "Towerdene", Bearsden, Glasgow. Joined 6th August 1914, as a Lieutenant.

MacDermott, Robert Wilson - Second Lieutenant
Royal Irish Rifles 8th Battalion *Age 25 Died in War on 8 January 1916*
AUCHONVILLERS MILITARY CEMETERY, France
B.A., LL B. Son of Rev John MacDermott, M.A., D.D., and Lydia Allan MacDermott, of Belmont Manse, Belfast. Educated at Campbell College. He was about to be called to the Bar when war broke out. He was the first 36th (Ulster) Division officer to be killed in the Somme area. His brother, Lord MacDermott, who also served, rose to be Lord Chief Justice of Northern Ireland.

MacDiarmuid, Seagon - Private
7956 Connaught Rangers 2nd Battalion *Age 32 Died in War on 14 September 1914*
VAILLY BRITISH CEMETERY, France
Son of William MacDiarmuid, husband of Margaret MacDiarmuid, of 3, Spencer Street, Belfast.

MacDonald, Walter - Private
875012 Canadian Infantry (Manitoba Regiment) 78th Battalion *Age 31 Died in War on 9 April 1917*
GIVENCHY-EN-GOHELLE CANADIAN CEMETERY, SOUCHEZ, France
Husband of Mrs. B. MacDonald, of 29, Roseberry Gardens, Belfast, Ireland. He was born in Liverpool and worked as a plumber. A Presbyterian, he had served for three years in the Canadian Militia.

MacDowell, Robert - Second Lieutenant
North Staffordshire Regiment *Died in War on 25 February 1917*
BASRA MEMORIAL, Iraq
17, Jocelyn Gardens, Belfast.

MacFarland, George Adams - Captain
5779 Royal Army Medical Corps *Age 44 Died in War on 17 October 1917*
ST. MARYLEBONE CEMETERY, United Kingdom
Son of the late Rev. George MacFarland. Born at Belfast.

MacIlwaine, Julian Mackay - Captain
Royal Irish Rifles 5th Battalion and Royal Flying Corps 12 Squadron *Age 29 Killed in Action on 22 March 1918*
ARRAS FLYING SERVICES MEMORIAL, France
Son of the late Edward Nangle MacIlwaine and Julia Alma Gaussen MacIlwaine, of Eglantine Avenue, Belfast. Educated at RBAI and a member of Queen's University OTC. Wounded in April, 1915, whilst serving with 1st Battalion Royal Irish Rifles. Thereafter was attached to the Royal Flying Corps as a pilot. He, his observer, and aircraft went missing in action, later presumed killed.

MacKay, James - Lieutenant
Gordon Highlanders 3rd Battalion attached 1st Battalion *Age 23 Died in War on 25 September 1915*
SANCTUARY WOOD CEMETERY, Belgium
A former pupil at RBAI and son of W. M. and Jessie Mackay, of 63, Castlereagh Street, Belfast. Born at Caithness, Scotland.

MacKenzie, John Cameron - Lance Corporal
2374 Australian Infantry 12th Battalion *Age 31 Killed in Action on 1 May 1918*
LE PEUPLIER MILITARY CEMETERY, CAESTRE, France
Son of William Gordon MacKenzie and Mary Gordon MacKenzie, of Cooroy, Queensland. Born in Belfast, Ireland.

MacMahon, Featherston - Private
3528 Royal Irish Fusiliers 1st Battalion *Died in War on 3 May 1917*
ARRAS MEMORIAL, France
Born and enlisted in Belfast.

MacMaster, William Graham - Lance Corporal
17/214 Royal Irish Rifles 10th Battalion *Age 27 Died in War on 13 October 1916*
ST. QUENTIN CABARET MILITARY CEMETERY, Belgium
Son of James Henry and Isabella MacMaster, of 81, Claremont Avenue, Montclair, New Jersey, U.S.A. Returned from the U.S.A. at outbreak of war and enlisted in the Ulster Division early in 1915. Born at Belfast.

MacRory, Samuel - Rifleman
395 Royal Irish Rifles 10th Battalion *Killed In Action on 1 July 1916*
THIEPVAL MEMORIAL, France
Born and enlisted in Belfast.

MacWhinnie, Norman Henry - Regimental Sergeant Major
5177 King's Own Scottish Borderers 2nd Battalion *Age 37 Killed in Action on 13 September 1914*
VAILLY BRITISH CEMETERY, *France*
Awarded the Medaille Militaire (France), the Military Cross, the Distinguished Conduct Medal and Mentioned in Despatches. Son of James Tait MacWhinnie and Elizabeth Carruthers MacWhinnie; husband of Caroline Christine MacWhinnie, of 38, Harcourt Street, Cliftonville, Belfast. Born at Dumfries, Scotland.

Maconachie, Samuel - Private
S3/030986 Army Service Corps Ulster Divisional Train *Age 21 Died after operation on 2 September 1915*
SEAFORD CEMETERY, *United Kingdom*
1, Greenmount, Ballygomartin Road, Belfast. Youngest son of the late Mr & Mrs John Maconachie. A member of the old UVF.

Madden, Francis - Lance Corporal
9973 Royal Irish Fusiliers 2nd Battalion *Died in War on 14 March 1915*
YPRES (MENIN GATE) MEMORIAL, *Belgium*
(served as CAMPBELL), 39, McDonnell Street, Belfast. Son of the late James Madden; husband of Josephine McIntyre (formerly Madden), of 2, Salisbury Square, Edinburgh.

Madden, William Henry - Captain
Royal Irish Rifles 16th (Pioneer) Battalion *Died in War on 24 March 1918*
NOYON NEW BRITISH CEMETERY, *France*
Born in Cork where his father was Dean of the Cathedral. Taught at Campbell College, Belfast.

Maddock, William - Private
1594 Highland Light Infantry 7th (Blythswood) Battalion (Territorial) *Died in War on 13 July 1915*
LANCASHIRE LANDING CEMETERY, *Turkey*
Born in Belfast, enlisted Glasgow.

Magee, Alexander - Private
S/6596 Army Ordance Corps *Died in War on 14 August 1916*
BAILLEUL COMMUNAL CEMETERY EXTENSION (NORD), *France*
123, Sandy Row, Belfast. Born in Dublin.

Magee, Alexander - Rifleman
13246 Royal Irish Rifles "C" Company 8th Battalion *Age 21 Died of Wounds on 19 November 1915*
MAILLY-MAILLET COMMUNAL CEMETERY EXTENSION, *France*
Son of Malcom McGacken Magee and Margaret Magee, of Gortmerron, Bloomfield, Belfast.

Magee, Arthur - Sergeant
8599 Royal Inniskilling Fusiliers *Died in War on 14 November 1914*
PLOEGSTEERT MEMORIAL, *Belgium*
72, Cheviot Avenue, Belfast.

Magee, David - Private
6242 Royal Inniskilling Fusiliers 8th Battalion *Died in War on 9 September 1916*
THIEPVAL MEMORIAL, *France*
Born in Belfast, enlisted Omagh.

Magee, David - Stoker First Class
SS/109577 Royal Navy HMS "Indefatigable" *Age 23 Killed in Action on 31 May 1916*
PLYMOUTH NAVAL MEMORIAL, *United Kingdom*
Son of James and Agnes Magee, of 2, Iris Street, Belfast. Native of Glastry, County Down.

Magee, Edward - Lance Corporal
357905 King's (Liverpool Regiment) 10th Battalion *Died in War on 30 November 1917*
CAMBRAI MEMORIAL, France
Born in Belfast. Lived in Liverpool when enlisted.

Magee, Edward - Private
8507 Princess Victoria's (Royal Irish Fusiliers) 1st Battalion *Died in War on 27 August 1914*
BANTOUZELL COMMUNAL CEMETERY, France
Born and enlisted in Belfast.

Magee, Edward - Rifleman
6157 Royal Irish Rifles 2nd Battalion *Age 23 Killed in Action on 24 March 1918*
SAVY BRITISH CEMETERY, France
Son of James and Sarah Magee, of 7, Malcolm Street, Belfast.

Magee, Edward G. - Private
28771 Royal Inniskilling Fusiliers "C" Company 7/8th Battalion *Age 25 Died in War on 21 March 1918*
POZIERES MEMORIAL, France
Son of Ephraim and Jane Magee, of 16, Beechfield Street, Belfast.

Magee, Edward James - Sergeant
50998 Machine Gun Corps (Cavalry) 14th Squadron *Died of Wounds on 29 March 1918*
ST. SEVER CEMETERY EXTENSION, ROUEN, France
Son of William John Magee, 45, Ottawa Street, Belfast. Two brothers also served.

Magee, Henry - Private
10318 Royal Inniskilling Fusiliers "D" Company 2nd Battalion *Age 20; Died in War on 10 November 1914*
BAILLEUL COMMUNAL CEMETERY (NORD), France
Son of James and Elizabeth Magee, of 13, Frere Street, Belfast.

Magee, Hugh - Lance Corporal
8862 Royal Irish Rifles 2nd Battalion *Age 29 Died of pneumonia on 27 September 1918*
SELESTAT (Schlestadt) COMMUNAL CEMETERY, France
Son of Hugh and Mary Magee, of Willowfield Street, Belfast; husband of Alice Magee, of 6, Canal Quay, Newry.

Magee, Hugh - Private
72971 Machine Gun Corps (Infantry) *Died in War on 17 August 1917*
MENDINGHEM MILITARY CEMETERY, Belgium
Born and enlisted in Belfast. Formerly 2466 Connaught Rangers.

Magee, James - Private
10333 Royal Inniskilling Fusiliers 2nd Battalion *Killed in Action on 1 April 1917*
ROUPY COMMUNAL CEMETERY, France
Born and enlisted in Belfast. Awarded the Military Medal.

Magee, James - Rifleman
6988 Royal Irish Rifles 1st Battalion *Killed in Action on 12 March 1915*
LE TOURET MEMORIAL, France
Born and resident in Belfast. Enlisted in Holywood.

Magee, James - Rifleman
8863 Royal Irish Rifles 1st Battalion *Died in War on 4 April 1915*
SAILLY-SUR-LA-LYS-CANADIAN CEMETERY, France
Born and enlisted in Belfast.

Magee, James Alexander - Rifleman
1517 Royal Irish Rifles 10th Battalion *Killed in Action on 1 July 1916*
THIEPVAL MEMORIAL, France
33, Richmond Street, Belfast.

Magee, John - Private
4070 Seaforth Highlanders "B" Company 1/4th Battalion *Age 28 Killed in Action on 17 November 1916*
FRANKFURT TRENCH BRITISH CEMETERY, BEAUMONT-HAMEL, France
Son of John and Jane Magee, of 3, Antigua Street, Belfast.

Magee, Joseph - Lance Corporal
1718 Connaught Rangers 6th Battalion *Died in War on 26 October 1916*
BAILLEUL COMMUNAL CEMETERY EXTENSION (NORD), France
Born at Belfast, enlisted Workington, Cumberland. Son of Edgar and Jemima Magee.

Magee, Joseph - Private
5031 Royal Munster Fusiliers 6th Battalion *Died in War on 15 August 1915*
HELLES MEMORIAL, Turkey
Son of John and Sarah Magee, of 4, Gibson Street, Belfast.

Magee, Joseph - Rifleman
9178 Royal Irish Rifles 1st Battalion *Killed in Action on 1 July 1916*
THIEPVAL MEMORIAL, France
Born and enlisted in Belfast.

Magee, Malcolm M - Private
3347658 Canadian Garrison Regiment 6th Battalion *Age 30 Died of influenza on 11 December 1918*
HALIFAX (FORT MASSEY) CEMETERY, Canada
Son of Malcolm McCracken Magee and Margaret Magee, of Gortmerror, Bloomfield, Belfast, Ireland. He worked as a teamster and was Presbyterian by religion.

Magee, Patrick - Private
20920 Royal Irish Fusiliers "C" Company 8th Battalion *Age 19 Killed in Action on 13 December 1916*
ST. POL COMMUNAL CEMETERY EXTENSION, France
Son of Patrick and Mary Ann Magee, of 12, Osman Street, Belfast.

Magee, Patrick - Sergeant
14352 Royal Inniskilling Fusiliers 7th Battalion *Died in War on 9 September 1916*
THIEPVAL MEMORIAL, France
Husband of Annie Magee, 48, Ton Street, Belfast.

Magee, Robert - Rifleman
19129 Royal Irish Rifles 12th Battalion *Died in War on 22 March 1917*
BAILLEUL COMMUNAL CEMETERY EXTENSION (NORD), France
Born in Belfast, lived in Ballymena, County Antrim when enlisted

Magee, Robert Henry - Private
528 Princess Partricia's Canadian Light Infantry *Age 18 Died in War on 8 May 1915*
YPRES (MENIN GATE) MEMORIAL, Belgium
Son of John Magee, 31, Eia Street, Belfast. Born at Whiteabbey.

Magee, William - Rifleman
13234 Royal Irish Rifles 9th Battalion *Died in War on 21 June 1917*
DERRY HOUSE CEMETERY No.2, Belgium
Son of Daniel Magee, Clovelly Street, Belfast. A member of the old UVF.

Magee, William John - Company Sergeant Major
6666 Royal Inniskilling Fusiliers "G" Company 1st Battalion *Age 35 Killed in Action on 17 May 1915*
TWELVE TREE COPSE CEMETERY, Turkey
Son of Francis James and Louisa F. Magee, of 80, Kimberley Street, Ballynafeigh, Belfast.
Awarded the Distinguished Conduct Medal.

Magill, Alexander - Corporal
S/6251 Argyll and Sutherland Highlanders 10th Battalion *Age 25 Died in War on 27 September 1915*
LOOS MEMORIAL, France
Son of Hugh Magill, of 2, Fedora Terrace, Skegoneill Avenue, Belfast.

Magill, Charles - Rifleman
49296 Rifle Brigade 1st Battalion *Age 20 Died in War on 1 November 1918*
PRESEAU COMMUNAL CEMETERY EXTENSION, France
Son of Samuel and Mary Magill, of 46, Dundela Street, Belfast. Formerly 4449 Seaforth Highlanders.

Magill, Frank - Rifleman
1833 Royal Irish Rifles 15th Battalion *Died in War on 21 March 1918*
POZIERES MEMORIAL, France
Born and enlisted in Belfast.

Magill, Harry - Lance Corporal
101102 Canadian Infantry (Alberta Regiment) 49th Battalion *Age 25 Died in War on 27 September 1918*
ONTARIO CEMETERY, SAINS-LES-MARQUION, France
Son of Robert and Agnes Magill. Native of Belfast, Ireland. A homesteader, he was Presbyterian by religion.

Magill, Hugh - Private
4351 Manchester Regiment 12th Battalion *Died in War on 26 August 1918*
VIS-EN-ARTOIS BRITISH MEMORIAL, HAUCOURT, France
Born in Belfast. Lived in Belfast when enlisted.

Magill, James - Corporal
2412 Australian Infantry 15th Battalion *Killed in Action on 17 October 1917*
TYNE COT CEMETERY, Belgium
Son of James and Elizabeth Magill. Native of Belfast, Ireland.

Magill, James - Private
522 Manchester Regiment 1st Battalion *Died in War on 20 December 1914*
LE TOURET MEMORIAL, France
Born in Belfast, enlisted Manchester.

Magill, James - Private
S/40512 Seaforth Highlanders 2nd Battalion *Died in War on 11 April 1917*
BROWN'S COPSE CEMETERY, ROEUX, France
29, Belmont Street, Belfast.

Magill, James - Rifleman
9149 Royal Irish Rifles 1st Battalion *Age 20 Killed in Action on 9 May 1915*
PLOEGSTEERT MEMORIAL, Belgium
Son of James and Annie Magill, of 50, Mayflower Street, Belfast.

Magill, John - Corporal
10015 Royal Inniskilling Fusiliers 1st Battalion *Age 26 Died in War on 27 January 1917*
THIEPVAL MEMORIAL, France
Son of William Magill, of 97, Melrose Street, Belfast, and the late Catherine Magill (née Wilson).

Magill, John - Rifleman
19684 Royal Irish Rifles 13th Battalion *Killed in Action on 1 July 1916*
THIEPVAL MEMORIAL, France
Born and enlisted in Belfast.

Magill, John - Rifleman
7916 Royal Irish Rifles 2nd Battalion *Killed in Action on 24 March 1918*
POZIERES MEMORIAL, France
Enlisted Larne, resident of Belfast.

Magill, Michael - Private
5033 Royal Munster Fusiliers 6th Battalion *Died in War on 15 August 1915*
HELLES MEMORIAL, Turkey
18, Ton Street, Belfast.

Magill, Richard - Private
2453 Leinster Regiment 7th Battalion *Died in War on 12 May 1916*
Born in Lancashire, enlisted and resident in Belfast.

Magill, Robert James - Rifleman
11012 Royal Irish Rifles 6th Battalion *Died in War on 29 November 1915*
DOIRAN MEMORIAL, Greece
Born and enlisted in Larne, resident of Belfast.

Magill, William - Private
8391 Royal Irish Fusiliers 1st Battalion *Died in War on 21 November 1914*
PLOEGSTEERT MEMORIAL, Belgium
10, Little Patrick Street, Belfast.

Magennis, Edward - Private
M/344863 Royal Army Service Corps 1019th M.T. Company *Age 23 Died as a result of war on 20 May 1919*
BAGHDAD (NORTH GATE) WAR CEMETERY, Iraq
Son of Edward and Martha Magennis, of 128, Divis Street, Belfast.

Maginnes, Archibald - Corporal
387 Royal Irish Rifles 15th Battalion *Died in War on 7 December 1915*
MESNIL RIDGE CEMETERY, MESNIL-MARTINSART, France
Husband of Sarah and father of five children, all boys. 44, Bracken Street, Belfast.

Maginnis, James Abraham - Able Seaman
223915 Royal Navy HMS "Bittern"
Age 33 Drowned through collision in English Channel on 4 April 1918
PLYMOUTH NAVAL MEMORIAL, United Kingdom
Son of Jane Maginnis, of Lismachan Cottages, Belmont, Strandtown, Belfast,
and the late John Maginnis.

Magookin, William Douglas - Second Lieutenant
Royal Irish Rifles 12th Battalion *Age 38 Killed in Action on 21 March 1918*
POZIERES MEMORIAL, France
Husband of Dorothea Magookin, of 28, Newport Street, Belfast. Had been a bricklayer in civilian life.
Had risen through the ranks to become a Company Sergeant Major and was then commissioned.
Awarded the Distinguished Conduct Medal for bravery.

Magowan, James - Sergeant
19526 Machine Gun Corps (Infantry) 201st Company *Age 22 Killed in Action on 28 November 1917*
CAMBRAI MEMORIAL, LOUVERVAL, France
Son of James and Victoria Magowan, of 30, Braemar Street, Belfast.

Magowan, John - Private
14075 Royal Inniskilling Fusiliers 7/8th Battalion *Died in War on 16 August 1917*
TYNE COT MEMORIAL, Belgium
Born in Belfast, enlisted Newtownards.

Magowan, Samuel - Rifleman
15336 Royal Irish Rifles 14th Battalion *Killed In Action on 1 July 1916*
THIEPVAL MEMORIAL, France
Born and enlisted in Belfast.

Magowan, Thomas - Private
T4/160022 Royal Army Service Corp *Died on 17 May 1918*
BELFAST (DUNDONALD) CEMETERY, United Kingdom
Born and enlisted in Belfast.

Maguire, Daniel Joseph - Private
3155269 Canadian Infantry (Quebec Regiment) "C" Company 22nd Battalion
Age 25 Killed in Action on 27 August 1918
QUEBEC CEMETERY, CHERISY, France
Son of John Maguire, of 8, Lucknow Street, Belfast, Ireland and the late Mary McCorry Maguire.
Born in Markethill, County Armagh, he was a Catholic, worked as an electrician and was a single man.

Maguire, James - Private
46649 Lancashire Fusiliers 18th Battalion *Died in War on 23 May 1918*
VARENNES MILITARY CEMETERY, France
Born and enlisted in Belfast. Formerly 205820 Royal Engineers.

Maguire, John - Private
23900 Royal Irish Fusiliers 1st Battalion *Age 19 Died in War on 11 April 1917*
ARRAS MEMORIAL, France
Son of Thomas and Annie Maguire, of 33, Parkview Street, Belfast.

Maguire, Samuel John - Gunner
77062 Royal Field Artillery 106th Brigade *Age 19 Died of Wounds on 7 June 1917*
BEDFORD HOUSE CEMETERY, Belgium
Son of Mrs. Maria Maguire, of 44, Weir Street, Belfast.

Maguire, T - Able Seaman
Mercantile Marine Reserve HMS "Vivid III" *Age 56 Died as a result of war on 3 July 1919*
BELFAST (MILLTOWN) ROMAN CATHOLIC CEMETERY, United Kingdom
Husband of Mrs. Mary Maguire, of 40, Colligan Street, Belfast.

Maguire, William - Private
2715 Royal Inniskilling Fusiliers 8th Battalion *Killed in Action on 19 September 1917*
COXYDE MILITARY CEMETERY, Belgium
Born and enlisted Belfast.

Magury, James - Deck Hand
2183SD Royal Naval Reserve "St. Seiriol" *Age 43 Killed by a mine explosion in North Sea on 25 April 1918*
PORTSMOUTH NAVAL MEMORIAL, United Kingdom
Son of William and Mary Ann Magury, of Belfast.

Mahaffey, Samuel - Rifleman
5995 Royal Irish Rifles "C" Company 1st Battalion *Age 26 Died in War on 9 May 1915*
PLOEGSTEERT MEMORIAL, Belgium
Son of Mr. and Mrs. Mahaffey, of 69, Urney Street, Belfast.

Mahaffy, Henry Emerson - Private
S/290876 Royal Army Service Corps *Died in War on 22 October 1918*
STE MARIE CEMETERY, LE HAVRE, France
Born in Belfast. Lived in Glasgow when enlisted.

Mahaffy, Thomas - Rifleman
20908 Royal Irish Rifles 12th Battalion *Died in War on 13 April 1918*
TYNE COT MEMORIAL, Belgium
29, Hugh Street, Belfast.

Mahaffy, William - Private
26234 Royal Inniskilling Fusiliers 8th Battalion *Killed in Action on 29 April 1916*
LOOS MEMORIAL, France
Born and enlisted in Belfast.

Mahaffy, William - Private
63586 Canadian Infantry (Central Ontario Regiment) "A" Company 4th Battalion
Age 21 Killed in Action at Festubert on 1 June 1915
VIMY MEMORIAL, France
Son of Mrs. Sarah Mahaffy, of 80, Ewarts Row, Belfast, Ireland. Employed in the Angus shops, Montreal. He was a Presbyterian and had trained as a boilermaker.

Maher, Henry - Corporal
10033 Royal Munster Fusiliers 2nd Battalion *Died in War on 9 May 1915*
GUARDS CEMETERY WINDY CORNER, CUINCHY, France
Born in Capetown, South Africa, enlisted and resident in Belfast.

Journey of Remembering

Mahon, David - Rifleman
8989 Royal Irish Rifles 2nd Battalion *Died in War on 25 October 1914*
LE TOURET MEMORIAL, France
Born and enlisted in Belfast.

Mahon, William John - Lance Bombardier
750117 Royal Horse Artillery and Royal Field Artillery Territorial Force
Died as a result of war on 30 November 1918
CAMBRAI MEMORIAL LOUVERVAL, France
Born in Belfast enlisted in Newcastle.

Mahony, James - Lance Corporal
13519 Royal Irish Fusiliers 1st Battalion *Age 32 Died in War on 3 May 1917*
ARRAS MEMORIAL, France
Son of Charles Mahony; husband of Maggie Mahony, of 3, Gracehill Street, Belfast.

Mahood, David Ellis - Rifleman
9/15540 Royal Irish Rifles 9th Battalion *Age 22 Died in War on 21 September 1916*
ST. QUENTIN CABARET MILITARY CEMETERY, Belgium
Son of Joseph and Fannie Mahood, of 67, Weir Street, Belfast.

Mahood, John - Assistant Steward
Mercantile Marine S.S. "Neuquen" (London)
Age 21 Drowned, as a result of an attack by an enemy submarine on 20 January 1917
TOWER HILL MEMORIAL, United Kingdom
Son of the late William John and Elizabeth Mahood. Born at Belfast.

Mailey, Francis John - Private
21274 Royal Irish Fusiliers 7th/8th Battalion *Died in War on 18 July 1917*
VLAMERTINGHE NEW MILITARY CEMETERY, Belgium
Brother of Minnie Mailey, 11, Elmfield Street, Belfast.

Mailey, John H - Lance Corporal
836 Royal Irish Rifles 9th Battalion *Killed in Action on 1 July 1916*
THIEPVAL MEMORIAL, France
Husband of Sarah Mailey, 15, Crosby Street, Belfast. A member of Belfast Temperance Orange Lodge 456.

Mairs, James - Sergeant
42524 Machine Gun Corps (Infantry) 183rd Company *Age 21 Died of Wounds on 5 December 1917*
ROCQUIGNY-EQUANCOURT ROAD BRITISH CEMETERY, MANANCOURT, France
Son of William John and Margaret Mairs, of Belfast.

Major, Charles - Rifleman
20271 Royal Irish Rifles 2nd Battalion *Age 19 Died of Wounds on 9 September 1918*
ARNEKE BRITISH CEMETERY, France
Son of George and Harriett Major, of 63, Minard Road, Crossmyloof, Glasgow. Native of Belfast.

Major, Samuel - Rifleman
845 Royal Irish Rifles 14th Battalion *Killed in Action on 7 October 1916*
POND FARM CEMETERY, Belgium
Born and enlisted in Belfast

Majury, William - Rifleman
2743 Royal Irish Rifles 14th Battalion *Killed in Action on 1 July 1916*
THIEPVAL MEMORIAL, France
Born and enlisted in Belfast.

Majury, William J - Rifleman
5745 Royal Irish Rifles 1st Battalion *Died in War on 11 April 1916*
BECOURT MILITARY CEMETERY, BECORDEL-BECOURT, France
Brother of Mrs Smith, 14, Hudson Street, Belfast.

Makemson, Frank Henry - Private
2812 Black Watch (Royal Highlanders) Mechanical Transport *Age 23 Died in War on 27 July 1916*
THIEPVAL MEMORIAL, France
Brother of Thomas Makemson, of 35, Roe Street, Cliftonville, Belfast.

Malcolm, Arthur - Lance Corporal
8848 Royal Inniskilling Fusiliers 1st Battalion *Age 26 Died in War on 28 April 1915*
HELLES MEMORIAL, Turkey
Son of James Malcolm, of 4, Fourth Street, Belfast, and the late Frances Ann Malcolm.

Mallon, Joseph - Private
9207 Princess Victoria's (Royal Irish Fusiliers) 1st Battalion *Died in War on 27 September 1914*
LEVALLOIS-PERRET COMMUNAL CEMETERY, PARIS, France
Born in Belfast, enlisted Ballykinler.

Mallon, Peter - Private
24217 Royal Inniskilling Fusiliers 7th Battalion *Died in War on 9 October 1917*
CROISILLES BRITISH CEMETERY, France
Born and enlisted in Belfast.

Mallon, Thomas - Private
2248 Connaught Rangers 6th Battalion *Died in War on 4 March 1916*
LOOS MEMORIAL, France
Born, enlisted and resident in Belfast .

Malloy, William John - Rifleman
9147 Royal Irish Rifles 1st Battalion *Died in War on 17 November 1914*
MERVILLE COMMUNAL CEMETERY, France
Son of Thomas Malloy, 2, Alexander Street, Belfast.

Malone, Bristow M - Second Lieutenant
Royal Irish Fusiliers 9th Battalion *Died in War on 16 August 1917*
TYNE COT MEMORIAL, Belgium
Son of John and Margaret Beck Malone of Fortwilliam Park Belfast, member of Belfast Masonic Lodge 262.

Malone, Hugh - Cooper
340469 Royal Navy HMS "Indefatigable" *Age 41 Killed in Action at Battle of Jutland on 31 May 1916*
PLYMOUTH NAVAL MEMORIAL, United Kingdom
Son of the late Hugh and Mary Malone, of 75, Brookfield Street, Crumlin Road, Belfast; husband of Maud Mary Malone, of 16, Townshend Avenue, Devonport.

Journey of Remembering

Malone, Hugh - Private
10919 Connaught Rangers 6th Battalion *Killed in Action on 23 March 1918*
ROYE BRITISH CEMETERY, France
Born in County Antrim, enlisted in Glasgow, resident of Belfast.

Malone, William Adolphe - Second Lieutenant
Cheshire Regiment 13th Battalion *Age 30 Died in War on 16 May 1917*
YPRES (MENIN GATE) MEMORIAL, Belgium
Son of John and Margaret B. Malone, of "Entroya", Fortwilliam Park, Belfast.
Member of Belfast Masonic Lodge No. 51.

Maloney, Thomas - Private
22734 Princess Victoria's (Royal Irish Fusiliers) 9th Battalion *Died in War on 28 March 1918*
ST SEVER CEMETERY EXTENSION ROUEN, France
Born and enlisted in Belfast.

Maltman, Joseph - Private
M2/105567 Royal Engineers Mechanical Transport Army Service Corps
Age 24 Died of disease on 10 December 1918
DOULLENS COMMUNAL CEMETERY EXTENSION No.2, France
Son of William James and Louise Maltman, of Belfast.

Mandall, Harry - Second Lieutenant
Royal Engineers *Age 24 Drowned on 18 May 1919*
CAIRO WAR MEMORIAL CEMETERY, Egypt
Son of Mrs. E. Grosse, of Rose Cottage, Shaw's Bridge, Belfast. Born in Lancashire.
Awarded the Military Medal.

Mann, Robert - Private
27233 Royal Inniskilling Fusiliers 11th Battalion *Age 35 Died in War on 27 April 1917*
POND FARM CEMETERY, Belgium
Son of Samuel Mann, of 58, Esmond Street, Shankill Road, Belfast.

Manning, Edward - Private
2800 Royal Inniskilling Fusiliers 2nd Battalion *Died in War on 14 May 1915*
RUE-DES-BERCEAUX MILITARY CEMETERY, RICHEBOURG-L'AVOUE, France
11, Sultan Street, Belfast.

Manning, William - Lance Sergeant
26268 Royal Dublin Fusiliers 10th Battalion *Killed in Action on 27 March 1918*
POZIERES MEMORIAL, France
11, Kashmir Road, Belfast.

Mansbridge, Richard - Private
55240 Royal Fusiliers 23rd Battalion *Age 40 Died in War on 17 January 1918*
H.A.C. CEMETERY, ECOUST-ST. MEIN, France
Son of the late John and Mary Mansbridge, of 54, Tower Street, Belfast; husband of Eleanor Mansbridge, of 16, Lisavon Street, Sydenham, Belfast.

Mansell, Matthew - Sergeant
1315 Royal Irish Rifles 1st Battalion *Killed in Action on 9 May 1915*
PLOEGSTEERT MEMORIAL, Belgium
Born in Belfast, enlisted Liverpool.

Manson, George Erskine - Rifleman
338 Royal Irish Rifles 9th Battalion *Died in War on 18 October 1917*
ARTILLERY WOOD CEMETERY, Belgium
99, Silvio Street, Belfast.

Manson, William J - Private
592032 Labour Corps 299th Company *Age 26 Died as a result of war on 19 February 1919*
CARNMONEY (HOLY EVANGELISTS) CHURCH OF IRELAND CHURCHYARD EXTENSION, United Kingdom
Son of John and Janet Manson, of 42, McTier Street, Belfast. Formerly 2625 Royal Inniskilling Fusiliers

Markey, William John - Private
373 Australian Infantry 7th Trench Mortar Battery *Age 23 Died in War on 5 August 1916*
VILLERS-BRETONNEUX MEMORIAL, France
Son of William and Ellen Markey, of 51, Annadale Street, Belfast, Ireland.

Marks, James Ganly - Lieutenant
Seaforth Highlanders 5th Battalion *Age 22 Killed in Action on 23 March 1918*
LEBUCQUIERE COMMUNAL CEMETERY EXTENSION, France
Son of James G. and Sophie Marks, of "Roselyn", Deramore Drive, Belfast.
Enlisted as a Private in October 1914, in the Black Watch.

Marks, Robert - Private
376427 Royal Scots (Lothian Regiment) 13th Battalion *Died in War on 22 August 1917*
TYNE COT MEMORIAL, Belgium
Born in Belfast, enlisted Glasgow.

Marks, Thomas - Rifleman
16862 Royal Irish Rifles 11th Battalion *Killed in Action on 1 July 1916*
THIEPVAL MEMORIAL, France
Born and enlisted in Belfast.

Marlowe, Robert - Private
25650 Royal Inniskilling Fusiliers Depot *Age 25 Died in War on 30 October 1918*
BELFAST (MILLTOWN) ROMAN CATHOLIC CEMETERY, United Kingdom
Son of Mrs. Mary Marlowe, of 36, Whiterock Crescent, Belfast.

Marr, Daniel - Private
12107 Royal Inniskilling Fusiliers 2nd Battalion *Died in War on 16 May 1915*
LE TOURET MEMORIAL, France
Soon of Maria Marrs, 27, Magnetic Street, Belfast.

Marsden, James - Rifleman
G/13256 Royal Irish Rifles 9th Battalion *Age 20 Died in War on 17 January 1916*
SUCRERIE MILITARY CEMETERY, COLINCAMPS, France
Son of John and Mary Jane Marsden, of Belfast.

Marsh, Walter Arthur - Private
13181 Essex Regiment 10th Battalion *Died in War on 20 July 1916*
THIEPVAL MEMORIAL, France
Born in Belfast, enlisted Camberwell, Surrey, England.

Journey of Remembering

Marshall, Aubrey Edgar Lacey - Private
66590 Machine Gun Corps (Infantry) *Died in War on 13 April 1917*
CROISILLES BRITISH CEMETERY, France
Born in Belfast, enlisted Glasgow. Formerly 10301 Royal Irish Regiment.

Marshall, Charles Dunlop - Rifleman
428 Royal Irish Rifles 11th Battalion *Age 34 Killed in Action on 1 July 1916*
THIEPVAL MEMORIAL, France
Son of Joseph and Matilda Marshall, of Primrose Villa, Ballylesson, County Antrim;
husband of Elizabeth Marshall, of 16, Rutland Street, Belfast.

Marshall, David - Rifleman
656 Royal Irish Rifles 16th Battalion *Age 23 Died in War on 2 July 1916*
THIEPVAL MEMORIAL, France
Son of Samuel and Annie Marshall, of Ivy Cottage, Newtownbreda, Belfast.

Marshall, David - Sergeant
16865 Royal Irish Rifles 14th Battalion *Age 28 Died of Wounds as a prisoner of war on 28 April 1918*
BERLIN SOUTH-WESTERN CEMETERY, Germany
Son of James and Jessie Marshall, of "Ardenlee", Ravenhill Road, Belfast. Native of Gourock, Scotland.

Marshall, Edward Leslie - Captain
Royal Inniskilling Fusiliers 9th Battalion *Age 26 Died in War on 1 September 1918*
METEREN MILITARY CEMETERY, France
Born in Belfast. the son of Andrew Chambers Marshall and Annie M. Marshall, of Holywood.
Educated Bangor Grammar School and Methodist College. Awarded the Military Cross, twice.

Marshall, Frederick - Lance Corporal
27831 Royal Inniskilling Fusiliers 9th Battalion *Killed in Action on 16 August 1917*
TYNE COT MEMORIAL, Belgium
66, Selby Street, Belfast.

Marshall, Isaiah - Stoker First Class
Royal Navy HMS "Cressy" *Died in War on 22 September 1914*
CHATHAM NAVAL MEMORIAL, United Kingdom
Son of Isaiah Marshall, 28, City Street, Belfast.

Marshall, James - Driver
76737 Royal Horse Artillery and Royal Field Artillery *Died in War on 20 November 1917*
VLAMERTINGHE NEW MILITARY CEMETERY, Belgium
Born and enlisted in Belfast.

Marshall, James - Fireman And Trimmer
Mercantile Marine S.S. "Teelin Head" (Belfast)
Age 45 Drowned, as a result of an attack by an enemy submarine on 21 January 1918
TOWER HILL MEMORIAL, United Kingdom
Son of Margaret and the late James Marshall; husband of Elizabeth Marshall (née Crothers),
of 127, Bloomfield Street, Belfast. Born at Belfast.

Marshall, James - Private
29916 Royal Inniskilling Fusiliers 1st Battalion *Age 19 Died in War on 19 May 1917*
ARRAS MEMORIAL, France
Son of William and Sarah Marshall, of 49, Sugarfield Street, Belfast.

Marshall, John - Private
3657 Royal Inniskilling Fusiliers 2nd Battalion *Died of Wounds on 2 April 1917*
FORESTE COMMUNAL CEMETERY, France
Born and enlisted in Belfast.

Marshall, John - Private
6963 Royal Munster Fusiliers 6th Battalion *Died of Wounds on 30 December 1917*
RAMLEH WAR CEMETERY, Israel
11, Colinpark Street, Belfast.

Marshall, William - Rifleman
132 Royal Irish Rifles 10th Battalion attached 21st Entrenching Battalion *Age 20 Died in War on 21 March 1918*
POZIERES MEMORIAL, France
Son of Mrs. Mary Jane Marshall, of 60, Braemar Street, Broadway, Belfast.

Marshall, William Albert - Drummer
33167 Royal Warwickshire Regiment 1st Battalion *Died as a result of War on 14 August 1919*
PORTSDOWN (CHRIST CHURCH) MILITARY CEMETERY, United Kingdom
Born in Belfast, enlisted in Dover.

Marsland, A V - Signaller
J/1007 Royal Navy HMS "Lord Nelson" *Died in War on 28 June 1915*
LANCASHIRE LANDING CEMETERY, Turkey
53, Paxton Street, Belfast.

Marsland, George William - Private
23662 Royal Inniskilling Fusiliers 1st Battalion *Killed in Action on 1 July 1916*
Y RAVINE CEMETERY, BEAUMONT-HAMEL, France
Born in Belfast, enlisted at Dover.

Martin, Charles William - Sapper
64461 Corps of Royal Engineers 150th Field Company *Died in War on 1 July 1916*
THIEPVAL MEMORIAL, France
Born in Belfast, enlisted Coleraine.

Martin, Daniel - Private
2391 Royal Inniskilling Fusiliers 2nd Battalion *Age 27 Died of bronchial pneumonia on 13 February 1917*
ETAPLES MILITARY CEMETERY, France
Husband of Hannah S. Martin, of 42, Solway Street, Belfast.

Martin, David - Private
7636 Royal Irish Fusiliers 1st Battalion *Died in War on 27 May 1916*
LE CATELET CHURCHYARD, France
Husband of Mary Martin of 2, Athens Street, Belfast. During the German advance into France in August 1914 David, with other soldiers, became separated from his unit. They were hidden from the Germans by the kind villagers of Le Catelet and remained so for almost two years. In May 1916 their hiding place was discovered. As they were dressed in civilian clothes the Germans considered them spies. David Martin and three others were shot dead by a firing squad.

Martin, David - Sapper
WR/310237 Royal Engineers *Age 30 Died in War on 5 July 1915*
CARNMONEY CEMETERY, United Kingdom
Son of Andrew and Elizabeth Martin; husband of Mary Martin, of Aughagegnan Cottage, Longford. Born in Belfast.

Martin, Eric Franklin - Private
47904 Machine Gun Corps (Cavalry) 16th Squadron *Age 28 Drowned in the Tigris on 28 October 1918*
BASRA MEMORIAL, Iraq
Son of the Rev. Pierce Martin and Rose Edith Martin, of 34, Bawnmore Road, Balmoral, Belfast.

Martin, Francis - Private
27811 Princess Victoria's (Royal Irish Fusiliers) 1st Battalion *Died in War on 28 November 1917*
ROCQUIGNY-EQUANCOURT ROAD BRITISH CEMETERY, MANANCOURT, France
Born in Monaghan, enlisted Lisburn, resident Belfast.

Martin, Francis - Rifleman
6592 Royal Irish Rifles 16th Battalion *Killed in Action on 7 July 1916*
THIEPVAL MEMORIAL, France
Born and enlisted in Belfast.

Martin, George - Rifleman
1004 Royal Irish Rifles 8th Battalion *Died in War on 25 March 1918*
ROYE NEW BRITISH CEMETERY, France
Lived at 19, East Bread Street Belfast.

Martin, George - Sapper
28418 Corps of Royal Engineers 112th Field Company *Died in War on 23 September 1916*
THIEPVAL MEMORIAL, France
Born and enlisted in Belfast.

Martin, Herbert - Rifleman
6395 Royal Irish Rifles 16th Battalion *Age 24 Died in War on 26 July 1917*
POPERINGHE NEW MILITARY CEMETERY, Belgium
Son of Mr. and Mrs. Thomas Martin, of Belfast.

Martin, James - Private
12951 Royal Irish Fusiliers 9th Battalion *Age 33 Died in War on 27 December 1918*
LES BARAQUES MILITARY CEMETERY, SANGATTE, France
Husband of Margaret Martin, of 9, Montreal Street, Belfast.

Martin, John - Private
L/7548 Royal Sussex Regiment 2nd Battalion *Killed in Action on 13 September 1914*
PRIEZ COMMUNAL CEMETERY, France
Husband of Sarah Martin, Upper Meenan Street, Belfast.

Martin, John - Private
PLY/17295 Royal Marine Light Infantry HMS "Carnarvon" *Age 22 Died in War on 20 October 1918*
HASLAR ROYAL NAVAL CEMETERY, United Kingdom
Son of Thomas and Margaret Martin, of 19, Ligoneil Road, Ballysillan, Belfast.

Martin, John - Rifleman
336 Royal Irish Rifles 16th Battalion *Died in War on 3 April 1918*
ST SEVER CEMETERY EXTENSION ROUEN, France
Born in Belfast, enlisted Lurgan.

Martin, John - Rifleman
17/57 Royal Irish Rifles 9th Battalion *Died in War on 25 December 1917*
Born and enlisted in Belfast.

Martin, John Sinclair - Lieutenant
Royal Irish Rifles "D" Company 1st Battalion *Age 19 Killed in Action on 9 May 1915*
PLOEGSTEERT MEMORIAL, Belgium
Son of Edith S. Martin, of 14, College Gardens, Belfast, and the late Robert T. Martin.

Martin, Joseph - Company Sergeant Major
16835 Royal Irish Rifles 9th Battalion *Age 35 Died in War on 1 July 1916*
THIEPVAL MEMORIAL, France
Husband of Eliza J. Martin, of 3, Parkview Terrace, Woodvale Road, Belfast.

Martin, Robert - Private
8757 Scots Guards 2nd Battalion *Age 21 Died in War on 17 October 1915*
LOOS MEMORIAL, France
Son of Mrs. Martin, of 6, Middlepath Street, Belfast.

Martin, Robert - Rifleman
9963 Royal Irish Rifles 2nd Battalion *Age 20 Killed in Action on 13 November 1914*
WIMEREUX COMMUNAL CEMETERY, France
Son of Alexander Martin, of 218, Castlereagh Road, Belfast.

Martin, Samuel - Rifleman
907 Royal Irish Rifles 16th Battalion *Died in War on 16 April 1918*
CANADA FARM CEMETERY, Belgium
Born in Belfast, enlisted in Lurgan.

Martin, Sidney Todd - Lieutenant
Royal Inniskilling Fusiliers 6th Battalion *Killed in Action on 1 July 1916*
THIEPVAL MEMORIAL, France
Member of Fitzroy Avenue Presbyterian Church.

Martin, Thomas - Driver
T/329783 Army Service Corps 2nd Cavalry Reserve Park *Died in War on 7 November 1918*
ST. POL BRITISH CEMETERY, ST. POL-SUR-TERNOISE, France
Son of James McLean, of 3, Bradburys Buildings, Lisburn Road, Belfast.

Martin, Thomas - Fitter
30694 Royal Field Artillery 123rd Brigade *Died in War on 25 August 1918*
BAGNEUX BRITISH CEMETERY, GEZAINCOURT, France
Resident and enlisted in Belfast.

Martin, Thomas - Private
29730 York and Lancaster Regiment 16th (Transport Workers) Battalion *Died in War on 27 September 1916*
BELFAST CITY CEMETERY, United Kingdom
Born in Carrickfergus, resident Belfast. Formerly 4048 Royal Field Artillery.

Martin, Thomas - Private
93 Royal Irish Regiment 8th Battalion *Age 32 Died in War on 26 September 1918*
LE GRAND BEAUMART BRITISH CEMETERY, STEENWERCK, France
Son of Agnes Martin, of 7, Hornby Street, Belfast.

Martin, Thomas - Private
9377 Royal Inniskilling Fusiliers 1st Battalion *Died of Wounds on 9 August 1916*
BEDFORD HOUSE CEMETERY, Belgium
Born in Belfast and the holder of the Distinguished Conduct Medal.

Journey of Remembering

Martin, Thomas - Rifleman
16869 Royal Irish Rifles 14th Battalion *Age 22 Died in War on 6 May 1916*
AUTHUILE MILITARY CEMETERY, France
Son of Samuel Alexander and Fanny Martin, of 314, Springfield Road, Belfast.

Martin, Thomas - Rifleman
6847 Royal Irish Rifles 2nd Battalion *Killed in Action on 20 September 1914*
LA FERTE-SOUS-JOUARRE MEMORIAL, France
Born and enlisted in Belfast.

Martin, Thomas J - Private
Lancashire Regiment *Died in War*
10, Southland Street, Belfast.

Martin, William - Private
54172 Canadian Infantry (Western Ontario Regiment) 18th Battalion *Age 27 Died in War on 26 August 1916*
BELFAST (BALMORAL) CEMETERY, United Kingdom
Son of Francis and Lucy Martin, of 7, Stranmillis Street, Belfast. He was an Anglican and worked as a butcher.

Martin, William - Private
9103 Connaught Rangers 5th Battalion *Died in War on 7 December 1915*
DOIRAN MEMORIAL, Greece
Born in Belfast enlisted in Glasgow. Awarded the Gold Medal, 1st Class, of the Order of Karageorge (Serbia).

Martin, William - Rifleman
1684 Royal Irish Rifles 12th Battalion *Age 18 Died in War on 22 November 1917*
CAMBRAI MEMORIAL, LOUVERVAL, France
Son of Samuel and Catherine Martin, of 20, Carew Street, Belfast.

Martin, William - Rifleman
6319 Royal Irish Rifles 2nd Battalion *Killed in Action on 16 June 1915*
YPRES (MENIN GATE) MEMORIAL, Belgium
64, Euston Street, Belfast.

Martin, William - Stoker First Class
K/11808 Royal Navy HMS "Aboukir"
Age 22 Killed in Action with submarine in North Sea on 22 September 1914
CHATHAM NAVAL MEMORIAL, United Kingdom
Son of William and Ellen Martin, of Belfast; husband of Isabella Martin, of 28, Waterford Street, Belfast.

Martin, William Henry - Private
PLY/13501 Royal Marines HMS "Lion" *Age 28 Killed in Action on 31 May 1916*
PLYMOUTH NAVAL MEMORIAL, United Kingdom
Son of the late Stewart Martin, of 24, Ballymena Street, Belfast; husband of Edith Maud Martin, of 71, Wellfield Road, Streatham, London.

Martin, William James - Private
240977 Seaforth Highlanders 1/5th Battalion *Age 20 Died of Wounds on 18 May 1917*
AUBIGNY COMMUNAL CEMETERY EXTENSION, France
Son of Joseph and Mary Martin, of 24, East Bread Street, Belfast.

Mason, Henry - Private
22619 Royal Inniskilling Fusiliers 9th Battalion *Age 26 Died of Wounds on 10th May 1916*
FORCEVILLE COMMUNAL CEMETERY AND EXTENSION, France
Son of David and Elizabeth Mason of Belfast.

Mason, Henry - Seaman
Mercantile Marine S.S. "Eveleen" (Belfast) *Age 62 Presumed drowned on 6 May 1918*
TOWER HILL MEMORIAL, United Kingdom
Son of the late Roland and Margaret Mason; husband of Mary Mason (née McKeating),
of 55, Stanhope Street, Belfast. Born at Portaferry.

Mason, William - Private
201159 Seaforth Highlanders 7th Battalion *Age 19 Died in War on 28 September 1918*
YPRES TOWN CEMETERY EXTENSION, Belgium
Son of William and Mary Mason; of 5, Rathcool Street, Lisburn Road, Belfast.

Mason, William Joseph - Rifleman
1104 Royal Irish Rifles "A" Company 14th Battalion *Age 21 Died of Wounds on 7 December 1917*
ST. SEVER CEMETERY EXTENSION, ROUEN, France
Son of James and Rachel Mason, of 60, Delhi Steet, Belfast.

Massey, W Alfred - Rifleman
14/7491 Royal Irish Rifles 14th Battalion *Died in War on 7 June 1917*
SPANBROEKMOLEN BRITISH CEMETERY, Belgium
Husband of Sarah Massey, of 19, City Street, Belfast. Son of Joseph John and Emma Massey,
1, Henderson's Row, Balmoral, Belfast.

Massey, William James - Private
12165 Royal Inniskilling Fusiliers 2nd Battalion *Died in War on 11 July 1916*
THIEPVAL MEMORIAL, France
Born Ballymacarrett, Belfast. Enlisted in Belfast. Son of the late Mrs Agnes Massey.

Masterson, Andrew - Private
6121 Royal Irish Rifles 2nd Battalion *Killed in Action on 25 October 1914*
LE TOURET MEMORIAL, France
Husband of Sarah Masterson, 18, Glenfarne Street, Belfast.

Matchett, Harry - Private
4499 The King's (Liverpool Regiment) 9th Battalion *Age 20 Died in War on 25 September 1916*
THIEPVAL MEMORIAL, France
Son of Elizabeth Matchett, of 28, North Ann Street, Belfast, and the late William Matchett.
Returned from Russia to enlist.

Mateer, John - Private
188249 Labour Corps formerly 19668 Royal Irish Rifles *Died on 28 August 1918*
BELFASTCITY CEMETERY, United Kingdom
Son of the late John and Mary Mateer; husband of Annie Mateer, of 51, Clementine Street, Belfast. Born at Belfast.

Mathers, Thomas W - Lance Corporal
3725 Royal Inniskilling Fusiliers 2nd Battalion *Died in War on 1 April 1917*
THIEPVAL MEMORIAL, France
Born and enlisted in Belfast. The son of John Mathers, of Ballymagarahan, Moira, County Down.

JOURNEY OF REMEMBERING

Matier, Samuel - Rifleman
9/15567 Royal Irish Rifles 9th Battalion *Age 21 Died in War on 7 June 1917*
LONE TREE CEMETERY, Belgium
Son of James and Sarah Matier, of 171, Ainsworth Avenue, Belfast.

Matier, William - Rifleman
12474 Royal Irish Rifles "B" Company 8th Battalion *Age 37 Died in War on 9 July 1916*
ST. SOUPLET BRITISH CEMETERY, France
Son of John Matier; husband of Catherine Hamilton (formerly Matier),
of 34, Walton Street, Crumlin Road, Belfast.

Meehan, Matthew - Private
6711 Canadian Infantry (Western Ontario Regiment) *Died in War on 15 June 1915*
VIMY MEMORIAL, France
Born in Belfast.

Matthews, Benjamin - Private
14888 Royal Inniskilling Fusiliers 11th Battalion *Killed in Action on 1 July 1917*
THIEPVAL MEMORIAL, France
Born and enlisted in Belfast.

Matthews, Robert Henry - Rifleman
19136 Royal Irish Rifles 8th Battalion *Age 39 Died of Wounds received at Thiepval on 2 July 1916*
FORCEVILLE COMMUNAL CEMETERY AND EXTENSION, France
Son of Thomas and Annie Matthews, of Belfast.

Matthews, Samuel - Private
13734 Royal Inniskilling Fusiliers 11th Battalion *Died in War on 16 August 1917*
TYNE COT MEMORIAL, Belgium
Husband of Maria Matthews, 94, Cupar Street, Belfast. Formerly employed in Harland and Wolff.

Matthews, Thomas - Rifleman
203 Royal Irish Rifles 12th Battalion *Died in War on 15 August 1917*
YPRES (MENIN GATE) MEMORIAL, Belgium
Born and enlisted in Belfast.

Matthews, William - Private
9/15566 Royal Irish Rifles 9th Battalion *Died in War on 25 December 1916*
ST. QUENTIN CABARET MILITARY CEMETERY, Belgium
18, Springfield Village, Belfast.

Maule, Robert - Private
8/31468 Royal Inniskilling Fusiliers 1st Battalion *Killed in Action on 20 October 1918*
HARLEBEKE NEW BRITISH CEMETERY, Belgium
21, Brennan Street, Belfast.

Maunsell, Douglas Slade - Lieutenant
Royal Munster Fusiliers 2nd Battalion attached 1st Battalion *Age 31 Killed in Action on 5 - 6 September 1916*
THIEPVAL MEMORIAL, FRANCE
Born at Belfast the son of Major Arthur Munro Maunsell and educated at Armagh Royal School.
Wounded and sent home in September 1915. Returned to the front in September 1916 and was killed
within four hours at the battle of Guillemont on the Somme.

Mawhinney, Alexander - Rifleman
46 Royal Irish Rifles 1st Battalion *Killed in Action on 27 March 1918*
POZIERES MEMORIAL, OVILLERS-LA BOISSELLE, France
Born and enlisted in Belfast.

Mawhinney, Arthur - Private
40878 Cameronians (Scottish Rifles) 2nd Battalion *Age 23 Died of Wounds on 27 August 1917*
MENDINGHEM MILITARY CEMETERY, Belgium
Son of James and Rebecca Mawhinney, of 102, Roden Street, Belfast.

Mawhinney, David - Sapper
12288 Royal Engineers *Died of Wounds on 5 October 1915*
CHOCQUES MILITARY CEMETERY, France
Son of James and Rebecca Mawhinney, of 102, Roden Street, Belfast.

Mawhinney, James - Trimmer
933111 Mercantile Marine Reserve HMS "Champagne"
Age 20 Killed in Action with submarine in Atlantic on 9 October 1917
PLYMOUTH NAVAL MEMORIAL, United Kingdom
Son of Hugh Mawhinney, of 49, Ship Street, Belfast, and the late Elizabeth Mawhinney.

Maxwell, David - Lance Corporal
11465 Royal Irish Rifles 6th Battalion *Died in War on 31 October 1916*
DOIRAN MEMORIAL, Greece
Born and enlisted in Belfast.

Maxwell, Edward Wallace - Carpenters Crew
347388 Royal Navy HMS "Formidable" *Died in War on 1 January 1915*
CHATHAM NAVAL MEMORIAL, United Kingdom
Victoria Road, Sydenham, Belfast. Served as "Leigh".

Maxwell, James - Rifleman
1413 Royal Irish Rifles "A" Company 10th Battalion *Age 27 Died in War on 1 July 1916*
THIEPVAL MEMORIAL, France
Son of Dunlop Maxwell, of 26, Hurst Street, Sandy Row, Belfast, and the late Margaret Maxwell; husband of Jane Maxwell, of 20, Abbott Street, Ormeau Road, Belfast.

Maxwell, James - Second Mate
Mercantile Marine S.S. "Garron Head" (Belfast) *Age 35 Killed by mine on 16 November 1917*
TOWER HILL MEMORIAL, United Kingdom
Son of Elizabeth Maxwell (née Leslie), of 8, Carrington Street, Belfast, and the late Arthur Maxwell.
Born in Donaghadee.

Maxwell, James - Stoker Second Class
K/24593 Royal Navy HMS "Princess Irene" *Age 20 Killed by internal explosion of vessel off Sheerness on 27 May 1915*
CHATHAM NAVAL MEMORIAL, United Kingdom
Son of Joseph and Catherine Maxwell, of 24, Barbour Street, Greencastle, Belfast.

Maxwell, James Davy - Corporal
19690 Royal Irish Rifles 14th Battalion *Died in War on 16 August 1917*
TYNE COT MEMORIAL, Belgium
James and Agnes Maxwell, Lisburn Road Belfast.

Maxwell, Ralph - Sergeant
13268 Royal Irish Rifles 15th Battalion *Age 27 Died of Wounds*
DERRYAGHY (CHRIST CHURCH) CHURCH OF IRELAND CHURCHYARD, *United Kingdom*
Son of Ralph and Jane Maxwell, of 88, Everton Street, Belfast.

Maxwell, Stanley Woods - Second Lieutenant
Royal Irish Rifles "B" Company 8th Battalion *Age 25 Died of Wounds while a Prisoner of War on 27 July 1916*
ST. SOUPLET BRITISH CEMETERY, *France*
Son of Mrs. Agnes Maxwell, of "Calloden", North Parade, Belfast, and the late Samuel Maxwell.

Maxwell, Thomas - Rifleman
15572 Royal Irish Rifles 2nd Battalion *Died in War on 6 September 1918*
WULVERGHEM-LINDENHOEK ROAD MILITARY CEMETERY, *Belgium*
Brother of Maggie Maxwell, of 32, Crosby Street, Belfast.

Maxwell, Thomas - Sapper
200521 Royal Engineers *Age 44 Died in War on 4 July 1918*
BELFAST CITY CEMETERY, *United Kingdom*
Husband of Catherine Maxwell. Born in Belfast.

Maxwell, William John - Rifleman
17/990 Royal Irish Rifles 15th Battalion *Age 22 Died in War on 21 November 1915*
MESNIL RIDGE CEMETERY, MESNIL-MARTINSART, *France*
Son of James Edward and Annabella Maxwell, of 59, Utility Street, Belfast.

May, James - Lance Corporal
9762 King's Own Scottish Borderers 2nd Battalion *Died in War on 18 October 1914*
LE TOURET MEMORIAL, *France*
63, Newcastle Street, Belfast. Born in Scotland.

Mayberry, Joseph - Private
5891 Australian Infantry 27th Battalion *Died in War on 4 October 1917*
YPRES (MENIN GATE) MEMORIAL, *Belgium*
184, Albertbridge Road, Belfast.

Mayes, James - Rifleman
5714 Royal Irish Rifles 1st Battalion *Age 18 Killed in Action on 16 June 1915*
PLOEGSTEERT MEMORIAL, *Belgium*
Son of James and A. Jane Mayes, of 42, Methuen Street, Belfast

Maynard, Samuel - Rifleman
8895 Royal Irish Rifles 2nd Battalion *Age 17 Died in War on 21 June 1915*
CALAIS SOUTHERN CEMETERY, *France*
Son of Robert and Ellen Maynard, of 99, Argyle Street, Belfast.

Mayne, Alex - Private
26326 Royal Inniskilling Fusiliers 8th Battalion *Died in War on 24 July 1916*
VERMELLES BRITISH CEMETERY, *France*
20, Ulverston Street, Belfast.

Mayne, David - Private
23981 Royal Inniskilling Fusiliers 7th Battalion *Age 21 Killed in Action on 7 June 1917*
LA LAITERIE MILITARY CEMETERY, *Belgium*
Son of Margaret Cain (formerly Mayne), of 13, Hanna Street, Belfast; step-son of the late Charles Cain.

Mayne, Joseph - Private
4583 Connaught Rangers 6th Battalion *Died in War on 10 January 1918*
TINCOURT NEW BRITISH CEMETERY, France
Born, enlisted and resident of Belfast. Son of James and Mary Mayne of Ardcumber, Cookstown.

Maze, William James - Private
2604 Royal Inniskilling Fusiliers 2nd Battalion *Age 23 Died in War on 16 May 1915*
LE TOURET MEMORIAL, France
Son of Mrs. Martha Maze, of 92, Crimea Street, Belfast.

McAdam, Alfred - Private
Royal Irish Fusiliers *Died in War on 9 August 1915*
Second son of Eliza McAdam, 186, Roden Street, Belfast.

McAdams, A - Rifleman
7394 Royal Irish Rifles "C" Company 1st Battalion *Age 35 Died as a result of war on 31 May 1920*
BELFAST CITY CEMETERY, United Kingdom
Son of David and Isabella McAdams, of 20, Fleming Street, Belfast.

McAdams, Charles - Private
5170 Royal Munster Fusiliers 6th Battalion *Died in War on 17 September 1915*
HELLES MEMORIAL, Turkey
Born and enlisted in Belfast. Awarded the Military Medal. Formerly 16749 Royal Inniskilling Fusiliers

McAdorey , Peter - Corporal
12174 The Norfolk Regiment 2nd Battalion *Died in War on 1 March 1917*
AMARA WAR CEMETERY, Iraq
Born in Sailortown, Belfast, the son of John McAdorey, of 23 Garmoyle Street. He served under the alias of "John Murray". His brother, John McAdorey, was killed serving with the Royal Navy.

McAdorey, John - Able Seaman
225486 Royal Navy HMS "Princess Irene"
Age 32 Killed by internal explosion of vessel off Sheerness on 27 May 1915
PORTSMOUTH NAVAL MEMORIAL, United Kingdom
Son of the late John McAdorey, of 23, Garmoyle Street, Belfast. His brother, Peter, who served under the alias of 'John Murray', died in Mesopotamia (Iraq) with 2nd Battalion Norfolk Regiment.

McAdorey, John - Sergeant
11700 Royal Irish Rifles 15th Battalion *Killed in Action on 1 July 1916*
THIEPVAL MEMORIAL, France
10, Clanmorris Street, Belfast.

McAfee, Johnston - Company Quartermaster Sergeant
6717 Royal Irish Fusiliers 2nd Battalion *Age 36 Died of Wounds (burns) on 3rd January 1917*
SALONIKA (LEMBET ROAD) MILITARY CEMETERY, Greece
Son of Mrs. McClatchey, of 111, Donegall Road, Belfast; husband of Elizabeth Jane McAfee, of Portland School House, Birr, County Offaly. Served in the South African Campaign

McAfee, Thomas - Private
20305 Royal Inniskilling Fusiliers 6th Battalion *Died in War on 7 September 1915*
HELLES MEMORIAL, Turkey
Born and enlisted in Belfast.

Journey of Remembering

McAlea, Bernard - Rifleman
7598 Royal Irish Rifles 2nd Battalion *Age 28 Killed in Action on 15 September 1914*
LA FERTE-SOUS-JOUARRE MEMORIAL, France
Son of Bernard and Jane McAlea, of 5, Cranford Street, Belfast; husband of Mary A. McAlea, of 118, New Lodge Road, Belfast.

McAleavey, Patrick Bernard - Private
23551 Princess Victoria's (Royal Irish Fusiliers) 1st Battalion *Died in War on 11 July 1917*
CRUMP TRENCH BRITISH CEMETERY FAMPOUX, France
Born in Belfast, enlisted in Glasgow. Formerly 21110 Royal Inniskilling Fusiliers.

McAleer, Owen - Trimmer
Mercantile Marine S.S. "Hunsdon" (London)
Age 25 Drowned, as a result of an attack by an enemy submarine on 18 October 1918
TOWER HILL MEMORIAL, United Kingdom
Son of Mary McAleer and the late Mr. McAleer; husband of Susan Mary McAleer (née Farlay), of 11, Jennymount Street, St. Joseph's, Belfast. Born in County Tyrone.

McAleer, William - Driver
80665 Royal Field Artillery 42nd Brigade *Died in War on 31 July 1916*
DANTZIG ALLEY BRITISH CEMETERY, MAMETZ, France
40, Boundary Street, Belfast.

McAleese, Daniel - Private
1177 Royal Munster Fusiliers 6th Battalion *Died in War on 15 August 1915*
HELLES MEMORIAL, Turkey
Born in Belfast, enlisted in Glasgow.

McAlinden, James - Private
4264 Royal Inniskilling Fusiliers 2nd Battalion *Killed in Action on 16 May 1915*
LE TOURET MEMORIAL, France
Born and enlisted in Belfast.

McAlinden, John - Able Seaman
Clyde Z/5173 Royal Naval Volunteer Reserve Anson Battalion Royal Naval Division
Age 19 Died in War on 28 April 1917
ARRAS MEMORIAL, France
Son of Joseph McAlinden, of 5, Majorca Street, Belfast.

McAlister, Alexander - Rifleman
13235 Royal Irish Rifles 15th Battalion *Died in War on 1 July 1916*
THIEPVAL MEMORIAL, France
Born and enlisted in Belfast.

McAlister, Robert - Bombardier
157634 Canadian Field Artillery Divisional Ammunition Column *Age 21 Died in War on 31 July 1917*
ERQUINGHEM-LYS CHURCHYARD EXTENSION, France
Son of Samuel and Edith McAlister. 535, Dupont Street, Toronto, Canada.
A clerk, he was born in Belfast, Ireland.

McAlister, Samuel - Lance Corporal
315954 Canadian Infantry (Central Ontario Regiment) "D" Company 20th Battalion
Age 26 Killed in Action on 11 October 1918
NIAGARA CEMETERY, IWUY, France
Son of Samuel and Edith McAlister, of 535, Dupont Street, Toronto, Ontario; husband of Selina McAlister. Native of Belfast, Ireland. A Presbyterian, he was employed as printer.

McAlister, William George - Corporal
10/15194 Royal Irish Rifles 15th Battalion *Age 36 Died in War on 23 March 1918*
ROYE NEW BRITISH CEMETERY, France
Son of Robert and Sarah McAlister; husband of Elizabeth McAlister, of 7, Gaffikin Street, Belfast Born at Tyrone.

McAllan, George Herbert - Lieutenant (Quartermaster)
South African Medical Corps *Age 39 Died as a result of war on 14 December 1918*
THABA TSHWANE MILITARY CEMETERY, South Africa
Born in Belfast the son of William, a bank manager, and Marion McAllan. Brought up in Monaghan and educated at the Royal School Dungannon. Played rugby for Ireland. Went to South Africa in 1901 and died from injuries incurred during the war.

McAllister, Alexander - Corporal
13235 Royal Irish Rifles 15th Battalion *Killed in Action on 1 July 1916*
THIEPVAL MEMORIAL, France
Born and enlisted in Belfast.

McAllister, Andrew - Sergeant
15325 Royal Irish Rifles 9th Battalion *Age 23 Died of Wounds on 25 February 1917*
ST. QUENTIN CABARET MILITARY CEMETERY, Belgium
Son of Andrew and Isabella McAllister, of Thornton, Belfast Road, Carrickfergus, County Antrim. Native of Belfast.

McAllister, Daniel - Private
3463 Royal Inniskilling Fusiliers 1st Battalion *Age 22 Killed in Action on 1 July 1916*
ANCRE BRITISH CEMETERY, BEAUMONT-HAMEL, France
Son of William John and Mary McAllister, of 101, Sydney Street West, Belfast.

McAllister, Ennis Alexander - Private
G/3480 Royal Irish Fusiliers 1st Garrison Battalion *Died in War on 8 April 1918*
TAUKKYAN WAR CEMETERY, Myanmar
Husband of Rachel McAllister, of 71, Hudson Street, Belfast.

McAllister, James - Private
21865 Royal Dublin Fusiliers 2nd Battalion *Age 35 Died of sickness whilst prisoner of war on 31 October 1918*
LE CATEAU MILITARY CEMETERY, France
Son of Alexander McAllister, of 1, Peters Hill, Belfast.

McAllister, James - Rifleman
7583 Royal Irish Rifles 2nd Battalion *Killed in Action on 27 October 1914*
LE TOURET MEMORIAL, France
Born and enlisted in Downpatrick, resident of Belfast.

McAllister, James - Sergeant
636633 Canadian Infantry (Central Ontario Regiment) 4th Battalion *Age 35 Died in War on 27 September 1918*
ONTARIO CEMETERY, SAINS-LES-MARQUION, France
Son of Mrs. Ellen Croll, of 24, Bentham Street, Belfast, Ireland. Native of Carrickfergus, County Antrim. He was a Presbyterian and was employed as a labourer. Had already spent three years in the United States Army.

Journey of Remembering

McAllister, John - Private
6343 Connaught Rangers 6th Battalion *Age 26 Died in War on 11 January 1917*
POND FARM CEMETERY, *Belgium*
Son of John and Charlotte McAllister, of 11, Emily Place, Belfast. Native of Ballymena, County Antrim.

McAllister, Joseph - Private
27558 Royal Irish Fusiliers 9th Battalion *Age 21 Died in War on 25 October 1918*
TYNE COT MEMORIAL, *Belgium*
Son of William and Matilda McAllister, of 92, Argyle Street, Shankill Road, Belfast.

McAllister, Joseph - Private
421489 Labour Corps formerly 20141 7th Battalion Royal Irish Rifles *Died suddenly on 24 January 1918*
BLEUET FARM CEMETERY, *Belgium*
82, Aberdeen Street, Belfast.

McAllister, Richard James Watson - Corporal
S/37281 Rifle Brigade 2nd Battalion *Age 38 Killed in Action on 21 August 1918*
LA TARGETTE BRITISH CEMETERY, NEUVILLE-ST. VAAST, *France*
Son of Robert and Susan McAllister, of Belfast; husband of Edith Frances McAllister,
of "Holford", Friern Park, North Finchley, London.

McAllister, Samuel - Private
52762 Royal Army Medical Corps 109th Field Ambulance *Age 20 Died while a Prisoner of War on 15 May 1918*
ROYE NEW BRITISH CEMETERY, *France*
Son of Samuel and Margaret McAllister, of 7, Fallswater Street, Belfast.

McAllister, William - Rifleman
8994 Royal Irish Rifles "A" Company 2nd Battalion *Age 25 Killed in Action on 21 September 1914*
LA FERTE-SOUS-JOUARRE MEMORIAL, *France*
Son of Mrs Rose McAllister, of 31, Emerson Row, Ligoniel, Belfast.

McAllister, William J - Private
S/10608 Seaforth Highlanders 2nd Battalion *Age 21 Died in War on 11 April 1917*
ARRAS MEMORIAL, *France*
Son of Mrs Mary McAllister, of 101, Sydney Street West, Belfast; husband of Martha Hanlon
(formerly McAllister), of 13, Springmount Street, Shankill Road, Belfast.

McAllister, William John - Pioneer
WR/353997 Royal Engineers *Age 52 Died of sickness on 2 January 1920*
CARNMONEY CEMETERY, *United Kingdom*
Husband of Mary McAllister, of 101, Sydney Street West, Belfast. Father of William J.

McAlonen, James - Gunner
70071 Royal Horse Artillery and Royal Field Artillery *Died in War on 9 April 1918*
ADELAIDE CEMETERY, VILLERS BRETONNEUX, *France*
Born and enlisted in Belfast.

McAloraum, Henry Joseph - Rifleman
9848 Royal Irish Rifles 1st Battalion *Died in War on 12 March 1915*
Born and enlisted in Belfast.

McAlpin, James - First Mate
Mercantile Marine S.S. "Stuart Prince" (Newcastle)
Age 40 Drowned, as a result of an attack by an enemy submarine on 22 March 1917
TOWER HILL MEMORIAL, United Kingdom
Son of the late William and Eliza McAlpin; husband of Edith McAlpin (née Redmond),
of 485, Cregagh Road, Belfast. Born at Carrickfergus.

McAnally, John - Stoker
1744U Royal Naval Reserve HMS "Goliath" *Age 45 Died in War on 13 May 1915*
PORTSMOUTH NAVAL MEMORIAL, United Kingdom
Son of John and Catherine McAnally, of Belfast; husband of Mary McAnally, of 1, Linen Street, Belfast.

McAneney, James - Private
10612 Royal Inniskilling Fusiliers 1st Battalion *Died in War on 24 December 1915*
LANCASHIRE LANDING CEMETERY, Turkey
Son of James McAneney, 21, Riga Street, Belfast.

McAnespie, Michael - Private
3063 Royal Munster Fusiliers 6th Battalion *Age 27 Died in War on 13 August 1915*
HELLES MEMORIAL, Turkey
Son of James and Martha McAnespie, of 48, New Lodge Road, Belfast.

McAree, James - Second Cook
Mercantile Marine S.S. "Bray Head" (Belfast) *Age 22 Drowned, as a result of an attack by an enemy submarine on 14 March 1917*
TOWER HILL MEMORIAL, United Kingdom
Son of James and the late Kate McAree; husband of Rachel McAree (née McCann), of 82, Nelson Street, Belfast.

McAree, Thomas - Private
172256 4th Canadian Mounted Rifles (Central Ontario Regiment) *Age 29 Died in War on 16 September 1916*
VIMY MEMORIAL, France
Son of Mrs. M. McAree, of 260, Donegall Road, Belfast, Ireland. He was single,
worked as a dairy man and was a Methodist.

McArthur, Alex - Private
9652 Royal Inniskilling Fusiliers 1st Battalion *Age 25 Killed in Action on 7 June 1915*
PINK FARM CEMETERY, HELLES, Turkey
Son of Robert McArthur, of 53, Boness Street, Belfast.

McArthur, George - Rifleman
13054 Royal Irish Rifles 8th Battalion *Died in War on 2 July 1916*
THIEPVAL MEMORIAL, France
Born and enlisted in Belfast.

McArthur, John - Gunner
38206 Royal Horse Artillery and Royal Field Artillery *Died in War on 30 September 1916*
LEEDS (LAWNS WOOD) CEMETERY, United Kingdom
Born and enlisted in Belfast.

McAteer, David - Private
4493 Royal Inniskilling Fusiliers 2nd Battalion *Died in War on 10 July 1916*
THIEPVAL MEMORIAL, France
Born in Belfast, enlisted Hamilton, Scotland.

McAteer, John - Rifleman
18181 Royal Irish Rifles "C" Company 14th Battalion
Age 23 Killed in Action on 16 August 1917
NEW IRISH FARM CEMETERY, Belgium
Son of Hugh and Margaret McAteer, of 4, Ariel Street, Belfast.

McAteer, John - Stoker Second Class
K/21873 Royal Navy HMS "Good Hope"
Age 17 Killed in Action at Battle of Coronel on 1 November 1914
PORTSMOUTH NAVAL MEMORIAL, United Kingdom
Brother of Mrs. Rachel Gillen, of 4, Irwin Street, Belfast.

McAteer, Patrick - Sergeant
846 Highland Light Infantry 10th (Service) Battalion
Died in War on 25 September 1915
CAMBRIN CHURCHYARD EXTENSION, France
Born in Belfast, enlisted Lanark, Scotland.

McAteer, Robert - Lance Corporal
10605 Royal Irish Rifles 6th Battalion *Died in War on 8 August 1915*
HELLES MEMORIAL, Turkey
Brother of Thomas, 50, Brownlow Street, Belfast.

McAteer, Thomas J - Rifleman
2303 Royal Irish Rifles 11/13th Battalion attached 22nd Entrenching Battalion
Died in War on 28 March 1918
POZIERES MEMORIAL, France
Husband of Mary McAteer, 50, Brownlow Street, Belfast.

McAughey, Herbert - Lance Corporal
350815 Royal Scots 9th Battalion *Age 25 Killed in Action on 23 April 1917*
BROWN'S COPSE CEMETERY, ROEUX, France
Son of Alfred and Margaret McAughey, of 73, Edinburgh Street, Belfast.

McAughey, Robert - Gunner
100692 Royal Field Artillery transferred to 474505 Labour Corps
Age 23 Died as a result of war on 1 November 1919
BELFAST (DUNDONALD) CEMETERY, United Kingdom
Son of Alfred and Margaret McAughey, of 73, Edinburgh Street, Lisburn Road, Belfast.

McAuley, Arthur - Lance Corporal
61988 Corps of Royal Engineers 87th Field Company *Died in War on 2 October 1915*
LOOS MEMORIAL, France
Born in Belfast enlisted Chatham, Kent.

McAuley, Charles - Rifleman
6793 Royal Irish Rifles 11th Battalion *Died in War on 1 July 1916*
THIEPVAL MEMORIAL, France
Born in Belfast, enlisted Clandeboye.

McAuley, Daniel - A/Bombardier
23772 Royal Horse Artillery and Royal Field Artillery *Died in War on 13 March 1915*
FROME (VALLIS) WALL, SOMERSET, United Kingdom
Born in Belfast, enlisted Glasgow.

McAuley, Edward - Private
G/20791 Royal Irish Fusiliers 2nd (Garrison) Battalion *Age 45 Died of malaria on 23 September 1917*
MIKRA BRITISH CEMETERY, KALAMARIA, Greece
Son of Charles and Catherine McAuley, of Belfast. Served in the South African War.

McAuley, Francis - Private
4078 Royal Inniskilling Fusiliers 2nd Battalion *Killed in Action on 19 November 1915*
SUZANNE COMMUNAL CEMETERY EXTENSION, France
Born and enlisted in Belfast.

McAuley, George - Private
Royal Inniskilling Fusiliers 9th Battalion *Died of Wounds on 17 August 1917*
LIJSSENTHOEK MILITARY CEMETERY, Belgium
152, Sugarfield Street, Belfast.

McAuley, James - Lance Corporal
9293 Royal Irish Rifles 2nd Battalion *Killed in Action on 30 August 1916*
POZIERES BRITISH CEMETERY, OVILLERS-LA BOISSELLE, France
16, Jude Street, Belfast.

McAuley, John - Private
355 Royal Irish Rifles 15th Battalion *Died in War on 1 July 1916*
THIEPVAL MEMORIAL, France
Husband of Jane McAuley, 34, Tobergill Street, Belfast.

McAuley, John - Rifleman
17/1676 Royal Irish Rifles 10th Battalion *Age 26 Died of Wounds received at the Battle of the Somme on 6 July 1916*
ST. SEVER CEMETERY, ROUEN, France
Son of Isaac and Maggie McAuley, of 11, Saunders Street, Belfast.

McAuley, Patrick Hugh - Leading Seaman
J/1215 Royal Navy HMS "Defence" *Age 29 Killed in Action at Battle of Jutland on 31 May 1916*
PLYMOUTH NAVAL MEMORIAL, United Kingdom
Son of Sarah McAuley, of 14, Benares Street, Belfast, and the late Patrick McAuley.

McAuley, Walter - Rifleman
8039 Royal Irish Rifles 2nd Battalion *Died of Wounds on 27 March 1918*
POZIERES MEMORIAL, France
Son of Robert and Annie McAuley, 102, Carnan Street, Belfast.

McAuley, William - Rifleman
8237 Royal Irish Rifles 1st Battalion *Age 28 Killed in Action on 11 March 1915*
LE TOURET MEMORIAL, France
Son of Mrs. Ann Jane McAuley, of 4, Mayfair Street, Belfast.

McAvoy, John - Private
15180 Royal Dublin Fusiliers 2nd Battalion *Age 23 Died in War on 9 September 1918*
VALENCIENNES (ST. ROCH) COMMUNAL CEMETERY, France
Son of James and Bridget McAvoy, of 4, Kerrera Street, Crumlin Road, Belfast.

McAvoy, Michael - Private
7/1729 Leinster Regiment 2nd Battalion *Died in War on 8 June 1917*
LIJSSENTHOEK MILITARY CEMETERY, Belgium
Son of Isabella McAvoy, of 28, Mary Street, Belfast.

McAvoy, Peter - Private
6278 Leinster Regiment 2nd Battalion *Died in War on 20 October 1914*
PLOEGSTEERT MEMORIAL, Belgium
Born in Londonderry, resident of Belfast.

McBay, Alexander - Private
9982 Royal Inniskilling Fusiliers 1st Battalion *Age 23 Died in War on 29 June 1915*
HELLES MEMORIAL, Turkey
Son of Alexander McBay, of 63, Wilton Street, Shankill Road, Belfast.

McBratney, John Harkness - Rifleman
18184 Royal Irish Rifles 1st Battalion *Died in War on 29 April 1918*
NEW IRISH FARM CEMETERY, Belgium
Born and enlisted in Belfast. Son the late T. H. B. and Lizzie McBratney

McBriar, James - Private
12519 Royal Scots (Lothian Regiment) 2nd Battalion *Age 33 Died in War on 18 July 1916*
THIEPVAL MEMORIAL, France
Born in Belfast, enlisted in Barrhead, Scotland.

McBride, Alexander - Fireman And Trimmer
Mercantile Marine S.S. "Glenfruin" (Glasgow) *Age 42 Presumed drowned on 26 January 1918*
TOWER HILL MEMORIAL, United Kingdom
Son of the late James and Ann Jane McBride; husband of Catherine McBride (née Campbell),
of 7, Milewater Street, Belfast. Born at Ballymena, County Antrim.

McBride, Arthur King - Captain
Royal Irish Rifles 12th Battalion *Age 36 Killed in Action on 7 June 1917*
POND FARM CEMETERY, Belgium
Son of Henry James McBride, of Hyde Park, Belfast; husband of Ruby McBride,
of Mervue, Waterloo, Larne, County Antrim.

McBride, Charles - Private
15071 Royal Irish Regiment 7th Battalion *Died as a result of war on 11 December 1918*
BERLIN SOUTHERN-WESTERN CEMETERY, Germany
Son of Mr A Bride, 85, Durham Street, Belfast.

McBride, David - Rifleman
12/47919 Royal Irish Rifles 1st Battalion *Killed in Action on 2 October 1918*
DADIZEELE NEW BRITISH CEMETERY, Belgium
Husband of Mrs. F. McBride, of 30, Gaffikin Street, Belfast. Formerly 206076 Royal Engineers

McBride, George - Private
22029 Princess Victoria's (Royal Irish Fusiliers) 9th Battalion *Died in War on 29 March 1918*
POZIERES MEMORIAL, France
Born and enlisted in Belfast.

McBride, George Alfred - Rifleman
211 Royal Irish Rifles 16th Battalion *Died in War on 17 March 1918*
ST SEVER CEMETERY EXTENSION ROUEN, France
Born in County Down, enlisted Lurgan, resident of Belfast.

McBride, Gilbert - Stoker First Class
SS/103628 Royal Navy HMS "Aboukir" *Age 26 Killed in Action with submarine in North Sea on 22 September 1914*
CHATHAM NAVAL MEMORIAL, United Kingdom
Son of Elizabeth McBride, of 28, Mayflower Street, Belfast, and the late William McBride; husband of the late Sarah McBride.

McBride, Joseph - Acting Corporal
9492 Royal Inniskilling Fusiliers 1st Battalion *Killed in Action on 1 July 1916*
ANCRE BRITISH CEMETERY, BEAUMONT-HAMEL, France
Born and enlisted in Belfast.

McBride, Joseph - Major
Royal Field Artillery 27th Brigade *Died in War on 23 April 1917*
VIMY COMMUNAL CEMETERY, France
Member of Westbourne Presbyterian Church, Belfast. Born at Downpatrick and husband of Mary McBride of Ballymaconnell, Bangor.

McBride, Kirker Gibson - Corporal
12015 Royal Irish Rifles 15th Battalion *Age 21 Died in War on 22 November 1917*
CAMBRAI MEMORIAL, LOUVERVAL, France
Son of James and Elizabeth McBride, of 41, Upper Charleville Street, Belfast.

McBride, Patrick - Private
7025 Royal Inniskilling Fusiliers 2nd Battalion *Age 32 Died in War on 20 October 1914*
PLOEGSTEERT MEMORIAL, Belgium
Husband of Mary Jane McBride, of 19, Stanfield Street, Belfast.

McBride, Samuel - Lance Sergeant
50042 Northumberland Fusiliers 3rd Battalion *Age 44 Died in War on 7 July 1917*
BELFAST (DUNDONALD) CEMETERY, United Kingdom
Husband of Jane McBride, of 98, Portallo Street, Belfast.

McBride, Victor William - Stoker
3726S Royal Navy HMS "Queen Mary" *Died in War on 31 May 1916*
PORTSMOUTH NAVAL MEMORIAL, United Kingdom
127, Alexander Park Avenue, Belfast.

McBride, William - Rifleman
794 Royal Irish Rifles 13th Battalion *Killed in Action on 16 August 1917*
TYNE COT MEMORIAL, Belgium
Born and enlisted in Belfast.

McBride, William - Stoker First Class
K/6288 Royal Navy HMS "Laforey" *Age 30 Killed by mine explosion in Straits of Dover on 23 March 1917*
CHATHAM NAVAL MEMORIAL, United Kingdom
Son of Samuel and Sarah McBride, of Belfast.

McBride, William Wilson - Second Lieutenant
Royal Garrison Artillery 229th Siege Battery *Age 20 Killed in Action on 5 December 1917*
GIAVERA BRITISH CEMETERY, ARCADE, Italy
Son of William Durham and Elizabeth Wallace McBride, of Malone, Belfast.

McBrinn, John Charles - Second Lieutenant
Royal Irish Regiment 5th Battalion attached 6th Battalion Connaught Rangers *Died in War on 3 September 1916*
DELVILLE WOOD CEMETERY, LONGUEVAL, France
Son of Head Constable Patrick McBrinn (Royal Irish Constabulary) and Mrs. M. E. McBrinn,
of 2, Roseleigh Street, Belfast.

McBroom, Walter - Private
2457 South African Infantry 3rd Regiment *Age 46 Died in War on 1 August 1916*
THIEPVAL MEMORIAL, France
Son of Walter McBroom, of Cave Hill, Belfast, Ireland. Served in the South African Campaign,
also served in German South West Africa.

McBurney, John - Gunner
45755 Royal Garrison Artillery *Died in War on 13 March 1918*
AUBIGNY COMMUNAL CEMETERY EXTENSION, France
Born in County Longford, enlisted Liverpool, resident of Belfast.

McBurney, William Busby - Sapper
57696 Royal Engineers Training Centre (Newark) *Age 41 Died in War on 21 April 1917*
LEEDS (LAWNS WOOD) CEMETERY, United Kingdom
Son of John and Sarah Busby McBurney, of Belfast; husband of Martha McBurney
of 46, Fife Street, Shore Road, Belfast.

McClurkin, Charles James - Stoker First Class
Royal Navy HMS "Formidable" *Died in War on 1 January 1915*
CHATHAM NAVAL MEMORIAL, United Kingdom
3, Broadbent Street, Belfast. Worked in the Brookfield Mill.

McCabe, John - Private
3452 Princess Victoria's (Royal Irish Fusiliers) 5th Battalion *Died in War on 7 November 1917*
GAZA WAR CEMETERY, Israel
Born and enlisted in Belfast.

McCabe, Robert - Sergeant
6654 Royal Inniskilling Fusiliers 2nd Battalion *Died in War on 27 March 1918*
SERRE ROAD CEMETERY No.2, France
Brother of Mrs Jane Green, 3, Rowan Street, Belfast.

McCabe, Thomas - Private
3432 Royal Inniskilling Fusiliers 8th Battalion *Killed in Action on 6 September 1916*
THIEPVAL MEMORIAL, France
Born and enlisted in Belfast.

McCabe, William John - Private
22554 Royal Dublin Fusiliers 2nd Battalion *Died Of Wounds on 31 October 1916*
ETAPLES MILITARY CEMETERY, France
Born and enlisted in Belfast.

McCabe, William John - Private
PLY/15918 Royal Marine Light Infantry HMS "Foresight" *Age 25 Died as a result of war on 29 March 1919*
MALTA (CAPUCCINI) NAVAL CEMETERY
Son of the late James and Lena McCabe, of Belfast.

McCafferty, John - Corporal
48061 Royal Field Artillery 43rd Battery *Killed in action on 23 April 1916*
VLAMERTINGHE NEW MILITARY CEMETERY, Belgium
11, Chater Street, Belfast.

McCafferty, Patrick - Second Steward
Mercantile Marine S.S. "War Clover" (London) *Age 18 Drowned, as a result of an attack by an enemy submarine on 19 October 1917*
TOWER HILL MEMORIAL, United Kingdom
Son of James McCafferty, of 39, Marine Street, Belfast, and the late Mary McCafferty.

McCafferty, Thomas - Gunner
5030 Royal Garrison Artillery *Died in War on 13 October 1917*
LIJSSENTHOEK MILITARY CEMETERY, Belgium
Born in Belfast, enlisted Carrickfergus.

McCaffery, William - Lance Corporal
10380 Royal Inniskilling Fusiliers 1st Battalion *Age 22 Killed in Action on 1 July 1916*
THIEPVAL MEMORIAL, France
Son of Mr. and Mrs. William John McCaffery, of 77, Wellesley Avenue, Malone Road, Belfast.

McCaffrey, Thomas - Rifleman
4767 Royal Irish Rifles 2nd Battalion *Age 33 Killed in Action on 5 January 1915*
YPRES (MENIN GATE) MEMORIAL, Belgium
Son of Bridget McCaffrey, of 7, Collyer Street, Belfast.

McCagherty, James - Rifleman
5452 Royal Irish Rifles 2nd Battalion *Age 24 Killed in Action on 28 August 1916*
POZIERES BRITISH CEMETERY, France
Born and enlisted in Belfast. Native of Tandragee, County Armagh.

McCahon, Robert - Lieutenant
Royal Engineers 69th Field Company *Died in War on 30 March 1918*
DOULLENS COMMUNAL CEMETERY, EXTENSION No 1, France
Member of Knock Presbyterian church. Son of John McCahon of Regent Street, Kilrea, County Derry.

McCall, Joe - Sapper
86132 Royal Engineers 258th Tunnelling Company *Died in War on 15 October 1916*
LOOS MEMORIAL, France
Brother of David McCall, of 511, Ormeau Road, Belfast.

McCall, Samuel - Private
16728 Royal Irish Rifles 14th Battalion *Killed in Action on 1 July 1916*
THIEPVAL MEMORIAL, France
Gainsbrough Drive, Belfast.

McCallam, William - Private
23524 Royal Inniskilling Fusiliers 9th Battalion *Age 39 Died in War on 29 March 1918*
POZIERES MEMORIAL, France
Son of the late Hugh and Eliza McCallam, of Sion Mills, County Tyrone; husband of Mary McCallam, of 17, Fifth Street, Shankill Road, Belfast.

JOURNEY OF REMEMBERING

McCallion, William - Private
16143 Cameronians (Scottish Rifles) 1st Battalion *Died in War on 25 December 1915*
GORRE BRITISH AND INDIAN CEMETERY, France
Born in Belfast. Lived in Nigg Camp, Rossshire, Scotland.

McCallum, Alexander - Trooper
4670 Guards Machine Gun Regiment 2nd Life Guards *Age 35 Died in War on 18 February 1919*
BELFAST CITY CEMETERY, United Kingdom
Husband of Ethel McCallum, of 8, Forth Glen, Ballygomartin Road, Belfast.
Formerly 5315 6th Dragoon Guards

McCallum, Frederick - Rifleman
6910 Royal Irish Rifles 2nd Battalion *Killed in action on 24 March 1918*
POZIERES MEMORIAL, France
Husband of Sarah McCallum, 40, Edith Street, Belfast.

McCallum, James - Rifleman
15342 Royal Irish Rifles 10th Battalion *Died in War on 24 November 1915*
SUCRERIE MILITARY CEMETERY, COLINCAMPS, France
Born and enlisted in Belfast.

McCallum, John - Private
4509 Seaforth Highlands 1st/6th Battalion transferred to 634882 Labour Corps
Died in War on 5 November 1918
TERLINCTHUN BRITISH CEMETERY, WIMILLE, France
Nephew of Mary Comiskey, Bridge End Belfast.

McCallum, John - Sergeant
12335 Royal Irish Rifles 8th Battalion *Age 23 Died in War on 21 June 1917*
YPRES (MENIN GATE) MEMORIAL, Belgium
Son of Margaret McCallum, of 26, Peveril Street, Ormeau Road, Belfast, and the late John McCallum.

McCallum, Robert Henry - Lance Corporal
8774 Royal Irish Rifles 1st Battalion *Age 27 Killed in Action on 9 May 1915*
PLOEGSTEERT MEMORIAL, Belgium
Son of Andrew and Sarah McCallum, of 26, Cuba Street, Belfast.

McCallum, William - Private
904 Princess Louise's (Argyll & Sutherland Highlanders) 1st Battalion *Died in War on 16 January 1915*
VOORMEZEELE ENCLOSURES No 1 and No 2, Belgium
Born in Belfast, enlisted in Glasgow.

McCalmont, James - Lance Corporal
10679 Royal Inniskilling Fusiliers 1st Battalion *Died in War on 26 April 1915*
HELLES MEMORIAL, Turkey
61, Woodvale Street, Belfast.

McCambley, James - Corporal
14492 Princess Victoria's (Royal Irish Fusiliers) 9th Battalion *Killed in Action on 1 July 1916*
ANCRE BRITISH CEMETERY, BEAUMONT-HAMEL, France
Born in Belfast, enlisted in Armagh.

BELFAST BOOK OF HONOUR

M

McCance, William - Private
22066 Royal Dublin Fusiliers 6th Battalion *Age 20 Died in War on 9 August 1915*
HELLES MEMORIAL, Turkey
Son of Margret McCance, of 115, Harding Street, Belfast, and the late John McCance.

McCandless, Adam - Rifleman
11196 Royal Irish Rifles 6th Battalion *Died in War on 30 August 1915*
BEACH CEMETERY ANZAC, Turkey
Born and enlisted in Belfast.

McCandless, Robert - Rifleman
307 Royal Irish Rifles 10th Battalion *Age 29 Killed in Action on 1 July 1916*
SERRE ROAD CEMETERY No.2, France
Son of the late William and Margaret McCandless, of Ballaney, Banbridge, County Down; husband of Mary Jane McCandless, of 60, Excise Street, Belfast.

McCann, Alexander - Rifleman
926 Royal Irish Rifles 14th Battalion *Killed in action on 24 March 1918*
POZIERES MEMORIAL, France
Son of Mrs Annie McCann, 130, Matilda Street, Belfast.

McCann, Edward - Private
12407 Royal Irish Fusiliers 5th Battalion *Age 33 Died in War on 25 June 1918*
TERLINCTHUN BRITISH CEMETERY, WIMILLE, France
Son of Edward M. and Sarah McCann, of Belfast.

McCann, Frederick - Lance Corporal
1524 Australian Infantry 15th Battalion *Age 27 Died of Wounds on 9 June 1918*
CROUY BRITISH CEMETERY, CROUY-SUR-SOMME, France
Son of Ellen J. and the late Samuel McCann, of 41, Hatfield Street, Belfast, Ireland.
Native of Ballycullen, Newtownards, County Down.

McCann, Henry - Private
592718 Labour Corps formerly 18201 Royal Irish Rifles *Died in War on 10 November 1918*
AGHALEE CEMETERY, COUNTY ANTRIM, United Kingdom
Born in Dunmurry, enlisted Holywood, resident of Belfast.

McCann, James - Corporal
2591 Connaught Rangers *Age 29 Died of Wounds on 21 September 1916*
BELFAST (MILLTOWN) ROMAN CATHOLIC CEMETERY, United Kingdom
Husband of Mary Agnes McCann, of 54, Vernon Street, Ormeau Road, Belfast.

McCann, James - Lance Corporal
2943 Royal Inniskilling Fusiliers 1st Battalion *Age 21 Killed in Action on 1 July 1916*
THIEPVAL MEMORIAL, France
Son of Mary McCann, of 25, Ritchie Street, Belfast, and the late William McCann.

McCann, John - Private
7236 South Lancashire Regiment 2nd Battalion *Age 29 Died in War on 25 December 1914*
YPRES (MENIN GATE) MEMORIAL, Belgium
(Served as BROWN), son of Edward and Jane McCann, of 74, Avon Street; husband of Sarah McCann, of 60, Avon Street, Ballymacarrett, Belfast.

Journey of Remembering

McCann, Matthew - Fireman
Mercantile Marine S.S. "California" (Glasgow) *Age 55 Drowned, as a result of an attack by an enemy submarine on 7 February 1917*
TOWER HILL MEMORIAL, *United Kingdom*
Son of the late James and Alice McCann; husband of Jane McCann (née Bevie),
of 14, Hamilton Street, Govan, Glasgow. Born in Belfast.

McCann, Thomas - Gunner
37431 Royal Garrison Artillery 27th Trench Mortar Battery *Age 20 Died of Wounds on 22 September 1915*
LIJSSENTHOEK MILITARY CEMETERY, *Belgium*
Son of John and Jane McCann, of Armaghbreague, Keady, County Armagh. Born Belfast.
One of the first to land in France, 13th August 1914.

McCann, William - Corporal
8845 Royal Irish Rifles "A" Company 2nd Battalion *Age 25 Killed in Action at Neuve Chapelle on 25 October 1914*
LE TOURET MEMORIAL, *France*
Son of the late John McCann, of 42, Greenville Road, Bloomfield, Belfast.

McCann, William - Rifleman
A/203561 King's Royal Rifle Corps 12th Battalion *Died in War on 11 October 1918*
HOUCHIN BRITISH CEMETERY, *France*
Son of Mrs M McCann, 37, Howe Street, Belfast.

McCann, William Robert - Second Lieutenant
Durham Light Infantry 7th Battalion *Age 19 Died in War on 11 October 1916*
BAZENTIN-LE-PETIT COMMUNAL CEMETERY EXTENSION, *France*
Son of Mr. and Mrs. James McCann, "Fernagh", Whiteabbey, Belfast.

McCardle, Thomas Henry - Sergeant
6757 Royal Irish Fusiliers 2nd Battalion *Died in War on 4 May 1915*
YPRES (MENIN GATE) MEMORIAL, *Belgium*
23, Harvey Street, Belfast. Born in County Down.

McCarrol, George - Rifleman
1491 Royal Irish Rifles "B" Company 9th Battalion *Age 20 Killed in Action on 1 July 1916*
THIEPVAL MEMORIAL, *France*
Son of Elizabeth Huddleston (formerly McCarrol), of 51, Cambrai Street, Crumlin Road, Belfast,
and the late George McCarrol.

McCarroll, Alexander - Rifleman
17/615 Royal Irish Rifles 16th Battalion *Age 36 Died of Wounds on 22 August 1917*
WIMEREUX COMMUNAL CEMETERY, *France*
Husband of Christina McCarroll, of 43, Hopewell Street, Belfast.

McCarroll, James - Rifleman
15350 Royal Irish Rifles 14th Battalion *Killed in Action on 24 March 1918*
POZIERES MEMORIAL, *France*
Born and enlisted in Belfast.

McCarroll, Thomas J - Private
5035 Royal Munster Fusiliers 1st Battalion *Killed in Action on 28 June 1918*
COUIN NEW BRITISH CEMETERY, *France*
Son of Mary McCarroll, of 14, Colchester Street, Donegall Road, Belfast.

McCartan, Francis - Private
4746 Connaught Rangers 6th Battalion *Age 23 Died in War on 3 September 1916*
BERNAFAY WOOD BRITISH CEMETERY, MONTAUBAN, France
Son of Hugh and Bridget McCartan, of 3, Smith Street, Belfast.

McCartan, William John - Private
4373 Connaught Rangers 6th Battalion *Died in War on 28 January 1916*
DUD CORNER CEMETERY, LOOS, France
Born in Belfast, enlisted in Belfast.

McCarthy, Daniel - Private
9818 Princess Victoria's (Royal Irish Fusiliers) 2nd Battalion *Died in War on 2 May 1915*
YPRES (MENIN GATE) MEMORIAL, Belgium
Born in Monaghan, enlisted in Enniskillen, resident of Belfast.

McCarthy, John - Private
4875 Corps of Lancers 5th Lancers (Royal Irish) *Died in War on 13 February 1916*
CALAIS SOUTHERN CEMETERY, France
Born in Antrim, enlisted Edinburgh, resident of Belfast.

McCarthy, William - Private
258 Royal Munster Fusiliers 2nd Battalion *Died in War on 11 September 1915*
VERMELLES BRITISH CEMETERY, France
Born in County Antrim, enlisted in Manchester, resident of Belfast.

McCarthy, William - Private
26068 Northumberland Fusiliers 12th/13th Battalion *Age 21 Died in War on 4 October 1917*
TYNE COT MEMORIAL, Belgium
Son of Mrs. Mary McCarthy, of 27, Arran Street, Belfast.

McCartney, Alexander - Private
DM2/224602 Royal Army Service Corps 1038th Mechanical Transport Company
Age 29 Died of pneumonia on 10 December 1918
ALEXANDRIA (HADRA) WAR MEMORIAL CEMETERY, Egypt
Son of Annie McCartney, of 42, Collyer Street, Limestone Road, Belfast.

McCartney, Alexander - Rifleman
13225 Royal Irish Rifles 8th Battalion *Died in War on 5 August 1917*
NEW IRISH FARM CEMETERY, Belgium
Born and enlisted in Belfast.

McCartney, Andrew - Private
16784 Corps of Dragoons Shorpshire Yeomanry *Died in War on 10 October 1918*
HOLLYBROOK CEMETERY, Southampton
Born in Belfast, enlisted Preston.

McCartney, Archibald - Acting Bombardier
52533 Royal Field Artillery "B" Battery *Age 24 Died in War on 2 June 1915*
HELLES MEMORIAL, Turkey
Son of Margaret McCartney, of 4, Sydney Street, Belfast.

McCartney, Daniel - Leading Stoker
K/3632 Royal Navy H.M. Submarine "G8" *Age 26 Killed in loss of vessel in North Sea on 3 January 1918*
CHATHAM NAVAL MEMORIAL, United Kingdom
Son of Daniel and Margaret McCartney, of 67, Wigton Street, Belfast.

McCartney, Henry - Rifleman
13223 Royal Irish Rifles 1st Battalion *Killed in Action on 21 March 1918*
POZIERES MEMORIAL, France
Born and enlisted in Belfast.

McCartney, James - Private
21120 Princess Victoria's (Royal Irish Fusiliers) 7/8th Battalion *Died in War on 19 November 1916*
Born and enlisted in Belfast. Formerly 2473 Connaught Rangers

McCartney, James - Rifleman
7252 Royal Irish Rifles 2nd Battalion *Age 29 Died in War on 11 November 1914*
YPRES (MENIN GATE) MEMORIAL, Belgium
Son of David and Margaret McCartney, of 2, Mashona Street, Belfast.

McCartney, John - Rifleman
341 Royal Irish Rifles 8/9th Battalion *Died in War on 8 August 1917*
NEW IRISH FARM CEMETERY, Belgium
Born and enlisted in Belfast.

McCartney, Robert Law - Rifleman
10310 Royal Irish Rifles 1st Battalion *Died in War on 11 March 1915*
LE TOURET MEMORIAL, France
His wife and son lived at 22, Arnon Street, Belfast.

McCartney, Samuel - Private
12886 Princess Victoria's (Royal Irish Fusiliers) 6th Battalion *Died in War on 15 August 1915*
HELLES MEMORIAL, Turkey
Born and enlisted in Belfast.

McCartney, Samuel - Rifleman
1198 Royal Irish Rifles 15th Battalion *Died in War on 23 January 1916*
MAILLY-MAILLET COMMUNAL CEMETERY EXTENSION, France
Born and enlisted in Belfast.

McCartney, Thomas - Lance Corporal
6586 Royal Irish Rifles 2nd Battalion *Died of Wounds on 3 April 1915*
BAILLEUL COMMUNAL CEMETERY (NORD), France
Born in Belfast, enlisted in Dublin.

McCartney, William - Rifleman
106 Royal Irish Rifles 15th Battalion *Died in War on 11 June 1916*
THIEPVAL MEMORIAL, France
Born and enlisted in Belfast.

McCartney, William - Rifleman
G/215 Royal Irish Rifles *Age 51 Died on 2 August 1917*
CARNMONEY CEMETERY, United Kingdom
Native of Belfast. Husband of Nellie McCartney, of Waringstown.

McCartney, William John - Lance Corporal
9225 Royal Irish Rifles 1st Battalion *Killed in Action on 26 October 1916*
GROVE TOWN CEMETERY MEAULTE, France
Born and enlisted in Belfast.

McCartney, William John - Lance Corporal
Canadian Army *Age 26 Died of Wounds on 26 October 1916*
47, Cambrai Street, Belfast. A Presbyterian, he worked as a teamster and in Ireland had served in the North Down Militia. Husband of Florence Beatrice McCartney, Winnipeg, Canada.

McCartney, William John - Private
8101 Princess Victoria's (Royal Irish Fusiliers) 1st Battalion *Died in War on 26 April 1916*
BERLES-AU-BOIS CHURCHYARD EXTENSION, France
Born and enlisted in Belfast. Formerly 6972 South Lancashire Regiment.

McCarton, Frank - Private
4746 Connaught Rangers 6th Battalion *Died in War on 3 September 1916*
BERNAFAY WOOD BRITISH CEMETERY MONTAUBAN, France
Born and enlisted in Belfast.

McCarty, William - Sapper
41472 Corps of Royal Engineers 144th Company *Died in War on 12 September 1916*
ETRETAT CHURCHYARD, France
Born and enlisted in Belfast.

McCashin, Henry - Rifleman
15351 Royal Irish Rifles 14th Battalion *Killed in Action on 1 July 1916*
THIEPVAL MEMORIAL, France
Dunluce Avenue, Belfast. A native of Galway.

McCaugherty, David - Able Seaman
176815 Royal Navy HMS "Hawke" *Age 37 Killed in Action with submarine in North Sea on 15 October 1914*
CHATHAM NAVAL MEMORIAL, United Kingdom
Son of William McCaugherty, of Belfast; husband of Martha McCaugherty, of 30, Hurst Street, Belfast. Awarded East and West Africa Medal (Benin expedition). Served in the South African War.

McCaugherty, James - Private
Royal Irish Rifles *Died in War*
24, Bowness Street, Belfast.

McCaughey, Charles - Lance Corporal
10252 Royal Inniskilling Fusiliers 1st Battalion *Age 23 Killed in Action on 22 May 1915*
TWELVE TREE COPSE CEMETERY, Turkey
6, Bloomfield Avenue. Son of the late John and Annie McCaughey, of Belfast.

McCauley, Alfred - Private
1235 Princess Louise's (Argyll & Sutherland Highlanders) 2nd Battalion *Died in War on 10 November 1914*
PLOEGSTEERT MEMORIAL, Belgium
Born in Belfast, enlisted Paisley, Scotland.

McCauley, Charles - Rifleman
6793 Royal Irish Rifles 11th Battalion *Age 18 Killed in Action on 1 July 1916*
THIEPVAL MEMORIAL, France
Son of James McCauley, of 19, McCleery Street, Belfast.

McCauley, George - Private
13620 Royal Inniskilling Fusiliers "C" Company 9th Battalion *Age 20 Died of Wounds on 17 August 1917*
LIJSSENTHOEK MILITARY CEMETERY, Belgium
Son of Samuel and Mary McCauley, of 152, Sugarfield Street, Shankill Road, Belfast.
Born Dungannon, County Tyrone.

McCauley, Robert - Rifleman
18207 Royal Irish Rifles 11th Battalion *Age 20 Died of Wounds on 17 June 1916*
WARLOY-BAILLON COMMUNAL CEMETERY EXTENSION, France
Son of Mary Elizabeth McConnell (formerly McCauley), of 2, Hill Street, Dunmurry, Belfast, and the late James McCauley.

McCausland, David - Rifleman
19/410 Royal Irish Rifles 12th Battalion *Age 20 Died of Wounds on 25 November 1918*
BELFAST CITY CEMETERY, United Kingdom
Son of Mr. and Mrs. W. J. McCausland, of 102, York Road, Belfast.

McCausland, Patrick - Private
22145 Royal Irish Fusiliers 7th Battalion *Age 17 Died of Wounds (gas) on 1 May 1916*
LILLERS COMMUNAL CEMETERY, France
Son of Edward and Elizabeth McCausland, of 88, Lepper Street, Belfast.

McCausland, William James - Private
PLY/17058 Royal Marine Light Infantry HMS "Indefatigable"
Age 19 Killed in Action at Battle of Jutland on 31 May 1916
PLYMOUTH NAVAL MEMORIAL, United Kingdom
Son of Charles and Elizabeth McCausland, of 36, Donegall Avenue, Belfast. Native of Newry.

McCavert, John - Private
6726 Cameronians (Scottish Rifles) 1st Battalion *Died in War on 20 July 1916*
THIEPVAL MEMORIAL, France
Born in Belfast, enlisted Coatbridge, Scotland.

McCaw, James - Private
11600 Royal Inniskilling Fusiliers 2nd Battalion *Died in War on 16 May 1915*
LE TOURET MEMORIAL, France
Son of William McCaw, 45, Cumberland Street, Belfast.

McCaw, Joseph - Sergeant
7699 North Staffordshire Regiment 1st Battalion *Killed in Action on 12 March 1915*
PLOEGSTEERT MEMORIAL, Belgium
Husband of Mary McCaw, of 50, Halcombe Street, Woodstock Road, Belfast.

McCaw, William George. - Sergeant
13228 Royal Irish Rifles 8th Battalion *Died in War on 2 July 1916*
MILL ROAD CEMETERY, THIEPVAL, France
47, Atlantic Avenue, Belfast.

McChesney, William - Rifleman
1941 Royal Irish Rifles 8/9th Battalion *Died in War on 23 November 1917*
CAMBRAI MEMORIAL, LOUVERVAL, France
59, Everton Street, Belfast.

McClarnon, John - Private
1847 Duke of Wellington's (West Riding Regiment) 1/4th Battalion *Died in War on 19 December 1915*
TALANA FARM CEMETERY, *Belgium*
Born in Belfast, enlisted Halifax, Yorkshire.

McClay, Thomas - Rifleman
15215 Royal Irish Rifles 9th Battalion *Age 43 Accidentally killed on 14 November 1914*
CARNMONEY CEMETERY, *United Kingdom*
Son of Andrew and Esther McClay; husband of Margaret McClay, of 7, Main Street, Whitehouse, Belfast.
Born at Belfast.

McClean, Abraham - Private
19523 Machine Gun Corps (Infantry) *Died in War on 15 June 1916*
THIEPVAL MEMORIAL, *France*
Born and enlisted in Belfast. Formerly 15445 Royal Irish Rifles

McClean, Alexander - Private
32697 Otago Regiment, New Zealand Expeditionary Force 2nd Battalion *Age 28 Died of Wounds on 17 June 1917*
TROIS ARBRES CEMETERY, STEENWERCK, *France*
Son of John and Mary A. McClean, of Belfast, Ireland; husband of Hilda McClean,
of St. Kilda, Dunedin, New Zealand.

McClean, John - Private
10260 Princess Victoria's (Royal Irish Fusiliers) 6th Battalion *Died in War on 31 October 1916*
LAHANA MILITARY CEMETERY, *Greece*
Born in Belfast, enlisted Armagh.

McClean, John W - Private
20795 Canadian Infantry (Alberta Regiment) *Died in War 23 April 1915*
POPERINGE OLD MILITARY CEMETERY, *Belgium*
32, Madison Avenue, Belfast. Born at Newry and had served in the Yeomanry in Ireland. A clerk in civilian life.

McClean, Joseph - Lance Corporal
18225 Royal Irish Rifles 14th Battalion *Killed in Action on 1 July 1916*
THIEPVAL MEMORIAL, *France*
Born and enlisted in Belfast.

McClean, Joseph - Lance Corporal
9389 Royal Irish Rifles 1st Battalion *Died in War on 10 March 1915*
LE TOURET MEMORIAL, *France*
36, Mersey Street, Belfast.

McClean, Joseph - Private
9823 East Lancashire Regiment 6th Battalion *Died in War on 25 January 1917*
AMARA WAR CEMETERY, *Iraq*
Born and enlisted in Belfast.

McClean, Joseph Henry - Private
29536 Royal Irish Fusiliers 9th Battalion *Age 19 Died of Wounds on 13 September 1918*
ARNEKE BRITISH CEMETERY, *France*
Son of William and Catherine McClean, of 78, Frome Street, Belfast.
Native of Brookhill, Lisburn, County Antrim.

JOURNEY OF REMEMBERING

McClean, R - Private
10731 Royal Inniskilling Fusiliers 2nd Battalion *Died in War on 27 September 1917*
COXYDE MILITARY CEMETERY, *Belgium*
Son of Mrs. Margaret Thornton, of 44, Boyne Square, Belfast.

McClean, Ramsay - Private
641 Royal Irish Rifles 16th Battalion *Died of Wounds on 11 June 1916*
STE. MARIE CEMETERY, LE HAVRE, *France*
5, Ohio Street, Belfast. A member of the old UVF.

McClean, Robert - Private
8746 Royal Inniskilling Fusiliers 2nd Battalion *Age 25 Killed in Action on 18 September 1914*
MONTBREHAIN COMMUNAL CEMETERY, *France*
Son of Sarah and Allan McClean, 22, Clementine Street, Belfast.

McClean, William - Able Seaman
J/10446 Royal Navy HMS "Princess Irene" *Died in War on 27 May 1915*
PORTSMOUTH MEMORIAL, *United Kingdom*
42, Turin Street, Belfast.

McClean, William - Rifleman
657 Royal Irish Rifles 10th Battalion *Died in War on 15 September 1916*
ST QUENTIN CABARET MILITARY CEMETERY, *Belgium*
Born Ballymacarrett, Belfast. Enlisted in Belfast.

McClean, William - Sergeant
6547 Royal Irish Regiment 2nd Battalion *Age 38 Killed in Action on 21 March 1918*
POZIERES MEMORIAL, *France*
Son of the late William and Margaret McClean, of Belfast.

McCleanghan, Alexander - Private
17199 Northumberland Fusiliers 2nd Battalion *Died in War on 8 May 1915*
YPRES (MENIN GATE) MEMORIAL, *France*
Born in Belfast, enlisted Durham, England.

McCleave, Edward - Rifleman
17/955 Royal Irish Rifles 15th Battalion *Died in War on 29 May 1918*
CANADA FARM CEMETERY, *Belgium*
51, Langford Street, Belfast.

McCleery, Austin - Private
15364 Royal Irish Rifles 14th Battalion *Killed in Action on 1 July 1916*
CONNAUGHT CEMETERY, THIEPVAL, *France*
44, Arkwright Street, Belfast.

McCleery, Samuel - Lance Corporal
19561 Machine Gun Corps 107th Company *Age 24 Killed in Action on 1 July 1916*
THIEPVAL MEMORIAL, *France*
Son of Mrs. McCleery, of 44, Perth Street, Belfast; husband of Margretta Barbour (formerly McCleery), of 8, Benwell Street, Belfast.

McCleery, William - Private
3482 Royal Inniskilling Fusiliers 1st Battalion *Age 22 Died in War on 9 August 1916*
POTIJZE CHATEAU WOOD CEMETERY, Belgium
Son of Mrs. A. McCleery, of 23, City Street, Belfast.

McClelland, Alfred - Second Lieutenant
Royal Irish Rifles 1st Battalion *Age 24 Died of Wounds on 13 October 1917*
TROIS ARBRES CEMETERY, STEENWERCK, France
Son of James and Charlotte Marion McClelland, of 105, Cavehill Road, Belfast.
Originally joined the North Irish Horse in the ranks, later commissioned into the Royal Irish Rifles.

McClelland, Arthur - Driver
T4/038840 Army Service Corps 4th Horse Transport Company *Age 28 Died in War on 10 November 1918*
CAMBRAI EAST MILITARY CEMETERY, France
Husband of Mary McClelland, of 23, Jennymount Terrace, Belfast.

McClelland, David - Rifleman
7678 Royal Irish Rifles 2nd Battalion *Age 30 Died in War on 17 October 1914*
BETHUNE TOWN CEMETERY, France
Brother of Robert McClelland, of 24, Merville Street, Belfast.

McClelland, John Caskey - Lance Sergeant
17080 Canadian Infantry (British Columbia Regiment) 7th Battalion *Age 32 Killed in Action on 5 May 1916*
CHESTER FARM CEMETERY, Belgium
Son of the late James and Annie Caskey McClelland, of Ballinteer, County Derry, Ireland; husband of Rosa McClelland, of Whitehall Terrace, 463, Ormeau Road, Belfast.
A Presbyterian, he was a farmer and had previous army service.

McClelland, Samuel - Corporal
13193 Royal Irish Rifles 15th Battalion *Killed in Action on 21 March 1918*
POZIERES MEMORIAL, France
Born and enlisted in Belfast.

McClelland, William - Rifleman
7507 Royal Irish Rifles 1st Battalion *Age 26 Died of Wounds on 26 March 1915*
GRANGEGORMAN MILITARY CEMETERY, Republic of Ireland
Son of James and Agnes McClelland, of 26, Cromwell Street, Belfast.

McClelland, William James - Private
481 Royal Irish Rifles "D" Company 8th Battalion *Age 19. Died in War on 20 June 1917*
YPRES (MENIN GATE) MEMORIAL, Belgium
Son of Moses and Mary McClelland, of 11, Bann Street, Oldpark Road, Belfast.

McClelland, William John - Rifleman
2832 Royal Irish Rifles 15th Battalion *Killed in Action on 14 December 1917*
THIEPVAL MEMORIAL, France
26, Meenan Street, Belfast.

McClements, Alexander - Rifleman
1300 Royal Irish Rifles 1st Battalion *Killed in Action on 23 March 1918*
POZIERES MEMORIAL, France
Born and enlisted in Belfast.

Journey of Remembering

McClements, Robert - Rifleman
489 Royal Irish Rifles 8th Battalion *Died in War on 2 July 1916*
THIEPVAL MEMORIAL, France
Lived at 7, Martin Street, Belfast.

McClements, William James - Rifleman
11715 Royal Irish Rifles 15th Battalion *Killed in Action on 21 March 1918*
POZIERES MEMORIAL, France
Husband of Ellen McClements, 21, Leadbetter Street, Belfast.

McClenaghan, George - Sergeant
11408 Royal Irish Rifles 2nd Battalion *Age 25 Died of Wounds on 17 October 1917*
BETHUNE TOWN CEMETERY, France
Husband of Mary E. McClenaghan, of 125, Newcome Road, Fratton, Portsmouth. Native of Belfast.

McClenaghan, John Henry - Rifleman
66 Royal Irish Rifles 15th Battalion *Age 21 Killed in Action on 21 March 1918*
POZIERES MEMORIAL, France
Son of Jane Robinson McClenaghan, of 2A, Greenmount Street, Belfast, and the late Thomas McClenaghan.

McClenaghan, Thomas - Private
22878 Royal Inniskilling Fusiliers 9th Battalion *Killed in Action on 1 July 1916*
THIEPVAL MEMORIAL, France
137, Snugville Street, Belfast.

McClinton, David - Sergeant
404004 Canadian Infantry 35th Battalion *Age 45 Died of sickness on 12 June 1916*
TORONTO (PROSPECT) CEMETERY, Canada
Son of the late Samuel and Rebecca McClinton, of Belfast, Ireland, husband of G. McClinton, of 105, Givens Street, Toronto, Canada. A former Regular soldier and a Presbyterian, he was employed as a prison guard.

McClinton, John Stuart - Captain
South Lancashire Regiment 7th Battalion *Died in War on 5 July 1916*
THIEPVAL MEMORIAL, France
Educated at RBAI and a member of the North of Ireland Cricket and Football Club.
Employed in his father's seed buiness in Great Victoria Street.

McClinton, Samuel - Private
4381 Irish Guards 1st Battalion *Died of Wounds on 18 November 1914*
POPERINGHE OLD MILITARY CEMETERY, Belgium
Son of John and Minnie McClinton, 18, Glenbank Place, Ballysillan, Belfast.

McCloskey, Alexander - Private
10173 Connaught Rangers 6th Battalion *Died in War on 21 March 1918*
POZIERES MEMORIAL, France
Born and enlisted in Belfast. Formerly 2867 Leinster Regiment

McCloskey, Thomas - Rifleman
2384 Royal Irish Rifles 13th Battalion *Died in War on 8 December 1917*
THIEPVAL MEMORIAL, France
Born and enlisted in Belfast.

McClughan, Robert - Rifleman
669 Royal Irish Rifles 11th Battalion *Age 28 Killed in Action on 1 July 1916*
THIEPVAL MEMORIAL, France
Son of George and Catherine McClughan; husband of Jeannie B. McClughan, of Hyde Park, Mallusk, Belfast.

McClune, George - Rifleman
6940 Royal Irish Rifles 1st Battalion *Died in War on 16 August 1917*
TYNE COT CEMETERY, Belgium
Born in Belfast, enlisted in Holywood.

McClune, Harry - Rifleman
8937 Royal Irish Rifles 6th Battalion *Age 18 Died of dysentery on 27 September 1915*
PIETA MILITARY CEMETERY, Malta
Son of William and Margaret McClune, of the Lodge, Riddel Hall, Stranmillis Road, Belfast.

McClune, William J - Private
1277 Royal Irish Fusiliers 3rd Battalion *Age 48 Died from the effects of heat on 15 August 1918*
BELFAST CITY CEMETERY, United Kingdom
Son of the late John and Elizabeth McClune. Born at Belfast.

McClure, Francis - Sapper
57758 Royal Engineers 121st Field Company *Died in War on 27 March 1918*
POZIERES MEMORIAL, France
Born and enlisted in Belfast.

McClure, Henry Alfred - Rifleman
772 Royal Irish Rifles 8th Battalion *Died in War on 24 August 1916*
DRANOUTRE MILITARY CEMETERY, Belgium
Born and enlisted in Belfast.

McClure, Hugh - Sapper
64264 Royal Engineers 150th Field Company *Age 30 Died in War on 6 October 1916*
POND PARK CEMETERY, Belgium
197, Crumlin Road, Belfast. Husband of Maude McClure.

McClure, James Henry - Private
25158 Royal Inniskilling Fusiliers 1st Battalion *Died in War on 25 June 1916*
MESNIL RIDGE CEMETERY, MESNIL-MARTINSART, France
Born in Salford, Lancashire, enlisted Inverkeithing, Scotland, resident of Belfast.

McClure, Samuel - Gunner
35693 Royal Field Artillery *Died in War on 24 June 1917*
POPERINGHE NEW MILITARY CEMETERY, Belgium
Eldest son of Samuel and Mary McClure of Whiteabbey. Member of Castleton Presbyterian Church Belfast.

McClurg, Francis - Lance Corporal
10099 Royal Irish Rifles 2nd Battalion *Killed in Action on 15 September 1914*
LA FERTE -SOUS-JOUARRE MEMORIAL, France
Born in Belfast, enlisted Newtownards.

McClurg, Hugh - Private
306573 Lancashire Fusiliers 1/8th Battalion *Died in War on 13 October 1917*
ZUYDCOOTE MILITARY CEMETERY, France
Born in Belfast enlisted in Manchester.

Journey of Remembering

McClurg, James - Private
241471 Highland Light Infantry 1/6th Battalion *Age 27 Died of Wounds on 28 August 1918*
BAGNEUX BRITISH CEMETERY, GEZAINCOURT, France
Son of James Kennedy McClurg and Annie McClurg, of 69, Cumberland Street, Belfast.
Employed by Workman Clark Shipyard.

McClurg, James - Rifleman
9873 Royal Irish Rifles 1st Battalion *Killed in Action on 14 January 1915*
MERVILLE COMMUNAL CEMETERY, France
Born and enlisted in Belfast.

McClurg, Nathaniel - Private
23681 Royal Irish Fusiliers 1st Battalion *Died in War on 5 November 1917*
ROCQUIGNY-EQUANCOURT ROAD BRITISH CEMETERY, MANANCOURT, France
Husband of Maggie McClurg, 177, Sidney Street West, Belfast.

McClurg, Thomas - Private
3566 Royal Inniskilling Fusiliers 2nd Battalion *Died in War on 11 July 1916*
LE TOURET MEMORIAL, France
Second son of William George and Matilda McClurg, 120, Fortingale Street, Belfast.
His brother was in the Seaforth Highlanders.

McClurg, Thomas - Private
4381 Royal Inniskilling Fusiliers 2nd Battalion *Died of Wounds on 16 May 1915*
LE TOURET MEMORIAL, France
Born in Belfast.

McClurg, William - Lance Corporal
5511 Royal Irish Rifles 2nd Battalion *Age 27 Died in War on 25 September 1915*
YPRES (MENIN GATE) MEMORIAL, Belgium
Husband of Minnie M'Clurg, of 118, Urney Street, Belfast. Served 5 years in the 1st Battalion
prior to the Great War, being invalided home from India.

McCluskey, James - Private
14902 Royal Inniskilling Fusiliers 11th Battalion *Killed in Action on 16 July 1917*
TYNE COT MEMORIAL, Belgium
Born in Belfast.

McCluskey, Thomas - Rifleman
2384 Royal Irish Rifles 13th Battalion *Age 23 Died in War on 8 December 1917*
THIEPVAL MEMORIAL, France
Brother of Miss Elizabeth McCluskey, of 38, Frederick Street, Belfast.

McColl, John - Rifleman
5736 Royal Irish Rifles 2nd Battalion *Age 25 Killed in Action on 5 May 1916*
ECOIVRES MILITARY CEMETERY, MONT-ST. ELOI, France
Son of Dugald and Elizabeth McColl, of 72, Parkmount Street, Belfast. Native of Scotland.

McColl, Malcolm - Rifleman
14/19640 Royal Irish Rifles 14th Battalion *Age 21 Died in War on 17 February 1917*
BERKS CEMETERY EXTENSION, Belgium
Son of John and Sarah McColl, of Rose Cottage, Finaghy, Belfast.

McCollom, Robert - Driver
76593 Royal Field Artillery 5th Battery *Died in War on 7 April 1917*
VILLERS-FAUCON COMMUNAL CEMETERY, France
Son of Mrs. F. McCollom, of 32, Crossley Street, Templemore Avenue, Belfast.

McComb, Hugh - Stoker First Class
SS/100505 Royal Navy HMS "Hawke" *Died in War on 15 October 1914*
CHATHAM NAVAL MEMORIAL, United Kingdom
Husband of Dorothy, 97, Ogilvie Street, Belfast.

McComb, John - Private
40940 Cameronians (Scottish Rifles) 9th Battalion *Died in War on 3 May 1917*
ARRAS MEMORIAL, France
Born in Belfast, enlisted Glasgow. Formerly 1823 Lanark Yeomanry.

McComb, Joseph - Private
10680 Royal Inniskilling Fusiliers 1st Battalion *Age 22 Died in War on 3 May 1915*
HELLES MEMORIAL, Turkey
Son of the late William John and Martha McComb.

McComb, Leonard - Rifleman
5480 Royal Irish Rifles 2nd Battalion *Killed in Action on 7 July 1916*
THIEPVAL MEMORIAL, France
Son of Sarah McComb, 19, Broadbent Street, Belfast.

McComb, Thomas - Lance Corporal
8850 Royal Irish Rifles 1st Battalion *Killed in Action on 26 October 1916*
THIEPVAL MEMORIAL, France
45, Richmond Street, Belfast.

McComb, William - Rifleman
15225 Royal Irish Rifles 9th Battalion *Age 30 Died in War on 5 August 1917*
YPRES (MENIN GATE) MEMORIAL, Belgium
Son of James McComb, of 21, North Howard Street, Belfast. A member of the old UVF.

McCombe, William Thomas - Rifleman
17/980 Royal Irish Rifles 10th Battalion *Age 17 Died in War on 22 December 1915*
SUCRERIE MILITARY CEMETERY, COLINCAMPS, France
Son of Joseph and Ada McCombe, of 36, Coolbeg Street, Donegall Road, Belfast.
One of the younger soldiers to perish - killed just before Christmas.

McComish, Daniel - Able Seaman (And Steward)
Mercantile Marine S.S. "Castlebar" (Belfast) *Presumed drowned 13 March 1918*
TOWER HILL MEMORIAL, United Kingdom
Son of Daniel and the late Catherine McComish; husband of Elizabeth McComish (née Kelly)
of 29, Wall Street, Belfast. Born at Dundee, Scotland.

McComiskey, John - Rifleman
15373 Royal Irish Rifles 9th Battalion *Killed in Action on 1 July 1916*
THIEPVAL MEMORIAL, France
52, Parkmount Street, Belfast.

Journey of Remembering

McConachy, Charles George - Able Seaman
234602 Royal Navy HMS "Amphion" *Age 25 Killed by mine explosion in North Sea on 6 August 1914*
PLYMOUTH NAVAL MEMORIAL, United Kingdom
Son of David and Margaret McConachy, of Strath House, Dungiven, Londonderry. Native of Belfast.

McConkey, John - Private
20431 Royal Inniskilling Fusiliers 7th Battalion *Died in War on 6 April 1916*
PHILOSOPHE BRITISH CEMETERY, MAZINGARBE, France
Born in Belfast enlisted Enniskillen.

McConkey, William - Private
17689 Royal Inniskilling Fusiliers 5th Battalion *Died in War on 10 September 1916*
STRUMA MILITARY CEMETERY, Greece
Born and enlisted in Belfast.

McConkey, William - Stoker First Class
K/20038 Royal Navy HMS "Natal" *Killed by internal explosion of vessel in Cromarty Firth on 30 December 1915*
CHATHAM NAVAL MEMORIAL, United Kingdom
Son of Margaret McConkey, of 7, Enniskillen Street, Belfast.

McConnell , Robert Wallace - Lieutenant
King's Own (Royal Lancaster Regiment) *Age 20 Died in War on 9 April 1916*
BASRA MEMORIAL, Iraq
Son the late Rev James McConnell, Megain Memorial Presbyterian Church, and Annie Duffield McConnell of "Ulidia", Holywood Road Belfast. Educated at Campbell College and Queen's University Belfast. Served at Gallipoli but lost his life in Mesopotamia (Iraq).

McConnell, Alexander - Private
10495 Royal Inniskilling Fusiliers 2nd Battalion *Killed in Action on 16 May 1915*
LE TOURET MEMORIAL, France
Born and enlisted in Belfast.

McConnell, Alexander - Rifleman
17/157 Royal Irish Rifles 15th Battalion *Age 21 Died in War on 2 October 1918*
MENIN ROAD SOUTH MILITARY CEMETERY, Belgium
Son of Alexander and Annie McConnell, of 10, Barbour Street, Greencastle, Belfast.

McConnell, Hugh - Private
18413 Canadian Infantry (Western Ontario Regiment) "C" Company 1st Battalion
Age 26 Died of Wounds, received at Vimy Ridge on 11 April 1917
LAPUGNOY MILITARY CEMETERY, France
Son of Hugh and Eliza McConnell, late of Boardmills, Lisburn; husband of Jane J. McConnell, of 227, Cregagh Street, Belfast, Ireland. A Presbyterian, he was employed as a labourer.

McConnell, Isaac - Lance Corporal
57588 Royal Engineers P Special Company *Killed in Action on 9 July 1917*
NEW IRISH FARM CEMETERY, Belgium
Husband of Jeannie McConnell, of 1, Roden Street, Belfast.

McConnell, James Wilfred - Private
EMT/43633 Army Service Corps Mechanical Transport Section *Age 18 Died as a result of war on 20 August 1919*
BELFAST CITY CEMETERY, United Kingdom
A young winner of the Military Medal. Son of Isaac and Jane McConnell, of 1, Roden Street, Belfast.

McConnell, John - Private
13202 Royal Irish Rifles 8th Battalion *Died in War on 7 June 1917*
LONE TREE CEMETERY, *Belgium*
77, Otawa Street, Belfast.

McConnell, John - Rifleman
7975 Royal Irish Rifles 1st Battalion *Died in War on 17 March 1915*
LE TOURET MEMORIAL, *France*
6, Lady Street, Belfast.

McConnell, John Wesley - Lance Sergeant
2313 Leinster Regiment 7th Battalion *Age 23 Died in War on 27 June 1916*
LOOS MEMORIAL, *France*
Son of Rose McConnell, of 169, Crimea Street, Belfast, and the late William McConnell.

McConnell, Reginald Brian - Second Lieutenant
King's Own Scottish Borderers 6th Battalion *Age 18 Killed in Action on 22 January 1917*
FAUBOURG D'AMIENS CEMETERY, ARRAS, *France*
Son of Thomas Edward McConnell, of 31/33, Chichester Street, Belfast.

McConnell, Robert - Private
41445 Royal Irish Fusiliers 9th Battalion *Age 23 Died in War on 19 April 1918*
TYNE COT MEMORIAL, *Belgium*
Son of Mary McConnell, of 11, High Street, Greencastle, Belfast.

McConnell, Samuel Morton - Lance Corporal
15374 Royal Irish Rifles 14th Battalion *Age 20 Died in War on 21 November 1917*
GREVILLERS BRITISH CEMETERY, *France*
Son of Alexander and Annie McConnell, of 198, My Lady's Road, Belfast. Awarded the Military Medal.

McConnell, Thomas - Sergeant
13541 Royal Inniskilling Fusiliers 9th Battalion *Died in War on 8 May 1916*
AUTHUILE MILITARY CEMETERY, *France*
Born in Belfast, enlisted Dublin.

McConnell, W C - Able Seaman
Royal Navy HMS "Hawke" *Died in War on 15 October 1914*
CHATHAM WAR MEMORIAL, *United Kingdom*
26, Foreman Street, Belfast.

McConnell, William - Private
18177 Connaught Rangers 6th Battalion *Died of Wounds on 25 March 1918*
ST. SEVER CEMETERY EXTENSION, ROUEN, *France*
1, Scotland Street, Belfast.

McConnell, William - Private
3589 Royal Irish Fusiliers 1st Battalion *Died of Wounds on 4 May 1917*
AUBIGNY COMMUNAL CEMETERY EXTENSION, *France*
Son of Rose McConnell, of 169, Olivia Terrace, Crimea Street, Belfast, and the late William McConnell. Formerly an apprentice with Harland and Wolff. One brother, John Wesley McConnell, was killed and another served.

Journey of Remembering

McConnell, William - Private
Royal Irish Rifles 9th Battalion *Died in War*
Second son of William McConnell, 6 Mountcashel Street, Belfast.

McConnell, William Clark - Lieutenant
Royal Irish Rifles 3rd Battalion attached 2nd Battalion *Age 31 Killed in Action on 9 July 1916*
THIEPVAL MEMORIAL, *France*
Youngest son of Robert John McConnell DL and Mary Elizabeth McConnell of Strandtown, Belfast. Educated in Hampshire, Germany and London. Qualified as an electrical engineer before being commissioned into the Army.

McConnell, William John - Lance Corporal
262 Royal Irish Rifles 16th Battalion *Died in War on 2 December 1917*
HERMIES BRITISH CEMETERY, *France*
Born in Belfast, enlisted Lurgan.

McConville, James - Private
423 Manchester Regiment 12th Battalion *Died in War on 4 August 1916*
THIEPVAL MEMORIAL, *France*
Born in Belfast, enlisted in Lancashire.

McConville, Matthew - Private
5726 Princess Victoria's (Royal Irish Fusiliers) 1st Battalion *Died in War on 28 April 1915*
YPRES (MENIN GATE) MEMORIAL, *France*
Born in Belfast, enlisted Lurgan.

McConville, Peter - Private
39778 Highland Light Infantry 2nd Battalion *Died in War on 1 October 1918*
SEQUEHART BRITISH CEMETERY No 2, *France*
Born in Belfast, enlisted Lurgan.

McCoo, Isaac - Rifleman
6930 Royal Irish Rifles 1st Battalion *Killed in Action on 10 March 1915*
LE TOURET MEMORIAL, *France*
Born in Belfast, enlisted Holywood.

McCool, Edward - Gunner
29627 Royal Garrison Artillery *Died in War on 3 August 1915*
REDOUBT CEMETERY HELLES, *Turkey*
Born and enlisted in Belfast.

McCord, David - Sapper
306326 Royal Engineers 1506th Artisan Works Company *Age 40 Died in War on 31 December 1917*
JANVAL CEMETERY, DIEPPE, *France*
Son of the late Henry and Melenia McCord, of Belfast.

McCormack , Harold H. P. - Sergeant
536 Royal Irish Rifles 13th Battalion *Killed in Action on 16 August 1917*
TYNE COT MEMORIAL, *Belgium*
Husband of Irene McCormack, 7, Monarch Street, Belfast.

McCormack, Alexander - Private
12714 Royal Inniskilling Fusiliers 6th Battalion *Died in War on 3 October 1918*
DOINGT COMMUNAL CEMETERY EXTENSION, France
Born and enlisted in Belfast.

McCormack, Jackson - Private
3639 Royal Inniskilling Fusiliers 1st Battalion *Died of Wounds on 1 May 1918*
DUHALLOW A.D.S. CEMETERY, Belgium
Born in Belfast.

McCormack, James - Rifleman
6101 Royal Irish Rifles 7th Battalion *Died in War on 31 July 1916*
MAZINGARBE COMMUNAL EXTENSION, France
Born and enlisted in Belfast.

McCormack, John - Rifleman
6399 Royal Irish Rifles 1st Battalion *Killed in Action on 6 May 1915*
BOULOGNE EASTERN CEMETERY, France
Born and enlisted in Belfast.

McCormack, Patrick - Private
3620 Connaught Rangers 6th Battalion *Died in War on 7 February 1916*
LOOS MEMORIAL, France
Son of James and Margaret McCormack, of 45, Carlisle Street, Belfast.

McCormick, Alexander - Private
12714 Royal Inniskilling Fusiliers 8th Battalion *Died in War on 2 October 1918*
DOINGT COMMUNAL CEMETERY EXTENSION, France
Son of Mr. A. McCormick, of 22, McMillan's Place, Belfast.

McCormick, Archibald - Private
7235 South Lancashire Regiment 2nd Battalion *Died in War on 14 October 1914*
LE TOURET MEMORIAL, France
29, Sanroft Street, Belfast.

McCormick, David - Rifleman
13316 King's Royal Rifle Corps 17th Battalion *Killed in Action on 21 March 1918*
POZIERES MEMORIAL, France
Born and enlisted in Belfast. Formerly T/26239, Army Servive Corps.

McCormick, Hugh Henry - Private
3466 Royal Irish Rifles 9th Battalion *Killed in Action on 1 July 1916*
TINCOURT NEW BRITISH CEMETERY, France
7, Anglesea Street, Belfast.

McCormick, Ian Campbell - Sub-Lieutenant
Royal Naval Volunteer Reserve Hood Battalion Royal Naval Division *Age 21 Died in War on 24 January 1917*
HAMEL MILITARY CEMETERY, BEAUMONT-HAMEL, France
Son of John and Margaret McCormick (née Campbell), of Craigroyston, Knock, Belfast.

McCormick, James - Rifleman
9/656 Royal Irish Rifles 9th Battalion *Age 33 Struck by rifle grenade on 11 January 1916*
SUCRERIE MILITARY CEMETERY, COLINCAMPS, France
Son of Samuel McCormick, of 24, Hutchinson Street, Belfast, and the late Mary Jane McCormick.

Journey of Remembering

McCormick, John - Private
3568 Seaforth Highlanders 1st/4th Battalion *Killed in Action on 8 June 1916*
LOUEZ MILITARY CEMETERY, DUISANS, France
Son of Cornelius and Annie McCormick, of Belfast; husband of Catherine McCormick, of 89, McDonnell Street, Belfast.

McCormick, John - Rifleman
6399 Royal Irish Rifles 1st Battalion *Age 42 Killed in Action on 6 May 1915*
BOULOGNE EASTERN CEMETERY, France
Son of Bernard and Jane McCormick, of 35, Weaver Street, York Road, Belfast.

McCormick, Joseph - Rifleman
6101 Royal Irish Rifles 7th Battalion *Died in War on 3 July 1916*
MAZINGARBE COMMUNAL CEMETERY EXTENSION, France
Husband of Annie McCormick, 64, Westland Street, Belfast.

McCormick, Thomas - Rifleman
13132 Royal Irish Rifles *Killed in Action on 1 July 1916*
THIEPVAL MEMORIAL, France
Husband of Sarah McCormick, 87, Glenwood, Street, Belfast.

McCormick, William - Private
11927 Royal Inniskilling Fusiliers 6th Battalion *Died in War on 26 March 1918*
JERUSALEM MEMORIAL, Israel
Born and enlisted in Belfast, the son of Mrs R. J. McCormick.

McCormick, William - Private
41075 Royal Army Medical Corps 109th Field Ambulance *Died in War on 17 August 1917*
TYNE COT MEMORIAL, Belgium
Adopted son of Jackson and Catherine McCormick, 35, Beverley Street, Belfast. Awarded the Military Medal. One brother also served.

McCormick, William - Private
41607 Royal Irish Fusiliers 9th (North Irish Horse) Battalion *Died of Wounds on 3 November 1918*
KEZELBERG MILITARY CEMETERY, Belgium
Son of Mr. M. McCormick, of 77, Tennent Street, Belfast.

McCormick, William - Private
Royal Irish Fusiliers *Died in War on 25 March 1918*
Son of Ellen and the late Robert McCormick, 30, McTier Street, Belfast.

McCormick, William - Rifleman
1053 Royal Irish Rifles 12th Battalion *Died in War on 15 April 1918*
TYNE COT MEMORIAL, Belgium
Son of the late Robert and Minnie McCormick.

McCormick, William - Rifleman
47194 Royal Irish Rifles 15th Battalion *Killed in Action on 23 November 1917*
THIEPVAL MEMORIAL, France
23, Leadbetter Street, Belfast.

McCorry, Charles - Private
21747 Royal Irish Fusiliers 7th Battalion *Age 19 Died in War on 20 May 1916*
BETHUNE TOWN CEMETERY, France
Son of Catherine and the late Charles McCorry, 79, Leeson Street, Belfast.

McCorry, William - Private
32986 Royal Irish Fusiliers 1st Battalion *Died as a result of war on 19 March 1920*
TEHRAN WAR CEMETERY, *Iran*
Son of Mr. J. McCorry, of 37, Abyssinia Street, Grosvenor Park, Belfast.

McCoskrie, John - Rifleman
7585 Royal Irish Rifles 2nd Battalion *Killed in Action on 26 August 1914*
LE FERTE-SOUS-JOUARRE MEMORIAL, *France*
Born and enlisted in Belfast.

McCoubrey, John - Rifleman
3782 Royal Irish Rifles 9th Battalion *Died in War on 26 December 1916*
ST QUENTIN CABARET MILITARY CEMETERY, *Belgium*
Born and enlisted in Belfast.

McCoubrey, John James - Sergeant
14/16739 Royal Irish Rifles "B" Company 14th Battalion *Age 28 Killed in Action on 23 June 1917*
MESSINES RIDGE BRITISH CEMETERY, *Belgium*
Son of John and Isabella McCoubrey, of 9, Abercorn Street, Lisburn Road, Belfast.

McCoubrie, Thomas - Sergeant
20826 Royal Inniskilling Fusilliers 6th Battalion formerly 457 Irish Guards *Died of Wounds on 4 October 1918*
DOINGT COMMUNAL CEMETERY EXTENSION, *France*
Born in Belfast. Husband of Margaret Ballantine (formerly McCoubrie), of Strabane.

McCoubrie, Thomas - Sergeant
5922 Royal Irish Rifles 1st Battalion *Age 31 Killed in Action on 9 May 1915*
PLOEGSTEERT MEMORIAL, *Belgium*
Husband of Mrs. Sarah McCoubrie, of 4, Roxburgh Street, Belfast.

McCoubrie, William J - Private
10119 Royal Irish Fusiliers *Died in War on 8 November 1917*
BELFAST CITY CEMETERY, *United Kingdom*
5, St Andrew's Square, Belfast.

McCourt, Peter - Private
27532 Royal Inniskilling Fusiliers 7th/8th Battalion *Age 38 Killed in Action on 29 March 1918*
NAMPS-AU-VAL BRITISH CEMETERY, *France*
Son of John and Elizabeth McCourt, of Belfast; husband of Rose Ann McCourt, of 9, Hardinge Street, North Queen Street, Belfast.

McCourt, Richard J - Private
11947 Royal Inniskilling Fusiliers 5th Battalion *Age 25 Died in War on 15 August 1915*
HELLES MEMORIAL, *Turkey*
Son of Mrs. Eliza McCourt, of 25, Upper Charleville Street, Belfast; husband of the late Charlotte McCourt.

McCoy, Francis - Private
6489 Connaught Rangers 6th Battalion *Died in War on 20 November 1917*
CROISILLES RAILWAY CEMETERY, *France*
Born in Lower Kileaney, County Armagh. Enlisted and resident in Belfast. Husband of Catherine and father of Josephine, Sissy and Ellen, 95, Brookfield Street, Belfast.

McCoy, James - Private
9248 Royal Irish Rifles 1st Battalion *Killed in Action on 10 March 1915*
LE TOURET MEMORIAL, France
10, Stanley Street, Belfast.

McCoy, James - Rifleman
6226 Royal Irish Rifles "D" Company 10th Battalion *Age 53 Killed in Action on 3 July 1916*
MARTINSART BRITISH CEMETERY, France
Son of Samuel and Mary McCoy, of Belfast; husband of Sarah Ellen McCoy, of 124, Disraeli Street, Belfast.

McCoy, James Joseph - Private
14094 Royal Inniskilling Fusiliers 1st Battalion *Died in War on 9 August 1916*
LIJSSENTHOEK MILITARY CEMETERY, Belgium
Born in Rosslea, enlisted Enniskillen, resident of Belfast.

McCoy, John - Corporal
10/15250 Royal Irish Rifles 10th Battalion *Age 27 Killed in Action on 1 July 1916*
CONNAUGHT CEMETERY, THIEPVAL, France
Son of Frederick McCoy, of 1, Walnut Street, Donegall Pass, Belfast.

McCoy, John - Lance Corporal
21353 Royal Dublin Fusiliers 8th Battalion *Age 28 Died in War on 9 September 1916*
THIEPVAL MEMORIAL, France
Son of Patrick McCoy, of 53, Chatham Street, Crumlin Road, Belfast.

McCoy, Joseph - Company Sergeant Major
1470 Royal Irish Rifles "C" Company 13th Battalion *Age 46 Killed in Action on 28 June 1916*
MARTINSART BRITISH CEMETERY, France
Son of the late Richard and Margaret McCoy, of County Monaghan; husband of Eliza McCoy, of 22, Blythe Street, Belfast. One of 14 men killed, (nine died of wounds later), when a powerful shell devastated a platoon preparing to move into the front line.

McCoy, Robert - Rifleman
11616 Royal Irish Rifles 2nd Battalion *Killed in Action on 24 March 1918*
AVESNES-SUR-HELPE COMMUNAL CEMETERY, France
Husband of Jennie McCoy, 10, Greenland Street, Belfast.

McCoy, William - Rifleman
2953777 Royal Irish Rifles 1st Battalion *Age 40 Died in War on 11 February 1918*
BELFAST CITY CEMETERY, United Kingdom
Son of Thomas and Esther McCoy. Born at Belfast.

McCoy, William - Steward
Mercantile Marine S.S. "Princess Caroline" (Glasgow) *Age 60 Killed by mine on 13 August 1915*
TOWER HILL MEMORIAL, United Kingdom
Husband of Frances McCoy, of 36, Wentworth Street, Everton. Born at Belfast.

McCracken, Alexander - Private
12468 Royal Irish Fusiliers 6th Battalion *Age 27 Died of Wounds on 25 August 1915*
ALEXANDRIA (CHATBY) MILITARY AND WAR MEMORIAL CEMETERY, Egypt
Son of William McCracken, of Belfast.

McCracken, Alfred - Private
10263 4th (Queen's Own) Hussars *Died in War on 14 May 1915*
BOULOGNE EASTERN CEMETERY, *France*
13, Vere Street, Belfast.

McCracken, Frederick - Rifleman
7243 Royal Irish Rifles 2nd Battalion *Killed in Action on 27 October 1914*
LE TOURET MEMORIAL, *France*
Son of Joseph and Mary McCracken, of 42, Crimea Street, Belfast. His brother, Joseph also fell.

McCracken, George - Private
85544 Durham Light Infantry 1/8th Battalion *Died in War on 12 October 1918*
GLAGEON COMMUNAL CEMETERY EXTENSION, *France*
Born and enlisted in Belfast. Formerly 200380 Royal Engineers.

McCracken, Henry Joy - Lieutenant
Royal Flying Corps and General List 111th Squadron *Age 21 Died in War on 17 October 1917*
KANTARA WAR MEMORIAL CEMETERY, *Egypt*
Son of Mr. H. J. McCracken, of Austinville, Bloomfield, Belfast. Signed the Ulster Covenant in 1912.

McCracken, James - Corporal
50611 East Yorkshire Regiment 1st Battalion *Age 23 Died in War on 15 August 1918*
VIS-EN-ARTOIS MEMORIAL, *France*
Son of William J. and Mary J. McCracken, of 19, Moorgate Street, Belfast.

McCracken, James - Private
8748 Machine Gun Corps (Infantry) 6th Battalion *Age 29 Died in War on 6 November 1918*
ST. SEVER CEMETERY EXTENSION, ROUEN, *France*
Son of the late William John and Jane Julia McCracken, of Belfast.

McCracken, John F - Rifleman
15/13211 Royal Irish Rifles 15th Battalion *Age 19 Died in War on 19 March 1916*
MAILLY-MAILLET COMMUNAL CEMETERY EXTENSION, *France*
A native of Belfast. Shot by firing squad for desertion.

McCracken, Joseph - Able Seaman
239868 Royal Navy HMS "Vanguard" *Killed by internal explosion of vessel at Scapa Flow on 9 July 1917*
CHATHAM NAVAL MEMORIAL, *United Kingdom*
Son of Joseph and Mary McCracken, of 42, Crimea Street, Belfast. His brother, Frederick also fell.

McCracken, Joseph - Rifleman
241 Royal Irish Rifles 14th Battalion *Killed in Action on 3 August 1917*
YPRES (MENIN GATE) MEMORIAL, *Belgium*
Born in Belfast.

McCracken, Samuel - Private
71828 Canadian Infantry (Manitoba Regiment) 27th Battalion *Age 19 Died of Wounds on 20 October 1915*
LOKER CHURCHYARD, *Belgium*
Son of Samuel and Elizabeth McCracken, of 359, Donegall Road, Belfast.
An Anglican, he worked as a labourer in Canada.

JOURNEY OF REMEMBERING

McCracken, William J - Rifleman
323120 Royal Irish Rifles 9th Battalion *Died in War on 7 June 1917*
SPANBROEKMOLEN BRITISH CEMETERY, Belgium
Husband of Mrs. M. McCracken, of 63, Matchett Street, Belfast.

McCrea, Albert - Private
12882 Royal Irish Fusiliers 6th Battalion *Died in War on 16 August 1915*
HELLES MEMORIAL, Turkey
3, Upper Malvern Street, Belfast.

McCrea, Alexander - Private
8534 Royal Irish Fusiliers 1st Battalion *Age 47 Died in War on 24 June 1915*
YPRES (MENIN GATE) MEMORIAL, Belgium
Son of Alexander McCrea, of 5, Little Patrick Street, Belfast.

McCrea, Charles - Private
3575 Royal Inniskilling Fusiliers 2nd Battalion *Age 21 Died in War on 10 July 1916*
THIEPVAL MEMORIAL, France
Son of the late Richard and Elizabeth McCrea, 56, Crosby Street, Belfast.

McCready, Alexander - Private
18328 Royal Dublin Fusiliers 8th Battalion *Killed In Action on 9 September 1916*
THIEPVAL MEMORIAL, France
Born in Belfast, enlisted in Hamilton, Scotland.

McCready, David - Private
9499 The King's (Liverpool Regiment) 4th Battalion *Age 35 Died in War on 1 May 1915*
YPRES (MENIN GATE) MEMORIAL, Belgium
(Served as BOYD), son of Joseph and Isabella McCready, of 64, Methuen Street, Belfast; husband of Ellen McCready, of 20, Templemore Street, Belfast.

McCready, George - Private
L/6353 Royal Sussex Regiment 2nd Battalion *Killed in Action on 30 October 1914*
YPRES (MENIN GATE) MEMORIAL, Belgium
Husband of Emily McCready, 90, Glenwood Street, Belfast.

McCready, James - Lance Corporal
Royal Irish Rifles 1st Battalion *Died in War on 9 May 1915*
15, Woodvale Street, Belfast. A member of the old UVF.

McCready, James - Private
17163 Princess Victoria's (Royal Irish Fusiliers) 8th Battalion *Killed in Action on 1 June 1916*
BOLTON (HEATON) CEMETERY, United Kingdom
Born in Belfast. Son of John William and Sarah Ellen McCready, of 23, Milford Road, Great Lever, Bolton.

McCready, Robert - Private
23973 Royal Inniskilling Fusiliers 7th Battalion *Killed in Action on 27 April 1916*
PHILOSOPHE BRITISH CEMETERY, MAZINGARBE, France
Born and enlisted in Belfast.

McCready, Robert - Private
H/71705 Nottinghamshire Yeomanry (Sherwood Rangers) *Age 20 Died in War on 6 August 1918*
ALEXANDRIA (HADRA) WAR MEMORIAL CEMETERY, Egypt
Son of William and Mary McCready, of 45, Sunnyside Street, Ormeau Road, Belfast.

McCreanor, Joseph - Second Lieutenant
783782 Auckland Regiment New Zealand Expeditionary Force 2nd Battalion
Age 35 Killed in Action on 1 September 1918
BANCOURT BRITISH CEMETERY, *France*
Son of Robert and Margaret McCreanor, of Belfast, Ireland.

McCreanor, Nicholas - Private
21389 Royal Scots (Lothian Regiment) 16th Battalion *Died in War on 16 April 1918*
Born in Belfast, enlisted Edinburgh.

McCreanor, Thomas - Private
A/38151 Canadian Infantry (Manitoba Regiment) 8th Battalion *Died in War on 26 September 1916*
VIMY MEMORIAL, *France*
32, Rosebank Street, Belfast.

McCreedy, Albert - Corporal
503095 Canadian Engineers Third Army Troops Company *Age 27 Died of influenza on 2 December 1918*
VALENCIENNES (ST. ROCH) COMMUNAL CEMETERY, *France*
Son of John and Lizzie McCreedy, of Belfast, Ireland; husband of Agnes McCreedy,
of 367, Charles Street, St. John's, Winnipeg. Worked as a mechanic, a Presbyterian.

McCreedy, John - Lance Corporal
6272 Royal Irish Rifles 1st Battalion *Killed in Action on 9 May 1915*
YPRES (MENIN GATE) MEMORIAL, *Belgium*
17, Fingal Street, Belfast.

McCreedy, Robert - Private
19494 Machine Gun Corps *Age 30 Died in War*
SHANKILL CEMETERY, *United Kingdom*
Son of Jane Eliza McCreedy and the late John McCreedy; husband of Margaret Jane McCreedy,
of 16, Caledon Street, Belfast. Born at Belfast.

McCreery, Thomas Henry - Rifleman
35 Royal Irish Rifles "A" Company 8th Battalion *Age 28 Died in War on 2 July 1916*
THIEPVAL MEMORIAL, *France*
Son of Thomas H. and Annie McCreery; husband of Rachel Lemon (formerly McCreery),
of 88, Church Street East, Belfast.

McCreight, George - Regimental Sergeant Major
41202 Royal Inniskilling Fusiliers 10th Battalion *Age 38 Died in War on 11 August 1917*
ETAPLES MILITARY CEMETERY, *France*
Son of George and Eliza McCreight, of Belfast; husband of Margaret McCreight,
of 15, Harrow Green, Leystonstone, London.

McCreight, John - Private
T/328358 Royal Army Service Corps Supply Reserve Depot (Basra) *Age 24 Died as a result of war on 26 March 1919*
SHANKILL CEMETERY, *United Kingdom*
Son of Elizabeth McCreight, of 5, Lisbon Street, Belfast, and the late John McCreight.

McCreight, William Nesbit - Private
15339 South African Infantry 4th Regiment (Infantry) *Age 38 Died in War on 11 April 1918*
YPRES (MENIN GATE) MEMORIAL, *Belgium*
Husband of Sarah McCreight, of 47, Shore Road, Belfast, Ireland.

McCrory, Henry - Corporal
13422 Royal Inniskilling Fusiliers 11th Battalion *Died of Wounds on 19 August 1917*
MENDINGHEM MILITARY CEMETERY, Belgium
Born and enlisted in Belfast.

McCrory, John - Private
3332 Leinster Regiment Depot *Age 19 Died in War on 26 July 1916*
BELFAST (MILLTOWN) ROMAN CATHOLIC CEMETERY, United Kingdom
Son of Thomas and Margaret McCrory, of Belfast.

McCrory, William - Rifleman
6890 Royal Irish Rifles 2nd Battalion *Died in War on 26 September 1915*
BRANDHOEK MILITARY CEMETERY, Belgium
Born in Belfast, enlisted in Holywood.

McCrory, William - Sergeant
7501 Royal Irish Rifles 2nd Battalion *Killed in Action on 25 September 1915*
YPRES (MENIN GATE) MEMORIAL, Belgium
Son of Elizabeth McCrory, 30, Oregon Street, Belfast. An Army Reservist who had worked in the Shipyard.

McCrossan, Francis - Private
4308 Connaught Rangers 6th Battalion *Died in War on 10 March 1916*
LOOS MEMORIAL, France
Husband of Catherine McCrossan 7, Bow Street, Belfast.

McCrossan, Robert James - A/Corporal
10049 Royal Inniskilling Fusiliers 1st Battalion *Age 29 Died of Wounds on 23 March 1918*
ST. SOUPLET BRITISH CEMETERY, France
Born and enlisted in Belfast.

McCrum, Alexander - Private
31034 Royal Inniskilling Fusiliers 7/8th Battalion formerly 19527 Royal Irish Fusiliers
Died of Wounds as a Prisoner of War on 26 May 1918
BERLIN SOUTH-WESTERN CEMETERY, Germany
Born in Belfast, served in the South African War.

McCue, James - Private
21659 Royal Irish Fusiliers 7th Battalion *Died in War on 21 June 1916*
BETHUNE TOWN CEMETERY, France
Native of Belfast. Son of the late James McCue.

McCue, James Ernest - Rifleman
1187 Royal Irish Rifles 8th Battalion *Died in War on 2 July 1916*
THIEPVAL MEMORIAL, France
Born and enlisted in Belfast.

McCue, John P - Rifleman
14/18251 Royal Irish Rifles Depot *Age 26 Died as a result of war on 6 February 1919*
BELFAST CITY CEMETERY, United Kingdom
Son of Elizabeth McCue, of 5, Willowfield Drive, Belfast, and the late Robert McCue.

McCullagh, Alexander Henry - Second Lieutenant
Royal Inniskilling Fusiliers 11th Battalion attached 109th Trench Mortar Battery
Age 21 Killed in Action on 16 August 1917
NEW IRISH FARM CEMETERY, *Belgium*
Son of William McCullagh, of 45, Ponsonby Avenue, Antrim Road, Belfast.

McCullagh, Edwin Samuel - Second Lieutenant
Cheshire Regiment 14th Battalion attached 13th Battalion *Age 23 Killed in Action on 7 June 1917*
MESSINES RIDGE BRITISH CEMETERY, *Belgium*
Son of Mr. and Mrs. S. W. McCullagh, of "Roselands", Rosetta Park, Belfast.

McCullough, Albert - Private
25038 Royal Irish Fusiliers 7/8th Battalion *Age 16 Killed in Action on 20 November 1917*
ST. MARTIN CALVAIRE BRITISH CEMETERY, ST. MARTIN-SUR-COJEUL, *France*
Son of William J. McCullough, of 8, Lower California Street, Belfast.

McCullough, Alfred - Rifleman
7529 Royal Irish Rifles 2nd Battalion *Killed in Action on 20 September 1914*
LE FERTE-SOUS-JOUARRE MEMORIAL, *France*
Born and enlisted in Belfast.

McCullough, Andrew - Rifleman
405 Royal Irish Rifles 1st Battalion *Age 21 Killed in Action on 4 October 1918*
TYNE COT MEMORIAL, *Belgium*
Step-son of Elizabeth McCullough, of 39, Keswick Street, Belfast.

McCullough, David - Rifleman
11702 Royal Irish Rifles 14th Battalion *Age 36 Killed in Action on 16 August 1917*
TYNE COT MEMORIAL, *Belgium*
Husband of Mrs. Sarah McCullough, of 11, Meenan Street, Belfast.

McCullough, Francis - Rifleman
8739 Royal Irish Rifles "C" Company 2nd Battalion *Age 24 Died in War on 15 September 1914*
LA FERTE-SOUS-JOUARRE MEMORIAL, *France*
Son of William James and Annie McCullough, of 42, Downing Street, Belfast;
husband of Catherine McCullough, of 42, Cavour Street, Belfast.

McCullough, Hugh - Rifleman
1206 Royal Irish Rifles 2nd Battalion *Age 35 Killed in Action on 10 May 1918*
DUHALLOW A.D.S. CEMETERY, *Belgium*
Son of the late Mr. McCullough, of Belfast; husband of Mary McCullough,
of 17, Fairymount, Carrickfergus, County Antrim.

McCullough, James - Able Seaman
17551 Royal Navy HMS "Princess Irene" *Died in War on 27 May 1915*
PORTMOUTH NAVAL MEMORIAL, *United Kingdom*
84, Donneybrook Street, Belfast.

McCullough, James - Rifleman
3213 Royal Irish Rifles 2nd Battalion *Killed in Action on 18 December 1914*
YPRES (MENIN GATE) MEMORIAL, *Belgium*
15, Oakley Street, Belfast.

Journey of Remembering

McCullough, James - Rifleman
354 Royal Irish Rifles "B" Company 10th Battalion *Age 22 Killed in Action on 7 June 1917*
YPRES (MENIN GATE) MEMORIAL, Belgium
Son of Sarah McCullough, of 19, Agincourt Avenue, Ormeau Road, Belfast, and the late Edward McCullough.

McCullough, John - Boy First Class
J/37462 Royal Navy HMS "Invincible" *Age 17 Killed in Action at Battle of Jutland on 31 May 1916*
PLYMOUTH NAVAL MEMORIAL, United Kingdom
Son of John and Mary McCullough, of 7, Southwell Street, Belfast.

McCullough, Joseph - Private
1438A Australian Infantry 13th Battalion *Age 23 Killed in Action on 3 May 1915*
LONE PINE MEMORIAL, Turkey
Son of William McCullough and Isabella McCullough, of Leigh, Auckland, New Zealand.
Native of Belfast, Ireland.

McCullough, Joseph C - Rifleman
15241 Royal Irish Rifles 9th Battalion *Killed in Action on 1 July 1916*
MILL ROAD CEMETERY, THIEPVAL, France
104, Canmore Street, Belfast.

McCullough, Robert - Sergeant
15244 Royal Irish Rifles 2nd Battalion *Died of Wounds on 23 September 1918*
LONGUENESSE (ST. OMER) SOUVENIR CEMETERY, France
Son of the late Charles and Mary McCullough, of Belfast; husband of Sarah McCullough,
of 63, Lanark Street, Belfast. Awarded the Distinguished Conduct Medal for gallantry.

McCullough, Samuel - Private
57202 Royal Welsh Fusiliers transferred to 620125 Labour Corps *Age 39 Died as result of War on 3 March 1919*
BELFAST CITY CEMETERY, United Kingdom
Husband of Agnes McCullough, of 6, Brussels Street, Belfast.

McCullough, Thomas - Rifleman
12030 Royal Irish Rifles 15th Battalion *Died in War on 24 December 1915*
SUCRERIE MILITARY CEMETERY, COLINCAMPS, France & Flanders
Born and enlisted in Belfast.

McCullough, William John - Rifleman
15385 Royal Irish Rifles 9th Battalion *Killed in Action on 1 July 1916*
THIEPVAL MEMORIAL
123, Cupar Street, Belfast.

McCullough, William Walter - Rifleman
11713 Royal Irish Rifles 15th Battalion *Age 28 Killed in Action on 1 July 1916*
THIEPVAL MEMORIAL, France
Son of the late Matthew and Margaret McCullough, of 9, Fleet Street, Belfast;
husband of Frances Kelso McCullough, of 19, Sandyfaulds Street, South Side, Glasgow.

McCully, John - Rifleman
1499 Royal Irish Rifles 1st Battalion *Killed in Action on 4 October 1918*
LIJSSENTHOEK MILITARY CEMETERY, Belgium
Born and enlisted in Belfast. Nephew of Sarah McCully, 19, Bisley Street, Belfast.

McCune, Edward - Gunner
133674 Royal Field Artillery 14th Brigade *Age 21 Killed in Action on 31 March 1918*
ARRAS MEMORIAL, *France*
Son of Agnes Butler (formerly McCune) and A. J. Butler (stepfather), of 23, Bank Street, Belfast.

McCune, James - Lance Corporal
15387 Royal IrishRifles 14th Battalion *Killed in Action on 1 July 1916*
THIEPVAL MEMORIAL, *France*
Born and enlisted in Belfast. Member of Fountainville Presbyterian Church.

McCune, Joseph - Private
21160 Princess Victoria's (Royal Irish Fusiliers) 8th Battalion *Died in War on 4 June 1916*
LOOS MEMORIAL, *France*
Born and enlisted in Belfast. Formerly 2375 Connaught Rangers

McCurdie, Archibald - Fourth Engineer Officer
Mercantile Marine S.S. "City of Glasgow" (Glasgow)
Age 26 Drowned, as a result of an attack by an enemy submarine on 1 September 1918
TOWER HILL MEMORIAL, *United Kingdom*
Son of Ellen McCurdie (née Twinet), of 7, Langside Road, Crosshill, Glasgow, and the late Archibald McCurdie. Born at Belfast.

McCurdy, Frederick - Lance Corporal
10718 Royal Irish Rifles 1st Battalion *Age 20 Killed in Action on 14 October 1918*
DADIZEELE NEW BRITISH CEMETERY, *Belgium*
Son of Archibald and Catherine McCurdy, of 52, Brougham Street, Belfast.

McCurdy, Robert - Private
100266 Canadian Infantry (Alberta Regiment) 49th Battalion *Age 19 Killed in Action on 15 September 1916*
VIMY MEMORIAL, *France*
Son of William McCurdy, of Belfast, Ireland. A Presbyterian, he was a farmer and had already served in the British Army.

McCurrie, John - Private
8154 Royal Irish Fusiliers 1st Battalion *Died in War on 26 August 1916*
RAILWAY DUGOUTS BURIAL GROUND, *Belgium*
171, Snugville Street, Belfast.

McCurrie, Robert - Private
DM2/161694 Army Service Corps Mechanical Transport Company *Died in War on 4 April 1918*
NOYON NEW BRITISH CEMETERY, *France*
Husband of Mrs M. A. McCurrie, of 70, Montreal Street, Belfast.

McCurrie, William - Lance Corporal
8797 Royal Irish Rifles Depot *Age 28 Died as result of War on 19 February 1919*
BELFAST CITY CEMETERY, *United Kingdom*
Son of William and Ellen McCurrie, of 171, Snugville Street, Belfast. Holder of the Silver War Badge,

McCurry, Alexander - Second Lieutenant
Machine Gun Corps (Infantry) 9th Battalion *Age 20 Died in War on 25 April 1918*
TYNE COT MEMORIAL, *Belgium*
Son of James Isaac and Bessie McCurry, of Lisnadill, Osborne Park, Belfast.
Joined Officer Training Corps at Queen's University, Belfast

JOURNEY OF REMEMBERING

McCurry, Thomas - Private
20262 Royal Inniskilling Fusiliers 9th Battalion *Killed in Action on 1 July 1916*
CONNAUGHT CEMETERY, THIEPVAL, France
Born and enlisted in Belfast.

McCurry, Walter Tennyson - Lieutenant
Royal Army Medical Corps *Age 22 Killed in Action at Ypres on 14 March 1915*
RAMPARTS CEMETERY, LILLE GATE YPRES, Belgium
Elder son of Joseph and Jessie Graham McCurry of Belfast Bank House, Shankill Road, Belfast.

McCusker, Henry - Private
4242 Connaught Rangers 6th Battalion *Died in War on 19 March 1916*
CALAIS SOUTHERN CEMETERY, France
Born in Belfast, enlisted in Lurgan.

McCusker, John - Acting Sergeant
15375 Princess Victoria's (Royal Irish Fusiliers) 7th Battalion *Died in War on 5 September 1916*
THIEPVAL MEMORIAL, France
Born in Belfast, enlisted in Portadown.

McCusker, Maurice - Private
43216 Royal Inniskilling Fusiliers Battalion *Died in War on 26 October 1916*
YPRES (MENIN GATE) MEMORIAL, Belgium
32, Pound Street, Belfast.

McCutcheon, George - Private
60241 Royal Welsh Fusiliers 2nd Battalion formerly 269479 Army Service Corps *Killed in Action on 22 June 1917*
CROISILLES BRITISH CEMETERY, France
Born and enlisted in Belfast.

McCutcheon, Herbert Victor - Private
2659 Royal Inniskilling Fusiliers 2nd Battalion *Age 21 Died in War on 11 July 1916*
THIEPVAL MEMORIAL, France
Son of Daniel and Sarah A. McCutcheon, of 8, Malcolm Lane, Belfast.

McCutcheon, John Cecil - Lieutenant
Royal Irish Fusiliers 6th Battalion *Age 24 Died of Wounds on 2 October 1916*
LAHANA MILITARY CEMETERY, Greece
Son of John B. and Mary H. McCutcheon, of Rineen, Annadale, Belfast.
Served in Queen's University Officer Training Corps. Late of the Chinese Customs Service.

McDade, James - Private
23284 Royal Irish Fusiliers "C" Company 9th Battalion *Age 33 Died of Wounds on 20 July 1916*
PORTSDOWN (CHRIST CHURCH) MILITARY CEMETERY, United Kingdom
Husband of Isabella McDade, of 4, Parkview Street, Belfast.

McDermott, (William) Henry - Private
25319 Royal Inniskilling Fusiliers 9th Battalion *Killed in Action on 16 August 1917*
TYNE COT MEMORIAL, Belgium
53, Cavour Street, Belfast.

BELFAST BOOK OF HONOUR

McDermott, John Harold - Sergeant
4752 16th Lancers (The Queen's) *Died in War on 21 November 1914*
YPRES (MENIN GATE) MEMORIAL, Belgium
Born in Belfast. Enlisted in Lurgan.

McDermott, Terence - Private
23377 Machine Gun Corps (Infantry) *Died in War on 23 October 1916*
CONTAY BRITISH CEMETERY, France
Born in Belfast, enlisted in Ballykinler. Awarded the Distinguished Conduct Medal.
Formerly 5094 Royal Irish Rifles

McDonagh, Patrick - Private
2351 Royal Irish Regiment 6th Battalion *Died of Wounds on 10 May 1916*
STRUMA MILITARY CEMETERY, Greece
139, Springfield Road, Belfast.

McDonald, Andrew - Private
25244 Highland Light Infantry 12th Battalion *Age 23 Killed in Action on 8 October 1918*
DADIZEELE NEW BRITISH CEMETERY, Belgium
Son of Margaret McDonald, Saul Street, Belfast and the late James McDonald. Born at Greenock, Scotland.

McDonald, Charles - Private
Royal Scots Fusiliers *Died in War on 26 September 1915*
Brother of Jane Tierney, 2 The Cottages, Falls Road, Belfast.

McDonald, Daniel - Rifleman
7137 Royal Irish Rifles "D" Company 2nd Battalion *Age 33. Died in War on 7 May 1915*
YPRES (MENIN GATE) MEMORIAL, Belgium
Son of William John McDonald, of 49, Tomb Street, Belfast.

McDonald, David - Lance Corporal
7578 Royal Irish Rifles 1st Battalion *Died in War on 9 May 1915*
PLOEGSTEERT MEMORIAL, Belgium
Born and enlisted in Belfast.

McDonald, James Alexander - Private
1687 Australian Infantry 59th Battalion *Age 39 Died of Wounds on 6 October 1918*
TINCOURT NEW BRITISH CEMETERY, France
Son of Thomas and Margaret McDonald; husband of Martha McDonald, of West Shore, Llandudno, Wales. Born at Belfast, Ireland.

McDonald, James F - Lance Sergeant
11439 Royal Inniskilling Fusiliers 6th Battalion *Killed in Action on 17 October 1918*
HIGHLAND CEMETERY, LE CATEAU, France
8, Israel Street, Belfast.

McDonald, John - Lance Sergeant
744 Army Cyclist Corps Depot *Age 37 Died of Wounds (gas) on 22 December 1918*
BELFAST (DUNDONALD) CEMETERY, United Kingdom
Husband of Martha Amelia McDonald, of 13, Lismain Street, Ravenhill Avenue, Belfast.
Holder of the Silver War Badge.

McDonald, John - Rifleman
20318 Royal Irish Rifles 1st Battalion *Killed in Action on 2 October 1918*
TYNE COT MEMORIAL, *Belgium*
Born in Belfast, enlisted Glasgow.

McDonald, John Riddell - Stoker First Class
SS/114477 Royal Navy HM Submarine "K.17" *Age 24 Drowned through collision in North Sea on 31 January 1918*
CHATHAM NAVAL MEMORIAL, *United Kingdom*
Son of Hugh G. and Sarah J. McDonald, of Central Fire Station, 82, Chichester Street, Belfast.

McDonald, Robert - Gunner
31099 Royal Horse Artillery and Royal Field Artillery *Died in War on 18 September 1917*
MENDINGHEM MILITARY CEMETERY, *Belgium*
Born and enlisted in Belfast.

McDonald, Robert - Sergeant
8005 Royal Field Artillery *Died in War on 29 April 1915*
IPSWICH CEMETERY, *United Kingdom*
47, Thorndyke Street, Belfast.

McDonald, Ronald - Private
25906 Royal Inniskilling Fusiliers 8th Battalion *Age 28 Died of Wounds on 7 October 1916*
BAILLEUL COMMUNAL CEMETERY EXTENSION (NORD), *France*
Son of Thomas Edward and Annie McDonald, of 15, Third Street, Shankill Road, Belfast.

McDonald, William - Private
23814 Lancashire Fusiliers 15th Battalion *Died in War on 16 December 1918*
THIEPVAL MEMORIAL, *France*
60, Rosapenna Street, Belfast.

McDonald, William - Private
8698 Royal Inniskilling Fusiliers 2nd Battalion *Died in War on 21 October 1914*
PLOEGSTEERT MEMORIAL, *Belgium*
11, Isthmus Street, Belfast.

McDonald, William - Rifleman
9022 Royal Irish Rifles "D" Company 1st Battalion *Age 41 Killed in Action on 1 July 1916*
THIEPVAL MEMORIAL, *France*
Son of William John and Sarah McDonald; husband of Ellen McDonald,
of 4, Ludlow Street, New Lodge Road, Belfast.

McDonald, William - Ship's Cook
Mercantile Marine S.S. "Garron Head" (Belfast) *Age 38 Killed by mine on 16 November 1917*
TOWER HILL MEMORIAL, *United Kingdom*
Son of John and Mary McDonald; husband of Elizabeth McDonald (née Hughes),
of 2, Seaview Terrace, Greencastle, Belfast. Born in Belfast.

McDonald, William Robert - Rifleman
1617 Royal Irish Rifles 12th Battalion *Age 32 Killed in Action on 1 July 1916*
THIEPVAL MEMORIAL, *France*
Son of Mrs. Fanny Hughes (formerly McDonald), of Rose's Lane Ends, Belfast;
husband of Susan Wilson (formerly McDonald), of Lower Darkley, Keady, County Armagh.

McDonnell, Alexander - Private
21161 Royal Irish Fusiliers 1st Battalion *Age 26 Died in War on 11 April 1917*
BROWN'S COPSE CEMETERY, ROEUX, *France*
Son of William and Ellen McDonnell, of 54, Conway Street, Belfast.

McDonnell, Patrick - Rifleman
11035 Royal Irish Rifles 6th Battalion *Age 20 Died of Wounds, received at the Dardanelles on 5 September 1915*
ALEXANDRIA (CHATBY) MILITARY AND WAR MEMORIAL CEMETERY, *Egypt*
Son of Edward and Elizabeth McDonnell, of 71, Hardinge Street, Belfast.

McDonnell, Thomas - Rifleman
8711 Royal Irish Rifles 1st Battalion *Age 24 Killed in Action on 9 May 1915*
PLOEGSTEERT MEMORIAL, *Belgium*
Son of John McDonnell, of 8, Murdoch Street, Belfast.

McDowell, Arthur - Private
46237 Royal Army Medical Corps 110th Field Ambulance *Killed in Action on 9 June 1917*
LINDENHOEK CHALET MILITARY CEMETERY, *Belgium*
114, McTier Street, Belfast.

McDowell, Daniel - Private
9112 Leinster Regiment 1st Battalion *Died in War on 14 February 1915*
YPRES (MENIN GATE) MEMORIAL, *France*
93, Chatham Street, Belfast.

McDowell, Edward - Private
4827 Royal Irish Rifles 7th Battalion *Died in War on 10 June 1916*
DUD CORNER CEMETERY, LOOS, *France*
74, Aberdeen Street, Belfast.

McDowell, Henry (Harry) - Rifleman
9115 Royal Irish Rifles 2nd Battalion *Age 24 Killed in Action 8 July 1916*
THIEPVAL MEMORIAL, *France*
Husband of Martha McDowell, of 13, Geoffrey Street, Belfast.

McDowell, Hugh - Private
18565 King's Own (Royal Lancaster Regiment) 6th Battalion *Died in War on 5 April 1916*
BASRA MEMORIAL, *Iraq*
Born in Belfast, enlisted in Barrow-in-Furness, England.

McDowell, James - Corporal
160 Royal Irish Rifles 19th Battalion *Died of Wounds on 23 March 1918*
POZIERES MEMORIAL, *France*
Born and enlisted in Belfast.

McDowell, James - Rifleman
17/525 Royal Irish Rifles 8th/9th Battalion *Age 22 Died in War on 11 April 1918*
ST. SEVER CEMETERY EXTENSION, ROUEN, *France*
Son of Daniel and Mary McDowell of 40, Israel Street, Belfast.

McDowell, John - Private
4186 Seaforth Highlanders 1st/5th Battalion *Died in War on 16 May 1916*
MAROEUIL BRITISH CEMETERY, *France*
Son of Margaret McDowell of 22, Erin Street, Belfast.

McDowell, John - Private
171250 Canadian Infantry (Quebec Regiment) 24th Battalion *Age 27 Died in War on 28 August 1918*
SUN QUARRY CEMETERY, CHERISY, France
Son of John and Martha McDowell, of 59, Bastedo Avenue, Toronto. Native of Belfast, Ireland.
A Methodist, he worked as a printer and had served in the militia.

McDowell, John - Private
20079 Royal Inniskilling Fusiliers 1st Battalion *Died in War on 21 August 1915*
HELLES MEMORIAL, Turkey
Born Edenderry, enlisted in Londonderry. A resident of Belfast.

McDowell, John - Rifleman
1073 Royal Irish Rifles 12th Battalion *Age 21 Killed in Action on 30 September 1918*
TYNE COT MEMORIAL, Belgium
Son of John and Margaret A. McDowell, of 15, Tennyson Street, Belfast.

McDowell, John Beck - Lance Corporal
5261 Royal Fusiliers(City of London Regiment) 20th Battalion *Killed in Action on 13 March 1916*
CAMBRIN CHURCHYARD EXTENSION, France
Son of Ada McDowell of 10, Malone Park, Belfast, and the late John McDowell.

McDowell, Matthew - Rifleman
2017 Royal Irish Rifles 15th Battalion *Age 21 Died in War on 2 December 1917*
ACHIET-LE-GRAND COMMUNAL CEMETERY EXTENSION, France
Brother of Mrs. Jennie McChesney, of 99, Mountcollyer Avenue, Belfast.

McDowell, Patrick - Private
22050 Royal Dublin Fusiliers 6th Battalion *Age 31 Died in War on 27 August 1915*
GREEN HILL CEMETERY, Turkey
Son of Robert and Mary McDowell; husband of Maria McDowell, of 64, Conway Street, Belfast.

McDowell, R - Lance Corporal
Royal Irish Rifles *Killed in Action*
7, Peter's Place, Belfast.

McDowell, Robert - Private
5087 Royal Munster Fusiliers 6th Battalion *Age 28 Died in War on 1 January 1918*
RAMLEH WAR CEMETERY, Israel
Son of Daniel and Mary McDowell, of 40, Israel Street, Belfast. Brother of James.

McDowell, Robert John - Stoker
2644S Royal Naval Reserve HMS "Goliath" *Age 22 Died in War on 13 May 1915*
PORTSMOUTH NAVAL MEMORIAL, United Kingdom
Son of James and Letitia McDowell, of 77, Leopold Street, Belfast.

McDowell, William - Corporal
8942 Royal Inniskilling Fusiliers "D" Company 1st Battalion *Age 27 Died in War on 27 January 1917*
THIEPVAL MEMORIAL, France
Son of William and Jane McDowell, of 25, Nevis Avenue, Belfast. Husband of Gertrude Mary McDowell, of 80, Wood Street, Rugby.

McDowell, William - Engineer
Mercantile Marine Reserve HMS "Warden" *Age 25 Accidentally Drowned on 30 September 1918*
TYNEMOUTH (PRESTON) CEMETERY, United Kingdom
Son of Allan and Mary Jane McDowell, of 34, Derg Street, Belfast.

McDowell, William - Lance Corporal
5120 Northumberland Fusiliers 1st Battalion *Age 24 Died in War on 26 June 1918*
SANDPITS BRITISH CEMETERY, FOUQUEREUIL, France
Son of William and Sarah McDowell, of Belfast.

McDowell, William - Private
11161 Royal Inniskilling Fusiliers 2nd Battalion *Age 19 Died in War on 16 May 1915*
LE TOURET MEMORIAL, France
Son of Robert and Maria McDowell, of 14, Frankfort Street, Belfast.

McDowell, William - Rifleman
273 Royal Irish Rifles 8th Battalion *Died in War on 17 August 1917*
TYNE COT MEMORIAL, Belgium
114, McTier Street, Belfast.

McDowell, William James - Private
G/14527 Royal Irish Fusiliers 9th Battalion *Died in War on 25 September 1917*
NEUVILLE-BOURJONVAL BRITISH CEMETERY, France
92, Selby Street, Belfast.

McElhagga, John - Sergeant
10814 Royal Dublin Fusiliers 1st Battalion *Age 30 Died in War on 8 July 1916*
DOULLENS COMMUNAL CEMETERY EXTENSION No.1, France
(Served as McFARLANE). Son of Margaret McElhagga, of 5, Azamar Street, Shankill Road, Belfast. Awarded the Military Medal.

McElrath, Robert Harper - Private
25459 Royal Dublin Fusiliers 1st Battalion *Age 32 Died in War on 21 October 1918*
DADIZEELE NEW BRITISH CEMETERY, Belgium
Born and enlisted in Belfast. Son of James and Mary McElrath of Mill Farm, County Antrim.

McElroy, Edward - Sergeant
3/6439 Princess Louise's (Argyll & Sutherland Highlanders) 1/5th Battalion *Age 38 Died in War on 13 November 1917*
DEIR EL BELAH WAR CEMETERY, Israel
Son of John and Ann McElroy; husband of Mrs McElroy of 25, Orr Street, Glasgow. Served in the South African War and a native of Belfast.

McElroy, James - Rifleman
8634 Royal Irish Rifles 2nd Battalion *Age 19 Died in War on 27 April 1915*
VOORMEZEELE ENCLOSURES No 1 and No2, Belgium
Resident of Belfast. Reported to have been shot in the chest and died within thirty minutes.

McElroy, William - Corporal
15400 Royal Irish Rifles 8th Battalion *Died in War on 2 July 1916*
THIEPVAL MEMORIAL, France
Enlisted in Belfast and born at Castleblaney, County Monaghan.
Member of Westbourne Presbyterian Church Belfast.

Journey of Remembering

McEntee, James - Private
12115 Cameronians (Scottish Rifles) 9th Battalion *Age 30 Died in War on 25 April 1918*
TYNE COT MEMORIAL, *Belgium*
Son of James J. McEntee; husband of Essie McEntee, of 24, Welland Street, Belfast.

McErlane, Harry - Fireman And Trimmer
Mercantile Marine S.S. "Dorothy" (Sunderland)
Age 34 Drowned, as a result of an attack by an enemy submarine on 24 February 1917
TOWER HILL MEMORIAL, *United Kingdom*
(Served as McILLVAIN). Son of Mary and the late John McErlane; husband of Mary McErlane (née McConney), of 28, Vulcan Street, Belfast. Born at Belfast.

McErlean, James - Private
10017 Irish Guards 1st Battalion *Age 42 Died in War on 27 March 1918*
DOUCHY-LES-AYETTE BRITISH CEMETERY, *France*
Son of John and Catherine McErlean, of Armoy, County Antrim; husband of Mary Kate McErlean, 10, Vicinage Park, Belfast.

McErvel, John Harold - Major
The King's (Liverpool Regiment) attached Manchester Regiment 1st Battalion *Age 32 Died in War on 8 August 1916*
BERNAFAY WOOD BRITISH CEMETERY, MONTAUBAN, *France*
Brother of Anna McErvel, of 110, Eglantine Avenue, Belfast. Educated at the Masonic School, Dublin and later in Queen's University OTC. He was a Mason and an active member of the Royal North of Ireland Yacht Club. Involved in the linen trade and, when killed, he was engaged to be married.

McEvoy, James Joseph - Lance Sergeant
20673 Royal Irish Fusiliers 9th Battalion *Age 19 Killed in Action on 16 August 1917*
TYNE COT MEMORIAL, *Belgium*
Son of James J. and Annabella Cosgrove McEvoy, of 41 and 43, Berry Street, Belfast.

McEvoy, Thomas - Rifleman
9685 Royal Irish Rifles 1st Battalion *Age 25 Died in War on 1 July 1916*
OVILLERS MILITARY CEMETERY, *France*
(Served as McDONALD). Son of Michael and Margaret McEvoy; husband of Elizabeth McEvoy, of 36, Balkan Street, Belfast.

McEvoy, William John - Private
3701 Royal Inniskilling Fusiliers 8th Battalion *Age 24 Died in War on 16 August 1917*
TYNE COT MEMORIAL, *Belgium*
Son of Thomas J. and Annie McEvoy, of 55A, Agnes Street, Belfast.

McEwan, David - Rifleman
8596 Royal Irish Rifles 2nd Battalion *Killed in Action on 10 March 1915*
YPRES (MENIN GATE) MEMORIAL, *Belgium*
Son of George and Annie McEwan, 34, Hardcastle Street, Belfast.

McFadden, James - Able Seaman
Mercantile Marine S.S. "Mangara" (Glasgow)
Age 26 Drowned, as a result of an attack by an enemy submarine on 28 July 1915
TOWER HILL MEMORIAL, *United Kingdom*
Son of Grace McFadden, of 272, Grosvenor Road, Belfast, and the late Charles McFadden. Born at Ramelton, County Donegal.

McFadden, Joseph - Private
1722 Leinster Regiment 2nd Battalion *Died in War on 27 March 1918*
POZIERES MEMORIAL, France
Born in Glasgow Lived in Belfast when enlisted.

McFadzean, William Frederick - Rifleman
18278 Royal Irish Rifles C Company 14th Battalion *Age 20 Killed in Action on 1 July 1916*
THIEPVAL MEMORIAL, France
Posthumously awarded the Victoria Cross for an act of supreme bravery and self sacifice.
Born in Lurgan he was the son of William and Annie Pedlow McFadzean, of "Rubicon", Cregagh, Belfast.

McFall, Alexander - Fireman And Trimmer
Mercantile Marine S.S. "War Clover" (London)
Age 32 Drowned, as a result of an attack by an enemy submarine on 19 October 1917
TOWER HILL MEMORIAL, United Kingdom
Husband of Esther McFall (née McKinley), of 43, Harland Street, Belfast. Born at Cork.

McFall, John - Private
5274 20th Hussars *Age 26 Died in War on 30 October 1914*
YPRES (MENIN GATE) MEMORIAL, Belgium
Son of John and Susan McFall of Ligoneil, Belfast.

McFall, Robert - Rifleman
15262 Royal Irish Rifles 9th Battalion *Age 37 Killed in Action on 7 August 1917*
YPRES (MENIN GATE) MEMORIAL, Belgium
Spamount Steet, Belfast. Husband of Ellen Bruce McFall, of Craigs Cottage, Mill Road, Whitehouse, Belfast.

McFall, Thomas Lamont - Second Lieutenant
Royal Inniskilling Fusiliers 9th Battalion *Age 22 Killed in Action on 7 August 1917*
POTIJZE CHATEAU GROUNDS CEMETERY, Belgium
Son of John and Elizabeth McFall, of Magherintendry, Bushmills, CountyAntrim. Belfast Banking Company official.

McFall, William John - Rifleman
9599 Royal Irish Rifles 1st Battalion *Died in War on 11 March 1915*
TYNE COT MEMORIAL, Belgium
Born and enlisted in Belfast.

McFarland, George - Rifleman
7518 Royal Irish Rifles 2nd Battalion *Age 28 Killed in Action on 14 January 1915*
YPRES (MENIN GATE) MEMORIAL, Belgium
Husband of Agnes McFarland, of 7, Rosebery Street, Connswater, Belfast.

McFarland, James - Private
18728 Machine Gun Corps (Infantry) 109th Company *Killed in Action on 1 July 1916*
THIEPVAL MEMORIAL, France
9, Dunmoyle Street, Belfast.

McFarland, John - Chief Petty Officer
F/2863 Royal Naval Air Service Royal Naval Armoured Cars Division *Age 36 Died in War on 1 July 1917*
POZNAN MEMORIAL, Poland
Holder of the Distinguished Service Medal. Also awarded the Medals of 2nd, 3rd and 4th Classes of the Order of St. George (Russia). Son of William and Jane McFarland; husband of Mary M. E. McFarland, of 90, Northumberland Street, Belfast.

McFarland, Robert - Lance Corporal
16566 Royal Inniskilling Fusiliers 5th Battalion *Died in War on 27 December 1917*
JERUSALEM WAR CEMETERY, Israel
Born in Belfast, enlisted Dublin.

McFarlane, Charles - Third Steward
Mercantile Marine S.S. "Bray Head" (Belfast)
Age 22 Drowned, as a result of an attack by an enemy submarine on 14 March 1917
TOWER HILL MEMORIAL, United Kingdom
Son of Bridget McFarlane (née Canavan), of 2, Weaver Street, St. Joseph's, Belfast, and the late Charles McFarlane.

McFarlane, Donald McVicor - Third Engineer
Mercantile Marine S.S. "Hungerford" (London)
Age 25 Drowned, as a result of an attack by an enemy submarine on 16 April 1918
TOWER HILL MEMORIAL, United Kingdom
Son of Colin and Wilhelmina McFarlane; husband of May McFarlane (née Booth), of Cumberland Hotel, 11, Dock Street, Belfast. Born in Lanark, Scotland.

McFarlane, George - Rifleman
1402 Royal Irish Rifles 8/9th Battalion *Died in War on 23 November 1917*
CAMBRAI MEMORIAL LOUVERVAL, France
Born and enlisted in Belfast.

McFarlane, John - Private
10719 Royal Inniskilling Fusiliers 1st Battalion *Died in War on 20 November 1917*
CAMBRAI MEMORIAL, LOUVERVAL, France
Husband of Alice McFarlane, 12, Fourth Street, Belfast.

McFarlane, Nicholas - Private
26/497 Northumberland Fusiliers Depot Battalion *Died in War on 1 February 1917*
JARROW CEMETERY, United Kingdom
Born in Belfast, enlsited in Newcastle-upon-Tyne.

McFarlane, William - Stoker First Class
SS/108637 Royal Navy HMS "Hawke"
Age 24 Killed in Action with submarine in North Sea on 15 October 1914
CHATHAM NAVAL MEMORIAL, United Kingdom
Son of William and Sarah McFarlane, of 24, Fifth Street, Belfast.

McFerran, Thomas - Aircraftman Second Class
304638 Royal Air Force Cadet College (Cranwell) *Age 19 Died as a result of war on 6 June 1920*
LARNE NEW CEMETERY, United Kingdom
Son of Mrs. Hester McFerran, of 20, Mountcollyer Street, Belfast. Born at Larne.

McFerran, Walter - Lance Corporal
24614 Royal Irish Fusiliers 1st Battalion *Age 19 Died in War on 23 November 1917*
CAMBRAI MEMORIAL, LOUVERVAL, France
Son of Robert and Elizabeth McFerran, of 73, Silver Street, Belfast.

McFerran, William James - Sapper
202406 Royal Engineers Inland Water Transport *Died in War on 3 December 1916*
LONGUENESSE (ST. OMER) SOUVENIR CEMETERY, *France*
Husband of Elizabeth McFerran, of 7, Lisavan Street, Strandtown, Belfast. Formerly 1003 North Irish Horse.

McGahan, Patrick John - Private
21413 Royal Irish Fusiliers 8th Battalion *Age 25 Died in War on 4 May 1916*
VERMELLES BRITISH CEMETERY, *France*
Son of Mrs. Mary McGahan, of 53, Chatham Street, Belfast.

McGahey, John - Private
27171 Royal Inniskilling Fusiliers 1st Battalion *Age 23 Died in War on 27 January 1917*
THIEPVAL MEMORIAL, *France*
Son of Henry McGahey, of 89, Saunders Street, Newtownards Road, Belfast.

McGarry, Alexander - Private
1416 Lancashire Fusiliers 1st Battalion *Died in War on 16 June 1915*
ALEXANDRIA (CHATBY) MILITARY AND WAR MEMORIAL CEMETERY, *Egypt*
Born in Belfast to Alexander and Lizzie McGarry, 57, Grove Street, Belfast.

McGarry, Charles - Private
12803 Royal Inniskilling Fusiliers 1st Battalion *Age 22 Killed in Action on 1 July 1916*
Y RAVINE CEMETERY, BEAUMONT-HAMEL, *France*
Son of John and Sarah J. McGarry, of 36, Parkview Street, Belfast.

McGarry, Gerald - Rifleman
7785 Royal Irish Rifles posted to 18th London Regiment *Died in War on 6 September 1918*
FINS NEW BRITISH CEMETERY, SOREL-LE-GRAND, *France*
Born and enlisted in Belfast.

McGarry, James - Private
186598 Royal Air Force *Age 20 Died as a result of war on 11 December 1918*
BELFAST (MILLTOWN) ROMAN CATHOLIC CEMETERY, *United Kingdom*
Son of John and Sarah J. McGarry, of 36, Parkview Street, Belfast.

McGarry, Joseph - Rifleman
2645 Royal Irish Rifles 7th Battalion *Died in War on 9 September 1916*
THIEPVAL MEMORIAL, *France*
Born in Belfast enlisted Airdrie, Scotland.

McGarry, Patrick - Private
5228 Connaught Rangers 1st Battalion *Died in War on 8 October 1916*
AMARA WAR CEMETERY, *Iraq*
Born in Belfast, enlisted Hamilton, Scotland.

McGarry, Peter - Private
26904 Royal Scots (Lothian Regiment) 12th Battalion *Died in War on 12 April 1917*
ATHIES COMMUNAL CEMETERY EXTENSION, *France*
Born in Belfast, enlisted Clydebank, Scotland.

McGarvey, John - Sergeant
11099 Royal Irish Rifles 6th Battalion *Age 38 Killed in Action on 11 August 1915*
HELLES MEMORIAL, *Turkey*
Son of the late Thomas McGarvey.

McGaughey, William - Private
26206 Royal Dublin Fusiliers 9th Battalion *Died of Wounds on 19 March 1917*
BAILLEUL COMMUNAL CEMETERY EXTENSION (NORD), France
7, Marchioness Street, Belfast.

McGeagh, James - Rifleman
7003 Royal Irish Rifles 1st Battalion *Age 19 Killed in Action on 25 October 1916*
GROVE TOWN CEMETERY, MEAULTE, France
Son of Sarah and the late Ambrose McGeagh, of 46, Euston Street, Belfast.

McGeary, John J - Private
PS/10100 Royal Fusiliers 9th Battalion *Age 18 Died in War on 5 August 1916*
THIEPVAL MEMORIAL, France
Son of Francis and Charlotte McGeary, of 31, Islandbawn Street, Belfast.

McGee, Hugh - Private
5742 Royal Army Medical Corps attached H.M.H.S. "Salta" *Age 26 Killed in Action on 10 April 1917*
SALTA MEMORIAL STE. MARIE CEMETERY, LE HAVRE, France
Lost at sea as a result of a mine explosion off Le Havre. Son of Hugh and Ellen McGee, of Belfast.

McGee, James - Rifleman
5474 Royal Irish Rifles *Age 17 Died in War on 21 December 1916*
CARNMONEY (HOLY EVANGELISTS) CHURCH OF IRELAND CHURCHYARD EXTENSION, United Kingdom
Son of Henry and Ann Jane McGee, of 10, New North Queen Street, Belfast.

McGee, James - Rifleman
6988 Royal Irish Rifles 1st Battalion *Killed in Action on 12 March 1915*
LE TOURET MEMORIAL, France
Born in Bond Street, in the Markets area of Belfast. Enlisted in Holywood.

McGee, Patrick - Private
7876 Cameronians (Scottish Rifles) 9th Battalion *Age 31 Died in War on 25 September 1915*
LOOS MEMORIAL, France
Son of John and Mary McGee, of 47, Churchill Street, Belfast; husband of Margaret Mary McGee, of 58, High Street, Kilkenny.

McGee, William - Lance Corporal
4095 Queen's Own Cameron Highlanders 5th Battalion *Died in War on 18 October 1916*
THIEPVAL MEMORIAL, France
Born in Belfast, lived in Glasgow when enlisted.

McGee, William - Private
9385 Royal Inniskilling Fusiliers 1st Battalion *Died of Wounds on 20 June 1915*
LANCASHIRE LANDING CEMETERY, Turkey
Born and enlisted in Belfast.

McGeough, Patrick - Lance Corporal
18946 Royal Dublin Fusiliers 2nd Battalion *Died in War on 5 November 1917*
CROISILLES BRITISH CEMETERY, France
Born in Belfast, enlisted Dublin.

McGeown, John - Private
49878 Royal Irish Fusiliers 1st Battalion *Age 20 Died in War on 22 October 1918*
DUHALLOW A.D.S. CEMETERY, Belgium
Son of John and Jennie McGeown, of 114, Mervue Street, Belfast.

McGibben, James - Driver
46917 Royal Field Artillery 34th Battery 38th Brigade *Age 27 Killed in Action on 24 August 1916*
FLATIRON COPSE CEMETERY, MAMETZ, France
Son of Mr. and Mrs. Edmond McGibben, of Belfast; husband of Sarah McGibben, of 6, Pembroke Street, Belfast.

McGibben, Samuel - Rifleman
432 Royal Irish Rifles 16th Battalion *Age 22 Killed in Action 21 March 1918*
POZIERES MEMORIAL, France
Son of Edmund and Bessie McGibben, of 25, Palestine Street, Belfast.

McGibbon, James - Private
7246 Royal Scots Fusiliers 1st Battalion *Died in War on 16 June 1915*
YPRES (MENIN GATE) MEMORIAL, Belgium
Born in Belfast, enlisted Glasgow.

McGibbon, John - Private
22781 Machine Gun Corps (Infantry) 57th Battalion *Age 25 Died of Wounds on 13 September 1918*
ST. SEVER CEMETERY EXTENSION, ROUEN, France
Son of Felix McGibbon; husband of Jane McGibbon, of 152, Falls Road, Belfast
Formerly 4054 6th Connaught Rangers.

McGill, Owen - Rifleman
6860 Royal Irish Rifles "B" Company 1st Battalion *Killed in Action on 25 September 1915*
PLOEGSTEERT MEMORIAL, Belgium
Husband of Jane McGill, of 21, St. James Place, Belfast.

McGill, William - Private
8003 Highland Light Infantry 10th (Service) Battalion *Died in War on 18 December 1915*
YPRES (MENIN GATE) MEMORIAL, Belgium
Born in Belfast, enlisted Glasgow.

McGilton, James - Rifleman
15/15409 Royal Irish Rifles 15th Battalion *Age 27 Killed in Action on 13 October 1916*
ST. QUENTIN CABARET MILITARY CEMETERY, Belgium
Son of Hugh and Jane McGilton, of 62, Henry Street, Belfast.

McGimpsey, Robert - Private
30881 Royal Inniskilling Fusiliers 8th Battalion *Died in War on 7 August 1917*
YPRES (MENIN GATE) MEMORIAL, Belgium
Native of Belfast, enlisted in Omagh.

McGimpsey, Samuel - Sergeant
524611 Canadian Army Medical Corps *Age 51 Died of sickness on 16 August 1921*
VICTORIA (ROSS BAY) CEMETERY, Canada
Son of Thomas and Mary McGimpsey, of 27, Oakland Avenue, Bloomfield, Belfast, Ireland; husband of Elsie McGimpsey, of 829, Short Street, Saanich, Victoria, British Columbia.
A Presbyterian who, in Canada, worked as salesman.

McGinley, Bernard - Private
3844 Royal Irish Fusiliers 1st Battalion *Age 21 Died of Wounds on 3 May 1917*
LEVEL CROSSING CEMETERY, FAMPOUX, France
Son of John and Sarah McGinley, of Belfast; husband of Mary McGinley, of 33, Lucknow Street, Belfast.

McGinn, David - Private
13182 Royal Inniskilling Fusiliers 5th Battalion *Died of Wounds on 27 October 1918*
ST. SEVER CEMETERY EXTENSION, ROUEN, *France*
39, Nail Street, Belfast.

McGinn, Hugh - Rifleman
9776 Royal Irish Rifles 2nd Battalion *Killed in Action on 24 March 1918*
POZIERES MEMORIAL, *France*
Born in Belfast, enlisted Newtownards.

McGinn, James - Private
2487 Irish Guards 1st Battalion *Died in War on 6 November 1914*
YPRES (MENIN GATE) MEMORIAL, *Belgium*
26, Lawnbrook Avenue, Belfast.

McGinney, Patrick Joseph - Private
2408 Connaught Rangers 6th Battalion *Age 23 Died in War on 3 September 1916*
DELVILLE WOOD CEMETERY, LONGUEVAL, *France*
Son of Mrs. Mary E. McGinney, of 34, Balham Street, Belfast.

McGinty, George - Private
23062 Royal Irish Fusiliers 9th Battalion *Died in War on 1 July 1916*
THIEPVAL MEMORIAL, *France*
113, Fortingale Street Belfast.

McGinty, Joseph - Private
Royal Irish Fusiliers *Died in War*
113, Fortingale Street Belfast.

McGivern, James - Driver
DM2/154881 Army Service Corps Y Siege Park *Accidentally killed while on active service on 5 October 1917*
LIJSSENTHOEK MILITARY CEMETERY, *Belgium*
35, Wall Street, Belfast.

McGivern, Michael - Corporal
6808 Royal Irish Rifles 2nd Battalion *Killed in Action on 17 December 1914*
YPRES (MENIN GATE) MEMORIAL, *Belgium*
Husband of Mary Anne McGivern, 38, Merrion Street, Belfast.

McGladdery, John - Rifleman
8821 Royal Irish Rifles 1st Battalion *Died in War on 28 March 1918*
Born and enlisted in Belfast.

McGlade, Daniel - Private
3490 Connaught Rangers 6th Battalion *Died in War on 31 July 1916*
LONGUENESSE (ST. OMER) SOUVENIR CEMETERY, *France*
Born and enlisted in Belfast.

McGlade, James - Private
10147 Royal Irish Rifles 2nd Battalion *Killed in Action on 27 October 1914*
LE TOURET MEMORIAL, *France*
Mother, brother and sister lived at 83, Argyle Street, Belfast.

McGlade, John - Private
24067 Princess Victoria's (Royal Irish Fusiliers) 1st Battalion *Died in War on 24 June 1917*
ARRAS MEMORIAL, France
Born and enlisted in Belfast.

McGladrigan, James - Private
15901 Royal Irish Fusiliers transferred to 498732 Labour Corps *Died in War on 28 September 1918*
BELFAST (MILLTOWN) ROMAN CATHOLIC CEMETERY, United Kingdom
Husband of M. McGladrigan, of 143, McDonald Street, Belfast.

McGlenaghan, John Henry - Rifleman
66 Royal Irish Rifles 15th Battalion *Killed in Action 21 March 1918*
POZIERES MEMORIAL, France
Born and enlisted in Belfast.

McGouran, George - Driver
T4/142506 Royal Army Service Corps *Died in War on 5 April 1916*
BELFAST(MILLTOWN) ROMAN CATHOLIC CEMETERY, United Kingdom
Born and enlisted in Belfast.

McGoveran, Patrick Joseph - Rifleman
O/711 Rifle Brigade 1st Battalion *Age 22 Died in War on 10 August 1918*
LOOS MEMORIAL, France
Son of Patrick Edward and Louisa McGoveran, of 89, Killowen Street, Belfast.

McGovern, James - Stoker First Class
SS/107748 Royal Navy HMS "Euryalus" *Died in War on 24 November 1916*
ISMAILIA WAR MEMORIAL CEMETERY, Egypt
Son of James McGovern, of 35, Winetavern Street, Belfast.

McGowan, Arthur Patrick - Lance Corporal
8217 Royal Irish Fusiliers 2nd Battalion *Died in War on 15 March 1915*
YPRES (MENIN GATE) MEMORIAL, Belgium
Lived on Antrim Road, Belfast. Born in Rathmullan, County Donegal.

McGowan, Frederick - Lance Corporal
10520 Royal Scots (Lothian Regiment) 2nd Battalion *Died in War on 7 November 1914*
LA GORGUE COMMUNAL CEMETERY, France
Born in Dover, enlisted and resident in Belfast.

McGowan, James - Private
6950 Connaught Rangers 5th Battalion *Died in War on 8 December 1917*
KANTARA WAR MEMORIAL CEMETERY, Egypt
Born and enlisted in Belfast.

McGowan, John - Private
30506 East Lancashire Regiment "Y" Company 11th Battalion *Age 20 Died in War on 27 March 1918*
ARRAS MEMORIAL, France
Son of James and Elizabeth McGowan, of 4, Comber Street, Belfast.

McGowan, Patrick - Private
4154 Manchester Regiment 12th Battalion *Died in War on 7 July 1916*
THIEPVAL MEMORIAL, France
28, Burnaby Street, Belfast.

Journey of Remembering

McGowan, Thomas - Private
4218 Seaforth Highlanders 5th Battalion *Age 24 Died of Wounds on 28 July 1916*
ST. SEVER CEMETERY, ROUEN, France
Son of Moses and Jane McGowan, of 37, New North Queen Street, Belfast.

McGowan, W J - Private
30834 Auckland Regiment New Zealand Expeditionary Force 2nd Battalion
Age 25 Killed in Action on 21 October 1917
TYNE COT MEMORIAL, Belgium
Son of Marianne McGowan, of 34A, Antrim Road, Belfast, Ireland, and the late George McGowan.

McGrady, Hugh - Rifleman
7045 Royal Irish Rifles 1st Battalion *Age 19 Died in War on 9 May 1915*
PLOEGSTEERT MEMORIAL, Belgium
Son of Hugh V. and Jane McGrady, of 50, Raglan Street, Belfast.

McGrady, James - Stoker First Class
K/21819 Royal Navy HMS "Gaillardia" *Age 24 Killed by mine explosion in North Sea on 22 March 1918*
CHATHAM NAVAL MEMORIAL, United Kingdom
Son of John and Ann Jane McGrady, of Belfast.

McGrady, John - Private
1599 Royal Munster Fusiliers 1st Battalion *Died in War on 17 October 1917*
BUCQUOY ROAD CEMETERY, FICHEUX, France
Born and enlisted in Belfast.

McGrady, William John - Stoker First Class
SS/110738 Royal Navy HMS "Cheerful" *Age 26 Killed by a mine explosion off Shetland Islands on 30 June 1917*
CHATHAM NAVAL MEMORIAL, United Kingdom
Son of John and Ann Jane McGrady, of 55, Grove Street, Belfast.

McGrath, Arthur - Private
4323 Royal Munster Fusiliers 8th Battalion *Died in War on 24 January 1916*
MAZINGARBE COMMUNAL CEMETERY, France
Born in Coleraine, enlisted and resident in Belfast. Formerly 2217 Royal Irish Regiment

McGrath, Charles - Private
26445 Royal Inniskilling Fusiliers 2nd Battalion *Died in War on 23 November 1916*
FRANKFURT TRENCH BRITISH CEMETERY, BEAUMONT-HAMEL, France
Born in Belfast, enlisted Antrim. Formerly 8/1566 Royal Munster Fusiliers

McGrath, David - Trimmer
7920TS Royal Naval Reserve H.M. Trawler "Thomas Cornwall"
Age 50 Drowned through collision off Flamborough Head on 29 October 1918
PORTSMOUTH NAVAL MEMORIAL, United Kingdom
Father of Evelyn McGrath, of 21, Lorton Street, Belfast.

McGrath, James - Private
24705 Royal Inniskilling Fusiliers 7th Battalion *Age 22 Died in War on 11 June 1916*
PHILOSOPHE BRITISH CEMETERY, MAZINGARBE, France
Son of James and Mary McGrath, of 24, Colligan Street, Belfast.

McGrath, James - Private
2967 Leinster Regiment 2nd Battalion *Killed in Action on 21 March 1918*
MEZIERES COMMUNAL CEMETERY EXTENSION, France
Born and enlisted in Belfast.

McGrath, James - Rifleman
375 Royal Irish Rifles 16th Battalion *Age 30 Died in War on 16 April 1918*
CANADA FARM CEMETERY, Belgium
Son of Mary Ann McGrath, of 64, Connaught Street, Belfast.

McGrath, John - Private
532318 London Regiment (Prince of Wales' Own Civil Service Rifles) 2nd/15th Battalion
Age 32 Died in War on 31 October 1917
BEERSHEBA WAR CEMETERY, Israel
Son of John and Mary E. McGrath, of 64, Cooke Street, Belfast.

McGrath, John Robert - Stoker First Class
SS/103926 Royal Navy HMS "Conquest" *Age 28 Died in War on 28 March 1916*
WALTON-ON-THE-NAZE (OR WALTON-LE-SOKEN) (ALL SAINTS) CHURCHYARD EXTENSION, United Kingdom
Son of Annie McGrath, of 6, Ludlow Street, Belfast, and the late Thomas McGrath.

McGrath, Joseph - Private
9702 Royal Inniskilling Fusiliers 2nd Battalion *Age 23 Died in War on 16 May 1915*
LE TOURET MEMORIAL, France
Son of Mrs. Margaret McGrath, of 128, Roseberry Road, Belfast.

McGreevy, Hugh - Rifleman
8250 Royal Irish Rifles 2nd Battalion *Killed in Action on 15 September 1914*
LA FERTE -SOUS-JOUARRE MEMORIAL, France
Born and enlisted in Belfast.

McGreevy, John - Fireman and Trimmer
Mercantile Marine S.S. "War Clover" (London)
Age 36 Drowned, as a result of an attack by an enemy submarine on 19 October 1917
TOWER HILL MEMORIAL, United Kingdom
Son of the late John and Margaret McGreevy; husband of Annie McGreevy (née Rice),
of 20, Moffat Street, Belfast.

McGreevy, Joseph - Private
29569 Royal Inniskilling Fusiliers 1st Battalion *Age 19 Died in War on 27 January 1917*
THIEPVAL MEMORIAL, France
Son of Mrs. Isabella McGreevy, of 18, Watson Street, Belfast.

McGregor, John - Private
6080 Princess Victoria's (Royal Irish Fusiliers) 1st Battalion *Died in War on 26 February 1916*
NEWRY OLD CHAPEL ROMAN CATHOLIC CEMETERY, United Kingdom
Born in Belfast, enlisted Newry.

McGregor, William - Corporal
11900 The King's (Liverpool Regiment) "C" Company 1st Battalion *Age 19 Died in War on 23 April 1916*
LOOS BRITISH CEMETERY, France
Son of William John McGregor, born in Belfast.

McGrillen, Francis A - Private
837 Australian Infantry A.I.F. 6th Battalion *Died in War on 8 May 1915*
HELLES MEMORIAL, *Turkey*
52, Lagan Street, Belfast.

McGroarty, Joseph - Lance Corporal
15281 Royal Irish Fusiliers 7th/8th Battalion *Age 20 Died in War on 21 July 1917*
MENDINGHEM MILITARY CEMETERY, *Belgium*
Son of Bernard and Elizabeth McGroarty, of 55, Gracehill Street, Belfast. Born Banbridge, County Down.

McGrogan, James - Stoker
Mercantile Marine HMS "Magic II" *Age 38 Died in War on 2 April 1916*
BURIED IN A FAMILY PLOT IN MILLTOWN CEMETERY, *United Kingdom*
Killed by a boiler explosion on board a Belfast Steamship Company vessel, the "Magic II",
which had been pressed into Admiralty service as a hospital ship.

McGrogan, John - Gunner
71706 Royal Horse Artillery and Royal Field Artillery *Died in War on 26 August 1914*
LA FERTE -SOUS-JOUARRE MEMORIAL, *France*
Born and enlisted in Belfast.

McGucken, William H - Private
12881 Royal Irish Fusiliers 1st Battalion *Died in War on 9 June 1915*
YPRES (MENIN GATE) MEMORIAL, *Belgium*
Son of Elizabeth McGucken, 96, McTier Street, Belfast. A brother, James, also served.

McGuffin, James - Sergeant
11163 Lancashire Fusiliers 15th Battalion *Died in War on 13 September 1917*
ZUYDCOOTE MILITARY CEMETERY, *France*
Born in Belfast, enlisted Salford, England.

McGuigan, Henry - Private
2505 Royal Inniskilling Fusiliers 1st Battalion *Age 28 Died in War on 21 August 1915*
HELLES MEMORIAL, *Turkey*
Husband of Annie McCabe (formerly McGuigan), of 25, Bow Street, Belfast.

McGuigan, John - Private
12102 Royal Inniskilling Fusiliers 3rd Battalion *Died in War on 2 October 1915*
BELFAST (MILLTOWN) ROMAN CATHOLIC CEMETERY, *United Kingdom*
Husband of Jane McGuigan, of 31, Bow Street, Belfast.

McGuigan, John - Rifleman
4605 Royal Irish Rifles 1st Battalion *Age 39 Killed in Action on 23 October 1916*
THIEPVAL MEMORIAL, *France*
Brother of Mrs. Ellen Graham, of 18, Alton Street, Belfast.

McGuigan, Patrick - Rifleman
8121 Royal Irish Rifles 2nd Battalion *Age 25 Died of Wounds on 28 November 1914*
STOKE (OR STOKE ROCHFORD) (SS. MARY AND ANDREW) CHURCHYARD, EASTON, *United Kingdom*
Husband of Lizzie McGuigan, of 27, Bow Street, Belfast.

JOURNEY OF REMEMBERING

McGuiggan, John - Rifleman
16751 Royal Irish Rifles 14th Battalion *Died in War on 15 August 1917*
YPRES (MENIN GATE) MEMORIAL, Belgium
9, Ceylon Street, Belfast.

McGuiggan, William - Rifleman
1355 Royal Irish Rifles 9th Battalion *Died in War on 8 July 1916*
CAUDRY OLD COMMUNAL CEMETERY, France
Son of Alexander and Mary, 9, Ceylon Street, Belfast.

McGuinn, John Francis - Sergeant
5097 Irish Guards 2nd Battalion *Age 23 Died of Wounds on 27 March 1916*
BRANDHOEK MILITARY CEMETERY, Belgium
Son of Thomas and Julia Ellen McGuinn, of Cashill, Tubbercurry, County Sligo.
Brother Charles lived at 34, Garfield Street, Belfast.

McGuinness, Daniel - Private
16352 Royal Irish Fusiliers 7th Battalion *Died in War on 12 November 1914*
TIPPERARY (ST. MICHAEL'S) NEW CEMETERY, Republic of Ireland
Husband of Mrs. McGuinness, of 7, Shamrock Terrace, Belfast.

McGuinness, Patrick - Private
7376 Cameronians (Scottish Rifles) 2nd Battalion *Died in War on 12 September 1916*
VERMELLES BRITISH CEMETERY, France
Born in Belfast, enlisted Hamilton, Scotland.

McGuinness, Philip - Private
T/307801 Army Service Corps 866th Company *Accidentally killed on 11 September 1917*
BELFAST (MILLTOWN) ROMAN CATHOLIC CEMETERY, United Kingdom
Husband of Margaret McGuinness, of 43, Raglan Street, Belfast. Born in Limavady.

McGuinnity, Charles - Steward
Mercantile Marine S.S. "Hesperian" (Glasgow) *Age 24 Drowned, as a result of an attack by an enemy submarine on 4 September 1915*
TOWER HILL MEMORIAL, United Kingdom
Son of Charles and Rose McGuinnity; husband of Emily McGuinnity (née Franson),
of 126, New Chester Road, Birkenhead. Born at Belfast and educated at Queen's College.

McGuirk, Charles - Private
2873 Irish Guards 1st Battalion *Age 25 Killed in Action on 4 September 1914*
GUARDS GRAVE, VILLERS COTTERETS FOREST, France
Son of of John F. McGuirk, of 17, Arizona Street, Belfast.

McGuirk, John - Private
5070 Connaught Rangers 5th Battalion *Died in War on 7 December 1915*
DOIRAN MEMORIAL CEMETERY, Greece
Born and enlisted in Belfast.

McGurk, Francis - Ordinary Seaman
Mercantile Marine S.S. "Teelin Head" (Belfast)
Age 20 Drowned, as a result of an attack by an enemy submarine on 21 January 1918
TOWER HILL MEMORIAL, United Kingdom
Son of James and Mary McGurk, of 13, Andrew Street, Belfast.

JOURNEY OF REMEMBERING

McGurk, James Joseph - Private
22695 Princess Victoria's (Royal Irish Fusiliers) 1st Battalion *Died in War on 23 November 1917*
CAMBRAI MEMORIAL LOUVERVAL, *France*
Born and enlisted in Belfast.

McGurk, Michael - Private
1732 Leinster Regiment 7th Battalion *Age 32 Died of Wounds on 18 April 1918*
WIMEREUX COMMUNAL CEMETERY, *France*
Son of Alice McGurk, of Belfast. Husband of Mary Ellen McGurk of 61, Norfolk Street, Belfast.

McHaffie, William - Private
19300 Royal Inniskilling Fusiliers 9th Battalion *Age 33 Killed in Action on 1 July 1916*
THIEPVAL MEMORIAL, *France*
Son of the late Peter and Isabel McHaffie, of Belmont, Belfast.

McHugh, William - Guardsman
3356 Scots Guards 1st Battalion *Died in War on 18 May 1916*
NIEDERZWEHREN CEMETERY, *Germany*
Born in Belfast, enlisted Hamilton, Scotland.

McIldoon, James - Rifleman
8699 Royal Irish Rifles 2nd Battalion *Age 27 Killed in Action on 2 May 1915*
RIDGE WOOD MILITARY CEMETERY, *Belgium*
Son of James and Margaret McIldoon, of 31, Oakley Street, Ballysillan, Belfast.

McIlheron, Daniel - Private
27563 Royal Inniskilling Fusiliers 7th Battalion *Age 35 Died in War on 20 August 1916*
PHILOSOPHE BRITISH CEMETERY, MAZINGARBE, *France*
Brother of Hugh McIlheron, of Glen Road Cottages, Andersonstown, Belfast.

McIlrath, James - Petty Officer Stoker
299009 Royal Navy HMS "Nottingham" *Age 32 Killed in Action with submarine in North Sea on 19 August 1916*
TYNEMOUTH (PRESTON) CEMETERY, *United Kingdom*
Son of John and Jane McIlrath, of Belfast; husband of Margaret McIlrath,
of 92, Riga Street, Belfast. Fifteen years' service.

McIlree, Henry - Rifleman
8/13191 Royal Irish Rifles 12th Battalion *Age 25 Died of Wounds on 25 October 1918*
HARLEBEKE NEW BRITISH CEMETERY, *Belgium*
Son of Mr. and Mrs. McIlree, of 60, Dundela Street, Strandtown, Belfast

McIlroy, David - Rifleman
1506 Royal Irish Rifles 2nd Battalion *Age 19 Killed in Action on 30 July 1918*
PLOEGSTEERT MEMORIAL, *Belgium*
Son of Mary McIlroy, of 11, St. Paul's Street, Belfast, and the late David McIlroy

McIlroy, David - Sergeant
6630 Royal Inniskilling Fusiliers 1st Battalion *Died of Wounds on 19 May 1915*
TWELVE TREE COPSE CEMETERY, *Turkey*
Son of Mrs McIlroy, 107, Silvio Street. Thought to be the brother-in-law of John Brown Savage
who was also killed with the 1st Inniskillings at the Dardanelles.

McIlroy, Samuel - Rifleman
1903 Royal Irish Rifles 14th Battalion *Age 26 Killed in Action on 1 July 1916*
CONNAUGHT CEMETERY, THIEPVAL, France
Son of David McIlroy, a cabinet maker who lived in Rugby Avenue. The family had emigrated to Blackstock, South Carolina, U.S.A. to run a cotton plantation.

McIlroy, Walter - Rifleman
5519 Royal Irish Rifles *Died in War on 11 March 1915*
BELFAST CITY CEMETERY, United Kingdom
41, Vernon Street, Belfast.

McIlroy, William - Lance Corporal
241159 Seaforth Highlanders 1st/5th Battalion *Age 33 Died in War on 9 April 1917*
ROCLINCOURT VALLEY CEMETERY, France
Son of Thomas Kelly, of 1, Emily Place, Belfast

McIlroy, William - Lance Corporal
9223 Royal Irish Rifles 2nd Battalion *Age 32 Killed in Action on 16 June 1915*
YPRES (MENIN GATE) MEMORIAL, Belgium
Son of the late William McIlroy; husband of Elizabeth McIlroy, of 31, Aberdeen Street, Belfast. An Orangeman and a member of the old UVF.

McIlveen, Robert - Stoker
2092U Royal Naval Reserve HMS"Juno" *Age 39 Died of heart disease on 23 November 1916*
PORTSMOUTH NAVAL MEMORIAL, United Kingdom
Son of William and Eliza McIlveen, of Belfast; husband of Agnes McIlveen, of 59, Cherryville Street, Belfast.

McIlveen, Thomas - Lance Corporal
460796 Canadian Infantry (Manitoba Regiment) 8th Battalion *Age 27 Died in War on 27 November 1916*
VILLERS STATION CEMETERY, VILLERS-AU-BOIS, France
Son of Joseph McIlveen, of Belfast, Ireland; husband of Mary McIlveen, of 245, Montrose Avenue, East Kildonan, Winnipeg. A Presbyterian, he had served in the Royal Irish Rifles and later worked as a salesman.

McIlveen, William - Company Sergeant Major
14/15416 Royal Irish Rifles15th Battalion *Died in War on 6 May 1918*
CANADA FARM CEMETERY, Belgium
Son of John McIlveen, 66, Westland Street, Belfast. Awarded the Distinguished Conduct Medal and Bar: "He won the D.C.M. at the capture of the Messines-Wytschaete Ridge, and gained a Bar to this decoration for gallantry during the opening of the German offensive."

McIlvenny, Peter - Private
267520 Seaforth Highlanders (Ross-shire Buffs, the Duke of Albany's) 6th Battalion
Died in War on 17 October 1917
ORPINGTON (ALL SAINTS) CHURCHYARD EXTENSION, United Kingdom
Son of Neil and Josephine McIlvenny, of 76, Hamilton Street, Govan, Glasgow. Born and enlisted in Belfast.

McIlvenny, Robert - Private
2502 Connaught Rangers 6th Battalion *Died in War on 9 October 1918*
MONS COMMUNAL CEMETERY, Belgium
Born and enlisted in Belfast.

McIlvenny, Samuel - Stoker First Class
SS/113434 Royal Navy HMS "Vanguard" *Age 22 Killed by internal explosion of vessel at Scapa Flow on 9 July 1917*
CHATHAM NAVAL MEMORIAL, *United Kingdom*
Son of W. H. and Elizabeth McIlvenny, of 22, Stratheden Street, Belfast.

McIlvenny, Thomas - Rifleman
15417 Royal Irish Rifles 9th Battalion *Age 38 Killed in Action on 1 July 1916*
THIEPVAL MEMORIAL, *France*
Son of Jane Beedham, of 8, McTier Street, Belfast.

McIlwaine, James C - Corporal
6992 South Lancashire Regiment 2nd Battalion *Died in War on 2 December 1914*
YPRES (MENIN GATE) MEMORIAL, *Belgium*
Son of William McIlwaine, 14, Acton Street, Belfast.

McIlwaine, John - Sergeant
18307 Royal Irish Rifles 12th Battalion *Killed in Action on 1 July 1916*
THIEPVAL MEMORIAL, *France*
Born Ballymacarrett, Belfast. Son of James and Annie McIlwaine of Carrickfergus.

McIlwaine, Samuel - Private
5122 Royal Munster Fusiliers 6th Battalion *Died in War on 15 August 1915*
HILL TEN CEMETERY, *Turkey*
Born and enlisted in Belfast. Formerly 13110 Royal Inniskilling Fusiliers

McIlwaine, William - Lance Corporal
8480 Royal Irish Rifles 2nd Battalion *Killed in Action on 7 July 1916*
THIEPVAL MEMORIAL, *France*
62, McDonnell Street, Belfast.

McIlwarth, John - Sergeant
6317 Royal Irish Rifles 1st Battalion *Killed in Action on 5 January 1915*
ROYAL IRISH RIFLES GRAVEYARD, LAVENTIE, *France*
Brother of William McIlwrath, of 109, Mayo Street, Belfast.

McIlwee, James - Private
7481 Connaught Rangers 6th Battalion *Died in War on 3 August 1917*
YPRES (MENIN GATE) MEMORIAL, *Belgium*
Resident of Belfast. Son of Patrick and Rose McIlwee and husband of Susan McIlwee, 2, Ballygolan Terrace. Born at Sion Mills, County Tyrone.

McIlwrath, Edward - Rifleman
G/15420 Royal Irish Rifles 15th Battalion *Age 29 Died of Wounds on 15 December 1917*
ROCQUIGNY-EQUANCOURT ROAD BRITISH CEMETERY, MANANCOURT, *France*
Son of James and Margaret McIlwrath, of Ligoniel, Belfast.

McIlwrath, James - Private
PLY/18372 Royal Marine Light Infantry 1st R.M. Battalion Royal Naval Division
Age 19 Died in War on 6 April 1918
POZIERES MEMORIAL, *France*
Son of Alexander and Sarah McIlwrath, of 8, Queen Victoria Street, Connswater, Belfast.

McIlwrath, James - Rifleman
1220 Royal Irish Rifles 9th Battalion *Died in War on 6 June 1916*
AUTHUILE MILITARY CEMETERY, France
Born and enlisted in Belfast.

McIlwrath, Martin - Rifleman
1658 Royal Irish Rifles 1st Battalion *Killed in Action on 13 August 1917*
MONT HOUN MILITARY CEMETERY, LE TREPORT, France
Born and enlisted in Belfast.

McIlwrath, Robert - Private
337 Royal Munster Fusiliers 2nd Battalion *Age 23 Died in War on 14 July 1916*
FRICOURT BRITISH CEMETERY, France
Son of James and Mary McIlwrath, of 12, Halliday's Road, Belfast.

McIlwrath, Samuel - Stoker
2045S Royal Naval Reserve HMS "Invincible" *Died in War on 31 May 1916*
PORTSMOUTH NAVAL MEMORIAL, United Kingdom
57, Hogarth Street, Belfast.

McIlwrath, William James - Rifleman
5893 Royal Irish Rifles 2nd Battalion *Age 32 Killed in Action on 27 October 1914*
LE TOURET MEMORIAL, France
Son of William John McIlwrath, of 20, Ardilaun Street, Belfast.

McIndoe, A - Rifleman
15/1001 Royal Irish Rifles 17th Battalion *Age 35 Died in War on 14 April 1917*
CARNMONEY CEMETERY, United Kingdom
Son of Alexander McIndoe; husband of Eliza McIndoe, of 1, Ivan Street, York Road, Belfast.

McIntee, Charles - Private
PLY/647(S) Royal Marine Light Infantry 2nd R.M. Battalion Royal Naval Division
Age 25 Died in War on 26 October 1917
TYNE COT MEMORIAL, Belgium
(Served as McCARTY), Son of Edward and Mary McIntee, of 17, Park Street, Belfast.

McIntosh, Archibald - Private
1310 Royal Irish Rifles 9th Battalion *Killed in Action on 1 July 1916*
THIEPVAL MEMORIAL, France
11 Edenderry Street, Belfast.

McIntosh, John - Rifleman
2849 Royal Irish Rifles "C" Company 15th Battalion *Age 20 Killed in Action on 7 June 1917*
YPRES (MENIN GATE) MEMORIAL, Belgium
Son of Harriett McIntosh, of 67, Meadow Street, Belfast.

McIntosh, John Campbell - Driver
101590 Royal Field Artillery 36th Battery 172nd Brigade *Age 18 Died in War on 12 June 1917*
BELFAST (DUNDONALD) CEMETERY, United Kingdom
Son of James and Lizzie McIntosh, of 163, Bloomfield Avenue, Belfast.

McIntyre, Daniel - Private
10327 Royal Inniskilling Fusiliers 1st Battalion *Died of Wounds on 29 July 1915*
TWELVE TREE COPSE CEMETERY, *Turkey*
Born and enlisted in Belfast.

McIntyre, Frederick - Rifleman
16755 Royal Irish Rifles "D" Company 14th Battalion *Age 19 Killed in Action on 1 July 1916*
THIEPVAL MEMORIAL, *France*
Son of William and Lizzie McIntyre, of 110, Ormeau Road, Belfast.

McIntyre, Gilbert - Private
11334 Royal Inniskilling Fusiliers 9th Battalion *Age 22 Killed in Action on 8 May 1916*
AUTHUILE MILITARY CEMETERY, *France*
Son of William and Catherine McIntyre, of 4, Bootle Street, Belfast.

McIntyre, John - Private
8288 Argyll & Sutherland Highlanders 2nd Battalion *Died in War on 30 April 1915*
RATION FARM MILITARY CEMETERY, LA CHAPELLE-D'ARMENTIERES, *France*
Born Ballymacarrett, Belfast, enlisted Paisley, Scotland. Resident Glasgow.

McIntyre, Robert - Private
S/20131 Cameron Highlanders 5th Battalion *Age 35 Died in War on 18 October 1916*
THIEPVAL MEMORIAL, *France*
Son of Annie McIntyre, and the late William McIntyre; husband of Eugenie McIntyre, of 4, Moore Street, Ravenhill Road, Belfast.

McIntyre, Robert William - Second Lieutenant
East Yorkshire Regiment 11th Battalion *Age 23 Died in War on 25 July 1918*
LE GRAND HASARD MILITARY CEMETERY, MORBECQUE, *France*
Son of Jeanie Isabel and the late John McIntyre, of Whittinghame Villa, 7, Knock Road, Knock, Belfast.
Awarded the MBE.

McIroy, Alfred - Private
14512 Princess Victoria's (Royal Irish Fusiliers) 1st Battalion *Died in War on 30 September 1918*
DADIZEELE NEW BRITISH CEMETERY, *Belgium*
Born in Belfast, enlisted Lurgan.

McIvers, Daniel - Lance Corporal
8945 Royal Irish Rifles 2nd Battalion *Killed in Action on 27 October 1914*
LE TOURET MEMORIAL, *France*
Raglan Street, Belfast.

McIvor, William - Rifleman
14/16756 Royal Irish Rifles 14th Battalion *Age 23 Killed in Action on 9 October 1916*
POND FARM CEMETERY, *Belgium*
Son of Hugh and Margery McIvor, of 176, Ainsworth Avenue, Belfast.

McIvor, William - Ship's Cook
Mercantile Marine S.S. "Teelin Head" (Belfast)
Age 26 Drowned, as a result of an attack by an enemy submarine on 21 January 1918
TOWER HILL MEMORIAL, *United Kingdom*
Son of Mrs. Susan McIvor, of 450, Oldpark Road, Belfast. Born in Antrim.

McKane, Adam - Sergeant
29286 Canadian Infantry (Manitoba Regiment) 16th Battalion *Died in War on 23 April 1915*
YPRES (MENIN GATE) MEMORIAL, Belgium
Husband of Mary E. McKane, of 6, Century Street, Belfast, Ireland.
A widower and a Presbyterian, he worked as a draughtsman.

McKay, Alexander - Gunner
10611 Royal Field Artillery 32nd Brigade *Age 35 Drowned on 19 June 1916*
DOULLENS COMMUNAL CEMETERY EXTENSION No.1, France
Son of John and Elizabeth McKay, of 34, Spamount Street, Belfast.

McKay, Edward - Private
21419 Royal Irish Fusiliers 8th Battalion *Died in War on 24 July 1916*
ST PATRICKS CEMETERY, LOOS, France
Born in Ardoyne, enlisted in Belfast.

McKay, Edward - Private
59966 Royal Scots (Lothian Regiment) 2nd Battalion *Died in War on 23 August 1918*
VIS-EN-ARTOIS MEMORIAL, HAUCOURT, France
Born and enlisted in Belfast.

McKay, Frank - Sergeant
242657 Royal Warwickshire Regiment 1st/6th Battalion *Age 22 Died of Wounds on 22 August 1917*
LIJSSENTHOEK MILITARY CEMETERY, Belgium
Son of Francis McKay, of 25, Plevna Street, Belfast. Won the Distinguished Conduct Medal

McKay, Joseph - Private
4418 Connaught Rangers 6th Battalion *Died in War on 20 November 1917*
CROISILLES RAILWAY CEMETERY, France
Brother of Mrs Johnston, 4 Cape Street, Belfast.

McKay, Patrick H. - Corporal
13168 Royal Irish Fusiliers 7th Battalion *Age 45 Died in War on 29 April 1916*
BETHUNE TOWN CEMETERY, France
Husband of E. McKay, of 1, Currell's Place, Belfast.

McKay, Robert - Rifleman
7476 Royal Irish Rifles 2nd Battalion *Killed in Action on 20 September 1914*
VAILLY BRITISH CEMETERY, France
Born and enlisted in Belfast.

McKean, James - Leading Seaman
209507 Royal Navy HMS "Laurentic" *Age 32 Killed by mine explosion off the north Irish coast on 25 January 1917*
PLYMOUTH NAVAL MEMORIAL, United Kingdom
Son of James and Mary Ann McKean, of 24, Canning Street, Belfast.

McKeaveney, Thomas - Private
156 Royal Army Medical Corps 17th Field Ambulance *Age 29 Died in War on 29 May 1916*
LIJSSENTHOEK MILITARY CEMETERY, Belgium
Son of John and Alice McKeaveney, of 175, Durham Street, Belfast; husband of Elizabeth McKeaveney, of Dunbought, Clough, County Antrim.

Journey of Remembering

McKechnie, Robert - Lance Corporal
18314 Royal Irish Rifles 11th Battalion *Age 21 Killed in Action on 1 July 1916*
THIEPVAL MEMORIAL, France
Son of James and Janet McKechnie, of Milfort Avenue, Dunmurry, Belfast.

McKee, Alexander - Lieutenant
Royal Irish Rifles 10th Battalion *Age 35 Killed in Action on 22 November 1917*
CAMBRAI MEMORIAL, LOUVERVAL, France
Son of Agnes McKee, of 20, Madison Avenue, Antrim Road, Belfast, and the late Alexander McKee.

McKee, Henry - Able Seaman
SS/3388 Royal Navy HMS "Natal" *Age 25 Killed by internal explosion of vessel in Cromarty Firth on 30 December 1915*
CHATHAM NAVAL MEMORIAL, United Kingdom
Son of John and Elizabeth McKee, of Beaumont Lodge, Malone Road, Belfast.

McKee, Hiram W. H. - Private
871945 Canadian Infantry 183rd Battalion *Age 44 Died in War on 29 November 1916*
BRANDON CEMETERY, Canada
Son of Jane Harvey McKee, of 19, Cavehill Road, Belfast, Ireland, and the late John Ritchie McKee.
A Presbyterian, he worked in Canada as an accountant.

McKee, James - Rifleman
19/351 Royal Irish Rifles 8th Battalion *Died in War on 7 June 1917*
LONE TREE CEMETERY, Belgium
Son of Mrs. A. McKee, of 46, Solway Street, Belfast.

McKee, John - Private
6546 Lancashire Fusiliers 1st Battalion *Died in War on 4 June 1915*
TWELVE TREE COPSE CEMETERY, Turkey
Born in Belfast, enlisted Salford, England.

McKee, Patrick Joseph - Lieutenant
Royal Irish Rifles 3rd Battalion attached 2nd Battalion *Age 28 Died in War on 10 August 1918*
YPRES (MENIN GATE) MEMORIAL, Belgium
Born in Belfast and baptized in St Mary's Catholic Church. Educated at St Mary's School and King's College London. Served with Queen's University Officer Training Corps and as a private soldier before being commissioned.

McKee, Robert - Private
6607 Royal Irish Regiment 4th Battalion *Died on 6 December 1917*
ROSSGLASS (ST. MARY STAR OF THE SEA) ROMAN CATHOLIC CHURCHYARD, COUNTY DOWN, United Kingdom
Born and enlisted in Belfast.

McKee, Thomas - Private
15269 Royal Irish Rifles 9th Battalion *Age 33 Died of Wounds on 6 June 1916*
FORCEVILLE COMMUNAL CEMETERY AND EXTENSION, France
Husband of Jane McKee, 44, Ashmore Street, Belfast.

McKee, Walter - Private
241071 Seaforth Highlanders 5th Battalion *Age 19 Killed in Action on 31 July 1917*
YPRES (MENIN GATE) MEMORIAL, Belgium
Son of Samuel and Mary McKee, of 153, Avoniel Road, Belfast.

McKee, William - Corporal
4885 Royal Irish Rifles 2nd Battalion *Died in War on 30 August 1916*
PUCHEVILLERS BRITISH CEMETERY, France
Born and enlisted in Downpatrick, resident of Belfast.

McKee, William - Private
10339 Royal Inniskilling Fusiliers 1st Battalion *Died in War on 21 August 1915*
HELLES MEMORIAL, Turkey
Son of Mary Jane McKee, of 134, Boundary Street, Shankill Road, Belfast, and the late William McKee.

McKee, William Dickson - Lieutenant
Royal Irish Rifles 12th Battalion *Age 22 Died in War on 11 August 1917*
YPRES (MENIN GATE) MEMORIAL, Belgium
Son of the late Samuel McKee, of 35, Cyprus Park, Bloomfield, Belfast. Mentioned in the London Gazette for "services rendered in Ireland in 1916".

McKeever, J - Rifleman
7189 Royal Irish Rifles 4th Battalion *Died in War on 14 March 1915*
BELFAST (MILLTOWN) ROMAN CATHOLIC CEMETERY, United Kingdom
Son of Mrs. C. McKeever, of 34, Plevna Street, Belfast.

McKegney, William Ernest - Private
404903 Canadian Infantry (Central Ontario Regiment) 20th Battalion
Age 24 Killed in Action on 28 August 1918
VIS-EN-ARTOIS BRITISH CEMETERY, HAUCOURT, France
Son of Adam and Mary McKegney, of 262, Woodstock Road, Belfast, Ireland.
A single man and a Anglican he had been born in the USA and had worked as a clerk.

McKelvey, Adam - Rifleman
15431 Royal Irish Rifles 9th Battalion *Died in War on 15 December 1917*
ST SEVER CEMETERY EXTENSION ROUEN, France
Born and enlisted in Belfast.

McKendrick, Andrew - Corporal
266783 Black Watch 6th Battalion *Died in War on 7 April 1917*
ARRAS MEMORIAL, France
Chichester Avenue, Belfast.

McKendry, Hugh - Private
6086 Royal Irish Rifles 7th Battalion *Died of Wounds on 25 July 1916*
LONGUENESSE (ST. OMER) SOUVENIR CEMETERY, France
Husband of Margaret McKendry, 7 Bracken Street, Belfast.

McKendry, James - Private
2798 Royal Irish Rifles 9th Battalion *Killed in Action on 1 July 1916*
CONNAUGHT CEMETERY, THIEPVAL, France
129, Bellevue Street, Belfast.

McKendry, William - Private (Signaller)
2815 Royal Inniskilling Fusiliers "D" Company 2nd Battalion *Age 24 Killed in Action on 23 March 1918*
POZIERES MEMORIAL, France
Son of Mrs. Margaret McKendry, of 125, Bellevue Street, Shankill Road, Belfast.

Journey of Remembering

McKenna, Charles - Lance Corporal
8415 Royal Irish Rifles 1st Battalion *Age 29 Died of Wounds on 26 September 1915*
LIJSSENTHOEK MILITARY CEMETERY, Belgium
Son of Charles and Elizabeth McKenna, of Belfast; husband of M. McKenna, of Chapel House, Bishopgate Street, Mullingar, County Westmeath.

McKenna, Daniel - Sergeant
2195 Connaught Rangers 6th Battalion *Died in War on 26 July 1916*
DUD CORNER CEMETERY, LOOS, France
Born, enlisted and resident in Belfast.

McKenna, Edward - Private
5174 Royal Munster Fusiliers 6th Battalion *Died in War on 9 August 1915*
HELLES MEMORIAL, Turkey
Born and enlisted in Belfast. Formerly 13789 Royal Inniskilling Fusiliers

McKenna, Henry - Private
4505 Royal Inniskilling Fusiliers 1st Battalion *Died in War on 19 June 1915*
TWELVE TREE COPSE CEMETERY, Turkey
Born and enlisted in Belfast.

McKenna, Hugh - Private First Class
231871 Royal Air Force (Eastern Mediterranean Group) *Age 24 Died of influenza on 10 December 1918*
LANCASHIRE LANDING CEMETERY, Turkey
Son of James McKenna, of 17, Martin Street, Belfast.

McKenna, James - Lance Corporal
10297 Royal Inniskilling Fusiliers 1st Battalion *Age 27 Died in War on 28 January 1917*
THIEPVAL MEMORIAL, France
Son of James McKenna; husband of Sarah McKenna, of 32, Maria Place, Belfast.

McKenna, James Joseph - Private
10411 Royal inniskilling Fusiliers 2nd Battalion *Died of Wounds on 14 December 1914*
BOULOGNE EASTERN CEMETERY, France
Born and enlisted in Belfast.

McKenna, John - Private
3641 Royal Inniskilling Fusiliers Depot *Died on 29 September 1916*
Born and enlisted in Belfast.

McKenna, John - Private
45029 Loyal North Lancashire Regiment 15th Battalion *Died in War on 13 September 1918*
HAGLE DUMP CEMETERY, Belgium
Born in Belfast, enlisted in Cardiff. Formerly 72745, Royal Welsh Fusiliers.

McKenna, John Henry - Private
2328 Connaught Rangers 6th Battalion *Died in War on 7 June 1917*
IRISH HOUSE CEMETERY, Belgium
Born, enlisted and resident in Belfast.

McKenna, Joseph - Corporal
13000 Royal Inniskilling Fusiliers "C" Company 8th Battalion *Age 31 Killed in Action on 16 August 1917*
TYNE COT MEMORIAL, Belgium
Son of Patrick and Catherine McKenna, of 122, New Lodge Road, Belfast; husband of Ellen McKenna, of 3, Union Place, Dungannon, County Tyrone.

McKenna, Patrick J - Gunner
119411 Royal Field Artillery 115th Brigade *Age 23 Killed in Action on 6 October 1918*
MIKRA BRITISH CEMETERY, KALAMARIA, Greece
Son of James and Susan McKenna, of 26, Peel Street, Belfast.

McKenna, Robert - Ordinary Seaman
J/31862 Royal Navy HMS "Invincible" *Age 18 Killed in Action at Battle of Jutland on 31 May 1916*
PLYMOUTH NAVAL MEMORIAL, United Kingdom
Ward of David McDowell, of School Buildings, Belfast Union, Belfast.

McKenna, William Dominick - Private
138491 Canadian Infantry (Central Ontario Regiment) 75th Battalion *Age 28 Died in War on 24 October 1916*
VIMY MEMORIAL, France
Son of William and Katherine McKenna, of Belfast, Ireland; husband of Sarah Gibson McKenna, of 119-08, Inwood Street, Ozone Park, New York, U.S.A.

McKenzie, Francis Murray - Sergeant
41084 Royal Army Medical Corps 66th General Hospital *Age 44 Died of accidental injuries on 1 January 1918*
BORDIGHERA BRITISH CEMETERY, Italy
Husband of Mary Elizabeth McKenzie, of 4, Finimore Street, Belfast.

McKenzie, Kenneth - Waiter
Mercantile Marine S.S. "Lusitania" (Liverpool)
Age 25 Drowned, as a result of an attack by an enemy submarine on 7 May 1915
COBH OLD CHURCH CEMETERY, Republic of Ireland
Son of the late Kenneth and Ellen McKenzie. Born at Belfast.

McKenzie, Maurice - Private
3602 Leinster Regiment 2nd Battalion *Died in War on 11 December 1916*
PHILOSOPHE BRITISH CEMETERY, MAZINGARBE, France
Born and enlisted in Belfast.

McKenzie, Robert - Private
8702 Durham Light Infantry 2nd Battalion *Died in War on 9 August 1915*
YPRES (MENIN GATE) MEMORIAL, Belgium
Born in Belfast, enlisted in Jarrow, England.

McKenzie, Thomas - Rifleman
10217 Royal Irish Rifles 2nd Battalion *Age 18 Died in War on 16 June 1915*
YPRES (MENIN GATE) MEMORIAL, Belgium
Son of George McKenzie, of 80, Convention Street, Belfast.

McKenzie, William - Private
14349 Royal Army Medical Corps *Age 20 Died as a result of war on 30 June 1920*
BAGHDAD (NORTH GATE) WAR CEMETERY, Iraq
Son of Robert and Elizabeth McKenzie, of 19, Upper Mervue Street, Belfast.

Journey of Remembering

McKeown, Daniel - Private
25203 Princess Victoria's (Royal Irish Fusiliers) 1st Battalion *Died in War on 11 April 1917*
BROWN'S COPSE CEMETERY, ROEUX, *France*
Born in Belfast enlisted Dublin.

McKeown, David - Private
14440 Royal Inniskilling Fusiliers 2nd Battalion *Died in War on 27 September 1916*
CAMBRIN CHURCHYARD EXTENSION, *France*
Born and enlisted in Belfast.

McKeown, Francis - Rifleman
G/638 Royal Irish Rifles 1st Garrison Battalion *Age 54 Died in War on 23 April 1918*
BELFAST (MILLTOWN) ROMAN CATHOLIC CEMETERY, *United Kingdom*
Son of James and Mary McKeown, of Belfast.

McKeown, James - Private
2425 Leinster Regiment 7th Battalion *Died in War on 12 May 1916*
PHILOSOPHE BRITISH CEMETERY, MAZINGARBE, *France*
Born and enlisted in Belfast.

McKeown, James - Sapper
10368 Royal Engineers *Killed in Action on 16 August 1917*
DOZINGHEM MILITIARY CEMETERY, *Belgium*
Born County Tyrone, enlisted and resident in Belfast.

McKeown, John - Private
3457 8th (King's Royal Irish) Hussars *Died in War on 22 March 1918*
POZIERES MEMORIAL, *France*
Born and enlisted in Belfast.

McKeown, John - Rifleman
5722 Royal Irish Rifles 2nd Battalion *Age 22 Killed in Action on 16 June 1915*
YPRES (MENIN GATE) MEMORIAL, *Belgium*
Son of Douglas McKeown, of 9, Conlig Street, Belfast; husband of Ellen McKeown,
of 59, Conlon Street, Belfast.

McKeown, John Harold - Second Lieutenant
Connaught Rangers 5th Battalion attached 1st Battalion *Age 22 Died in War on 5 October 1917*
BAGHDAD (NORTH GATE) WAR CEMETERY, *Iraq*
Born the son of Captain John and Eleanor McKeown of Glantane Street, Belfast. Educated privately
and a member of Queen's University, Belfast. A former choir boy in Belfast Cathedral.

McKeown, Joseph - Lance Corporal
2256 Connaught Rangers 6th Battalion *Died in War on 17 May 1917*
LEICESTER (WELFORD ROAD) CEMETERY, *United Kingdom*
Born, enlisted and resident in Belfast.

McKeown, Joseph Bernard - Ship's Cook
Mercantile Marine S.S. "Clearfield" (Newcastle) *Age 25 Presumed drowned on 23 October 1916*
TOWER HILL MEMORIAL, *United Kingdom*
Son of Felix and Mary McKeown, of 3 & 5, Dock Street, Belfast.

McKeown, Terence - Private
231799 Labour Corps *Died in War on 6 January 1918*
BELFAST (MILLTOWN) ROMAN CATHOLIC CEMETERY, *United Kingdom*
Born and enlisted in Belfast. Formerly 10641 Royal Irish Fusiliers.

McKeown, William - Lance Corporal
17344 Highland Light Infantry 10th (Service) Battalion *Died in War on 25 September 1915*
LOOS MEMORIAL, *France*
Born in Belfast, enlisted Rutherglen, Scotland.

McKeown, William - Lance Corporal
18320 Royal Irish Rifles 14th Battalion *Age 24 Died in War on 1 July 1916*
THIEPVAL MEMORIAL, *France*
Son of F. R. and A. McKeown, of 6, Cregagh Road, Belfast.

McKeown, William - Rifleman
2997 Royal Irish Rifles 11th Battalion *Killed in Action on 1 July 1916*
THIEPVAL MEMORIAL, *France*
Born in Belfast, enlisted Lisburn.

McKernan, Edward - Sergeant
21108 Royal Inniskilling Fusiliers 7th Battalion *Age 35 Died in War on 16 August 1917*
TYNE COT MEMORIAL, *Belgium*
Husband of Annie M. McKernan, of 8, Devonshire Street, Belfast. Awarded the Military Medal.

McKernan, James - Rifleman
5699 Royal Irish Rifles "C" Company 7th Battalion *Age 17 Died in War on 9 September 1916*
THIEPVAL MEMORIAL, *France*
Son of George and Mary A. McKernan, of 15, Convention Street, Belfast.

McKernan, Thomas H - Sergeant
8/13162 Royal Irish Rifles "D" Company 8th Battalion *Age 21 Killed in Action on 30 November 1916*
RATION FARM (LA PLUS DOUVE) ANNEXE, *Belgium*
Son of George and M. A. McKernan, of 15, Convention Street, Belfast. Mentioned in Despatches

McKernon, John - Private
2437 Connaught Rangers 6th Battalion *Age 20 Died of Wounds (gas) on 29 April 1916*
BETHUNE TOWN CEMETERY, *France*
Son of Annie McKernon, of Collinward Terrace, Whitewell, Belfast, and the late John McKernon. A native of Crumlin, County Antrim.

McKevitt, Patrick - Private
1653 Leinster Regiment 2nd Battalion *Killed in Action on 27 March 1918*
POZIERES MEMORIAL, *France*
Born in Newry, enlisted and resident in Belfast.

McKibbin, Hugh - Private
3207 Australian Infantry 52nd Battalion *Age 21 Died of Wounds on 27 August 1917*
TROIS ARBRES CEMETERY, STEENWERCK, *France*
Son of Martha McKibbin, of 184, Templemore Street, Belfast, Ireland, and the late James McKibbin.

McKibbin, Robert - Rifleman
1813005 Royal Irish Rifles 11th Battalion *Age 27 Died of Wounds on 1 July 1916*
FORCEVILLE COMMUNAL CEMETERY AND EXTENSION, France
Son of James and Mary McKibbin, of Belfast.

McKievor, B - Sergeant
Supply & Transport Corps *Died in War*
McDonnell Street, Belfast.

McKillen, Charles - Lance Corporal
27036 Royal Dublin Fusiliers 9th Battalion *Age 18 Died on 18 August 1917 of Wounds received 16 August*
LIJSSENTHOEK MILITARY CEMETERY, Belgium
Son of James and Frances McKillen, of Belfast.

McKillen, George Wallace - Rifleman
1512 Royal Irish Rifles 10th Battalion *Killed In Action on 1 July 1916*
MILL ROAD CEMETERY, THIEPVAL, France
Born and enlisted in Belfast.

McKillen, Patrick - Lance Corporal
2394 Connaught Rangers 6th Battalion *Died in War on 7 August 1917*
BRANDHOEK NEW MILITARY CEMETERY, Belgium
Son of John and Catherine McKillen, of 60, Oranmore Street. Employed in Clonard Mills and a member of the Belfast Regiment of the Irish National Volunteers. Commended by General Hickie for devotion to duty while under sustained attack.

McKimm, James - Private
M2/193481 Royal Army Service Corps *Died in War on 12 October 1916*
NEWTOWNARDS (MOVILLA) CEMETERY, United Kingdom
Born in Newtownards, enlisted and resident in Belfast.

McKinley, George Thomas - Lance Corporal
9471 Royal Irish Rifles 2nd Battalion *Killed in Action on 23 August 1914*
LA FERTE-SOUS-JOUARRE MEMORIAL, France
Son of John and Jane McKinley of 79, Upper Meadow Street. Possibly the first Belfast soldier to be killed in the Great War. He was riddled with German machine gun bullets.

McKinley, Hugh - Rifleman
9220 Royal Irish Rifles 1st Battalion *Age 22 Killed in Action on 26 October 1916*
THIEPVAL MEMORIAL, France
Son of Elizabeth Young (formerly McKinley), of "Wynella", 117, Cregagh Road, Belfast, and the late John McKinley.

McKinley, James - Rifleman
5874 Royal Irish Rifles 2nd Battalion *Killed in Action on 7 July 1916*
THIEPVAL MEMORIAL, France
Born and enlisted in Belfast.

McKinney, Felix - Private
2386 Connaught Rangers 6th Battalion *Died in War on 5 March 1916*
QUARRY CEMETERY VERMELLES, France
Born, enlisted and resident in Belfast.

McKinney, James - Staff Sergeant
TS/10610 Royal Army Service Corps *Died in War on 12 July 1918*
BELFAST (MILLTOWN) ROMAN CATHOLIC CEMETERY, *United Kingdom*
Born in Belfast, enlisted in Aldershot, England.

McKinney, William Finlay - Carpenter
Mercantile Marine Reserve HMS "Andes" *Age 27 Accidentally drowned on 16 December 1916*
PLYMOUTH NAVAL MEMORIAL, *United Kingdom*
Son of Samuel Moore McKinney and Margaret McKinney, of 44, Cheviot Avenue, Belfast.
Native of Carrickfergus.

McKinstry, James - Sergeant
327 Royal Irish Rifles 15th Battalion *Died in War on 26 March 1918*
POZIERES MEMORIAL, *France*
18, Lisavon Street, Belfast.

McKinstry, James McNeill - Second Lieutenant
Royal Inniskilling Fusiliers 2nd Battalion *Age 21 Died of Wounds, received at Beaumont Hamel on 2 December 1916*
WARLOY-BAILLON COMMUNAL CEMETERY EXTENSION, *France*
Son of A. R. and the late Robert McKinstry, of 16, Rugby Road, Belfast. Born in Cookstown, County Tyrone.

McKinstry, William - Private
28938 Royal Scots (Lothian Regiment) 1st G.N. Battalion *Died in War on 3 May 1916*
ALEXANDRIA (HADRA) WAR MEMORIAL CEMETERY, *Egypt*
Born in Belfast, enlisted in Hampshire, England. Formerly 3350, Highland Light Infantry

McKinstry, William - Rifleman
15304 Royal Irish Rifles 9th Battalion *Died in War on 10 February 1915*
BELFAST (DUNDONALD) CEMETERY, *United Kingdom*
Son of the late William and Elizabeth McKinstry; husband of Agnes McKinstry, of 53, Snugville Street, Belfast.

McKirdy, Alexander - Chief Engineer
Mercantile Marine Reserve HM Tug "Sonia" *Died as result of War on 23 February 1919*
CARNMONEY CEMETERY, *United Kingdom*
63, Gainsborough Drive, Belfast.

McKisack, Lawrence Hill Wilson - Lieutenant
Royal Flying Corps and 5th (Royal Irish) Lancers *Age 23 Killed in a flying accident at Thetford on 13 November 1916*
BELFAST CITY CEMETERY, *United Kingdom*
Son of Dr. H. L. McKisack, M.D., and Emily McKisack, of 88, University Road, Belfast. Born at Belfast.
Formerly served in the Royal Garrison Artillery and Royal Engineers.

McKissick, Thomas James - Rifleman
10/19624 Royal Irish Rifles 10th Battalion *Killed by shellfire on 13 August 1917*
YPRES (MENIN GATE) MEMORIAL, *Belgium*
Lived at 71, Clementine Street, Belfast. He left a wife and three children.
The family later emigrated to Canada.

McKnight, Alexander - Rifleman
15441 Royal Irish Rifles 9th Battalion *Age 20 Died in War on 7 June 1917*
LIJSSENTHOEK MILITARY CEMETERY, *Belgium*
Husband of Alice Crawford (formerly McKnight), of 30, Barrington Street, Belfast.

McKnight, David - Private
42302 Royal Irish Fusiliers 1st Battalion *Age 20 Died in War on 24 October 1918*
TYNE COT MEMORIAL, Belgium
Son of James McKnight, of 64, Hatton Drive, Belfast.

McKnight, James - Rifleman
13163 Royal Irish Rifles 9th Battalion *Died in War on 9 February 1916*
SUCRERIE MILITARY CEMETERY, COLINCAMPS, France
Youngest son of Samuel and Ellen McKnight, 236, Cupar Street, Belfast.

McKnight, Tom - Second Lieutenant
Royal Inniskilling Fusiliers 10th Battalion *Age 28 Killed in Action on 21 February 1917*
BERKS CEMETERY EXTENSION, Belgium
Son of Matilda McKnight, of 71, Alexandra Park Avenue, Belfast, and the late John McKnight.
Born Tillinkisy, Castledawson, County Londonderry.

McLarnen, Patrick James - Private
5087 Australian Infantry 49th Battalion *Age 25 Killed in Action on 21 October 1916*
RIDGE WOOD MILITARY CEMETERY, Belgium
Son of James and Rose Ann McLarnen; husband of Beatrice McLarnen,
of Upper Mongogarie, New South Wales. Native of Belfast, Ireland.

McLarnon, Francis - Rifleman
8670 Royal Irish Rifles 2nd Battalion *Died in War on 2 March 1915*
KEMMEL CHATEAU MILITARY CEMETERY, Belgium
18, Grosvenor Place, Belfast.

McLarnon, George - Rifleman
7286 Royal Irish Rifles 11th Battalion *Age 24 Killed in Action on 1 July 1916*
A.I.F. BURIAL GROUND, FLERS, France
Son of John and Ellen McLarnon, of Dunmurry, Belfast.

McLarnon, John - Private
1847 Duke of Wellington's (West Riding Regiment) "D" Company 1st/4th Battalion *Age 45 Killed in Action on 19 December 1915*
TALANA FARM CEMETERY, Belgium
Son of Michael and Margaret McLarnon, late of Marchioness Street, Belfast; husband of Agnes Cecelia
McLarnon, of 27, Launds, Golcar, Huddersfield. Served in the South African Campaign.

McLarnon, Michael Hugh - Gunner
1622 Australian Field Artillery 14th Brigade *Age 32 Died of Wounds on 16 August 1917*
VLAMERTINGHE NEW MILITARY CEMETERY, Belgium
Son of Henry and Mary McLarnon, of 26, Shore Street, Shore Road, Belfast, Ireland.

McLarnon, Robert - Bombardier
77073 Royal Field Artillery 149th Battery *Died in War on 10 September 1916*
STRUMA MILITARY CEMETERY, Greece
Son of Robert McLarnon, of 7, Sidney Street West, Belfast.

McLaughlan or McLoughlin, Thomas - Private
3/7410 Princess Louise's (Argyll & Sutherland Highlanders) 11th Battalion *Died in War on 22 May 1918*
CAMELON CEMETERY, United Kingdom
Born in Belfast, enlisted Falkirk, Scotland.

JOURNEY OF REMEMBERING

McLaughlin, Arthur M - Lieutenant
Royal Irish Rifles 3rd Battalion attached 1st Battalion *Age 20 Died in War on 9 May 1915*
PLOEGSTEERT MEMORIAL, *Belgium*
Born in Belfast, the son of William Henry McLaughlin, of McLaughlin & Harvey, and Emily Sophia McLaughlin. One brother also served and a second was killed in the Boer War. Educated at Monkton Combe School, Bath, and Jesus College, Cambridge.

McLaughlin, Charles - Rifleman
12042 Royal Irish Rifles 15th Battalion *Died in War on 22 November 1917*
THIEPVAL MEMORIAL, *France*
Born and enlisted in Belfast.

McLaughlin, John - Leading Seaman
176819 Royal Navy HMS "Hampshire" *Age 40 Killed by mine explosion off Orkneys on 5 June 1916*
PORTSMOUTH NAVAL MEMORIAL, *United Kingdom*
Son of John and Rachel McLaughlin; husband of Sarah McLaughlin, of 12, Hillview Street, Belfast. Served in the Naval Brigade under Sir George White at the Siege of Ladysmith.

McLaughlin, John - Private
1517 Princess Patricia's Canadian Light Infantry (Eastern Ontario Regiment) *Age 26 Died in War on 27 February 1915*
VOORMEZEELE ENCLOSURE No.3, *Belgium*
Son of Hugh and Agnes McLaughlin, of 61, South Parade, Belfast, Ireland.
A Presbyterian, he had already served in the Irish Yeomanry.

McLaughlin, John - Private
3331 Irish Guards 1st Battalion *Killed in Action on 3 November 1914*
YPRES TOWN CEMETERY EXTENSION, *Belgium*
Husband of Maggie McLaughlin, 23, Massereene Street, Belfast.

McLaughlin, John - Rifleman
11131 Royal Irish Rifles "A" Company 6th Battalion *Age 25 Died in War on 10 August 1915*
HELLES MEMORIAL, *Turkey*
Son of Mrs. Mary McLaughlin, of 8, Meadowbank Place, Lisburn Road, Belfast.

McLaughlin, John - Rifleman
11237 Royal Irish Rifles 6th Battalion *Age 19 Died of Wounds (soldier, buried at sea) on 22 September 1915*
HELLES MEMORIAL, *Turkey*
Son of James and Sarah McLaughlin, of 139, Leeson Street, Grosvenor Road, Belfast.

McLaughlin, M P - Deck Hand
1321/DA Royal Naval Reserve H.M. Drifter "Alfred" *Age 40 Died in War on 4 January 1918*
BELFAST (MILLTOWN) ROMAN CATHOLIC CEMETERY, *United Kingdom*
Husband of Margaret McLaughlin, of 102, Bridge End, Belfast.

McLaughlin, R - Rifleman
231796 Labour Corps formerly Royal Irish Rifles *Age 42 Died as a result of war on 16 November 1918*
BELFAST (MILLTOWN) ROMAN CATHOLIC CEMETERY, *United Kingdom*
Husband of Elizabeth McLaughlin, of 4, Clyde Street, Belfast.

McLaughlin, Samuel - Rifleman
D/10022 Royal Irish Rifles 6th Battalion *Age 21 Died in War on 1 May 1918*
JERUSALEM WAR CEMETERY, *Israel*
Son of James and Elizabeth McLaughlin, of 93, Bridge End, Belfast.

McLaughlin, William - Rifleman
15442 Royal Irish Rifles 10th Battalion *Died in War on 18 December 1914*
BELFAST CITY CEMETERY, *United Kingdom*
Son of the late William McLaughlin. Born at Belfast.

McLean, Albert - Stoker First Class
SS/112148 Royal Navy HMS "Bittern" *Age 25 Drowned through collision in English Channel on 4 April 1918*
PLYMOUTH NAVAL MEMORIAL, *United Kingdom*
Son of Mr. and Mrs. Robert McLean, of 55, Coolfin Street, Belfast.

McLean, Charles Stuart - Private
17479 Highland Light Infantry 10th Battalion *Died in War on 25 September 1915*
LOOS MEMORIAL, *France*
55, Dunmore Street, Belfast.

McLean, Henry - Sapper
WR/342441 Corps of Royal Engineers Inland Water Transport *Died on 2 August 1918*
CHEPSTOW CEMETERY, *United Kingdom*
Born and enlisted in Belfast.

McLean, John - Rifleman
7494 Royal Irish Rifles 1st Battalion *Killed in Action on 23 October 1916*
THIEPVAL MEMORIAL, *France*
Born and enlisted in Belfast.

McLean, John Beattie - Private
3093 Royal Inniskilling Fusiliers 5th Battalion *Killed in Action on 10 October 1918*
ST. SOUPLET BRITISH CEMETERY, *France*
Born and enlisted in Belfast.

McLean, John Warnock - Lance Corporal
9240 Royal Irish Rifles 1st Battalion *Age 21 Killed in Action on 1 January 1915*
LE TOURET MEMORIAL, *France*
Son of James Johnston and Emily Young McLean, of 36, Mersey Street, Belfast.

McLean, Robert - Corporal
T4/111300 Queen's Own (Royal West Kent Regiment) 11th Battalion
Age 21 Killed in Action on 7 April 1917
DICKEBUSCH NEW MILITARY CEMETERY, *Belgium*
Son of Robert and Eliza McLean, of 42, College Park Avenue, Belfast.
Also served with the Army Service Corps

McLean, Robert George - Rifleman
995 Royal Irish Rifles 10th Battalion *Age 21 Died in War on 6 August 1917*
YPRES (MENIN GATE) MEMORIAL, *Belgium*
Son of Annie McLean, of 34, Fortuna Street, Donegall Road, Belfast, and the late Thomas McLean.

McLean, Thomas - Rifleman
13094 Royal Irish Rifles "C" Company 15th Battalion *Age 41 Died of pneumonia on 20 December 1914*
CARNMONEY CEMETERY, *United Kingdom*
Husband of Jane McLean, of 43, Osborne Street, Belfast.

McLean, W - Engineman
4163/ES Royal Naval Reserve H.M. Drifter "Expectation" *Age 46 Died in War on 30 March 1918*
CARNMONEY CEMETERY, *United Kingdom*
Son of the late Thomas and Julia McLean; husband of Agnes McLean,
of 42, Cheviot Avenue, Belfast. Born at Coleraine, County Londonderry.

McLean, William Alexander - Private
11332 Royal Inniskilling Fusiliers 9th Battalion *Age 22 Died in War on 29 March 1918*
POZIERES MEMORIAL, *France*
Brother of Samuel McLean, of 39, Danube Street, Belfast.

McLean, William James - Private
21886 Royal Dublin Fusiliers 8th Battalion *Age 18 Died in War on 27 April 1916*
LOOS MEMORIAL, *France*
Son of Jane McLean, of 43, Osborne Street, Belfast, and the late William James McLean.

McLenaghen, Daniel - Private
553776 Labour Corps 324th Company *Age 50 Died as a result of war on 3 March 1920*
BELFAST (MILLTOWN) ROMAN CATHOLIC CEMETERY, *United Kingdom*
Husband of Eliza Ann McLenaghen, of 5, Stanhope Street, Belfast.

McLennan, John - Private
10942 Royal Scots (Lothian Regiment) 1st Battalion *Died in War on 12 May 1915*
YPRES (MENIN GATE) MEMORIAL, *Belgium*
Born in Belfast, enlisted Glengorse, Scotland.

McLeod, Albert Edward - Private
67538 Devonshire Regiment 5th Battalion (Territorials) *Died in War on 28 July 1918*
THIEPVAL MEMORIAL, *France*
Born in Belfast, enlisted Manchester.

McLester, James - Private
1533 Irish Guards 1st Battalion *Age 34 Killed in Action on 22 June 1915*
LE TOURET MEMORIAL, *France*
Son of the late James and Mary McLester, of 47, Churchill Street, Belfast; husband of Antonia McLester,
of 16, Iris Street, Springfield Road, Belfast.

McLoughlin, Andrew - Private
45680 Northumberland Fusiliers 24th (Tyneside Irish) Battalion *Died in War on 6 June 1917*
FAUBOURG D'AMIENS CEMETERY, ARRAS, *France*
94, Leopold Street, Belfast.

McLoughlin, Frederick - Guardsman
7312 Scots Guards 1st Battalion *Died in War on 11 November 1914*
YPRES (MENIN GATE) MEMORIAL, *Belgium*
Born in Belfast, enlisted Hamilton, Scotland.

McLoughlin, Patrick - Private
1659 Leinster Regiment 7th Battalion *Age 24 Died of Wounds on 7 June 1917*
BAILLEUL COMMUNAL CEMETERY EXTENSION (NORD), *France*
Son of James Margaret McLoughlin, of 137, McDonnell Street, Belfast.

JOURNEY OF REMEMBERING

McLoughlin, William - Lance Sergeant
14530 Duke of Wellington's (West Riding Regiment) "C" Company 10th Battalion *Age 26 Died in War on 5 July 1916*
THIEPVAL MEMORIAL, *France*
Brother of R. McLoughlin, of 45, Newry Street, Castlereagh Road, Belfast.

McLurg, George - Able Seaman
215399 Royal Navy HMS "Formidable"
Age 30 Killed in Action with submarine in English Channel on 1 January 1915
CHATHAM NAVAL MEMORIAL, *United Kingdom*
Son of the late James and Anna Maria Fleeten McLurg. Born in Belfast.

McMahon, Alfred - Rifleman
6115 Royal Irish Rifles 7th Battalion *Age 20 Died in War on 9 September 1916*
THIEPVAL MEMORIAL, *France*
Son of Martha McMahon, of 144, Leopold Street, Belfast, and the late Alfred McMahon.

McMahon, J - Assistant Steward
Mercantile Marine S.S. "Eskmere" (Liverpool)
Age 32 Drowned, as a result of an attack by an enemy submarine on 13 October 1917
TOWER HILL MEMORIAL, *United Kingdom*
Son of Peter Patrick and Mary McMahon; husband of Catherine McMahon (née Gangbran), of Hostel 16, Government Housing Colony, Holbrook Lane, Coventry. Born at Belfast.

McMahon, John - Private
6486 Royal Inniskilling Fusiliers 2nd Battalion *Died of Wounds on 8 November 1914*
NETLEY MILITARY CEMETERY, *United Kingdom*
Born and enlisted in Belfast.

McMahon, John - Rifleman
7502 Royal Irish Rifles 1st Battalion *Age 20 Killed in Action on 9 May 1915*
PLOEGSTEERT MEMORIAL, *Belgium*
Son of James and Elizabeth McMahon, of 25, Short Strand, Belfast.

McMahon, Joseph - Private
7426 Cameronians (Scottish Rifles) 2nd Battalion *Age 22 Died of Wounds on 5 June 1915*
SAILLY-SUR-LA-LYS-CANADIAN CEMETERY, *France*
Son of Patrick and Mary McMahon, of 16, Townsend Street, Belfast.

McMahon, Peter - Private
14218 Royal Inniskilling Fusiliers 5th Battalion *Age 23 Died of Wounds on 9 October 1918*
TINCOURT NEW BRITISH CEMETERY, *France*
Son of James and Mary Ann McMahon, of 50, Clyde Street, Belfast.

McMahon, Robert - Private
29373 Royal Inniskilling Fusiliers 1st Battalion *Killed in Action on 19 April 1917*
ARRAS MEMORIAL, *France*
Born and enlisted in Belfast.

McMahon, Thomas - Private
4539 Royal Inniskilling Fusiliers "A" Company 1st Battalion *Age 29 Died of Wounds on 4 July 1915*
LANCASHIRE LANDING CEMETERY, *Turkey*
Brother of James McMahon, of 131, Millfield, Belfast.

McMahon, Thomas - Private
664 Princess Patricia's Canadian Light Infantry (Eastern Ontario Regiment) *Died in War on 19 March 1915*
VOORMEZEELE ENCLOSURES NO 2, Belgium
40 Teutonic Street, Belfast. Born at Lurgan, County Armagh. An Anglican, he had worked as a labourer and spent eight years in the Royal Inniskilling Fusiliers. He was described as being "fully tattooed on chest and arms."

McMahon, Thomas - Private
9238 Cameronians (Scottish Rifles) 8th Battalion *Died in War on 30 November 1915*
REDOUBT CEMETERY HELLES, Turkey
Born in Belfast, enlisted Glasgow. Formerly 12460, King's Own Scottish Borderers, awarded the Military Medal.

McMann, Joseph - Rifleman
1938 Royal Irish Rifles 1st Battalion *Age 19 Killed in Action on 27 April 1918*
NEW IRISH FARM CEMETERY, Belgium
Son of William and Lizzie McMann, of 16, Klondyke Street, Belfast.

McMann, Patrick - Private
3903 Royal Garrison Artillery 22nd Heavy Battery transferred to 633150 Labour Corps
Age 42 Died in War on 11 February 1919
LONGUEAU COMMUNAL CEMETERY, France
Son of Peter and Margaret McMann, of 1, Matilda Street, Belfast.

McManus, Edward - Rifleman
2/8174 Royal Irish Rifles 2nd Battalion *Age 27 Died of Wounds on 19 May 1916*
AUBIGNY COMMUNAL CEMETERY EXTENSION, France
Husband of Margaret McManus, of 5, Sherriff Street, Belfast.

McManus, Hugh - Private
14 Irish Guards 1st Battalion *Died in War on 18 May 1915*
LE TOURET MEMORIAL, France
Son of Elizabeth McManus of 8, Lonsdale Street, Belfast.

McManus, James - Private
23046 Princess Victoria's (Royal Irish Fusiliers) 8th Battalion *Died in War on 6 September 1916*
THIEPVAL MEMORIAL, France
Born in Loughgall, enlisted Armagh, resident Belfast.

McManus, John - Company Sergeant Major
G/15309 Royal Irish Rifles 18th Battalion *Age 64 Died in War on 11 September 1916*
BELFAST (MILLTOWN) ROMAN CATHOLIC CEMETERY, United Kingdom
Long Service and Good Conduct Medal. Husband of Hannah McManus, of 16, Majorca Street, Belfast.

McManus, Patrick - Private
1615 Leinster Regiment 7th Battalion *Died in War on 28 September 1917*
ST SEVER CEMETERY EXTENSION ROUEN, France
Born and enlisted in Belfast.

McManus, Terence - Sergeant
77189 Royal Field Artillery 153rd Brigade *Died in War on 2 August 1917*
BRANDHOEK NEW MILITARY CEMETERY, Belgium
44, Stanhope Street, Belfast.

McManus, Thomas - Private
27681 Royal Dublin Fusiliers 9th Battalion *Age 20 Killed in Action on 8 June 1917*
YPRES (MENIN GATE) MEMORIAL, Belgium
Brother of Mrs. Betty Hughes, of 24, Penrose Street, Rugby Avenue, Belfast.

McManus, William Johnstone - Private
202152 Canadian Infantry (Central Ontario Regiment) 20th Battalion *Died in War on 15 August 1917*
LOOS BRITISH CEMETERY, France
8, Rushholme Street, Belfast.

McMaster, Charles - Captain
Royal Irish Rifles 7th Battalion attached Trench Mortar Battery *Age 35 Killed in Action on 16 August 1917*
TYNE COT MEMORIAL, Belgium
Son of John and Mary McMaster, of Rose Lodge, Bloomfield, Belfast; husband of Maude Evelyn McMaster, of Mount Royal, Banbridge, County Down. Awarded the Military Cross.

McMaster, David - Private
M/341498 Army Service Corps 62nd Division Mechanical Transport *Age 21 Died in War on 21 November 1918*
ST. SEVER CEMETERY EXTENSION, ROUEN, France
Son of Anna M. McMaster, of 94, Castlereagh Road, Belfast, and the late David McMaster.

McMaster, James Andrew - Private
PLY/17781 Royal Marine Light Infantry 2nd R.M. Battalion Royal Naval Division
Age 20 Died in War on 17 September 1916
BULLY-GRENAY COMMUNAL CEMETERY, BRITISH EXTENSION, France
Son of Thomas and Mary Jane McMaster, of 11, Wayland Street, Belfast.

McMaster, John - Sailor
Mercantile Marine S.S. "Inishowen Head" (Belfast) *Age 17 Died in War on 14 February 1917*
TOWER HILL MEMORIAL, United Kingdom
Son of William and Jane McMaster, Gransha, Islandmagee, County Antrim. Native of Belfast.

McMaster, John Charles - Private
1193 Australian Machine Gun Corps 4th Brigade *Age 20 Died of Wounds on 9 August 1916*
WARLOY-BAILLON COMMUNAL CEMETERY EXTENSION, France
Son of John and Mary McMaster, of 48, Frederick Street, Maylands, South Australia. Native of Belfast, Ireland.

McMaster, Robert - Lance Corporal
8302 Royal Inniskilling Fusiliers 2nd Battalion *Died in War on 10 July 1916*
THIEPVAL MEMORIAL, France
34, Elizabeth Street, Belfast. Employed in the Shipyard.

McMaster, William Graham - Lance Corporal
214 Royal Irish Rifles 10th Battalion *Died in War on 13 October 1916*
ST. QUENTIN CABARET MILITARY CEMETERY, Belgium
Son of James Henry and Isabella McMaster, of 81, Claremont Avenue, Montclair, New Jersey, U.S.A. Returned from U.S.A. at outbreak of war and enlisted in the Ulster Division early in 1915. Born in Belfast.

McMeekan, William - Private
13001 Royal Irish Fusiliers 2nd Battalion *Age 29 Died in War on 15 May 1915*
YPRES (MENIN GATE) MEMORIAL, Belgium
Son of Mrs. Sarah Jane McMeekan, of 40, Bentham Street, Belfast.

McMeekin, Samuel - Sergeant
32119 Royal Field Artillery 3rd Battery 45th Brigade *Age 33 Killed in Action on 13 April 1918*
BOUCHOIR NEW BRITISH CEMETERY, France
Son of Joseph and Mary McMeekin, of Belfast; husband of Annie McMeekin, of 19, Geoffrey Street, Belfast.

McMeekin, Thomas - Rifleman
10971 Royal Irish Rifles 6th Battalion *Age 18 Died in War on 11 August 1915*
HELLES MEMORIAL, Turkey
59 Brownlow Street, Belfast.

McMeekin, Thomas - Rifleman
36 Royal Irish Rifles "D" Company 15th Battalion *Age 22 Killed in Action on 21 March 1918*
POZIERES MEMORIAL, France
Son of Thomas McMeekin, of 44, Mountcollyer Street, Belfast.

McMenamin, Patrick - Private
4255 Royal Inniskilling Fusiliers 1st Battalion *Died in War on 21 October 1916*
THIEPVAL MEMORIAL, France
8, Garnet Street, Belfast.

McMenamy, Thomas - Private
8419 Irish Guards 2nd Battalion *Died in War on 12 September 1917*
TYNE COT MEMORIAL, France
36, Marchioness Street, Belfast.

McMichael, Daniel - Private
19464 Lancashire Fusiliers 9th Battalion *Died in War on 26 September 1916*
THIEPVAL MEMORIAL, France
Born in Londonderry, enlisted in Wallsend, England, resident of Belfast.
Formerly 8296, Northumberland Fusiliers.

McMichael, Joseph - Private
11689 Royal Inniskilling Fusiliers 2nd Battalion *Died in War on 26 February 1917*
FOUQUESCOURT BRITISH CEMETERY, France
Born in Belfast, enlisted in Rutherglen, Scotland.

McMillan, Duncan - Private
22843 Alexandra, Princess of Wales's Own (Yorkshire Regiment) 9th Battalion *Died in War on 7 October 1916*
THIEPVAL MEMORIAL, France
Born in Belfast, enlisted in Motherwell, Scotland.

McMillan, Michael - Private
48141 Machine Gun Corps (Infantry) 8th Battalion *Age 26 Killed in Action on 26 June 1919*
ARCHANGEL ALLIED CEMETERY (buried Ust-Vaga Burial Ground), Russian Federation
Son of Andrew and Mary McMillan, of 30, Greenville Street, Connswater, Belfast. Born at Bloomfield, Belfast.
Formerly 11599 Royal Inniskilling Fusiliers.

McMillen, Richard - Sergeant
12045 Royal Irish Rifles 15th Battalion *Killed in Action on 1 July 1916*
VILLERS-BRETONNEUX MILITARY CEMETERY, France
Son of Mrs McMillen, 2 Shipbouy Street, Belfast.

McMillan, Robert - Private
2327 Irish Guards 1st Battalion *Age 28 Died in War on 1 November 1914*
YPRES (MENIN GATE) MEMORIAL, Belgium
Husband of Margaret McMillan, of 59, Convention Street, Belfast.

McMillan, Robert James - Rifleman
13170 Royal Irish Rifles 15th Battalion *Age 22 Died in War on 22 November 1917*
THIEPVAL MEMORIAL, France
Son of Mrs. Jane McMillan, of 10, Oldpark Road, Belfast.

McMinn, John - Captain
Royal Irish Rifles 5th Battalion attached 14th Battalion Secondary Regiment: Durham Light Infantry
Age 32 Killed in Action on 27 May 1918
SEZANNE COMMUNAL CEMETERY, France
Husband of Isabella McMinn, of 16, Crumlin Gardens, Woodvale Road, Belfast.

McMinn, John - Rifleman
8181 Royal Irish Rifles 1st Battalion *Died in War on 13 March 1915*
LE TOUQUET-PARIS PLAGE COMMUNAL CEMETERY, France
56, Little York Street, Belfast.

McMinn, William J - Rifleman
14/6401 Royal Irish Rifles 14th Battalion *Age 18 Died in War on 24 November 1916*
POND FARM CEMETERY, Belgium
Brother of Samuel McMinn, of "Parkview", Newtownbreda, Belfast.

McMordie, James - Rifleman
15315 Royal Irish Rifles 9th Battalion *Died in War on 6 August 1917*
YPRES (MENIN GATE) MEMORIAL, Belgium
13, Lower Urney Street, Belfast.

McMordie, James Wilson - Second Lieutenant
King's Shropshire Light Infantry attached King's Own Yorkshire Light Infantry *Age 19 Died in War on 18 November 1916*
THIEPVAL MEMORIAL, France
Son of Agnes Elizabeth McMordie, of 30, South Parade, Ormeau Road, Belfast, and the late Francis McMordie, of Crossgar, County Down.

McMordie, Leslie William Watt - First Mate
Mercantile Marine S.S. "Garron Head" (Belfast) *Age 28 Killed by mine on 16 November 1917*
TOWER HILL MEMORIAL, United Kingdom
Son of Elizabeth McMordie (née Watt), of Dundella, Larne Harbour, County Antrim, and the late James McMordie. Born in Belfast.

McMorran, John - Private
10741 Royal Inniskilling Fusiliers 2nd Battalion *Died in War on 16 May 1915*
LE TOURET MEMORIAL, France
Born Ballymacarrett, Belfast. Enlisted in Belfast.

McMullan, Charles - Private
3054 Royal Inniskilling Fusiliers 2nd Battalion *Age 28 Died of Wounds on 6 June 1915*
LE TREPORT MILITARY CEMETERY, France
Son of Francis McMullan, of 5, Norfolk Street, Belfast.

McMullan, George - Private
3087 Royal Inniskilling Fusiliers 1st Battalion *Killed in Action on 21 August 1915*
HELLES MEMORIAL, *Turkey*
Born in Belfast.

McMullan, James - Private
2005036 Canadian Army Medical Corps 13th Field Ambulance *Age 48 Died in War on 5 July 1918*
BELFAST (MILLTOWN) ROMAN CATHOLIC CEMETERY, *United Kingdom*
Son of George and Mary Ann McMullan; husband of Catherine McMullan, of 12, Marchioness Street, Born in Belfast, a career soldier.

McMullan, John - Able Seaman
214958 Royal Navy HMS "Monmouth" *Died in War on 1 October 1914*
PLYMOUTH NAVAL MEMORIAL, *United Kingdom*
9, Derwent Street, Belfast. Son of George and Rose Mullan, Downpatrick, County Down.

McMullan, John - Sergeant
15457 Royal Irish Rifles 10th Battalion *Age 21 Died in War on 3 April 1918*
AVESNES-SUR-HELPE COMMUNAL CEMETERY, *France*
Brother of Letitia McMullan, of 191, Sandy Row, Belfast.

McMullan, Robert - Lance Corporal
6587 Royal Irish Rifles 1st Battalion *Shot dead just bfore leaving the trenches on 6 February 1915*
ROYAL IRISH RIFLES GRAVEYARD, LAVENTIE, *France*
Brother of Mrs. C. Walsh, of 26, Outram Street, Belfast.

McMullan, Robert - Private
27192 Royal Inniskilling Fusiliers 10th Battalion *Age 36 Died of Wounds on 3 July 1916*
PUCHEVILLERS BRITISH CEMETERY, *France*
Husband of Agnes McMullan, of 31, Queensland Street, Belfast.

McMullan, Samuel - Gunner
34652 Royal Garrison Artillery *Died in War on 11 April 1918*
ST NICHOLAS BRITISH CEMETERY, *France*
Born in Belfast, enlisted London.

McMullan, William - Private
10271 Irish Guards 2nd Battalion *Died in War on 22 July 1917*
DOZINGHEM MILITARY CEMETERY, *Belgium*
Born and enlisted in Belfast.

McMullan, William - Private
3162 Royal Inniskilling Fusiliers 2nd Battalion *Died of Wounds on 22 July 1915*
BETHUNE TOWN CEMETERY, *France*
37 Glenwood Street, Belfast.

McMullen, E H - Corporal
73125 Royal Engineers 1st Division Signal Company *Age 20 Died of accidental injuries on 15 December 1915*
NOEUX-LES-MINES COMMUNAL CEMETERY, *France*
Son of Mackenzie and Margaret McMullen, of 62, Eglantine Avenue, Belfast.

Journey of Remembering

McMurdie, John - Private
3531 Royal Inniskilling Fusiliers 1st Battalion *Died in War on 8 August 1916*
YPRES (MENIN GATE) MEMORIAL, Belgium
141, Urney Street, Belfast.

McMurray, Charles - Private
3966 Seaforth Highlanders 4th Battalion *Age 29 Died in War on 26 July 1916*
DAOURS COMMUNAL CEMETERY EXTENSION, France
Son of George and Matilda McMurray; brother of Mrs. E. J. Harris, of 15, Springmount Street, Belfast.

McMurray, James - Sergeant
6833 Royal Horse and Field Artillery *Died in War on 3 November 1914*
WULVERGHEM-LINDENHOEK ROAD MILITARY CEMETERY, Belgium
Born in Ballysillan, Belfast, enlisted in Belfast.

McMurray, William - Private
5039 Royal Munster Fusiliers "W" Company 1st Battalion *Age 27; Died of Wounds on 9 May 1918*
COUIN NEW BRITISH CEMETERY, France
Son of William and Elizabeth McMurray, of 1, Nile Street, Belfast.

McMurray, William T - Private
10615 Royal Irish Fusiliers 1st Battalion *Killed in Action on 15 April 1915*
SEAFORTH CEMETERY, CHEDDAR VILLA, Belgium
255, Oldpark Road, Belfast.

McMurtry, Matthew - Sapper
WR/302045 Royal Engineers Inland Waterways and Docks *Age 29 Died as a result of war on 31 March 1919*
PORTIANOS MILITARY CEMETERY, Greece
Son of Robert and Jane McMurtry, of 6, Fleet Street, Belfast.

McMurtry, William J - Rifleman
19/20860 Royal Irish Rifles 12th Battalion *Age 19 Died in War on 27 May 1918*
CANADA FARM CEMETERY, Belgium
Son of W. J. and Ellen McMurtry, of 34, Linwood Street, Belfast.

McNair, Donald - Private
4206 Seaforth Highlanders 1/5th Battalion *Age 24 Died in War on 13 November 1916*
HAWTHORN RIDGE CEMETERY No.1, AUCHONVILLERS, France
Son of John and Margaret McNair, of 10, Ferguson Drive, Strandtown, Belfast.

McNally, Charles - Private
4609 Connaught Rangers 6th Battalion *Died in War on 18 July 1916*
BETHUNE TOWN CEMETERY, France
Born in County Antrim, enlisted and resident in Belfast. Son of Hugh and Sarah McNally of Randalstown.

McNally, Charles - Rifleman
10461 Royal Irish Rifles 2nd Battalion *Age 26 Killed in Action on 19 May 1916*
ECOIVRES MILITARY CEMETERY, MONT-ST. ELOI, France
Son of David and Mary McNally, of Castle Lane, Lurgan; husband of Sarah McNally, of 226, Leeson Street, Belfast.

Journey of Remembering

McNally, Hugh Francis - Surgeon
Royal Navy HMS "Hampshire" *Age 24 Killed by mine explosion off Orkneys on 5 June 1916*
PORTSMOUTH NAVAL MEMORIAL, *United Kingdom*
Son of Nicholas and Elizabeth McNally, of "The Shore" Portaferry, County Down. Born at Belfast. Lord Kitchener was the principal passenger on the ship en route to Russia. He also perished.

McNally, James - Private
21654 Royal Irish Fusiliers 9th Battalion *Age 24 Killed in Action on 1 July 1916*
THIEPVAL MEMORIAL, *France*
Son of George H. and Jane McNally, of 24, Tobergill Street, Belfast.

McNally, James - Rifleman
8335 Royal Irish Rifles 2nd Battalion *Age 23 Killed in Action on 27 October 1914*
LE TOURET MEMORIAL, *France*
Son of John and Margaret McNally, of 28, Lagan Street, Belfast; husband of May C. McNally, of 10, Thomas Street, Belfast.

McNally, James - Stoker First Class
SS/107103 Royal Navy HMS "Hawke" *Age 23 Killed in Action with a submarine in North Sea on 15 October 1914*
CHATHAM NAVAL MEMORIAL, *United Kingdom*
Son of Joseph and Elizabeth McNally, of Belfast.

McNally, Joseph - Private
10683 Royal Irish Regiment 7th (South Irish Horse) *Died of Wounds on 31 August 1918*
CABARET-ROUGE BRITISH CEMETERY, SOUCHEZ, *France*
Native of Belfast.

McNally, Joseph - Private
22160 Royal Irish Fusiliers "D" Company 8th Battalion *Age 23 Died in War on 2 April 1916*
DUD CORNER CEMETERY, LOOS, *France*
Son of Patrick and Bridget McNally, of 66, Raglan Street, Belfast.

McNally, Thomas John - Private
13/455 East Yorkshire Regiment 13th Battalion *Age 22 Died in War on 13 November 1916*
EUSTON ROAD CEMETERY, COLINCAMPS, *France*
Son of Martina Long, of 4, Parkend Street, Belfast.

McNamara, Richard - Rifleman
15461 Royal Irish Rifles "B" Company 10th Battalion *Age 22 Killed in Action on 1 July 1916*
THIEPVAL MEMORIAL, *France*
Son of Richard Johnston McNamara and Catherine McNamara, of Ardoyne Tramway Depot, Crumlin Road, Belfast.

McNamee, Edward - Private
11380 Cameronians (Scottish Rifles) 9th Battalion *Died of gas poisoning on 18 July 1916*
THIEPVAL MEMORIAL, *France*
Born in Cookstown, enlisted Hamilton, Scotland, resident of Belfast.

McNamee, Peter - Lance Corporal
9819 Royal Inniskilling Fusiliers 1st Battalion *age 24 Died of gas poisoning on 9 August 1916*
BEDFORD HOUSE CEMETERY, *Belgium*
75 Hawthorn Street, Belfast.

Journey of Remembering

McNeff, Edward F - Sergeant
20697 Royal Inniskilling Fusiliers 8th Battalion *Age 21 Died in War on 29 April 1916*
VERMELLES BRITISH CEMETERY, France
Son of James and Mary A. McNeff, of Short Strand, Belfast.

McNeice, Henry - Rifleman
13140 Royal Irish Rifles 15th Battalion *Killed in Action on 1 July 1916*
THIEPVAL MEMORIAL, France
Born and enlisted in Belfast.

McNeill, George - Private
G/50895 Duke of Cambridge's Own (Middlesex Regiment) 19th Battalion *Died in War on 30 July 1917*
KLEIN-VIERSTRAAT BRITISH CEMETERY, Belgium
Born Cheshire, enlisted London, resident of Belfast.

McNeill, Hugh - Private
17904 Machine Gun Corps (Infantry) *Died in War on 10 November 1916*
THIEPVAL MEMORIAL, France
Born and enlisted in Belfast. Formerly10642 Royal Irish Rifles

McNeill, Samuel Alexander - Private
12/184 York and Lancaster Regiment 12th Battalion *Died in War on 27 July 1916*
RUE-DU-BACQUEROT NO. 1 MILITARY CEMETERY LAVENTIE, France
Born in Belfast, enlisted Sheffield, Yorkshire.

McNeilly, David - Private
457666 Canadian Infantry 60th Battalion *Age 21 Died of Wounds on 3 June 1916*
LIJSSENTHOEK MILITARY CEMETERY, Belgium
Son of David and Agnes McNeilly, of 42, De Normanville Street, Montreal. Native of Belfast, Ireland and a Presbyterian.

McNiece, Alexander - Rifleman
448 Royal Irish Rifles 10th Battalion *Died in War on 1 July 1916*
THIEPVAL MEMORIAL, France
Son of James McNiece, of Glenavy, County Antrim; husband of Mrs McNiece, of 24, Haldane Street, Belfast.

McParland, John - Private
4463 Royal Inniskilling Fusiliers 2nd Battalion *Age 19 Died in War on 11 July 1916*
THIEPVAL MEMORIAL, France
Son of Patrick and Ellen McParland, of 57, Ross Street, Belfast.

McPherson, Duncan - Private
254869 Labour Corps transferred from West Yorkshire Regiment *Age 36 Died in War on 13 April 1918*
BELFAST (MILLTOWN) ROMAN CATHOLIC CEMETERY, United Kingdom
Husband of Mary McPherson, of 10, Stratheden Street, Belfast.

McPherson, John - Private
14826 Royal Irish Fusiliers 6th Battalion *Died of Wounds on 26 August 1915*
EAST MUDROS MILITARY CEMETERY, Greece
121, Grosvenor Road, Belfast. Had served in the Boer War.

McPhillips, James - Private
14006 Royal Inniskilling Fusiliers 6th Battalion *Died of Wounds on 4 February 1917*
STRUMA MILITARY CEMETERY, Greece
Born in Belfast.

McPoland, Michael - Sergeant
20701 Royal Inniskilling Fusiliers 8th Battalion *Age 22 Died of Wounds (gas) on 1 May 1916*
VERMELLES BRITISH CEMETERY, France
Son of John and Annie McPoland, of Erinvale, Finaghy, Belfast.

McQuade, Alexander - Stoker First Class
277718 Royal Navy HMS "Laurentic" *Age 50 Killed by mine explosion on 25 January 1917*
PLYMOUTH NAVAL MEMORIAL, United Kingdom
Son of William and Martha McQuade; husband of Annie Jane McQuade, of 27, Wimbledon Street, Belfast.

McQuade, Henry - Private
20637 Royal Scots (Lothian Regiment) 2nd Battalion *Died in War on 13 November 1916*
THIEPVAL MEMORIAL, France
Born in Belfast, enlisted Edinburgh.

McQuade, James - Private
2452 King's Own (Royal Lancaster Regiment) 1/4th Battalion *Died in War on 18 December 1915*
MILLENCOURT COMMUNAL CEMETERY EXTENSION, France
Born in St Peter's Belfast, enlisted Ulverton, England.

McQuade, John - Gunner
56494 Royal Horse Artillery and Royal Field Artillery *Died in War on 15 October 1916*
BAGHDAD (NORTH GATE) WAR CEMETERY, Iraq
Born and enlisted in Belfast.

McQuade, John - Private
40012 Royal Dublin Fusiliers 2nd Battalion *Died in War on 4 October 1917*
ARRAS MEMORIAL, France
Born in Belfast, enlisted Glasgow. Formerly 12460, King's Own Scottish Borderers, awarded the Military Medal.

McQuade, William - Private
12220 Royal Irish Fusiliers "D" Company 5th Battalion *Age 40 Died in War on 10 August 1915*
HELLES MEMORIAL, Turkey
Husband of Mary McQuade, of 4, Britton Street, Belfast.

McQuillan, John - Lance Corporal
8454 Highland Light Infantry 2nd Battalion *Died in War on 25 September 1915*
ST HILAIRE CEMETERY EXTENSION, FREVENT, France
Born in Belfast, enlisted Glasgow.

McQuillan, Robert - Corporal
15253 Royal Scots (Lothian Regiment) 2nd Battalion *Killed in Action on 21 March 1918*
ARRAS MEMORIAL, France
Born in Belfast, enlisted Glasgow.

McQuillan, William - Stoker First Class
SS/100594 Hood Battalion 2nd Naval Brigade *Age 36 Died in War on 4 June 1915*
HELLES MEMORIAL, Turkey
Husband of Sarah A. McQuillan.

McQuiston, Samuel - Rifleman
11195 Royal Irish Rifles 6th Battalion *Age 19 Died in War on 11 August 1915*
HELLES MEMORIAL, Turkey
Son of Mr. and Mrs. James McQuiston, of 91, Clementine Street, Belfast.

McQuoid, James Bailie - Corporal
9681 Royal Inniskilling Fusiliers 1st Battalion *Age 24 Died of Wounds on 3 May 1915*
SHRAPNEL VALLEY CEMETERY, Turkey
Son of William and Elizabeth McQuoid, of 94, Chief Street, Belfast.

McReavie, William John - Rifleman
7528 Royal Irish Rifles 15th Battalion *Age 25 Died in War on 31 October 1916*
PONT-DU-HEM MILITARY CEMETERY, LA GORGUE, France
Son of Hugh and Elizabeth McReavie, of 10, Weir Street, Belfast.

McReynolds, Hugh L. - Lance Corporal
32240 Highland Light Infantry 16th (Service) Battalion (2nd Glasgow) *Died in War on 7 April 1918*
BIENVILLERS MILITARY CEMETERY, France
Born in Belfast, enlisted Glasgow.

McReynolds, John Archibald - Sergeant
15468 Royal Irish Rifles 10th Battalion *Age 20 Died in War on 22 December 1915*
SUCRERIE MILITARY CEMETERY, COLINCAMPS, France
Son of John J. and Mary J. McReynolds, of 2, Chlorine Gardens, Belfast.

McRoberts, Alexander - Rifleman
6916 Royal Irish Rifles 2nd Battalion *Age 18 Killed in Action on 7 July 1916*
OVILLERS MILITARY CEMETERY, France
Native of Ballymacarrett. Son of Malcolm and Agnes McRoberts, of 22, Welland Street, Newtownards Road, Belfast.

McRoberts, Hugh - First Mate
Mercantile Marine S.S. "Dowlais" Cardiff
Age 54 Drowned, as a result of an attack by an enemy submarine on 3 December 1917
TOWER HILL MEMORIAL, United Kingdom
Son of Rose McRoberts and the late Bryce McRoberts; husband of Elizabeth McRoberts (née Neill), of 21, Clifton Crescent, Belfast. Born at Larne.

McRoberts, James - Private
3009 Irish Guards 1st Battalion *Age 30 Died in War on 14 January 1915*
RUE-DES-BERCEAUX MILITARY CEMETERY, RICHEBOURG-L'AVOUE, France
Son of Thomas and Annie McRoberts, of 128, Bristol Street, Belfast. An Army Reservist he was empoyed in Greeve's Mill and a member of the old UVF. His brother also served.

McRoberts, James - Rifleman
13147 Royal Irish Rifles 9th Battalion *Died in War on 1 July 1916*
THIEPVAL MEMORIAL, France
Son of John and Jane McRobert, 127 Leopold Street, Belfast.

McRoberts, William - Lance Corporal
15469 Royal Irish Rifles 9th Battalion *Age 25 Died in War on 11 July 1916*
CAUDRY OLD COMMUNAL CEMETERY, France
Son of Mrs. Annie McRoberts, of 128, Bristol Street, Belfast. His brother was also killed.

McShane, Arthur - Private
12583 Machine Gun Corps 148th Company *Age 20 Died of Wounds on 1 November 1917*
WIMEREUX COMMUNAL CEMETERY, France
Son of Arthur and Jane McShane, of 8, Garnet Street, Belfast.

McShane, John - Private
12403 Royal Irish Fusiliers 5th Battalion *Died in War on 8 August 1915*
HELLES MEMORIAL, Turkey
14, Gibson Street, Belfast.

McShane, Joseph L - Lance Corporal
7200 Royal Irish Rifles 1st Battalion *Killed in Action on 1 July 1916*
THIEPVAL MEMORIAL, France
16, Servia Street, Belfast.

McShane, Thomas - Private
27210 Machine Gun Corps (Infantry) formerly 3388,Royal Irish Fusiliers *Killed in Action on 2 August 1917*
YPRES (MENIN GATE) MEMORIAL, Belgium
Born in Belfast.

McSherry, John - Private
50265 Prince of Wales's Own (West Yorkshire Regiment) 12th Battalion *Died in War on 3 May 1917*
ARRAS MEMORIAL, France
Born in Govan, Scotland, enlisted Huddersfield Yorkshire, resident of Belfast.

McTaggart, David - Rifleman
3036 Royal Irish Rifles 14th Battalion attached 23rd Entrenching Battalion *Died in War on 24 March 1918*
POZIERES MEMORIAL, France
(served as CURRIE). Son of Daniel and Alice McTaggart, of 52, Clonallon Street, Belfast.

McTaggart, William - Rifleman
122 Royal Irish Rifles 16th Battalion formerly Royal Irish Fusiliers *Age 44 Died in War on 21 March 1918*
BOUCHOIR NEW BRITISH CEMETERY, France
Husband of Agnes McTaggart and father of six children, 25 Richmond Street, Belfast.

McTaggart, William McClelland - Private
9851 East Lancashire Regiment 2nd Battalion *Killed in Action on 9 May 1915*
PLOEGSTEERT MEMORIAL, Belgium
Born Ballymacarrett, Belfast. Enlisted in Belfast. Son of Robert and Mary McTaggart.

McTeague, John - Private
24329 Royal Irish Fusiliers 2nd Battalion attached 9th Battalion *Age 19 Killed in Action on 16 August 1917*
TYNE COT MEMORIAL, Belgium
Son of Thomas Patrick McTeague, of 7, Edward Street, Belfast.

McTicr, Frank - Rifleman
528 Royal Irish Rifles 2nd Battalion *Killed in Action on 24 March 1918*
SAVY BRITISH CEMETERY, France
Brother of Mrs McMurray, 264, Crumlin Road, Belfast.

McTier, J - Stoker
Royal Navy HMS "Good Hope" *Died in War on or before August 1915*
4, Irwin Street, Belfast.

McVarnick, James M - Private
24014 Royal Irish Fusiliers 1st Battalion *Died in War on 11 April 1917*
BROWN'S COPSE CEMETERY, ROEUX, France
13, Duffy Street, Belfast.

McVea, John - Private
71473 North Irish Horse *Age 23 Died in War on 26 August 1918*
VIS-EN-ARTOIS MEMORIAL, France
Son of James and Mary J. McVea, of 28, Cedar Avenue, Belfast.

McVeigh, Alexander - Rifleman
7213 Royal Irish Rifles 1st Battalion *Killed in Action on 18 July 1915*
Y FARM MILITARY CEMETERY, BOIS-GRENIER, France
Born and enlisted in Belfast.

McVeigh, James - Private
40295 Royal Inniskilling Fusiliers 8th Battalion formerly 32177 Notts and Derby Regiment
Died as a Prisoner of War on 3 November 1918
NIEDERZWEHREN CEMETERY, Germany
Born in Belfast.

McVeigh, John Marmion - Stoker First Class
MC/433 Royal Navy (Mine Clearance Service) HMS "Gentian"
Age 22 Killed by mine explosion in the Baltic on 15 July 1919
CHATHAM NAVAL MEMORIAL, United Kingdom
Son of John and Jane McVeigh, of 70, Forthbank Terrace, Bo'ness, West Lothian. Native of Belfast.

McVeigh, Richard (Dick) - Corporal
2816 Royal Irish Rifles 15th Battalion *Age 19 Killed in Action on 24 March 1918*
POZIERES MEMORIAL, France
Son of William John and Mary Ann McVeigh, of 346, Crumlin Road, Belfast.

McVeigh, Robert - Lance Sergeant
477 Cameronians (Scottish Rifles) 8th Battalion *Died in War on 28 June 1915*
HELLES MEMORIAL, Turkey
Husband of Maggie McVeigh, 4 Peter's Place, Belfast.

McVeigh, Samuel - Corporal
12050 Royal Irish Rifles 15th Battalion *Died in War on 26 July 1916*
ST SOUPLET BRITISH CEMETERY, France
Born and enlisted in Belfast.

McVeigh, William - Private
39867 Gloucestershire Regiment 1st Battalion *Age 24 Died in War on 4 October 1918*
UNICORN CEMETERY, VEND'HUILE, France
Son of the late Richard and Rebecca McVeigh, of Belfast.
Formerly 25857 Duke of Wellington's (West Riding) Regiment.

McVeigh, William Thomas - Pioneer
57500 Royal Engineers 122nd Field Company *Killed in Action on 1 July 1916*
THIEPVAL MEMORIAL, France
132, Dee Street, Belfast.

McVey, James - Gunner
RMA/11425 Royal Marine Artillery HMS "Good Hope" *Age 25 Killed in Action at Battle of Coronel on 1 November 1914*
PORTSMOUTH NAVAL MEMORIAL, United Kingdom
Son of Elizabeth McVey, of 67, Burmah Street, Belfast, and the late Robert McVey.

McVicker, John - Private
11709 Canterbury Regiment New Zealand Expeditionary Force 2nd Battalion
Age 24 Killed in Action on 1 October 1916
WARLENCOURT BRITISH CEMETERY, France
Son of William and Margaret McVicker, of Belfast, Ireland; husband of Jessie McVicker,
of 250, Gloucester Street, Christchurch, New Zealand.

McVicker, John Henry - Corporal
64636 Royal Engineers 121st Field Company *Died in War on 5 July 1916*
FORCEVILLE COMMUNAL CEMETERY AND EXTENSION, France
Born Ballymacarrett, Belfast. Enlisted in Belfast.

McWilliam, Robert - Private
1442 Manchester Regiment 1/7th Battalion *Died in War on 4 June 1915*
HELLES MEMORIAL, Turkey
Born in Belfast, enlisted Manchester.

McWilliams, Andrew - Rifleman
4837 Royal Irish Rifles 7th Battalion *Died in War on 9 September 1916*
THIEPVAL MEMORIAL, France
Born in Dumbarton, Scotland, enlisted in Barrow, resident of Belfast.

McWilliams, Andrew - Rifleman
26 Royal Irish Rifles 1st Battalion *Age 20 Killed in Action on 24 March 1918*
POZIERES MEMORIAL, France
Born and enlisted in Belfast. Son of Ben and Ellen McWilliams, of 42, Manor Street, Donaghadee.

McWilliams, Herbert - Rifleman
17/1344 Royal Irish Rifles 8th Battalion *Age 19 Died in War on 10 February 1916*
AUCHONVILLERS MILITARY CEMETERY, France
Son of Ellen McWilliams, of 9, Abingdon Street, Belfast.

McWilliams, Hugh Stewart - Private
10387 Royal Inniskilling Fusiliers 2nd Battalion *Age 21 Died of Wounds on 25 July 1916*
ETAPLES MILITARY CEMETERY, France
Son of Hugh and Margaret McWilliams, of 2, Coyle's Place, Belfast.

McWilliams, James - Rifleman
15472 Royal Irish Rifles *Died in War on 2 September 1916*
YPRES (MENIN GATE) MEMORIAL, Belgium
Born and enlisted in Belfast.

McWilliams, John - Donkeyman
Mercantile Marine S.S. "Dunbarmoor" (London) *Age 41 Killed, as a result of an attack by an enemy submarine on 8 March 1917*
TOWER HILL MEMORIAL, United Kingdom
Son of the late Thomas and Elizabeth McWilliams; husband of Martha McWilliams (née Taggart),
of 1, Vicarage Street, Belfast. Born in Belfast.

Journey of Remembering

McWilliams, John - Private
446223 Canadian Infantry (Alberta Regiment) 31st Battalion *Died in War on 7 April 1916*
YPRES (MENIN GATE) MEMORIAL, Belgium
Upper Charleville Street, Belfast. A Presbyterian, he had worked as a clerk in Canada.

McWilliams, John - Private
9642 Irish Guards 1st Battalion *Killed in Action on 25 September 1916*
THIEPVAL MEMORIAL, France
32, Panton Street, Belfasrt.

McWilliams, John - Rifleman
15473 Royal Irish Rifles 10th Battalion *Killed in Action on 1 July 1916*
THIEPVAL MEMORIAL, France
Born and enlisted Belfast.

McWilliams, Robert - Gunner
23250 Royal Garrison Artillery *Died in War on 28 July 1917*
COXYDE MILTARY CEMETERY, Belgium
Born in Belfast.

McWilliams, Robert - Sapper
57734 Corps of Royal Engineers 121st Field Company *Killed in Action on 27 December 1916*
ST. QUENTIN CABARET MILITARY CEMETERY, Belgium
Born in Belfast.

McWilliams, Samuel - Rifleman
1177 Royal Irish Rifles 15th Battalion *Killed in Action on 1 July 1916*
THIEPVAL MEMORIAL, France
Born and enlisted in Belfast.

McWilliams, William - Private
14359 Royal Inniskilling Fusiliers "B" Company 2nd Battalion *Age 47 Killed in Action on 26 April 1916*
AUTHUILE MILITARY CEMETERY, France
Husband of Abigail McWilliams, of 13, Glenwherry Street, Belfast.

McMillan, Samuel - Rifleman
13171 Royal Irish Rifles 8th Battalion *Died in War on 2 July 1916*
THIEPVAL MEMORIAL, France
52, McMaster Street, Belfast. Born at Newtownards.

McMillan, William - Private
M/316460 Royal Army Service Corps *Died in War on 13 December 1918*
PEMBA (FORMERLY PORT AMELIA) CEMETERY, Mozambique
38, Fox Street, Belfast.

Meaney, Thomas - Sergeant
10504 Royal Irish Rifles 10th Battalion *Killed in Action on 1 July 1916*
THIEPVAL MEMORIAL, France
47, Unity Street, Belfast.

Mearnes, Alistair - Rifleman
7164 Royal Irish Rifles 2nd Battalion *Died in War on 26 October 1914*
LE TOURET MEMORIAL, France
90 Selby Street, Belfast.

Meechan, Alexander M - Private
7931 Argyll & Sutherland Highlanders *Died in War on 26 August 1916*
LA FERTE-SOUS-JOUARRE MEMORIAL, France
Born in Dundee, resident in Ardoyne, Belfast. Killed in the first few days of the war.

Meehan, John - Lance Corporal
10755 Royal Dublin Fusiliers 2nd Battalion *Age 22 Killed in Action on 1 July 1916*
THIEPVAL MEMORIAL, France
Son of Mrs. Isabella Fennelly, of 4, Lady Street, Belfast.

Megaw, Edward - Fireman And Trimmer
Mercantile Marine S.S. "Glenfruin" (Glasgow) *Age 36 Presumed drowned on 26 January 1916*
TOWER HILL MEMORIAL, United Kingdom
Son of the late James and Ann Jane Megaw; husband of Margaret Megaw (née McWhirter), of 11, Hanna Street, Belfast. Born in Belfast.

Megaw, William - Rifleman
5006 Royal Irish Rifles 2nd Battalion formerly 32177 Notts and Derby Regiment
Died of Wounds on 10 September 1915
LIJSSENTHOEK MILITARY CEMETERY, Belgium
Husband of Margaret Megaw, 86 Selby Street, Belfast.

Megraw, Henry - Seaman
Mercantile Marine S.S. "Eveleen" (Belfast) *Age 59 Presumed drowned on 6 May 1918*
TOWER HILL MEMORIAL, United Kingdom
Son of the late Richard and Mary Megraw; husband of Mary Megraw (née Flynn), of 2, Young Row, Belfast. Born at Ardglass, County Down.

Mehaffey, John - First Steward
Mercantile Marine S.S. "Bray Head" (Belfast)
Age 44 Drowned, as a result of an attack by an enemy submarine on 14 March 1917
TOWER HILL MEMORIAL, United Kingdom
Husband of Emma Beatrice Mehaffey (née Vosper), of 287, Skegoniell Avenue, Belfast. Born at Belfast.

Meharg, Robert - Private
200525 The King's (Liverpool Regiment) 1st/5th Battalion *Age 28 Died as a result of war on 25 January 1919*
TERLINCTHUN BRITISH CEMETERY, WIMILLE, France
Son of William John and Sarah Ann Meharg, of Belfast.

Meharry, Samuel - Rifleman
17/823 Royal Irish Rifles "B" Company 9th Battalion *Age 20 Killed in Action on 1 July 1916*
THIEPVAL MEMORIAL, France
Son of the late William and Isabella Meharry, of 49, Donegall Pass, Belfast.

Meighton, Thomas - Rifleman
5556 Royal Irish Rifles 1st Battalion *Killed in Action on 10 March 1915*
LE TOURET MEMORIAL, France
Born and enlisted in Belfast.

Mellin, John - Private
6499 Connaught Rangers 6th Battalion *Died in War on 20 November 1917*
CROISILLES RAILWAY CEMETERY, France
Born in Fintona County Tyrone, enlisted and resident in Belfast.

Melough, James - Private
2596 Black Watch (Royal Highlanders) 6th (Perthshire) Battalion (Territorial) *Died in War on 30 November 1915*
AVELUY COMMUNAL CEMETERY EXTENSION, France
Born and enlisted in Belfast.

Melville, Robert - Private
3284 Royal Inniskilling Fusiliers 4th Battalion *Died in War on 31 August 1914*
LONDONDERRY CITY CEMETERY, United Kingdom
Born and enlisted in Belfast.

Melville, William - Sergeant
2374 Royal Inniskilling Fusiliers 1st Battalion *Died of Wounds on 4 April 1917*
CAYEUX MILITARY CEMETERY, France
Born in Belfast.

Mendon, James - Private
22702 Royal Inniskilling Fusiliers 9th Battalion *Died in War on 23 April 1918*
NESLE COMMUNAL CEMETERY, France
Born and enlisted in Belfast. Awarded the Military Medal.

Meneely, James - Private
4792 South African Infantry 8th Regiment *Age 24 Killed in Action on 21 March 1916*
MOSHI CEMETERY, Tanzania
Son of John and Margaret Meneely, of 117, Oak Avenue, Premier Mine, Transvaal. Born at Belfast, Ireland.

Meneilly, James - Sergeant
9983 Royal Inniskilling Fusiliers 1st Battalion formerly 32177 Notts and Derby Regiment
Age 21 Died of Wounds on 1 January 1916
HELLES MEMORIAL, Turkey
Son of Thomas Meneilly, 65 Downing Street, Belfast.

Meneilly, William J - Gunner
81852 Royal Field Artillery 15th Brigade *Died in War on 25 July 1916*
DANTZIG ALLEY BRITISH CEMETERY, MAMETZ, France
65, Downing Street, Belfast.

Mercer, Samuel - Lance Corporal
18464 Royal Irish Rifles 14th Battalion formerly 32177 Notts and Derby Regiment *Killed in Action on 1 July 1916*
THIEPVAL MEMORIAL, France
Son of Eliza and the late James, 163 Snugville Street, Belfast.

Mercer, Thomas - Stoker First Class
304608 Royal Navy HM Mine-sweeper "Nasturtium"
Age 32 Killed by mine explosion in Mediterranean on 27 April 1916
PLYMOUTH NAVAL MEMORIAL, United Kingdom
Son of James Mercer, of 62, Westmoreland Street, Belfast; husband of Mary H. White (formerly Mercer), of Prospect Terrace, St. Ann's Chapel, Gunnislake, Tavistock, England.

Midgley, Alexander Alex - Corporal
130627 Royal Engineers "G" Special Company *Age 22 Died in War on 6 July 1917*
HERMIES BRITISH CEMETERY, France
Son of Alexander and Elizabeth Midgley, of 59, Crosscollyer Street, Belfast.

Miles, Richard - Private
12641 Royal Inniskilling Fusiliers 1st Battalion *Age 16 (Soldier, buried at sea) on 30 August 1915*
HELLES MEMORIAL, Turkey
Son of William Miles, of 6, Edith Street, Belfast.

Miles, Samuel - Private
47294 Royal Army Medical Corps *Age 38 Died as a result of war on 15 December 1918*
BELFAST CITY CEMETERY, United Kingdom
Son of Thomas and Ellen Miles. Born at Belfast.

Millar, Arthur James - Captain
Royal Irish Fusiliers 3rd Battalion attached 1st Battalion *Age 24 Died in War on 25 April 1915*
YPRES (MENIN GATE) MEMORIAL, Belgium
Son of James Millar FCIS and Jane Isabella, 87 Eglantine Avenue, Belfast. Formerly attended Methodist College and Queen's University. A former member of the Officer Training Corps.

Millar, George - Sergeant
35603 Duke of Cornwall's Light Infantry 8th Battalion *Age 31 Killed in Action on 4 September 1917*
DOIRAN MILITARY CEMETERY, Greece
Son of Mrs. A. Millar, of 7, Innes Place, Belfast.

Millar, James - Rifleman
8/15592 Royal Irish Rifles 8th Battalion *Age 19 Died in War on 21 June 1916*
AUTHUILE MILITARY CEMETERY, France
Son of Mrs. Mary Millar, of 19, Pitt Street, Belfast.

Millar, John - Greaser
Mercantile Marine S.S. "Setter" (Glasgow) *Age 58 Killed in Action on 21 March 1918*
TOWER HILL MEMORIAL, United Kingdom
Son of the late Robert and Fanny Millar (née O'Neill); husband of the late Margaret Millar (formerly Welsh, née Murphy). Born at Belfast.

Millar, John - Quartermaster Sergeant Saddler
1574 Royal Field Artillery 13th Brigade Ammunition Column *Age 38 Died of sun-stroke on 29 June 1916*
AMARA WAR CEMETERY, Iraq
Husband of Annie Millar, of 26, Parkmount Street, Belfast.

Millar, John - Rifleman
7102 Royal Irish Rifles "D" Company 2nd Battalion *Age 23 Died of Wounds on 2 July 1917*
ETAPLES MILITARY CEMETERY, France
Son of Alexander and Anna Millar, of Belfast; husband of Martha Millar, of 144, East Bread Street, Belfast.

Millar, Robert - Rifleman
7417 Royal Irish Rifles 2nd Battalion *Age 17 Killed in Action on 9 May 1915*
YPRES (MENIN GATE) MEMORIAL, Belgium
Son of Matilda Freel (formerly Millar), of 14, Harrison Street, Belfast.

Millar, Robert - Sergeant
7445 Royal Irish Rifles 1st Battalion *Killed in Action on 1 July 1916*
THIEPVAL MEMORIAL, France
Son of Joshua and Elizabeth Millar, 19 Beit Street, Belfast.

Millar, Thomas - Able Seaman
165506 Royal Navy HMS "Majestic" *Died in War on 27 May 1915*
PLYMOUTH NAVAL MEMORIAL, *United Kingdom*
28 Broadway, Belfast. A member of Broadway Presbyterian Church.

Millar, Thomas - Private
12405 Royal Irish Fusiliers 1st Battalion *Age 32 Killed in Action on 24 March 1918*
POZIERES MEMORIAL, *France*
Son of the late Thomas and Mary Millar; husband of Alice Millar, of 3, Taylor Street, Belfast.

Millar, Thomas - Rifleman
17/409 Royal Irish Rifles 8th Battalion *Killed in Action on 7 June 1917*
LONE TREE CEMETERY, *Belgium*
Son of Mr. Millar, of 61, Thorndyke Street, Belfast.

Millar, Thomas - Sergeant
15499 Royal Irish Rifles 8th Battalion *Died in War on 12 July 1916*
THIEPVAL MEMORIAL, *France*
Belmont Street, Belfast.

Millar, William - Private
20215 Cheshire Regiment 25th Battalion *Died in War on 20 August 1918*
THIEPVAL MEMORIAL, *France*
68, Fleet Street, Belfast.

Millar, William - Rifleman
5/5549 Royal Irish Rifles 2nd Battalion *Age 36 Died of Wounds on 12 May 1916*
LE TREPORT MILITARY CEMETERY, *France*
Son of Alexander and Malia Millar Belfast.

Millar, William - Rifleman
5729 Royal Irish Rifles 1st Battalion *Age 26 Died in War on 18 July 1915*
Y FARM MILITARY CEMETERY, BOIS-GRENIER, *France*
Son of Annie Millar, of 19, Fifth Street, Belfast, and the late William Millar.

Millen, Herbert - Rifleman
12068 Royal Irish Rifles 15th Battalion *Killed in Action on 1 July 1916*
THIEPVAL MEMORIAL, *France*
Son of Mrs. Agnes Millen, of 23, Charleville Street, Belfast.

Miller, David - Lance Corporal
Royal Irish Rifles 1st Battalion *Age 24 Died in War on 21 December 1914*
RUE-DU-BACQUEROT (13th LONDON) GRAVEYARD, LAVENTIE, FRANCE.
10 Cumberland Street, Belfast.

Miller, David - Private
1716 Australian Infantry 25th Battalion *Age 27 Killed in Action on 22 April 1917*
NOREUIL AUSTRALIAN CEMETERY, *France*
Son of David and Agnes Miller, of 27, Annalee Street, Belfast, Ireland.

Miller, Frederick William - Lance Corporal
9023 Royal Irish Rifles 1st Battalion *Killed in Action on 29 July 1915*
MERVILLE COMMUNAL CEMETERY, *France*
Born and enlisted in Belfast.

Miller, Henry - Private
12808 Royal Inniskilling Fusiliers 2nd Battalion *Age 35 Died in War on 28 November 1917*
TYNE COT MEMORIAL, *Belgium*
Son of James and Catherine McNary, of 57, Roundhill Street, Belfast.

Miller, John - Private
566 Princess Louise's (Argyll & Sutherland Highlanders) 10th Battalion *Died in War on 15 October 1915*
YPRES (MENIN GATE) MEMORIAL, *Belgium*
Born in Londonderry, enlisted Dublin, resident Belfast.

Miller, Robert - Private
17574 Princess Victoria's (Royal Irish Fusiliers) 1st Battalion *Died in War on 23 November 1917*
CAMBRAI MEMORIAL LOUVERVAL, *France*
Born and enlisted in Belfast.

Miller, Thomas - Private
12405 Princess Victoria's (Royal Irish Fusiliers) 1st Battalion *Killed in Action on 24 March 1918*
POZIERES MEMORIAL *France*
Born and enlisted in Belfast.

Miller, William - Private
31387 Royal Inniskilling Fusiliers 9th Battalion *Age 19 Died in War on 24 May 1918*
ESQUELBECQ MILITARY CEMETERY, *France*
Son of William Miller, of 21A, Ayr Street, York Road, Belfast.

Miller, William - Private
9740 Royal Inniskilling Fusiliers 1st Battalion *Age 26 Died in War on 4 June 1915*
HELLES MEMORIAL, *Turkey*
Son of Robert and Mary Jane Miller, of 12, Taylor Street, Belfast.

Milligan, David - Private
11333 Royal Inniskilling Fusiliers 9th Battalion *Killed in Action on 1 July 1916*
THIEPVAL MEMORIAL, *France*
Husband of Isabella Milligan, 16 Jersey Street, Belfast.

Milligan, Oliver - Private
8033 Royal Irish Rifles 2nd Battalion *Killed in Action on 9 July 1916*
THIEPVAL MEMORIAL, *France*
Resident of Belfast.

Milligan, Robert - Rifleman
143 Royal Irish Rifles "B" Company 15th Battalion *Age 21 Died in War on 22 August 1918*
PLOEGSTEERT MEMORIAL, *Belgium*
Son of Samuel Milligan, of 21, Outram Street, Ormeau Road, Belfast.

Milligan, William - Private
1324 Royal Irish Rifles 9th Battalion *Killed in Action on 1 July 1916*
THIEPVAL MEMORIAL, *France*
Husband Arabella Milligan, 106, Silvio Street, Belfast.

Milligan, William - Rifleman
15505 Royal Irish Rifles 10th Battalion *Killed in Action on 1 July 1916*
THIEPVAL MEMORIAL, *France*
Born and enlisted in Belfast.

Milliken, John - Private
12708 King's Own Scottish Borderers 6th Battalion *Died on 25 September 1915*
LOOS MEMORIAL, France
Born in Belfast, enlisted in Glasgow.

Milliken, William - Rifleman
813 Royal Irish Rifles "C" Company 10th Battalion *Age 23 Killed in Action on 1 July 1916*
THIEPVAL MEMORIAL, France
Son of David and Martha Milliken, of 25, Rowland Street, Belfast.

Mills, Alexander - Private
1994 Irish Guards 1st Battalion *Died in War on 1 November 1914*
YPRES (MENIN GATE) MEMORIAL, Belgium
16, Silvergrove Grove Street, Belfast. Born in County Tyrone.

Mills, Charles J - Private
41057 Royal Army Medical Corps *Age 24 Died as a result of war on 24 January 1919*
BELFAST CITY CEMETERY, United Kingdom
Son of Mrs. M. A. Mills, of 63, Newcastle Street, Belfast.

Mills, James - Rifleman
8513 Royal Irish Rifles 2nd Battalion *Age 24 Killed in Action on 13 May 1915*
BAILLEUL COMMUNAL CEMETERY EXTENSION (NORD), France
Son of the late James Mills, of Belfast.

Mills, James - Rifleman
888 Royal Irish Rifles 16th (Pioneer) Battalion *Age 20 Killed in Action on 21 June 1917*
WYTSCHAETE MILITARY CEMETERY, Belgium
Son of Margaret J. Mills, of 41, Majestic Street, Belfast, and the late Henry Mills.

Mills, John - Rifleman
1810 Royal Irish Rifles 10th Battalion *Killed in Action on 1 July 1916*
THIEPVAL MEMORIAL, France
91, Ardenvohr Street, Belfast.

Mills, John - Stoker First Class
SS/106665 Royal Navy HMS "Hawke" *Age 25 Killed in Action with submarine in North Sea on 15 October 1914*
CHATHAM NAVAL MEMORIAL, United Kingdom
Husband of Mary Mills, of 26, Coolderry Street, Donegall Road, Belfast.

Mills, Robert - Rifleman
1752 Royal Irish Rifles 15th Battalion attached 107th Trench Mortar Battery
Age 23 Died in War on 29 March 1918
POZIERES MEMORIAL, France
Son of James and Eliza J. Mills, of 68, Joseph Street, Belfast.

Mills, Samuel - Private
A/20424 Canadian Infantry (Manitoba Regiment) 16th Battalion *Age 25 Died of Wounds on 17 August 1915*
BAILLEUL COMMUNAL CEMETERY EXTENSION (NORD), France
Son of the late William and Mary Mills, of Belfast, Ireland. A Prebyterian, he was born at Cookstown, County Tyrone and worked as a labourer.

Millsop, Thomas James - Private
4906 Royal Irish Fusiliers 2nd Battalion *Age 25 Died of Wounds on 30 May 1915*
SEAGOE CEMETERY, *United Kingdom*
Son of Robert and Mary A. Millsop.

Milne, Ashley Albert - Rifleman
17/2247 Royal Irish Rifles 15th Battalion *Died while Prisoner of War on 19 July 1918*
BERLIN SOUTH-WESTERN CEMETERY, *Germany*
Son of Thomas and Caroline Milne of 107, Roden Street, Belfast. His father and two brothers also served. His last letter to his mother arrived after she had received the notification of his death.

Minnis, Andrew - Private
7909 Royal Inniskilling Fusiliers 1st Battalion *Died of Wounds on 27 July 1916*
LE CATEAU MILITARY CEMETERY, *France*
Born in Belfast.

Miskelly, John - Rifleman
6833 Royal Irish Rifles 2nd Battalion *Age 27 Killed in Action on 26 April 1917*
ST. QUENTIN CABARET MILITARY CEMETERY, *Belgium*
Son of John and Susanah Miskelly; husband of Mary Miskelly, of 4, Bloomfield Street, Belfast.

Miskelly, Samuel - Rifleman
15602 Royal Irish Rifles 8th Battalion *Age 22 Died in War on 2 July 1916*
THIEPVAL MEMORIAL, *France*
Son of Mary Norris (formerly Miskelly), of 7, Bangor Street, Belfast, and the late John Miskelly.

Miskimmon, Samuel - Private
23691 Hampshire Regiment 2nd Battalion *Age 26 Died in War on 4 September 1918*
PLOEGSTEERT MEMORIAL, *Belgium*
Son of Mary Ann McCourt (formerly Miskimmon), of 17, Singleton Street, Belfast, and the late Jonathan Miskimmon.

Mitchell, Alexander - Rifleman
838 Royal Irish Rifles 13th Battalion *Killed in Action on 1 July 1916*
THIEPVAL MEMORIAL, *France*
Born in Belfast, enlisted Banbridge.

Mitchell, Arthur Gorman - Second Lieutenant
Royal Irish Rifles 5th Battalion attached 2nd Battalion *Age 19 Killed in Action - shot by a sniper on 13 May 1916*
ECOIVRES MILITARY CEMETERY, MONT-ST. ELOI, *France*
A medical student he was the son of Arthur B. Mitchell (Lieutenant Colonel Royal Army Medical Corps) and Agnes C Mitchell of 18, University Square, Belfast.

Mitchell, George Smith - Rifleman
1628 Royal Irish Rifles 8th Battalion *Died in War on 5 July 1916*
THIEPVAL MEMORIAL, *France*
16, Abington Street, Belfast. Born in South Africa.

Mitchell, Hamilton Trelford - Private
781425 Canadian Infantry (Saskatchewan Regiment) 28th Battalion *Age 21 Killed in Action on 12 May 1918*
BELLACOURT MILITARY CEMETERY, RIVIERE, *France*
Son of the late Robert Wesley Stuart Mitchell and Isabella Mitchell, of Belfast, Ireland. His brother Hugh Brown also fell. Was a farmer in Canada. Anglican in religion and awarded the Military Medal.

Journey of Remembering

Mitchell, Henry Joseph - Lance Corporal
683 Royal Irish Rifles 10th Battalion *Age 24 Died in War on 22 November 1917*
CAMBRAI MEMORIAL,LOUVERVAL,France
Husband of Elizabeth Mitchell, née Garrett, of 147, Manor Street, Belfast.

Mitchell, Hugh Brown - Private
781187 Canadian Infantry (Saskatchewan Regiment) 128th Battalion *Killed in Action on 6 November 1917*
YPRES (MENIN GATE) MEMORIAL, France
300, Springfield Road Belfast. A Methodist, he worked as a farmer in Canada. His brother also fell.

Mitchell, James - Private
17658 Machine Gun Corps (Infantry) *Killed in Action on 7 June 1917*
VOORMEZEELE ENCLOSURES No 3, Belgium
Born in Belfast, enlisted Glasgow. Formerly 7199 Scottish Rifles.

Mitchell, James - Private
5980 Royal Munster Fusiliers 8th Battalion *Age 22 Died of Wounds on 2 September 1918*
BELFAST (MILLTOWN) ROMAN CATHOLIC CEMETERY, United Kingdom
Son of James and Margaret Mitchell, of 33, Jonesboro' Street, Belfast.

Mitchell, James - Private
922 Highland Light Infantry 10/11th Battalion *Died in War on 9 April 1917*
CABARET-ROUGE BRITISH CEMETERY, SOUCHEZ, France
Born in Belfast. Lived in Kilmarnock, Scotland on enlistment.

Mitchell, James - Rifleman
17/267 Royal Irish Rifles 8/9th Battalion *Died in War on 23 October 1917*
ROCQUIGNY-EQUANCOURT ROAD BRITISH CEMETERY, MANANCOURT, France
Son of Allan and Ellen Mitchell, 34 Fifth Street, Belfast.

Mitchell, John Howard - Sergeant
79804 Machine Gun Corps (Motors) Royal Navy Armoured Car Section *Age 29 Died in War on 14 September 1918*
BASRA MEMORIAL, Iraq
Son of the late Isaac and Isabella Mitchell, of Belfast. Also served in Belgium and Russia.

Mitchell, Robert Hugh - Private
G/1321 Princess Victoria's (Royal Irish Fusiliers) 2nd Garrison Battalion *Died in War on 3 August 1918*
MIKRA BRITISH CEMETERY, KALAMARIA, Greece
Born and enlisted in Belfast. Formerly 706 Royal Irish Rifles.

Mitchell, S - Private
4554 Australian Infantry, A.I.F. 6th Battalion *Died in War on 4 October 1917*
YPRES (MENIN GATE) MEMORIAL, Belgium
19, Perth Street, Belfast.

Mitchell, Samuel - Lance Corporal
17530 King's Own Scottish Borderers 2nd Battalion *Age 22 Died in War on 30 July 1916*
THIEPVAL MEMORIAL, France
Son of Mrs. Margaret Mitchell, of 49, London Street, Belfast.

Mitchell, Walter - Corporal
11871 Royal Dublin Fusiliers 2nd Battalion *Age 32 Died in War on 24 May 1915*
YPRES (MENIN GATE) MEMORIAL, Belgium
Son of the late Thomas and Jane Mitchell, of Belfast. Served in the South African Campaign. Also in India and Egypt.

Mitchell, William Hamilton - Lieutenant
Canadian Infantry (Manitoba Regiment) 8th Battalion *Age 29 Died in War on 27 November 1916*
VILLERS STATION CEMETERY, VILLERS-AU-BOIS, France
Son of John and Margaret Mitchell. A career soldier, both in the British and Canadian armies. Had been in Canada for eleven years. Twice wounded prior to his death.

Moan, James Leo - Rifleman
8807 Royal Irish Rifles 2nd Battalion *Age 22 Killed in Action on 25 September 1915*
YPRES (MENIN GATE) MEMORIAL, Belgium
Son of Francis Joseph and Mary Jane Moan, of 7, Anderson Street, Belfast.

Moffat, Andrew Watson - Rifleman
40263 Royal Irish Rifles 12th Battalion *Age 21 Died in War on 9 April 1918*
BOULOGNE EASTERN CEMETERY, France
Son of William and Margaret Moffat, of 40, Avon Street, Belfast.

Moffatt, W - Rifleman
15/12077 Royal Irish Rifles 15th Battalion *Age 21 Died in War on 29 May 1918*
CANADA FARM CEMETERY, Belgium
Son of Mr. Moffatt, of 9, Ligoniel Road, Belfast.

Moffett, Alexander - Rifleman
13284 Royal Irish Rifles Depot *Age 27 Died of influenza on 2 July 1918*
CARNMONEY CEMETERY, United Kingdom
Son of Robert Moffett; husband of Elizabeth Moffett, of 26, Fox Street, Belfast.

Moffett, Hugh - Private
12288 Royal Inniskilling Fusiliers 9th Battalion *Killed in Action on 1 July 1916*
CONNAUGHT CEMETERY, THIEPVAL, France
17, Gawn Street, Belfast.

Mohan, Joseph - Private
17202 Duke of Wellington's (West Riding Regiment) 2/7th Battalion *Died in War on 27 November 1917*
ARRAS MEMORIAL, France
Born in Ballybay, enlisted in Cavan, resident of Belfast.

Molloy, Charles - Chief Petty Officer
171847 Royal Navy HMS "Hawke" *Died in War on 15 October 1914*
CHATHAM NAVAL MEMORIAL, United Kingdom
Son of Charles Malloy, 76, Clementine Street, Belfast.

Molloy, Lawrence - Lance Corporal
2891 Leinster Regiment 2nd Battalion *Died in War on 4 September 1918*
PLOEGSTEERT MEMORIAL, Belgium
Born and enlisted in Belfast.

Molloy, Michael - Private
2222 Royal Irish Regiment 6th Battalion *Age 30 Died of pneumonia on 31 October 1915*
BELFAST (MILLTOWN) ROMAN CATHOLIC CEMETERY, United Kingdom
Husband of Margaret Molloy, of 34, Balaclava Street, Belfast. Born at Belfast.

Molloy, William - Private
1696 Leinster Regiment 2nd Battalion *Died in War on 27 March 1918*
POZIERES MEMORIAL, OVILLERS-LA BOISSELLE, France
Born in Londonderry, enlisted and resident Belfast.

Molloy, William - Sapper
57479 Royal Engineers 122nd Field Company *Killed in Action on 1 July 1916*
THIEPVAL MEMORIAL, France
20 Christopher Street, Belfast.

Molloy, William John - Rifleman
9147 Royal Irish Rifles 1st Battalion *Age 25 Died of Wounds on 17 November 1914*
MERVILLE COMMUNAL CEMETERY, France
Son of Thomas Molloy, of 2, Alexander Street, Belfast.

Monaghan, Bernard - Greaser
Mercantile Marine S.S. "War Clover" (London)
Age 49 Drowned, as a result of an attack by an enemy submarine on 19 October 1917
TOWER HILL MEMORIAL, United Kingdom
Son of the late Bernard and Martha Monaghan; husband of Margaret Monaghan (née McGregor), of 23, Lancaster Street, York Street, Belfast. Born at Belfast.

Montgomery, Alexander - Lance Corporal
S/40511 Seaforth Highlanders 2nd Battalion *Age 18 Died in War on 3 May 1917*
ARRAS MEMORIAL, France
Son of Johnston and Elizabeth Montgomery, of 59, Dundee Street, Belfast.

Montgomery, Alexander - Private
17105 Princess Victoria's (Royal Irish Fusiliers) 6th Battalion *Died in War on 9 August 1915*
HELLES MEMORIAL, Turkey
Born in Belfast, enlisted Dublin.

Montgomery, Alexander - Rifleman
850 Royal Irish Rifles 11th Battalion *Died in War on 10 August 1917*
YPRES (MENIN GATE) MEMORIAL, Belgium
Born in Belfast, enlisted Ballymena.

Montgomery, Charles Hill - Corporal
20183 Canadian Infantry (Alberta Regiment) *Died in War on 23 April 1915*
YPRES (MENIN GATE) MEMORIAL, Belgium
Lough Villas, Shore Road, Belfast. A single man he was an Anglican who worked as a carpenter.

Montgomery, Frederick Alexander - Second Lieutenant
King's Own Scottish Borderers 6th Battalion *Age 24 Died in War on 19 October 1916*
THIEPVAL MEMORIAL, France
Son of Frederick Alexander and Jane Montgomery, of 8, Sandhurst Road, Belfast.

Montgomery, George - Lance Corporal
26039 Royal Inniskilling Fusiliers 7th Battalion *Died in War on September 1916*
THIEPVAL MEMORIAL, France
Brother of Alfred T Montgomery 41, Grosvenor Road, Belfast.

Montgomery, James - Private
17156 Highland Light Infantry 10th (Service) Battalion *Killed in Action on 25 September 1915*
LOOS MEMORIAL, France
Born in Belfast, enlisted Glasgow.

Montgomery, James - Private
1910 North Irish Horse *Age 25 Died as a result of war on 17 June 1919*
BELFAST (DUNDONALD) CEMETERY, United Kingdom
Son of James and Martha Montgomery, of 2, Forth Glen, Ballygomartin Road, Belfast.

Montgomery, James - Rifleman
3778 Royal Irish Rifles 9th Battalion transferred to 333801 Labour Corps 421st Agricultural Company
Died of pneumonia on 31 October 1918
CARNMONEY CEMETERY, United Kingdom
Son of Alexander and Jane Montgomery, of Belfast.

Montgomery, James - Rifleman
3905 Royal Irish Rifles 15th Battalion *Died in War on 11 June 1916*
HAMEL MILITARY CEMETERY, BEAUMONT-HAMEL, France
Son of Mrs. Annie Montgomery, of 68, Church Street East, Newtownards Road, Belfast.

Montgomery, James - Rifleman
406 Royal Irish Rifles 16th Battalion *Died in War on 2 June 1916*
FORCEVILLE COMMUNAL CEMETERY AND EXTENSION, France
Born in Belfast, enlisted in Lurgan.

Montgomery, John - Private
PLY/17190 Royal Marine Light Infantry HMS "Defence" *Killed in Action at Battle of Jutland on 31 May 1916*
PLYMOUTH NAVAL MEMORIAL, United Kingdom
Son of Isaac Montgomery, of 26, Mill Street, Belfast.

Montgomery, John - Sergeant
12094 Royal Irish Rifles "C" Company 15th Battalion *Age 24 Killed in Action on 1 July 1916*
SERRE ROAD CEMETERY No.2, France
Son of Edward and Agnes Montgomery, of 12, Mountcollyer Avenue, Belfast.

Montgomery, Joseph - Rifleman
14/15509 Royal Irish Rifles 10th Battalion *Age 39 Killed in Action on 27 August 1916*
ST. QUENTIN CABARET MILITARY CEMETERY, Belgium
Son of Andrew Montgomery, of Ballyvasey, Carnmoney, Belfast; husband of Elizabeth Montgomery, of 64, Braemar Street, Broadway, Belfast.

Montgomery, Robert - Sergeant
420082 Canadian Infantry (Manitoba Regiment) 16th Battalion *Killed in Action on 16 August 1917*
LIEVIN COMMUNAL CEMETERY EXTENSION, France
Son of Mr. and Mrs. R. Montgomery, of 58, Hillview Street, Oldpark Road, Belfast, Ireland.
A Unitarian, he had worked as a farmer and was a member of the militia.

Montgomery, Robert - Sergeant
57586 Royal Engineers 122nd Field Company *Age 37 Killed in Action on 7 June 1917*
BAILLEUL COMMUNAL CEMETERY EXTENSION (NORD), France
A carpenter, he was the son of Robert and Margaret Montgomery, of 47, Castlereagh Place, Belfast.

Journey of Remembering

Montgomery, Robert George Donaldson - Private
40655 Royal Inniskilling Fusiliers 2nd Battalion formerly (2192) North Irish Horse
Died in War on 31 August 1918
BERTENACRE MILITARY CEMETERY, FLETRE, France
Son of Robert and Eliza D. Montgomery, of 148, Ormeau Road, Belfast.

Montgomery, Samuel - Private
2482 Royal Irish Fusiliers 1st Battalion *Killed in Action on 2 September 1918*
LINDENHOEK CHALET MILITARY CEMETERY, Belgium
Husband of R. Montgomery of 38, Crosby Street, Belfast.

Montgomery, Thomas Rutherford - Private
225284 Canadian Infantry (Central Ontario Regiment) 102nd Battalion *Killed in Action at Cambrai on 1 October 1918*
CANADA CEMETERY, TILLOY-LES-CAMBRAI, France
Son of William and Sarah B. Montgomery, of 48, Castlereagh Street, Belfast, Ireland. Lived in Chicago, USA, before enlisting. An Anglican, he had worked as a book keeper.

Montgomery, William - Private
10861 Royal Inniskilling Fusiliers 2nd Battalion *Age 23 Died in War on 16 May 1915*
LE TOURET MEMORIAL, France
Son of James and Martha Montgomery, of 160, Snugville Street, Belfast.

Mooney, Charles - Sapper
113781 Royal Engineers 78th Field Company *Died in War on 14 October 1917*
TYNE COT MEMORIAL, Belgium
Husband of Mary Jane Mooney, of 73, Upper Meadow Street, Belfast.

Mooney, Edward - Lance Corporal
15617 Royal Irish Rifles 9th Battalion *Died in War on 6 June 1916*
AUTHUILE MILITARY CEMETERY, France
Husband of Elizabeth Mooney, 11, Third Street, Belfast. A veteran of the Boer War. Thereafter joined the old UVF and became a drill instructor. Worked in the New Northern Spinning and Weaving Company.

Mooney, James Alexander - Rifleman
7005 Royal Irish Rifles 2nd Battalion *Killed in Action on 14 May 1916*
ECOIVRES MILITARY CEMETERY, MONT-ST. ELOI, France
Born and enlisted in Belfast.

Mooney, John - Private
3194 Royal Inniskilling Fusiliers 2nd Battalion *Died in War on 22 July 1915*
BETHUNE TOWN CEMETERY, France
27, Belgrade Street, Belfast.

Mooney, John - Rifleman
8016 Royal Irish Rifles 2nd Battalion *Died in War on 27 October 1914*
LE TOURET MEMORIAL, France
Husband of Margaret Mooney, of 94, Ardilea Street, Belfast.

Mooney, John Leo - Private
10513 Royal Inniskilling Fusiliers 2nd Battalion *Killed in Action on 16 May 1915*
LE TOURET MEMORIAL, France
Born in Belfast.

Moore, Alexander - Chief Steward
Mercantile Marine S.S. "Garron Head" (Belfast) *Age 37 Killed by mine on 16 November 1917*
TOWER HILL MEMORIAL, United Kingdom
Son of the late Thomas and Catherine Moore; husband of Kathleen Isabella Moore (née Maguire), of 3, Orwell Terrace, Ballygomartin Road, Belfast. Born in Rathdrum, County Wicklow.

Moore, Archibald - Rifleman
11036 Royal Irish Rifles 2nd Battalion *Died in War on 21 May 1916*
AUBIGNY COMMUNAL CEMETERY EXTENSION, France
Born and enlisted in Belfast.

Moore, Charles - Rifleman
13288 Royal Irish Rifles 8th Battalion *Died in War on 27 January 1917*
CARNMONEY CEMETERY, United Kingdom
Born and enlisted in Belfast.

Moore, David Sidney - Private
1896 Royal Scots 9th Battalion *Died in War on 9 May 1915*
SANCTUARY WOOD CEMETERY, Belgium
University Street, Belfast.

Moore, Edward - Rifleman
9176 Royal Irish Rifles 1st Battalion *Died in War on 8 February 1916*
SAILLY-SUR-LA-LYS-CANADIAN CEMETERY, France
Son of Henry Moore, of 30, Hunter Street, Belfast.

Moore, Francis Wright - Lance Corporal
2264 London Regiment 2nd (City of London) Battalion (Royal Fusiliers) *Died in War on 15 September 1916*
GROVE TOWN CEMETERY, MEAULTE, France
Resident of Belfast, enlisted in Lurgan.

Moore, Harry - Corporal
57655 Royal Engineers "Q" Depot Company *Age 29; Died in War on 1 November 1918*
BELFAST CITY CEMETERY, United Kingdom
Husband of Emma Moore, of 15, Eureka Street, Belfast. Awarded the Military Medal.

Moore, Harry Havelock - Private
1018287 Canadian Infantry (Saskatchewan Regiment) 28th Battalion
Age 21 Killed in Action on 6 November 1917
YPRES (MENIN GATE) MEMORIAL, Belgium
Son of Thomas John and Jeanie Stuart Moore, of Merton, Cregagh, Belfast, Ireland. An Anglican, he had worked as a bank clerk.

Moore, James - Private
G/925 Buffs (East Kent Regiment) 2nd Battalion *Died in War on 28 September 1915*
LOOS MEMORIAL, France
Born in Belfast, enlisted in London.

Moore, James Henry - Private
3222 Royal Inniskilling Fusiliers 1st Battalion *Age 21 Died in War on 21 August 1915*
HELLES MEMORIAL, Turkey
Son of Robert and Catherine Moore, of 57, Ashmore Street, Belfast.

Moore, John - Able Seaman
229507 Royal Navy HMS "Indefatigable" *Age 28 Killed in Action at Battle of Jutland on 31 May 1916*
PLYMOUTH NAVAL MEMORIAL, United Kingdom
Native of Belfast. Half-brother of Selina Moore, of 24, Rowland Street, Belfast.

Moore, John - Private
48247 Royal Warwickshire Regiment 16th Battalion formerly S/4/127965 Royal Army Service Corps
Died in War on 23 August 1918
VIS-EN-ARTOIS MEMORIAL, France
Born in Belfast.

Moore, John - Rifleman
10/15624 Royal Irish Rifles 10th Battalion *Killed in Action on 28 June 1917*
DERRY HOUSE CEMETERY No.2, Belgium
Brother of Mrs. J. Dickson, of 19, City Street, Belfast.

Moore, John Alexander - Rifleman
1112371 Royal Irish Rifles 15th Battalion *Age 19 Died in War on 6 May 1918*
CANADA FARM CEMETERY, Belgium
Born in Belfast the son of John and Margaret Moore.

Moore, John Henry - Private
26103 Royal Inniskilling Fusiliers 8th Battalion *Age 31 Died in War on 5 October 1916*
KEMMEL CHATEAU MILITARY CEMETERY, Belgium
Son of Henry and Agnes Moore, of Belfast.

Moore, John Reid - Sergeant
15627 Royal Irish Rifles 14th Battalion attached 109th Light Trench Mortar Battery *Age 22 Killed in Action on 1 July 1916*
CONNAUGHT CEMETERY, THIEPVAL, France
Son of Thomas G. and Susan Moore, of 19, Baltic Avenue, Belfast. An Orangeman he was also a member of the Young Citizen Volunteers. His brother, William, also served.

Moore, Joseph - Private
12804 Royal Inniskilling Fusiliers 6th Battalion *Died of dysentery on 28 August 1915*
HELLES MEMORIAL, Turkey
Husband of Margaret Moore, 76, Beresford Street, Belfast.

Moore, Joseph - Private
27092 Royal Inniskilling Fusiliers 8th Battalion *Killed in Action on 4 August 1917*
YPRES (MENIN GATE) MEMORIAL, Belgium
Born in Belfast.

Moore, Joseph - Private
76576 Royal Defence Corps *Age 46 Died in War on 19 September 1920*
BREANDRUM CEMETERY, United Kingdom
Son of William and Elizabeth Moore; husband of Margaret Moore, of 18, Spring Street, Belfast.
Born in Londonderry.

Moore, Patrick - Private
23310 Princess Victoria's (Royal Irish Fusiliers) 7th Battalion *Died in War on 5 September 1916*
THIEPVAL MEMORIAL, France
Born in Belfast, enlisted in Glasgow.

Moore, Peter - Private
15085 Cameronians (Scottish Rifles) 11th Battalion *Died in War on 1 October 1915*
THIEPVAL MEMORIAL, France
Born in Belfast, enlisted in Glasgow.

Moore, Richard - Corporal
19529 Machine Gun Corps (Infantry) 107th Company *Age 23 Died in War on 6 June 1917*
POND FARM CEMETERY, Belgium
Son of Robert and Mary Anne Moore, of 8, Kenmare Street, Belfast.

Moore, Richard - Private
2206 North Irish Horse *Died in War on 6 May 1917*
ANNAHILT PRESBYTERIAN CHURCH, United Kingdom
Born in Belfast, enlisted in Antrim.

Moore, Robert McConnell - Second Lieutenant
Royal Irish Rifles 1st Battalion *Age 23 Killed in Action on 27 March 1918*
MEZIERES COMMUNAL CEMETERY EXTENSION, France
Son of Thomas and Sarah Moore, of 227, Springfield Road, Belfast. Born on the Shankill Road he had been a fitter by trade. Promoted Sergeant he was awarded the Military Medal for bravery. Commissioned in 1917 he was confirmed killed the following year after being posted wounded and missing.

Moore, Samuel - Driver
25832 Royal Engineers 63rd Field Company *Age 23 Killed in Action on 21 April 1918*
LA CLYTTE MILITARY CEMETERY, Belgium
Son of Hugh and Mary Moore, of 7, Belmont Street, Woodstock Road, Belfast. Born at Ballynahinch, County Down.

Moore, Samuel - Private
34885 Royal Scots Fusiliers 6/7th Battalion *Killed in Action on 31 July 1917*
YPRES (MENIN GATE) MEMORIAL, Belgium
Born in Belfast, enlisted Beith, Ayrshire, Scotland.

Moore, Samuel - Sergeant
12070 Princess Victoria's (Royal Irish Fusiliers) 5th Battalion *Died in War on 29 September 1918*
SAILLY-LABOURSE COMMUNAL CEMETERY, France
Born and enlisted in Belfast.

Moore, T - Seaman
Mercantile Marine S.S. "Thracia" (Liverpool)
Age 22 Drowned, as a result of an attack by an enemy submarine, or killed by mine on 27 March 1917
TOWER HILL MEMORIAL, United Kingdom
Born in Belfast.

Moore, Thomas - Driver
35697 Royal Field Artillery 36th Division Ammunition Column *Age 26 Died in War on 8 September 1918*
BERTENACRE MILITARY CEMETERY, FLETRE, France
Son of Margaret Moore, of 63, Sandy Row, Belfast, and the late Robert Moore.

Moore, Thomas - Rifleman
12084 Royal Irish Rifles 15th Battalion *Died in War on 31 January 1916*
SUCRERIE MILITARY CEMETERY, COLINCAMPS, France
Born and enlisted in Belfast.

Moore, Thomas - Sergeant
48899 Machine Gun Corps (Infantry) *Died in War on 5 October 1916*
MIKRA BRITISH CEMETERY, KALAMARIA, Greece
Born in Belfast, enlisted in Glasgow. Formerly 10016 Argyll and Sutherland Highlanders.

Moore, Thomas George - Second Lieutenant
Royal Irish Rifles 17th Battalion attached 8th Battalion *Killed in Action on 1 July 1916*
THIEPVAL MEMORIAL, France
Educated at the Model School and at RBAI. He was the son of Head Constable G Moore of York Street Royal Irish Constabulary.

Moore, William - Second Lieutenant
Royal Irish Fusiliers 10th Battalion *Age 24 Killed in Action on 16 August 1917*
TYNE MEMORIAL, Belgium
Son of Elizabeth R. Moore, of Ashley House, Albertbridge Road, Belfast, and the late Dr A Moore.

Moore, William - Sergeant
12087 Royal Irish Rifles 15th Battalion *Killed in Action on 1 July 1916*
THIEPVAL MEMORIAL, France
Born and enlisted in Belfast.

Moore, William John - Private
11946 Royal Inniskilling Fusiliers 1st Battalion *Killed in Action on 1 July 1916*
Y RAVINE CEMETERY, BEAUMONT-HAMEL, France
Born in Belfast.

Moorhead, Henry - Rifleman
51 Royal Irish Rifles 16th Battalion *Died in War on 19 August 1916*
BERKS CEMETERY EXTENSION, Belgium
Born in Belfast enlisted in Lurgan.

Moorhead, James - Rifleman
6855 Royal Irish Rifles 4th Battalion *Age 20 Died of Wounds on 21 March 1915*
BELFAST CITY CEMETERY, United Kingdom
Son of Annie Moorhead, of 18, Bright Street, Belfast, and the late William Moorhead.

Moran, Bryan - Driver
T/33084 Royal Army Service Corps *Died in War on 15 May 1917*
BASRA MEMORIAL, Iraq
Born in Sligo, enlisted Glasgow, resident of Belfast. Formerly 4545 Connaught Rangers

Moran, Patrick Joseph - Gunner
5314 Royal Garrison Artillery *Age 27 Died of Wounds on 11 January 1917*
BELFAST (MILLTOWN) ROMAN CATHOLIC CEMETERY, United Kingdom
(Served as LAVERY) Son of James and Sophia Moran, of Belfast; husband of E A Moran, of 10, Sackville Street, Belfast.

Moran, Thomas - Private
5542 Royal Irish Regiment 1st Garrison Battalion *Age 45 Died as a result of War on 9 April 1919*
CAIRO WAR MEMORIAL CEMETERY, Egypt
Husband of Agnes Moran, of 5, Tyrone Street, Belfast.

Moreland, Robert - Lance Corporal
44141 Royal Army Medical Corps 110th Field Ambulance *Age 23 Died of Wounds on 9 June 1917*
LONGUENESSE (ST. OMER) SOUVENIR CEMETERY, France
Son of Robert and Mary Moreland, of 54, Sydney Street West, Belfast.

Moreland, Robert - Private
225614 Canadian Infantry (Western Ontario Regiment) 18th Battalion *Died in War on 13 April 1917*
VIMY MEMORIAL, France
Son of William and Charlotte, 168, Cambrai Street, Belfast.

Moreland, Thomas - Private
3290 Royal Inniskilling Fusiliers 1st Battalion *Died in War on 19 June 1915*
TWELVE TREE COPSE CEMETERY, Turkey
145, Bellevue Street, Belfast. A former member of the old UVF. His brother also served.

Morell, James - Carpenter
Mercantile Marine S.S. "Arab" (Shanghai)
Age 65 Drowned, as a result of an attack by an enemy submarine on 7 January 1918
TOWER HILL MEMORIAL, United Kingdom
Son of the late James and Mary Morell; husband of Sarah Ann Morell (née McKee), of 154, Corporation Street, Belfast. Born at Picton, Nova Scotia.

Morell, Robert - Rifleman
666 Royal Irish Rifles 16th Battalion *Died in War on 4 July 1916*
THIEPVAL MEMORIAL, France
Born in Ballymena, enlisted Lurgan, resident of Belfast.

Morgan , James Finlay - Corporal
18508 Royal Irish Rifles 12th Battalion *Age 20 Killed in Action on 1 July 1916*
THIEPVAL MEMORIAL, France
Born in Belfast, enlisted in Carrickfergus.

Morgan, Frank - Corporal
10112 Royal Irish Fusiliers 2nd Battalion *Died in War on 14 March 1915*
YPRES (MENIN GATE) MEMORIAL, Belgium
54, Middlepath Street, Belfast. Born in County Down.

Morgan, George - Corporal
7017 Royal Irish Rifles 2nd Battalion *Age 30 Killed in Action on 16 June 1915*
YPRES (MENIN GATE) MEMORIAL, Belgium
Son of the late Albert and Elizabeth Morgan; husband of Jane Morgan, of 13, Chamberlain Street, Belfast.

Morgan, John - Able Seaman
Clyde Z/6053 Royal Naval Volunteer Reserve HMS "Black Prince"
Killed in Action at Battle of Jutland on 31 May 1916
PORTSMOUTH NAVAL MEMORIAL, United Kingdom
Son of John and Mary Morgan, of Belfast.

Morgan, Malachy - Private
13746 Royal Inniskilling Fusiliers 7th Battalion *Died of Wounds on 10 March 1916*
PHILOSOPHE BRITISH CEMETERY, MAZINGARBE, France
Born in Belfast.

Morgan, Patrick Lawrence - Private
S/23658 Seaforth Highlanders 1st Garrison Battalion *Age 37 Died in War on 28 November 1917*
STRUMA MILITARY CEMETERY, Greece
Educated by the Christian Brothers. Married his wife Margaret in St Joseph's Chruch and his death left her a widow with three children. Formerly 3651 Highland Light Infantry.

Morgan, Robert - Private
3819 Royal Irish Fusiliers 7/8th Battalion *Age 26 Died in War on 4 January 1918*
UNICORN CEMETERY, VEND'HUILE, France
Son of Robert and Annie Morgan, of 21, Stratheden Street, Belfast.

Morgan, Robert - Private
643673 Canadian Infantry (Central Ontario Regiment) 19th Battalion *Age 26 Died in War on 9 May 1917*
VIMY MEMORIAL, France
Son of William and Rachel Morgan, of 52, Ottawa Street, Belfast, Ireland.
A Presbyterian, he had worked in Canada as a labourer.

Morgan, Robert - Sergeant
9931 Royal Inniskilling Fusiliers 1st Battalion *Died in War on 28 January 1917*
CATERPILLAR VALLEY CEMETERY LONGUEVAL, France
Born and enlisted in Belfast.

Morgan, William - Rifleman
594534 London Regiment 18th (County of London) Battalion (London Irish Rifles)
Killed in Action on 16 August 1917
LOOS MEMORIAL, France
Born in Belfast, enlisted in London.

Morgan, William - Second Lieutenant
Royal Inniskilling Fusiliers 7th Battalion *Age 25 Died in War on 9 September 1916*
THIEPVAL MEMORIAL, France
Son of the late Francis Morgan and of Sarah Morgan (stepmother), of 147, University Street, Belfast; husband of the late Annie Rodgers (formerly Morgan).

Morgan, William J P - Sergeant Major
1655 Leinster Regiment 7th Battalion *Died in War on 8 March 1917*
POND FARM CEMETERY, Belgium
Brother of Mrs Spears, 13, Abyssinia Street, Belfast.

Moroney, Joseph Austin - Gunner
L/20942 Royal Horse Artillery and Royal Field Artillery *Died in War on 27 April 1918*
GROOTEBEEK BRITISH CEMETERY, Belgium
Born and enlisted in London, resident of Belfast.

Morris, George Herbert - Private
11889 Gloucestershire Regiment 2nd Battalion *Age 22 Died in War on 7 February 1915*
YPRES (MENIN GATE) MEMORIAL, Belgium
Son of Joseph and Anna Maria Morris, of 32, Vicinage Park, Belfast.

Morris, John - Rifleman
1236 Royal Irish Rifles 7th Battalion *Age 43 Died in War on 9 September 1916*
THIEPVAL MEMORIAL, France
Son of John and Maryanne Morris, of Elizabeth Street, Belfast. A railway clerk.

Morris, Thomas - Rifleman
7276 Royal Irish Rifles 1st Battalion *Killed in Action on 9 May 1915*
PLOEGSTEERT MEMORIAL, Belgium
Husband of Rose Morris, of 15, Cinnamond Street, Belfast.

Morrison, Albert Lowry - Stoker First Class
SS/113067 Royal Navy HMS "Queen Mary" *Killed in Action on 31 May 1916*
PORTSMOUTH NAVAL MEMORIAL, United Kingdom
Died along with his friend and fellow Belfast man, Robert O'Neill, when the battleship HMS "Queen Mary" exploded.

Morrison, Albert Victor - Second Lieutenant
Royal Scots Fusiliers 2nd Battalion *Age 21 Died in War on 30 July 1916*
THIEPVAL MEMORIAL, France
Son of Alexander and Margaret Elizabeth Morrison, of 38, Hopefield Avenue, Antrim Road, Belfast.

Morrison, Alexander Thompson - Corporal
PO/16397 Royal Marine Light Infantry 1st R.M. Battalion Royal Naval Division
Age 24 Died in War on 6 October 1918
HERMIES HILL BRITISH CEMETERY, France
Son of James and Emily Morrison, of 7, My Lady's Road, Belfast. Awarded the Military Medal.

Morrison, Cyril Aubrey - Rifleman
40933 Royal Irish Rifles 1st Battalion formerly North Irish Horse *Age 18 Killed in Action on 16 August 1917*
TYNE COT MEMORIAL, Belgium
Son of William Todd Morrison and Madeline M. Morrison, of Atlantic House, 101, Limestone Road, Belfast.

Morrison, David - Corporal
13117 Royal Irish Rifles 9th Battalion *Died in War on 16 January 1916*
SUCRERIE MILITARY CEMETERY, COLINCAMPS, France
Husband of Jessie Morrison, 13, Southland Street, Belfast.

Morrison, Douglas St. George - Lieutenant
Royal Field Artillery attached "R" Anti-Aircraft Battery *Died in War on 3 September 1917*
ACHIET-LE-GRAND COMMUNAL CEMETERY EXTENSION, France
Son of Robert Douglas Morrison (County Inspector Royal Irish Constabulary) and Henrietta Maria Langrishe Morrison (née St. George), of "Dunsona" 28, Derryvolgie Avenue, Belfast.

Morrison, Fraser - Lance Corporal
7/1219 Royal Irish Rifles 7th Battalion *Age 22 Killed in Action on 6 August 1916*
VERMELLES BRITISH CEMETERY, France
Son of Francis and Susanna Morrison, of 36, McDonnell Street, Belfast.

Morrison, George - Private
21311 Princess Victoria's (Royal Irish Fusiliers) 7th Battalion *Died in War on 9 September 1916*
THIEPVAL MEMORIAL, France
Born in Belfast, enlisted Glasgow. Formerly 17011, Royal Dublin Fusiliers

Morrison, George - Rifleman
8705 Royal Irish Rifles 2nd Battalion *Age 22 Killed in Action on 27 October 1914*
LE TOURET MEMORIAL, France
Son of George and Ann Morrison, of 20, Parkview Street, Belfast.

Morrison, John - Private
9894 Manchester Regiment 18th Battalion *Died in War on 30 July 1916*
THIEPVAL MEMORIAL, France
Born and enlisted Belfast.

Morrison, John - Rifleman
6400 Royal Irish Rifles 2nd Battalion *Died in War on 5 May 1916*
ECOIVRES MILITARY CEMETERY, MONT-ST. ELOI, France
Husband of Catherine Morrison, of 41, Hamill Street, Belfast.

Morrison, John Graham - Private
160239 Canadian Infantry (Central Ontario Regiment) *Died in War on 22 October 1916*
ADANAC MILITARY CEMETERY, MIRAUMONT, FRANCE.
1, Lombard Avenue, Belfast.

Morrison, Joseph - Private
3351 Royal Irish Regiment *Age 20 Died as a result of war on 27 December 1920*
BELFAST CITY CEMETERY, United Kingdom
Husband of Mrs. Mary Morrison, of 19, Boyne Square, Sandy Row, Belfast.

Morrison, Patrick - Rifleman
9078 Royal Irish Rifles 2nd Battalion *Age 19 Died in War on 1 August 1916*
BRIGHTON (BEAR ROAD) BOROUGH CEMETERY, United Kingdom
Son of the late Thomas and Jane Morrison, of 50, Main Street, Greencastle, Belfast.

Morrison, Robert - Private
13112 Royal Scots Fusiliers 7th Battalion *Died in War on 26 September 1915*
LOOS MEMORIAL, France
Born in Belfast, enlisted Irvine, Scotland.

Morrison, Robert - Private
42398 Royal Irish Fusiliers 1st Battalion *Age 20 Died of Wounds on 1 October 1918*
DADIZEELE NEW BRITISH CEMETERY, Belgium
Son of Joseph and Annie Morrison, of 118, Riga Street, Belfast.

Morrison, Thomas - Private
10215 Royal Inniskilling Fusiliers 1st Battalion *Age 22 Killed in Action on 22 May 1915*
TWELVE TREE COPSE CEMETERY, Turkey
Son of William and Ellen Morrison, of Belfast.

Morrison, Thomas - Private
PLY/17545 Royal Marine Light Infantry 2nd R.M. Battalion Royal Naval Division *Died of Wounds on 22 February 1917*
DERNANCOURT COMMUNAL CEMETERY EXTENSION, France
2a, Tobergill Street, Belfast.

Morrison, Thomas - Rifleman
1392 Royal Irish Rifles 2nd Battalion *Killed in Action on 24 March 1918*
NOYON NEW BRITISH CEMETERY, France
Born and enlisted in Belfast.

Morrison, Thomas - Sergeant
9401 Royal Inniskilling Fusiliers 6th Battalion *Age 29 Killed in Action on 3 October 1918*
TEMPLEUX-LE-GUERARD BRITISH CEMETERY, France
Son of George and Mary A. Morrison, of 212, Templemore Street, Beersbridge Road, Belfast.

Morrison, Thomas William - Able Seaman
J/20256 Royal Navy HMS "Queen Mary" *Killed in Action on 31 May 1916*
PORTSMOUTH NAVAL MEMORIAL, United Kingdom
A native of Belfast.

Morrison, William John - Corporal
7134 Royal Inniskilling Fusiliers 1st Battalion *Age 35 Died in War on 1 February 1917*
YPRES (MENIN GATE) MEMORIAL, Belgium
Son of the late James A. and Charlotte Morrison. An Apprentice Boy, he was also member of the old UVF.

Morrison, William Ross - Private
9966 Hampshire Regiment 2nd Battalion *Age 20 Died in War on 8 January 1916*
HELLES MEMORIAL, Turkey
Son of Thomas Ross Morrison and Jane Long Morrison, of 152, Nelson Street, Belfast.

Morrow, Adam - Private
PLY/13542 Royal Marine Light Infantry HMS "Monmouth"
Age 28 Killed in Action at Battle of Coronel on 1 November 1914
PLYMOUTH NAVAL MEMORIAL, United Kingdom
Native of Parkmore, Belfast. Son of James and Margaret Morrow, of Issbawn, Cushendall, County Antrim.

Morrow, Alexander - Sergeant
7338 Lancashire Fusiliers 1/6th Battalion *Died in War on 8 August 1915*
REDOUBT CEMETERY HELLES, Turkey
Born in Belfast, enlisted in Middleton Lancashire.

Morrow, Andrew - Private
200490 King's Own (Royal Lancaster Regiment) 1/4th Battalion *Died in War on 29 September 1917*
TYNE COT MEMORIAL, Belgium
Born in Belfast, enlisted in Ulverston, England.

Morrow, Arthur Galway - Rifleman
16894 Royal Irish Rifles 14th Battalion *Age 19 Killed in Action on 1 July 1916*
CONNAUGHT CEMETERY, THIEPVAL, France
Son of John J. and Mary Morrow, of 10, India Street, Belfast.

Morrow, Frederick Roulstone - Acting Sergeant
Royal Field Artillery D Battery 174th Brigade *Age 21 Died in War 17 September 1917*
OUTTERSTEENE COMMUNAL CEMETERY EXTENSION, France
Born in Belfast the son of Mrs and Mrs Alexander Morrow of Sandymount, Dublin. A law clerk in civilian life, he was a former junior Irish international football player.

Morrow, Hugh Gelston - Captain
Royal Irish Rifles 15th Battalion *Age 24 Died in War on 20 October 1918*
HARLEBEKE NEW BRITISH CEMETERY, Belgium
Son of Andrew J. Morrow, of 2, Avonmore Terrace, Balmoral, Belfast. He was unmarried, and worked as a warehouseman before enlisting as a private soldier and was later commissioned. Awarded the Military Cross for bravery.

Morrow, James - Lance Corporal
9074 Royal Irish Rifles 1st Battalion *Killed in Action on 9 May 1915*
PLOEGSTEERT MEMORIAL, Belgium
Born and enlisted in Belfast.

Morrow, James - Rifleman
8731 Royal Irish Rifles 2nd Battalion *Killed in Action on 16 June 1915*
YPRES (MENIN GATE) MEMORIAL, Belgium
Husband of Nellie Morrow, Coates Street, Belfast.

Morrow, James Foster - Rifleman
658 Royal Irish Rifles 8th Battalion *Died in War on 20 June 1917*
CABIN HILL CEMETERY, Belgium
Born and enlisted in Belfast.

Morrow, John Bennett - Rifleman
13332 Royal Irish Rifles "D" Company 8th Battalion *Age 23 Died in War on 2 July 1916*
THIEPVAL MEMORIAL, France
Son of John Morrow and Martha Breeze Morrow, of 47, Rushfield Avenue, Ormeau Road, Belfast.

Morrow, R - Private
4677 Royal Inniskilling Fusiliers 6th Battalion *Age 26 Died in War on 3 October 1918*
GUIZANCOURT FARM CEMETERY, GOUY, France
Son of Andrew and Lizzie Morrow, of 18, Excise Street, Grosvenor Road, Belfast.

Morrow, Robert - Rifleman
1916 Royal Irish Rifles 14th Battalion *Age 20 Killed in Action on 16 August 1917*
TYNE COT MEMORIAL, Belgium
Son of Thomas R. and Christiana Morrow, of 63, Ormeau Road, Belfast.

Morrow, Robert - Sapper
57552 Royal Engineers 126th Field Company *Age 38 Killed in Action on 20 April 1918*
THE HUTS CEMETERY, Belgium
Husband of Mary Ann Morrow, of 24, Central Street, Belfast.

Morrow, Stewart - Sergeant
12483 Royal Irish Rifles 8th Battalion *Died of Wounds on 10 July 1916*
BELFAST (DUNDONALD) CEMETERY, United Kingdom
Husband of Sarah Morrow, of 19, Rathmore Street, Belfast.

Morrow, Thomas - Private
2467 Royal Inniskilling Fusiliers 7th/8th Battalion *Died in War on 8 August 1917*
TYNE COT CEMETERY, Belgium
Husband of Mary Morrow, 30 Wilton Street, Belfast.

Morrow, W - Private
28284 New Zealand Machine Gun Corps *Killed in Action on 23 July 1917*
MUD CORNER CEMETERY, Belgium
Son of Mr. and Mrs. S. Morrow, of 14, Brussels Street, Belfast.

Morrow, William Alexander - Private
H/71123 North Irish Horse *Age 38 Died of Wounds on 9 April 1918*
HINGES MILITARY CEMETERY, France
Son of Mrs. Agnes Jane Morrow, of 1, Little Grosvenor Street, Belfast. Born at Rathfriland, County Down.

Morrow, William Breeze - Lance Corporal
64081 Royal Engineers *Age 28 Died of pneumonia on 20 March 1919*
BELFAST (DUNDONALD) CEMETERY, United Kingdom
Son of John Morrow; husband of Margaret Morrow (née Fisher), of Belfast. Born at Belfast.

Mortimer, Bernard - Private
18908 Royal Scots Fusiliers 10th Works Battalion transferred to TR/2/20882 77th Battalion, Training Reserve *Age 28 Died in War on 6 December 1916*
DUNDEE (BALGAY) CEMETERY, United Kingdom
Son of Arthur and Marget Mortimer, of 83, Unity Street, Belfast.

Mortimer, Robert - Second Lieutenant
3351 Royal Irish Rifles *Age 25 Died in War on 27 October 1918*
BELFAST CITY CEMETERY, United Kingdom
Son of John Charles and Martha A. Mortimer. Born at Belfast.

Morton, H - Engineer
Mercantile Marine S.S. "Cymric" (Liverpool) *Age 23 Killed, as a result of an attack by an enemy submarine on 8 May 1916*
TOWER HILL MEMORIAL, United Kingdom
Son of John Morton, of "Rossmoyne", Winston Gardens, Knock, Belfast. Born at Belfast.

Morton, Henry - Private
27971 Leinster Regiment 1st Battalion *Age 28 Died in War on 19 October 1918*
RAMLEH WAR CEMETERY, Israel
Son of Robert M. Morton, of 38, Stranmillis Gardens, Belfast.

Morton, James Alexander - Sergeant
5845 Royal Irish Rifles 2nd Battalion *Shot by a Sniper on 27 May 1915*
RIDGE WOOD MILITARY CEMETERY, Belgium
4 Anglesea Street, Belfast, a younger brother also served.

Morton, James Lorimer - Private
S4/060470 Army Service Corps G.H.Q. 3rd Echelon *Age 26 Died of pneumonia on 24 October 1918*
STE. MARIE CEMETERY, LE HAVRE, France
Son of Robert M. and Isabella A. Morton, of 38, Stranmillis Gardens, Stranmillis, Belfast.

Morton, Nathaniel - Lance Corporal
18/250 Royal Irish Rifles 18th Battalion *Age 19 Died of Wounds on 29 April 1916*
GRANGEGORMAN MILITARY CEMETERY, Republic of Ireland
Son of James Morton, of 22, Woodvale Street, Belfast.

Motherwell, James - Private
202542 Dorsetshire Regiment 1st/4th Battalion *Age 41 Died of cholera on 18 November 1917*
BAGHDAD (NORTH GATE) WAR CEMETERY, Iraq
Son of William Gemmell Motherwell and Mary Motherwell, of Belfast; husband of Marie Motherwell, of 20, Locket Road, Wealdstone, Harrow, Middesex. Member of No 29 Masonic Lodge Belfast.

Motherwell, John Ernest - Captain
Royal Irish Rifles 9th Battalion attached The Loyal North Lancashire Regiment 3rd Battalion *Age 29 Died in War on 21 October 1916*
REGINA TRENCH CEMETERY, GRANDCOURT, France
Son of David and Catherine Motherwell, of 7, Somerset Terrace, Belfast.

Moutray, Alexander - Rifleman
15/15522 Royal Irish Rifles 15th Battalion *Age 43 Died in War on 11 February 1918*
BELFAST (DUNDONALD) CEMETERY, United Kingdom
Husband of Mary Moutray, of 25, Annadale Street, Belfast.

Moygannon, James Alexander - Private
11151 Royal Irish Fusiliers 5th Battalion *Died in War on 8 December 1915*
DOIRAN MEMORIAL, *Greece*
Son of David and Martha Moygannon 13, Lindsay Street, Belfast.

Muir, Alexander - Private
26002 Princess Victoria's (Royal Irish Fusiliers) 1st Battalion *Died in War on 1 October 1917*
ROCQUIGNY-EQUANCOURT ROAD BRITISH CEMETERY, MANANCOURT, *France*
Born in Belfast, enlisted Newry.

Mulcahy, Daniel Howard - Rifleman
19906 Royal Irish Rifles 7th Battalion *Died in War on 30 September 1917*
COJEUL BRITISH CEMETERY, ST. MARTIN-SUR-COJEUL, *France*
Husband of Mary Mulcahy and father of eight children. 1, Milford Street, Belfast.

Mulgrew, Edward - Private
24691 Princess Victoria's (Royal Irish Fusiliers) 1st Battalion *Killed in Action on 24 March 1918*
POZIERES MEMORIAL, *France*
Born and enlisted in Belfast.

Mulgrew, John - Rifleman
9054 Royal Irish Rifles 2nd Battalion *Killed in Action on 27 October 1914*
LE TOURET MEMORIAL, *France*
39, Malt Street, Belfast.

Mulhern, P J - Private
S/29909 Argyll and Sutherland Highlanders 3rd Battalion *Age 27 Died as a result of war on 19 March 1919*
BELFAST (MILLTOWN) ROMAN CATHOLIC CEMETERY, *United Kingdom*
Son of Daniel and Ellen McManus Mulhern, of 32, Queen Street, Govan, Glasgow. Born at Belfast.

Mulheron, Andrew - Rifleman
5955 Royal Irish Rifles 6th Battalion *Died in War on 20 September 1916*
LAHANA MILITARY CEMETERY, *Greece*
Resident of Belfast, enlisted in Glasgow.

Mulheron, Daniel - Private
23082 Royal Irish Fusiliers 7th/8th Battalion *Age 36 Killed in Action on 6 September 1916*
FLATIRON COPSE CEMETERY, MAMETZ, *France*
Son of John and Sarah Mulheron; husband of Mary Mulheron, of 25, Vulcan Street, Belfast.

Mulholland, Daniel - Driver
69500 Royal Field Artillery 119th Battery *Age 24 Died as a result of war on 14 November 1918*
NIEDERZWEHREN CEMETERY, *Germany*
Brother of Patrick Mulholland, of 43, Church Road, Garston, Liverpool. Native of Belfast.

Mulholland, David - Lance Corporal
19141 Royal Irish Rifles A Company 9th Battalion *Age 20 Died of Wounds on 16 January 1916*
FORCEVILLE COMMUNAL CEMETERY AND EXTENSION, *France*
Son of John and Bessie Mulholland, of Belfast.

Mulholland, Frank - Private
2155 Lancashire Fusiliers 1/7th Battalion *Died in War on 23 August 1915*
ALEXANDRIA (CHATBY) MILITARY AND WAR MEMORIAL CEMETERY, *Egypt*
Born in Belfast, enlisted Salford, England.

Mulholland, Henry - Private
15083 Connaught Rangers 5th Battalion *Died as a result of war on 14 November 1918*
BUSIGNY COMMUNAL CEMETERY EXTENSION, *France*
Born in Lisburn, enlisted and resident of Belfast. Formerly 1642 Leinster Regiment

Mulholland, Hugh - Private
4656 Royal Inniskilling Fusiliers 5th Battalion *Age 22 Died in War on 15 August 1915*
HELLES MEMORIAL, *Turkey*
Son of Henry and Mary Mulholland, of 47, Milford Street, Belfast.

Mulholland, James - Private
3/7400 Royal Inniskilling Fusiliers 3rd Battalion *Age 32 Died in War on 17 June 1918*
BELFAST (MILLTOWN) ROMAN CATHOLIC CEMETERY, *United Kingdom*
Husband of S. Mulholland, of 50, Chemical Street, Belfast. Discharged as unfit for war service and awarded the Silver War Badge.

Mulholland, John - Boy
28750 Royal Irish Fusiliers 3rd Battalion *Age 16 Died in War on 26 September 1918*
BELFAST (DUNDONALD) CEMETERY, *United Kingdom*
Son of Joseph and Elizabeth Mulholland, of 20, Boyne Square, Sandy Row, Belfast.

Mulholland, John - Lance Corporal
14462 Scots Guards *Died in War on 31 July 1917*
YPRES (MENIN GATE) MEMORIAL, *Belgium*
Born in Belfast, enlisted Glasgow.

Mulholland, Robert - Private
23575 Royal Irish Fusiliers 1st Battalion *Age 20 Died in War on 9 July 1917*
CRUMP TRENCH BRITISH CEMETERY, FAMPOUX, *France*
Son of Mr. and Mrs. Patrick Mulholland, of 34, Glenview Street, Belfast.

Mulholland, Samuel - Private
117318 Machine Gun Corps (Infantry) formerly 49997 Welsh Regiment *Killed in Action on 21 March 1918*
POZIERES MEMORIAL, *France*
Born in Belfast the only son of Captain Mulholland and Rosena Muholland, of 27, Malefant Street, Cathays, Cardiff.

Mulholland, Samuel - Private
3561 Royal Irish Rifles 12th Battalion *Died of Wounds on 1 July 1916*
THIEPVAL MEMORIAL
59, Denmark Street, Belfast.

Mulholland, William Andrew - A/Lance Corporal
201796 Prince of Wales's Own (West Yorkshire Regiment) 2/5th Battalion *Died in War on 20 November 1917*
ROCQUIGNY-EQUANCOURT ROAD BRITISH CEMETERY, MANANCOURT, *France*
Born in Belfast, enlisted in Leeds, Yorkshire.

Mulholland, William J - Sergeant
13419 Royal Inniskilling Fusiliers 7th Battalion *Died in War on 6 March 1916*
PHILOSOPHE BRITISH CEMETERY, MAZINGARBE, *France*
Husband of M. Gillespie (formerly Mulholland), of 18, Castlereagh Road, Belfast.

Journey of Remembering

Mulholland, William P. - Private
2280 Irish Guards 1st Battalion *Age 27 Died in War on 6 November 1914*
YPRES (MENIN GATE) MEMORIAL, *Belgium*
Son of William John and Mary Mulholland, of 136, Cavendish Street. Formerly Royal Irish Constabulary.

Mullaly, Frank - Private
Connaught Rangers *Died in War*
8, Cavour Street, Belfast.

Mullan, Bernard - Rifleman
8240 Royal Irish Rifles 2nd Battalion *Died in War on 18 March 1915*
BELFAST (MILLTOWN) ROMAN CATHOLIC CEMETERY, *United Kingdom*
Born and enlisted in Belfast.

Mullan, Charles - Private
9420 Irish Guards 2nd Battalion *Age 31 Died in War on 25 September 1916*
GUARDS' CEMETERY, LESBOEUFS, *France*
Son of Charles and Mary Ann Mullan, of 66, Hawthorn Street, Belfast. Native of Caledon, County Tyrone.

Mullan, David - Rifleman
3707 Royal Irish Rifles 8th Battalion *Age 17 Died in War on 2 July 1916*
THIEPVAL MEMORIAL, *France*
Son of David Mullan, of 61, Witham Street, Belfast.

Mullan, Edward - Stoker First Class
SS/106287 Royal Navy HMS "Hawke" *Age 26 Lost at sea on 15 October 1914*
CHATHAM NAVAL MEMORIAL, *United Kingdom*
Son of William and Jane Mullen, of 76, Sugarfield Street, Belfast.

Mullan, John - Private
10474 Royal Inniskilling Fusiliers 2nd Battalion *Age 20 Died in War on 16 May 1915*
LE TOURET MEMORIAL, *France*
Son of Mrs. Alice Mullan, of 26, Artillery Street, Belfast.

Mullan, John - Private
7551 Royal Inniskilling Fusiliers 2nd Battalion *Age 31 Died in War on 21 October 1914*
PLOEGSTEERT MEMORIAL, *Belgium*
Son of Patrick and Margaret Mullan, of Lincoln Avenue, Belfast; husband of Margaret Mullan, of 3, Dawson Street, Belfast.

Mullan, Thomas - Private
18188 Leinster Regiment "D" Company 2nd Battalion *Age 28; Died of Wounds on 17 September 1918*
TERLINCTHUN BRITISH CEMETERY, WIMILLE, *France*
Husband of Mary Ann Mullan, of 50, Sultan Street, Belfast.

Mullan, Thomas - Rifleman
5542 Royal Irish Rifles 2nd Battalion *Age 29 Killed in Action on 16 June 1915*
YPRES (MENIN GATE) MEMORIAL, *Belgium*
Son of the late Henry and Catherine Mullan; husband of Ellen J. Beattie (formerly Mullan), of 10, Genoa Street, Grosvenor Road, Belfast.

Mullen, Edward - Stoker First Class
SS/106287 Royal Navy HMS "Hawke" *Age 26 Killed in Action with a submarine in North Sea on 15 October 1914*
CHATHAM NAVAL MEMORIAL, United Kingdom
Son of William and Jane Mullen, of 76, Sugarfield Street, Belfast.

Mullen, George William - Rifleman
9/421 Royal Irish Rifles 9th Battalion *Killed in Action on 1 July 1916*
THIEPVAL MEMORIAL, France
Only son of James and Maraget Jane Mullen, 135 Westmoreland Street, Belfast.

Mullen, Hugh - Lance Sergeant
27764 Royal Inniskilling Fusiliers 9th Battalion *Killed in Action on 16 August 1917*
TYNE COT MEMORIAL, Belgium
Born in Belfast, enlisted Coleraine.

Mullen, James - Rifleman
15652 Royal Irish Rifles 9th Battalion *Killed in Action on 1 July 1916*
THIEPVAL MEMORIAL, France
Born and enlisted in Belfast.

Mullen, Patrick - Private
7370 Princess Louise's (Argyll & Sutherland Highlanders) 2nd Battalion *Died in War on 29 October 1918*
THIEPVAL MEMORIAL, France
Born in Dungannon, enlisted Glasgow, resident of Belfast.

Mullen, Patrick - Rifleman
6694 Royal Irish Rifles 1st Battalion *Age 30 Killed in Action on 11 April 1916*
BECOURT MILITARY CEMETERY, BECORDEL-BECOURT, France
Son of John and Grace Mullen, of Newtownards, County Down; husband of Ellen Mullen, of 22, Ton Street, Belfast. Three brothers served.

Mullheron, Joseph - Private
11950 Cheshire Regiment 2nd Battalion *Age 24 Died in War on 5 October 1915*
LOOS MEMORIAL, France
Son of John and Sarah Mullheron, of 36, Kilmood Street, Ballymacarrett, Belfast.

Mulligan, Francis William - Rifleman
9386 Royal Irish Rifles 2nd Battalion *Killed in Action on 7 June 1917*
WULVERGHEM-LINDENHOEK ROAD MILITARY CEMETERY, Belgium
Born and enlisted in Belfast.

Mulligan, John - Private
3632 Royal Inniskilling Fusiliers 1st Battalion *Killed in Action on 19 June 1915*
TWELVE TREE COPSE CEMETERY, Turkey
Born in Belfast. Son of John Mulligan; husband of Mary Mulligan, of 2, Head Street, Enniskillen, County Fermanagh.

Mullin, Joseph - Gunner
90856 Royal Field Artillery 13th Brigade *Age 22 Died on active service on 7 May 1916*
AMARA WAR CEMETERY, Iraq
Born and enlisted in Belfast, the son of Thomas and Susan Mullin, of 48, North Strand Road, Dublin.

Mullins, Thomas - Sergeant
6719 King's Shropshire Light Infantry 5th Battalion *Died in War on 18 March 1917*
ARRAS MEMORIAL, France
38, California Street, Belfast.

Mulvenny, John - Private
20684 Princess Victoria's (Royal Irish Fusiliers) 8th Battalion *Died in War on 8 July 1916*
ST PATRICK'S CEMETERY LOOS, France
Born in Belfast, enlisted in Liverpool.

Mumford, Henry Walter - Rifleman
392488 London Regiment 9th Battalion *Died in War on 29 August 1917*
WANCOURT BRITISH CEMETERY, France
Born Belfast 1897 the son of Reverend Henry and his wife Ethel. History student at the University of Belfast. Enlisted 1916.

Munce, G A - Private
Cameron Highlanders 2nd Battalion *Died in War on or before August 1915*
239, Shankill Road Belfast.

Munce, George - Rifleman
15653 Royal Irish Rifles 15th Battalion *Killed in Action on 1 July 1916*
THIEPVAL MEMORIAL, France
67, Tobergill Street, Belfast.

Munn, John - Private
9060 Royal Fusiliers (City of London Regiment) 7th Battalion *Died in War on 13 November 1916*
ANCRE BRITISH CEMETERY, BEAUMONT-HAMEL, France
Born and enlisted in Belfast.

Munn, Robert - Rifleman
708 Royal Irish Rifles 8th Battalion *Died in War on 2 July 1916*
THIEPVAL MEMORIAL, France
Born and enlisted in Belfast.

Munro, William James - Gunner
39728 Royal Garrison Artillery *Died in War on 29 July 1917*
BAILLEUL COMMUNAL CEMETERY EXTENSION (NORD), France
Born in County Down, enlisted Omagh, resident of Belfast.

Munster, John - Rifleman
13922 Royal Irish Rifles "C" Company 1st Battalion *Age 34 Died of Wounds on 28 February 1915*
ESTAIRES COMMUNAL CEMETERY, France
Son of John Munster, of Drogheda; husband of R A. Munster, of 44, Seaforde Street, Belfast. Mortally wounded by shellfire.

Murdoch, Ross - Private
12568 Royal Irish Fusiliers 1st Battalion *Age 38 Died in War on 12 October 1916*
THIEPVAL MEMORIAL, France
Son of Nathaniel and Ann Murdoch, of 36, Trillick Street, Belfast; husband of Elizabeth Cavan (formerly Murdoch), of 56, Trillick Street, Belfast.

Murdock, James Gabriel - Rifleman
19706 Royal Irish Rifles 2nd Battalion *Age 24 Killed in Action on 1 October 1918*
DADIZEELE NEW BRITISH CEMETERY, Belgium
Son of William James Murdock, of Belfast.

Murdock, James Stanley - Rifleman
18351 Royal Irish Rifles 14th Battalion *Died in War on 1 September 1916*
YPRES (MENIN GATE) MEMORIAL, Belgium
Born and enlisted in Belfast.

Murdock, John - Rifleman
879 Royal Irish Rifles 15th Battalion *Killed in Action on 1 July 1916*
THIEPVAL MEMORIAL, France
Born and enlisted in Belfast. Member of Castleton Presbyterian Church.

Murdock, William Andrew - Lance Corporal
15656 Royal Irish Rifles 15th Battalion *Age 23 Died as a Prisoner of War on 20 July 1918*
BERLIN SOUTH-WESTERN CEMETERY, Germany
Son of Charlotte Murdock, of 6, Canmore Street, Belfast, and the late William Andrew Murdock.

Murdock, William Francis - Rifleman
12097 Royal Irish Rifles 15th Battalion *Killed in Action on 1 July 1916*
THIEPVAL MEMORIAL, France
Born and enlisted in Belfast.

Murdock, William Henry - Sergeant
8294 Royal Inniskilling Fusiliers 1st Battalion *Died in War on 23 May 1915*
HELLES MEMORIAL, Turkey
86 Mountpottinger Road Belfast. The son of Company Sergeant Major Patrick Murdock and Annie Murdock, 8, Ely Place Dublin.

Murphy, Alexander - Private
1662 Leinster Regiment 7th Battalion *Died in War on 3 September 1916*
THIEPVAL MEMORIAL, France
Born and enlisted in Belfast.

Murphy, Alexander - Sergeant
13723 Royal Scots Fusiliers 6/7th Battalion *Died in War on 21 October 1916*
THIEPVAL MEMORIAL, France
Born in Belfast, enlisted in Paisley, Scotland.

Murphy, Christopher - Rifleman
20258 Royal Irish Rifles 1st Battalion *Killed in Action on 15 April 1918*
ST SEVER CEMETERY EXTENSION ROUEN, France
Born and enlisted in Dublin, resident of Belfast.

Murphy, Francis - Private
4826 Leinster Regiment 2nd Battalion *Died in War on 28 September 1918*
HOOGE CRATER CEMETERY, Belgium
Born in Brookeborough, Fermanagh, enlisted and resident in Belfast.

JOURNEY OF REMEMBERING

Murphy, Henry - Corporal
12387 Royal Irish Rifles 8th Battalion *Died in War on 8 January 1916*
AUCHONVILLERS MILITARY CEMETERY, France
Born and enlisted in Belfast.

Murphy, Hugh - Rifleman
15/12099 Royal Irish Rifles "D" Company 15th Battalion *Age 29 Killed in Action on 7 June 1917*
LINDENHOEK CHALET MILITARY CEMETERY, Belgium
Son of James and Elizabeth Murphy, of Belfast; husband of Ellen Murphy, of 24, Nile Street, Belfast.

Murphy, James - Sergeant
5/12045 Royal Irish Fusiliers 5th Battalion *Age 23 Died of Wounds on 10 March 1918*
JERUSALEM WAR CEMETERY, Israel
Son of Mrs. Elizabeth Murphy, of 23, Jennymount Terrace, York Road, Belfast.

Murphy, James A - Private
21176 Royal Irish Fusiliers 1st Battalion *Died in War on 24 August 1918*
PLOEGSTEERT MEMORIAL, Belgium
Brother of Miss A Murphy, 8 Bedeque Street, Belfast.

Murphy, John - Lance Corporal
9017 Royal Irish Rifles 2nd Battalion *Killed in Action on 27 October 1914*
LE TOURET MEMORIAL, France
Born and enlisted in Belfast.

Murphy, John - Private
16600 Royal Dublin Fusiliers 8th Battalion *Age 19 Killed in Action on 27 April 1916*
LOOS MEMORIAL, France
Son of Malachy and Lizzie Murphy, of 8, New Lodge Place, Belfast.

Murphy, John - Sergeant
8263 Royal Irish Rifles "A" Company 1st Battalion *Age 28 Killed in Action on 16 August 1917*
TYNE COT MEMORIAL, Belgium
Son of Mary Ann Murphy, of 8, Lawyer Street, Sandy Row, Belfast.

Murphy, John Joseph - Carpenter
Mercantile Marine S.S. "Huntsmoor" *Age 27 Died in War on 20 February 1918*
DOVER (ST. JAMES'S) CEMETERY, United Kingdom
Son of John Murphy, of 31, Lowry Street, Belfast.

Murphy, John Patrick - Corporal
62866 Royal Army Medical Corps *Age 43 Died of pneumonia on 25 May 1915*
CARNMONEY CEMETERY, United Kingdom
Son of John and Isabella Murphy; husband of Mary Murphy, of 133, Fortingale Street, Belfast. Born at Belfast.

Murphy, John Samuel - Fireman
Mercantile Marine S.S. "Arabic" (Liverpool) *Age 29 Drowned, as a result of an attack by an enemy submarine on 19 August 1915*
TOWER HILL MEMORIAL, United Kingdom
Brother of Mrs. Mary Quinn, of 58, Christian Street, Liverpool. Born in Belfast.

Murphy, Joseph - Gunner
5311 Royal Garrison Artillery 37th Siege Battery *Age 36 Died in War on 22 July 1916*
DANTZIG ALLEY BRITISH CEMETERY, MAMETZ, France
Son of Francis Murphy, of 21, Bow Street, Belfast.

Murphy, Joseph P - Lance Sergeant
6430 Irish Guards 1st Battalion *Died in War on 30 March 1918*
DOUCHY-LES-AYETTE BRITISH CEMETERY, France
Born in Clogher, County Tyrone, enlisted in Liverpool, resident of Belfast.

Murphy, Matthew - Rifleman
15661 Royal Irish Rifles 10th Battalion *Age 21 Killed in Action on 1 July 1916*
CONNAUGHT CEMETERY, THIEPVAL, France
Son of Henry and Elizabeth Murphy, of 21, Excise Street, Belfast.

Murphy, P - Private
316840 Argyll and Sutherland Highlanders 2nd Battalion *Age 22 Killed in Action on 26 February 1917*
PERONNE COMMUNAL CEMETERY EXTENSION, France
Son of Patrick and Rose McAuley, of 12, Fairfield Street, Crumlin Road, Belfast.

Murphy, Thomas James - Rifleman
5565 Royal Irish Rifles 2nd Battalion *Died in War on 10 June 1917*
YPRES (MENIN GATE) MEMORIAL, Belgium
Husband of Mrs S J Murphy, 5 Joy Street, Belfast.

Murphy, William - Rifleman
5331 Royal Irish Rifles 2nd Battalion *Killed in Action on 9 July 1916*
POZIERES BRITISH CEMETERY, OVILLERS-LA BOISSELLE, France
Born and enlisted in Belfast.

Murphy, William J - Rifleman
840 Royal Irish Rifles 9th Battalion *Age 26 Died in War on 2 July 1916*
SERRE ROAD CEMETERY No.2, France
Son of the late Mr. and Mrs. Samuel Murphy, of Westmoreland Street, Belfast; husband of Mrs. McPherson (formerly Murphy), of 15, North King Street, Belfast.

Murray, Alexander - Rifleman
8709 Royal Irish Rifles 1st Battalion *Killed in Action on 10 March 1915*
LE TOURET MEMORIAL, France
Born and enlisted in Belfast.

Murray, Daniel - Lance Corporal
18128 Royal Irish Regiment 2nd Battalion *Age 23 Killed in Action on 16 August 1917*
TYNE COT MEMORIAL, Belgium
Husband of Mrs. A. Murray, of 40, Barrack Street, Belfast.

Murray, David - Rifleman
11369 Royal Irish Rifles 2nd Battalion *Age 26 Killed in Action on 24 March 1918*
POZIERES MEMORIAL, France
Son of Henry and Jane Murray, of 25, Ewart's Row, Belfast.

Murray, Frank - Rifleman
7475 Royal Irish Rifles 1st Battalion *Killed in Action on 9 May 1915*
PLOEGSTEERT MEMORIAL, Belgium
Born and enlisted in Belfast.

Journey of Remembering

Murray, George H - Private
M2/080359 Royal Army Service Corps 619th Mechanical Transport Company
Age 34 Died in War on 29 December 1918
MIKRA BRITISH CEMETERY, KALAMARIA, Greece
Husband of M. Murray, of 30, Springfield Village, Belfast.

Murray, George Turkington - Private
25637 Royal Irish Regiment 7th (South Irish Horse) Battalion *Age 25 Died in War on 12 December 1917*
TEMPLEUX-LE-GUERARD BRITISH CEMETERY, France
Son of Thomas David and Ann Jane Murray, of 474, Oldpark Road, Belfast.

Murray, Henry - Private
4517 Connaught Rangers 5th Battalion *Age 37 Died in War on 22 August 1915*
HELLES MEMORIAL, Turkey
Husband of Catherine Murray, of 7, Grove Street, Belfast.

Murray, Hugh - Corporal
6095 Royal Irish Rifles "C" Company 2nd Battalion *Age 24 Killed in Action on 16 June 1915*
YPRES (MENIN GATE) MEMORIAL, Belgium
Son of Mary Murray, of 20, Seaforde Street, Belfast, and the late James Murray.

Murray, Hugh - Rifleman
3/7431 Royal Irish Rifles 6th Battalion attached Machine Gun Corps (Infantry)
Age 29 Died of wounds accidentally received on 3 June 1918
JERUSALEM WAR CEMETERY, Israel
Husband of Rose Ann Murray, of 5, Sydney Street, Belfast.

Murray, Hugh Robert - Naval Schoolmaster
M/14912 Royal Navy HMS "Vanguard" *Age 22 Killed by internal explosion of vessel at Scapa Flow on 9 July 1917*
PORTSMOUTH NAVAL MEMORIAL, United Kingdom
Son of Samuel and Mary Murray, of 23, Halliday's Road, Belfast.

Murray, J. Henry - Private
GS/16109 Lancers 5th (Royal Irish) *Age 22 Died in War on 22 June 1917*
UNICORN CEMETERY, VEND'HUILE, France
Son of Mary Murray, of 20, Seaforde Street, Belfast, and the late James Murray.

Murray, James - Able Seaman
172205 Royal Navy HMS "Majestic" *Age 40 Killed in Action with submarine off Dardanelles on 27 May 1915*
PLYMOUTH NAVAL MEMORIAL, United Kingdom
Son of Richard Loughlin Murray and Eliza Murray, of 61, Mountpottinger Road, Belfast.

Murray, James - Private
631962 Royal Inniskilling Fusiliers 1st Battalion *Age 17 Died in War on 9 August 1916*
LIJSSENTHOEK MILITARY CEMETERY, Belgium
Son of Patrick and Agnes Murray, of 28, Wallace's Row, Ravenhill Road, Belfast.

Murray, Jim - Lance Corporal
45428 Northumberland Fusiliers 9th Battalion *Age 20 Died of Wounds on 11 April 1918*
LIJSSENTHOEK MILITARY CEMETERY, Belgium
Son of David and Margaret Murray, of 14, Adelaide Avenue, Belfast.

Murray, John - Private
1777 Royal Munster Fusiliers 2nd Battalion *Age 29 Killed in Action on 4 October 1918*
TEMPLEUX-LE-GUERARD BRITISH CEMETERY, France
Son of Patrick and Sarah Murray, of 100, Chatham Street, Belfast.

Murray, Joseph - Private
3630 Royal Inniskilling Fusiliers 1st Battalion *Died in War on 9 August 1916*
LIJSSENTHOEK MILITARY CEMETERY, Belgium
Born and enlisted in Belfast.

Murray, Joseph - Private
3743 Princess Victoria's (Royal Irish Fusiliers) 1st Battalion *Died in War on 14 April 1918*
TYNE COT MEMORIAL, Belgium
Born and enlisted in Belfast.

Murray, Joseph - Private
9715 Royal Irish Regiment 6th Battalion *Age 25 Died in War on 3 September 1916*
THIEPVAL MEMORIAL, France
Son of William and Sarah Murray, of Shamrock Street, Belfast; husband of Mary Murray, of Sallins Road, Naas, County Kildare.

Murray, Patrick - Private
12619 Cameronians (Scottish Rifles) 2nd Battalion *Age 37 Killed in Action on 25 September 1916*
SAILLY-LABOURSE COMMUNAL CEMETERY, France
Son of Constantine and Eliza Murray, of 124, Great George's Street, Belfast.
Native of Greencastle, Londonderry.

Murray, Patrick Joseph - Private
G/18524 Royal Sussex Regiment 11th Battalion *Age 16 Died in War on 24 September 1917*
TYNE COT MEMORIAL, Belgium
Son of Mrs. Mary Murray, of 12, Colin Street, Falls Road, Belfast.

Murray, Peter - Driver
25545 Royal Engineers 57th Field Company *Age 22 Died in War on 2 March 1918*
NINE ELMS BRITISH CEMETERY, Belgium
Brother of Catherine Murray, of 51, Park View Street, Oldpark Road, Belfast.

Murray, Thomas - Private
7100 Royal Inniskilling Fusiliers 2nd Battalion *Died in War on 26 August 1914*
LE FERTE-SOUS -JOUARRE MEMORIAL, France
Born in County Antrim, enlisted Coatbridge, Scotland, resident of Belfast.

Murray, Thomas - Rifleman
6605 Royal Irish Rifles 1st Battalion *Killed in Action on 9 May 1915*
PLOEGSTEERT MEMORIAL, Belgium
Born in Newry, enlisted Newtownards, resident of Belfast.

Murray, William - Rifleman
7759 Royal Irish Rifles 2nd Battalion *Age 29 Killed in Action on 14 October 1914*
LE TOURET MEMORIAL, France
Husband of Mrs. S. Cunningham (formerly Murray), of 76, Weir Street, Belfast.

Journey of Remembering

Murray, William - Rifleman
9363 Royal Irish Rifles 1st Battalion *Killed in Action on 9 May 1915*
PLOEGSTEERT MEMORIAL, Belgium
Born and enlisted in Belfast.

Murray, William - Second Lieutenant
Middlesex Regiment 1st Battalion *Age 25 Killed in Action on 24 April 1917*
COJEUL BRITISH CEMETERY, ST. MARTIN-SUR-COJEUL, France
Son of William and Mary Eliza Murray, of 120, University Avenue, Belfast.

Mussen, Richard - Rifleman
11378 Royal Irish Rifles 1st Battalion *Age 23 Killed in Action on 21 March 1918*
POZIERES MEMORIAL, France
Son of Richard Mussen, of 89, Canmore Street, Belfast.

Mussen, William J - Private
402796 Canadian Infantry (Western Ontario Regiment) 18th Battalion *Age 27 Died in War on 19 March 1916*
BAILLEUL COMMUNAL CEMETERY EXTENSION (NORD), France
145 Cupar Street, Belfast. An Anglican, he had worked as a blacksmith's assistant.

Myers, Walter Gardner - Sapper
4825 Royal Engineers *Age 34 Died in War on 8 October 1916*
BELFAST CITY CEMETERY, United Kingdom
Husband of Annie Myers, of 171, York Road, Belfast

Myles, James - Rifleman
199 Royal Irish Rifles 8th Battalion *Age 40 Killed in Action on 5 December 1917*
ROCQUIGNY-EQUANCOURT ROAD BRITISH CEMETERY, MANANCOURT, France
Husband of Rose Myles, of 48, Sheriff Street, Belfast.

McAleer, Charles - Private
3033177 Canadian Infantry (Central Ontario Regiment) *Died in War on 1 October 1918*
SANCOURT BRITISH CEMETERY, France
Resident of New York, USA but born in the Brown Square area of Belfast, Ireland.

McGuckin, Robert James - Private
20970 Royal Irish Fusiliers 7/8th Battalion *Died in War on 14 January 1917*
BAILLEUL COMMUNAL CEMETERY EXTENSION (NORD), France
His wife, Rosina, and sons, Robert and Bernard, lived at St James Drive, Belfast.

Nabney, Hugh - Rifleman
9274 Royal Irish Rifles 1st Battalion *Age 25 Killed in Action on 9 May 1915*
PLOEGSTEERT MEMORIAL, Belgium
Son of Margaret Nabney, of 42, Central Street, Ballymacarrett, Belfast, and the late Thompson Nabney.

Nabney, William - Private
14751 Royal Inniskilling Fusiliers 11th Battalion attached 23rd Battalion
Age 30 Killed in Action on 25 March 1918
POZIERES MEMORIAL, France
Son of Thomas and Margaret Nabney, of 42, Central Street, Ballymacarrett, Belfast;
husband of the late Margaret Jane Nabney.

Nalty, Frederick William - Corporal
10401 Royal Irish Rifles 2nd Battalion *Killed in Action on 12 March 1915*
YPRES (MENIN GATE) MEMORIAL, Belgium
Born in Malta, enlisted in Naas, Kildare, resident of Belfast.

Nannery, Thomas - Company Sergeant Major
7721 Royal Irish Rifles 1st Battalion *Killed in Action on 31 July 1917*
YPRES (MENIN GATE) MEMORIAL, Belgium
Born and enlisted in Belfast.

Napier, Jonathan - Second Lieutenant
King's Own Yorkshire Light Infantry 7th Battalion *Age 23 Killed in Action on 16 August 1917*
TYNE COT MEMORIAL, Belgium
Son of Mrs. E. C. Napier, of 21, Lincoln Avenue, Belfast, and the late William Napier.

Napier, Joseph - Rifleman
689 Royal Irish Rifles 10th Battalion *Age 19 Died in War on 6 August 1917*
YPRES (MENIN GATE) MEMORIAL, Belgium
Son of Johanan and Sarah Napier, of 132, Beersbridge Road, Belfast.

Néeson, Charles - Sergeant
10345 Royal Inniskilling Fusiliers 1st Battalion *Died of Wounds on 23 April 1917*
ARRAS MEMORIAL, France
Born in Belfast.

Neeson, Joseph - Private
28138 Royal Inniskilling Fusiliers 1st Battalion *Killed in Action on 1 July 1916*
THIEPVAL MEMORIAL, France
Born in Belfast.

Neill, Alfred - Private
769 Royal Irish Rifles 9th Battalion *Age 27 Killed in Action on 1 July 1916*
THIEPVAL MEMORIAL, France
Son of the late William and Eleanor Neill.

Neill, Charles - Stoker First Class
SS/106586 Royal Navy HMS "Cressy" *Age 26 Killed in Action with submarine in North Sea on 22 September 1914*
CHATHAM NAVAL MEMORIAL, United Kingdom
Son of the late Mr. and Mrs. W. Neill, of Belfast; husband of Annie Anderson White (formerly Neill),
of 135, York Road, Belfast.

Neill, Dermot - Lieutenant
Machine Gun Corps (Infantry) 108th Company *Age 29 Killed in Action on 1 July 1916*
THIEPVAL MEMORIAL, France
One of the first to join the 13th Battalion of the Royal Irish Rifles before his transfer to the Machine Gun Corps. A keen yachtsman and golfer he was educataed at RBAI and Alderham School Hertfordshire. Eldest son of Mr Sharman D Neill, a noted jeweller, of Donegall Place, Belfast and Cultra. His brother, Robert was also killed.

Neill, Edmund - Private
21361 Royal Inniskilling Fusiliers 1st Battalion *Died in War on 1 July 1916*
ANCRE BRITISH CEMETERY, BEAUMONT-HAMEL, France
Born in St Mary's, Belfast, enlisted in Dublin.

Neill, George - Rifleman
7231 Royal Irish Rifles 2nd Battalion *Age 32 Died in War on 19 September 1914*
LA FERTE-SOUS-JOUARRE MEMORIAL, France
Son of Thomas and Elizabeth Neill, of 9, Surrey Street, Belfast; husband of Margaret Neill, of 67, Abingdon Street, Donegall Road, Belfast.

Neill, Henry - Private
S/393090 Royal Army Service Corps *Died in War on 13 April 1918*
STE MARIE CEMETERY, LE HAVRE, France
Resident of Belfast. Formerly 19/144 Royal Irish Rifles

Neill, James - Private
201272 Highland Light Infantry 5th (City of Glasgow) Battalion (Territorial) *Died in War on 25 August 1918*
VIS-EN-ARTOIS BRITISH MEMORIAL, HAUCOURT, France
Born in Belfast, enlisted in Glasgow.

Neill, James - Rifleman
1361 Royal Irish Rifles 8th Battalion *Died in War on 2 September 1916*
YPRES (MENIN GATE) MEMORIAL, Belgium
Born and enlisted in Belfast.

Neill, John - Rifleman
12100 Royal Irish Rifles 15th Battalion *Age 24 Died in War on 6 August 1917*
YPRES (MENIN GATE) MEMORIAL, Belgium
Son of John and Annie Neill, of The Lane, Whitehouse, Belfast.

Neill, Robert - Private
8123 Irish Guards 2nd Battalion *Age 18 Died of Wounds on 24 September 1916*
ETAPLES MILITARY CEMETERY, France
Son of Robert Neill, of 8, College Place, Belfast.

Neill, Robert - Rifleman
12104 Royal Irish Rifles 15th Battalion *Died in War on 2 July 1916*
THIEPVAL MEMORIAL, France
9, Ballymoney Street, Belfast.

Neill, Robert - Rifleman
428 Royal Irish Rifles 10th Battalion *Killed in Action on 1 July 1916*
THIEPVAL MEMORIAL, France
145, Durham Street, Belfast.

Neill, Robert Larmour - Lieutenant
Royal Irish Rifles 5th Battalion attached 1st Battalion *Age 21 Died in War on 9 May 1915*
PLOEGSTEERT MEMORIAL, *Belgium*
Younger son of Sharmon Dermot Neill, a well known jeweller of Donegall Place Belfast and Annie Symonds Neill. Robert has been educated at Campbell College where he had been in the school OTC. Was a company commander in the UVF. Subsequently commissioned into the Royal Irish Rifles.

Neill, Thomas - Lance Corporal
3210 Royal Inniskilling Fusiliers "C" Company 2nd Battalion *Age 20 Killed in Action on 1 July 1916*
LONSDALE CEMETERY, AUTHUILE, *France*
Son of Mrs. Annie Cathcart (formerly Neill) and Thomas Cathcart (stepfather), of 85, Donegall Road, Belfast.

Neill, Thomas - Rifleman
20/20172 Royal Irish Rifles 1st Battalion attached 18th Battalion London Regiment *Died in War on 3 October 1918*
Born and enlisted in Belfast.

Neill, William - Private
3450 Royal Inniskilling Fusiliers 1st Battalion *Age 45 Died in War on 21 August 1915*
HELLES MEMORIAL, *Turkey*
Son of Mrs. John Neill, of Drumbeg, Dunmurry, Belfast; husband of Maggie Neill, of Sandymount, Ballyskeagh, Lambeg, Lisburn.

Nelson, Albert Ernest - Lance Corporal
6322 Royal Irish Rifles 4th Battalion *Age 21 Killed in Action on 1 July 1916*
CONNAUGHT CEMETERY, THIEPVAL, *France*
Son of Albert Edward and Mary A. Nelson, of 96, Bryson Street, Belfast. Holder of the Military Medal.

Nelson, Charles - Private
20255 Royal Inniskilling Fusiliers 7/8th Battalion *Killed in Action on 29 July 1918*
GODEWAERSVELDE BRITISH CEMETERY, *France*
Husband of Mrs. M. Nelson, of 15, Fifth Street, Shankill Road, Belfast.

Nelson, David - Private
420210 Canadian Infantry (Manitoba Regiment) 43rd Battalion *Died in War on 2 June 1916*
YPRES (MENIN GATE) MEMORIAL, *Belgium*
Son of Annie Nelson, of 32, Marsden Gardens, Cavehill Road, Belfast, Ireland, and the late Samuel Nelson; husband of Margaret Kelly (formerly Nelson). A Presbyterian he was a cabinet maker with former military service.

Nelson, David - Rifleman
222 Royal Irish Rifles 1st Garrison Battalion *Died in War on 26 May 1918*
MADRAS 1914-18 WAR MEMORIAL CHENNAI, *India*
Born and enlisted in Belfast.

Nelson, Frederick J - Rifleman
14/671 Royal Irish Rifles 14th Battalion *Age 23 Killed in Action on 1 July 1916*
TINCOURT NEW BRITISH CEMETERY, *France*
Son of Mrs. S. Nelson, of 9, Clara Park, Knock, Belfast.

Nelson, George - Lance Corporal
8705 Royal Irish Rifles 2nd Battalion *Killed in Action on 9 May 1915*
YPRES (MENIN GATE) MEMORIAL, *Belgium*
8, St Paul's Street, Belfast.

Nelson, Hugh - Corporal
10498 Royal Irish Regiment 1st Battalion *Age 20 Killed in Action on 2 October 1918*
CEMENT HOUSE CEMETERY, *Belgium*
Son of Annie Nelson, of Belfast.

Nelson, Joseph - Private
3108 Royal Inniskilling Fusiliers "D" Company 2nd Battalion *Age 20 Died in War on 16 May 1915*
LE TOURET MEMORIAL, *France*
Son of Mrs. Emily Nelson, of 40, Mount Pottinger Road, Belfast.

Nelson, Redmond - Rifleman
17/1243 Royal Irish Rifles "B" Company 8th Battalion *Age 22 Died of Wounds on 7 November 1916*
KANDAHAR FARM CEMETERY, *Belgium*
Son of Eliza Jane Nelson, of 36, Belvoir Street, Belfast, and the late Samuel Nelson.

Nelson, Robert - Rifleman
1157 Royal Irish Rifles 16th Battalion *Age 42 Died in War on 11 August 1917*
YPRES (MENIN GATE) MEMORIAL, *Belgium*
Husband of Mrs. J. E. Nelson, of 2, Dickson Street, Belfast.

Nelson, Robert - Rifleman
3036 Royal Irish Rifles 2nd Battalion *Died of Wounds on 5 October 1918*
LIJSSENTHOEK MILITARY CEMETERY, *Belgium*
Husband of S. E. Nelson, of 12, Brookfield Street, Belfast.

Nelson, Robert B - Rifleman
8/13357 Royal Irish Rifles 15th Battalion *Age 24 Killed in Action on 21 April 1918*
BARD COTTAGE CEMETERY, *Belgium*
Son of William and Margaret Nelson of 6, New Street, Ballyhackamore, Belfast.

Nelson, Samuel - Driver
60189 Royal Horse Artillery and Royal Field Artillery *Died in War on 15 October 1914*
LA FERTE -SOUS-JOUARRE MEMORIAL, *France*
Born and enlisted in Belfast.

Nelson, Samuel - Rifleman
6917 Royal Irish Rifles 2nd Battalion *Age 28 Died in War on 19 July 1918*
ESQUELBECQ MILITARY CEMETERY, *France*
Son of Mr. and Mrs. William Nelson, of Ballymagee Street, Bangor, County Down; husband of Madge Nelson, of 22, Thorndyke Street, Belfast.

Nelson, Samuel - Rifleman
8180 Royal Irish Rifles 2nd Battalion *Age 30 Died of Wounds on 12 December 1914*
BOULOGNE EASTERN CEMETERY, *France*
Son of Samuel and Catherine Nelson; husband of Margaret Nelson, of 8, North Ann Street, Belfast. Native of Ballymena, County Antrim. Had been wounded at Mons in August and had recovered and returned to the front.

Nelson, William - Rifleman
A/201947 King's Royal Rifle Corps 2nd Battalion *Age 19 Died of Wounds (gas) on 7 September 1918*
TERLINCTHUN BRITISH CEMETERY, WIMILLE, *France*
Son of William and Margaret Nelson, of Belfast.

Nelson, William John Charles - Second Engineer
Mercantile Marine S.S. "Earl of Elgin" (Glasgow)
Age 38 Drowned, as a result of an attack by an enemy submarine, or killed by mine on 7 December 1917
TOWER HILL MEMORIAL, United Kingdom
Son of Robert and Elizabeth Nelson; husband of Annie Nelson (née McArthur) of 6 Lowther Street, Belfast.

Nelson, William Robert - Sapper
97485 Royal Engineers 91st Field Company *Age 38 Died in War on 14 July 1917*
YPRES TOWN CEMETERY EXTENSION, Belgium
Son of James and the late Maggie Nelson, of North Queen Street, Belfast; husband of Margaret Nelson, of 71, Seaview Street, Belfast.

Nesbit, William - Private
22802 Royal Scots (Lothian Regiment) 11th Battalion *Died in War on 13 May 1916*
RIFLE HOUSE CEMETERY, Belgium
Born in Belfast enlisted in Edinburgh.

Nesbitt, Francis - Sergeant
5124 Royal Irish Rifles 7th Battalion *Died in War on 16 August 1917*
TYNE COT MEMORIAL, Belgium
Born in Belfast, enlisted in Waringstown, County Down.

Nesbitt, Hugo - Lance Corporal
4502 London Irish Rifles 1/18th Battalion *Died in War on 15 September 1916*
THIEPVAL MEMORIAL, France
Born in Belfast, son of Lieutenant Commander and Mrs Mary Catherine Nesbitt of West Brompton London. Educated at Skegoniel and Kelvin House School. Came back from South America to enlist. One of two brothers to perish.

Nesbitt, James - Private
2488 Royal Inniskilling Fusiliers 2nd Battalion *Died in War on 26 May 1915*
LONGUENESSE (ST. OMER) SOUVENIR CEMETERY, France
87, Euston Street, Belfast. Enlisted in Belfast.

Nesbitt, Noble - Rifleman
19710 Royal Irish Rifles 8th Battalion *Killed in Action on 1 July 1916*
SERRE ROAD CEMETERY No.2, France
Born and enlisted in Belfast.

Nesbitt, Robert Matthew - Private
30054 Lancashire Fusiliers 16th Battalion *Age 36 Killed in Action on 4 November 1918*
PREMONT BRITISH CEMETERY, France
Son of Samuel Nesbitt, of Belfast, and the late Mary Nesbitt.

Nesbitt, Robert W - Sapper
WR/260378 Royal Engineers *Age 25 Died as a result of war on 11 November 1919*
BELFAST CITY CEMETERY, United Kingdom
Son of Joseph and Charlotte Nesbitt, of 6, Athol Street, Belfast.

Nesbitt, Samuel - Private
13151 Royal Inniskilling Fusiliers 1st Battalion *Age 44 Died of Wounds on 3 August 1916*
BELFAST (DUNDONALD) CEMETERY, United Kingdom
Son of Samuel and Mary Nesbitt, of Wilson Street, Belfast; husband of Mary Nesbitt, of 36, Campbell Street, Belfast.

Nesbitt, Terence Beale - Second Lieutenant
The Dorsetshire Regiment 3rd Battalion attached 2nd Battalion *Age 18 Died of Wounds on 24 April 1916*
BASRA MEMORIAL, *Iraq*
Born in Belfast, son of Lieutenant Commander and Mrs Mary Catherine Nesbitt of West Brompton London. Educated at Belfast Academy and at schools in England. Died of wounds received in Mesopotamia (Iraq). One of two brothers to perish.

Neville, John - Shipwright Second Class
345486 Royal Navy HMS "Vanguard" *Age 36 Killed by internal explosion of vessel at Scapa Flow on 9 July 1917*
CHATHAM NAVAL MEMORIAL, *United Kingdom*
Son of Charles and Mary Jane Neville, of 493, Cregagh Road, Belfast. Native of Dundalk, County Louth.

Neville, Robert James - Private
41092 Royal Army Medical Corps *Died in War on 6 March 1918*
BELFAST CITY CEMETERY, *United Kingdom*
Husband of Margaret Neville, 138 Mervue Street, Belfast.

Nevin, William - Company Sergeant Major
15696 Royal Irish Rifles 14th Battalion *Age 22 Killed in Action on 16 August 1917*
TYNE COT MEMORIAL, *Belgium*
Son of Mr. and Mrs. S. Nevin, of "Beaumaris", Finaghy Park, Belfast.

Newall, Thomas - Private
3452 Royal Scots (Lothian Regiment) 1st Battalion *Died in War on 8 February 1915*
YPRES (MENIN GATE) MEMORIAL, *Belgium*
Born in Belfast, enlisted Haddington.

Newberry, Robert - Rifleman
2329 Royal Irish Rifles 11/13th Battalion *Died in War on 8 December 1917*
SUNKEN ROAD CEMETERY, VILLERS-PLOUICH, *France*
Born and enlisted in Belfast.

Newel, David Lumsden - Private
PS/5390 Royal Fusiliers 20th Battalion Royal Fusiliers *Age 21 Killed in Action on 13 March 1916*
CAMBRIN CHURCHYARD EXTENSION, *France*
Son of Henry Arthur and Helen H. Newel, of 362, Antrim Road, Belfast. One of three brothers killed.

Newel, George Frank - Company Quartermaster Sergeant
12102 Royal Irish Rifles 15th Battalion *Age 26 Died in War on 6 August 1917*
WIELTJE FARM CEMETERY, *Belgium*
Son of Henry Arthur and Helen Hunter Newel, of 362, Antrim Road, Belfast. One of three bothers killed.

Newel, Walter - Lance Corporal
1765 Black Watch (Royal Highlanders) "A" Company 1/6th Battalion *Age 26 Killed in Action on 10 July 1915*
RUE-DAVID MILITARY CEMETERY, FLEURBAIX, *France*
Son of Henry Arthur and Helen Newel, of 362, Antrim Road, Belfast. One of three brothers killed.

Newell, Joseph - Private
3430 Royal Irish Regiment *Age 47 Died as a result of War on 5 November 1919*
BELFAST (MILLTOWN) ROMAN CATHOLIC CEMETERY, *United Kingdom*
Son of Robert and Mary Newell of Belfast; husband of Mary Ann Newell, of 11, Sultan Street, Belfast.

Newell, Thomas - Stoker First Class
SS/114489 Royal Navy HMS "Natal" *Age 21 Killed by internal explosion of vessel in Cromarty Firth on 30 December 1915*
CHATHAM NAVAL MEMORIAL, *United Kingdom*
Son of Thomas and Mary Jane Newell, of 2, Lackagh Street, Belfast.

Newell, Thomas Brennan - Private
23977 Royal Irish Fusiliers 1st Battalion *Age 17 Died in War on 18 October 1916*
GROVE TOWN CEMETERY, MEAULTE, *France*
Son of the late John and Catherine Newell, of Belfast.

Newell, William John - Private
CH/17878 Royal Marine Light Infantry *Died in War on 1 January 1915*
CHATHAM WAR MEMORIAL, *United Kingdom*
2, Lackagh Street, Belfast.

Newton, George William - Lance Corporal
10960 Cheshire Regiment 1st Battalion *Died in War on 5 September 1916*
THIEPVAL MEMORIAL, *France*
Born in Belfast, enlisted Birkenhead, England.

Niblock, John - Corporal
21361 Cheshire Regiment 16th Battalion *Killed In Action on 19 July 1916*
THIEPVAL MEMORIAL, *France*
Born and enlisted in Belfast.

Niblock, Robert Douglas - Private
421 Australian Infantry 8th Battalion *Age 32 Died of Wounds received on 25 April 1915 on 3 May 1918*
ALEXANDRIA (CHATBY) MILITARY AND WAR MEMORIAL CEMETERY, *Egypt*
Son of James and Agnes Niblock; husband of Louisa E. D. Niblock,
of 275, Hyde Street, Yarraville, Victoria, Australia. Born in Belfast, Ireland.

Niblock, William - Private
Royal Irish Rifles 1st Battalion *Died in War on 17 December 1914*
11, Maria Street, Belfast.

Nichol, James Patrick - Private
49418 King's (Liverpool Regiment) 4th Battalion *Died in War on 3 February 1917*
THIEPVAL MEMORIAL, *France*
Born in Belfast, enlisted Seaforth, Lancashire, resident of Belfast.

Nicholl, Alfred Ernest - Second Lieutenant
Royal Irish Rifles 13th Battalion *Age 27 Died in War on 3 February 1917*
BAILLEUL COMMUNAL CEMETERY EXTENSION (NORD), *France*
Son of Samuel and Annie E. Nicholl, of 3, St. Jude's Avenue, Belfast.

Nicholl, Edward - Private
145478 Canadian Infantry 77th Battalion *Died of sickness on 10 January 1918*
OTTAWA (BEECHWOOD) CEMETERY, *Canada*
Son of Mrs. B. Nicholl, of 14, Napier Street, Belfast, Ireland.

Nicholl, James - Gunner
60179 Royal Horse Artillery and Royal Field Artillery *Died in War on 14 September 1917*
BELFAST CITY CEMETERY, United Kingdom
Born and enlisted in Belfast.

Nicholl, Robert George - Lance Corporal
10000 Royal Inniskilling Fusiliers 2nd Battalion *Age 22 Killed in Action on 16 September 1914*
LA FERTE-SOUS-JOUARRE MEMORIAL, France
Son of Thomas and Agnes Nicholl, of 29, Danube Street, Belfast.

Nicholl, William - Corporal
13358 Royal Irish Rifles "B" Company 15th Battalion *Age 23 Killed in Action on 1 July 1916*
THIEPVAL MEMORIAL, France
Son of Agnes Cunningham Nicholl, of 27, Legane Street, Ballysillan, Belfast, and the late William Nicholl.

Nichols, Herbert Spencer - Sapper
548799 Royal Engineers 126th Field Company *Age 26 Died in War on 7 October 1917*
TYNE COT MEMORIAL, Belgium
Son of John J. Nichols; husband of Mrs E Downie (formerly Nichols), of 13, Keswick Street, Belfast.

Nicholson, Hugh - Rifleman
15711 Royal Irish Rifles 10th Battalion *Killed in Action on 1 July 1916*
THIEPVAL MEMORIAL, France
Ferndale Place Belfast.

Nicholson, Hugh - Steward
Mercantile Marine Steam Trawler "Fanny" (Fleetwood) *Age 40 Presumed drowned on 1 February 1917*
TOWER HILL MEMORIAL, United Kingdom
Son of Edward Nicholson, of 11, Byron Street, Fleetwood. Born in Belfast.

Nicholson, John - Corporal
6357 Army Cyclist Corps *Died in War on 27 September 1915*
LOOS MEMORIAL, France
Born in Belfast, enlisted Glasgow. Formerly 17354 Royal Scots Fusiliers.

Nickell, James - Sapper
25042 Royal Engineers 7th Field Company *Died in War on 16 January 1916*
PERTH CEMETERY (CHINA WALL), Belgium
Born and enlisted in Belfast.

Nicol, Harry - Lance Corporal
13361 Royal Irish Rifles 14th Battalion attached Fifth Army Infantry School
Age 20 Died in War on 30 March 1918
POZIERES MEMORIAL, France
Son of Alexander and Emily Nicol, of 20, Hopefield Avenue, Belfast.

Nixon, Charles - Rifleman
17/1829 Royal Irish Rifles "B" Company 17th Battalion *Age 19 Killed in Action on 1 July 1916*
THIEPVAL MEMORIAL, France
Son of Margaret Ann Nixon, of 13, Curzon Street, Belfast, and the late William John Nixon.

Nixon, Edward - Lance Corporal
3086 Irish Guards 1st Battalion *Age 26 Died in War on 1 November 1914*
YPRES (MENIN GATE) MEMORIAL, Belgium
Son of Mrs Mary Nixon, of 161, Bellevue Street, Belfast.

Nixon, Edward - Private
2068 Australian Infantry 6th Battalion *Age 26 Died of Wounds at sea on 27 April 1915*
LONE PINE MEMORIAL, Turkey
Son of James and Margaret Nixon, of 21, Eccles Street, Belfast, Ireland.

Nixon, Harold Perceval - Second Lieutenant
Wiltshire Regiment 6th (Wiltshire Yeomanry) Battalion *Age 22 Died in War on 26 October 1918*
WARCOING CHURCHYARD, Belgium
Son of Alexander and Annie Nixon, of 12, Hopefield Avenue, Belfast.

Nixon, John - Rifleman
151468 Royal Irish Rifles 15th Battalion *Age 19 Died of Wounds on 28 December 1917*
ETAPLES MILITARY CEMETERY, France
Son of John and Agnes Vance Nixon, of 50, Israel Street, Belfast. Educated at Townsend Street School and was then apprenticed as a linen lapper.

Nixon, Robert - Private
7561 5th Dragoon Guards (Princess Charlottte's Own) *Killed in Action on 25 March 1918*
POZIERES MEMORIAL, France
Served under the alias of "Joseph Irvine". Born and enlisted in Belfast.

Nixon, Robert - Rifleman
7294 Royal Irish Rifles 1st Battalion *Killed in Action on 1 July 1916*
THIEPVAL MEMORIAL, France
Born Downpatrick, enlisted Newtownards, resident Belfast.

Nixon, Stanley - Lieutenant
Princess Patricia's Canadian Light Infantry (Eastern Ontario Regiment) 11th Battalion attached 55th Squadron Royal Air Force *Age 26 Died in War on 1 January 1919*
FILLIEVRES BRITISH CEMETERY, France
Son of the late James Nixon, J.P., of Glenbrook House, Cliftonville Road, Belfast.
A Methodist and accountant he was later commissioned.

Nixon, William - Rifleman
16901 Royal Inniskilling Fusiliers 9th Battalion *Age 20 Killed in Action on 1 July 1916*
THIEPVAL MEMORIAL, France
Lisburn Road, Belfast. Son of James Nixon of 11 Campsie, Omagh, County Tyrone.

Nixon, William Henry - Lance Corporal
19822 Royal Irish Fusiliers 7th Battalion *Age 26 Killed in Action on 6 April 1916*
ST. PATRICK'S CEMETERY, LOOS, France
Son of Robert and Elizabeth Nixon, of 251, Woodstock Road, Belfast.

Noble, Charles - Rifleman
17/1178 Royal Irish Rifles 15th Battalion *Age 21 Killed in Action on 31 May 1918*
DUHALLOW A.D.S. CEMETERY, Belgium
Son of Robert and Elizabeth Noble, of Ballymacarrett, Belfast.

Noble, James - Rifleman
13364 Royal Irish Rifles 8th Battalion *Died in War on 2 July 1916*
STUMP ROAD CEMETERY, GRANDCOURT, France
Born and enlisted in Belfast.

Noble, Wesley Alexander Fraser - Corporal
5497 Rifle Brigade 12th Battalion *Age 22 Died of Wounds on 29 October 1916*
BELFAST (DUNDONALD) CEMETERY, United Kingdom
Youngest Son of Wesley and Elizabeth Noble, of 9, Albertville Drive, Crumlin Road, Belfast.

Noble, William H - Private
5089 Royal Munster Fusiliers 2nd Battalion *Killed in Action on 4 October 1918*
PROSPECT HILL CEMETERY, GOUY, France
Son of Mr. N. Noble, of 11, Clanmorris Street, Belfast.

Noblett, Edward William - Private
51255 Cheshire Regiment 1st Battalion *Age 27 Died in War on 14 April 1918*
LONGUENESSE (ST. OMER) SOUVENIR CEMETERY, France
Son of Edward and Mary Noblett, of 147, The Mount, Belfast.

Noblett, Robert James - Private
28188 Royal Inniskilling Fusiliers 2nd Battalion *Age 27 Died in War on 1 April 1917*
SAVY BRITISH CEMETERY, France
Son of Edward and Mary Noblett, of 147, The Mount, Belfast.

Nolan, Archie - Lance Corporal
18391 Royal Munster Fusiliers 1st Battalion formerly 10th Battalion Royal Dublin Fusiliers
Age 21 Died in War on 28 August 1916
VIS-EN-ARTOIS MEMORIAL, France
Brother of Mrs. Jennie Graves, of 144, Donegall Avenue, Belfast, and Mrs Kathleen Guilfayle, of 26 Albert Place, East Dublin.

Nolan, John Joseph - Sapper
150938 Royal Engineers Inland Water Transport *Died in War on 11 November 1917*
AIRE COMMUNAL CEMETERY, France
Born Ballymacarrett, Belfast. Son of Henry and Agnes Nolan of Dublin.
Husband of Alice Nolan, Eccles Street, Dublin.

Norney, Thomas Joseph - Private
3286 Royal Inniskilling Fusiliers 7th Battalion *Died in War on 16 July 1917*
YPRES (MENIN GATE) MEMORIAL, Belgium
Son of William Norney, of 115, Millfield, Belfast. Awarded the Military Medal.

Norris, Francis - Private
11137 Royal Irish Fusiliers 1st Battalion *Age 25 Died in War on 11 April 1917*
ARRAS MEMORIAL, France
Son of Mrs. Margaret Jane McIlroy, of 107, Church Street East, Belfast.

Norris, Thomas - Private
23066 Royal Inniskilling Fusiliers "D" Company 9th Battalion *Age 18 Killed in Action on 1 July 1916*
THIEPVAL MEMORIAL, France
Son of Henry and Margaret Norris, of 9, Kingswood Street, Belfast.

Norris, William James - Rifleman
10419 Royal Irish Rifles 1st Battalion *Age 18 Killed in Action on 9 May 1915*
PLOEGSTEERT MEMORIAL, Belgium
Son of Mrs. Marget McElroy, of 107, Church Street East, Belfast.

Northcote, George - Driver
91280 Royal Engineers 108th Field Company *Age 31 Died of dysentery on 31 August 1916*
SALONIKA (LEMBET ROAD) MILITARY CEMETERY, Greece
Husband of Mary Northcote, of 20, Christopher Street, Belfast.

Norton, James - Rifleman
9343 Royal Irish Rifles 1st Battalion *Killed by shellfire on 9 February 1916*
SAILLY-SUR-LA-LYS-CANADIAN CEMETERY, France
26, Cullingtree Road, Belfast.

Norton, Nathaniel - Lance Corporal
250 Royal Irish Rifles 18th Battalion *Died on 29 April 1916*
Born and enlisted in Belfast.

Norwood, James - Rifleman
8463 Royal Irish Rifles 1st Battalion *Age 25 Killed in Action on 9 May 1915*
PLOEGSTEERT MEMORIAL, Belgium
Son of Robert and Mary Ann Norwood, of 37, Willow Street, Belfast.

Norwood, James Hamilton - Corporal
53605 Canadian Infantry (Western Ontario Regiment) 18th Battalion
Age 23 Died in War on 15 September 1916
SERRE ROAD CEMETERY No.2, France
Son of Samuel and Alice Norwood, of 62, Ravenhill Road, Belfast, Ireland.
He was a farmer and Methodist in religion.

Nugent, Garrett P - Rifleman
10816 Royal Irish Rifles 7th Battalion *Age 20 Died in War on 3 October 1917*
ST. MARTIN CALVAIRE BRITISH CEMETERY, ST. MARTIN-SUR-COJEUL, France
Son of Patrick Nugent and Ellen McCandless.

Nugent, James - Private
11162 Royal Inniskilling Fusiliers 2nd Battalion *Age 18 Presumed killed on 16 May 1915*
LE TOURET MEMORIAL, France
Son of Sarah and William Nugent, 31, Percy Street, Belfast. His brother, Robert, was killed two years later.

Nugent, Robert - Private
9836 Royal Inniskilling Fusiliers 1st Battalion *Died in War on 15 February 1917*
ST. SEVER CEMETERY EXTENSION, ROUEN, France
Son of Sarah and William Nugent, 31, Percy Street, Belfast. His brother, James, also fell.

Nutt, Mark - Rifleman
15703 Royal Irish Rifles 10th Battalion *Age 20 Killed in Action on 1 July 1916*
THIEPVAL MEMORIAL, France
Son of Mrs. Jane Nutt, of 36, Ulsterville Gardens, Belfast.

O'Boyle, Francis Alexander - Private
2053 Leinster Regiment "B" Company 7th Battalion *Age 24 Died in War on 12 July 1916*
PHILOSOPHE BRITISH CEMETERY, MAZINGARBE, France
Son of Alexander and Mary O'Boyle, of 35, Fort Street, Belfast.

O'Boyle, James - Private
3384 Royal Inniskilling Fusiliers 4th Battalion *Age 21 Died in War on 30 May 1915*
BELFAST (MILLTOWN) ROMAN CATHOLIC CEMETERY, United Kingdom
Son of Mrs. Annie O'Boyle, of 85, Ardilea Street, Belfast.

O'Boyle, John - Private
20480 Royal Irish Fusiliers "C" Company 1st Battalion *Age 21 Died in War on 15 July 1918*
PLOEGSTEERT MEMORIAL, Belgium
Son of Elizabeth Scott (formerly O'Boyle), of 12, Vulcan Street, Belfast, and the late John O'Boyle.

O'Boyle, Michael - Private
38693 South Wales Borderers 10th Battalion *Age 20 Died in War on 24 August 1918*
FRANVILLERS COMMUNAL CEMETERY EXTENSION, France
Son of John and Mary O'Boyle, of 78, Alfred Street, Wavertree, Liverpool. Native of Belfast.

O'Boyle, Peter - Private
21415 Royal Irish Fusiliers 7th Battalion *Age 22 Died in War on 5 September 1916*
THIEPVAL MEMORIAL, France
Son of Mrs. Annie O'Boyle, of 85, Ardilea Street, Belfast. His brother, James, also fell.

O'Brien, Michael - Gunner
31259 Royal Garrison Artillery *Died in War on 12 November 1917*
VLAMERTINGHE NEW MILITARY CEMETERY, Belgium
Born and enlisted in Belfast.

O'Callaghan, Bernard - Private
13231 Royal Irish Fusiliers 9th Battalion *Died in War on 16 August 1917*
TYNE COT CEMETERY, Belgium
Son of Mrs Mary O'Callaghan, 7 Butler Street, Belfast.

O'Connor, Christopher - Rifleman
7430 Royal Irish Rifles 1st Battalion *Died in War on 16 May 1916*
LURGAN (DOUGHER) ROMAN CATHOLIC CEMETERY, United Kingdom
Born in Belfast, enlisted Portadown.

O'Connor, David - Private
51654 East Yorkshire Regiment 1st Battalion *Died in War on 10 September 1918*
VIS-EN-ARTOIS MEMORIAL, HAUCOURT, France
Born and enlisted in Belfast. Formerly 3/10497, Royal Irish Rifles

O'Connor, John - Private
28825 Royal Irish Fusiliers 11th Battalion *Died in War on 7 June 1917*
IRISH HOUSE CEMETERY, Belgium
17 Bantry Street, Belfast.

O'Connor, Patrick - Corporal
10354 Royal Irish Rifles 1st Battalion *Killed in Action on 4 September 1918*
WULVERGHEM-LINDENHOEK ROAD MILITARY CEMETERY, Belgium
Born and enlisted in Belfast.

Journey of Remembering

O'Donnell, Hubert - Sergeant
3025 Royal Irish Fusiliers 7/8th Battalion *Died in War on 20 November 1917*
ST. MARTIN CALVAIRE BRITISH CEMETERY, ST. MARTIN-SUR-COJEUL, France
Son of Mrs H O'Donnell, 15 Brassey Street, Belfast.

O'Donnell, John - Acting Sergeant
10487 Princess Victoria's (Royal Irish Fusiliers) 2nd Battalion *Died in War on 14 March 1915*
YPRES (MENIN GATE) MEMORIAL, Belgium
Born in County Antrim, enlisted Newtownards, resident of Belfast.

O'Donnell, John - Private
16731 Royal Dublin Fusiliers 8th Battalion *Died in War on 27 April 1916*
LOOS MEMORIAL, France
Born and enlisted in Belfast, resident of Belfast.

O'Donnell, John - Private
7020 Royal Munster Fusiliers 2nd Battalion *Died in War on 4 October 1918*
TEMPLEUX-LE-GUERARD BRITISH CEMETERY, France
Born in Belfast, enlisted in Inverkeithing, Scotland.

O'Donnell, John - Private
G/125 Royal Irish Fusiliers formerly 5707 Royal Irish Rifles 1st Garrison Battalion *Age 38 Died of sickness on 14 December 1915*
DRUMBO (HOLY TRINITY) CHURCH OF IRELAND CHURCHYARD, United Kingdom
Son of John O'Donnell; husband of Jane O'Donnell, of Carolan Road, Belfast. Born at Ballylesson.

O'Donnell, Patrick - Private
116853 Machine Gun Corps *Died in War on 17 September 1918*
GLAGEON COMMUNAL CEMETERY EXTENSION, France
Born in Belfast, enlisted in Dublin. Formerly 655956 London Regiment

O'Donohoe, Patrick Joseph - Rifleman
7505 Royal Irish Rifles 2nd Battalion *Age 20 Killed in Action on 7 June 1917*
YPRES (MENIN GATE) MEMORIAL, Belgium
Nephew of Eliza Monaghan, of 16, Waterford Street, Belfast.

O'Flaherty, Douglas Hill - Captain
Royal Irish Rifles 15th Battalion *Age 36 Killed in Action on 1 July 1916*
THIEPVAL MEMORIAL, France
Son of Mr. and Mrs. Francis Hill Hale O'Flaherty, of Belfast; husband of Beatrice O'Flaherty, of 31, Myrtlefield Park, Belfast.

O'Flaherty, James   Private
Royal Irish Fusiliers *Died of illness*
13, Garnet Street, Belfast.

O'Hagan, James - Private
12972 Princess Victoria's (Royal Irish Fusiliers) 1st Battalion *Died in War on 11 April 1917*
ARRAS MEMORIAL, France
Born in Belfast, enlisted in Sheffield.

O'Hagan, John - Company Sergeant Major
8618 Royal Irish Fusiliers 2nd Battalion *Age 29 Died in War on 14 March 1915*
YPRES (MENIN GATE) MEMORIAL, Belgium
Son of John O'Hagan, of 44, Frederick Street, Belfast.

Journey of Remembering

O'Halloran, Patrick - Private
22082 Royal Dublin Fusiliers 6th Battalion *Age 23 Killed in Action on 8 October 1918*
BEAUREVOIR BRITISH CEMETERY, France
Son of Patrick O'Halloran, of 87, Hardinge Street, North Queen Street, Belfast.

O'Hanlan, Owen - Rifleman
11494 Royal Irish Rifles 6th Battalion *Died in War on 10 March 1918*
RAMLEH WAR CEMETERY, Israel
Born and enlisted in Belfast.

O'Hara, Arthur - Private
11475 Royal Irish Rifles 1st Battalion *Killed in Action on 1 July 1916*
THIEPVAL MEMORIAL, France
7 Wall Street, Belfast.

O'Hara, Charles - Private
10013 Royal Irish Fusiliers 2nd Battalion *Age 33 Died in War on 10 November 1917*
BEERSHEBA WAR CEMETERY, Israel
Son of John and Elizabeth O'Hara, of 12, Getty Street, Belfast.

O'Hara, John - Private
3070 Royal Scots (Lothian Regiment) 11th Battalion *Died in War on 17 October 1915*
PHALEMPIN COMMUNAL CEMETERY, France
Born in Belfast, enlisted in Leith, Scotland.

O'Hara, Michael - Private
24624 Royal Irish Fusiliers 1st Battalion *Age 23 Died in War on 9 April 1917*
ARRAS MEMORIAL, France
Only son of James and Ellen O'Hara, of 17, Oranmore Street, Belfast.

O'Hara, Michael - Rifleman
5818 Royal Irish Rifles 2nd Battalion *Died in War on 7 May 1915*
YPRES (MENIN GATE) MEMORIAL, Belgium
Born in Belfast, enlisted Ballykinler.

O'Hara, Robert James - Private
8161 Princess Victoria's (Royal Irish Fusiliers) 1st Battalion *Died in War on 28 March 1915*
LES GONARDS CEMETERY, VERSAILLES, France
Born and enlisted in Belfast.

O'Hara, Samuel - Sergeant
5353 Royal Irish Rifles 2nd Battalion *Killed in Action on 13 May 1916*
ECOIVRES MILITARY CEMETERY, MONT-ST. ELOI, France
Son of James and Mary Ann O'Hara, of 12, Lower California Street, Belfast; husband of Elizabeth O'Hara, of 11, Arnon Street, Belfast.

O'Hara, Thomas - Rifleman
11301 Royal Irish Rifles 1st Battalion *Died in War on 9 May 1915*
PLOEGSTEERT MEMORIAL, Belgium
Born and enlisted in Belfast.

Belfast Book of Honour

O'Hare, H - Private
10943 Inns of Court Officer Training Corps *Age 19 Died of German measles on 28 November 1917*
BROOKWOOD MILITARY CEMETERY, United Kingdom
Son of John and the late Emily O'Hare, of Belfast.

O'Hare, James - Private
2465 Royal Irish Rifles 2nd Battalion *Killed in Action on 15 July 1916*
THIEPVAL MEMORIAL, France
14 Peel Street, Belfast.

O'Hare, John - Private
27629 Royal Inniskilling Fusiliers 8th Battalion *Died in War on 29 April 1916*
LOOS MEMORIAL, France
Born and enlisted in Belfast. Formerly 1745 Leinster Regiment

O'Hare, Robert James - Private
8161 Royal Irish Fusiliers 1st Battalion *Died in War on 28 March 1915*
LES GONARDS CEMETERY, VERSAILLES, France
35, Eureka Street, Belfast.

O'Leary, Patrick - Able Seaman
Mercantile Marine S.S. "Bristol City" (Bristol) *Age 53 Drowned, as a result of an attack by an enemy submarine on 16 December 1917*
TOWER HILL MEMORIAL, United Kingdom
Son of the late Patrick and Ann O'Leary. Born at Belfast.

O'Lone, Robert James - Captain
Royal Irish Rifles 2nd Battalion *Age 31 Killed in Action on 11 November 1915*
TANCREZ FARM CEMETERY, Belgium
Son of John and Mary O'Lone, of Belfast; husband of Gladys Louise O'Lone, of 11, Grove Avenue, Twickenham, London. Mentioned in Despatches

O'Lone, Walter Percy - Captain
Royal Irish Rifles 2nd Battalion *Age 25 Died in War on 25 September 1915*
YPRES (MENIN GATE) MEMORIAL, BELGIUM
Born in Belfast. his brother, Captain Robert James O'Lone, was also killed. Enlisted in 1905 and rose through the ranks, received the Distinguished Conduct Medal for gallantry and was commissioned. He was the son of a Quartmaster Sergeant and his wife, Annie O'Lone, lived in Ballynahinch.

O'Neil, John - Gunner
42944 Royal Garrison Artillery *Died in War on 24 September 1918*
TINCOURT NEW BRITISH CEMETERY, France
Born and enlisted in Belfast.

O'Neil, Patrick - Private
13673 Royal Scots Fusiliers 7th Battalion *Died in War on 26 September 1915*
LOOS MEMORIAL, France
Born in Belfast, enlisted in Greenock, Scotland.

O'Neill - ALIAS - family name "Tohill", Patrick - Rifleman
6915 Royal Irish Rifles 1st Battalion *Died in War on 9 May 1915*
PLOEGSTEERT MEMORIAL, Belgium
Born in Belfast, enlisted Banbridge.

O'Neill, Alfred - Private
8011 Royal Irish Fusiliers 1st Battalion *Age 46 Died in War on 21 October 1914*
PLOEGSTEERT MEMORIAL, Belgium
Brother of Mary E. O'Neill, of 31, Malt Street, Belfast.

O'Neill, Anthony - Rifleman
22346 Royal Irish Rifles 1st Battalion *Age 16 Killed in Action on 1 October 1918*
MENIN ROAD SOUTH MILITARY CEMETERY, Belgium
Son of Jane O'Neill, of 3, King's Court, Lancaster Street, Belfast.

O'Neill, Christopher - Rifleman
8973 Royal Irish Rifles 1st Battalion *Killed in action on 21 March 1918*
GRAND-SERAUCOURT BRITISH CEMETERY, France
Husband of Maggie O'Neill, Belfast.

O'Neill, Daniel - Lance Corporal
4342 Royal Inniskilling Fusiliers 1st Battalion *Age 19 Died in War on 22 May 1915*
HELLES MEMORIAL, Turkey
Son of Mary Catherine O'Neill, of 29, New Lodge Road, Belfast, and the late John O'Neill.
Awarded the Distinguished Conduct Medal.

O'Neill, Daniel - Rifleman
740 Royal Irish Rifles 7th Battalion *Died in War on 21 April 1916*
DUD CORNER CEMETERY, LOOS, France
Born in Belfast, enlisted Newtownards.

O'Neill, David - Horseman
Mercantile Marine S.S. "Anglo Californian" (London) *Age 45 Killed as a result of an attack by an enemy submarine on 4 July 1915*
COBH OLD CHURCH CEMETERY, Republic of Ireland
Born in Belfast.

O'Neill, Francis - Private
21004 Princess Victoria's (Royal Irish Fusiliers) 8th Battalion *Died in War on 1 June 1916*
ST PATRICK'S CEMETERY, LOOS, France
Born and enlisted in Belfast. Formerly 3556, Connaught Rangers.

O'Neill, Harry - Private
21088 Princess Victoria's (Royal Irish Fusiliers) 7/8th Battalion *Died in War on 1 January 1917*
KEMMEL CHATEAU MILITARY CEMETERY, Belgium
Born and enlisted in Belfast. Formerly 2862, Connaught Rangers

O'Neill, Hugh - Private
5631 Royal Irish Rifles 2nd Battalion *Killed in Action on 21 March 1918*
POZIERES MEMORIAL, France
Son of Matthew and Elizabeth O'Neill, 152 Ross Street, Belfast.

O'Neill, James - Greaser
Mercantile Marine H.M.H.T. "Justicia" (Liverpool)
Age 51 Drowned, as a result of an attack by an enemy submarine on 19 July 1918
TOWER HILL MEMORIAL, United Kingdom
Son of the late Peter and Mary O'Neill; husband of Elizabeth Rachell O'Neill
(formerly Thistlewood, née Hooper), of 7, Davy Street, Everton, Liverpool. Born at Belfast.

Journey of Remembering

O'Neill, James - Private
3408 Royal Inniskilling Fusiliers 1st Battalion *Died in War on 30 January 1917*
THIEPVAL MEMORIAL, France
Born and enlisted in Belfast.

O'Neill, James - Private
8443 7th Dragoon Guards (Princess Royal) *Died in War on 8 August 1918*
VIS-EN-ARTOIS MEMORIAL, HAUCOURT, France
Born in Belfast.

O'Neill, James - Rifleman
9183 Royal Irish Rifles 2nd Battalion *Killed in Action on 27 October 1914*
LE TOURET MEMORIAL, France
Born and enlisted in Belfast.

O'Neill, John - Private
16802 Loyal North Lancashire Regiment 10th Battalion *Died in War on 27 March 1916*
BOLTON (TONGUE) CEMETERY, Lancahsire
Born in Belfast, enlisted Bolton, England.

O'Neill, John - Private
24780 Royal Scots 17th Battalion *Died in War on 26 July 1916*
CORBIE COMMUNAL CEMETERY EXTENSION, France
Divis Street, Belfast.

O'Neill, John - Private
3652 Royal Irish Fusiliers 5th Battalion *Died in War on 27 February 1917*
MIKRA BRITISH CEMETERY, KALAMARIA, Greece
Son of Mrs. Mary O'Neill, of Belfast.

O'Neill, John S - Rifleman
19/578 Royal Irish Rifles 12th Battalion *Age 19 Died as a result of war on 27 December 1918*
HAMBURG CEMETERY, Germany
Son of John and Sarah O'Neill, of 16, Christopher Street, Belfast.

O'Neill, Malachy - Rifleman
8691 Royal Irish Rifles "G" Company 1st Battalion *Age 29 Died as a result of war on 18 November 1918*
BELFAST (MILLTOWN) ROMAN CATHOLIC CEMETERY, United Kingdom
Husband of Mary Ellen O'Neill, of 98, Balkan Street, Falls Road, Belfast.
Discharged and awarded the Silver War Badge.

O'Neill, Maurice - Private
DM2/209980 Royal Army Service Corps *Died in War on 19 July 1918*
TEHRAN MEMORIAL, Iran
Born and enlisted in Belfast.

O'Neill, Robert - Stoker First Class
2088U Royal Navy HMS "Queen Mary" *Killed in Action on 31 May 1916*
PORTSMOUTH NAVAL MEMORIAL, United Kingdom
Lived at Fife Street, Shore Road. Left behind a wife, Sarah, and two daughters. Robert, a Catholic, was killed when, during the Battle of Jutland, a German shell pierced the deck of his battleship. The vessel exploded killing over 1200 men. Only nine survived. With Robert O'Neill was his best friend and fellow Stoker, Albert Morrison, a Protestant from the Antrim Road who also died.

O'Neill, Samuel - Driver
58806 Royal Field Artillery 29th Division Ammunition Column *Age 29 Died in War on 31 May 1918*
CINQ RUES BRITISH CEMETERY, HAZEBROUCK, France
Son of Samuel and Jane O'Neill, of Belfast; husband of Mrs. M. O'Neill, of 20, Mayfair Street, Belfast.

O'Neill, Thomas - Private
17099 Princess Victoria's (Royal Irish Fusiliers) 6th Battalion *Died in War on 9 August 1915*
HELLES MEMORIAL, Turkey
Born in Belfast. enlisted Coatbridge, Scotland.

O'Neill, William - Lance Corporal
1735 Leinster Regiment 2nd Battalion *Died in War on 26 March 1918*
POZIERES MEMORIAL, France
13 Bombay Street, Belfast.

O'Neill, William - Private
35647 Royal Inniskilling Fusiliers 4th Battalion formerly 7/24746, Alexandra Princess of Wales's Own (Yorkshire Regiment) *Died on 4 October 1918*
GLAGEON COMMUNAL CEMETERY EXTENSION, France
Born at Belfast.

O'Neill, William - Rifleman
10466 Royal Irish Rifles 6th Battalion *Died in War on 11 August 1915*
HELLES MEMORIAL, Turkey
Born in Belfast, enlisted Lurgan.

O'Neill, William Woods - Rifleman
435 Royal Irish Rifles 12th Battalion *Age 24 Died as a Prisoner of War on 29 June 1918*
BERLIN SOUTH-WESTERN CEMETERY, Germany
Son of Agnes O'Neill, of 3, Hanwood Street, Memel Street, Belfast, and the late Joseph Craig O'Neill. Born at Ballyclare, County Antrim.

O'Rawe, Edward - Private
9807 Princess Victoria's (Royal Irish Fusiliers) 1st Battalion *Died in War on 2 March 1916*
HENU CHURCHYARD, France
Born in Belfast, enlisted Portadown.

O'Reilly, Joseph - Lance Corporal
9021 Royal Irish Rifles 2nd Battalion *Died Of Wounds on 6 August 1917*
MENIN ROAD SOUTH MILITARY CEMETERY, Belgium
Husband of Nellie Bushell (formerly O'Reilly), of The Dolphin Inn, Boughton, Faversham, Kent.

O'Reilly, Thomas - Rifleman
9955 Royal Irish Rifles 2nd Battalion *Killed in Action on 25 October 1914*
LE TOURET MEMORIAL, France
56 Crumlin Street, Belfast.

O'Rorke, Robert James - Private
6762 Royal Inniskilling Fusiliers 2nd Battalion *Died in War on 1 May 1915*
LE TOURET MEMORIAL, France
Born in Monkstown, County Antrim. Enlisted at Finner Camp, County Donegal, resident of Belfast.

JOURNEY OF REMEMBERING

O'Rorke, Thomas - Sergeant
8851 Royal Irish Rifles 2nd Battalion *Age 19 Killed by Shellfire on 28 August 1915*
YPRES (MENIN GATE) MEMORIAL, Belgium
Son of Catherine O'Rorke, of 18, Osman Street, Belfast, and the late Francis O'Rorke.

O'Shea, Thomas - Private
21537 Royal Irish Fusiliers 7/8th Battalion *Died in War on 10 August 1917*
YPRES (MENIN GATE) MEMORIAL, Belgium
26, Palmer Street, Belfast.

O'Sullivan, James Eugene - Private
62946 Machine Gun Corps (Infantry) 118th Company *Age 34 Killed in Action on 31 July 1917*
YPRES (MENIN GATE) MEMORIAL, Belgium
Son of Mrs. Kate O'Sullivan, of Waterford, and the late P. J. O'Sullivan. B.A. (Queen's College, Belfast).

Officer, Arthur - Private
63694 Canadian Infantry (Central Ontario Regiment) 3rd Battalion *Age 22 Died in War on 17 June 1915*
VIMY MEMORIAL, France
Son of Arthur and Margaret Officer, of 135, Manor Street, Belfast, Ireland.
An Anglican, he was employed as a tinsmith before enlisting.

Officer, William - Private
25625 Canadian Infantry (Quebec Regiment) 14th Battalion *Age 28 Killed in Action on 3 June 1916*
YPRES (MENIN GATE) MEMORIAL, Belgium
Son of Arthur and Margaret Officer, of 135, Manor Street, Belfast, Ireland.

Ogden, Frank - Rifleman
45718 King's Royal Rifle Corps 9th Battalion *Died in War on 16 July 1918*
PERNOIS BRITISH CEMETERY, HALLOY-LES-PERNOIS, France
Born in Belfast, enlisted Leeds, Yorkshire. Formerly 912225 Royal Army Service Corps.

Ogle, Josias Johnston - Private
769669 Canadian Infantry (Western Ontario Regiment) 18th Battalion *Age 24 Died in War on 9 April 1917*
VIMY MEMORIAL, France
Son of John and Harriet Ogle, of 42, Witham Street, Belfast, Ireland. Employed as a labourer and was a member of the Church of Ireland.

Ogle, Thomas Hugh - Second Engineer
Mercantile Marine S.S. "Kenmare" (Cork) *Age 23 Drowned, as a result of an attack by an enemy submarine on 2 March 1918*
TOWER HILL MEMORIAL, United Kingdom
Son of Thomas Henry Ogle, of 10, Kenilworth Street, Bootle, Lancs, and the late Margaret Ann Ogle.
Born in Belfast.

Ogle, William Robert - Lance Corporal
2105 Black Watch (Royal Highlanders) 6th (Perthshire) Battalion (Territorial) *Died in War on 30 July 1916*
THIEPVAL MEMORIAL, France
Born in Belfast, enlisted in Perth, Scotland.

Oliver, Frank Albert - Gunner
184254 Royal Garrison Artillery *Died in War on 30 November 1917*
LIJSSENTHOEK MILITARY CEMETERY, Belgium
Born in Belfast, enlisted in Warwick, England.

BELFAST BOOK OF HONOUR

Oliver, Richard Henry - Lance Corporal
3/9605 Duke of Wellington's (West Riding Regiment) 2nd Battalion *Age 22 Died in War on 6 May 1915*
YPRES (MENIN GATE) MEMORIAL, Belgium
Son of George and Margaret Oliver, of 47, Cannon Street, Regent Street, Leeds. Born in Belfast.

Oliver, Robert - Rifleman
11210 Royal Irish Rifles "D" Company 6th Battalion *Age 27 (Soldier, buried at sea) on 17 August 1915*
HELLES MEMORIAL, Turkey
Son of Mary E. Oliver, of Bangor, County Down, and the late Captain Gilbert Oliver;
husband of Margaret Oliver, of 9, Chater Street, Belfast.

Oliver, Samuel - Private
41351 Royal Army Medical Corps attached Transport Troops Base Depot Calais
Age 44 Drowned on 1 March 1919
ETAPLES MILITARY CEMETERY, France
Son of Robert and Emma Oliver; husband of Mary Ellen Oliver, of 37, Tyne Street, Belfast.

Orr, Burrell - Private
5393 Regiment Corp Royal Fusiliers (City of London Regiment) 20th Battalion *Died in War on 14 February 1916*
CAMBRIN CHURCHYARD EXTENSION, France
Born in Enniskerry, lived in Belfast when enlisted.

Orr, David Edward - Private
CH/340(S) Royal Marine Light Infantry Chatham Battalion Royal Naval Division *Age 22 Naval, died ashore on 8 May 1915*
HELLES MEMORIAL, Turkey
Son of the late William John and Margaret Orr of Belfast.

Orr, Frank - Rifleman
8298 Royal Irish Rifles 1st Battalion *Age 24 Killed in Action on 5 May 1915*
ROYAL IRISH RIFLES GRAVEYARD, LAVENTIE, France
Son of Mrs. E. Orr, of 278, Crimea Street, Belfast.

Orr, Hugh - Private
9285 Highland Light Infantry 2nd Battalion *Died in War on 17 May 1915*
LE TOURET MEMORIAL, France
Born in Belfast, enlisted Edinburgh.

Orr, James - Private
241920 Cheshire Regiment 1/5th Battalion *Died in War on 25 June 1917*
DUISANS BRITISH CEMETERY, ETRUN, France
Born in Belfast, enlisted in Birkenhead, England.

Orr, Robert Clifford - Captain
Somerset Light Infantry 3rd Battalion attached 1st Battalion *Age 34 Killed in Action on 19 December 1914*
PLOEGSTEERT WOOD MILITARY CEMETERY, Belgium
Son of Robert Harrison Orr and Cassandra Marchaise Orr, of 1, Lombard Street, Belfast. A solicitor who with his brother practised in Belfast and Ballymena. He was killed attacking the German lines. His body was recovered by the Germans who returned it to the British lines on 25 December during the Christmas truce.

Orr, Samuel - Private
35891 King's Own (Royal Lancaster Regiment) 1st Battalion *Age 19 Died in War on 28 March 1918*
ROCLINCOURT VALLEY CEMETERY, France
Son of Samuel and Sarah E. Orr, of 12, Beresford Street, Belfast.

JOURNEY OF REMEMBERING

Orr, William - Private
8481 Irish Guards 2nd Battalion *Age 32 Died of Wounds on 10 October 1916*
LEEDS (HAREHILLS) CEMETERY, United Kingdom
Son of William and Ellen Orr, of 8, Howe Street, Belfast.

Orr, William - Sergeant
432 Royal Irish Rifles 10th Battalion *Age 40 Died in War on 4 August 1917*
YPRES (MENIN GATE) MEMORIAL, Belgium
Son of Alexander and Sarah Orr; husband of Robina Orr, of 33, Belvoir Street, Belfast.

Osborne, Hugh - Private
29310 Yorkshire Regiment 13th Battalion *Age 20 Died in War on 4 March 1917*
THIEPVAL MEMORIAL, France
Son of Mrs. Elizabeth Osborne, of 15, Eliza Street, Belfast.

Osborne, Hugh Corry - Second Lieutenant
West Yorkshire Regiment 12th Battalion *Died in War on 23 July 1916*
THIEPVAL MEMORIAL, France
Son of Joseph Osborne, Hopefield Crescent, Belfast. An accountant he had been educated at RBAI and worked in his father's business.

Oswald, Joseph - Rifleman
13371 Royal Irish Rifles 8th Battalion *Died in War on 4 April 1916*
LE TREPORT MILITARY CEMETERY, France
Brother of Elizabeth, University Road, Belfast.

Owens, Alfred - Sergeant
18704 Machine Gun Corps (Infantry) 109th Company *Age 24 Killed in Action on 1 July 1916*
THIEPVAL MEMORIAL, France
Son of Mrs. Jane Owens, of 4, University Street Belfast. Employed by Workman and Clark shipyard, he was a noted cricket and rugby player.

Owens, James - Rifleman
8287 Royal Irish Rifles 1st Battalion *Age 25 Died in War on 9 May 1915*
PLOEGSTEERT MEMORIAL, Belgium
Son of Mrs. Annie Owens, of 58, North Boundary Street, Belfast.

Owens, John - Private
799098 Canadian Infantry (Central Ontario Regiment) 15th Battalion *Age 20 Died in War on 9 April 1917*
NINE ELMS MILITARY CEMETERY, THELUS, France
Son of William and Marion Owens, of 133, Berkely Street, Toronto, Ontario. Born at Belfast, Ireland. A box folder by trade, he was a member of the Presbyterian Church.

Owens, Samuel James - Able Seaman
J/31624 Royal Navy HMS "Formidable"
Age 21 Killed in Action with submarine in the English Channel on 1 January 1915
CHATHAM NAVAL MEMORIAL, United Kingdom
Son of the late Thomas and Letitia Owens, of Belfast.

Pace, Charles William - Private
44368 Royal Scots 9th Battalion *Age 19 Died in War on 1 August 1918*
SOISSONS MEMORIAL, France
Son of George and Alice Pace, of 310, Woodstock Road, Belfast.

Pace, John - Private
7158 Army Cyclist Corps X Corps, Cyclist Battalion *Age 22 Died of Wounds on 18 August 1917*
BRANDHOEK NEW MILITARY CEMETERY No.3, Belgium
Son of the late Henry and Mary Pace, of Belfast.

Paisley, David Gordon - Private
265817 Black Watch (Royal Highlanders) 6th (Perthshire) Battalion (Territorial) *Died in War on 1 April 1917*
MAROEUIL BRITISH CEMETERY, France
Born in Belfast, enlisted in Perth, Scotland.

Paisley, George - Lance Corporal
19719 Royal Irish Rifles 14th Battalion *Age 21 Killed in Action on 16 August 1917*
TYNE COT MEMORIAL, Belgium
Son of William and Isabella Paisley, of 20, Ulsterdale Street, Belfast.

Paisley, William - Lieutenant
Royal Naval Reserve HMS "Africa" *Age 29 Died of influenza on 18 September 1918*
FREETOWN (KING TOM) CEMETERY, Sierra Leone
Son of Catherine Paisley, of 2, Oak Terrace, Beech Street, Liverpool, and the late John Paisley. Born in Belfast.

Palmer, Benjamin Norman - Private
SS/1462 Royal Army Service Corps *Died in War on 19 September 1914*
SOUTH STOKE (ST ANDREW) CHURCHYARD, OXFORDSHIRE, United Kingdom
Born in Dublin, enlisted and resident in Belfast.

Palmer, Henry - Gunner
319 Royal Horse Artillery and Royal Field Artillery Territorial Force *Killed in Action on 1 July 1916*
THIEPVAL MEMORIAL, France
Born in Belfast. Enlisted in Bradford, Yorkshire.

Palmer, John - Private
17/63 Royal Irish Rifles 15th Battalion *Killed in Action on 1 July 1916*
CONNAUGHT CEMETERY, THIEPVAL, France
8 Pernau Street, Belfast.

Palmer, John - Sergeant
8014 Royal Irish Rifles 1st Battalion *Age 30 Drowned in the River Lys on 28 October 1915*
SAILLY-SUR-LA-LYS-CANADIAN CEMETERY, France
Husband of Agnes Palmer, of 73, Glasgow Street, Belfast.

Palmer, Joseph - Lance Corporal
8712 Royal Irish Rifles "D" Company 1st Battalion *Age 25 Killed in Action on 1 April 1917*
FINS NEW BRITISH CEMETERY, SOREL-LE-GRAND, France
Son of John and Tresa Palmer, of Belfast.

Parfitt, William George - Lance Corporal
314 Rifle Brigade 3rd Battalion *Age 30 Died in War on 6 July 1915*
DUHALLOW A.D.S. CEMETERY, Belgium
23 Oakley Street, Ballysillan, Belfast. Husband of Mary Jane Parfitt.

Park, Jacob - Private
4595 Seaforth Highlanders 5th Battalion *Age 22 Died of Wounds on 13 June 1916*
ST. POL COMMUNAL CEMETERY EXTENSION, France
Son of Mr. and Mrs. T. Park, of "Dochrie", Belmont Church Road, Belfast.

Park, James - Rifleman
15735 Royal Irish Rifles 10th Battalion *Killed in Action on 1 July 1916*
THIEPVAL MEMORIAL, France
Born and enlisted in Belfast.

Parker, Albert - Rifleman
14/3090 Royal Irish Rifles "D" Company 14th Battalion *Age 18 Killed in Action on 16 November 1916*
POND FARM CEMETERY, Belgium
Son of George J. and Jane Parker, of 71, Castlereagh Street, Belfast.

Parker, Edwin - Private
4242 Seaforth Highlanders 1/5th Battalion *Died in War on 16 September 1916*
CITE BONJEAN MILITARY CEMETERY, ARMENTIERES, France
Son of Joseph, 54 Glenbrook Avenue, Belfast.

Parker, Isaac - Private
19532 Machine Gun Corps formerly Royal Irish Rifles *Killed in Action on 8 August 1917*
YPRES (MENIN GATE) MEMORIAL, Belgium
71, Howard Street South, Belfast.

Parker, James - Rifleman
5/5749 Royal Irish Rifles *Age 23 Died as a result of war on 22 March 1919*
CARNMONEY CEMETERY, United Kingdom
Son of James Parker, of 18, Jennymount Street, Belfast.

Parker, Ralph - Rifleman
3139 Royal Irish Rifles 8/9th Battalion *Died in War on 11 April 1918*
HARINGHE (BANDAGHEM) MILITARY CEMETERY, Belgium
Born and enlisted in Belfast.

Parker, Robert John - Rifleman
10/15758 Royal Irish Rifles 15th Battalion *Age 24 Killed in Action on 19 August 1918*
BERTENACRE MILITARY CEMETERY, FLETRE, France
Son of Margaret Parker, of 11, City Street, Belfast, and the late John Parker.

Parker, Samuel - Rifleman
18/400 Royal Irish Rifles 13th Battalion *Age 18 Killed in Action on 1 July 1916*
ANCRE BRITISH CEMETERY, BEAUMONT-HAMEL, France
Son of Thomas and Ellen Parker, of 59, Tower Street, Belfast.

Parker, Thomas - Gunner
91466 Royal Field Artillery "D" Battery 57th Brigade *Age 30 Died of pneumonia on 29 September 1918*
TARANTO TOWN CEMETERY EXTENSION, Italy
Son of Annie and the late Thomas Parker, of Belfast.

Parkes, James - Fireman
Mercantile Marine HMS "Perth" *Age 36 Died in War on 23 October 1915*
ARDROSSAN CEMETERY, United Kingdom
Husband of Sarah Parkes, of 71, Vere Street, Belfast.

Parkes, James Patterson - Piper
16926 Royal Irish Rifles 14th Battalion *Killed in Action on 1 July 1916*
THIEPVAL MEMORIAL, France
Eldest son of Mr and Mrs James Parkes, 154, Snugville Street, Belfast.

Parkhill, James - Sergeant
8706 Royal Irish Rifles 1st Battalion *Age 27 Killed in Action on 28 October 1916*
A.I.F. BURIAL GROUND, FLERS, France
Son of Mr. and Mrs. William Parkhill, of 113, Ewarts Row, Belfast.

Parks, Thomas - Lance Corporal
24388 Royal Inniskilling Fusiliers 1st Battalion formerly 76683 Royal Field Artillery
Killed in Action on 6 July 1917
BARD COTTAGE CEMETERY, Belgium
Born in Belfast.

Parry, William - Rifleman
127 Royal Irish Rifles 15th Battalion *Age 27 Died in War on 31 October 1916*
YPRES (MENIN GATE) MEMORIAL, Belgium
Brother of John Parry, of 105, Upper Canning Street, Belfast.

Partridge, Patrick - Rifleman
8972 Royal Irish Rifles 2nd Battalion *Age 38 Killed in Action on 26 October 1914*
LE TOURET MEMORIAL, France
Resident at 10, Albert Place, Belfast. Husband of Ellen Partridge, of 4, High Street, Bessbrook, County Armagh. Served in the South African Campaign.

Partridge, Thomas - Rifleman
18604 Royal Irish Rifles 12th Battalion *Killed in Action on 1 July 1916*
THIEPVAL MEMORIAL, France
Born in Belfast.

Pascoe, Henry - Sapper
112368 Royal Engineers *Age 37 Died in War on 14 May 1918*
BELFAST (DUNDONALD) CEMETERY, United Kingdom
Son of the late John H. and Mrs. Pascoe; husband of Sarah Pascoe, of 53, Canton Street, Belfast. Born in Belfast.

Pass, Alec - Private
11291 King's Own (Royal Lancaster Regiment) 6th Battalion *Died in War on 9 February 1917*
BASRA MEMORIAL, Iraq
Born in Belfast, enlisted in Lancaster, England.

Patchell, William Neville - Private
5435 Royal Fusiliers 20th Battalion *Age 25 Died in War on 16 July 1916*
THIEPVAL MEMORIAL, France
Son of William Anderson Patchell and Alice Louisa Patchell, of 45, Malone Avenue, Belfast.

Paton, Norman Giles - Sub-Lieutenant
Royal Naval Volunteer Reserve H.M.M.L No. " 403"
Age 32 Killed while salving German torpedo in Runswick Bay on 22 August 1918
CHATHAM NAVAL MEMORIAL, United Kingdom
Son of John and Maggie Paton, of "Ardmore", Bangor, County Down. Native of Belfast.

Paton, William McClimon - Lance Sergeant
14891 Worcestershire Regiment 9th Battalion *Died in War on 10 August 1915*
HELLES MEMORIAL, *Turkey*
Born in Belfast, enlisted in Birmingham.

Patrick, John - Lance Sergeant
13004 Royal Inniskilling Fusiliers 11th Battalion *Killed in Action on 1 July 1916*
THIEPVAL MEMORIAL, *France*
80, Cosgrave Street, Belfast.

Pattenden, William - Private
L/7711 Royal Sussex Regiment 2nd Battalion *Killed in Action on 31 October 1914*
YPRES (MENIN GATE) MEMORIAL, *Belgium*
13, Third Street, Belfast. Worked in the Northern Bank.

Patterson, Aubrey - Rifleman
10523 Royal Irish Rifles 2nd Battalion *Age 18 Killed in Action on 6 September 1918*
PLOEGSTEERT MEMORIAL, *Belgium*
Son of Robert Patterson, of 5, Ambleside Street, Belfast.

Patterson, Ernest - Private
3015 Royal Inniskilling Fusiliers 2nd Battalion *Age 19 Died in War on 16 May 1915*
LE TOURET MEMORIAL, *France*
Son of Robert and Sarah Patterson, of 27, Denmark Street, Belfast. A Special Reservist.

Patterson, Harold Jamison - Lance Corporal
16931 Royal Irish Rifles 14th Battalion *Age 19 Killed in Action on 16 August 1917*
TYNE COT MEMORIAL, *Belgium*
Son of Mr. J. W. and Margaret Patterson, of 5, South Parade, Belfast.

Patterson, Hugh - Private
4314 Seaforth Highlanders 1/5th Battalion *Age 20 Killed in Action on 27 July 1916*
DARTMOOR CEMETERY, BECORDEL-BECOURT, *France*
Son of George and Sarah Patterson, of 85, Walmer Street, Belfast.

Patterson, James - Private
7124 Royal Irish Regiment 2nd Battalion *Killed in Action on 9 May 1915*
YPRES (MENIN GATE) MEMORIAL, *Belgium*
53 Devonshire Street, Belfast.

Patterson, James Alexander - Lance Corporal
G/12323 Duke of Cambridge's Own (Middlesex Regiment) 19th Battalion *Died in War on 28 January 1917*
DICKEBUSCH NEW MILITARY CEMETERY, *Belgium*
Born in Belfast, enlisted in London, resident in Liverpool.

Patterson, John - Lance Corporal
10224 Royal Inniskilling Fusiliers 2nd Battalion *Killed in Action on 17 September 1918*
BAILLEUL COMMUNAL CEMETERY EXTENSION (NORD), *France*
Born in Belfast.

Patterson, John - Sergeant
35006 Northumberland Fusiliers 14th Battalion *Died as a result of war on 22 October 1920*
LISBURN CEMETERY, *United Kingdom*
Husband of Matilda Patterson, of 88, Tate's Avenue, Belfast.

Patterson, John - Sergeant
PO/11550 Royal Naval Division Royal Marine Light Infantry Portsmouth Battalion
Age 29 Died in War on 20 July 1915
ALEXANDRIA (CHATBY) MILITARY AND WAR MEMORIAL CEMETERY, Egypt
Son of John Patterson; husband of L. M. Patterson, of "Leahurst", Milton Road, Cowes, Isle of Wight. Born in Belfast.

Patterson, R C - Private
351424 Argyll and Sutherland Highlanders 5th Battalion *Age 26 Died as a result of War on 30 November 1918*
BELFAST (DUNDONALD) CEMETERY, United Kingdom
Son of Alexander and Elizabeth Patterson. Born in Belfast.

Patterson, Robert - Corporal
8902 Royal Irish Rifles 2nd Battalion *Age 28 Killed in Action on 22 March 1918*
SAVY BRITISH CEMETERY, France
Son of William Patterson, of 54, Foundry Street, Belfast.

Patterson, Robert - Private
8401 Royal Inniskilling Fusiliers "C" Company 1st Battalion *Age 26 Died in War on 29 June 1915*
HELLES MEMORIAL, Turkey
Son of Mrs. J. McDonald (formerly Patterson), of 47, Thorndyke Street, Albert Bridge Road, Belfast, and the late John Patterson.

Patterson, Robert - Private
S/16086 Black Watch 10th Battalion *Died in War on 9 May 1917*
DOIRAN MEMORIAL, Greece
Member of Fountainville Presbyterian Church, Belfast.

Patterson, Robert - Rifleman
18613 Royal Irish Rifles 13th Battalion *Killed in Action on 1 July 1916*
THIEPVAL MEMORIAL, France
Born Purdysburn, enlisted Comber, resident of Belfast.

Patterson, Robert - Rifleman
863 Royal Irish Rifles 8th Battalion *Age 36 Died in War on 2 July 1916*
THIEPVAL MEMORIAL, France
Son of W. J. and Charlotte Patterson, of Dromore, County Down; husband of Mary E. Patterson, of 9, Wayland Street, Belfast.

Patterson, Robert J - Private
21923 Royal Inniskilling Fusiliers 10th Battalion *Age 18 Died in War on 28 March 1918*
NAMPS-AU-VAL BRITISH CEMETERY, France
Son of Rachel Patterson, of 91, Donegall Road, Belfast.

Patterson, Thomas James - Private
41239 Royal Army Medical Corps 109th Field Ambulance *Age 20 Died in War on 8 August 1916*
BERKS CEMETERY EXTENSION, Belgium
Son of James and Annie Patterson, of 14, Glasgow Street, Belfast. Born Antrim.

Patterson, William - Corporal
15760 Royal Irish Rifles 10th Battalion *Killed in Action on 7 June 1917*
WULVERGHEM-LINDENHOEK ROAD MILITARY CEMETERY, Belgium
Brother of Eva Patterson, 73 Pine Street, Belfast.

Patterson, William - Private
28464 Royal Inniskilling Fusiliers 1st Battalion *Died in War on 9 August 1916*
POTIJZE CHATEAU WOOD CEMETERY, Belgium
Born and enlisted in Belfast.

Patterson, William Alexander Duncan - Sergeant
6669 Royal Irish Rifles 1st Battalion *Age 27 Killed in Action on 21 March 1918*
POZIERES MEMORIAL, France
Son of Robert and Phoebe Patterson, of 19, South Parade, Belfast; husband of Mary Josephine Patterson, of 5, Sion Hill Avenue, Harold's Cross, Dublin.

Patterson, William James - Corporal
18606 Royal Irish Rifles "B" Company 13th Battalion *Killed in Action on 1 July 1916*
THIEPVAL MEMORIAL, France
Husband of Mary Patterson, of 278A, Newtownards Road, Belfast.

Patton, Arthur - Sergeant
3482 Royal Irish Rifles 14th Battalion *Killed In Action on 27 June 1917*
MESSINES RIDGE BRITISH CEMETERY, Belgium
Born and enlisted in Belfast.

Patton, Edwin Millikin - Private
38598 King's Own Yorkshire Light Infantry 10th Battalion *Age 23 Died in War on 4 October 1917*
TYNE COT MEMORIAL, Belgium
Son of Mrs. A. F. Patton, of 34, Lendrick Street, Newtownards Road, Belfast, and the late Samuel Patton.

Patton, George Henry - Able Seaman
J/6183 Royal Navy HMS "Monmouth" *Killed in Action at Battle of Coronel on 1 November 1914*
PLYMOUTH NAVAL MEMORIAL, United Kingdom
Son of George H. and Christina Patton, of 62, Everton Street, Belfast.

Patton, James - Rifleman
6612 Royal Irish Rifles 2nd Battalion *Killed in Action on 1 December 1914*
YPRES (MENIN GATE) MEMORIAL, Belgium
Husband of Emily Patton, 15 Douglas Street, Belfast.

Patton, John - Rifleman
4785 Royal Irish Rifles 3rd Battalion *Died in War on 27 December 1914*
GRANGEGORMAN MILITARY CEMETERY, Republic of Ireland
Born in Portadown, enlisted at Ballykinler, resident of Belfast.

Patton, Leslie - Drummer
15732 Royal Irish Rifles 10th Battalion *Age 32 Died of Wounds on 10 August 1917*
MENDINGHEM MILITARY CEMETERY, Belgium
Son of Mr. and Mrs. L. Patton, of Belfast; husband of Evelyn Patton, of 55, Abingdon Street, Belfast.

Patton, Samuel - Private
3422 Royal Inniskilling Fusiliers 2nd Battalion *Killed in Action on 16 May 1915*
LE TOURET MEMORIAL, France
Born in Belfast.

Journey of Remembering

Patton, Thomas James - Rifleman
15730 Royal Irish Rifles 10th Battalion *Killed In Action on 1 July 1916*
CONNAUGHT CEMETERY, THIEPVAL, *France*
Born and enlisted in Belfast.

Patton, William - Private
17460 Durham Light Infantry 22nd Battalion *Age 38 Died in War on 7 July 1917*
BELGIAN BATTERY CORNER CEMETERY, *Belgium*
Son of John Patton, of 53, Cambrai Street, Belfast.

Patton, William John - Private
3411 Royal Inniskilling Fusiliers 2nd Battalion *Died in War on 16 May 1915*
LE TOURET MEMORIAL, *France*
145, Snugville Street, Belfast.

Paul, John McNeil - Driver
318978 Canadian Field Artillery *Died in War on 7 May 1917*
STOCKPORT (WILLOW GROVE) CEMETERY, *United Kingdom*
Born in Belfast the son of Thomas Paul of Wine Street, Sligo. Held a First Class degree in Engineering from Univerity College Galway. Died of pnemonia after service at Vimy Ridge.

Paul, Joseph - Private
PLY/17320 Royal Marine Light Infantry Plymouth Royal Naval Division *Age 18 Died of Wounds on 14 July 1915*
LANCASHIRE LANDING CEMETERY, *Turkey*
Son of Agnes Paul, of 41, Bann Street, Oldpark Road, Belfast, and the late Robert Paul. Worked for Combe Barbour's Mill.

Payne, Henry - Rifleman
958 Royal Irish Rifles 9th Battalion *Age 18 Died in War on 2 July 1916*
THIEPVAL MEMORIAL, *France*
Son of William Payne, of 13, Vistula Street, Belfast.

Payne, Thomas - Able Seaman
234604 Royal Navy HMS "Torrent" *Age 27 Killed by mine explosion in North Sea on 23 December 1917*
PLYMOUTH NAVAL MEMORIAL, *United Kingdom*
Son of Thomas and Maria Payne; brother of Mrs. Harriette Lutton, of 14, Franklin Street, Weymouth 88, Massachussetts, USA. A native of Belfast.

Paysden, George - Rifleman
19720 Royal Irish Rifles 14th Battalion *Died in War on 11 October 1916*
BAILLEUL COMMUNAL CEMETERY EXTENSION (NORD), *France*
Born and enlisted in Belfast.

Peacock, Walter - Second Lieutenant
Royal Irish Fusiliers "A" Company 9th Battalion *Age 20 Killed in Action on 22 December 1916*
RAMPARTS CEMETERY, LILLE GATE, *Belgium*
Son of George Henry and Annie Peacock, of 17, Dromore Street, Cregagh, Belfast.

Pearce, William Nelson - Private
2897 Royal Inniskilling Fusiliers 1st Battalion *Age 21 (Soldier, buried at sea) on 24 August 1915*
HELLES MEMORIAL, *Turkey*
Son of William and Mary Ann Pearce, of 68, Carnan Street, Shankill Road, Belfast.

Peden, James - Drummer
G/1393 Royal Irish Fusiliers 2nd Garrison *Age 41 Died of malaria fever on 3 November 1918*
KIRECHKOI-HORTAKOI MILITARY CEMETERY, Greece
Husband of Sarah Peden, of 23, Tyne Street, Belfast.

Peel, Samuel - Rifleman
15773 Royal Irish Rifles 10th Battalion *Died in War on 14 August 1917*
YPRES (MENIN GATE) MEMORIAL, Belgium
Born and enlisted in Belfast.

Pelan, William James - Corporal
48110 Royal Garrison Artillery *Died in War on 29 September 1916*
LONSDALE CEMETERY, AUTHUILE, France
Born and enlisted in Belfast. Awarded the Distinguished Conduct Medal.

Penman, Charles - Lance Sergeant
16936 Royal Irish Rifles 14th Battalion *Age 19 Died in War on 15 March 1916*
HAMEL MILITARY CEMETERY, BEAUMONT-HAMEL, France
Son of Mrs. A. Penman, of 10, Lyle Street, Belfast.

Penn, William - Private
5320 Royal Munster Fusiliers 7th Battalion *Age 18 Died in War on 8 August 1915*
HELLES MEMORIAL, Turkey
Son of William and Mary Penn, of 73, Hardinge Street, Belfast.

Pennal, William - Private
668608 Canterbury Regiment New Zealand Expeditionary Force 2nd Battalion
Age 17 Killed in Action on 16 September 1916
THISTLE DUMP CEMETERY, HIGH WOOD, LONGUEVAL, France
Son of Thomas Pennal, of Belfast, Ireland.

Pennell, George - Private
42531 Royal Irish Fusiliers 9th Battalion *Age 19 Killed in Action on 25 October 1918*
TYNE COT MEMORIAL, Belgium
Son of Thomas and Mary Pennell, of Pernau Street, Belfast.

Pentland, William - Rifleman
9080 Royal Irish Rifles 1st Battalion *Died of Wounds on 26 August 1916*
CANTERBURY CEMETERY, KENT, United Kingdom
Born and enlisted in Belfast.

Pepper, Andrew - Private
41427 Royal Irish Fusiliers 9th Battalion *Age 34 Died in War on 12 August 1918*
PLOEGSTEERT MEMORIAL, Belgium
Son of James and Mary Pepper, of 21, Greenville Terrace, Bloomfield, Belfast.

Percy, David Black - Lance Corporal
16165 Norfolk Regiment 8th Battalion *Killed in Action on 1 July 1916*
THIEPVAL MEMORIAL, France
Born in Belfast, enlisted in London.

Percy, Thomas James - Private
746088 Canadian Infantry (Eastern Ontario Regiment) 2nd Battalion *Age 26 Died of Wounds on 9 April 1917*
LAPUGNOY MILITARY CEMETERY, France
Son of Edward and Elizabeth Percy; husband of Elizabeth Raike (formerly Percy),
of 125, Alice Street, Oshawa, Ontario, Canada. Native of Belfast, Ireland.

Perris, Charles Hind - Staff Sergeant
S4/045458 Army Service Corps 1st Company 7th Divisonal Train *Age 37 Died in War on 6 October 1917*
LIJSSENTHOEK MILITARY CEMETERY, Belgium
Son of George Henry and Annie Perris, of Manchester; husband of Margaret Perris,
of 22, Powerscourt Street, Belfast.

Perry, James - Private
2275 Royal Irish Fusiliers 2nd Battalion *Died of Wounds on 29 March 1915*
BOULOGNE EASTERN CEMETERY, France
Brother of Robert Perry, of 106, Upper Canning Street, Belfast.

Perry, John - Rifleman
7942 Royal Irish Rifles 2nd Battalion *Killed in Action on 25 October 1914*
LE TOURET MEMORIAL, France
Born and enlisted in Belfast.

Petticrew, Alexander - Private
10193 Royal Inniskilling Fusiliers 2nd Battalion *Killed in Action on 11 July 1916*
THIEPVAL MEMORIAL, FRANCE
Born in Belfast. Husband of May McCarthy (formerly Petticrew), of 2, Chapel Court, Snargate Street, Dover, Kent.

Pettigrew, Patrick - Private
22628 Princess Victoria's (Royal Irish Fusiliers) 1st Battalion *Died in War on 11 April 1917*
FAMPOUX BRITISH CEMETERY, France
Born and enlisted in Belfast. The son of Patrick and Annie Pettigrew of 21 Hill Street, Holywood, County Down.

Pettigrew, Robert McCalmont - Second Lieutenant
Royal Irish Rifles "C" Company 8th Battalion *Age 20 Killed in Action at Thiepval on 10 June 1916*
AUTHUILE MILITARY CEMETERY, France
Only son of the late John Graham Pettigrew and of Matilda Pettigrew, of 19, Eglantine Avenue, Belfast.

Pettigrew, William J - Private
S/2390 Argyll and Sutherland Highlanders 1st Battalion *Age 32 Killed in Action on 17 March 1915*
BOULOGNE EASTERN CEMETERY, France
Son of William and Agnes Pettigrew, of 39, Apsley Street, Belfast.

Petty, William J. - Private
41406 Royal Irish Fusiliers 9th (North Irish Horse) Battalion *Age 26 Died in War on 22 November 1917*
CAMBRAI MEMORIAL, LOUVERVAL, France
Son of Francis Petty, of 32, Agincourt Avenue, Belfast, and the late Marion Petty.

Phair, George - Rifleman
8723 Royal Irish Rifles 8th Battalion *Age 22 Died in War on 8 August 1917*
YPRES (MENIN GATE) MEMORIAL, Belgium
Son of George and Susan Phair, of 20, Laganvale Street, Stranmillis Road, Belfast.

Philips, Thomas McCann - Captain
Royal Army Medical Corps *Age 24 Died in War on 4 November 1914*
POPERINGE COMMUNAL CEMETERY, Belgium
A graduate of Queen's University he was born in Damascus, Syria, the son of the Rev J G Philips and Annie Phillips. Attended both RBAI and Campbell College. He then qualified as a doctor, worked at the Royal Victoria Hospital before being commissioned into the Royal Army Medical Corps.

Philips, William - First Engineer
Mercantile Marine "Eveleen" (Belfast) *Age 53 Presumed drowned on 6 May 1918*
TOWER HILL MEMORIAL, United Kingdom
Son of George Philips and the late Helen Murdoch Philips; husband of Catherine Philips (née Cochrane), of 82, Castlereagh Road, Belfast. Born at Glasgow.

Phillips, Robert - Rifleman
12112 Royal Irish Rifles 15th Battalion *Died in War on 20 January 1916*
MIRAUMONT COMMUNAL CEMETERY, France
Born and enlisted in Belfast.

Phillips, William John - Private
12586 Princess Victoria's (Royal Irish Fusiliers) 1st Battalion *Died in War on 19 April 1917*
POINT-DU-JOUR MILITARY CEMETERY, ATHIES, France
Born and enlisted in Belfast.

Philpott, George - Sergeant
15055 Royal Inniskilling Fusiliers 8th Battalion *Died in War on 2 May 1916*
LILLERS COMMUNAL CEMETERY, France
Son of Robert and Matilda Philpott; husband of Elizabeth Philpott, of 182, Conway Street, Belfast. Served in the South African Campaign. Native of Belfast.

Pickering, Ernest Edward - Private
2606 Black Watch (Royal Highlanders) 1/6th Battalion *Age 19 Died in War on 25 July 1916*
FLATIRON COPSE CEMETERY, MAMETZ, France
Son of George and Elizabeth Pickering, of 8, Evelyn Gardens, Antrim Road, Belfast.

Pickup, Joseph - Private
40292 Lancashire Fusiliers 15th Battalion *Died in War on 26 September 1917*
COXYDE MILITARY CEMETERY, Belgium
Born in Accrington, enlisted in Barrow, both Lancashire, resident of Belfast.

Pierce, Joseph - Gunner
19893 Royal Garrison Artillery *Died in War on 26 September 1917*
WIELTJE FARM CEMETERY, Belgium
Born in Belfast, enlisted in Hamilton, Scotland.

Pilson, Samuel - Sapper
57510 Royal Engineers 121st Field Company *Died in War on 16 October 1918*
KORTRIJK (ST JAN) COMMUNAL CEMETERY, Belgium
Born in Banbridge, County Down. 125, Canmore Street, Belfast. Member of Argyle Place Presbyterian Church.

Pinkerton, Matthew - Private
2634 Royal Inniskilling Fusiliers 6th Battalion *Died in War on 31 October 1916*
DOIRAN MEMORIAL, Greece
Son of the late William and Catherine Pinkerton of Belfast.

Journey of Remembering

Pinkerton, Robert - Chief Baker
Mercantile Marine S.S. "Lusitania" (Liverpool) *Age 50 Drowned, as a result of an attack by an enemy submarine on 7 May 1915*
TOWER HILL MEMORIAL, United Kingdom
Son of the late Robert and Margaret Jane Pinkerton; husband of Eliza Jane Pinkerton (née Clokey), of 40, Linacre Road, Liverpool. Born in Belfast.

Pirret, James Kay - Second Lieutenant
King's Royal Rifle Corps 1th Battalion *Died in War on 4 April 1917*
METZ-EN-COUTURE COMMUNAL CEMETERY BRITISH EXTENSION, France
43 Ardenlee Avenue, Belfast.

Pitkethly, William Lawrence - Corporal
5939 Royal Irish Rifles 2nd Battalion *Age 19 Killed in Action on 10 June 1917*
MESSINES RIDGE BRITISH CEMETERY, Belgium
Son of Mr. W. H. and Mrs. M. R. Pitkethly, of 174, Ravenhill Avenue, Belfast.

Poag, James Stevinson - Lance Corporal
7170 Royal Irish Rifles 2nd Battalion *Age 27 Killed in Action on 23 October 1914*
LE TOURET MEMORIAL, France
Son of Robert Poag; husband of Mary Poag, of 3, William Street, Donaghadee, County Down.
A Belfast City Tramway employee his brother, also a native of Belfast, was also killed.

Poag, Robert - Bombardier
32049 Royal Garrison Artillery 67th Anti-Aircraft Battery *Age 26 Died in War on 5 September 1916*
MESNIL COMMUNAL CEMETERY EXTENSION, France
Son of Robert and Rachel Poag, of 103, Woodstock Road, Belfast. His brother, James, was also killed.

Pollard, Patrick - Private
12195 Royal Irish Fusiliers 1st Battalion *Died in War on 11 April 1917*
BROWN'S COPSE CEMETERY, ROEUX, France
65, Sultan Street, Belfast.

Pollard, Thomas - Private
6733 Royal Irish Fusiliers 1st Battalion *Killed in Action on 18 October 1914*
PLOEGSTEERT MEMORIAL, Belgium
Husband of Mary Pollard, 45 McDonnell Street, Belfast.

Pollen, Edward - Boy Second Class
J/92860 Royal Navy HMS "Impregnable" *Age 15 Died in War on 22 October 1918*
FORD PARK CEMETERY (FORMERLY PLYMOUTH OLD CEMETERY) (PENNYCOMEQUICK), United Kingdom
Son of John and Ellen Pollen, of 90, Portallo Street, Belfast.

Pollin, Robert Kelly - Second Lieutenant
Royal Irish Rifles 4th Battalion attached 1st Battalion *Age 20 Killed in Action on 31 July 1917*
YPRES (MENIN GATE) MEMORIAL, Belgium
Son of James Moore Pollin and Martha Pollin (née Corbitt), of "Westhoek", Taunton Avenue, Belfast.
Articled to a solicitor. Had joined as a private soldier and later commissioned.

Pollins, William - Gunner
38197 Royal Field Artillery "B" Battery 60th Brigade *Age 33 Died in War on 17 October 1916*
POZIERES BRITISH CEMETERY, OVILLERS-LA BOISSELLE, France
Son of William Pollins, of 72, Stranmillis Gardens, Belfast.

Pollock, Alexander - Lance Corporal
14/15779 Royal Irish Rifles "D" Company 14th Battalion *Age 19 Killed in Action on 5 May 1917*
POND FARM CEMETERY, Belgium
Son of John and Maggie Pollock, of 105, Saunders Street, Belfast. Native of Govan, Glasgow.

Pollock, David - Rifleman
1100 Royal Irish Rifles 15th Battalion *Died in War on 5 February 1916*
SUCRERIE MILITARY CEMETERY, France
Born and enlisted in Belfast.

Pollock, James - Lance Corporal
19548 Machine Gun Corps (Infantry) 107th Company *Age 22 Died in War on 15 June 1916*
THIEPVAL MEMORIAL, France
Son of David and Letitia Pollock, of 55, Ligoniel Place, Belfast.

Pollock, John - Rifleman
5885 Royal Irish Rifles 5th Battalion *Died in War on 10 January 1916*
BELFAST CITY CEMETERY, United Kingdom
Born and enlisted in Belfast.

Pollock, Joseph - Ordinary Seaman
J/25436 Royal Navy HMS "Defence" *Age 18 Killed in Action at Battle of Jutland on 31 May 1916*
PLYMOUTH NAVAL MEMORIAL, United Kingdom
Son of Elizabeth Pollock, of 31, Epworth Street, Belfast.

Pollock, Paul G - Lance Corporal
Royal Irish Rifles 14th Battalion *Died in War on 1 July 1916*
7 Glandore Park, Belfast.

Pollock, Thomas - Driver
T3/031010 Royal Army Service Corps *Died in War on 18 July 1915*
SEAFORD CEMETERY, SUSSEX
Born in Glenarm, Antrim, enlisted and resident in Belfast.

Pollock, William - Private
29379 Royal Inniskilling Fusiliers "C" Company 2nd Battalion *Age 20 Died in War on 21 March 1918*
POZIERES MEMORIAL, France
Son of Mrs. Margaret Pollock, of 130, Boundary Street, Belfast.

Polly, William Alexander - Private
4321 Seaforth Highlanders 1/5th Battalion *Age 22 Died of Wounds on 28 July 1916*
DARTMOOR CEMETERY, BECORDEL-BECOURT, France
Son of Richard Polly, of Belfast.

Ponise, William - Private
20868 Royal Inniskilling Fusiliers *Died in War on 21 August 1917*
BELFAST (MILLTOWN) ROMAN CATHOLIC CEMETERY, United Kingdom
Husband of Mary Ann Ponise, of 27, Jetty Street, Belfast. Served on the North-West Frontier and in the South African Campaign.

Poots, Robert - Private
9472 Royal Inniskilling Fusiliers 1st Battalion *Age 24 Died in War on 21 August 1915*
HELLES MEMORIAL, Turkey
Son of Robert and Mary Pootes, of 43, Pernau Street, Belfast. His father served throughout the war in the Seaforth Highlanders and his brother with the Royal Navy - both survived.

Poots, William John - Rifleman
798 Royal Irish Rifles 15th Battalion *Killed in Action on 21 March 1918*
POZIERES MEMORIAL, France
Born in Banbridge, resident of Belfast.

Porter, Alexander - Private
7825 1st Canadian Mounted Rifles (Saskatchewan Regiment) *Age 22 Died in War on 2 June 1916*
YPRES (MENIN GATE) MEMORIAL, Belgium
Son of Mrs. Elizabeth Porter, of 9, Geoffrey Street, Belfast, Ireland.
An Anglican, he was born in Portadown and worked as a rivetter.

Porter, Ernest - Lance Corporal
8123 Royal Irish Rifles 1st Battalion *Killed in Action on 3 March 1917*
THIEPVAL MEMORIAL, France
Born and enlisted in Belfast.

Porter, George - Rifleman
5821 Royal Irish Rifles 7th Battalion *Died in War on 26 April 1916*
DUD CORNER CEMETERY, LOOS, France
Born and enlisted in Belfast.

Porter, J - Private
3744 Royal Irish Fusiliers 4th Battalion *Died in War on 9 June 1916*
BELFAST CITY CEMETERY, United Kingdom
Husband of Annie Porter, of 42, Crosby Street, Belfast.

Porter, James - Private
S/2015 Seaforth Highlanders (Ross-shire Buffs, the Duke of Albany's) 7th Battalion
Died in War on 25 September 1915
LOOS MEMORIAL, France
Born in Belfast, enlisted Fort George, Scotland.

Porter, John - Private
7181 Princess Victoria's (Royal Irish Fusiliers) 1st Battalion *Died in War on 11 April 1917*
FAMPOUX BRITISH CEMETERY, France
Born and enlisted in Belfast.

Porter, John - Private
S/12474 Black Watch (Royal Highlanders) 2nd Battalion *Died on 14 July 1916*
AMARA WAR CEMETERY, Iraq
Son of John Porter, 97 Hillman Street, Belfast.

Porter, John - Sergeant
538 Royal Irish Rifles 1st Battalion *Died in War on 27 March 1917*
BELFAST CITY CEMETERY, United Kingdom
Born and enlisted in Belfast.

Porter, Joseph - Private
11674 Royal Inniskilling Fusiliers 6th Battalion *Died of Wounds on 18 August 1915*
CAIRO WAR MEMORIAL CEMETERY
Born in Belfast.

Journey of Remembering

Porter, Leslie - Captain
Royal Flying Corps 45th Squadron *Age 34 Died in War on 24 October 1916*
ARRAS FLYING SERVICES MEMORIAL France
Husband of Kathleen Porter, of Tordeerna, Helen's Bay, Belfast, native of Belfast and member of Belfast Masonic Lodge No. 154.

Porter, Robert John - Private
550116 Otago Regiment New Zealand Expeditionary Force 3rd Battalion
Age 20 Killed in Action on 24 November 1917
TYNE COT CEMETERY, Belgium
Son of Christopher and Martha Porter, of 6, Gibson Street, Timaru, New Zealand. Native of Belfast, Ireland.

Porter, Samuel - Sergeant
13398 Royal Irish Rifles 15th Battalion *Age 23 Killed in Action on 1 July 1916*
THIEPVAL MEMORIAL, France
Son of William Porter, of 17, Albertville Drive, Belfast.

Porter, Thomas - Private
6567 Royal Inniskilling Fusiliers 2nd Battalion *Presumed dead on 16 May 1915*
LE TOURET MEMORIAL, France
Husband of Edith Porter, 111 Sugarfield Street, Belfast.

Porter, William - Corporal
8552 Royal Irish Rifles 2nd Battalion *Killed in Action on 17 May 1915*
RIDGE WOOD MILITARY CEMETERY, Belgium
Husband of Mary Porter, of Belfast.

Porter, William - Private
865 Royal Irish Rifles 9th Battalion *Killed in Action on 1 July 1916*
THIEPVAL MEMORIAL, France
111 Sugarfield Street, Belfast.

Porter, William - Private
S/13421 Gordan Highlanders 1st Battalion *Killed in Action on 18 July 1916*
THIEPVAL MEMORIAL, France
Son of John Porter, 97 Hillman Street.

Porter, William - Second Lieutenant
Royal Inniskilling Fusiliers 6th Battalion attached 1st Battalion *Age 31 Killed in Action on 1 July 1916*
ANCRE BRITISH CEMETERY, BEAUMONT-HAMEL, France
Son of William and Mary Porter, of "Beechview", Balmoral Avenue, Belfast.

Porter, William Edgar Walsh - Corporal
1284 Australian Infantry 14th Battalion *Age 33 Died in War on 21 October 1917*
YPRES (MENIN GATE) MEMORIAL, Belgium
Son of James and Isabel Porter. Native of Belfast, Ireland. Holder of the Military Medal.

Porterfield, Thomas - Private
16878 Highland Light Infantry 10th (Service) Battalion *Died in War on 25 September 1915*
LOOS MEMORIAL, France
Born in Belfast, enlisted Neilson, Scotland.

Journey of Remembering

Portis, John George - Private
7722 Royal Inniskilling Fusiliers 2nd Battalion *Died on 14 January 1915*
STE. MARIE CEMETERY, LE HAVRE, *France*
Born in Belfast.

Potter, James Alexander - Private
16240 Royal Inniskilling Fusiliers "C" Company 11th Battalion *Age 27 Killed in Action on 1 July 1916*
A.I.F. BURIAL GROUND, FLERS, *France*
Son of Robert and Maggie E. Potter, of 81, Snugville Street, Belfast.

Potts, Alexander - Private
13116 Royal Inniskilling Fusiliers 11th Battalion *Killed in Action on 1 July 1916*
THIEPVAL MEMORIAL, *France*
Born in Belfast.

Potts, Andrew - Able Seaman
228087 Royal Navy HMS "Defence" *Age 30 Killed in Action at Battle of Jutland on 31 May 1916*
PLYMOUTH NAVAL MEMORIAL, *United Kingdom*
Son of John and Annie Potts, of 8, Christopher Street, Belfast.

Potts, John - Private
13075 Royal Inniskilling Fusiliers 11th Battalion *Killed in Action on 1 July 1916*
THIEPVAL MEMORIAL, *France*
21 Israel Street, Belfast.

Poulter, Alexander - Private
27947 Royal Inniskilling Fusiliers 9th Battalion *Age 24 Killed in Action on 16 August 1917*
TYNE COT MEMORIAL, *Belgium*
Son of Lewis George and Margaret Poulter, of 43, Kilton Street, Battersea, London. Born in Belfast.

Power, Thomas - Rifleman
5859 Royal Irish Rifles 6th Battalion *Died in War on 3 October 1916*
STRUMA MILITARY CEMETERY, *Greece*
Born and enlisted in Belfast.

Poynter, George - Gunner
63239 Royal Horse Artillery and Royal Field Artillery *Died in War on 6 September 1916*
BAGHDAD (NORTH GATE) WAR CEMETERY, *Iraq*
Born in Belfast, enlisted in India.

Pratt, Thomas - Private
7725 Royal Irish Fusiliers 1st Battalion *Died in War on 26 August 1914*
LA FERTE-SOUS-JOUARRE MEMORIAL, *France*
Resident and enlisted in Belfast.

Preece, Samuel Charles - Stoker First Class
SS/103563 Royal Navy HMS "Majestic" *Died in War on 27 May 1915*
PLYMOUTH NAVAL MEMORIAL, *United Kingdom*
Husband of Jennie, 46 Upper Townsend Street, Belfast.

Prenter, Dalton - Second Lieutenant
Royal Irish Fusiliers 9th (North Irish Horse) Battalion *Age 27 Killed in Action on 21 March 1918*
POZIERES MEMORIAL, *France*
Son of James B. and Clara E. A. Prenter, of 123, Fitzroy Avenue, Belfast.
Had served in the ranks before being commissioned.

Prenter, Joseph - Private
6693 King's Shropshire Light Infantry 1st Battalion *Age 25 Died in War on 9 August 1915*
YPRES (MENIN GATE) MEMORIAL, *Belgium*
Son of Samuel Prenter, of Snugville Street, Crumlin Road, Belfast.

Prenter, Patrick James - Private
195924 Connaught Rangers 6th Battalion *Age 26 Died as a result of war on 17 March 1920*
BELFAST (MILLTOWN) ROMAN CATHOLIC CEMETERY, *United Kingdom*
Son of Mrs. Prenter, of 15, Bombay Street, Kashmir Road, Belfast.

Prenter, W J - Private
11672 Royal Inniskilling Fusiliers 6th Battalion
Age 33 Died of Wounds received at the Dardanelles on 28 March 1918
BELFAST CITY CEMETERY, *United Kingdom*
Son of Samuel Prenter, of 51, Silvio Street, Belfast; husband of Margaret Prenter,
of 51, Hooker Street, Crumlin Road, Belfast.

Prentice, David - Able Seaman
231155 Royal Navy HMS "Monmouth" *Died in War on 1 November 1914*
PLYMOUTH NAVAL MEMORIAL, *United Kingdom*
36 Charles Street South, Belfast. Son of William Prentice of Gallows Street, Dromore, County Down.

Prentice, George - Private
9/13945 Royal Inniskilling Fusiliers 9th Battalion *Died in War on 9 May 1916*
GEZAINCOURT COMMUNAL CEMETERY EXTENSION, *France*
Son of Henry and the late Elizabeth Prentice of 39, Westmoreland Street, Belfast.

Prentice, Patrick - Private
2115 Royal Irish Regiment 8th Battalion *Died in War on 23 August 1918*
BAGNEUX BRITISH CEMETERY, GEZAINCOURT, *France*
Son of Mrs Mary Prentice, Castlereagh, Belfast.

Preshur, Matthew - Rifleman
18/744 Royal Irish Rifles 8th Battalion *Age 20 Killed in Action on 20 June 1917*
POND FARM CEMETERY, *Belgium*
Son of Elizabeth Preshur, of 57, Langford Street, Belfast, and the late William Preshur.

Preshur, Robert - Rifleman
15744 Royal Irish Rifles 10th Battalion *Killed In Action on 1 July 1916*
THIEPVAL MEMORIAL, *France*
Born and enlisted in Belfast.

Preshur, William - Rifleman
15/3066 Royal Irish Rifles 9th Battalion *Age 32 Killed in Action on 8 September 1916*
ST. QUENTIN CABARET MILITARY CEMETERY, *Belgium*
Son of Elizabeth Preshur, of 57, Longford Street, Belfast, and the late William Preshur.

Journey of Remembering

Press, Victor John - Rifleman
450 Royal Irish Rifles "B" Company 8th Battalion *Age 19 Died of gastritis on 10 May 1915*
BELFAST (DUNDONALD) CEMETERY, United Kingdom
Son of James S. and Margaret F. Press, of 16, Clara Street, Castlereagh Road, Belfast.

Pressdee, John - Rifleman
17/679 Royal Irish Rifles 9th Battalion *Killed in Action on 1 July 1916*
THIEPVAL MEMORIAL, France
31 Paris Street, Belfast.

Price, Hugh Bernard - Private
3490 Royal Inniskilling Fusiliers 1st Battalion *Killed in Action on 21 August 1915*
HELLES MEMORIAL, Turkey
10 Merrion Street, Belfast.

Price, Joseph - Private
9047 Royal Irish Rifles 1st Battalion *Killed in Action on 1 July 1916*
OVILLERS MILITARY CEMETERY, France
20 Symons Street, Belfast.

Price, Michael - Rifleman
4432 Royal Irish Rifles 2nd Battalion *Age 40 Died in War on 29 May 1918*
POZIERES MEMORIAL, France
Husband of Margaret Price, of 23, Altcar Street, Mountpottinger, Belfast.

Price, Patrick - Private
2801 Royal Inniskilling Fusiliers 6th Battalion *Age 24 Killed in Action on 3 October 1918*
PROSPECT HILL CEMETERY, GOUY, France
Son of James and Alice Price, of 10, Merrion Street, Belfast.

Price, Samuel - Private
41167 Royal Irish Fusiliers 9th Battalion *Died in War on 23 November 1917*
CAMBRAI MEMORIAL, LOUVERVAL, France
Born Ballymacarrett, Belfast. Enlisted in Belfast. Formerly North Irish Horse.

Price, William - Acting Bombardier
66133 Royal Field Artillery "B" Battery 63rd Brigade *Age 22 Died in War on 14 April 1917*
CAGNICOURT BRITISH CEMETERY, France
Son of Mrs. Elizabeth Price of 4, Brookfield Street, Belfast.

Price, William - Private
1277 Royal Army Medical Corps 6th Battalion *Died in War on 15 October 1917*
HOOGE CRATER CEMETERY, Belgium
Born and enlisted in Belfast.

Priestly, John Arthur - Private
PLY/15258 Royal Marine Light Infantry *Died in War on 13 May 1918*
BROOKWODD (UNITED KINGDOM 1914-1918) MEMORIAL
Son of Samuel Priestly, 371 Woodstock Road, Belfast.

Printer, William - Corporal
9414 Royal Irish Rifles 1st Battalion *Died in War on 25 December 1915*
STE MARIE CEMETERY, LE HAVRE, France
Born and enlisted in Belfast.

Pritchard, Alexander - Rifleman
9387 Royal Irish Rifles 1st Battalion *Killed in Action on 11 March 1915*
LE TOURET MEMORIAL, France
4, Hope's Place, Belfast.

Pritchard, John - Private
12896 King's Own Scottish Borderers 6th Battalion *Died in War on 25 September 1915*
LOOS MEMORIAL, France
Born in Belfast, enlisted at Dunbar, Haddington.

Pritchard, John - Rifleman
17/132 Royal Irish Rifles 9th Battalion *Died in War on 23 December 1915*
MIRAUMONT COMMUNAL CEMETERY, France
Husband of Margaret Pritchard, 15, Little Sackville Street, Belfast.

Proctor, John William - Gunner
169823 Royal Garrison Artillery 164th Siege Battery *Age 30 Died as a result of war on 31 July 1919*
DRUMBO PRESBYTERIAN CHURCHYARD, United Kingdom
Husband of Lily Proctor, of "Rea Anna" Marlborough Park, Belfast.

Proctor, Thomas - Sergeant (Observer)
212137 Royal Air Force 88th Squadron *Died in War on 27 September 1918*
ARRAS FLYING SERVICES MEMORIAL, France
Son of Elizabeth Proctor, of 47, Lanark Street, Belfast.

Prunty, James - Private (Signaller)
17024 Royal Irish Fusiliers 7th Battalion *Age 21 Died in War on 29 April 1916*
LOOS MEMORIAL, France
(Served as PRENDER). Son of James Prunty, of 30, McDonnell Street, Belfast.

Pryce, William Henry - Private
3760 Cameron Highlanders 4th Battalion *Age 21 Died in War on 10 July 1916*
GORDON DUMP CEMETERY, OVILLERS-LA BOISSELLE, France
Son of William and Charlotte Pryce, of 45, Alexandra Park Avenue, Belfast.

Purdy, Henry - Rifleman
1999 Royal Irish Rifles 12th Battalion *Age 19 Died in War on 11 April 1918*
TYNE COT MEMORIAL, Belgium
Son of William and Annabella Purdy, of 15, Thames Street, Broadway, Belfast.

Purdy, James Hamilton - Rifleman
15790 Royal Irish Rifles 14th Battalion *Killed in Action on 1 July 1916*
THIEPVAL MEMORIAL, France
Born and enlisted in Belfast.

JOURNEY OF REMEMBERING

Purdy, Richard - Stoker First Class
SS/104630 Royal Navy HMS "Hawke" *Killed in Action on 15 October 1914*
CHATHAM NAVAL MEMORIAL, United Kingdom
35 Argyle Street, Belfast.

Purdy, Richard Shaw - Second Lieutenant
Royal Inniskilling Fusiliers 6th Battalion attached 8th Battalion *Age 25 Died of Wounds on 11 September 1916*
CORBIE COMMUNAL CEMETERY EXTENSION, France
Son of Joseph and Mary Hannah Purdy; husband of Annie Maud Purdy, of 131, Ormeau Road, Belfast. Had been married, on home leave, only a few weeks before he was killed.

Purdy, Samuel - Rifleman
18643 Royal Irish Rifles 11th Battalion *Killed In Action on 16 August 1917*
TYNE COT MEMORIAL, Belgium
Son of Margaret Purdy, of 22, Canal Street, Lisburn. Born in Belfast

Pursley, William - Private
7759 East Lancashire Regiment 1st Battalion *Died in War on 13 May 1915*
YPRES (MENIN GATE) MEMORIAL, Belgium
Born and resident in Belfast, enlisted in Blackburn, England.

Purvis, James - Private
12500 Royal Irish Fusiliers 6th Battalion *Age 24 Died in War on 7 August 1915*
HELLES MEMORIAL, Turkey
Son of James and Rachel Purvis, of 64, Wilton Street, Belfast.

Pyke, William Robert - Rifleman
7200 Royal Irish Rifles 6th Battalion *Died in War on 21 July 1916*
DOIRAN MEMORIAL, Greece
Son of Mrs Margaret Pyke, 38 Eureka Street, Belfast.

Pyper, Albert Ernest - Private
S/14922 Seaforth Highlanders 2nd Battalion *Age 33 Died of dysentery on 16 February 1917*
ST. SEVER CEMETERY EXTENSION, ROUEN, France
Son of John and Dorothy Pyper, of Belfast; husband of Ivy Crafter Turner or Pyper, of 24, Braid Crescent, Edinburgh.

Pyper, Archibald - Private
17074 Royal Irish Fusiliers 6th Battalion *Age 29 Died in War on 7 August 1915*
HELLES MEMORIAL, Turkey
Son of John and Dorothy Pyper, of 238, Newtownards Road, Belfast.

Pyper, Robert Wilfred - Private
37187 Royal Welsh Fusiliers 16th Battalion *Died in War on 12 May 1916*
RUE-DU-BACQUEROT (13th LONDON) GRAVEYARD, LAVENTIE, France
Born in Belfast, enlisted in Liverpool.

Journey of Remembering

Quail, Thomas - Rifleman
9016 Royal Irish Rifles 2nd Battalion *Age 48 Killed in Action on 27 October 1914*
LE TOURET MEMORIAL, France
Husband of the late Sarah Quail, of 66, Foreman Street, Belfast. Served in the South African Campaign. A Reservist he had worked as a boilermaker in the shipyard. Left behind four daughters and one son.

Quail, Wesley - Rifleman
1750 Royal Irish Rifles 8/9th Battalion *Age 19 Died of Wounds on 3 April 1918*
ST. SEVER CEMETERY EXTENSION, ROUEN, France
Resided in Hounslow. Son of the late James and Selina Quail, of Belfast. Holder of the Military Medal.

Quarry, William H - Corporal
5491 Royal Fusiliers 20th Battalion *Age 25 Killed in Action on 17 August 1916*
FLATIRON COPSE CEMETERY, MAMETZ, France
Son of the late George Henry and May Quarry, of Belfast.

Quate, William - Lance Corporal
12120 Royal Irish Rifles 15th Battalion *Killed accidently on 16 October 1918*
DADIZEELE NEW BRITISH CEMETERY, Belgium
Son of Mr. W. Quate, of 56, Regent Street, Belfast.

Quigley, Alfred - Private
20797 Royal Dublin Fusiliers 8th Battalion *Killed in Action on 7 June 1917*
YPRES (MENIN GATE) MEMORIAL, Belgium
Born in Belfast, enlisted Glasgow.

Quigley, John - Sergeant
9493 Highland Light Infantry 2nd Battalion *Died in War on 21 March 1916*
ST SEVER CEMETERY EXTENSION, ROUEN, France
Born in Belfast, enlisted Cambuslang, Scotland.

Quinlan, John - Private
27778 Royal Dublin Fusiliers 9th Battalion *Age 17 Killed in Action on 17 August 1917*
TYNE COT MEMORIAL, Belgium
Son of Andrew and Rose Anne Quinlan, of 130, Oldpark Road, Belfast.

Quinn, Albert - Private
22474 Royal Inniskilling Fusiliers 9th Battalion *Age 19 Killed in Action on 1 July 1916*
THIEPVAL MEMORIAL, France
Son of William Quinn, of Carlow Street, Belfast, and the late Martha Quinn.

Quinn, Alexander - Private
S/8426 Seaforth Highlanders "B" Company 3rd Reserve Battalion *Age 51 Died of pneumonia on 20 February 1917*
BELFAST (MILLTOWN) ROMAN CATHOLIC CEMETERY, United Kingdom
Son of Mr. and Mrs. Quinn, of Belfast; husband of Mary Quinn, of 52, McDonnell Street, Belfast.

Quinn, Charles Wesley - Sergeant
11734 Royal Irish Rifles 20th Battalion transferred to 109527 60th Company Chinese Labour Corps
Age 47 Died in War on 19 March 1918
DOZINGHEM MILITARY CEMETERY, Belgium
Son of Charles Henry and Jane Isabella Quinn; husband of Sarah Quinn,
of 82, Broom Street, Woodvale Road, Belfast.

Journey of Remembering

Quinn, Frank - Private
9803 Royal Munster Fusiliers 1st Battalion *Died in War on 28 June 1915*
HELLES MEMORIAL, Turkey
Born in Belfast, enlisted in Greenock, Scotland.

Quinn, Henry - Private
6598 Royal Inniskilling Fusiliers 2nd Battalion *Age 35 Died in War on 13 September 1914*
LA FERTE-SOUS-JOUARRE MEMORIAL, France
Husband of Sarah Elizabeth Quinn, of 45, Hanna Street, Belfast. Served in the South African War.

Quinn, Hugh - Private
21183 Royal Irish Fusiliers 7/8th Battalion *Age 37 Died in War on 20 November 1917*
ARRAS MEMORIAL, France
Son of James and Alice Quinn; husband of Ann Jane Quinn, of 9, Rosetta Cottages, Ormeau Road, Belfast.

Quinn, James - Corporal
2494 Leinster Regiment 7th Battalion *Age 20 Died in War on 1 February 1917*
POND FARM CEMETERY, Belgium
Son of Joseph Quinn, of 3, Granville Street, Belfast. Holder of the Military Medal.

Quinn, James - Lance Corporal
9423 East Lancashire Regiment 11th Battalion *Died in War on 8 March 1917*
AUCHONVILLERS MILITARY CEMETERY, France
Born and enlisted in Belfast.

Quinn, James - Rifleman
13407 Royal Irish Rifles 9th Battalion *Killed in Action on 1 July 1916*
THIEPVAL MEMORIAL, France
Husband of Maggie Quinn, 280, Conway Street, Belfast.

Quinn, James A - Private
10064 Royal Inniskilling Fusiliers 1st Battalion *Age 22 Died in War on 22 May 1915*
TWELVE TREE COPSE CEMETERY, Turkey
Son of the late Robert and Ruth Quinn of Belfast.

Quinn, James P - Private
11828 Irish Guards 2nd Battalion *Died in War on 13 April 1918*
PLOEGSTEERT MEMORIAL, Belgium
Born in North Shields, enlisted in Dudley, both England, resident in Belfast.

Quinn, Joseph - Lance Corporal
25 Royal Irish Rifles 1st Battalion *Killed in Action on 21 March 1918*
POZIERES MEMORIAL, France
Born and enlisted in Belfast.

Quinn, Michael - Lance Corporal
2497 Leinster Regiment 7th Battalion *Died of Wounds on 21 February 1917*
BOULOGNE EASTERN CEMETERY, France
Husband of Hannah Quinn, of 5, Cape Street, Belfast.

Journey of Remembering

Quinn, Patrick - Rifleman
6081 Royal Irish Rifles 2nd Battalion *Killed In Action on 15 October 1914*
LE TOURET MEMORIAL, France
Born and enlisted in Belfast.

Quinn, Richard - Lance Corporal
2325 Royal Irish Rifles 17th Battalion *Age 40 Died in War on 24 September 1917*
BELFAST (DUNDONALD) CEMETERY, United Kingdom
Son of the late John and Mary Quinn. Born in Belfast.

Quinn, Robert - Private
7338 South Lancashire Regiment 2nd Battalion *Age 29 Died of Wounds as a Prisoner of War on 21 May 1915*
HAMBURG CEMETERY, Germany
Son of Sarah Quinn, of 51, Fifth Street, Belfast, and the late Hugh Quinn.

Quinn, Robert G - Private
3308 Royal Inniskilling Fusiliers 2nd Battalion *Died in War on 1 April 1917*
SAVY BRITISH CEMETERY, Belgium
15, North Boundary Street, Belfast.

Quinn, Samuel - Private
7362 South Lancashire Regiment 2nd Battalion *Killed in Action on 24 October 1914*
LE TOURET MEMORIAL, France
Born and enlisted in Belfast. The son of the late Hugh and Sarah Quinn.

Quinn, Samuel - Rifleman
3526 Royal Irish Rifles 8th Battalion *Died in War on 2 July 1916*
THIEPVAL MEMORIAL, France
Born Cromac, Belfast, enlisted in Belfast, resident in Kent.

Quinn, Thomas - Private
49752 Princess Victoria's (Royal Irish Fusiliers) 1st Battalion *Died in War on 24 August 1918*
PLOEGSTEERT MEMORIAL, Belgium
Born and enlisted in Belfast. Formerly 21758 Royal Inniskilling Fusiliers

Quinn, Thomas - Stoker First Class
SS/100714 Royal Navy HMS "Abokir" *Age 29 Killed in Action with submarine in North Sea on 22 September 1914*
CHATHAM NAVAL MEMORIAL, United Kingdom
Son of Thomas and Susan Quinn; husband of Annie Quinn, of 19, Avoneil Street, Belfast. Native of Belfast.

Quinn, Thomas H - Private
18549 Royal Irish Regiment 2nd Battalion *Age 20 Killed in Action on 14 July 1918*
LOUVENCOURT MILITARY CEMETERY, France
Son of Robert and the late Ruth Quinn, of Shankill Road, Belfast and nephew of Eliza J. Mateer, of 15, North Boundary Street, Belfast. Robert was one of three Quinn brothers, the others being James A and William John, killed in the war. All three had been brought up by their aunt after their mother died.

Quinn, Thomas H - Rifleman
16923 Royal Irish Rifles 14th Battalion *Died in War on 27 March 1918*
HAM BRITISH CEMETERY, MUILLE-VILLETTE, France
Son of Mrs M Quinn, 112, Utility Street, Belfast.

Quinn, William - Private
11610 Royal Inniskilling Fusiliers 2nd Battalion *Age 18 Died in War on 16 May 1915*
LE TOURET MEMORIAL, France
Son of John Thomas Quinn, of 17, Distillery Street, Belfast.

Quinn, William - Rifleman
9135 Royal Irish Rifles 2nd Battalion *Killed in Action on 23 March 1915*
KEMMEL CHATEAU MILITARY CEMETERY, Belgium
55, Walton Street, Belfast.

Quinn, William George - Rifleman
8/12406 Royal Irish Rifles 8th Battalion *Died in War on 10 June 1916*
AUTHUILE MILITARY CEMETERY, France
33, Hornby Street, Belfast.

Quinn, William J - Rifleman
3590 Royal Irish Rifles "C" Company 9th Battalion *Age 22 Killed in Action on 6 June 1916*
AUTHUILE MILITARY CEMETERY, France
Son of Mrs. Mary Quinn, of 27, Little Sackville Street, Belfast, and the late James Quinn.

Quinn, William John - Private
10502 Royal Inniskilling Fusiliers 2nd Battalion *Age 20 Died of Wounds on 4 November 1914*
BAILLEUL COMMUNAL CEMETERY (NORD), France
Son of Robert Quinn, North Boundary Street, Belfast.

Quirey, Frank - Private
G/80 Royal Irish Fusiliers 1st Garrison Battalion *Age 21 Died in War on 20 September 1918*
TAUKKYAN MEMORIAL, Myanmar
Son of Mrs. Jane Williamson, of 40, Mackey Street, Lowther Street, Belfast.

Quirk, John - Private
2495 Leinster Regiment 7th Battalion *Age 19 Died of Wounds on 27 October 1916*
BELFAST (MILLTOWN) ROMAN CATHOLIC CEMETERY, United Kingdom
Son of William and Mary Quirk, of 19, Colinward Street, Belfast.

Quirk, John Edward - Private
33792 Machine Gun Corps (Infantry) *Died in War on 9 October 1917*
TYNE COT CEMETERY, Belgium
Born in Belfast. Lived in Liverpool when enlisted. Formerly 5184, Liverpool Regiment.

Quirke, William Gomartin - Driver
97497 Royal Horse Artillery and Royal Field Artillery *Died in War on 21 August 1917*
BARD COTTAGE CEMETERY, Belgium
Born in Belfast, enlisted Woolwich, London.

Radcliffe, Charles - Lance Corporal
90024 The King's (Liverpool Regiment) Depot formerly 1st Battalion Royal Irish Fusiliers
Age 33 Died of sickness on 23 March 1919
BELFAST CITY CEMETERY, United Kingdom
Son of Mary Radcliffe; husband of Ann J. Hillen (formerly Radcliffe), of 11, Gay Street, Belfast.

Rafferty, Edward H - Lance Corporal
12578 Royal Dublin Fusiliers 5th Battalion *Died on 29 September 1916*
CURRAGH MILITARY CEMETERY, Republic of Ireland
Born and enlisted in Belfast.

Rafferty, John - Private
8751 Royal Inniskilling Fusiliers 2nd Battalion *Age 26 Died in War on 26 August 1914*
LA FERTE-SOUS-JOUARRE MEMORIAL, France
Son of Peter and Mary Ann Rafferty, of 58, Butler Street, Belfast.

Rafferty, William - Private
8336 Royal Irish Fusiliers 1st Battalion *Age 26 Died in War on 6 May 1915*
YPRES (MENIN GATE) MEMORIAL, Belgium
Brother of Mrs. M. Lenaghan, of 8, Lower Clonard Street, Falls Road, Belfast.

Rainey, Alexander - Private
47932 Northamptonshire Regiment 7th Battalion *Died in War on 25 March 1918*
PARGNY BRITISH CEMETERY, France
72, Limestone Road, Belfast.

Rainey, Charles - Rifleman
7163 Royal Irish Rifles "A" Company 1st Battalion *Age 25 Died of Wounds on 6 June 1915*
IPSWICH CEMETERY, United Kingdom
Husband of Frances Johnston (formerly Rainey), of 24, Crumlin Street, Crumlin Road, Belfast.

Rainey, Edward - Private
24524 Canadian Highlanders 13th Battalion *Age 32 Died in War on 22 May 1915*
HINGES MILITARY CEMETERY, France
Son of Joseph and Elisabeth Rainey, of 49, Tenth Street, Belfast, Ireland.
A Prebyterian, he worked as a labourer before enlisting.

Rainey, James - Private
71838 Canadian Infantry (Manitoba Regiment) 27th Battalion *Age 32 Died in War on 15 September 1916*
COURCELETTE BRITISH CEMETERY, France
Son of James and Margaret Rainey, of Glencoe, Dumurry, County Antrim, Ireland. Native of Belfast, Ireland.
An iron moulder, he was a member of the Prebyterian Church.

Rainey, James Henry - Sergeant
13414 Royal Irish Rifles 15th Battalion *Age 35 Killed in Action on 1 July 1916*
SERRE ROAD CEMETERY No.2, France
Son of Joseph Rainey, of Albert Bridge Road, Belfast; husband of Agnes M. Rainey, of 30, Cyprus Avenue, Belfast.

Rainey, John - Private
364473 Labour Corps 17th Company *Died of Wounds on 27 April 1918*
LIJSSENTHOEK MILITARY CEMETERY, Belgium
Husband of M. E. Rainey, of 15, James Street, Belfast.

Rainey, Robert - Rifleman
3591 Royal Irish Rifles 9th Battalion *Age 22 Died of Wounds on 11 July 1916*
DOULLENS COMMUNAL CEMETERY EXTENSION No.1, France
Son of George and Mary Rainey, of Belfast.

Rainey, Robert - Rifleman
6523 Royal Irish Rifles 2nd Battalion *Killed In Action on 7 July 1916*
THIEPVAL MEMORIAL, France
Born in Belfast, enlisted Ballykinler.

Rainey, Thomas - Rifleman
6165 Royal Irish Rifles 2nd Battalion *Age 33 Killed in Action on 26 August 1914*
LA FERTE-SOUS-JOUARRE MEMORIAL, France
Husband of Jane Rainey, of 11, Osborne Street, Limestone Road, Belfast.

Rainey, William - Second Lieutenant
Royal Irish Rifles 2nd Battalion *Died in War on 23 November 1917*
CAMBRAI MEMORIAL, LOUVERVAL, France
Born Christopher Street, Belfast. Married to Sarah (née Dempsey) three children: William Henry, Sarah Adeline and Warren Dempsey. A regular soldier he was twice wounded and had reached the rank of Sergeant before being commissioned.

Ralph, Charles Bernard - Lance Corporal
8531 Dorsetshire Regiment 1st Battalion *Died in War on 22 October 1914*
LE TOURET MEMORIAL, France
Born in Belfast. Enlisted in Gosport, England.

Ralph, Edward - Private
413764 Labour Corp formerly 12730 Royal Irish Fusliers *Died of Wounds on 11 April 1918*
PICQUIGNY BRITISH CEMETERY, France
Born in Belfast.

Ramage, George Norris - Commander
Royal Naval Reserve HMS "Duke of Albany"
Age 45 Killed in Action with submarine in North Sea on 24 August 1916
PLYMOUTH NAVAL MEMORIAL, United Kingdom
Son of William and Jane Ramage, of Westruther, Berwickshire; husband of Annie Amelia Ramage, of "Bromsgrove", Bloomfield, Belfast.

Ramsay, John - Corporal
11676 Royal Inniskilling Fusiliers 1st Battalion *Age 23 Killed in Action on 1 July 1916*
THIEPVAL MEMORIAL, France
Son of Annie Ramsay, of 22, Wilmont Terrace, Lisburn Road, Belfast, and the late John Ramsay. Enlisted August 1914, also served at Gallipoli and was wounded.

Ramsay, Thomas Laing - Private
8358 Cameron Highlanders 2nd Battalion *Age 24 Died in War on 28 April 1915*
YPRES (MENIN GATE) MEMORIAL, Belgium
Son of Jessie McMillan Ramsay, of 37, Harrybrook Street, Belfast, and the late Thomas Alexander Ramsay. Military Telegraphist at Bangalore, India. Re-joined his Battalion in India October 1914.

Ramsey, Robert - Private
21482 Royal Irish Fusiliers 7th Battalion *Killed in Action on 30 April 1916*
BETHUNE TOWN CEMETERY, *France*
26 Sidney Street West, Belfast.

Ramsey, Robert - Sergeant
18672 Royal Irish Rifles 12th Battalion *Died in War on 23 August 1916*
RATION FARM (LA PLUS DOUVE) ANNEXE, *Belgium*
Born in Kilrea, enlisted Ballymoney, resident of Belfast.

Ramsey, William - Private
64 Princess Victoria's (Royal Irish Fusiliers) 1st Garrison Battalion *Died in War on 12 October 1916*
KIRKEE 1914-1918 MEMORIAL, *India*
Born in Belfast, enlisted Ballymoney. Formerly 9406, Royal Irish Rifles.

Ramshaw, William Greenwall - Sergeant
3221 Durham Light Infantry 1/7th Battalion *Died in War on 24 May 1915*
YPRES RESERVOIR CEMETERY, *Belgium*
Native of Belfast.

Rankin, Christopher - Private
40745 Cameronians (Scottish Rifles) 2nd Battalion *Killed in Action on 16 August 1917*
TYNE COT MEMORIAL, *Belgium*
Born in Belfast, enlisted Glasgow. Formerly 19888 King's Own Scottish Borderers.

Rankin, John - Rifleman
5454 Royal Irish Rifles 1st Battalion *Died in action during a German raid on his trench on 11 April 1916*
BECOURT MILITARY CEMETERY, BECORDEL-BECOURT, *France*
Born and enlisted in Belfast.

Rankin, John Alexander - Private
11677 Royal Inniskilling Fusiliers 6th Battalion *Age 23 Killed in Action on 17 October 1918*
HIGHLAND CEMETERY, LE CATEAU, *France*
Son of David and Annie Rankin. Native of Belfast.

Rankin, Robert Herbert - Second Lieutenant
Royal Irish Rifles 15th Battalion *Age 23 Died in War on 23 November 1917*
CAMBRAI MEMORIAL, LOUVERVAL, *France*
Son of John A. and M. C. Rankin, of Stockman's Lane, Belfast.

Ranson, Andrew - Rifleman
4745 Royal Irish Rifles "A" Company 8th Battalion *Age 29 Died of Wounds on 2 July 1916*
GRANDCOURT ROAD CEMETERY, GRANDCOURT, *France*
Son of Susan and the late Andrew Ranson, of 53, Ravenhill Road, Belfast.

Ravey, William - Rifleman
853 Royal Irish Rifles "D" Company 8th Battalion *Age 26 Died in War on 2 July 1916*
THIEPVAL MEMORIAL, *France*
Son of John Ravey, of 133, Parkgate Avenue, Belfast; husband of Agnes Ravey, of 34, Glenvarlock Street, Belfast.

Journey of Remembering

Rawe, William James - Fireman And Trimmer
Mercantile Marine S.S. "Rathlin Head" (Belfast)
Age 37 Killed, as a result of an attack by an enemy submarine on 26 May 1918
TOWER HILL MEMORIAL, United Kingdom
Son of Eliza Rawe, and the late William Rawe; husband of Ellen Rawe (née Cason), of 5, Edward Street, Belfast.

Rea, Allen - Rifleman
13433 Royal Irish Rifles 8th Battalion *Age 24 Died in War on 2 July 1916*
SERRE ROAD CEMETERY No.2, France
Son of John Alexander Rea, of 9, Fitzroy Avenue, Belfast.

Rea, Daniel - A/Corporal
10135 Hampshire Regiment 10th Battalion *Died in War on 21 August 1915*
HELLES MEMORIAL, Turkey
Born in Newtownards, enlisted Southampton, resident of Belfast.

Rea, James - Private
31914 7th (Queen's Own) Hussars *Died in War on 24 October 1918*
BASRA MEMORIAL, Iraq
Born and enlisted in Belfast.

Rea, James - Rifleman
3/11302 Royal Irish Rifles "B" Company 8th Battalion *Age 25 Killed in Action on 2 September 1916*
RATION FARM (LA PLUS DOUVE) ANNEXE, Belgium
Son of James and Elizabeth Rea, of 187, Beersbridge Road, Belfast.

Rea, John - Private
6273 Machine Gun Corps (Infantry) 57th Battalion *Age 22 Killed in Action on 26 March 1918*
PLOEGSTEERT MEMORIAL, Belgium
Son of Francis and Sarah Rea, of Clarke Lodge, Craigarogan, Mallusk, Belfast.

Rea, Robert Morrow - Company Sergeant Major
26106 The King's (Liverpool Regiment) 17th Battalion *Died in War on 27 June 1916*
CERISY-GAILLY MILITARY CEMETERY, France
Born in Lisburn, enlisted and resident in Belfast.

Rea, Vivian Trevor Tighe - Lieutenant
Royal Irish Rifles 4th Battalion attached 2nd Battalion *Age 23 Died of Wounds on 25 October 1914*
GUARDS CEMETERY, WINDY CORNER, CUINCHY, France
Born in Argentina, where his father was the vice-Consul, the only son of Henry Tighe and Clare Tighe Rea, of 1, Glandore Park, Belfast.

Rea, William - Private
145229 Royal Army Medical Corps *Died in War on 6 October 1918*
MIKRA BRITISH CEMETERY, KALAMARIA, Greece
Born and enlisted in Belfast. Formerly 15801 Royal Irish Rifles

Rea, William - Stoker First Class
289073 Royal Navy HMS "Invincible" *Age 37 Killed in Action at Battle of Jutland on 31 May 1916*
PORTSMOUTH NAVAL MEMORIAL, United Kingdom
Son of William and Mary Rea, of County Antrim; husband of Mary Rea, of Belfast.

Reaney, Edward Thomas - Private
9467 Princess Victoria's (Royal Irish Fusiliers) 1st Battalion *Died in War on 25 April 1915*
YPRES (MENIN GATE) MEMORIAL, Belgium
Born in Belfast, enlisted in Armagh.

Reaney, Robert - Private
18070 Royal Irish Fusiliers 9th Battalion *Died of Wounds on 12 October 1916*
RATION FARM (LA PLUS DOUVE) ANNEXE, Belgium
141 Silvio street, Belfast.

Reardom, Joseph - Rifleman
1587 Royal Irish Rifles 6th Battalion *Died in War on 11 August 1915*
HELLES MEMORIAL, Turkey
Born and enlisted in Dublin, resident of Belfast.

Reavey, Henry - Rifleman
8577 Royal Irish Rifles 1st Battalion *Killed in Action on 9 May 1915*
PLOEGSTEERT MEMORIAL, Belgium
Born and enlisted in Belfast.

Reavey, William - Rifleman
9504 Royal Irish Rifles 2nd Battalion *Killed in Action on 26 January 1916*
PLOEGSTEERT MEMORIAL, Belgium
A native of Belfast and enlisted in the city.

Redford, Joseph - Private
7717 Royal Inniskilling Fusiliers 2nd Battalion *Died on 26 August 1914*
NORWICH CEMETERY, NORFOLK, United Kingdom
Born in Belfast. Husband of Mary Crosby Morrison Redford, of 117, Northcote Avenue, Toronto, Canada.

Redmond, Edward - Rifleman
465 Royal Irish Rifles 2nd Battalion *Age 26 Killed in Action on 24 March 1918*
POZIERES MEMORIAL, France
Son of Henry and Elizabeth Redmond, of 14 Canmore Street, Belfast.

Redmond, Walter Henry - Sergeant
65813 Canadian Infantry (Quebec Regiment) 24th Battalion *Age 26 Died in War on 22 May 1916*
YPRES (MENIN GATE) MEMORIAL, Belgium
Son of John and Sarah Redmond, of 10, Parkgate Avenue, Belfast, Ireland. A clerk in Molson's Bank, Montreal. An Anglican, he had served in the militia.

Redmond, William Joseph - Stoker First Class
SS/104015 Royal Navy HMS "Cressy" *Age 29 Killed in Action from submarine in North Sea on 22 September 1914*
CHATHAM NAVAL MEMORIAL, United Kingdom
Husband of Annie Redmond, of 99, Gracehill Street, Belfast.

Reel, Hugh - Private
14497 Royal Dublin Fusiliers 8th Battalion *Died in War on 27 April 1916*
LOOS MEMORIAL, France
Born and enlisted in Belfast

Journey of Remembering

Regan, John - Private
11813 Royal Scots Fusiliers 6th Battalion *Died in War on 26 September 1915*
LOOS MEMORIAL, France
Husband of Annie, 11 Chatham Street, Belfast.

Reid , William - Private
6007 Royal Inniskilling Fusiliers 2nd Battalion *Killed in Action on 7 November 1914*
PLOEGSTEERT MEMORIAL, Belgium
Born in Belfast.

Reid, Alexander - Lance Corporal
6419 Royal Inniskilling Fusiliers 2nd Battalion *Killed in Action on 21 March 1918*
POZIERES MEMORIAL, France
Born in Belfast.

Reid, Alfred - Rifleman
17/215 Royal Irish Rifles *Age 21 Died as a result of War on 16 September 1919*
CARNMONEY CEMETERY, United Kingdom
Son of William and Grace Reid, of 32, Lilliput Street, Belfast. Discharged as unfit for war service. Awarded the Silver War Badge.

Reid, Arthur - Rifleman
1817 Royal Irish Rifles 1st Battalion *Died in War on 23 March 1918*
POZIERES MEMORIAL, France
Husband of Mrs S E Reid, 29 Legnevea Street, Belfast.

Reid, Charles - Rifleman
6810 Royal Irish Rifles 2nd Battalion *Died in War on 9 July 1916*
THIEPVAL MEMORIAL, France
Husband of Margaret Reid, 42 Constance Street, Belfast.

Reid, Edward - Rifleman
19949 Royal Irish Rifles 1st Battalion *Killed in Action on 21 March 1918*
POZIERES MEMORIAL, France
Born in Belfast, enlisted in Hamilton, Scotland.

Reid, Edward - Sergeant
15849 Royal Irish Rifles 9th Battalion *Age 23 Died in War on 7 August 1917*
AEROPLANE CEMETERY, Belgium
Son of Mary Ann Reid, 52 Stratheden Street, Belfast. Awarded the Military Medal.

Reid, Henry - Lance Corporal
13419 Royal Irish Rifles 8th Battalion *Age 23 Died in War on 10 July 1916*
CAUDRY OLD COMMUNAL CEMETERY, France
Son of Martha Ann Reid, of 46, Roxburgh Street, Ballymacarrett, Belfast, and the late John Reid.

Reid, Herbert George - Private
27757 Canadian Infantry (Central Ontario Regiment) 15th Battalion *Age 24 Died in War on 24 April 1915*
YPRES (MENIN GATE) MEMORIAL, Belgium
Only son of John and Jane Reid, of 236, Cliftonville Road, Belfast, Ireland. A single man and an Anglican he had worked as a fitter.

Reid, Jack Reginald - Private
1587 King's Own (Royal Lancaster Regiment) 1/4th Battalion *Died in War on 20 July 1915*
ROYAL IRISH RIFLES GRAVEYARD, LAVENTIE, France
Born and enlisted in Barrow, England, resident of Belfast.

Reid, James - Lance Corporal
9574 Royal Irish Rifles 2nd Battalion *Age 24 Killed in Action on 26 April 1916*
ECOIVRES MILITARY CEMETERY, MONT-ST. ELOI, France
Son of Henry and Margaret Reid, of Belfast.

Reid, James - Private
13006 Royal Inniskilling Fusiliers 1st Battalion *Killed in Action on 1 July 1916*
THIEPVAL MEMORIAL, France
Born Maryhill, Glasgow. Resident at 28, Rowan Street, Belfast.

Reid, John - Corporal
19544 Machine Gun Corps (Infantry) *Killed in Action on 1 July 1916*
THIEPVAL MEMORIAL, France
Born in Belfast. Formerly 13435 Royal Irish Rifles.

Reid, John - Lance Corporal
18677 Royal Irish Rifles 11/13th Battalion attached 22nd Entrenching Battalion
Age 23 Died in War on 28 March 1918
POZIERES MEMORIAL, France
Son of George and Ann Jane Reid, of 103, Dee Street, Belfast.

Reid, Joseph - Private
436 Irish Guards 1st Battalion *Age 26 Died of Wounds on 20 February 1915*
CAMBRIDGE CITY CEMETERY, United Kingdom
Son of William Nelson Reid and Annie Reid, of Glennavy, County Antrim; husband of Sarah Reid, of 121, Argyle Street, Belfast. Employed in the Shipyard, and a member of the old UVF.

Reid, Joseph - Rifleman
3/20115 Royal Irish Rifles 1st Battalion *Killed in Action on 14 October 1918*
DADIZEELE NEW BRITISH CEMETERY, Belgium
Son of Mrs. C. Reid, of 32, Massareene Street, Cullingtree Road, Belfast.

Reid, Moses Alexander - Seaman
Mercantile Marine S.S. "Bray Head" (Belfast)
Age 18 Drowned, as a result of an attack by an enemy submarine on 14 March 1917
TOWER HILL MEMORIAL, United Kingdom
Son of Emma Reid (née McCann), of 11A, Fleet Street, Belfast, and the late Thomas Andrew Reid.

Reid, Richard - Corporal
8527 Royal Inniskilling Fusiliers 1st Battalion *Age 29 Died in War on 6 August 1915*
HELLES MEMORIAL, Turkey
Husband Agnes Reid, Westmoreland Street, Belfast. An Army Reservist who had worked on the city tram system.

Reid, Robert - Private
11172 Royal Dublin Fusiliers 1st Battalion *Age 27 Died in War on 29 March 1918*
EPEHY WOOD FARM CEMETERY, EPEHY, France
Son of James and Sarah Jane Reid, of 17, Powerscourt Street, Ormeau Road, Belfast. Born in Londonderry.

Reid, Robert - Rifleman
17/131 Royal Irish Rifles "D" Company 10th Battalion *Age 34 Died of Wounds on 6 September 1918*
BELFAST (BALMORAL) CEMETERY, United Kingdom
Son of David and Annie Reid. Born in Belfast.

Reid, Samuel - Rifleman
19189 Royal Irish Rifles 1st Battalion *Killed in Action on 21 October 1918*
TYNE COT CEMETERY, Belgium
Born and enlisted in Belfast.

Reid, Thomas - Rifleman
15844 Royal Irish Rifles 9th Battalion *Age 20 Killed in Action on 1 July 1916*
THIEPVAL MEMORIAL, France
Son of James Reid, 51 Bellevue Street, Belfast.

Reid, Thomas Jackinson - Rifleman
165 Royal Irish Rifles 15th Battalion *Age 19 Died in War on 12 December 1917*
THIEPVAL MEMORIAL, France
Son of George Reid, of 46, Silvergrove Street, Belfast.

Reid, William - Flight Sergeant
142596 Royal Field Artillery transferred to the Royal Air Force *Age 38 Died of Wounds on 30 October 1919*
WANDSWORTH (STREATHAM) CEMETERY, United Kingdom
Son of Robert and Margaret Reid, of Ballyhackamore, Belfast; husband of Ethel Margaret Agnes Reid, of 208, Coteford Street, Tooting, London. 16 years service.

Reid, William - Private
2835 Connaught Rangers 1st Battalion *Died in War on 18 November 1918*
DEIR EL BELAH WAR CEMETERY, Israel
Native of Belfast.

Reid, William - Private
6007 Royal Inniskilling Fusiliers 2nd Battalion *Died in War on 7 November 1914*
PLOEGSTEERT MEMORIAL, Belgium
Husband of Catherine, 31, Emerson Street, Belfast. Employed in the Shipyard he was a Orangeman and a member of the old UVF.

Reid, William - Private
S/43613 Seaforth Highlanders 1/5th Battalion *Age 23 Died in War on 13 October 1918*
AVESNES-LE-SEC COMMUNAL CEMETERY EXTENSION, France
Son of Mary Jane Reid, of 201, Grosvenor Road, Belfast, and the late George Reid.

Reid, William George - Stoker First Class
SS/113428 Royal Navy HMS "Vanguard" *Age 22 Killed by internal explosion of vessel at Scapa Flow on 9 July 1917*
CHATHAM NAVAL MEMORIAL, United Kingdom
Husband of Susan McIlvenny (formerly Reid), of 65, Upper Mervue Street, Belfast.

Reid, William Henry - Rifleman
18678 Royal Irish Rifles 14th Battalion *Age 24 Killed in Action on 6 April 1916*
HAMEL MILITARY CEMETERY, BEAUMONT-HAMEL, France
Son of the late William Reid, of Bloomfield, Belfast.

Reid, William James - Sergeant
13417 Royal Irish Rifles "B" Company 9th Battalion *Age 39 Died in War on 23 November 1917*
CAMBRAI MEMORIAL, LOUVERVAL, France
Son of the late William and Annie Reid; husband of Ellen Jane Cooke (formerly Reid),
of 177, Agnes Street, Belfast.

Reid, William John - Sergeant
15841 Royal Irish Rifles 14th Battalion *Age 21 Killed in Action on 16 August 1917*
TYNE COT MEMORIAL, Belgium
Son of William John and Mary Ann Reid, of 6, New North Queen Street, Belfast.

Reid, William Robert - Private
2414 Manchester Regiment 1/8th Battalion *Died in War on 4 June 1915*
HELLES MEMORIAL, Turkey
Born in Belfast, enlisted Manchester.

Reilly, Alfred - Rifleman
8393 Royal Irish Rifles 2nd Battalion *Died in War on 27 October 1914*
LE TOURET MEMORIAL, France
9 Avoniel Street, Belfast.

Reilly, James - Private
22620 Royal Inniskilling Fusiliers 10th Battalion *Died in War on 10 August 1917*
YPRES (MENIN GATE) MEMORIAL, Belgium
41 Sugarfield Street, Belfast.

Reilly, James - Rifleman
10003 Royal Irish Rifles 2nd Battalion *Killed In Action on 9 July 1916*
POZIERES BRITISH CEMETERY, OVILLERS-LA BOISSELLE, France
Born at Belfast, wife resided at 38 Carlisle Street, Belfast.

Reilly, James Henry - Private
12830 Machine Gun Corps (Infantry) 137th Company *Age 23 Killed in Action on 11 August 1916*
DE CUSINE RAVINE BRITISH CEMETERY, BASSEUX, France
Son of Mary Reilly of Belfast, and the late John Reilly; husband of Isabella Reilly,
of 75, King Street, Belfast.

Reilly, James Patrick - Able Seaman
J/10246 Royal Navy HMS "Indefatigable" *Age 23 Killed in Action at Battle of Jutland on 31 May 1916*
PLYMOUTH NAVAL MEMORIAL, United Kingdom
Son of Elizabeth Reilly, of 13, Ballycastle Street, Belfast, and the late William Reilly.

Reilly, John - Private
956023 Royal Irish Rifles 7th Battalion *Died of Wounds on 29 June 1916*
BETHUNE TOWN CEMETERY, France
38 Carlisle Street, Belfast.

Reilly, John - Private
S/1974 Seaforth Highlanders (Ross-shire Buffs, the Duke of Albany's) 7th Battalion
Died in War on 25 September 1915
LOOS MEMORIAL, France
Born in Belfast, enlisted Glasgow.

Reilly, Michael - Fireman And Trimmer
Mercantile Marine S.S. "War Clover" (London)
Age 40 Drowned, as a result of an attack by an enemy submarine on 19 October 1917
TOWER HILL MEMORIAL, United Kingdom
Son of the late William and Rose Reilly; husband of Rose Ann Reilly (née Creaney), of 36, Gordon Street, Belfast. Born in County Meath

Reilly, Michael - Private
7655 Cameronians (Scottish Rifles) 1st Battalion *Age 21 Killed in Action on 26 September 1915*
CAMBRIN CHURCHYARD EXTENSION, France
Son of Edward and Margret Reilly, of Belfast.

Reilly, Peter - Private
7046 Princess Victoria's (Royal Irish Fusiliers) 1st Battalion *Died in War on 12 October 1916*
THIEPVAL MEMORIAL, France
Born and enlisted in Belfast.

Reilly, William - Lance Corporal
5055 Leinster Regiment 2nd Battalion *Died in War on 20 June 1918*
CINQ RUES BRITISH CEMETERY, HAZEBROUCK, France
Born in Portrush, resident of Belfast.

Reilly, William George - Rifleman
4931 Royal Irish Rifles 2nd Battalion *Died as a Prisoner of War on 22 June 1918*
COLOGNE SOUTHERN CEMETERY, Germany
Born in Belfast, enlisted Waringston.

Rentoul, James Lawrence - Private
129116 Royal Army Medical Corps 91st Field Ambulance *Age 33 Died in War on 30 September 1918*
LA BARAQUE BRITISH CEMETERY, BELLENGLISE, France
Son of Rev and Mrs Rentoul of Clonard, County Tipperary. Husband of B Eileen Rentoul, Hawthornden Road, Belfast. He was the former assistant minister of Rosemary Street Presbyterian Church.

Renwick, William - Sergeant
6444 Royal Irish Rifles "E" Company 1st Battalion *Age 36 Killed in Action on 24 March 1918*
POZIERES MEMORIAL, France
Husband of Anne Renwick, of 18, Fife Street, Belfast.

Reynolds, George - Sergeant
7442 Royal Irish Rifles 2nd Battalion *Killed in Action on 27 October 1914*
LE TOURET MEMORIAL, France
Husband of Maggie Reynolds, 16 Cavour Street, Belfast.

Reynolds, John - Private
13941 Loyal North Lancashire Regiment 6th Battalion *Died in War on 9 August 1915*
HELLES MEMORIAL, Turkey
Born in Belfast, enlisted Preston.

Reynolds, Robert - Rifleman
11054 Royal Irish Rifles 6th Battalion *Age 23 Died in War on 7 August 1915*
HELLES MEMORIAL, Turkey
Son of Robert Reynolds, of 47, Beit Street, Belfast, and the late Alice Reynolds.

Reynolds, William - Corporal
5817 Royal Garrison Artillery 4th Siege Battery *Age 44 Died as a result of war on 18 April 1920*
BELFAST (DUNDONALD) CEMETERY, United Kingdom
Husband of Elizabeth Reynolds, of 132, Roseberry Road, Belfast.

Rice, Alfred James - Junior Second Engineer Officer
Mercantile Marine S.S. "Hungerford" (London)
Age 26 Drowned, as a result of an attack by an enemy submarine on 16 April 1918
TOWER HILL MEMORIAL, United Kingdom
Son of Laurence and Agnes Rice (formerly Edmonds), of 107, Ogilvie Street, Belfast.
Born in Newtownards, County Down.

Rice, Archibald - Private
12672 Royal Irish Fusiliers 6th Battalion *Age 24 Died in War on 7 August 1915*
HELLES MEMORIAL, Turkey
Son of William John and Annie Rice, of 13, Glenalpin Street, Belfast.

Rice, J - Lance Corporal
2500 Leinster Regiment "D" Company 7th Battalion *Age 45 Killed in Action on 21 May 1916*
NOEUX-LES-MINES COMMUNAL CEMETERY, France
Husband of Mary Ann Rice, of 17, Alton Street, Old Lodge Road, Belfast.

Rice, James - Lance Corporal
8602 Highland Light Infantry 1/6th Battalion *Died of Wounds on 24 November 1917*
JERUSALEM WAR CEMETERY, Israel
17 Alton Street, Belfast.

Rice, Joseph - Private
16974 Princess Victoria's (Royal Irish Fusiliers) 6th Battalion *Died in War on 15 August 1915*
HELLES MEMORIAL, Turkey
Born in Belfast. Enlisted in Lisburn.

Rice, Joseph - Private
3484 Royal Inniskilling Fusiliers 1st Battalion *Died on 15 July 1918*
SAINS-DU-NORD COMMUNAL CEMETERY, France
Born in Belfast.

Rice, Samuel - Private
13060 Royal Scots (Lothian Regiment) 2nd Battalion *Died in War on 14 July 1916*
THIEPVAL MEMORIAL, France
Born in Belfast.

Rice, Thomas (Tom) - Corporal
57697 Royal Engineers 122nd Field Company *Age 23 Died of Wounds on 7 August 1917*
HOP STORE CEMETERY, Belgium
Son of James and Mary Jane Rice, of 23, Geoffrey Street, Belfast.

Rice, William - Gunner
195981 Royal Field Artillery 190th Brigade *Died in War on 26 September 1917*
LARCH WOOD (RAILWAY CUTTING) CEMETERY, Belgium
64 Carlow Street, Belfast.

Rice, William - Private
1763 Leinster Regiment 7th Battalion *Killed in Action on 1 July 1916*
ST PATRICK'S CEMETERY, LOOS, *France*
Born and enlisted in Belfast.

Rice, William Henry - Private
393571 Labour Corps *Died as a result of war on 18 November 1918*
BELFAST CITY CEMETERY, *United Kingdom*
Brother of Eva Rice, 143 Sidney Street West, Belfast.

Richards, Ernest Henry - Lance Corporal
10151 Alexandra, Princess of Wales's Own (Yorkshire Regiment) 2nd Battalion *Killed in Action on 11 March 1915*
LE TOURET MEMORIAL, *France*
Born in Belfast, enlisted in Richmond, Yorkshire.

Richardson, George - Sapper
57751 Royal Engineers 122nd Field Company *Age 44 Died of illness contracted on active service on 17 November 1917*
BROOKWOOD MILITARY CEMETERY, *United Kingdom*
Son of the late William John and Agnes Richardson, of Grosvenor Road, Belfast.

Richardson, Isaac - Rifleman
17/51 Royal Irish Rifles 10th Battalion *Age 36 Killed in Action on 1 July 1916*
CONNAUGHT CEMETERY, THIEPVAL, *France*
Husband of Elizabeth Richardson, of 39, Abingdon Street, Donegall Road, Belfast.

Richardson, Robert Andrew - Rifleman
10986 Royal Irish Rifles 1st Battalion *Age 19 Killed in Action on 21 October 1918*
HARLEBEKE NEW BRITISH CEMETERY, *Belgium*
Son of Mrs. Agnes Moffatt (formerly Richardson), of 236, Matilda Street, Belfast,
and the late Pte. Robert Richardson, Imperial Yeomanry.

Riddall, Robert - Lance Corporal
64242 Royal Engineers 150th Field Company *Age 26 Died of Wounds on 27 June 1916*
FORCEVILLE COMMUNAL CEMETERY AND EXTENSION, *France*
Son of Jane and the late R. Robert Riddall, of Armagh; husband of Ethel Riddall,
43, Third Street, Conway Street, Belfast.

Riddell, David Moore - Second Lieutenant
The King's (Liverpool Regiment) *Age 27 Died of Wounds received in June 1916 on 23 September 1917*
BELFAST CITY CEMETERY, *United Kingdom*
Son of Henry and Mary Jane Riddell, of 51, Myrtlefield Road, Belfast.

Riddell, James - Lance Corporal
6502 Royal Irish Rifles 2nd Battalion *Age 43 Killed in Action on 9 May 1915*
YPRES (MENIN GATE) MEMORIAL, *Belgium*
Husband of Ellen Riddell, of 2, Bathurst Court, Belfast. Served in the South African Campaign.

Riddick, Alexander - Sergeant
38984 Royal Garrison Artillery 46th Siege Battery *Killed in Action on 21 March 1918*
FEUCHY BRITISH CEMETERY, *France*
72 Unity Street, Belfast.

Riddles, John - Private
8132 Royal Inniskilling Fusiliers 2nd Battalion *Age 27 Died of Wounds on 28 April 1916*
WARLOY-BAILLON COMMUNAL CEMETERY, France
Son of James and Elizabeth Riddles, of Londonderry. Resident of Belfast.

Ridgway, William H - Rifleman
18681 Royal Irish Rifles 14th Battalion *Killed in action on 1 July 1916*
A.I.F. BURIAL GROUND, FLERS, France
Son of Mrs Mary E Ridgway, 56 Vernon Street, Belfast.

Rigby, Henry George - Private
G/69283 Royal Fusiliers (City of London Regiment) *Killed in Action on 21 March 1918*
POZIERES MEMORIAL, France
Born in Liverpool, enlisted and resident in Belfast. Formerly SE/030929 Army Service Corps

Rigby, William John - Lance Corporal
17/870 Royal Irish Rifles 8/9th Battalion *Died in War on 25 January 1918*
HAM BRITISH CEMETERY, MUILLE-VILLETTE, France
40 Little Georges Street, Belfast.

Ringland, William - Pioneer
328717 Royal Engineers 1st Reserve Battalion *Age 19 Died of pneumonia on 10 February 1919*
BELFAST (DUNDONALD) CEMETERY, United Kingdom
Son of William and Martha Ringland, of 135, Euston Street, Belfast.

Rippard, John T - Driver
12647 Royal Engineers Raynes Park Signal Depot *Died of Wounds on 6 October 1916*
ST. ALBANS CEMETERY, United Kingdom
65 Paris Street, Belfast.

Rippard, Thomas - Rifleman
13441 Royal Irish Rifles 8th Battalion *Died in War on 2 July 1916*
GRANDCOURT ROAD CEMETERY, GRANDCOURT, France
Born and enlisted in Belfast.

Risk, William - Private
10244 South Lancashire Regiment 2nd Battalion *Age 22 Killed in Action on 5 January 1916*
LONDON RIFLE BRIGADE CEMETERY, Belgium
Son of William and Annie Risk, of 13, Major Street, Belfast.

Ritchie, Edward - Rifleman
5829 Royal Irish Rifles 15th Battalion *Died in War on 21 January 1916*
RUE PETILLON MILITARY CEMETERY FLEURBAIX, France
Born in Belfast, enlisted Ballykinler.

Ritchie, George - Private
S/8351 Black Watch (Royal Highlanders) 1st Battalion *Age 34 Killed in Action on 25 September 1915*
DUD CORNER CEMETERY, LOOS, France
Son of George and Helen Ritchie, of 64, Carnie Street, Arbroath, Forfarshire; husband of Mary Anna Ritchie, of 91, St. Leonard Street, Belfast.

Journey of Remembering

Ritchie, James - Rifleman
3231 Royal Irish Rifles 14th Battalion *Killed in Action on 1 July 1916*
THIEPVAL ANGLO-FRENCH CEMETERY, AUTHUILE, *France*
Born and enlisted in Belfast.

Ritchie, John - Rifleman
13443 Royal Irish Rifles 8th Battalion *Age 22 Killed in Action on 2 July 1916*
CONNAUGHT CEMETERY, THIEPVAL, *France*
Foster son of Mrs. M. Hibbs, of 30, Moorfield Street, Belfast.

Ritchie, John - Sapper
64682 Royal Engineers 554th Company *Accidently killed on 13 February 1919*
KORTRIJK (ST. JAN) COMMUNAL CEMETERY, *Belgium*
Husband of Agnes Ritchie 87 Silvio Street, Belfast.

Ritchie, William Morgan - Rifleman
114 Royal Irish Rifles "A" Company 13th Battalion *Age 20 Killed in Action on 16 August 1917*
NEW IRISH FARM CEMETERY, *Belgium*
Son of Charles Hanston Ritchie and Lucy A. Ritchie, of 5, Eblana Street, Belfast.
Native of Bloomfield, Belfast.

Robb, Arthur Charles - Private
28991 Canadian Infantry (Manitoba Regiment) 16th Battalion *Died in War 23 April 1915*
YPRES (MENIN GATE) MEMORIAL, *Belgium*
Born in Holywood and lived in Belfast. An Anglican and a bookkeeper by profession.
Son of John McLorinan Robb and Charlotte, of 11, Whitley Wood Road, Shinfield, Reading, England.

Robb, David - Private
3765 Princess Victoria's (Royal Irish Fusiliers) 5th Battalion *Died in War on 26 October 1918*
THIEPVAL MEMORIAL, *France*
Born, resided and enlisted in Belfast. Formerly 4003 Royal Garrison Artillery

Robb, John James - Sergeant
10089 Lancashire Fusiliers 15th Battalion *Age 29 Died of Wounds on 12 April 1918*
DOULLENS COMMUNAL CEMETERY, EXTENSION *No.1, France*
Son of James and Elizabeth Ann Robb, of Belfast.

Robb, Victor Harold - Lieutenant
Royal Irish Rifles 14th Battalion *Died in War on 3 July 1916*
BELFAST CITY CEMETERY, *United Kingdom*
Member of Fortwilliam Presbyterian Church.

Robb, William - Private
31782 Duke of Cornwall's Light Infantry 1st Battalion *Died in War on 17 December 1916*
ST VAAST POST MILITARY CEMETERY RICHEBOURG-L'AVOUE, *France*
Born in Belfast, enlisted Southampton. Formerly 4068295 Army Service Corps

Robbins, William - Company Quartermaster Sergeant
L/5857 Royal Sussex Regiment 7th Battalion *Age 32 Died in War on 25 November 1917*
CAMBRAI MEMORIAL, LOUVERVAL, *France*
Long Service and Good Conduct Medal. Husband of Margaret Robbins,
of 29, Sandymount Street, Stranmillis Road, Belfast.

Journey of Remembering

Roberts, John - Rifleman
419012 London Regiment 9th (County of London) Battalion (Queen Victoria's Rifles) *Died in War on 23 October 1917*
Born in Belfast, enlisted Stratford, England. Formerly 595945, 18th London Regiment.

Roberts, Walter Edward - Corporal
16880 Royal Garrison Artillery *Died in War on 27 May 1916*
GUARDS CEMETERY, WINDY CORNER, CUINCHY, France
Born in Belfast, enlisted Lurgan.

Robertson, James - Corporal
58824 Royal Fusiliers (City of London Regiment) 11th Battalion *Died in War on 16 August 1918*
VIGNACOURT BRITISH CEMETERY, France
Born in Belfast, enlisted London.

Robertson, John - Private
26416 Machine Gun Corps (Infantry) *Died in War on 4 February 1917*
BELFAST CITY CEMETERY, United Kingdom
Born in Belfast, enlisted Jarrow, England. "Clarke" was the true family name. Formerly 16515 King's Royal Rifle Corps.

Robinson, Albert - Private
8164 The King's (Liverpool Regiment) 1st Battalion *Age 28 Died in War on 19 May 1915*
LE TOURET MEMORIAL, France
Son of Mr. and Mrs. Kelso Robinson, of 32, Roe Street, Belfast.

Robinson, Alexander - Acting Regimental Sergeant Major
6733 Seaforth Highlanders (Ross-shire Buffs, the Duke of Albany's) 9th Battalion *Killed in Action on 22 March 1918*
POZIERES MEMORIAL, France
Born in Belfast, enlisted Glasgow.

Robinson, Arthur - Private
28520 Royal Inniskilling Fusiliers 9th Battalion *Age 39 Died in War on 29 March 1918*
POZIERES MEMORIAL, France
Son of Arthur and Margaret Robinson, of 11, Langley Street, Belfast; husband of the late Louisa Robinson, of Midland Street, Shankill Road, Belfast.

Robinson, Arthur Gunning - Private
PS/10184 Royal Fusiliers 8th Battalion *Age 19 Died in War on 7 October 1916*
THIEPVAL MEMORIAL, France
Son of John J. and Margaret H. Robinson, of 43, Cliftonville Road, Belfast.

Robinson, Charles W - Corporal
18084 Royal Inniskilling Fusiliers 9th Battalion *Age 21 Killed in Action on 7 June 1917*
SPANBROEKMOLEN BRITISH CEMETERY, Belgium
Son of Captain Thomas and Mrs. Agnes Robinson, of "Ivy Dean", Wandsworth Road, Knock, Belfast.

Robinson, Daniel - Rifleman
8262 Royal Irish Rifles 2nd Battalion *Killed in Action on 25 October 1914*
LE TOURET MEMORIAL, France
Brother of James Robinson of 218 Matilda Street, Belfast.

Robinson, David - Corporal
15864 Royal Irish Rifles 21st Entrenching Battalion late 10th Battalion *Killed in action on 21 March 1918*
POZIERES MEMORIAL, France
Sister of Mary Robinson, 47 Abbot Street, Belfast.

Journey of Remembering

Robinson, David - Rifleman
7296 Royal Irish Rifles 2nd Battalion *Killed in Action on 26 October 1914*
LE TOURET MEMORIAL, *France*
Born and enlisted in Belfast.

Robinson, Ernest Cecil - Private
1810 Suffolk Regiment 4th Battalion *Died in War on 12 March 1915*
GUARDS' CEMETERY, WINDY CORNER CUINCHY, *France*
Born in Belfast, enlisted Ipswich.

Robinson, George - Private
10221 Royal Inniskilling Fusiliers 1st Battalion *Age 23 Died in War on 27 January 1917*
THIEPVAL MEMORIAL, *France*
Son of Joseph and Lizzie Robinson, of 2, Cairo Street, Belfast.

Robinson, James - Lance Corporal
12411 Royal Irish Rifles "D" Company 8th Battalion *Age 34 Died in War on 2 July 1916*
THIEPVAL MEMORIAL, *France*
Son of the late John and Sarah Robinson; husband of Sarah Robinson, of 4, Saunders Street, Belfast.

Robinson, James - Lance Corporal
31013 Royal Dublin Fusiliers 1st Battalion *Died in War on 27 May 1918*
AIRE COMMUNAL CEMETERY, *France*
Native of Belfast. Son of the late James Robinson.

Robinson, James - Private
1760 Leinster Regiment 2nd Battalion *Age 31 Killed in Action on 18 June 1918*
CINQ RUES BRITISH CEMETERY, HAZEBROUCK, *France*
Nephew of Miss Jane Morgan, of 14, Linden Street, Belfast.

Robinson, James - Rifleman
15818 Royal Irish Rifles 9th Battalion *Died in War on 23 August 1916*
ST QUENTIN CABARET MILITARY CEMETERY, *Belgium*
Born and enlisted in Belfast.

Robinson, James G - Rifleman
19/122 Royal Irish Rifles 14th Battalion *Died in War on 9 October 1916*
POND FARM CEMETERY, *Belgium*
Son of Mr. R. G. Robinson, of 342, Springfield Road, Belfast. A member of the old UVF.

Robinson, James Henry - Lance Corporal
10677 Royal Irish Rifles "C" Company 6th Battalion *Age 17 Died in War on 10 August 1915*
HELLES MEMORIAL, *Turkey*
Son of William John and Sarah Robinson, of The Chief Fire Station, Belfast.

Robinson, James Thomas - Engineer Sub-Lieutenant
Royal Naval Reserve M.F.A. "Whitehead"
Age 29 Killed in Action with submarine in the Mediterranean on 15 October 1917
PORTSMOUTH NAVAL MEMORIAL, *United Kingdom*
Son of the late James and Annie Robinson, of 14, Stranmillis Park, Belfast.

Robinson, James Thompson - Lieutenant
Royal Welsh Fusiliers 24th (Denbighshire Yeomanry) Battalion *Age 25 Died in War on 8 September 1916*
BAILLEUL COMMUNAL CEMETERY EXTENSION (NORD), France
Son of John Clarke Graham Robinson and Lizzie Robinson, of "Mynsbella" Chichester Park, Belfast.

Robinson, John Thomas - Lance Corporal
26174 Royal Inniskilling Fusiliers 8th Battalion *Age 27 Killed in Action on 16 August 1917*
TYNE COT MEMORIAL, Belgium
Husband of Mary Elizabeth Robinson, of 4, Ardgreenan Place, Belmont Church Road, Belfast.

Robinson, Joseph - Private
8336 Royal Irish Rifles 2nd Battalion *Age 32 Killed in Action on 24 October 1914*
LE TOURET MEMORIAL, France
Son of the late James Robinson of Belfast.

Robinson, Joseph - Rifleman
1257 Royal Irish Rifles 7th Battalion *Died in War on 6 September 1916*
THIEPVAL MEMORIAL, France
Born and enlisted in Belfast.

Robinson, Robert - Private
GS/471 Royal Sussex Regiment 9th Battalion *Died in War on 27 May 1916*
LA CLYTTE MILITARY CEMETERY, Belgium
Born in Belfast, enlisted in Hove, England.

Robinson, Thomas - Private
12453 Royal Inniskilling Fusiliers 2nd Battalion *Died as a result of war on 19 November 1918*
NIEDERZWEHREN CEMETERY, Germany
Born and enlisted in Belfast.

Robinson, Thomas - Private
9843 Royal Inniskilling Fusiliers 8th Battalion *Killed in Action on 16 August 1917*
TYNE COT MEMORIAL, France
Born Belfast.

Robinson, Thomas - Rifleman
12124 Royal Irish Rifles 15th Battalion *Killed In Action on 1 July 1916*
THIEPVAL MEMORIAL, France
Born and enlisted in Belfast. Family lived in Cosgrave Street.

Robinson, Thomas - Rifleman
15866 Royal Irish Rifles 10th Battalion *Killed in Action on 1 July 1916*
THIEPVAL MEMORIAL, France
Born and enlisted in Belfast.

Robinson, Thomas - Sapper
64354 Royal Engineers 150th Field Company *Age 32 Killed in Action on 16 August 1917*
TYNE COT MEMORIAL, Belgium
Husband of Edith Robinson, of 44, Tennent Street, Belfast.

Robinson, William - Private
6815 South Lancashire Regiment 2nd Battalion *Age 30 Died in War on 24 October 1914*
LE TOURET MEMORIAL, France
Son of Mr. and Mrs. Kelso Robinson, of 32, Roe Street, Belfast.

Journey of Remembering

Robinson, William James - Private
10388 Royal Inniskilling Fusiliers 1st Battalion *Killed in Action on 1 July 1916*
THIEPVAL MEMORIAL, *France*
Born in Belfast.

Robinson, William John Reynolds - Fireman
Mercantile Marine S.S. "Castlebar" (Belfast) *Age 23 Presumed drowned on 13 March 1918*
TOWER HILL MEMORIAL, *United Kingdom*
Son of Thomas and the late Rose Robinson; husband of Sarah Robinson (née McLenaghan), of 61, Bann Street, Belfast. Born in Belfast.

Rochester, James - Rifleman
191309 Royal Irish Rifles 12th Battalion *Age 23 Died as a POW on 23 June 1918*
BERLIN SOUTH-WESTERN CEMETERY, *Germany*
Son of James and Elizabeth Rochester, of 184, Ravenhill Avenue, Belfast. Native of Gateshead.

Rocks, Patrick - Rifleman
6974 Royal Irish Rifles 1st Battalion *Killed in Action on 21 March 1918*
POZIERES MEMORIAL, *France*
Born in Belfast, enlisted Ballykinler.

Roddy, William - Rifleman
15869 Royal Irish Rifles 14th Battalion *Killed in Action on 1 July 1916*
THIEPVAL MEMORIAL, *France*
Member of Townsend Presbyterian Church, Belfast. Son of Joseph and Mary Ellen Roddy of Keady, County Armagh.

Rodgers, Adam - Sergeant
17880 Machine Gun Corps (Infantry) formerly 8th Battalion Royal Irish Rifles *Age 28 Died in War on 24 April 1918*
POZIERES MEMORIAL, *France*
Son of George and Margaret Rodgers, of Kersland Crescent, Knock, Belfast; husband of Dorothy Emily Gregory (formerly Rodgers), of 14, Blucher Street, Dover. Twice previously wounded

Rodgers, Alexander - Able Seaman
232035 Royal Navy HMS "Monmouth" *Age 26 Killed in Action at Battle of Coronel on 1 November 1914*
PLYMOUTH NAVAL MEMORIAL, *United Kingdom*
Son of Nathaniel Grant Rodgers and Ellen Jane Rodgers, of 70, Bentinck Street, Belfast.

Rodgers, Benjamin - Rifleman
7012 Royal Irish Rifles 2nd Battalion *Killed In Action on 25 September 1915*
YPRES (MENIN GATE) MEMORIAL, *Belgium*
Born and enlisted in Belfast.

Rodgers, Daniel - Rifleman
7026 Royal Irish Rifles 2nd Battalion *Died as a Prisoner of War on 5 June 1918*
NIEDERZWEHREN CEMETERY, *Germany*
Born Ballymacarrett, Belfast. Enlisted in Newtownards.

Rodgers, Frederick George - Sailor
Mercantile Marine S.S. "Teelin Head" (Belfast) *Age 16 Drowned, as a result of an attack by an enemy submarine on 21 January 1918*
TOWER HILL MEMORIAL, *United Kingdom*
Son of John and Martha Rodgers, of 170, Nelson Street, Belfast.

Rodgers, George - Gunner
32466 Royal Garrison Artillery 59th Siege Battery *Died in War on 19 September 1915*
VERMELLES BRITISH CEMETERY, France
Brother of Isaac Rodgers, 60, Connaught Street, Belfast.

Rodgers, James - Sapper
64393 Royal Engineers 150th Field Company *Age 35 Killed in Action on 30 April 1918*
DUHALLOW A.D.S. CEMETERY, Belgium
Son of James and Agnes Rodgers, of 18, Evelyn Avenue, Belfast; husband of Emily Rodgers, of 20, Hollycroft Avenue, Belfast.

Rodgers, James - Sergeant
70773 Machine Gun Corps (Infantry) *Died in War on 6 May 1918*
LOOS MEMORIAL, France
Born and enlisted in Belfast. Formerly 9148 Royal Irish Fusiliers

Rodgers, James Grant - Stoker First Class
229527 Royal Navy HMS "Queen Mary" *Age 29 Killed in Action at Battle of Jutland on 31 May 1916*
CHATHAM NAVAL MEMORIAL, United Kingdom
Son of James and Jane Rodgers, of 71, City Street, Belfast.

Rodgers, James Joseph - Lance Corporal
10076 Royal Inniskilling Fusiliers 1st Battalion formerly 8550 Royal Irish Rifles *Died in War on 7 June 1915*
HELLES MEMORIAL, Turkey
17, Middlepath Street, Belfast (Formerly 8550 Royal Irish Rifles).

Rodgers, James Joseph - Private
441570 British Columbia Regiment 2nd Canadian Mounted Rifles *Age 24 Died in War on 13 October 1916*
COURCELETTE BRITISH CEMETERY, France
Son of Thomas James Rodgers, of 43, Rosapenna Street, Belfast, Ireland.
An Anglican he had gone to farm in Canada.

Rodgers, John - Private
201360 Cameronians (Scottish Rifles) 5th Battalion *Died in War on 20 July 1916*
THIEPVAL MEMORIAL, France
Born in Belfast, enlisted Glasgow.

Rodgers, Robert - Rifleman
15870 Royal Irish Rifles "A" Company 4th Battalion *Age 27 Killed in Action on 1 July 1916*
CONNAUGHT CEMETERY, THIEPVAL, France
Son of James and Agnes Rodgers, of 18, Evelyn Avenue, Bloomfield, Belfast.

Rodgers, Thomas - Lance Corporal
15823 Royal Irish Rifles "C" Company 9th Battalion *Killed in Action on 1 July 1916*
THIEPVAL MEMORIAL, France
Son of Thomas and Annie Rodgers, of 42, Northumberland Street, Belfast; husband of Sarah Rodgers, of 80, Sugarfield Street, Belfast.

Rodgers, William - Private
1211 Royal Irish Rifles 10th Battalion attached 21st Entrenching Battalion *Killed in Action on 21 March 1918*
POZIERES MEMORIAL, France
Enlisted and resident in Belfast. May have resided in the Donegall Pass area.

Rodgers, William Herbert - Corporal
8690 Royal Irish Rifles 1st Battalion *Killed in Action on 16 June 1916*
PLOEGSTEERT MEMORIAL, *Belgium*
Born and enlisted in Belfast.

Rodgerson, Henry Cooke - Rifleman
15824 Royal Irish Rifles 15th Battalion *Killed in Action on 1 July 1916*
THIEPVAL MEMORIAL, *France*
Born and enlisted in Belfast.

Rogan, Herbert John - Private
2609 Black Watch (Royal Highlanders) 6th Battalion *Age 23 Died in War on 30 July 1916*
THIEPVAL MEMORIAL, *France*
Son of John, a former Royal Irish Constabulary Sergeant and Catherine Rogan, of 4, Victoria Terrace, Cregagh, Belfast; husband of Catherine Rogan (née McCord), of Willow House, Trummery, County Down. He had just completed his apprenticeship in the linen business when he enlisted.

Rogan, James - Private
5827 Royal Munster Fusiliers 9th Battalion *Died in War on 27 April 1916*
LOOS MEMORIAL, *France*
Born in County Down, enlisted and resident in Belfast.

Rogers, George Murray - Lieutenant
Royal Irish Rifles 13th Battalion *Age 24 Killed in Action on 1 July 1916*
MILL ROAD CEMETERY, THIEPVAL, *France*
Son of George M. and Nellie Rogers, of "Dalkeith" Hawthornden Road, Knock, Belfast.
Native of Banbridge, County Down.

Rogers, Maurice Croston - Second Lieutenant
Royal Engineers 59th Field Company *Age 24 Died in War on 25 February 1915*
NIEUWKERKE CHURCHYARD, *Belgium*
Born at Belfast and educated at Campbell College. Only son of John Croston and Leily Rogers of Ellersie, Athlone. His father was the Inspector of National Schools in Ireland.

Rogers, Samuel Bertie - Private
7567 Royal Irish Fusiliers 1st Battalion *Age 38 Died in War on 31 May 1915*
BOULOGNE EASTERN CEMETERY, *France*
20 Houston Street, Belfast.

Rollins, George - Private
201382 Leicestershire Regiment 1st Battalion *Age 27 Killed in Action on 22 March 1918*
ARRAS MEMORIAL, *France*
Son of William B. Rollins, of 50, Rainey Street, Belfast.

Rollins, George - Private
292658 Gordon Highlanders 2nd Battalion *Age 29 Died in War on 26 October 1917*
TYNE COT MEMORIAL, *Belgium*
Son of Alexander and Margaret Anne Rollins, of 18, Brennan Street, Belfast.

Ronaldson, James Gray - Second Lieutenant
Queen's West Surrey Regiment 10th Battalion *Died in War on 20 September 1917*
TYNE COT MEMORIAL, *Belgium*
Cliftonville Circus, Belfast.

Rooney, James - Bombardier
17703 Royal Garrison Artillery 4th Siege Battery *Age 32 Killed in Action on 28 October 1918*
TAINTIGNIES COMMUNAL CEMETERY, *Belgium*
Son of Bernard and Margaret Rooney; husband of Margaret Rooney, of 59, Sheriff Street, Belfast.

Rooney, Patrick - Sapper
WR/504252 Royal Engineers Inland Water Transport *Age 38 Died as a result of war on 24 February 1919*
BELFAST (MILLTOWN) ROMAN CATHOLIC CEMETERY, *United Kingdom*
Husband of Mary Rooney, of 11, Crawford Street, Belfast.

Rooney, Peter - Rifleman
18704 Royal Irish Rifles "A" Company 14th Battalion *Age 20 Killed in Action on 1 July 1916*
THIEPVAL MEMORIAL, *France*
Son of Lawrence and S. Rooney, of 43, Kilmood Street, Belfast.

Rooney, Thomas - Private
3527 Leinster Regiment 7th Battalion *Died in War on 4 September 1916*
LA NEUVILLE BRITISH CEMETERY, CORBIE, *France*
Born and enlisted in Belfast.

Rosbotham, Samuel - Corporal
3390 Royal Inniskilling Fusiliers 7th Battalion *Age 19 Died in War on 9 August 1917*
YPRES (MENIN GATE) MEMORIAL, *Belgium*
Son of Stewart and Sarah Rosbotham, of 32, Woodvale Avenue, Belfast. Enlisted at the age of 16, and had been an apprentice in Workman Clarke Shipyard.

Rosbotham, Thomas - Lance Corporal
37961 Lancashire Fusiliers 2nd Battalion *Died in War on 3 May 1917*
ARRAS MEMORIAL, *France*
Born in Belfast, enlisted in Salford, England.

Rosbotham, William - Private
102754 Royal Army Medical Corps 20th Company *Age 57 Died in War on 8 April 1916*
TIDWORTH MILITARY CEMETERY, *United Kingdom*
Son of Mathew and Elizabeth Rosbotham; husband of Annie Rosbotham, of 22, Greenland Street, Belfast.

Rosbottam, William - Lance Corporal
3388 Royal Inniskilling Fusiliers 2nd Battalion *Killed in Action on 3 January 1916*
AUTHILLE MILITARY CEMETERY, *France*
Born in Belfast.

Rose, John Carson - Private
515 King's Own Scottish Borderers 1/4th Battalion *Age 23 Died in War on 12 July 1915*
HELLES MEMORIAL, *Turkey*
Son of the late Mr. and Mrs. Thomas Henry Rose, of Whitewell, Belfast.

Ross, (Robert) Rex - Lance Corporal
9323 Royal Irish Rifles 1st Battalion *Killed in Action on 11 March 1915*
LE TOURET MEMORIAL, *France*
Son of Robert and Julia Ross, of 20, Linview Street, Grosvenor Road, Belfast.

Journey of Remembering

Ross, Daniel - Private
13373 Royal Inniskilling Fusiliers 8th Battalion *Age 24 Died in War on 6 April 1916*
PHILOSOPHE BRITISH CEMETERY, MAZINGARBE, France
Son of Daniel Ross, of 3, McDonnell Street, Belfast.

Ross, George - First Mate
Mercantile Marine SS "Teelin Head" (Belfast)
Age 31 Drowned, as a result of an attack by an enemy submarine on 21 January 1918
TOWER HILL MEMORIAL, United Kingdom
Son of Mary and the late Robert Ross; husband of Essie Eva Ross (née Mckee), of 82, Woodvale Avenue, Belfast. Born at Islandmagee.

Ross, George Raphael - Private
446990 Canadian Infantry (Alberta Regiment) *Died in War on 14 June 1916*
YPRES (MENIN GATE) MEMORIAL, Belgium
Henderson Avenue, Belfast.

Ross, James Graham - Private
862556 Canadian Pioneers 123rd Battalion *Age 32 Died in War on 30 August 1917*
AIX-NOULETTE COMMUNAL CEMETERY EXTENSION, France
Son of Alexander and Mary Ross, of Edgar Avenue, Yonge Street, Richmond Hill, York County, Ontario, Canada. Born at Belfast, Ireland. A Methodist and a carpenter by trade.

Ross, John - Private
1/17489 Royal Dublin Fusiliers 7th Battalion *Died of Wounds on 28 December 1917*
JERUSALEM WAR CEMETERY, Israel
3 McDonnell Street, Belfast.

Ross, John - Rifleman
13455 Royal Irish Rifles "C" Company 8th Battalion
Age 34 Died of Wounds received on the Somme on 7 July 1916
PUCHEVILLERS BRITISH CEMETERY, France
Son of the late George and Mary Ross, of Ballynafeigh, Belfast; husband of Frances Ross, of 77, Ardenmoor Street, Belfast. Served 12 years in Royal Field Artillery in India; also took part in the South African campaign.

Ross, Robert - Lance Corporal
9323 Royal Irish Rifles 1st Battalion *Killed in Action on 11 March 1915*
LE TOURET MEMORIAL, France
Son of Robert and Julia Ross, of 20, Linview Street, Grosvenor Road, Belfast.

Ross, Robert - Private
71579 North Irish Horse *Age 25 Killed in Action on 21 August 1918*
ANCRE BRITISH CEMETERY, BEAUMONT-HAMEL, France
Son of J and Elizabeth Ross, of 318, Springfield Road, Belfast.

Ross, Robert Campbell - Rifleman
14/15878 Royal Irish Rifles 14th Battalion *Age 19 Killed in Action on 7 June 1917*
SPANBROEKMOLEN BRITISH CEMETERY, Belgium
Son of Robert John and Caroline Ross, of 6, Cameron Street, Belfast.

Ross, Robert Campbell - Rifleman
15878 Royal Irish Rifles 14th Battalion *Killed In Action on 7 June 1917*
SPANBROEKMOLEN BRITISH CEMETERY, Belgium
Son of the late Mr and Mrs Thomas Henry Ross, of Whitewell, Belfast.

Ross, Robert Simmie - Second Lieutenant
King's Own Scottish Borderers *Age 25 Died in War on 3 September 1916*
DELVILLE WOOD CEMETERY, LONGUEVAL, France
Son of Helena and George Ross of Aberdeen. Native of Belfast, educated at Campbell College and a member of Knock Rugby Club.

Ross, Samuel - Rifleman
553 Royal Irish Rifles 8th Battalion *Died in War on 26 October 1917*
RUYAULCOURT MILITARY CEMETERY, France
Born and enlisted in Belfast.

Ross, William - Private
3091 Royal Inniskilling Fusiliers 1st Battalion *Died in War on 22 May 1915*
HELLES MEMORIAL, Turkey
134, Mervue Street, Belfast.

Ross, William James - Able Seaman
SS/2905 Royal Navy HMS "Hawke"
Age 23 Killed in Action with submarine in North Sea on 15 October 1914
CHATHAM NAVAL MEMORIAL, United Kingdom
Son of Robert and Sarah Ross, of 234, Newtownards Road, Belfast.

Ross, William Samuel Baird - Second Lieutenant
Royal Irish Rifles 15th Battalion *Killed in Action on 21 March 1918*
POZIERES MEMORIAL, France
Gainsborough Drive, Belfast.

Routledge, Harry - Private
12282 Alexandra Princess of Wales's Own (Yorkshire Regiment) 13th Battalion
Died in War on 23 November 1917
CAMBRAI MEMORIAL, France
Born in Belfast, enlisted in Leeds.

Rowan, Archibald - Rifleman
19/504 Royal Irish Rifles 3rd Battalion *Age 21 Died in War on 4 November 1918*
BELFAST (DUNDONALD) CEMETERY, United Kingdom
Son of William Rowan, of 28, Athens Street, Belfast.

Rox, Arthur - Private
22090 Royal Dublin Fusiliers "D" Company 6th Battalion *Age 34 Killed in Action on 2 - 4 October 1916*
STRUMA MILITARY CEMETERY, Greece
Son of John and Ann Rox, of 36, Chapel Street, Hamilton; husband of Sarah Rox, of 14, John Street, Belfast.

Journey of Remembering

Roy, Archibald - Lance Corporal
4933 Rifle Brigade 18th Battalion *Died in War on 1 November 1918*
VILLERS-EN-CAUCHIES COMMUNAL CEMETERY, France
Son of Mrs J Roy, 49 Moore Street, Belfast.

Roy, Joseph - Rifleman
13457 Royal Irish Rifles 15th Battalion *Died in War on 24 June 1918*
SARRALBE MILITARY CEMETERY, France
Born and enlisted in Belfast.

Ruddell, William Alexander - Sergeant
8941 Royal Inniskilling Fusiliers 1st Battalion *Died in War on 14 May 1915*
HELLES MEMORIAL, Turkey
86 Donegall Avenue, Belfast. Born in County Armagh.

Ruddock, James - Sergeant
6561 Royal Irish Rifles 2nd Battalion *Killed in Action on 12 October 1914*
LE TOURET MEMORIAL, France
Husband of Agnes Ruddock, 51 Fourth Street, Belfast.

Ruddock, Robert - Rifleman
15881 Royal Irish Rifles 9th Battalion *Killed in Action on 1 July 1916*
255, Conway Street, Belfast.

Ruddy, William - Private
10410 Royal Inniskilling Fusiliers 2nd Battalion *Age 22 Killed in Action on 26 August 1914*
LA FERTE-SOUS-JOUARRE MEMORIAL, France
Son of William Ruddy, of 17, Ardgowan Street, Belfast.

Runaghan, James - Private
2499 Leinster Regiment 7th Battalion *Died in War on 3 September 1916*
THIEPVAL MEMORIAL, France
Born and enlisted in Belfast.

Runaghan, John - Private
2329 Connaught Rangers 6th Battalion *Killed, with others, by a shell explosion on 28 March 1916*
DUD CORNER CEMETERY, LOOS, France
Husband of Mary Ann Runaghan, 13 Milton Street, Belfast. Worked in the street cleaning section of Belfast Corporation.

Runeghan, James - Private
2329 Connaught Rangers 6th Battalion *Died in War on 28 March 1916*
DUD CORNER CEMETERY, LOOS, France
3, Milton Street, Belfast.

Runnette, William John - Carpenter
Mercantile Marine S.S. "Garron Head" (Belfast) *Age 28 Killed by mine on 16 November 1917*
TOWER HILL MEMORIAL, United Kingdom
Son of John and Maggie Runnette; husband of Daisy Edith Runnette (née Backler), of 456, Cregagh Road, Belfast. Born at Brooklyn, New York.

Rush, Frank - Private
6956 Royal Inniskilling Fusiliers 1st Battalion *Died in War on 20 November 1917*
CAMBRAI MEMORIAL, LOUVERVAL, France
Son of Sarah Rush, 33 Little May Street, Belfast.

Rush , James - Private
4632 Royal Inniskilling Fusiliers 4th Battalion *Died on 5 May 1915*
GRANGEGORMAN MILITARY CEMETERY, DUBLIN, Republic of Ireland
Born and enlisted in Belfast.

Rush, Bernard - Private
5180 Royal Munster Fusiliers 2nd Battalion *Died in War on 10 November 1917*
TYNE COT MEMORIAL, Belgium
Born in Glasgow, enlisted and resident in Belfast. Formerly 13050 Royal Inniskilling Fusiliers

Rush, John - Private
2759 Connaught Rangers 6th Battalion *Died in War on 5 May 1916*
DUD CORNER CEMETERY, LOOS, France
Born in Sion Mills, enlisted and resident in Belfast.

Rusk, Francis - Rifleman
19/234 Royal Irish Rifles 8th Battalion *Age 20 Died in War on 27 October 1916*
RATION FARM (LA PLUS DOUVE) ANNEXE, Belgium
Son of David and Jane Rusk, of Craigarogan, Mallusk, Belfast.

Russell, Andrew - Private
6693 Cameron Highlanders 1st Battalion *Age 30 Died in War on 22 September 1914*
NETLEY MILITARY CEMETERY, United Kingdom
Husband of Mary Russell, of 56, Templemore Street, Belfast.

Russell, Archibald - Sergeant
8216 Royal Irish Rifles 1st Battalion *Killed in Action on 13 April 1916*
BECOURT MILITARY CEMETERY, BECORDEL-BECOURT, France
Born and enlisted in Belfast.

Russell, Edmund - Driver
38199 Royal Field Artillery 2nd Brigade *Age 34 Died of Wounds on 8 November 1916*
GROVE TOWN CEMETERY, MEAULTE, France
Son of Benjamin and Susannah Russell; husband of Elizabeth Russell, of 40, Selby Street, Belfast. Native of Belfast.

Russell, James - Private
3595 Royal Inniskilling Fusiliers 1st Battalion *Age 27 Died in War on 2 May 1915*
TWELVE TREE COPSE CEMETERY, Turkey
Husband of Jane Russell, of 6, Coates Street, Belfast. Worked in York Street Flax Spinning Mill.

Russell, Joseph - Lance Corporal
30280 Dublin Fusiliers 1st Battalion *Died in War on 5 May 1918*
BELFAST CITY CEMETERY, United Kingdom
Son of Mrs Hessie Russell, 64, Mayo Street, Belfast.

Russell, Patrick - Private
7526 Cameronians (Scottish Rifles) 2nd Battalion *Age 20 Died in War on 3 February 1915*
LE TOURET MEMORIAL, *France*
Son of Patrick and Rose A. Russell, of 32, Plevna Street, Belfast.

Russell, Robert - Corporal
59859 Canadian Infantry (Eastern Ontario Regiment) 21st Battalion
Age 20 Killed in Action on 20 June 1918
BELLACOURT MILITARY CEMETERY, RIVIERE, *France*
Son of Mrs. James Chambers (formerly Russell), of Richmond Lodge, Knocknagoney, Strandtown, Belfast, Ireland, and the late Robert Russell.

Russell, Robert Evans - Private
12753 Canadian Infantry (Saskatchewan Regiment) 5th Battalion *Age 38 Died in War on 24 May 1915*
VIMY MEMORIAL, *France*
Son of Thomas and Elizabeth Russell, of 3, Eblana Street, Belfast, Ireland.
An Anglican he had seen previous regular service in the South Lancashire Regiment.

Russell, Thomas - Gunner
31179 Royal Horse Artillery and Royal Field Artillery *Died in War on 4 February 1916*
STE MARIE CEMETERY, LE HAVRE, *France*
Born and enlisted in Belfast.

Russell, Thomas - Rifleman
10737 Royal Irish Rifles 1st Battalion *Killed in Action on 16 August 1917*
TYNE COT MEMORIAL, *Belgium*
Born and enlisted in Belfast.

Russell, William - Lance Corporal
5843 Royal Irish Rifles 2nd Battalion *Age 18 Died of Wounds on 3 October 1918*
HARINGHE (BANDAGHEM) MILITARY CEMETERY, *Belgium*
Son of Catherine Russell, of 6, Jennymount Street, Belfast.

Russell, William - Private
S/11780 Seaforth Highlanders 1st Battalion *Age 24 Died of Wounds on 25 January 1917*
AMARA WAR CEMETERY, *Iraq*
Son of William and Margaret Russell, of 20, Loftus Street, Belfast.

Russell, William James - Rifleman
17/729 Royal Irish Rifles 10th Battalion *Age 21 Died of Wounds on 28 August 1916*
BAILLEUL COMMUNAL CEMETERY EXTENSION (NORD), *France*
Son of Andrew and Elizabeth E. Russell (née Moore), of Belfast.

Russell, William James - Rifleman
593 Royal Irish Rifles 16th Battalion *Age 24 Died in War on 7 July 1916*
THIEPVAL MEMORIAL, *France*
Son of William and Annie Liza Russell, of 30, Central Street, Belfast.

Rutherford, William McConnell - Second Lieutenant
East Yorkshire Regiment 10th Battalion *Age 37 Died of Wounds on 19 April 1918*
WIMEREUX COMMUNAL CEMETERY, France
Son of William and Lily Rutherford, of College Green, Belfast. Enlisted as private in the Royal Army Medical Corps in October 1914. Served in Egypt. Received Commission in East Yorks Regiment, June, 1917. Serving in France at the time of death.

Ryan, Edward - Rifleman
10146 Royal Irish Rifles 2nd Battalion *Killed in Action on 15 September 1914*
LA FERTE-SOUS-JOUARRE MEMORIAL, France
Born and enlisted in Dublin, resident of Belfast.

Ryce, James - Private
4317 Highland Light Infantry 18th Battalion (4th Glasgow) *Died in War on 30 September 1918*
LIJSSENTHOEK MILITARY CEMETERY, Belgium
Born in Belfast, enlisted Glasgow.

Ryding, William Henry - Master
Mercantile Marine "Castlebar" *Age 46 Died in War on 13 March 1918*
TOWER HILL MEMORIAL, United Kingdom
Son of the late Henry William and Maria Ryding; husband of Mary Elizabeth Ryding, of 28, Colvil Street, Strandtown, Belfast.

Sadlier, William Armstrong - Private
1144 South Irish Horse *Died in War on 22 December 1915*
CHAPELLE-D'ARMENTIERES NEW MILITARY CEMETERY, France
Born in Belfast, enlisted in Dublin.

Sales, John - Sergeant
2261 Irish Guards 1st Battalion *Age 27 Died in War on 18 May 1915*
LE TOURET MEMORIAL, France
Son of Mr. and Mrs. Sales, of 18, March Street, Belfast; husband of Dorothy Georgina Sales, of 7J, Lewis Dwellings, Chelsea, London.

Sales, Malcolm - Corporal
10412 Royal Inniskilling Fusiliers 2nd Battalion *Killed in Action on 11 July 1916*
CONNAUGHT CEMETERY, THIEPVAL, France
Born in Belfast.

Sales, Thomas - Private
PLY/14074 Royal Marine Light Infantry HMS "Lion" *Died in War on 31 May 1916*
PLYMOUTH NAVAL MEMORIAL, United Kingdom
Son of Robert Sales, 12, March Street.

Sampson, Francis Robert - Rifleman
15930 Royal Irish Rifle 14th Battalion attached 109th Battery *Age 19 Killed in Action on 1 July 1916*
THIEPVAL MEMORIAL, France
Son of Captain H. Sampson, Military Medal, and Mary Sampson, of 25, Willowbank Gardens, Belfast.

Sanders, Thomas - Petty Officer
300974 Royal Navy HMS "Vivid" *Died as a result of war on 16 September 1919*
FORD PARK CEMETERY, PLYMOUTH, United Kingdom
26 Bristol Street, Belfast.

Sanderson, Harry - Private
466024 Canadian Infantry (Saskatchewan Regiment) "C" Company 5th Battalion
Age 33 Died in War on 27 September 1916
VIMY MEMORIAL, France
Son of the late William and Mary Jane Sanderson, of 27, Kimona Street, Belfast, Ireland.
A farmer and a Presbyterian, he was born in England.

Sanderson, James A. M. - Lance Corporal
17/219 Royal Irish Rifles 15th Battalion *Age 23 Died in War on 23 November 1917*
ROCQUIGNY-EQUANCOURT ROAD BRITISH CEMETERY, MANANCOURT, France
Son of Samuel Sanderson, of 4, Chichester Terrace, Antrim Road, Belfast.

Sanderson, William - Rifleman
710 Royal Irish Rifles 10th Battalion *Killed in Action on 1 July 1916*
THIEPVAL MEMORIAL, France
Born and enlisted in Belfast.

Sands, Henry - Rifleman
386 Royal Irish Rifles 10th Battalion *Died of Wounds on 14 August 1917*
BRANDHOEK NEW MILITARY CEMETERY, Belgium
Born and enlisted in Belfast.

Sands, Hugh - Stoker First Class
SS/109990 Royal Navy HMS "Aboukir" *Age 24 Killed in Action with submarine in North Sea on 22 September 1914*
CHATHAM NAVAL MEMORIAL, United Kingdom
Son of the late John and Mary Sands. Native of Belfast.

Sands, Peter - Lance Corporal
8225 Royal Irish Rifles 1st Battalion *Age 27 Died in War on 15 September 1915*
CABARET-ROUGE BRITISH CEMETERY, SOUCHEZ, France
Husband of Elizabeth Sands, of 74, Abyssinia Street, Belfast. A soldier since 1906 he was arrested in Belfast after being absent from his battalion for four months having failed to return from home leave.
After his arrest he was sent back to France and tried by Court Martial on the grounds that he "when on active service deserted His Majesty's service". The verdict was guilty and Peter Sands was shot by firing squad.

Sands, William - Lance Corporal
5803 Royal Irish Rifles 7th Battalion *Died in War on 16 September 1916*
THIEPVAL MEMORIAL, France
Born and enlisted in Belfast.

Sansome, William - Private
L/6597 Royal; Sussex Regiment 2nd Battalion *Died in War on 27 September 1914*
VENDRESSE BRITISH CEMETERY, France
Husband of Bridget Todd (formerly Sansome), 5 Burke Street, Belfast.

Sargaison, William Henry - Second Lieutenant
Royal Dublin Fusiliers 7th Battalion *Age 22 Died in War on 6 December 1915*
DOIRAN MEMORIAL, Greece
Son of Walter and Elizabeth Sargaison, of 8, Clara Park, Neill's Hill, Belfast.

Saulters, Samuel - Rifleman
5779 Royal Irish Rifles 2nd Battalion *Age 45 Died of Wounds on 27 November 1915*
SOUTHEND-ON-SEA (SUTTON ROAD) CEMETERY, United Kingdom
Son of Mrs. Isabella Saulters; husband of Elizabeth Saulters, of 26, Weir Street, Belfast.

Saulters, William - Private
10639 Royal Inniskilling Fusiliers 2nd Battalion *Killed in Action on 31 October 1914*
PLOEGSTEERT MEMORIAL, Belgium
Born in Belfast.

Saunders, John Albert - Sergeant
6065 Royal Irish Rifles 2nd Battalion *Age 21 Killed in Action on 30 September 1918*
DADIZEELE NEW BRITISH CEMETERY, Belgium
Son of Mr. J. Saunders, of 127, Oldpark Road, Belfast.

Savage, Alfred - Rifleman
5507 Royal Irish Rifles 2nd Battalion *Died of Wounds on 26 March 1918*
POZIERES MEMORIAL, France
Born in Belfast.

Savage, Edgar - Rifleman
15931 Royal Irish Rifles 14th Battalion *Killed in Action on 1 July 1916*
THIEPVAL MEMORIAL, France
Son of Mrs J Savage, Ardoyne Fire Station Belfast.

Savage, Francis - Rifleman
10858 Royal Irish Rifles 6th Battalion *Died in War on 4 April 1918*
RAMLEH WAR CEMETERY, Israel
Born and enlisted in Belfast.

Savage, Frank - Rifleman
13538 Royal Irish Rifles 10th Battalion *Age 22 Died of Wounds 15 February 1916*
FORCEVILLE COMMUNAL CEMETERY AND EXTENSION, France
Son of Minnie and the late Frank Savage, of Mountpottinger, Belfast.

Savage, John Ardkeen - Captain
Northamtonshire Regiment 1st Battalion *Age 31 Died in War on 17 September 1914*
LA FERTE-SOUS-JOUARRE MEMORIAL, France
A veteran of the Boer War and resident of Belfast. Son of Rev and Mrs Ethel Savage of Falmouth, Cornwall.

Savage, John Brown - Private
3162 Royal Inniskilling Fusiliers 1st Battalion *Died in War on 21 August 1915*
HELLES MEMORIAL, Turkey
A pre-war Regular soldier he was the brother of Mrs. Edith McIlroy, of 32, Wimbledon Street, Belfast. He landed with his battalion at Cape Helles in the Dardanelles and was killed during an attack on Scimitar Hill, an operation which destoyed three quarters of the soldiers in his unit. His sister Edith wrote, for the *Belfast Evening Telegraph* - 'A brother true, a soldier brave. He now sleeps in a heroes grave.' The husband of his sister, Sergeant David McIlroy, was also killed with the same Battalion.

Savage, Joseph - Rifleman
12417 Royal Irish Rifles "B" Company 8th Battalion *Age 42 Died in War on 2 July 1916*
THIEPVAL MEMORIAL, France
Son of James Savage, of 22, High Street, Holywood and the late Eliza Savage; husband of Annie Savage, of 42, Epworth Street, Belfast.

Savage, Joseph Samuel - Rifleman
13534 Royal Irish Rifles 8th Battalion *Age 21 Died in War on 8 June 1917*
BAILLEUL COMMUNAL CEMETERY EXTENSION (NORD), France
Son of Robert and Eliza Savage, of 32, Parker Street, Belfast.

Savage, Matthew - Lance Corporal
27574 Royal Inniskilling Fusiliers 7th Battalion formerly 3503, Leinster Regiment
Killed in Action on 9 September 1916
LA NEUVILLE BRITISH CEMETERY, CORBIE, France
Born in Belfast.

Savage, Patrick - Private
3256 Leinster Regiment 2nd Battalion *Died in War on 29 September 1918*
HOOGE CRATER CEMETERY, Belgium
Born and enlisted in Belfast.

Savage, Robert - Rifleman
1340 Royal Irish Rifles 9th Battalion *Age 18 Killed in Action on 1 July 1916*
THIEPVAL MEMORIAL, France
Son of Robert and Elizabeth Jane Savage, of 32, Parker Street, Belfast.

Savage, Thomas - Driver
77174 Royal Horse Artillery and Royal Field Artillery *Died in War on 25 May 1915*
YPRES (MENIN GATE) MEMORIAL, Belgium
Born in Belfast, enlisted in Glasgow.

Scollan, John - Private
20545 Royal Scots Fusiliers 1st Battalion *Died in War on 25 October 1916*
EUSTON ROAD CEMETERY, COLINCAMPS, France
Born in Belfast, enlisted in Paisley, Scotland.

Scott, Alexander - Private
16994 Royal Inniskilling Fusiliers 11th Battalion *Age 42 Killed in Action on 16 August 1917*
TYNE COT MEMORIAL, Belgium
Son of Alexander and Margaret Redmond, of 4, Ballymoney Street, Belfast.

Scott, Alexander - Rifleman
13572 Royal Irish Rifles 8th Battalion *Died of Wounds on 7 July 1916*
ST. SEVER CEMETERY, ROUEN, France
Son of Mrs. Isabella Scott, of Belfast.

Scott, Alexander - Rifleman
7840 Royal Irish Rifles 2nd Battalion *Age 27 Killed in Action on 6 September 1918*
WULVERGHEM-LINDENHOEK ROAD MILITARY CEMETERY, Belgium
Son of Alexander Scott; husband of Catherine Scott, of 20, Dundee Street, Belfast.

Scott, Edward Allan - Lance Corporal
320 Seaforth Highlanders (Ross-shire Buffs, the Duke of Albany's) 1st Battalion
Died in War on 4 November 1914
LE TOURET MEMORIAL, France
Born in Belfast, enlisted in Poona, India.

Scott, Frederick - Private
20098 Northumberland Fusiliers 12th Battalion *Age 21 Died in War on 30 September 1915*
LAPUGNOY MILITARY CEMETERY, France
Son of Robert and Abigail Scott, of 45, Spencer Street, Belfast.

Scott, George Alexander - Rifleman
1462 Royal Irish Rifles 12th Battalion *Died in War on 11 April 1918*
TYNE COT MEMORIAL, Belgium
164 Argyle Street, Belfast.

Scott, Hugh Cecil - Rifleman
10186 Royal Irish Rifles 2nd Battalion *Age 22 Died of pneumonia on 22 August 1918*
VEVEY (ST. MARTIN'S) CEMETERY, Switzerland
Son of Hugh and Isabella Scott, of 10, Larkstone Street, Lisburn Road, Belfast.

Scott, Hugh Gault - Private
492 Canadian Infantry (Manitoba Regiment) 8th Battalion *Age 29 Died in War on 14 June 1916*
YPRES (MENIN GATE) MEMORIAL, Belgium
Son of Sarah Scott, of 2, Gainsborough Drive, Belfast, Ireland, and the late Samuel Scott.

Journey of Remembering

Scott, James - Company Sergeant Major
14/15892 Royal Irish Rifles 14th Battalion *Age 35 Killed in Action on 22 January 1917*
LA PLUS DOUVE FARM CEMETERY, Belgium
Husband of Jane Duffy (formerly Scott), of Finaghy Halt, Balmoral, Belfast.

Scott, James - Engine Room Artificer
M/4198 Royal Navy HMS "Recruit" *Died in War on 1 May 1915*
CHATHAM NAVAL MEMORIAL, United Kingdom
Brookside, Oldpark Road, Belfast.

Scott, James - Private
203129 Royal Scots Fusiliers 1/4th Battalion *Died in War on 23 April 1917*
ALEXANDRIA (HADRA) WAR MEMORIAL CEMETERY, Egypt
Born in Belfast. Enlisted in Kilmarnock Scotland.

Scott, James - Private
PLY/16410 Royal Marine Light Infantry Plymouth Battalion Royal Naval Division
Age 19 Naval, died ashore on 4 March 1915
HELLES MEMORIAL, Turkey
Son of William and Margaret Scott, of 42, Cheviot Avenue, Belfast.

Scott, James - Rifleman
4353 Royal Irish Rifles 2nd Battalion *Age 46 Killed in Action on 20 September 1914*
LA FERTE-SOUS-JOUARRE MEMORIAL, France
Son of Margaret Scott, of 25, Wilton Street, Belfast, and the late William John Scott.
A Presbyterian, he had previous military service.

Scott, James - Rifleman
78 Royal Irsh Rifles 15th Battalion *Killed in Action on 6 August 1917*
WIELTJE FARM CEMETERY, Belgium
Born and enlisted in Belfast.

Scott, John - Private
21418 Canadian Infantry (Manitoba Regiment) 8th Battalion *Age 22 Died in War on 19 May 1915*
VIMY MEMORIAL, France
Son of John and Alexina Scott, previously of Stranmillis Gardens, Belfast, Ireland,
later of Suite 19, Thelmo Mansions, Winnipeg, Canada.

Scott, John - Rifleman
456 Royal Irish Rifles posted to 1/8th London Regiment *Died in War on 6 September 1918*
VIS-EN-ARTOIS MEMORIAL, France
Born in Belfast, enlisted Dunfermline, Scotland.

Scott, John - Rifleman
8857 Royal Irish Rifles 2nd Battalion *Age 26 Killed in Action on 20 September 1914*
LA FERTE-SOUS-JOUARRE MEMORIAL, France
Son of William Scott, of 258, Woodstock Road, Belfast.

Scott, John C - Corporal
57522 Royal Engineers 122nd Field Company *Age 29 Died of Wounds on 12 May 1916*
GEZAINCOURT COMMUNAL CEMETERY EXTENSION, France
Son of Matilda and the late John Scott, of 37, Bedeque Street, Belfast.

BELFAST BOOK OF HONOUR

Scott, John N - Private
Royal Irish Rifles transferred to Machine Gun Corps *Age 21 Died in War on 10 August 1917*
YPRES (MENIN GATE) MEMORIAL, Belgium
28, Sherbrook Street, Belfast.

Scott, Kennedy - Rifleman
907 Royal Irish Rifles 15th Battalion *Died in War on 6 April 1918*
ROYE NEW BRITISH CEMETERY, France
Husband of Annie Scott, 36 Blythe Street, Belfast.

Scott, Matthew - Rifleman
8400 Royal Irish Rifles 2nd Battalion *Age 21 Killed in Action on 26 October 1914*
LE TOURET MEMORIAL, France
Son of Matthew and Mary Scott; husband of Jane McCrory (formerly Scott), of 21, Gertrude Street, Belfast.

Scott, Ninian Robinson - Private
996 Australian Infantry 20th Battalion *Age 39 Died in War on 7 April 1918*
VILLERS-BRETONNEUX MEMORIAL, France
Son of John Alexander Scott and Margaret Robinson Scott of 48, Eglantine Avenue, Belfast, Ireland.

Scott, Richard - Private
10089 Royal Inniskilling Fusiliers 2nd Battalion *Died in War on 1 November 1914*
PLOEGSTEERT MEMORIAL, Belgium
Son of James and Margaret Scott 133, Frenchpark Street, Belfast.

Scott, Robert - Lance Corporal
8896 Royal Irish Rifles 1st Battalion *Killed in Action on 10 December 1914*
RUE-DU-BOIS MILITARY CEMETERY, FLEURBAIX, France
3, Charlotte Street, Belfast.

Scott, Robert - Private
8493 Royal Inniskilling Fusiliers 2nd Battalion *Killed in Action on 26 August 1914*
LA FERTE-SOUS-JOUARRE MEMORIAL, France
15 Oregon Street, Belfast.

Scott, Robert - Rifleman
7126 Royal Irish Rifles 2nd Battalion *Killed In Action on 7 July 1916*
THIEPVAL MEMORIAL, France
Born and enlisted in Belfast.

Scott, Robert J - Rifleman
1151 Royal Irish Rifles 10th Battalion *Age 22 Died in War on 26 June 1917*
BELFAST (DUNDONALD) CEMETERY, United Kingdom
Son of Robert and Mary Jane Scott, of 58, Fraser Street, Belfast.

Scott, Robert James - Rifleman
6101 Royal Irish Rifles 2nd Battalion *Age 32 Killed in Action on 27 October 1914*
PONT-DU HEM MILITARY CEMETERY, LA GORGUE, France
Husband of Alexandrina Scott, of 71, Island Street, Belfast.

Scott, Samuel A - Sergeant
19542 Machine Gun Corps 107th Brigade *Died of Wounds on 2 July 1916*
FORCEVILLE COMMUNAL CEMETERY AND EXTENSION, France
62, Orkney Street, Belfast.

Scott, Stewart - Rifleman
13473 Royal Irish Fusiliers 1st Battalion *Died of Wounds on 18 April 1918*
MONT HUAN MILITARY CEMETERY, LE TREPORT, *France*
65, Dundee Street, Belfast.

Scott, Thomas - Private
G/52344 Middlesex Regiment 13th Battalion *Age 40 Died in War on 27 August 1917*
TYNE COT MEMORIAL, *Belgium*
Son of Thomas and Ellen Scott, of 54, Lawnbrook Avenue, Belfast; husband of Margaretta Scott, of 91, Lawnbrook Avenue, Belfast.

Scott, Walter - Rifleman
13569 Royal Irish Rifles 8th Battalion *Age 29 Died of Wounds on 1 July 1916*
BOUZINCOURT COMMUNAL CEMETERY EXTENSION, *France*
Son of Ellen Scott (née East), of 10, Calvin Street, Mountpottinger, Belfast, and the late William John Scott.

Scott, Walter Alexander - Second Lieutenant
Royal Irish Rifles 10th Battalion *Age 27 Died in War on 22 November 1917*
CAMBRAI MEMORIAL, LOUVERVAL, *France*
Son of Samuel Scott, of 16, Dunluce Avenue, Belfast; husband of Minnie Scott, of 14, Botanic Avenue, Belfast.

Scott, William - Private
3095 Royal Inniskilling Fusiliers 1st Battalion *Killed in Action on 1 July 1916*
Y RAVINE CEMETERY, BEAUMONT-HAMEL, *France*
21, Huss Street, Belfast.

Scott, William - Rifleman
12418 Royal Irish Rifles 15th Battalion *Died in War on 21 March 1918*
GRAND-SERAUCOURT BRITISH CEMETERY, *France*
Born and enlisted in Belfast.

Scott, William - Sapper
97996 Royal Engineers 281st Army Troops Company *Died in War on 7 November 1918*
VIS-EN-ARTOIS MEMORIAL, *France*
Coniston Street, Belfast.

Scott, William John - Rifleman
2293 Royal Irish Rifles 12th Battalion *Age 19 Died in War on 11 April 1918*
TYNE COT MEMORIAL, *Belgium*
Son of James and Margaret Scott, of 98, Crimea Street, Belfast.

Scott, William John - Rifleman
7510 Royal Irish Rifles 7th Battalion *Died in War on 16 August 1917*
TYNE COT MEMORIAL, *Belgium*
Born and enlisted in Belfast.

Scott, William John - Sergeant
15937 Royal Irish Rifles "A" Company 14th Battalion *Age 27 Killed in Action on 1 July 1916*
THIEPVAL MEMORIAL, *France*
Husband of Charlotte Scott, of 66, Sunnyside Street, Belfast.

Scullion, John - Rifleman
20876 Royal Irish Rifles 2nd Battalion *Killed In Action on 1 October 1918*
TYNE COT MEMORIAL, Belgium
Born in Belfast, son of the late Patrick Scullion.

Scullion, Richard - Rifleman
11336 Royal Irish Rifles 2nd Battalion *Age 19 Died in War on 16 October 1918*
DUHALLOW A.D.S. CEMETERY, Belgium
Son of Arthur and Mary Scullion, of 9, Wolfhill Lane, Ligoneil, Belfast.

Seaver, Charles - Captain
Royal Inniskilling Fusiliers 8th Battalion *Age 22 Died in War on 3 October 1916*
ST. SEVER CEMETERY, ROUEN, France
Son of Henry Seaver, of Lisroyan, Malone, Belfast. Educated at Wellington College and the University of Cambridge.

Seawright, James - Rifleman
8738 Royal Irish Rifles 1st Battalion *Age 25 Killed in Action on 3 April 1915*
PLOEGSTEERT MEMORIAL, Belgium
Son of Mr. and Mrs. James Seawright, of Belfast.

Seeds, Thomas - Private
3507 Royal Inniskilling Fusiliers "B" Company 1st Battalion *Age 17 Died in War on 21 August 1915*
HELLES MEMORIAL, Turkey
Nephew of Mrs. Hamilton, of 13, Crosby Street, Belfast.

Seeley, William - Rifleman
10151 Royal Irish Rifles 2nd Battalion *Killed in Action on 24 March 1918*
POZIERES MEMORIAL, France
Enlisted Glasgow, resident of Belfast.

Sefton, John - Private
8804 Royal Inniskilling Fusiliers 1st Battalion *Died in War on 27 May 1915*
ALEXANDRIA (CHATBY) MILITARY AND WAR MEMORIAL CEMETERY, Egypt
39, Paris Street, Belfast.

Sefton, Thomas H - Stoker First Class
SS/103314 Royal Navy HMS "Hawke" *Killed in Action on 15 October 1914*
CHATHAM NAVAL MEMORIAL, United Kingdom
20, Kendal Street, Belfast.

Selby, Joseph - Private
15855 Princess Victoria's (Royal Irish Fusiliers) 9th Battalion *Killed in Action on 1 July 1916*
THIEPVAL MEMORIAL, France
Born and enlisted in Belfast.

Selby, William George - Private
L/8311 Royal Sussex Regiment 2nd Battalion *Killed in Action on 30 October 1914*
YPRES (MENIN GATE) MEMORIAL, Belgium
Son of the late Henry and Susan Selby, of Brook Street, Cuckfield, Sussex; husband of Sarah Selby, of 45, Sixth Street, Shankill Road, Belfast.

Semple, John - Rifleman
6013 Royal Irish Rifles "A" Company 1st Battalion *Age 36 Killed in Action on 29 October 1917*
BERKS CEMETERY EXTENSION, Belgium
Son of William John and Ellen Semple, of 7, Wolfhill Lane, Ligoneil, Belfast.

Seymour, Samuel H - Private
19466 Machine Gun Corps (Infantry) 17th Company *Age 24 Died in War on 19 August 1917*
YPRES (MENIN GATE) MEMORIAL, Belgium
Son of John H. Seymour, of 3, Blackwood Street, Belfast. Formerly 13582 Royal Irish Rifles.

Seymour, William Matthew - Second Lieutenant
Royal Irish Fusiliers 10th Battalion *Killed in Action on 16 August 1917*
TYNE COT MEMORIAL, Belgium
Son of William and Lydia Seymour, of 56, Glen Road, Belfast.

Shane, Samuel - Private
1457 Royal Irish Rifles 9th Battalion *Died of Wounds on 2 July 1916*
SERRE ROAD CEMETERY No.2, France
Only son of Ellen and the late George Shane of 94, Cambrai Street, Belfast.

Shanks, Charles - Lance Corporal
8492 Irish Guards 2nd Battalion *Died in War on 5 July 1916*
FERME-OLIVER CEMETERY, France
Born Ballymacarrett, Belfast. Enlisted Greypoint, County Down.

Shanks, James - Lance Corporal
10610 Royal Irish Rifles 6th Battalion *Died in War on 11 August 1915*
HELLES MEMORIAL, Turkey
Born and enlisted in Belfast.

Shanks, James - Stoker
7131S Royal Naval Reserve HMS "Black Prince" *Age 35 Killed in Action at Battle of Jutland on 31 May 1916*
PORTSMOUTH NAVAL MEMORIAL, United Kingdom
Son of Mr. and Mrs. Shanks, of Belfast; husband of Annie Shanks (née Pratt), of 234, North Woodside Road, Glasgow.

Shanks, John - Rifleman
7775 Royal Irish Rifles 2nd Battalion *Age 28 Killed in Action on 26 October 1914*
LE TOURET MEMORIAL, France
Brother of Mrs. A. Graham, of 11, Hills Avenue, Sydenham, Belfast.

Shanks, John James - Rifleman
4640 Royal Irish Rifles "C" Company 14th Battalion *Age 19 Killed in Action on 1 July 1916*
THIEPVAL MEMORIAL, France
Son of John and Elizabeth Shanks, of 36, Hillview Street, Belfast.

Shanks, William - Lance Corporal
15997 Mercantile Marine formerly Royal Inniskilling Fusiliers 2nd Battalion *Killed In Action on 21 March 1918*
TOWER HILL MEMORIAL, United Kingdom
Born in Belfast, enlisted in Castledawson.

Shanks, William Taylor - Rifleman
253 Royal Irish Rifles 8th Battalion *Age 56 Died in War on 2 July 1916*
THIEPVAL MEMORIAL, France
Husband of Mrs. E. Maynes (formerly Shanks), of 66, Trillick Street, Belfast.

Shannon, Alexander - Sergeant
19996 3rd Dragoon Guards (Prince of Wales' Own) *Died in War on 5 April 1918*
ABBEVILLE COMMUNAL CEMETERY EXTENSION, France
Born in Belfast, enlisted in Greenock, Scotland.

Shannon, Edward - Private
24968 Royal Inniskilling Fusiliers 1st Battalion *Age 22 Died in War on 9 August 1916*
POTIJZE CHATEAU WOOD CEMETERY, Belgium
Son of Joseph and Elizabeth Shannon, of 42, Hillview Street, Belfast.

Shannon, George Moorhead - Private
41428 Royal Irish Fusiliers "C" Company 9th (North Irish Horse) Battalion *Age 25 Killed in Action on 25 October 1918*
HARLEBEKE NEW BRITISH CEMETERY, Belgium
Son of Francis and Rebecca Shannon, of Belfast.

Shannon, James - Sergeant
2518 Leinster Regiment 7th Battalion *Age 28 Killed in Action on 7 June 1917*
LA LAITERIE MILITARY CEMETERY, Belgium
Son of John and Margaret Shannon, of 142, Oldpark Road, Belfast.

Shannon, John - Private
147866 Canadian Infantry (Saskatchewan Regiment) 5th Battalion *Died in War on 22 July 1916*
YPRES (MENIN GATE) MEMORIAL, Belgium
Son of Richard and Eleanor Shannon, of "Greystones" Antrim Road, Belfast, Ireland.
A grocer and a Prebyterian, he had previous military service.

Shannon, John - Private
297604 Canadian Forestry Corps 30th Company *Age 35 Died in War on 14 April 1918*
ALENCON (ST. LEONARD) CEMETERY, France
Son of Robert J. and Martha Shannon, of 43, Kansas Avenue, Belfast.
A Presbyterian he had previous military service and worked as a lumberjack.

Shannon, John Francis - Private
3327 Irish Guards 1st Battalion *Age 29 Killed in Action on 15 September 1917*
CANADA FARM CEMETERY, Belgium
Son of Thomas Shannon, of 21, Calvin Street, Belfast. Native of Bawnboy, County Cavan.

Shannon, Joseph James - Rifleman
13583 Royal Irish Rifles 9th Battalion *Killed in Action on 1 July 1916*
THIEPVAL MEMORIAL, France
Son of Joseph and Eliza Jane Shannon. Also served in the South African Campaign, and the Boxer Rebellion, with the Royal Garrison Artillery.

Shannon, Patrick M - Sergeant
2490 Connaught Rangers 6th Battalion *Age 22 Died of Wounds on 6 June 1916*
LE TREPORT MILITARY CEMETERY, France
Son of Dominick and Margaret Shannon, of 17, Gotha Street, Belfast, Ireland.
Born in County Louth, he was solicitor's clerk.

Shannon, Robert - Rifleman
18745 Royal Irish Rifles "A" Company 14th Battalion *Age 22 Killed in Action on 1 July 1916*
THIEPVAL MEMORIAL, France
Son of Alexander and Sarah Shannon, of 194, Cliftonville Road, Belfast.

Journey of Remembering

Shannon, Thomas - Private
PLY/17502 Royal Marine Light Infantry *Age 24 Died as a result of war on 8 August 1921*
BROOKWOOD (UNITED KINGDOM 1914-1918) MEMORIAL
Native of Belfast.

Sharkey, Edward - Corporal
2945 Leinster Regiment 7th Battalion *Age 28 Died of Wounds on 4 September 1916*
DERNANCOURT COMMUNAL CEMETERY EXTENSION, France
Husband of Amelia Sharkey, of 8, Colligan Street, Belfast.

Sharkey, Frank - Private
9110 Manchester Regiment 1st Battalion *Died in War on 25 March 1917*
BASRA MEMORIAL, Iraq
Born in St Patrick's Belfast, enlisted in Fleetwood, Lancashire.

Sharkey, John - Private
2350 Australian Infantry A.I.F. 1st Battalion *Age 32 Died of Wounds received on 5 May on 8 May 1917*
VILLERS-BRETONNEUX MEMORIAL, France
(Served as John DEVLIN). Son of James and Jane Sharkey. Born in Belfast, Ireland.

Sharkey, John - Private
2522 Leinster Regiment 7th Battalion *Died in War on 2 September 1916*
THIEPVAL MEMORIAL
31 Lucknow Street, Belfast.

Sharland, Herbert - Private
7007 Regiment Corp Royal Fusiliers (City of London Regiment) 3rd Battalion *Died in War on 24 May 1915*
YPRES (MENIN GATE) MEMORIAL, Belgium
Born in Belfast, enlisted in Hounslow, London.

Sharpe, Charles E - Sapper
871455 Canadian Engineers "C" Company 2nd Battalion *Age 22 Died of accidental injuries on 8 October 1918*
QUEANT COMMUNAL CEMETERY BRITISH EXTENSION, France
Eldest son of Mr. and Mrs. R. Sharpe, of 1322, Arlington Street, Winnipeg. Native of Belfast, Ireland.
An Anglican, he was a single man and worked as a clerk.

Sharpe, Peter - Rifleman
9236 Royal Irish Rifles "B" Company 1st Battalion *Age 26 Killed in Action on 29 January 1915*
ROYAL IRISH RIFLES GRAVEYARD, LAVENTIE, France
Killed by the same bullet which badly wounded another soldier. Son of Mrs. Sharpe, of Sheriff Street, Belfast.

Shaw, Alexander - Rifleman
952 Royal Irish Rifles 9th Battalion transferred to 376251 760th Company Labour Corps
Age 42 Killed in Action on 27 April 1918
ESQUELBECQ MILITARY CEMETERY, France
Son of Robert Shaw, of Belfast.

Shaw, Andrew - Private
7231 Gordon Highlanders 1st Battalion *Age 36 Died in War on 13 October 1914*
LE TOURET MEMORIAL, France
Son of Alexander and Sarah Jane Shaw; husband of Mary Shaw, of 49, Coolfin Street, Belfast.

Shaw, George - Gunner
51511 Royal Horse Artillery and Royal Field Artillery *Died in War on 22 July 1916*
DANTZIG ALLEY BRITISH CEMETERY MAMETZ, France
Born and enlisted in Belfast.

Shaw, James McCandless - Private
21647 The Loyal North Lancashire Regiment 6th Battalion *Age 20 Died in War on 10 June 1916*
AMARA WAR CEMETERY, Iraq
Son of William James and Agnes Shaw, of 20, Laburnum Street, Belfast.

Shaw, John Westleigh - Gunner
448 Royal Garrison Artillery 125th Heavy Battery *Age 22 Died in War on 8 November 1916*
THISTLE DUMP CEMETERY, HIGH WOOD, LONGUEVAL, France
Son of Mrs Elizabeth Wylie Shaw, of 350, Shankill Road, Belfast.

Shaw, Robert Hayes - Rifleman
4903 Royal Irish Rifles 10th Battalion *Died in War on 22 November 1917*
CAMBRAI MEMORIAL, LOUVERVAL, France
91, Egmont Street, Belfast.

Shaw, Robert Norton - Corporal
5548 Princess Victoria's (Royal Irish Fusiliers) 7/8th Battalion *Died in War on 15 August 1917*
YPRES (MENIN GATE) MEMORIAL, Belgium
Born and enlisted in Newry, resident of Belfast.

Shaw, Thomas Moran - Rifleman
4035 Royal Irish Rifles "D" Company 9th Battalion *Age 35 Killed in Action on 1 July 1916*
THIEPVAL MEMORIAL, France
Son of John and Elizabeth Shaw, of 7, Linwood Street, Belfast.

Shaw, William - Rifleman
1382 Royal Irish Rifles 1st Battalion *Died in War on 9 May 1915*
PLOEGSTEERT MEMORIAL, Belgium
103, St Leonard's Street, Belfast.

Shaw, William - Sergeant
11335 King's Own (Yorkshire Light Infantry) 6th Battalion *Died in War on 5 August 1915*
SANCTUARY WOOD CEMETERY, Belgium
Born in Belfast, enlisted Dewsbury, England.

Shaw, William J - Private
10272 Irish Guards 1st Battalion *Age 24 Died in War on 9 October 1917*
RUISSEAU FARM CEMETERY, Belgium
Son of James B. Shaw; husband of Agnes McRoberts (formerly Shaw), of 17, Eastland Street, Belfast.

Shaw, William Lindsay - Major
Royal Engineers 228th Field Company *Age 32 Died in War on 16 April 1918*
DUHALLOW A.D.S. CEMETERY, Belgium
Son of Martin McKnight Shaw and Jane Elizabeth Shaw, of 13, Chlorine Gardens, Belfast; husband of Beatrice Margaret Shaw, of 32, Milton Park, Highgate, London. Awarded the Military Cross.

Sheals, Terence Edward - Private
20205 East Lancashire Regiment 8th Battalion *Died in War on 3 September 1916*
THIEPVAL MEMORIAL, France
Born in Belfast, enlisted in London, resident in Liverpool.

Shearer, John - Private
16399 Royal Scots 2nd Battalion *Died in War on 17 June 1915*
YPRES (MENIN GATE) MEMORIAL, *Belgium*
Born in Belfast, enlisted Glasgow.

Shearer, William - Sergeant
6055 Royal Irish Rifles 2nd Battalion *Died in War on 25 September 1915*
YPRES (MENIN GATE) MEMORIAL, *Belgium*
His wife, Sarah, lived at 29 Seventh Street. Belfast. He had been an instructor with the old UVF.
On the 23 September he had written to his wife, anticipating his own death.
Awarded the Distinguished Conduct Medal for his "absolute fearlessness in dangerous situations".

Sheehy, Henry - Private
7417 Leinster Regiment 2nd Battalion *Died in War on 20 October 1914*
CANADIAN CEMETERY No.2, NEUVILLE-ST. VAAST, *France*
Husband of F. Sheehy (now Jones), of 175, Upper Meadow Street, Belfast, Ireland.

Sheen, William - Lance Corporal
21647 Royal Dublin Fusiliers 1st Battalion *Killed In Action on 18 August 1917*
TYNE COT MEMORIAL, *Belgium*
Born in Belfast.

Sheridan, John - Private
27614 Royal Inniskilling Fusiliers 1st Battalion *Killed in Action on 22 March 1918*
POZIERES MEMORIAL, *France*
Born and enlisted in Belfast. Formerly 2572, 7th Leinster Regiment

Sheridan, Joseph - Private
23132 Royal Inniskilling Fusiliers 7th Battalion *Died in War on 28 May 1916*
PHILOSOPHE BRITISH CEMETERY, MAZINGARBE, *France*
193, Canmore Street, Belfast.

Sherlin, John - Private
8238 Royal Inniskilling Fusiliers 2nd Battalion *Died in War on 16 May 1915*
Born in Belfast, enlisted in Derry.

Sherlock, George - Private
7319 Royal Inniskilling Fusiliers 2nd Battalion *Died in War on 21 September 1915*
ST. BRIEUC (ST. MICHEL) CEMETERY, *France*
Born and enlisted in Belfast, lived in Howard Street.

Sherman, Nelson - Private
8495 Royal Inniskilling Fusiliers "A" Company 2nd Battalion *Age 26 Died in War on 21 October 1914*
PLOEGSTEERT MEMORIAL, *Belgium*
Son of Mrs. Margaret Sherman, of 6, Madison Avenue East, Strandtown. Belfast.

Sherman, William - Corporal
51723 Royal Army Medical Corps 16th General Hospital *Age 35 Died of accidental injuries on 15 March 1916*
LE TREPORT MILITARY CEMETERY, *France*
Son of Sarah and the late Thomas Sherman, of Belfast. Served in the South African Campaign, 1901-2.

Sherriff, Edwin Percival - Private
17914 Princess Victoria's (Royal Irish Fusiliers) 9th Battalion *Killed in Action on 1 July 1916*
THIEPVAL MEMORIAL, *France*
Born in Belfast, enlisted in Cootehill, County Cavan.

Sherrington, Robert Joseph - Private
2717 Royal Inniskilling Fusiliers 2nd Battalion *Age 22 Died in War on 11 September 1916*
BETHUNE TOWN CEMETERY, *France*
Husband of Elizabeth Sherrington, of 52, Cullingtree Road, Belfast.

Shevlin, John - Private
8238 Royal Inniskilling Fusiliers 2nd Battalion *Age 29 Died in War on 16 May 1915*
LE TOURET MEMORIAL, *France*
Son of Edward and Elizabeth Shevlin of Belfast.

Shields, Arthur - Private
26052 Royal Inniskilling Fusiliers 7th Battalion *Age 17 Died in War on 25 September 1916*
KEMMEL CHATEAU MILITARY CEMETERY, *Belgium*
Son of Arthur and Jane Shields, of 38, Dunvegan Street, Belfast.

Shields, Daniel - Gunner
31775 Royal Field Artillery 47th Ammunition Supply Column *Age 22 Died of Wounds on 2 June 1917*
DUISANS BRITISH CEMETERY, ETRUN, *France*
Son of John and Janet Shields, of 96, Dunraven Avenue, Belfast. Native of Greenock.

Shields, James - Rifleman
4424 Royal Irish Rifles 7th Battalion *Died in War on 23 February 1916*
BETHUNE TOWN CEMETERY, *France*
Born in Port Glasgow, enlisted Preston, Lancashire, resident Belfast.

Shields, James - Rifleman
Royal Irish Rifles *Died in War on 4 August 1915*
Born Belfast. Son of James and Mary (née Hamill) and husband of Ellen (née Morgan) of Ton Street. Two children, Elizabeth and James.

Shields, John - Lance Corporal
10609 Royal Irish Rifles 9th Battalion *Age 28 Killed in Action on 1 July 1916*
THIEPVAL MEMORIAL, *France*
Son of John and Elizabeth Shields, of 56, Pitt Street, Belfast.

Shields, John - Rifleman
9033 Royal Irish Rifles 1st Battalion *Age 26 Killed in Action on 12 March 1915*
LE TOURET MEMORIAL, *France*
Son of James and Margaret Shields, of 5, Barbour Street, Greencastle, Belfast.

Shields, Patrick - Rifleman
9672 Royal Irish Rifles 1st Battalion *Killed in Action on 16 August 1917*
TYNE COT MEMORIAL, *Belgium*
Born and enlisted in Belfast. Awarded the Military Medal.

Shields, R - Private
33242 Royal Irish Fusiliers 1st Battalion *Age 23 Died in War on 9 November 1919*
KUT WAR CEMETERY, *Iraq*
Son of Mrs. C. J. Shields, of 4, Cliftonville Street, Belfast, and the late Robert Shields.

Shields, Samuel - Sergeant
13588 Royal Irish Rifles 8th Battalion *Age 23 Died in War on 2 July 1916*
THIEPVAL MEMORIAL, France
Son of Samuel and Sarah Shields, of 33, Upper Frank Street, Belfast. Awarded the Military Medal.

Shields, Thomas Orr Simpson - Second Corporal
23171 Royal Engineers 49th Air Line Section *Age 25 Died of influenza on 8 December 1918*
DAR ES SALAAM (UPANGA ROAD) CEMETERY, Tanzania
Son of Robert and Ellen Shields, of 32, North Boundary Street, Belfast. Born at Portstewart.

Shields, William - Lieutenant
Royal Flying Corps 45th Squadron and Manchester Regiment *Age 28 Killed in air combat on 5 September 1917*
VLAMERTINGHE NEW MILITARY CEMETERY, Belgium
Son of Samuel and Sarah Shields, of 33, Upper Frank Street, Belfast.

Shirlow, William - Rifleman
3995 Royal Irish Rifles 2nd Battalion *Age 37 Killed in Action on 27 October 1914*
LE TOURET MEMORIAL, France
Brother of Mrs. A. Magee, of 67, Grove Street, North Queen Street, Belfast.

Sholdis, James - Gunner
31159 Royal Horse Artillery and Royal Field Artillery *Died in War on 10 June 1916*
NORFOLK CEMETERY, BECORDEL-BECOURT, France
Born in Belfast, enlisted Dundalk.

Short, Andrew George - Corporal
M2/073628 Royal Army Service Corps *Died in War on 30 September 1917*
LOCRE HOSPICE CEMETERY, Belgium
Born in Belfast.

Short, Clement - Sapper
156986 Corps of Royal Engineers *Died on 26 August 1916*
LONGUENESSE (ST. OMER) SOUVENIR CEMETERY, France
Born in Belfast.

Short, John - Private
3977 Connaught Rangers 6th Battalion *Died in War on 23 November 1917*
BUCQUOY ROAD CEMETERY, FICHEUX, France
Born, enlisted and resident in Belfast.

Short, Joseph - Private
21638 King's Own(Royal Lancaster Regiment) 1st Battalion *Killed in Action on 12 October 1917*
TYNE COT MEMORIAL, Belgium
Born in Belfast.

Short, Robert - Lance Corporal
13485 Royal Irish Rifles 9th Battalion *Killed in Action on 1 July 1916*
THIEPVAL MEMORIAL, France
Husband of Ethel Short 54, Dundee Street, Belfast.

Shortt, Alexander - Private
4069 Connaught Rangers 6th Battalion *Age 19 Killed in Action on 29 April 1916*
VERMELLES BRITISH CEMETERY, France
Son of Alexander and Ellen Shortt, of 71, Elizabeth Street, Grosvenor Road, Belfast.
Native of Banbridge, County Down.

Sillars, Thomas - Lance Corporal
17/1301 Royal Irish Rifles 8th Battalion *Died in War on 2 July 1916*
GRANDCOURT ROAD CEMETERY, GRANDCOURT, France
Husband of Mrs. A. Sillars, of 3, Ballyclare Street, Belfast.

Sillery, Robert - Rifleman
13486 Royal Irish Rifles 15th Battalion *Killed in Action on 1 July 1916*
THIEPVAL MEMORIAL, France
Husband of Sarah Sillery, 11 Oregon Street, Belfast.

Silvey, William John - Rifleman
469 Royal Irish Rifles 8th Battalion *Died in War on 2 July 1916*
THIEPVAL MEMORIAL, France
Inverary Avenue, Belfast.

Simmons, Simpson - Lance Corporal
20608 Princess Victoria's (Royal Irish Fusiliers) 8th Battalion *Died in War on 6 September 1916*
THIEPVAL MEMORIAL, France
Enlisted in Glasgow, resident in Belfast.

Simms, A - Private
20983 Royal Inniskilling Fusiliers 2nd Battalion *Age 19 Died in War on 6 June 1916*
AUTHUILE MILITARY CEMETERY, France
Son of Daniel and Margaret Simms, of 508, Dumbarton Road, Glasgow. Born in Belfast.

Simms, John McKeen - Private
10437 Royal Inniskilling Fusiliers 2nd Battalion *Killed in Action on 26 August 1914*
ESNES COMMUNAL CEMETERY, France
69, Victoria Road, Belfast. A native of Carrickfergus, County Antrim.
Killed at the Battle of Le Cateau, a delaying Action at the beginning of the war.

Simms, Robert - Lance Sergeant
4209 Royal Irish Rifles 2nd Battalion *Died of Wounds on 30 August 1918*
BELFAST CITY CEMETERY, United Kingdom
Husband of Annie Simms, of 6, Annalee Street, Belfast.

Simms, Thomas - Rifleman
47448 Royal Irish Rifles 1st Battalion *Age 28 Died in War on 22 November 1917*
TYNE COT MEMORIAL, Belgium
Son of Henry Simms, of 29, Malvern Street, Belfast.

Simonton, Mason - Private
5634 Royal Fusiliers 20th Battalion *Age 21 Died in War on 20 July 1916*
SERRE ROAD CEMETERY No.2, France
Son of William D. and Jenny Simonton, of 1, Malone Park, Belfast.

Simpson, Alexander McDonald - Rifleman
20654 Royal Irish Rifles 1st Battalion *Age 19 Killed in Action on 14 October 1918*
DADIZEELE NEW BRITISH CEMETERY, Belgium
Son of David and Lily Simpson, of 119, Rosebery Road, Belfast.

Simpson, David - Private
14435 Cameronians (Scottish Rifles) 11th Battalion *Died of Wounds on 8 May 1917*
DOIRAN MEMORIAL, Greece
Born in Belfast, enlisted in Port Glasgow.

Simpson, George - Stoker
1947U Royal Navy HMS "Goliath" *Died in War on 13 May 1915*
CHATHAM NAVAL MEMORIAL, United Kingdom
Belmont, Belfast.

Simpson, George Charles - Second Steward
Mercantile Marine S.S. "Bray Head" (Belfast) *Age 26 Drowned, as a result of an attack by an enemy submarine on 14 March 1917*
TOWER HILL MEMORIAL, United Kingdom
Son of the late John and Rosetta Simpson. Born in Belfast.

Simpson, Johnston Hill - Rifleman
19/448 Royal Irish Rifles 14th Battalion *Age 27 Killed in Action on 7 June 1917*
SPANBROEKMOLEN BRITISH CEMETERY, Belgium
Son of Robert H. and Sarah Simpson, of Creeveytenant, Ballynahinch, County Down; husband of Isabella Simpson, of 62, Battenberg Street, Belfast.

Simpson, Joseph - Rifleman
5121 London Regiment 18th (County of London) Battalion (London Irish Rifles)
Killed in Action on 16 September 1916
HEILLY STATION CEMETERY, MERICOURT-L'ABBE, France
Enlisted and resident in Belfast.

Simpson, Robert Greer - Private
2137487 Canadian Infantry (British Columbia Regiment) 7th Battalion *Age 30 Killed in Action on 8 April 1918*
ECOIVRES MILITARY CEMETERY, MONT-ST. ELOI, France
Born in Belfast, Ireland the son of Mrs Robert Simpson of Los Angeles, USA.
Trained as a nurse and was Presbyterian in religion.

Simpson, William - Private
8800 Royal Inniskilling Fusiliers 1st Battalion *Died in War on 21 August 1915*
HELLES MEMORIAL, Turkey
Born and enlisted in Belfast.

Sinclair, Andrew - Sergeant
13590 Royal Irish Rifles 15th Battalion *Died in War on 22 November 1917*
THIEPVAL MEMORIAL, France
Born and enlisted in Belfast.

Sinclair, Edward - Rifleman
9318 Royal Inniskilling Fusiliers 1st Battalion *Died in War on 1 July 1915*
HELLES MEMORIAL, Turkey
16 Beggs Street, Belfast. Awarded the Distinguished Conduct Medal.

Sinclair, George Stanley - Second Lieutenant
Royal Irish Rifles 1st Battalion *Age 20 Died in War on 28 May 1917*
PERONNE COMMUNAL CEMETERY EXTENSION, France
Son of Samuel and Edith M. Sinclair, of "Inglewood", Adelaide Park, Belfast. Educated at Castle Park Dublin and RBAI. Enrolled as a medical student at Queen's University to study medicine. Trained with the university OTC and was commissioned into the Royal Irish Rifles. Killed 'accidently' by a grenade while supervising a training session.

Sinclair, John - Lance Corporal
16534 Royal Inniskilling Fusiliers 8th Battalion *Age 22 Killed in Action on 27 December 1916*
KEMMEL CHATEAU MILITARY CEMETERY, Belgium
Son of Robert and Emma Sinclair, of 76, Chadolly Street, Belfast.

Sinclair, William - Rifleman
3550 Royal Irish Rifles 11th Battalion *Age 38 Died in War on 10 May 1916*
AUTHUILE MILITARY CEMETERY, France
Husband of Annie Sinclair, of 37, Beech Street, Donegall Pass, Belfast. A plasterer by trade.

Sinclaire, Ivan Harwood - Sergeant
7794 Royal Munster Fusiliers 2nd Battalion *Died in War on 22 August 1916*
FLATIRON COPSE CEMETERY, MAMETZ, France
Born in Belfast, enlisted in Plymouth.

Singleton, George - Corporal
57527 Royal Engineers 122nd Field Company *Killed in Action on 21 March 1918*
POZIERES MEMORIAL, France
38 Lanark Street, Belfast.

Singleton, John Robertson - Private
1573 King's Own (Royal Lancaster Regiment) 4th Battalion *Died in War on 19 November 1914*
BARROW-IN-FURNESS CEMETERY, United Kingdom
Born in Belfast, enlisted in Barrow.

Sittlington, Hugh - Petty Officer Stoker
276560 Royal Navy HMS "Defence" *Killed in Action on 31 May 1916*
PLYMOUTH NAVAL MEMORIAL, United Kingdom
Son of the late Hugh and Annie Sittlington, of Larne, County Antrim; husband of Elizabeth Wilson Sittlington, of 10, Eighth Street, Belfast. Served for more than 22 years.

Skeats, Alexander - Private
5266 Royal Munster Fusiliers 7th Battalion *Age 24 Died in War on 9 August 1915*
HELLES MEMORIAL, Turkey
Son of Archibald and Mary Skeats, of 63, Tower Street, Belfast.

Skeats, Samuel - Lance Corporal
T/33113 Royal Army Service Corps *Age 23 Died in War on 12 July 1918*
ST. HILAIRE CEMETERY EXTENSION, FREVENT, France
Born and enlisted in Belfast.

Skeffington, Francis - Private
2519 Leinster Regiment 2nd Battalion *Age 43 Killed in Action on 11 May 1918*
MORBECQUE BRITISH CEMETERY, France
Son of Francis and Mary Skeffington, of 10, Bow Street, Belfast.

Skellern, William - Company Quartermaster Sergeant
240030 Loyal North Lancashire Regiment 1/5th Battalion (Territorial Force) *Died in War on 30 November 1917*
CAMBRAI MEMORIAL, France
Born in Belfast, enlisted in Hindley, Lancashire.

Skelly, Robert - Gunner
302447 Canadian Field Artillery 10th Brigade *Age 41 Died of sickness on 7 February 1920*
TORONTO (PROSPECT) CEMETERY, Canada
Son of the late William and Mary Skelly, of 6, Wellington Park Avenue, Belfast, Ireland.
Served in the Boer War and then worked as a labourer, a Presbyterian.

Skelly, Robert - Rifleman
11744 Royal Irish Rifles 15th Battalion *Died in War on 1 July 1916*
A.I.F. BURIAL GROUND, FLERS, France
Born and enlisted in Belfast.

Skelly, Samuel - Private
5381 6th Dragoons (Inniskilling) attached 1st Life Guards *Age 31 Died in War on 30 October 1914*
YPRES (MENIN GATE) MEMORIAL, Belgium
Son of William Skelly, of 65, Farnham Street, Belfast.

Skillen, John - Lance Corporal
3391 Royal Inniskilling Fusiliers 2nd Battalion *Died in War on 28 September 1917*
COXYDE MILITARY CEMETERY, Belgium
Brother of James Skillen, of 15, Eighth Street, Belfast.

Skillen, Robert - Rifleman
13491 Royal Irish Rifles 10th Battalion *Age 26 Killed in Action on 1 July 1916*
THIEPVAL MEMORIAL, France
Son of David Skillen, of 18, Posnett Street, Belfast; husband of Annetta Skillen, of 10, Ebor Street, Donegall Avenue, Belfast.

Skillen, Robert C. - Rifleman
18/324 Royal Irish Rifles 12th Battalion *Age 28 Died of dysentery on 13 October 1918*
TERLINCTHUN BRITISH CEMETERY, WIMILLE, France
Husband of Margaret Skillen, of 16, Gertrude Street, Belfast.

Skilling, James - Lance Corporal
Argyll and Sutherland Highlanders *Died of Wounds*
Formerly of Shankill Road, Belfast.

Slacke, Charles Owen - Captain
Royal Irish Rifles 14th Battalion *Age 44 Killed in Action on 1 July 1916*
CONNAUGHT CEMETERY, THIEPVAL, France
Wheatfield, Belfast. Son of Sir Owen Randal Slacke. He was the grandson of the architect, Charles Lanyon.

Slavin, James - Able Seaman
Mercantile Marine S.S. "Vedamore" (Liverpool)
Age 43 Drowned, as a result of an attack by an enemy submarine, or killed by mine on 7 February 1917
TOWER HILL MEMORIAL, United Kingdom
Born in Belfast.

Sleator, James - Private
41418 Royal Irish Fusiliers 9th (North Irish Horse) Battalion *Age 22 Died in War on 23 November 1917*
CAMBRAI MEMORIAL, LOUVERVAL, France
Son of James and Elizabeth Sleator, of 6, Cappy Street, Ravenhill Road, Belfast.

Sloan, Albert E. - Company Quartermaster Sergeant
21191 Royal Irish Fusiliers 8th Battalion *Age 32 Died in War on 5 September 1916*
THIEPVAL MEMORIAL, France
Husband of Catherine Sloan, of 106, Leeson Street, Falls Road, Belfast.

Sloan, David James - Lance Corporal
18723 Royal Irish Rifles "A" Company 14th Battalion *Age 26 Killed in Action on 24 October 1916*
BAILLEUL COMMUNAL CEMETERY EXTENSION (NORD), France
Son of John and Agnes Sloan, of Belfast; husband of May Ethel Sloan,
of 7, Ash Grove, Wright Street, Birmingham.

Sloan, Jack - Corporal
700687 Canadian Engineers 1st Tramway Company *Age 26 Died of Wounds on 20 August 1918*
BOVES WEST COMMUNAL CEMETERY EXTENSION, France
Son of John and Martha Sloan, of 685, Home Street, Winnipeg. Native of Belfast, Ireland

Sloan, John - Private
PLY/17737 Royal Marine Light Infantry 2nd R.M. Battalion Royal Naval Division
Age 20 Killed in Action on 13 November 1916
THIEPVAL MEMORIAL, France
Son of Mrs. Jane Sloan, of 4, Ballycarry Street, Belfast.

Sloan, John - Rifleman
10110 Royal Irish Rifles 2nd Battalion *Died in War on 16 July 1916*
BOULOGNE EASTERN CEMETERY, France
Nephew of Mrs. Grace Harrison, of 28, Albert Bridge Road, Belfast.

Sloan, William - Private
2997 Royal Inniskilling Fusiliers 1st Battalion *Died of Wounds on 23 July 1917*
DOZINGHEM MILITARY CEMETERY, Belgium
Husband of Elizabeth Sloan, of 180, Sugarfield Street, Belfast.

Sloan, William - Private
412868 Canadian Infantry (Quebec Regiment) 13th Battalion *Age 30 Killed in Action on 27 June 1916*
YPRES (MENIN GATE) MEMORIAL, Belgium
Son of William and Margaret Sloan, of 170, Donegall Road, Belfast; husband of Annie Sloan,
of 12, Boyne Square, Belfast, Ireland.

Sloan, William - Rifleman
7094 Royal Irish Rifles 2nd Battalion *Killed in Action on 7 May 1915*
YPRES (MENIN GATE) MEMORIAL, Belgium
Born and enlisted in Belfast.

Sloane, Douglas - Able Seaman
J/10191 Royal Navy HMS "Indefatigable" *Age 21 Killed in Action at Battle of Jutland on 31 May 1916*
PLYMOUTH NAVAL MEMORIAL, United Kingdom
Son of Robert and Jane Sloane, of 22, Nile Street, off York Street, Belfast.

Sloane, Joseph W - Rifleman
15949 Royal Irish Rifles "C" Company 14th Battalion *Age 25 Killed in Action on 6 August 1916*
BERKS CEMETERY EXTENSION, Belgium
Son of Mrs. Sloane, of 16, Malone Avenue, Belfast, and the late Joseph Sloan, born Lisburn.

Sloane, Thomas George - Rifleman
18780 Royal Irish Rifles 14th Battalion *Age 26 Died in War on 6 May 1916*
AUTHUILE MILITARY CEMETERY, France
Son of Benjamin and Harriet E. Sloane, of 9, Elswick Street, Belfast.

Small, John Wesley - Rifleman
7190 Royal Irish Rifles 1st Battalion *Died in War on 11 March 1915*
LE TOURET MEMORIAL, France
Brother of Hannah Meighan, of 9, Walbeck Street, Belfast. Served in the South African Campaign

Smeaton, Robert - Rifleman
8206 Royal Irish Rifles 2nd Battalion *Killed in Action on 20 September 1914*
LA FERTE-SOUS-JOUARRE MEMORIAL, France
15 Harrybrook Street, Belfast.

Smeeth, James Burrows - Rifleman
1105 Royal Irish Rifles Battalion 15th Battalion *Age 41 Killed in Action on 21 March 1918*
POZIERES MEMORIAL, France
Husband of Mary Ann Smeeth, of 7, Malvern Street, Belfast.

Smeeth, Roland - Private
11445 Royal Inniskilling Fusiliers 5th Battalion *Age 20 Died of Wounds (soldier, buried at sea) on 25 August 1915*
HELLES MEMORIAL, Turkey
Son of the late Rowland and Catherine Smeeth; husband of Jane Smeeth,
of 69, Paris Street, Belfast. Served in the Sudan Campaign.

Smiles, Samuel - Second Lieutenant
Royal Irish Rifles 1st Battalion *Age 36 Killed in Action on 16 August 1917*
TYNE COT CEMETERY, Belgium
Son of Mrs. Lucy Smiles (half- sister of the famous cook Mrs Beeton), Strandtown, Belfast. His father had been a founder of Belfast Rope Works. Educated at English public schools, he qualified as a solicitor.
Volunteered directly the war broke out and killed in 1916. His brother, William, was also killed.

Smiles, William Alan - Captain
Royal Irish Rifles 2nd Battalion *Age 34 Killed in Action on 9 July 1916*
THIEPVAL MEMORIAL, France
Son of William Holmes Smiles and Lucy Smiles, of Westbank, Strandtown, Belfast.
A solicitor by profession his bother, Samuel, also fell.

Smiley, George - Able Seaman
231456 Royal Navy HMS "Black Prince" *Age 27 Killed in Action at Battle of Jutland on 31 May 1916*
PLYMOUTH NAVAL MEMORIAL, United Kingdom
Son of Samuel and Emily Smiley, of Belfast; husband of Mabel Smiley, of 6, Lanark Street, Belfast.

Smiley, George - Lance Corporal
8448 Royal Irish Rifles 1st Battalion *Killed in Action on 9 May 1915*
PLOEGSTEERT MEMORIAL, Belgium
1 Tavanagh Street, Belfast.

Smiley, Samuel Thomas - Sub-Lieutenant
Royal Naval Reserve HMS "Arabis" *Age 35 Killed in Action with destroyer in North Sea on 11 February 1916*
PLYMOUTH NAVAL MEMORIAL, *United Kingdom*
Son of Samuel and Jennie Smiley, of 18, Chichester Avenue, Belfast. A former officer in the Merchant Navy.

Smith, John - Private
4279 Royal Irish Regiment 8th Battalion formerly 785 Royal Irish Rifles *Killed In Action on 6 September 1918*
PLOEGSTEERT MEMORIAL, *Belgium*
Born and enlisted in Belfast.

Smith, Thomas - Rifleman
648978 Royal Irish Rifles 11th Battalion *Died in War on 2 September 1916*
BAILLIEUL COMMUNAL CEMETERY EXTENSION (NORD), *France*
Born in Belfast, enlisted Lisburn. Son of Thomas Smith, of Dollingstown, Lurgan, and the late Julia Smith.

Smith, Albert Arthur - Private
Royal Irish Fusliers *Died in War*
13 Acton Street, Belfast.

Smith, Alec Park - Private
8049 Royal Inniskilling Fusiliers "B" Company 2nd Battalion *Age 28 Killed in Action on 21 October 1914*
PLOEGSTEERT MEMORIAL, *Belgium*
Husband of Margaret Jane Nicholl (formerly Smith), of 82, Elizabeth Street, Belfast.

Smith, Alexander Ferguson - Rifleman
14/18783 Royal Irish Rifles 14th Battalion *Age 22 Died of Wounds on 11 July 1916*
ETAPLES MILITARY CEMETERY, *France*
Son of Alexander and Jane Smith, of Belfast.

Smith, Benjamin - Private
8630 The King's (Liverpool Regiment) 1st Battalion *Age 30 Died in War on 15 September 1914*
LA FERTE-SOUS-JOUARRE MEMORIAL, *France*
Son of Thomas and the late Catherine Smith; husband of Charlotte Smith, of 119, Herschell Street, Anfield, Liverpool. Born in Belfast.

Smith, Bernard - Private
11215 Royal Irish Regiment 2nd Battalion *Died in War on 3 September 1916*
THIEPVAL MEMORIAL, *France*
Lived, as one of a family of fourteen, the son of Daniel and Mary, in Roden Street.
His brother, Daniel also served and died in 1919 as a result of gassing.

Smith, Charles - Private
13809 Royal Scots Fusiliers 7th Battalion *Died in War on 26 September 1915*
LOOS MEMORIAL, *France*
32 Gibson Street, Belfast.

Smith, Charles - Rifleman
1708 Royal Irish Rifles 8th Battalion *Age 19 Died of Wounds on 7 June 1917*
DRANOUTRE MILITARY CEMETERY, *Belgium*
Son of Jack and Sarah Smith, of 69, Crimea Street, Belfast.

Journey of Remembering

Smith, Daniel - Private
28882 Royal Irish Fusiliers 2nd Battalion *Died as a result of war on 22 January 1919*
BELFAST (MILLTOWN) ROMAN CATHOLIC CEMETERY, United Kingdom
Son of Daniel and Mary Smith. Died as a result of gassing. His brother, Bernard, was killed in 1916.

Smith, Daniel - Rifleman
11861 Royal Irish Rifles 7th Battalion *Killed in Action on 7 June 1917*
YPRES (MENIN GATE) MEMORIAL, Belgium
Born and enlisted in Belfast.

Smith, George - Rifleman
9/13613 Royal Irish Rifles 8/9th Battalion *Died in War on 24 November 1917*
GREVILLERS BRITISH CEMETERY, France
36 Argyle Street, Belfast.

Smith, Herbert - Rifleman
7372 Royal Irish Rifles 2nd Battalion *Age 17 Died in War on 26 April 1916*
ECOIVRES MILITARY CEMETERY, MONT-ST. ELOI, France
Son of Alfred and Jane Smith, 28 Heather Street, Belfast. Worked in Ewarts Mill before enlisting.

Smith, Hugh - Private
10390 Royal Inniskilling Fusiliers 1st Battalion *Age 21 Died in War on 28 April 1915*
HELLES MEMORIAL, Turkey
Son of Mrs. Agnes Smith, of 4, Belgrave Street, Belfast. His brother also served.

Smith, Hugh Mckeown - Lance Corporal
8039 Princess Victoria's (Royal Irish Fusiliers) 2nd Battalion *Died in War on 5 February 1915*
LONGUENESSE (ST OMER) SOUVENIR CEMETERY, France
Born and enlisted in Belfast.

Smith, James - Driver
36179 New Zealand Army Service Corps H.Q. Divisional Train *Age 22 Killed in Action on 17 May 1918*
LOUVENCOURT MILITARY CEMETERY, France
Son of Margaret J. and the late Cornelius Smith, of 19, Albert Street, Belfast, Ireland.

Smith, James - Lance Corporal
7175 Royal Irish Rifles 8th Battalion *Died in War on 2 July 1916*
Born and enlisted in Belfast.

Smith, James - Rifleman
8913 Royal Irish Rifles 1st Battalion *Killed in Action on 9 May 1915*
PLOEGSTEERT MEMORIAL, Belgium
Born and enlisted in Belfast.

Smith, James P - Private
10319 Royal Irish Rifles 2nd Battalion *Died in War on 12 June 1915*
PERTH CEMETERY (CHINA WALL), Belgium
10 St Peter's Place, Belfast. A married man and an Army Reservist.

Smith, John - Private
16380 Royal Welsh Fusiliers 9th Battalion *Died in War on 24 July 1917*
LOCRE HOSPICE CEMETERY, Belgium
Born in Belfast, enlisted in Staffordshire.

Smith, John - Private
17/471 Royal Irish Rifles 10th Battalion transferred to 379708 Labour Corps
Age 45 Died in War on 21 June 1918
TERLINCTHUN BRITISH CEMETERY, WIMILLE, France
Son of David and Catherine Smith, of 111, Bray Street, Belfast.

Smith, John - Private
25232 Royal Inniskilling Fusiliers *Died of Wounds on 29 April 1916*
2b Aberdeen street, Belfast. Son of Margaret and Arthur Smith; two brother were also in the Army.

Smith, John - Private
379708 Labour Corps *Died in War on 21 June 1918*
Born and enlisted in Belfast. Formerly 471 Royal Irish Rifles

Smith, John - Private
5002 Royal Irish Rifles 2nd Battalion *Died of Wounds on 14 October 1914*
LE TOURET MEMORIAL, France
8 Kildare Street, Belfast. A soldier for 18 years.

Smith, John - Rifleman
13614 Royal Irish Rifles "B" Company 10th Battalion *Age 22 Killed in Action on 1 June 1916*
HAMEL MILITARY CEMETERY, BEAUMONT-HAMEL, France
Son of Mrs. S. Smith, of 61, Blythe Street, Belfast.

Smith, John - Rifleman
40917 Royal Irish Rifles 1st Battalion *Killed in Action on 6 September 1917*
PLOEGSTEERT MEMORIAL, Belgium
Born in Belfast, enlisted in Antrim. Formerly 2108 North Irish Horse

Smith, John Edward - Private
23223 Royal Inniskilling Fusiliers 1st Battalion *Died in War on 23 April 1917*
ARRAS MEMORIAL, France
Born Ballymacarrett, Belfast, enlisted Warrington. Husband of Esther Smith, 115 Mersey Street, Warrington.

Smith, John Frederick - Rifleman
B/201747 Rifle Brigade (The Prince Consort's Own) 9th Battalion *Died in War on 24 March 1918*
POZIERES MEMORIAL, France
Born and enlisted in Belfast formerly T/3/031120 Army Service Corps.

Smith, John Joseph - Driver
58574 Royal Field Artillery 34th Brigade H.Q *Age 25 Died in War on 3 August 1916*
LA NEUVILLE BRITISH CEMETERY, CORBIE, France
Son of Patrick and Annie Smith, of Belfast.

Smith, Joseph - Lance Corporal
S/6812 Black Watch (Royal Highlanders) 9th (Service) Battalion *Died in War on 25 September 1915*
Born in Belfast, enlisted in Leicester.

Journey of Remembering

Smith, Patrick J - Private
2913 Leinster Regiment 7th Battalion *Age 23 Died in War on 13 May 1916*
BETHUNE TOWN CEMETERY, *France*
Nephew of Sarah McAlister, of 23, Hamill Street, Belfast.

Smith, Robert - Rifleman
3653 Royal Irish Rifles 1st Battalion *Killed in Action on 9 May 1915*
PLOEGSTEERT MEMORIAL, *Belgium*
Born in Blaris, Lisburn. Enlisted Ballykinler, resident of Belfast.

Smith, Robert - Rifleman
839 Royal Irish Rifles 15th Battalion *Died in War on 2 November 1917*
METZ-EN-COUTURE COMMUNAL CEMETERY BRITISH EXTENSION, *France*
Born and enlisted in Belfast.

Smith, Samuel James - Private
9263 Argyll and Sutherland Highlanders 11th Battalion *Age 30 Died in War on 16 September 1916*
MILLENCOURT COMMUNAL CEMETERY EXTENSION, *France*
Son of James and Isabella Smith, of Belfast.

Smith, Thomas - Able Seaman
Mercantile Marine S.S. "Sea Gull" (London) *Age 39 Drowned, as a result of an attack by an enemy submarine on 16 March 1918*
TOWER HILL MEMORIAL, *United Kingdom*
Son of the late Thomas and Bridget Smith. Born in Belfast.

Smith, Thomas - Rifleman
4766 Royal Irish Rifles 2nd Battalion *Age 21 Died in War on 31 July 1915*
NETLEY MILITARY CEMETERY, *United Kingdom*
Son of Mrs. Sarah Andrews, of 21, Coolbeg Street, Donegall Road, Belfast.

Smith, Thomas - Rifleman
Royal Irish Rifles *Died in War*
Burnaby Street, Belfast.

Smith, William - Private
IL/357 Royal Irish Regiment transferred to 109036 182nd Company Labour Corps *Age 30 Died of Wounds on 29 January 1918*
ETAPLES MILITARY CEMETERY, *France*
Son of the late William and Annie Smith. Native of Belfast.

Smith, William - Private
S/18692 Queen's Own Cameron Highlanders 5th Battalion *Died in War on 5 November 1917*
DOZINGHEM MILITARY CEMETERY, *Belgium*
Born in Belfast, enlisted Glasgow.

Smith, William - Rifleman
13603 Royal Irish Rifles 15th Battalion *Killed In Action on 21 March 1918*
POZIERES MEMORIAL, *France*
Born and enlisted in Belfast.

Smith, William - Rifleman
2322 Royal Irish Rifles 6th Battalion *Died in War on 11 August 1915*
HELLES MEMORIAL, *Turkey*
88 Oregon Street, his sister lived at 3 Mossvale Street.

Smith, William Ernest - Private
34857 Northumberland Fusiliers 26th (Tyneside Irish) Battalion *Age 35 Died in War on 5 June 1917*
ARRAS MEMORIAL, France
Son of John Perry Smith, of Belfast; husband of Millicent Winifred Smith,
of 142, Brighton Street, Egremont, Wallasey, Cheshire.

Smullen, Abraham - Private
33847 Manchester Regiment 16th Battalion *Killed in Action on 21 March 1918*
POZIERES MEMORIAL, France
Born in Belfast, enlisted Manchester.

Smylie, Robert - Private
11697 Royal Inniskilling Fusiliers 9th Battalion *Age 24 Died in War on 7 August 1916*
BELFAST CITY CEMETERY, United Kingdom
Son of the late David Smylie; husband of Minnie Carroll (formerly Smylie), of 10, Pakenham Street, Belfast.

Smylie, William J. - Private
23209 Royal Irish Fusiliers 9th Battalion *Age 18 Killed in Action on 1 July 1916*
THIEPVAL MEMORIAL, France
Son of Mrs. Elizabeth Smylie, of 66, Hillview Street, Belfast.

Smylie, William Millar - Private
537 Australian Infantry 10th Battalion *Age 22 Killed in Action on 25 April 1915*
LONE PINE MEMORIAL, Turkey
Son of Joseph and Anna Maria Smylie, of 59, Burmah Street, Belfast, Ireland.

Smyth , George - Rifleman
9001 Royal Irish Rifles 2nd Battalion *Died of Wounds on 30 December 1914*
ROYAL IRISH RIFLES GRAVEYARD, LAVENTIE, France
Born and enlisted in Belfast. Husband of E. Evans (formerly Smyth),
of 6, George Street, Newtownards, County Down.

Smyth, Abraham - Rifleman
13619 Royal Irish Rifles 15th Battalion *Died in War on 7 June 1916*
HAMEL MILITARY CEMETERY, BEAUMONT-HAMEL, France
21 Rusholme Street, Belfast. Survived by his mother and was a former employee of Brookfield Mill.

Smyth, Albert George - Private
17497 Royal Inniskilling Fusiliers "B" Company 6th Battalion *Age 31 Died in War on 10 September 1916*
DOIRAN MEMORIAL, Greece
Son of Hugh and Elizabeth Smyth, of 13, Acton Street, Belfast

Smyth, Alfred John - Private
49714 Durham Light Infantry 14th Battalion *Died in War on 6 March 1917*
PHILOSOPHE BRITISH CEMETERY, MAZINGARBE, France
Member of Townsend Presbyterian Church, Belfast. Son of Thomas and Margaretta Smyth of Ballymena.

Smyth, Daniel - Rifleman
18803 Royal Irish Rifles 13th Battalion *Died in War on 1 July 1916*
THIEPVAL MEMORIAL, France
42 Bracken Street, Belfast. Son of Hugh Smyth, of Bridge Street Comber, County Down.

Journey of Remembering

Smyth, Edmund - Private
Royal Irish Rifles 14th Battalion *Died of Wounds*
75 Emerson Street, Belfast.

Smyth, Edward - Private
77067 Canadian Infantry (British Columbia Regiment) 7th Battalion *Age 29 Died of sickness on 4 October 1917*
HALIFAX (FORT MASSEY) CEMETERY, *Canada*
Son of Thomas and Susan Smyth, of 87, Woodstock Road, Belfast, Ireland.
An Anglican, he had served in the militia and worked as a clerk.

Smyth, Edward - Rifleman
6176 Royal Irish Rifles 2nd Battalion *Killed in Action on 27 October 1914*
LE TOURET MEMORIAL, *France*
Born and enlisted in Belfast.

Smyth, Fredrick John - Rifleman
7053 Royal Irish Rifles "A" Company 7th Battalion *Age 26 Died of Wounds on 5 October 1917*
BUCQUOY ROAD CEMETERY, FICHEUX, *France*
Son of Fredrick and Elizabeth Smyth of Belfast.

Smyth, George - Corporal
15952 Royal Irish Rifles 10th Battalion *Killed In Action on 1 July 1916*
THIEPVAL MEMORIAL, *France*
Born and enlisted in Belfast.

Smyth, George - Rifleman
18/173 Royal Irish Rifles 9th Battalion *Died of Wounds on 4 March 1917*
BAILLEUL COMMUNAL CEMETERY EXTENSION (NORD), *France*
19 Hudson Street, Belfast.

Smyth, Gordon Dill Long - Second Lieutenant
Royal Irish Rifles *Age 21 Killed in Action on 16 August 1917*
TYNE COT MEMORIAL,, *Belgium*
Son of Mrs. M. F. D. Smyth, of 111, University Street, Belfast, and the late Rev. James Smyth.

Smyth, Hugh - Private
5176 Highland Light Infantry 18th Battalion (4th Glasgow) *Died in War on 18 July 1916*
THIEPVAL MEMORIAL, *France*
Born in Belfast, enlisted in Hamiliton, Scotland.

Smyth, Irvine Johnston - Second Lieutenant
Royal Inniskilling Fusiliers 6th Battalion *Age 23 Killed in Action on 3 September 1915*
GREEN HILL CEMETERY, *Turkey*
Son of William Henry and Mary J. R. Smyth, of The Manse, Green Road, Knock, Belfast.
Enlisted originally in the 6th Battalion Black Watch.

Smyth, Isaac - Rifleman
15957 Royal Irish Rifles "D" Company 14th Battalion *Age 23 Died in War on 11 August 1917*
YPRES (MENIN GATE) MEMORIAL, *Belgium*
Son of Mr. and Mrs. Alex Smyth, of 11, James Street, Belfast.

Smyth, James - Private
7641 Royal Inniskilling Fusiliers 2nd Battalion *Age 37 Killed in Action on 26 August 1914*
LESDAIN CHURCHYARD, France
Son of James and Barbara Smyth, of 68, Louisa Street, Belfast.

Smyth, James - Second Lieutenant (Pilot)
Royal Flying Corps 2nd Squadron *Died in War on 11 March 1917*
CABARET-ROUGE BRITISH CEMETERY, SOUCHEZ, France
Son of William Ferguson Smyth and I. Smyth of Belfast; husband of Ethel Smyth,
of Herbert Road, Plumstead, London.

Smyth, James J. - Private
17731 Royal Inniskilling Fusiliers 1st Battalion *Died in War on 19 April 1917*
ARRAS MEMORIAL, France
Born in Belfast.

Smyth, John - Private
31062 The Loyal North Lancashire Regiment "A" Company 2/4th Battalion
Age 21 Died in War on 2 October 1918
CAMBRAI EAST MILITARY CEMETERY, France
Lived at 51, Bow Lane, Preston. Born at Belfast.

Smyth, John - Rifleman
18786 Royal Irish Rifles 13th Battalion *Age 21 Died in War on 6 August 1917*
POTIJZE CHATEAU GROUNDS CEMETERY, Belgium
Native of Comber, County Down. Son of David and Elizabeth Smyth, of 49, Beersbridge Road, Belfast.

Smyth, John - Second Lieutenant
Royal Irish Rifles 9th Battalion *Died in War on 23 November 1917*
CAMBRAI MEMORIAL, LOUVERVAL, France
Member of Ulsterville Presbyterian Church, Belfast. Son of William and
Margareeta Smyth of Clough, County Antrim.

Smyth, John - Stoker First Class
SS/104254 Royal Navy HMS "Hawke" *Died in War on 15 October 1914*
CHATHAM NAVAL MEMORIAL, United Kingdom
Husband of Annie Smyth, 26 Coningsby Street, Belfast.

Smyth, Joseph - Private
1773 Leinster Regiment 2nd Battalion *Died in War on 31 July 1917*
BEDFORD HOUSE CEMETERY, Belgium
Husband of Maggie Smyth, of 26, Benares Street, Belfast.

Smyth, Joseph - Private
706 Australian Infantry 24th Battalion *Age 21 Died of Wounds on 12 August 1916*
ST. SEVER CEMETERY, ROUEN, France
Son of Joseph and Emily Smyth, of 8, Union Dale Street, Belfast.

Smyth, Joseph - Rifleman
3467 Royal Irish Rifles "D" Company 9th Battalion *Age 19 Killed in Action on 1 July 1916*
THIEPVAL MEMORIAL, France
Son of James and Agnes Jane Smyth, of 21, Dunmoyle Street, Belfast.

Smyth, Joseph Bammer - Lance Corporal
S/6812 Black Watch (Royal Highlanders) 9th Battalion *Age 25 Died in War on 25 September 1915*
LOOS MEMORIAL, France
Son of the late Joseph and Isabella Smyth, of 49, Great Patrick Street, Belfast, an artist.

Smyth, Marshall - Private
159636 4th Canadian Mounted Rifles (Central Ontario Regiment) *Age 33 Died in War on 9 April 1917*
VIMY MEMORIAL, France
Son of John and Sarah Smyth, of Upper Ballysillan, Ligoneil, Belfast, Ireland; husband of Sarah McQuillan Smyth, of 287, Chisholm Avenue, East Toronto, Ontario. Worked as a watchman, a Presbyterian.

Smyth, Matthew - Rifleman
15906 Royal Irish Rifles 9th Battalion *Killed by a Sniper on 3 January 1916*
SUCRERIE MILITARY CEMETERY, COLINCAMPS, France
5 Gardiner Street, Belfast. Husband of Charlotte and a member of 457 Star of the North Lodge.

Smyth, Patrick - Private
2913 Leinster Regiment 7th Battalion *Died in War on 13 May 1916*
BETHUNE TOWN CEMETERY, France
Born in Belfast. Lived in Belfast when enlisted.

Smyth, Patrick - Rifleman
8297 Royal Irish Rifles 2nd Battalion *Age 28 Died in War on 21 October 1914*
RUE-PETILLON MILITARY CEMETERY, FLEURBAIX, France
Son of Mrs. Catherine Smyth, of 10, New Lodge Place, Belfast.

Smyth, Patrick - Sergeant
8513 Royal Irish Rifles 6th Battalion *Died in War on 10 September 1915*
HELLES MEMORIAL, Turkey
Born and enlisted in Belfast.

Smyth, Richard Simpson - Private
5329 Royal Irish Rifles 2nd Battalion *Age 20 Died of Wounds on 24 April 1915*
BAILLEUL COMMUNAL CEMETERY (NORD), France
Son of Mr. W. J. and Elizabeth Smyth, of 54, Leadbetter Street, Belfast.

Smyth, Robert A - Private
24943 Royal Dublin Fusiliers 6th Battalion *Killed in Action on 8 October 1918*
SERAIN COMMUNAL CEMETERY EXTENSION, France
88 Woodvale Road, Belfast. Husband of Ena, he had two brothers serving in the Navy. Employed by the Irish Land Commission.

Smyth, Robert - Lance Corporal
15954 Royal Irish Rifles 9th Battalion *Killed in Action on 1 July 1916*
THIEPVAL MEMORIAL, France
Son of James L. and Jane Smyth, of 42, Perth Street, Belfast.

Smyth, Robert - Private
20741 Royal Inniskilling Fusiliers 7/8th Battalion *Killed in Action on 9 October 1918*
Born in Belfast.

Smyth, Robert - Rifleman
15/12431 Royal Irish Rifles 19th Battalion *Age 38 Died in War on 25 September 1919*
SHANKILL CEMETERY, United Kingdom
Husband of Maggie Smyth, of 139, Leopold Street, Belfast.

Smyth, Robert - Rifleman
8997 Royal Irish Rifles 2nd Battalion *Killed in Action on 18 March 1915*
KEMMEL CHATEAU MILITARY CEMETERY, Belgium
196 Leopold Street, Belfast. Worked at Ewarts Mill.

Smyth, Robert - Rifleman
9891 Royal Irish Rifles 1st Battalion *Killed in Action on 12 November 1915*
SAILLY-SUR-LA-LYS CANADIAN CEMETERY, France
Born in Dromore, enlisted in Banbridge, resident of Belfast.

Smyth, Samuel - Rifleman
15955 Royal Irish Rifles 10th Battalion *Died in War on 15 March 1918*
THIEPVAL MEMORIAL, France
Born Ballymacarrett, Belfast. Enlisted in Belfast.

Smyth, Samuel - Rifleman
4229 Royal Irish Rifles 1st Battalion *Killed in Action on 17 March 1915*
ESTAIRES COMMUNAL CEMETERY AND EXTENSION, France
Born in Dromore, enlisted in Ballykinler, resident in Belfast.

Smyth, Thomas - Lance Corporal
58992 Royal Fusiliers 7th Battalion *Age 19 Died in War on 5 February 1918*
ETRETAT CHURCHYARD EXTENSION, France
Son of Robert and Frances Smyth, of 27, Peveril Street, Belfast.

Smyth, Thomas Mercer - Private
4363 Seaforth Highlanders 1/5th Battalion *Killed in Action on 18 September 1916*
CITE BONJEAN MILITARY CEMETERY, ARMENTIERES, France
(Served as MERCER). Son of Isaac and Martha Smyth, of 57, Weir Street, Shankill Road, Belfast.

Smyth, William - Private
CH/960(S) Royal Marine Light Infantry 1st R.M. Battalion Royal Naval Division
Age 25 Died in War on 28 April 1917
ARRAS MEMORIAL, France
Son of John Smyth; husband of Annie Smyth, of 43, Mackey Street, Belfast.

Smyth, William James - Rifleman
5964 Royal Irish Rifles 14th Battalion *Died in War on 9 February 1918*
GRAND-SERAUCOURT BRITISH CEMETERY, France
Born and enlisted in Belfast.

Smyth, William John - Rifleman
9441 Royal Irish Rifles 1st Battalion *Age 26 Killed in Action on 21 March 1918*
POZIERES MEMORIAL, France
Son of David and Margaret Smyth, of 3, Eastland Street, Belfast.

Smyth, William Woods - Driver
77563 Royal Field Artillery *Age 21 Died of Wounds on 6 September 1918*
ST. SEVER CEMETERY EXTENSION, ROUEN, *France*
123, Sidney Street West. Son of Matilda and the late Edmund Smyth, Heather Street, Belfast. Had worked in Ewarts Mill and had two brothers also serving.

Smyth, Wilson - Corporal
42167 Royal Irish Fusiliers 9th (North Irish Horse) Battalion *Age 25 Died in War on 25 August 1918*
MONT NOIR MILITARY CEMETERY, ST. JANS-CAPPEL, *France*
Husband of Elizabeth Smyth, of 6, Brenda Street, Belfast. Native of Belfast.

Smythe, Philip - Driver
6695 Royal Horse Artillery and Royal Field Artillery *Died in War on 18 July 1917*
DICKEBUSCH NEW MILITARY CEMETERY EXTENSION, *Belgium*
Born in Belfast.

Snoddy, Thomas - Rifleman
47481 Royal Irish Rifles 1st Battalion *Died in War on 19 December 1917*
BAILLEUL COMMUNAL CEMETERY EXTENSION (NORD), *France*
Born and enlisted in Belfast. Formerly 091287 Army Service Corps

Snowden, George - Corporal
12765 King's (Liverpool Regiment) 11th Battalion *Died in War on 23 March 1918*
POZIERES MEMORIAL, *France*
Born in Newcastle-on-Tyne, enlisted in Liverpool, resident of Belfast.

Snowden, John - Corporal
14/6325 Royal Irish Rifles "C" Company 14th Battalion *Age 22 Killed in Action on 5 May 1917*
POND FARM CEMETERY, *Belgium*
Son of Matthew T. and Mary Snowden, of 14, Carlton Street, Belfast.

Snowden, William - Corporal
8727 Royal Irish Rifles 1st Battalion *Died of Wounds received at Neuve Chapelle on 4 April 1915*
BELFAST (DUNDONALD) CEMETERY, *United Kingdom*
Son of Thomas and Margaret Snowden, 1, Wauchope Street, Belfast.

Somers, William John Reeves - Corporal
6660 Royal Sussex Regiment 2nd Battalion *Died in War on 9 May 1915*
LE TOURET MEMORIAL, *France*
32, Selby Street, Belfast. Son of the late Mr. and Mrs. Somers, of Glenfarg Road, Catford, London; husband of Kate Annie Somers, of 4, Bridge Place, St. James' Road, Croydon.

Somerville, George - Rifleman
7087 Royal Irish Rifles "D" Company 2nd Battalion *Age 18 Killed in Action on 25 September 1915*
YPRES (MENIN GATE) MEMORIAL, *Belgium*
Son of William and Margaret Somerville, of 99, St. Leonard's Street, Belfast.

Somerville, Richard Newman - Lieutenant
Royal Engineers 94th Field Company *Age 28 Died in War on 9 October 1915*
ST. VAAST POST MILITARY CEMETERY, RICHEBOURG-L'AVOUE, *France*
Son of Mr. R. N. and Mrs. J. D. Somerville, of "Atbara", Osborne Park, Belfast. Born at Galway and a graduate of Trinity College Dublin.

Sparrow, Henry Ambrose - Sergeant
8746 Cheshire Regiment 1st Battalion *Age 27 Killed in Action on 25 May 1915*
TUILERIES BRITISH CEMETERY, Belgium
Son of John Ambrose and Sarah Ann Sparrow, of Birkenhead; husband
of Mary Holt (formerly Sparrow), of 8, Kensington Street, Belfast.

Spedding, Charles Rodney - Major
Royal Irish Rifles 2nd Battalion *Age 43 Died in War on 19 September 1914*
LA FERTE-SOUS-JOUARRE MEMORIAL, France
Son of Dr. and Mrs. H. B. Spedding, of Belfast; husband of Mrs. C. M. E. Spedding, of "Hawani",
Totland Bay, Isle of Wight. A Regular soldier he took part in the Boer War. In this he was twice Mentioned
in Despatches and awarded the Distinguished Service Order (DSO). He was again Mentioned in Despatches
in the first weeks of the Great War before being posted missing and, much later, confirmed killed.

Speers, John - Private
3317 Royal Inniskilling Fusiliers 2nd Battalion *Killed in Action on 23 November 1916*
THIEPVAL MEMORIAL, France
Born in Belfast.

Speers, John - Private
Leinster Regiment *Died of Wounds on 3 August 1917*
23 Massereene Street, Street.

Speers, William - Private
2888 Guards Machine Gun Regiment *Died in War on 20 July 1918*
BAGNEUX BRITISH CEMETERY, GEZAINCOURT, France
Son of Mrs. A. J. Russell, of 7, Auburn Street, Donegall Pass, Belfast. Formerly 5877 Irish Guards.

Speight, John - Private
25536 West Yorkshire Regiment (Prince of Wales's Own) 2nd Battalion *Age 21 Died in War on 10 October 1916*
PHILOSOPHE BRITISH CEMETERY, MAZINGARBE, France
Native of Belfast; the husband of Rhoda Speight, of 43, Devon Street, Pontefract Lane, Leeds.

Spence, Joseph - Rifleman
15962 Royal Irish Rifles 13th Battalion *Killed in Action on 16 August 1917*
TYNE COT MEMORIAL, Belgium
Born and enlisted in Belfast.

Spence, Robert - Private
24747 Royal Inniskilling Fusiliers 7th Battalion *Killed in Action on 15 August 1916*
PHILOSOPHE BRITISH CEMETERY, MAZINGARBE, France
Son of John and Mary Spence, 83 Devonshire Street, Belfast.

Spence, Robert - Rifleman
22325 Royal Irish Rifles 12th Battalion *Age 33 Died in War on 15 October 1918*
TYNE COT MEMORIAL, Belgium
Son of James Given Spence and Agnes Spence, of 2, Bellevue Terrace, Shore Road, Belfast.

Spence, Thomas - Rifleman
17/195 Royal Irish Rifles "D" Company 14th Battalion *Age 37 Killed in Action on 23 - 25 March 1918*
POZIERES MEMORIAL, France
Son of Edward and Margaret Spence, of Collyer Street, Belfast; husband of Annie Spence, of 29, Mervue Street, Belfast.

Spence, Thomas H - Rifleman
13637 Royal Irish Rifles 9th Battalion *Killed in Action on 1 July 1916*
MILL ROAD CEMETERY, THIEPVAL, France
14, Wilton Square, North Belfast. Parents Robert and Athelia. A member of the old UVF and an employee of Mackie's Foundry.

Spence, William - Private
19749 Royal Irish Fusiliers 9th Battalion *Killed in Action on 1 July 1916*
THIEPVAL MEMORIAL, France
11 Brookmount Street. Sister Mary and bother-in-law Robert Watson.

Spence, William - Private
3171 Royal Inniskilling Fusiliers 2nd Battalion *Age 20 Died of Wounds on 18 March 1916*
MILLENCOURT COMMUNAL CEMETERY EXTENSION, France
Son of William and Elizabeth Spence, of 58, Church Street East, Belfast.

Spence, William - Rifleman
17010 Royal Irish Rifles "D" Company 14th Battalion *Age 20 Killed in Action on 7 June 1917*
LONE TREE CEMETERY, Belgium
Son of Anna Spence, of 203, Albert Bridge Road, Belfast, and the late Samuel Spence.

Spence, William - Rifleman
7172 Royal Irish Rifles 1st Battalion *Age 32 Killed in Action on 9 May 1915*
PLOEGSTEERT MEMORIAL, Belgium
Husband of Annie Spence, of 22, Stanhope Street, Belfast.

Spence, William - Rifleman
Royal Irish Rifles *Killed in Action on 1 July 1916*
16 Ashmore Street, Belfast.

Spence, William J - Private
13775 Royal Inniskilling Fusiliers 11th Battalion *Killed in Action on 1 July 1916*
CONNAUGHT CEMETERY, THIEPVAL, France
24 Keswick Street, Belfast. Left a wife, Maggie, and two small children.

Spencer, Frank - Private
9038 Cheshire Regiment 1st Battalion *Age 25 Died of Wounds on 11 October 1915*
CORBIE COMMUNAL CEMETERY, France
Son of Edwin and Elizabeth Spencer, of Burland, Nantwich, Cheshire; husband of Mrs. S. E. Spencer, of 71, St. Kilda Street, Belfast.

Spencer, John - Acting Bombardier
20815 Royal Garrison Artillery *Died in War on 1 November 1914*
YPRES (MENIN GATE) MEMORIAL, Belgium
Born in Belfast, enlisted in Singapore.

Spiers, Charles - Trimmer
478728 Mercantile Marine HMS "Ophi" *Age 32 Died in War on 16 July 1918*
BELFAST CITY CEMETERY, United Kingdom
Son of Mrs. E. Spiers, of 67, Hudson Street, Belfast. Born at Glasgow.

Spratt, Robert - Lance Corporal
72808 Machine Gun Corps (Infantry) Formerly 5825 Royal Irish Rifles
Killed in Action on 23 March 1918
ARRAS MEMORIAL, *France*
Born in Belfast.

Spratt, Robert - Sergeant
6484 South Wales Borderers 3rd Battalion *Died in War on 15 October 1917*
DAR ES SALAAM WAR CEMETERY, *Tanzania*
Born and enlisted in Belfast.

Spratt, Samuel - Lance Corporal
8185 Royal Irish Rifles 2nd Battalion *Age 23 Killed in Action on 26 October 1914*
LE TOURET MEMORIAL, *France*
Husband of Elizabeth Spratt, of 30, Lecale Street, Donegall Road, Belfast.

Spratt, Thomas - Stoker First Class
298606 Royal Navy Nelson Battalion Royal Naval Division *Died in War on 15 July 1915*
LANCASHIRE LANDING CEMETERY, *Turkey*
Brother of Mrs. Patterson, of 30, Witham Street, Belfast.

Spurr, George Albert - Rifleman
R/5184 King's Royal Rifle Corps 2nd Battalion *Age 37 Killed in Action on 11 August 1915*
CAMBRIN CHURCHYARD EXTENSION, *France*
Husband of Elizabeth Spurr, of 75, Clementine Street, Belfast.

Squires, Ernest S. - Lance Corporal
57963 Royal Engineers *Age 47 Died in War on 13 April 1919*
BELFAST (DUNDONALD) CEMETERY, *United Kingdom*
Son of William and Lucinda Squires, of Stockport, Cheshire; husband of Jane Squires,
of 25, Emerald Street, Belfast. Served in the South African Campaign.

Stafford-King-Harman, Edward Charles - Captain
Irish Guards 1st Battalion *Age 23 Died in War on 6 November 1914*
YPRES (MENIN GATE) MEMORIAL, *Belgium*
Born in Belfast, the son of the Rt Hon Sir Thomas and Lady Stafford, Boyle, County Roscommon.
Husband of Olive Stafford-King-Harman of Strokestown Park, Longford.

Stainer, Albert H - Private
18172 Dorsetshire Regiment 5th Battalion *Died in War on 11 February 1917*
ETAPLES MILITARY CEMETERY, *France*
Husband of Charlotte E. Stainer, of Primrose Villa, Shore Road, Belfast.

Stanfield, Thomas - Rifleman
303 Royal Irish Rifles 1st Garrison Battalion
Age 38 Died at sea en route to India on H.M.T. "Franconia" on 29 February 1916
HOLLYBROOK MEMORIAL, SOUTHAMPTON, *United Kingdom*
Husband of Margaret Stanfield, of 25, Hanover Street, Belfast.

Journey of Remembering

Stanfield, William Hughes - Private
CH/282(S) Royal Marine Light Infantry Chatham Battalion Royal Naval Division *Age 30 Died of Wounds on 14 May 1915*
GIBRALTAR (NORTH FRONT) CEMETERY
Son of the late William and Mary Josephine Stanfield. Born in Belfast.

Stanley, Robert Oliver - Second Lieutenant
Royal Welsh Fusiliers 12th Battalion *Died in War on 9 April 1916*
BASRA MEMORIAL, Iraq
Knockbreda Road, Belfast.

Stannage, Robert - Corporal
6226 Royal Irish Rifles 2nd Battalion *Killed in Action on 16 November 1914*
PONT-DU-HEM MILITARY CEMETERY, LA GORGUE, France
86, Mountjoy Street, left a widow and young daughter, Selina.

Stark, Thomas - Private
1319 Highland Light Infantry 5th (City of Glasgow) Battalion (Territorial) *Died in War on 4 September 1915*
LANCASHIRE LANDING CEMETERY, Turkey
Born and enlisted in Belfast.

Starrett, James - Rifleman
45548 Royal Irish Rifles 12th Battalion *Died in War on 21 March 1918*
POZIERES MEMORIAL, France
104 Fortingale Street. Left a widow and five children.

Startup, Robert George - Private
180506 Machine Gun Corps (Infantry) "C" Training Battalion *Age 28 Died as a result of war on 15 November 1918*
ST. PANCRAS CEMETERY, United Kingdom
Husband of Agnes Startup, of 75, Manor Street, Belfast.

Staunton, Albert - Rifleman
40019 Royal Irish Rifles 2nd Battalion *Killed in Action on 24 March 1918*
POZIERES MEMORIAL, France
Son of Mr. and Mrs. Staunton, of 52, Heather Street, Belfast. Formerly 3496 Royal Irish Fusiliers

Stead, Thomas - Sergeant
11748 Royal Irish Rifles 15th Battalion *Died in War on 22 November 1917*
THIEPVAL MEMORIAL, France
Native of Lanark, Scotland and a holder of the Distinguished Conduct Medal he was a member of St Enoch's Presbyterian Church, Belfast. He had first joined his regiment in 1898 and fought in the Boer War, including at the relief of Ladysmith. Thereafter he left the Army and, an Orangeman, was politically active. He was involved in the formation of the old UVF before returning to the Army at the beginning of the war. He left behind a widow, Sarah Jane, and four surviving children. The youngest, Margaret, he was never to see.

Steel, James - Rifleman
15967 Royal Irish Rifles 15th Battalion *Died in War on 22 October 1918*
HARLEBEKE NEW BRITISH CEMETERY, Belgium
Born and enlisted in Belfast.

Steele, Alexander - Private
6177 The Loyal North Lancashire Regiment 1st Battalion *Died in War on 23 October 1914*
YPRES (MENIN GATE) MEMORIAL, Belgium
Son of Agnes Steele, of 26, Isabella Street, Belfast, and the late John Steele.

Steele, David - Rifleman
5543 Royal Irish Rifles 1st Battalion *Age 30 Killed in Action on 25 September 1915*
BOIS GRENIER COMMUNAL CEMETERY, France
Husband of Elizabeth Steele, of 4, Rowan Street, Belfast.

Steele, James - Private
75932 Royal Fusiliers (City of London Regiment) *Died in War on 24 April 1918*
POZIERES MEMORIAL, France
Born in Belfast, enlisted in Hove. Formerly 11625 Royal West Surry Regiment

Steele, James - Rifleman
10/15967 Royal Irish Rifles 15th Battalion *Died in War on 22 October 1918*
HARLEBEKE NEW BRITISH CEMETERY, Belgium
9 Perry Street, Belfast.

Steele, John M - Driver
64176 Royal Engineers 469th Field Company *Age 20 Died of Wounds on 19 April 1918*
MENDINGHEM MILITARY CEMETERY, Belgium
Son of Mrs. Steele, of 57, Silvergrove Street, Belfast.

Steele, Robert George - Lieutenant
Royal Naval Reserve HMS "Polandia" *Age 43 Drowned on 10 March 1917*
PLYMOUTH NAVAL MEMORIAL, United Kingdom
Son of Samuel and Anna Steele, of Belfast; husband of Lilian Smith (formerly Steele).

Steen, Alfred - Rifleman
9326 Royal Irish Rifles 1st Battalion *Killed in Action on 9 May 1915*
PLOEGSTEERT MEMORIAL, Belgium
Born and enlisted in Belfast.

Steenson, Alexander - Private
3579 Connaught Rangers 6th Battalion *Age 48 Died in War on 30 May 1916*
LOOS MEMORIAL, France
Son of Alexander and Mary Steenson, of Cookstown, County Tyrone; husband of Jane Steenson, of 59, Cawnpore Street, Belfast.

Steenson, Alfred - Rifleman
9396 Royal Irish Rifles 1st Battalion *Killed in Action on 9 May 1915*
PLOEGSTEERT MEMORIAL, Belgium
Born in Belfast, the son of Mr and Mrs William Steen.

Steenson, Charles - Rifleman
6676 Royal Irish Rifles 1st Battalion *Killed in Action on 9 May 1915*
PLOEGSTEERT MEMORIAL, Belgium
2, Millview Place, Belfast.

Steenson, Robert - Private
45288 Cameronians (Scottish Rifles) 16th Battalion *Died in accident while on active service on 19 May 1918*
GLASLOUGH CHURCH OF IRELAND NEW CEMETERY, Republic of Ireland
49, Montreal Street, Belfast. Son of Mary Steenson.

Steenson, Robert - Private
9823 Princess Victoria's (Royal Irish Fusiliers) 2nd Battalion *Died in War on 19 May 1918*
CAIRO WAR MEMORIAL CEMETERY, *Egypt*
Born in Dungannon, enlisted in Armagh, resident of Belfast.

Steenson, William John - Private
241005 Seaforth Highlanders "C" Company 1st/5th Battalion *Age 21 Killed in Action on 9 April 1917*
ROCLINCOURT VALLEY CEMETERY, *France*
Son of John and Isabella Steenson, of 161, Madrid Street, Belfast.

Stephenson, Thomas John - Sergeant
G/29856 Royal Irish Fusiliers *Age 46 Died of sickness on 2 March 1919*
BELFAST CITY CEMETERY, *United Kingdom*
Son of Robert and Ellen Stephenson; husband of Margaret M. Stephenson (née Cupples), of 280, Cupar Street, Springfield Road, Belfast. Born in Falls Park, Belfast. Twenty seven years service including in the South African Campaign

Stephenson, William - Sergeant
19849 Royal Irish Rifles 14th Battalion *Age 25 Killed in Action on 6 April 1916*
HAMEL MILITARY CEMETERY, BEAUMONT-HAMEL, *France*
Son of William R. and Fanny Stephenson, of 26, Fitzwilliam Street, Belfast.

Sterling, J - Private
PLY/13644 Royal Marine Light Infantry 2nd R.M. Battalion Royal Naval Division
Age 30 Killed in Action on 3 August 1916
TRANCHEE DE MECKNES CEMETERY, AIX-NOULETTE, *France*
Son of Elizabeth J. Sterling, of 2, Well Street, Woodstock Road, Belfast, and the late Robert Sterling.

Sterling, Samuel Young - Private
12465 Irish Guards 1st Battalion *Age 20 Died in War on 7 March 1918*
BROMPTON CEMETERY, *United Kingdom*
Son of Mary J. Sterling, of 70, Cedar Avenue, Belfast, and the late James Sterling. A medical student.

Sterling, Walter Ambrose - Private Second Class
310462 Royal Air Force *Age 14 Died of pneumonia on 5 November 1918*
SHANKILL CEMETERY, *United Kingdom*
Son of Wesley and Margaret Sterling, of 68, Newport Street, Belfast.

Sterrett, Thomas - Private
39755 Machine Gun Corps (Cavalry) *Died in War on 24 November 1917*
CAMBRAI MEMORIAL, *France*
Born in Belfast, enlisted in Bristol.

Stevens, Francis Henry - Sapper
13071 Corps of Royal Engineers 9th Field company *Died in War on 16 January 1915*
BAILLEUL COMMUNAL CEMETERY (NORD), *France*
Born in Belfast, enlisted in Dublin.

Stevenson, Aubrey - Sergeant
17012 Royal Irish Rifles 14th Battalion *Killed in Action on 1 July 1916*
THIEPVAL MEMORIAL, *France*
Born Ballymacarrett, Belfast. Enlisted in Belfast.

Stevenson, Harold George - Second Lieutenant
York and Lancaster Regiment 13th Battalion *Age 21 Died in War on 25 June 1917*
ORCHARD DUMP CEMETERY, ARLEUX-EN-GOHELLE, France
Educated at RBAI, Belfast.

Stevenson, Hugh - Private
19861 Highland Light Infantry 11th Battalion *Age 31 Died in War on 25 September 1915*
LOOS MEMORIAL, France
Husband of Margaret Stevenson (née Craig), of 7, Ninth Street, Belfast.

Stevenson, Hugh - Private
3330 Royal Inniskilling Fusiliers 1st Battalion *Age 21 Died in War on 21 August 1915*
HELLES MEMORIAL, Turkey
Son of Alexander and Mary Stevenson, of 61, Methuen Street, Belfast.

Stevenson, Hugh - Rifleman
6480 Royal Irish Rifles 1st Battalion *Killed in Action on 21 March 1918*
POZIERES MEMORIAL, France
Born in Belfast, enlisted in Newtownards.

Stevenson, Joseph - Lance Corporal
13512 Royal Irish Rifles 9th Battalion *Killed in Action on 1 July 1916*
THIEPVAL MEMORIAL, France
31, Tennent Street, Belfast. Husband of Sarah Stevenson.

Stevenson, Joseph - Rifleman
13646 Royal Irish Rifles 9th Battalion *Died in War on 20 September 1916*
BAILLEUL COMMUNAL CEMETERY EXTENSION (NORD), France
Born and enlisted in Belfast.

Stevenson, Robert - Corporal
41628 Royal Engineers 71st Field Company *Died in War on 1 May 1918*
BASRA MEMORIAL, Iraq
Born and enlisted in Belfast.

Stevenson, Thomas - Private
267495 Seaforth Highlanders 6th Battalion *Killed in Action on 31 July 1917*
YPRES (MENIN GATE) MEMORIAL, Belgium
A native of Belfast and enlisted in the city.

Stewart, Albert Lewis - Major
Machine Gun Corps (Infantry) 22nd Battalion *Age 28 Died in War on 4 October 1917*
HOOGE CRATER CEMETERY, Belgium
Awarded the Distinguished Service Order. Son of Mrs Stewart of 101 Wellesley Avenue, Belfast; and the late James Stewart (Solicitor).

Stewart, Alfred - Private
Royal Inniskilling Fusiliers 2nd Battalion *Died in War on 16 May 1915*
LE TOURET MEMORIAL, France
59 Canmore Street the son of May and the late John Stewart. His brother was also killed.

Stewart, Arthur - Private
L/9858 Royal Fusiliers 1st Battalion *Age 30 Died of Wounds on 19 October 1914*
CHAPELLE-D'ARMENTIERES OLD MILITARY CEMETERY, France
Son of Arthur Stewart, of London; husband of Laura Pritchard (formerly Stewart), of 6, Selina Street, Grosvenor Road, Belfast.

Stewart, Charles - Corporal
8396 Royal Irish Rifles 1st Battalion *Age 38 Died as a result of war on 14 December 1918*
BELFAST (MILLTOWN) ROMAN CATHOLIC CEMETERY, United Kingdom
Son of John and Mary Stewart 3, Legmail Street, Ballysillan Road, Belfast.

Stewart, Charles - Greaser
Mercantile Marine S.S. "Howth Head" (Belfast)
Age 28 Killed, as a result of an attack by an enemy submarine on 19 April 1917
TOWER HILL MEMORIAL, United Kingdom
Son of Rachel Stewart, of 21, Carnmoney Street, Belfast, and the late Mr. Stewart; husband of the late Jane Stewart (née Rolston). Born in Belfast.

Stewart, Eric Hilton - Corporal
5676 Royal Fusiliers 20th Battalion *Age 21 Died in War on 16 July 1916*
THIEPVAL MEMORIAL, France
Son of H. Hilton Stewart and Maude M. Stewart, of, Chattenden, Chichester Park, Belfast.

Stewart, George - Private
2978 Australian Infantry 46th Battalion *Age 38 Died in War on 1 October 1917*
YPRES (MENIN GATE) MEMORIAL, Belgium
Son of George and Martha Stewart; husband of Martha Maria Stewart, of 13, Gosford Road, Adamstown, New South Wales. Native of Belfast, Ireland.

Stewart, Hugh Henry - Rifleman
8/13657 Royal Irish Rifles 8th Battalion *Died in War on 2 July 1916*
GRANDCOURT ROAD CEMETERY, GRANDCOURT, France
Son of Henry Stewart, of 28, Belvoir Street, Belfast.

Stewart, Hugh James - Private
A/22156 Canadian Infantry (Manitoba Regiment) 8th Battalion *Age 24 Died of Wounds on 8 September 1916*
PUCHEVILLERS BRITISH CEMETERY, France
Son of Hugh and Alice Stewart, of Cregagh Belfast, Ireland. He worked as a clerk, a Presbyterian.

Stewart, James Andrew - Rifleman
19861 Royal Irish Rifles 14th Battalion *Age 24 Died in War on 15 February 1917*
BAILLEUL COMMUNAL CEMETERY EXTENSION (NORD), France
Son of James and Jane Stewart, of 3, Virginia Street, Belfast.

Stewart, James - Private
12267 Royal Inniskilling Fusiliers 5th Battalion *Killed in Action on 15 August 1915*
HELLES MEMORIAL, Turkey
Born in Belfast.

Stewart, James - Private
4227 Seaforth Highlanders attached 185th Tunnelling Company Royal Engineers *Died in War on 4 August 1916*
LOUEZ MILITARY CEMETERY, DUISANS, France
Husband of Mrs. M. Stewart of 88, Island Street, Belfast.

Stewart, James - Private
51441 Princess Patricia's Canadian Light Infantry (Eastern Ontario Regiment) *Died in War on 4 May 1915*
YPRES (MENIN GATE) MEMORIAL, Belgium
224 Hillman Street, Belfast. Born at Lisburn, a Presbyterian, he was a steel worker before joining the Army.

Stewart, James - Rifleman
9357 Royal Irish Rifles 1st Battalion *Age 25 Died of Wounds on 11 May 1915*
BOULOGNE EASTERN CEMETERY, *France*
Son of John and Mary Stewart, of 20, Ballycarry Street, Oldpark Road, Belfast.

Stewart, James Alexander - Rifleman
8264 Royal Irish Rifles 2nd Battalion *Killed in Action on 11 November 1914*
YPRES (MENIN GATE) MEMORIAL, *Belgium*
Born and enlisted in Belfast.

Stewart, John - Corporal
9299 Connaught Rangers 5th Battalion *Age 26 Died in War on 7 December 1915*
HELLES MEMORIAL, *Turkey*
Son of Sophia Stewart, of 388, Beersbridge Road, Bloomfield, Belfast, and the late John Stewart.

Stewart, John - Private
3044 Irish Guards 1st Battalion *Died in War on 1 November 1914*
YPRES (MENIN GATE) MEMORIAL, *Belgium*
56, Carmel Street, Belfast. Born in County Monaghan.

Stewart, John - Rifleman
243 Royal Irish Rifles 15th Battalion *Killed in Action on 1 July 1916*
THIEPVAL MEMORIAL, *France*
Son of John and Rebecca Stewart, Shankill Road, Belfast.

Stewart, Joseph - Private
4167 Royal Irish Rifles 2nd Battalion *Died of Wounds on 25 September 1915*
LIJSSENTHOEK MILITARY CEMETERY, *Belgium*
45, Urney Street, Belfast. Husband of May and father of three young children.
An Army Reservist he was a member of Nelson Temperance Flute Band .

Stewart, Patrick - Corporal
191 Royal Irish Fusiliers 1st Garrison Battalion *Age 31 Drowned on 4 April 1918*
TAUKKYAN MEMORIAL, *Myanmar*
Son of Michael and Ellen Stewart; husband of Alice Stewart, of 9, Fort Street, Springfield Avenue, Belfast.

Stewart, R - Rifleman
1091316 Royal Irish Rifles 12th Battalion *Age 19 Died in War on 8 March 1917*
ST. QUENTIN CABARET MILITARY CEMETERY, *Belgium*
Son of James and Martha Stewart, of Hydepark, Mallusk, Belfast.

Stewart, Robert - Private
11889 Royal Dublin Fusiliers 6th Battalion *Died in War on 15 August 1915*
HELLES MEMORIAL, *Turkey*
Born in Belfast, enlsited in Naas.

Stewart, Robert - Private
1282 Seaforth Highlanders 2nd Battalion *Died in War on 5 May 1915*
YPRES (MENIN GATE) MEMORIAL, *Belgium*
5 Manderson Street, Belfast.

Journey of Remembering

Stewart, Robert - Rifleman
13542 Royal Irish Rifles 2nd Battalion *Killed in Action on 6 September 1918*
PLOEGSTEERT MEMORIAL, *Belgium*
Born in Belfast, enlisted in Lisburn.

Stewart, Robert Hanna - Captain
Canadian Infantry (Alberta Regiment) 10th Battalion (Western Canada Regiment) *Died in War on 22 May 1915*
BROWN'S ROAD MILITARY CEMETERY, FESTUBERT, *France*
His father, William John, lived at 39 Distillery Street, Belfast, Ireland. Married to Margaret and an accountant by profession. He was a Presbyterian and had previously served with the Manchester Regiment.

Stewart, Samuel - Private
PLY/15164 Royal Marine Light Infantry HMS "Indefatigable" *Age 24 Killed in Action at Battle of Jutland on 31 May 1916*
PLYMOUTH NAVAL MEMORIAL, *United Kingdom*
Son of William and Ann Jane Stewart, of 3, Woodstock Place, Woodstock Road, Belfast. Native of Castlereagh, Belfast.

Stewart, Samuel - Rifleman
12440 Royal Irish Rifles 15th Battalion *Died in War on 10 January 1917*
ST. QUENTIN CABARET MILITARY CEMETERY, *Belgium*
Son of Matthew and Catherine Stewart, of Ballymena, County Antrim; husband of Annie Stewart, of 3, Lower Urney Street, Belfast.

Stewart, Thomas - Corporal
43967 Machine Gun Corps (Infantry) *Died in War on 24 September 1918*
BELLICOURT BRITISH CEMETERY, *France*
Born in Belfast, enlisted Holywood. Son of John and Mary, 29, Canmore Street, Belfast. Formerly 6152 Royal Irish Fusiliers

Stewart, Thomas - Private
43518 Cameronians (Scottish Rifles) 9th Battalion *Died in War on 21 October 1916*
THIEPVAL MEMORIAL, *France*
Born in Belfast, enlisted in Hamilton, Scotland.

Stewart, Thomas - Private
5451 Royal Irish Rifles 2nd Battalion *Killed in Action on 25 September 1915*
YPRES (MENIN GATE) MEMORIAL, *Belgium*
Son of Mrs. Louisa Stewart, of 65, Brownlow Street, Shankill Road, Belfast, and the late James Stewart.

Stewart, Thomas George - Lance Corporal
8/13653 Royal Irish Rifles 8th Battalion *Age 23 Killed in Action on 8 December 1916*
ST. QUENTIN CABARET MILITARY CEMETERY, *Belgium*
Son of James and Sarah Stewart, of 23, Lower Mount Street, Albert Bridge Road, Belfast.

Stewart, Thomas James - Private
2935 Royal Inniskilling Fusiliers 4th Battalion *Age 26 Died in War on 19 May 1919*
BELFAST (DUNDONALD) CEMETERY, *United Kingdom*
Son of Thomas J. and Elizabeth Stewart, of 165, Park Avenue, Sydenham, Belfast.

Stewart, Wesley - Rifleman
491 Royal Irish Rifles 15th Battalion *Age 21 Killed in Action on 21 March 1918*
POZIERES MEMORIAL, *France*
Son of Elizabeth Stewart, of 165, Park Avenue, Sydenham, Belfast, and Thomas Stewart.

Stewart, William - Private
24200 Royal Irish Fusiliers 1st Battalion *Died in War on 3 May 1917*
ARRAS MEMORIAL, France
Mother Elizabeth lived at 54 Carlow Street, Belfast.

Stewart, William - Rifleman
13663 Royal Irish Rifles 9th Battalion *Age 18 Died in War on 5 February 1915*
LISBURN CEMETERY, United Kingdom
Son of Andrew and Mary Stewart, of 155, Mayo Street, Belfast.

Stewart, William - Rifleman
163 Royal Irish Rifles 13th Battalion *Age 20 Killed in Action on 16 August 1917*
TYNE COT MEMORIAL, Belgium
Son of John Alexander Stewart and Sarah Stewart, of 112, Ravenhill Road, Belfast.

Stewart, William - Rifleman
2551 Royal Irish Rifles 11th Battalion *Killed in Action on 1 July 1916*
THIEPVAL MEMORIAL, France
Born in Belfast, enlisted Randalstown.

Stewart, William - Rifleman
4964 Royal Irish Rifles 7th Battalion *Died in War on 26 April 1916*
VERMELLES BRITISH CEMETERY, France
Born in Belfast, enlisted in Waringstown, County Down.

Stewart, William - Sergeant
41320 Royal Army Medical Corps 92nd Field Ambulance *Killed in Action on 9 November 1918*
MAZINGHIEN COMMUNAL CEMETERY, Belgium
6 Malt Street, Belfast.

Stewart, William A - Private
54914 Highland Light Infantry 1st/7th Battalion *Died in War on 21 September 1918*
SUNKEN ROAD CEMETERY, BOISLEUX-ST. MARC, France
Son of Mr. T. Stewart, of 46, North Boundary Street, Belfast.

Stewart, William M H - Second Lieutenant
Royal Inniskilling Fusiliers 11th Battalion *Killed in Action on 16 August 1917*
TYNE COT MEMORIAL, Belgium
Member of Fortwilliam Presbyterian Church.

Stirling, Robert - Rifleman
45858 Royal Irish Rifles 1st Battalion *Killed in Action on 3 June 1918*
HOOGSTADE BELGIAN MILITARY CEMETERY, Belgium
Born in County Durham, enlisted Sunderland, resident of Belfast. Formerly 4449 Durham Light Infantry.

Stitt, Francis - Sergeant
5156 Royal Irish Rifles 7th Battalion *Died in War on 11 September 1916*
BOIS GUILLAUME COMMUNAL CEMETERY, France
Born in Lisburn, enlisted in Waringstown, County Down. Resident of Belfast.

Stitt, John - Bombardier
35877 Royal Field Artillery 36th Trench Mortar Battery *Died of Wounds on 7 January 1917*
BAILLEUL COMMUNAL CEMETERY EXTENSION (NORD), France
20, Sixth Street, Belfast. Sister and brother in law were Maggie and James McWha.
An Orangeman and member of the old UVF he was also a member of the Wellington Flute Band.

Stitt, John Reid - Rifleman
8560 Royal Irish Rifles 2nd Battalion *Age 24 Died of dysentery on 29 September 1914*
LES GONARDS CEMETERY, VERSAILLES, France
Son of William and Agnes Stitt, of 8, Parker Street, Newtownards Road, Belfast.

Stitt, Robert - Rifleman
1458 Royal Irish Rifles 15th Battalion *Died in War on 22 November 1917*
THIEPVAL MEMORIAL, France
Son of Robert Henry and Margaret Stitt, of 13, Broom Street, Woodvale Road, Belfast.

Stockman, Henry - Rifleman
12151 Royal Irish Rifles 15th Battalion *Killed in Action on 1 July 1916*
THIEPVAL MEMORIAL, France
Born and enlisted in Belfast.

Stormonth, Alexander - Private
10203 Argyll and Sutherland Highlanders "D" Company 2nd Battalion
Age 28 Died in War on 10 November 1914
PLOEGSTEERT MEMORIAL, Belgium
Son of Thomas and Margaret Stormonth, of 16, Grove Street, Belfast; husband of
Margaret Cowan Stormonth, of 17 Stanners Street, Greenock.

Story, Louis Percival St. John - Surgeon Probationer
Royal Naval Volunteer Reserve HMS "Opal" *Age 22 Drowned in wreck of vessel off Orkneys on 12 January 1918*
PORTSMOUTH MEMORIAL, United Kingdom
Son of Rev. Lawrence Parsons Story, and Katharine Evelyn Story, of 41, Ulsterville Avenue, Belfast.

Stouppe, William - Private
18036 Border Regiment 2nd Battalion *Died in War on 25 September 1915*
LOOS MEMORIAL, France
Born in Belfast, enlisted in Cumberland, England.

Strahan, Henry - Corporal
16981 Royal Irish Rifles 3rd Battalion *Died in War on 31 January 1916*
BELFAST CITY CEMETERY, United Kingdom
Born and enlisted in Belfast.

Strain, John - Gunner
44805 Royal Field Artillery 82nd Battery *Age 27 Died as a Turkish Prisoner of War on 4 August 1916*
BAGHDAD (NORTH GATE) WAR CEMETERY, Iraq
Son of John and Margaret Ann Strain, of 33, North Thomas Street, Belfast.

Strain, John - Private
6315 Royal Inniskilling Fusiliers 2nd Battalion *Died in War on 15 May 1915*
LE TOURET MEMORIAL, France
Born and enlisted in Belfast.

Journey of Remembering

Strain, Robert George - Corporal
84945 King's (Liverpool Regiment) 7th Battalion formerly M/286463 Army Service Corps
Died in War on 27 September 1918
MOEUVRES COMMUNAL CEMETERY EXTENSION, France
Born and enlisted in Belfast. Awarded the Military Medal

Strain, William - Private
12821 Royal Inniskilling Fusiliers 6th Battalion *Age 19 Killed in Action on 7 December 1915*
DOIRAN MEMORIAL, Greece
Son of David and Mary Strain, of 3, Urney Street, Shankill Road, Belfast.

Stranaghan, Robert - Private
7955 Royal Inniskilling Fusiliers 3rd Battalion *Age 34 Died in War on 20 November 1914*
CLACTON CEMETERY, United Kingdom
Son of the late Andrew and Mary Stranaghan. Born at Belfast.

Straney, James - Private
5096 Dorsetshire Regiment 2nd Battalion *Died in War on 1 December 1915*
BASRA MEMORIAL, Iraq
Born in Belfast, enlisted in London.

Strange, Samuel - Stoker
326V Royal Navy HMS "Queen Mary" *Died in War on 31 May 1916*
PORTSMOUTH MEMORIAL, United Kingdom
Coventry Street, Belfast.

Stranney, James - Private
1580 Royal Munster Fusiliers 8th Battalion *Died in War on 4 September 1916*
THIEPVAL MEMORIAL, France
Born in Belfast.

Stringer, John - Private
2242 Royal Irish Regiment 6th Battalion *Killed in Action on 25 October 1916*
LA LAITERIE MILITARY CEMETERY, Belgium
Son of Mr. T. Stringer, of 96, Maryville Street, Belfast.

Stuart, Daniel - Rifleman
8956 Royal Irish Rifles 2nd Battalion *Age 40 Killed in Action on 25 September 1915*
YPRES (MENIN GATE) MEMORIAL, Belgium
Son of Patrick Stuart; husband of the late Bridget Stuart, of 4, Alexander Street, Belfast.

Stuart, Herbert W - Corporal
49655 Royal Army Medical Corps 73rd Field Ambulance *Age 28 Died in War on 19 August 1916*
BRONFAY FARM MILITARY CEMETERY, BRAY-SUR-SOMME, France
Son of James and Fannie Stuart, of 20, Ravenhill Gardens, Belfast.

Stuart, John - Private
20412 Royal Dublin Fusiliers 2nd Battalion *Age 34 Died whilst prisoner of war on 29 October 1918*
LE CATEAU MILITARY CEMETERY, France
Husband of Jane Stuart, of 48, Forest Street, Belfast.

Stuart, William Isaac - Private
PO/16616 Royal Marine Light Infantry HMS "Black Prince" *Age 21 Killed in Action at Battle of Jutland on 31 May 1916*
PORTSMOUTH NAVAL MEMORIAL, United Kingdom
Son of William and Marion Stuart; brother of Marion Franaitis, of 29, Hart Street, London Road, Liverpool. Native of Belfast.

Stuart, William Patrick - Private
41598 Royal Irish Fusiliers 9th (North Irish Horse) Battalion *Age 29 Died of Wounds on 30 March 1918*
HAM BRITISH CEMETERY, MUILLE-VILLETTE, France
Son of Andrew and Mary Stuart, of 6, New Bond Street, Belfast.

Sturgeon, William - Rifleman
8827 Royal Irish Rifles "B" Company 1st Battalion *Age 25 Killed in Action on 12 March 1915*
LE TOURET MEMORIAL, France
Son of Mrs. Mary Thompson, of 37, Montreal Street, Belfast.

Suffern, Robert - Master
Mercantile Marine "Teelin Head"
Age 56 Drowned, as a result of an attack by an enemy submarine on 21 January 1918
TOWER HILL MEMORIAL, United Kingdom
Son of the late Robert and Mary Suffern, of Balmoral, Belfast; husband of Elizabeth Eleanor Suffern, of "Martells", Holywood, County Down. Educated at Belfast Royal Academy.

Sullivan, Bernard - Rifleman
7797 Royal Irish Rifles 2nd Battalion *Killed in Action on 26 October 1914*
LE TOURET MEMORIAL, France
33, Cupar Street, Belfast.

Sullivan, James - Ordinary Signalman
J/43884 Royal Navy HMS "Laforey" *Age 25 Killed by mine explosion in Straits of Dover on 23 March 1917*
CHATHAM NAVAL MEMORIAL, United Kingdom
Son of John and Jane Sullivan, of 37, Fallswater Street, Belfast.

Sullivan, John - Private
3749 Irish Guards 1st Battalion *Died as a Prisoner of War on 28 July 1915*
NIEDERZWEHREN CEMETERY, Germany
Born in Lismore, County Waterford, enlisted in Dublin, resident of Belfast.

Sullivan, Thomas - Private
9793 Princess Charlotte of Wales's (Royal Berkshire Regiment) 2nd Battalion *Died in War on 25 September 1915*
WHITE CITY BOIS GRENIER COMMUNAL CEMETERY, France
Born in Belfast. Enlisted in Reading, England. Resident in Toronto, Canada.

Surgenor, Leslie - Private
6276 Royal Warwickshire Regiment 2/6th Battalion *Died in War on 19 July 1916*
LOOS MEMORIAL, France
Enlisted in Bournemouth, resident of Belfast. Formerly 2151 Hampshire Regiment.

Surgenor, Robert - Lance Corporal
19784 Royal Irish Rifles 8th Battalion *Died in War on 3 November 1917*
METZ-EN-COUTURE COMMUNAL CEMETERY BRITISH EXTENSION, France
Born and enlisted in Belfast.

Surgenor, Thomas - Private
S/10591 Black Watch (Royal Highlanders) 2nd Battalion *Died in War on 15 July 1916*
BASRA WAR CEMETERY, Iraq
Born in Belfast, enlisted in Irvine, Scotland. Formerly 21445 Cameron Highlanders.

Sutherland, Edward - Lance Corporal
7655 Royal Irish Rifles 1st Battalion *Age 28 Killed by shellfire on 1 July 1916*
AVELUY COMMUNAL CEMETERY EXTENSION, France
Son of the late Edward Sutherland, of Shankill Road, Belfast; husband of Mary Sutherland, of 1, Lisbon Street, Albertbridge Road, Belfast.

Swain, George - Rifleman
948 Royal Irish Rifles 9th Battalion *Died in War on 1 July 1916*
CONNAUGHT CEMETERY, THIEPVAL, France
12, Kenswick Street, Belfast. Husband of Mary Jane and father of a small son.

Swain, John - Gunner
30323 Royal Garrison Artillery *Died in War on 8 May 1916*
AMARA WAR CEMETERY, Iraq
Born and enlisted in Belfast.

Swain, Samuel - Private
24811 Machine Gun Corps (Infantry) 107th Company *Died of Wounds on 17 August 1917*
LIJSSENTHOEK MILITARY CEMETERY, Belgium
Son of George and the late Annie Swain, of Shankill Road, Belfast. A member of the old UVF.

Swain, William Steadman - Able Seaman
Mersey Z/57 Royal Naval Volunteer Reserve Howe Battalion Royal Naval Division *Age 23 Died in War on 5 July 1915*
SKEW BRIDGE CEMETERY, Turkey
Son of Henry and Annie Swain, of 70, Monfa Road, Orrell, Bootle, Liverpool. Native of Belfast.

Swan, Andrew - Rifleman
908 Royal Irish Rifles 15th Battalion *Died in War on 11 June 1916*
HAMEL MILITARY CEMETERY, BEAUMONT-HAMEL, France
Born and enlisted in Belfast.

Swan, J - Stoker
Royal Navy HMS "Pathfinder" *Died in War on 15 May 1915*
2, Orchard Street, Belfast.

Sweeney, Charles - Able Seaman
Mercantile Marine S.S. "Wyndhurst" (Swansea)
Age 17 Drowned, as a result of an attack by an enemy submarine on 6 December 1917
TOWER HILL MEMORIAL, United Kingdom
Son of the late John and Elizabeth Sweeney. Born in Belfast.

Sweeney, Edward - Acting Lance Corporal
T/25543 Royal Army Service Corps *Died in War on 6 April 1917*
BELFAST CITY CEMETERY, United Kingdom
Born and enlisted in Dublin, resident of Belfast.

Journey of Remembering

Sweeney, John - Private
2197 Connaught Rangers 6th Battalion *Died in War on 31 January 1916*
BETHUNE TOWN CEMETERY, France
Husband of Sarah Sweeney, of 36, Stanhope Street, Belfast. His newspaper memorial said, 'Oh Immaculate Heart of Mary, / Your prayers on him extol; / Oh Sacred Heart of Jesus, / Have mercy on his soul.'

Sweeney, Michael - Private
2511 Leinster Regiment 6th Battalion *Died from dysentery on 4 September 1918*
ALEXANDRIA (HADRA) WAR MEMORIAL CEMETERY, Egypt
92, Cupar Street. His brother John was killed in action 17 Aug 1917. Elizabeth, his wife, lost her brother in action and another was wounded. Michael had worked in Craig's Mill on the Falls Road.

Sweeney, Patrick - Private
3396 Princess Victoria's (Royal Irish Fusiliers) 1st Battalion *Died in War on 1 October 1918*
TYNE COT MEMORIAL, Belgium
Born and enlisted in Belfast.

Sweeney, Robert - Rifleman
9592 Royal Irish Rifles 1st Battalion *Killed in Action on 10 March 1917*
THIEPVAL MEMORIAL, France
Born and enlisted in Belfast. Formerly 45163 Cheshire Regiment

Swindle, John - Rifleman
18/908 Royal Irish Rifles 12th Battalion *Died in War on 29 May 1917*
POND FARM CEMETERY, Belgium
Born and enlisted in Belfast.

Swinfen, Percy Courtney - Second Lieutenant
Royal Flying Corps and General List *Age 18 Killed whilst flying (crashed) on 20 September 1917*
HULL WESTERN CEMETERY, United Kingdom
Son of Charles Percy and Milly Lucy Swinfen, of 49, Lyndhurst Drive, Leyton, London. Born at Belfast.

Symington, Charles - Rifleman
11234 Royal Irish Rifles 6th Battalion *Died in War on 11 August 1915*
HELLES MEMORIAL, Turkey
Brother of Mrs. Margaret Hughes, of 55, Rockville Street, Belfast.

Symons, John - Rifleman
Z/1032 Rifle Brigade 1st Battalion *Died in War on 3 April 1915*
PLOEGSTEERT MEMORIAL, Belgium
Born in Belfast, enlisted in Manchester.

Journey of Remembering

Taggart, John - Rifleman
19788 Royal Irish Rifles 13th Battalion *Killed in Action on 16 August 1917*
TYNE COT MEMORIAL, Belgium
Born and enlisted in Belfast.

Taggart, William - Gunner
1343 Royal Horse Artillery "A" Battery - 282nd Brigade *Died in War on 8 April 1917*
BOIS-LE-NOULETTE BRITISH CEMETERY, AIX-NOULETTE, France
Born and enlisted in Belfast.

Taggart, William - Rifleman
12162 Royal Irish Rifles 15th Battalion *Age 19 Killed in Action on 1 July 1916*
THIEPVAL MEMORIAL, France
Son of James and Matilda Taggart, of 54, Jaffa Street, Belfast.

Tate, Charles - Private
12465 Manchester Regiment 19th Battalion *Died in War on 30 March 1917*
BELLACOURT MILITARY CEMETERY, RIVIERE, France
Born in Belfast.

Tate, Charles Bernard - Captain
Royal Irish Rifles 15th Battalion *Age 27 Died in War on 1 July 1916*
THIEPVAL MEMORIAL, France
Son of the late Jon Tate of Rantalard, Belfast. Member of Masonic Lodge No. 7.

Tate, Frank - Private
41195 Princess Victoria's (Royal Irish Fusiliers) 9th Battalion *Killed in Action on 21 March 1918*
NOYON NEW BRITISH CEMETERY, France
Born in Belfast, enlisted in Antrim. Formerly 2119 North Irish Horse.

Tate, Hugh - Rifleman
12443 Royal Irish Rifles "A" Company 8th Battalion *Age 30 Killed in Action on 7 June 1917*
LONE TREE CEMETERY, Belgium
Husband of Sarah J. Tate, of 9, Mersey Street, Belfast.

Tate, James - Private
13943 Royal Irish Fusiliers 6th Battalion *Age 39 Died as a result of war on 10 February 1920*
BELFAST CITY CEMETERY, United Kingdom
Husband of Annie Tate, of 60, Claremont Lane, Albertbridge Road, Belfast.

Tate, Johnston - Second Lieutenant
Royal Irish Fusiliers 5th Battalion *Age 27 Died in War on 7 November 1917*
GAZA WAR CEMETERY, Israel
Son of the late Robert and Esther Tate of Belfast.

Taylor, Alfred Squire - Captain
Royal Army Medical Corps attached 10/11th Battalion Highland Light Infantry *Age 29 Killed in Action on 31 July 1917*
YPRES TOWN CEMETERY EXTENSION, Belgium
Son of the Rev David A Taylor, D.D., of "Eastbourne", Windsor Avenue North, Belfast.

Taylor, Arthur - Corporal
8922 Cheshire Regiment 1st Battalion *Died of Wounds on 4 June 1916*
LES BARAQUES MILITARY CEMETERY, SANGATTE, France
A married man, he had spent ten years in the Army. Two brothers also served.

Journey of Remembering

Taylor, Charles - Chief Engine Room Artificer
271165 Royal Navy HMS "Defence" *Killed in Action at Battle of Jutland on 31 May 1916*
PLYMOUTH NAVAL MEMORIAL, *United Kingdom*
Son of Margaret Taylor, of 23, Melrose Street, Belfast, and the late John Taylor.

Taylor, Charles Victor - Corporal
570 Royal Irish Rifles 16th Battalion *Died in War on 14 March 1918*
GRAND SERAUCOURT BRITISH CEMETERY, *France*
Born in Belfast, enlisted in Lurgan.

Taylor, George - Lieutenant
Royal Engineers 517th Field Company *Age 28 Died in War on 23 March 1918*
ASSEVILLERS NEW BRITISH CEMETERY, *France*
Son of Mrs. Jane Grey Taylor, of 63, Kansas Avenue, Belfast, and the late George Taylor.

Taylor, James - Private
268801 Sherwood Foresters (Nottinghamshire and Derbyshire Regiment) 2/7th Battalion *Died in War on 26 September 1917*
TYNE COT CEMETERY, *Belgium*
Born in Belfast, enlisted Derby, England.

Taylor, James Riddell - Lance Corporal
1116 Royal Irish Rifles 14th Battalion *Age 31 Died as a result of war on 22 December 1918*
RISEBERGA CHURCHYARD, *Sweden*
Son of Alexander and Sarah Taylor, of 77, South Parade, Belfast.

Taylor, John - Private
43463 Royal Scots Fusiliers 1st Battalion *Died in War on 21 August 1918*
RAILWAY CUTTING CEMETERY COURSELLES-LE-COMTE, *France*
Born in Belfast, enlisted Hamilton, Scotland.

Taylor, John Charles Alfred - Corporal
9295 Prince of Wales's (North Staffordshire Regiment) 1st Battalion *Killed in Action on 18 August 1916*
THIEPVAL MEMORIAL, *France*
Born in Belfast, enlisted Mill Hill, London.

Taylor, Samuel - Rifleman
16008 Royal Irish Rifles 12th Battalion *Age 21 Died in War on 14 April 1918*
TYNE COT MEMORIAL, *Belgium*
Son of John and Mary Ann Taylor, of 221, Ligoneil Road, Belfast.

Taylor, William Henry - Leading Stoker
4395 Royal Australian Navy HMAS "Penguin" *Died in War on 30 December 1917*
ROOKWOOD NECROPOLIS, SYDNEY, *Australia*
18, Newry Street, Belfast.

Taylor, William J - Rifleman
15989 Royal Irish Rifles 9th Battalion *Killed in Action on 1 July 1916*
CONNAUGHT CEMETERY, THIEPVAL, *France*
47, Turin Street. He left a wife, Annie and a young son.

Teeney, Samuel - Private
3158 Royal Inniskilling Fusiliers 2nd Battalion *Died in War on 1 April 1917*
SAVY BRITISH CEMETERY, *France*
17, Alma Street, Belfast. Youngest son of Mary and the late Alexander Teeney.

Journey of Remembering

Teeney, Samuel - Private
4943 Royal Munster Fusiliers 8th Battalion *Died in War on 28 June 1916*
ST PATRICK'S CEMETERY, LOOS, France
Born in Belfast, enlisted in Cork.

Tees, Percy Miller - Lance Corporal
16408 Royal Irish Regiment 2nd Battalion *Age 20 Died of Wounds on 4 November 1918*
TERLINCTHUN BRITISH CEMETERY, WIMILLE, France
Son of David and Jane Tees, of 80, North Parade, Belfast.

Telford, Robert - Rifleman
8422 Royal Irish Rifles 1st Battalion attached 25th Light Trench Mortar Battery
Age 27 Killed in Action on 30 August 1916
VERMELLES BRITISH CEMETERY, France
Husband of Mrs. Telford, of 20, Broadbent Street, Belfast.

Telford, Thomas Samuel - Sergeant
79840 Machine Gun Corps (Motors) *Age 19 Died of pneumonia on 12 March 1919*
BELFAST CITY CEMETERY, United Kingdom
Son of Thomas and Mary E. Telford, of 88, University Avenue, Belfast.

Templeton, Andrew - Rifleman
15/13715 Royal Irish Rifles 15th Battalion *Age 18 Died of Wounds on 8 November 1915*
FORCEVILLE COMMUNAL CEMETERY AND EXTENSION, France
Son of Margaret and the late Captain John Templeton, of 11, Upper Meadow Street, Belfast.

Templeton, James - Private
09770 Royal Army Ordnance Corps *Died in War on 10 May 1917*
ACTON CHURCH OF IRELAND CHURCHYARD, COUNTY ARMAGH, United Kingdom
Born in Belfast, enlisted in Newry.

Templeton, James - Private
3855 Seaforth Highlanders (Ross-shire Buffs, the Duke of Albany's) 4th Battalion *Died in War on 9 June 1916*
AUBIGNY COMMUNAL CEMETERY EXTENSION, France
Born and enlisted in Belfast.

Templeton, James - Private
7613 Royal Inniskilling Fusiliers 2nd Battalion *Killed in Action on 26 August 1914*
LA FERTE-SOUS-JOUARRE MEMORIAL, France
Husband of Susan Templeton, of 327, Cupar Street, Belfast.

Templeton, James - Private
8417 Royal Irish Rifles 2nd Battalion *Killed in Action on 25 October 1914*
LE TOURET MEMORIAL, France
Born and enlisted in Belfast the son of Robert and Martha Templeton; husband of Catherine Yendall, (formerly Templeton), of 15, The Avenue, Teesville, South Bank, Yorkshire.

Templeton, James - Rifleman
15/890 Royal Irish Rifles 15th Battalion *Age 20 Died in War on 19 March 1916*
MAILLY-MAILLET COMMUNAL CEMETERY EXTENSION, France
Son of William and Mary Ann Templeton, of 12, Enfield Street, Belfast.
Executed by firing squad for desertion.

Journey of Remembering

Templeton, Robert Miller - Private
5555 Royal Irish Rifles 2nd Battalion *Died of Wounds on 18 July 1916*
PUCHEVILLERS BRITISH CEMETERY, *France*
Born and enlisted in Belfast, son of George and Agnes Miller Templeton, of Ballymena, County Antrim.

Tennant, Thomas - Lieutenant
Australian Machine Gun Corps 5th Company *Age 29 Killed in Action on 14 November 1916*
WARLENCOURT BRITISH CEMETERY, *France*
Son of Robert and Elizabeth Tennant; husband of M. Tennant, of 4, Lothair Avenue, Belfast, Ireland. Native of Ballymena, County. Antrim.

Thomas, Charles - Rifleman
524 Royal Irish Rifles 12th Battalion *Died as a Prisoner of War on 25 July 1918*
BERLIN SOUTHERN-WESTERN CEMETERY, *Germany*
Born Ballymacarrett, Belfast. Enlisted in Carrickfergus. Brother of Mrs Mary Chambers, Sailors Row, Carrickfergus.

Thomas, David - Rifleman
19/58 Royal Irish Rifles 15th Battalion *Age 43 Died in War on 10 August 1916*
RATION FARM (LA PLUS DOUVE) ANNEXE, *Belgium*
Husband of Mary Thomas, of 57, Sussex Street, Belfast.

Thompson, Albert - Private
4033 Argyll & Sutherland Highlanders 1/8th Battalion *Died in War on 7 July 1916*
NORTH WALSHAM NEW CEMETERY, *United Kingdom*
Born in Belfast, enlisted in Argyl, Scotland.

Thompson, Alexander - Private
10507 Royal Inniskilling Fusiliers 2nd Battalion *Killed in Action on 20 October 1914*
PLOEGSTEERT MEMORIAL, *Belgium*
Born and enlisted in Belfast.

Thompson, Alexander - Private
6805 Royal Scots Fusiliers 1st Battalion *Age 19 Killed in Action on 14 March 1915*
TUILERIES BRITISH CEMETERY, *Belgium*
Son of Mrs. Margaret Thompson, of 86, Walton Street, Crumlin Road, Belfast.

Thompson, Alexander - Rifleman
1623 Royal Irish Rifles 8th/9th Battalion *Died in War on 23 November 1917*
CAMBRAI MEMORIAL, LOUVERVAL, *France*
Son of Mrs. Sarah Thompson, of 110, Woodvale Avenue, Belfast.

Thompson, Andrew - Private
4310 Seaforth Highlanders "C" Company 1/5th Battalion *Age 30 Died of Wounds on 17 May 1916*
AUBIGNY COMMUNAL CEMETERY EXTENSION, *France*
Son of John and Jane Thompson; husband of Ellen Thompson, of 22, Primrose Street, Ballynafeigh, Belfast.

Thompson, Archer - Stoker First Class
SS/104956 Royal Navy HMS "Hawke" *Killed in Action on 15 October 1914*
CHATHAM NAVAL MEMORIAL, *United Kingdom*
16, Selby Street, Belfast.

Belfast Book of Honour

JOURNEY OF REMEMBERING

Thompson, Arthur - Private
288960 Canadian Infantry (Manitoba Regiment) 78th Battalion *Age 34 Died in War on 7 August 1917*
MAROC BRITISH CEMETERY, GRENAY, France
Son of Agnes Harper, of 24, Glenbank Place, Ballysillan, Belfast. He worked as a boilermaker, and was a Presbyterian.

Thompson, Charles - Rifleman
7944 Royal Irish Rifles 13th Battalion *Killed in Action on 1 July 1916*
THIEPVAL MEMORIAL, France
Born in Donaghadee, County Down. Enlisted in Antrim and resident of Belfast.

Thompson, Charles Wesley - Rifleman
7549 Royal Irish Rifles 11th Battalion *Died in War on 9 August 1917*
YPRES (MENIN GATE) MEMORIAL, Belgium
Born in Belfast, enlisted in Lisburn.

Thompson, David - Private
3113 Royal Inniskilling Fusiliers 1st Battalion *Age 18 Died in War on 21 August 1915*
HELLES MEMORIAL, Turkey
Son of William and Catherine Thompson, of 14, Dunbar Street, Belfast.

Thompson, David - Rifleman
7868 Royal Irish Rifles 7th Battalion *Age 20 Killed in Action on 16 August 1917*
TYNE COT MEMORIAL, Belgium
Son of William A. Thompson, of 59, Craigmore Street, Belfast.

Thompson, David - Rifleman
8548 Royal Irish Rifles 1st Battalion *Killed in Action on 12 May 1915*
MERVILLE COMMUNAL CEMETERY, France
Husband of A. Thompson, of 35, Brownlow Street, Belfast. An Army Reservist he had worked in the Shipyard.

Thompson, Edward J - Private
8/26181 Royal Inniskilling Fusiliers 1st Battalion *Died of Wounds on 6 July 1917*
LIJSSENTHOEK MILITARY CEMETERY, Belgium
Son of the late James and Margaret Thompson of Wilton Street.

Thompson, Ernest - Private
53079 Manchester Regiment 2nd Battalion *Age 29 Died in War on 1 October 1918*
JONCOURT EAST BRITISH CEMETERY, France
Son of Anna Thompson, of 2A, Bedeque Street, Belfast.

Thompson, Ezekeil - Rifleman
4872 Royal Irish Rifles 1st Battalion *Killed in Action on 25 September 1915*
YPRES (MENIN GATE) MEMORIAL, Belgium
Born in Belfast, enlisted in Waringstown, County Down.

Thompson, Frank - Private
8823 Cheshire Regiment 1st Battalion *Died in War on 27 July 1916*
THIEPVAL MEMORIAL, France
Lived with his wife Laura and son Frankie at 42, Fortingale Street, Belfast.

Thompson, Fred - Private
15258 Royal Inniskilling Fusiliers 11th Battalion *Killed in Action on 1 July 1916*
CONNAUGHT CEMETERY, THIEPVAL, France
62, Hopewell Street, Belfast.

Journey of Remembering

Thompson, George - Private
10772 9th (Queen's Royal) Lancers *Died in War on 20 May 1915*
YPRES (MENIN GATE) MEMORIAL, Belgium
12, Emerald Street, Belfast.

Thompson, George - Private
2940 Royal Inniskilling Fusiliers 2nd Battalion *Died in War on 9 March 1915*
BETHUNE TOWN CEMETERY, France
Born and enlisted in Belfast, lived in 5, Rowan Street.

Thompson, Gordon - Lance Corporal
40606 Highland Light Infantry 15th Battalion (1st Glasgow) *Died in War on 3 April 1918*
BIENVILLERS MILITARY CEMETERY, France
Born in Islandmagee, County Antrim, enlisted in Glasgow, resident of Belfast.

Thompson, Herbert - Driver
T3/031111 Royal Army Service Corps *Died in War on 28 May 1918*
DUISANS BRITISH CEMETERY, ETRUN, France
Born and enlisted in Belfast.

Thompson, Hugh - Private
WR/42791 Royal Engineers *Age 44 Died as a result of War on 22 January 1919*
CARNMONEY (HOLY EVANGELISTS) CHURCH OF IRELAND CHURCHYARD EXTENSION, United Kingdom
Husband of Rebecca Smyth (formerly Thompson) 183, Crimea Street, Belfast.

Thompson, Hugh James - Private
2846 Royal Inniskilling Fusiliers 1st Battalion *Died of Wounds on 11 July 1915*
HELLES MEMORIAL, Turkey
57, Carnon Street, Belfast. His brother, John, was also killed.

Thompson, James - Gunner
1257958 Canadian Field Artillery Reserve Brigade *Age 20 Died in War on 20 April 1918*
BELFAST (DUNDONALD) CEMETERY, United Kingdom
Son of Thomas and Elizabeth Thompson, of 57, Hornby Street, Belfast. A Methodist, he had worked as a shipbuilder.

Thompson, James - Lance Corporal
30907 Royal Inniskilling Fusiliers "B" Company 2nd Battalion *Age 22 Died in War on 28 November 1917*
TYNE COT MEMORIAL, Belgium
Son of James and Margaret J. Thompson, of 11, Southland Street, Belfast.

Thompson, James - Private
739157 Canadian Infantry (Central Ontario Regiment) 4th Battalion *Age 21 Died of Wounds on 2 October 1918*
BUCQUOY ROAD CEMETERY, FICHEUX, France
Brother of Mary Jane Thompson, of 64, Joseph Street Belfast. An Anglican and a farmer.

Thompson, James - Private
7407 Royal Inniskilling Fusiliers 2nd Battalion *Died in War on 7 November 1914*
PLOEGSTEERT MEMORIAL, Belgium
Born and enlisted in Belfast.

Thompson, James - Rifleman
12971 Royal Irish Rifles 15th Battalion *Age 21 Killed in Action on 22 November 1917*
MOEUVRES COMMUNAL CEMETERY EXTENSION, France
Son of Andrew and Catherine Thompson, of 33, Limestone Road, Belfast.

Thompson, James Henry - Private
6615 South Lancashire Regiment 2nd Battalion *Age 32 Killed in Action on 24 October 1914*
LE TOURET MEMORIAL, *France*
Son of Charles and Teresa Thompson, of 37, Annadale Street, Antrim Road, Belfast. One of 5 brothers who served.

Thompson, John - Lance Corporal
16526 Princess Victoria's (Royal Irish Fusiliers) 7/8th Battalion *Died in War on 5 June 1917*
LA LAITERIE MILITARY CEMETERY, *Belgium*
Born in Belfast. Enlisted in Maryborough, Queen's County, resident of Belfast. Formerly 1857, Royal Irish Regiment.

Thompson, John - Private
10468 Royal Dublin Fusiliers 1st Battalion *Died in War on 25 April 1915*
V BEACH CEMETERY, *Turkey*
Son of Mr. J. Thompson, of 57, Carnan Street, Belfast. His brother, Hugh, was also killed.

Thompson, John - Private
16752 Royal Scots Fusiliers 6th Battalion *Died in War on 16 September 1915*
LOOS MEMORIAL, *France*
Born in Belfast, enlisted in Hamilton, Scotland.

Thompson, John - Private
9928 Princess Victoria's (Royal Irish Fusiliers) 1st Battalion *Died in War on 19 October 1916*
THIEPVAL MEMORIAL, *France*
Born in Templepatrick, enlisted in Lurgan, resident of Belfast.

Thompson, John - Rifleman
18/868 Royal Irish Rifles 12th Battalion *Age 22 Killed in Action on 1 July 1916*
HAMEL MILITARY CEMETERY, BEAUMONT-HAMEL, *France*
Son of the late Thomas Thompson and of Matilda Thompson, of The Cottages, Ballybeen, Dundonald, Belfast.

Thompson, John Crawford - Second Lieutenant
Royal Irish Rifles 5th Battalion attached 1st Battalion *Age 19 Killed in Action on 21 March 1918*
POZIERES MEMORIAL, *France*
Only son of Mrs. O. G. Thompson, of 7, Chlorine Gardens, Belfast, and the late James B. Thompson. He and another soldier were killed by shellfire. An observer noted that what was left of the two men "could be put on a shovel".

Thompson, John Lawless - Rifleman
17/217 Royal Irish Rifles 15th Battalion *Age 28 Died in War on 20 October 1918*
HARLEBEKE NEW BRITISH CEMETERY, *Belgium*
Son of Robert James Thompson, of 47, Enfield Street, Woodvale Road, Belfast, and the late Letitia Thompson. Holder of the Military Medal.

Thompson, John Wallace - Able Seaman
189958 Royal Navy HMS "Turbulent" *Killed in Action on 1 June 1916*
CHATHAM NAVAL MEMORIAL, *United Kingdom*
Son of Jacob and Mary Thompson, of 11, Forsythe Street, Belfast.
Served in the South African War and awarded the China Medal, 1900.

Thompson, Joseph - Private
7039 Irish Guards 2nd Battalion *Died in War on 30 September 1916*
THIEPVAL MEMORIAL, *France*
Husband of Eliza Jane Thompson, of 81, Solway Street, Belfast.

Journey of Remembering

Thompson, M - Rifleman
17021 Royal Irish Rifles 10th Battalion *Age 39 Died in War on 12 February 1915*
DROMARA FIRST PRESBYTERIAN CHURCHYARD, United Kingdom
Son of Robert and Annie Thompson (née Scott); husband of Martha Thompson, of 14, Balmoral Street, Belfast. Born at Dromara County Down.

Thompson, Richard - Rifleman
15094 Royal Irish Rifles 10th Battalion *Died of Wounds received on 1st July on 28 August 1916*
BELFAST CITY CEMETERY, United Kingdom
Husband of May Thompson, 36, Peveril Street, Belfast.

Thompson, Robert - Lance Corporal
5295 Royal Irish Rifles 1st Battalion *Killed in Action on 11 March 1915*
LE TOURET MEMORIAL, France
Born and enlisted in Belfast.

Thompson, Robert - Lance Corporal
6512 Royal Irish Rifles "C" Company 1st Battalion *Age 30 Killed in Action on 1 July 1916*
THIEPVAL MEMORIAL, France
Son of David and Hannah Thompson, of 77, Glasgow Street, Belfast.

Thompson, Robert - Private
12328 Royal Irish Regiment 8th Battalion *Died in War on 15 October 1918*
HOUPLINES COMMUNAL CEMETERY EXTENSION, France
Born and enlisted in Belfast. Formerly 8768 Royal Inniskilling Fusiliers

Thompson, Robert - Rifleman
17023 Royal Irish Rifles "B" Company 8th Battalion *Age 23 Killed in Action on 1 July 1916*
THIEPVAL MEMORIAL, France
Son of John Thompson, of 56, Constance Street, Belfast; husband of Annie Thompson, of 38, Frome Street, Belfast.

Thompson, Robert - Sergeant
201703 King's Own (Royal Lancaster Regiment) 1/4th Battalion *Died in War on 20 September 1917*
TYNE COT MEMORIAL, Belgium
Born and enlisted in Belfast. Formerly 9001 Hussars

Thompson, Robert James - Rifleman
3408 Royal Irish Rifles 15th Battalion *Died in War on 22 November 1917*
THIEPVAL MEMORIAL, France
Son of James and Mary Ann Thompson, of 35, Hanover Street, Belfast.

Thompson, Robert Lloyd - Major
Royal Field Artillery "C" Battery 173rd Brigade *Age 29 Died in War on 1 December 1917*
HERMIES HILL BRITISH CEMETERY, France
Awarded the Military Cross. The son of James Armstrong Thompson and Sara Thompson, of "Penrhyn", Strandtown, Belfast.

Thompson, Samuel - Private
46086 London Regiment East Surrey Regiment posted to 2/23rd Battalion *Age 23 Died in War on 1 November 1918*
TYNE COT MEMORIAL, Belgium
Son of Samuel and Mary Thompson, of 63, Donard Street, Ravenhill Road, Belfast.

Thompson, Samuel - Rifleman
21945 Royal Irish Rifles *Died in War on 5 September 1918*
FINS NEW BRITISH CEMETERY, SOREL-LE-GRAND, France
Son of William and Margaret Thompson of 3, Dagmar Street, Belfast.

Thompson, Shepherd - Rifleman
10/16015 Royal Irish Rifles 15th Battalion *Died in War on 5 October 1918*
DADIZEELE NEW BRITISH CEMETERY, Belgium
Son of Mr. J. Thompson, of 56, Constance Street, Belfast.

Thompson, Thomas - Boatswain's Mate
Mercantile Marine S.S. "Ivernia" (Liverpool)
Age 40 Drowned as a result of an attack by an enemy submarine on 1 January 1917
TOWER HILL MEMORIAL, United Kingdom
Son of Eliza Thompson, of 181, North Queen Street, Belfast, and the late Thomas Thompson.
Born in Carrickfergus.

Thompson, Thomas - Lance Corporal
14596 Royal Scots 11th Battalion *Age 24 Died in War on 26 January 1917*
CATHCART CEMETERY, United Kingdom
Son of the late John and Margaret Thompson of Belfast.

Thompson, Thomas - Private
2444 Royal Inniskilling Fusiliers *Died in War on 16 May 1915*
LE TOURET MEMORIAL, France
Born Ballymacarrett, Belfast. Enlisted in Belfast.

Thompson, Thomas - Private
3512 Seaforth Highlanders 4th Battalion *Age 31 Died in War on 19 November 1916*
THIEPVAL MEMORIAL, France
Son of Mrs. Ellen Thompson, of 35, Lilliput Street, Belfast.

Thompson, Thomas - Private
36441 Royal Army Medical Corps *Died in War on 1 November 1917*
BELFAST CITY CEMETERY, United Kingdom
Son of Thomas and Margaret Thompson; husband of Alice Thompson, of 7, Bann Street, Belfast.
Born at Belfast. 18 years' service. Served in the Chitral Expedition (1895), Punjab Frontier
and Tirah Expeditions (1897-8), and in the South African Campaign.

Thompson, Thomas - Sergeant
4457 Royal Irish Rifles 3rd Battalion *Died in War on 23 July 1915*
GRANGEGORMAN MILITARY, DUBLIN, Republic of Ireland
Born and enlisted in Belfast.

Thompson, William - Sergeant
6994 Royal Inniskilling Fusiliers *Age 33 Died in War on 13 December 1916*
LONDONDERRY CITY CEMETERY, United Kingdom
Son of John and Margaret Foy Thompson, of 544, Princess Street, Kingston, Ontario, Canada.
Born at Belfast, Ireland.

Thompson, William David - Private
135403 Canadian Infantry (Central Ontario Regiment) 19th Battalion *Age 22 Died in War on 11 June 1916*
BEDFORD HOUSE CEMETERY, *Belgium*
Son of Thomas Robert and Margaret Thompson, of 22, Iona Avenue, Toronto.
Born at Belfast, Ireland. A Presbyterian, he worked in the rubber industry.

Thompson, William Edward - Lance Corporal
1642 Royal Irish Rifles 1st Battalion *Age 21 Died of Wounds on 27 March 1918*
GRAND-SERAUCOURT BRITISH CEMETERY, *France*
Son of William Edward and the late Mary A. Thompson, of 49, Belmont Road, Strandtown, Belfast.

Thompson, William Henry - Private
Royal Munster Fusiliers 6th Battalion *Died in War on 9 August 1915*
2, Matlock Street, Belfast. A native of Newtownards, he was survived by his sister.

Thompson, William Thomas - Rifleman
7156 Royal Irish Rifles 1st Battalion *Killed in Action on 9 May 1915*
PLOEGSTEERT MEMORIAL, *Belgium*
Son of William and Mary Ann, 48, Brown Street, Belfast.

Thomson, Alfred Maurice - Captain
Royal Army Merdical Corps attached 7th Battalion Royal Sussex Regiment *Age 30 Died in War on 7 July 1916*
THIEPVAL MEMORIAL, *France*
Son of Alfred and Florence Thomson of Marlborough Park, Belfast. Educated at RBAI and
Queen's University. Killed whilst bringing in a wounded officer.

Thomson, Roland Francis Croasdaile - Private
629566 Canadian Infantry (Quebec Regiment) 14th Battalion *Age 41 Died in War on 26 September 1916*
VIMY MEMORIAL, *France*
Son of William Lisle Thompson and Mrs Thompson of Fountainville, Belfast, Ireland. Educated at RBAI
and the High School, Dublin. Served in the Boer War and afterwards became a poultry farmer in Canada.
Joined the Canadian Forces in 1915. An Anglican, he was also a member of the Canadian Militia.

Thomson, William Kerr - Squadron Quartermaster Sergeant
4703 13th Hussars *Age 34 Died in War on 25 July 1916*
BASRA WAR CEMETERY, *Iraq*
Son of Mary Thomson, of 56, Elm Row, Edinburgh, and the late J. K. Thomson. Native of Belfast.

Thornbury, James - Rifleman
6057 Rifle Brigade 2nd Battalion *Died in War on 6 October 1915*
Y FARM MILITARY CEMETERY, BOIS-GRENIER, *France*
Son of the late James and Agnes Thornbury, of Belfast.

Thornton, George William - Corporal
15418 Machine Gun Corps (Infantry) *Died in War on 26 May 1918*
MONT HUON MILITARY CEMETERY, LE TREPORT, *France*
Born in Belfast, enlisted in Hounslow, England. Formerly 12355, Royal Fusiliers

Thorpe, Alfred Victor - Rifleman
11428 Royal Irish Rifles 6th Battalion *Age 38 Killed in Action on 16 May 1917*
STRUMA MILITARY CEMETERY, *Greece*
Son of the late James and Mary Thorpe, of Belfast.

Tiffin, George Frederick Henry - Lance Corporal
544 Royal Irish Rifles 15th Battalion *Died in War on 7 June 1917*
YPRES (MENIN GATE) MEMORIAL, Belgium
31, Hopefield Street, Belfast.

Tiffin, James - Rifleman
17/176 Royal Irish Rifles 10th Battalion *Died in War on 23 December 1915*
MAILLY-MAILLET COMMUNAL CEMETERY EXTENSION, France
Son of Mr. Tiffin, of 3, Kavanagh Street, Belfast.

Tildesley, Percy - Rifleman
6721 Royal Irish Rifles 1st Battalion *Killed in Action on 6 March 1917*
THIEPVAL MEMORIAL, France
Born in Boosley, Shropshire, enlisted Birmingham, resident of Belfast.

Timbey, William Fairburn - Private
41232 Royal Irish Fusiliers 9th Battalion *Age 22 Died in War on 4 September 1918*
PLOEGSTEERT MEMORIAL, Belgium
Son of John and Eliza Jane Timbey, of 18, Athol Street, Belfast.

Tindall, John Ernest - Private
4473 Duke of Cornwall's Light Infantry 1/4th Battalion *Died in War on 3 October 1915*
BASRA MEMORIAL, Iraq
Born in Belfast, enlisted in Cornwall.

Tipping, William James - Rifleman
9615 Royal Irish Rifles 1st Battalion *Killed in Action on 1 July 1916*
OVILLERS MILITARY CEMETERY, France
Born and enlisted in Belfast.

Toal, Daniel - Gunner
187720 Royal Garrison Artillery 103rd Company *Age 38 Died in War on 5 March 1918*
ALEXANDRIA (CHATBY) MILITARY AND WAR MEMORIAL CEMETERY, Egypt
Son of Daniel and Jane Toal, of Belfast. Formerly 4382 Royal Irish Regiment.

Toal, J - Driver
1853833 Royal Engineers 55th Field Company *Age 40 Died as a result of war on 7 March 1921*
HAIDAR PASHA CEMETERY, Turkey
Son of James Toal, husband of Mary Toal, of 16, Seventh Street, Belfast. Born at Lurgan

Todd, (William Francis) Frank - Private
7305 Royal Irish Fusiliers 1st Battalion *Killed in Action on 22 October 1914*
HOUPLINES COMMUNAL CEMETERY EXTENSION, France
Son of the late William James and Harriett Todd, of Belfast. A member of the old UVF and the John Kensit Memorial Orange Lodge 869

Todd, Harold Edwin - Private
33568 Yorkshire Regiment 2nd Battalion *Died in War on 2 August 1917*
YPRES (MENIN GATE) MEMORIAL, Belgium
Son of James and Elizabeth Todd, of Claremount, Andersonstown, Belfast.

Journey of Remembering

Todd, Hugh - Engineer
Royal Naval Reserve No. 3 Special Service Squadron *Died in War on 3 July 1915*
CARNMONEY CEMETERY, United Kingdom
Brougham Street, Belfast.

Todd, John - Rifleman
15998 Royal Irish Rifles 15th Battalion *Died in War on 28 March 1918*
BOUCHOIR NEW BRITISH CEMETERY, France
Born and enlisted in Belfast.

Todd, John - Seaman
3767C Royal Naval Reserve HMS "Bayano" *Age 35 Killed in Action with submarine off the Clyde on 11 March 1915*
PORTSMOUTH NAVAL MEMORIAL, United Kingdom
Son of Mrs. George Todd, of Belfast; husband of Sarah Todd, of 22, Earl Lane, Belfast.

Todd, Robert - Driver
64272 Royal Engineers 150th Field Company *Killed in Action on 16 August 1917*
WHITE HOUSE CEMETERY, Belgium
Husband of Mrs. E. Todd, of 48, Wolff Street, Belfast.

Todd, Robert James - Rifleman
9241 Royal Irish Rifles 1st Battalion *Age 19 Killed in Action on 9 May 1915*
PLOEGSTEERT MEMORIAL, Belgium
Nephew of Susan Keeves, of 27, Jennymount Street, Belfast.

Todd, Robert John - Rifleman
20021 Royal Irish Rifles 1st Battalion *Died in War on 29 August 1918*
STE. MARIE CEMETERY, LE HAVRE, France
Son of Mrs Todd, 1, Greenville Avenue, Belfast.

Todd, Samuel - Rifleman
17/748 Royal Irish Rifles 9th Battalion *Died in War on 6 June 1916*
AUTHUILE MILITARY CEMETERY, France
Son of Stephen and Maggie Todd, of 36, Chief Street, Belfast.

Todd, Thomas - Rifleman
11537 Royal Irish Rifles 1st Battalion *Killed in Action on 11 April 1916*
BECOURT MILITARY CEMETERY, BECORDEL-BECOURT, France
Born in Belfast, enlisted Newtownards.

Todd, Thomas McQuilty - Fireman And Trimmer
Mercantile Marine S.S. "Bray Head" (Belfast) *Age 31 Drowned, as a result of an attack by an enemy submarine on 14 March 1917*
TOWER HILL MEMORIAL, United Kingdom
Son of James and Isabella Todd, of 39, Lilliput Street, Belfast. Born at Carrickfergus.

Todd, Victor
Wellington Regiment New Zealand Expeditionary Force 3rd Battalion *Died in War 4 October 1917*
TYNE COT MEMORIAL, Belgium
Son of John Todd and a former pupil of RBAI.

Todd, William - Private
9/27261 Royal Dublin Fusiliers 9th Battalion *Died in War on 18 July 1916*
MAZINGARBE COMMUNAL CEMETERY EXTENSION, France
77, Hawthorn Street, Belfast.

Todd, William - Rifleman
19/826 Royal Irish Rifles 15th Battalion *Died in War on 14 October 1918*
DADIZEELE NEW BRITISH CEMETERY, *Belgium*
Husband of Mrs I. Todd, of 6, Grace Avenue, Bloomfield, Belfast.

Todd, William Francis - Private
7365 Royal Irish Fusiliers 1st Battalion *Age 33 Killed in Action on 22 October 1914*
HOUPLINES COMMUNAL CEMETERY EXTENSION, *France*
Son of the late William James and Harriett Todd, of Belfast.

Tohill, John Patrick - Private
M1/08974 Royal Army Service Corps *Died in War on 26 January 1916*
ALBERT COMMUNAL CEMETERY EXTENSION, *France*
Born in Belfast, enlisted in London.

Tolland, Hugh - Sergeant
8900 Argyll & Sutherland Highlanders) 2nd Battalion *Died in War on 25 September 1915*
CAMBRIN CHURCHYARD EXTENSION, *France*
Born in Belfast, enlisted in Glasgow.

Toner, Christopher - Private
18511 Royal Irish Regiment 2nd Battalion *Killed in Action on 21 August 1918*
CAGNICOURT BRITISH CEMETERY, *France*
374, Ligoneil Road, Belfast.

Toner, James - Private
9303 Highland Light Infantry 1st Battalion *Died in War on 27 April 1915*
YPRES (MENIN GATE) MEMORIAL, *Belgium*
Born in Belfast.

Toner, John - Private
19295 Royal Dublin Fusiliers 8th Battalion *Died in War on 9 September 1916*
THIEPVAL MEMORIAL, *France*
Born in Belfast. enlisted in Dublin.

Toner, Patrick - Sergeant
1786 Leinster Regiment 7th Battalion *Age 29 Died of Wounds on 28 June 1916*
ST. PATRICK'S CEMETERY, LOOS, *France*
Son of Mrs. Elizabeth Toner, of 10, Smith Street, Belfast.

Toner, Thomas - Private
21039 Royal Irish Fusiliers 7th/8th Battalion *Age 19 Died in War on 24 July 1917*
VLAMERTINGHE NEW MILITARY CEMETERY, *Belgium*
Son of James and Isabella Toner, of 15, Limepark Street, Ballysillan, Belfast. Native of Moira, County Down.

Toner, William - Private
4698 Connaught Rangers 5th Battalion *Age 24 Killed in Action on 8 October 1918*
SERAIN COMMUNAL CEMETERY EXTENSION, *France*
Husband of Emile Toner, of 48, Hardinge Street, Belfast.

Toole, William - Corporal
8916 Royal Irish Rifles 2nd Battalion *Killed In Action on 25 September 1915*
YPRES (MENIN GATE) MEMORIAL, *France*
Born and enlisted in Belfast.

Toomath, James - Second Engineer
Mercantile Marine S.S. "Eveleen" (Belfast) *Age 29 Presumed drowned on 6 May 1918*
TOWER HILL MEMORIAL, *United Kingdom*
Son of Richard Toomath and the late Anna Toomath; husband of Elizabeth Toomath (née Steele), of 17, Kensington Avenue, Bloomfield, Belfast. Born in Belfast.

Topping, Allan - Corporal
15/16020 Royal Irish Rifles 15th Battalion *Age 22 Died in War on 28 September 1918*
HOOGE CRATER CEMETERY, *Belgium*
Son of Mrs. Elizabeth Topping, of 145, Mayo Street, Belfast.

Topping, Isaac - Rifleman
2398 Royal Irish Rifles 13th Battalion *Killed in Action on 8 December 1917*
THIEPVAL MEMORIAL, *France*
29, Unity Street, Belfast.

Topping, William - Rifleman
5554 Royal Irish Rifles 2nd Battalion *Killed in Action on 21 March 1918*
POZIERES MEMORIAL, *France*
79, Hudson Street, Belfast.

Torbitt, William - Private
12684 Royal Irish Fusiliers 6th Battalion *Age 35 Died in War on 15 August 1915*
HELLES MEMORIAL, *Turkey*
Son of Arthur and Agnes Torbitt, of 46, Summer Street, Belfast.

Torrans, Samuel - Rifleman
40229 Royal Irish Rifles "A" Company 10th Battalion *Age 22 Killed in Action on 7 June 1917*
YPRES (MENIN GATE) MEMORIAL, *Belgium*
Son of Thomas Torrans, of 17, Schomberg Street, Belfast.

Torrens, James - Second Lieutenant
Machine Gun Corps (Infantry) "B" Company 19th Battalion *Age 27 Died in War on 30 May 1918*
SEZANNE COMMUNAL CEMETERY, *France*
Son of James Torrens, of Everton, Knock, Belfast.

Totten, William - Rifleman
6407 Royal Irish Rifles 11th Battalion *Killed in Action on 1 July 1916*
THIEPVAL MEMORIAL, *France*
Born in Belfast, enlisted in Lisburn.

Totton, Archie - Private
12420 Royal Irish Fusiliers 5th Battalion *Died in War on 24 August 1915*
HELLES MEMORIAL, *Turkey*
Survived by his sister, Sarah Totton, of 35, Grosvenor Road, Belfast.

Totton, George - Private
3229 Royal Inniskilling Fusiliers 3rd Battalion *Age 24 Accidentally killed on 15 October 1919*
BELFAST (DUNDONALD) CEMETERY, *United Kingdom*
Son of Mary Totton, of 16, Convention Street, Belfast, and the late George Totton.

Totton, Herbert - Lance Corporal
2117 Black Watch (Royal Highlanders) 1/6th Battalion *Died in War on 18 February 1916*
CHIPILLY COMMUNAL CEMETERY, *France*
Son of Jackson Totton, Clara Park, Knock Belfast.

Totton, William - Rifleman
13742 Royal Irish Rifles 10th Battalion *Age 21 Killed in Action on 1 July 1916*
THIEPVAL MEMORIAL, *France*
Son of William and Charlotte Totton, of 13, Riversdale Street, Shankill Road, Belfast.

Toward, Louis Ormston - First Engineer
Mercantile Marine S.S. "Cairndhu" (Newcastle)
Age 43 Drowned, as a result of an attack by an enemy submarine on 15 April 1917
TOWER HILL MEMORIAL, *United Kingdom*
Husband of Isabel Dixon Toward (née Rutherford), of 5, Clovelly Gardens, Whitley Bay, Northumberland.
Born at Belfast.

Towe, John - Private
18731 Machine Gun Corps (Infantry) 109th Company *Age 25 Killed in Action on 1 July 1916*
THIEPVAL MEMORIAL, *France*
Son of Jane Towe, of 54, Richardson Street, Belfast, and the late Hugh Towe.

Towell, Henry - Driver
T1/3398 Royal Army Service Corps *Died in War on 8 July 1916*
AMARA WAR CEMETERY, *Iraq*
Born in Belfast, enlisted in Guildford, England.

Towell, William - Stoker First Class
SS/100382 Royal Navy HMS "Raglan" *Age 32 Killed in Action at Imbros with "Goeben" and "Breslau" on 20 January 1918*
PLYMOUTH NAVAL MEMORIAL, *United Kingdom*
Son of James and Lizzie Towell, of Belfast; husband of Annie Towell, of 7, St. Leonard Street, Belfast.

Townley, James - Rifleman
597 Royal Irish Rifles 8th Battalion *Died in War on 19 December 1915*
MAILLEY-MAILLET COMMUNAL CEMETERY EXTENSION, *France*
Born and enlisted in Belfast.

Tracey, John - Bandsman
9028 Royal Dublin Fusiliers 2nd Battalion *Died in War on 6 August 1917*
YPRES TOWN CEMETERY EXTENSION, *Belgium*
Had served in the Army for twenty five years and held the Long Service and Good Conduct Medal
Sister, Mrs Campbell lived at 108, Palmer Street, Belfast.

Trainor, Archie - Private
DM2/168399 Army Service Corps attached 10th Cavalry Brigade *Died in War on 16 October 1918*
DAMASCUS COMMONWEALTH CEMETERY, *Syria*
Born Ballymacarrett, Belfast. Enlisted in Belfast and resident of Holywood.

Trainor, Bernard John - Corporal
3524 Royal Irish Fusiliers 1st Battalion *Died in War on 7 May 1917*
FEUCHY CHAPEL BRITISH CEMETERY, WANCOURT, *France*
Son of James and Mary 12, Hartley Street, Belfast.

Journey of Remembering

Trainor, Francis - Private
23479 Royal Dublin Fusiliers 8th Battalion *Died in War on 29 April 1916*
LOOS MEMORIAL, France
Born in Belfast enlisted in Dublin.

Trainor, J - Sapper
33881 Royal Engineers 613th Fortress Company *Age 58 Died as a result of war on 19 December 1918*
BELFAST (MILLTOWN) ROMAN CATHOLIC CEMETERY, United Kingdom
Husband of Mrs Maria Trainor, of 33, Alexander Street, Belfast.

Trainor, John - Able Seaman
SS/374 Royal Navy HMS "Fauvette" *Died in War on 9 March 1916*
BELFAST (MILLTOWN) ROMAN CATHOLIC CEMETERY, United Kingdom
Husband of Jeanie Trainor, of 23, Rockville Street, Falls Road, Belfast. Worked as a postman, he had previously served twelve years in the Army and was a Reservist.

Trainor, John - Corporal
3524 Princess Victoria's (Royal Irish Fusiliers) 1st Battalion *Died in War on 7 May 1917*
FEUCHY CHAPEL BRITISH CEMETERY, WANCOURT, France
Born and enlisted in Belfast.

Trainor, Thomas - Lance Corporal
1121 Royal Army Medical Corps 99th Field Ambulance *Died suddenly while on active service on 26 July 1917*
OISSY CHURCHYARD, France
11, Canmore Street, Belfast.

Traynor, C - Fireman and Trimmer
Mercantile Marine S.S. "Waverley" (West Hartlepool)
Age 29 Drowned, as a result of an attack by an enemy submarine on 20 December 1917
TOWER HILL MEMORIAL, United Kingdom
Son of Mary Anne Traynor, of Crossmaglen, County Armagh, Ireland. Born at Belfast.

Treanor, James - Rifleman
8923 Royal Irish Rifles 1st Battalion *Killed in Action on 24 August 1917*
LIJSSENTHOEK MILITARY CEMETERY, Belgium
Born and enlisted in Belfast.

Trew, John - Rifleman
689 Royal Irish Rifles 12th Battalion *Age 23 Died in War on 25 July 1918*
PLOEGSTEERT MEMORIAL, Belgium
Son of Arthur and Annie Trew, of 15, Clovelly Street, Belfast.

Trimble, David Ditty - Private
7287 Royal Irish Rifles 2nd Battalion *Died of Wounds on 5 July 1915*
ETAPLES MILITARY CEMETERY, France
66, Belgrave Street, Belfast. Survived by his sister.

Trimble, William - Assistant Storekeeper
723122 Royal Navy HMS "Hilary" *Died in War on 26 May 1917*
PLYMOUTH NAVAL MEMORIAL, United Kingdom
Lived at Excise Street, Belfast, the son of Robert and Catherine Trimble, of 3, Lonsdale Street, Armagh.

Troland, Daniel - Chief Engineer
Mercantile Marine S.S. "Dingle" (Liverpool) *Age 40 Killed by mine on 20 February 1916*
TOWER HILL MEMORIAL, United Kingdom
Son of the late Hugh and Martha Donnelly Troland; husband of Mary Jane Troland (née Rooney), of 32, New Dock Street, Belfast. Born at Belfast. Father of James Troland.

Troland, James - Fireman
Mercantile Marine S.S. "Dingle" (Liverpool) *Age 18 Killed by mine on 20 February 1916*
TOWER HILL MEMORIAL, United Kingdom
Son of Mary Jane Troland, of 32, New Dock Street, Belfast, and the late Daniel Troland.

Truesdale, John - Rifleman
6/11558 Royal Irish Rifles 6th Battalion *Age 23 Killed in Action on 16 May 1917*
STRUMA MILITARY CEMETERY, Greece
Son of William and Ellen Truesdale, of 70, Moyola Street, Belfast.

Tullock, David - Rifleman
310 Royal Irish Rifles 8th Battalion *Died in War on 21 September 1916*
RATION FARM (LA PLUS DOUVE) ANNEXE, Belgium
Born and enlisted in Belfast.

Tully, David - Stoker First Class
SS/107383 Royal Navy HMS "Hawke" *Killed in Action with submarine in North Sea on 15 October 1914*
CHATHAM NAVAL MEMORIAL, United Kingdom
Son of George and Susannah Tully of 95, Bristol Street, Belfast.

Tully, William - Private
3239 Royal Inniskilling Fusiliers *Killed in Action on 16 August 1917*
TYNE COT CEMETERY, Belgium
Born and enlisted in Belfast.

Tumblety, William - Rifleman
8619 Royal Irish Rifles 2nd Battalion *Killed in Action on 25 October 1914*
PONT-DU-HEM MILITARY CEMETERY, LA GORGUE, France
Born and enlisted in Belfast.

Turkington, William James - Private
41173 Royal Irish Fusiliers 9th (North Irish Horse) Battalion *Age 26 Died in War on 23 November 1917*
CAMBRAI MEMORIAL, LOUVERVAL, France
Son of William James and Hannah Turkington, of 10, University Avenue, Belfast.

Turley, Francis Joseph - Corporal
13/745 East Yorkshire Regiment "B" Company 13th Battalion *Age 34 Died in War on 13 November 1916*
QUEENS CEMETERY, PUISIEUX, France
Son of Robert and Eliza Turley, of Belfast; husband of Florence May Turley, of 11, Pelham Terrace, Beaumont Street, Hull.

Turley, John - Rifleman
3932 Royal Irish Rifles 1st Battalion *Age 34 Killed in Action on 31 July 1917*
YPRES (MENIN GATE) MEMORIAL, Belgium
Husband of Annie Turley of 107, Cyprus Street, Belfast.

Turley, Martin - Rifleman
8977 Royal Irish Rifles 2nd Battalion *Died Of Wounds on 7 May 1916*
AUBIGNY COMMUNAL CEMETERY EXTENSION, France
Born and enlisted in Belfast.

Turnbull, Alexander - Lance Corporal
3572 Lancashire Fusiliers 1st Battalion *Died in War on 25 April 1917*
TILLOY BRITISH CEMETERY, TILLOY-LES-MOFFLAINES, France
Born in Belfast, enlisted in Belfast.

Turnbull, Alexander Miller - Second Lieutenant
Royal Flying Corps 12th Squadron and General List *Age 24 Died in War on 25 April 1917*
VIS-EN-ARTOIS BRITISH CEMETERY, HAUCOURT, France
Son of Martin Harper Turnbull and Agnes Edgar Turnbull, of Belfast.

Turner, Clement Douglas - Private
1978 North Irish Horse *Killed in Action on 20 July 1917*
VLAMERTINGHE NEW MILITARY CEMETERY, Belgium
Son of Robert J. Turner, of Earl Street, Longford; husband of Annabella Turner, of 111, Ulsterville Avenue, Belfast.

Turner, Samuel - Rifleman
8441 Royal Irish Rifles 2nd Battalion *Killed In Action on 27 October 1914*
LE TOURET MEMORIAL, France
Born and enlisted in Belfast.

Turner, Stewart Lyttle - Lance Corporal
1656 North Irish Horse *Age 24 Died in War on 20 July 1917*
VLAMERTINGHE NEW MILITARY CEMETERY, Belgium
Son of Robert Turner, of 279, Springfield Road, Belfast; husband of Margaret Turner.

Turner, Theophilus - Rifleman
5245 Royal Irish Rifles 7th Battalion *Died in War on 3 June 1916*
DUD CORNER CEMETERY, LOOS, France
Born in Belfast, enlisted in Belfast.

Turner, Thomas J - Private
17/1028 Royal Irish Rifles 15th Battalion *Died in War on 20 December 1916*
RATION FARM (LA PLUS DOUVE) ANNEXE, Belgium
4, Penrith Street, Belfast.

Turtle, John - Corporal
19572 Machine Gun Corps (Infantry) 62nd Battalion *Age 22 Died in War on 20 July 1918*
SOISSONS MEMORIAL, France
Son of James and Mary Jane Turtle, of 37, Mountcollyer Road, Belfast.

Tushingham, William - Sergeant
43488 Royal Dublin Fusiliers 1st Battalion *Age 47 Died of Wounds on 24 October 1918*
DOVER (ST. JAMES'S) CEMETERY, United Kingdom
Son of Willie Tushingham, of Manchester; husband of Margaret Tushingham, of 14, Townsend Street, Belfast.

Twaddell, Maude Elizabeth - Worker
50290 Queen Mary's Army Auxiliary Corps *Died in War on 17 October 1918*
CARNMONEY CEMETERY, United Kingdom
Born and enlisted in Belfast.

Tweedie, Charles - Rifleman
120 Royal Irish Rifles 15th Battalion *Killed in Action on 21 March 1918*
POZIERES MEMORIAL, France
Born and enlisted in Belfast.

Tyler, Albert Cecil - Gunner
121370 Royal Garrison Artillery 99th Siege Battery *Age 35 Died of Wounds on 30 May 1915*
AIRE COMMUNAL CEMETERY, France
Born in Chester, England and enlisted in Monaghan. Husband of Sara Tyler,
of Upper Crescent Nursing Home, Belfast.

Tyndall, William - Private
3683 Royal Inniskilling Fusiliers 1st Battalion *Age 18 Died in War on 14 August 1915*
HELLES MEMORIAL, Turkey
Son of James Tyndall, of 30, Connswater Street, Belfast.

Tyrrell, John Marcus - Captain
Royal Irish Fusiliers 3rd Reserve Battalion and Royal Air Force *Age 23 Died in War on 20 June 1918*
BOULOGNE EASTERN CEMETERY, France
Son of John Tyrrell, J.P., and Mrs. Tyrrell, of "The Cairn", Ballyholme, Bangor, County Down.
Native of Belfast.

Tyrrell, Walter Alexander - Captain
Royal Flying Corps 32nd Squadron *Age 19 Killed in Action on 9 June 1918*
BEAUVAIS COMMUNAL CEMETERY, France
Son of John and Jeannie Tyrell, Fairview Buildings, Crumlin Road, Belfast, later of Bangor. Educated at
RBAI he was a former member of Queen's University Officer Training Corps. Originally had served in the
Royal Navy before being commissioned into the Royal Flying Corps. A very skilled pilot he had destroyed
a total of seventeen German aircraft and was awarded the Military Cross before his own death.
His brother Marcus, was also a pilot and he too lost his life.

Unsworth, J - Private
G/23131 Royal Sussex Regiment 11th Battalion *Age 19 Died in War on 31 October 1917*
BEDFORD HOUSE CEMETERY, *Belgium*
Son of Joseph and Ellen Unsworth, of Tennent Street, Belfast.

Unsworth, W. Hubert - Engineer Sub-Lieutenant
Royal Navy HMS "Invincible" *Killed in Action at Battle of Jutland on 31 May 1916*
PORTSMOUTH MEMORIAL, *United Kingdom*
Son of William Thomas and Margaret Unsworth, of Taymount, Bloomfield, Belfast.
Had signed the 1912 Ulster Covenant. He was an engineering draughtsman by training.

Uprichard, Charles Edward - Stoker First Class
SS/108911 Royal Navy HMS "Hawke" *Killed in Action in a submarine attack in the North Sea on 15 October 1914*
CHATHAM NAVAL MEMORIAL, *United Kingdom*
Son of John and Elizabeth Uprichard, of 12, Rosebank Street, Belfast.

Uprichard, James Henry - Rifleman
1164 Royal Irish Rifles 12th Battalion *Died on 22 November 1917*
CAMBRAI MEMORIAL, LOUVERVAL, *France*
Born and enlisted in Belfast.

Uprichard, Joseph - Rifleman
75 Royal Irish Rifles 2nd Battalion *Age 33 Killed in Action on 6 September 1918*
PLOEGSTEERT MEMORIAL, *Belgium*
Son of William and Jane Uprichard, of Moira, County Down; husband of Margaret Uprichard, of 24, Templemore Street, Belfast.

Uprichard, Thomas John - Rifleman
8947 Royal Irish Rifles 7th Battalion *Died in War on 8 August 1917*
YPRES (MENIN GATE) MEMORIAL, *Belgium*
Born in Waringstown, County Down, enlisted in Lisburn, resident of Belfast.

Upstall, Frederick John - Stoker First Class
K/20211(Dev) Royal Navy HMS "Sandhurst" *Age 23 Died of burns on 27 February 1917*
LYNESS ROYAL NAVAL CEMETERY, *United Kingdom*
Son of James C. and Elizabeth Upstall, of 67, Connsbrook Avenue, Strandtown, Belfast.
Possibly killed in an accidental engine room explosion or fire.

Ussher, Archibald (Archie) - Private
31509 Royal Inniskilling Fusiliers 6th Battalion *Died of influenza on 2 November 1918*
ROISEL COMMUNAL CEMETERY EXTENSION, *France*
Stepson of Mrs. Elizabeth Ussher, of 18, Jersey Street, Belfast. Born at Belfast.

Ussher, James - Lance Corporal
182 Royal Irish Rifles 15th Battalion *Age 19 Killed in Action on 1 July 1916*
THIEPVAL MEMORIAL, *France*
Stepson of Mrs. Elizabeth Ussher, of 18, Jersey Street, Belfast.

Vallely, John - Private
16428 Princess Victoria's (Royal Irish Fusiliers) 9th Battalion *Killed in Action on 1 July 1916*
THIEPVAL MEMORIAL, France
Born and enlisted in Belfast.

Vance, Henry - Rifleman
13764 Royal Irish Rifles 12th Battalion *Died in War on 25 October 1918*
HARLEBEKE NEW BRITISH CEMETERY, Belgium
Born and enlisted in Belfast.

Vance, James - Corporal
57950 Royal Engineers *Age 43 Accidentally killed on 18 July 1919*
CARNMONEY CEMETERY, United Kingdom
Husband of Margaret Vance, of 147, Garmoyle Terrace, York Road, Belfast.

Vance, Joseph - Rifleman
11474 Royal Irish Rifles 6th Battalion *Age 24 Died in War on 11 August 1915*
HELLES MEMORIAL, Turkey
Son of Catherine Vance, of 2, Irvine Street, Ballyhackamore, Belfast, and the late James Vance.

Vance, William - Lance Corporal
3393 Royal Inniskilling Fusiliers 1st Battalion *Age 22 Died in War on 28 February 1917*
THIEPVAL MEMORIAL, France
Son of William Vance, of 50, Lindsay Street, Belfast; husband of Jane Vance, of 16, Glentilt Street, Belfast.

Vance, William Frederick - Rifleman
20817 Royal Irish Rifles *Died in War on 5 September 1918*
PERONNE COMMUNAL CEMETERY EXTENSION, France
Son of William J. and Maude Vance, of 5, Battenberg Street, Belfast.

Veighey, Andrew - Lance Corporal
532 Royal Irish Rifles 10th Battalion attached 21st Entrenching Battalion
Age 21 Killed in Action on 21 March 1918
POZIERES MEMORIAL, France
Son of William and Martha Veighey, of 28, Hutchinson Street, Belfast.

Verner, Thomas - Rifleman
19238 Royal Irish Rifles 12th Battalion *Died of Wounds on 28 October 1918*
THIEPVAL MEMORIAL, France
Resident of Belfast, the son of Joseph and Elizabeth Verner, of Halftown, Hillsborough, County Down.

Verner, William Martin - Private
26375 Royal Inniskilling Fusiliers 9th Battalion *Age 18 Killed in Action on 16 August 1917*
TYNE COT MEMORIAL, Belgium
Son of Samuel and Jane Verner, of 13, Fourth Street, Belfast.

Victor, Henry Edward - Private
G/7574 Duke of Cambridge's Own (Middlesex Regiment) 2nd Battalion *Killed in Action on 1 July 1916*
THIEPVAL MEMORIAL, France
Born in Belfast, enlisted Plymouth, Devon.

Vint, William Percival - Captain
Machine Gun Corps "C" Company 6th Battalion *Age 33 Killed in Action on 5 August 1918*
LIJSSENTHOEK MILITARY CEMETERY, Belgium
Son of William and Eleanor Vint, of Belfast. Educated at Bedford School, and thereafter spent nine years in a Nitrate Works in Chile. Recommended twice for the Albert Medal.

Vinters, John - A/Corporal
23867 Princess Victoria's (Royal Irish Fusiliers) 1st Battalion *Died in War on 16 February 1917*
SAILLY-SAILLISEL BRITISH CEMETERY, France
Born in Belfast, enlisted Glasgow.

Vogan, Robert - Private
18521 Royal Irish Regiment 2nd Battalion *Died in War on 27 September 1918*
MOEUVRES COMMUNAL CEMETERY EXTENSION, France
Son of Samuel and M. A. Vogan, of 135, Silvio Street, Crumlin Road, Belfast. Awarded the Military Medal.

Vogan, Samuel - Bugler
5898 Royal Irish Rifles 2nd Battalion *Died on 24 March 1918*
POZIERES MEMORIAL, France
Survived by his mother at 7, Vistula Street, Belfast.

Vogan, Samuel - Mess Room Steward
Mercantile Marine S.S. "Forestmoor" (London)
Age 17 Drowned, as a result of an attack by an enemy submarine on 6 October 1917
TOWER HILL MEMORIAL, United Kingdom
Son of Robert and Annie Vogan (née Burns), of 26, Lothair Avenue, Belfast.

Waddell, Frederick William - Rifleman
13768 Royal Irish Rifles "A" Company 8th Battalion *Age 36 Died of sickness on 20 September 1915*
BELFAST CITY CEMETERY, United Kingdom
Son of Robert Henry and Mary J. Waddell; husband of Margaret Waddell,
of 14, Brandon Avenue, Toronto, Canada. Born at Belfast.

Waddell, George - Rifleman
553 Royal Irish Rifles 18th Battalion *Died on 14 October 1915*
BORDON MILITARY CEMETERY, HAMPSHIRE, United Kingdom
Born in Belfast, the son of Robert and Elizabeth Ann Waddell, of Cogry Square, Doagh, County Antrim.

Waddell, James - Corporal
57542 Royal Engineers 99th Tunnelling Company *Died in War on 15 September 1916*
KARASOULI MILITARY CEMETERY, Greece
Son of Martha and Robert Waddell, 58, Bright Street, Belfast.

Wade, William - Rifleman
6949 Royal Irish Rifles 1st Battalion *Age 22 Killed in Action on 12 March 1915*
BOULOGNE EASTERN CEMETERY, France
Son of Thomas and Margaret Wade, of 57, Brownlow Street, Belfast.

Wadsworth, Stanley - Rifleman
5349 Royal Irish Rifles 7th Battalion *Killed in Action on 16 August 1917*
TYNE COT MEMORIAL, Belgium
Son of George and Mrs A Wadsworth of 37, Joseph Street, Belfast.

Wagland, George - Lance Corporal
3616 Royal Inniskilling Fusiliers 1st Battalion *Killed in Action on 20 May 1917*
ARRAS MEMORIAL, France
Born in Belfast.

Waite, James - Private
451425 Labour Corps formerly 7349 Royal Irish Fusiliers *Age 35 Died of Wounds (gas) on 23 March 1920*
BELFAST CITY CEMETERY, United Kingdom
Son of the late Felix and Sarah Waite; husband of Rachel Waite, of 16, James Street, Belfast. Born at Belfast.

Wakeham, James Edward - Sergeant
6258 Essex Regiment 1st Battalion *Age 30 Died in War on 6 June 1915*
HELLES MEMORIAL, Turkey
Husband of Martha Annie Moffatt (formerly Wakeham), of 40, Whitehall Parade, Belfast.

Wales, Samuel - Rifleman
607 Royal Irish Rifles 9th Battalion *Age 19 Died in War on 23 November 1917*
CAMBRAI MEMORIAL, LOUVERVAL, France
Son of James Wales, of 10, McIvor's Place, Belfast.

Wales, William - Rifleman
8359 Royal Irish Rifles 2nd Battalion *Died in War on 24 November 1917*
GREVILLERS BRITISH CEMETERY, France
Born and enlisted in Belfast.

Walker, Andrew - Sapper
57543 Royal Engineers 121st Company *Age 23 Died of meningitis on 19 April 1916*
VILLERS-BOCAGE COMMUNAL CEMETERY EXTENSION, France
Son of John and Agnes Walker, of 31, Glasgow Street, Belfast. Holder of the Military Medal.

Walker, Arthur James - Rifleman
47470 Royal Irish Rifles 1st Battalion formerly 128731 Army Service Corps
Age 28 Killed in Action on 28 March 1918
POZIERES MEMORIAL, France
Son of Samuel and Ellen Walker, of 3, Marlborough Avenue, Lisburn Road, Belfast.

Walker, Claud Arthur Leonard - Second Lieutenant
Royal Inniskilling Fusiliers *Age 21 Died in War on 11 July 1916*
BOUZINCOURT COMMUNAL CEMETERY EXTENSION, France
Originally joined the Public Schools Corps, attended Sandhurst and was commissioned into the Inniskillings.
Son of the Rev R Walker, Rector of St Matthew's, Shankill, Belfast and Mrs L J T Walker.

Walker, Cornwall Nathaniel Brownlow - Captain
Royal Inniskilling Fusiliers 7th Battalion *Age 19 Killed in Action on 16 August 1917*
TYNE COT MEMORIAL,, Belgium
Son of Adaline C. Walker, of 103, Fitzroy Avenue, Belfast, and the late Cornwall Walker.

Walker, Frederick Ramsay - Second Lieutenant
Argyll and Sutherland Highlanders 2nd Battalion *Age 21 Died in War on 6 January 1917*
EDINBURGH (DALRY) CEMETERY, United Kingdom
Husband of Josephine Margaret Walker, of 107, Donegall Street, Belfast. Awarded Medaille Militaire (France).

Walker, George - Rifleman
12450 Royal Irish Rifles 8/9th Battalion *Killed in Action on 21 March 1918*
POZIERES MEMORIAL, France
Born and enlisted in Belfast.

Walker, Hugh - Rifleman
8079 Royal Irish Rifles 2nd Battalion *Killed In Action on 27 October 1914*
LE TOURET MEMORIAL, France
Born in Belfast.

Walker, J - Gunner
Royal Garrison Artillery *Died in War*
62 Aberdeen Street, husband of Ellen and father of a young daughter.

Walker, James - Lance Corporal
10479 East Lancashire Regiment 2nd Battalion *Died in War on 27 August 1916*
VERMELLES BRITISH CEMETERY, France
Son of John and Mary Walker, of 32, Mayo Street, Belfast. His brother, William was also killed
with the same regiment. His father also served.

Walker, James - Private
16175 Royal Irish Fusiliers 6th Battalion *Age 35 Died in War on 9 August 1915*
HELLES MEMORIAL, Turkey
Son of Thomas Walker, of 28, Ballycastle Street, Belfast, and the late Mary Ellen Walker;
husband of Margaret Walker, of 42, Ballarat Street, Belfast.

Walker, James - Rifleman
19275 Royal Irish Rifles 12th Battalion *Died in War on 29 January 1917*
ST. QUENTIN CABARET MILITARY CEMETERY, *Belgium*
Born Ballymacarrett, Belfast. Enlisted in Larne. Son of James and Charlotte Walker of "The Laurels", Larne.

Walker, James Henry - Private
11095 Royal Inniskilling Fusiliers 9th Battalion *Died in War on 1 July 1916*
THIEPVAL MEMORIAL, *France*
Born in Belfast, enlisted Omagh.

Walker, John - Boatswain (Bosun)
Mercantile Marine S.S. "Normandiet" (London)
Age 44 Drowned as a result of an attack by an enemy submarine on 21 April 1918
TOWER HILL MEMORIAL, *United Kingdom*
Son of the late Andrew Graham Walker and Jane Walker; husband of Ellen Walker (née Wright),
of 9, Lumsden Street, Glasgow. Born in at Belfast.

Walker, John - Private
511 Royal Irish Regiment 2nd Garrison Battalion formerly 7217 Royal Irish Rifles *Died on 10 November 1916*
BELFAST (MILLTOWN) ROMAN CATHOLIC CEMETERY, *United Kingdom*
Born in Belfast.

Walker, John - Rifleman
2316 Royal Irish Rifles 2nd Battalion *Died in War on 24 March 1918*
PLAINE FRENCH NATIONAL CEMETERY, *France*
Born and enlisted in Belfast.

Walker, John Charles - Sapper
428155 Corps of Royal Engineers 420th Field Company *Died in War on 24 February 1918*
STRUMA MILITARY CEMETERY, *Greece*
Enlisted in St Helens, Lancashire. Resident in Belfast

Walker, John J - Lance Corporal
11/22587 Royal Inniskilling Fusiliers 11th Battalion *Died in War on 4 November 1916*
POND FARM CEMETERY, *Belgium*
Son of James and Ellen Walker, of Belfast.

Walker, John Porter - Corporal
8/957 Royal Irish Rifles 8th Battalion transferred to 109056 182nd Company Labour Corps as a Sergeant
Age 25 Died of Wounds on 21 March 1918
FAUBOURG D'AMIENS CEMETERY, ARRAS, *France*
Husband of Sarah Jane Walker, of 29, Foxglove Street, Belfast.

Walker, Joseph - Private
19153 South Wales Borderers 1st Battalion *Died in War on 2 April 1916*
ST PATRICK'S CEMETERY, LOOS, *France*
Born in Belfast, lived in Newport, Monmouthshire.

Walker, Joseph Henry - Lance Corporal
22436 Gloucestershire Regiment 10th Battalion *Age 26 Died of Wounds on 25 September 1916*
STE. MARIE CEMETERY, LE HAVRE, *France*
Son of James Foster Walker and Ellen Walker, of Belfast; husband of Annie Louisa Walker, of 4, Doone Road, Horfield, Bristol.

Journey of Remembering

Walker, Robert - Driver
T/32628 Army Service Corps attached 14th Brigade *Died in War on 27 August 1914*
ANGRE COMMUNAL CEMETERY, Belgium
Son of Thomas Walker, of 33, Mossvale Street, Belfast.

Walker, Ronald McDonald - Rifleman
11758 Royal Irish Rifles 15th Battalion *Age 30 Died in War on 22 November 1917*
THIEPVAL MEMORIAL, France
Husband of Sarah J. Walker, of 5, Salisbury Place, Ligoneil, Belfast.

Walker, Samuel Hugh - Second Lieutenant
Royal Irish Rifles 14th Battalion *Age 26. Died in War on 16 August 1917*
TYNE COT MEMORIAL, Belgium
Son of Samuel and Eliza Ann Walker, of 5, Dee Street, Belfast.

Walker, Thomas - Private
22183 Cameronians (Scottish Rifles) 10th Battalion *Age 21 Killed in Action on 13 June 1916*
VERMELLES BRITISH CEMETERY, France
Son of Mary and the late William John Walker, of 399, Woodstock Road, Belfast.

Walker, Thomas - Rifleman
12492 Royal Irish Rifles 1st Battalion *Killed in Action on 9 May 1915*
PLOEGSTEERT MEMORIAL, Belgium
Son of the late Thomas and Elizabeth Walker. His brother and sister lived at 96, Bristol Street, Belfast.

Walker, William Bill - Private
10905 East Lancashire Regiment 1st Battalion *Died in War on 22 August 1918*
PLOEGSTEERT MEMORIAL, BELGIUM
Resident in Belfast. His brother, James, was killed with the same regiment.

Walkington, Charles Edward - Captain
Royal Irish Rifles 2nd Battalion *Age 38 Died in War on 14 October 1918*
DADIZEELE NEW BRITISH CEMETERY, Belgium
Son of the late Mr Dolway Walkington and his wife Maria, Thornhill, Belfast.

Wallace, George - Lance Corporal
14/13813 Royal Irish Rifles 8th Battalion *Age 25 Died in War on 17 August 1917*
YPRES RESERVOIR CEMETERY, Belgium
Son of Mrs. Margaret Wallace, of 1, St. Leonard's Street, Belfast.

Wallace, James - Rifleman
1733 Royal Irish Rifles 1st Battalion *Killed in Action on 2 October 1918*
YPRES RESERVOIR CEMETERY, Belgium
Born and enlisted in Belfast.

Wallace, James - Rifleman
6023 Royal Irish Rifles 7th Battalion *Died in War on 7 September 1916*
THIEPVAL MEMORIAL, France
Son of Robert and the late Mary Ann Wallace, Canmore Street.

Wallace, James Leahy - Rifleman
914 Royal Irish Rifles 8th Battalion *Age 19 Died in War on 2 July 1916*
SERRE ROAD CEMETERY No.2, France
Son of William and Margaret Wallace, of 24, Riverview Street, Belfast.

Wallace, Joseph - Rifleman
894 Royal Irish Rifles 11th Battalion *Killed in Action on 1 July 1916*
THIEPVAL MEMORIAL, France
14, Limestone Road, Belfast.

Wallace, Patrick Joseph - Rifleman
19811 Royal Irish Rifles 14th Battalion *Age 23 Died of Wounds on 20 July 1916*
CAUDRY OLD COMMUNAL CEMETERY, France
Son of P. Wallace, of 114, Duncairn Gardens, Belfast, and the late Mary Wallace.

Wallace, Robert - Private
3792 Seaforth Highlanders 4th Battalion *Age 19 Died in War on 16 November 1916*
THIEPVAL MEMORIAL, France
Son of William John and Margaret Jane Wallace, of 268, Springfield Road, Belfast.

Walls, Andrew - Corporal
53793 Royal Engineers 13th Signal Company *Age 27 Killed in Action on 25 February 1917*
BASRA MEMORIAL, Iraq
Brother of Mrs. Margaret Patterson, of 56, Saunders Street, Belfast.

Walls, John - Rifleman
11108 Royal Irish Rifles 1st Battalion *Killed in Action on 26 October 1916*
THIEPVAL MEMORIAL, France
Born and enlisted in Belfast.

Walsh, David - Rifleman
1484 Royal Irish Rifles 8th Battalion *Died in War on 2 July 1916*
THIEPVAL MEMORIAL, France
Born and enlisted in Belfast.

Walsh, Edward - Private
9879 Hampshire Regiment 2nd Battalion *Died in War on 18 September 1916*
VLAMERTINGHE NEW MILITARY CEMETERY, Belgium
Born on the Isle of Wight, enlisted Southampton, resident of Belfast.

Walsh, George - Corporal
6964 Royal Irish Rifles "A" Company 2nd Battalion *Age 18 Died in War on 20 October 1916*
THIEPVAL MEMORIAL, France
Son of William Henry and Margret Jane Walsh, of 13, Apsley Street, Belfast.

Walsh, John - Private
20847 Royal Inniskilling Fusiliers 9th Battalion *Age 19 Killed in Action on 23 October 1918*
TERLINCTHUN BRITISH CEMETERY, WIMILLE, France
Son of James and Emmie H. Walsh, of 4, Magdala Street, Belfast.

Walsh, John Herbert - Rifleman
1840 Royal Irish Rifles 15th Battalion *Died in War on 4 August 1917*
YPRES (MENIN GATE) MEMORIAL, Belgium
Born in Hillsborough, enlisted in Belfast. Member of Fisherwick Presbyterian Church.

Walsh, Michael - Private
17142 Princess Victoria's (Royal Irish Fusiliers) 2nd Battalion *Died in War on 14 February 1915*
YPRES (MENIN GATE) MEMORIAL, Belgium
Born and enlisted in Belfast.

Walsh, Patrick - Corporal
10382 Royal Irish Rifles 1st Battalion *Killed in Action on 21 March 1918*
POZIERES MEMORIAL, France
Born in Belfast, enlisted in Dublin.

Walsh, Patrick - Lance Corporal
26463 Royal Inniskilling Fusiliers 7th Battalion *Died of Wounds on 28 April 1916*
PHILOSOPHE BRITISH CEMETERY, MAZINGARBE, France
Survived by his sister, Mrs Wylie, 38, Dunlewey Street, Belfast.

Walsh, Patrick - Private
3669 Royal Irish Fusiliers 1st Battalion *Age 30 Died in War on 3 May 1917*
ARRAS MEMORIAL, France
Son of John and Elizabeth Walsh, of 17, Saul Street, Belfast.

Walsh, Robert - Private
27795 Leinster Regiment 1st Battalion *Age 26 Died in War on 25 May 1919*
CAIRO WAR MEMORIAL CEMETERY, Egypt
Son of John and Eliza Walsh, of 17, Saul Street, Belfast.

Walsh, Stanley - Private
240187 Border Regiment 6th Battalion *Age 20 Died of Wounds on 9 October 1917*
DOZINGHEM MILITARY CEMETERY, Belgium
Son of Thomas J. and A. Walsh, of 146, Manor Street, Belfast. Born Cockermouth, Cumberland.

Walsh, Thomas - Lance Corporal
9141 Royal Irish Rifles 1st Battalion *Killed in Action on 31 July 1917*
YPRES (MENIN GATE) MEMORIAL, Belgium
Husband of Georgina Walsh, of 6, Gilbert Street, Belfast.

Ward, James - Private
3417 Royal Inniskilling Fusiliers 1st Battalion *Died in War on 30 June 1915*
PINK FARM CEMETERY, HELLES, Turkey
His Grandmother lived at 11, Concord Street, Belfast.

Ward, Patrick Joseph - Private
8921 Royal Irish Rifles 1st Battalion *Killed in Action on 9 May 1915*
PLOEGSTEERT MEMORIAL, Belgium
77, Smithfield, Belfast.

Ward, Stephen Henry - Petty Officer
199275 Royal Navy HMS "London" *Age 36 Died in War on 31 August 1915*
CARNMONEY CEMETERY, United Kingdom
Husband of Caroline E. Ward, of 226, Old Lodge Road, Belfast. Born in Belfast.

Ward, Thomas - Rifleman
10683 Royal Irish Rifles 1st Battalion *Age 19 Killed in Action on 31 July 1917*
TYNE COT CEMETERY, Belgium
Son of Samuel and Annie Ward, of 2, Cameron Court, Anderston, Glasgow. Born at Belfast.

JOURNEY OF REMEMBERING

Ward, William Albert Victor - Lance Corporal
8665 Royal Inniskilling Fusiliers 1st Battalion *Age 25 Died in War on 22 May 1915*
TWELVE TREE COPSE CEMETERY, Turkey
Son of Stephen and Margaret Jane Ward, of 10, Eastland Street, Belfast.

Wardlow, James - Private
S/21503 Seaforth Highlanders 8th Battalion *Age 33 Died in War on 22 July 1918*
ROYALLIEU FRENCH NATIONAL CEMETERY, COMPIEGNE, France
Son of Thomas and Margaret Wardlow, of 10, Henryville Street, Ravenhill Road, Belfast; husband of Annie Wardlow.

Wardlow, Thomas - Driver
T4/124969 Army Service Corps 1st Horse Transport Company 36th Division Train *Age 31 Died in War on 18 June 1915*
BELFAST (DUNDONALD) CEMETERY, United Kingdom
Son of Thomas Wardlow; husband of Elizabeth Wardlow, of 155, Beersbridge Road, Belfast. Born at Belfast.

Wardlow, William V. - Private
142186 Canadian Infantry (Central Ontario Regiment) 4th Battalion *Age 27 Died in War on 3 May 1917*
VIMY MEMORIAL, France
(served as BURNS). Son of the late John and Annie Wardlow, of Belfast, Ireland.

Waring, Robert - Private
432504 Canadian Infantry (Alberta Regiment) 49th Battalion *Age 29 Died in War on 2 - 5 June 1916*
TYNE COT CEMETERY, Belgium
Husband of Isabella Waring, of 3, Everton Street, Crumlin Road, Belfast. He was an Anglican and boat builder and was born at Dunmurry.

Warke, Thomas - Rifleman
13774 Royal Irish Rifles 8th Battalion *Age 32 Died in War on 2 July 1916*
THIEPVAL MEMORIAL, France
Son of Mrs. Jane Warke; husband of Sarah Ann Warke, of 26, Downpatrick Street, Belfast.

Warlow, Andrew - Private
10284 Irish Guards 2nd Battalion *Died in War on 11 October 1917*
DOZINGHEM MILITARY CEMETERY, Belgium
Born in Belfast, enlisted in Boyle, County Roscommon.

Warnock, Charles - Private
10000 Royal Irish Fusiliers 2nd Battalion *Died in War on 25 March 1918*
JERUSALEM WAR CEMETERY, Israel
70, Beresford Street, Belfast.

Warnock, John - Private
2268 4th (Queen's Own) Hussars *Died in War on 31 October 1914*
YPRES (MENIN GATE) MEMORIAL, Belgium
45, Lindsay Street, Belfast. Born in Dublin the son of William and Margaret Warnock.

Warnock, Robert - Private
PLY/16727 Royal Marine Light Infantry Plymouth Battalion Royal Naval Division
Age 18 Naval, died ashore on 4 March 1915
HELLES MEMORIAL, Turkey
Son of the late Hugh and Margaret Warnock, of 12, Westcott Street, Connswater, Belfast.

JOURNEY OF REMEMBERING

Warnock, Thomas - Stoker
1079U Royal Naval Reserve HMS "Goliath" *Died in War on 13 May 1915*
PLYMOUTH NAVAL MEMORIAL, United Kingdom
North Ann Street, Belfast.

Warnock, William - Private
6699 Royal Inniskilling Fusiliers 2nd Battalion *Age 32 Died in War on 26 August 1914*
LA FERTE-SOUS-JOUARRE MEMORIAL, France
Son of Sarah Warnock, of 1, Richmond Street, Belfast, and the late James Warnock.

Warren, Samuel - Rifleman
696 Royal Irish Rifles 13th Battalion *Age 21 Killed in Action on 1 July 1916*
A.I.F. BURIAL GROUND, FLERS, France
Son of Mrs. Mary Jane Bayliss, of Glen House, Strandtown, Belfast.

Wasson, Albert - Rifleman
13821 Royal Irish Rifles "B" Company 8th Battalion *Age 19 Died in War on 2 July 1916*
THIEPVAL MEMORIAL, France
Son of Alfred and Eleanor Wasson, of 72, Convention Street, Belfast.

Wasson, Henry - Stoker First Class
SS/103313 Royal Navy HMS "Hawke" *Lost at sea on 15 October 1914*
CHATHAM NAVAL MEMORIAL, United Kingdom
Husband of Annie Wasson, 33, Emerson's Row, Belfast.

Waterman, Ronald - Lance Corporal
210 Royal Irish Rifles 12th Battalion *Age 19 Killed in Action on 1 July 1916*
THIEPVAL MEMORIAL, France
Son of Samuel and Elsie Waterman, of 8, Glencollyer Street, Belfast.

Waterworth, Thomas - Lance Corporal
9128 Royal Inniskilling Fusiliers 1st Battalion *Killed in Action on 1 July 1916*
THIEPVAL MEMORIAL, France
Brother of Mrs. A. Smith, of 15, Aberdeen Street, Shankill Road, Belfast. Awarded the Military Medal.

Watson, Charles - Sergeant
5336 Coldstream Guards *Died in War on 21 November 1916*
GUARDS' CEMETERY, LESBOEUFS, France
Born in Belfast, enlisted in Sheffield, Yorkshire.

Watson, George - Corporal
21555 Royal Garrison Artillery 111th Heavy Battery *Age 30 Died in War on 20 June 1917*
VOORMEZEELE ENCLOSURE No.3, Belgium
Husband of Mary Watson, of 11, Schomberg Street, Belfast.

Watson, George - Lance Corporal
9171 Royal Inniskilling Fusiliers 2nd Battalion *Died in War on 16 May 1915*
LE TOURET MEMORIAL, France
Born and enlisted in Belfast.

Watson, George - Private
CH/465(S) Royal Marine Light Infantry *Age 19 Died in War on 17 November 1915*
BROOKWOOD (UNITED KINGDOM 1914-1918) MEMORIAL
Born in Belfast.

Watson, Gilbert - Private
33520 Royal Scots Fusiliers 1st Battalion *Died in War on 23 December 1916*
EUSTON ROAD CEMETERY, COLINCAMPS, France
Born and enlisted in Belfast.

Watson, James - Private
10056 East Yorkshire Regiment 1st Battalion *Died in War on 18 October 1914*
PLOEGSTEERT MEMORIAL, Belgium
Born in Belfast, enlisted Beverley, Yorkshire.

Watson, James - Private
49874 Royal Irish Fusiliers 1st Battalion *Age 20 Killed in Action on 1 October 1918*
DADIZEELE NEW BRITISH CEMETERY, Belgium
Son of Mrs. J. Watson, of 40, Gertrude Street, Belfast.

Watson, James - Rifleman
1425 Royal Irish Rifles 12th Battalion *Age 19 Killed in Action on 21 March 1918*
POZIERES MEMORIAL, France
Brother of Mrs. Agnes Black, of 11, Hemp Street, Belfast.

Watson, James - Rifleman
6604 Royal Irish Rifles 10th Battalion *Died in War on 1 July 1916*
THIEPVAL MEMORIAL, France
Husband of Margaret 70, Carlow Street, Belfast.

Watson, James - Second Lieutenant
Royal Irish Rifles 14th Battalion *Died in War on 9 July 1916*
BAPAUME POST MILITARY CEMETERY, France
Botanic Avenue Belfast. Son of Alexander and Sarah Watson, Ashfield, Portadown.

Watson, James Furness - Private
13728 King's Liverpool Regiment 14th Battalion *Died in War on 14 September 1917*
DOIRAN MEMORIAL, Greece
Born Belfast, enlisted Liverpool, resident Moose Jaw, Canada.

Watson, James Joseph - Private
21187 Princess Victoria's (Royal Irish Fusiliers) 8th Battalion *Died in War on 6 September 1916*
THIEPVAL MEMORIAL, France
Born and enlisted in Belfast. Formerly 2510 Connaught Rangers.

Watson, John - Private
21403 Royal Irish Fusiliers 9th Battalion *Age 19 Killed in Action on 1 July 1916*
HAMEL MILITARY CEMETERY, BEAUMONT-HAMEL, France
Son of Edwin and Mary Watson, of 150, Earl Street, Belfast.

Watson, John - Rifleman
12195 Royal Irish Rifles 15th Battalion *Died in War on 16 February 1916*
SUCRERIE MILITARY CEMETERY, COLINCAMPS, FRANCE
51, Mervue Street, Belfast.

Watson, John - Rifleman
1427 Royal Irish Rifles 10th Battalion *Killed In Action on 1 July 1916*
CONNAUGHT CEMETERY, THIEPVAL, France
Son of Edward and the late Sarah Jane Watson, of 46, Combermere Street, Belfast.

Watson, John - Rifleman
16082 Royal Irish Rifles 14th Battalion *Died in War on 20 June 1917*
MESSINES RIDGE BRITISH CEMETERY, Belgium
Born and enlisted in Belfast.

Watson, John - Rifleman
47449 Royal Irish Rifles 12th Battalion *Age 27 Died in War on 22 November 1917*
CAMBRAI MEMORIAL, LOUVERVAL, France
Son of Agnes Watson, of 52, Egmont Street, Belfast, and the late John Watson.

Watson, John Graham - Trimmer
G/9218 Mercantile Marine Reserve HMS "Stonecrop" *Age 16 Killed in Action with submarine in Atlantic on 18 September 1917*
PLYMOUTH NAVAL MEMORIAL, United Kingdom
Son of William and Marion Watson, of 36, Bentinck Street, Belfast.

Watson, John Hyndman - Lance Sergeant
20076 Royal Scots 15th Battalion *Age 27 Died in War on 16 April 1918*
PLOEGSTEERT MEMORIAL, Belgium
Son of the Rev. John Watson, B.A. and Elizabeth Watson, of Drumderrig, Boyle, County Roscommon. Educated at Campbell College, Belfast. Student of Medicine, Edinburgh University. Officer Training Corps Medical Cadet Corporal, 1912. Enlisted December 1914. Previously wounded at Arras in 1917.

Watson, Joseph - Private
19896 Highland Light Infantry 11th Battalion *Killed in Action on 19 July 1915*
LE TOURET MILITARY CEMETERY, RICHEBOURG-L'AVOUE, France
Born in County Antrim, enlisted in Hamilton, Scotland, resident of Belfast

Watson, Matthew James - Rifleman
10123 Royal Irish Rifles 2nd Battalion *Killed in Action on 19 January 1916*
PLOEGSTEERT MEMORIAL, Belgium
Born and enlisted in Belfast.

Watson, The Rev. John Edmund Malone - Chaplain
Army Chaplains' Department attached Middlesex Regiment 21st Battalion *Age 31 Died in War on 10 April 1918*
HAVERSKERQUE BRITISH CEMETERY, France
Son of The Rev. John Watson, of Charlemont Rectory, County Tyrone; husband of Mary K. Watson, of "Ard-Stratha" Antrim Road, Belfast. Awarded the Military Cross.

Watson, Thomas - Rifleman
13824 Royal Irish Rifles 15th Battalion *Killed in Action on 21 March 1918*
POZIERES MEMORIAL, France
Born and enlisted in Belfast.

Watson, Thomas - Rifleman
16083 Royal Irish Rifles 10th Battalion *Killed in Action on 1 July 1916*
THIEPVAL MEMORIAL, France
Born and enlisted in Belfast.

Watson, Victor Charles - Private
22988 Princess Victoria's (Royal Irish Fusiliers) 9th Battalion *Died in War on 15 January 1918*
ETRETAT CHURCHYARD EXTENSION, France
Born in Belfast, enlisted in Lurgan.

Watson, William - Lance Corporal
33520 Royal Irish Regiment 2nd Battalion *Died in War on 3 September 1916*
THIEPVAL MEMORIAL, France
Born and enlisted in Belfast.

Watson, William - Private
12248 Royal Inniskilling Fusiliers 5th Battalion *Age 18 Died in War on 15 August 1915*
HELLES MEMORIAL, Turkey
Only son of James Henry and Margaret Watson, of 16, Beggs Street, Belfast.

Watson, William Gilbert - Sapper
28898 Royal Engineers 11th Pack Wireless Squadron *Age 21 Died of pneumonia on 19 May 1917*
MIKRA BRITISH CEMETERY, KALAMARIA, Greece
Son of James and Sara Watson, of 111, Madrid Street, Belfast.

Watson, William J - Private
86869 Machine Gun Corps (Infantry) 16th Company *Age 20 Killed in Action on 20 November 1917*
RIBECOURT BRITISH CEMETERY, France
Son of James and Sarah Ann Watson, of 78, Church Street East, Belfast.

Watson, William John - Lance Corporal
14759 Princess Victoria's (Royal Irish Fusiliers) 9th Battalion *Killed in Action on 16 August 1917*
DOCHY FARM NEW BRITISH CEMETERY, Belgium
Born and enlisted in Belfast.

Watson, William T - Sergeant
19/140 Royal Irish Rifles 8th Battalion *Age 33 Died in War on 7 June 1917*
LONE TREE CEMETERY, Belgium
Son of Samuel John and Isabella Watson, of 4 and 6, Maxwell Street, Sandy Row, Belfast.

Watt, David - Private
7619 Argyll and Sutherland Highlanders 2nd Battalion *Age 34 Died in War on 13 August 1916*
THIEPVAL MEMORIAL, France
Son of Mrs. Jane Watt, of 143, Kitchener Street, Belfast. His brother, Robert, was also killed.

Watt, Herbert - Lance Corporal
11772 Irish Guards 2nd Battalion *Age 24 Died in War on 27 November 1917*
CAMBRAI MEMORIAL, LOUVERVAL, France
Son of William and Mary Watt, of "Maryville", Springfield Road, Belfast.

Watt, James - Private
M2/114952 Army Service Corps attached XVIII Corps Heavy Artillery "S" Siege Park
Age 34 Killed in Action on 26 July 1917
MENDINGHEM MILITARY CEMETERY, Belgium
Son of David and Essie Watt, of Ballynefearn, County Down; husband of Marion Watt, of 36, Kilronan Street, Duncairn Gardens, Belfast.

Watt, John - Rifleman
Royal Irish Rifles *Died in War on 12 October 1917*
Husband of Dora and father of a young son, 53, Braemar Street, Belfast.

Watt, Robert - Rifleman
13791 Royal Inniskilling Fusiliers 1st Battalion *Killed in Action on 1 July 1916*
Y RAVINE CEMETERY, BEAUMONT HAMEL, France
Son of Mrs Jane Watt, 143, Kitchener Street, Belfast. His brother, David, was also killed.

Watters, Charles - Private
41372 King's Own Scottish Borderers 2nd Battalion *Age 19 Killed in Action on 11 June 1918*
TANNAY BRITISH CEMETERY, THIENNES, France
Son of John and Elizabeth Watters, of 17, Ewarts Row, Belfast.

Watters, James - Private
41144 King's Own Scottish Borderers 1st Battalion formerly 46061 Royal Scots *Died in War on 5 October 1917*
TYNE COT MEMORIAL, Belgium
Born in Belfast, enlisted in Glasgow.

Watters, James - Sergeant
348677 Canadian Field Artillery 10th Battery 3rd Brigade *Age 27 Killed in Action on 27 September 1918*
MOEUVRES COMMUNAL CEMETERY EXTENSION, France
Son of George and Rachel Watters. A Presbyterian, he was born in Belfast.

Watters, John - Rifleman
8270 Royal Irish Rifles 2nd Battalion *Age 27 Killed in Action on 27 October 1914*
LE TOURET MEMORIAL, France
Husband of Matilda Watters, of 13, Renfrew Street, Belfast.

Watters, Samuel - Private
S/22531 Argyll and Sutherland Highlanders 10th Battalion *Died in War on 15 August 1918*
CROUY BRITISH CEMETERY, CROUY-SUR-SOMME, France
Husband of Isabella Watters, of 5, Wigton Street, Belfast.

Watters, Thomas - Rifleman
2710 The King's (Liverpool Regiment) 5th Battalion *Age 23 Died in War on 2 July 1916*
WAILLY ORCHARD CEMETERY, France
Son of William Nassau Watters and Mary Watters, of 2, Mill Cottage, Woolton Road, Wavertree, Liverpool. Native of Belfast.

Watterson, George - Rifleman
1171 Royal Irish Rifles 5th Battalion *Age 22 Died in War on 17 April 1916*
BELFAST (DUNDONALD) CEMETERY, United Kingdom
Son of Mary Watterson, of 28, Carew Street Belfast and the late John Watterson.

Watterson, Joseph - Private
4640 Royal Inniskilling Fusiliers 6th Battalion *Died of Wounds on 11 November 1918*
BUSIGNY COMMUNAL CEMETERY EXTENSION, France
Born in Belfast.

Wauchope, George William Alfred - Sub-Lieutenant
Royal Naval Volunteer Reserve Anson Battalion Royal Naval Division *Age 32 Died in War on 13 November 1916*
THIEPVAL MEMORIAL, FRANCE
3, Oakland Avenue Belfast. Son of Joseph and Mrs J Wauchope of Newry.

Waugh, Hugh Henry - Company Sergeant Major
8214 Royal Inniskilling Fusiliers 1st Battalion *Died in War on 20 November 1917*
CAMBRAI MEMORIAL, LOUVERVAL, France
Born and enlisted in Belfast.

Waugh, John Brennan - Private
648945 Central Ontario Regiment 4th Canadian Mounted Rifles *Age 33 Died of sickness on 29 September 1920*
NEWTOWNARDS (MOVILLA) CEMETERY, United Kingdom
Son of Mrs. Elizabeth Jane Waugh, of 81, High Street, Belfast. Born at Mountstewart, Newtownards.
A druggist, he was a Presbyterian, a single man and had previously served in the Canadian militia.

Waugh, Thomas - Private
18636 Royal Irish Regiment 2nd Battalion *Died in War on 23 August 1918*
VIS-EN-ARTOIS MEMORIAL, France
23, Ninth Street, Belfast.

Waugh, Thomas - Sergeant
7873 Royal Inniskilling Fusiliers 2nd Battalion *Age 31 Died in War on 16 May 1915*
LE TOURET MEMORIAL, France
Son of John and Ann Jane Waugh, of 55, Epworth Street, Belfast; husband of Maggie Waugh,
of Ballykeel, Ardaragh, Newry.

Weatherall, Albert - Private
26325 Royal Inniskilling Fusiliers 8th Battalion *Age 17 Killed in Action on 16 August 1917*
TYNE COT MEMORIAL, Belgium
Son of William John and Ann Jane Weatherall, of 10, Kendal Street, Belfast. Awarded the Military Medal.

Weatherall, James - Rifleman
Royal Irish Rifles
85, Sidney Street West, Belfast.

Webb, Francis - Private
21485 Royal Irish Fusiliers "A" Company 7th Battalion *Age 18 Died in War on 9 September 1916*
THIEPVAL MEMORIAL, France
Son of James and Rose Webb, of 10, Arran Street, Belfast.

Webb, Gilbert Watson - Captain (Pilot)
Royal Irish Rifles and Royal Flying Corps 22nd Squadron *Age 26 Killed whilst flying in battle on 1 July 1916*
ACHIET-LE-GRAND COMMUNAL CEMETERY EXTENSION, France
Son of Richard Thomas and Blanche Louise Webb, of Rath House, Knock, Belfast. Native of County Down.
His brother, Karl also served, both had signed the 1912 Ulster Covenant.

Webb, James - Private
29394 Royal Inniskilling Fusiliers 7th/8th Battalion *Died of Wounds on 8 December 1917*
TINCOURT NEW BRITISH CEMETERY, France
57, Iris Street, Belfast.

Webster, Joseph - Sergeant
7389 King's Own Scottish Borderers 6th Battalion *Died in War on 7 July 1916*
THIEPVAL MEMORIAL, France
Born at Kirkcudbright, Scotland, lived in Britannic Street, Belfast.

Webster, William - Rifleman
13827 Royal Irish Rifles 10th Battalion *Killed in Action on 1 July 1916*
CONNAUGHT CEMETERY, THIEPVAL, France
Born and enlisted in Belfast.

Wedgwood, Gilbert Colclough - Lieutenant
Machine Gun Corps (Infantry) 109th Company *Age 22 Killed in Action on 1 July 1916*
THIEPVAL MEMORIAL, France
Son of Elizabeth Wedgwood, of "Egerton", 76, North Road, Bloomfield, Belfast, and the late Rev. George Ryles Wedgwood.

Wedgwood, Philip Egerton - Second Lieutenant
Royal Irish Rifles 16th Battalion *Killed in Action on 1 July 1916*
MILL ROAD CEMETERY, THIEPVAL, France
A former pupil of Methodist College he had worked for the Ulster Bank. A brother, Gilbert, was killed with the Machine Gun Corps and another brother served with the Royal Navy. Their father was the Rev George Ryles Wedgwood of University Road Methodist Church.

Weir, Albert - Private
65057 Royal Fusiliers (City of London Regiment) 13th Battalion formerly M2/196703 Army Service Corps *Died in War on 28 April 1917*
ARRAS MEMORIAL, France
Born and enlisted in Belfast.

Weir, Armour - Private
8992 Royal Inniskilling Fusiliers 2nd Battalion *Age 24 Died as a prisoner of War on 2 September 1914*
PORTE-DE-PARIS CEMETERY, CAMBRAI, France
Son of Mrs. Isabella Weir, of 38, Tyne Street, Belfast.

Weir, B - Private
Royal Irish Fusiliers *Died in War*
97, Enfield Street, Belfast.

Weir, Charles - Private
19883 Highland Light Infantry 11th Battalion *Died in War on 25 September 1915*
LOOS MEMORIAL, France
Born in Belfast, enlisted in Port Glasgow.

Weir, Hugh - Rifleman
5795 Royal Irish Rifles 2nd Battalion *Killed in Action on 9 July 1916*
POZIERES BRITISH CEMETERY, OVILLERS-LA BOISSELLE, France
Son of Mrs. Isabella Weir, of 37, Linwood Street, Belfast.

Weir, James - Acting Regimental Sergeant Major
10838 King's Own Scottish Borderers 6th Battalion *Died in War on 9 April 1917*
TILLOY BRITISH CEMETERY, TILLOY-LES-MOFFLAINES, France
Born in Belfast, enlisted in London.

Weir, James - Private
10491 Royal Inniskilling Fusiliers 1st Battalion *Died in War on 26 February 1917*
THIEPVAL MEMORIAL, France
Son of Samuel and Sarah Weir, of 12, Woodvale Street, Belfast.

Weir, James - Private
M2/020754 Army Service Corps *Age 33 Died in War on 19 May 1918*
BELFAST (DUNDONALD) CEMETERY, United Kingdom
Husband of Catherine R. Weir, of 42, London Road, Belfast.
Discharged as unfit for war service and awarded the Silver War Badge

Weir, James - Rifleman
13835 Royal Irish Rifles 8th Battalion *Died in War on 4 December 1916*
BAILLEUL COMMUNAL CEMETERY EXTENSION (NORD), France
Born and enlisted in Belfast.

Weir, John - Corporal
9826 Royal Inniskilling Fusiliers 1st Battalion *Died in War on 30 November 1917*
CAMBRAI MEMORIAL, LOUVERVAL, France
Son of Samuel and Sarah Weir, of 12, Woodvale Street, Belfast.

Weir, Joseph - Private
25397 Border Regiment 11th Battalion *Age 31 Killed in Action on 18 November 1916*
WAGGON ROAD CEMETERY, BEAUMONT-HAMEL, France
Son of Joseph and Annie Maria Weir, of "River View", Shaw's Bridge, Belfast.

Weir, Joseph - Rifleman
8962 Royal Irish Rifles 1st Battalion *Killed in Action on 9 May 1915*
PLOEGSTEERT MEMORIAL, Belgium
Born and enlisted in Belfast.

Weir, Matthew - Boilermaker
Mercantile Marine S.S. "Minneapolis" (Belfast)
Age 26 Drowned, as a result of an attack by an enemy submarine on 23 March 1916
TOWER HILL MEMORIAL, United Kingdom
Son of Annie Magill (formerly Weir), of 1, Ivanhoe Street, Belfast.

Weir, Noble - Rifleman
16090 Royal Irish Rifles 9th Battalion *Killed in Action on 1 July 1916*
THIEPVAL MEMORIAL, France
55, Mayo Street, Belfast.

Weir, Patrick - Rifleman
4770 Royal Irish Rifles 3rd Battalion *Age 31 Died of Wounds on 19 May 1915*
BRISTOL (ARNOS VALE) ROMAN CATHOLIC CEMETERY, United Kingdom
Son of Patrick and Mary Weir; husband of Mary Weir, of 86, Lepper Street, Belfast.

Weir, Robert - Corporal
15/13832 Royal Irish Rifles 15th Battalion *Killed in Action on 7 June 1917*
WULVERGHEM-LINDENHOEK ROAD MILITARY CEMETERY, Belgium
97, Enfield Street, Belfast

Weir, Samuel - Rifleman
13831 Royal Irish Rifles 8th Battalion *Died in War on 2 July 1916*
THIEPVAL MEMORIAL, France
Born Ballymacarrett, Belfast. Enlisted in Belfast. Son of W. T. and Isabella Weir,
of Upper Clara Crescent, Bloomfield, Belfast.

Weir, William - Lance Corporal
9/13829 Royal Irish Rifles 9th Battalion *Died in War on 22 June 1917*
DERRY HOUSE CEMETERY No.2, Belgium
Son of Mrs. S. Weir, of 87, Brookmount Street, Belfast. Worked for Combe Barbour before enlisting.

Welby, John Arthur - Captain
Worcestershire Regiment 11th Battalion *Age 44 Died of Wounds on 17 March 1917*
VARENNES MILITARY CEMETERY, France
Son of John and Mary Welby, of Southsea; husband of Olivia Florence J. Welby,
of 38, Knutsford Drive, Cliftonville, Belfast. Served in the South African Campaign

Welch, Jack - Private
404233 Canadian Infantry (Central Ontario Regiment) 3rd Battalion *Age 21 Died in War on 3 May 1917*
ORCHARD DUMP CEMETERY, ARLEUX-EN-GOHELLE, France
Son of John and Margaret Welch, of 31, Park Parade, Belfast, Ireland. A Prebyterian, he worked in the shipping industry.

Welch, Robert - Rifleman
915 Royal Irish Rifles 8th Battalion *Age 21 Died in War on 5 December 1917*
CAMBRAI MEMORIAL, LOUVERVAL, France
Son of David and Mary Welch, of 48, Eia Street, Belfast.

Wells, Joseph - Rifleman
1501 Royal Irish Rifles 12th Battalion *Age 34 Died in War on 4 September 1918*
AULNOYE COMMUNAL CEMETERY, France
Husband of Margaret Wells, of 102, Hillman Street, Belfast.

Welsh, Michael - Private
Royal Irish Fusiliers
22, Arnon Street, Belfast.

Welton, Samuel - Private
20387 Royal Inniskilling Fusiliers 9th Battalion *Died in War on 29 March 1918*
HAM BRITISH CEMETERY, MUILLE-VILLETTE, France
Born and enlisted in Belfast.

West, Andrew - Stoker First Class
K/3964 Royal Navy HMS "Pathfinder" *Killed in Action on 5 September 1914*
CHATHAM NAVAL MEMORIAL, United Kingdom
Son of Mrs Teresa West, 50, Tobergill Street, Belfast.

West, Isaac - Private
17/961 Royal Irish Rifles 8th Battalion *Died in War on 7 June 1917*
LONE TREE CEMETERY, Belgium
Son of David and Mary John West, of 65, Fortingale Street, Belfast.

West, James - Private
22224 Royal Inniskilling Fusiliers 5th Battalion formerly 088834 Army Service Corps *Died in War on 8 October 1918*
PROSPECT HILL CEMETERY, GOUY, France
Son of Mrs. M. West, of 140, Fortingale Street, Belfast.

Wetherall, James - Rifleman
8878 Royal Irish Rifles 1st Battalion *Killed in Action on 9 May 1915*
PLOEGSTEERT MEMORIAL, Belgium
Born and enlisted in Belfast.

Whearty, John - Private
11763 Royal Inniskilling Fusiliers 2nd Battalion *Died in War on 16 May 1915*
LE TOURET MEMORIAL, France
Brother of Miss Whearty, 2, Grosvenor Place, Belfast.

Whelan, John Percy - Captain
Royal Irish Rifles 2nd Battalion *Age 35 Killed in Action on 11 December 1914*
YPRES (MENIN GATE) MEMORIAL, Belgium
Son of Joseph Whelan of Osborne Park, Belfast he was educated at Loretto School, Edinburgh.
First commissioned in 1902.

Whelan, Robert Selkirk - Company Sergeant Major
10/16093 Royal Irish Rifles 10th Battalion *Age 25 Killed in Action on 29 August 1917*
METZ-EN-COUTURE COMMUNAL CEMETERY BRITISH EXTENSION, France
Son of John Edward Whelan, of Ravenhill Road, Belfast, and the late Elizabeth Whelan.
Awarded the Military Cross and Military Medal.

Whelan, Samuel - Rifleman
1417 Royal Irish Rifles 8th Battalion *Died in War on 21 June 1917*
YPRES (MENIN GATE) MEMORIAL, Belgium
Son of Mrs Charles Whelan, 16, Ewart's Row, Belfast.

Whelan, Timothy - Private
2360 Royal Munster Fusiliers 1st Battalion *Age 33 Killed in Action on 23 March 1918*
BRONFAY FARM MILITARY CEMETERY, BRAY-SUR-SOMME, France
Son of Sarah and the late Timothy Whelan; husband of Sarah Agnew (formerly Whelan),
of 14, Fairfield Street, Crumlin Road, Belfast.

Whelehan, Christopher - Private
11496 Royal Irish Fusiliers 1st Battalion *Died in War on 13 April 1915*
PLOEGSTEERT MEMORIAL, Belgium
Resident of Belfast. Brother of Thomas Whelehan, of 3, Bishopsgate Street, Mullingar, County Westmeath.
Two brothers also served.

Wherry, James - Private
6940 Royal Irish Rifles 1st Battalion *Died of enteric fever in hospital at Le Havre, post-wounds on 30 April 1915*
STE. MARIE CEMETERY, LE HAVRE, France
30, Thames Street, Belfast.

Whisker, Alexander Newman - Private
5130 Australian Infantry 17th Battalion *Age 25 Died in War on 3 May 1917*
VILLERS-BRETONNEUX MEMORIAL, France
Son of James and Eliza Mary Whisker, of 28, Stranmillis Gardens, Stranmillis Road, Belfast, Ireland.
Born in Crossgar, County Down, Ireland.

White, John - Rifleman
751 Royal Irish Rifles 14th Battalion *Killed in Action on 7 December 1917*
CAMBRAI MEMORIAL LOUVERVAL, France
Born and enlisted in Belfast.

White, Patrick - Rifleman
9157 Royal Irish Rifles 2nd Battalion *Killed in Action on 26 April 1916*
ECOIVRES MILITARY CEMETERY, MONT-ST. ELOI, France
Born and enlisted in Belfast.

White, Cecil Godfrey - Captain
Royal Air Force 53rd Squadron and Royal Field Artillery *Age 26 Died in War 21 April 1918*
SANCTUARY WOOD CEMETERY, *Belgium*
Awarded the Military Cross, the son of Dr. Robert Godfrey White, F.R.C.P., F.R.C.S.,
and Minnie Moore White, of Lonsdale, Strandtown, Belfast.

White, Edward T - Private
10650 Royal Irish Fusiliers 1st Battalion *Killed in Action on 3 May 1917*
ARRAS MEMORIAL, *France*
Brother of Mrs M Crymble 18, Mountjoy Street, Belfast.

White, Hugh - Lance Corporal
16095 Royal Irish Rifles 10th Battalion *Died in War on 13 August 1917*
YPRES (MENIN GATE) MEMORIAL, *Belgium*
49, Severn Street, Belfast. Enlisted in Belfast.

White, James - Private
10379 Royal Inniskilling Fusiliers 2nd Battalion *Age 21 Died in War on 16 May 1915*
LE TOURET MEMORIAL, *France*
Son of Mrs. E. White, of 1, Havelock Cottage, Ormeau Road, Belfast.

White, James - Private
31543 Royal Inniskilling Fusiliers "C" Company 5th Battalion *Age 20 Killed in Action on 8 October 1918*
PROSPECT HILL CEMETERY, GOUY, *France*
Son of Mrs. Margaret White, of 45, Seventh Street, Belfast.

White, James - Private
4489 Connaught Rangers 5th Battalion formerly 13857 Royal Inniskillling Fusiliers
Died in War on 22 August 1915
7th FIELD AMBULANCE CEMETERY, *Turkey*
Born and enlisted in Belfast.

White, John - Private
9408 Royal Scots Fusiliers 2nd Battalion *Died in War on 8 November 1914*
NETLEY MILITARY CEMETERY, *United Kingdom*
Born and enlisted in Belfast.

White, John - Sapper
57701 Royal Engineers 154th Field Company *Died in War on 14 November 1916*
THIEPVAL MEMORIAL, *France*
Born Ballymacarrett, Belfast. Enlisted in Belfast.

White, Joseph - Rifleman
6521 Royal Irish Rifles 1st Battalion *Killed in Action on 12 March 1915*
LE TOURET MEMORIAL, *France*
Mother, brother and sister lived at 35, Elm Street.

White, Patrick - Rifleman
9157 Royal Irish Rifles 2nd Battalion *Died in War on 26 April 1916*
ECOIVRES MILITARY CEMETERY, MONT-ST. ELOI, *France*
30, Getty Street, Belfast.

White, Robert - Private
9127 Royal Inniskilling Fusiliers 2nd Battalion *Age 24 Died in War on 20 October 1914*
PLOEGSTEERT MEMORIAL, Belgium
Son of the late Robert and Sarah White, of 92, Wilton Street, Shankill Road, Belfast.

White, Thomas - Rifleman
6358 Royal Irish Rifles 2nd Battalion *Killed in Action on 20 December 1914*
LA FERTE-SOUS-JOUARRE MEMORIAL, France
Born and enlisted in Belfast.

White, Thomas - Second Lieutenant
The Loyal North Lancashire Regiment 2nd Battalion attached 8th Battalion *Died in War on 8 July 1916*
THIEPVAL MEMORIAL, France
Educated at RBAI he was the son of W. J. White, Winston Gardens, Knock, Belfast.
Joined the Inns of Court Training Corps before being commissioned into his regiment.

White, W C - Engineer Sub-Lieutenant
Royal Naval Reserve HMS "Snaefell" *Died in War on 15 June 1918*
MALTA (CAPUCCINI) NAVAL CEMETERY
Son of Patrick and A. P. M. White, of Carlton. Carolan Road, Belfast.

White, William - Driver
102237 Royal Horse Artillery and Royal Field Artillery *Died in War on 3 January 1916*
SALISBURY (DEVIZES ROAD) CEMETERY, WILTSHIRE, United Kingdom
Resident in Belfast, enlisted in Bristol.

White, William - Private
54192 Royal Army Medical Corps *Died in War on 7 July 1918*
BELFAST (DUNDONALD) CEMETERY, United Kingdom
Husband of Emma White, of 20, Sylvan Street, Belfast.

White, William - Rifleman
15/568 Royal Irish Rifles 15th Battalion *Age 22 Killed in Action on 13 October 1916*
ST. QUENTIN CABARET MILITARY CEMETERY, Belgium
Son of William and Ellen Jane White, of 31, Great George's Street, Belfast.

Whitehill, Thomas - Private
S/4301 Seaforth Highlanders (Ross-shire Buffs, the Duke of Albany's) 2nd Battalion
Died in War on 28 May 1915
LEWISHAM (LADYWELL) CEMETERY LONDON, United Kingdom
Born in Belfast, enlisted in Lanarkshire, Scotland.

Whiteside, David John - Private
5429 Royal Irish Rifles 2nd Battalion *Killed in Action on 4 May 1916*
ECOIVRES MILITARY CEMETERY, MONT-ST. ELOI, France
Son of David and Eliza Whiteside, of 58, Canmore Street, Belfast.

Whiteside, James - Rifleman
17/1240 Royal Irish Rifles 8th Battalion *Age 18 Died in War on 2 July 1916*
MILL ROAD CEMETERY, THIEPVAL, France
Son of Thomas Whiteside, of 27, Keswick Street, Belfast.

Whiteside, Joseph - Sapper
WR/355331 Royal Engineers Inland Waterways and Docks *Age 22 Died in War on 19 November 1917*
MINSTER (THANET) CEMETERY, United Kingdom
Son of Mary Whiteside, of 5, Reid's Place, Belfast, and the late Joseph Whiteside.

Whiteside, William - Rifleman
6120 Royal Irish Rifles 2nd Battalion *Died in War on 15 January 1916*
BELFAST (DUNDONALD) CEMETERY, United Kingdom
Son of William and Jane Whiteside; husband of Sarah Ferrin (formerly Whiteside),
of 3, Ardilaun Street, Belfast.

Whitley, Andrew - Rifleman
9862 Royal Irish Rifles 7th Battalion *Age 18 Killed in Action on 16 August 1917*
TYNE COT MEMORIAL, Belgium
Son of Andrew and Kathleen Hopkins, of 73, Byron Street, Belfast.

Whitley, George - Private
42304 Royal Irish Fusiliers 1st Battalion formerly 22479 Royal Irish Rifles *Died in War on 6 October 1918*
HARINGE (BANDAGHEM) MILITARY CEMETERY, Belgium
Born Ballymacarrett, Belfast. Enlisted in Belfast.

Whitley, William George - Second Lieutenant
The King's (Liverpool Regiment) 13th Battalion *Age 22 Died in War on 16 August 1916*
GUILLEMONT ROAD CEMETERY, GUILLEMONT, France
Son of Henry and Annie Whitley, of "Florida", Ardenlee Parade, Belfast.

Whyte, Alexander - Private
S/21404 Seaforth Highlanders (Ross-shire Buffs, the Duke of Albany's) 4th Battalion
Died in War on 30 May 1918
ANZIN-ST AUBIN BRITISH CEMETERY, France
Born and enlisted in Belfast.

Whyte, James - Rifleman
8738 Royal Irish Rifles "B" Company 1st Battalion *Age 27 Killed in Action on 9 May 1915*
PLOEGSTEERT MEMORIAL, Belgium
Brother of Mrs. Elizabeth Beattie, of 17, Glentoran Street, Belfast.

Wickson, Frederick Charles - Private
5106 3rd Dragoon Guards (Prince of Wales' Own) *Died in War on 31 October 1914*
YPRES (MENIN GATE) MEMORIAL, Belgium
Born and enlisted in Monmouthshire, Wales, resident of Belfast.

Wightman, Henry - Stoker First Class
K/21030 Royal Navy HMS "Arethusa" *Age 21 Killed by mine explosion in North Sea on 11 February 1916*
CHATHAM NAVAL MEMORIAL, United Kingdom
Son of Isabella Gillespie (formerly Wightman), of 18, Newcastle Street, Belfast, Ireland,
and the late Robert Wightman.

Wightman, Herbert - Rifleman
13852 Royal Irish Rifles 10th Battalion *Age 19 Killed in Action on 23 November 1915*
SUCRERIE MILITARY CEMETERY, COLINCAMPS, France
Brother of Harold T. Wightman, of 133, Ormeau Road, Belfast.

Wigley, William Robert - Private
66925 Northumberland Fusiliers 12/13th Battalion *Died in War on 6 August 1918*
SISSONNE BRITISH CEMETERY, France
Born in Belfast, enlisted in Leeds.

Wigson, Joseph - Sapper
24936 Royal Engineers 102nd Field Company *Died as a result of war on 20 February 1919*
DUEVILLE COMMUNAL CEMETERY EXTENSION,, Italy
Napier Street, Belfast. Son of Joseph and Martha Wigson of Clandeboye.

Wigston, William - Rifleman
9209 Royal Irish Rifles 2nd Battalion *Died in War on 10 November 1914*
POPERINGHE OLD MILITARY CEMETERY, Belgium
Husband of Sarah Jane Wigston, of 33, Bradford Street, Belfast. Father of a young son.
His brother also served. An Orangeman, his lodge was Sons of Ulster 759.

Wilkin, George Henry - Sergeant
8209 Norfolk Regiment 1st Battalion *Age 24 Died in War on 23 April 1917*
ARRAS MEMORIAL, France
Son of Robert and Sarah Wilkin, of 52, Diamond Street, King's Lynn, Norfolk.
Husband of Eliza Jane Wilkin, of 49, Moscow Street, Belfast.

Wilkin, John - Corporal
493 Royal Irish Rifles 12th Battalion *Killed in Action on 22 November 1917*
CAMBRAI MEMORIAL, LOUVERVAL, France
59, Hanover Street, Belfast. His brother also fell.

Wilkin, Thomas - Sergeant
15/13855 Royal Irish Rifles 15th Battalion *Died in War on 23 November 1917*
THIEPVAL MEMORIAL, France
Son of James Wilkin, of 9, Derwent Street, Sunderland. Born in Belfast. His brother also fell.

Wilkins, Alfred - Leading Seaman
297237 Royal Navy Nelson Battalion Royal Naval Division *Age 34 (Naval, died ashore) on 3 May 1915*
HELLES MEMORIAL, Turkey
Husband of Minnie Wilkins, of 7, Kathleen Street, Templemore Avenue, Belfast.

Wilkinson, Albert - Corporal
S4/127937 Army Service Corps 254th Company *Died of pneumonia on 3 December 1915*
ST. SEVER CEMETERY, ROUEN, France
Son of Thomas Wilkinson; husband of Mrs. Wilkinson, of 86, Conway Street, Belfast.

Wilkinson, Bernard - Private
2988 Royal Inniskilling Fusiliers 2nd Battalion *Age 20 Died of Wounds on 22 July 1915*
BETHUNE TOWN CEMETERY, France
Son of Richard Wilkinson, of Maguire's Bridge, County Fermanagh; husband of
Rose Smyth (formerly Wilkinson), of 135, Oldpark Avenue, Belfast.

Wilkinson, James - Private
9615 Connaught Rangers 1st Battalion *Killed in Action on 18 July 1916*
BASRA MEMORIAL, Iraq
Resident of Belfast, the son of Mrs. Jane Taylor, of The Gatehouse, Poyntzpass, County Armagh.

Wilkinson, Joseph James - Private
1747 Australian Infantry 49th Battalion *Age 19 Died in War on 15 August 1916*
VILLERS-BRETONNEUX MEMORIAL, *France*
Son of Joseph and Agnes Beattie Wilkinson, of Smyth Avenue, Wynnum, Queensland, Australia.
Born in Belfast, Ireland.

Wilkinson, Kennedy - Rifleman
9389 Royal Irish Rifles formerly Army Cyclist Corps 2nd Battalion *Killed in Action on 10 August 1917*
YPRES (MENIN GATE) MEMORIAL, *Belgium*
Son of the late William John and Elizabeth Wilkinson, of 1, Bristol Street, Belfast.

Wilkinson, Walter - Rifleman
6310 Royal Irish Regiment 2nd Battalion *Died in War on 15 September 1914*
LE-FERTE-SOUS-JOUARRE MEMORIAL, *France*
Born and enlisted in Belfast. Husband of Mrs B Wilkinson of Inchicore, Dublin.

Wilkinson, William J - Sapper
WR/505299 Royal Engineers Inland Water Transport (Aire) *Accidentally drowned on 26 December 1918*
LONGUENESSE (ST. OMER) SOUVENIR CEMETERY, *France*
Husband of Elizabeth Wilkinson, of 16, Burton Street, Belfast.

Wilkinson, William John - A/Corporal
42052 South Wales Borderers 1st Battalion formerly 10182 Cheshire Regiment *Died in War on 27 August 1916*
ADANAC MILITARY CEMETERY, MIRAUMONT, *France*
Born in Belfast, enlisted in Chester, England.

Willey, Joseph - Lance Corporal
9347 Royal Inniskilling Fusiliers 2nd Battalion *Age 21 Killed in Action on 26 August 1914*
BEVILLERS COMMUNAL CEMETERY, *France*
Son of Mr. and Mrs. J. Willey, of 14, Christopher Street, Belfast.

Williams, Charles Henry - Boatswain (Bosun)
Mercantile Marine S.S. "Forestmoor" (London) *Age 31 Drowned as a result of an attack by an enemy submarine on 6 October 1917*
TOWER HILL MEMORIAL, *United Kingdom*
Son of the late Charles Walter and Alice Williams; husband of Mary Annie Williams (née Hunt),
of 4, Station Street, Barry Dock, Glamorgan, Wales. Born in Belfast.

Williams, Daniel - Private
637806 Royal Inniskilling Fusiliers 1st Battalion *Killed in Action on 1 July 1916*
KNIGHTSBRIDGE CEMETERY, MESNIL-MARTINSART, *France*
Brother of Annie Williams, 3 North Ann Street, Belfast.

Williams, David Albert - Corporal
60836 Royal Field Artillery 12th Battery 35th Brigade *Age 28 Killed in Action on 22 October 1917*
THE HUTS CEMETERY, *Belgium*
Son of Richard and Mary A. Williams, of 164, Ravenhill Road, Belfast.

Williams, Frank Leonard - Captain
Machine Gun Corps (Infantry) attached 8th Battalion Border Regiment *Age 28 Died in War on 30 May 1918*
TERLINCTHUN BRITISH CEMETERY, WIMILLE, *France*
Son of Alfred and Isabelle Williams, of Hatton, Warwick; husband of Norah M. Williams,
of 83, Malone Avenue, Belfast. Awarded the Military Cross.

Journey of Remembering

Williams, Frederick - Lieutenant
Royal Air Force 22nd Squadron *Age 23 Died in War on 2 April 1918*
ARRAS FLYING SERVICES MEMORIAL, France
Born in Belfast, the son of Frederick and Emmie Williams. Educated at Larne Grammar School and thereafter was in the motor business. Joined the Royal Engineers in 1915 as a dispatch rider. Transferred to the Royal Flying Corps and obtained his pilots wings in 1917.

Williams, J - Able Seaman
Mercantile Marine S.S. "Mirlo" (London)
Age 51 Drowned, as a result of an attack by an enemy submarine on 16 August 1918
TOWER HILL MEMORIAL, United Kingdom
Husband of Isabella Williams, of 262, Castlereagh Road, Belfast. Born in Kingston.

Williams, Richard - Rifleman
6390 Royal Irish Rifles 2nd Battalion *Age 28 Died of Wounds on 6 September 1918*
WULVERGHEM-LINDENHOEK ROAD MILITARY CEMETERY, Belgium
Son of Thomas and Annie Williams, of 14, Westland Gardens, Belfast.

Williams, Robert John - Private
2501 6th Inniskilling Dragoons *Died in War on 11 February 1915*
YPRES TOWN CEMETERY EXTENSION, Belgium
The Chief Fire Station, Belfast.

Williamson, (Francis) Frank - Rifleman
9088 Royal Irish Rifles 2nd Battalion *Killed in Action on 11 November 1914*
YPRES (MENIN GATE) MEMORIAL, Belgium
Son of William John and Mary Jane Williamson, of 31, Kendal Street, Belfast.

Williamson, Archie - Private
19/550 Royal Irish Rifles 12th Battalion *Age 20 Killed in Action on 21 March 1918*
POZIERES MEMORIAL, France
Son of David and Jane Eliza Williamson, of 108, Crumlin Road, Belfast.

Williamson, Francis - Rifleman
9088 Royal Irish Rifles 2nd Battalion *Age 38 Killed in Action on 11 November 1914*
YPRES (MENIN GATE) MEMORIAL, Belgium
Son of William John and Mary Jane Williamson, of 31, Kendal Street, Belfast.

Williamson, Frederick - Lieutenant
4th Gurkha Rifles Indian Army Reserve of Officers attached 1st Battalion *Age 18 Died in War on 10 May 1917*
STRUMA MILITARY CEMETERY, Greece
Son of John and Jane Williamson of 22, Stranmillis Road, Belfast.

Williamson, George - Gunner
279817 Royal Garrison Artillery 14th Company *Age 55 Died as a result of war on 28 June 1919*
BELFAST CITY CEMETERY, United Kingdom
Husband of Patience Williamson, of 40, Coolfin Street, Belfast.

Williamson, Hugh - Rifleman
16096 Royal Irish Rifles 9th Battalion *Killed in Action on 1 July 1916*
THIEPVAL MEMORIAL, France
21, Broadbent Street, Belfast.

Journey of Remembering

Williamson, J - Private
M/320090 Army Service Corps 648th Mechanical Transport Company *Age 19 Died in War on 18 July 1918*
LUMBO BRITISH CEMETERY, Mozambique
Son of Mrs. A. Williamson, of 30, Cumbermere Street, Belfast.

Williamson, James - Private
3363 Royal Inniskilling Fusiliers "C" Company 7th Battalion *Age 20 Died of Wounds on 8 June 1917*
BAILLEUL COMMUNAL CEMETERY EXTENSION (NORD), France
Son of John and Sarah Anne Williamson of Belfast.

Williamson, John - Gunner
47678 Royal Field Artillery 35th Brigade *Died in War on 20 September 1916*
DELVILLE WOOD CEMETERY, LONGUEVAL, France
24, Crosby Street, Belfast.

Williamson, Joseph - Private
22712 King's Own (Yorkshire Light) 2nd Battalion formerly10931 Durham Light Infantry *Died in War on 27 June 1916*
BOUZINCOURT COMMUNAL CEMETERY EXTENSION, France
Born in Belfast, enlisted in Gateshead, England.

Williamson, Martin - Rifleman
320 Royal Irish Rifles 8th Battalion *Killed in Action on 7 June 1917*
LONE TREE CEMETERY, Belgium
Born and enlisted in Belfast.

Williamson, R - Rifleman
6787 Royal Irish Rifles 7th Battalion *Age 19 Died in War on 3 June 1916*
DUD CORNER CEMETERY, LOOS, France
Son of Ellen Williamson, of 36, Upton Street, Belfast.

Williamson, Samuel - Rifleman
2789 Royal Irish Rifles 9th Battalion *Age 16 Killed in Action on 29 March 1916*
SUCRERIE MILITARY CEMETERY, COLINCAMPS, France
Son of Samuel and Mary Williamson of 62, Dee Street, Belfast. One of the youngest to die on the Somme.

Williamson, Thomas (Tom) - Rifleman
17/1104 Royal Irish Rifles 15th Battalion *Age 18 Died of Wounds on 23 November 1915*
GEZAINCOURT COMMUNAL CEMETERY, France
Eldest son of James Porter Williamson and Edith Richardson Williamson, of 7, Hazelnut Street, Belfast.

Williamson, Thomas - Private
13703 Royal Inniskilling Fusiliers 11th Battalion *Killed in Action on 1 July 1916*
THIEPVAL MEMORIAL, France
Husband of Maggie Williamson, 31, Fortingale Street, Belfast.

Williamson, Thomas - Rifleman
13861 Royal Irish Rifles 9th Battalion *Killed in Action on 1 July 1916*
THIEPVAL MEMORIAL, France
Son of Charles and Mary Jane Williamson, of 28, Ruskin Street, Belfast.

Williamson, Thomas Henry - Private
6529 Royal Inniskilling Fusiliers 3rd Battalion *Age 43 Died as a result of war on 15 November 1918*
BELFAST CITY CEMETERY, United Kingdom
Son of Thomas and Sarah Ann Williamson; husband of Jeannie Williamson, of 22, Brittanic Street, Belfast.

Williamson, William - Private
4553 Royal Inniskilling Fusiliers 2nd Battalion *Died in War on 16 May 1915*
GUARDS' CEMETERY, WINDY CORNER, GUINCHY, France
Born and enlisted in Belfast.

Williamson, William - Rifleman
13789 Royal Irish Rifles 9th Battalion *Age 41 Died of accidental injuries on 10 May 1916*
BEAUVAL COMMUNAL CEMETERY, France
Husband of Mary Williamson, of 179, Canmore Street, Belfast.

Williamson, William James - Private
3523 Royal Inniskilling Fusiliers 7th Battalion *Killed in Action on 9 September 1916*
THIEPVAL MEMORIAL, France
Born in Belfast.

Willis, Howard - Rifleman
19341 Royal Irish Rifles 12th Battalion *Killed in Action on 1 July 1916*
THIEPVAL MEMORIAL, France
Born and enlisted in Belfast.

Willis, James Denning - Lance Corporal
2551 Black Watch (Royal Highlanders) 2nd/6th Battalion *Age 24 Killed in Action on 10 July 1915*
RUE-DAVID MILITARY CEMETERY, FLEURBAIX, France
Son of William and Margaret Willis, of Belfast.

Willis, Philip - Gunner
1978 South African Heavy Artillery *Age 26 Died of meningitis on 18 August 1918*
STE. MARIE CEMETERY, LE HAVRE, France
Only son of Philip and Isabella Willis, of 13, Glandore Gardens, Belfast, Ireland.

Willis, Thomas Bell - Company Sergeant Major
6220 Royal Irish Rifles 2nd Battalion *Age 20 Killed in Action on 5 October 1918*
TYNE COT MEMORIAL, Belgium
Brother of Mrs. G. Allen, of 22, Rosewood Street, Belfast.

Wilson, Albert Patterson - Able Seaman
224462 Royal Navy HMS "Hawke" *Killed in acton with submarine in North Sea on 15 October 1914*
CHATHAM NAVAL MEMORIAL, United Kingdom
Son of Mr. and Mrs. Richard Wilson, of Belfast, husband of May Wilson,
of The Square, Maynooth, County Kildare.

Wilson, Alexander Simms - Private
12717 Royal Irish Fusiliers 5th Battalion *Age 21 Died in War on 16 August 1915*
HELLES MEMORIAL, Turkey
Son of William and Elizabeth Wilson, of 140, Earl Street, Belfast.

Wilson, Andrew - Rifleman
9/16104 Royal Irish Rifles 9th Battalion *Age 21 Died of Wounds on 17 January 1916*
FORCEVILLE COMMUNAL CEMETERY AND EXTENSION, France
Only son of Edward and Susan Wilson, of 42, Mervue Street, Belfast.

Journey of Remembering

Wilson, Andrew - Rifleman
9262 Royal Irish Rifles 13th Battalion *Died in War on 2 July 1916*
THIEPVAL MEMORIAL, France
Son of Mrs A. Wilson, of 20, Riga Street, Belfast.

Wilson, Charles - Private
125781 Royal Army Medical Corps *Died in War on 28 October 1918*
DIED OF NATURAL CAUSES IN INDIA
Born and enlisted in Belfast.

Wilson, Christopher - Rifleman
7154 Royal Irish Rifles "B" Company 2nd Battalion *Age 29 Killed in Action on 27 October 1914*
LE TOURET MEMORIAL, France
Son of the late Christopher and Elizabeth Wilson, of 34, East Street, Belfast.

Wilson, Edmund - Private
2614 Black Watch (Royal Highlanders) 6th Battalion *Age 25 Killed in Action on 22 October 1916*
FORCEVILLE COMMUNAL CEMETERY AND EXTENSION, France
Son of Henrietta and the late Thomas Wilson, of 59, Devonshire Street, Grosvenor Road, Belfast.

Wilson, Edward - Rifleman
12182 Royal Irish Rifles 15th Battalion *Age 23 Killed in Action on 1 July 1916*
THIEPVAL MEMORIAL, France
Son of Samuel and Jane Wilson, of 38, Carnalea Street, Belfast.

Wilson, George - Private
11005 Royal Inniskilling Fusiliers 2nd Battalion *Died in War on 20 March 1915*
POST OFFICE RIFLES CEMETERY, FESTUBERT, France
Only son of Sarah of 31, Brussels Street, Belfast.

Wilson, H - Lance Sergeant
Royal Irish Rifles *Killed in Action*
49, Tobergill Street, Belfast.

Wilson, Harold - Private
11126 Black Watch (Royal Highlanders) *Age 20 Struck on head by a piece of exploding shell on 15 March 1916*
ST PATRICK'S CEMETERY, LOOS, France
A teacher, he had been educated and later taught at Townsend Street National School.
The son of James and Margaret Wilson of Tennent Street, Belfast.

Wilson, Hill - Rifleman
6921 Royal Irish Rifles 12th Battalion *Killed in Action on 3 September 1918*
NIEUWKERKE CHURCHYARD, Belgium
Born and enlisted in Belfast.

Wilson, Hugh - Rifleman
13868 Royal Irish Rifles 1st Battalion *Killed in Action on 21 March 1918*
POZIERES MEMORIAL, France
Born and enlisted in Belfast.

Journey of Remembering

Wilson, James - Lance Sergeant
871485 Canadian Pioneers 107th Brigade *Died of Wounds on 15 August 1917*
MAROC BRITISH CEMETERY, GRENAY, *France*
Husband of Margaret Wilson, of 503, Sherbrook Street, Winnipeg, Manitoba, Canada.
Native of Belfast, Ireland. An Anglican, he worked as a machinist.

Wilson, James - Private
15749 Royal Irish Fusiliers 6th Battalion *Age 28 Died in War on 7 August 1915*
HELLES MEMORIAL, *Turkey*
Husband of Rose Wilson, of 57, Massareene Street, Cullingtree Road, Belfast.

Wilson, James - Private
201518 Canadian Infantry (Central Ontario Regiment) 4th Battalion *Died in War on 8 October 1916*
VIMY MEMORIAL, *France*
Son of the late George and Mary Jane Wilson, of Woodvale Road, Belfast, Ireland.
He worked as a labourer in Canada, a Presbyterian.

Wilson, James - Private
333905 Royal Engineers formerly East Surrey Regiment *Killed in Action on 4 October 1918*
Born in Belfast.

Wilson, James - Sergeant
1167 Lanarkshire Yeomanry *Age 34 Died in War on 9 January 1917*
JERUSALEM MEMORIAL, *Israel*
Son of Mrs. Eliza Wilson, of 37, Fort William Parade, Belfast.

Wilson, James - Stoker First Class
SS/108189 Royal Navy HMS "Hawke" *Died in War on 15 October 1914*
CHATHAM NAVAL MEMORIAL, *United Kingdom*
53, Brittanic Street, Belfast.

Wilson, James Harold - Private
S/11126 Black Watch (Royal Highlanders) 1st Battalion *Age 20 Died in War on 18 March 1916*
ST. PATRICK'S CEMETERY, LOOS, *France*
Son of James F. Wilson, of 40, Tennent Street, Belfast.

Wilson, James Renwick - Private
S/43192 Black Watch (Royal Highlanders) 9th Battalion *Age 20 Died in War on 31 March 1918*
ARRAS MEMORIAL, *France*
Son of Adam Renwick Wilson and Barbara Wilson, of 20, Deacon Street, Belfast.

Wilson, John - Lance Corporal
267736 Seaforth Highlanders 6th Battalion *Age 22 Killed in Action on 9 April 1917*
HIGHLAND CEMETERY, ROCLINCOURT, *France*
Son of Mrs Wilson, of 8, Diamond Street, Belfast.

Wilson, John - Petty Officer Stoker
K/9455 Royal Navy HMS "Kale" *Died in War on 27 March 1918*
CHATHAM NAVAL MEMORIAL, *United Kingdom*
Son of Thomas Wilson of Maymount Street, Belfast. Husband of Maggie Shaw (formerly Wilson)
of Derryboy, Crossgar, County Down.

Wilson, John - Private
1437 Australian Infantry 51st Battalion *Age 27 Died in War on 15 August 1916*
VILLERS-BRETONNEUX MEMORIAL, France
Son of William and Elizabeth Wilson, of 140, Earl Street, Belfast, Ireland.

Wilson, John - Rifleman
13878 Royal Irish Rifles 15th Battalion *Age 24 Killed in Action on 7 June 1917*
YPRES (MENIN GATE) MEMORIAL, Belgium
Son of William and Jane Wilson, of 9, Linwood Street, Belfast. Awarded the Military Medal.

Wilson, John - Rifleman
6072 Royal Irish Rifles 7th Battalion *Age 37 Died in War on 15 August 1917*
YPRES (MENIN GATE) MEMORIAL, Belgium
Husband of Agnes Wilson, of 17, Tyrone Street, Belfast.

Wilson, John W. C. - Private
24255 Royal Irish Fusiliers 9th Battalion *Age 19 Killed in Action on 20 August 1917*
WIMEREUX COMMUNAL CEMETERY, France
Son of Hugh and the late Jane Wilson, of Belfast.

Wilson, Joseph - Sergeant
7836 King's Royal Rifles 3rd Battalion *Killed in Action on 8 May 1915*
YPRES (MENIN GATE) MEMORIAL, Belgium
Eldest son of Joseph and Nina Wilson of 335, Donegall Road. Had settled in Rhodesia after the Boer War but returned to Belfast to re-enlist.

Wilson, Lawrence - Sergeant
10929 The King's (Liverpool Regiment) *Died in War on 10 March 1915*
LE TOURET MEMORIAL, France
Shaftesbury Avenue, Belfast. Born in Middlesex, enlisted Warrington, England.

Wilson, John - Lance Corporal
9101 Royal Irish Rifles 2nd Battalion *Died in War on 24 March 1918*
POZIERES MEMORIAL, France
Husband of Mrs Rose Wilson, Scotch Street, Belfast.

Wilson, Matthew - Private
49873 Royal Irish Fusiliers 1st Battalion *Killed in Action on 21 October 1918*
HARLEBEKE NEW BRITISH CEMETERY, Belgium
81, Hopeton Street, Belfast.

Wilson, Robert - Driver
T3/030917 Army Service Corps (36th Division) Horse Transport *Accidentally drowned on 18 July 1915*
SEAFORD CEMETERY, United Kingdom
40 Roden Street, Belfast. Lost his life before the Division arrived in France.

Wilson, Robert - Lance Corporal
9889 Royal Irish Rifles *Died in War on 28 April 1915*
HELLES MEMORIAL, Greece
109, Charles Street South, Belfast.

Wilson, Robert - Private
19471 Machine Gun Corps (Infantry) 107th Company *Age 19 Died in War on 10 June 1916*
THIEPVAL MEMORIAL, France
Son of Agnes Wilson, of 87, Hornby Street, Belfast, and the late William Wilson.

Wilson, Robert - Private
SS/25945 Royal Army Service Corps *Died in War on 2 December 1915*
Born in Belfast.

Wilson, Samuel - Private
1738 6th Dragoons (Inniskilling) *Died in War on 2 July 1917*
TINCOURT NEW BRITISH CEMETERY, France
Born and enlisted in Belfast.

Wilson, Samuel - Rifleman
8143 Royal Irish Rifles 1st Battalion *Killed in Action on 9 May 1915*
PLOEGSTEERT MEMORIAL, Belgium
Born and enlisted in Belfast.

Wilson, The Rev. William Andrew - Chaplain
Young Men's Christian Association *Died of accidental injuries (motor accident) on 20 March 1918*
STE. MARIE CEMETERY, LE HAVRE, France
M.A. Born in Minterburn County Tyrone, 1869. Son of the Rev. A. J. Wilson, D.D., Belfast; husband of Ellen F. Wilson, of Ashbrook, Coleraine, Londonderry. Presbyterian Minister of New Row, Coleraine, 1896-1918.

Wilson, Thomas - Corporal
23138 Royal Inniskilling Fusiliers 7th Battalion *Age 29 Died in War on 28 May 1916*
PHILOSOPHE BRITISH CEMETERY, MAZINGARBE, France
Husband of Elizabeth Hogg (formerly Wilson), of 30, Grove Street, Belfast.

Wilson, Thomas - Gunner
17379 Royal Garrison Artillery 12th Siege Battery *Age 38 Died of Wounds on 1 April 1916*
LIJSSENTHOEK MILITARY CEMETERY, Belgium
Son of Thomas and Christina Wilson. Born Belfast.

Wilson, Thomas - Gunner
40176 Royal Garrison Artillery 1st Essex Battery *Age 23 Died in War on 26 October 1918*
BUSIGNY COMMUNAL CEMETERY EXTENSION, France
Son of Thomas and Isabella Wilson, of 46, Thorndale Avenue, Belfast.

Wilson, Thomas - Private
25 Highland Light Infantry 10th Battalion *Died in War on 25 September 1915*
LOOS MEMORIAL, France
Born Enniskillen, enlisted Hampshire, resident of Belfast.

Wilson, Thomas - Private
PLY/11164 Royal Marine Light Infantry HMS "Invincible"
Age 29 Killed in Action at Battle of Jutland on 31 May 1916
PLYMOUTH NAVAL MEMORIAL, United Kingdom
Son of Thomas and Annie J. Wilson, of 24, Bentinck Street, Belfast.

Wilson, W - Private
21562 Royal Irish Fusiliers *Age 49 Died in War on 11 January 1917*
BELFAST (DUNDONALD) CEMETERY, United Kingdom
Husband of Annie Wilson, of 20, Roseberry Gardens, Woodstock Road, Belfast.

Wilson, William - Able Seaman
J/4776 Royal Navy HMS "Monmouth" *Age 19 Killed in Action at Battle of Coronel on 1 November 1914*
PLYMOUTH NAVAL MEMORIAL, United Kingdom
Son of William Robert and Mary Wilson, of Plumas, Manitoba, Canada. Native of Belfast.

Wilson, William - Boatswain (Bosun)
Mercantile Marine S.S. "Dunbarmoor" (London)
Age 37 Killed as a result of an attack by an enemy submarine on 8 March 1917
TOWER HILL MEMORIAL, United Kingdom
Son of the late Robert and Eliza Wilson; husband of Sarah Jane Wilson (née Gray), of 10, Southwell Street, Belfast.

Wilson, William - Corporal
47013 Royal Garrison Artillery *Died in War on 3 August 1918*
HOLLYBROOK MEMORIAL SOUTHAMPTON, United Kingdom
Born and enlisted in Belfast

Wilson, William - Private
10349 Royal Inniskilling Fusiliers "B" Company 3rd Battalion *Age 24 Died of sickness on 21 April 1917*
BELFAST (DUNDONALD) CEMETERY, United Kingdom
Son of Mrs. Annie Wilson, of 20, Roseberry Gardens, Belfast, and the late W. Wilson.
Discharged as unfit for war service and awarded the Silver War Badge.

Wilson, William - Private
9986 Irish Guards 1st Battalion *Died in War on 14 September 1917*
MENDINGHEM MILITARY CEMETERY, Belgium
Son of Thomas and Alice Wilson, of Andersonstown, Belfast.

Wilson, William - Rifleman
1276 Royal Irish Rifles 15th Battalion *Died in War on 13 October 1916*
ST QUENTIN CABARET MILITARY CEMETERY, Belgium
Born and enlisted in Belfast.

Wilson, William - Rifleman
13872 Royal Irish Rifles 10th Battalion *Age 23 Died in War on 1 July 1916*
THIEPVAL MEMORIAL, France
Son of Mrs. Rebecca Wilson, of 27, Dover Street, Belfast.

Wilson, William - Rifleman
13880 Royal Irish Rifles "B" Company 8th Battalion *Age 36 Died of influenza while a POW on 18 October 1918*
COLOGNE SOUTHERN CEMETERY, Germany
Son of the late John and Jane Wilson, of Belfast.

Wilson, William - Rifleman
5433 Royal Irish Rifles *Died in War on 4 January 1915*
BELFAST CITY CEMETERY, United Kingdom
Born in Belfast, the son of Isaac Wilson. Died as a result of a shooting accident.

Wilson, William - Rifleman
6758 Royal Irish Rifles 15th Battalion *Died in War on 27 June 1917*
MESSINES RIDGE BRITISH CEMETERY, Belgium
Born and enlisted in Belfast.

Wilson, William Bell - Private
523966 Canadian Infantry (Manitoba Regiment) 8th Battalion *Age 33 Died in War on 2 September 1918*
DOMINION CEMETERY, HENDECOURT-LES-CAGNICOURT, France
Son of James and Susan Wilson, of 43, Rugby Road, Belfast, Ireland. A Presbyterian, he had pre-war military experience.

Wilson, William James - Private
49290 East Surrey Regiment 12th Battalion *Killed in Action on 4 October 1918*
DADIZEELE NEW BRITISH CEMETERY, Belgium
Son of William James and Agnes Wilson, of 96, Dundee Street, Belfast.

Wilson, William John - Private
26848 Royal Inniskilling Fusiliers 2nd Battalion *Killed in Action on 21 March 1918*
POZIERES MEMORIAL, France
Born and enlisted in Belfast.

Winter, Albert Arthur - Sergeant
549 Royal Irish Rifles 8/9th Battalion *Died in War on 2 July 1916*
THIEPVAL MEMORIAL, France
Born and enlisted in Belfast.

Wisely, Francis Joseph - Lieutenant
Royal Army Medical Corps *Died of Wounds on 14 September 1915*
ALEXANDRIA (CHATBY) MILITARY AND WAR MEMORIAL CEMETERY, Egypt
An old boy of St Malachy's and a university medical student. As a young doctor he was a houseman at the Mater Hospital, Belfast. Landed in Gallipoli as Medical Officer of the 1st Battalion Lancashire Fusiliers. Mortally wounded whilst tending the wounded under fire and evacuated. Died in a military hospital in Egypt. Francis Wisely was the uncle of Monsignor Tom Toner formerly of St Peter's Cathedral, Falls Road, Belfast.

Wiseman, Joseph - Private
S/15853 Black Watch (Royal Highlanders) 2nd Battalion *Died in War on 14 March 1917*
BASRA MEMORIAL, Iraq
Husband of Mrs Isabella Wiseman, Edenbank, Knutsford Drive, Belfast.

Withers, Edmond James - Private
22806 Alexandra, Princess of Wales's Own (Yorkshire Regiment) 6th Battalion *Killed in Action on 9 April 1918*
SAILLY-LABOURSE COMMUNAL CEMETERY, France
Born in Belfast, enlisted Pontefract, Yorkshire.

Wood, Joseph - Leading Stoker
305734 Royal Navy HMS "Good Hope" *Age 30 Killed in Action at Battle of Coronel on 1 November 1914*
PORTSMOUTH NAVAL MEMORIAL, United Kingdom
Son of Mr. and Mrs. Matthews Wood, of Failsworth, Manchester; husband of Elizabeth Wood, of 6, Hatton Drive, Belfast.

Woodburn, William A. - Private
57864 Highland Light Infantry 18th Battalion (4th Glasgow) *Died in War on 17 October 1918*
LIJSSENTHOEK MILITARY CEMETERY, Belgium
Born in Belfast, enlisted Glasgow.

Journey of Remembering

Woodhouse, Thomas - Private
8355 Royal Irish Fusiliers *Died in War on 21 October 1914*
HOUPLINES COMMUNAL CEMETERY EXTENSION, France
7 Dargle Street Belfast.

Woodney, Robert (Bob) - Boy First Class
J/39160 Royal Navy HMS "Natal" *Age 17 Killed by internal explosion of vessel in Cromarty Firth on 30 December 1915*
PLYMOUTH NAVAL MEMORIAL, United Kingdom
Only son of Robert and Elizabeth Woodney, of 64, Queensland Street, Belfast and originally from County Louth.

Woodrow, Robert - Private
3249 Royal Inniskilling Fusiliers 1st Battalion *Died in War on 21 August 1915*
HELLES MEMORIAL, Turkey
Born and enlisted in Belfast.

Woods, Claude William - Private
9002 Cameron Highlanders 1st Battalion *Killed in Action on 25 September 1914*
LA FERTE-SOUS-JOUARRE MEMORIAL, France
Ravenhill Road, Belfast..

Woods, James - Major
Indian Medical Service *Age 38 Died in War on 9 May 1915*
ST. VAAST MILITARY POST CEMETERY, RICHENBOURG, France
The youngest son of William and Isabella Woods, Waring Street Belfast.

Woods, James - Second Lieutenant
King's Own (Royal Lancaster Regiment) 10th Battalion attached 1st Battalion *Age 29 Died in War on 23 October 1916*
THIEPVAL MEMORIAL, France
Son of James and Margaret Woods, of 24, Wellesley Avenue, Belfast; husband of Marjorie Woods, of 28, Glenshiel Road, Eltham Park, London.

Woods, James Arthur - Pioneer
313004 Royal Engineers "H" Special Company *Age 23 Died of Wounds on 20 April 1918*
PERNES BRITISH CEMETERY, France
Son of James and Charlotte Woods, of Belfast.

Woods, James Edwin - Lieutenant
Royal Inniskilling Fusiliers 9th Battalion *Died in War on 6 December 1917*
CAMBRAI MEMORIAL, France
Son of Mr and Mrs Frederick W Woods, 6, St John's Park, Knockbreda Road, Belfast

Woods, John - Private
18295 Leinster Regiment 2nd Battalion *Died in War on 13 August 1918*
BORRE BRITISH CEMETERY, France
Born in Belfast enlisted in Ardrossan, Scotland. Formerly 5045 Connaught Rangers.

Woods, Neil - Private
Royal Irish Rifles *Died in War*
Survived by his mother at 41, Alexander Street West, Belfast. His twin bother also served and was wounded.

Woods, Norman Hill - Lieutenant
Royal Inniskilling Fusiliers 3rd Battalion attached 7th Battalion *Died in War on 16 July 1917*
TYNE COT MEMORIAL, BELGIUM
Holywood, County Down. Holder of the Military Cross.

Woods, Samuel - Rifleman
1037 Royal Irish Rifles 8/9th Battalion *Died in War on 21 June 1917*
MESSINES RIDGE BRITISH CEMETERY, Belgium
Born and enlisted in Belfast.

Woods, Samuel - Rifleman
8/4262 Royal Irish Rifles 8/9th Battalion *Killed in Action on 2 July 1916*
THIEPVAL MEMORIAL, France
Born and enlisted in Belfast.

Woods, Thomas - Private
7787 Royal Irish Rifles 2nd Battalion *Killed in Action on 25 October 1914*
LE TOURET MEMORIAL, France
Born and enlisted in Belfast. Husband of Elizabeth McCauley (formerly Woods), of Toronto, Canada.

Woods, William J - Corporal
64336 Royal Engineers 43rd Broad Gauge Railway Operating Company *Age 30 Died of Wounds on 28 March 1918*
ABBEVILLE COMMUNAL CEMETERY EXTENSION, France
Native of Carrickfergus, enlisted Belfast.

Woods, William - Lance Corporal
14140 Royal Inniskilling Fusiliers 11th Battalion *Age 36 Died of Wounds on 1 August 1916*
DERRYVOR (OR CROM) (HOLY TRINITY) CHURCH OF IRELAND CHURCHYARD, United Kingdom
Son of Andrew and Mary Woods; husband of Harriet A. Woods, of 59, Balfour Avenue, Belfast.
Born in County Fermanagh.

Woodside, Charles Richard - Private
71563 North Irish Horse *Died in War on 8 November 1918*
ROCQUIGNY-EQUANCOURT ROAD BRITISH CEMETERY, MANANCOURT, France
Born in Antrim, resident of Belfast. Died three days before the end of the war.

Woodside, Wallace McMullan - Corporal
14/16107 Royal Irish Rifles 14th Battalion *Age 26 Died of Wounds, received at the Battle of the Somme on 5 July 1916*
PUCHEVILLERS BRITISH CEMETERY, France
Son of John T. Woodside, M.D., and Maria Woodside, of Belfast.

Woodward, James - Leading Stoker
K/9273 Royal Navy HMS "Defence" *Age 24 Killed in Action at Battle of Jutland on 31 May 1916*
PLYMOUTH NAVAL MEMORIAL, United Kingdom
Son of Ellen Woodward, of 66, Fraser Street, Belfast; and the late John Woodward.

Worke, Patrick - Ordinary Seaman
Clyde 2/2480 Royal Naval Volunteer Reserve HMS "Bayano" *Died in War on 11 March 1915*
PORTSMOUTH NAVAL MEMORIAL, United Kingdom
Husband of Catherine, 30, Durham Street, Belfast.

Workman, Edward - Lieutenant
Royal Irish Rifles 2nd Battalion
Age 29 Died of Wounds received while leading a trench raid at Le Touquet, River Lys, on 26 January 1916
ETAPLES MILITARY CEMETERY, France
Only son of Frank and Sara Workman, of "The Moat", Strandtown. Native of Belfast.
Educated at Charterhouse and B.A. of Trinity College, Cambridge. Awarded the Military Cross.

Workman, John - Gunner
46955 Royal Garrison Artillery 115th Heavy Battery *Died in War on 1 November 1917*
MINTY FARM CEMETERY, Belgium
Son of Mrs. E. Workman, of 88, Disraeli Street, Belfast.

Worth, Arthur - Lance Corporal
7764 Royal Inniskilling Fusiliers 2nd Battalion *Died in War on 9 December 1917*
TYNE COT MEMORIAL, Belgium
Husband of Elizabeth Worth, of 51, Pine Street, Donegall Pass, Belfast.

Worthington, David - Sapper
57633 Royal Engineers 150th Field Company *Age 22 Died in War on 7 July 1916*
THIEPVAL MEMORIAL, France
Husband of Evelyn Worthington, of 12, Ballymoney Street, Oldpark Road, Belfast.

Worthington, Hugh - Private
6980 Irish Guards 2nd Battalion *Killed in Action on 27 September 1916*
GUARDS' CEMETERY, LESBOEUFS, France
Born in Belfast.

Wortley, Thomas George - Sergeant
14/17063 Royal Irish Rifles "D" Company 14th Battalion *Age 33 Killed in Action at Messines Ridge on 7 June 1917*
SPANBROEKMOLEN BRITISH CEMETERY, Belgium
Son of John and Isabella Wortley, of Belfast; husband of Hannah Wortley, of 2, Fleet Street, Belfast.

Wotherspoon, Walter Biggar - Third Engineer
Mercantile Marine S.S. "Reventazon" (Manchester)
Age 31 Drowned, as a result of an attack by an enemy submarine on 5 October 1918
TOWER HILL MEMORIAL, United Kingdom
Son of Annie Wotherspoon (née Biggar), of 30, Tate's Avenue, Belfast, and the late William Wotherspoon.
Born in Belfast.

Wright, Alexander Allen - Captain
King's Own (Royal Lancaster Regiment) 1/4th Battalion *Age 29 Died in War on 8 August 1916*
THIEPVAL MEMORIAL, France
Son of Joseph S. Wright, of Belfast. Played rugby for Collegians and worked in the Audit Office in the City Hall.

Wright, Charles Seabourne - Rifleman
3796 Royal Irish Rifles 12th Battalion *Age 19 Died in War on 22 November 1917*
CAMBRAI MEMORIAL, LOUVERVAL, France
Son of Charles Seabourne Wright and Letitia Wright, of 14, Coburg Street, Belfast.

Wright, Frederick James - Private
H/24512 8th (King's Royal Irish) Hussars *Age 23 Died in War on 30 November 1917*
GOUZEAUCOURT NEW BRITISH CEMETERY, France
Son of Ex-Sergeant Major Joseph Wright; husband of Ellen Dunbar Wright,
of 116, East Bread Street, Connswater, Belfast.

Wright, George - Private
7126 West Yorkshire Regiment (Prince of Wales's Own) "B" Company 3rd Battalion *Age 39 Died in War on 31 May 1915*
SHEFFIELD (CITY ROAD) CEMETERY, United Kingdom
Son of B. Wright; husband of Agnes Wright, of 24, Stonyford Street, Belfast.
Served in the South African Campaign. Born at Sheffield.

JOURNEY OF REMEMBERING

Wright, George - Private
9055 Royal Inniskilling Fusiliers 2nd Battalion *Died in War on 16 May 1915*
LE TOURET MEMORIAL, France
105, St Leonards Street, Belfast. Originally from Aughnacloy, County Tyrone. Husband of Isabella.

Wright, James - Private
9631 Princess Victoria's (Royal Irish Fusiliers) 1st Battalion *Died in War on 25 April 1915*
YPRES (MENIN GATE MEMORIAL), Belgium
Born and enlisted in Belfast.

Wright, James Woodside - Rifleman
12187 Royal Irish Rifles 15th Battalion *Age 26 Killed in Action on 1 July 1916*
THIEPVAL MEMORIAL, France
Son of Mrs. Mary Wright, of 19, Derg Street, Belfast.

Wright, John - Rifleman
796 Royal Irish Rifles 9th Battalion *Died in War on 18 March 1916*
THIEPVAL MEMORIAL, France
105, St Leonards Street, Belfast.

Wright, John - Sergeant
30/162 Northumberland Fusiliers 1st/4th Battalion *Age 22 Died in War on 10 April 1918*
PLOEGSTEERT MEMORIAL, Belgium
Son of Mrs. Margaret Wright, of 38, Seaview Street, York Road, Belfast.

Wright, John Bremner - Private
43657 Machine Gun Corps (Infantry) *Age 25 Died of Wounds on 11 November 1917*
BELFAST CITY CEMETERY, United Kingdom
Born at Belfast the son William and Mary Bremner of 107, Agincourt Avenue, Belfast.
Died of his injuries in a hospital in Halifax, Yorkshire.

Wright, Robert - Second Lieutenant
Royal Irish Rifles 18th Battalion attached 2/5th Royal Irish Fusiliers *Age 21 Killed in Action on 7 November 1918*
GAZA WAR CEMETERY, Israel
Born in Scotland he was the son of Davis and Marion Wright, of the "Moat", Dundonald, Belfast.
Killed during the third battle of Gaza.

Wright, Robert - Sergeant
17772 Machine Gun Corps (Infantry) 217th Battalion *Died of Wounds on 2 September 1917*
ST. SEVER CEMETERY EXTENSION, ROUEN, France
Husband of Martha Wright, of 9, Roxburgh Street, Belfast.

Wright, Robert Sinclair - Private
147680 Canadian Machine Gun Corps 4th Battalion *Age 30 Died in War on 13 December 1918*
MAUBEUGE-CENTRE CEMETERY, France
Son of John and Jane Wright, of 263, Greenmount Road, Belfast. An Anglican, he had been born at Ballyclare, County Antrim, Ireland. Worked as a clerk and had previously served in the militia.

Wright, Samuel - Gunner
100664 Royal Field Artillery "D" Battery 186th Brigade *Age 19 Died in War on 1 October 1917*
LA CLYTTE MILITARY CEMETERY, Belgium
Son of the late Samuel and Mary Wright, of 10, Glencollyer Street, Belfast.

Wright, Samuel - Private
10095 Royal Irish Fusiliers 6th Battalion *Age 33 Accidentally killed on 4 December 1915*
DOIRAN MEMORIAL, *Greece*
Son of Mrs. Catherine Wright. Born at Belfast.

Wright, Samuel - Private
4165 Royal Inniskilling Fusiliers 2nd Battalion *Died in War on 16 May 1915*
BETHUNE TOWN CEMETERY, *France*
Born and enlisted in Belfast.

Wright, Samuel - Rifleman
17065 Royal Irish Rifles 10th Battalion *Killed in Action on 7 December 1915*
THIEPVAL MEMORIAL, *France*
Born and enlisted in Belfast, husband of Jane Wright, of North Road, Carrickfergus.

Wright, Samuel Keer - Private
66123 Canadian Infantry (Quebec Regiment) 24th Battalion *Died in War on 4 June 1916*
LIJSSENTHOEK MILITARY CEMETERY, *Belgium*
Son of Robert Wright, 42, Sunnyside Street, Belfast.

Wright, Thomas - Private
17095 King's Own (Royal Lancaster Regiment) 2nd Battalion *Died in War on 8 May 1915*
YPRES (MENIN GATE) MEMORIAL, *Belgium*
Born in Belfast, enlisted in Manchester.

Wright, Thomas Henry - Private
8108 4th Dragoon Guards (Royal Irish) *Age 25 Killed in Action on 1 July 1917*
BULLY-GRENAY COMMUNAL CEMETERY, BRITISH EXTENSION, *France*
Native of Belfast.

Wright, William - Engine Room Artificer
425EB Royal Navy HMS "Cressy" *Died in War on 22 September 1914*
PORTSMOUTH NAVAL MEMORIAL, *United Kingdom*
Husband of Sarah Wright, 31, Glenrosa Street, Belfast.

Wright, William Henry - Private
13704 Royal Inniskilling Fusiliers 11th Battalion *Killed in Action on 1 July 1916*
THIEPVAL MEMORIAL, *France*
Brother of Mr E Killen, 14, Barrington Street, Belfast.

Wright, William J - Sergeant
12/19265 Royal Irish Rifles 14th Battalion *Age 27 Died of Wounds on 18 August 1917*
BRANDHOEK NEW MILITARY CEMETERY No.3, *Belgium*
Son of William John and Elizabeth Wright, of Belfast; husband of Catherine Jane Wright, of Ballycushion, Templepatrick, County Antrim.

Wright, William John - Lance Corporal
29614 Worcestershire Regiment 4th Battalion *Died in War on 9 October 1917*
TYNE COT MEMORIAL, *Belgium*
Born in Belfast, enlisted in Birmingham.

JOURNEY OF REMEMBERING

Wylie, Edward - Sapper
64006 Royal Engineers 121st Field Company *Died in War on 5 July 1916*
THIEPVAL MEMORIAL, *France*
Rose Cottage, Finaghy, Belfast.

Wylie, James Randolph - Second Lieutenant
Royal Air Force *Age 23 Died in War on 23 April 1918*
URMSTON CEMETERY, *United Kingdom*
Son of James and Lizzie Grayson Wylie of 17, Oak Avenue, Urmston, Manchester.
Born in Belfast. Commissioned from the Royal Dublin Fusiliers.

Wylie, John - Private
13837 Royal Inniskilling Fusiliers 2nd Battalion *Age 34 Died in War on 28 April 1918*
TYNE COT MEMORIAL, *Belgium*
Brother of Mrs. Jane Boyd, of 107, East Bread Street, Beersbridge Road, Belfast.

Wylie, S D - Private
19461 Royal Inniskilling Fusiliers *Age 29 Died of phthisis on 25 February 1918*
BELFAST CITY CEMETERY, *United Kingdom*
(Served as DAVISON). Son of Samuel and Sarah Wylie, of 16, Hunter Street, Belfast;
husband of Lizzie McCullogh (formerly Wylie), of 82, Hunter Street, Belfast.

Wylie, Thomas - Private
18330 Leinster Regiment 2nd Battalion formerly 4694 Connaught Rangers.*Died in War on 4 September 1918*
NIEUWKERKE CHURCHYARD, *Belgium*
Born and enlisted in Belfast.

Wylie, William Smyth - Private
9319 Royal Inniskilling Fusiliers 2nd Battalion *Age 25 Died in War on 16 May 1915*
LE TOURET MEMORIAL, *France*
Son of William James and Sarah Wylie, of 43, Lecale Street, Belfast.

Wynne, Alfred - Rifleman
5811 Royal Irish Rifles 14th Battalion *Age 18 Killed in Action on 20 October 1916*
POND FARM CEMETERY, *Belgium*
Son of Walter and Sarah Wynne, of 80, Lepper Street, Belfast.

Wynne, Thomas - Corporal
8099 Royal Dublin Fusiliers 2nd Battalion *Died in War on 14 December 1914*
PROWSE POINT MILITARY CEMETERY, *Belgium*
Born in Belfast, enlisted in Dublin.

Wynne, William John - Rifleman
54213 King's Royal Rifle Corps 2nd Battalion *Age 19 Killed in Action on 17 October 1918*
BUSIGNY COMMUNAL CEMETERY EXTENSION, *France*
Son of Francis and Agnes Wynne, of 13, Greenville Terrace, Bloomfield, Belfast.

Journey of Remembering

Yardley, Thomas - Rifleman
490 Royal Irish Rifles 16th (Pioneer) Battalion *Age 19 Died in War 4 July 1916*
THIEPVAL MEMORIAL, France
Son of James and Eleanor Yardley, 21, Kimona Street, Belfast.

Yarr, William Robert - Rifleman
10303 Royal Irish Rifles 1st Battalion *Died in War on 16 August 1917*
TYNE COT MEMORIAL, Belgium
Born in Barrow, Lancashire, enlisted Newtownards, resident of Belfast.

Yates, John - Stoker First Class
SS/100526 Royal Navy HMS "Hawke" *Lost at sea on 15 October 1914*
CHATHAM NAVAL MEMORIAL, United Kingdom
Son of Thomas Yates, 25, Springmount Street. An Orangeman, he was a member of Crystal Spring Lodge 903.

Yeates, Andrew - Sergeant
16112 Royal Irish Rifles 14th Battalion *Age 31 Killed in Action on 16 August 1917*
NEW IRISH FARM CEMETERY, Belgium
Son of the late Henry and Mary Jane Yeates, of Belfast.

Yorke, Robert - Lance Corporal
19362 Royal Irish Rifles 14th Battalion *Age 22 Died in War on 15 August 1917*
NEW IRISH FARM CEMETERY, Belgium
Son of Robert and Agnes Yorke, of 197, Upper Meadow Street, Belfast

Young, Alfred - Acting Sergeant
17175 Highland Light Infantry 10th Battalion *Died in War on 25 September 1915*
LOOS MEMORIAL, France
Born in Belfast, enlisted in Rutherglen, Scotland.

Young, Archibald - Rifleman
7312 Royal Irish Rifles 2nd Battalion *Died in War on 28 June 1915*
BOULOGNE EASTERN CEMETERY, France
59, Short Strand Belfast.

Young, Charles - Sergeant
706672 Canadian Infantry "D" Company 103rd Battalion *Died in War on 6 August 1917*
BELFAST CITY CEMETERY, United Kingdom
Son of John and Agnes Young, of 17, Lawnview Street, Woodvale Road, Belfast.
A Presbyterian who served in the militia prior to the war.

Young, David - Private
11009 Royal Inniskilling Fusiliers 2nd Battalion *Killed in Action on 16 May 1915*
LE TOURET MEMORIAL, France
Born in Belfast.

Young, Edward - Private
8508 Royal Inniskilling Fusiliers 1st Battalion *Age 26 Died in War on 10 May 1915*
HELLES MEMORIAL, Turkey
Son of James and Maggie Young, of 61, Wilton Street, Belfast. Had nine years service, mostly in India.

Young, Frederick - Rifleman
A/204347 King's Royal Rifles 7th Battalion *Killed in Action on 4 April 1918*
POZIERES MEMORIAL, *France*
81, Brookmount Street, Belfast.

Young, Henry - Private
5746 Royal Army Medical Corps attached H.M.H.S. "Galeka"
Age 23 Lost at sea (mine explosion), five miles N.W. from Cape la Hague on 28 October 1916
THE SHIP'S MEMORIAL IS IN STE. MARIE CEMETERY, LE HAVRE, *France*
Son of John and Mary Jane Young, of 105, Bray Street, Belfast.

Young, Herbert - Private
10157 Royal Inniskilling Fusiliers 1st Battalion *Died in War on 26 March 1915*
POELCAPELLE BRITISH CEMETERY, *Belgium*
77, St Leonard's Street. Enlisted in Belfast.

Young, Herbert - Private
L/76749 Middlesex Regiment 4th Battalion *Died in War on 16 February 1915*
YPRES (MENIN GATE) MEMORIAL, *Belgium*
23, Beersbridge Road, Belfast.

Young, James - Corporal
13929 Royal Irish Rifles 9th Battalion *Died in War on 3 January 1916*
SUCRERIE MILITARY CEMETERY, COLINCAMPS, *France*
Born and enlisted in Belfast.

Young, James - Private
3376 4th Dragoon Guards (Royal Irish) *Age 25 Died in War on 5 March 1915*
YPRES (MENIN GATE) MEMORIAL, *Belgium*
Son of John Young, of 65, Westbourne Street, Belfast, and the late Elizabeth Young.

Young, James Murray - Rifleman
837 Royal Irish Rifles 12th Battalion *Age 21 Killed in Action on 1 July 1916*
THIEPVAL MEMORIAL, *France*
Son of William John and Jane Johnston Young, of 8, Madrid Street, Belfast.

Young, John - Rifleman
571 Royal Irish Rifles 15th Battalion *Age 31 Died of Wounds on 23 December 1915*
STE. MARIE CEMETERY, LE HAVRE, *France*
Son of Mr. and Mrs. James Young, of Belfast; husband of Agnes Young, of 1, Valentine Street, Belfast.

Young, Margaret Cameron - Nurse
British Red Cross Society 2nd General Hospital Voluntary Aid Detachment
Age 25 Died of disease on 30 July 1918
TERLINCTHUN BRITISH CEMETERY, WIMILLE, *France*
Daughter of Amelia and the late Thomas Young, of 37, Newington Avenue, Belfast.

Young, Robert - Private
22726 King's Own (Royal Lancaster Regiment) 1st Battalion *Killed in Action on 13 October 1916*
GUARDS' CEMETERY, LESBOEUFS, *France*
Born in Belfast.

Young, Robert - Rifleman
13907 Royal Irish Rifles 1st Battalion *Killed in Action on 21 March 1918*
GRAND-SERAUCOURT BRITISH CEMETERY, France
Born and enlisted in Belfast.

Young, Samuel - Rifleman
869 Royal Irish Rifles 2nd Battalion *Died in War on 24 March 1918*
POZIERES MEMORIAL, France
Son of Mr and Mrs Samuel Young, 162, Sugarfield Street, Belfast.

Young, Thomas - Private
29466 Royal Irish Fusiliers 1st Battalion *Age 23 Died of Wounds on 3 September 1918*
BAILLEUL COMMUNAL CEMETERY EXTENSION (NORD), France
Son of Thomas and Violet Young, of 77, St. Leonard's Street, Newtownards Road, Belfast.

Young, William - Rifleman
1196 Royal Irish Rifles 9th Battalion *Age 21 Died in War on 7 October 1918*
BELFAST CITY CEMETERY, United Kingdom
Son of Mr. and Mrs. William Young, of 11, Beresford Street, Belfast.

Younger, Robert Boyd - Lance Corporal
21541 Royal Irish Fusiliers "D" Company 7th Battalion *Age 18 Died in War on 7 September 1916*
THIEPVAL MEMORIAL, France
Son of John Younger, of 6, Little Brunswick Street, Belfast.

Zachary, John - Private
830497 Canadian Infantry (Manitoba Regiment) 8th Battalion *Age 32 Died in War on 5 August 1917*
BULLY-GRENAY COMMUNAL CEMETERY, BRITISH EXTENSION, France
Son of John George and Jane Goodwin Zachary, of "Norbrae", 37, Kirkliston Drive, Bloomfield, Belfast, Ireland.

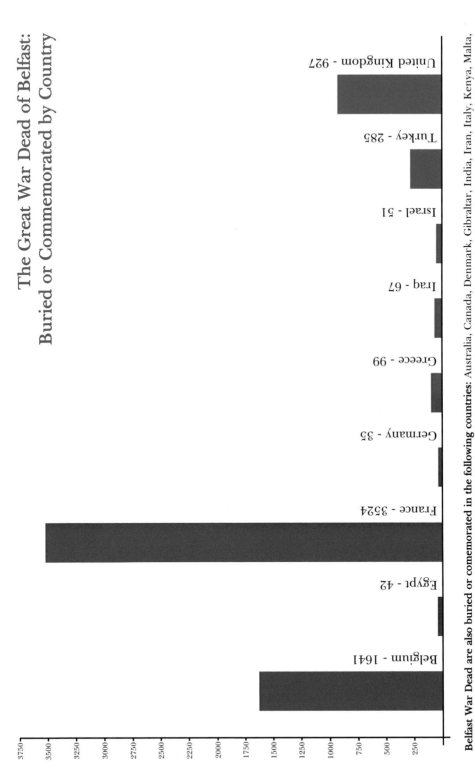

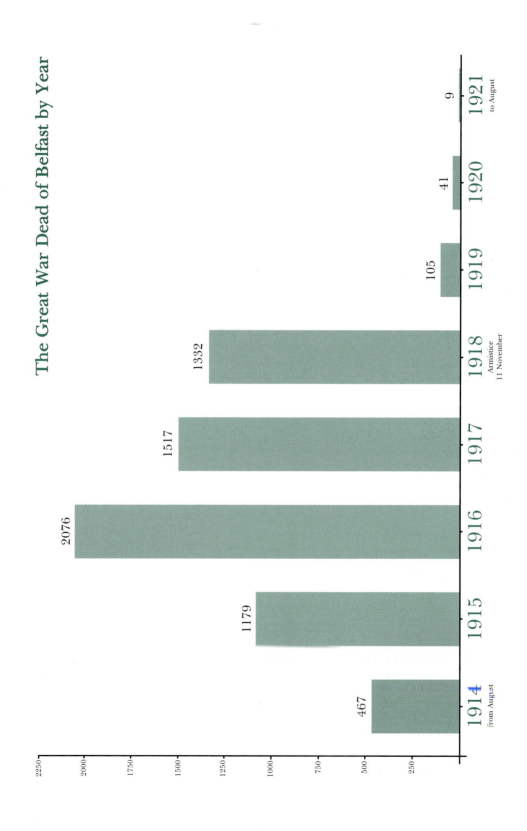

Some Military Terms

Regiment (Infantry): In normal conditions an infantry regiment usually consisted of two, peacetime regular battalions. One of these would remain at home and the other serve abroad, often in India. When the war began each regiment raised a number of new battalions specifically for war service. These were known as "service" battalions and would be disbanded at the end of hostilities.

Battalion: Battalions of infantry, when at full strength, mustered just over one thousand officers and men and were commanded by a Lieutenant Colonel. Battalions were then sub-divided into four companies of 220 commanded by a Captain or Major. Companies were further divided into platoons and sections. As the war progressed some battalions were merged or disbanded altogether. Soldiers were sometimes attached or transferred to other units.

Brigade (Infantry): A Brigade consisted of four battalions, reduced to three in 1918, and was commanded by a Brigadier General.

Division (Infantry): A Division was commanded by a Major General and mustered, in three Brigades, nineteen thousand men. It had twelve infantry battalions, a pioneer battalion, specialist engineers, signallers, medical and supply troops, a squadron of cavalry and, crucially, artillery. Although Belfast men served in every division in the Army three infantry divisions were formed in Ireland. They were the 10th (Irish) the 16th (Irish) and the 36th (Ulster) Divisions.

Regiments (Cavalry): Cavalry regiments were smaller, 550 strong and did not have battalions.

Battery: A battery was a group of artillery guns and soldiers. Several batteries would be grouped, confusingly, into an artillery brigade, the equivalent of a regiment. There were three branches in the Royal Artillery, Horse, Field and Garrison.

Mentioned in Despatches: Recognition of good service which falls below the status of a gallantry medal. The recipient wore an oak leaf on the appropriate campaign medal or the Victory Medal.

POW: Prisoner of War, Over 180,000 British soldiers became prisoners during the great war.

Silver War Badge: A badge to be worn on civilian clothes by former soldiers discharged because of wounds, illness or age. It bore the words; "For King and Empire – Services Rendered"

Court Martial: - A Military court made up of officers and without a jury. There were four types of courts martial depending on the severity of the charge.

Croix de Guerre: - A French and Belgian bravery medal sometimes awarded to British soldiers. Other allied countries, including Russia, also bestowed decorations.